MW01180709

ITALIAN WINES 2001

LE GUIDE
DEL GAMBERO ROSSO

Gambero Rosso Editore

Slow Food Arcigola Editore

italianwines

2001

ITALIAN WINES 2001

IS THE ENGLISH LANGUAGE EDITION OF VINI D'ITALIA 2001 BY
GAMBERO ROSSO EDITORE AND SLOW FOOD EDITORE

GAMBERO ROSSO EDITORE
VIA A. BARGONI, 8 - 00153 ROMA
TEL. 39-6-5852121 - FAX 39-6-58310170
E-MAIL: gambero@gamberorosso.it

SLOW FOOD ARCIGOLA EDITORE
VIA MENDICITÀ ISTRUITA, 45 - 12042 BRA (CN)
TEL. 39-172-412519 - FAX 39-172-411218
E-MAIL: info@slowfood.it

EDITORIAL STAFF FOR THE ORIGINAL EDITION

CHIEF EDITORS
DANIELE CERNILLI AND CARLO PETRINI

SENIOR EDITORS
GIGI PIUMATTI AND MARCO SABELLICO

TECHNICAL SUPERVISION
GIANNI FABRIZIO, ERNESTO GENTILI, VITTORIO MANGANELLI, FABIO RIZZARI

MEMBERS OF THE FINAL TASTING PANELS
MARCO BOLASCO, DARIO CAPPELLONI, GIULIO COLOMBA,
EGIDIO FEDELE DELL'OSTE, CRISTIANA LAURO, GIACOMO MOJOLI,
MARCO OREGGIA, SILVANO PROMPICAI, PIERO SARDO

CONTRIBUTORS
NINO AIELLO, FRANCESCO ANNIBALI, GILBERTO ARRU, STEFANO ASARO, ANTONIO ATTORRE,
PAOLO BATTIMELLI, ENRICO BATTISTELLA, ALBERTO BETTINI, WALTER BORDO,
MICHELE BRESSAN, DARIO CAPPELLONI, ROBERTO CHECCHETTO, DANIELE CERNILLI,
VALERIO CHIARINI, ANTONIO CIMINELLI, GIULIO COLOMBA, EGIDIO FEDELE DELL'OSTE,
MASSIMO DI CINTIO, MASSIMO DOGLIOLO, GIANNI FABRIZIO, MAURIZIO FAVA,
NICOLA FRASSON, LUCA FURLOTTI, ERNESTO GENTILI, FABIO GIAVEDONI, VITO LACERENZA,
GIANCARLO LO SICCO, ALBERTO MALLARINO, VITTORIO MANGANELLI, GIACOMO MOJOLI,
MARCO OREGGIA, DAVIDE PANZIERI, MARIO PAPANI, STEFANO PASTOR, NEREO PEDERZOLLI,
CARLO PETRINI, GUIDO PIRAZZOLI, GIGI PIUMATTI, MARIO PLAZIO, PIERPAOLO RASTELLI,
GABRIELE RICCI ALUNNI, FABIO RIZZARI, LEONARDO ROMANELLI, GIOVANNI RUFFA,
FABRIZIO RUSSO, MARCO SABELLICO, PIERO SARDO, DIEGO SORACCO, HERBERT TASCHLER,
MASSIMO TOFFOLO, PAOLO VALDASTRI, ANDREA VANNELLI,
RICCARDO VISCARDI, MASSIMO VOLPARI, ALBERTO ZACCONE

WITH SPECIAL THANKS TO
ALBERTO AROSSA, BRUNO BEVILACQUA, MARCO BOLASCO, ALESSANDRO BULZONI,
TEODOSIO BUONGIORNO, REMO CAMURANI, DARIO CAPPELLONI, SERGIO CECCARELLI,
ENZO CODOGNO, IAN DOMENICO D'AGATA, ANGELO DAL BON, AURELIO DAMIANI,
MARINO DEL CURTO, STEFANO FERRARI, DAVIDE GANDINO, CRISTIANA LAURO, MARCO LISI,
ENZO MERZ, DANNY MURARO, DUILIO MURARO, GIOVANNI NORESE, UGO ONGARETTO,
ROBERTO PALMIERI, NICOLA PERULLO, LIANO PETROZZI, SILVANO PROMPICAI,
MARINO POERIO, FRANCESCO PENSOVECCHIO, VALENTINO RAMELLI,
GABRIELE RICCI ALUNNI, HELMUT RIEBSCHLEGER, MAURIZIO ROSSI, PAOLO VALDASTRI,
GIULIANA VELISCECH, VALERIO ZORZI

EDITORIAL ASSISTANTS
MARCO OREGGIA AND UMBERTO TAMBURINI

EDITORIAL COORDINATOR
GIORGIO ACCASCINA

TRANSLATIONS COORDINATED AND EDITED BY
GILES WATSON

TRANSLATORS
MAUREEN ASHLEY, MICHAEL BENSON, KAREN CHRISTENFELD, HELEN DONALD, STEPHEN
HOBLEY, STEPHEN JACKSON, ANDREW L. MILLER, GILES WATSON

PUBLISHER
GAMBERO ROSSO, INC.
636 BROADWAY - SUITE 1219 - NEW YORK, NY 10012
TEL. 212- 253-5653 FAX 212 253-8349 - E-MAIL: gamberousa@aol.com

DISTRIBUTION:
USA AND CANADA BY ANTIQUE COLLECTOR'S CLUB, MARKET STREET INDUSTRIAL PARK,
WAPPINGER FALLS, NY 12590, USA;
UK AND AUSTRALIA BY GRUB STREET, THE BASEMENT, 10 CHIVALRY ROAD,
LONDON SW11 1HT, UK.

ITALIAN WINES 2001 WAS CLOSED SEPTEMBER 30, 2000

PRINTED IN ITALY BY ROTOLITO LOMBARDA - VIA ROMA, 115/A - PIOLTELLO (MILANO)

CONTENTS

INTRODUCTION

The year 2001 brings with it not only a new century – this time the old millennium is well and truly behind us – but also the fourteenth edition of Italian Wines, hot off the presses of, in strictly alphabetical order, Gambero Rosso and Slow Food. As usual, it has been a challenging task, involving about a hundred people including editorial staff, contributors, tasting panel co-ordinators and so on. Roughly 20,000 wines were tasted by more than 30 panels of at least four members each. Finally, we gathered together about 800 wines selected during the first round and subjected them to further scrutiny at a final tasting, in which all the Guide's main contributors took part. The reason for this is that the Guide, unlike other superficially similar publications, is a collective effort. The editors' responsibility is limited to liaison with producers, the selection of contributors and the overall supervision of the project. The panel assessments and the award of our top accolade, the now-legendary Three Glasses, are the outcome of discussions in which all the main contributors take part after tastings have been completed, including – naturally – the final round. All tastings are comparative and blind, which means in effect that tasters on our panels will know the type and vintage of the wines being assessed, but nothing more. This is a guarantee for producers, who thus have a level playing field, and for Guide readers, who can rest assured that our evaluations do not depend on any other factors apart from the intrinsic quality of the products being tested. Or at least of our perception of that quality, because while we think we can claim to be reasonably competent, we, too, are human, and therefore fallible. It must be said, and we do so with no little pride, that this approach has won our readers' trust. Today, the Guide is no longer a manual of interest only to experts or wine professionals. Almost 80,000 copies are sold throughout Italy, and that number rises to nearly 150,000 if you add in the German and English-language editions that have carved out a considerable niche for themselves in the world's markets. All this means that the guide has become the international voice of Italian wine, a development that has surprised us as much as anyone else. But the figures speak for themselves. We acknowledge our responsibilities and the pressures to which this success now exposes us. Nowadays, a winery that wins a Three Glass rating also has an endorsement that earns respect anywhere on the planet. Our "Three Glass" system has become a benchmark for assessing the merits of a wine. The Glasses have acquired a life of their own, quite apart from the Guide, so that a "Three Glass wine" has the same status in popular parlance as a Three Star (Michelin ones, obviously) restaurant or a Five Star hotel, which is a source of great satisfaction for those who invented the system fourteen long years ago. But let's come back to the present, and this year's Guide. We have frequently explained how the Three Glass awards are made and this year there are fully 230 of them. But, as the ancient Romans used to say, "repetita iuvant", so we'll take their advice and recap briefly. The assessments of the individual panels take no account of the absolute merit of the various wines. Instead, they evaluate how well the product reflects the best features of its wine type and the technical skill with which it was vinified, as well as the balance of its various components during visual, olfactory and gustatory examination. Evaluations should therefore be seen as the outcome of a series of rounds held in parallel, since we do not think it is particularly useful to compare wines of completely different types, or from dissimilar vintages, varieties or regions. Balance in the tasting profile, adherence to the characteristics of terroir and grape type, and well-managed vinification, cask conditioning and bottle-ageing are the foundation for the assessments made by our panels of all the wines tasted. The extreme flexibility of the process, which can easily be fine-tuned to suit each category, enables our tasters to take due consideration of all the many variables that the vast differences in the wines tested call into play. It is in this perspective that the Three Glass awards should be seen, for the process is more complex, and rather less mechanical, than it might at first appear. We mentioned earlier how many Three Glass winners there are – fully 230 – in this year's edition of the Guide. That number reflects developments in the overall quality of Italian wines as well as the simultaneous release of major wines from particularly exciting vintages, and in some of the most significant categories. We had a big batch of '96 Barolos, '97 Barbarescos, and Chianti Classico Riservas and Supertuscans from '97 and '98. But there was also a raft of Amarones from '95 and '97, a flood of Friulian whites from '99 and a horde of heavy-duty '97s and '98s from the south of Italy. Close behind were large numbers of well-made, well-typed, terroir-driven products. The quality gap continues to narrow and it is becoming increasingly arduous to make meaningful distinctions. Unless, of course, we were to descend to the level of "ideology", a stance that we respectfully and resolutely reject. We are not looking to express a judgement on the personality of a producer, or how effective a cellar's advertising campaigns have been. We make no distinction between the great and the humble, the traditionalists and the innovators, the celebrated and the obscure. We strive simply to evaluate the quality of the wines that are presented to us with all the intellectual honesty and knowledge of the territory that we can muster. And we set particular store by that local knowledge. Many of our contributors are members of Slow Food, and careful readers of Gambero Rosso, who live in the winegrowing areas. They have a very detailed understanding of the territory and the seasonal cycle, and often also have an intimate knowledge of the wineries themselves, since they are regular visitors. This is a tremendous advantage that enables us to keep bang up to date with the latest news, among other things. It means that we can procure tasting samples from little known, or new, producers, and from cellars that we previously disregarded but which might now be producing serious products as a result of structural improvements. In short, it is unlikely that any interesting winery or new, top-flight product will escape our notice. Or at least, our unique testing structure makes such a lapse less likely than in the case of our rivals. Finally, a brief mention of the other Italian Wines 2001 nominations. For the past three years, we have been flanking the classic Three Glass ratings with other awards and here they are. Cellar of the Year for 2001 is the La Spinetta winery, owned by the Rivetti family, at Castagnole Lanze. La Spinetta swept up four Three Glass accolades and almost picked up a further two, an exploit that merits appropriate recognition. Oenologist of the Year is Riccardo Cotarella, 11 of whose wines won Three Glasses. Riccardo's international reputation has made him a celebrity, bringing him to the attention of four producers in Saint-Emilion, in Bordeaux, who have asked for and obtained his services as consultant. The Sparkler of the Year award goes to a magisterial Giulio Ferrari '92 while the White of the Year is Leonildo Pieropan's Soave Classico Superiore La Rocca '98. Red of the Year is the awesome Montepulciano d'Abruzzo Villa Gemma '95 from Gianni Masciarelli and, in conclusion, the Sweet Wine of the Year is the Alto Adige Gewürztraminer Passito Terminum '98 from the Cantina Produttori di Termeno. Four wines that get the 21st century off to a truly delicious start.

Daniele Cernilli and Carlo Petrini

THREE GLASS AWARDS 2001

VALLE D'AOSTA
VALLÉE D'AOSTE CHARDONNAY CUVÉE FRISSONIÈRE
LES CRÊTES CUVÉE BOIS '98	LES CRÊTES	17

PIEDMONT
BARBARESCO '97	GAJA	31
BARBARESCO BRICCO ASILI BRICCO ASILI '97	BRICCO ROCCHE - BRICCO ASILI	56
BARBARESCO BRICCO LIBERO '97	RINO VARALDO	36
BARBARESCO COLE '97	MOCCAGATTA	33
BARBARESCO COPAROSSA '97	BRUNO ROCCA	35
BARBARESCO COTTÀ VIGNA BRICHET '97	SOTTIMANO	113
BARBARESCO GAIUN '97	CISA ASINARI DEI MARCHESI DI GRESY	30
BARBARESCO ROMBONE '97	FIORENZO NADA	134
BARBARESCO SERRABOELLA '97	F.LLI CIGLIUTI	110
BARBARESCO SORÌ PAITIN '97	PAITIN	113
BARBARESCO VANOTU '97	PELISSERO	135
BARBARESCO VIGNA BORGESE '97	PIERO BUSSO	109
BARBARESCO VIGNETO BRICH RONCHI '97	ALBINO ROCCA	35
BARBARESCO VIGNETO GALLINA '97	LA SPINETTA	52
BARBARESCO VIGNETO STARDERI '97	LA SPINETTA	52
BARBERA D'ALBA BRIC LOIRA '98	CASCINA CHICCO	46
BARBERA D'ALBA SUPERIORE '98	HILBERG - PASQUERO	119
BARBERA D'ALBA VIGNA VIGIA '98	BRICCO MAIOLICA	66
BARBERA D'ALBA VIGNETO GALLINA '98	LA SPINETTA	52
BARBERA D'ALBA VITTORIA '98	GIANFRANCO ALESSANDRIA	95
BARBERA D'ASTI BRICCO DELL'UCCELLONE '98	BRAIDA	120
BARBERA D'ASTI SUPERIORE LA VIGNA DELL'ANGELO '98	CASCINA LA BARBATELLA	115
BARBERA DEL MONFERRATO SUPERIORE BRICCO BATTISTA '98	GIULIO ACCORNERO E FIGLI	138
BAROLO BRIC DËL FIASC '96	PAOLO SCAVINO	59
BAROLO BRICCO FIASCO '96	AZELIA	56
BAROLO BRICCO LUCIANI '96	SILVIO GRASSO	83
BAROLO BRUNATE '96	ROBERTO VOERZIO	89
BAROLO BUSSIA '96	PRUNOTTO	27
BAROLO BUSSIA VIGNA MUNIE '96	ARMANDO PARUSSO	101
BAROLO CA' MIA '96	BROVIA	57
BAROLO CANNUBI '96	E. PIRA & FIGLI - CHIARA BOSCHIS	38
BAROLO CEREQUIO '96	MICHELE CHIARLO	44
BAROLO CEREQUIO '96	ROBERTO VOERZIO	89
BAROLO ENRICO VI '96	MONFALLETTO CORDERO DI MONTEZEMOLO	85
BAROLO FALLETTO '96	BRUNO GIACOSA	111
BAROLO FOSSATI '96	ENZO BOGLIETTI	81
BAROLO LA SERRA '96	GIANNI VOERZIO	89
BAROLO PARAFADA '96	VIGNA RIONDA - MASSOLINO	130
BAROLO PERCRISTINA '95	DOMENICO CLERICO	96
BAROLO VIGNA CAPPELLA DI SANTO STEFANO '96	PODERE ROCCHE DEI MANZONI	102
BAROLO VIGNA CONCA '96	MAURO MOLINO	85
BAROLO VIGNA DEL GRIS '96	CONTERNO - FANTINO	98
BAROLO VIGNETO ROCCHE '96	ANDREA OBERTO	86
BAROLO VIGNETO ROCCHE '96	MAURO VEGLIO	88
COLLI TORTONESI BIGOLLA '98	VIGNETI MASSA	104
DOLCETTO DI DOGLIANI SAN FEREOLO '99	SAN FEREOLO	69
DOLCETTO DI DOGLIANI SIRI D'JERMU '99	F.LLI PECCHENINO	68
DOLCETTO DI DOGLIANI VIGNA DEL PILONE '99	SAN ROMANO	70
GAVI DEL COMUNE DI GAVI MONTE ROTONDO '99	VILLA SPARINA	78
HARYS '98	GIOVANNI BATTISTA GILLARDI	71
LANGHE ARBORINA '98	ELIO ALTARE	80
LANGHE LARIGI '98	ELIO ALTARE	80
LANGHE NEBBIOLO SPERSS '96	GAJA	31
LANGHE ROSSO BRIC DU LUV '98	CA' VIOLA	105
LANGHE ROSSO LUIGI EINAUDI '98	PODERI LUIGI EINAUDI	68
LANGHE ROSSO MONPRÀ '98	CONTERNO - FANTINO	98
LOAZZOLO PIASA RISCHEI '97	FORTETO DELLA LUJA	91
MINAIA '98	FRANCO M. MARTINETTI	133
MONFERRATO ROSSO PIN '98	LA SPINETTA	52
MONFERRATO ROSSO SONVICO '98	CASCINA LA BARBATELLA	115
ROERO RÒCHE D'AMPSÈJ '97	MATTEO CORREGGIA	47
ROERO SUPERIORE '97	MALVIRÀ	49
ROERO SUPERIORE '98	FILIPPO GALLINO	48
SPUMANTE METODO CLASSICO BRUT RISERVA GIUSEPPE CONTRATTO '96	GIUSEPPE CONTRATTO	50

9

THE STARS

For the past three years, we have been flanking our Glass symbols with a new mark of distinction that indicates Italy's very finest producers – the Guide Star. It is awarded to all those wineries that have received a Three Glass rating at least ten times. We think the Star is an effective visual signal of a producer's reliability and quality over time. Angelo Gaja is our only Two Star producer, with the rest of this illustrious field some way behind. Ca' del Bosco and Elio Altare have 18 Three Glass awards and One Star each. At 16, after a spectacular surge this year, is La Spinetta, followed at 15 by La Spinetta and at 14 by three more great names, Castello di Fonterutoli, Fattoria di Felsina and Vinnaioli Jermann. Next is Paolo Scavino with 13 while Domenico Clerico and Marchesi Antinori move up to 12. Behind them are 11 wineries with 11 Three Glass ratings each, including Ruffino, Mario Schiopetto, Poliziano and Fontodi, then with 10 we find Castello Banfi, Edoardo Valentini, Isole e Olena, Livio Felluga, Roberto Voerzio, Tasca d'Almerita and Tenuta San Guido. A couple of remarks in conclusion. The first is that if we added together the Three Glass scores achieved by Antinori and Castello della Sala, the total would easily be enough to earn Two Stars. Our other observation is that there are a lot of producers who are very close to winning their first Star.

★ ★

27
GAJA (Piedmont)

★

18
CA' DEL BOSCO (Lombardy)
ELIO ALTARE (Piedmont)

16
LA SPINETTA (Piedmont)

15
ALLEGRINI (Veneto)

14
CASTELLO DI FONTERUTOLI
(Tuscany)
FATTORIA DI FELSINA (Tuscany)
VINNAIOLI JERMANN
(Friuli Venezia Giulia)

13
PAOLO SCAVINO (Piedmont)

12
DOMENICO CLERICO (Piedmont)
MARCHESI ANTINORI (Tuscany)

11
BELLAVISTA (Lombardy)
CASCINA LA BARBATELLA
(Piedmont)
CASTELLO DELLA SALA (Umbria)
FERRARI (Trentino)
GIROLAMO DORIGO
(Friuli Venezia Giulia)
MARIO SCHIOPETTO
(Friuli Venezia Giulia)
PODERI ALDO CONTERNO
(Piedmont)
POLIZIANO (Tuscany)
TENIMENTI RUFFINO (Tuscany)
TENUTA DI FONTODI (Tuscany)
VIE DI ROMANS (Friuli Venezia Giulia)

10
CASTELLO BANFI (Tuscany)
CASTELLO DI AMA (Tuscany)
EDOARDO VALENTINI (Abruzzo)
GIACOMO CONTERNO (Piedmont)
ISOLE E OLENA (Tuscany)
JOSKO GRAVNER
(Friuli Venezia Giulia)
LIVIO FELLUGA (Friuli Venezia Giulia)
ROBERTO VOERZIO (Piedmont)
TASCA D'ALMERITA (Sicily)
TENUTA SAN GUIDO (Tuscany)
VILLA RUSSIZ (Friuli Venezia Giulia)

A GUIDE TO VINTAGES, 1971-1998

	BARBARESCO	BRUNELLO DI MONTALCINO	BAROLO	CHIANTI CLASSICO	VINO NOBILE DI MONTEPULCIANO	AMARONE
1971	●●●●	●●●	●●●●●	●●●●●	●●●●	●●●●
1972	●	●	●	●●	●	●
1973	●●	●●●	●●	●●	●●●	●●
1974	●●●●	●●	●●●●	●●●	●●●	●●●●
1975	●●	●●●●●	●●	●●●●	●●●●	●●●
1976	●●	●	●●	●●	●●	●●●●
1977	●●	●●●●	●●	●●●●	●●●●	●●●
1978	●●●●●	●●●●	●●●●●	●●●●●	●●●●●	●●●
1979	●●●●	●●●●	●●●	●●●●	●●●●	●●●●
1980	●●●●	●●●●	●●●●	●●●●	●●	●●●
1981	●●●	●●●	●●●	●●●	●●●	●●●
1982	●●●●●	●●●●●	●●●●●	●●●●	●●●●	●
1983	●●●●	●●●●	●●●●	●●●●	●●●●	●●●●●
1984	●	●●	●●	●	●	●●
1985	●●●●●	●●●●●	●●●●●	●●●●●	●●●●●	●●●●
1986	●●●	●●●	●●●	●●●●	●●●●	●●●
1987	●●	●●	●●	●●	●●	●●
1988	●●●●●	●●●●●	●●●●●	●●●●●	●●●●●	●●●●●
1989	●●●●●	●●	●●●●●	●	●	●●
1990	●●●●●	●●●●●	●●●●●	●●●●●	●●●●●	●●●●●
1991	●●●	●●●	●●●	●●●	●●●	●●
1992	●●	●●	●●	●	●	●
1993	●●●	●●●●	●●●	●●●●	●●●●●	●●●●
1994	●●	●●●	●●	●●	●●	●●
1995	●●●●●	●●●●●	●●●●●	●●●●●	●●●●●	●●●●
1996	●●●●●	●●●	●●●●●	●●●	●●●	●●●
1997	●●●●●	●●●●●	●●●●●	●●●●●	●●●●●	●●●●●
1998	●●●●●	●●●●	●●●●●	●●●●	●●●●	●●●●

HOW TO USE THE GUIDE

KEY

○ WHITE WINES
● RED WINES
⊙ ROSÉ WINES

RATINGS

LISTING WITHOUT A GLASS SYMBOL:
A WELL MADE WINE
REPRESENTATIVE OF ITS CATEGORY

🍷
ABOVE AVERAGE TO GOOD IN ITS CATEGORY, EQUIVALENT TO 70-79/100

🍷🍷
VERY GOOD TO EXCELLENT IN ITS CATEGORY, EQUIVALENT TO 80-89/100

🍷🍷🍷
OUTSTANDING WINE IN ITS CATEGORY, EQUIVALENT TO 90-99/100

(, , 🍷🍷🍷) THE WHITE GLASSES REFER TO RATINGS GIVEN IN PREVIOUS EDITIONS OF THE GUIDE, AND WHICH ARE CONFIRMED WHERE THE WINES IN QUESTION ARE STILL DRINKING AT THE LEVEL FOR WHICH THE ORIGINAL AWARD WAS MADE

STAR ★

GIVEN TO ALL THOSE ESTATES WHICH HAVE WON AT LEAST TEN THREE GLASS AWARDS

GUIDE TO PRICES (1)

1 UP TO $ 8 AND UP TO £6
2 FROM $ 8 TO $ 12 AND FROM £ 6 TO £ 8
3 FROM $ 12 TO $ 18 AND FROM £ 8 TO £ 11
4 FROM $ 18 TO $ 27 AND FROM £ 11 TO £ 15
5 FROM $ 27 TO $ 40 AND FROM £ 15 TO £ 20
6 MORE THAN $ 40 AND MORE THAN £ 20
(1)Approx. retail prices in USA and UK

ASTERISK *

INDICATES ESPECIALLY GOOD VALUE FOR MONEY

NOTE

PRICES REFER TO RETAIL AVERAGES. INDICATIONS OF PRICES FOR OLDER VINTAGES INCLUDE APPRECIATION WHERE APPROPRIATE

ABBREVIATIONS

A.A.	Alto Adige
Cl.	Classico
C.S.	Cantina Sociale
Cant.	Cantina
Cast.	Castello
C. Am.	Colli Amerini
COF	Colli Orientali del Friuli
Cons.	Consorzio
Coop.Agr.	Cooperativa Agricola
DOC:	initials standing for Denominazione di Origine Controllata. The term refers to classic quality wines made in traditional wine-making areas where production is regulated by law.
DOCG:	initials standing for Denominazione di Origine Controllata e Garantita. Like DOC, but subject to more rigorous governmental controls. The wines are tasted before bottling, and numbered official seals are applied to each bottle.
M.	Metodo
M.to	Monferrato
O. P.	Oltrepò Pavese
P.R.	Peduncolo Rosso
P. d. V.	Prosecco di Valdobbiadene
Rif. Agr.	Riforma Agraria
Sel.	Selezione
Sup.	Superiore
T.	Terre
T.d.F.	Terre di Franciacorta
Ten.	Tenute
Tenim.	Tenimenti
V.	Vigna
Vign.	Vigneto
V. T.	Vendemmia Tardiva

VALLE D'AOSTA

For the second year running, the Valle d'Aosta can point to a Three Glass wine. The award-winning bottle and, particularly, the winery that produced it come as no surprise. We are talking here about one of Italy's very finest Chardonnays, made by Les Crêtes, unquestionably the best producer in the region and one of Italy's finest in absolute terms. The wine in question – fermented and aged in barrique for a good 12 months – reconfirms Costantino Charrère's adroitness in dealing with this variety and style. The '98 Chardonnay lacks a little bit of weight compared to the previous vintage but makes up for it handsomely in finesse and elegance. This white does credit to its excellent producer and to the Valle d'Aosta winemaking scene as a whole. This year, Les Crêtes also released two fine red wines that got through to the final taste-off for the Guide's top accolade. You really should try the '99 Coteau La Tour (100 percent syrah) and the '98 Fumin. Remaining in the zone around Aymavilles, we would draw your attention to Costantino Charrère's family winery, to the Lo Triolet estate, which also offers holiday accommodation, and to Renato Anselmet. Charrère confirms his instinct for making red wines, Lo Triolet makes the most of the experience gained over the last few years by presenting an excellent Pinot Grigio, and Anselmet proves that there is room in this region for the small producer who is prepared to put in the work. The region's smaller estates are in fact taking the initiative in an attempt to break the monopoly of the co-operative wineries that until now dominated the scene in this tiny region. The Associazione Piccoli Produttori Vini Valdostani "Viticulteur Encaveur" has been founded to bring together 20 producers, some of which are already reviewed in this Guide. Many make fewer than 10,000 bottles a year. Some produce wine to supply the restaurant they run alongside their winery, others because they have inherited a family tradition. Today, however, the small fry feel a need to band together, to be able to have an exchange of opinions about wine and to grow in terms of both quality and quantity. The estates that belong to this association have an emblem that they display at the entrance to each of their wineries. Amidst this flurry of initiatives that attest the spirit of change that is in the air, the Institut Agricole Régional at Aosta remains Valle d'Aosta's benchmark for quality. Here, study and research are carried out into new and better clones of the regional grape varieties and into increasingly avant-garde vinification techniques. The Regional Institute is also itself responsible for some very interesting wines. In particular, we would draw your attention to the barrique-aged selections which, unfortunately, are produced in strictly limited quantities. No more than two barriques of each type of wine are made, which is rather too little for them to become better known. If you get the chance, try the syrah-based Trésor du Caveau, a truly exceptional red. There is no real news from the co-operatives. As usual, it is La Crotta di Vegneron at Chambave which offers the best wines.

AOSTA

INSTITUT AGRICOLE RÉGIONAL
REG. LA ROCHERE, 1/A
11100 AOSTA
TEL. 0165/553304

Founded in 1982 with the aim of maintaining the high standards of Valle d'Aosta agricultural products, the Institut Agricole Régional, which is following in the footsteps of the Agricultural College set up 30 years earlier, has made a name for itself both in Italy and around the world for the quality of its wines. The new millennium begins in the best possible way. Many of the wines presented obtained Two Glass ratings, and the new label designs, which now show greater differentiation of the various selections, have been a success. There are two lines on offer: wines produced without any use of oak and in reasonably large quantities, and the experimental barrique-aged products, of which only a relatively small number of bottles are made. In the unoaked range, it is the whites that catch the eye. The Müller Thurgau is excellent. Elegant both in its aromatic bouquet and on the palate, it offers a long fruity finish. The Petite Arvine is also very sound. Very bright in colour, it proffers hints of pears and other ripe fruits on the nose and is reasonably fleshy on the palate. There is considerable finesse in its crisply acidulous finish. The Pinot Gris scores a shade lower. Even its deep golden colour displays notes of over-ripeness, which are abundantly evident in the intense bouquet. Its flavour is powerful rather than elegant and a faintly bitter tone detracts from the long finish. The reds made from pinot noir and petite rouge are pleasant. In contrast, we definitely preferred the reds in the wood-aged range. The Trésor du Caveau, one of the best Syrahs of the vintage, is as exceptional as ever and this year it is approached in quality by the Vin du Prévôt (50 percent cabernet sauvignon, 25 percent each of cabernet franc and merlot). The viognier-based Élite and the barrique-matured Chardonnay are both very good.

○	Élite '98	▼▼	4
●	Trésor du Caveau '98	▼▼	4
○	Vallée d'Aoste Müller Thurgau '99	▼▼	3*
○	Vallée d'Aoste Petite Arvine '99	▼▼	3*
●	Vin du Prévôt '98	▼▼	4
●	Rouge du Prieur '98	▼	4
●	Sang des Salasses '98	▼	4
○	Vallée d'Aoste Chardonnay Barrique '98	▼	4
○	Vallée d'Aoste Pinot Gris '99	▼	3
●	Vallée d'Aoste Petit Rouge '99		3
●	Vallée d'Aoste Pinot Noir '99		3
●	Trésor du Caveau '97	▽▽	4
●	Vin du Prévôt '97	▽▽	4

AYMAVILLES (AO)

COSTANTINO CHARRÈRE
FRAZ. DU MOULINS, 28
11010 AYMAVILLES (AO)
TEL. 0165/902135

From a pre-phylloxera vineyard that has not been grafted onto American rootstock, Costantino Charrère obtains the grapes for one of the Valle d'Aosta's most distinctive wines, the Vin de La Sabla. This is a red made from equal parts of petite rouge, fumin and barbera, plus ten percent of mayolet, a typical variety of the zone rediscovered by this extraordinary "vigneron". A wine of great character and personality, it is produced using cutting-edge systems in the vineyard, planted at 8,000 vines per hectare, while vinification is carried out using more traditional techniques, such as prolonged fermentation. Then there are the old vines, planted on sandy soil at an altitude of 600 metres above sea level where the sun shines from dawn until dusk. These very special plants offer Costantino the opportunity to produce this choice red wine, dedicated to his father Antoine. The '99 Vin Les Fourches is also excellent. In this case, it is grenache (70 percent) which accounts for the lion's share, while the rest of the blend is made up of various local varieties, such as gros rouge, vien de nus and dolcetto. The wine is an almost opaque purple in appearance, with exuberant scents of super-ripe red berry fruits, spices and vanilla. The overall impression is of finesse and complexity. On the palate, the fruit is seriously potent and so generous you can practically chew it. The Torrette is good (70 percent petit rouge, plus mayolet, tinturier and cornalin making up the other 30 percent) and the Prëmetta is very distinctive. In a sense, this is the flagship wine of the estate, which has always tried to champion traditional grape varieties. Prëmetta, in fact, has been cultivated in the Valle d'Aosta since time immemorial and Costantino intends to show it to its best advantage.

●	Vallée d'Aoste Torrette '99	▼▼	4
●	Vin de La Sabla '99	▼▼	4
●	Vin Les Fourches '99	▼▼	4
●	Vallée d'Aoste Prëmetta '99	▼	4
●	Vin de La Sabla '98	▽▽	4
●	Vin Les Fourches '98	▽▽	4
●	Vallée d'Aoste Prëmetta '98	▽	4
●	Vallée d'Aoste Torrette '98	▽	3

AYMAVILLES (AO)

LES CRÊTES
LOC. VILLETOS, 50
11010 AYMAVILLES (AO)
TEL. 0165/902274

Les Crêtes has seven different wines, all of them of excellent quality, and at least three of them can compete with the very best that Italy has to offer. This year, we again gave our preference to the Chardonnay Cuvée Bois, a white that has acquired legendary status. This wine, which is increasingly reminiscent of the great wines of Burgundy both in terms of style and quality, more than merits our Three Glass accolade. If the '97 impressed us with the almost overwhelming richness of its body, this version of Costantino Charrère's Chardonnay excited us with its elegance and finesse. It is vinified in barrique using "bâtonnage", or stirring, to keep the fine lees, on which it spends a considerable period of time, in suspension. The resulting wine has a brilliant golden straw-yellow colour and a complex bouquet of musk, honey and toasted oak. The vigorous, buttery flavour is wonderfully sustained and long, and the fruit is soft and elegant. The second wine is an excellent '98 Fumin, with spices and pepper on the nose, and rich, velvety tannins on the palate which guarantee outstanding ageing potential. The Coteau La Tour (100 percent syrah) is equally outstanding. It is made from grapes grown in one of the Valle d'Aosta's most stunningly beautiful vineyards, which also gives its name to the wine. The purplish colour is almost impenetrable and the fragrances of blackberries and bilberries give way to subtle gamey scents. On the palate, it still tastes a little too young, even if the texture of its tannins and its structure are very impressive. The estate's other two whites, the unusual and appealing Petite Arvine and the well-balanced, full-flavoured Chardonnay, are very creditable. A Torrette and a Pinot Noir complete the range. Our congratulations to Costantino and his staff!

CHAMBAVE (AO)

LA CROTTA DI VEGNERON
P.ZZA RONCAS, 2
11023 CHAMBAVE (AO)
TEL. 0166/46670

Chambave has a vine-growing tradition that dates as far back as the 13th century, as is testified by a bequest to the parish at that time. But reliable historical data go back to 1494 and Charles Passerin d'Entreves, who reports that Charles VIII, King of France, and George de Challant visited this area, tasting the Clairet and the Passito di Chambave. The famous Moscato Passito is still made at Chambave even today and La Crotta di Vegneron is its best producer. The selection we tasted this year – the '98 – is , as usual, very good indeed, and can hold its own against many of Italy's finest dessert wines. It has a lustrous, intense golden colour, introducing a nose that unfurls elegant raisiny sensations while also offering the aromatic notes that are typical of moscato. It is oily, very potent and well-balanced on the palate, with a wonderfully discreet touch of sweetness. Also on top form is the Nus Malvoisie Flétri, another wine made from partially dried grapes from the lower valley and the pride of the little village of Nus. After drying, its pinot grigio grapes give a bright golden wine with perfumes of plump raisins, incense and wax and the palate is rich and long. Best of the dry white wines is the Nus Malvoisie whereas the standard Müller Thurgau earns no more than a Guide listing. The Fumin, an indigenous red which could have an important future in the viticulture of the Valle d'Aosta, is excellent. This particular version is aged in barrique and has a purplish colour. The nose offers intense aromas that give way to the notes of game, pepper and black berry fruits that are typical of the variety. The palate has great structure and plenty of tannins but has yet to knit. The Chambave Rouge and the Nus Rouge are both worthy of an honourable mention in the Guide.

O	Vallée d'Aoste Chardonnay Cuvée		
	Frissonière Les Crêtes Cuvée Bois '98	🍷🍷🍷	5
●	Coteau La Tour '99	🍷🍷	5
O	Vallée d'Aoste Chardonnay		
	Cuvée Frissonière Les Crêtes '99	🍷🍷	4
●	Vallée d'Aoste Fumin		
	Vigne La Tour '98	🍷🍷	4
O	Vallée d'Aoste Petite Arvine		
	Vigne Champorette '99	🍷🍷	4
●	Vallée d'Aoste Torrette		
	Vigne Les Toules '99	🍷🍷	4
●	Vallée d'Aoste Pinot Noir		
	Vigne La Tour '99	🍷	4
O	Vallée d'Aoste Chardonnay Cuvée		
	Frissonière Les Crêtes Cuvée Bois '97	🍷🍷🍷	5

O	Vallée d'Aoste Chambave		
	Moscato Passito '98	🍷🍷	5
●	Vallée d'Aoste Fumin '98	🍷🍷	4
O	Vallée d'Aoste Nus		
	Malvoisie Flétrì '98	🍷🍷	4
O	Vallée d'Aoste Chambave		
	Muscat '99	🍷	3
O	Vallée d'Aoste Nus Malvoisie '98	🍷	3
●	Vallée d'Aoste Chambave		
	Rouge '99		3
O	Vallée d'Aoste Müller Thurgau '99		3
●	Vallée d'Aoste Nus Rouge '99		3
O	Vallée d'Aoste Chambave		
	Moscato Passito '97	🍷🍷	5
●	Vallée d'Aoste Fumin '97	🍷	3

INTROD (AO)

MORGEX (AO)

LO TRIOLET - EMILIA MILLET
FRAZ. JUNOD, 4
11010 INTROD (AO)
TEL. 0165/95067 - 0165/95437

CAVE DU VIN BLANC DE MORGEX
ET DE LA SALLE
CHEMIN DES ILES, 19
FRAZ. LA RUINE
11017 MORGEX (AO)
TEL. 0165/800331

The estate of Emilia Millet and her son Marco Martin, an agronomist who works for the regional authority, has changed its official title. The owner's name has joined that of the residential facility that the family has opened in the same building as the small winery, Lo Triolet. This attractive estate with tourist accommodation lies outside the built-up area of Introd, on the road that leads to Cogne, at an altitude of 700–800 metres above sea level. There are two apartments and a garden to relax in, perhaps while sipping a glass of Pinot Grigio. It is at these altitudes that Marco Martin cultivates half a hectare of vineyard, split into two plots (one lower down and the other at around 900 metres). The two parcels are planted with pinot grigio, a variety that offers good yields even when grown well above sea level. The wine presented this year is impressive and earns our Two Glass distinction. We are talking about a Pinot Grigio that will get even better with time, when a little bottle-age will have softened some of the harsh acidic edges still present at the moment. On the nose, varietal aromas dominate the fruity notes while the fleshy, rounded attack of the fruit on the palate gives the wine considerable personality. The finish is reasonably long. Marco Martin, not content with the 3,000 bottles he produces at present, is already thinking ahead to the future. Part of the Pinot Grigio he makes now will spend some time in wood while a small plot he has bought at the bottom of the valley will enable him to produce a red from fumin grapes.

At the beginning of the 80s, the growers at Morgex and La Salle joined together to create the Cave du Vin Blanc, with the intention of keeping alive the viticultural tradition of a mountainous zone where the rigid climate and altitude would seem to militate against viticulture. This means that we have not lost one of Italy's most individual wines and at the same time, one of the country's most beautiful and uncontaminated areas has been saved from rampant building development. In fact, the blanc de Morgex vineyards in the final part of the Valle d'Aosta, where the majestic Valdigne begins and from where the magnificent spectacle of the Mont Blanc massif is visible. Here, at almost 1,300 metres above sea level, around 100 farmers continue to cultivate vines in tiny allotments rarely even one hectare in area. The modern vinification plant is located on the main Aosta-Courmayeur road, at the junction where the "autostrada" begins. At the plant, which is surrounded by a pretty flower-filled garden, there is also a cellar door sales outlet and a restaurant. Five wines are produced in all but only two are DOC products. The Blanc de Morgex e de La Salle charms with its attractively inviting style and is made particularly refreshing by an acidulous note that lingers on the finish. The Brut Metodo Classico, made from the same variety, has a straw colour and a perlage of medium-sized but persistent bubbles. The palate is soft on entry and is noteworthy for its restrained carbon dioxide. The finish, however, is a little bit rustic.

○ Vallée d'Aoste Pinot Gris Lo Triolet '99	▼▼ 3*

○ Vallée d'Aoste Blanc de Morgex et de La Salle '99	▼ 3
○ Vallée d'Aoste Blanc de Morgex et de La Salle Metodo Classico '96	▼ 5

QUART (AO)

VILLENEUVE (AO)

F.LLI GROSJEAN
FRAZ. OLLIGNAN, 1
11020 QUART (AO)
TEL. 0165/765283

RENATO ANSELMET
FRAZ. LA CRÊTE, 46
11018 VILLENEUVE (AO)
TEL. 0165/95217

The Grosjean brothers, Vincenzo, Piergiorgio, Marco, Fernando and Eraldo, earned a full Guide profile for the second time, after last year's debut, with some absolutely excellent wines. The estate, inherited from their still active father Delfino, is at Quart on the outskirts of Aosta, at an altitude that varies between 500 and 650 metres above sea level. From six hectares of family-owned vineyards, plus some grapes purchased from other growers in the zone, the Grosjeans make around 45,000 bottles a year, split into six different types of wine. Of the wines we tasted this year, two obtained Two Glass ratings and another came very close. Again, the Fumin is the cellar's most interesting product and goes to show that this variety is a heritage that the growers of the Valle d'Aosta cannot afford to lose. The Grosjean version is an oak-aged red whose nose is dominated by gamey scents and hints of leather and spices. On the very long finish, there emerge notes of redcurrants and blackberries. It is rich and powerful on the palate, with loads of personality and character. The barrique-aged Pinot Nero is also rather successful. A deep, vibrant ruby in colour, it displays a bouquet characterized by a nice touch of oak melding with the underlying spicy, smoky and fruity notes. The palate is rich and complex but it is still trying to find the balance of tannins and acidity that would give it real complexity. One Glass goes to the easy-drinking, well-balanced Torrette while the Gamay gets an honourable mention. The Petite Arvine, the Grosjean brothers' well-structured white, is good. Fruity on the nose, broad and rich on the palate, it has an attractively zesty, well-balanced flavour.

The wines produced by Renato Anselmet this year are very good and some of them had no trouble in scoring Two Glass ratings. This small estate is run by Renato with the assistance of his son, Giorgio, who works at the Cooperativa Onze Communes. The Anselmets have little over a hectare and a half of vines on the well-exposed slopes lying between the communes of Saint-Pierre and Villeneuve. Apart from his own grapes, Renato buys some fruit from trusted suppliers to bring annual production to around 12,000 bottles, divided up between the wines typical of this part of the Valle d'Aosta. The barrique-aged Chardonnay is among the best of the year from the entire region. A straw-yellow shading into gold in colour, it offers intense, elegant perfumes in which oak-derived toastiness is kept under control, and where hints of vanilla, spices and tropical fruits emerge. The entry on the palate is butter-rich, and has good depth, but the fruit has not yet found an ideal point of equilibrium with the oak. It is still a young wine but will probably improve with age. The other Anselmet whites include an appealing Chardonnay vinified in stainless steel and a very few bottles – only 300 – of an excellent dessert wine called Declivium, produced from pinot grigio grapes left to dry on the vine and harvested in late autumn. It has a bright golden colour that leads in to citrus fruit aromas nicely backed up by toasty oak. The palate reveals a good balance of sweetness and acidity. Renato also produces three reds. His two Torrettes both earned One Glass ratings, although we preferred the barrique-aged one by a whisker, while the Pinot Noir, also cask-conditioned, is still a little short on balance, although it has impressive structure.

● Vallée d'Aoste Fumin '98	🍷🍷	4
● Vallée d'Aoste Pinot Noir Élevé en Barrique '98	🍷🍷	4
○ Vallée d'Aoste Petite Arvine '99	🍷	3
● Vallée d'Aoste Torrette '99	🍷	3
● Vallée d'Aoste Gamay '99		3
● Vallée d'Aoste Fumin '97	🍷🍷	4

○ Declivium '99	🍷🍷	6
○ Vallée d'Aoste Chardonnay Élevé en Fût de Chêne '99	🍷🍷	4
● Vallée d'Aoste Pinot Noir Élevé en Fût de Chêne '99	🍷	4
○ Vallée d'Aoste Chardonnay '99	🍷	3
● Vallée d'Aoste Torrette '99	🍷	3
● Vallée d'Aoste Torrette Sup. Élevé en Fût de Chêne '99	🍷	4
○ Vallée d'Aoste Chardonnay Élevé en Fût de Chêne '98	🍷🍷	4

OTHER WINERIES

The following producers obtained good scores in our tastings with one or more of their wines:

PROVINCE OF AOSTA

Dino Bonin, Arnad, tel. 0125/966067
Vallée d'Aoste Arnad-Montjovet Sup. '98

Cooperativa La Kiuva,
Arnad, tel. 0125/966351
Vallée d'Aoste Arnad-Montjovet '99,
Vallée d'Aoste Petite Arvine '99

Cooperativa Caves des Onze Communes,
Aymavilles, tel. 0165/902912
Vallée d'Aoste Torrette Sup. '98,
Vallée d'Aoste Müller Thurgau '99

Ezio Voyat,
Chambave, tel. 0166/46139
La Gazzella Moscato '98,
Vino Passito Le Muraglie

Caves Cooperatives de Donnas,
Donnas, tel. 0125/82096
Vallée d'Aoste Donnas Barrique '97,
Vallée d'Aoste Donnas '97

Diego Curtaz,
Gressan, tel. 0165/251079
Vallée d'Aoste Torrette '99

Maison Albert Vevey,
Morgex, tel. 0165/808930
Vallée d'Aoste Blanc de Morgex
et de La Salle '99

PIEDMONT

After last year's dazzling performance when 50 vintages obtained the Three Glass grading, Piedmont comes back in grand style to sweep the board with a record 64 top awards. Or rather, 64 Three Glasses and a whole slew of others jostling to be included in the honours list. This reconfirms Piedmont as the top region in Italy, the selection of very high quality bottles appearing even more impressive when you consider the wide range of wine types embraced. Long gone are the years when only the Barolos and the Barbarescos had any hope of taking on the world's best wines. Today, varieties once considered less noble, notably barbera, have scaled dizzying heights in terms of quality. Along with moscato, barbera is the most widely planted variety in the region and has become an extremely important resource for Piedmont, producing magnificent wines when cultivated with care. But dolcetto, cortese and other "foreign" varieties that contribute to Piedmont blends also give first-class results. And that's not all. The vintages we tasted are among the best of the last few decades. Never before have we seen four such magnificent years. The Barolo reaches its zenith with the '96, an exceptional year which produced powerful, austere wines. The Barbaresco '97 took full advantage of an historic vintage that have given us mature, eminently drinkable wines brimming with fruit. The '98 Barbera, although rarely matching the quality of the previous vintage, possesses a deeply satisfying palate that is alcohol-rich, at times rather rugged and on occasion over-ripe but always interesting. Dolcetto has rarely had such a high alcohol content as in '99 but more experienced cellarmasters exercised their skills to the utmost to keep the vinification process under control. Among the region's winemakers, Giorgio Rivetti and his family once more stood out from the rest and this year took home to La Spinetta the remarkable total of four Three Glass ratings. This outstanding achievement has won La Spinetta the Cellar of the Year award as the top-scoring winery. This year, the Rivettis will include Barolo in their range of wines after the purchase of an additional six hectares at Grinzane Cavour in June 2000. The Barbaresco estates have also enjoyed excellent results and Bruno Giacosa has come back to carry off Three Glasses. And the cortese grape has zoomed up the charts to net Three Glass awards. We were privileged to taste two exceptional whites in the Gavi Monte Rotondo from Villa Sparina and Martinetti's Minaia, even if a technicality in the regulations, which do not permit oak-ageing, meant that the Martinetti were unable to register the latter as a DOCG wine. For the first time, the Colli Tortonesi won a Three Glass award for Bigolla, a superb Barbera from Walter Massa. As well as bringing credit to Massa's cellar – a steadily rising star over the last few years – the rating is final proof of the renaissance of the entire province of Alessandria. Remember that until a short time ago, Alessandria was struggling to produce even the odd Two Glass wine. Finally, we are particularly delighted to see the return of the Bricco dell'Uccellone, the Barbera d'Asti created in 1982 by the great Giacomo Bologna.

AGLIANO TERME (AT)

Dacapo
S.da Asti Mare, 4
14041 Agliano Terme (AT)
tel. 0141/964921

What's in a name? In this case, the whole story. With the experience gleaned over a lifetime spent working in the major Asti wineries, Paolo Dania and Dino Riccomagno have started from scratch, "da capo", this time on their own. They have set themselves up in Agliano Terme, heart of one of the finest Barbera-producing areas, where they bought a farm with a vineyard, rolled up their sleeves, and set to work. They renewed the existing vine stock, comprising approximately one and a half hectares of barbera, and planted an additional half a hectare of merlot. Already up and running for the harvest of 2000, the Dacapo winery is a modern outfit that blends in with the local environment. One of the old brick and stone farm buildings has been converted into an attractive barrique cellar. And this is only the beginning for Dania and Riccomagno. Next year, they will have the grapes from three hectares of barbera and ruché vines in Castagnole Monferrato. For the time being, they have released two '98 Barbera d'Astis. Sanbastiàn, a lustrous, medium-intensity ruby in colour, has an attractive, if not overly complex, nose of strawberry laced with spices. The palate is interesting and well-balanced, with decent body, making it a good all-round food wine. The Barbera d'Asti Vigna Dacapo is the jewel in the Dacapo crown. Thanks to barrique ageing, it is a much more impressive, challenging wine. Dense, almost opaque, ruby with violet highlights, it unfolds well-defined cherry aromas with spicy, smoky nuances that enhance its complexity. The palate is harmonious and full of character, with a good fruity finish.

● Barbera d'Asti Vigna Dacapo '98	🍷🍷	5
● Barbera d'Asti Sanbastiàn '98	🍷	3

AGLIANO TERME (AT)

Roberto Ferraris
Via Dogliani, 33
14041 Agliano Terme (AT)
tel. 0141/954234

Roberto Ferraris runs this estate of approximately six hectares of vineyards, all in Agliano, with his parents, Achille and Bruna Molinari. Every year, 90 percent of the 20,000 bottles they produce go for export, including three Barberas and less than 1,000 bottles of Grignolino. Giuliano Noe is their technical consultant. The Ferraris' Barbera Nobbio, featured in the Guide for the first time last year, promises to be excellent this year, too. It is vinified and aged entirely in stainless steel with the deliberate intention of highlighting the strong personality of the fruit from this vineyard. Deep ruby with garnet highlights, it reveals a generous array of aromas. This is all the more impressive when you consider that it is not cask-conditioned and that barbera usually has a fairly compact range of aromas. The fruity notes are clear and sharp while hints of cocoa and mint combine to produce a satisfying overall complexity. Entry on the palate is succulent, opening out to reveal the variety's sinewy character, and there is a long, invigorating finish that deliciously echoes the palate's attractive fruit. The Barbera la Cricca is a new barrique-aged selection, first produced in 1997 to flank the estate's Nobbio label. Its ruby colour shades into quite a deep garnet and the nose is strongly redolent of the variety's trademark fruit but is slightly compromised by poorly defined notes of oak. In contrast, the solid weight and convincing follow through on the palate are well-defined, to be rounded off by an attractive, lingering finish with a slightly bitterish note.

● Barbera d'Asti Sup. Nobbio '98	🍷🍷	3*
● Barbera d'Asti La Cricca '97	🍷	4
● Barbera d'Asti Nobbio '97	🍸🍸	3

AGLIANO TERME (AT)

AGLIANO TERME (AT)

AGOSTINO PAVIA E FIGLI
FRAZ. BOLOGNA, 33
14041 AGLIANO TERME (AT)
TEL. 0141/954125

TENUTA GARETTO
S.DA ASTI MARE, 30
14041 AGLIANO TERME (AT)
TEL. 0141/954068

This is an area to keep an eye on. Among the small producers that work side by side with the big names, both locals and outsiders who moved into the Langhe some time ago, we find Agostino Pavia and his sons, Giuseppe and Mauro. In step with the overall improvements seen in Barbera d'Asti, the Pavias have taken great strides on the quality front. From their seven hectares under vine, mostly barbera, they produce 45,000 bottles of good quality, reasonably priced wines. The three Barberas they release each year differ in terms of vineyard location, vinification and ageing technique employed. This year, the Pavias can offer some interesting '98 vintages. The Marescialla is a cut above the others. It's a Barbera Superiore that was aged in barriques for one year and possesses clear notes of red fruit combined with toasty hints of coffee. The entry on the palate is thoroughly satisfying, whose already good breadth, body and length will only improve with cellaring. The Barbera d'Asti Moliss, aged in barrels and then 500-litre casks, boasts warm fruity aromas and appreciable structure on the palate but has a certain lack of polish in the finish. However, the Pavia Blina, vinified and aged entirely in stainless steel, is a fine example of just what this area can produce. From its brilliant colour to its fresh cherry nose, this is an agreeable, no-nonsense wine. Rounding off the Pavias' selection is the Grignolino d'Asti '99, with its nose of roses and white pepper. Despite a slightly tart palate, it has a satisfying enough finish.

The young Alessandro Garetto has only recently taken over this 13-hectare property. He plans to expand the estate by three hectares, which are currently being replanted. Garetto's philosophy is based solidly on quality and his success is witnessed by the excellence of his wines, the product of the relatively low estate yield of approximately 50 quintals per hectare. He also plays an active role in the local Associazione Vigne del Nizza that unites 12 producers from the Monferrato area under the common banner of promoting this zone to its best advantage. The propitious '98 harvest enabled Alessandro to create Favà, a truly great Barbera d'Asti. Ruby red with intense violet highlights, it tempts the nose with heady fragrances of fruit and spice enriched by the vanilla aromas of its 13-month sojourn in new wood. The gentle tannins are buttressed by typical Barbera acidity while the finish lingers. The robust 14.5-degree alcohol content is sustained by a more than adequate structure. One step down from Favà we have Garetto's other two Barberas. Of the two, we preferred Tra Neuit e Dì, aged partly in stainless steel and partly in wood. It is pleasant, if lacking in body. In Pectore, aged in large casks and barriques, lost points for a certain lack of definition on the nose. Finally, we sampled the varietal Chardonnay Diversamente, which strikes a nice balance between notes of fruit and oak-derived vanilla.

● Barbera d'Asti		
La Marescialla '98	▼▼	4
● Barbera d'Asti Bricco Blina '98	▼	3
● Barbera d'Asti Moliss '98	▼	3
● Grignolino d'Asti '99	▼	3
● Barbera d'Asti		
La Marescialla '96	▽▽	4
● Barbera d'Asti Bricco Blina '97	▽	3
● Barbera d'Asti Moliss '97	▽	3
● Barbera d'Asti		
La Marescialla '97	▽	4

● Barbera d'Asti Sup. Favà '98	▼▼	4
● Barbera d'Asti Sup. In Pectore '98	▼	4
● Barbera d'Asti Tra Neuit e Dì '98	▼	3
○ Piemonte Chardonnay		
Diversamente '99	▼	4
● Barbera d'Asti Sup. Favà '97	▽▽	4
● Barbera d'Asti Sup. In Pectore '97	▽▽	3
● Barbera d'Asti Tra Neuit e Dì '97	▽	3

AGLIÈ (TO)

CIECK
S.DA BARDESONO
FRAZ. S. GRATO
10011 AGLIÈ(TO)
TEL. 0124/32225 - 0124/330522

ALBA (CN)

SILVANO E ELENA BOROLI
LOC. MADONNA DI COMO, 34
12051 ALBA (CN)
TEL. 0173/35865

The Cieck estate became a commercial venture some 15 years ago when Remo Falconieri and Lodovico Bardesono renovated the old family farmhouse that nestles among the foothills of the Canavese DOC zone. They were joined by Domenico Caretto in 1999. The property has approximately 15 hectares planted to vine, not all of which are currently producing, and straddles the municipalities of Agliè, Cuceglio and San Giorgio. The three partners concentrate their efforts on developing the considerable potential of the local varieties, in particular erbaluce, from which they obtain four labels, Erbaluce Vigna Misobolo, Calliope (aged in barriques), San Giorgio Spumante Brut (Metodo Classico) and Passito Alladium. The Passito is a wine with a very special vinification process. After raisining, which takes place from harvest time to early March in well-aired attics, comes the "schiccatura", a process whereby each berry is individually selected and plucked from the stem by hand. This has become a bit of a tradition on the estate and sees everyone gathered together in the large courtyard in front of the farmhouse, usually at the beginning of March. Cieck's '95 Passito has a lovely rich golden colour and a nose redolent of raisins and caramel. The palate is full and rich, backed up by a crisp acidity that blends smoothly into its sweetness. We also liked the Erbaluce Calliope. Aged in barriques, it has a complex nose and a succulent palate underpinned by good solid character. The '95 Spumante Brut is excellent while the San Giorgio has a more delicate style. However, the Erbaluce Vigna, while full-bodied and agreeable on the palate, disappoints in the finish, which tends to peter out. Best of the reds were the Canavese Rosso Cieck and the Neretto di San Giorgio, a monovarietal Canavese DOC wine that since the 1999 vintage has been aged in barriques.

A big name in the Italian publishing world, the Boroli family has decided to branch out into the wine business. In 1998, they bought two farms in the Langhe, the Cascina Bompé at Madonna di Como near Alba, and the Cascina Brunella in Castiglione Falletto, in the Villero subzone. Although the properties were already planted to vine, the Borolis have done a lot of work. They have extended the vineyards, increased the number of varieties, and renovated the old cellars to the best modern standards. Enzo Alluvione, an oenologist of many years' standing, runs the technical side of things with the Borolis' son, Daniele. These two are ably supported by consultants Curtaz, Romana and Caviola. Cascina Bompé's 11.5 hectares yield mainly moscato and dolcetto, the traditional varieties of the area, with a little barbera and about three hectares of cabernet sauvignon and merlot that are soon to go into production. Cascina Brunella has six hectares of nebbiolo and two of chardonnay. In these, the winery's teething years, the Borolis have limited themselves to bottling their best selections, but they anticipate that they will eventually top 100,000 bottles. This year they offered us an excellent Moscato d'Asti, which enchanted with its aromas of ripe peach and apple, and a buttery richness that gives it length and balance. We found the Dolcetto d'Alba and the Barolo to be just as good. The Dolcetto astonishes with its sweet nose and full body, and the Barolo with its complex range of aromas and its aristocratically austere palate. Also good, albeit with a little room for improvement, are the Borolis' Barbera, Langhe Nebbiolo, and the chardonnay-based Langhe Bianco.

O Caluso Passito Alladium Vigneto Runc '95	♟♟	6
O Erbaluce di Caluso Calliope '98	♟♟	4
O Erbaluce di Caluso Spumante Brut S. Giorgio '95	♟♟	5
● Canavese Rosso Cieck '98	♟	4
O Erbaluce di Caluso Spumante Brut S. Giorgio	♟	5
O Erbaluce di Caluso Vigna Misobolo '99	♟	3
● Canavese Rosso Neretto di S. Giorgio '98		4
O Erbaluce di Caluso Calliope '97	♟♟	4
O Caluso Passito Alladium Vigneto Runc '94	♟	6

● Barolo La Brunella '96	♟♟	6
● Dolcetto d'Alba Madonna di Como '99	♟♟	4
O Moscato d'Asti Aureum '99	♟♟	4
● Barbera d'Alba Bricco Quattro Fratelli '98	♟	4
O Langhe Bianco Bel Amì '99	♟	4
● Langhe Nebbiolo Terranìn '98	♟	5

ALBA (CN)

CERETTO
LOC. S. CASSIANO, 34
12051 ALBA (CN)
TEL. 0173/282582

Of all the jewels in the Ceretto family's crown, which include the Bricco Roche and Bricco Asili estates, none shines brighter than La Bernardina, birthplace of the Cerettos' most innovative wines as well as their classic Dolcetto. We shall start with the Blangé, a white much favoured by younger wine drinkers. Obtained from 31 hectares planted to arneis in the municipalities of Vezza and Castellinaldo, this is a good quality wine. The '99 vintage stands out for its perky aromas of hawthorn and iris, as well as fresh, reasonably long notes of pear and apple. From the vineyards of Sinio and Albaretto Torre at an altitude of 600 metres above sea level comes Arbarei, obtained from riesling renano. The '98 vintage is a lovely golden straw-yellow colour, releasing aromas of flowers and toasted hazelnuts. The entry on the palate reveals a strong acid vein and its fruity overtones hint at apricot and peach. From La Bernardina, we tasted the Cerettos' Brut Metodo Classico '95, made from chardonnay and pinot nero grapes. After a delicate bouquet of spring flowers, the palate is well-structured and lively, with luscious, pleasantly aroma-rich fruit. The new Monsordo '97 selection is obtained from a blend of all the major red varieties cultivated at La Bernardina and the Cerettos are releasing it for the first time this year. The deep warm colour ushers in the trademark red pepper notes of cabernet sauvignon and the aromas of merlot, here blended with nebbiolo and pinot nero, which are joined by hints of raspberry and mulberry. On the palate, stewed fruit, toasty oak and coffee come through and the texture is very attractive. The offerings from the Rossana estate are not quite so good this year. The panel were unconvinced by the nose of the Barbera d'Alba Piana '98 and felt that the Nebbiolo d'Alba Lantasco '98, with its only moderate structure, lacked balance. The Dolcetto d'Alba '99 has a vibrant colour and good, fresh fruit.

○	La Bernardina Brut '95	🍷🍷	6
○	Langhe Arbarei '98	🍷🍷	5
●	Langhe Rosso Monsordo La Bernardina '97	🍷🍷	6
●	Barbera d'Alba Piana '98	🍷	5
●	Dolcetto d'Alba Rossana '99	🍷	4
○	Langhe Arneis Blangé '99	🍷	4
●	Nebbiolo d'Alba Lantasco '98	🍷	5
○	La Bernardina Brut '94	YY	6
●	Langhe Cabernet La Bernardina '95	YY	6
●	Langhe Cabernet La Bernardina '96	YY	6

ALBA (CN)

GIANLUIGI LANO
S.DA BASSO, 38
FRAZ. S. ROCCO SENO D'ELVIO
12051 ALBA (CN)
TEL. 0173/286958

Gianluigi Lano and his wife Daniela Marcarino have planted their seven and a half hectares of Guyot-trained vines with grass between the rows. They produce about 23,000 bottles a year and this number is set to increase when they plant 4,000 barbera vines at Altavilla. Gianluigi, who is advised by Gianfranco Cordero, offered us an exciting selection of wines this year, including a truly excellent Barbera Fondo Prà and an equally good Barbaresco. The quality of the Barbera is immediately apparent from the rich colour. An elegant wine with impressive breadth on the nose, its range of fruit encompasses ripe redcurrant and bilberry combined with balsamic hints of mint and juniper and subtle earthy nuances. The texture on the palate is rich and firm, generously sustained by the tannins. An attractive note of liquorice comes through in the long lingering finish. Ruby tending to garnet in the glass, the Barbaresco has a refined nose that hints at mulberry, raspberry, leather and brine. Its concentrated palate displays a wealth of fine tannins that round out the lasting liquorice and leaf finish. We awarded two glasses to the Dolcetto Ronchella for its solid colour and rich nose that releases notes of strawberry and raspberry over complex undertones of autumn leaves, cream and mint. The body and length are compromised somewhat by a barely discernible bitterness in the finish. We also liked the Dolcetto and the estate's second-label Barbera. The former has a nice range of flowery, fruity and balsamic aromas and a satisfyingly broad palate that smacks of sweet almonds. In contrast, the Barbera's nose embraces notes of cherries to cocoa and green leaves, which lead into a vigorous, robust palate.

●	Barbaresco '97	🍷🍷	5
●	Barbera d'Alba '98	🍷🍷	3*
●	Barbera d'Alba Fondo Prà '98	🍷🍷	4
●	Dolcetto d'Alba Ronchella '99	🍷🍷	3*
●	Dolcetto d'Alba '99	🍷	2*
●	Barbera d'Alba Fondo Prà '97	YY	4
●	Dolcetto d'Alba Ronchella '98	YY	3
●	Barbaresco '96	Y	4
●	Barbera d'Alba Fondo Prà '96	Y	4

ALBA (CN)

ALBA (CN)

PIO CESARE
VIA CESARE BALBO, 6
12051 ALBA (CN)
TEL. 0173/440386

PODERI COLLA
FRAZ. S. ROCCO SENO D'ELVIO, 82
12051 ALBA (CN)
TEL. 0173/290148

The range of wines made by Pio Cesare is very extensive. The panel began with the Barolo Ornato, which impressed with its admirable structure backed up by a firm structure of sweet tannins. Aromas of stewed cherries and liquorice emerge strongly in the broad range of aromas while there is satisfying length and an abundance of ripe fruit on the palate. The Barolo '96 flaunts a fine range of heady aromas that lead into an fruit so luscious it is almost sweet. Moderate acidity and understated tannins round off the palate. A cut above the preceding products we have the Barbaresco Il Bricco '96, which regales the nose with sumptuous notes of plum preserve. Its wonderfully intense, rich nose ushers in floral notes on a palate redolent of rose, raspberry and peach. The tannins are just right and add verve to an already vigorous body. The Pio Cesare Barbaresco '97 brings together all the best qualities of the vintage and his Barbera d'Alba Fides '97 is a fascinating wine, from its complex nose to its lingering notes of marinated fruit. On the palate, its exuberant acidity is mellowed by sweet fruit and warm alcohol. Cellaring will further enhance its appeal and, in our opinion, will make it the best wine of the year from the estate. The pleasant, alcohol-rich Langhe Il Nebbio '99 has overtones of dried mulberries and redcurrant syrup. We liked the Dolcetto d'Alba's rich, lustrous violet colour and its fresh, concentrated and attractively integrated hints of roses. The front palate is full-bodied and warm while its dry follow-through is attractively veined with sweet notes. The estate's two Chardonnays are also good. The PiodiLei '98 hints at camomile and macaroons on the palate and the Altro '99 is crisp and tangy. Finally, the Nebbiolo d'Alba '98 and the Barbera d'Alba '98 serve to confirm the quality of the wines this estate produces.

The Colla family winery, in San Rocco Seno d'Elvio, has a truly comprehensive range of products. Their wines are of good quality, made in the Langhe tradition, and include the satisfying Barolo Dardi Le Rose '96, a wine with a well-developed mineral nose and austere palate. Ruby red with garnet highlights, paling a little at the rim, it has a slightly rustic nose that is not lacking in character. The aromas of red berry jam are enhanced by hints of mint over a backdrop of damp earth. The palate has good structure but follows through a touch austerely because of the prominent tannins, which tend to make the otherwise attractive and long finish a little dry. The Collas' Barbaresco Tenuta Roncaglia '97 has a lovely rich colour and aromas that suggest liqueur cherries and cocoa over pot pourri. Well-balanced on the palate, it offers convincing thrust, opening out into a consistent, reasonably long finish. The Langhe Bianco Sanrocco, obtained from pinot nero, chardonnay and riesling, is a rich straw-yellow. The distinctive nose hints at plums, apricots, wild flowers and roasted hazelnuts while the substantial palate flows through seamlessly to a finish that may lack a little length but echoes the nose and has good balance. The moscato-based Bonmé has a restrained bouquet redolent of apple tart and fruit preserved in syrup. Distinct sweet notes come through on the elegant palate, which mirrors the aromas of the nose well. We found the Bricco del Drago to be an excellent wine, offering balsamic aromas and a robust, austere and still rather tannic palate, while the Dolcetto and the Barbera are very pleasant, and the Nebbiolo and the Freisa are well-managed.

● Barbaresco '97	♟♟	6
● Barbaresco Il Bricco '96	♟♟	6
● Barbera d'Alba Fides '97	♟♟	5
● Barolo '96	♟♟	6
● Barolo Ornato '96	♟♟	6
○ Langhe Chardonnay PiodiLei '98	♟♟	5
● Barbera d'Alba '98	♟	4
● Dolcetto d'Alba '99	♟	4
● Langhe Rosso Il Nebbio '99	♟	4
● Nebbiolo d'Alba '98	♟	4
○ Piemonte Chardonnay L'Altro '99	♟	4
● Barolo Ornato '85	♟♟♟	6
● Barolo Ornato '89	♟♟♟	6
● Barbaresco Il Bricco '95	♟♟	6
● Barolo Ornato '95	♟♟	6

● Barbaresco Tenuta Roncaglia '97	♟♟	6
● Barolo Bussia Dardi Le Rose '96	♟♟	6
● Langhe Bricco del Drago '97	♟♟	5
○ Bonmé	♟♟	5
● Barbera d'Alba Tenuta Roncaglia '98	♟	4
○ Langhe Bianco Sanrocco '99	♟	3
● Dolcetto d'Alba '99	♟	3
● Nebbiolo d'Alba '98		4
● Langhe Freisa '99		3
● Barbaresco Tenuta Roncaglia '93	♟♟	6
● Barbaresco Tenuta Roncaglia '95	♟♟	6
● Barbaresco Tenuta Roncaglia '96	♟♟	6
● Barolo Bussia Dardi Le Rose '93	♟♟	6
● Barolo Bussia Dardi Le Rose '95	♟♟	6
● Langhe Bricco del Drago '96	♟♟	4

ALBA (CN)

PRUNOTTO
REG. S. CASSIANO, 4/G
12051 ALBA (CN)
TEL. 0173/280017

ALFIANO NATTA (AL)

TENUTA CASTELLO DI RAZZANO
FRAZ. CASARELLO, 2
15021 ALFIANO NATTA (AL)
TEL. 0141/922124 - 0141/922426

This year, Prunotto offered us two '96 Barolo crus, the Cannubi and the Bussia. Both give impressions of damp earth, autumn leaves, and freshly mown grass, but there is an enticing hint of truffle in the Cannubi while the Bussia puts the accent on fruit and a touch of liquorice in the finish to give it a fuller range of aromas. On the palate, both are full bodied and robust, the Cannubi having greater acidity in contrast with the Bussia's more prominent tannins. In fact, it was the elegant, blue-blooded Bussia that earned the estate our Three Glass award. The Barbaresco '97 Bric Turot follows in the footsteps of the Barolo but differs in that it foregrounds red berry aromas. Its rich fruit is slightly compromised by a note of unripe peach. On the palate, it is luscious and has plenty of vigour. We liked the Barbera d'Asti Costamiòle whose impenetrable ruby colour immediately tells you it is a well-rounded, full-flavoured wine. The bouquet is rich, deep and very elegant while the palate is so concentrated as to seem almost unctuous. An outstanding Barbera. Prunotto's Nebbiolo d'Alba Occhetti has yet to disappoint and the '98 vintage promises to live up to its usual standard. An elegant, gracious wine, its nose has no great length but does manage to captivate with overtones of roses and spice against an aromatic backdrop. The Barbera d'Alba '98 Pian Romualdo has a lingering nose of concentrated floral notes over ripe mulberries and cassis. Firm on the palate, it is harmonious, full-flavoured and tannic, with discreet acidity. We concluded our tasting with Prunotto's Barolo '96 and Barbaresco '97, both well-structured, graceful and stylish; the Dolcetto d'Alba '99, an upfront, agreeable wine; and the Barbera d'Alba '98 and Barbera d'Asti '99 Fiulot, which are uncomplicated and a tad unsophisticated.

Augusto Olearo is both owner and oenologist at this magnificent old estate centred around the 18th-century castle of Razzano. The romantic stone cellars are now home to the state-of-the-art equipment responsible for the estate's vinification processes and immaculately kept barrels. Olearo has 30 hectares under vine and a further eight, planted mainly with barbera, that will soon go into production. Of the wines he presented for tasting this year, we were particularly struck by Augusto's Barbera Campasso, obtained from grapes grown in an old vineyard that faces east. Vinified with a long maceration at controlled temperatures, it is left to age for 18 months in big French oak barrels. A lush ruby with garnet highlights in the glass, its nose is redolent of cherry and walnut that return on the palate, which has great body and the invigorating finish of a classic Barbera. Olearo's Leona, a Barbera from this year's vintage, is a good everyday food wine. Ruby tending to violet, it possesses a straightforward, in-your-face nose that highlights black cherry, and a lovely fruit-rich, uncomplicated palate. Finally, there is the Grignolino whose geranium, rose, redcurrant and almond notes herald a palate dominated by acidity. Unfortunately for us, we were unable to taste the estate's two most important bottles, the Barbera d'Asti Vigna del Beneficio '98 and the pinot nero-based Monferrato Onero '98, as the winery's new policy involves a long period of bottle-ageing for both products. We look forward to tasting them next year.

● Barolo Bussia '96	YYY	6
● Barbaresco '97	YY	6
● Barbaresco Bric Turot '97	YY	6
● Barbera d'Alba Pian Romualdo '98	YY	5
● Barbera d'Asti Costamiòle '98	YY	6
● Barolo '96	YY	6
● Barolo Cannubi '96	YY	6
● Nebbiolo d'Alba Occhetti '98	YY	5
● Barbera d'Alba '98	Y	3
● Barbera d'Asti Fiulot '99	Y	3
● Dolcetto d'Alba '99	Y	3
● Barbera d'Asti Costamiòle '96	YYY	6
● Barbera d'Asti Costamiòle '97	YYY	6
● Barolo Bussia '85	YYY	6
● Barolo Cannubi '85	YYY	6

● Barbera d'Asti Sup. Campasso '98	YY	3*
● Barbera d'Asti La Leona '99	Y	2*
● Grignolino del M.to Casalese '99		2
● Barbera d'Asti Sup. Vigna del Beneficio '97	YY	4
● Barbera d'Asti Sup. Campasso '97	Y	3
● Barbera d'Asti Sup. Vigna del Beneficio '96	Y	4

ALICE BEL COLLE (AL)   ASTI

CA' BIANCA
REG. SPAGNA, 58
15010 ALICE BEL COLLE (AL)
TEL. 0144/55843

F.LLI ROVERO
FRAZ. S. MARZANOTTO, 218
14050 ASTI
TEL. 0141/592460

Alice Bel Colle lies in an area planted intensively to vine that straddles the territories of Asti and Acqui. Set up in the 50s, Ca' Bianca was originally a family concern but was taken over by the Gruppo Italiano Vini in 1997. They export 70 percent of the wine produced, the equivalent of about 1,000,000 bottles a year. The 45-hectare estate also owns the two vineyards of La Morra in the Langhe, and Novi Ligure in Gavi. Two Glasses go to their Barolo, aged partly in large barrels and partly in barriques. Its colour is intense, its nose elegant and complex with overtones of tar, rose and violet, and the palate is juicy and well-balanced. In short, a pleasant, well-managed and very typical Barolo. The winery uses 20 percent late-vintage grapes to make the cask-conditioned Gavi, which is one of the best we tasted. Pale gold flecked with green in the glass, it releases persistent aromas of pineapple, tangerine and hedgerow with a discreet dash of vanilla. The palate is well-structured and nicely balanced, with an elegant background of ripe fruit and an attractive freshness that is always under control. Ca' Bianca's Barbera is deep ruby tinged with garnet. Its toasty oak brings out the varietal barbera notes of cherry and raspberry but after a promising entry on the palate it fades away a little in the finish. The estate sets great store by barbera and is replanting many of its vineyards with this variety. Starting with the '99 vintage, the cellar will be making a Barbera selection. The pale gold Moscato has intense, varietal aromas and a sweet but not cloying palate. The Dolcetto d'Acqui, aged for eight months in large barrels, is also worth a Guide mention.

Take 16 hectares planted to vine, thin them out rigorously, shun weed killers, throw in plenty of technology, experience and passion, and you have the Rovero brothers' estate, a concern that produces about 80,000 bottles a year. A first sniff of their Monferrato Rosso Pinot Nero '98 reveals a certain lack of harmony, but after swirling in the glass the pungent gamey overtones dissipate to leave behind a complex range of cocoa, coffee and red fruit aromas. On the palate, it is sweetish and nicely balanced and follows through to a soft, caressing finish. The richly coloured Cabernet '97 flaunts notes of ripe fruit, green pepper, freshly cut hay and tar. The palate, although well-rounded, is compromised by its soft but rather bossy tannins. The Roveros produce two Sauvignons but have only released the Monferrato Bianco '99 this year. Vinified entirely in stainless steel, this is a truly splendid vintage. Its varietal notes hint at elderflower and tomato leaf while the lip-smacking palate boasts solid structure, good alcohol, and lots of style. We felt this wine merited a full Two Glasses. The two Barberas do not quite attain these giddy heights, but are nevertheless well put together. The generous Rouvé '97 is deep garnet in colour with a fruity, cherry jam nose. Uncompromisingly rich, it has vanilla notes that bear witness to its long sojourn in barriques. The Vigneto Gustin '98, not quite so evolved or opulent, oozes freshness from every pore with crisp floral and plum aromas. The elegant palate borne up by a strong but not overwhelming acidity.

● Barolo '96	▼▼	6
○ Gavi '99	▼▼	3*
● Barbera d'Asti '98	▼	3
● Dolcetto d'Acqui '98	▼	3
○ Moscato d'Asti '99	▼	3
● Barbera d'Asti '97	▽▽	3
● Barolo '95	▽	6

○ Monferrato Bianco Sauvignon '99	▼▼	3*
● Monferrato Rosso Cabernet '97	▼▼	4
● Barbera d'Asti Rouvé '97	▼	5
● Barbera d'Asti Vigneto Gustin '98	▼	3
● Monferrato Rosso Pinot Nero '98	▼	3
● Barbera d'Asti Rouvé '95	▽	5
● Barbera d'Asti Rouvé '96	▽	5
● Monferrato Rosso Cabernet '96	▽	4

BARBARESCO (CN)

BARBARESCO (CN)

CA' ROME' - ROMANO MARENGO
VIA RABAJÀ, 36
12050 BARBARESCO (CN)
TEL. 0173/635126

CANTINA DEL PINO
VIA OVELLO, 15
12050 BARBARESCO (CN)
TEL. 0173/635147

The Marengo family's wines just get better and better. Romano and his children Paola and Giuseppe are renovating the estate and have acquired new plots that will enable them to vinify solely their own grapes. A run of good vintages has earned many wines, such as the Barbaresco Maria di Brun and Barbera La Gamberaja, a high score. The first of these is a fairly deep ruby garnet and the nose suggests red fruit jam, violet and liquorice on a mineral base. The palate is succulent, with firm tannins that do not in any way impinge on its structure and the broad progression leads into a long finish that satisfyingly echoes nose and palate. The Barbera is dense garnet with a distinctive nose redolent of redcurrant and bilberry, enhanced by balsamic notes of resin and mint. It is concentrated on the palate, leading harmoniously and powerfully through to a finish reminiscent of cocoa and liquorice. The Marengos' second-label Barbera is a nicely structured wine with a good strong colour and aromas of brine and pot pourri over notes of slightly over-evolved fruit, rosemary and cocoa. A little austere on the palate, the range of flavours grows impressively, leading into a spirited finish. The Rosso Da Pruvé, obtained from nebbiolo and barbera, is garnet ruby with a youthful rim. The nose presents nuances of mulberry and raspberry, followed by vegetable and dried flower notes, which introduce a spunky, robust palate and a satisfying finish. We liked the Rapet best of the Marengo Barolos for its rather evolved nose and complex palate but were less impressed by the Vigna Cerretta which, despite its quality, is perhaps less inviting.

The Vacca family's estate has been included in the Guide for the first time this year with a selection of remarkably characterful wines. Renato is an oenologist and spends most of his time running the cellar while his father, Adriano, devotes his energies to the vineyards. Most of their six hectares lie in the Ovello di Barbaresco subzone, although a small proportion is located in Gallina di Neive. Cantina del Pino, which produces 30,000 bottles a year, was bought by Renato's grandfather in 1925 and has been vinifying its own grapes since 1997. Prior to this, the family sold its harvest to the Cantina dei Produttori del Barbaresco. The offerings of this young winery are the fruit of a happy marriage between tradition and technology. The Barbaresco Ovello '97 is obtained with brief maceration and ageing in both barriques and large barrels, a combination that really works. Its lush garnet colour immediately reveals the wine's potential, confirmed by aromas of black berries and autumn leaves over elegant balsamic notes. The wine's trademark juicy flesh is immediately obvious on the palate, which progresses generously yet softly to explode in a powerful crescendo that ushers in complex finish which combines suggestions of mint, confectioner's cream and fruit. The youthful colour of the Barbera hints at a wine of substance. Its cherry aromas combine with pepper, hay and green leaf notes and the palate is both full bodied and very satisfying, with a dignified, lingering finish. The Dolcetto d'Alba, the wine that has made the estate's name over the last few years, is excellent, among the best we tasted. La Freisa is slightly fizzy and pleasantly rustic, with a wild berry, pepper and tangerine nose, an agreeable, easy-to-drink palate, and a hint of bitterness in the finish.

● Barbaresco '97	♟♟	6
● Barbaresco Maria di Brun '97	♟♟	6
● Barbera d'Alba La Gamberaja '98	♟♟	4
● Barolo Rapet '96	♟♟	6
● Barolo Vigna Cerretta '96	♟	6
● Da Pruvé '98	♟	5
● Barbaresco Maria di Brun '95	♟♟	6
● Barbaresco Maria di Brun '96	♟♟	6
● Barbera d'Alba La Gamberaja '97	♟♟	5
● Barbaresco '96	♟	6
● Barolo Rapet '95	♟	6
● Barolo Vigna Cerretta '95	♟	6
● Da Pruvé '97	♟	5

● Barbaresco Ovello '97	♟♟	5
● Barbera d'Alba '98	♟♟	4
● Dolcetto d'Alba '99	♟♟	3*
● Langhe Freisa '99	♟	3

CASCINA LUISIN

Loc. Rabajà, 23
12050 Barbaresco (CN)
tel. 0173/635154

Luigi Minuto, his wife, Ines, and their qualified viticulturist son, Roberto, have five hectares planted to vine spread across the municipalities of Barbaresco, Neive and Alba. They use the grapes from a 60-year-old vineyard at San Rocco Seno d'Elvio to make their Nebbiolo d'Alba, released for the first time in December 2000. This year's Barbera Asili comes minus the wording "barrique" on the label and is very good. The ruby shades into a dense garnet, with a narrow, compact edge, while the nose regales you with its concentrated, fragrant mulberry and redcurrant fruit, enhanced by perfectly judged new oak and alluring green notes of bramble. The palate is complex right from the start, opening out steadily and generously to reveal a wonderfully harmonious structure. The lingering finish, too, is firm and perfectly balanced. The Minutos' Barbaresco Rabajà has a rich colour and a gamut of aromas ranging from red fruit jam through to hints of mineral. The palate is well-sustained and lively, revealing a warm, imposing texture. Firm tannins perk up the lingering finish. Sorì Paolin, the other Barbera selection, is less convincing. The Barbera Magiur, almost as good as the Asili, is an eminently satisfying wine, its intense, youthful colour introducing aromas of wild berries, confectioner's cream and damp earth. The succulent, well-sustained palate is rounded off by a long fruit-rich finish. Finally, the Dolcetto Bric Trifüla '99, ruby in colour with garnet highlights and a purple edge, displays the typical black cherry fruit of the variety hand in hand with rustic mineral tones. The palate is smooth and the tannins well to the fore.

●	Barbaresco Rabajà '97	▼▼	6
●	Barbera d'Alba Asili '98	▼▼	5
●	Barbera d'Alba Magiur '99	▼▼	3*
●	Barbaresco Sorì Paolin '97	▼	6
●	Dolcetto d'Alba Bric Trifüla '99	▼	3
●	Barbera d'Alba Asili Barrique '97	▽▽▽	5
●	Barbaresco Rabajà '95	▽▽	6
●	Barbaresco Rabajà '96	▽▽	6
●	Barbaresco Sorì Paolin '96	▽▽	6
●	Barbera d'Alba Asili Barrique '96	▽▽	5
●	Barbaresco Sorì Paolin '95	▽	6

BARBARESCO (CN)

TENUTE CISA ASINARI DEI MARCHESI DI GRESY

Via Rabajà, 43
12050 Barbaresco (CN)
tel. 0173/635222

The historic Tenute Cisa Astinari estate well deserves its acclaim for the never-failing quality of its wines and the success it regularly enjoys abroad. To add to its glory, this year it is the proud holder of a Three Glass award for its Barbaresco Gaiun '97. Marco Dotta's technical expertise and Alberto di Gresy's personality, combined with the vine stock at their disposal, make a winning team. The estate has 30 hectares under vine and several more soon to go into production, at Treiso (Monte Aribaldo), Cassine in the province of Alessandria (La Serra), and the famed Martinenga subzone in Barbaresco whose two selections open our profile. The Gaiun '97 carried off our highest award for its sheer character and the elegant sophistication of its aromas. The Camp Gros '97 also boasts complex notes of mulberry and tobacco and offers a full, well-rounded palate with a crisp, clean-tasting finish. The series is completed by the Martinenga '97, with its clean aromas redolent of fresh spices and balanced, stylish, tangy palate. Then came the two red blends. The first of these is the Langhe Rosso Virtus '97, 40 percent cabernet and 60 percent barbera, a sophisticated fruit-rich glass with just the right dash of oak. The second, the Langhe Rosso Villa Martis '97, is obtained from barbera and nebbiolo, and has a more mature bouquet. The panel also liked the Dolcetto and the Langhe Nebbiolo Martinenga '99 while the Sauvignon '99 is particularly good, with its grassy varietal notes. It is a wine that flatters the taste buds, picking up the aromas of the nose on the palate and signing off with a seductive finish. Other wines of character were the Moscato d'Asti La Serra '99, with a sage and flower nose and a creamy, nicely balanced, aroma-rich palate. Last but not least are the two Chardonnays. The Langhe Gresy '98 is fruit-rich and oaky while the Langhe Chardonnay '99 has an elegant nose and a very pleasant finish.

●	Barbaresco Gaiun '97	▼▼▼	6
●	Barbaresco Camp Gros '97	▼▼	6
●	Barbaresco Martinenga '97	▼▼	6
●	Langhe Rosso Virtus '97	▼▼	5
○	Langhe Sauvignon '99	▼▼	4
●	Dolcetto d'Alba Monte Aribaldo '99	▼	4
○	Langhe Chardonnay '99	▼	4
○	Langhe Chardonnay Gresy '98	▼	5
●	Langhe Nebbiolo Martinenga '99	▼	4
●	Langhe Rosso Villa Martis '97	▼	4
○	Moscato d'Asti La Serra '99	▼	3
●	Barbaresco Gaiun '85	▽▽▽	6
●	Barbaresco Camp Gros '96	▽▽	6
●	Barbaresco Martinenga '96	▽▽	6

BARBARESCO (CN)

BARBARESCO (CN)

GIUSEPPE CORTESE
LOC. RABAJÀ, 35
12050 BARBARESCO (CN)
TEL. 0173/635131

★ ★ GAJA
VIA TORINO, 36/A
12050 BARBARESCO (CN)
TEL. 0173/635158

Although traditionalists at heart, preferring to age their Nebbiolo in large barrels rather than barriques, Giuseppe Cortese and his son Piercarlo have opened the door a crack to an innovation or two. They have put back by a year the release date of their Chardonnay, a wine that in the past has been less than convincing. In response to past criticism, the Corteses have for the first time changed their basic production methods. Rigorous thinning and limited yields have produced an ambitious response to criticism that may well hold a few surprises. Their Barbera Morassina has splendid concentration and solid character but is a tad unpolished and fails to conceal a rustic note. There is a fine range of aromas, proffering fruity notes that blend attractively with the barrique-derived vanilla. Well-integrated acidity and robust alcohol are bolstered by a more than adequate structure and good balance. The Dolcetto d'Alba Trifolera, vinified and aged entirely in stainless steel, is deep violet with a ripe fruit-and-jam nose. On the palate, juicy fruit and a marked tannic note come through. Once again, we were very impressed by the Nebbiolo, made with grapes from the Rabajà cru after a first selection has been made for the Barbaresco. On the nose there are notes of berry fruit, toastiness and spices. While the entry on the palate is a little unsophisticated, the concentration and extract indicate that this is a wine with a future. The Cortese Barbaresco '97 is more evolved and readier for drinking than the '96. Its bouquet is intense, varietal, and generous but not overly complex and its palate is velvety, chewy, and rounded with a long, bitterish finish.

In a revolutionary year, masterminded by Angelo Gaja, that saw the demise of the Barbaresco Sorì San Lorenzo, Costa Russi and Sorì Tildin labels, we were only able to taste five of this estate's wines. Of these, we awarded two our maximum Three Glass award and all the others Two Glasses. From this year, Gaja has decided to axe production of his famous Barbaresco selections and to opt for the Langhe designation. Nor has the Barolo escaped unscathed. Gaja has announced that he will no longer make this king of wines but instead will use his Serralunga nebbiolo grapes to produce the Langhe Nebbiolo Sperss. Almost everyone has had something to say about this dramatic turnaround in company policy, not least Angelo himself. He thinks everyone is free to draw his or her own conclusions. Hats off to the stunning Barbaresco '97. Angelo and his trusty oenologist Guido Rivella have produced a wine of exceptional quality that easily matches previous vintages in terms of character and personality. Encouragingly, the estate produces many thousands of bottles of this wine, a worthy winner of our prestigious Three Glass award. Not to be outdone is the austere Langhe Nebbiolo Sperss '96, also a Three Glass winner. Its sumptuous richness is immediately evident from the dense ruby colour while the nose exalts all the characteristics of the variety. The stunningly long, mouth-filling palate perfectly blends oak-derived notes with ripe fruit. Excellent, too, are the cabernet sauvignon-based Langhe Darmagi '97 and the Langhe Nebbiolo Conteisa '96, the estate's newest release. In the absence of the Sauvignon Alteni di Brassica and the Chardonnay Gaja & Rey, the coherent, attractive Rossj-Bass cuts a fine figure on the white front.

● Barbaresco Rabajà '97	▼▼	5
● Langhe Nebbiolo '98	▼▼	4
● Barbera d'Alba Morassina '98	▼	4
● Dolcetto d'Alba Trifolera '99	▼	3
● Barbaresco Rabajà '95	♀♀	5
● Barbaresco Rabajà '96	♀♀	5
● Barbera d'Alba Morassina '97	♀	4

● Barbaresco '97	▼▼▼	6
● Langhe Nebbiolo Sperss '96	▼▼▼	6
● Langhe Nebbiolo Conteisa '96	▼▼	6
● Langhe Rosso Darmagi '97	▼▼	6
○ Langhe Rossj-Bass '99	▼▼	6
● Barbaresco Costa Russi '95	♀♀♀	6
● Langhe Rosso Costa Russi '96	♀♀♀	6
● Barbaresco Sorì S. Lorenzo '95	♀♀♀	6
● Langhe Rosso Sorì S. Lorenzo '96	♀♀♀	6
● Barbaresco Sorì Tildìn '93	♀♀♀	6
● Barolo Sperss '93	♀♀♀	6
● Barolo Sperss '95	♀♀♀	6
○ Chardonnay Gaia & Rey '94	♀♀♀	6
● Langhe Rosso Darmagi '94	♀♀♀	6
● Langhe Rosso Darmagi '96	♀♀♀	6

BARBARESCO (CN)

BARBARESCO (CN)

CARLO GIACOSA
VIA OVELLO, 8
12050 BARBARESCO (CN)
TEL. 0173/635116

I PAGLIERI
VIA RABAJÀ, 8
12050 BARBARESCO (CN)
TEL. 0173/635109

Previously run by father Donato, and now by son Carlo, the Giacosa estate makes a triumphant re-entry into the Guide this year with three Two Glass awards. Most of their vines lie on the best slopes in Barbaresco - Montefico, Cole, Asili, Ovello – and it is therefore natural that they should specialise in excellent nebbiolo-based wines. Carlo, his wife, Carla, and daughter, Maria Grazia, offered us two great Barbarescos this year. Their Montefico and the Narin, obtained by blending the estate's other grapes and dedicated to Carlo's father, Donato. The Montefico, aged in Slavonian oak, is the more traditional of the two. Its dried herbs and liquorice notes mingle with a suggestion of liqueur cherries, and a rather unsophisticated, tannic palate that will mellow with time in the cellar. The softer, fruitier Narin was aged in both new and old barriques and is drinking well even now, without however compromising on complexity. These classic wines are flanked by the Mary Grace '99, a table wine in the local tradition obtained from Barbaresco nebbiolo grapes. It is aged for a shorter period with the deliberate intention of bringing out the personality of the fruit. The result is a very soft red with a wide range of complex aromas. A sort of miniature Barbaresco. Less complex, but also very good, are the alcohol-rich, eminently drinkable Dolcetto d'Alba, and the fruity, rustic Barbera d'Alba Mucin, both made in part with fruit from the vineyards that the Giacosas have recently rented in Neive. The barrique-conditioned Barbera Lina has good colour and an attractive nose but does not quite hit the mark in terms of the weight and structure of the palate.

Alfredo Roagna has no time for fashion. For the last 20 years, he has been making wine as he sees fit, relying on the experience he has picked up along the way. He and his 19-year-old son, Luca, follow fairly traditional vinification methods that include slow maceration and lengthy ageing in oak, with judicious use of large and small barrels of varying age and origin. Alfredo prefers to devote his time to his land rather than to public relations. His 15 hectares are spread across Barbaresco, Castiglione Falletto and Priocca, the village his family originally came from. Several of his labels are missing from the Guide this year. The Barbaresco Crichët Pajé '97 and Opera Prima XIV have yet to mature, and the Dolcetto '99 fell victim to a heavy hailstorm. Of the wines we did taste, the most impressive were the Barolo La Rocca and La Pira, and the Barbaresco Riserva, already bottled but ready for release in January 2001. The Barolo La Rocca offers a full, elegant nose featuring balsam and fruit notes while the palate has a noble, close-knit tannic structure. The La Pira boasts an extremely full-bodied, fleshy palate and an intensely fruit-rich, spicy nose loaded with plum and liquorice against a backdrop of dried flowers. Despite its fairly evolved nose, the Barbaresco '97 lacks fullness and is a little too austere in the finish. The 95-percent chardonnay Solea astonishes with its almost burgundy-style bouquet redolent of super-ripe fruit, toasted hazelnuts and honey but fails to live up to its promise on the palate, where it falls short of the requisite richness and length.

● Barbaresco Montefico '97	🍷🍷	5
● Barbaresco Narin '97	🍷🍷	5
● Mary Grace '99	🍷🍷	4
● Barbera d'Alba Lina '98	🍷	4
● Barbera d'Alba Mucin '99	🍷	3
● Dolcetto d'Alba Cuchet '99	🍷	2*

● Barbaresco Ris. '96	🍷🍷	6
● Barolo La Rocca e La Pira '96	🍷🍷	6
● Barbaresco '97	🍷	6
○ Langhe Solea '98	🍷	5
● Barbaresco '96	🍷🍷	6
● Barbaresco Crichët Pajé '96	🍷🍷	6
● Barbaresco Ris. '93	🍷🍷	6
● Barolo La Rocca e La Pira Ris. '93	🍷🍷	6
● Crichët Pajé '89	🍷🍷	6
● Opera Prima XIII	🍷🍷	6
● Barolo La Rocca e La Pira '95	🍷	6

BARBARESCO (CN)

BARBARESCO (CN)

MOCCAGATTA
VIA RABAJÀ, 24
12050 BARBARESCO (CN)
TEL. 0173/635152 - 0173/635228

MONTARIBALDI
VIA RIO SORDO, 30/A
FRAZ. TRE STELLE
12050 BARBARESCO (CN)
TEL. 0173/638220

The Minuto brothers have exploited the great 1997 vintage to the very last grape and gave us three stunning Barbarescos to taste, winning Three Glasses for the Cole. For the award, they can thank the high quality of their wine and a responsible company policy in which the whole family has a say. Cole is a traditional Barbaresco whose aromas will undoubtedly benefit from cellaring. As yet, they struggle to emerge for a short time but then open out sure-footedly into complex, enfolding notes of berry fruit and intriguing hints of balsam and liquorice. Sumptuous in its concentration on the palate, this is a generously structured wine that fills the mouth superbly. The Barbaresco Bric Balin, a bit more upbeat and international than the previous bottle, is also exciting. The agreeable Basarin is the least complex of the Minutos' three Barbarescos. Elegant and very drinkable, it offers nice fruit-rich texture and good freshness but is let down by a nose that fails to find a point of balance for its oaky notes, sweetness and a faintly cloying hint of vanilla. The Barbera d'Alba Basarin '98 is, as ever, excellent, and the standard '99 Barbera and Dolcetto are also agreeable. On the white front, the Chardonnay Buschet '98 is particularly good. A lustrous yellow in the glass, it proffers apple, banana and distinct notes of toasty oak and then a rich, well structured palate that ends on a lingering note of fruit. The less demanding Langhe Chardonnay '99 is nicely balanced. A deep, green-flecked straw-yellow colour ushers in a yeasty, tropical fruit nose and a well-rounded palate with crisp acidity and moderate length.

Originally hailing from Montà d'Alba, in Roero, Giuseppe Taliano and his wife, Carla, moved to the Langhe way back in 1968 when they bought three hectares of barbaresco. Aided by their two sons, Luciano and Roberto, the Talianos have gradually added to their estate by both buying and renting. Today, they have 17 hectares in Barbaresco, Treiso, Alba, Trezzo Tinella, Costigliole d'Asti, Montà and Monteu. Between 1991 and 1994, they began to bottle a certain percentage of their own wines with the intention of gradually giving up the most distant and least suitable, rented vineyards to concentrate on vinifying their best quality grapes. Today, the estate offers an eclectic range of more than ten labels, but plans to reduce this number over the next few years. The Talianos make their first entry in the Guide this year with five selections: the Barbaresco Sörì Montaribaldi, aged for about 12 months in brand new and one-year-old barriques; the Barbera d'Alba dü Gir, aged for one year in new barriques; the Langhe Chardonnay Stissa d'le Favole, fermented and conditioned for nine months in new barriques; the Dolcetto d'Alba Nicolini; and the Roero Arneis. The Barbaresco '97 is lovely and fresh, with concentrated, tangy, berry fruit aromas, a soft, lingering palate and attractively balanced acidity. Oak-ageing lends the Barbera dü Gir balance while the nose offers nuances of incense, resin and sweet spices. The almost buttery richness of the Chardonnay nevertheless tends to be overwhelmed by the oak-derived toastiness. Finally, the reasonably concentrated Dolcetto and the Arneis are very easy to drink.

● Barbaresco Cole '97	▼▼▼	6
● Barbaresco Basarin '97	▼▼	6
● Barbaresco Bric Balin '97	▼▼	6
● Barbera d'Alba Basarin '98	▼▼	5
○ Langhe Chardonnay Buschet '98	▼▼	5
● Barbera d'Alba '99	▼	4
● Dolcetto d'Alba '99	▼	3
○ Langhe Chardonnay '99	▼	3
● Barbaresco Bric Balin '90	♈♈♈	6
● Barbaresco Bric Balin '93	♈♈	6
● Barbaresco Bric Balin '96	♈♈	6
● Barbaresco Cole '93	♈♈	6
● Barbaresco Cole '96	♈♈	6
● Barbera d'Alba Basarin '97	♈♈	5
● Barbaresco Basarin '96	♈	6

● Barbaresco Sörì Montaribaldi '97	▼▼	6
● Barbera d'Alba dü Gir '98	▼▼	4
● Dolcetto d'Alba Nicolini '99	▼	4
○ Langhe Chardonnay Stissa d'le Favole '98	▼	4
○ Roero Arneis '99	▼	3

BARBARESCO (CN)

Cascina Morassino

Via Ovello, 32
12050 Barbaresco (CN)
tel. 0173/635149

Qualified oenologist Roberto Bianco and his father, Mauro, are the owners of four and half hectares planted with 70 percent nebbiolo, as well as dolcetto and barbera. Their Ovello Ventimesi '97, obtained from the prestigious Ovello cru and aged in barriques, is the pick of the estate's Barbaresco crop. The high quality of the grapes and the controlled maceration on their skins with frequent pumping of the wine over the cap, give this wine a lush garnet colour that speaks volumes for its structure. Opening on a note of fresh hay, the nose then proposes violet, liquorice and peach with faint gamey overtones. On the palate, the generous progression is bolstered by robust, mature tannins that lend appropriate austerity to its lingering cocoa and liquorice finish. The Biancos' Ovello '97 is aged in large barrels and has a slightly less intense colour with an orange rim and a more traditional nose redolent of berry fruit, leather and pepper set against a vaguely minerally backdrop. The structure is solid, if not up to the standards of the Ventimesi, but its finish is marred by a faintly bitterish final note. The Barbaresco Morassino, aged in large split-stave barrels, makes its debut with the '97 vintage. Its ruby-garnet colour with an orange rim leads into aromas that range from wild berries to spices, to dried flowers, but has a less complex palate than the wines discussed above. The garnet-tinged ruby of the Barbera Vignot '98 introduces firm, fruit-rich aromas, notably black cherry, that are masked somewhat by the oak, and a palate lacking a little structure. Finally the Nebbiolo '98 is well-managed and pleasantly rustic.

●	Barbaresco Ovello Ventimesi '97	▼▼	6
●	Barbaresco Morassino '97	▼	5
●	Barbaresco Ovello '97	▼	6
●	Barbera d'Alba Vignot '98	▼	5
●	Langhe Nebbiolo '98	▼	4
●	Barbaresco Ovello Ventimesi '96	▽▽	6
●	Barbera d'Alba '97	▽▽	5
●	Barbaresco '96	▽	5
●	Barbaresco Ovello '95	▽	6
●	Barbaresco Ovello '96	▽	6

BARBARESCO (CN)

Produttori del Barbaresco

Via Torino, 52
12050 Barbaresco (CN)
tel. 0173/635139

The Cantina dei Produttori del Barbaresco vinifies the grapes of 60 member growers that together have about 100 hectares planted to vine in Barbaresco and Neive. They produce a grand total of 420,000 bottles a year. Flanking their basic Barbaresco is a Nebbiolo and nine prestigious Barbaresco selections, all known and acclaimed both in Italy and overseas. Gianni Testa, the oenologist in charge of the technical side of operations, sticks to traditional production techniques. These include extended maceration, the exclusive use of large barrels, and much longer ageing periods than regulations require for the selections. The base Barbaresco '97 is quite a deep ruby, verging on garnet, with a seductive but not excessively complex nose that flaunts refined fruit notes of wild berries over hints of creaminess. The austerity of the nebbiolo grape comes through on the palate in a body with decent structure that leads into a satisfying finish. The Montestefano and the Pajé stand out among the '95 vintages presented for tasting this year. The first is ruby red with an orange rim. The nose evinces mature, minerally notes and the palate is vigorous, with good structure and a measured elegance. The Pajé, however, has a rather one-dimensional nose that has yet to hit the right note, and a harsh palate with tannins that still need time to mellow. Ageing will do great things for this wine. The Pora '95 is not quite up to the standard set by the others. Its palate, dominated by hard tannins that dry out the finish, fails to echo its liquorice and tobacco nose.

●	Barbaresco Vigneti in Montestefano Ris. '95	▼▼	6
●	Barbaresco Vigneti in Pajé Ris. '95	▼▼	6
●	Barbaresco '97	▼	5
●	Barbaresco Vigneti in Pora Ris. '95	▼	6
●	Barbaresco Vigneti in Moccagatta Ris. '90	▽▽	6
●	Barbaresco Vigneti in Moccagatta Ris. '95	▽▽	6
●	Barbaresco Vigneti in Rio Sordo Ris. '95	▽▽	6
●	Barbaresco '96	▽	5
●	Barbaresco Vigneti in Montefico Ris. '95	▽	6
●	Barbaresco Vigneti in Ovello Ris. '95	▽	6
●	Barbaresco Vigneti in Rabajà Ris. '95	▽	6

BARBARESCO (CN)

BARBARESCO (CN)

ALBINO ROCCA
VIA RABAJÀ, 15
12050 BARBARESCO (CN)
TEL. 0173/635145

BRUNO ROCCA
VIA RABAJÀ, 29
12050 BARBARESCO (CN)
TEL. 0173/635112

Angelo Rocca imbues his wines with remarkable personality and style that come through in the balanced complexity of each and every bottle, from the most challenging to the humblest. He currently has ten hectares planted to vine and makes 65,000 bottles, 22,000 of which are Barbaresco. His Brichi Ronchi, aged in new barriques and with a dense, almost impenetrable colour in the glass, unfurls a bouquet of very ripe mulberry and cassis over tobacco leaf and toastiness. There is impressive power and concentration on the well-sustained palate, which reveals good breadth as it progresses through to a long, well-defined finish of fruit and cocoa. Another deserved Three Glasses for this vintage to add to the awards from previous years. Hot on its heels we have the elegant and authoritative Barbaresco Loreto, aged in large barrels. Deep garnet in colour, it has a crisply sumptuous nose whose fruit comes through in notes of redcurrant and bilberry, followed by resin, roasted coffee and rosemary, all served up against a delicate minerally backdrop. The palate is velvety and concentrated, growing in intensity thanks to the warm alcohol of the body and the vivacious tannins. The lingering finish is resplendent in a fine range of well-defined, varietal aromas. Almost opaque in the glass, Rocca's Barbera Gepin abounds in fruit aromas, notably redcurrant and black cherry, which blend with green leaf notes over a suggestion of toastiness. The succulent palate is underpinned by firm tannins that give depth to the long lingering finish. The cortese-based Bianco La Rocca has good breadth on a nose bursting with fresh and dried fruit, aromatic herbs and cakes. The silky palate has loads of length and class. The Chardonnay is soft and ripe, and the Dolcetto concentrated and elegant.

What a great year for Bruno Rocca. Of the two outstanding Barbarescos he presented, we went for the Coparossa in a big way and awarded it Three Glasses. His other five selections, including the Barbaresco Rabajà all went home with Two Glasses. Rocca has seven and a half hectares planted to vine, most of which lie in Barbaresco with the remainder in Neive, where he grows chardonnay and barbera, and Treiso. Barbaresco accounts for over half of his approximately 40,000 bottles a year. The estate, once again in a phase of expansion, has a distinctly modern approach to vinification but refuses to compromise on the high quality of its grapes. The Barbaresco Rabajà, a dense garnet ruby with the narrowest of rims, offers a vanilla and spice oak-derived nose that leads into the clean, fragrant, fruity notes of raspberry. The palate immediately signals the wine's solid personality, and the follow-through is coherent and stylish, finishing on a typically lingering note. The Coparossa is even better, flaunting an alluringly intense colour and a very elegant nose. Its chocolate and vanilla cream nuances enhance sweet oak-derived notes and herald hints of cherry, cocoa and green leaf. The palate is complex and vigorous, the finish long and satisfying. The deep garnet Barbera entices with its aromas of marinated fruit and wax on balsamic notes. The palate is well-sustained and full-bodied and the finish refreshing. Rocca's almost opaque Dolcetto Trifolé regales the nose with aromas of plum, mulberry and mint and the palate progresses triumphantly through to a lingering liquorice finish. Generous and well-structured, the cabernet, barbera and nebbiolo-based Rabajolo proffers aromas of sun-baked herbs and dry earth over fruit. Finally, the mature, elegant Chardonnay has a rich, well-rounded palate.

● Barbaresco Vigneto Brich Ronchi '97	♟♟♟	6
● Barbaresco Loreto '97	♟♟	6
● Barbera d'Alba Gepin '98	♟♟	4
● Dolcetto d'Alba Vignalunga '99	♟♟	3*
○ Langhe Bianco La Rocca '99	♟♟	4
○ Langhe Chardonnay da Bertu '99	♟	3
● Barbaresco Loreto '95	♛♛♛	6
● Barbaresco Vigneto Brich Ronchi '93	♛♛♛	6
● Barbaresco Vigneto Brich Ronchi '96	♛♛♛	6
● Barbaresco Loreto '96	♛♛	6
● Barbaresco Vigneto Brich Ronchi '95	♛♛	6
● Barbera d'Alba Gepin '97	♛♛	4

● Barbaresco Coparossa '97	♟♟♟	6
● Barbaresco Rabajà '97	♟♟	6
● Barbera d'Alba '98	♟♟	5
● Dolcetto d'Alba Vigna Trifolé '99	♟♟	4
○ Langhe Chardonnay Cadet '99	♟♟	5
● Langhe Rosso Rabajolo '97	♟♟	5
● Barbaresco Rabajà '88	♛♛♛	6
● Barbaresco Rabajà '89	♛♛♛	6
● Barbaresco Rabajà '93	♛♛♛	6
● Barbaresco Rabajà '96	♛♛♛	6
● Barbaresco Coparossa '95	♛♛	6
● Barbaresco Coparossa '96	♛♛	6
● Barbaresco Rabajà '95	♛♛	6

BARBARESCO (CN)

BAROLO (CN)

RINO VARALDO
VIA SECONDINE, 2
12050 BARBARESCO (CN)
TEL. 0173/635160

GIACOMO BORGOGNO & FIGLI
VIA GIOBERTI, 1
12060 BAROLO (CN)
TEL. 0173/56108

The estate of Mario Varaldo and his sons Rino and Michele has been in the spotlight for some time and is emerging as one of the most interesting wineries in this part of the Langhe. As in years past, their Barbaresco Bricco Libero earned an outstanding score at our tasting, confirming it as a wine of the highest calibre. Modern in style, this Barbaresco presents a strong varietal personality in a modern style. Intense garnet with a generous, enticing nose, the aromas marry fruit notes of mulberry, cassis and strawberry with complex overtones of tobacco leaf and herbs. All these are nicely set off by the touch of sweet spices from ageing in new oak. The palate starts out rich and concentrated, progressing steadily and sure-footedly, well supported by sweet tannins. The finish is well-balanced, with the sensations on the olfactory and taste receptors combining to produce an impressive overall experience. Three well-deserved Glasses for an estate that continues to improve. The Varaldos' Sorì Loreto has a solid colour with an orange-tinged rim, and aromas of liqueur cherries, cocoa, spice and caramel that combine to lend complexity and elegance. The palate is robust and slightly severe in character but with a satisfying finish. Of the other selections presented by this great winery, the Barbera d'Alba and the contemporary Langhe Nebbiolo Sorì Loreto shine through. The Barbera is an almost opaque violet, with cherry and balsamic aromas that harmonise perfectly and a complex, zesty, full-bodied palate. The Nebbiolo, more aggressively tannic, is every bit as good. The Varaldo Dolcetto is pleasant and the Freisa well-managed.

Giorgio, Cesare, Franco and Chiara Boschis put their all into their winery. They make a Barolo Classico according to traditional methods from a blend of grapes from several vineyards scattered over zones that include Cannubi Boschis, Liste, Brunate and San Pietro. Their '96 vintage has earned the Boschis Two Glasses for its impressive, elegant array of aromas and its full, satisfying body. Deep garnet in colour, its fruit-rich nose is redolent of strawberry and raspberry, backed up by complex undertones of toastiness, mint, confectioner's cream and chocolate. The front palate immediately announces a generous flavour that opens out into a slightly austere manner. The finish is lingering and harmonious. One Glass goes to the Boschis base Barolo with its deep garnet colour and faintly orange rim. Wild berries, mint, liquorice and leather aromas delight the nose while the palate is rounded, with well-defined phenols that lend volume to an appreciably long floral finish. The Barbaresco '97 offers hints of raspberry and mulberry that are only marginally compromised by a vaguely discordant toastiness. The palate is warm and bolstered by firm tannins that give a nice dryness to the finish. The Dolcetto is garnet-ruby with a violet rim, yielding trademark black cherry and peach fruit over attractive peppery notes. The chewy palate reveals a hint of sinew. Finally, we tasted the simple, gutsy Barbera '99 with its candied cherry aromas and vibrant character.

● Barbaresco Bricco Libero '97	♟♟♟	6
● Barbaresco Sorì Loreto '97	♟♟	6
● Barbera d'Alba '98	♟♟	5
● Langhe Nebbiolo '98	♟♟	5
● Dolcetto d'Alba '99	♟	3
● Langhe Freisa '99		4
● Barbaresco Bricco Libero '96	♟♟	6
● Barbaresco Sorì Loreto '96	♟♟	6
● Barbera d'Alba '97	♟♟	5
● Barolo Vigna di Aldo '95	♟♟	6

● Barolo Classico '96	♟♟	6
● Barbaresco '97	♟	6
● Barbera d'Alba '99	♟	3
● Barolo '96	♟	6
● Dolcetto d'Alba '99	♟	3
● Barolo Classico '93	♟♟	6
● Barolo '95	♟	6
● Barolo Classico '95	♟	6
● Barolo Classico Ris. '90	♟	6
● Barolo Liste '88	♟	6
● Barolo Liste '89	♟	6

BAROLO (CN)

Giacomo Brezza & Figli
Via Lomondo, 4
12060 Barolo (CN)
Tel. 0173/56354 - 0173/56191

This Barolo estate, founded in 1885, offers fine examples of the typical Langhe wines, turning out about 100,000 bottles a year. The Brezzas' Dolcetto d'Alba San Lorenzo '99 impressed us with its colour, ruby tending to garnet with a violet rim, and a nose that introduces the wine's great balance and intensity. Strong notes of grass and pepper pave the way for assertive fruit that comes through in overtones of morello cherry and bilberry, enhanced by a touch of juniper. The full body is apparent the minute it hits the palate and its follow-through brings out its robust phenols. The finish resoundingly reprises the forthright concentration of the fruit. We awarded Two Glasses to the Barolo Sarmassa. Fairly deep garnet in colour, it has a sweet, lingering nose with hints of vanilla and chocolate flanking roasted coffee and wild berries. Velvety and substantial in the mouth, it tends to fade slightly in mid palate but those wonderful hints of chocolate come through again in the finish. The Castellero is a bit more austere. It has a concentrated colour with a faint orange rim, proffering aromas of jam and vanilla over hints of dried flowers. The forward tannins compromise the depth of the palate and render the finish dryish. Ruby red with garnet highlights, the Barbera Cannubi Muscatel '97 has a straightforward nose and a palate that lacks length. Finally, the Barbera Cannubi is well-made, if slightly oak-dominated.

BAROLO (CN)

Marchesi di Barolo
Via Alba, 12
12060 Barolo (CN)
Tel. 0173/564400

The Marchesi di Barolo estate offers a huge range of products. Barolo is its flagship wine and the '96 vintage has great promise. Let's start with the highly acclaimed Cannubi vineyard selection whose palate displays its character and length. A first hint of roses and violets is followed by solid, complex fruit backed up by concentrated tannins. Although sincere and elegant, the nose is still a little closed. The slightly more open and lively Sarmassa possesses complex aromas of ripe fruit, notably mulberry and cherry preserve, and a full body. A notch or two down the scale, the Coste di Rose lacks complexity and excitement. In contrast, the Estate Vineyard is a well-balanced wine with liquorice and vanilla notes following hot on the heels of great fruit aromas, and preceding a full-flavoured, tangy, attractive palate. Our pick of the Riserva wines is the Barolo '93, witness to the fact that this estate can produce outstanding wines in less than excellent years. The lively nose and palate usher in rich flavours and a robust tannic structure. The well-made Barbaresco Creja '96 is velvety on the palate, which offers lingering notes of berry fruit. The Barbera d'Alba Pajagal '97 shows its hand in its violet-ruby colour. Nose and palate offer a heady range of intense fragrances and aromas, among which black cherry and raspberry stand out. The Barbera d'Alba Ruvei '98 lacks the power of the Pajagal wine but nevertheless reveals enticingly ripe fruit. The estate obtains its Dolcetto d'Alba '99 from two vineyard selections, Madonna di Como and Boschetti. The former is agreeable and fruity, while the Boschetti is darker in appearance and fuller bodied thanks to remarkable tannic structure. As always, the Moscato Zagara is well-made.

● Barolo Sarmassa '96	YY	6
● Dolcetto d'Alba S. Lorenzo '99	YY	4
● Barbera d'Alba Cannubi '97	Y	4
● Barbera d'Alba Cannubi Muscatel '97	Y	4
● Barolo Castellero '96	Y	6
● Barbera d'Alba Cannubi '96	YY	4
● Barolo Cannubi '90	YY	6
● Barolo Cannubi '93	YY	6
● Barolo Castellero Ris. '90	YY	6
● Barolo Sarmassa '94	YY	6
● Barolo Sarmassa Ris. '90	YY	6
● Barolo Bricco Sarmassa '93	Y	6
● Barolo Cannubi '95	Y	6

● Barbera d'Alba Pajagal '97	YY	4
● Barolo Cannubi '96	YY	6
● Barolo Estate Vineyard '96	YY	6
● Barolo Ris. '93	YY	6
● Barolo Sarmassa '96	YY	6
● Dolcetto d'Alba Boschetti '99	YY	3*
● Dolcetto d'Alba Madonna di Como '99	YY	3*
● Barbaresco Creja '96	Y	5
● Barbera d'Alba Ruvei '98	Y	3
● Barolo Coste di Rose '96	Y	6
○ Moscato d'Asti Zagara '99	Y	3
● Barolo Estate Vineyard '90	YYY	6
● Barolo Cannubi '95	YY	6
● Barolo Estate Vineyard '95	YY	6

BAROLO (CN)

BARTOLO MASCARELLO
VIA ROMA, 15
12060 BAROLO (CN)
TEL. 0173/56125

BAROLO (CN)

E. PIRA & FIGLI - CHIARA BOSCHIS
VIA VITTORIO VENETO, 1
12060 BAROLO (CN)
TEL. 0173/56247

Bartolo Mascarello's Barolo brings to mind the words of journalist Paolo Monelli: "Its colour takes me back to the towers of Bologna burning against the setting sun unexpectedly revealed by a stormy sky. It persuasively yet forcefully takes possession of the palate with its mouth-filling rotundity and its dry vigour". Bartolo is an important, charismatic figure in the Langhe and has made a Barolo that reflects his personality – seductive, with a wide range of flavours and aggressively vibrant notes. His Barolo '96 is worth every point of its Two Glass score. An austere wine, it owes its refined elegance to a precise discipline that respects the old winemaking traditions. Brilliant garnet with an orange rim, it abounds in intense, harmonious aromas that linger warmly. The aristocratic palate unveils muscular tannins and sustained acidity. Its elegance shines through in the well-balanced finish that lingers satisfyingly. We also gave Bartolo's Barbera d'Alba '98 Two Glasses. Made with fruit from the San Lorenzo vineyard, it has a pervasive nose of fresh fruit, red berries and roses. The palate is warm and enticing, with juicy fruit, and the finish is reminiscent of black cherry syrup. The Dolcetto d'Alba '98, obtained from the grapes of the Monrobiolo and Ruè vineyards, is not up to the standard of the preceding wines, perhaps because it has not yet spent much time in the bottle. Disappointing on the nose, it nevertheless has a rich, refreshing palate backed up by up-front acidity and tannins.

Young entrepreneur Chiara Boschis, who holds a degree in Economics and Business Studies, has been running this historic, early 20th-century estate in the heart of Barolo country full-time since 1990. Credit should go to Chiara for the successful relaunching of an estate whose full-bodied, characterful wines are today up there with the biggest names in the international wine market. The estate adopts modern winemaking methods, including brief maceration on the skins that give its products a lovely velvet smoothness. This does not, however, detract from nebbiolo's gutsy grip, which is enhanced by the skilful use made of the estate's technology. The quality of the grapes more than justifies the use of new barriques. Even in difficult years, when rigorous thinning of the vines and strict selections are necessary, the structure generated by the fruit is sufficient to benefit from a sojourn in oak – remember that fabulous Barolo of '94. The grapes for this Barolo come exclusively from the prestigious Cannubi subzone, famed for the delicacy of its wine which in this vintage also has remarkable power. The Cannubi '96 has swept back to reclaim its Three Glass. The firm ruby colour shades into garnet and the nose offers warm, fruit-rich notes that come through in the crisp aromas of very ripe wild berries. Undertones of roasted coffee and cakes add to its complex allure. The entry on the palate is full-bodied, revealing the wine's firm texture, before it opens out to reveal generous phenols that underpin the intriguing palate and lend weight to the long finish. Well-judged oak lingers to add a note of sweetness.

● Barolo '96	♟♟	6
● Barbera d'Alba		
Vigna S. Lorenzo '98	♟♟	4
● Dolcetto d'Alba		
Monrobiolo e Ruè '98	♟	4
● Barolo '83	♟♟♟	6
● Barolo '84	♟♟♟	6
● Barolo '85	♟♟♟	6
● Barolo '89	♟♟♟	6
● Barolo '88	♟♟	6
● Barolo '90	♟♟	6
● Barolo '93	♟♟	6
● Barolo '95	♟	6

● Barolo Cannubi '96	♟♟♟	6
● Barolo '94	♟♟♟	6
● Barolo Ris. '90	♟♟♟	6
● Barolo '93	♟♟	6
● Barolo Cannubi '95	♟♟	6

BAROLO (CN)

GIUSEPPE RINALDI
VIA MONFORTE, 3
12060 BAROLO (CN)
TEL. 0173/56156

Giuseppe Rinaldi has just added several new underground cellars to the beautiful winery where he employs traditional production methods with a class and a style that reflect the man himself. Large barrels and slow maceration bring out his nebbiolo's strong personality, which comes through in the robust tannins and full body. Giuseppe obtains fruit from some of the most legendary subzones, including Cannubi and Brunate. He also takes a traditional approach in choosing to vinify grapes from several different crus to obtain a greater complexity in his wines. This year we found ourselves favouring the Cannubi San Lorenzo-Ravera, whose '96 vintage is a lovely garnet-ruby edged with orange. Its rich, fascinating nose is full of fruit that comes through in vivid notes of redcurrant and mulberry. Interesting green notes of bramble overlay complex hints of leather and liquorice to round out this seductive nose. The wine's class is evident the moment it hits the palate as the mature, robust tannins back up the complex structure. The follow-through is well-sustained, progressing steadily to a finish that, although not particularly powerful, has great style. The fairly deep garnet-ruby Barolo Brunate-Le Coste possesses a more discreet nose, proffering notes of raspberry and bilberry that emerge against hints of hay and camomile. The palate is well-structured, with beautiful balance that lasts right through to the orderly, lingering, liquorice-tinged finish.

BAROLO (CN)

LUCIANO SANDRONE
VIA PUGNANE, 4
12060 BAROLO (CN)
TEL. 0173/560021

A solid family-based approach to business has given this very able Barolo producer just the shot of energy and self-confidence it needed. Witness the comprehensive renovation that the estate has just undergone. At the foot of the magnificent Cannubi hills they have built a cellar-residence that manages to be both beautiful and practical, traditional yet modern. Their big, bold, brassy Barolo Cannubi Boschis '96 bowled us over. A beautifully intense ruby wine, it proffers limpid, complex aromas of cocoa and red fruit preserve. The palate is full of character, with solid structure and excellent balance. The finish is very long indeed. The Barolo Le Vigne '96, obtained from a blend of grapes from Barolo, Monforte and Serralunga, has a gamey, balsamic bouquet with hints of plum and elder. The palate is generous and stylish, but a tad weak on the personality front. The Nebbiolo d'Alba Valmaggiore '98, its tannins and body perfectly judged, releases pleasant notes of liquorice and spice. The Barbera d'Alba '98, from the Barolo and Monforte vineyards, continues to provide all the pleasures of a full, well-rounded wine with polish, poise and character. To round off this prestigious selection, the panel sampled a superb Dolcetto d'Alba. Luciano Sandrone has always distinguished himself with this vintage, and here he has produced a red that, contrary to expectations, is not at all simple, but full-bodied and rendered beautifully smooth by an elegant, fruit-rich nose.

● Barolo Brunate-Le Coste '96	♟♟	6
● Barolo Cannubi		
S. Lorenzo-Ravera '96	♟♟	6
● Barolo Brunate '90	♟♟	6
● Barolo Brunate '91	♟♟	6
● Barolo Brunate '92	♟♟	6
● Barolo Brunate-Le Coste '94	♟♟	6
● Barolo Brunate-Le Coste '95	♟♟	6
● Barolo Brunate-Le Coste '93	♟♟	6
● Barolo Cannubi		
S. Lorenzo-Ravera '95	♟♟	6
● Barolo Cannubi		
S. Lorenzo-Ravera '93	♟	6

● Barbera d'Alba '98	♟♟	5
● Barolo Cannubi Boschis '96	♟♟	6
● Barolo Le Vigne '96	♟♟	6
● Dolcetto d'Alba '99	♟♟	4
● Nebbiolo d'Alba Valmaggiore '98	♟	5
● Barolo '83	♟♟♟	6
● Barolo '84	♟♟♟	6
● Barolo Cannubi Boschis '85	♟♟♟	6
● Barolo Cannubi Boschis '86	♟♟♟	6
● Barolo Cannubi Boschis '87	♟♟♟	6
● Barolo Cannubi Boschis '89	♟♟♟	6
● Barolo Cannubi Boschis '90	♟♟♟	6
● Barbera d'Alba '97	♟♟	5
● Nebbiolo d'Alba Valmaggiore '97	♟	5

BAROLO (CN)

Giorgio Scarzello e Figli
Via Alba, 29
12060 Barolo (CN)
tel. 0173/56170

Giorgio Scarzello, his wife, Gemma, and their son, Federico, who has just gained his oenology diploma at Alba, produce 22,000 bottles from their four and a half hectares in Barolo's Merenda subzone and the one and a half hectares they rent in Monteu Roero. This year, for the first time, they have released a Barbera Superiore, a '97 vintage with a limited production of 3,000 bottles, which we liked very much. Aged in six-hectolitre casks, it has a very dense, concentrated garnet colour. Its generous nose fascinates with aromas of cherry and leaves over complex toast and mineral undertones. The palate flaunts its breadth and weight right from entry, progressing sure-footedly and kept well in hand by the robust sinew. The lingering finish satisfyingly echoes the concentrated fruit and green notes. One Glass goes to the Dolcetto '98 for the medium intensity of the colour and a nose themed around a flower-and-fruit combination of violets and berries. The palate is well-structured while the finish is concentrated and gratifying. Fairly intense garnet-ruby in colour with a palish rim, the Barolo '96 offers an interesting nose with notes of fruit preserve and cocoa slightly marred by a hint of dryness. The entry on the palate is quite soft and vigorous, following through steadily into a long finish. The simple, uncomplicated Nebbiolo '98 is well put together with its raspberry and rhubarb nose and a fairly vigorous palate that finishes on a satisfying note of liquorice. The Barbera '98 is a happy-go-lucky and pleasantly rustic tipple.

● Barbera d'Alba Sup. '97	🍷🍷	4
● Barolo '96	🍷🍷	6
● Barbera d'Alba '98	🍷	3
● Dolcetto d'Alba '98	🍷	3
● Langhe Nebbiolo '98	🍷	4
● Barbera d'Alba '97	ΥΥ	4
● Barolo '93	ΥΥ	6
● Barolo '95	ΥΥ	6
● Barolo Vigna Merenda '90	ΥΥ	6

BAROLO (CN)

Tenuta La Volta - Cabutto
Loc. La Volta, 13
12060 Barolo (CN)
tel. 0173/56168

The wines of the Tenuta La Volta are traditional, which is just the way owners Osvaldo and Bruno Cabutto like them. The Cabuttos macerate the fruit for a fairly long period and subject their all wines, with the exception of the red Vendemmiaio, to a long ageing process in large barrels rather than barriques. They only make their Barolo Riserva del Fondatore in the very best years and we shall have to wait until 2002 to taste the '96 vintage. The last vintage released was the '90. The Barbera Bricco delle Viole '98 impressed us with its concentrated garnet colour and wide range of aromas, highlighting mulberry and raspberry notes that harmonize nicely with more complex hints of almond paste, fig leaf and toastiness. The palate is juicy and broad with strong tannins that shadow the wine's stay with the progression through to the vigorous cocoa and liquorice-themed finish. The Barolo Vigna La Volta '96 has a concentrated colour and a distinctive, well-sustained nose redolent of berry fruit jam, almond and cocoa over interesting green notes. The palate opens out solidly and seamlessly, becoming a little austere in mid palate before culminating in a tangy, lingering finish with a complex after-aroma. We also liked the Dolcetto Vigna La Volta for its agreeable colour, raspberry and cassis nose masking notes of pepper, and the full-bodied palate with a lingering finish that lays the focus on the up-front tannins. Lastly, the Vendemmiaio has a bright colour and an appealing nose of peach and vanilla. The palate has power and concentration while there are hints of liquorice in the finish.

● Barbera d'Alba Sup. Bricco delle Viole '98	🍷🍷	4
● Barolo Vigna La Volta '96	🍷🍷	6
● Dolcetto d'Alba Vigna La Volta '99	🍷	3
● Langhe Vendemmiaio '97	🍷	5
● Barolo Riserva del Fondatore '90	ΥΥ	6
● Barbera d'Alba Sup. Bricco delle Viole '97	Υ	4
● Barolo Vigna La Volta '95	Υ	6
● Langhe Vendemmiaio '96	Υ	5

BAROLO (CN)

BAROLO (CN)

TERRE DA VINO
VIA BERGESIA, 6
12060 BAROLO (CN)
TEL. 0173/564611

G. D. VAJRA
VIA DELLE VIOLE, 25
LOC. VERGNE
12060 BAROLO (CN)
TEL. 0173/56257

Here we have a new address for the Terre da Vino estate that has moved from Moriondo Torinese to Barolo. The estate offers a wide, good-quality selection from many different kinds of wine. We gave a very high score to two of their Barberas, the Croere '97 and La Luna e i Falò '98. The former has a vibrant garnet colour with a firm, narrow rim and a mature, fruity nose proffering balsamic notes of fresh pine resin. The palate is full-bodied, robust and well-sustained, and the finish lingers. La Luna e i Falò is deep ruby in colour and the nose is redolent of fruit with a sweet note of oak, vanilla, toastiness and hay. On the palate, it has a slightly sinewy character offset by good concentration and tannins that back up the long finish. The Barolo Poderi Parussi '96 is garnet with a slightly orange rim and offers ripe fruit aromas reminiscent of jam. The well-structured palate culminates in a satisfying finish. The dense colour of the Barbaresco La Casa in Collina releases notes of redcurrant, strawberry, vanilla and toastiness. Full on entry, the texture of the palate is slightly compromised by the effect of the tannins, but the finish lingers. Turning to the whites, the Chardonnay Tenuta Magnona flaunts a rich, straw-yellow colour shading into gold and a banana and cream nose with unusual vegetable notes. The palate is effortlessly soft. The Monferrato Bianco Tra Donne Sole is silky and rich in fruit while the two Gavis are very drinkable and have uncomplicated, approachable bouquets. The Chardonnay Rocche di Ricaldone is straightforward and well-made. And to complete the tasting, we have two dessert wines, the Malvasia Vezzolano and the Moscato Passito La Bella Estate.

The vineyards of this 20-year-old estate, highly acclaimed for the quality of its wines, lie in Vergne, La Morra, Fossati and on the Bricco delle Viole. They are located near the top of the altitude range for Barolo nebbiolo grapes, so an experienced hand is required to tend the vineyards and to run the cellar. For the dolcetto variety, however, the height is perfect. Barolo Bricco delle Viole '96 goes home with Two Glasses this year for its elegance and sheer force. Dense ruby in colour with a blood-red rim, its aromas are varied and persistent. The warm, pervasive fruit notes are redolent of stewed plums and morello cherry, with faintly exotic notes of spice. The '99 Dolcetto, obtained from the estate's Coste and Fossati plots, is every bit as good as the Barolo. Ruby red with deep purple and violet highlights, it has a generous, alcohol-rich nose nuanced with berry fruit and raspberries. The palate is warm, rich in succulent fruit, and followed up by just the right balance of tannins and acidity. To round things off, the finish is sumptuous. The Barbera d'Alba Bricco delle Viole '98 is utterly delicious. Its aromas are intense, vibrant, and fresh, suggesting vanilla and black cherry jam. The warm palate is substantial, sweet and well-rounded, offering crisp notes of strawberry and raspberry with an elegant finish. The Langhe Freisa Kyè '99 is an aristocrat, its alcohol-rich nose revealing more complex notes of hazelnut. Well-structured and fresh-tasting, it unveils a finish with a hint of acidity that lends character. The riesling-based Langhe Bianco is very interesting, offering us a good example of the personality that the Langhe vineyards can bring to the variety.

● Barbera d'Alba Croere '97	▼▼	4
● Barbera d'Asti La Luna e i Falò '98	▼▼	4
● Barolo Poderi Parussi '96	▼▼	6
● Barbaresco La Casa in Collina '97	▼	5
○ Gavi Masseria dei Carmelitani '99	▼	3
● Malvasia di Castelnuovo		
Don Bosco Vezzolano '99	▼	3
○ Monferrato Bianco Tra Donne Sole '99	▼	4
○ Piemonte Chardonnay		
Rocche di Ricaldone '99	▼	3
○ Piemonte Chardonnay		
Tenuta Magnona '99	▼	3
○ Gavi Ca' da Bosio '99		3
● Barbera d'Asti La Luna e I Falò '97	♈♈	4
● Langhe Rosso La Malora '97	♈♈	4

● Barbera d'Alba		
Bricco delle Viole '98	▼▼	5
● Barolo Bricco delle Viole '96	▼▼	6
● Dolcetto d'Alba		
Coste & Fossati '99	▼▼	5
● Langhe Freisa Kyè '99	▼▼	5
○ Langhe Bianco '99	▼▼	5
● Barbera d'Alba		
Bricco delle Viole '93	♈♈	5
● Barolo '93	♈♈	6
● Barolo Bricco delle Viole '94	♈♈	6
● Barolo Bricco delle Viole '95	♈♈	6

BASTIA MONDOVÌ (CN)

BRICCO DEL CUCÙ
FRAZ. BRICCO, 21
12060 BASTIA MONDOVÌ (CN)
TEL. 0174/60153

Dario Sciolla has transformed this estate radically over the last few years and today bottles every single one of the approximately 40,000 units produced. Dario's father, Giuseppe, who is in his 80s, has more or less retired and in his place Dario has taken on two new employees to look after his eight hectares. He grows almost exclusively dolcetto, but also has 1,500 arneis vines from which he produces 2,500 bottles of Langhe Bianco. This white, an outsider in red territory, has such a strong personality that it appeals mainly to connoisseurs. The full body, enhanced by a high alcohol level, tends to suggest oxidisation and brings to mind a Vin Jaune del Jura, another characteristically tangy wine. If you like wines in the Vin Jaune style, you'll love Langhe Bianco. Of the Dolcettos presented, the Langhe is naturally enough the one with least structure and complexity but one sip is enough to realize how deliciously drinkable it actually is. The Dolcetto di Dogliani, of which Dario produces 20,000 bottles, has a very dense, almost opaque colour and explosive aromas of ripe fruit – mulberry jam – and almond overlying elegant spicy notes. The palate is so muscular that its overall balance is compromised but the lingering finish tells you that this is a wine with a very good future. Dario has decided to postpone releasing his Bricco San Bernardo, an exceptionally juicy Dolcetto, until the spring of next year, to give it time to develop the balance it currently lacks. We could not agree more with this move. All that remains to point out is that the winery has invested this year in a small cooling system and that all the Dolcettos are now fermented and aged in wooden barrels.

●	Dolcetto di Dogliani '99	🍷🍷	3*
○	Langhe Bianco '99	🍷	3
●	Langhe Dolcetto '99	🍷	2*
●	Dolcetto di Dogliani Sup. Bricco S. Bernardo '98	🍸🍸	3

BORGONE SUSA (TO)

CARLOTTA
VIA CONDOVE, 61
10050 BORGONE SUSA (TO)
TEL. 011/9646150

The Carlotta estate, with its family home, winery and beautiful, terraced Costadoro vineyards, lies at the side of the SS 24 road just outside Borgonet. The estate is named after Carla Cornetto, who in 1991, together with her husband, began to improve the quality of her family's wines by applying modern oenological techniques. Ten years on, Carlotta produces 6,000 bottles a year and has become a shining example of the valley's new viticultural potential. Several years ago, the estate, which has about one hectare under vine, was awarded Valsusa DOC status. In addition to Costadoro, it has the Vignecombe and Roche du Bau (formerly known as Rocca del Lupo), a lovely terraced vineyard lying just below Ramats di Chiomonte, high in the hills at an altitude of over 700 metres. This year, Carlotta released its wines without DOC labelling but they are exactly the same categories of wine we noted and called to your attention in the Guide last year. The Roche du Bau '99, obtained from barbera, avanà, and a small proportion of gamay, has good structure and acidity. This year, the Costadoro has been released under the Il Conte label in honour of Conte Groppello di Borgone Susa, the finance minister of the royal house of Savoy, who terraced the vineyard at the beginning of the 18th century. Obtained from barbera, ciliegiolo and neretta cuneese grapes, it reveals notes of wild berries introducing a deliciously soft palate. This is Carlotta's pièce de résistance. The Roceja, known as Vignecombe until last year, is still young but has a deep ruby red colour with floral, grassy aromas. Definitely not a wine to cellar. It will be drinking wonderfully next spring.

●	Il Conte '99	🍷🍷	4
●	Roche du Bau '99	🍷	3
●	Roceja '99	🍷	3
●	Valsusa Costadoro '98	🍸🍸	3
●	Valsusa Rocca del Lupo '98	🍸	3
●	Valsusa Vignacombe '98	🍸	4

BRA (CN)

BRIGNANO FRASCATA (AL)

ASCHERI
VIA PIUMATI, 23
12042 BRA (CN)
TEL. 0172/412394

PAOLO POGGIO
VIA ROMA, 67
15050 BRIGNANO FRASCATA (AL)
TEL. 0131/784650 - 0131/784929

Matteo Ascheri has a style that manages to combine both tradition and innovation. In 1993, he chose to plant his Montalupa plot at Bra with non-traditional unusual varieties, a move that has amply demonstrated his vocation for both vineyard management and for the cellar, where his close attention to obtaining just the right balance in his wines is bearing fruit. Matteo's viognier-based Montalupa Bianco '99 shows an improvement in his use of oak and in the overall harmony of the product. Medium straw-yellow in colour, its nose initially releases faint vegetable aromas but then opens out to reveal notes of flowers and fruit. The seamless, silky, well-sustained palate culminates in a lovely long finish of apple and apricot. The Barolo Sorano from Serralunga flaunts a vibrant colour and aromas that gradually unfold to reveal redcurrant, green leaf, toastiness and menthol. The palate, elegant and vibrant, is underpinned by fine tannins as it progresses to a vigorous finish with hints of liquorice. The Barolo Vigna dei Pola is almost as good, with its bouquet of dried flowers and rustic notes of warm earth. The palate has good texture, although only moderate breadth. The Barbera Fontanelle has a vaguely mineral nose with overtones of almond, ripe berry fruit and pepper, while the palate is vigorous and well-balanced. The Dolcetto Vigna Nirane has a smooth, complex palate that echoes the slightly unsophisticated nose. The Nebbiolo Bricco San Giacomo proffers faintly balsamic aromas and a reasonable body on the palate. But we shall have to wait until the next issue of the Guide to review the Montalupa Rosso '98, as Matteo has decide to extend its sojourn in the cellar.

This small estate in the Colli Tortonesi area attracted our attention last year with its high-scoring Barbera Derio. While it caught our eye again this year, the estate's other wines were also rather good and, we feel, justify the promotion of the winery from a mere mention to a full Guide profile. The Poggio family has been making wine for three generations and Paolo, the latest in the line, is taking full advantage of his vineyards in the Tortone area. He has changed the way the vineyard is run and has invested money in the small winery itself. The grapes at his disposal are of very good quality, for the vines are over 50 years old and have modest yields. Paolo's Colli Tortonesi Derio, obtained from a selection of the very best barbera grapes, is almost impenetrably dark and the concentrated, very full-bodied palate has just the right amount of varietal acidity to back it up. The black cherry aromas mingle deliciously with the light toasty oak lent by a 12-month sojourn in small casks. The Timorasso, a variety Paolo has always grown and one that is emblematic of the zone, unveils camomile and citrus, blending with the mineral tones characteristic of the variety. The palate is well-structured and mirrors the nose while the colour is a moderately intense straw-yellow. A lowish One Glass score goes to Paolo's base Barbera for its vibrant colour and ripe black cherry nose. Its fruit-rich palate fades a little towards the rather short, dryish finish. The moscato-based Moscatè is also very pleasant, tempting the eye with a lovely golden colour, the nose with fresh, varietal aromas, and the palate with good weight, length and just the right degree of sweetness. A Guide mention also goes to the uncomplicated but very drinkable Cortese.

● Barolo Sorano '96	🍷🍷	6
○ Montalupa Bianco '99	🍷🍷	6
● Barbera d'Alba		
Vigna Fontanelle '99	🍷	4
● Barolo Vigna dei Pola '96	🍷	6
● Dolcetto d'Alba Vigna Nirane '99	🍷	3
● Nebbiolo d'Alba		
Bricco S. Giacomo '98	🍷	4
● Montalupa Rosso '97	🍷🍷	6
● Barolo Vigna dei Pola '95	🍷	6
● Barolo Sorano '95	🍷	6

● Colli Tortonesi Barbera Derio '98	🍷🍷	4
○ Timorasso '98	🍷🍷	3*
● Colli Tortonesi Barbera '99	🍷	2*
○ Moscatè '99	🍷	2*
○ Colli Tortonesi Cortese '99		1

CALAMANDRANA (AT)   CALOSSO (AT)

MICHELE CHIARLO
S. DA NIZZA CANELLI, 99
14042 CALAMANDRANA (AT)
TEL. 0141/769030

SCAGLIOLA
FRAZ. S. SIRO, 42
14052 CALOSSO (AT)
TEL. 0141/853183

Basking in the glow of the acclaim he has received for his wines, Michele Chiarlo continues to forge ahead in the quality stakes. His Barbera d'Asti Cipressi della Court '98, released for the first time this year, parades a plethora of aroma, from berry fruit and flowers to vanilla, an intense palate, well-handled acidity, and a strong finish. We awarded Two full Glasses to the more ambitious, purple-hued La Court '97 which boasts a nose of cherry preserve, cocoa and coffee and a warm, tangy palate with great texture. The stylish Barbera Valle del Sole is good again this year. The previous vintage had more structure but its balance is thoroughly convincing, despite the marked acidity. We also liked the Gavi Fornaci di Tassarolo '97, obtained from a 100-year-old vineyard with a very limited yield. Who would have guessed that this wine would turn out to be so cellarable? Aromas of peach and spring flowers dominate the cortese, chardonnay and sauvignon-based Plenilunio '98, a tangy, well-structured product. The Moscato Rocca delle Uccellette '99 surprises with its balance and elegance. Both the Countacc! '97, a blend of barbera, nebbiolo and cabernet sauvignon, and the rounded, mouth-filling Barilot '97 with its fruit-rich aromas, are both excellent. Chiarlo's garnet Barbaresco Asili '97 has a berry fruit and spice nose while the palate is well-structured, with good complexity and length. The Barolo Cannubi '96 has a modern slant, a generous nose of liquorice, blackberry and dried roses, and a soft, sweet palate. However, it lacks the sheer oomph of the top-notch Barolos. The panel thought that the Cerequio was one of the finest Barolos of its vintage, and accordingly gave it Three Glasses. The sumptuous aromas embrace blackcurrant, cherry, spice and mint, ushering in a close-knit palate with great structure, velvet-smooth tannins and a warm, lingering finish made with a master's touch.

The Scagliola brothers, who are becoming technically more and more reliable, came up with a selection of exceptional, characterful wines for our tasting. This year, for the first time, they have released their stunning Barbera SanSì Selezione '97, aged unhurriedly in the finest Sansì barriques. A dense, almost opaque ruby in colour with a youthful rim, it unleashes crisp, varietal cherry aromas that blend with notes of leather, cakes, and thyme. The entry on the palate is firm and rich, progressing to reveal considerable sinew kept in check by the wine's solid texture. The subtle understated tannins enhance a long, concentrated finish. Marginally lower down the scale, but still worth Two Glasses, is the vibrant-hued Barbera SanSì '98. In the generous wide array of aromas on the nose, berry fruit and vanilla come through over a distinctly balsamic vein. The palate offers good texture and plenty of energy, ensured by the prominent tannins and alcohol. Less complex and a bit more rustic is the Scagliolas' Barbera Frem '99, whose attractive nose is redolent of cherries, cloves, and warm earth. The palate has admirable texture and a vibrant, thoroughly satisfying finish. The excellent Moscato Volo di Farfalle proffers elderflower, pear and peach fragrances against a backdrop of fresh aromatic herbs. The palate mirrors these aromas perfectly, with a refreshing prickle and a complex, lingering finish. The Chardonnay '99 has a honey and fruit-in-syrup nose as well as an admirably full palate. Last on the list was the robust, personable Dolcetto Busiord.

● Barolo Cerequio '96	♈♈♈	6
● Barbaresco Asili '97	♈♈	6
● Barbera d'Asti Sup. Cipressi della Court '98	♈♈	4
● Barbera d'Asti Sup. La Court '97	♈♈	5
● Barbera d'Asti Sup. Valle del Sole '97	♈♈	5
● Barolo Cannubi '96	♈♈	6
○ Gavi Fornaci di Tassarolo '97	♈♈	5
● Langhe Barilot '97	♈♈	5
● Monferrato Countacc! '97	♈♈	6
○ Monferrato Plenilunio '98	♈	5
○ Moscato d'Asti Rocca delle Uccellette '99	♈	4
● Barolo Cerequio '95	♈♈♈	6

● Barbera d'Asti SanSì '98	♈♈	5
● Barbera d'Asti SanSì Sel. '97	♈♈	5
○ Moscato d'Asti Volo di Farfalle '99	♈♈	3*
● Barbera d'Asti Frem '99	♈	3
● Langhe Dolcetto Busiord '99	♈	3
○ Piemonte Chardonnay '99	♈	4
● Barbera d'Asti SanSì '96	♈♈	5
● Barbera d'Asti SanSì '97	♈♈	5
● Barbera d'Asti SanSì '95	♈	5

CALOSSO (AT)

CAMINO (AL)

TENUTA DEI FIORI
VIA VALCALOSSO, 3
REG. RODOTIGLIA
14052 CALOSSO (AT)
TEL. 0141/826938 - 0141/966500

TENUTA GAIANO
VIA TRINO, 8
15020 CAMINO (AL)
TEL. 0142/469440

Walter Bosticardo, an inspired eclectic of a winemaker from Calosso, surprises us every year with something new. The first to promote Asti made using the "metodo classico", he has moved on to pastures new, namely the Gamba di Pernice, a vine and a wine produced exclusively in this town near Asti. Ever on the crest of the innovation wave, in the mid 80s Walter released Rairì, a Moscato d'Asti made in the traditional manner, and hot on its heels, the barrique-aged Chardonnay Al Sole. This year, he presented us with a fascinating new white, Il Vento, the latest in a long line of wines that embody their inventor's best qualities. To make this wine, which has 14.5-percent alcohol, Walter used chardonnay grapes picked when very ripe, and the result is extremely interesting. A vibrant straw-yellow in colour, Il Vento abounds in fruit aromas of ripe apple and pear over lingering mineral notes. Entry on the palate is buttery, juicy and perfectly balanced by a vein of acidity that gives the wine length and delicacy. The lingering finish is exalted by delicious notes of honey. Also worth a mention is the Barbera d'Asti Is, a product of the exceptional '97 harvest. Absent for some time, the moscato-based Rairì makes its comeback this year. It is a wine that can only be made in years when the vintage offers healthy, ripe bunches of grapes. A wonderful sweet wine, it reveals the flower and peach aromas typical of a Moscato and a mouth-filling finish. The rich, lingering palate perfectly echoes the nose. Finally, the Dolcetto earned its One Glass very comfortably.

On his estate on the righthand bank of the Po, Gigi Lavandar continues to produce excellent wines with his oenologist, Giovanni Bailo, and his partner, Pier Iviglia, who takes care of public relations. Their wines, all labelled Monferrato, bring out the personality of native Piedmont vines that are frequently misunderstood in their own territory. This year, the Vigna della Torretta '97 selection is superb. A mighty, uncompromising Barbera with great structure, it owes as much to the vineyard as it does to the cellar. The impenetrable black hue anticipates a concentrated nose with all the aromas of a great red – stewed fruit, spices, Peruvian bark and cocoa. The palate is full-bodied and persistent, exploding in a wealth of juicy fruit. We were treated to an early taste of Lavandar's other Barbera, the Gallianum '98. A vibrant purplish ruby in colour, its has a nose of berry fruit and jam while its palate reveals warmth, power, and length. It will improve with cellaring, but even now it is a fine example of how to vinify and age a wine exclusively in stainless steel. The Grignolino '99's solid structure won it Two Glasses. Much darker in colour than most wines in its category, it has a rich nose of fruit and spices, particularly pepper while its close-to-perfect palate displays a lovely balance of freshness, warmth and tannins, all of which combine to make the finish long and satisfyingly full. The Birbarossa, obtained from a blend of aromatic red Piedmont varieties, intrigued us. A lovely purple ruby in colour, it offers aromatic notes of berry fruit laced with bitterish notes and spices. The freisa and ruché varieties used make their presence felt in the wine's aromas, basic freshness and astringency. A mention also goes to the estate's standard-label Barbera del Monferrato '98, a perfectly decent every-day tipple.

● Barbera d'Asti Is '97	♟♟	4
O Il Vento Chardonnay '99	♟♟	3*
O Rairì Moscato '99	♟♟	3*
● Monferrato Dolcetto '99	♟	3
● Monferrato Rosso '95	♟♟	5
● Monferrato Rosso Cabernet '96	♟♟	4
● Barbera d'Asti Vigneto del Tulipano Nero '96	♟	4
● Gamba di Pernice '97	♟	3

● Barbera del M.to Gallianum '98	♟♟	3*
● Barbera del M.to Vigna della Torretta '97	♟♟	4
● Grignolino del M.to Casalese '99	♟♟	3*
● Birbarossa '99	♟	3
● Barbera del M.to '98		2
● Barbera del M.to Gallianum '97	♟♟	3
● Barbera del M.to Vigna della Torretta '96	♟♟	4

CANALE (CN)

CANALE (CN)

CASCINA CA' ROSSA
LOC. CASE SPARSE, 56
12043 CANALE (CN)
TEL. 0173/98348 - 0173/98201

CASCINA CHICCO
VIA VALENTINO, 144
12043 CANALE (CN)
TEL. 0173/979069

With a series of small but shrewd acquisitions, Angelo Ferrio has managed to almost double his estate. Today it boasts 15 hectares planted to vine in comparison with the eight hectares owned in 1996. Many of these plots must be tended by hand as they lie on steep slopes. Over the last few years, the passion and dedication Angelo has lavished on his winery have increased not just the number of bottles produced, now about 70,000, but also their quality. His Roero Audinaggio, a ruby wine that shades into garnet, unveils a wide array of stylish aromas featuring ripe fruit laced with notes of red and black fruit preserves, cakes and spices. The entry on the palate is warm, and up-front tannins lead the wine through to a finish in which tactile and taste sensations linger long and deliciously in the mouth. The final note is an explosive echo of the initial fruit. The deep ruby Barbera Vigna Mulassa has a faintly orange rim and a generous nose whose balance is only faintly disturbed by marked oak-derived notes but there are also crisp hints of berry fruit and juniper coming through over sweet spices. The palate is close-knit, with slightly austere tannins and a very satisfying finish. Both of the Arneis, the Merica and the second-label version, are good. The Merica is medium straw-yellow in colour with a fruit-rich nose, good texture on the palate, and a tangy, complex finish. The standard version has a paler colour and a nose of banana, apricot and spring flowers. Its silky palate leads through to a lively finish. Finally, Angelo's base Barbera is uncomplicated and very drinkable.

Cascina Chicco has expanded progressively over the years to its present size of 20 hectares, which produce 100,000 bottles a year. Work has only recently finished on the beautiful, spacious cellar which offers the Faccendas the perfect environment in which to work comfortably and efficiently. The winery is now complete. The quality of their wines has kept pace with expansion and this year we were excited by the selection they presented for tasting. For the second successive vintage, the Barbera Bric Loira '98 wins our Three Glass award. An almost impenetrable garnet in colour, with a narrow rim, this Barbera has a rich, tempting nose brimming with raspberry, bilberry and peach that merge with toasty oak, mint and white pepper. Its powerful palate is well supported by robust tannins which also bolster the long fruit and spice finish. The Roero Valmaggiore, ruby shading into garnet in colour, has a broad, elegant nose of raspberry, confectioner's cream, mint and nutmeg. The palate develops slowly to unleash an astonishing array of flavours that combine to explode in a delicious chorus. The estate's vibrant-hued Nebbiolo Mompissano, aged partly in casks and partly in large barrels, is also very good. The crisp nose embraces notes of black cherry, redcurrant, vanilla and leather while its the generous palate has rather a severe personality and a fruit-rich finish. Replacing the basic Barbera this year we have the Barbera Granera Alta, a prime example of a robust, well-focused wine. The Favorita has a jolly, fruit-rich nose and an uncomplicated but convincing palate. The varietal aromas of brachetto come through loud and clear in both the Secco and the Dolce Birbét, while the Arneis is tangy and very tempting.

● Barbera d'Alba		
Vigna Mulassa '98	♈♈	4
● Roero Vigna Audinaggio '98	♈♈	5
● Barbera d'Alba '99	♈	3
○ Roero Arneis '99	♈	3
○ Roero Arneis Merica '99	♈	3
● Roero Vigna Audinaggio '96	♈♈♈	5
● Barbera d'Alba		
Vigna Mulassa '97	♈♈	4
● Roero Vigna Audinaggio '97	♈♈	5

● Barbera d'Alba Bric Loira '98	♈♈♈	5
● Nebbiolo d'Alba Mompissano '98	♈♈	5
● Roero Valmaggiore '98	♈♈	5
● Barbera d'Alba Granera Alta '99	♈	3
● Birbét Dolce '99	♈	3
● Birbét Secco '99	♈	3
○ Langhe Favorita '99	♈	3
○ Roero Arneis '99		3
● Barbera d'Alba Bric Loira '97	♈♈♈	5
● Barbera d'Alba Bric Loira '96	♈♈	5
● Nebbiolo d'Alba Mompissano '97	♈♈	4
● Roero Valmaggiore '97	♈♈	4

CANALE (CN)

CANALE (CN)

MATTEO CORREGGIA
VIA S. STEFANO ROERO, 124
12043 CANALE (CN)
TEL. 0173/978009

DELTETTO
C.SO ALBA, 33
12043 CANALE (CN)
TEL. 0173/979383

Matteo Correggia, flanked by his wife Ornella and mother Severina, has finally got the splendid, spacious, well-equipped cellar he wanted. The changes he has made are not just cosmetic for they affect the entire structure of the winery. We start our tasting with the newest wine in the selection Matteo offered us this year, his Langhe Bianco, of which he has produced 2,000 bottles. It was an impressive debut for a product that has great personality and superb balance. Deep straw-yellow in the glass, its complex, generous bouquet is rich in ripe, fragrant fruit. Hints of pineapple, grapefruit, sage and tomato blossom blend with a touch of vanillaed cream that testifies to Matteo's expert use of oak. His intensely coloured Ròche d'Ampsèj offers up notes of berry fruit, vanilla, toastiness, and citron with delicate mineral overtones. The entry on the palate is soft and full of flavour, revealing lively tannins that melt into a warm, lingering finish. This powerful wine highlights the strong personality of the nebbiolo variety and more than deserves another Three Glass distinction. As concentrated and as fascinating as ever, the impenetrable garnet Barbera Marun has a blackberry and cherry nose, well supported by discreet oak. The palate displays the customary fullness of flavour, its underlying softness braced by imperious yet perfectly integrated tannins. The Nebbiolo La Val dei Preti, ruby red with a narrow orange rim, delightfully blends mulberry and cassis with a suggestion of balsam and cakes. The complexity of the concentrated, well-sustained palate is ennobled by assertive tannins. Matteo's base Barbera is velvety and seductive, his Roero flaunts structure and personality, the Anthos, a brachetto, is spicy and aromatic, and his fresh-tasting Arneis is eminently drinkable.

Antonino Deltetto offered us an excellent range of wines this year. His whites, a category in which he has achieved great things in recent years, are every bit as good as the reds and he has managed to bridge the gap between the two by exploiting good vintages to the last grape. His Arneis Daivej is one of the best we tasted. A lustrous straw-yellow, it releases lovely aromas of banana, apple, apricot and spring flowers. The palate is well-balanced, with good thrust through to a complex finish that mirrors the fruit and flowers of the nose. Deltetto's sauvignon and chardonnay-based Langhe Bianco Suasì debuts this year (approximately 2,000 bottles were released). An intense straw-yellow introduces a bouquet nicely poised between wood and fruit. Overtones of vanilla, apricot, and exotic fruits come through. The palate is fleshy and soft while oak-derived aromas tend to prevail in the finish. The Favorita San Michele enchants and the base Arneis is a very attractive tipple. Moving on to the reds, we particularly liked the two Roeros, vinified with modern techniques and aged in barriques. The moderately dark ruby Braja '98 offers aromas that integrate well with the oak. It is still a bit rough on the palate but already shows good complexity and length. The Madonna dei Boschi, also '98, has regained its former glory. A slight note of super-ripeness lends it serious roundness and austerity. A Glass apiece to the Barbera d'Alba Bramè '98 and the Roero Arneis San Michele.

● Roero Ròche d'Ampsèj '97	♟♟♟	6
● Barbera d'Alba '99	♟♟	3*
● Barbera d'Alba Marun '98	♟♟	5
○ Langhe Bianco '99	♟♟	5
● Nebbiolo d'Alba		
La Val dei Preti '98	♟♟	5
● Roero '99	♟♟	3*
● Anthos '99	♟	3
○ Roero Arneis '99	♟	3
● Barbera d'Alba Bricco Marun '95	♟♟♟	5
● Barbera d'Alba Marun '96	♟♟♟	5
● Barbera d'Alba Marun '97	♟♟♟	5
● Nebbiolo d'Alba		
La Val dei Preti '96	♟♟♟	5
● Roero Ròche d'Ampsèj '96	♟♟♟	6

○ Langhe Bianco Suasì '98	♟♟	4
○ Roero Arneis Daivej '99	♟♟	3*
● Roero Braja '98	♟♟	4
● Roero Madonna dei Boschi '98	♟♟	4
● Barbera d'Alba Bramè '98	♟	4
○ Roero Arneis S. Michele '99	♟	3
○ Langhe Favorita S. Michele '99	♟	3
○ Roero Arneis '99		3
● Roero Braja '97	♟♟	4
● Roero Madonna dei Boschi '97	♟♟	4

CANALE (CN)

CANALE (CN)

FUNTANIN
VIA TORINO, 191
12043 CANALE (CN)
TEL. 0173/979488

FILIPPO GALLINO
FRAZ. VALLE DEL POZZO, 63
12043 CANALE (CN)
TEL. 0173/98112

Bruno and Piercarlo Sperone are going for structure. They have adopted techniques, including reasonably long macerations, which allow the full force of their extremely high quality grapes to come through in their wines. Prime examples of the approach are the Roero Bricco Barbisa and the Barbera Ciabot Pierin, which replaces the Sperones' Barbera Superiore. The Bricco Barbisa has a rich garnet-ruby hue and a generous nose with notes of berry fruit, juniper and aromatic herbs. The concentrated palate highlights the strong personality of the nebbiolo's mature tannins, and muscular alcohol puts the final touch to a poised, convincing wine that finishes in an explosion of elegant aromas. The Barbera is almost as impressive. Deep in colour, with a narrow rim, it flaunts satisfying, fragrant aromas of cherry, ripe mulberry, menthol, juniper and liquorice. Pleasantly zesty, the palate culminates in a long, complex and intense finish, borne up by soft yet beefy tannins. The estate's spunky, robust base Barbera proffers berry fruit and aromatic herb fragrances, and a substantial, nicely balanced palate. The Arneis Pierin di Soc's fruit-rich nose is shot through with fresh aromas of citrus fruit and the tangy, inviting palate leads through to a satisfying finish. The base Arneis is also good, unveiling a frank nose and smooth, well-structured palate. The chardonnay-based Papé Bianc tempts with fresh aromas of peaches in syrup, confectioner's cream and cakes, revealing good weight on the palate. Lastly, the fresh-tasting Favorita hints at medlar and peach.

Basking in the glow of the Three Glasses they won last year for their Barbera '97, Maria and Gianni Gallino are determined to maintain the same level of quality. Their two big reds, the Roero Superiore and the Barbera Superiore, are both once again excellent but the Roero has truly surpassed itself. Intense ruby red with garnet highlights in the glass, it is blessed with the wealth of aromas and personality that only great nebbiolo fruit can confer. A suggestion of liqueur fruit blends with mouth-watering notes of coffee, while enticing hints of spice and citrus wood lift this wine to dizzying heights. The entry on the palate is broad and full, with a powerful follow-through bolstered by heavy-duty tannins. The finish is warm, vigorous and long-lasting. Three very well-deserved Glasses for a serious estate that continues to set itself ever more ambitious goals. The Gallinos' Barbera is an impenetrably deep garnet with a brief, firm rim. The wide array of well-defined aromas includes black berry fruit, cocoa, vanilla and autumn leaves. The palate is complex, opening with warm alcohol that is kept in check by delicious tannins, and the long finish echoes the nose satisfyingly. The estate Arneis is a fairly pale straw-yellow with green highlights. Its nose hints at apple and camomile, and the smooth, refreshing palate concludes with a reasonably satisfying finish.

● Barbera d'Alba Ciabot Pierin '98	▾▾	5
● Roero Sup. Bricco Barbisa '98	▾▾	5
● Barbera d'Alba '99	▾	3
○ Langhe Favorita '99	▾	3
○ Papé Bianc '98	▾	4
○ Roero Arneis '99	▾	3
○ Roero Arneis Pierin di Soc '99	▾	3
● Barbera d'Alba Sup. '97	♈♈	4
● Roero Sup. Bricco Barbisa '97	♈♈	5

● Roero Sup. '98	▾▾▾	5
● Barbera d'Alba Sup. '98	▾▾	5
○ Roero Arneis '99	▾	3
● Barbera d'Alba Sup. '97	♈♈♈	5
● Barbera d'Alba Sup. '96	♈♈	4
● Roero Sup. '96	♈♈	4
● Roero Sup. '97	♈♈	4

CANALE (CN)

CANALE (CN)

MALVIRÀ
VIA S. STEFANO ROERO, 144
LOC. CASE SPARSE
12043 CANALE (CN)
TEL. 0173/978145

MONCHIERO - CARBONE
VIA S. STEFANO ROERO, 2
12043 CANALE (CN)
TEL. 0173/95568

Roberto and Massimo Damonte, together with their wives, Patrizia and Federica, are leading lights in the Roero renaissance, proving that great wines can be obtained even from sandy terrain. This year's Roero Superiore selection, the '97, is outstanding, just as robust and full-bodied as any of the big Barolos. A rich ruby red with a faintly orange rim, it offers a fruit and flower nose enhanced by hints of balsam and elegant creamy overtones. It opens out slowly on the palate and follows steadily through, underpinned by well-judged tannins. There was no way we could refuse the Damonte brothers Three Glasses for this superb vintage. Their standard-label Roero is of unusually high quality for a wine with a production of 30,000 bottles. It has good colour and a nose of strawberry and raspberry over mineral notes. On the palate, there is attractive structure, beefy tannins and a lingering finish. The Tre Uve, from 60 percent chardonnay and 20 percent each of sauvignon and arneis, is a rich straw-yellow. Its nose is redolent of banana, peach and peach blossom. Full-flavoured and broad on the palate, it revels in a zesty vein and a deliciously satisfying finish. The arneis-based wines are all good. The Saglietto takes home Two Glasses for its rounder and more intriguingly complex structure. The Renesio is full and silky smooth, the Trinità is enhanced by a sojourn in oak and even the standard-label Arneis is lip-smackingly coherent. The Damontes' Favorita is among the best in its category and should not be missed. Their San Guglielmo '98, 65 percent barbera, 30 percent nebbiolo, and five percent bonarda, will be released next year.

Marco Monchiero, flanked by wife, Lucia Carbone, and son, Francesco, have for years offered us selections of good solid wines made in a balanced, modern style from high quality grapes. Marco, who also finds the time to serve as mayor of Canale, is an expert technician and the quality of his wines bears witness to his skill. This year, in addition to his superb Srü, he presented us with another Roero, the Printi, also an excellent wine. Dense, almost opaque, ruby with a narrow orange rim, its generous nose tempts with clean fruity aromas of bilberry and mulberry that melt into hints of violets, cocoa and juniper over a delicately briny base. Its palate has great texture, with a nice tanginess, and opens out steadily, well supported by sweet tannins that give volume to the lingering cocoa and black fruit finish. The Srü is a lovely deep colour and a bouquet of wild berry fragrances set against a background of sweet spice and balsamic notes from the oak. The palate has admirable texture and the robust tannins complement the warmth of the body. The finish is typically long and lingering. The vibrant straw-yellow Bianco Tamardì '98 has floral aromas through which filter a suggestion of smoke and minerals. Its strong personality is evident on the palate and the warmth of the alcohol is well balanced by acidity. Overall, a very harmonious wine. The Monchieros' Barbera MonBirone has a slightly wood-dominated nose that reveals nuances of fruit and flowers. The tannins are a bit harsh, rendering the palate rather dry and decisive. Another newcomer this year is the Arneis Re Cit, an uncomplicated, well-managed wine.

● Roero Sup. '97	▼▼▼	5
○ Langhe Bianco Tre Uve '98	▼▼	4
● Roero '98	▼▼	4
○ Roero Arneis Saglietto '99	▼▼	4
○ Langhe Favorita '99	▼	3
○ Roero Arneis Renesio '99	▼	3
○ Roero Arneis Trinità '99	▼	3
○ Roero Arneis '99	▼	3
● Roero Sup. '90	♈♈♈	6
● Roero Sup. '93	♈♈♈	6
● Langhe Rosso S. Guglielmo '97	♈♈	5
● Roero Sup. '95	♈♈	5
● Roero Sup. '96	♈♈	5

○ Langhe Bianco Tamardì '98	▼▼	4
● Roero Srü '98	▼▼	5
● Roero Sup. Printi '97	▼▼	5
● Barbera d'Alba MonBirone '98	▼	5
○ Roero Arneis Re Cit '99	▼	3
● Barbera d'Alba MonBirone '97	♈♈	5
● Roero Srü '96	♈♈	5
● Roero Srü '97	♈♈	5
● Roero Sup. '95	♈♈	5

CANELLI (AT)

CANELLI (AT)

CASCINA BARISEL
REG. S. GIOVANNI, 2
14053 CANELLI (AT)
TEL. 0141/824849

GIUSEPPE CONTRATTO
VIA G. B. GIULIANI, 56
14053 CANELLI (AT)
TEL. 0141/823349

The Cascina Barisel produces a total of 20,000 bottles, split between Moscato and two types of Barbera. This year, they presented us with three very nice wines. Their Barbera La Cappelletta is a magnificent vintage and once again takes home Two Glasses, while the Barbera Barisel and a Moscato d'Asti earn One Glass apiece. These are the crowning glories of the estate belonging to the Penna family, comprising Enrico, wife Elda, and sons Franco and Fiorenzo. The Barbera La Cappelletta '97 is an intense ruby with garnet highlights and a slightly paler rim. Its wide range of aromas display varietal fruity notes, notably cherry and wild berries, which blend with hints of pepper and fresh aromatic herbs. Entry on the palate is full-bodied and its follow-through is nicely sustained, with good structure and a barely discernible varietal hint of acidity. Its complex, balanced finish has a lingering after-aroma that echoes the nose. Moderately intense ruby red, the Barbera Barisel's frank nose would be even more pleasing with just a touch more freshness. Nevertheless, its ripe fruit mingles well with notes of coffee and spice and the well-structured palate has nice sinew and a satisfying finish. The Moscato is a rich straw-yellow. Its complex, slightly evolved bouquet is redolent of the aromatic tones of its variety and offers very ripe fruity notes of peach and apple, with a faint suggestion of sage and hedgerow. Nicely balanced, its palate is agreeably prickly and its finish refreshing.

The Contratto estate in Canelli reaffirms its position as regional spumante leader with two excellent offerings, the Asti De Miranda and the Brut Riserva Giuseppe Contratto. Its other selections are also very respectable. Credit for the winery's winning approach goes to brother-and-sister team Antonella and Carlo Bocchino, who are ably supported by expert oenologist, Giancarlo Scaglione. Their De Miranda, straw-yellow with green highlights, flaunts enticing aromas of sage and aniseed and a creamy palate, sweet but not too sweet, with fabulous length. Their Brut '96 is every bit as good as the previous vintage and is an exemplary high-quality Contratto spumante. A lovely rich golden colour, it vaunts a dense, persistent perlage and a bouquet that introduces elegant notes of ripe fruit, hedgerow and toast that are fully echoed on the palate. Here, they blend with citrus and biscuity hints to lend elegance to this very classy wine. Three well-deserved Glasses, then, for one of the best sparkling wines in Italy. In the estate's deep ruby Barolo Tenuta Secolo, varietal touches of mint come through flanked by heady notes of berry fruit and part-dried roses. The sweet tannins bolster a palate that has a great future, but is drinking very nicely now. The estate's two Barbera d'Asti wines come from the superb barbera zones of Agliano and Nizza Monferrato. The Panta Rei is the simpler of the two and boasts the acidity typical of the variety in a full body. The fuller and more complex Solus Ad is a dark violet-ruby and offers a berry fruit, vanilla and spice bouquet. The palate is bolstered smooth acidity and exceptional structure. Finally, the Sabauda, a Chardonnay, is excellent, with crisp notes of vanilla and ripe fruit.

● Barbera d'Asti Sup. La Cappelletta '97	❢❢	5
● Barbera d'Asti Barisel '99	❢	3
○ Moscato d'Asti Barisel '99	❢	3
● Barbera d'Asti Sup. La Cappelletta '96	♀♀	4
● Barbera d'Asti Barisel '98	♀	3

○ Spumante Metodo Classico Brut Ris. Giuseppe Contratto '96	❢❢❢	5
○ Asti De Miranda Metodo Classico '98	❢❢	5
● Barbera d'Asti Solus Ad '98	❢❢	6
● Barolo Cerequio Tenuta Secolo '96	❢❢	6
○ Piemonte Chardonnay La Sabauda '98	❢❢	5
● Barbera d'Asti Panta Rei '98	❢	4
○ Asti De Miranda Metodo Classico '96	♀♀♀	5
○ Asti De Miranda Metodo Classico '97	♀♀♀	5
○ Spumante Metodo Classico Brut Ris. Giuseppe Contratto '95	♀♀♀	5
● Barbera d'Asti Solus Ad '96	♀♀	6
● Barbera d'Asti Solus Ad '97	♀♀	6
● Barolo Cerequio Tenuta Secolo '95	♀♀	6

CANELLI (AT)

Luigi Coppo e Figli

Via Alba, 66
14053 Canelli (AT)
tel. 0141/823146

When the renovation and expansion of their cellars - they have tunnelled into the rock to create galleries where thousands of bottles already lie ageing - is finished, the Coppo brothers will be the proud owners of a beautiful, functional winery that will make their work much easier. In the meantime, this year's range of offerings, led by their Barbera, is very good indeed. Credit for the quality also goes to Riccardo Cotarella, the estate's consultant. The style of the Coppo wines favours elegance and balance over muscle. We started with their Pomorosso '98, a wine whose nose gradually opens to reveal considerable charm and complexity, as well as a masterful use of new oak that blends seamlessly with the elegant fruit. The palate flaunts fine balance and persistence while the '97 vintage is almost as good. The less complex Barbera Camp du Rouss '98 is very agreeable, and its younger sister, the Barbera L'Avvocata, boasts a typically varietal personality. The Mondaccione '98 is superb while the Alterego '97 parades pepper and vegetable fragrances with a subtle, velvety palate. We also very much liked the two Chardonnays. The Monteriolo, a golden yellow with green highlights, can offer aromas of toast, vanilla, melon, tangerine and flowers and a fresh, seductive palate. The Costebianche, vinified partly in stainless steel and partly in wood, has a great attack and a very pleasant palate of some complexity. In our opinion, the better of the two spumantes is the straw-yellow Riserva '90. Its aromas of yeast, toast and citrus fruit are accompanied by a palate nicely backed up by crisp acidity.

●	Barbera d'Asti Camp du Rouss '98	▼▼	4
●	Barbera d'Asti Pomorosso '97	▼▼	6
●	Barbera d'Asti Pomorosso '98	▼▼	6
●	Mondaccione '98	▼▼	5
●	Alterego '97	▼▼	5
○	Piemonte Chardonnay Costebianche '99	▼▼	4
○	Piemonte Chardonnay Monteriolo '98	▼▼	5
○	Piero Coppo Brut Ris. del Fondatore '90	▼▼	6
●	Barbera d'Asti L'Avvocata '98	▼	3
○	Brut Ris. Coppo '95	▼	5
●	Barbera d'Asti Pomorosso '90	▽▽▽	6
●	Barbera d'Asti Pomorosso '96	▽▽	6

CANELLI (AT)

Villa Giada

Reg. Ceirole, 4
14053 Canelli (AT)
tel. 0141/831100

The Barbera d'Asti Superiore Bricco Dani is the jewel in the Faccio family's crown. They grow the grapes on their farm, the Cascina Dani, where they also offer holiday accommodation. The quality of the fruit grown in this zone, which is particularly suited to barbera, has produced a wine that wins the Faccios Two Glasses. The vibrant ruby of their '98 vintage anticipates the wine's impressive texture. Its broad, complex nose has notes of bilberry and blackcurrant fruit which blend with captivating hints of dried flowers, juniper berry and fig leaf. The palate is rich and concentrated, with a satisfying follow-through. The firm tannins lend potency to the long, warm finish, which is laced with cocoa. The Faccios' moderately intense ruby Barbera La Quercia proffers up interesting, if slightly evolved, aromas of liqueur fruit, leather and mint with vegetal nuances. The palate shows good texture and reasonable structure but tends to fade in the finish, which is however satisfying and nicely reflects the aromas of the nose. The Moscato Ceirole excites with its rich straw-yellow and elegant, unmistakable nose of peach, rose, grapefruit and mint. Its sustained effervescence mitigates the sweetness of the palate and the finish is refreshing and well-balanced. The Barbera Ajan '98 is the least complex of the Villa Giada selection but still has plenty of beef on the palate. To round off, the Chardonnay Bricco Mané is also very drinkable.

●	Barbera d'Asti Sup. Bricco Dani '98	▼▼	5
○	Moscato d'Asti Ceirole '99	▼▼	3*
●	Barbera d'Asti Sup. Vigneto La Quercia '98	▼	4
●	Barbera d'Asti Sup. Ajan '98	▼	3
○	Piemonte Chardonnay Bricco Mané '99		3
●	Barbera d'Asti Sup. Vigneto La Quercia '97	▽▽	4
●	Barbera d'Asti Sup. Bricco Dani '97	▽▽	5
○	Val di Gala Passito	▽	5

CAREMA (TO)

Cantina dei Produttori Nebbiolo di Carema

Via Nazionale, 28
10010 Carema (TO)
tel. 0125/811160

The zone that lies between the Canavese DOC zone in Piedmont and the Valle d'Aosta has always posed its own peculiar set of problems to viticulturists. Not least of these is the tiny parcels of terraced vineyards clinging to rocky outcrops which must be tended by hand, and the rigorous, Alp-influenced climate mercifully mitigated by the location of the vineyards. All of the approximately 40 members of the Cantina dei Produttori di Nebbiolo – except for one – have well under a hectare planted to vine at an altitude that varies from 300 to 600 metres. Their combined production of Carema amounts to around 56,000 bottles. This year they have released their cream of the crop, the Carema Carema '95, which is every bit as good as some of the previous vintages. The wine is aged for a minimum of four years, at least two of which it passes in oak barrels, and then ages for one year in the bottle. Starting with the '98 vintage, the producers have adopted a policy of vineyard selection. Prior to that vintage, the selection was made in the winery from the best batches of grapes. The Carema '96 is also pleasant on the nose and on the palate. In exceptional years, a limited quantity – about 3,000 bottles – of a barrique-aged Carema is also produced. Like the other nebbiolo-based wines, it has great ageing potential and could easily be cellared for ten years or more. Luciano Clerin runs the cellars with the assistance of Manlio Muggianu. Attached to the winery is a shop offering other labels, including both a red and a rosé Canavese DOC obtained from nebbiolo and vernassa.

● Carema Carema '95	**YY**	4
● Carema '96	**Y**	4
● Carema Carema '90	YY	5
● Carema Carema '93	YY	5
● Carema '95	Y	4

CASTAGNOLE LANZE (AT)

★ La Spinetta

Via Annunziata, 17
14054 Castagnole Lanze (AT)
tel. 0141/877396

Back in 1987, who would ever have guessed that Giuseppe Rivetti's small winery would become one of Italy's brightest stars? Today, his sons Bruno, Carlo and Giorgio have about 80 hectares planted to vine in the Langhe hills, straddling the provinces of Asti and Cuneo. The range the trio offered us this year features an outstanding quartet of Three Glass giants, from the two extraordinary years of 1997 and 1998. Like all the estate's great reds, the Rivettis' three Barbarescos are aged entirely in new barriques. The two Neive selections are more balanced than the Valeirano di Treiso, whose tannins are still a bit harsh. The Gallina, the most delicate and stylish of the three, has a sublime bouquet of berry fruit, mint and dried flowers, and a soft, silky palate of fabulous persistence. The Starderi, which combines potency and beefy tannins with a less generous range of fruit aromas, overlaid with spice, has a very long future ahead of it. Of the '98 Barberas, the explosive Gallina surpasses the Asti version thanks to its fuller, almost chewy, body and fine balance. The Pin manages to combine with rare harmony the austere tannins of nebbiolo, the soft fruity fleshiness of ripe barbera and cabernet sauvignon's complex spiciness. The two Moscatos and the Barbera Ca' di Pianare are, as ever, pleasant and refreshing. Given the estate's near-perfect performance, we cannot wait to sample its new wines, a Moscato Passito, a barrique-conditioned Sauvignon, the Chardonnay Lidia and the Barolo 2000, obtained from the grapes of the Rivettis' newly acquired vineyards in Grinzane Cavour.

● Barbaresco Vigneto Gallina '97	**YYY**	6
● Barbaresco Vigneto Starderi '97	**YYY**	6
● Barbera d'Alba Vigneto Gallina '98	**YYY**	6
● Monferrato Rosso Pin '98	**YYY**	6
● Barbera d'Asti Ca' di Pian '99	**YY**	4
● Barbera d'Asti Sup. '98	**YY**	6
● Barbaresco Vigneto Valeirano '97	**YY**	6
○ Moscato d'Asti Biancospino '99	**YY**	4
○ Moscato d'Asti Bricco Quaglia '99	**YY**	4
● Barbaresco Vigneto Gallina '96	YYY	6
● Barbera d'Alba Vigneto Gallina '96	YYY	6
● Barbera d'Alba Vigneto Gallina '97	YYY	6
● Monferrato Rosso Pin '95	YYY	6
● Monferrato Rosso Pin '96	YYY	6
● Monferrato Rosso Pin '97	YYY	6

CASTEL BOGLIONE (AT)

CASTEL BOGLIONE (AT)

ARALDICA VINI PIEMONTESI
V.LE LAUDANO, 2
14040 CASTEL BOGLIONE (AT)
TEL. 0141/762354

CASCINA GARITINA
VIA GIANOLA, 20
14040 CASTEL BOGLIONE (AT)
TEL. 0141/762162

This winery has the best wines on offer from the Antica Contea di Castelvero, Cantina di Mombaruzzo and Cantina di Ricaldone estates. The pale straw-yellow Moscato d'Asti releases notes of pear, peach and flowers enhanced by the merest suspicion of super-ripeness. Its sweet, full palate is well supported by a moderate effervescence and the initial fruit aromas come through again in the elegant finish. The Nebbiolo Castellero, vibrant ruby with garnet highlights, has cherry, chocolate and resin aromas, a somewhat austere palate, and a warm finish that smacks of liquorice and is well supported by the tannins. The estate produces two Arneis wines. The first, the Roero Arneis Sorilaria, has a lustrous straw-yellow hue, a very refined nose that suggests medlar, banana and dried aromatic herbs, and a persistent finish. The Langhe Arneis Alasia is medium straw-yellow in colour and has an uncomplicated bouquet that includes notes of apple, caramel and freshly mown grass. The palate is fresh-tasting and full-bodied and the finish, which echoes the nose perfectly, is very satisfying indeed. The ruby Barbera Croja tempts the nose with notes of jam and dry earth. Robust on the palate, it finishes on a note of cocoa. The Barbera Ceppi Storici has a rustic nose and a well-sustained palate with good progression through to a moderately long finish. The Spumante Metodo Classico '96 has a straw-yellow colour and moderate perlage. Its notes of yeast, apricot and apple accompany a fresh palate and bright effervescence. The very pale Bianco Camillona has a vaguely aromatic nose and a smooth, balanced palate. Lastly, the Muscaté Sec is very attractive with its varietal moscato bouquet and bright palate.

Pasquale Morino and his oenologist son, Luca, produce 70,000 bottles a year from their 13 hectare estate. Their wines, dominated by Barberas, are once again tip-top. The Barbera Neuvsent '98 has a dark garnet-ruby in colour that tells you all you need to know about the structure. Its complex, generous bouquet abounds with very ripe black berry notes of mulberry and cherry, autumn leaves, toasty oak and menthol. Entry on the palate is full and juicy while robust tannins underpin a solid follow-through that ushers in a lingering finish. The Morinos' Rosso Amis '98, obtained from 50 percent barbera, 40 percent pinot nero, and 10 percent cabernet sauvignon, is a lovely deep ruby red with garnet highlights and a narrow, youthful rim. Its fascinating bouquet offers assorted wild berry and spice aromas lifted by clear floral notes and complex gamey undertones. Its close-knit texture is apparent the minute it hits the palate, where it gradually acquires a delicate austerity. Well supported by robust tannins, the finish is lengthy and coherent with a barely discernible touch of bitterness. The Bricco Garitta is a simple, straightforward Barbera that would make a wonderful accompaniment to meat dishes or pasta served with a bolognese sauce. Its colour is moderately intensity, and its fruity nose has fairly marked balsamic notes. The full-bodied palate heralds an eminently satisfying finish. The estate's last offering, the Barbera Il Morinaccio, is a lively, very well-crafted wine whose clean, easy drinkability is a tribute to the Morinos' technical expertise.

O Moscato d'Asti Alasia '99	♥♥	3*
● Barbera d'Asti Sup. Ceppi Storici '98	♥	2*
● Barbera d'Asti Vigneti Croja '97	♥	3
O Langhe Arneis Alasia '99	♥	3
● Langhe Nebbiolo Castellero		
Poderi Alasia '98	♥	4
O Monferrato Bianco Camillona		
Poderi Alasia '99	♥	4
O Muscaté Sec Alasia '99	♥	2
O Piemonte Brut Poderi		
Alasia Metodo Classico '96	♥	4
O Roero Arneis Sorilaria		
Poderi Alasia '99	♥	4
● Langhe Nebbiolo Castellero		
Poderi Alasia '97	♥♥	4

● Barbera d'Asti Sup. Neuvsent '98	♥♥	4
● Monferrato Rosso Amis '98	♥♥	4
● Barbera d'Asti Bricco Garitta '98	♥	3
● Barbera del M.to Vivace		
Il Morinaccio '99	♥	2*
● Barbera d'Asti Sup. Neuvsent '96	♥♥	4
● Monferrato Rosso Amis '97	♥♥	4
● Barbera d'Asti Bricco Garitta '97	♥	3
● Barbera d'Asti Sup. Neuvsent '95	♥	4

CASTELLINALDO (CN)

CASTELLINALDO (CN)

TEO COSTA
VIA S. SALVARIO, 1
12050 CASTELLINALDO (CN)
TEL. 0173/213066

STEFANINO MORRA
VIA CASTAGNITO, 22
12050 CASTELLINALDO (CN)
TEL. 0173/213489

The Costa brothers, Marco and Roberto, produce about 100,000 bottles a year from their 26 hectares. Their two labels, the Giobbe and the premium Teo Costa, offer a fine interpretation of the typical wines of Roero, on the Castellinaldo side. The Costas' Nebbiolo Ligabue impressed us this year with its medium garnet ruby colour and elegant berry fruit nose. It has a firm palate and follows through steadily to culminate in a warm, aromatic finish of medium length. The ruby red Barbera Castelli di Castellinaldo has a lovely nose of wild berries, almonds and cakes. A slight bitterness tends to emerge in the progression but the tannins are robust and the lingering finish is dry and attractive. The Roero Batajot '98 has a fairly concentrated colour and a rather less than frank nose. It can still offer a very satisfying, if not exceptional, palate. The nose of the lustrous straw-yellow Arneis Ajnaldi Bianc '98 blends hints of super-ripeness with varietal fruit. The admirable texture of the palate has a silky dynamism, ushering in a long, refreshing finish where the fruit returns. One notch down is the Serramiana. Its reasonably well-defined nose evokes overtones of apple and dried grass. It has reasonable weight in the mouth and a moderately full, complex finish. The Birbét, pale ruby with violet tinges, offers aromas of roses and a balanced, tangy palate.

Stefanino Morra presented us with a good selection of wines this year, but it was his two Barberas, the Castellinaldo and the standard label, that scored highest at our tasting. The Castellinaldo is a rich ruby red with a nicely balanced nose where its pervasive fruit and vanilla are shot through with faint, complex mineral notes. It is substantial on the palate with a hint of acidity to support its progression through to a very satisfying finish. The base Barbera is medium ruby red with a slightly paler rim. Its interesting nose has ripe fruit and fresh aromatic herbs over sweet, oak-derived spices. The palate has good presence, adequately supported by attractive tannins, and the finish lingers. One notch or two below Barberas came the Roero, its garnet-ringed ruby hue ushering in aromas of wild berries and cocoa, which are still a little closed. The palate is full, if rather severe, and finishes on a lovely liquorice note. The Roero Arneis San Pietro, aged in large barrels, is a vibrant straw-yellow and reveals hints of apples, pears and coffee in rather a rustic nose. Velvety on the palate, it offers good body and a seamless progression. Morra's base Arneis is a very pale straw-yellow with a nose that hints at super-ripeness against a backdrop of fruit. The palate is approachable and refreshing.

● Birbét '99	♙	3
● Castellinaldo Barbera d'Alba		
Castelli di Castellinaldo '98	♙	4
● Nebbiolo d'Alba		
Ligabue Bric Costa '98	♙	4
○ Roero Arneis Ajnaldi Bianc '98	♙	4
● Roero Sup. Vigneto Batajot '98	♙	3
○ Roero Arneis Serramiana '99		3
● Castellinaldo Barbera d'Alba '95	♙♙	4
● Castellinaldo Barbera d'Alba '96	♙♙	4
● Castellinaldo Barbera d'Alba '97	♙	4
● Roero Sup. Vigneto Batajot '97	♙	3

● Castellinaldo Barbera d'Alba '98	♙♙	5
● Barbera d'Alba '98	♙	4
○ Roero Arneis '99	♙	4
○ Roero Arneis Vigna S. Pietro '98	♙	4
● Roero Sup. '98	♙	4
● Castellinaldo Barbera d'Alba '97	♙♙	5
● Roero Sup. '97	♙♙	4
● Barbera d'Alba '97	♙	4

CASTELLINALDO (CN)

FABRIZIO PINSOGLIO
FRAZ. MADONNA DEI CAVALLI, 8
12050 CASTELLINALDO (CN)
TEL. 0173/213078

CASTELNUOVO DON BOSCO (AT)

CASCINA GILLI
VIA NEVISSANO, 36
14022 CASTELNUOVO DON BOSCO (AT)
TEL. 011/9876984

Like many families in the Roero region, the Pinsoglios used to run a mixed farm with a few animals, some vines, and an orchard. Two things happened to change this. At the end of the 80s, Oreste Pinsoglio started to bottle his Arneis and in 1997, Fabrizio, following in the footsteps of his father and of Matteo Correggia, produced the estate's first big reds and tried his luck in the challenging world of quality wines. The Pinsoglios are in the process of building a new winery, an investment which shows just how committed Fabrizio is. It will be ready for the 2001 vintage. Fabrizio and his mother, Maria, tend the vines themselves and are particularly zealous in pruning and limiting yields. They have seven hectares of vineyards in Canale, Castellinaldo, and Priocca, on white tufa terrain, and grow equal amounts of barbera, nebbiolo and arneis. Fabrizio produces five labels to make a total of 20,000 bottles, and sells the remainder of his wine in bulk. The estate enters the Guide for the first time this year with two elegant, modern reds which are well worth their Two Glasses. The Barbera Bric La Rondolina, from forty-year-old vines, has a fine, complex bouquet redolent of berry fruit, notably cherries, and sweet spicy notes of cinnamon. Its palate, soft, rather than powerful, leads through to a long, lingering, velvety finish. Fabrizio ages his Roero, the second of the winners, for one year in new and one-year-old barriques. This wine enchanted us with its elegant aromas of raspberry and vanilla, and with the sweet juicy fruit that mellows the persistent finish. His Arneis and Barbera are not so richly extracted, but still very drinkable.

The vineyards of Cascina Gilli, run by Gianni Vergnano with the support of Carlo Feyes in the cellar, are situated in the valley on the road leading up to Albugnano from Castelnuovo Don Bosco. Three years ago, the estate built new cellars next to the original 18th-century structure. The winery lies in the middle of the vineyards which extend over the hills of white earth, a sharp contrast to the tufa common to the Basso Monferrato area. Cascina Gilli has 24 hectares at its disposition. Ten of these belong to the estate and spill over into neighbouring Moncucco and Cinzano. For years now, Vergnano has concentrated his efforts on earning the typical wines of this zone the recognition they deserve. Once again, his Malvasia and two Freisas stand out from the crowd, along with the Barbera d'Asti Vigna delle More '98 which merits Two Glasses this year. This new vintage confirms Vergnano's skill with the barbera variety. He has produced a vigorous Barbera d'Asti which impresses with its open, fruit-rich aromas laced with spice. His Malvasia di Castelnuovo is up to its usual standards, and both the Freisa Vivace Luna di Maggio '99 and the still Vigna del Forno match the quality that last year won One Glass. A good year, too, for the Monferrato Rosso, a blend of 30 percent barbera and 70 percent freisa.

● Barbera d'Alba		
Bric La Rondolina '98	▼▼	4
● Roero '98	▼▼	5
● Barbera d'Alba '99	▼	3
○ Roero Arneis Vigneto Malinat '99	▼	3

● Barbera d'Asti		
Vigna delle More '99	▼▼	3*
● Malvasia di Castelnuovo		
Don Bosco '99	▼▼	3*
● Freisa d'Asti Vigna del Forno '99	▼	3
● Freisa d'Asti Vivace		
Luna di Maggio '99	▼	3
● Monferrato Rosso '99	▼	3
● Barbera d'Asti		
Vigna delle More '98	♀♀	3
● Monferrato Rosso '98	♀	3

CASTIGLIONE FALLETTO (CN) CASTIGLIONE FALLETTO (CN)

AZELIA
VIA ALBA-BAROLO, 53
12060 CASTIGLIONE FALLETTO (CN)
TEL. 0173/62859

BRICCO ROCCHE - BRICCO ASILI
VIA MONFORTE, 63
12060 CASTIGLIONE FALLETTO (CN)
TEL. 0173/282582

Over the last few years, Luigi Scavino has shown himself adept at turning even difficult years to his advantage and has produced some truly excellent wines, notably Barolos. In good years, such as those that have favoured the Langhe since 1996, Scavino's skills really come to the fore. His base Barolo, obtained from a blend of grapes grown in Castiglione and Falletto, offers a fine example of the potential of this vintage and the two estate crus, the San Rocco and the Bricco Fiasco, both aged in new and used barriques, show what Scavino can do. The San Rocco, whose young tannins and still-assertive oak render it a tad aggressive, opens out slowly to reveal notes of fruit, balsam and spice over a hint of tobacco and liquorice. The attack on the palate is powerful, warm and mirror the nose generously. Like all the Serralunga Barolos, this wine has a great future. Obtained from Castiglione Falletto grapes, the already beautifully balanced Bricco Fiasco offers nicely judged oak that blends with notes of ripe fruit, spice and liquorice. Cellaring will only enhance the complexity of this superb bottle, which once again collected Three Glasses. The Dolcetto Bricco dell'Oriolo is also very good this year. The fruit, grown in the prestigious zone of Montelupo Albese, guarantees it structure and weight. A dark violet in the glass, it overwhelms nose and palate with its wonderful aromas. Drinking delightfully now, it will be even better if left to age in the bottle. This year, Scavino has released the '98 vintage of his trusty old warhorse, the Barbera Vigneto Punta. Powerful and well balanced, it has been well worth the wait.

Bruno and Marcello Ceretto have grouped their most prestigious wines under two labels that take their names from the vineyards of Rocche di Castiglione Falletto and Asili di Barbaresco. We shall open our tasting notes with the Cerettos' great Barolo '96, the Bricco Rocche. This vintage delivers aromas of sweet black cherry, bramble and vanilla, and a palate that seesaws between velvet fruit and rugged tannins. The follow-through is well-sustained and the finish smacks faintly, and very pleasantly, of redcurrants. The Brunate has a more austere, concentrated nose with hints of dried aromatic herbs and mint that melt into fruit, liquorice and coffee. The palate is firm and fleshy, focusing on plum jam. Good, solid tannins lead into a long, satisfying finish. The Prapò is notable for its scents of freshly cut grass and pot pourri but the palate is a little overstretched, despite a firm tannic structure. The Barbaresco '97 trio hits the jackpot with the Bricco Asili, a thumping Three Glass giant that regales the senses with a sumptuous range of aromas. Its bouquet is up-front, intense and never-ending, unfurling notes of mint, thyme, and wild strawberries. As it opens out, liquorice, pepper and vanilla notes join the chorus. Then the soft, succulent palate is packed full of sweet, lively fruit that emerges in notes of ripe cherries. At first, the Faset and the Bernardot have an identical grassy note but then the Faset introduces bright peach fruit while the Bernadot reveals more evolved notes of very ripe fruit. Both are full-bodied and backed up by a successful marriage of acidity and tannins.

Wine	Rating	Score
● Barolo Bricco Fiasco '96	▼▼▼	6
● Barbera d'Alba Vigneto Punta '98	▼▼	5
● Barolo S. Rocco '96	▼▼	6
● Dolcetto d'Alba Bricco dell'Oriolo '99	▼▼	3*
● Barolo '96	▼	6
● Barolo '91	♉♉♉	6
● Barolo Bricco Fiasco '93	♉♉♉	6
● Barolo Bricco Fiasco '95	♉♉♉	6
● Barbera d'Alba Vigneto Punta '97	♉♉	5
● Barolo Bricco Fiasco Ris. '90	♉♉	6
● Barolo S. Rocco '95	♉♉	6
● Barolo '95	♉	6

Wine	Rating	Score
● Barbaresco Bricco Asili Bricco Asili '97	▼▼▼	6
● Barbaresco Bernardot Bricco Asili '97	▼▼	6
● Barbaresco Faset Bricco Asili '97	▼▼	6
● Barolo Bricco Rocche Bricco Rocche '96	▼▼	6
● Barolo Brunate Bricco Rocche '96	▼▼	6
● Barolo Prapò Bricco Rocche '96	▼▼	6
● Barbaresco Bricco Asili Bricco Asili '85	♉♉♉	6
● Barbaresco Bricco Asili Bricco Asili '86	♉♉♉	6
● Barbaresco Bricco Asili Bricco Asili '88	♉♉♉	6
● Barbaresco Bricco Asili Bricco Asili '89	♉♉♉	6
● Barbaresco Bricco Asili Bricco Asili '96	♉♉♉	6
● Barolo Bricco Rocche Bricco Rocche '89	♉♉♉	6
● Barolo Brunate Bricco Rocche '90	♉♉♉	6
● Barolo Prapò Bricco Rocche '83	♉♉♉	6

CASTIGLIONE FALLETTO (CN) CASTIGLIONE FALLETTO (CN)

BROVIA
VIA ALBA-BAROLO, 54
12060 CASTIGLIONE FALLETTO (CN)
TEL. 0173/62852

CANTINA TERRE DEL BAROLO
VIA ALBA-BAROLO, 5
12060 CASTIGLIONE FALLETTO (CN)
TEL. 0173/262053

Raffaele and Giacinto Brovia, supported by Giacinto's daughters, Elena and Cristina, offered us an outstanding selection of vintage '96 Barolos. First off the bat, we have the Ca' Mia, made with grapes from the Brovias' Serralunga vineyards. Garnet, with a slightly orangey rim, it has an elegantly pervasive nose with hints of bilberry, redcurrant, juniper and cocoa. The palate is broad and vibrant, progressing firmly and austerely to a long, satisfying finish. Three full-bodied and very muscular Glasses. The Rocche dei Brovia, from the sandy terrain in the estate's Rocche di Castiglione Falletto cru, is ruby red, shading into garnet. Its raspberry, strawberry and fig aromas are thrown into relief by discreet briny and balsamic notes. The palate is soft and full, nicely held in check by its fine tannins, and finishes on a refreshing note. The Villero has a medium colour with a slightly paler rim. Wild berry and violet aromas layered over hints of wild fennel give it a faintly evolved note, while the palate is well structured and the finish gratifying. These three Barolos are traditional in style, well put together, and benefit from an excellent year. The lush garnet-ruby colour of the Brovias' Dolcetto Solatìo anticipates its character. Its fruit-rich nose is concealed beneath a layer of oak that introduces coffee and vanilla overtones. The rich palate flaunts assertive tannins that exalt its opulent flavours before toasty notes of oak come back to dominate the finish. The estate's Barbera Sorì del Drago proffers earthy, herbal aromas against a backdrop of moderate fruit and has an agreeably complex palate of reasonable length.

Over 800 hectares planted to vine, production of 1,800,000 bottles, variety, quality, and value for money. That's the formula of this co-operative winery. The location of the vineyards ensures that the reds reap all the benefits of the good years for varieties such as nebbiolo, dolcetto and barbera. We liked the Dolcetto di Diano d'Alba '99 wines. The very reasonably priced base selection and the Sorì Bricco del Ciabot both have zest and a structure that attests to their rich extract. Of the two, we preferred the Sorì Bricco. We found the Sorì Montagrillo to be a little evolved while the less richly extracted Dolcetto d'Alba Le Passere '99 offers heady aromas and fragrant, fruity notes. The Terre di Barolo Barberas are solid and traditional. The Valdisera '98 flaunts a full, generous nose and the powerful Barbera d'Albi Sorì Roncaglia '98 was marked down for its youthful astringency and exuberant acidity. The Barbera d'Alba Superiore '98, aged in large barrels and one-year-old barriques, is more closed on the nose and less elegant. Only One Glass. The Langhe Le Terre '97, obtained from barrique-aged pinot nero, is straightforward and convincing. Barolos account for over 50 percent of the winery's total production and the panel awarded One Glass to the Castiglione Falletto '96 for its pale hue, complex aromas and uncomplicated palate. The Codana '95 is excellent, with intriguing hints of liquorice and mint leaf in addition to good weight on the palate, which echoes the aromas on the nose very satisfyingly. The warm finish is lifted by silky, sweet tannins. Another One Glass goes to the Monvigliero '95, more interesting on the palate than the nose, which is still a bit closed. Finally, the pale red Pelaverga di Verduno '99 possesses a geranium and white pepper bouquet and a dry, spicy finish.

● Barolo Ca' Mia '96	♈♈♈	6
● Barolo Rocche dei Brovia '96	♈♈	6
● Barolo Villero '96	♈♈	6
● Dolcetto d'Alba Solatìo '98	♈♈	5
● Barbera d'Alba Sorì del Drago '97	♈	4
● Barolo Monprivato '90	♈♈♈	6
● Barolo Ca' Mia '95	♈♈	6
● Barolo Rocche dei Brovia '90	♈♈	6
● Barolo Rocche dei Brovia '93	♈♈	6
● Barolo Villero '93	♈♈	6
● Barolo Villero '95	♈♈	6
● Barolo Rocche dei Brovia '95	♈	6

● Barbera d'Alba Valdisera '98	♈♈	3*
● Barolo Codana '95	♈♈	6
● Diano d'Alba Sorì		
Bricco del Ciabot '99	♈♈	3*
● Barbera d'Alba Sorì Roncaglia '98	♈	3
● Barbera d'Alba Sup. '98	♈	3
● Barolo di Castiglione Falletto '96	♈	6
● Barolo Monvigliero '95	♈	6
● Diano d'Alba Sorì Montagrillo '99	♈	3
● Dolcetto d'Alba Le Passere '99	♈	3
● Dolcetto di Diano d'Alba '99	♈	3*
● Langhe Le Terre '97	♈	5
● Pelaverga di Verduno '99		4
● Barbera d'Alba Sorì Roncaglia '97	♈♈	3
● Barolo di Castiglione Falletto '95	♈	5

CASTIGLIONE FALLETTO (CN)

CASCINA BONGIOVANNI
VIA ALBA-BAROLO, 4
12060 CASTIGLIONE FALLETTO (CN)
TEL. 0173/262184

Davide Mozzone is a passionate, enthusiastic winemaker who obtained his diploma at Alba's School of Oenology. From three hectares of vines belonging to his aunt, Olga Bongiovanni, and a further hectare he has rented, he produces a scant 25,000 bottles a year of excellent wines. That quality comes from a modern cellar, the skilled use of oak and, of course, outstandingly good grapes. The apple of Davide's eye is his Barolo Pernanno. It is a rich, deep garnet in colour and possesses an incredible bouquet in which the aromas are overlaid in the characteristic fashion of a truly great Barolo. Redcurrant and cherry emerge in the concentrated, seductive fruit and delicious hints of chocolate contrast perfectly with pot pourri and gamey undertones. The attack on the palate is juicy, opening out in a broad, soft progression. Perfectly judged fine tannins lend volume and power to the long, lingering finish, with its fruity, balsamic hints. Mozzone's standard-label Barolo is almost as good. The moderately intense colour ushers in aromas of wild berries, hay, leather and dried flowers. The palate is slightly austere, reveals robust structure and has a long finish that mirrors the nose. The Dolcetto d'Alba '99 is a delight and earns Two Glasses for its notes of fruit in syrup and alcohol-rich palate with a faintly bitter note in the finish. The Langhe Faletto '98, a blend of barbera, nebbiolo and cabernet sauvignon, has a dark, almost opaque, colour that hints at its solid structure. The nose blends spices and toastiness deliciously while the palate is generous and beefy.

CASTIGLIONE FALLETTO (CN)

F.LLI CAVALLOTTO
TENUTA BRICCO BOSCHIS
VIA ALBA-MONFORTE
LOC. BRICCO BOSCHIS
12060 CASTIGLIONE FALLETTO (CN)
TEL. 0173/62814

Dedicated viticulturists of many years' standing, the Cavallottos have always limited their production to the 23 hectares planted to vine that have been in the family for five generations now. Their wines bring out the characteristics of the Castiglione Falletto terroir and are seriously structured, full-bodied and very cellarable. To maintain this level of quality, the Cavallottos only release their wines in favourable years and never before they are properly aged. They have excellent quality fruit at their disposition, including the grapes from the magnificent Bricco Boschis, and have chosen to vinify and age their wines in stainless steel and oak barrels, rather than barriques. The estate's Barolo Vigna San Giuseppe '95 bowled us over with its mulberry and liquorice nose, its full body, its harmony and its length. The Barolo Bricco Boschis '96 is also a winner, proffering warm aromas of fresh plum and raspberry, and delighting the palate with an exquisitely lingering flavour. Staying with the same variety, the Langhe Nebbiolo '98 displays a smooth, stylish palate which attractively foregrounds the character of the grape. The very interesting Barbera d'Alba Vigna del Cuculo '98 has crisp notes of red berry jam and offers a broad, well-structured and nicely balanced palate. This year, the Cavallottos' Barbera d'Alba, which has disappointed in the past, is very good indeed. Their Dolcetto d'Alba Scot '99, with its trademark violet hue, unveils balanced acidity and a full-bodied, zesty palate. The Dolcetto d'Alba Vigna Melera '98, possesses a lovely, alcohol-rich nose of cherry and is eminently drinkable. All in all, a very impressive selection from this estate, which deserves particular praise for the longevity of its Barolos.

● Barolo '96	ŶŶ	6
● Barolo Pernanno '96	ŶŶ	6
● Dolcetto d'Alba '99	ŶŶ	3*
● Langhe Rosso Faletto '98	ŶŶ	5
● Barolo Pernanno '95	ȲȲ	6
● Barolo '93	ȲȲ	6
● Langhe Rosso Faletto '97	ȲȲ	5
● Barolo '95	Ȳ	6

● Barbera d'Alba		
Vigna del Cuculo '98	ŶŶ	4
● Barolo Bricco Boschis '96	ŶŶ	6
● Barolo Vigna S. Giuseppe '95	ŶŶ	6
● Dolcetto d'Alba Vigna Scot '99	Ŷ	3
● Dolcetto d'Alba Vigna Melera '98	Ŷ	3
● Langhe Nebbiolo '98	Ŷ	4
● Barolo Vigna S. Giuseppe Ris. '89	ȲȲȲ	6
● Barolo Bricco Boschis '95	ȲȲ	6
● Barolo Colle Sud-Ovest Ris. '90	ȲȲ	6
● Barolo Colle Sud-Ovest Ris. '91	ȲȲ	6
● Barolo Vigna S. Giuseppe Ris. '90	ȲȲ	6
● Barolo Vigna S. Giuseppe Ris. '93	ȲȲ	6
● Barolo Vignolo Ris. '90	ȲȲ	6
● Barolo Vignolo Ris. '93	ȲȲ	6

CASTIGLIONE FALLETTO (CN) CASTIGLIONE FALLETTO (CN)

★ PAOLO SCAVINO
VIA ALBA-BAROLO, 59
12060 CASTIGLIONE FALLETTO (CN)
tel. 0173/62850

VIETTI
P.ZZA VITTORIO VENETO, 5
12060 CASTIGLIONE FALLETTO (CN)
TEL. 0173/62825

Enrico Scavino, his wife, Annamaria, and daughter Enrica, have just over 15 hectares, some their own property and some rented. They produce a truly outstanding range of wines whose character owes much to Enrico himself, an extremely diligent, painstaking winemaker. His well-balanced, attractively structured Barolo Bric dël Fiasc '96 has an impenetrably deep garnet colour and a generous array of complex aromas. Clean notes of redcurrant and raspberry fruit are offset by understated confectioner's cream and coffee from the new oak. A seductive touch of leather adds the final note to this chorus of classic Barolo aromas. The palate is soft, full, and very broad. It opens out gradually to become more austere, highlighting the rugged force of the variety which, however, in no way compromises its sumptuous body. Three resounding Glasses. Enrico's deep-hued Cannubi flaunts a wonderfully generous nose that blends notes of bilberry and raspberry with mint, coffee and cocoa. On the palate, it has a slightly nervous character, impressive structure and a finish with lashings of fruit. The Carobric, a nebbiolo blend with 65 percent from the Rocche di Castiglione cru, 20 percent from the Bric del Fiasc and 15 percent from the Cannubi, makes its debut this year. The colour is lustrous, the nose suggests hay, then opens out into notes of fruit, balsam and tobacco. The palate impresses more with its marvellous balance than with its strength. In addition to the Barolos, which include a very nice base version, Enrico offered us the superb '97 Barbera d'Alba Affinata in Carati and an excellent Langhe Rosso Corale, obtained from nebbiolo, barbera and cabernet. To finish off this year's range, there was a new release, the sauvignon and chardonnay Sorriso, and a Dolcetto d'Alba.

Luca Currado, ably assisted by Mario Cordero, runs a historic winery near Castiglione Falletto, an estate of 22 hectares under vine which he has extended by planting new plots. Currado produces an enormous range of wines which, in addition to their varietal characteristics, bear the hallmark of the estate. Wines from special vineyard selections flank a standard range that already has a high level of quality. Of the wines Currado presented this year, we particularly like the Barolo Lazzarito '96. It has an elegant nose of spice and understated oak, while the balanced, lingering palate progresses through to an elegant finish. The Rocche and the Brunate, both '96 vintages, offer lovely austere notes of ripe plum and decent structure on the palate but are still a tad harsh, although the assertive tannins and acidity promise well for the future. The Barbaresco Masseria '97 has great personality and a fine bouquet of well-rounded aromas, distinctive body and fine tannins. Once again the Tre Vigne is the pick of the Barberas. The '98 unfurls a generous array of well-matched fragrances, great persistence and lots of character. The Scarrone '98 is mature, complex and satisfying on the palate. The Vigna Vecchia '98 offers a crisper note of cherry and a better balanced, more convincing body. The Roero Arneis pitches in with a varietal, floral bouquet and a fragrant, fruity palate. Finally, we have the Dolcetto d'Albas. The Lazzarito is very good – fat, rich and fruity. We'll be back for another look at the still hard and unbottled Sant'Anna next year.

● Barolo Bric dël Fiasc '96	♟♟♟	6
● Barbera d'Alba Affinata in Carati '97	♟♟	6
● Barolo Cannubi '96	♟♟	6
● Barolo Carobric '96	♟♟	6
● Langhe Rosso Corale '97	♟♟	6
● Barolo '96	♟	6
● Dolcetto d'Alba '99	♟	4
○ Sorriso	♟	5
● Barolo Bric dël Fiasc '90	♟♟♟	6
● Barolo Bric dël Fiasc '93	♟♟♟	6
● Barolo Bric dël Fiasc '95	♟♟♟	6
● Barolo Rocche dell'Annunziata '93	♟♟♟	6
● Barolo Rocche dell'Annunziata Ris. '90	♟♟♟	6

● Barbaresco Masseria '97	♟♟	6
● Barbera d'Alba Scarrone Vigna Vecchia '98	♟♟	5
● Barbera d'Asti Tre Vigne '98	♟♟	4
● Barolo Brunate '96	♟♟	6
● Barolo Lazzarito '96	♟♟	6
● Barolo Rocche '96	♟♟	6
● Dolcetto d'Alba Lazzarito '99	♟♟	4
● Barbera d'Alba Scarrone '98	♟	5
○ Roero Arneis '99	♟	4
● Barolo Rocche di Castiglione '85	♟♟♟	6
● Barolo Rocche di Castiglione '88	♟♟♟	6
● Barolo Villero '82	♟♟♟	6
● Barbera d'Asti La Crena '97	♟♟	5

CASTIGLIONE TINELLA (CN)

CASTIGLIONE TINELLA (CN)

CAUDRINA - ROMANO DOGLIOTTI
S.DA CAUDRINA, 20
12053 CASTIGLIONE TINELLA (CN)
TEL. 0141/855126

ICARDI
VIA BALBI, 30
LOC. S. LAZZARO
12053 CASTIGLIONE TINELLA (CN)
TEL. 0141/855159

Romano Dogliotti runs a family business. One son, Alessandro, looks after the cellar while Sergio and Marco take care of the vineyards and Romano's wife, Bruna, deals with administration. They have 28 hectares and produce 150-160,000 bottles a year of Moscato, Asti, Barbera and Chardonnay. The first vintage of Romanos' Barbera La Solista was the '98 and we will be tasting barrique-aged Barbera d'Asti and Chardonnay for the next edition of the Guide. The three moscato-based offerings are all very good. The Asti La Selvatica, with a label designed by Romano Levi, is a pale straw-yellow flecked with green in the glass. Its bouquet offers crisp, pervasive notes of fresh peach and banana fruit with mint and sage. The palate has a tangy prickle to liven up the sweet, rich-textured body. Interesting hints of ripe grapes come through in the lengthy finish. The Moscato La Galeisa is a rich straw-yellow of medium intensity and has a ripe nose of peach and pear over hints of elderflower. The full, buttery palate is brought to life by jolly effervescence that keeps it nice and fizzy. The finish is attractively aromatic. The Moscato La Caudrina is more subtle and delicate, just as Romano intended. It has a bright straw-yellow colour and elegant aromas of apple, pear and sage. The palate has wonderful, delicate balance while the finish could perhaps have been just a tiny bit longer. Finally, the rich ruby Barbera La Solista unveils cherry and strawberry aromas over warm earth on the nose and the rather rustic, robust palate has good grip.

Claudio Icardi, an energetic producer and consultant to various wineries, never lets up his frenetic pace for a minute. Aided by his associates and his wife, Ornella, who is also responsible for the striking estate labels, he is just putting the finishing touches to a modern, well-organised cellar. Icardi has added new varieties to the range of wines, which now has greater personality and quality, as witnessed by the two most interesting wines of this year's wide selection. They are the Langhe Rosso Nej and the Cascina Bricco del Sole, both '98 vintages. The first of these, a monovarietal Pinot Nero, tempts with refined, penetrating aromas of spice and red berry fruit, a complex, well-balanced palate, and an elegant, rounded finish. The Cascina Bricco del Sole, a masterly blend of barbera, nebbiolo and cabernet sauvignon, has structure and character. The palate shows all its balance and length in a fragrant crescendo of flavours. Of Icardi's two Nebbiolos, we preferred the Pafoj '99, a fresh-tasting stylish wine with good structure. The Surìsjvan '98 is attractively clean while the Nuj Suj '98 stands out among the Barberas for its fresh fruit bouquet and full, fleshy palate. The Barolo Parej '96, released for the second year, does not entirely convince and lacks the personality we expect in a Barolo. We finished our tasting with the whites. The Pafoj '99, a blend of chardonnay and sauvignon, is particularly good. It has pleasant citrus tones which carry over onto the palate, and a pervasive, fresh nose. The Surìssara '99 and the Rosa Selvatica are headily fragrant and clean-tasting, faithfully expressing the qualities of the grapes they were made with.

○	Asti La Selvatica '99	♟♟	4
○	Moscato d'Asti La Galeisa '99	♟♟	4
●	Barbera d'Asti La Solista '99	♟	3
○	Moscato d'Asti La Caudrina '99	♟	3

●	Barbera d'Alba Nuj Suj '98	♟♟	5
●	Barbera d'Alba Surì di Mù '98	♟♟	5
●	Langhe Rosso Nej '98	♟♟	5
●	Langhe Rosso Pafoj '99	♟♟	6
○	Monferrato Bianco Pafoj '99	♟♟	5
●	Monferrato Rosso		
	Cascina Bricco del Sole '98	♟♟	6
●	Barolo Parej '96	♟	6
●	Langhe Nebbiolo Surìsjvan '98	♟	5
○	Moscato d'Asti		
	La Rosa Selvatica '99	♟	3
○	Piemonte Chardonnay		
	Surìssara '99	♟	4
●	Langhe Rosso Nej '97	♕♕	5
●	Langhe Rosso Pafoj '98	♕♕	6

CASTIGLIONE TINELLA (CN) CASTIGLIONE TINELLA (CN)

LA MORANDINA
VIA MORANDINI, 11
12053 CASTIGLIONE TINELLA (CN)
TEL. 0141/855261

ELIO PERRONE
S.DA S. MARTINO, 3/BIS
12053 CASTIGLIONE TINELLA (CN)
TEL. 0141/855803

Paolo and Giulio Morando, aided by their parents, Emma and Corrado, and by Paolo's wife, Giuliana, have vineyards at Castiglione Tinella, Montegrosso and Costigliole. We'll begin our review with their Barberas. The barrique-aged Varmat is a dense garnet in colour and has a nose bursting with personality in which hints of cocoa, mint and earth filter through overtones of black berry fruit and green leaves. The richly extracted palate reveals firm tannins and robust alcohol that back up the well-balanced, liquorice finish. Not quite as elegant but extremely satisfying nonetheless, the Barbera Zucchetto has a lovely rich colour and aromas of cherry and ripe mulberry over spicy, vegetal notes. The attractive palate unveils robust tannins that give weight to a finish with a bitter twist. The Costa del Sole, obtained from 60 percent moscato and 40 percent riesling renano raisined on the vine and fermented in barriques, is an outstanding product. A lustrous pale gold in the glass, it has a stylish nose of dried prunes and apricots, leather and saffron with a fascinating grace note of noble rot. The delicately sweet the palate has notable structure – broad but not opulent. The Moscato is pale straw-yellow and tempts the nose with vegetal aromas, including sage and tomato leaf, which highlight its apricot and citron overtones. The lively effervescence tempers the sweetness of a palate that culminates in a complex finish where the aromas of the nose return. The Chardonnay has a nice bouquet but still lacks balance on the palate.

The selection offered for tasting by this estate was large, including sweet wines and, in particular, Moscatos, which are about as good as any you will find. There are two versions, the Clarté and the Sourgal, both outstanding. The rich straw-yellow Clarté has an elegant, graceful bouquet of varietal aromas in which peach, pear and banana go hand in hand with flowers, notably roses. Full and generous on the palate, it has a well-defined sweet vein, nicely kept in check by a strong but not overpowering prickle of effervescence. It progresses smoothly through to a long, richly satisfying finish that mirrors the nose. One notch down from this, we have the pale Sourgal, its ripe, fairly elegant, nose redolent of fruit and flowers. The tangy effervescence marries well with the wine's sweetness, and the finish displays grace and complexity. The fairly pale ruby Barbera Grivò '98 proffers a bouquet which is initially a little surly but which then settles down to introduce balsamic and fruity aromas. The palate behaves a little better, showing structure, strong varietal backbone, and a lingering finish. The estate's deep straw-yellow Chardonnay Char-de S. '98 has an apricot and peach fruit bouquet echoed in its bitterish finish. The Bigarò, a brachetto and moscato blend, is light, aromatic and pleasantly sweet while the Dolcetto Giulin is simple and hearty.

●	Barbera d'Asti Varmat '98	ᵧᵧ	5	○	Moscato d'Asti Clarté '99	ᵧᵧ	3*
○	Costa del Sole '98	ᵧᵧ	5	●	Barbera d'Asti Grivò '98	ᵧ	4
○	Moscato d'Asti '99	ᵧᵧ	3*	●	Bigarò '99	ᵧ	3
●	Barbera d'Asti Zucchetto '98	ᵧ	3	○	Char-de S. '98	ᵧ	4
○	Langhe Chardonnay '99	ᵧ	3	○	Moscato d'Asti Sourgal '99	ᵧ	3
●	Barbera d'Asti Varmat '96	ᵧᵧ	4	●	Dolcetto d'Alba Giulin '99		3
●	Barbera d'Asti Varmat '97	ᵧᵧ	5	●	Barbera d'Asti Grivò '97	ᵧᵧ	4
●	Barbera d'Asti Zucchetto '97	ᵧ	4				

CASTIGLIONE TINELLA (CN)   COCCONATO D'ASTI (AT)

PAOLO SARACCO
VIA CIRCONVALLAZIONE, 6
12053 CASTIGLIONE TINELLA (CN)
TEL. 0141/855113

BAVA
S.DA MONFERRATO, 2
14023 COCCONATO D'ASTI (AT)
TEL. 0141/907083

Since the beginning of the 1980s, Paolo Saracco has been at the helm of this beautiful estate in Castiglione Tinella, a superb zone for the production of Moscato d'Asti. It is this variety, in fact, that has brought Paolo and his family success from both a commercial and a quality point of view. At least 90 percent of the Saraccos' 30 hectares is given over to moscato. They produce 250,000 bottles a year under five different labels, two Moscato d'Astis and three dry whites. Most of the Saraccos' attention is focused on Moscato d'Asti, and they are now among the top producers of this wine. This year they did not disappoint us and all credit goes to Paolo for his outstanding vinification skills, which are even more impressive when you consider how difficult it is to maintain such a high level of quality over 200,000 bottles of a single wine. Of the two Moscatos, we preferred the Autunno again this year. Its rich straw-yellow, almost golden, colour introduces a full body and elegant, varietal hints of ripe peach over flowers on the nose, laced with lingering nuances of honey. On the palate, it is rich, balanced and creamy with a long, satisfying finish. An excellent buy for the money. The Moscato d'Asti '99 lacks the complexity of its big brother but is nonetheless very good. As for the still whites, the Chardonnay Bianch del Luv '98 shows character while minerally riesling notes prevail in the Graffagno, a blend of 50 percent riesling with chardonnay and sauvignon, and the Chardonnay Prasuè is very pleasant.

The Bava family, today headed by Piero and sons, Roberto, Giulio and Paolo, have been oenologists for four generations. They produce 600,000 bottles a year of a wide variety of wines but still manage to score well in the quality stakes. Cocconato is in Barbera territory and the Bavas naturally dedicate themselves to this tradition, frequently excelling in recent years. Limited yields have lifted the quality of the family's crus and they also plan to replant fully 45 hectares in the Basso Monferrato, 20 of which lie in Cocconato. Released for the second time, their '97 Barbera Piano Alto reaffirms the quality of this wine. Deep violet in colour, it presents ripe red fruit aromas and a very elegant palate with a long finish that echoes the ripe fruit, mingled with over-generous alcohol. The Bavas have also released the '97 vintage of their Arbest, another Barbera d'Asti Superiore, from a seriously good harvest. But of all the Bavas' Barberas it is the Barbera d'Asti Stradivario that impresses most. It has a deep colour and a pervasive nose of plum and cherry jam nuanced with oak. Its tangy, velvety palate leads through to a satisfying finish. The estate's flagship white, the chardonnay-based Alteserre '98, is in its sixth vintage and bears testimony to the improvements in quality the estate has made over this last year. Finally, a well-deserved mention for the Malvasia di Castelnuovo Don Bosco '99 Rosa Canina, which is a fine reward for the estate's efforts to relaunch this traditional local wine. Nor must we forget the historic Giulio Cocchi label, taken over by the Bavas in the 70s, the Spumantes and the Barolo Chinato.

O	Langhe Bianco Graffagno '98	♥♥ 4	●	Barbera d'Asti Sup. Arbest '97	♥♥ 4
O	Langhe Chardonnay		●	Barbera d'Asti Sup. Piano Alto '97	♥♥ 5
	Bianch del Luv '98	♥♥ 5	●	Barbera d'Asti Sup. Stradivario '97	♥♥ 5
O	Moscato d'Asti '99	♥♥ 3*	O	Monferrato Bianco Alteserre '98	♥♥ 4
O	Moscato d'Asti		●	Malvasia di Castelnuovo	
	Moscato d'Autunno '99	♥♥ 3*		Don Bosco Rosa Canina '99	♥ 3
O	Langhe Chardonnay Prasuè '99	♥ 3	●	Barbera d'Asti Sup. Piano Alto '96	♛♛ 5
O	Langhe Bianco Graffagno '97	♛♛ 4	●	Barbera d'Asti Sup. Stradivario '96	♛♛ 5
O	Langhe Chardonnay		●	Barbera d'Asti Sup. Stradivario '95	♛ 5
	Bianch del Luv '97	♛♛ 5	O	Giulio Cocchi Brut '90	♛ 4

COSSOMBRATO (AT)

CARLO QUARELLO
VIA MARCONI, 3
14020 COSSOMBRATO (AT)
TEL. 0141/905204

COSTA VESCOVATO (AL)

LUIGI BOVERI
VIA XX SETTEMBRE, 6
FRAZ. MONTALE CELLI
15050 COSTA VESCOVATO (AL)
TEL. 0131/838165

Carlo Quarello has done much to restore the dignity of Grignolino with his austere, important wine which is a far cry from the poor, thinly coloured products that often line wine merchants' shelves. In creating their Grignolino, Carlo, a man of great culture and experience, his son, Valerio, and wife Bianca, have demonstrated not so much obstinacy as a sense of responsibility towards preserving an important piece of Monferrato's viticultural history and culture. And they have done this at no little risk to themselves. The quality of the wines we tasted this year, however, vindicates them fully. We start with the estate's flagship wine, the Marcaleone '99, which takes its name from an old local expression used to refer to something of exceptional quality and power. Obtained from 100 percent grignolino grapes, it is only produced in the very best vintages. Again this year, it flaunts all its personality. Unusually dark in colour, it releases elegant, crisp aromas of flowers and spice. The substantial structure does not detract from its freshness or drinkability for it achieves a truly remarkable balance of acidity, tannins and alcohol, concluding in a warm, mouth-filling finish. The Crebarné, of which the Quarellos produce 1,500 bottles, proves to be up to the same standard. A blend of 80 percent barbera with nebbiolo, it is aged in barriques. In this it differs from the Cré Marcaleone which is not vinified in wood. The Crebarné boasts a crisp, well-defined nose with understated oak and hints of morello cherry and berry fruit. While not particularly complex on the palate, it is full-flavoured, nicely balanced and lingers attractively on the palate.

Luigi Boveri is one of the finest wineries in the area around Tortona. This part of the province of Alessandria is at a crucial point in the development of its viticulture as many of the area's small producers have opted to go for quality, inspired by the collective realization that these hills possess all the ingredients for international success – exceptional site climates, good soil, and the barbera and timorasso varieties. We had a welcome sample of this commitment when we were tasting. Unfortunately the dreaded mycoplasma disease, flavescence dorée, has also hit the eastern slopes of Piedmont hard, creating a real nightmare for the local viticulturists. Luigi Boveri did not escape unscathed but so far his vineyards have not been too badly damaged. The deep-hued Vignalunga, 100 percent barbera, bears proud witness to the quality of the estate's wines. It boasts elegant aromas of cherry and plum and a full, lingering palate. The almost opaque Poggio delle Amarene offers up heady notes of ripe black cherry. Its fruity palate is less complex than that of the Vignalunga, but still has loads of character. The well-made Boccanera is uncomplicated and agreeable while the Timorasso, making its debut this year, has yet to find a balance with its oak, which tends to overwhelm the varietal aromas. It has a good future though. Finally, a mention for the tangy Cortese Vigna del Prete.

● Grignolino del M.to Casalese Cré Marcaleone '99	♟♟	3*
● Monferrato Rosso Crebarné '98	♟♟	4
● Grignolino del M.to Casalese Cré Marcaleone '98	♟♟	3
● Monferrato Rosso Crebarné '97	♟♟	4

● Colli Tortonesi Barbera Vignalunga '98	♟♟	4
● Colli Tortonesi Barbera Poggio delle Amarene '98	♟♟	3*
○ Colli Tortonesi Bianco Filari di Timorasso '98	♟♟	4
● Colli Tortonesi Barbera Boccanera '99	♟	3
○ Colli Tortonesi Cortese Vigna del Prete '99		2
● Colli Tortonesi Barbera Vignalunga '97	♟♟	4
● Colli Tortonesi Barbera Poggio delle Amarene '97	♟	3

COSTIGLIOLE D'ASTI (AT) COSTIGLIOLE D'ASTI (AT)

PIETRO BENOTTO
FRAZ. S. CARLO, 52
14055 COSTIGLIOLE D'ASTI (AT)
TEL. 0141/966406

PODERI BERTELLI
FRAZ. S. CARLO, 38
14055 COSTIGLIOLE D'ASTI (AT)
TEL. 0141/966137

The Benotto brothers run this estate, which dates back to 1917 and is situated at San Carlo in the municipality of Costiglione d'Asti. They produce a range of traditional Piedmont wines but concentrate principally on Barbera. This year, they offered us three superb products, their Superiori Rupestris, the Balau and the Casot. The Superiori Rupestris is ruby, tending to deep garnet, and possesses a generous, very elegant nose of redcurrant, cherry, fig leaf and liquorice shot through with intriguing hints of balsam and toastiness. The entry on the palate is richly extracted, and progresses solidly and smoothly through to a long fruit and liquorice finish. The Barbera Balau is every bit as good. Its rich colour ushers in a nose of black berry fruit, leather and spices. The excellent texture of the body is apparent from the first sip before the thrust takes you through to a lingering, very faintly bitter finish that mirrors the nose. The Benottos' vivid garnet Barbera Casot offers up mouth-watering aromas of fruit and oak layered over intriguing hints of eucalyptus and earth. It is robust on the palate, the tannins underpinning the leisurely finish. The Bonarda is deep, dark ruby with a young rim and has a nose of ripe black fruit and cakes. The palate is undemanding but holds up well and reveals lovely tannins. One Glass also goes to the Cortese Lacrime di Gioia for its medium straw-yellow colour, rather evolved but broad bouquet, and a fresh, tangy palate.

The Bertelli estate's six and a half hectares of vine are divided between clones of both international and traditional varieties, such as barbera, and their many wines are almost always excellent. Oenologist Maurizio Nervi runs the show and elects to use new wood right from the fermentation stage. He also likes to macerate his reds on the skins for a fairly long time. The ageing process is quite prolonged as the estate does not filter its wines and the result is a modern, rich and very distinctive range. Their deep garnet Barbera Montetusa has a generous, fascinating nose with concentrated fruit and notes of eucalyptus, toast, almond and tar. The entry on the palate is concentrated, leading into a fabulously extracted follow-through, well sustained by its delicious tannins, and the long finish hints at violet and cocoa. The Barbera Sant'Antonio, a dark garnet-ruby, is very good and unveils a wide array of aromas. Touches of balsam and aromatic woods give way to black berry fruit, almonds and autumn leaves. The concentrated palate is gutsy, zesty and satisfyingly mirrors the palate, while the lingering finish mingles fruit and spices. The Mon Mayor, obtained from cabernet and Costiglole's traditional nebbiolo, has a lovely dark hue and aromas that range from raspberry and cherry fruit to hay and green leaves. Attractive tannins bolster the round, elegant texture. The delicious Sauvignon I Fossaretti is noteworthy for its tomato leaf and wild flower nose and a soft, silky palate. Finally, the Chardonnay Giarone is well structured but could do with a bit more tang.

● Barbera d'Asti Sup. Balau '98	♈♈	3*
● Barbera d'Asti Sup. Rupestris '98	♈♈	5
● Barbera d'Asti Sup. Vigneto Casot '98	♈♈	3*
● Piemonte Bonarda '98	♈	2
○ Piemonte Cortese Lacrime di Gioia '99	♈	3
● Barbera d'Asti Sup. Rupestris '96	♉♉	4
● Barbera d'Asti Sup. Rupestris '97	♉♉	4
● Barbera d'Asti Sup. Vigneto Casot '97	♉♉	3

● Barbera d'Asti Montetusa '98	♈♈	5
● Barbera d'Asti S. Antonio Vieilles Vignes '98	♈♈	5
○ Monferrato Bianco I Fossaretti '98	♈♈	5
● Monferrato Rosso Mon Mayor '98	♈♈	5
○ Piemonte Chardonnay Giarone '98	♈	5
● Barbera d'Asti Giarone '97	♉♉	5
○ Piemonte Chardonnay Giarone '97	♉♉	5
● Barbera d'Asti Montetusa '97	♉	5
● Barbera d'Asti S. Antonio Vieilles Vignes '97	♉	5
● Monferrato Cabernet Fossaretti '97	♉	5

COSTIGLIOLE D'ASTI (AT)

COSTIGLIOLE D'ASTI (AT)

CASCINA CASTLÈT
S.DA CASTELLETTO, 6
14055 COSTIGLIOLE D'ASTI (AT)
TEL. 0141/966651

SCIORIO
VIA ASTI NIZZA, 87
14055 COSTIGLIOLE D'ASTI (AT)
TEL. 0141/966610

Mario Borio has 16 hectares planted to vine in Costigliole and a production of 120-130,000 bottles per year. With the technical support of oenologist Giorgio Gozzelino, he naturally concentrates his efforts on Barbera. In addition, Experimental Institute of Viticulture at Asti is using the estate to study ways to save the uvalino variety, which is close to extinction. Of the wines they offered for tasting this year, we liked the Monferrato Rosso Policalpo, a barbera-based wine with a small proportions of cabernet. Moderately intense ruby in colour, it proffers notes of ripe berry fruit and pepper with distinctive earthy mineral tones which add to the complexity of the nose. The palate has good weight and breadth and the finish echoes the nose satisfyingly. Borio's Barbera d'Asti Superiore Litina is aged in traditional barrels and has a fairly broad, quite elegant nose of jam with balsamic and metallic nuances. The palate is fairly full-bodied but the finish fades out just a little too early. The garnet-flecked ruby Barbera '99 unfurls notes of cherry and almond on the nose and a strong hint of acidity on the palate, before the finish picks up the aromas of the bouquet. The Barbera Vivace Goj is a jolly, light-hearted offering with a simple, varietal bouquet, a tangy palate and a pleasant finish. We also liked the Moscato '99. It is a bright, pale straw-yellow and possesses a subtle nose with hints of pear and peach. The sweetish palate has a lively prickle of effervescence.

Mauro and Giuseppe Gozzelino's estate was first featured in the Guide last year and comes back again this year to reaffirm its status as one of the most interesting wineries of the Asti region. Their almost opaque garnet-ruby Barbera d'Asti Beneficio has a narrow, firm rim and a nose that stands out for the complexity and clarity of its aromas. Its fruit notes range from mulberry to redcurrant and blend with touches of confectioner's cream, liquorice, juniper and aromatic herbs to produce a truly fascinating bouquet. The palate is richly extracted, following through solidly in a crescendo of tannins which render the long cocoa and fruit finish a touch dry. The estate's Monferrato Reginal '97, a barbera and cabernet sauvignon blend, has a rich hue and unveils notes of black berry fruit, coffee cream and cocoa. The palate has a sure-footed progression, thanks to its firm sinew, while a fine array of tannins lifts the lingering balsam and fruit finish. The Barbera Sciorio '97 also has a sumptuous colour and considerable structure. Its potent citrus notes stand out against a background of cocoa and berry fruit. The palate has a close-knit texture and buoyant tannins that provide balance and lead into a warm, lingering finish. The rich-hued Monferrato Rosso Antico Vitigno has a slightly aggressive nose revealing hints of bilberry, cocoa, spice and earth laced with barely discernible green notes. It has a fleshy, well-structured palate and a finish that echoes the bouquet. The Chardonnay Vigna Levi '98 does not quite live up to last year's promise, and succumbs to the over-assertive oak.

● Monferrato Rosso Policalpo '98	🍷🍷	5
● Barbera d'Asti '99	🍷	3
● Barbera d'Asti Sup. Litina '98	🍷	3
○ Moscato d'Asti '99	🍷	3
● Barbera del M.to Vivace Goj '99		3
● Monferrato Rosso Policalpo '97	🍷🍷	4
○ Piemonte Moscato Passito		
Avié '97	🍷🍷	5
● Barbera d'Asti Sup. Passum '96	🍷	5
● Barbera d'Asti Sup. Passum '97	🍷	5
● Monferrato Rosso Policalpo '96	🍷	4

● Barbera d'Asti Beneficio '97	🍷🍷	5
● Monferrato Rosso Reginal '97	🍷🍷	5
● Barbera d'Asti Sciorio '97	🍷🍷	4
● Monferrato Rosso		
Antico Vitigno '97	🍷	5
○ Piemonte Chardonnay		
Vigna Levi '98		5
● Barbera d'Asti '96	🍷🍷	4
● Barbera d'Asti Barrique '96	🍷🍷	5

66

DIANO D'ALBA (CN)

CLAUDIO ALARIO
VIA SANTA CROCE, 23
12055 DIANO D'ALBA (CN)
TEL. 0173/231808

Claudio Alario, with his wife and parents, puts his heart and soul into his eight hectares, producing 35,000 bottles a year. He has reaped success by scrupulously selecting his vines, religiously tending his vineyards, and limiting his yields to let the grapes mature fully. In the cellar, Claudio's modern style brings out the personality of the fruit, while brief macerations and small barrels, or stainless steel in the case of the Dolcetto, give his wines a lovely roundness. His two Dianos are richly extracted and excitingly fragrant while the deep garnet Costa Fiore offers mulberry, cherry, fresh hay and cocoa aromas over an intriguing mineral base. The texture vies with the robust structure to dominate the palate, combining to usher in a long finish of fruit and spice. Claudio's lustrous Montagrillo is redolent of grass and almonds. It has solid weight and tannins which lend volume to its lingering finish. The Barbera Valletta is also rather special. A rich garnet-ruby, it proffers a generous, complex nose with notes of mulberry and redcurrant alongside mint, almond paste and fig leaf. The palate is big and mouth-filling but not in the least flabby or obvious while the finish has good length and complexity. The Nebbiolo Cascinotto regales the nose with hints of leather and rosemary that enhance the rich fruit. The palate is even more concentrated, its well-integrated, delicate tannins ushering in a finish redolent of liquorice. The Barolo Riva is very well put together, with notable structure and elegance.

DIANO D'ALBA (CN)

BRICCO MAIOLICA
VIA BOLANGINO, 7
FRAZ. RICCA
12055 DIANO D'ALBA (CN)
TEL. 0173/612049

Beppe Accomo is a passionate, ambitious viticulturist and produces wines of excellent quality on his 20 hectare estate. He is ably assisted by his wife, Loredana, and his parents. We were very impressed this year by the Barbera Vigna Vigia. For the first time, Beppe has added to this vintage a barbera clone from old vines which produces tiny bunches of grapes. He planted these vines, which came on-stream in 1998, himself. The result is a deep, almost opaque garnet Barbera with the narrowest of rims. Its wide array of elegant aromas includes the fragrant black cherry and redcurrant fruit with complex hints of pepper, green leaf, and autumn leaves. The impressively flavoursome front palate opens out into a broad, juicy mid palate with very fine tannins. There are sweet hints of chocolate in the lingering finish. This exceptional vintage has earned Beppe his place among the select group of wineries that can boast a Three Glass award. His Dolcetto Sörì Bricco Maiolica is also superb. Top quality fruit and a skilful mix of barrique and stainless steel give this wine an impenetrable hue and a lovely dark, fruity nose of ripe morello cherries and mulberries. These are joined by hints of confectioner's cream, mint and thyme. Beppe's Lorié, obtained from pinot nero aged in used barriques, has achieved a perfect balance of fruit and wood in only its third vintage. Ruby with garnet highlights, it proffers strawberry and cake aromas over hints of wet dog. The Bianco Rolando has a nose of peaches-in-syrup and apples and a lingering, silky texture. The Nebbiolo Cumot is chock full of raspberry, bilberry and peach fruit over a balsamic, mineral base. The palate has outstanding structure and loads of interest. A veritable triumph!

● Barbera d'Alba Valletta '98	ŸŸ	5
● Barolo Riva '96	ŸŸ	6
● Dolcetto di Diano d'Alba Costa Fiore '99	ŸŸ	3*
● Dolcetto di Diano d'Alba Montagrillo '99	ŸŸ	3*
● Nebbiolo d'Alba Cascinotto '98	ŸŸ	5
● Barbera d'Alba Valletta '96	♀♀	5
● Barolo Riva '95	♀♀	6
● Dolcetto di Diano d'Alba Costa Fiore '98	♀♀	3
● Nebbiolo d'Alba Cascinotto '97	♀♀	5

● Barbera d'Alba Vigna Vigia '98	ŸŸŸ	4
● Dolcetto di Diano d'Alba Sörì Bricco Maiolica '99	ŸŸ	3*
○ Langhe Bianco Rolando '99	ŸŸ	3*
● Langhe Rosso Lorié '97	ŸŸ	5
● Nebbiolo d'Alba Cumot '98	ŸŸ	4
● Dolcetto di Diano d'Alba '99	Ÿ	3
● Dolcetto di Diano d'Alba Sörì Bricco Maiolica '98	♀♀	3
● Langhe Rosso Lorié '96	♀♀	5
● Nebbiolo d'Alba Cumot '97	♀	5

DOGLIANI (CN)

DOGLIANI (CN)

MARZIANO ED ENRICO ABBONA
VIA TORINO, 242
12063 DOGLIANI (CN)
TEL. 0173/70484 - 0173/721317

QUINTO CHIONETTI E FIGLIO
B.TA VALDIBERTI, 44
12063 DOGLIANI (CN)
TEL. 0173/71179

Once again, Marziano Abbona presented us with an excellent selection of wines that hover around the Three Glass threshold. The only criticism of this estate is perhaps that it spreads itself too thin and produces too many wines, but the potential is there. The Abbonos have 32 hectares planted to vine and plan to increase the figure to 36 over the next few years. Their vineyards lie mostly in Dogliani, but they also have plots in Barolo and Barbaresco and it is with these two wines that we open our review. Made with fruit from the Terlo Ravera vineyard, the Abbonos' Barolo is bright ruby in appearance. Its intense bouquet of balsam and cloves is lifted by hints of liquorice and liqueur fruit. The palate is wonderfully soft, lingering and full of personality. The Barbaresco, made with the grapes from Faset, one of the zone's most important crus, is every bit as good. We awarded Two Glasses to two of this estate's three Dolcettos, and the third, the Vigneto Muntâ, came very close. Yet again, the selection named after Papà Celso, made with grapes from the Doriolo vineyard, is a star thanks to its well-sustained body and full-flavoured drinkability. The Due Ricu is also very interesting. A cabernet sauvignon and barbera blend, its impenetrable, almost opaque garnet ushers in a complex bouquet. A first impression of slightly vegetal notes opens out into delicious fruit notes of blackcurrant and toast, while the muscular, juicy palate takes you through to a long, well-balanced and rather characterful finish. The Cinerino, a white making its debut this year, is obtained from oak-aged viognier and already shows great personality on its first outing.

This beautiful estate has 15 hectares of vines boasting prime positions in Dogliani, all dedicated to the zone's traditional variety – dolcetto. Quinto Chionetti, the owner, is a staunch traditionalist and has remained deaf to the siren calls of other varieties. He produces only two wines, which differ in that they are made from the fruit of two different crus. The estate's flagship wine, the Dolcetto di Dogliani Briccolero, once again proves to be one of the year's most interesting Dolcettos. Ruby red shading into garnet, it proffers a nose of almond and mulberry laced with minerals and spice. The austere palate has plenty of backbone but its rather astringent finish still lacks a little balance. This Dogliano Dolcetto is a superb example of its type and displays all the variety's trademark characteristics. Previous vintages have already shown how well it cellars, and this year's offering is no exception. We expect to savour it for years to come. Then there is the San Luigi, the less demanding of Chionetti's two Dolcettos. Notable for its balance and elegance, it is full-flavoured and lingering. The bitter almond finish is typical of a Dogliano Dolcetto and lives up to expectations.

● Barbaresco Faset '97	ΥΥ	6
● Barolo Vigneto Terlo Ravera '96	ΥΥ	6
O Cinerino '99	ΥΥ	4
● Dolcetto di Dogliani Bricco S. Bernardo '99	ΥΥ	3*
● Dolcetto di Dogliani Papà Celso '99	ΥΥ	4
● Langhe Rosso I Due Ricu '98	ΥΥ	5
● Dolcetto di Dogliani Vigneto Muntâ '99	Υ	3
● Barbaresco Faset '96	ΥΥ	6
● Barbera d'Alba Rinaldi '98	ΥΥ	4
● Barolo Vigneto Terlo Ravera '95	ΥΥ	6
● Dolcetto di Dogliani Papà Celso '98	ΥΥ	4
● Langhe Rosso Rico '97	Υ	5

● Dolcetto di Dogliani Briccolero '99	ΥΥ	4
● Dolcetto di Dogliani S. Luigi '99	ΥΥ	4
● Dolcetto di Dogliani Briccolero '98	ΥΥ	4
● Dolcetto di Dogliani S. Luigi '98	ΥΥ	4

DOGLIANI (CN)

DOGLIANI (CN)

PODERI LUIGI EINAUDI
B.TA GOMBE, 31/32
CASCINA TECC
12063 DOGLIANI (CN)
TEL. 0173/70191

F.LLI PECCHENINO
B.TA VALDIBERTI, 59
12063 DOGLIANI (CN)
TEL. 0173/70686

Here we have a genuine Langhe "Château". In a few short years, Giorgio Ruffo and his wife Paola Einaudi have transformed this estate into one of the most impressive wineries in the zone. Luigi Einaudi, first president of the Italian republic and Paola's uncle, could not have hoped for worthier heirs. The family motto could well be "Innovation with Tradition" and Paola is no exception. Ninety-eight of the estate's 104 hectares are in San Luigi, Gombe and Santa Lucia in the hills of Dogliani. Six more lie in Barolo, between the legendary Cannubi and Terlo Vie Nuove crus. Of the 13 wines Giorgio and Paola produce, the Langhe Luigi Einaudi leads the field out yet again. A blend of cabernet, merlot, barbera and nebbiolo, this rich, austere wine is one of the best reds in Italy and for the second year running wins a resounding Three Glasses. For some time now, the estate has only presented wines of the highest quality. Witness their two Barolos. The first, from Cannubi, is remarkable for its complexity and wealth of noble tannins. The second, the Costa Grimaldi, is obtained from the fruit of vineyards in Terlo Vie Nuove and is potent and aggressive. In fact, it has still to be released. The Einaudi white, the Langhe Vigna Meira '99, is not to be missed. It is obtained from an unusual variety for the Langhe, tocai-pinot gris. Two Glasses apiece go to the Dogliani Vigna Tecc '98 and the Dolcetto di Dogliani '99 but we shall have to wait one more year to taste their new barrique-conditioned I Filari selection. The Barbera is a muscular, very traditional offering with marked acidity while the Langhe Nebbiolo and standard-label Barolo carry off One Glass each. The estate also features a guesthouse, the Foresteria dei Poderi, comprising three bedrooms and one suite.

From its lofty position on Bricco Botti, the Pecchenino estate looks out over the valley of San Luigi. Here, Orlando and Attilio Pecchenino inaugurated their new winery with last year's harvest. They used the fruit of the surrounding vineyards to produce a Dolcetto di Dogliani Superiore which is aged in barriques for a longer period than most other selections before being bottled. This year they presented us with their Bricco Botti '98, of which they have made 7,500 bottles, and we were most impressed. Its aromas are still very fresh, despite the mystique added by fascinating fumé nuances. On the palate, it comes across as less forward than the vintage Dolcettos for the acidity and tannins have mellowed. The finish is long and mouth-filling. Even better was the Dolcetto di Dogliani Sirì d'Jermu, which flaunts all the fresh acidity and alcohol of a young Dolcetto. An intense, dark, almost opaque ruby in the glass, it proffers austere, lingering aromas of spice, walnut and ripe berry fruits. Mellow and seductive, it leaves the palate clean and a-tingle with rich, almost minerally, sensations. The Peccheninos have produced 32,000 bottles of this Dolcetto. All credit to this family for all their effort in the vineyard to produce a wine of this quality. There or thereabouts, too, is the San Luigi, made with fruit from the zone of the same name. What should have been a standard-label selection once more comes out right at the top of its category. Production runs to 15,000 bottles. The Pecchenino estate has not released its Chardonnay Vigna Maestro this year but the Langhe La Castella '97, a blend of 75 percent barbera, 15 percent nebbiolo, and 10 percent cabernet sauvignon, is proof of Orlando's mastery of the art of making red wine.

● Langhe Rosso Luigi Einaudi '98	▮▮▮	6
● Barolo Costa Grimaldi '96	▮▮	6
● Barolo nei Cannubi '96	▮▮	6
● Dolcetto di Dogliani '99	▮▮	3*
● Dolcetto di Dogliani Vigna Tecc '98	▮▮	4
○ Langhe Bianco Vigna Meira '99	▮▮	4
● Piemonte Barbera '98	▮▮	4
● Barolo '96	▮	6
● Langhe Nebbiolo '98	▮	4
● Langhe Rosso Luigi Einaudi '97	♈♈♈	6
● Barolo nei Cannubi '95	♈♈	6
● Dolcetto di Dogliani I Filari '97	♈♈	4

● Dolcetto di Dogliani Sirì d'Jermu '99	▮▮▮	4
● Dolcetto di Dogliani S. Luigi '99	▮▮	3*
● Dolcetto di Dogliani Sup. Bricco Botti '98	▮▮	5
● Langhe La Castella '97	▮▮	5
● Dolcetto di Dogliani Sirì d'Jermu '96	♈♈♈	4
● Dolcetto di Dogliani Sirì d'Jermu '97	♈♈♈	4
● Dolcetto di Dogliani Sirì d'Jermu '98	♈♈♈	4
● Dolcetto di Dogliani Sup. Bricco Botti '97	♈♈	5
● Langhe La Castella '95	♈♈	5
● Langhe La Castella '96	♈♈	5

DOGLIANI (CN)

DOGLIANI (CN)

PIRA
B.TA VALDIBERTI, 69
12063 DOGLIANI (CN)
TEL. 0173/78538

SAN FEREOLO
B.TA VALDIBÀ, 59
12063 DOGLIANI (CN)
TEL. 0173/742075

The vineyards of the Pira family are on the border of the municipalities of Dogliani and Monforte d'Alba, whose appellations they carry. The Piras do not, however, produce Barolo as their part of Monforte falls outside DOCG zone. That's why they concentrate their efforts on Dolcetto, both at Dogliani and Alba, and on Barbera d'Alba. This year, they have added a new selection obtained from raisined grapes. We'll kick off our review with this new offering, the unusual Barbera d'Alba V. T. '98, from grapes harvested late in the season and left to raisin on rush mats. Its vibrant, impenetrable red hue ushers in pervasive aromas of roasted hazelnuts mingling with spice, chocolate and fruit in syrup. The close-knit, full-bodied palate rounds off with an attractively mature finish. This excellent wine bears witness to the flexibility of one of Piedmont's trademark varieties. Matteo Pira seems to have a bent for vinifying very ripe fruit. His Langhe Rosso Briccobotti is made from late-vintage barbera grapes. It is powerful and opulent but never cloys. The Piras' other Barbera, the Vigna Fornaci '98, is almost as good. We awarded Two Glasses to their Dogliani Vigna Landes '99 for its juicy fruit, fabulous structure and sweet mulberry and almond aromas. Its stablemate, the Dolcetto d'Alba Vigna Fornaci '99, is a tad less stylish.

Nicoletta Bocca has raised the stakes. For the third year, she has pocketed a Three Glass award. Three years ago, it was the Dolcetto di Dogliani San Fereolo '97, last year it was the Langhe Brumaio '97, and now there's no stopping her. Her magnificent Dogliani San Fereolo '99 carries off this year's top prize. It is a wine of extraordinary elegance and longevity, from of the fruit of six hectares planted with 30 to 60-year-old vines and vinified with great skill. In addition, the estate's vineyards nestle among the hills of Valdiberti and Santa Lucia in one of the most favoured zones for the cultivation of dolcetto. Careful thinning and the low output of the old vines make for a very limited yield per hectare. Nicoletta Bocca leaves the fruit to mature on the vine and allows the wine to age much longer than is usual for a Dolcetto. She ages part of her San Fereolo '99, of which she has produced 20,000 bottles, in one-year-old barriques and a smaller percentage in new casks. The result is a dark wine with an alcohol-rich nose which opens out gradually to reveal fruit and mineral notes. The palate offers rich fruit and a wealth of extract with impressive aromas that lend the wine warmth and length. Nicoletta continues to experiment with the Dolcetto di Dogliani Superiore, which she ages for even longer than its predecessor. Finally, the 1593 '97 is excellent and the Brumaio '98 and the base Dolcetto di Dogliani are both very good.

● Barbera d'Alba V. T. '98	ỸỸ 6
● Dolcetto di Dogliani Vigna Landes '99	ỸỸ 3*
● Langhe Rosso Briccobotti '98	ỸỸ 5
● Barbera d'Alba Vigna Fornaci '98	Ỹ 4
● Dolcetto d'Alba Vigna Fornaci '99	Ỹ 3
● Barbera d'Alba V. T. '97	♈♈ 5
● Dolcetto di Dogliani Vigna Bricco dei Botti '98	♈♈ 4
● Barbera d'Alba Vigna Fornaci '97	♈ 4
● Piemonte Barbera Briccobotti '97	♈ 4

● Dolcetto di Dogliani S. Fereolo '99	ỸỸỸ 4
● Dolcetto di Dogliani '99	ỸỸ 3*
● Dolcetto di Dogliani Sup. 1593 '97	ỸỸ 4
● Langhe Rosso Brumaio '98	ỸỸ 5
● Dolcetto di Dogliani S. Fereolo '97	♈♈♈ 4
● Langhe Rosso Brumaio '97	♈♈♈ 5
● Dolcetto di Dogliani S. Fereolo '98	♈♈ 4
● Il Brumaio '95	♈♈ 5
● Langhe Rosso Brumaio '96	♈♈ 5

DOGLIANI (CN)

SAN ROMANO
B.TA GIACHELLI, 8
12063 DOGLIANI (CN)
TEL. 0173/76289

FARA NOVARESE (NO)

DESSILANI
VIA CESARE BATTISTI, 21
28073 FARA NOVARESE (NO)
TEL. 0321/829252

It has only been five years since Bruno Chionetti gave up a career in graphics for viticulture but he has certainly made the right move. This year, he makes his fourth appearance in the Guide. Not content with the Three Glass awards he won for his Dolcetto Vigna del Pilone '97 and '98, this year he adds the '99 vintage to his trophy cupboard, having taken full advantage of a very good harvest. He runs the San Romano winery with his wife, Sabina Bosio, and his brother-in-law, Enrico Durando. They have seven hectares planted to vine but only three and a half are currently producing. The rest will come on-stream over the next few years and should increase the current 25-30,000 bottles a year to 50,000. In addition to dolcetto, the traditional Dogliani variety, San Romano grows barbera and pinot nero. Once again, it is the Vigna del Pilone, a classic dolcetto, that stands out from the pack. Its robust 14.5 percent alcohol very nicely sets off the full body and tannins, which harmonise perfectly with the acidity. Drinking nicely right now, it is still a long way off its best and will benefit from ageing in the bottle. Bruno and a local group of producers have every faith in the potential of this variety and have experimented with extreme vinification methods, including a more prolonged ageing in wood. The estate's Dolcetto di Dogliani Superiore Dolianum '98 has been aged in stainless steel as well as in barriques and in casks. It may lack a little harmony but the resulting wine is nevertheless well worth investigating. Finally, the base Dogliani is very decent. Summer thinning and a low yield have produced a wine of 13.5 percent alcohol.

With a production of almost 400,000 bottles, this is a major winery both in terms of quantity and, after recent efforts, in terms of quality. Quality is the name of the game for Enzio Lucca, the ninth in a long line of oenologists to come from the Dessilani family. Agronomists Giampiero Romana and Federico Curtaz, with oenologist Beppe Caviola, have been collaborating with the Dessilanis for the last two years to improve the quality of the estate's wines. The Dessilanis' best vineyards lie in the Lochera area on the morainic Fara hillslope, and in the Caramino zone at Briona. From fairly low yields of less than 60 quintals per hectare and a careful selection of grapes, the team obtain two serious Faras, both aged in barriques for a minimum of 18 months. The Caramino '97 is excellent, with its deep garnet colour, its rich, fruity, elegant bouquet, and its succulent, velvety palate with a lingering finish of sweet tannins. The Lochera '97 is also very good. It is a tad more aggressive than the Caramino but fascinates with its rounded, silky structure. From a less favourable vintage, the Gattinara '94 is still good and is also proving to be very cellarable. The Nebbiolo '97 is also made with grapes grown in the Fara, Ghemme and Sizzano zones. Its nine-month barrique ageing has endowed it with a very successful marriage of berry fruit and toasty oak aromas.

● Dolcetto di Dogliani		
Vigna del Pilone '99	♟♟♟	4
● Dolcetto di Dogliani '99	♟♟	3*
● Dolcetto di Dogliani Sup.		
Dolianum '98	♟♟	5
● Dolcetto di Dogliani		
Vigna del Pilone '97	♟♟♟	4
● Dolcetto di Dogliani		
Vigna del Pilone '98	♟♟♟	4
● Langhe Rosso '98	♟♟	4

● Fara Caramino '97	♟♟	5
● Fara Lochera '97	♟♟	5
● Colline Novaresi Nebbiolo '97	♟	5
● Gattinara '94	♟	5
● Fara Lochera '95	♟♟	5
● Fara Caramino '95	♟♟	5

FARIGLIANO (CN)

Anna Maria Abbona

Fraz. Moncucco, 21
12060 Farigliano (CN)
tel. 0173/797228

Young Anna Maria and Franco Abbona have gained entry to the Dogliani élite by sticking to their watchword of quality. Healthy competition and astute collaboration with other noted wine makers in the area provide the stimulus that ensures their wines get better each year. They have eight hectares planted to vine, seven of which are currently in production, and bottle about 40,000 units a year. They have recently planted less than half a hectare to barbera on the lowest slopes with best exposure. In a few years time, the fruit of these vines will go to make their Langhe Rosso Cadò, whose production currently totals a scant 4,500 bottles. Underpinning the Abbona range is a Langhe Dolcetto, obtained from the youngest vines and boasting a refreshing, heady nose reminiscent of strawberries. Simple and very drinkable, it possesses a lively, tannic palate that brings out the personality of the fruit, grown at an altitude of around 550 metres above sea level. The almost opaque Dolcetto di Dogliani Sorì dij But accounts for approximately half of the Abbonas' production. This classic Dolcetto di Dogliani is potent and fragrant. As yet, it is a little closed but its length and complexity on the palate augur well for the future. The Sorì dij But's big brother, the Maioli, is a product of the estate's oldest vines. Ink-black in the glass, it unveils a very intense bouquet of mulberry jam and cocoa. The powerful palate reveals close-knit tannins which are nicely set off by the juicy fruit. The Cadò, 90 percent barbera and 10 percent dolcetto, is aged in casks of French oak for 18 months. It has less heft but more elegance than the previous vintage, and has a strong suit in its balance.

● Dolcetto di Dogliani Maioli '99	🍷🍷	4
● Dolcetto di Dogliani Sorì dij But '99	🍷🍷	3*
● Langhe Rosso Cadò '98	🍷🍷	5
● Langhe Dolcetto '99		2
● Dolcetto di Dogliani Maioli '98	YY	4
● Langhe Rosso Cadò '97	YY	5

FARIGLIANO (CN)

Giovanni Battista Gillardi

Cascina Corsaletto, 69
12060 Farigliano (CN)
tel. 0173/76306

We wrote in the Guide last year that the Gillardi wines were all very sound but none merited the hallowed Three Glass distinction. One year later, we are opening the account with the Harys '98, the first wine from the estate to win the top Guide award. This is the least traditional of all Gillardi products but it is worth every point of its Three Glass score, which pays homage not only to the estate itself but also to Giovanni Gillardi and his wife, Pinuccia, two unique, self-effacing wine makers. The Gillardis, who look after their vineyards as if they were a private garden, work with their son, Giacolino, who has brought to the property many years of professional experience gained from working at the Ceretto winery and now acts as oenologist and manager on the family estate. It was a magnificent insight to plant syrah in this zone, on the highest hilltop at Farigliano, as the variety has flourished and is now robust and mature enough to produce a great wine. A dash of cabernet – 15 percent – lifts the syrah and gives it the veneer of elegance and polish that the variety tends to lack, especially when young. The wine is ruby red, tending to dark violet, with an intense, complex bouquet of spice, leather and tobacco. These positively inebriating aromas herald a staggeringly huge, persistent palate that echoes each aroma faithfully. A veritable triumph. Of the two superb Dolcetto di Doglianis, we preferred the Cursalet sul Vigneto Maestra.

● Harys '98	🍷🍷🍷	6
● Dolcetto di Dogliani Cursalet '99	🍷🍷	4
● Dolcetto di Dogliani Vigneto Maestra '99	🍷🍷	3*
● Dolcetto di Dogliani Cursalet '98	YY	4
● Dolcetto di Dogliani Vigneto Maestra '98	YY	3
● Harys '96	YY	6
● Harys '97	YY	6

FRASSINELLO M.TO (AL)   GATTINARA (VC)

CASTELLO DI LIGNANO
REG. LIGNANO
15035 FRASSINELLO M.TO (AL)
TEL. 0142/334529 - 0142/925326

ANTONIOLO
C.SO VALSESIA, 277
13045 GATTINARA (VC)
TEL. 0163/833612 - 0163/826112

The mediaeval castle of Lignano was erected on the top of a hill amidst vineyards that had already been cultivated for centuries. In 1988, the Gaiero family of iron and steel industrialists from Casale took over the 85-hectare estate. There are 15 hectares under vine, nestling on the slopes surrounding the castle. Of the selection the Gaieros offered for tasting this year, we particularly liked the Barbera Vigna Stramba. Rich ruby red in the glass, it proffers clean, lingering aromas of cherry, vanilla and coffee. The palate opens out to become soft and fleshy then the finish reveals a typical Barbera tanginess. A blend of 60 percent barbera, 30 percent cabernet and 10 percent freisa, the Lhennius '98 is aged in large barrels and also wins Two Glasses. It boasts a dark colour, a bouquet of dried flowers, cherry and plum over a grassy background and great structure. The Freisa is interesting, its lustrous ruby colour introducing fragrances of raspberry and black cherry laced with spice. The palate has medium length and good balance. The Grignolino Vigna Tufara, a bright cherry red, offers up clean aromas of almond, redcurrant, green pepper and cloves. Its varietal palate avoids excessive austerity and leads into a lovely bitterish finish. Obtained from a 60-40 blend of cortese and sauvignon, the Grisello is part-aged (20 percent) in large oak casks. Elegant notes of tangerine and tomato leaf herald a coherent, well-balanced palate with a delicately citric finish. The Valisenda, barbera with a touch of freisa, is also enjoyable.

Established in 1949, this estate deserves much of the credit for the acclaim Gattinara has received on the international as well as the domestic front. This is a family-run enterprise: Rosanna Antoniolo, often cited in the Guide, has been joined by her son, Alberto, who helps her to run the winery with his sister, Lorella, who takes care of the administrative side of things. From their 12 hectares planted to vine, they produce 70,000 bottles a year, 40,000 of which are dedicated to Gattinara. The vineyards that have made the Antoniolos their name, however, are San Francesco (about 4,000 bottles), Osso San Grato (5,000 bottles) and Castelle (4,000 bottles). Their other two vineyards, Borelle and Valferana, produce the grapes that go to make Juvenia, their young Nebbiolo, released for the first time in 1987, and their white and rosé wines. The estate's Erbaluce is well worth a mention. They buy in the grapes from Caluso to make this wine, for which Rosanna has a particular fondness. Of the '96 Gattinara vintages presented, the Vigneto Osso San Grato is head and shoulders above the rest. Dark garnet in colour, it already possesses an intense bouquet despite its youth. Hints of leather, aniseed and brandied fruit assail the nose and the austere palate is shot through with elegant, velvety tannins. The barrique-conditioned Gattinara Vigneto Castelle's initial aromas open out to embrace sweet, pleasant balsamic tones. The palate is full-bodied with a wealth of extract and tannins, and oak that returns in the final note. The Gattinara San Francesco '96 is very good if a little evolved while the basic Gattinara easily merits One Glass along with the Juvenia, which is notable for its agreeable fruity palate.

● Barbera d'Asti		
Vigna Stramba '98	❡❡	4
● Monferrato Rosso Lhennius '98	❡❡	5
● Barbera del M.to Valisenda '98	❡	3
● Grignolino del M.to Casalese		
Vigna Tufara '99	❡	3
○ Monferrato Casalese Grisello '99	❡	3
● Monferrato Freisa '98	❡	3
● Barbera d'Asti		
Vigna Stramba '97	♀♀	4
● Monferrato Rosso Lhennius '97	♀♀	5

● Gattinara Vigneto Castelle '96	❡❡	6
● Gattinara		
Vigneto Osso S. Grato '96	❡❡	6
● Gattinara Vigneto S. Francesco '96	❡❡	6
● Coste della Sesia Nebbiolo		
Juvenia '99	❡	3
● Gattinara '96	❡	5
○ Erbaluce di Caluso '99		3
● Gattinara Vigneto Castelle '95	♀♀	5
● Gattinara		
Vigneto Osso S. Grato '93	♀♀	5
● Gattinara		
Vigneto Osso S. Grato '95	♀♀	5
● Gattinara Vigneto S. Francesco '95	♀	5

GATTINARA (VC)

GATTINARA (VC)

NERVI
C.SO VERCELLI, 117
13045 GATTINARA (VC)
TEL. 0163/833228

GIANCARLO TRAVAGLINI
S.DA DELLE VIGNE, 36
13045 GATTINARA (VC)
TEL. 0163/833588

Nervi is a name that will go down in the history of Gattinara. Established by Luigi Nervi in the early 20th century, the estate then passed to his son, Italo, who ran it for 30 years and launched it internationally. In 1991, it was taken over by the Bocciolone family who started out in the metallurgical industry. They have introduced a series of important innovations, both in the vineyards and in the cellar, and are in the process of converting the estate's beautiful 19th-century headquarters on the fringe of Gattinara into a small museum dedicated to local viticulture, which will also feature tasting rooms. The estate is run with genial enthusiasm by Giorgio Aliata, with the support of Carla Ferrero and the oenological expertise of Giorgio Barbero. The jewel in their crown is still the Gattinara Vigneto Molsino, of which they make an average of 25-30,000 bottles. This wine is only produced in the best years from the fruit of the best vineyards on the Gattinara slopes, where long exposure to the sun and shelter from the coldest winds provides the perfect environment for the nebbiolo grapes to reach full maturity. Their Molsino '96 is one of the most interesting Gattinaras we have ever had the pleasure of tasting. Its bright garnet appearance hints at the fabulous concentration that comes into its own on the palate where velvet tannins provide a wonderful counterpoint for the full body. The spicy nose blends hints of dried flowers and forest floor. The estate's output of its standard Gattinara totals 30,000 bottles and the wine is aged for a minimum of three years in oak casks. The '95 vintage is good, even if it lacks the complexity of the '96. To finish off the range we have Amore, a blend of nebbiolo with cabernet and merlot from other regions.

Giancarlo Travaglini continues his quest to modernise his cellars, plant new vineyards, and market wines with a much more modern style than the traditional northern Piedmont Nebbiolos. Nine out of ten of the 300,000 bottles he produces from his 39-hectare estate are destined for the overseas markets, mainly the United States, but also Brazil, Japan and Finland. Of the wines Travaglini offered for tasting this year, it was the new Gattinara Tre Vigne '97 selection (25,000 bottles) that Giancarlo was most excited about, and we share his enthusiasm. Obtained from the grapes of the Permolone, Lurghe and Alice vineyards, it is a deep, dark, almost opaque ruby colour. It possesses a complex bouquet of spice and alcohol-preserved red berry fruit and a truly fascinating palate whose soft, dense tannins open out into a rich, fleshy fruitiness that bottle age will refine and harmonise. This is an outstanding wine, one of the best in the zone and beyond. The Gattinara Riserva '96 is also very impressive. From time immemorial the flagship wine of this estate, the '96 version has a colour to rival that of its predecessor. In fact, it may even be just a shade more intense. The nose and the palate are both very satisfying, complementing each other to highlight the wine's full body. Two resounding Glasses for this wine which has never come so close to the Guide's top grading. To round off the Gattinara trilogy we have the basic '97 selection, slightly inferior to previous vintages but still nicely expressive. A round of applause for Giancarlo Travaglini who has managed to change the face of his winery in the space of a few short years by introducing changes which have enhanced the vigour of his wines.

● Gattinara '95	▓▓	5
● Gattinara Vigneto Molsino '96	▓▓	5
● Amore		3
● Gattinara Vigneto Molsino '93	♟♟	5
● Gattinara Vigneto Molsino '95	♟♟	5
● Gattinara '93	♟	5

● Gattinara Ris. '96	▓▓	6
● Gattinara Tre Vigne '97	▓▓	6
● Gattinara '97	▓	4
● Gattinara Ris. '93	♟♟	6
● Gattinara Ris. '95	♟♟	6
● Gattinara Ris. Numerata '88	♟♟	6
● Gattinara Ris. Numerata '89	♟♟	6
● Gattinara Ris. Numerata '90	♟♟	6

GAVI (AL)

NICOLA BERGAGLIO
LOC. PEDAGGERI, 59
FRAZ. ROVERETO
15066 GAVI (AL)
TEL. 0143/682195

If Rovereto is rightly considered to be one of the "grands crus" of Gavi, then owner Gianluigi Bergaglio is one of the celebrated grower-producers in the zone. His wines enjoy all the advantages of a winemaking and bottling tradition that goes back to 1969, and his labels are widely appreciated and respected for their solid reliability. Bergaglio's 12 hectares are dedicated solely to the production of cortese which go to make the estate's two historic lines, the standard label and the Minaia. The standard Gavi '99 is a pale, intense, lustrous straw-yellow flecked with clear green highlights. It offers clear floral and golden delicious fruit aromas over a hint of hay and a fresh, tangy palate that displays marked acidity. The Minaia '99 is a lovely, moderately intense straw-yellow with vibrant green highlights. It boasts a full, rich bouquet of wild flowers, hawthorn and apple over a minerally base. Entry on the palate is very satisfying and succulent, opening out into a soft, well-structured mid palate with enjoyable vanilla sensations. Strong acidity ensures the wine will age comfortably.

○	Gavi del Comune di Gavi '99	🍷	3
○	Gavi del Comune di Gavi Minaia '99	🍷	3

GAVI (AL)

GIAN PIERO BROGLIA
TENUTA LA MEIRANA
LOC. LOMELLINA, 14
15066 GAVI (AL)
TEL. 0143/642998 - 0143/743267

Piero Broglia, who this year has taken over as president of the Consorzio di Tutela del Gavi, has just inaugurated the very functional renovated headquarters of the 1000-year-old Meirana winery, the first "cascina", or "farm", documented as producing wine in the area. It dates all the way back to 972 AD and today lies at the heart of a beautiful estate on the panoramic Lomellina road. New vineyards, some planted with black varieties, are constantly coming into production and others are being planted as part of an forward-looking investment scheme intended to lay increasingly solid foundations for the future. Broglia's wines continue to maintain their high standards in terms of quality, starting with his Gavi Bruno Broglia '98. One of the estate's top selections, it is right up there with the best Italian whites this year. A blend of steel and wood-vinified Gavi, it unveils a rich, green-flecked straw-yellow colour and flaunts a sophisticated, complex nose blending notes of flowers, butter, ripe apples and pears, and spices. The attack on the palate is firm and nicely balanced, displaying softness, succulence and fabulous length. The Gavi La Meirana '99, a rich straw-yellow with flecks of green, also merits Two Glasses for its refined, complex nose of ripe fruit, citrus and spices. Its palate is typically varietal with a firm, lively tanginess and solid structure. The estate's refreshing, very drinkable Gavi Spumante Roverello '99 sparkler has structure and character. The rich, bright violet ruby Monferrato Rosso '98 also makes an impressive debut. Its nose is every bit as rich as its colour, showing complexity and elegance with hints of earth, spices and minerals, while on the palate it reveals power, weight, and moderate persistence.

○	Gavi del Comune di Gavi La Meirana '99	🍷🍷	3*
○	Gavi del Comune di Gavi Bruno Broglia '98	🍷🍷	5
●	Monferrato Rosso '98	🍷🍷	5
○	Gavi del Comune di Gavi Roverello '99		3
○	Gavi del Comune di Gavi Bruno Broglia '96	🍸🍸	5
○	Gavi del Comune di Gavi Bruno Broglia '97	🍸🍸	5
○	Gavi Spumante Extra Brut '92	🍸	4

GAVI (AL)

CASTELLARI BERGAGLIO
FRAZ. ROVERETO, 136
15066 GAVI (AL)
TEL. 0143/644000

Marco Bergaglio is in the process of renovating his beautiful estate at Rovereto di Gavi on the Pessenti coast. He has decided to make serious structural investments in his cellars and in his reception area and, on the wine front, in single-variety vineyards of Gavi, the cortese grape. There is the odd blot on the landscape, however. His Pilìn, jewel in the estate's crown and, for some time, the pride of the appellation, is not called Gavi this year but goes out under the label of table wine. This change has come about thanks to a strict interpretation of production regulations, which question the use of wood, even if the text allows "traditional methods" and, in our experience, wood is about as traditional as it gets in the cellar! The toastiness of the Pilìn '97 dominates the notes of jasmine, spice, and balsam and the other tertiary aromas, which are developing nicely. It is an intense, lustrous straw-gold in appearance and boasts a complex, full-flavoured palate with a long finish whose oak gives it a bitter final twist. The Vignavecchia is also obtained from a low yield - 50 quintals per hectare – of well-ripened fruit pre-raisined in cases for one month then vinified entirely in stainless steel. Vivid straw-yellow in colour, it releases floral, fruity aromas with a hint of wax and is fresh, tangy and structured on the palate. The Fornaci, an impressive cru, is a lovely rich greenish straw-yellow colour with a nice mineral nose laced with honey and fruit. It develops softly and refreshingly on the palate, culminating in a lingering finish which is both tangy and harmonious. But the ace up Bergaglio's sleeve is the Rolona '99. Intense and vibrant in the glass, it offers a generous, elegant nose redolent of apples and pears over an attractive mineral vein. This classy product is full and intense on the palate, following through satisfyingly to a long mineral finish.

○	Gavi del Comune di Gavi Rolona '99	🍷🍷	3*
○	Gavi Fornaci '99	🍷🍷	3*
○	Gavi Rovereto Vignavecchia '99	🍷🍷	4
○	Pilìn '97	🍷	5
○	Gavi Rovereto Pilìn '96	ΥΥ	4

GAVI (AL)

IL ROCCHIN
LOC. VALLEMME, 39
15066 GAVI (AL)
TEL. 0143/642228

Rocchin is an ancient property that lies on the right bank of the Lemme river near the old Lemurina church. Its inclusion in the Guide for the second year running is proof that the strategy it has adopted and the investments made in the cellars are having their effect. The estate, run by the Zerbo family with the support of oenologist, Mario Ronco, continues to improve in terms of quality thanks to lower yields and good-quality fruit, although it has not fully realised the promise of the previous year. Rocchin produces two whites from its cortese vines at Gavi and a single red from its vineyards in the Dolcetto di Ovada DOC zone. The Gavi '99 possesses a truly fascinating nose with notes of hay and flowers over a pleasant mineral base but the palate falls a bit short of expectations. Although fresh and tangy, it lacks complexity and finishes on an almondy note. The Gavi Vigna del Bosco '99 also parades a range of complex aromas and a pleasing palate. We liked the Dolcetto di Ovada '98 and gave it One full Glass for its red hue with violet-ruby lights and its interesting aromas of berry fruit, redcurrants and hay. It is attractive and nicely refreshing on the palate despite its ripe, moderately persistent tannins.

●	Dolcetto di Ovada '99	🍷	3
○	Gavi del Comune di Gavi '99	🍷	3
○	Gavi del Comune di Gavi Vigna del Bosco '99	🍷	4

GAVI (AL)

LA CHIARA
LOC. VALLEGGE, 24/2
15066 GAVI (AL)
TEL. 0143/642293

GAVI (AL)

LA GIUSTINIANA
FRAZ. ROVERETO, 5
15066 GAVI (AL)
TEL: 0143/682132

You can bank on the quality of the wines produced by Roberto Bergaglio's winery, located at the foot of the sandstone ridge which narrows the Lemme Valley as it heads towards the centre of Gavi. This year is no exception. His crowning glory is still the Vigneto Groppella, vinified and fermented in small barrels in the Burgundian style, or rather, traditionally, since wood was the only material used to make cellar containers in these parts until about ten years ago. Indeed, this wine has become a benchmark for the entire DOC zone. The '98 vintage favoured the cortese variety and the resulting wine is a deep, vivid, golden straw-yellow with a generously complex nose hinting at apple, ripe banana, vanilla and almond. The palate is impressive, fleshy and well structured, with nice harmony and persistence, so we are very happy to confirm the Two Glasses we awarded to the wine in last year's Guide profile. The Gavi La Chiara '99, vinified in stainless steel, takes home One well-deserved Glass for its vibrantly lustrous straw-yellow colour and aromas of apple, exotic and citrus fruits with a hint of mineral. It is on the palate, however, that it comes into its own, unfolding a wonderfully fresh, full-flavoured and complex progression with remarkable length in the finish.

Giustiniana is the largest estate in Gavi. The Lombardini family, entrepreneurs whose interests extend to other areas of Italy including Strevi, have owned it for years and today it is run with panache by Enrico Tomalino. This time, they offered us a new table wine, Just, in white and red versions. This estate label, pronounced with an initial "y" sound, stakes its claim to a position at the top end of the market. The Bianco, from cortese grapes harvested in 1998, has been partially aged in wood and sports a golden straw-yellow colour. The spicy, minerally notes of melted butter, honey and vanilla come through on the intense, generous nose while the palate is fat and harmonious. The tangy, velvety finish lingers temptingly. We had a preview taste of the dense, inky black, monovarietal barbera Rosso but will review it in depth next year. Strawberry and wild berry preserve dominate the bouquet, and the still soft palate leads into a tannic finish that promises well for the future. Among the estate's Gavis, the bright, green-flecked straw-yellow Lugarara offers strong, vegetal aromas while the palate is tangy with good length. The greenish, straw-yellow Montessora '99 flaunts a floral, citrus fruit nose and a full-bodied palate that is both refreshing and persistent. The Lombardinis' Contero di Strevi estate is the source of their versions of Piedmont's two sweet DOCG wines. The Brachetto '99, bottled with a standard cork, is somewhere between ruby and cherry red in colour and its carbon dioxide erupts in a wonderful rosy foam of medium persistence. Hints of roses and wild berries mingle on the sweet, refreshing palate. The Brachetto Spumante '99 is more upbeat with intense aromas of violet and rose and fine perlage and the Asti Spumante is elegant and nicely balanced. The standard-cork version displays the typical butteriness of Moscato di Strevis without being overly sweet.

O Gavi del Comune di Gavi Vigneto Groppella '98	♀♀	4
O Gavi del Comune di Gavi La Chiara '99	♀	3
O Gavi del Comune di Gavi Vigneto Groppella '97	♀♀	4

O Just Bianco '98	♀♀	5
O Asti Contero '99	♀	3
● Brachetto d'Acqui Contero '99	♀	4
● Brachetto d'Acqui Spumante Contero '99	♀	4
O Gavi del Comune di Gavi Lugarara '99	♀	3
O Gavi del Comune di Gavi Montessora '99	♀	4
O Moscato d'Asti Contero '99		3

GAVI (AL)

LA SCOLCA
FRAZ. ROVERETO
15066 GAVI (AL)
TEL. 0143/682176

GAVI (AL)

MORGASSI SUPERIORE
LOC. CASE SPARSE SERMORIA, 7
15066 GAVI (AL)
TEL. 0143/642007

There is news at this historic Gavi estate. Giorgio Soldati has been joined by his daughter and they are looking to the future with renewed enthusiasm, continuing to invest in the estate and moving toward a "Château"-style organisation. Yet again, the perlage of this year's Scolca is on a par with any international product, and their new selection of rosés is very good indeed. The Soldati Brut '87 comes to us in a new bottle which marks it out as a wine of distinction, and boasts a straw-yellow colour and a fine, persistent perlage. The bouquet is complex and generous, offering aromas of yeast and crusty bread, which are mirrored on the long, gratifying palate. The pale salmon pink Brut Rosé unveils a delicate, lingering perlage and aromas that hint at berry fruit and yeast as well as a palate that is pleasant and discreet. We have a newcomer among the still Gavis in the form of the d'Antàn '91, which is aged in stainless steel for nine years before bottling. It is a lustrous, vibrant straw yellow and unveils tertiary aromas, with notes of mineral and bitter almond. Entry on the palate is full and tangy, and the finish is strong and solid. The golden straw-yellow Gavi dei Gavi '99 possesses a classic, varietal nose redolent of flowers, citrus fruits and bitter almonds that introduces a soft, warm, refreshing, nicely rounded palate. The Soldatis' white-label Gavi La Scolca '99 is straw-yellow with green highlights and proffers clean aromas leading in to a soft, lengthy palate. We awarded One Glass to the straw-yellow Gavi Villa Scolca '99 for its bouquet of apples and pears, flowers and fine herbs and its tangy, complex and persistent palate.

The Morgassi Superiore winery was set up in 1990 by the dynamic Piacitelli family. Its current 13 hectares – soon to become 20 – were planted to vine between 1992 and 1993 on plots of land that enjoy a good position but that had been allowed to run wild. The Piacitellis initially dabbled in both international and native varieties but, although their experiments proved interesting, did not follow through on all of them. The grapes they chose to develop today provide the basis for the wide range of wines produced by the estate. The modern, well-equipped cellars are run by Massimo Azzolini, the consultant oenologist who took over from Scaglione in 1998. All their wines are stamped with the same clean, elegant style and aim for an almost impossible level of concentration. The syrah-based Tamino boasts a deep, seductive ruby-tending-to-violet hue and clear varietal aromas of black pepper, burnt rubber, coffee, plum and mulberry. It is well-balanced and persistent on the palate. The estate's Sarastro, a classic and beautifully orchestrated blend of barbera and cabernet, is also deep, dark and vivid in appearance. Of the estate's whites, we liked the Timorasso and the Cherubino. The Timorasso's typical mineral overtones enhance its notes of pineapple and apricot, and its full-bodied palate ushers in a long finish that echoes the nose. The Cherubino displays just the right dose of oak, which in no way overwhelms the hints of tangerine and white peach. One full Glass goes to the Gavi for its clean, varietal aromas and its refreshing, zesty palate, which revels in an agile structure. Finally, a mention for the Pistrice, a chardonnay and cortese blend, which is consistent if a little bland.

○ Gavi d'Antàn '91	ΥΥ	6	
○ Gavi dei Gavi Etichetta Nera '99	ΥΥ	5	
○ Soldati La Scolca Brut '87	ΥΥ	6	
○ Gavi La Scolca '99	Υ	4	
○ Gavi Villa Scolca '99	Υ	3	
⊙ Soldati La Scolca Brut Rosé	Υ	5	
○ Soldati La Scolca Brut '90	ΨΨ	6	
⊙ Soldati La Scolca Brut 2000 Rosé	Ψ	5	
○ Soldati La Scolca Brut Nature '87	Ψ	5	

○ Cherubino '98	ΥΥ	5	
● Sarastro '97	ΥΥ	5	
● Tamino '98	ΥΥ	5	
○ Timorasso '98	ΥΥ	4	
○ Gavi del Comune di Gavi '99	Υ	4	
○ Pistrice '99		4	
● Arbace '96	ΨΨ	5	
● Tamino '97	ΨΨ	5	
○ Cherubino '97	Ψ	5	

GAVI (AL)

GAVI (AL)

SAN BARTOLOMEO
CASCINA S. BARTOLOMEO, 26
LOC. VALLEGGE
15066 GAVI (AL)
TEL. 0143/643180

VILLA SPARINA
FRAZ. MONTE ROTONDO, 56
15066 GAVI (AL)
TEL. 0143/633835

The year 1999 was a difficult one for the Bergaglios. Teresina Carrea's son had an accident and spent a long time convalescing and this took the shine off the opening of their brand new cellars, creating problems for the estate in planning its work. But they rallied and with the strength, passion and pride of a family that has been self-sufficient for generations, they came through this difficult period and are now looking to the future on the San Bartolomeo estate. It was a good year for cortese and for DOCG Gavi, though, and we were able to confirm the judgement we expressed in last year's Guide profile. Of the three labels that make up the range offered by the estate, we liked the partially wood-conditioned Gavi Cappello del Diavolo '99. A lovely rich straw yellow with bright gold highlights, it has a full, complex, elegant bouquet whose oak imbues it with aromas of ripe fruit and vanilla laced with spice. The palate is full and distinctive, offering good balance and persistence with an agreeable bitterish note. San Bartolomeo's Gavi Etichetta Nera flaunts a lustrous, deep golden straw-yellow hue and an intense nose of apple, wild flowers, honey, vanilla and citrus fruit. It is refreshing, harmonious and nicely balanced on the palate with a bitterish finish of medium length. The bright straw-yellow Gavi '99 proffers rather closed aromas of dried flowers and vanilla with a suggestion of wax but comes across fresher and younger on the medium-length palate.

"Château" Villa Sparina is consolidating its position thanks to the initiative of Massimo Moccagatta, the youngest member of the family, while Mario takes on other responsibilities and Stefano deals with overseas PR. The winery atmosphere is charged with a tangible electricity and the soft, mellow style of their wines, after a rigorous selection process by Curtaz and Caviola who were going for structure, is strongly in evidence. Villa Sparina's Gavi Monte Rotondo '99 is the at the very top of the DOC's production and carries off a triumphant Three Glasses. Obtained from partially raisined grapes harvested in mid-October, it revels in a lustrous straw-yellow colour and a bouquet rich in super-ripe pear, spice and citrus fruits, laced with notes of botrytis and oak. These fragrances carry over onto the palate, which is full of flavour, tangy and full-bodied, achieving a perfect harmony between the fruit and the wood. A real eye-opener for the critics of cortese. The Rivalta '98 is a deep, vivid ruby red with a bouquet of berry fruit, Peruvian bark, spice and vanilla from the oak. The estate's golden straw-yellow Müller Thurgau has notes of biscuit, vanilla, yeast, orange blossom and jasmine on the nose. Its warm, zesty, well-balanced palate leads into a long, pleasantly bitterish finish. The Bric Maioli '99 also bears witness to the estate's quest for structure and body. Ruby red with youthful violet highlights, it regales the nose with aromas of berry fruit and bilberry. Entry on the palate is warm, and the progression is dry, tannic, full-bodied and persistent. The Gavi '99 has a strong greenish straw-yellow hue and a soft, sweet nose introducing an impressive structure that could do with a little more tang. The Spumante Brut '95, too, is an outstanding sparkler.

○ Gavi del Comune di Gavi	
Cappello del Diavolo '99	▼▼ 3*
○ Gavi del Comune di Gavi '99	▼ 3
○ Gavi del Comune di Gavi	
Etichetta Nera '99	▼ 3

○ Gavi del Comune di Gavi	
Monte Rotondo '99	▼▼▼ 6
● Dolcetto d'Acqui Bric Maioli '99	▼▼ 3*
○ Villa Sparina Brut	
Metodo Classico '95	▼▼ 5
○ Monferrato Müller Thurgau '99	▼▼ 4
● Monferrato Rosso Rivalta '98	▼▼ 6
○ Gavi del Comune di Gavi '99	▼ 3
● Barbera del M.to Rivalta '97	♈♈♈ 6
● Barbera del M.to Rivalta '96	♈♈ 6
● Dolcetto d'Acqui Sup.	
d'Giusep '98	♈♈ 4
○ Gavi Cremant Pas Dosé '92	♈♈ 5
○ Gavi del Comune di Gavi	
Monte Rotondo '97	♈♈ 6

GHEMME (NO)

INCISA SCAPACCINO (AT)

ANTICHI VIGNETI DI CANTALUPO
VIA MICHELANGELO BUONARROTI, 5
28074 GHEMME (NO)
TEL. 0163/840041

ERMANNO E ALESSANDRA BREMA
VIA POZZOMAGNA, 9
14045 INCISA SCAPACCINO (AT)
TEL. 0141/74019 - 0141/74617

Alberto Arlunno, a passionate winemaker and expert on local history, has given a Latin name to almost every one of the wines he makes on the alluvial-morainic slopes above the town of Ghemme. He has chosen to use Latin because the winemaking tradition goes back to Roman times in this area dedicated to nebbiolo, known locally as "spanna", a grape mentioned by Pliny in the first century AD. The Arlunnos have been tending vines in Ghemme since 1550, and this alone would be enough to explain their deep love of the territory, attested by the grandiloquent appellations of their products. The two estate selections, the Collis Breclemae and Collis Carellae, are named after the two hills where the Breclema, a village belonging to the counts of Biandrate destroyed at the time of Barbarossa, and the Carella vineyards lie. The family produces an average of about 23,000 bottles of these two crus out of an annual total of 150,000. The Collis Carellae '96 is truly excellent. It boasts a nose of wild berries and cocoa and a palate which reveals a full-bodied, powerful structure. The barrique-conditioned Ghemme Signore di Bayard '95 selection is also outstanding. It has a spicy, balsamic nose and impressive complexity on the palate. The Ghemme Signore di Bayard '96 is less intriguing but also takes home Two Glasses, even if it didn't tickle the panel's fancy quite as much as its big brother. The fairly rich basic Ghemme rounds off the estate's range of offerings with the rather lighter Colline Novaresi Agamium and two young vespolina-based reds, the Primigenia and the Villa Horta. The white Carolus, obtained from greco di Ghemme, arneis and chardonnay grapes is interesting, as is the nebbiolo-based rosé, Mimo.

The quality of the wide range of wines offered by this estate is proof of Ermanno Brema's and oenologist Giancarlo Scaglione's skill and dedication to their vineyards and cellar. The estate's vines are planted in excellent locations and are subject to rigorous thinning to obtain more concentrated fruit. These two factors combine to produce raw material of outstanding structure that expresses its personality in cellarable wines of character and distinction. This year, again, the Barbera Bricconizza stands out from the crowd. Ruby shading into violet with dark bluish highlights, it has a nose that gradually unfolds to reveal notes of cherry and berry fruit mingling with oak-derived hints of vanilla, toastiness and spice. It opens on the palate to reveal hints of pepper, balsam and liquorice. Brema's latest Barbera d'Asti, the Bricco della Volpettona, is also very good. Its bouquet has yet to develop fully but it offers an interesting palate where the acidity offers a fine contrast to the full body. The Barbera Le Cascine is rather austere at the moment but augurs well for the future. Definitely a wine to watch. The lovely violet-ruby Barbera Cascina Croce unveils a luscious berry fruit and vanilla nose and moderate structure nicely offset by the acidity. Brema's traditional Grignolino Brich Le Roche has a deep, varietal onion-skin colour and proffers aromas of wild rose and pepper, leading into a slightly astringent, tannic palate. The rich, violet Dolcetto Vigna Impagnato unleashes crisp, heady, fruit-rich notes and then shows good concentration and persistence on the palate.

● Ghemme Collis Carellae '96	♟♟	5
● Ghemme Signore di Bayard '95	♟♟	5
● Ghemme Signore di Bayard '96	♟♟	5
○ Carolus '99	♟	2
● Colline Novaresi Agamium '98	♟	3
☉ Colline Novaresi Il Mimo '99	♟	2
● Ghemme '96	♟	4
● Villa Horta '99	♟	2
● Primigenia '99		2
● Ghemme Collis Breclemae '91	♟♟	4
● Ghemme Signore di Bayard '93	♟♟	5
● Ghemme Collis Breclemae '94	♟	5
● Ghemme Collis Carellae '91	♟	4
● Ghemme Collis Carellae '94	♟	5

● Barbera d'Asti Sup. Bricco della Volpettona '98	♟♟	5
● Barbera d'Asti Sup. Bricconizza '98	♟♟	5
● Barbera d'Asti Sup. Cascina Croce '98	♟	3
● Barbera d'Asti Sup. Le Cascine '98	♟	4
● Dolcetto d'Asti Vigna Impagnato '98	♟	3
● Grignolino d'Asti Brich Le Roche '99	♟	3
● Barbera d'Asti Sup. Bricconizza '97	♟♟	5 ●
● Barbera d'Asti Sup. Le Cascine '97	♟♟	4

IVREA (TO)

FERRANDO E C.
VIA TORINO, 599/A
10015 IVREA (TO)
TEL. 0125/641176 - 0125/633550

The Ferrandos have been making and trading wine for five generations. Today, Luigi Ferrando heads the family business and is flanked by his sons Roberto, who runs the cellars, and Andrea, who takes care of the commercial side of things. In 1999, they transferred production to their new premises on the outskirts of Ivrea but their cellars at Carema are still operational and they continue to make and age their Carema selection there. Their specialist "enoteca" retail outlet at Ivrea is still open, too. The Ferrandos have been making Carema since 1957. They release the best vintages under their black label and in the past this selection has justly received wide recognition and Two Glasses from the Guide. Neither does the '96 version disappoint. A rich garnet in the glass, it releases fruity, balsamic notes on the nose and while it is still a little rough on the palate, its robust tannins are nicely complemented by the solid structure. The Caluso Passito Cariolo, another of the estate's flagship wines from the grapes of a vineyard on the Serra di Ivrea plateau at Viverone, is missing from the ranks this year. But from the same vineyard, which the Ferrandos have recently replanted and where they have adopted an innovative planting density for the Canavese DOC zone (4,500 vines per hectare), we have the green and the black Erbaluce di Caluso labels. The green is the simpler of the two, straw-yellow in colour with a spring flower and ripe pear bouquet. On the palate, it is full-bodied and well-rounded in an elegant overall framework. The Erbaluce Etichetta Nera is more succulent and complex, buttressed by its oak-ageing and a late vintage. Finally, the fragrant Solativo '98 is from a very late harvest.

●	Carema Etichetta Nera '96	🍷🍷	6
○	Erbaluce di Caluso Cariola Etichetta Verde '99	🍷🍷	4
○	Erbaluce di Caluso Etichetta Nera '98	🍷🍷	5
●	Carema Etichetta Bianca '96	🍷	5
○	Solativo '98	🍷	6
○	Canavese Bianco Castello di Loranzé '99		3
○	Erbaluce di Caluso '99		3
○	Caluso Passito Vigneto Cariola '94	🍷🍷 (outline)	6
●	Carema Etichetta Nera '90	🍷🍷 (outline)	6
●	Carema Etichetta Nera '95	🍷🍷 (outline)	6
●	Carema Etichetta Bianca '95	🍷 (outline)	5
○	Solativo '97	🍷 (outline)	5

LA MORRA (CN)

★ ELIO ALTARE
CASCINA NUOVA, 51
FRAZ. ANNUNZIATA
12064 LA MORRA (CN)
tel. 0173/50835

Hats off to Elio Altare for persevering with his own personal philosophy in the face of severe opposition. Today, his style is recognised and emulated. His wines, born of his genius and determination, enjoy world-wide acclaim. The jewel of Altare's outstanding selection is the stylish, near-perfect Barolo Vigneto Arborina '96. Dense garnet-ruby with a narrow rim, it parades a cornucopia of aromas with clear, fragrant notes of mulberry. The wine's incredibly solid structure comes through on the palate and the progression is full-bodied and mouth-filling, bolstered by the sweetest of tannins right through to its long, elegant, balanced finish. Just as concentrated in appearance, Altare's Barolo Brunate reveals a generous nose that unleashes notes of redcurrant, raspberry, eucalyptus, aromatic herbs and tobacco. The attack on the palate is proudly austere, heralding the sheer force of the wine's structure. This is a magnificent Barolo, unfortunately only produced in limited quantities and all of it for export. The estate's standard Barolo is excellent, the initial note of oak opening to reveal lively fruit aromas and a well-rounded bouquet. The Insieme, on which Altare collaborated with six other leading producers, is an exquisite table wine obtained by blending the finest selections of native Piedmont and international grapes. The Larigi and the Arborina, both from the '98 vintage, are at their peak and the panel could only award them Three Glasses each. The Larigi is an object lesson in the many-sided powers of the barbera grape while the Arborina is a celebration of nebbiolo at the highest possible level. As ever, Elio Altare's simpler offerings, his Barbera and Dolcetto d'Alba, are also very good.

●	Langhe Arborina '98	🍷🍷🍷	6
●	Langhe Larigi '98	🍷🍷🍷	6
●	Barbera d'Alba '99	🍷🍷	4
●	Barolo '96	🍷🍷	6
●	Barolo Brunate '96	🍷🍷	6
●	Barolo Vigneto Arborina '96	🍷🍷	6
●	Dolcetto d'Alba '99	🍷🍷	4
●	L'Insieme	🍷🍷	6
●	Langhe La Villa '98	🍷🍷	6
●	Barolo Vigneto Arborina '93	🍷🍷🍷 (outline)	6
●	Langhe Arborina '96	🍷🍷🍷 (outline)	6
●	Langhe Arborina '97	🍷🍷🍷 (outline)	6
●	Langhe Larigi '95	🍷🍷🍷 (outline)	6
●	Langhe Larigi '97	🍷🍷🍷 (outline)	6
●	Barolo Vigneto Arborina '95	🍷🍷 (outline)	6

LA MORRA (CN)

BATASIOLO
FRAZ. ANNUNZIATA, 87
12064 LA MORRA (CN)
TEL. 0173/50130 - 0173/50131

LA MORRA (CN)

ENZO BOGLIETTI
VIA ROMA, 37
12064 LA MORRA (CN)
TEL. 0173/50330

The range of Barolos offered by the Batasiolo estate is very good indeed. The Barolo Corda della Briccolina '96 is their flagship selection with its warm, generous palate where acidity, alcohol and tannins all combine in perfect harmony. This is a complex wine with a lingering finish redolent of raisined fruit, whose nose opens gradually to reveal aromas of thyme and aromatic herbs, then hints of black cherry jam. Batastiolo's Barolo Boscareto '96 has a more open, immediately approachable nose that suggests rich fruit and ripe red berry fruit. Powerful and mouth-filling on the palate, it signs off with a note of dry tannins. A little less forthcoming in character, the Barolo Bofani '96 has clean aromas and a reserved elegance which hint pleasantly at mint and dry grass. Its soft palate displays up-front tannins and attractive notes of caramel and redcurrant in the finish. At first, the Barbaresco '97's bouquet comes across as rather confused but a little aeration in the glass softens it. A warm, discreet wine, it has a sweetish, very persuasive palate. The estate's powerful, dark Barbera d'Alba Sovrana '98 has a rose, cassis and bramble nose laced with coffee. Its palate flaunts a warm, sensuous body that revels in the succulence of black cherry and sun-ripened gooseberry. An intense violet-ruby in hue, the Dolcetto d'Alba Bricco Vergne '99 releases strong varietal aromas of roses and violets, followed up by a distinct, soft, refreshing palate. Finally, the Langhe Chardonnay Morino '97 is tangy and very pleasant.

The Bogliettis, Enzo and Gianni, have renovated and expanded their Via Roma cellars and intend to carry out further work, perhaps next year. In the meantime, they presented us with a fine trio of Barolos from three adjacent south-facing vineyards situated on one of the most beautiful slopes of La Morra. We'll open our tasting notes with the Barolo Brunate '96, which impressed us with its strong, earthy character, typical of an outstanding cru. Like all young blue-blooded wines, it does not open up immediately on the nose but prefers to play hide-and-seek with aromas of thyme, mint, plum jam and oak-derived liquorice. It lets itself go a little bit more on the palate, where it displays an opulent body with hints of roses and a well-defined tannic framework. The palate gradually unfolds to reveal sweet, austere fruit and a round, tangy fullness. Not to be outdone, the Bogliettis' Barolo Case Nere '96 offers wonderful, clean notes of mulberry and raspberry and an attractive, elegant palate. It is, however, slightly less structured than the other two wines presented. The best of the three is the Fossati, which carries off a splendid Three Glasses. Its generous, complex bouquet of dried flowers melts into notes of ripe cherry and vanilla while its full-bodied, beautifully poised palate offers attractive tannins and a particularly lingering finish which smacks of black cherry syrup. Two Glasses go to the Barbera d'Alba Vigna dei Romani and the Dolcetto d'Alba Tigli Neri as well as the Langhe Buio for their structure and elegance. But the quality of the Bogliettis' wines perhaps comes through best in their simple Barbera d'Alba '99, which stands out for its lovely violet colour and a nose with strong varietal notes of dried roses. Its full-bodied, on occasion taut, structure ushers in a slow, satisfying finish.

Wine	Rating	Score
● Barbera d'Alba Sovrana '98	♖♖	4
● Barolo Bofani '96	♖♖	6
● Barolo Boscareto '96	♖♖	6
● Barolo Corda della Briccolina '96	♖♖	6
● Barbaresco '97	♖	6
● Dolcetto d'Alba Bricco Vergne '99	♖	4
○ Langhe Chardonnay Morino '97	♖	6
● Barolo Corda della Briccolina '88	♛♛♛	6
● Barolo Corda della Briccolina '89	♛♛♛	6
● Barolo Corda della Briccolina '90	♛♛♛	6
● Barbera d'Alba Sovrana '97	♛♛	4
● Barolo Boscareto '95	♛♛	6
● Barolo Corda della Briccolina '93	♛♛	6
● Barolo Corda della Briccolina '95	♛♛	6
● Barolo Bofani '93	♛	6

Wine	Rating	Score
● Barolo Fossati '96	♖♖♖	6
● Barbera d'Alba '99	♖♖	4
● Barbera d'Alba Vigna dei Romani '98	♖♖	5
● Barolo Brunate '96	♖♖	6
● Dolcetto d'Alba Tigli Neri '99	♖♖	4
● Langhe Rosso Buio '98	♖♖	5
● Barolo Case Nere '96	♖	6
● Barbera d'Alba Vigna dei Romani '94	♛♛♛	5
● Barbera d'Alba Vigna dei Romani '97	♛♛	5
● Barolo Case Nere '95	♛♛	6
● Langhe Rosso Buio '97	♛♛	5
● Barolo Brunate '95	♛	6

LA MORRA (CN)

LA MORRA (CN)

GIANFRANCO BOVIO
B.TA CIOTTO, 63
FRAZ. ANNUNZIATA
12064 LA MORRA (CN)
TEL. 0173/50190 - 0173/50604

GIOVANNI CORINO
FRAZ. ANNUNZIATA, 24
12064 LA MORRA (CN)
TEL. 0173/50219 - 0173/509452

In addition to his considerable skills as a winemaker, Gianfranco Bovio is also noted as an expert on Piedmontese cuisine. His beautiful restaurant offers dishes that celebrate traditional, local cooking and excellent wines from all over the world are available from his splendid cellar to go with them. He offered the panel his usual high-quality selection for tasting this year and we'll start with two Barolos. The deep ruby-garnet Vigneto Arborina has a narrow rim and fascinating aromas of slightly evolved fruit, hay, cocoa and liquorice set off by mineral tones of rain-soaked earth. The wine's soft, wide-ranging palate has a full body nicely buttressed by strong tannins and its rich, varied finish lingers satisfyingly on the palate. Bovio's Vigneto Gattera boasts a lovely rich colour and a seductive nose of liqueur fruit, mint, pepper and dried flowers over a tempting chocolate base. Well structured on the palate, it follows through nicely to reveal solid tannins backing up a long finish that echoes the earlier fragrances. The Dolcetto d'Alba Dabbene is enjoyable, offering a varietal bouquet of ripe raspberry and a solid if rather rustic palate. We very much liked the estate's new Barbera Regia Veja. Deep ruby, it unfurls notes of spice that blend with toastiness from the oak and fruity notes. The palate is nicely structured and the acid vein apparent in its finish contrasts well with its body. This wine also has remarkable length. Bovio's Chardonnay, with its apple and hazelnut nose, is also very attractive.

The Corino family, consisting of father Giovanni and sons Renato and Silvano, have three nebbiolo crus at Annunziata in La Morra, a stone's throw from their winery. With their dolcetto and barbera vineyards, these plots bring the estate total to 15 hectares. Their Barolo Vigna Giachini '96 proffers a wide range of aromas, starting with herbaceous notes of mint, thyme and oregano, then moving on to fermented red berry fruit. This wine stands out for its immediacy and elegance. It offers a palate that is full of sweet, concentrated, fleshy fruit with a hint of stewed black cherries in the finish. The Corinos' deep-hued Barolo Vigneto Rocche '96 has an intense nose of peonies, roses and fermenting wild berries, then the entry on the palate reveals a wonderful harmony of acidity, tannins and alcohol. The Barolo Arborina '96 is every bit as good as these two. The oak tends to dominate the nose but the palate has a full-bodied, solid fruitiness and the finish satisfies with its sweet note of ripe fruit. The standard Barolo '96 proffers slightly acidulous fragrances of medium intensity which recall wild strawberries. Lighter in colour than the vineyard selections, it has respectable structure even if it appears to lack power. The Barbera Pozzo is solid but not up to '97 standards while the Barbera d'Alba has good persistence and the Dolcetto is harmonious. The Insieme, a full-bodied red making its debut this year, brings to a close the range of Corino offerings. A final note. The estate is collaborating with six other local producers on the Insieme (which means "Together") winemaking project.

● Barbera d'Alba Regia Veja '98	▼▼	5
● Barolo Vigneto Arborina dell'Annunziata '96	▼▼	6
● Barolo Vigneto Gattera dell'Annunziata '96	▼▼	6
● Barbera d'Alba Il Ciotto '99	▼	3
● Dolcetto d'Alba Vigneto Dabbene dell'Annunziata '99	▼	3
○ Langhe Chardonnay '99	▼	5
● Barolo Vigneto Arborina dell'Annunziata '90	▼▼▼	6
● Barolo Vigneto Gattera dell'Annunziata '95	▼▼	6
● Barbera d'Alba Regia Veja '97	▼	5

● Barbera d'Alba Pozzo '98	▼▼	5
● Barolo Arborina '96	▼▼	6
● Barolo Vigna Giachini '96	▼▼	6
● Barolo Vigneto Rocche '96	▼▼	6
● L'Insieme	▼▼	6
● Barbera d'Alba '99	▼	3
● Barolo '96	▼	6
● Dolcetto d'Alba '99	▼	3
● Barbera d'Alba Vigna Pozzo '96	▼▼▼	5
● Barbera d'Alba Vigna Pozzo '97	▼▼▼	5
● Barolo Vigna Giachini '89	▼▼▼	6
● Barolo Vigneto Rocche '90	▼▼▼	6
● Barolo Arborina '95	▼▼	6
● Barolo Vigneto Rocche '95	▼▼	6
● Barolo Vigna Giachini '95	▼	6

LA MORRA (CN)

LA MORRA (CN)

GIANNI GAGLIARDO
B.TA SERRA DEI TURCHI, 88
FRAZ. SANTA MARIA
12064 LA MORRA (CN)
TEL. 0173/50829

SILVIO GRASSO
CASCINA LUCIANI, 112
FRAZ. ANNUNZIATA
12064 LA MORRA (CN)
TEL. 0173/50322

Gianni Gagliardo and his sons Stefano and Alberto run this 250,000 bottle-a-year estate with the help of Daniele Benevello and Dario Poddana. Three wines from the selection they presented to the panel this year stand out: two Barolos, the Preve and the standard-label version, and their Dolcetto Paulin. The Preve is a blend of nebbiolo fruit from La Morra and Castiglione Falletto vinified separately. Dense garnet in hue, it reveals a nose of rhubarb, wild berries, cocoa and violet while the palate displays solid character and decisive tannins. The basic Barolo is deep in colour, proffering aromas of redcurrant and bilberry through which filter notes of autumn leaves and tar. It is soft on the palate, with sweet tannins and a good finish. The Gagliardos' Dolcetto Paulin is ruby tending to garnet, with a redcurrant and ripe blackberry nose over a hint of balsam. Its robust, harmonious and persistent palate ushers in a finish with a faint hint of almonds. The standard Dolcetto is deep and dark in the glass, introducing a slightly rustic bouquet that mingles fruit and earthy fragrances while the tannins lift the palate. The estate's Favorita Neirole is redolent of caramel and exotic fruit leading in to a refreshing, rather lightweight palate with a final note of hay. The Nebbiolo Batié has a reasonably elegant nose, a smooth, coherent palate and barely discernible tannins. The Favorita Casà is a happy-go-lucky, very quaffable bottle and the Barolo Chinato has a range of powerful aromas that in no way compromise the notes of jam and long-dried violets. The strength of its alcohol and the well-sustained texture are to the fore on the palate but the finish is a tad bitter due to the strong note of Peruvian bark.

The '96 vintage Barolos proposed by Silvio and Marilena Grasso are superb. Their Ciabot Manzoni, Bricco Luciani and standard Barolo easily surpass the Two Glass level, displaying a modern style that highlights the personality of the grape. The Bricco Luciani is a weighty example of the genre and rivals the dizzying heights of the '90 and '95 vintages. An intense garnet ruby, it has a clean, pervasive fruity nose that hints at redcurrant, raspberry, toastiness and coffee, with intriguing touches of Peruvian bark, all combining in supreme elegance. The entry on the palate is soft and succulent, becoming more austere as it follows through steadily to culminate in a finish that lingers on notes of fruit and cocoa over attractive tannins. Three well deserved Glasses. The Grassos' deep-hued Ciabot Manzoni boasts a complex, harmonious array of aromas marginally compromised by a rather strong note of oak. This does not, however, mask the hints of redcurrant, blackberry, toastiness and vanilla with their attractive nuances of thyme. The fullness of the body is obvious the moment it hits the palate and the wide-ranging progression is kept in check by assertive tannins that enhance the finish, which signs off with a lingering note of fruit and spice. Very much in the same mould as these two heavyweights is the estate's basic Barolo. The Barbera d'Alba Fontanile '98 also takes home Two Glasses, as does the Insieme, a new offering from a group of seven winemakers who have used both local and international varieties in the blend. The Barbera d'Alba is mellow and very drinkable, and the Dolcetto d'Alba is also fairly good.

● Barolo '96	🍷🍷	6
● Barolo Preve '96	🍷🍷	6
● Dolcetto d'Alba Paulin '99	🍷🍷	4
● Barolo Chinato	🍷	6
○ Langhe Favorita Neirole '99	🍷	5
● Langhe Nebbiolo Batié '96	🍷	5
● Dolcetto d'Alba '99		3
○ Langhe Favorita Casà '99		4
● Barolo Preve '95	🍷🍷	6
● Batié '95	🍷🍷	5

● Barolo Bricco Luciani '96	🍷🍷🍷	6
● Barbera d'Alba Fontanile '98	🍷🍷	5
● Barolo '96	🍷🍷	6
● Barolo Ciabot Manzoni '96	🍷🍷	6
● L'Insieme	🍷🍷	6
● Barbera d'Alba '99	🍷	3
● Dolcetto d'Alba '99	🍷	3
● Barolo Bricco Luciani '90	🍷🍷🍷	6
● Barolo Bricco Luciani '95	🍷🍷🍷	6
● Barbera d'Alba Fontanile '97	🍷🍷	5
● Barolo Ciabot Manzoni '90	🍷🍷	6
● Barolo Ciabot Manzoni '93	🍷🍷	6
● Barolo Ciabot Manzoni '94	🍷🍷	6
● Barolo Ciabot Manzoni '95	🍷🍷	6
● Barolo Bricco Luciani '94	🍷	6

LA MORRA (CN)

LA MORRA (CN)

MARCARINI
P.ZZA MARTIRI, 2
12064 LA MORRA (CN)
TEL. 0173/50222

MARIO MARENGO
VIA XX SETTEMBRE, 32
12064 LA MORRA (CN)
TEL. 0173/50127

The lovely Brunate and Serra vineyards used to belong to the Marcarini family of doctors and notaries. In their day, the cellars, which have now been enlarged, lay under the main residence at La Morra. Today, the 12-hectare estate is run by Luisa Bava and her husband, Manuel Marchetti, who grow mainly nebbiolo destined for Barolo. Brunate and Serra, two of La Morra's best crus, supply the couple with two Barolo selections. The '96 vintages are superb and both merit a Two Glass rating. The Brunate combines power with elegance and its fruity flesh recalls plum jam and blackberry. This is something of an austere wine with aristocratic pretensions. Bava's Barolo La Serra is more refined with its hints of mentholated herbs and faint spicy aromas. Its pleasant, persistent palate ushers in a satisfying finish. The Dolcetto d'Alba Boschi di Berri is up to its usual standards and the '99 is a great vintage. A dark ruby shot through with violet, it flaunts a veritable cornucopia of generous, complex aromas and a warm, full-bodied, mouth-filling palate rich in flamboyant red berry fruit. The Dolcetto d'Alba Fontanazza '99 also has a vibrant hue. The nose has generous notes of heady alcohol and morello cherry but prominent tannins make the palate a little harsh. Cellaring will give this bottle the harmony it lacks at the moment. We liked the ruby Barbera d'Alba Ciabot Camerano '98 and its intense raspberry and vanilla nose, even though its acidity tends to overwhelm the fruit. The Langhe Nebbiolo Lasarin '99 is also enjoyable.

Mario Marengo and his son, Marco, divide their time between their ironmongery business and this small estate which, given the zone it lies in, has turned out to be much more than just a hobby for them. Marco is determined to exploit this valuable property to the full and for the 2000 vintage will produce a small but significant amount of Nebbiolo using grapes from a rented vineyard at Valmaggiore in Vezza d'Alba. Of the wines he presented to the panel for tasting this year, his Barolo Brunate '96 (5,000 bottles) is balanced and modern in style with a palate worthy of its noble origins. Moderately intense ruby tending to garnet with quite a narrow rim, it offers a beautifully harmonious range of fruit aromas on the nose including well-defined notes of bilberry and raspberry. Subtle hints of wood come through in overtones of coffee and vanilla cream. The rich texture of the vintage is apparent the minute it hits the palate, where the progression is steady and solid, revealing all the bite of the nebbiolo tannins. The finish is tidy and persistent. One generous Glass goes to the Marengos' Dolcetto '99, aged in large casks and only 1,500 bottles of which were released. It is a lovely deep ruby and has a distinctive nose of strawberry, cherry and peach over a mineral base. The palate has good structure but tends to peter out and doesn't take the delicious fruit right through to the finish.

● Barolo Brunate '96	ŸŸ	6
● Barolo La Serra '96	ŸŸ	6
● Dolcetto d'Alba Boschi di Berri '99	ŸŸ	4
● Barbera d'Alba Ciabot Camerano '98	Ÿ	4
● Dolcetto d'Alba Fontanazza '99	Ÿ	3
● Langhe Nebbiolo Lasarin '99	Ÿ	4
● Barolo Brunate Ris. '85	ŸŸŸ	6
● Dolcetto d'Alba Boschi di Berri '96	ŸŸŸ	5
● Barbera d'Alba Ciabot Camerano '97	ŸŸ	4
● Barolo La Serra '95	ŸŸ	6
● Dolcetto d'Alba Boschi di Berri '98	ŸŸ	4
● Barolo Brunate '95	Ÿ	6

● Barolo Brunate '96	ŸŸ	6
● Dolcetto d'Alba '99	Ÿ	3
● Barolo Brunate '95	ŸŸ	6

LA MORRA (CN)

LA MORRA (CN)

MAURO MOLINO
B.TA GANCIA, 111
FRAZ. ANNUNZIATA
12064 LA MORRA (CN)
TEL. 0173/50814

MONFALLETTO
CORDERO DI MONTEZEMOLO
FRAZ. ANNUNZIATA, 67/BIS
12064 LA MORRA (CN)
TEL. 0173/50344

Mauro Molino continues in his quest for quality. He is expanding his estate with new nebbiolo vines for Barolo and is also in the process of building new cellars. It will be some time before we can taste the fruits of these labours so in this edition of the Guide we shall take a look at the wines he released in 2000. His Barolo Vigna Conca '96, which takes its name from its vineyard of origin just a few hundred metres from the winery, boasts an impressive hue of lush ruby with peony highlights. The bouquet releases aromas of mint, plum and peach jams with vanilla and the warm, mouth-filling palate has firm, juicy fruit laced with lingering notes of berry fruit and tobacco. The tannins are very well orchestrated, keeping the acidity and alcohol in check. The panel had no difficulty in awarding Three Glasses to this smooth, elegant vintage. Molino's Barolo Vigna Gancia '96 has complex, tangy, penetrating aromas of black cherry and liquorice to take you in to a palate where the rich, well-rounded flesh smacks of wild strawberry and redcurrant, culminating in a long, satisfying finish. This austere, elegant wine is made with fruit from the vineyard that lies at the foot of the estate. The basic Barolo '96 is much simpler, proffering clean fragrances of dried aromatic herbs and cherry jam and then a refreshing, lively palate. The compact, sober Acanzio '98 weds the power of nebbiolo to barbera's vivacity while the Barbera d'Alba Vigna Gattere is one of the best we tasted, although it does not quite match previous vintages. The estate's Chardonnay Livrot '99 comes across as elegant and beautifully poised, with hints of banana and citrus fruits. The Insieme, a red blend of nebbiolo, barbera, merlot and cabernet sauvignon, was a pleasant surprise and we found it to be balanced, intriguing and dynamic, with a complex, array of aromas and a succulent palate.

The Cordero di Montezemolo estate's newly restructured cellars offer Gianni and Enrico Cordero all the space they need to store hundreds of barrels. Their selection has made great strides on the quality front, but this year the estate has surpassed itself with the Barolo Vigna Enrico VI '96 and, hot on its heels, the Barolo Monfalletto '96 and the fabulous Barbera Funtanì '98. The last of these, released for the first time (5,000 bottles), bowled us over with its structure and the sweetness of its tannins, as well as the ripe fruit that comes through in notes of marmalade and Peruvian bark, and the perfectly integrated, well-judged oak. The magnificent Barolo Vigna Enrico VI '96, vinified entirely in new barriques, is a deep, dark garnet and reveals spicy aromas of vanilla, pepper and chocolate mingling with the fruit. It explodes onto the palate with a wealth of boisterous tannins that only a truly noble vineyard such as the Villero di Castiglione Falletto can provide in an outstanding year. This Barolo has a long future ahead of it but is already well worth Three Glasses. The Monfalletto '96 is not quite such a blockbuster but is still notable for its elegance and finesse. The Corderos' pinot nero-based Langhe Nebbiolo '99 and Curdè '98 are very good indeed. The first has great structure, unveiling a nose of raspberry and fresh grass, and the second, with its rich varietal aromas, is the most interesting Curdè this estate has produced for several years. We finished our tasting with the very creditable Dolcetto, the warm Arneis and the toasty Chardonnay.

● Barolo Vigna Conca '96	ŶŶŶ	6
● Barbera d'Alba Vigna Gattere '98	ŶŶ	5
● Barolo Vigna Gancia '96	ŶŶ	6
● L'Insieme	ŶŶ	6
○ Langhe Chardonnay Livrot '99	ŶŶ	4
● Langhe Rosso Acanzio '98	ŶŶ	5
● Barolo '96	Ŷ	6
● Dolcetto d'Alba '99	Ŷ	3
● Barbera d'Alba Vigna Gattere '96	ŶŶŶ	5
● Barbera d'Alba Vigna Gattere '97	ŶŶŶ	5
● Barolo Vigna Conca '95	ŶŶ	6
● Barolo Vigna Gancia '95	ŶŶ	6
● Langhe Rosso Acanzio '97	ŶŶ	5

● Barolo Enrico VI '96	ŶŶŶ	6
● Barbera d'Alba Sup. Funtanì '98	ŶŶ	5
● Barolo Monfalletto '96	ŶŶ	6
● Langhe Nebbiolo '99	ŶŶ	4
● Langhe Rosso Curdè '98	ŶŶ	5
● Dolcetto d'Alba '99	Ŷ	3
○ Langhe Arneis '99	Ŷ	3
○ Langhe Chardonnay Elioro '98	Ŷ	4
● Barolo Enrico VI '90	ŶŶ	6
● Barolo Enrico VI '93	ŶŶ	6
● Barolo Enrico VI '95	ŶŶ	6
● Barolo Monfalletto '90	ŶŶ	6
● Barolo Monfalletto '93	ŶŶ	6
● Barolo Monfalletto '95	ŶŶ	6

LA MORRA (CN)

LA MORRA (CN)

ANDREA OBERTO
VIA G. MARCONI, 25
12064 LA MORRA (CN)
TEL. 0173/509262

F.LLI ODDERO
VIA S. MARIA, 28
12064 LA MORRA (CN)
TEL. 0173/50618

Andrea Oberto and his son, Fabio, have been producing excellent wines for some time now and this year is no exception. We were privileged to taste some very exciting wines, including the Barolo Vigneto Rocche '96 which elbowed aside the Barbera Giada for a Three Glass award this time. A remarkably intense ruby with garnet highlights in the glass, its alluringly complex nose offers opulent fruit with evident notes of very ripe mulberries. The generous bouquet adds hints of vanilla and mint to the dominant fruit, lacing the whole with subtle notes of autumn leaves. After a sumptuous entry, the palate opens out, its breadth and power supported by serious extract that provides plenty of power and grip on the very long, liquorice finish that echoes the nose. The Barolo Albarella, obtained from vineyards at Barolo, has a dense, close-knit colour and a bouquet of liqueur fruit, coffee and mint in a well-balanced whole. Solid and well-sustained on the palate, it has an austere style and a satisfying finish. The Obertos' basic Barolo does not aspire to such dizzying heights but does follow through well on the palate. The Barbera d'Alba Giada fulfils expectations and, although not as impressive as the previous vintage, has lots of weight. The Fabio '98, a barbera and nebbiolo blend, and the Dolcetto d'Alba Vantrino Albarella '99 are both excellent while the Dolcetto San Francesco '99 is a little uninteresting. Work is under way on a new structure in the zone of Loreto between La Morra and Verduno which, when finished, will provide Fabio and Andrea with better equipped cellars.

With the assistance of Cristina, the Oddero brothers, Luigi and Giacomo, run this estate which has existed for more than 100 years. The winery's spiritual home is still in the original cellars of Bricco Chiesa at Santa Maria in La Morra, but the family has expanded into the neighbouring territories of Serralunga, Monforte and Castiglione Falletto, buying up choice Barolo plots. Their Serralunga Barolo Vigna Rionda '96 possesses a lovely, intense nose redolent of aromatic herbs with faint gamey tones. On the palate, it shows good structure, although it has yet to knit fully, and the tangy acidity keeps the tannins in check. The Monforte Barolo Mondoca di Bussia Soprana '96 comes across rather aggressive but displays all the characteristics of a great vintage. Cellaring will smooth out and balance its tart fruit and still mellowing structure. The Barbaresco '97 gradually opens out to unfold notes of berry fruit and cherry that are delicately mirrored on the palate. More colourful and fuller bodied, the Furesté '98 is an innovative wine and by definition unusual (its name means "stranger") for this estate, which has always been staunchly traditional in style. Made with fruit from a small cabernet sauvignon vineyard not far from the Bricco Chiesa cellars, it possesses varietal aromas of red pepper which meld with coffee overtones while the palate is full and well-rounded. The deep violet-ruby Dolcetto '99 has a lingering bouquet of raspberry and wild strawberry and is pleasantly refreshing on the palate.

● Barolo Vigneto Rocche '96	♟♟♟	6
● Barbera d'Alba Giada '98	♟♟	5
● Barolo '96	♟♟	6
● Barolo Vigneto Albarella '96	♟♟	6
● Dolcetto d'Alba Vigneto Vantrino Albarella '99	♟♟	4
● Langhe Fabio '98	♟♟	6
● Dolcetto d'Alba Vigneto S. Francesco '99	♟	3
● Barbera d'Alba Giada '96	♟♟♟	6
● Barbera d'Alba Giada '97	♟♟♟	6
● Barolo Vigneto Albarella '95	♟♟	6
● Barolo Vigneto Rocche '95	♟♟	6
● Langhe Fabio '97	♟♟	6

● Barolo Vigna Rionda '96	♟♟	6
● Langhe Furesté '98	♟♟	4
● Barbaresco '97	♟	6
● Barolo Mondoca di Bussia Soprana '96	♟	6
● Dolcetto d'Alba '99	♟	3
● Barolo Vigna Rionda '89	♟♟♟	6
● Barolo '95	♟♟	6
● Barolo Vigna Rionda '90	♟♟	6
● Barolo Vigna Rionda '93	♟♟	6
● Barolo Vigna Rionda '95	♟♟	6
● Langhe Furesté '97	♟♟	4
● Barolo Rocche dei Rivera '93	♟	6

LA MORRA (CN)

LA MORRA (CN)

RENATO RATTI ANTICHE CANTINE
DELL'ABBAZIA DELL'ANNUNZIATA
FRAZ. ANNUNZIATA, 7
12064 LA MORRA (CN)
TEL. 0173/50185

F.LLI REVELLO
FRAZ. ANNUNZIATA, 103
12064 LA MORRA (CN)
TEL. 0173/50276

The prestigious estate belonging to Renato Ratti is located in the amphitheatre of vineyards, known as Conca dell'Annunziata, given over to nebbiolo for Barolo. Unfortunately, neither the Barolo '96 from this cru nor the Nebbiolo Ochetti, another of the estate's important labels, was available for this tasting. Their fine Barolo Rocche Marcenasco '96, however, went a long way towards making up for our disappointment. The aromas of strawberries in syrup, blackberry jam and liquorice mingling with tobacco herald a moderately robust, close-knit structure and good alcohol content. Far from being aggressive, this is a very satisfying wine. The Barolo Marcenasco '96 lacks the potency of its sibling. The lightweight body has a brilliant ruby colour with a pale orange rim taking you in to a moderately full, persistent bouquet redolent of mint leaves and violet petals. On the palate, it reveals well-orchestrated acidity, tannins and alcohol with overtones of stewed black cherries lacing its spicy finish. Compliments are due for Ratti's Dolcetto d'Alba Colombé '99 and Monferrato Villa Pattono '98. The dark ruby Dolcetto is flecked with violet and leads in to a rich, heady bouquet and dry palate with pleasant acidity, moderate tannins and lovely notes of crushed fruit. The Villa Pattono offers sweet fruity aromas tinged with black cherry and on the palate hints of cassis veil the grassy undertones. The balanced Barbera d'Alba Torriglione '98 has prominent wild berry fruit.

Beppe Caviola lends his support to brothers Carlo and Enzo Revello in the running of their approximately nine hectares planted to vine. Their property is split up across plots that they own and rent, and yields a total of about 35,000 bottles a year. Best of the wines they offered for tasting this year was the Barolo Vigna Giachini, a dense garnet in the glass with a narrow orange rim. Barrique-ageing imbues this wine with sweet spicy aromas that open out into a generous, evocative bouquet blending clean fruit notes of blackberry and raspberry with fascinating undertones of earth and liquorice, the whole being attractively veined with delicious chocolate. The palate immediately reveals its fullness of flavour and develops robustly, almost austerely, with good structure to culminate into a long, cocoa-nuanced finish. Making its debut appearance, the Barolo Rocche dell'Annunziata has an intense colour and a narrow rim before unveiling a seductive nose of raspberry, redcurrant and rhubarb over notes of Peruvian bark and toastiness. Robust tannins render the palate a tad severe but the full body comes through in the long finish, which mirrors the aromas of the nose. Also very good were the standard Barolo and the Barbera d'Alba Ciabot du Re. The Insieme, a nebbiolo, barbera and cabernet blend released for the first time this year, is a lovely intense colour and proffers a complex array of aromas which include eucalyptus, jam, rhubarb and caramel. Full-bodied and well-structured on the palate, its fine tannins back up the solid follow-through to a warm, long, vigorous finish. To finish off the range, the basic Dolcetto and Barbera d'Alba selections are very decent, offering great flavour and equally good value for money.

● Barolo Rocche Marcenasco '96	ŸŸ	6
● Dolcetto d'Alba Colombé '99	ŸŸ	3*
● Monferrato Villa Pattono '98	ŸŸ	5
● Barbera d'Alba Torriglione '98	Ÿ	4
● Barolo Marcenasco '96	Ÿ	6
● Barolo Rocche Marcenasco '83	ŸŸŸ	6
● Barolo Rocche Marcenasco '84	ŸŸŸ	6
● Barolo Conca Marcenasco '93	ŸŸ	6
● Barolo Rocche Marcenasco '90	ŸŸ	6
● Monferrato Villa Pattono '97	ŸŸ	5
● Nebbiolo d'Alba Ochetti '97	ŸŸ	4
● Barolo Rocche Marcenasco '95	Ÿ	6
● Monferrato I Cedri '97	Ÿ	5
● Monferrato Rosso '97	Ÿ	5

● Barbera d'Alba '99	ŸŸ	3*
● Barbera d'Alba Ciabot du Re '98	ŸŸ	5
● Barolo '96	ŸŸ	6
● Barolo Giachini '96	ŸŸ	6
● Barolo Rocche dell'Annunziata '96	ŸŸ	6
● Dolcetto d'Alba '99	ŸŸ	3*
● L'Insieme	ŸŸ	6
● Barolo '93	ŸŸŸ	6
● Barbera d'Alba Ciabot du Re '96	ŸŸ	5
● Barbera d'Alba Ciabot du Re '97	ŸŸ	5
● Barolo '95	ŸŸ	6
● Barolo Giachini '95	ŸŸ	6
● Barolo Vigna Giachini '94	ŸŸ	6

LA MORRA (CN)

LA MORRA (CN)

MAURO VEGLIO
LOC. CASCINA NUOVA, 50
12064 LA MORRA (CN)
TEL. 0173/509212

ERALDO VIBERTI
B.TA TETTI, 53
FRAZ. SANTA MARIA
12064 LA MORRA (CN)
TEL. 0173/50308

Mauro Veglio has made his name with a range of outstanding, characterful wines. In addition to his own very considerable skills, he also takes full advantage of the advice of his close friend Elio Altare. We were very impressed with Veglio's Barolo Rocche and for the first time awarded it Three Glasses. Dark garnet with a narrow orange rim, it delights the nose with aromas of crushed raspberries and balsamic notes of menthol, juniper, earth and green leaf. The attack on the palate is concentrated and the progression full-bodied, buttressed by strong, noble tannins, while the lingering finish is richly nuanced. Veglio's Insieme, a product made in collaboration with six other winemakers and whose profits will go towards protecting the environment, is a blend of nebbiolo, barbera and cabernet. Its deep, rich colour anticipates an opulent wine with well-defined, fragrant fruit evident in notes of blackberry and cherry highlighted by complex touches of liquorice, spice and leaves. It develops wonderfully on the palate and its density is borne up by lovely noble tannins. Another newcomer, the Barolo Castelletto, comes from the fruit of a vineyard belonging to the parents of Daniela, Mauro's wife. Its strong fruit aroma is joined by a chorus of leather, mint and cocoa, while the palate displays body and an agreeably austere character. The estate's Gattera offers sweet oaky notes and a succulent palate with a floral finish. The Arborino has a subtler nose that opens out gradually, and a weighty, well-articulated palate that culminates in a warm, vigorous finish. Up there with it is the very fine Barbera d'Alba Cascina Nuova '98, one of the best of its category. The Dolcetto d'Alba and the Barbera d'Alba are, as usual, good and anything but one-dimensional.

Not for the first time, Eraldo Viberti's Barbera Vigna Clara carries off a triumphant Two Glasses this year. Viberti tends his vines with passionate care and they reward him with high quality fruit. He has very clear ideas on vinification and limits his range of offerings to a technically irreproachable selection of the zone's classics. His '97 vintage Barbera Vigna Clara – last year, there was a misprint in our profile; the "'97" Barbera Vigna Clara reviewed was actually the '96 – has a lovely intense garnet colour. Its bouquet initially suggests subtle oaky tones of toastiness, pastries and vanilla but these give way to rich, distinctive fruit that unfurls notes of cherry, raspberry and sweet almond. Entry on the palate immediately reveals the wine's full body and the progression is well-sustained and elegant, rather than powerful, through to a lingering finish that echoes generous fruit of the nose, mingling this with spicy touches of oak. Viberti's fairly intense garnet-ruby Barolo is also impressive with its well-focused berry fruit and spice nose. On the palate, it is even richer and more convincing, the mid palate being firmly backed up by robust, fine tannins that lend volume and vigour to the tidy, lingering finish with its subtle bitterish note. The estate's Dolcetto merits One Glass for its medium dark ruby tending to garnet and the refined, intriguing bouquet of very ripe wild berries, hay and aromatic herbs over faint minerally notes of earth. The tannins are evident on the well-structured palate, which is followed by a fruity finish.

● Barolo Vigneto Rocche '96	䷀ 6	
● Barbera d'Alba Cascina Nuova '98	䷀ 5	
● Barolo Arborina '96	䷀ 6	
● Barolo Castelletto '96	䷀ 6	
● Barolo Gattera '96	䷀ 6	
● Dolcetto d'Alba '99	䷀ 3*	
● L'Insieme	䷀ 6	
● Barbera d'Alba '99	䷀ 3	
● Barbera d'Alba Cascina Nuova '96	䷀ 5	
● Barbera d'Alba Cascina Nuova '97	䷀ 5	
● Barolo Gattera '95	䷀ 6	
● Barolo Arborina '95	䷀ 6	
● Barolo Vigneto Rocche '95	䷀ 6	

● Barbera d'Alba Vigna Clara '97	䷀ 5	
● Barolo '96	䷀ 6	
● Dolcetto d'Alba '99	䷀ 3	
● Barolo '93	䷀ 6	
● Barbera d'Alba Vigna Clara '96	䷀ 5	
● Barolo '94	䷀ 6	
● Barolo '95	䷀ 6	

LA MORRA (CN)

LA MORRA (CN)

GIANNI VOERZIO
S.DA LORETO, 1/BIS
12064 LA MORRA (CN)
TEL. 0173/509194

★ ROBERTO VOERZIO
LOC. CERRETO, 1
12064 LA MORRA (CN)
TEL. 0173/509196

Gianni Voerzio's winemaking style is born of a clear vision and the project he has in mind is finally being realized. He aims to create a wine that, above all, will possess a serious fine tannic structure with no trace of roughness. Such a wine requires high-quality grapes and skilful cellar technique, including maceration at fairly high temperatures to produce the right balance between anthocyans and tannins, and racking without aeration to preserve the freshness of the fruit. Voerzio has realised in full that objective with his Barolo La Serra '96, which the panel rewarded with its first Three Glass accolade. Dense ruby tending to garnet with a narrow rim, it flaunts a broad, complex bouquet of fresh black berry fruit with fascinating hints of tobacco and liquorice. Velvet-soft on the palate, it has a rich personality that burgeons in a crescendo of flavours that are carried through to its long, complex finish. As if that were not excitement enough, Voerzio's Barbera Ciabot della Luna obtains a very high score for a nose that beautifully balances notes of redcurrant and cherry with toasty, oak-derived vanilla. On the palate, it is full-bodied and juicy, its tannins bolstering the very long finish. The nebbiolo and barbera-based Serrapiù is up to its usual excellent standards. It has a complex bouquet and a well-sustained, beautifully co-ordinated palate with a nice note of toastiness. The Dolcetto d'Alba Rocchettevino is not overly powerful on the palate but does have structure and balance. The almond-nuanced Freisa is pleasant and the Arneis is mature and forthright.

In his 15-year career as a winemaker, Roberto Voerzio has never once veered from his mission of pushing back the frontiers of quality. Indeed, on the rare occasions he has felt that he had achieved the quality he sought but not the recognition, he has changed direction. His success is evident not only in his Barolo selections but also in his now widely known Barbera Vigneto Pozzo, which is available only in magnums. His now famous limited yields have meant that production has yet to reach 50,000 bottles a year but the foundations have been laid and future harvests will produce a Barolo from Rocche dell'Annunziata in La Morra. Voerzio's '96 Barolos are exceptional. The Cerequio is a veritable monument of complexity, sumptuously fruit-rich, wonderfully fresh-tasting and nuanced with oak-derived toastiness. The Brunate is every bit as impressive. Its very rich, sophisticated aromas are just a touch sweeter than those of the Cerequio and herald a great future for this wine. These two monsters had no difficulty in securing Three Glass scores and the admiration of our tasting panel. The La Serra has slightly less structure while the Dolcetto and the Vignaserra are both very respectable, offering an intense nose of hay and freshly mown grass. The estate's latest Chardonnay is good and very buttery. The success of his superlative Barbera Pozzo has encouraged Voerzio to carry on in the same vein. He has released a limited selection of his superb '95 vintage Barolo Vecchie Viti dei Capalotti e delle Brunate. This is a masterly wine, austere and complex, and again is only available in magnums.

● Barolo La Serra '96	♟♟♟	6
● Barbera d'Alba Ciabot della Luna '98	♟♟	5
● Langhe Rosso Serrapiù '98	♟♟	5
● Dolcetto d'Alba Rocchettevino '99	♟	4
● Langhe Nebbiolo Ciabot della Luna '98	♟	5
○ Roero Arneis Bricco Cappellina '99	♟	4
● Langhe Freisa Sotti I Bastioni '99		4
● Barbera d'Alba Ciabot della Luna '97	♟♟	5
● Barolo La Serra '93	♟♟	6
● Barolo La Serra '95	♟♟	6
● Langhe Rosso Serrapiù '97	♟♟	5
● Barolo La Serra '94	♟	6

● Barolo Cerequio '96	♟♟♟	6
● Barolo Brunate '96	♟♟♟	6
● Barbera d'Alba Vigneto Pozzo dell'Annunziata Ris. '97	♟♟	6
● Barolo La Serra '96	♟♟	6
● Dolcetto d'Alba Priavino '99	♟♟	4
○ Langhe Chardonnay Fossati Roscaleto '99	♟♟	5
● Langhe Rosso Vignaserra '98	♟♟	5
● Barbera d'Alba Vigneto Pozzo dell'Annunziata Ris. '96	♟♟♟	6
● Barolo Brunate '89	♟♟♟	6
● Barolo Brunate '93	♟♟♟	6
● Barolo Cerequio '90	♟♟♟	6
● Vignaserra '96	♟♟♟	6

LESSONA (BI)

SELLA

VIA IV NOVEMBRE, 110
13853 LESSONA (BI)
TEL. 015/99455

Lying at an altitude of over 300 metres, the Lessona vineyards stand on the hillslopes around Biella between the Rivers Cervo and Sesia. In 1671, the Sella family began to buy up terrain in this zone and the family home is still to be found on their San Sebastiano allo Zoppo vineyard, which produces one of the estate's best crus. Today, Fabrizio Sella heads the business, supported on the technical side by Giancarlo Scaglione. The cellars where the wine is aged are lower down on the Piccone estate, and offer tasting facilities and the opportunity to buy the full range of Sella wines, of which 60-70,000 bottles a year are produced. Nebbiolo, the variety traditional to these hills, is present in both DOC wines. The Lessona is 75 percent nebbiolo and the rest is mainly bonarda with a little vespolina, and the Bramaterra is a blend of 50-70 percent nebbiolo, 20-30 percent croatina, and 10-20 percent of bonarda and vespolina. The Bramaterra takes its name from the vineyards where the fruit is grown at Villa del Bosco. The Sellas introduced viticulture to this estate at the end of the 19th century. Of the wines they offered for tasting this year, two merit Two Glasses, the Il Chioso, a Lessona selection, and the Lessona San Sebastiano allo Zoppo. The first of these, a '96 vintage, is garnet in colour and proffers intense balsamic aromas lifted by hints of spice and autumn leaves. It is fleshy on the palate and offers well-sustained tannins. Balsamic notes also dominate the nose of the San Sebastian allo Zoppo '95 but on the palate its structure and tannins give it length. The admirable fruit is slightly compromised by exuberant oak. One Glass apiece goes to the standard Lessona and the Bramaterra while the Orbello wins an honourable mention.

●	Lessona Il Chioso '96	🍷🍷	5
●	Lessona S. Sebastiano allo Zoppo '95	🍷🍷	5
●	Bramaterra '96	🍷	4
●	Lessona '96	🍷	5
●	Coste della Sesia Orbello '98		3
●	Bramaterra '95	🍸🍸	5
●	Lessona Il Chioso '95	🍸🍸	5
●	Lessona S. Sebastiano allo Zoppo '93	🍸	5

LOAZZOLO (AT)

BORGO MARAGLIANO

REG. S. SEBASTIANO, 2
14050 LOAZZOLO (AT)
TEL. 0144/87132

Giuseppe and Carlo Galliano run their small winery with passion and vision. Their love of Loazzolo, where their family has lived since the mid-18th century, is evident, as is their determination to produce wines other than those traditional to the area. Witness their foray into spumante. The Gallianos' classic method Brut Giuseppe Galliano '96, an 80 percent pinot nero and 20 percent chardonnay blend of which they have produced 1,500 bottles, is a balanced, sophisticated Pas Dosé. It flaunts lovely buttery aromas with hints of toasted hazelnut which are satisfyingly echoed on the palate, and culminates in a very elegant finish. Their Brut Chardonnay, a persistent cuve close sparkling wine that proffers notes of yeast mingling with apples and pears, is clean on the palate and full of delicious flavours. But it is their Loazzolo Vendemmia Tardiva that is the cream of the crop. This bottle is made with selected fruit from a south-facing vineyard, 15-20 percent of which is raisined on rush mats while the remainder is harvested in the second half of November. The lustrous gold hue ushers in fragrant aromas of apricot and dark honey. These are picked up on the palate, which also has measured acidity. A touch more robustness in the body would put this spumante at the top of its class. The estate's Moscato d'Asti La Caliera '99 is coming on well, showing refined hints of rose and sage, and a silky aromatic profile on the palate. The El Calié, obtained from part-fermented grape must, is simple and fragrant. The Chardonnay Marajan '98 does not fully live up to expectations, presenting faint, fresh aromas and a nicely balanced, if not overly complex, palate. The clean-tasting Crevoglio '99, named after another of the family's estates, convinces with its well-structured aromas.

○	Giuseppe Galliano Brut '96	🍷🍷	5
○	Loazzolo Borgo Maragliano V. T. '97	🍷🍷	5
○	El Calié '99	🍷	3
○	Giuseppe Galliano Chardonnay Brut	🍷	3
○	Moscato d'Asti La Caliera '99	🍷	3
○	Piemonte Chardonnay Crevoglio '99	🍷	3
○	Piemonte Chardonnay Marajan '98	🍷	4
○	Giuseppe Galliano Brut '95	🍸🍸	5
○	Loazzolo Borgo Maragliano V. T. '96	🍸🍸	5

LOAZZOLO (AT)

LU MONFERRATO (AL)

FORTETO DELLA LUJA
CASA ROSSO, 4
REG. BRICCO
14050 LOAZZOLO (AT)
TEL. 0141/831596

CASALONE
VIA MARCONI, 92
15040 LU MONFERRATO (AL)
TEL. 0131/741280

Giancarlo Scaglione's technical expertise and highly attuned oenological skills have made him an important figure in the Piedmont winemaking world and beyond. As far as his own small, beautiful estate is concerned, Scaglione puts his faith in his children and the results are excellent. Yet again, Gianni and Silvia have produced a range of very high quality wines that bear witness to their own skills. Their Loazzolo Piasa Rischei '97 has become a point of reference in the world of Moscato. Its clear gold highlights hint at the citrus fruit, ripe yellow peach and raisiny aromas to come. A skilful and patient hand with the oak has lent a well-balanced complexity to the palate and the lingering finish is subtle and elegant. This is a great spumante which owes perhaps more to its character than its strength. The Scagliones take home another Three Glass award for a fabulous dessert wine which is among the best both in Italy and abroad. Next, the panel tried the Monferrato Rosso Le Grive '98, a blend of barbera and pinot nero. This rich ruby wine offers a bouquet of fresh spices and succulent berry fruit whose fragrances are mirrored on the balanced, concentrated palate. Last but not least, we have the Brachetto Pian dei Sogni '98, another outstanding selection. A brilliant garnet in hue, its rose and raspberry nose anticipates a elegant attack, enhanced by a well-gauged balance of tannins and characteristic varietal aromas. The Moscato Piasa San Maurizio, a product of the Scagliones' Santo Stefano Belbo vineyard, was unavailable for tasting as it was already sold out.

This lovely Monferrato estate enjoys a winemaking tradition that goes all the way back to 1734. The current owner, Paolo Casalone, manages the 10 acres, cellar and marketing of the wines with the help of his father, his brother, and oenologist, Giovanni Bailo. Casalone's straw-yellow Piemonte Chardonnay '99 has a bouquet of flowers and tropical fruit and citrus. It is agreeable on the palate, showing medium length and persistence and a barely discernible prickle. Given its quality, we consider this to be a very good buy. His Barbera d'Asti '98 is also good and almost won a Two Glass rating for its dark ruby colour and marked berry fruit aromas. The masculine palate has a solid structure and well-sustained progression. The estate's Piemonte Grignolino '99 carries off Two Glasses for its spice and berry fruit nose, and succulent, lingering palate dominated by notes of pepper and cloves. The Barbera d'Asti Rubermillo '98 is another Two Glass winner. Its distinguishing features are its garnet-ruby hue and its intense blackberry, redcurrant and dried rose aromas against a backdrop of balsamic notes. This impressive offering has an explosive, awesomely concentrated palate with marked, satisfying acidity. Equally good is the Rubermillo Selezione '98, a masterpiece of balance in a Barbera d'Asti. The deep, dark, almost opaque ruby colour introduces a dense balsamic nose redolent of berry fruit and flowers. Its warm, velvety palate finds a perfect point of equilibrium between the marked acidity and the tannins. A mention also goes to Casalone's Cortese Piemonte '99, his 100-percent pinot nero Monferrato Chiaretto La Rosella '99, and his satisfying Freisa del Monferrato.

	Wine	Glasses	Score
O	Loazzolo Piasa Rischei '97	♛♛♛	6
●	Monferrato Rosso Le Grive '98	♛♛	5
●	Piemonte Brachetto Forteto Pian dei Sogni '98	♛♛	6
O	Loazzolo Piasa Rischei '93	♀♀♀	6
O	Loazzolo Piasa Rischei '94	♀♀♀	6
O	Loazzolo Piasa Rischei '95	♀♀♀	6
O	Loazzolo Piasa Rischei '96	♀♀♀	6
●	Piemonte Brachetto Forteto Pian dei Sogni '95	♀♀	6
●	Piemonte Brachetto Forteto Pian dei Sogni '97	♀♀	6

	Wine	Glasses	Score
●	Barbera d'Asti Rubermillo '98	♛♛	4
●	Barbera d'Asti Rubermillo Sel. '98	♛♛	5
●	Piemonte Grignolino '99	♛♛	3*
●	Barbera d'Asti '98	♛	3
O	Piemonte Chardonnay '99	♛	2*
⊙	Monferrato Chiaretto La Rosella '99		2
●	Monferrato Freisa '99		2
O	Piemonte Cortese '99		2

LU MONFERRATO (AL)   MANGO (CN)

TENUTA S. SEBASTIANO
CASCINA S. SEBASTIANO, 41
15040 LU MONFERRATO (AL)
TEL. 0131/741353 - 0131/749984

CASCINA FONDA
LOC. CASCINA FONDA, 45
12056 MANGO (CN)
TEL. 0173/677156

Roberto De Alessi's passion for wine is beginning to win out over his passion for flying (he pilots a helicopter for the emergency services in Milan). He has recently refurbished his cellars with additional temperature-controlled stainless steel vats and is in the process of revamping his barrique cellars and reception area. This year, he has taken Mario Ronco on board as oenologist. The estate is going from strength to strength and bowled us over with an extremely unusual offering, the Lu. Obtained from moscato grapes with a light dusting of botrytis harvested late in the season, it seduced us with its opulent varietal aromas and characteristic notes of noble rot over discreet oak. A beautiful lustrous gold in colour, it fills the palate with moderately sweet aromas that echo the nose but fade a little towards the finish which, perhaps because of the wine's youth, is rather short and dry. De Alessi's rich ruby Mepari scored well again. It proffers a cherry, plum and spice nose and a full, vigorous palate which reveals that lovely underlying vein of acidity typical of a true Barbera, and just the right amount of wood. The estate's standard Barbera is a little simple but has a nice tang to it. The Grignolino is well put together and can offer clean, pervasive varietal notes of geranium, sweet spices and roses which are picked up by the palate. Its tannins are nicely balanced and the colour is attractive. We awarded One Glass to the refreshing Cortese for its lustrous straw-yellow colour and inviting floral bouquet.

The Barberos, Secondino and Maria, and their sons, Massimo and Marco, uncorked for the panel four Moscatos bursting with personality, despite their well-defined aromatic profile. We tasted them all – a rich Vendemmia Tardiva, a delicate Asti, a complex Driveri Metodo Classico and a no-nonsense Moscato d'Asti – and enjoyed every single one of them. The Vendemmia Tardiva has a fairly pale straw-yellow colour and a nose that blends notes of ripe fruit with fresh touches of mint and elder. It is fat on the palate but nice acidity and restrained effervescence give it balance and remarkable grace. It finishes on a lovely fruity note. The Barberos' Driveri Metodo Classico revels in aromas of super-ripeness, croissants, raisins, vanilla and jam and has a wide-ranging palate nicely bolstered by an extremely fine perlage. It culminates in a wonderfully long finish which unveils a succession of elegant varietal fragrances. The straw-yellow Asti is flecked with shimmering green highlights and reveals a nose with subtle notes of apricots in syrup, grapefruit and vanilla, enhanced by nuances of super-ripeness. The broad palate has good thrust and a barely marked prickle that take you through to a satisfying finish that echoes the notes of ripe fruit. The Moscato d'Asti is limpid in the glass, presenting a nose of pear, peach and elderflower while the sweet palate is nicely perked up by the effervescence. The Barbera Bruseisa is a medium ruby red and offers aromas of wild berries and resin leading in to an uncomplicated but well-structured palate. The estate's Brachetto suggests black cherries in rather a too ripe aromatic profile but is refreshing and easy to drink.

● Barbera del M.to Mepari '98	♟♟	4
○ Lu '99	♟♟	4
● Barbera del M.to '99	♟	2*
○ Monferrato Casalese Cortese '99	♟	2*
● Piemonte Grignolino '99	♟	3
● Barbera del M.to Mepari '97	♟♟	4

○ Asti '99	♟♟	3
○ Asti Driveri		
Metodo Classico '98	♟♟	5
○ Vendemmia Tardiva '99	♟♟	3*
● Barbera d'Alba		
Vigna Bruseisa '98	♟	3
○ Moscato d'Asti '99	♟	3
● Dolcetto d'Alba Brusalino '99		3
● Piemonte Brachetto '98		4

MANGO (CN)

MOASCA (AT)

DEGIORGIS
VIA CIRCONVALLAZIONE, 3
12056 MANGO (CN)
TEL. 0141/89107

PIETRO BARBERO
CASCINA LA GHERSA
V.LE S. GIUSEPPE, 19
14050 MOASCA (AT)
TEL. 0141/856012

Sergio Degiorgis and his wife Patrizia run this lovely Mango estate which offers a range of products with notable personality. The jewel in the Degiorgis' impressive crown is without a doubt their Dolcetto d'Alba Bricco Peso, an intense, structured wine that foregrounds the varietal characteristics of the grape. Hints of very ripe black berry fruit herald a truly sumptuous varietal note while delicious undertones of menthol, eucalyptus and cocoa lend fullness and complexity to the whole. The entry on the palate immediately tells you this wine is concentrated and full of flavour, its generous, solid follow-through unfolding an array of powerful tannins that invigorate the long, liquorice finish. The Moscato Sorì del Re is a rich straw-yellow and proffers a nose of apples, pears, peaches, apricots and elderflower. The palate is perked up by a balanced effervescence that lingers on through to the lovely, eminently satisfying, finish. The estate's Barbera has a medium ruby red hue that introduces a fairly delicate nose with clear notes of cherry and cakes. The robust palate reveals slightly forward tannins and a moderately long finish that echoes the fruit and is nuanced with cocoa. The freisa and barbera-based Langhe Rosso Riella has yet to find balance. The rich, clean bouquet is followed by a disappointing body. Finally, the straw-yellow Accordo has an evanescent nose of spring flowers, yeast and fruit. The palate is full-flavoured, with sweet, succulent fruit, and the finish offers a note of toasty oak.

Young Massimo Barbero has a tight grip on the reins of this estate, which has years of tradition behind it and which is determined to exploit barbera, undisputed queen of the Asti region, to its full potential. Not for the first time, the Barbera La Vignassa is the pick of the estate's offerings this year. A lovely, rich ruby violet colour, it has a complex nose dominated by notes of berry fruit and tobacco with attractive hints of spice and vanilla. On the palate, it can point to great structure, combining the elegance and balance that are the trademarks of a major Barbera. The estate's white Sivoj is also very inviting, marrying the strength and vanilla fragrances of its chardonnay and barrique-conditioned sauvignon with the zest and aromatic range of the cortese grape that makes up 60 percent of this wine's blend. The result is an original, delicious straw-yellow glass that unveils fresh fruity and floral aromas and a palate bolstered by good acidity. The Gavi Il Poggio is a fine example of its kind, its green-flecked straw-yellow introducing well-articulated notes of fruit and a clean, well-structured palate with medium body. The Barbera Camparò also impressed us with the harmony of its varietal components. It lacks only a little concentration and complexity to take it up to the level of its elder sister. Massimo's Barbera Filere Longhe is a bright wine and his Piagé, a blend of 60 percent barbera plus merlot and syrah, is well worth tasting. Rich ruby red, it boasts elegant aromas of ripe cherry and berry fruit laced with spice. Its great personality and well-rounded flavour come out on the palate, together with prominent but unassertive tannins.

O	Accordo	🍷🍷 4	●	Barbera d'Asti Sup.	
●	Dolcetto d'Alba Bricco Peso '99	🍷🍷 4		La Vignassa '98	🍷🍷 5
O	Moscato d'Asti Sorì del Re '99	🍷🍷 3*	O	Monferrato Bianco Sivoj '98	🍷🍷 3*
●	Barbera d'Alba '98	🍷 5	●	Monferrato Rosso Piagé '98	🍷🍷 3*
●	Langhe Rosso Riella '98	🍷 4	●	Barbera d'Asti Sup. Camparò '98	🍷 3
●	Dolcetto d'Alba Bricco Peso '98	🍷🍷 4	●	Barbera del M.to Filere Longhe '99	🍷 3
			O	Gavi di Rovereto	
				Vigna Il Poggio '99	🍷 3
			●	Barbera d'Asti Sup.	
				La Vignassa '96	🍷🍷 5
			●	Barbera d'Asti Sup.	
				La Vignassa '97	🍷🍷 5

MONCALVO (AT)

MONCHIERO (CN)

CASCINA ORSOLINA
VIA CAMINATA, 28
14036 MONCALVO (AT)
TEL. 0141/917277

GIUSEPPE MASCARELLO E FIGLIO
VIA BORGONUOVO, 108
12060 MONCHIERO (CN)
TEL. 0173/792126

The Denegris' Cascina Orsolina estate excels at producing Barberas and under the expert guidance of oenologist, Donato Lanati, the quality of its wines gets better every year. They have recently rented three and a half hectares from the Locanda del Sant'Uffizio at Cioccaro di Penango to give them a total of 15 hectares planted to vine. Of the wide range of wines the Denegris offered to the panel this year, two Barberas stand out, the Bricco dei Cappuccini and the Caminata (30,000 bottles have been produced of each), along with their Monferrato Rosso Sole (7,000 bottles), a barbera, merlot and pinot nero blend, their Grignolino (6,000 bottles), and their Chardonnay Rosanna (6,000 bottles). The Bricco dei Cappuccini is aged in new and once-used barriques and is very dark in appearance. It has an intense, fruity nose veined with very toasty oak and on the palate its marked tanginess and robust acidity are mellowed by a substantial alcohol content. The Caminata, aged in large barrels, proffers the classic varietal aromas of cherry and a tangy, harmonious palate but falls slightly short in terms of structure. The estate's dense, inky-black Sole is excellent, revealing complex notes of toastiness, balsam and fruit and an almost chewy palate. Wonderfully powerful, it never goes too far thanks to its refreshing acid vein. The Grignolino is nicely put together, showing very subtle spicy and peppery aromas and a softness rare for this variety. The Chardonnay is not quite up to this standard, let down by an oak which overwhelms the fruit and renders its final note bitter.

Mauro Mascarello, supported by his wife and son, continues to run the family estate passed down to him by his father as it has always been run, producing wines full of character and personality. He both buys in grapes from the best zones of Barolo and Barbaresco and uses those he grows himself on the Monprivato di Castiglione Falletto cru, a historic Langhe vineyard. This magnificent plot gives Mauro Mascarello the nebbiolo grapes which go to make his finest Barolo selections, labelled Giuseppe Mascarello. This year he has released a new Barolo label, from Ca' d' Morissio, a small vineyard at Monprivato. There are 1,000 bottles of this austere, full-bodied red, which promises great longevity. The estate's Barolo Monprivato '95 is not quite as structured, but is still up there with the best of the great, traditional Barolos. The fragrant Nebbiolo San Rocco '98 is complex and varietal and can only improve with more time in the cellar. We liked the Codana '97 best of the Barberas we tasted. It has good acidity, a fruit-rich nose and an agreeable palate, while the Barbera from the historic Santo Stefano di Perno cru in Monforte d'Alba is powerful but still a bit closed on the nose. The Dolcetto d'Alba Bricco '98 is worth investigating for its striking floral notes and its tangy vitality. The Dolcetto from Santo Stefano has very robust tannins but the Freisa Toetto lacks a little definition on the nose.

● Barbera d'Asti Sup. Bricco dei Cappuccini '98	▼▼	5
● Monferrato Rosso Sole '98	▼▼	5
● Barbera d'Asti Caminata '98	▼	3
● Grignolino d'Asti S. Giacu '99	▼	3
○ Piemonte Chardonnay Rosanna '98		4
● Barbera d'Asti Sup. Bricco dei Cappuccini '97	♀♀	5
● Monferrato Rosso Sole '97	♀♀	5

● Barbera d'Alba Codana '97	▼▼	5
● Barolo Monprivato '95	▼▼	6
● Barolo Monprivato Ca' d' Morissio '93	▼▼	6
● Barbera d'Alba S. Stefano di Perno '97	▼	5
● Dolcetto d'Alba Bricco '98	▼	4
● Dolcetto d'Alba S. Stefano di Perno '98	▼	3
● Nebbiolo d'Alba S. Rocco '98	▼	5
● Langhe Freisa Toetto '98		3
● Barolo Monprivato '85	♀♀♀	6
● Barolo Monprivato '90	♀♀	6
● Barolo Villero '93	♀♀	6
● Barolo S. Stefano di Perno '93	♀	6

MONDOVI (CN)

MONFORTE D'ALBA (CN)

IL COLOMBO - BARONE RICCATI
VIA DEI SENT, 2
12084 MONDOVI (CN)
TEL. 0174/41607

GIANFRANCO ALESSANDRIA
LOC. MANZONI, 13
12065 MONFORTE D'ALBA (CN)
TEL. 0173/78576 - 0173/787222

Adriana and Carlo Riccati just failed to repeat the triumphs of their two previous vintages, the '97 and the '98. This year they miss out on a Three Glass award, but only by a whisker. Their Dolcetto delle Langhe Monregalesi pays tribute to all their hard work, including pruning back the vines to limit yields and traditional vinification methods, with the aim of getting the maximum quality out of their fruit. Under-rated until the mid 90s, this DOC zone owes much of the international standing it enjoys today to the Riccatis' perseverance and determination. The Dolcetto Il Colombo is still one of the best of its vintage, even if it did not win our top prize this time around. The fullness of its body is immediately evident from the colour, a deep, almost opaque, violet. An initial heady sensation of fruit gives way to notes of morello cherry, cherry and redcurrant while the palate is still a bit inflexible and lacks harmony. Tannins, alcohol and acidity have yet to find a meeting point they can all agree on. However, a final period of ageing in the bottle will smooth out its youthful rough edges. The estate's Vigna della Chiesetta is also worthy of note. It is marginally lighter than the house selection, but offers excellent value for money.

The addition of one and a half hectares of nebbiolo soon to go into production will give Gianfranco Alessandria a total of five and a half hectares under vine. In terms of quantity, Gianfranco is a small winemaker as he produces little more than 20,000 bottles a year but in quality he is anything but. His products are outstanding and seem to get better every year. His Barbera Vittoria '98 is the fabulous child of a variety that Gianfranco is obviously passionate about. Dark and very, very dense in the glass, it unveils a nose of morello cherry and berry fruit that mingle to perfection with touches of oak (90 percent new barriques) and are further exalted by a mineral note. It is sweet on the palate, possessing a rare fullness and softness with a hint of tanginess betraying its terror. The finish just goes on and on forever. The richness and elegance of this show-stopping wine won it Three resounding Glasses. The standard '99 version has just as deep a hue with violet highlights and a formidable but subtle range of aromas. On the palate, it is broad, full-bodied and deliciously drinkable, thanks to the nice acidity that draws out the finish. Between them, the two Barolos account for a production of 8,500 bottles. The standard '96 selection has a typical Barolo ruby-with-garnet-highlights appearance, the characteristic mentholated overtones of the Monforte region, and rather a hard palate with robust tannins ending with a finish that echoes the balsamic tones. The San Giovanni is darker in colour and its sweet aromas hint at its sojourn in new barriques but do not impinge on its glorious fruit. Entry on the palate is sweet with a lovely roundness in mid palate and a fabulously long finish. A very classy wine. Gianfranco's fairly simple Dolcetto offers clean aromas that hint at almond and a satisfying quaffability on the palate. His Insieme, a red obtained from a blend of several varieties, makes an impressive debut.

● Dolcetto delle Langhe		
Monregalesi Il Colombo '99	ΨΨ	4
● Dolcetto delle Langhe		
Monregalesi		
Vigna della Chiesetta '99	ΨΨ	3*
● Dolcetto delle Langhe		
Monregalesi Il Colombo '97	ΨΨΨ	4
● Dolcetto delle Langhe		
Monregalesi Il Colombo '98	ΨΨΨ	4

● Barbera d'Alba Vittoria '98	ΨΨΨ	5
● Barbera d'Alba '99	ΨΨ	3*
● Barolo '96	ΨΨ	6
● Barolo S. Giovanni '96	ΨΨ	6
● L'Insieme	ΨΨ	6
● Dolcetto d'Alba '99	Ψ	3*
● Barbera d'Alba Vittoria '96	ΨΨΨ	5
● Barbera d'Alba Vittoria '97	ΨΨΨ	5
● Barolo '93	ΨΨΨ	6
● Barolo S. Giovanni '95	ΨΨ	6
● Barolo '95	Ψ	6

MONFORTE D'ALBA (CN)   MONFORTE D'ALBA (CN)

BUSSIA SOPRANA
LOC. BUSSIA, 81
12065 MONFORTE D'ALBA (CN)
TEL. 039/305182

★ DOMENICO CLERICO
LOC. MANZONI, 67
12065 MONFORTE D'ALBA (CN)
TEL. 0173/78171

Silvano Casiraghi and Guido Rossi came up with some good wines for this edition of the Guide. Their Barbera d'Alba Vin del Ross has great texture and personality while the '97 vintage (here we would like to apologise for erroneously labelling the '96 a '97 in last year's edition) has a dense garnet colour that speaks volumes for the quality of its fruit. And that rich, concentrated fruit comes across in hints of blackberry, cherry and cassis in an aromatic profile lent complexity by attractive mineral and gamey nuances. The entry on the palate is succulent and the progression opens out to take you through to finish in a superbly balanced array of aromas. The estate's Barolo Mosconi is ruby red tending to garnet with an orange rim and rolls out a nose redolent of coffee, red berry fruit, menthol, cakes and spice. On the palate, balanced tannins buttress its broad yet dense progression, which ends in a well-orchestrated fruit-and-spice finish. The deep-hued Barolo Bussia has a firm, narrow rim and aromas of wild berries, vanilla and caramel, laced with a suspicion of earth. It is strong, soft and big on the palate, with tannins that invigorate the lingering finish, where aromas of mint, cocoa and bramble emerge. Almost as good is the Barolo Vigna Colonnello. A fairly dark ruby in the glass, with an orange rim, its nose vacillates between fruit and green tones, with touches of leather and liquorice. It is solid and a tad austere on the palate, finishing on a spicy, vegetal note.

We could only open our tasting notes with the Barolo Percristina '95, the most interesting newcomer in the range offered to the panel by the dynamic Domenico Clerico and the capable young Massimo Conterno. Clerico's 5,500-bottle beauty is produced in the subzone of Mosconi di Monforte and earns our unalloyed admiration, as well as a triumphant Three Glass distinction. A rich, intense red, this Barolo offers classic varietal aromas lifted by very subtle oak, and has a sweet, moderately full palate that leads in to a rather long finish. This is a superb success and is even more impressive when you consider the vintage. Clerico's two '96 Barolos are magnificent. The Pajana is very dark in appearance and has an oaky nose which opens out to embrace classic notes of grape. It is wonderfully sweet on the palate, gathering momentum in the mid palate, and signing off with a lingering finish. We liked the estate's dark, vividly hued Ciabot Mentin Ginestra '96 even better. It enfolds the nose with inebriating aromas of violets, roses and tar. Although more austere than the Pajana, it can point to a magnificent palate with sweet yet powerful tannins and a very, very long, succulent finish. This wine has a very exciting future. The Arte '98 lives up to its reputation. A blend of 85 percent nebbiolo with barbera and cabernet sauvignon, it offers a complex nose, excellent tannic structure which in no way compromises its eminent drinkability, and a satisfying finish. Clerico's first-rate Dolcetto '99 has a clean, intense nose and a lovely rich palate which reaffirm the quality of last year's version. His Barbera '98 is also very good. It has an intense yet subtle nose and a sweet, soft palate packed with smooth fruit and bolstered by just the right dose of acidity.

● Barbera d'Alba Vin del Ross '97	♟♟	5
● Barolo Bussia '96	♟♟	6
● Barolo Mosconi '96	♟♟	6
● Barolo Vigna Colonnello '96	♟	6
● Barbera d'Alba Vin del Ross '96	♟♟	5
● Barolo Mosconi '95	♟♟	6
● Barolo Vigna Colonnello '93	♟♟	6
● Barolo Bussia '93	♟	6
● Barolo Bussia '95	♟	6

● Barolo Percristina '95	♟♟♟	6
● Barbera d'Alba Trevigne '98	♟♟	4
● Barolo Ciabot Mentin Ginestra '96	♟♟	6
● Barolo Pajana '96	♟♟	6
● Langhe Arte '98	♟♟	6
● Langhe Dolcetto Visadì '99	♟♟	3*
● Arte '90	♟♟♟	6
● Arte '93	♟♟♟	6
● Barolo Ciabot Mentin Ginestra '85	♟♟♟	6
● Barolo Ciabot Mentin Ginestra '89	♟♟♟	6
● Barolo Pajana '90	♟♟♟	6
● Barolo Pajana '91	♟♟♟	6
● Barolo Pajana '93	♟♟♟	6
● Barolo Pajana '95	♟♟♟	6
● Langhe Arte '96	♟♟♟	6

MONFORTE D'ALBA (CN)   MONFORTE D'ALBA (CN)

★ GIACOMO CONTERNO
LOC. ORNATI, 2
12065 MONFORTE D'ALBA (CN)
TEL. 0173/78221

PAOLO CONTERNO
VIA GINESTRA, 34
12065 MONFORTE D'ALBA (CN)
TEL. 0173/78415

Giovanni Conterno is true to the nature of his Langhe home, a land that can be generous or miserly, sometimes harsh and other times gentle. Giovanni's wines have the same quixotic personality, and each new bottle that was opened unfailingly amazed the panel. We were anxiously looking forward to the Barolo Monfortino, released only in exceptional vintages or when Giovanni considers it up to his exalted standards. So, after the Three Glass '90, we were keen to sample the '93. Although not as good as its predecessor, the new vintage is austere and utterly convincing. The intense garnet reveals a slightly forward wine, preceding a broad, complex nose of dry grass, tobacco and liquorice. A powerful palate is underpinned by serious tannins, signing off with a lingering finish. This is an uncompromisingly dry Barolo with a noble soul. The Barolo Cascina Francia '96 thoroughly deserved its Two Glasses. It is another aristocrat with a moderately intense garnet ruby hue. Stewed fruit and spice on the nose lead in to an austerely dry, robust and complex structure on the palate. The fruit comes from the Francia vineyard where, as can be seen from the Slow Food Atlas of Langhe Vineyards, the rich soil yields uncompromising, highly tannic wines destined for a lengthy stay in the cellar. When young, they are potent, long-limbed and dry but over the years, they gain in elegance and fullness of flavour. The Barolo di Conterno is a typical example. The traditional style of the Barbera d'Alba '99 is expressed in a nose of roses and red berries, and an attractive palate of stewed fruit and mulberry jam with a deliciously long finish. In contrast, the Dolcetto d'Alba '99 is a much more straightforward wine.

Le Ginestre is one of Monforte's most historic crus and the Barolo it yields is a very superior product indeed. That was the opinion of Lorenzo Fantini, who contributed to the Jacini report on agriculture in the late 19th century. All of the vineyards cultivated by Paolo Conterno and his son Giorgio bask in the sun at Le Ginestre and again this year, in the fields and in the cellar, the pair have shown the worth of this generous Langhe soil. We'll start with the Barolo Ginestra '96, which impressed us with its bearing. The nose has power and breadth, revealing tempting liquorice with attractive spice blending subtly with hints of red berry fruit, dry flowers and incense. As you would expect from a '96, the tannins are massive and the finish goes on forever. This is an outstanding wine of exceptional nobility and austerity. The Langhe Bric Ginestra '98 also combines power with breeding. Its brilliant, eye-catching ruby colour takes you into a delicate, leisurely nose. On the palate, this Nebbiolo is a welter of superb fruit-rich aromas while the juicy mature fruit mellows the concentration of the tannins. The Dolcetto d'Alba Ginestra '99 is a deep, dark purple whose unfathomable depths are illuminated by occasional flashes of light. The nose has yet to find a length but the classic Dolcetto vinosity and red berry fruit are already there. Good concentration and remarkable structure are evident on the palate. The Barbera d'Alba Ginestra '98 was still rather closed when we tasted it but a few months in the bottle will ensure it expresses its full potential.

● Barbera d'Alba '99	▼▼	5
● Barolo Cascina Francia '96	▼▼	6
● Barolo Monfortino Ris. '93	▼▼	6
● Dolcetto d'Alba '99	▼	4
● Barolo Cascina Francia '85	♀♀♀	6
● Barolo Cascina Francia '87	♀♀♀	6
● Barolo Cascina Francia '89	♀♀♀	6
● Barolo Cascina Francia '90	♀♀♀	6
● Barolo Monfortino Ris. '82	♀♀♀	6
● Barolo Monfortino Ris. '85	♀♀♀	6
● Barolo Monfortino Ris. '87	♀♀♀	6
● Barolo Monfortino Ris. '88	♀♀♀	6
● Barolo Monfortino Ris. '90	♀♀♀	6
● Barolo Cascina Francia '95	♀♀	6

● Barolo Ginestra '96	▼▼	6
● Dolcetto d'Alba Ginestra '99	▼▼	4
● Langhe Brich Ginestra '98	▼▼	6
● Barbera d'Alba Ginestra '98	▼	4
● Barolo Ginestra '95	♀♀	6
● Barolo Ginestra Ris. '93	♀♀	6
● Barbera d'Alba Ginestra '97	♀	4

MONFORTE D'ALBA (CN) MONFORTE D'ALBA (CN)

★ PODERI ALDO CONTERNO
LOC. BUSSIA, 48
12065 MONFORTE D'ALBA (CN)
TEL. 0173/78150

CONTERNO - FANTINO
VIA GINESTRA, 1
LOC. BRICCO BASTIA
12065 MONFORTE D'ALBA (CN)
TEL. 0173/78204

A few hours spent in the company of Aldo Conterno are a memorable experience. The charm with which he puts forward his convictions regarding wine, his competence in every area of winemaking and the sincere respect he has for the opinions and policies of other producers can only elicit our admiration and, we would like to add, our sincere affection. But now for the wines. Thanks to the excellent '96 vintage, Aldo's Barolo Cicala is outstanding. The textbook colour in the glass ushers in bright, intense, exquisitely clean aromas with distinct notes of violets and mint. The mid palate is powerful and lively, the tannins – awesome but not dry – coming through the wine's rich, full flavour while the finish shows good length. The Barolo Colonnello is equally traditional in colour and in its intense fruit aromas. Perhaps a little closed on the palate, it has good breadth of flavour, nice tannins and will certainly improve in the cellar. This year, the standard Barolo '96 bears the indication Bussia Soprana only on the back-label. Its fruit aromas nuanced with menthol and rain-soaked grass lead in to a potent, tannin-rich palate that has less complexity than the premium bottles. The Favot is a nice wine with notes of violets and a fairly juicy finish. The newcomer on the Conterno estate is Quartetto, a blend of nebbiolo, barbera, cabernet sauvignon and merlot. Dark in the glass, it offers intense berry aromas, a full, close-knit palate and length in the finish. The Chardonnay Bussiador is also excellent. In fact, it is one of the best ever, even though the wood is still a little too prominent. As usual, the Contorno Barbera is good, the Printanié quaffably fruity, and the Dolcetto delicious.

There is news of a major reshuffle at the Conterno Fantino winery. Diego Conterno has handed over to Claudio Conterno, who looks after the vineyards, and Guido Fantino, in charge of the cellars. The 34 hectares under vine, of which 24 belong to the property, produce 130-140,000 bottles and the flagship wines are the two Barolos from the Monforte vineyard. In fact, the '96 Vigna del Gris is, in our opinion, one of the finest versions of the wine. Its colour is dark and profound, and thanks to ageing in 100 percent new wood, it has a wealth of aromas, an exceptionally full flavour and magnificent length. Three Glasses for a wine whose '96 vintage is actually superior to the more celebrated Sorì Ginestra. But that wine, too, is magnificently muscular, its tannins robust but never aggressive. The supreme richness of the palate is sustained through to the leisurely finish with its notes of spice and sweet liquorice. The winery's third great red, the Monprà, is a blend of Barolo nebbiolo from Castiglione Falletto, barbera and cabernet sauvignon. As ever, it is superb. Delicate aromas strike a delicious balance of fruit and wood on the nose. The palate has length and can already offer remarkable complexity. That was why the panel gave Conterno Fantino its second Three Glass award for this consistently excellent Langhe blend. Cellar ageing can only improve these three magnificent wines. The '99 Dolcetto confirms last year's turn-around. and the Chardonnay Bricco Bastia '98 is also attractive and less oak-dominated than in the past. finally, the '99 Barbera has many virtues but we were hoping for a little more complexity.

● Barbera d'Alba Conca Tre Pile '98	🍷🍷	5
● Barolo Bussia Soprana '96	🍷🍷	6
● Barolo Cicala '96	🍷🍷	6
● Barolo Colonnello '96	🍷🍷	6
○ Langhe Chardonnay Bussiador '98	🍷🍷	6
● Langhe Nebbiolo Favot '98	🍷🍷	6
● Langhe Rosso Quartetto '98	🍷🍷	6
● Dolcetto d'Alba '99	🍷	4
○ Langhe Bianco Printanié '99	🍷	4
● Barolo Gran Bussia Ris. '88	🍷🍷🍷	6
● Barolo Gran Bussia Ris. '89	🍷🍷🍷	6
● Barolo Gran Bussia Ris. '90	🍷🍷🍷	6
● Barolo Vigna Colonnello '88	🍷🍷🍷	6
● Barolo Vigna Colonnello '89	🍷🍷🍷	6
● Barolo Vigna Colonnello '90	🍷🍷🍷	6

● Barolo Vigna del Gris '96	🍷🍷🍷	6
● Langhe Rosso Monprà '98	🍷🍷🍷	6
● Barolo Sorì Ginestra '96	🍷🍷	6
● Dolcetto d'Alba Bricco Bastia '99	🍷🍷	3*
○ Langhe Chardonnay Bastia '98	🍷🍷	5
● Barbera d'Alba Vignota '99	🍷	4
● Barolo Sorì Ginestra '86	🍷🍷🍷	6
● Barolo Sorì Ginestra '90	🍷🍷🍷	6
● Barolo Sorì Ginestra '91	🍷🍷🍷	6
● Langhe Rosso Monprà '95	🍷🍷🍷	6
● Langhe Rosso Monprà '97	🍷🍷🍷	6
● Monprà '94	🍷🍷🍷	6
● Barolo Sorì Ginestra '95	🍷🍷	6
● Barolo Vigna del Gris '93	🍷🍷	6
● Barolo Vigna del Gris '95	🍷🍷	6

MONFORTE D'ALBA (CN)   MONFORTE D'ALBA (CN)

ALESSANDRO E GIAN NATALE FANTINO
VIA G. SILVANO, 18
12065 MONFORTE D'ALBA (CN)
TEL. 0173/78253

ATTILIO GHISOLFI
REG. BUSSIA, 27
CASCINA VISETTE
12065 MONFORTE D'ALBA (CN)
TEL. 0173/78345

Alessandro and Gian Natale Fantino have completed work on their elegant cellars, located in a lovely palazzo in the historic centre of Monforte d'Alba, only 100 metres from the main square. Two ancient wells ensure constant humidity and cool temperatures in the ageing cellars, where their Barolos and Barberas wait to be released. These make up the bulk of the 30-35,000 bottles the brothers produce from their seven hectares under vine at Bussia. Alessandro is a passionate vineyard manager who shuns all chemical products, including fertilizer, because he believes that a great red can only come from great grapes. Cellar technology can work miracles but risks jeopardising the final product's identity. That is the philosophy behind the '96 Barolo Vigna dei Dardi and the '98 Barbera d'Alba Vigna dei Dardi. The Barolo is garnet with an orange edge, showing delicate, complex aromas and an austere, remarkably long palate. In contrast, the Barbera is elegantly sophisticated rather than powerful. The brother's other great passion is Passito di Nebbiolo, a wine they make only in the best vintages, harvesting the fruit about 15 days before the nebbiolo that will go into their Barolo. The grapes are then laid out on cane racks to raisin until the end of January, when they are pressed. After fermentation, the Passito spends three years in small oak casks before being bottled unfiltered. The Fantinos suggest trying this wine with game but it can also be a delightfully unusual aperitif.

Gian Marco Ghisolfi is at the helm of this six-hectare estate, which he runs with a little help from his parents. They produce about 30,000 bottles and this year there is a newcomer to the range. It's the Langhe Rosso Alta Bussia, a blend of 80 percent barbera with 20 percent nebbiolo, and 2,500 bottles have been released. The dense garnet colour introduces a broad, intriguing nose with ripe notes of cassis, bilberry, spices and crusty bread. On entry, the rich, full-bodied palate reveals stylish, tight-knit tannins that invigorate the long, well-balanced finish. The Rosso Carlin, a blend of 60 percent nebbiolo and 40 percent freisa, unveils a satisfyingly deep colour and a fascinating nose of vanilla, mint, redcurrant, raspberry and cocoa, brought together in a stupendous chorus. The wine's austere, but never harsh, personality comes out on the palate, where up-front tannins back up the chewy fruit. Elegant notes of liquorice emerge in the warm dry finish. The concentrated colour of the Barolo Visette highlights a nose of cocoa, jam and sweet spices over leather and camomile. The palate has a firm texture and a slightly severe character tempered by the warmth and vigour of the finish. The Barber and the Dolcetto are outstanding. The intense colour of the Barbera heralds a fruit and balsam nose and a broad, full-bodied body held firmly together by elegant tannins. The equally intense Dolcetto adds cream to the wild berry and cherry fruit on the nose, going on to develop remarkable complexity in a muscular, well-balanced palate.

● Barolo Vigna dei Dardi '96	♟♟	6
● Nebbiolo Passito		
Vigna dei Dardi '97	♟♟	6
● Barbera d'Alba		
Vigna dei Dardi '98	♟	4
● Barolo Vigna dei Dardi '93	♕♕	6
● Barolo Vigna dei Dardi '95	♕♕	6
● Nebbiolo Passito		
Vigna dei Dardi '96	♕♕	6
● Barbera d'Alba		
Vigna dei Dardi '97	♕	4

● Barbera d'Alba Vigna Lisi '98	♟♟	5
● Barolo Bricco Visette '96	♟♟	6
● Dolcetto d'Alba '99	♟♟	3*
● Langhe Rosso Alta Bussia '98	♟♟	5
● Langhe Rosso Carlin '98	♟♟	5
● Barbera d'Alba Vigna Lisi '96	♕♕	4
● Barbera d'Alba Vigna Lisi '97	♕♕	4
● Barolo Bricco Visette '93	♕♕	6
● Barolo Bricco Visette '95	♕♕	6
● Langhe Rosso Carlin '97	♕♕	4

MONFORTE D'ALBA (CN)

ELIO GRASSO
LOC. GINESTRA, 40
12065 MONFORTE D'ALBA (CN)
TEL. 0173/78491

MONFORTE D'ALBA (CN)

GIOVANNI MANZONE
VIA CASTELLETTO, 9
12065 MONFORTE D'ALBA (CN)
TEL. 0173/78114

Marina and Elio Grasso's property, set among the vineyards of Ginestra in the Langhe hills of Monforte and Serralunga, is well worth a visit, as is their modern cellar, which produces 60,000 bottles every year. We'll begin with the wine that most took our fancy. The elegant, potent Barolo Runcot '95 is blood-red in the glass, with faintly orange highlights, and proffers a nose of red roses, raspberries and blackcurrant, ending on a delicately spicy note. The tannins are well to the fore on the full-bodied palate and the complex fruit aromas hint pleasantly at menthol, tobacco and liquorice. The Barolo Gavarini Vigna Chiniera '96 has elegance, length, warmth, harmony and sincerity in its favour. The aromas of grass and dry aromatic flowers immediately grab your attention, taking you into the ripe, sweet fruit of the firm-textured palate. The Barolo Ginestra Vigna Casa Maté '96 is less of a heavyweight that the previous two but its colour is markedly subtler. The roses on the nose overlay mint in an appealing weave while the body is in thrall to the lively acidity and tannins for the time being. Age will, however, ensure a better balance. Also in search of equilibrium is the vibrant, ruby and deep-violet, Barbera Vigna Martina '97. Its warm vinosity masks the nose of macerated fruit and rose petals with assertive alcohol but the palate is dense, revealing raspberry and strawberry aromas. Hawthorn and iris are the keynotes of the Langhe Chardonnay Educato '98 on the nose while ripe, sweet fruit mingles with toasty notes on the palate. And to finish, we enjoyed the purple-hued Dolcetto d'Alba Vigna dei Grassi.

Giovanni Manzone's Barolo delle Gramolere is strongly redolent of dry aromatic herbs, combining mint and thyme before adding nuances of incense and spices. Of the '96s, we preferred the balanced, ripe fruit and convincingly rich, almost chewy structure of the Bricat. Somewhat lighter in texture, and with less intense aromas, was the standard Gramolere Barolo. But the Riserva '95 scored well, despite a vintage that was far from exciting. The nose opens with mint, hay and crushed fruit, leading into a full body with substantial acidity and tannins before the finish rounds off with a hint of black cherry. The Barbera d'Alba La Serra '97 has a potent peach and apricot nose with a hint of spices in the tail while the palate is soft and warm, with sweet, ripe and fairly chewy fruit. The Tris '97, a blend of nebbiolo, barbera and dolcetto, soon has you reaching for another glass thanks to a warm, smooth presence on the palate, although the nose has yet to reach its peak. We were astonished at the dark purple colour and syrupy consistency of the Dolcetto d'Alba '99. Sadly, its relative youth means that nose and palate have yet to reach full maturity. To round off our tasting, we tried the Rosserto, a white table wine from rossese grapes. This is an experiment, or perhaps a gamble, to demonstrate the potential of the Langhe terroir. Whatever the case, the wine is elegantly subtle, offering attractive nuances of gooseberry.

● Barbera d'Alba Vigna Martina '97	🍷🍷	5
● Barolo Gavarini Vigna Chiniera '96	🍷🍷	6
● Barolo Ginestra		
Vigna Casa Maté '96	🍷🍷	6
● Barolo Runcot '95	🍷🍷	6
● Dolcetto d'Alba Gavarini		
Vigna dei Grassi '99	🍷	3
○ Langhe Chardonnay Educato '98	🍷	4
● Barolo Gavarini Vigna Chiniera '89	🍷🍷🍷	6
● Barolo Ginestra Vigna Casa Maté '90	🍷🍷🍷	6
● Barolo Ginestra Vigna Casa Maté '93	🍷🍷🍷	6
● Barbera d'Alba Vigna Martina '96	🍷🍷	5
● Barolo Gavarini Vigna Chiniera '93	🍷🍷	6
● Barolo Gavarini Vigna Chiniera '95	🍷🍷	6
● Barolo Ginestra Vigna Casa Maté '95	🍷🍷	6

● Barbera d'Alba La Serra '97	🍷🍷	4
● Barolo Gramolere Bricat '96	🍷🍷	6
● Barolo Gramolere Ris. '95	🍷🍷	6
● Langhe Rosso Tris '97	🍷🍷	5
○ Rosserto '97	🍷🍷	4
● Barolo Gramolere '96	🍷	6
● Dolcetto d'Alba '99	🍷	3
● Barolo Gramolere '93	🍷🍷	6
● Barolo Gramolere '95	🍷🍷	6
● Barolo Gramolere Bricat '94	🍷🍷	6
● Barolo Gramolere Bricat '95	🍷🍷	6
● Barolo Gramolere Ris. '90	🍷🍷	6
● Langhe Rosso Tris '96	🍷🍷	5
● Barolo Gramolere Ris. '93	🍷	6

MONFORTE D'ALBA (CN)

MONTI
LOC. S. SEBASTIANO, 39
FRAZ. CÀMIA
12065 MONFORTE D'ALBA (CN)
TEL. 0173/78391

MONFORTE D'ALBA (CN)

ARMANDO PARUSSO
LOC. BUSSIA, 55
12065 MONFORTE D'ALBA (CN)
TEL. 0173/78257

As you leave Monforte on the road to Dogliani, two kilometres from the town you will see the indication for Càmia Benenti on the left. Here, in a farmhouse that was completely renovated in 1986, Pier Paolo Monti, a young building contractor from Turin, has set in motion his carefully planned winemaking strategy. The first fruits of Monti's efforts could be appreciated in his Barbera d'Asti '97, which easily scored high enough to earn Two Glasses last year. But the 2000 vintage brought the estate up to speed for it is now turning out just over 30,000 bottles from about five and a half hectares under vine. Standing beside the farmhouse are the chardonnay and riesling renano vineyards that produce the exciting Langhe Bianco L'Aura '99, an original wine thanks to the German variety included in its blend. Straw-yellow with greenish highlights, it displays minerally notes on the nose, with a hint of flowers providing added finesse. The palate is sure-footed, muscular and soft-textured, signing off with a lingering almondy aftertaste. We'll have to wait until June 2001 to sample the Langhe Rosso, a blend of nebbiolo, cabernet and merlot grapes, and the first of the Barolos should be released in 2003. For now, Monti and Roberto Gervino, a young wine technician from Alba and Monti's righthand man in vineyard and cellar, are banking on their Barbera d'Alba '98. It's not quite as good as the '97 but it is still a very attractive and thoroughly serious bottle.

The upward march of the Parusso family to the heights of Piedmontese winemaking continues apace. This year, they have inaugurated a spacious and very functional modern cellar, where Marco and Tiziana will have more room to work on the grapes from the property's vineyards. The '96 vintage was a promising one and the Parussos took full advantage. Their Vigna Munie is a magnificent Barolo with a deep, lustrous garnet-ruby colour and still youthful but already stylishly complex fruit aromas. The rich, powerful texture in the mouth reveals great balance and has a full, lingering finish. So the Parusso family has a Three Glass wine again. But it wasn't the only product to honour the cellar's name for the Barolo Mariondino is also beautifully made. The colour is a little forward but its oak-rich nose hints at spices and menthol, while the weight and structure on the palate are exemplary. A touch austere, perhaps, but those beefy tannins are out of the top drawer. The Barolo Vigna Rocche has a similarly rich colour but is less evolved. The nose is even more oak-dominated, with nuances of sweet spices coming through, and the palate is full-flavoured, rich in juicy fruit and lingering, if less well-structured than the Mariondino. The Piccole Vigne, the estate's second-label Barolo has nice presence in the mouth and is very drinkable. Other wines we tried include the Bricco Rovella '98, a blend of nebbiolo, barbera and cabernet sauvignon. Attractively mouth-filling, it displays excellent structure and sweet tannins, as well as a seductively lazy finish. Both the Barbera and the Dolcetto, aged in two and three-year-old barrels, are well worth their One Glass rating. All in all, a memorable vintage for the Parussos.

● Barbera d'Alba '98	▼	5
○ Langhe Bianco L'Aura '99	▼	4
● Barbera d'Alba '97	▼▼	5

● Barolo Bussia Vigna Munie '96	▼▼▼	6
● Barolo Bussia Vigna Rocche '96	▼▼	6
● Barolo Mariondino '96	▼▼	6
● Langhe Rosso Bricco Rovella '98	▼▼	5
● Barbera d'Alba Ornati '99	▼	4
● Barolo Piccole Vigne '96	▼	6
● Dolcetto d'Alba Piani Noci '99	▼	3
● Langhe Rosso Bricco Rovella '96	▽▽▽	5
● Barolo Bussia Vigna Munie '95	▽▽	6
● Barolo Bussia Vigna Rocche '94	▽▽	6
● Barolo Bussia Vigna Rocche '95	▽▽	6
○ Langhe Bianco Bricco Rovella '98	▽▽	5
● Langhe Rosso Bricco Rovella '97	▽▽	5
● Barolo Mariondino '95	▽	6

MONFORTE D'ALBA (CN)

PODERE ROCCHE DEI MANZONI
LOC. MANZONI SOPRANI, 3
12065 MONFORTE D'ALBA (CN)
TEL. 0173/78421

Valentino Migliorini has now built his property up to 40 hectares but above all, he has proved that he is now part of the Langhe landscape. His Barolo '96 Vigna Cappella di Santo Stefano is the child of a perfect marriage of terroir and cellar: austere, elegant and rich in fragrances of roses and violets that meld with complex notes of ripe fruit. The wood has yet to integrate but the structure promises that this will turn out to be a monster Barolo in a few years' time. Even today, it has all the style we are looking for in a Three Glass wine. The Barolo Vigna Big mingles raspberries, strawberries, thyme, sage, roast hazelnuts and vanilla on the nose while black cherry emerges on the soft, creamy palate. Next, the nose of the Vigna d'la Roul reveals menthol, progressing into plum jam and coffee. But it is the Quatr Nas '97 that shows just how good a winemaker Valentino is. Herbs, flowers and red berries are evident on the nose from entry and the palate releases all the power of nebbiolo. His stylish nebbiolo and barbera Bricco Manzoni '97 is a balanced, full-flavoured bottle and his Barbera Sorito Mosconi '98 offers an intriguing nose reminiscent of cherry jam. The fruit on the palate is almost big enough to chew while the lingering aromas are laced with characteristic barbera acidity. The Barbera La Cresta '98 is a decent product, but a notch or two below the previous wine. A lovely ruby hue and fragrances of cassis and mulberry introduce the Pinònero '96, leading into a warm, full-bodied palate. The Chardonnay L'Angelica '97 has attractive hedgerow aromas and impressive texture. It's a pity the oak is so assertive. Finally, the estate's sparklers include a rich, creamy, delicately fragranced Brut Zero '96 and the rather brighter Brut Riserva Elena '97, which has a more open bouquet.

MONFORTE D'ALBA (CN)

FERDINANDO PRINCIPIANO
VIA ALBA, 19
12065 MONFORTE D'ALBA (CN)
TEL. 0173/787158

"Modern" and "measured" are the adjectives that best describe Ferdinando Principiano's wines. He strives to bring out their varietal character without jeopardising balance. His most successful wine this year is the Barolo Boscareto '96. Rich garnet-ruby, shading into a paler orange at the edge, it successfully plays vibrant cassis and raspberry fruit off against oak-derived cream, toastiness and hay on a nose enticingly veined with a subtle vegetal note of dark leaves. There is plenty of juicy fruit on the palate. Serious structure gives the wine a slightly aloof air in the mouth but it mellows as it follows through beautifully to a finish that adds nuances of cocoa to the fruit. The Barolo Le Coste, of which the '96 is the first vintage, has a deep garnet-tinged colour, paling a little at the rim. Coffee, vanilla and cakes are still the prevailing notes on the nose but the fragrant, nicely expressed red berry fruit will make its presence felt before long. The entry in the mouth is a little heavy but the wine gains breadth in mid palate, underpinned by the extract, while the finish, its after-aroma redolent of menthol, fruit and toastiness, is well-managed and not without vigour. Another winner is the rich-hued Barbera La Romualda. Warm notes of ripe wild berries meld deliciously with sweet, oak-derived nuances on the nose. In the mouth, it has breadth, fullness of flavour and plenty of vigour, taking you through to a lingering finish that closes on hints of liquorice.

● Barolo Vigna		
Cappella di S. Stefano '96	♛♛♛	6
● Barbera d'Alba Sorito Mosconi '98	♛♛	5
● Barolo Vigna Big '96	♛♛	6
● Barolo Vigna d'la Roul '96	♛♛	6
● Bricco Manzoni '97	♛♛	6
○ Langhe Chardonnay L'Angelica '97	♛♛	6
● Langhe Rosso Pinònero '96	♛♛	6
● Langhe Rosso Quatr Nas '97	♛♛	6
○ Valentino Brut Ris. Elena '97	♛♛	5
○ Valentino Brut Zero Ris. '96	♛♛	6
● Barbera d'Alba		
Vigna La Cresta '98	♛	5
● Langhe Rosso Quatr Nas '96	♛♛♛	6

● Barbera d'Alba La Romualda '97	♛♛	5
● Barolo Boscareto '96	♛♛	6
● Barolo Le Coste '96	♛♛	6
● Barolo Boscareto '93	♛♛♛	6
● Barbera d'Alba La Romualda '96	♛♛	5
● Barbera d'Alba		
Pian Romualdo '95	♛♛	5
● Barolo Boscareto '94	♛♛	6
● Barolo Boscareto '95	♛♛	6

MONFORTE D'ALBA (CN) MONFORTE D'ALBA (CN)

FLAVIO RODDOLO
LOC. SANT'ANNA, 5
BRICCO APPIANI
12065 MONFORTE D'ALBA (CN)
TEL. 0173/78535

F.LLI SEGHESIO
FRAZ. CASTELLETTO, 20
12065 MONFORTE D'ALBA (CN)
TEL. 0173/78108

Flavio Roddolo, a winemaker of immense skill, has recently planted some new vineyards to bring his estate to six hectares, producing 18-20,000 bottles. For years, Flavio has been regaling wine-lovers with delights such as his Bricco Appiani '97, a monovarietal cabernet sauvignon of which only 1,300 bottles are available at the moment. However, some of the new rows will soon be coming onstream to boost the total. This close-knit garnet wine has an elegant, characterful nose that enhances its beautifully handled fruit, where the ripe notes of mulberry, cassis, sweet tobacco and green leaves are stylish and crystal clear over a basso continuo of wood-derived liquorice. "Concentration" is the first impression on the palate, which then progresses to reveal the fine tannins that back up the structure and sweep you through to a fruit and liquorice finish. There are 3,000 bottles available of the Barolo '96, a ruby wine with the characteristic intense, fruit-rich nebbiolo nose over sweeter notes from the superbly judged oak. The palate is broad, deep and soft, the wild berry fruit lingering lazily over the vibrant tannins. To round off, the Dolcetto '98 has good colour and a clean, complex nose where black cherry and cherry mingle with sweet spices. The palate has loads of weight and grip, which comes out in the attractively dry tannins of the consistent and satisfying finish.

The estate run by Aldo and Riccardo Seghesio is worth a visit even if you have no interest at all in wine. The setting is breathtakingly beautiful, the Serralunga valley providing a backdrop for the La Villa and Chiesa vineyards that lead gently down to a country chapel dedicated to Our Lady of the Assumption. The brothers began to bottle only in 1990 but their Barolo Vigneto La Villa '91, aged in the wood for 18 months, won Three Glasses in the 1996 Guide. Their nine hectares under vine will be expanded with a further two next year and currently they are producing about 55,000 bottles a year, including 21,000 of Barolo and 15,000 of Barbera. The Seghesio Barbera has always been notable for its skilful use of new barriques, where the wine stays for 18 months, acquiring great balance and enhancing its varietal personality. This year the panel did not award Three Glasses to any of the brothers' wines but the overall total of four Two Glass wines and one One Glass product is convincing proof of the range's quality. In particular, the muscular Barbera Vigneto della Chiesa is again very good, its luscious fruit melding faultlessly into the wood, and the austere Barolo La Villa reveals sweet tannins in the finish. Both are emblematic of the serious work done by an estate that remains firmly attached to its roots despite deserved commercial success. Also worth sampling are the Bouquet, a blend of merlot, cabernet sauvignon and nebbiolo grapes, and the Dolcetto Vigneto della Chiesa. The Barbera d'Alba '99 is more straightforward but still very drinkable.

● Barolo '96	❑❑	6
● Bricco Appiani '97	❑❑	6
● Dolcetto d'Alba Sup. '98	❑❑	3*
● Barbera d'Alba '97	❑❑	4
● Barolo '93	❑❑	6
● Bricco Appiani '96	❑❑	6
● Nebbiolo d'Alba '96	❑❑	4
● Nebbiolo d'Alba '97	❑❑	4
● Barolo '95	❑	6

● Barbera d'Alba Vigneto della Chiesa '98	❑❑	5
● Barolo Vigneto La Villa '96	❑❑	6
● Langhe Rosso Bouquet '98	❑❑	5
● Dolcetto d'Alba Vigneto della Chiesa '99	❑❑	3*
● Barbera d'Alba '99	❑	3
● Barbera d'Alba Vigneto della Chiesa '97	❑❑❑	5
● Barolo Vigneto La Villa '91	❑❑❑	6
● Barolo Vigneto La Villa '90	❑❑	6
● Barolo Vigneto La Villa '93	❑❑	6
● Barolo Vigneto La Villa '95	❑❑	6
● Bouquet '97	❑❑	5

MONLEALE (AL)

VIGNETI MASSA
P.ZZA G. CAPSONI, 10
15059 MONLEALE (AL)
TEL. 0131/80302

It's not difficult to see what Walter Massa is up to. When he started out, many thought he was just an obstinate romantic and we years ago called his estate a "beacon in the mists of Tortona". Now it has to be admitted that he has extended the boundaries of premium winemaking in Piedmont. Walter's non-too-secret agenda was to use barbera to make world-quality reds and leave timorasso, a grape other producers were to take up later on, as an exciting discovery. Walter's reds won their first Three Glass rating with the Colli Tortonesi-labelled Bigolla '98. And it's no flash in the pan for the Monreale '97 – the version we reviewed last year was the '96, wrongly reported as '97 – is in the same class. These are two genuinely interesting reds that express, albeit with contrasting approaches, the very highest levels of Barbera winemaking. The first is coal-black, potent and velvet-smooth while the second is tauter and more complex, with delicious spicy aromas and a mouth-filling palate. You don't have to be an expert to predict a great future for both. The Timorasso will definitely improve with bottle ageing but its nose already offers minerally notes with hints of camomile and lime blossom. The palate echoes the same aromas with plenty of body, grip and length. This year's surprise is the Muscaté, a 100 percent moscato wine, that reveals heady varietal aromas and a long, full-bodied palate that is sweet but never cloying. Walter's Cerretta was still a little closed when we sampled it but its traditional elegance and complexity were again in evidence. The Freisa Pietra del Gallo and Croatina Pertichetta are both good wines, while the Barbera Sentieri and Cortese Casareggio are well worth uncorking.

●	Colli Tortonesi Bigolla '98	▼▼▼	5
●	Colli Tortonesi Cerreta '98	▼▼	5
●	Colli Tortonesi Monleale '97	▼▼	5
○	Colli Tortonesi Timorasso Costa del Vento '98	▼▼	5
○	Muscaté '99	▼▼	3*
●	Colli Tortonesi Croatina Pertichetta '98	▼	4
●	Colli Tortonesi Freisa Pietra del Gallo '99	▼	4
●	Piemonte Barbera Sentieri '99	▼	3
○	Piemonte Cortese Casareggio '99	▼	3
●	Piemonte Barbera Campolungo Vivace '99		3
●	Colli Tortonesi Bigolla '97	▽▽	6
●	Colli Tortonesi Cerreta '97	▽▽	6
●	Colli Tortonesi Monleale '96	▽▽	5

MONTÀ D'ALBA (CN)

GIOVANNI ALMONDO
VIA S. ROCCO, 26
12052 MONTÀ D'ALBA (CN)
TEL. 0173/975256

Giovanni Almondo's Roero Superiore, dedicated to his father Domenico and only available in magnums, impressed our panel as one of the most distinctive Nebbiolos from the lefthand side of the Tanaro. The wine perfectly reflects the style of its maker, the mayor of Montà, mixing modern elements with tradition. New wood is not allowed to overwhelm the fruit and maceration on the skins is skilfully judged to achieve the right balance between the personality of the fruit and the character of the wine. A rich garnet-ruby hue tells you all you need to know about the structure and the nose mingles hints of hay, vanilla, pepper and red berries against a pleasant background note of balsam. The enticing front palate is soft, broadening out into a long, beautifully balanced finish where the austerity of the nebbiolo is offset by warm, rich alcohol in a veritable clash of the titans. The Roero Valdiana is rather predictable. The well-defined nose hints at vanilla, violets and raspberry while the soft, fluent palate concludes on a stylishly understated note of phenolics. The deep ruby of the Barbera Valbianchera is tinged with garnet, heralding an excitingly rich nose of cherry, mint, cocoa and cloves. A wine that offers good solid texture, its fruit and spice aromas linger nicely on the palate. The '99 version of the Arneis Bricco delle Ciliegie has lost a little of its usual breadth of palate. Straw-yellow with greenish highlights, it reveals elegant notes of banana, hedgerow and tomato leaf on the nose while the palate is clean, consistent and refreshing. The workhorse Arneis Vigne Sparse is also well up to standard. Its medium straw-yellow introduces notes of ripe apricot, spring flowers and a fresh-tasting finish with just a hint of bitterness.

●	Barbera d'Alba Valbianchera '98	▼▼	4
○	Roero Arneis Bricco delle Ciliegie '99	▼▼	4
●	Roero Bric Valdiana '98	▼▼	5
●	Roero Sup. Giovanni Almondo '97	▼▼	6
○	Roero Arneis Vigne Sparse '99	▼	3
●	Barbera d'Alba Valbianchera '97	▽▽	4
●	Roero Bric Valdiana '96	▽▽	5
●	Roero Bric Valdiana '97	▽▽	5

MONTEGROSSO D'ASTI (AT)

TENUTA LA MERIDIANA

Fraz. Tana, 5
14048 Montegrosso d'Asti (AT)
tel. 0141/956172 - 0141/956250

This year, the wines presented by Giampiero Bianco achieved distinctly good results, thanks in part to their outstanding vintages and even more so to Bianco's ability to get the best out of already excellent raw material. The estate owns 12 hectares of vines, eight planted to barbera, and annual production hovers around 85,000 bottles, most of it going for export. We particularly admired the Barbera d'Asti Bricco Sereno, an elegant interpretation of a wine that is coming increasingly to be regarded as one of Piedmont's - and indeed Italy's – major league reds. The entry on the nose is leisurely, then red berries emerge, together with hints of spices and pepper mingling with vanilla. In the mouth, the dominant impression is one of softness and balance, the extract and alcohol providing a sufficient counterpoint for the wine's acidity. The finish, too, is long and satisfying. The Rivaia, a 60-30-10 blend of nebbiolo, barbera and cabernet sauvignon, scored equally well. A red that strives for elegance rather than power, it offers a nose only slightly influenced by the cabernet, which nonetheless successfully enhances the colour of the two local varieties, combining to produce a very drinkable bottle in which fruit wins out over wood. The Barbera Le Gagie has no pretensions to complexity but does clearly express all the variety's characteristics. And to round off the tasting there was an onion skin-coloured Grignolino with lovely notes of wild roses on the nose and tannins to the fore in the mouth as well as the Malaga, a heady, deliciously sweet dessert wine.

● Barbera d'Asti Sup. Bricco Sereno '97	🍷🍷	4
● Monferrato Rosso Rivaia '97	🍷🍷	5
● Barbera d'Asti Le Gagie '98	🍷	3
● Grignolino d'Asti Vignamaestra '99	🍷	3
● Vigneto del Malaga '99	🍷	4
● Barbera d'Asti Sup. Bricco Sereno '95	🍸	4
● Barbera d'Asti Sup. Bricco Sereno '96	🍸	4
● Monferrato Rosso Rivaia '96	🍸	5

MONTELUPO ALBESE (CN)

CA' VIOLA

Via Langa, 17
12050 Montelupo Albese (CN)
tel. 0173/617570

In addition to running a small farm at Montelupo Albese with the help of Maurizio Anselma, Beppe Caviola is also one of the finest oenologists in the Langhe, or indeed the region. He collaborates with a number of Piedmontese estates and for several years has been casting his net further afield. The results speak for themselves, both at Montelupo Albese and elsewhere. As usual, "stunning" was the word that first sprang to mind at our tasting and this year the Bric du Luv has taken over as Ca' Viola's top wine from the magnificent Barturot, one of the finest Dolcettos around. It was Three Glasses to one of the Langhe's great reds, the Bric du Luv. Its deep, vibrant colour promises solid structure and firm extract while the nose is an object lesson in how to bring out the fruit without burying it in oak-derived toastiness (Beppe uses new and used barriques for ageing). The luscious, opulent palate is elegant as well as concentrated, filling the mouth with silky, sweet caresses that continue into the effortlessly long finish. Tannins and acidity perfectly enhance the massive structure. This has to be a world-beater. Thanks to this estate, Montelupo Albese, a tiny Langhe village whose territory lies outside the major DOC zones, has become a name recognised by wine-lovers everywhere and today is widely held to lead the field for the quality of its Dolcetto d'Alba. Beppe Caviola's Barturot was the forerunner of the category and is outstanding again this year, even though the panel did not award Three Glasses. Finally, his Rangone is one of the most convincing Pinot Neros in Italy and the Dolcetto Vilot turns out to be a satisfyingly fruit-rich bottle.

● Langhe Rosso Bric du Luv '98	🍷🍷🍷	6
● Dolcetto d'Alba Barturot '99	🍷🍷	4
● Dolcetto d'Alba Vilot '99	🍷🍷	3
● Langhe Rosso Rangone '98	🍷🍷	5
● Dolcetto d'Alba Barturot '96	🍸🍸🍸	4
● Dolcetto d'Alba Barturot '98	🍸🍸🍸	4
● Langhe Rosso Bric du Luv '95	🍸🍸🍸	5
● Langhe Rosso Bric du Luv '96	🍸🍸🍸	5
● Langhe Rosso Bric du Luv '97	🍸🍸	5
● Langhe Rosso Rangone '97	🍸🍸	5

MONTELUPO ALBESE (CN)

DESTEFANIS
VIA MORTIZZO, 8
12050 MONTELUPO ALBESE (CN)
TEL. 0173/617189

Marco Destefanis has amply confirmed the excellent impression he made last year, both for his ambition of making great Dolcettos and in his intention of emulating his consultant – and outstanding producer, Beppe Caviola. The Montelupo terroir and the estate's superb vine stock – many of the plants are very old – have enabled Marco to achieve his goal, starting with the base Dolcetto that accounts for about two thirds of production. Its intense ruby colour is tinged with purple and the nose has the trademark fresh Dolcetto notes of black berries and almond nuanced with chocolate. The lively, juicy palate reveals a long finish that already has good balance. This year, the estate rented the four-hectare Cascina Vigna vineyards at Alba. Some of the plots will be planted to Dolcetto to produce a major new selection. Unfortunately, the quality of this year's crop was compromised by a summer whirlwind. But there was no problem with the Monia Bassa '99, a few bottles of which are made from the estate's oldest, lowest-yielding plants. It's a Dolcetto that will stand comparison with any other. The colour is black and already almost impenetrable. Elegant and well-balanced on the nose, it is truly enormous on the palate, its mouth-filling softness discreetly masking the robust, close-knit tannins in the fruit-rich finish. While we wait for the few bottles of the new Barbera '99 selection to emerge from the barrel cellar, we tasted the admirable standard Barbera, whose delightful fruit is its most enticing feature. The '98 Nebbiolo, aged part in small and large oak barrels and part in stainless steel, was even better, proving to be an austere, well-managed red. And to conclude, the skilfully oaked Chardonnay is definitely appealing.

● Dolcetto d'Alba '99	🍷🍷	3*
● Dolcetto d'Alba Vigna Monia Bassa '99	🍷🍷	4
● Nebbiolo d'Alba '98	🍷🍷	4
● Barbera d'Alba '99	🍷	3
○ Langhe Chardonnay Barrique '99	🍷	3
● Dolcetto d'Alba Vigna Monia Bassa '98	🍸🍸	3
● Nebbiolo d'Alba '97	🍸🍸	4

MONTEU ROERO (CN)

CASCINA PELLERINO
FRAZ. S. ANNA
12040 MONTEU ROERO (CN)
TEL. 0173/978171 - 0173/979083

Cristian Bono, with the capable help of his father Luciano, produces a series of good-quality Roero wines that combine a touch of modernity with solidly focused typicity. It was the Roero Vicot '98 that stood out among the wines Cristian presented this year. Its garnet-tinged ruby colour pales a little at the rim while the nose mingles oak-derived sweet spices and hay with crisply defined fruit over a note of violets. The palate has nice weight, progressing firmly and sure-footedly through to an admirable lingering finish. The Barbera d'Alba Gran Madre '98 has a fairly deep colour tinged with orange at the rim while the notes of red berries and vanilla on the nose are laced with slight hints of pot pourri. The mouth-filling palate has attractive texture and is underpinned by adequate structure. Fruit and spices in the after-aroma provide the keynotes of a long, warm, dry finish that echoes the nose and palate precisely. Next, we tasted the excellent base Roero, which has a fairly deep, garnet-tinged ruby colour. There are notes of strawberry and quince jam over spices on the rather elegant nose. A touch rustic on the palate, it is not the broadest of wines but offers excellent texture and a reasonably long finish. Finally, there was One Glass for the Arneis Boneur. A pale straw-yellow in the glass, the nose comes up with hints of apples and pears over faint notes of spring flowers. The fresh-tasting, uncomplicated palate closes with a decently long, well-managed finish.

● Barbera d'Alba Sup. Gran Madre '98	🍷🍷	4
● Roero Vicot '98	🍷🍷	4
● Roero '98	🍷	3
○ Roero Arneis Boneur '99	🍷	3
● Barbera d'Alba Sup. Gran Madre '97	🍸🍸	4
● Roero Vicot '97	🍸🍸	4
○ Arneis Passito Poch ma Bon '97	🍸	4

MONTEU ROERO (CN)   MORSASCO (AL)

ANGELO NEGRO & FIGLI
CASCINA RIVERI
FRAZ. S. ANNA, 1
12040 MONTEU ROERO (CN)
TEL. 0173/90252

LA GUARDIA
REG. LA GUARDIA
15010 MORSASCO (AL)
TEL. 0144/73076

If we say "50 hectares under vine producing over 300,000 bottles a year" you'll get an idea of the size of this constantly expanding estate. Giovanni Negro, who is also mayor of Monteu Roero, runs things with the very competent assistance of his family. Son Gabriele looks after the vineyards while his brother Angelo is the wine technician and their sister Emanuela takes care of the commercial side. Giuseppe, Giovanni's youngest son, is still studying. Their Roero Superiore Sodisfà '97 has spent some time in the wood. It has a deep garnet colour, with a faintly orange rim. There is good balance of wood-derived vanilla and toastiness with the fruit on the nose while the solid, slightly austere palate loosens up in the very satisfying finish. Another wine that we liked was the Barbera Bric Bertu '98, whose garnet ruby holds firm almost to the edge of the glass. The balmy notes of rosemary and pine resin in the entry on the nose give way to wild berries and cocoa while the palate displays admirable texture, taking you smoothly through to a warm, leisurely finish. Next came the delightful and nicely balanced Perdaudin Passito. The deep amber colour tempts the nose with hints of apricots, dried figs, walnut and noble rot while the well-defined sweetness is kept in check by the vigorous thrust of its development on the palate. One Glass went to the Roero Prachiosso: Oak tends to get the upper hand on the nose but the tannins in the mouth integrate well into the overall balance. Of the two arneis-based wines, we thought the Gianat had the fuller-flavoured palate, as well as a distinctly intriguing nose of banana, peach, hedgerow and citron. In contrast, the Perdaudin has less concentration.

Set in its 30 hectares of vineyards, the Priarone estate is one of the Ovada area's landmarks. Superb winemaking terrain, outstandingly located plots, ability, hard work and sheer love of the land have prompted the family, among other things, to restore the 17th-century Villa Delfini and drive Graziella's activities as chair of the Consorzio Ovada. We would like to give a special mention to the two '98 Dolcettos we tasted, the Two Glass Bricco Riccardo and the Gamondino. The rich purple-red Bricco Riccardo has a red berry and elderflower nose leading in to a serious, flavoursome palate with loads of fine tannins that guarantee its future in the cellar. The Gamondino, too, has a close-knit colour, differing in its more mature aromas and sweeter, fruitier tannins. "Impressive" is the word for the Monferrato Rosso Sacro e Profano '98, a 65-35 blend of cabernet sauvignon and barbera that spent a full 18 months in small oak casks. Its dark ruby leads into a broad nose of berries, spices, dried roses and vanilla. The warm, mouth-filling front palate explodes in a concentration of fruit, backed up by mouth-watering acidity. The Barbera del Monferrato '98 Ornovo is also a delight, combining variety and terroir with skill. Great red berry fruit is underpinned by stunning acidity. Moving on to the attractive Chardonnay Butàs '99, partially fermented in new wood, we found nuances of citrus and tropical fruit on the nose, mirrored faithfully on the long and seriously good palate, which adds hazelnut for good measure. Altogether more approachable, but nice nevertheless, are the Gavi '99 Camghé and the '98 Il Bacio Dolcetto. Concluding the Priarone offerings this year was the '99 Figlio di un Bacco Minore, from the part-fermented must of brachetto grapes.

● Barbera d'Alba Bric Bertu '98	▼▼	4
○ Perdaudin Passito '97	▼▼	5
● Roero Sup. Sodisfà '97	▼▼	5
○ Roero Arneis Gianat '99	▼	4
● Roero Prachiosso '98	▼	4
○ Roero Arneis Perdaudin '99		4
● Barbera d'Alba Bric Bertu '97	♀♀	4
● Roero Sup. Sodisfà '96	♀♀	4
● Barbera d'Alba Nicolon '97	♀	3

● Barbera del M.to Ornovo '98	▼▼	4
● Dolcetto di Ovada Sup. Vigneto Bricco Riccardo '98	▼▼	4
● Monferrato Rosso Sacro e Profano '98	▼▼	5
○ Piemonte Chardonnay Butàs '99	▼▼	4
● Dolcetto di Ovada Il Bacio '98	▼	4
● Dolcetto di Ovada Sup. Il Gamondino '98	▼	4
○ Gavi Camghé '99	▼	4
● Figlio di un Bacco Minore '99		4
● Monferrato Rosso Sacro e Profano '97	♀♀	5
● Dolcetto di Ovada Sup. Vigneto Bricco Riccardo '97	♀	4

MURISENGO (AL)

MURISENGO (AL)

ISABELLA
VIA GIANOLI, 64
FRAZ. CORTERANZO
15020 MURISENGO (AL)
TEL. 0141/693000

LA ZUCCA
VIA SORINA, 53
FRAZ. SORINA
15020 MURISENGO (AL)
TEL. 011/8193343

Gabriele Calvo is the well-mannered and friendly owner of this lovely property at Murisengo, where he looks after the winemaking in person. The 18th-century building has marvellous cellars which today house new barriques alongside time-worn oak barrels. There are 50 hectares all told on the property and 27 of them are planted to vine. Once upon a time, this corner of Monferrato was covered in vineyards but since the Second World War, the move to the cities has led to a major drop in production. Moving over to this year's wines, we thought the Bric Stupui performed well. This Barbera is one quarter aged in new wood and walked away with Two well-merited Glasses. Its intense ruby releases notes of cherry, violet and understated vanilla while the fruit-rich palate has great structure and a characteristically tangy finish. The Barbera Truccone, aged in large barrels, is a simpler wine for everyday consumption at table. Bright ruby in colour, its red berry nose is echoed well on the palate and there is a lovely bitterish note in the finish. The Chardonnay has an unexpected hint of pear that brings to mind certain late-harvest wines. Good balance, great structure make it an excellent wine all round. Gabriele's Sobric, Freisa Vivace, is a translucent ruby with youthful purple highlights. On the nose, there are notes of strawberry, redcurrant and pepper while the very drinkable palate takes you through to a bitterish finish where the spices emerge again. Finally, the well-managed, instantly approachable Barbera Vivace Bricco Montemà is worth a mention.

Ester Accornero is a an enthusiastic, dynamic producer who has never lost her desire to learn. Her property lies on the border of the Casale and Asti parts of Monferrato. Currently, she has five hectares under vine with another four in the pipeline. This will enable her to diversify her range with a new wine, which will be a blend of local and international varieties. The estate's consultant winemaker is Donato Lanati. this year, we were particularly impressed by the Barbera Martizza, which came within a whisker of Three Glasses. Obtained from a careful selection of grapes grown on the property's core vineyards, it matures after fermentation for about 14 months in large barrels and small casks, only some of which are new. The result is a concentrated product, as can be seen from the impenetrable, almost black colour with its bright ruby rim. The close-textured aromas evoke cherry and bilberry as well as toastiness on the nose before the rich, warm, lingering palate fills your mouth. Ca' di Sru is the name of La Zucca's number one vineyard. Located near Murisengo, its 50-60 year-old vines enjoy a south-facing aspect. Fruit from Ca' di Sru goes into the Barbera 'l Sulì, vinified exclusively in stainless steel. Less ambitious and less demanding than the previous product, Barbera 'l Sulì is a reasonably intense ruby in colour, releasing notes of walnut, cherry and fig on the nose, followed by an attractive if unsophisticated palate.

● Barbera d'Asti Bric Stupui '98	▼▼	4
● Barbera d'Asti Truccone '98	▼	3
● Monferrato Freisa Vivace Sobric '99	▼	3
○ Piemonte Chardonnay '97	▼	4
● Barbera del M.to Vivace Bricco Montemà '99		3
● Barbera d'Asti Bric Stupui '97	▽▽	4
● Barbera d'Asti Truccone '97	▽	3

● Barbera d'Asti Martizza '98	▼▼	5
● Barbera d'Asti 'l Sulì '98	▼	4
● Barbera del M.to Martizza '97	▽▽	5
● Barbera del M.to 'l Sulì '97	▽	4

NEIVE (CN)

NEIVE (CN)

PIERO BUSSO
VIA ALBESANI, 8
12057 NEIVE (CN)
TEL. 0173/67156

CASCINA VANO
VIA RIVETTI, 9
12057 NEIVE (CN)
TEL. 0173/677705 - 0173/67263

Piero Busso, his wife Lucia, and their son, Pierguido, currently studying at Alba to qualify as a wine technician, run a property that produces about 25-30,000 bottles a year from just under seven hectares of vineyards, of which three are owned by the family. Barbaresco accounts for about half of their output and comes in two versions, the Bricco Mondino and the Vigna Borgese. Bricco Mondino, aged in two-year-old wood, has a vibrant garnet-ruby colour with a narrowish orange rim. The intriguing nose offers aromas of jam, mint and cream over enticing nuances of leather and dry earth. There is plenty of rich fruit in the mouth, where the slightly nervous front palate moves on sure-footedly, its vigorous tannins enhancing the long, cocoa-nuanced finish. Vigna Borgese ages in large barrels and has a slightly less intense colour than the Bricco Mondino. The nose is broad and firm, yielding aromas of raspberry, morello cherry and almond complemented by pepper and dried herbs. Clean and forthright in the mouth, it holds its balance through to the leisurely finish; redolent of cocoa over fruit. A thoroughbred nebbiolo-based wine, its sheer wealth of aromas and superb balance earned it Three Glasses from the panel. The Dolcetto Vigna Majano has a vibrant colour and a generous range of fruit notes on the nose, blending raspberry, morello cherry and peach with fleeting hints of mint and macaroon. The palate has admirable structure and the finish satisfies. Bianco di Busso is straw-yellow in the glass with elegant golden highlights. Its broad nose alternates vanilla, tomato leaf, peach and butter over discreet hints of super-ripeness. Full-flavoured and broad on the palate, it develops consistently through to the vigorous, vegetable and spice-themed finish.

Beppe Rivetti and his son, Bruno, tend about eight hectares of vines, most of which lie within the municipal boundaries of Nieve. Their very contemporary winemaking style involves fairly short maceration and skilful use of new wood. In this way, they turn out a range that is noteworthy for its rich, juicy fruit and irresistible personality. From the estate's offerings this year, it was the Barbera '98 that caught the panel's eye, with its deep garnet edged by a close-knit, youthful rim. Crisp, clean, strawberry and mulberry fruit mingles superbly on the nose with intriguingly complex pepper, green leaves and steak tartare. The weight in the mouth is obvious on entry and the palate continues well-sustained by fine tannins that give volume to the long, satisfying finish of elegantly balanced fruit and spice. The Langhe Rosso Duetto is another fine wine. Its garnet-tinged ruby, shading into purple at the rim, ushers in a broad nose that creeps up on you with lovely nuances of mulberry, strawberry, cocoa and coffee over attractive vegetal notes of green leaves. Concentrated yet soft on the palate, it builds up beautifully to a long, liquorice-themed finish. We were less convinced by the '97 Barbaresco. Quite honestly, we were looking for more from the vintage.

●	Barbaresco Vigna Borgese '97	❢❢❢	6
●	Barbaresco Bricco Mondino '97	❢❢	6
●	Dolcetto d'Alba Vigna Majano '99	❢❢	3*
○	Langhe Bianco di Busso '98	❢❢	4
●	Barbaresco Vigna Borgese '95	♈♈	5
●	Barbaresco Vigna Borgese '96	♈♈	5
●	Barbera d'Alba Vigna Majano '97	♈♈	4
●	Barbaresco Bricco Mondino '96	♈	5

●	Barbaresco '97	❢❢	5
●	Barbera d'Alba '98	❢❢	4
●	Langhe Rosso Duetto '98	❢❢	4
●	Barbaresco '96	♈♈	5
●	Barbera d'Alba '97	♈♈	4

NEIVE (CN)

NEIVE (CN)

F.LLI CIGLIUTI
VIA SERRABOELLA, 17
12057 NEIVE (CN)
TEL. 0173/677185

FONTANABIANCA
FRAZ. BORDINI, 15
12057 NEIVE (CN)
TEL. 0173/67195

For the umpteenth time, Renato Cigliuti has come up with a great range of wines but then the fruit comes from Serraboella, a superb subzone near the famous Bricco di Nieve. Of course, the producer's expert hand is also obvious in the reliability of these wines, not to mention their great personality. In the glass, the Rosso Bricco Serra '98 has a youthful rim around its intense colour. The irresistibly harmonious nose focuses on very ripe wild berries, cocoa, dark leaves and aromatic wood, notably cedar. Full-flavoured and very compact in the mouth, its muscular fine tannins set the pace for a broad, solid follow-through into a lingering finish that builds up to a thrillingly dynamic finish. Next came the intensely garnet-hued Barbera d'Alba Serraboella '98, with a nicely judged nose of mulberry and cherry combined with alluring hints of green leaves, autumn leaves and mint to give complexity to the whole. The beefy texture and sheer power of the structure come through clearly on the palate. It holds up well on the palate, with a nice breadth of aroma, while the ample finish echoes the aromas on the nose. Renato's Barbaresco '97 has a concentrated garnet-ruby colour with a firm rim. To follow, there is a delightfully broad nose elegantly proposing notes of red berry jam, toastiness, hay and violets, all laced with warm nuances of chocolate. On the palate, it has loads of juicy fruit, although the progression is rendered slightly austere by the forthright tannins that give the leisurely finish plenty of welcome grip. The well-merited Three Glasses this time are for a wine that is only slightly softer and full-flavoured than the top-scoring '96. And to round off, the Dolcetto d'Alba, also from the Serraboella vineyard, is as good as ever.

The Pola and Ferro families, who own this property at Bordini near Neive, have shown they have what it takes. Since they were first included in the Guide two years, they have been constantly improving quality. The estate turns out about 50,000 bottles a year from its 12 hectares under vine, two of which are rented. All the vineyards are located within the municipal boundaries of Neive. The '97 vintage produced such awesome nebbiolo fruit that the two families decided not to release a second-label Barbaresco but instead limited production to 12,000 bottles of an excellent Sorì Burdin. Its intense garnet hue is edged by the narrowest of rims, offering a wonderfully balanced nose of clean, concentrated fruit that highlights crisp notes of raspberry and cherry over an intricate basso continuo of confectioner's cream, cocoa and dry flowers. The confident palate flaunts its rich pulp right from the attack, revealing very fine tannins and a long finish centred on mint and cocoa. You really must try the Fontanabianca Barbera d'Alba. Its profound and almost impenetrable colour offers a fruit-rich nose with hints of spice in the finish while the palate has lovely concentration and balance. The Dolcetto Bordini '99 is reasonably intense in colour and sweet and fruity on the nose, which yields up stylishly fragrant notes of black berries and almond paste. There is plenty of weight in the front palate before the nose is mirrored attractively in the long, tannic finish. Medium straw-yellow in the glass, the Arneis parades aromas of apple and spring flowers tinged with notes of super-ripeness before the soft, silky palate reveals reasonable vigour in a tidy, well-balanced whole.

● Barbaresco Serraboella '97	￥￥￥	6
● Barbera d'Alba Serraboella '98	￥￥	4
● Langhe Rosso Bricco Serra '98	￥￥	6
● Dolcetto d'Alba Serraboella '99	￥	3
● Barbaresco Serraboella '90	￥￥￥	6
● Barbaresco Serraboella '96	￥￥￥	6
● Barbaresco Serraboella '93	￥￥	6
● Barbaresco Serraboella '95	￥￥	6
● Barbera d'Alba Serraboella '97	￥￥	4
● Langhe Rosso Bricco Serra '97	￥￥	6
● Langhe Rosso Bricco Serra '96	￥	6

● Barbaresco Sorì Burdin '97	￥￥	6
● Barbera d'Alba '99	￥￥	4
● Dolcetto d'Alba Bordini '99	￥	3
○ Langhe Arneis '99	￥	3
● Barbaresco '96	￥￥	5
● Barbaresco Sorì Burdin '95	￥￥	5
● Barbaresco Sorì Burdin '96	￥￥	5

NEIVE (CN)

NEIVE (CN)

GASTALDI
VIA ALBESANI, 20
12057 NEIVE (CN)
TEL. 0173/677400

BRUNO GIACOSA
VIA XX SETTEMBRE, 52
12057 NEIVE (CN)
TEL. 0173/67027

Dino Gastaldi is one of the most representative of the new generation of producers. He is so self-critical that although he has 15 hectares under vine at Rodello (planted to chardonnay, sauvignon and dolcetto), Neive and Monforte, he bottles only the very best of his wine, releasing about 35,000 units a year. The Bianco Gastaldi, a blend of 80 percent sauvignon with 20 percent chardonnay, is fermented and aged in stainless steel, with extended fine lees contact. One of the finest whites you will find in Piedmont, it has a rich colour and an intense, complex nose of ripe fruit and honey complemented by the freshness of the sauvignon. The full-flavoured buttery palate has plenty of finesse and balance, which are sustained through to the long finish. You can see straight away that the Chardonnay has less complexity and maturity. Its attractive minerally notes are still a little harsh but the long, elegant finish bodes well for the future. Next came the truly admirable Moriolo, also aged in stainless steel. The rich nose conjures up mature, elegant chocolate, mulberry and strawberry before the palate delights you with its sophisticated harmony of fruit, tannins and acidity. Gastaldi's new wine is from the Castlè vineyard at Monforte. The nebbiolo-based Rosso Castlè is an austere and thoroughly aristocratic wine aged in French oak that regales the nose with hints of fruit and spices nuanced with balsam. For the time being, close-knit, powerful tannins keep the delicious fruit under wraps. This year, Dino did not present any of his reds from Neive. The Barbaresco '96 will be tasted in time for the next edition of the Guide while – alas – the Rosso Gastaldi is only released after genuinely exceptional vintages (the last version was the '93).

Bruno Giacosa is legendary figure in Langhe winemaking and this time round, he has presented an extensive range of high-profile bottles. Top of the class is a magnificent Barolo Falletto di Serralunga '96 that inspires a passionate response while faithfully interpreting its terroir. This is tradition with a capital "T". The aromas of still-latent violets, mulberries and red berries are austere and invitingly complex. In the mouth, the broad, vibrantly intense palate is quite impeccable. It is a Barolo that has remained absolutely true the traditional style yet manages to be readier-to-drink and better-balanced than previous versions. The blue-blooded tannins are lively but well under control and the finish triumphantly marries power with subtlety. Three effortless Glasses for one of Piedmont's most skilled and respected winemakers. Bruno's Barbaresco Santo Stefano '97 is also out of the top drawer. The pale garnet colour has hints of orange on the rim. The nose is endlessly rich and leads into a full, firmly textured palate. Giacosa has been making Arneis consistently well for ages and his Roero Arneis '99 is easily one of the best in its class. Its deep straw-yellow introduces an enticingly fresh-tasting wine whose palate faithfully mirrors the nose before giving way to a fruity banana and peach finish. The Dolcetto d'Alba Basarin di Neive '99 is well-made and appealing. It offers a chewy palate and well-defined flavour that is inevitably characterised for the time being by the excesses of youth. Finally, the Spumante Extra Brut '96, obtained from pinot nero grapes grown in the Oltrepò Pavese, wasn't quite up to past heights and neither was the Nebbiolo d'Alba Valmaggiore '98.

● Dolcetto d'Alba Moriolo '99	♟♟	4
○ Langhe Bianco '98	♟♟	5
● Langhe Rosso Castlè '96	♟♟	6
○ Langhe Chardonnay '98	♟	5
● Dolcetto d'Alba Sup.		
Moriolo '90	♟♟♟	5
● Gastaldi Rosso '89	♟♟♟	6
● Gastaldi Rosso '88	♟♟♟	6
● Gastaldi Rosso '93	♟♟	6
○ Langhe Bianco '97	♟♟	5
● Barbaresco '95	♟	6

● Barolo Falletto '96	♟♟♟	6
● Barbaresco S. Stefano '97	♟♟	6
○ Roero Arneis '99	♟♟	4
● Dolcetto d'Alba Basarin '99	♟	4
● Nebbiolo d'Alba Valmaggiore '98		5
● Barolo Collina Rionda '82	♟♟♟	6
● Barolo Rocche di Castiglione		
Falletto '85	♟♟♟	6
● Barbaresco S. Stefano '95	♟♟	6
● Barbaresco S. Stefano '96	♟♟	6
● Barolo Collina Rionda '93	♟♟	6
● Barolo Falletto '93	♟♟	6
● Barolo Falletto '95	♟♟	6

NEIVE (CN)

NEIVE (CN)

F.LLI GIACOSA
VIA XX SETTEMBRE, 64
12057 NEIVE (CN)
TEL. 0173/67013

UGO LEQUIO
VIA DEL MOLINO, 10
12057 NEIVE (CN)
TEL. 0173/677224

The range offered by this winery, run by Valerio and Silverio Giacosa with their respective sons, Maurizio and Paolo, is very reliable. Their Barolo Vigna Mandorlo and Barbaresco Rio Sordo both earned excellent marks, the Barolo beating out its stablemate by a hair. Its close-knit garnet ruby has a firm, narrow rim of orange. The nose opens unhurriedly to reveal delightfully clean fruit where nuances of redcurrant, raspberry, liquorice, autumn leaves and menthol come together in a enthralling chorus. On the slightly austere palate, the good texture holds up well, leading into a never-ending finish that closes on notes of liquorice and cocoa. Its partner, the Barbaresco Rio Sordo '97 has a fine ruby colour that pales only slightly at the rim. Aromas of strawberry jam, dry flowers, aromatic herbs and leather tempt you into a fairly austere palate whose up-front tannins are never aggressive. In the finish, lip-smacking hints of chocolate emerge over a balmy keynote. We liked the two Chardonnays, the cask-conditioned Ca' Lunga and the unpretentious, well-managed Roera. Ca' Lunga is a lustrous straw-yellow and has a fairly stylish nose of apple, apricot and sweet spices. There's nice weight on the palate and the wood is a little too apparent in the finish. The vibrant colour of the Roera offers up the characteristic varietal aromas of banana, hazelnut and apple while the clean, uncomplicated palate has a finish that perhaps lacks length but satisfies to the hilt. Finally, there was One Glass for the Rosso Connubio, a blend of barbera, nebbiolo and pinot nero in equal proportions.

Since 1986, Ugo Lequio has been vinifying at his well-equipped cellar the grapes he buys in mainly from the Gallina cru. He presented us with a top-quality Barbera and an equally good Barbaresco, both in a whistle-clean style firmly rooted in the Langhe tradition. His Barbera d'Alba Gallina '98 has a firm ruby colour with a compact purple rim, heralding an entrancingly broad nose that opens in the glass with an aristocratic lack of hurry. Crisp strawberry and cherry fruit mingles with notes of fresh-baked cakes and cocoa powder, all laced with an evocative minerally note of rain-soaked earth. The front palate makes it clear that this is a feather-soft wine with big structure and serious texture to match. It moves on to a discreet, nicely judged accompaniment of tannins before the endless finish slowly dies away in a cascade of fruit fragrances. In contrast, the Barbaresco Gallina '97 is ruby shading into garnet, with a narrow orange rim while its crystal-clear, beautifully orchestrated nose reveals all the finesse of the great Barbaresco tradition. The clear notes of red berry preserve and violets meld seamlessly with the notes of earth, leather and spices that add complexity to the nose. The entry makes no secret of the palate's rich texture and weight. Then the wine acquires austerity from the nebbiolo's tannins in the mid palate before the long, tactile finish elegantly mirrors the nose, modulating the aromas with stylish notes of cocoa. Finally, the '99 Arneis is pleasant and drinkable.

● Barbaresco Rio Sordo '97	♟♟	6
● Barolo Vigna Mandorlo '96	♟♟	6
○ Langhe Chardonnay Ca' Lunga '98	♟	4
○ Langhe Chardonnay Roera '99	♟	3
● Langhe Rosso Connubio '97	♟	4
● Barbaresco Rio Sordo '95	♟♟	6
● Barbaresco Rio Sordo '96	♟♟	6
● Barolo Vigna Mandorlo '95	♟♟	6
● Barbera d'Alba Maria Gioana '97	♟	4
● Barolo Bussia '95	♟	6

● Barbaresco Gallina '97	♟♟	6
● Barbera d'Alba Gallina '98	♟♟	4
○ Langhe Arneis '99	♟	4
● Barbaresco Gallina '96	♟♟	5
● Barbera d'Alba Gallina '97	♟♟	4

NEIVE (CN)

NEIVE (CN)

PAITIN
VIA SERRABOELLA, 20
12057 NEIVE (CN)
TEL. 0173/67343

SOTTIMANO
LOC. COTTÀ, 21
12057 NEIVE (CN)
TEL. 0173/635186

The wines from this lovely estate at Nieve are stunners. By combining modernity with tradition – their barrique cellars date from the 16th century – the Pasquero Elia family have reached the goals they set out to achieve. In contrast with past vintages, their Campolive Bianco, from sauvignon and chardonnay, was vinified in stainless steel and has shed its toasty vanilla aromas to leave more scope for its fruit and fresh notes of balsam and spices. The Dolcetto d'Alba Sorì Paitin comes up with leisurely alcohol-rich aromas and hints of red berries and mulberry. In fact, it's a perfect example of the variety's potential. The brilliant ruby colour of the Barbera Serra Boella introduces outstandingly well-defined aromas and a temptingly drinkable palate. But the Barbera Campolive '98 is rather more interesting and complex. The best-ever version of the wine, it has a ruby hue and an elegant nose that foregrounds sage and mint. Full-flavoured in the mouth, it makes up what it lacks in power in a stunningly well-balanced palate. The palish Barbaresco Sorì Paitin shades into garnet at the rim while the nose sets out notes of spices, liquorice and tobacco. The palate mirrors the nose well, following through delightfully to a warm, nicely balanced finish on the back of sweet silky tannins. All in all, a fine wine that thoroughly deserved its Three Glasses. There is class and personality a-plenty in the Langhe Paitin '98, obtained from barrique-aged nebbiolo, barbera, cabernet sauvignon and syrah. You can see it means business from the intense, ruby colour and a many-faceted nose that makes no secret of its aromas. On the palate, it is sure-footed and confident, as it should be with its soft tannins and irresistibly soft, well-rounded flavour. The exuberant finish lingers delightfully.

Rino and Andrea Sottimano have increased production slightly to just under 60,000 bottles this year, obtained from the property's ten hectares under vine. All of the many wines they presented were at the top of their respective categories. We'll start with the Dolcetto Bric del Salto. It is a better product than the Cottà, which suffers from poorly defined aromas, offering instead a complex, potent nose, serious structure and admirable length. The Barbera Pairolero is still a little closed on the nose so the aromas of bilberry, cherry and vanilla will need time to come through but the palate is luscious, unveiling fruit, decent acidity, tannins and notes of new wood. The Sottimano Brachetto Secco Maté is a precise expression of the entire taste profile of its variety but the lion's share of the range is reserved, as usual, for Barbaresco, which the winery proposes in four different, but equally impressive, selections. The best this year is the Cottà Vigna Brichet. It has all the austerity of a great Langhe red wine, warm and pervasive on the nose with the trademark aromas of rose, berry fruit and liquorice while the tannins on the palate are silky smooth, albeit still slightly astringent given the wine's youth. The finish is quite incredibly, awesomely long, making this one of the very finest wines in its category. The Three Glass rating was a mere formality. The other Sottimano Barbarescos scored slightly lower but are nonetheless very characterful wines. The Currà Vigna Masué is more open on the nose and softer on the palate, the Pajoré Vigna Lunetta is mouth-filling and very stylish, and the Fausoni Vigna del Salto stands out for its balmy nuances and more insistent tannins. But if you didn't know, you wouldn't guess that any of them had seen new wood.

● Barbaresco Sorì Paitin '97	♟♟♟	6
● Barbera d'Alba Campolive '98	♟♟	5
○ Campolive Bianco '98	♟♟	4
● Dolcetto d'Alba Sorì Paitin '99	♟♟	3*
● Langhe Paitin '98	♟♟	5
● Barbera d'Alba Serra Boella '98	♟	4
● Barbaresco Sorì Paitin '95	♟♟♟	6
● Langhe Paitin '97	♟♟♟	5
● Barbaresco Sorì Paitin '96	♟♟	6
● Langhe Paitin '96	♟♟	5

● Barbaresco Cottà		
Vigna Brichet '97	♟♟♟	6
● Barbaresco Currà Vigna Masué '97	♟♟	6
● Barbaresco Fausoni		
Vigna del Salto '97	♟♟	6
● Barbaresco Pajoré		
Vigna Lunetta '97	♟♟	6
● Barbera d'Alba Pairolero '98	♟♟	5
● Dolcetto d'Alba Bric del Salto '99	♟♟	3*
● Dolcetto d'Alba Cottà '99	♟	3
● Maté '99	♟	3
● Barbaresco Fausoni		
Vigna del Salto '96	♟♟♟	6
● Barbaresco Cottà Vigna Brichet '96	♟♟	5
● Barbaresco Currà Vigna Masué '96	♟♟	5

NEVIGLIE (CN)

NIZZA M.TO (AT)

F.LLI BERA
CASCINA PALAZZO, 12
12050 NEVIGLIE (CN)
TEL. 0173/630194

BERSANO
P.ZZA DANTE, 21
14049 NIZZA M.TO (AT)
TEL. 0141/720211

Walter Brera is a tireless champion of the territory and the DOC wines of the area he lives in, especially Moscato d'Asti. Walter's contributions to the solution of Moscato d'Asti-related problems are increasingly significant, especially since he was elected mayor of Neviglie, many of whose residents make their living from the variety. With barbera, it is the most widely cultivated vine type in the area. In addition, Walter has diversified his range, which still comprises mostly Moscato and Asti wines, by expanding his reds. In only a few years, he has managed to make his mark with an excellent Langhe Rosso selection. Sassisto, a 75-25 blend of barbera and nebbiolo, has a dark, close-knit colour and a nose that mingles sweet notes of ripe fruit with toasty oak that is never too assertive. In the mouth, the full, well-rounded flavour is delightful. We found the same qualities in Walter's '98 Barbera d'Alba Superiore, a dense, palate-thrilling wine that has even better balance than its stablemate. The Barbera d'Alba '98 is a less complex but eminently drinkable wine that allows the grape's varietal characteristics to shine through. There was a slight lack of vigour about the Langhe Nebbiolo '96 but the Dolcetto has an attractive note of bitter almonds in the finish. Best of the sweet wines, in our opinion, was Walter's Moscato d'Asti Su Reimond, with its golden hue and almost super-ripe aromas of apricot and peach. The buttery, oily palate is a stunner, finishing on a note of camomile. Bera is one of the few small producers to make his own Asti. Our tasters found the 2000 selection to be an alluring product with notes of resin on the nose and a sweet but not cloying palate. The Bera Brut '93 was past its best but to round off this year's offerings, there was a fresh, fruity Moscato d'Asti Cascina Palazzo.

Bersano is an excellent example of how commitment and shrewd management policies can combine high-volume production with outstanding quality and this year, the range is as good as ever. The top-notch in-house professionals, Nico Conta, Piersandro Sandri, Filippo Mobrici and Massimiliano Diotto, can call on the consultancy services of leading oenologist, Giuliano Noè, and the company is firmly oriented towards the ongoing enhancement of quality, with premium-quality reds as well-as whites. Let's start with Barbera d'Asti, the flagship Bersano product, and specifically with the Gerenala '98. Its spice-rich nose with clear notes of ripe fruit easily earned it Two Glasses. The palate picks up the same attractive aromas in a long, elegant progression through to the finish. The Cremosina '98, aged for 12 months in large oak casks, is mouth-filling, releasing intense notes of fruit on a meaty, well-balanced and whistle-clean palate. Next in line is the well-managed Pomona '98, a blend of cabernet and barbera in equal proportions. Delicate grassy nuances and red berry preserve on the nose lead into an enfolding palate with a soft finish. Another Two Glass product was the irresistibly elegant Gavi Marchese Raggio '99, with its aromas of flowers and characteristic but discreetly restrained acidity. Don't snub the Brachetto d'Acqui Castelgaro '99, either, even though its attractive notes of roses are let down by a slight lack of body. And finally, the Albaluce '98 is an Erbaluce di Caluso from a vineyard overlooking the lake at Viverone. It has style, appeal and a note of roasted hazelnuts on the nose.

● Barbera d'Alba Sup. '98	🍷🍷	3*
● Langhe Sassisto '97	🍷🍷	4
○ Moscato d'Asti Su Reimond '99	🍷🍷	3*
○ Asti Cascina Palazzo Sel. 2000 '99	🍷	3
● Barbera d'Alba '98	🍷	3
● Langhe Nebbiolo '96	🍷	5
○ Moscato d'Asti Cascina Palazzo '99	🍷	3
○ Bera Brut '93		5
● Dolcetto d'Alba '99		3
● Barbera d'Alba '97	🍷🍷	3
● Langhe Sassisto '96	🍷🍷	4

● Barbera d'Asti Cremosina '98	🍷🍷	5
● Barbera d'Asti Sup. Generala '98	🍷🍷	6
○ Gavi del Comune di Gavi Marchese Raggio '99	🍷🍷	4
● Monferrato Pomona '98	🍷🍷	6
● Brachetto d'Acqui Castelgaro '99	🍷	4
○ Erbaluce di Caluso Albaluce '98	🍷	5
● Barbera d'Asti Sup. Generala '97	🍷🍷🍷	6
● Barbera d'Asti Sup. Generala '96	🍷🍷	6
● Monferrato Pomona '97	🍷🍷	6
● Barbera d'Asti Cremosina '97	🍷	4
● Pomona '96	🍷	6

NIZZA M.TO (AT)

★ Cascina La Barbatella
S.da Annunziata, 55
14049 Nizza M.to (AT)
TEL. 0141/701434

Yet again this year, Angelo Sonvico and Giuliano Noè have taken full advantage of a series of excellent vintages to make some very superior wines. Their Barbera La Vigna dell'Angelo and Sonvico have been released in new versions that demonstrate the skill of a small winery that has made a decisive contribution to the resurgence of premium-quality winemaking in Monferrato. Not content with this success, Angel and Giuliano have announced that the '99 vintage will herald the arrival of new red. The barbera, cabernet sauvignon and pinot nero-based wine is bound to be a stunner. But now for this year's wines. The Noè white has a fine yellow colour with greenish highlights, leading into a pleasant nose and a delicate palate of fruit backed up by refreshing acidity. The second-label Barbera is purplish ruby in the glass while nose and palate are utterly true to barbera type. As ever, the Vigna dell'Angelo is one of the best bottles of Barbera d'Asti around. Its deep, dark ruby red shades into purple, introducing a nose of wild berries, vanilla, cocoa and coffee. Alluringly soft on the palate, it keeps the characteristic barbera acidity well under control with a subtle yet muscular structure that enhances the aromas in the mouth. Length and balance are beyond reproach. The impressively dense colour of the Sonvico '98 is followed up by a veritable explosion of mulberry, redcurrant, pepper and cocoa on the nose. There is no mistaking the contribution of new wood but it exalts rather than masks the vegetal aromas, complementing them with toasty oak and vanilla. In the mouth it has power, polish and plenty of flesh, showing how much potential there is in this partnership of cabernet sauvignon and barbera. There was no denying Three Glasses to either Sonvico or Vigna dell'Angelo.

NIZZA M.TO (AT)

Scarpa - Antica Casa Vinicola
Via Montegrappa, 6
14049 Nizza M.to (AT)
TEL. 0141/721331

Wine fads, fashions and even sea changes have never altered Mario Pesce's philosophy. For Mario, a great wine never drinks well when young. A well-organized traditionalist who shuns barriques in favour of large casks, Mario insists on extended maturing in the wood followed by years of bottle ageing. A sprightly 70-odd years old, Pesce has always resisted the trend towards the globalization of taste, defending the use of local vine types. We have already reviewed his '94 La Freisa Selva di Moirano selection but according to Mario, it is only now ready to be uncorked. Indeed, this thrillingly lively, fresh-tasting bottle is enjoying an exciting phase of development. Liquorice on the palate and crisp raspberry aromas on the nose make it a tempting proposition. The Dolcetto d'Acqui La Selva di Moirano '98 is also a very convincing red but we had to knock a mark or two off for the rather over-abundant acidity. However, Mario's rich-hued Grignolino San Defendente '98 offers robust tannins to underpin its surprising punch. As usual, the Brachetto Secco and the now hard-to-find Rouchet were exciting. The Brachetto, fewer than 2,000 bottles of which are made, is a garnet-coloured wine to serve with strawberries or fruit tart. The nose is redolent of the characteristic strawberries and the finish, although a touch powdery, has decent balance. The entrancing Rouchet mingles notes of balsam and rose petals with a bitterish twist in the tail while of the two acidity-rich Barberas, we preferred the more discreet and approachable La Bogliona '97 to the Bricchi di Castelrocchero. The new Barolos and Barbarescos will see the light of day in couple of years. For the time being, they rest peacefully in Pesce's cellars at Nizza Monferrato with other prestigious vintages from the recent and distant past.

● Barbera d'Asti Sup.		
La Vigna dell'Angelo '98	♟♟♟	6
● Monferrato Rosso Sonvico '98	♟♟♟	6
● Barbera d'Asti La Barbatella '99	♟♟	4
O Monferrato Bianco Noè '99	♟	4
● Barbera d'Asti Sup.		
La Vigna dell'Angelo '96	♟♟♟	6
● La Vigna di Sonvico '90	♟♟♟	6
● La Vigna di Sonvico '93	♟♟♟	6
● La Vigna di Sonvico '94	♟♟♟	6
● La Vigna di Sonvico '95	♟♟♟	6
● La Vigna di Sonvico '96	♟♟♟	6
● Monferrato Rosso Sonvico '97	♟♟♟	6
● Barbera d'Asti Sup.		
La Vigna dell'Angelo '97	♟♟	6

● Barbera d'Asti Sup.		
La Bogliona '97	♟♟	6
● Barbera d'Asti Sup.		
I Bricchi di Castelrocchero '97	♟	6
● Brachetto Secco La Selva di Moirano '99	♟	6
● Dolcetto d'Acqui La Selva di Moirano '98	♟	5
● Grignolino d'Asti S. Defendente '98	♟	5
● Rouchet Bricco Rosa '99	♟	6
● Rouchet Bricco Rosa '90	♟♟♟	6
● Barbera d'Asti Sup. La Bogliona '95	♟♟	6
● Barolo Tettimora '88	♟♟	6
● Rouchet Bricco Rosa '98	♟♟	6
● Barbera d'Asti Sup.		
I Bricchi di Castelrocchero '96	♟	5
● Barbera d'Asti Sup. La Bogliona '96	♟	6

NIZZA M.TO (AT)

FRANCO E MARIO SCRIMAGLIO
VIA ALESSANDRIA, 67
14049 NIZZA M.TO (AT)
TEL. 0141/721385 - 0141/727052

NOVELLO (CN)

ELVIO COGNO
LOC. RAVERA, 2
12060 NOVELLO (CN)
TEL. 0173/744006

The Scrimaglio winery at Nizza Monferrato produces a vast range of exceptional wines. Vincenzo Munì keeps an ever-watchful eye on everything that goes on, from vineyard – some of the plots are owned by the estate – to vinification. This year's newcomer is called Il Sogno, which means "The Dream". It's a Barbera d'Asti obtained thanks to the collaboration of Scrimaglio, Fontanafredda and the two co-operative wineries of Nizza Monferrato and Vinchio e Vaglio Serra. The aim is to make 150,000 bottles of excellent but affordable wine. The '98 Il Sogno, made under the supervision of Giuliano Noè, is a convincingly true-to-type Barbera. The style is distinctly modern for the variety's trademark acidity has been kept in check to bring out the lovely, contrasting notes of fruit and oak. Next we tried the Acsé, which year after year is one of the estate's leading products. The '98 vintage confirms that you can bank on its structure and the intriguing complexity of nose and palate. Up there with Acsé for quality is another new red, the Tantra. Obtained from barbera and cabernet sauvignon fruit, Tantra is a textbook example of what this blend can do, the refreshing acidity of the barbera melding with the cabernet tannins into a convincing mix of fruit and vegetal notes, attractively underpinned by the discreet presence of oak. Both the Barbera Bricco Sant'Ippolito and the RoccaNivo are well-made and true to type while the Croutin, with its subtle balmy fragrance, is a notch or two higher up the scale. We liked the bright, cheerful Barbera Il Matto and the Bianco Sant'Ippolito, a skilful interpretation of sauvignon that opens on the nose with crisp citrus fruit and elegant vegetal nuances.

Walter Fissore and his equally capable wife, Nadia, make a range of very dependable wines whose strong point is a consistent quality wine-lovers can rely on. The house style, modern but not fanatically so, puts the spotlight on the juicy, ripe fruit. The '96 is the first vintage for Fissore's Barolo Le Coste, which has a concentrated garnet-tinged ruby colour. You're sure to be won over by the broad nose with its wealth of contrasts, setting elegant hints of fruit and dried flowers against complex nuances of leather, liquorice and tar to bring out all the facets of the aristocratic progression that Barolos can on occasion unveil. On the palate, its full texture is obvious on entry while graceful, fine yet compact tannins sustain it effortlessly through to the leisurely finish, which signs off with a stylish aroma of flowers. Next in line was the vibrantly coloured Barbera Bricco dei Merli, its warm, mature nose hinting at morello cherry and mulberry over autumn leaves and menthol, the whole being laced with enticing nuances of tar. Firm, juicy flesh is obvious on the front palate while the development is seamless, revealing a touch of tension, before the tannins kick in on the utterly satisfying finish. Dark and compact in colour, the Dolcetto Vigna del Mandorlo tempts you with ripe notes of plum, mulberry and fig over resin and cocoa powder. The full palate is nicely backed up by well-amalgamated tannins and a structure of commendable breadth. The Rosso Montegrilli reveals aromas of wild berries, rhubarb and wild fennel on the nose, echoed by the bright, lively palate. Finally, the Bianco Nas-Cetta, from the rare local vine type of the same name, proffers a subtle nose of apricot and aromatic herbs, leading in to a soft palate that conceals a pleasant tangy note.

● Barbera d'Asti Sup. Acsé '98	🍷🍷	6
● Barbera d'Asti Sup. Il Sogno '98	🍷🍷	5
● Monferrato Rosso Tantra '98	🍷🍷	5
● Barbera d'Asti Sup. Bricco S. Ippolito '98	🍷	4
● Barbera d'Asti Sup. Croutin '97	🍷	5
● Barbera d'Asti Sup. Vigneto RoccaNivo '98	🍷	3
● Barbera del M.to Vivace Il Matto '99	🍷	3
○ Monferrato Bianco Bricco S. Ippolito '99	🍷	4
● Barbera d'Asti Sup. Acsé '97	🍷🍷	6
● Barbera d'Asti Sup. Croutin '95	🍷	5
● Barbera d'Asti Sup. Croutin '96	🍷	5

● Barbera d'Alba Bricco dei Merli '98	🍷🍷	5
● Barolo Ravera '96	🍷🍷	6
● Dolcetto d'Alba Vigna del Mandorlo '99	🍷🍷	3*
● Langhe Rosso Montegrilli '98	🍷	5
○ Nas-Cetta '99	🍷	4
● Barbera d'Alba Bricco dei Merli '97	🍷🍷	5
● Barolo Ravera '93	🍷🍷	5
● Barolo Ravera '95	🍷🍷	6
● Dolcetto d'Alba Vigna del Mandorlo '98	🍷🍷	3
● Langhe Rosso Montegrilli '97	🍷🍷	5

NOVI LIGURE (AL)

NOVI LIGURE (AL)

CASCINA DEGLI ULIVI
S.DA MAZZOLA, 12
15067 NOVI LIGURE (AL)
TEL. 0143/744598

IL VIGNALE
VIA GAVI, 130
15067 NOVI LIGURE (AL)
TEL. 0143/72715

All Stefano Bellotti's hard work in the past is bearing fruit. Having got his country holiday facilities up and running, he then built a cellar at Tassarolo on the hill at Montemarino, right in the middle of the estate's finest vineyards. Reds are more important than whites at Cascina degli Ulivi and one of them is the Monferrato Dolcetto Nibiò '98, made from the rare, red-stalked local variety called "nibiò" in these parts. The vibrant ruby is enlivened by youthful purple highlights, introducing a nose that is a little dumb to begin with before it explodes into fragrant fruit after being allowed to breathe. The magnificently soft, round, full-bodied palate, with its sweet tannins and appreciable length, confirms just how good this wine is. It's a wager Bellotti has undoubtedly won, demonstrating that this dolcetto clone has plenty of quality as well as a long history. Staying with the reds, Stefano's Barbera Piemonte Mounbè has a bright, reasonably intense ruby hue. A little closed on the nose, it releases heady aromas of ripe fruit before delivering a zesty, fresh-tasting palate that has you enquiring after a second glass. New this year is the second-label Barbera Venta Quemada. Among the whites, it was the Gavi I Filagnotti '99 that caught our attention. Pale straw-yellow with green highlights, it offers a fairly intense nose of apple, tropical fruit and spices, nuanced with a minerally note, while the soft, buttery palate has good balanced and decent length, with a bitterish twist in the finish. The Montemarino '98 is labelled as Monferrato Bianco. Vibrant straw-yellow in the glass, it is a little closed and hard to pin down on the nose, despite hints of apple, while the palate is bursting with power and freshness. As always, the partially fermented L'Amoroso red is seriously good. An ideal wine for your dessert.

Piero and Vilma Cappelletti are chemists by profession and winemakers by choice who continue to earn their place in the Guide with a range of wines in an instantly recognizable style. Expert oenologist Giuseppe Bassi contributes his knowledge, experience and professional competence to the team. Our favourite from their range was the Gavi Vigne Alte '99. Its lively straw-yellow colour heralds a low-key nose that opens gently in aromas of flowers and apple, with a fresh balmy note that adds vibrancy. Despite its fresh taste and acidity, the palate has plenty of structure, which comes out in the warm, full-flavoured and fairly long finish. The Vilma Cappelletti '99 selection spent a long time on the fine lees before part went into large oak barrels. Its straw-yellow hue is brightened by youthful greenish highlights, which usher in a delicately understated nose nuanced with citrus. Tangily fresh and acidic on the front palate, it mellows delightfully into a satisfyingly long finish. Bassi's long experience with pinot nero grapes has been put to good use in the Monferrato Rosso di Malì '98, where it is blended with cabernet sauvignon. The pinot nero variety is not an easy grape. It demands scrupulous care and attention, particularly as it is uncommon in Gavi. But the results are excellent. The lovely ruby colour introduces fairly well-defined varietal aromas while the skilfully handled wood adds hints of vanilla. On the palate it is dry, with decent structure and length.

● Monferrato Dolcetto Nibiô '98	▼▼	4
○ Gavi I Filagnotti '99	▼	3
● Piemonte Barbera Mounbè '98	▼	4
○ Monferrato Bianco Montemarino '98	▼	4
● L'Amoroso '99		3
● Piemonte Barbera Venta Quemada '99		3
● Monferrato Dolcetto Nibiô '97	▼▼	4

○ Gavi Vigne Alte '99	▼▼	4
○ Gavi Vilma Cappelletti '99	▼	4
● Monferrato Rosso di Malì '98	▼	4
○ Gavi Vigne Alte '98	▼▼	4
● Monferrato Rosso di Malì '97	▼	4

NOVI LIGURE (AL)

PIOBESI D'ALBA (CN)

VIGNE DEL PARETO
VIA GAVI, 105
15067 NOVI LIGURE (AL)
TEL. 0143/2900 - 010/8398776

TENUTA CARRETTA
LOC. CARRETTA, 2
12040 PIOBESI D'ALBA (CN)
TEL. 0173/619119

The road from Novi Ligure to Gavi is called "della Lomellina", after the Genoese family whose country estate was located here. It wends its way through the hills of what for many centuries was the most important route from the Po valley flatlands to the port of Genoa. Pietro Occhetti is a businessman from Genoa who has always loved the area and indeed is emblematic of its historic links. His lovely residence has been transformed into a delightful winery that we have been following with approval for some time. This year, at last, Vigne del Pareto is in the Guide. The new, breathtakingly located cellars were inaugurated last year and is now ready to receive fruit from the new vineyards, which have been replanted in terrain that traditionally yields superb black grapes. At the moment, Occhetti has seven hectares under vine and while we are waiting for his barbera and other red varieties, we can enjoy his two admirable Gavis. The '99 Gavi Il Pareto has a pale straw-yellow colour with youthful reflections of green, followed up by a herb and flower nose that opens out into a minerally, spicy finish. Fresh, full-bodied and vigorous on the well-balanced palate, it takes its unhurried leave with an almondy note. We had no hesitation in awarding Two Glasses. The '99 Ricella Alta vineyard selection was equally good. Its bright, straw-yellow colour is tinged with green while the nose brings out all the finesse and well-rounded aroma of the cortese grape. The apple, lemony, mineral and bitter almond notes are reflected deliciously on the fresh-tasting, mellow palate whose full, tangy, well-judged flavour reveals admirable length. Our compliments to Mario Ronco, the highly competent winemaker who supervises activities in the cellar.

The Miroglio family's winery is on a roll at the moment and several of their wines won Two Glasses. The most impressive of the bottles we tasted for the Guide this year was the Langhe Rosso Bric Quercia. Its garnet-tinged ruby colour is dark to the point of impenetrable and the nose has both style and personality. Notes of deliciously ripe, fruity raspberry and cassis mingle with rosemary, rhubarb and minerally hints to be followed by a mouth-fillingly rich, dense palate whose fine tannins lead you through sedately and confidently to a long, long finish that mirrors the aromas of the nose. Fruit for the Carretta Barolo comes from the legendary Cannubi vineyard at Barolo. The wine itself has the narrowest of rims and an enticingly deep colour. Balmy aromas on the nose give way to crisp, clean notes of bilberry and ripe raspberries. Firm and consistent in the mouth, it offers a long finish that picks up the menthol of the nose over attractive fruit. We liked the deep colour and narrow orange rim of the Barbaresco Cascina Bordino. On the nose, we found cherry, cocoa, woodsmoke and sun-dried hay while the only moderately powerful palate has great balance, following through nicely to a finish that lacks just a touch of length. Equally well-managed is the Roero Bric Paradiso, which offers a fruit-rich nose and plenty of body on the palate. True to type, the Dolcetto Tavoleto has a nose dominated by black cherries, nicely complemented by notes of violets and hay. It could do with a little more breadth but the structure is decent and it has a lively finish. Finally, the two Arneis wines and the Favorita are all well-made.

O	Gavi Vigne del Pareto '99	🍷🍷	3*
O	Gavi Ricella Alta '99	🍷🍷	4

●	Barolo Vigneti in Cannubi '96	🍷🍷	6
●	Langhe Bric Quercia '98	🍷🍷	4
●	Roero Sup. Bric Paradiso '98	🍷🍷	4
●	Barbaresco Cascina Bordino '97	🍷	6
●	Dolcetto d'Alba Vigna Tavoleto '99	🍷	4
O	Roero Arneis Vigna Canorei '99	🍷	4
O	Langhe Favorita '99		3
O	Roero Arneis '99		4
●	Barbaresco Cascina Bordino '96	♀♀	6
●	Barolo Vigneti in Cannubi '95	♀♀	6
●	Langhe Bric Quercia '97	♀♀	4
●	Roero Sup. Bric Paradiso '97	♀	4

PRIOCCA (CN)

PRIOCCA (CN)

CASCINA VAL DEL PRETE
S.DA SANTUARIO, 2
12040 PRIOCCA (CN)
TEL. 0173/616534

HILBERG - PASQUERO
VIA BRICCO GATTI, 16
12040 PRIOCCA (CN)
TEL. 0173/616197

Our compliments to the Roagna family, who produce a fine range of typical wines on their eight-hectare property, located on the lefthand bank of the river Tanaro. Bartolomeo and his wife Carolina spend some of their time running a livestock farm while their sons Mario and Luigi look after winemaking with a dedicated passion. It was their excellent Nebbiolo Vigna di Lino that particularly took our fancy. Rich and concentrated, right from its garnet colour, it conjures up a broad, complex nose of raspberry and peaches mingling with elegant hints of autumn leaves and mint. The attack on the palate is equally concentrated, broadening out over robust tannins that add attractive volume and ending in a long, fruit-rich finish. Next, we tasted the moderately deep ruby Barbera Carolina, which has an intriguing nose of bilberry, raspberry, fresh, aromatic herbs and violets. The sumptuous texture of the palate is offset by confident tannins that lend a dry note to the long finish with its after-aromas of cocoa powder and fruit. The Roero '98 has a close-knit colour and an exciting nose that finds a wonderful balance of wood and fruit. In the mouth, the breadth and concentration of the palate are vigorously backed up aristocratic tannins that also enhance the gratifying finish. For the lustrous straw-yellow Arneis Luet, the panel noted ripe fruit on the nose and a silky, beautifully managed palate. Finally, there was the Favorita '99, which has fair depth of colour and a nose that blends elegant hints of pear, apple and country herbs. The palate is tangy and only too drinkable.

Michele Pasquero, his wife Annette Hilberg, and mother Clementina are looking to expand the current production of about 11,000 bottles from this three-hectare estate without jeopardizing quality. After their sensational – and thoroughly deserved – Three Glass awards last year, the Barbera d'Alba Superiore has done it again, confirming that is one of the best in its class. It's a Barbera with attitude, aged in new barriques and vinified with fairly brief periods of maceration. The '98 version, of which 4,000 bottles have been released, has a deep ruby colour that shades into garnet and a rich, concentrated nose with utterly delicious hints of violets, wild berries, mint, liquorice, leather and autumn leaves. The breadth of texture on the palate is obvious on entry, then firm, aristocratic tannins sustain the progression towards a long, vigorous finish that mirrors the nose and palate. The reasonably dense ruby colour of the Nebbiolo '98 heralds clean, well-balanced notes of raspberry and morello cherry, exalted by complex overtones of fresh-baked cakes and hay. Its smooth palate is underpinned by forthright tannins that take it through to a finish of exemplary length that is redolent of liquorice. Then we tasted the second-label Barbera, a reasonably deep coloured wine with an attractive, unsophisticated nose of berry fruit, cocoa and earth. The palate has good grip and a distinct note of acidity. The last wine this time round was the Vareij, a 30-70 blend of barbera and brachetto. It has a satisfyingly deep colour, an alluring nose of berry fruit, sweet almonds and pepper, and a bright lively palate.

● Barbera d'Alba Sup. Carolina '98 ▼▼ 5	● Barbera d'Alba Sup. '98 ▼▼▼ 5
● Nebbiolo d'Alba Vigna di Lino '98 ▼▼ 5	● Nebbiolo d'Alba '98 ▼▼ 5
● Roero '98 ▼▼ 5	● Barbera d'Alba '99 ▼ 4
○ Langhe Favorita '99 ▼ 2*	● Vareij '99 ▼ 4
○ Roero Arneis Luet '99 ▼ 3	● Barbera d'Alba Sup. '97 ♀♀♀ 5
● Barbera d'Alba Sup. Carolina '97 ♀♀ 4	● Nebbiolo d'Alba '97 ♀♀ 5
● Nebbiolo d'Alba Vigna di Lino '97 ♀ 4	● Barbera d'Alba '97 ♀ 4

ROCCAGRIMALDA (AL)

ROCCHETTA TANARO (AT)

CASCINA LA MADDALENA
LOC. PIANI DEL PADRONE, 258
15078 ROCCAGRIMALDA (AL)
TEL. 0143/876074

BRAIDA
VIA ROMA, 94
14030 ROCCHETTA TANARO (AT)
TEL. 0141/644113

Making premium-quality wine in "minor" zones is not an easy task, especially if the winery is a new one. But that is precisely the challenge that Anna Poggio, Cristina Bozzano and Marilena De Gasperi have set themselves. With the aid of oenologist Giovanni Bailo, they want to show that the Ovada area can turn out great wines. The '99 version of their second-label Dolcetto was well worth its Glass. Bright ruby with a violet rim, it has a berry fruit nose with faint hints of flowers and a palate whose abundant sweet tannins are nicely offset by acidity. Next, their Barbera Monferrato '98 was equally well-made and very quaffable. In contrast, the Dolcetto Bricco del Bagatto '99 is a much more serious wine. Contact with the fine lees and controlled oxidation during fermentation have endowed it with outstanding complexity on the nose and exceptional structure. Its dull, purplish ruby colour ushers in a fruit and elderflower nose that has still to open fully while the palate is big, full-flavoured and gratifyingly long. Two Glasses with marks to spare. Expectations regarding the monovarietal barbera Bricco Maddalena '98 were high and the wine, aged in small oak casks, was just as good as the '97 version, although this time the accent is on balance rather than power. Our panel noted the almost impenetrably dark garnet-ruby colour and the enormous complexity of the nose, which combines flowers, fruit and spices. The palate is simply spectacular, echoing the berry fruit and spice in the finish while the acidity and up-front but elegant tannins tell you this is a wine for the cellar. And this year, La Maddalena has released Barbera Rocca d'Ocra, part aged in small, one-year-old casks. The enticing fruit, well-supported by toasty oak on the nose, leads into an tangy palate with good structure.

Today, Barbera d'Asti is acquiring an ever more prominent place in the world of Italian wine so we can now truly appreciate the insight of Giacomo Bologna, the first man to free this wine of its traditional down-market image. Giacomo's wife and family are continuing in his footsteps and this year's wines are particularly good. In some cases, they are world-beaters. The '98 Bricco dell'Uccellone and Ai Suma Barberas are marvellous. The first fills your glass with a deep, vibrant ruby, offering up a stylish blend of red berries, vanilla, spices and cocoa on the nose before broadening out into a soft, beautifully balanced palate that is backed up by the variety's trademark mouth-watering acidity. A wine that demands Three Glasses for the Bolognas. The Ai Suma has a similar personality and well-defined notes of ripe fruit thanks to its late-harvest grapes. In contrast, the Uccellone '97 isn't up to the high standards of the '98. Less complex, it nonetheless offers a convincing overall balance. Both the '97 and the '98 Bricco della Bigotta are excellent wines, with the '98 just winning out. It has rich notes of spices, pepper and ripe berry fruit. The Bacialé '99, a blend of 30 percent pinot nero and 70 percent barbera, also convinces while the Barbera La Monella is lively and fragrant. Even the "second-string" wines – a Grignolino, a Brachetto and a Moscato d'Asti – are very well-typed and enticingly drinkable. Finally, the Serra dei Fiori estate at Trezzo Tinella, co-managed by the Giacosa family, has contributed a pleasantly vinous Dolcetto d'Alba and a captivatingly fresh-tasting white, Il Fiore, from an interesting blend of chardonnay and riesling.

● Dolcetto di Ovada		
Bricco del Bagatto '99	🍷🍷	3*
● Monferrato Rosso		
Bricco Maddalena '98	🍷🍷	5
● Barbera del M.to '98	🍷	3
● Barbera del M.to		
Rossa d'Ocra '98	🍷	3
● Dolcetto di Ovada '99	🍷	2
● Monferrato Rosso		
Bricco Maddalena '97	🍷🍷	5
● Barbera del M.to		
La Maddalena '97	🍷	3

● Barbera d'Asti		
Bricco dell'Uccellone '98	🍷🍷🍷	6
● Barbera d'Asti Ai Suma '98	🍷🍷	6
● Barbera d'Asti		
Bricco dell'Uccellone '97	🍷🍷	6
● Barbera d'Asti		
Bricco della Bigotta '97	🍷🍷	6
● Barbera d'Asti		
Bricco della Bigotta '98	🍷🍷	6
● Barbera del M.to La Monella '99	🍷	3
● Dolcetto d'Alba Serra dei Fiori '99	🍷	3
○ Langhe Bianco Il Fiore '99	🍷	3
● Monferrato Rosso Il Bacialé '99	🍷	4
● Barbera d'Asti Ai Suma '89	🍷🍷🍷	6
● Bricco dell'Uccellone '91	🍷🍷🍷	6

ROCCHETTA TANARO (AT)   RODELLO (CN)

HASTAE
P.ZZA ITALIA, 1/BIS
14030 ROCCHETTA TANARO (AT)
TEL. 0141/644113

F.LLI MOSSIO
VIA MONTÀ, 12
12050 RODELLO (CN)
TEL. 0173/617149

The "Quorum project" continues to gain momentum. Promoted by six wineries – Coppo, Braida, Chiarlo, Vietti, Antinori and Berti – it aims to produce a great Barbera d'Asti that will be able to stand shoulder to shoulder with Italy's finest reds and thus boost the fortunes of this DOC zone. The '98 vintage was the second for Quorum, which for the first time was made under the sole supervision of Riccardo Cotarella, one of the country's most successful winemakers and an established name outside Italy. Each of the six contributors selects one hectare of the property's finest vines and delivers the fruit to a cellar that has an in-house laboratory for grape analysis. Cotarella oversees work in the vineyards and all the subsequent stages. The grapes are vinified separately and the wine is then aged in barriques for varying periods before being assembled to make the final wine. Yields per hectare are kept very low, averaging 40-45 quintals. But the end result is a Barbera that even in its first vintage – the '97 – reached an outstanding level. And the '98 looks even better. It purple-tinged colour is deep and vibrant while the nose offers clear, elegant notes of wild berries, enhanced by hints of cocoa and coffee over toasty oak and vanilla from the new wood. Palate mirrors nose perfectly, keeping the variety's characteristic acidity well under control, melding it with elegant tannins in a soft, silky overall structure. And the finish goes on forever.

The lack of competition from barbera and nebbiolo in the zone and the welcome quality consciousness that has hit the Langhe have enabled Dolcetto to move up the scale from being an everyday tipple to enjoy at table and become a powerful, complex red with serious structure. And, despite some family resistance, the Mossios are going for quality. Consultancy advice from Beppe Caviola, careful vineyard management, low yields and scrupulous vinification have allowed them to make three very different Dolcettos that can all boast remarkable concentration and a superb breadth of aromas. Their eight or so hectares of vineyards produce 35,000 bottles of second-label Dolcetto and the two crus, Bricco Caramelli and Piano delli Perdoni. This year's newcomer is the Piano delli Perdoni. Its ruby colour shades into purple with some bluish highlights, introducing a nose that is still a little latent but offers plum, cherry and attractive notes of toastiness. On the palate, there is massive structure, more than enough to offset the more than 14° alcohol content, and the finish is very leisurely. Equally attractive is the Bricco Caramelli. Already sufficiently open to reward attention, it has a nose that is less closed and at the same time is more balanced and elegant, the ripe berry fruit mingling perfectly with the assertive tannins. And the second-label Dolcetto has no reason to be shy alongside these two big boys. Its deep, purple-highlighted colour is followed up by fruit-rich aromas and a full-bodied, mouth-filling flavour. More straightforward than the other two, certainly, but still a treat for nose and palate.

● Barbera d'Asti Quorum '98	ㅜㅜ	6
● Barbera d'Asti Quorum '97	♀♀	6

● Dolcetto d'Alba		
Bricco Caramelli '99	ㅜㅜ	3*
● Dolcetto d'Alba		
Piano delli Perdoni '99	ㅜㅜ	4
● Dolcetto d'Alba '99	ㅜ	3
● Dolcetto d'Alba		
Bricco Caramelli '98	♀♀	3

ROSIGNANO M.TO (AL)

S. GIORGIO CANAVESE (TO)

VICARA
CASCINA MADONNA DELLE GRAZIE, 5
15030 ROSIGNANO M.TO (AL)
TEL. 0142/488054

ORSOLANI
VIA MICHELE CHIESA, 12
10090 S. GIORGIO CANAVESE (TO)
TEL. 0124/32386

Vicara is the acronym of Visconti, Cassinis and Ravizza, the owners of the three independent wineries that since 1992 have been a single entity. All their wines share the same elegance and whistle-clean style. The Rubello is a blend of 80 percent barbera, 15 percent cabernet and 5 percent nebbiolo. Deep red in colour, it offers notes of mulberry, plum and coffee on the nose, and a satisfying follow-through on the palate with plenty of mouth-filling fruit. Cantico della Crosia, the flagship Barbera, is aged in barriques for about 15 months. The colour is vibrant while the nose yields intense aromas of cherry and mulberry over faint grassy notes. The palate is intriguing, with plenty of depth and a warm finish of cocoa powder and red berries. The Barbera Superiore, aged in large barrels, is reliably traditional. We were pleasantly surprised by the Sarnì, a barrique-aged Chardonnay with a production of 4,000 half-litre bottles. A lustrous golden straw-yellow in colour, it offsets the exuberance of the oak with quite remarkable structure and butteriness. The varietal and very well-made Grignolino is one of the best wines in its category. The bright cherry hue introduces notes of strawberry, spices, geraniums and roses and a very easy-drinking style. Airales, from chardonnay, cortese and sauvignon grapes, releases delicately fresh aromas in which the three varieties achieve a splendid harmony. The palate, while not particularly muscular, has loads of style and zest. Monferrato Rosso l'Uccelletta is an unusual blend of barrique-aged grignolino (75 percent) and pinot nero. A translucent ruby red in the glass, it offers aromas of raspberry, wild strawberries and spices on the nose while the clean, fruit-rich palate closes with a faint burning sensation. Finally, a well-merited mention goes to the Volpuva.

The Orsolanis are firm believers in the potential of the erbaluce grape. Although they release in excess of 100,000 bottles every year, all their attention is focused on the local variety whose grapes produce spumante, "passito"dried-grape wines and whites. Gian Francesco Orsolani has been joined by his son, Gigi, who has brought a new enthusiasm for innovation to the cellar. The results look distinctly interesting. Indeed, as the new vintages come on-stream, the Orsolanis are confirming their position as the leading makers of erbaluce-based wines with a thoroughly reliable range of exciting bottles. The '99 Erbaluce di Caluso La Rustia (the name means "roast" in the local dialect, indicating that the grapes were harvested when "sunbaked" and very ripe) is a delicious white. And the traditional Erbaluce has been flanked for some years by Caluso Bianco Vignot Sant'Antonio, available in the '98 vintage. It is white that is part fined in barriques and then left to age for eight or nine months in the bottle. The Spumante Metodo Classico Cuvée Storica '96 is a stylish sparkler, headily aromatic with a generous perlage. It is the fitting culmination to over 30 years' work by the Orsolanis in sparkling winemaking. Even better is the '95 Gran Riserva selection, an excellent wine and indeed one of the finest spumantes in Piedmont. The estate's best known and loved wines also of course include Caluso Passito Sulé '95, the new name for Passito La Rustia, which confirms the Orsolanis as masters of the art of making dried-grape wines. Old gold in colour, it offers nuances of spices and toasty oak against a backdrop of plums and candied peel that lead in to a long, full palate

● Barbera del M.to Sup.		
Cantico della Crosia '98	🍷🍷	5
○ Monferrato Bianco Sarnì '98	🍷🍷	5
● Monferrato Rubello '98	🍷🍷	5
● Barbera del M.to Sup. '98	🍷	3
● Grignolino del M.to Casalese '99	🍷	3
○ Monferrato Bianco Airales '99	🍷	3
● Monferrato Rosso l'Uccelletta '98	🍷	4
● Barbera del M.to Volpuva '99		3
● Barbera del M.to Sup.		
Cantico della Crosia '97	🍷🍷	4
● Monferrato Rubello '96	🍷🍷	5
● Monferrato Rubello '97	🍷🍷	4

○ Cuvée Storica		
Spumante Metodo Classico '96	🍷🍷	4
○ Cuvée Storica Spumante		
Metodo Classico Gran Riserva '95	🍷🍷	5
○ Caluso Bianco		
Vignot S. Antonio '98	🍷🍷	4
○ Caluso Passito Sulé '95	🍷🍷	5
○ Erbaluce di Caluso La Rustìa '99	🍷	3
○ Brut Nature Cuvée '94	🍷🍷	5
○ Caluso Passito La Rustìa '93	🍷🍷	5
○ Caluso Passito La Rustìa '94	🍷🍷	5

S. MARTINO ALFIERI (AT)   S. MARZANO OLIVETO (AT)

MARCHESI ALFIERI
CASTELLO ALFIERI
14010 S. MARTINO ALFIERI (AT)
TEL. 0141/976288

ALFIERO BOFFA
VIA LEISO, 50
14050 S. MARZANO OLIVETO (AT)
TEL. 0141/856115

At Castello Alfieri in San Martino, history, art and wine fuse together into a single, irresistible whole. Before tasting or purchasing the wines, visitors who book in advance can view the castle's Baroque halls, its magnificent gardens, laid out by Xavier Kurten in 1815, of cedars, limes, beeches and elms, with one awe-inspiringly majestic oak tree, or the elegant semi-circular lines of the lemon grove planted over the winery's barrique cellar. The estate's oldest vineyards take their names from the farmsteads of Tanarella, Alfiera and La Tota. They were planted in the 40s and then gradually replanted from 1990 onwards with mainly south-facing rows. Now, they boast the estate's finest Barbera d'Asti vines. The San Germano sisters, who own the property, and their winemaker, Mario Olivero, have an unshakeable faith in the variety, and indeed have plans to plant a further two and a half hectares. At present, the estate has 18 hectares under vine, of which 12 are planted to barbera, a little over two to pinot nero, two and a half to grignolino and just over one hectare to riesling italico. Annual production is 80,000 bottles. The wine that most appealed to us was the Barbera d'Asti Alfiera. Thanks to the excellent vintage, it has impressive concentration and balance. It is beyond doubt the best Barbera the Marchesi Alfieri estate has ever released. The Monferrato Rosso San Germano, obtained from pinot nero, and the Piemonte Grignolino Sansoero are also excellent wines. In particular, the Sansoero stands out for its peppery aromas and juicy fruit body, which mellows the typically beefy grignolino tannins. Finally, the Barbera La Tota was also well worth its Glass.

Rossano and Alfiero Boffa are at the helm of this San Marzano-based winery, turning out about 100,000 bottles every year from their 25 hectares of estate-owned and rented vineyards at San Marzano and Nizza Monferrato. Some of their wines earned Two Glasses, among them the Barbera Collina della Vedova '97 Vigne Uniche. Its intense garnet is firm almost to the edge of the glass while the nose hints at bilberry, cherry and green leaves over subtle hints of rhubarb and pepper. The soft, concentrated palate is backed up by delicate tannins and there are notes of liquorice and cocoa in the lingering finish. Velo di Maya is a 70 percent barbera-based table wine with an attractively intense garnet ruby hue. On the nose, there are notes of black berry preserve and violets, enhanced by spicy, smoky nuances in a delicate and nicely balanced whole. The palate has good breadth and depth, with a counterpoint of robust tannins leading into a satisfying, liquorice-themed finish. There are garnet on ruby highlights in the Barbera Cua Longa that introduce a no-nonsense nose of blackcurrant and raspberry with earthy and balmy overtones. The firm, moderately sinewy palate is mirrored nicely in the finish. In contrast, the Barbera Vigna Ronco is palish with a nose that is not entirely convincing while the palate offers moderate weight. Barbera Vigna delle More has an uncomplicated nose of berry fruit and rosemary with a delightfully invigorating palate to follow. Next, the nose of the Barbera Muntrivé is dominated by sweet spices but the palate is powerful and dry. Finally, Barbera Testimonium, made with more protracted maceration and no filtration, has a moderately elegant nose and a palate that guarantees satisfaction.

● Barbera d'Asti Sup. Alfiera '97	ΥΥ	5
● Monferrato Rosso S. Germano '97	ΥΥ	5
● Barbera d'Asti La Tota '98	Υ	4
● Piemonte Grignolino Sansoero '99	Υ	3
● Barbera d'Asti Sup. Alfiera '96	ΥΥ	5
● Barbera d'Asti La Tota '97	ΥΥ	4
● Monferrato Rosso S. Germano '95	Υ	5

● Barbera d'Asti Collina della Vedova '97	ΥΥ	5
● Velo di Maya '97	ΥΥ	5
● Barbera d'Asti Testimonium '96	Υ	5
● Barbera d'Asti Vigna Cua Longa '98	Υ	4
● Barbera d'Asti Vigna delle More '98	Υ	4
● Barbera d'Asti Vigna Muntrivé '98	Υ	4
● Barbera d'Asti Vigna Ronco '97	Υ	4
● Barbera d'Asti Vigna delle More '97	ΥΥ	4
● Barbera d'Asti Vigna Muntrivé '97	ΥΥ	4
● Barbera d'Asti Collina della Vedova '96	Υ	5
● Barbera d'Asti Vigna Cua Longa '97	Υ	4

S. MARZANO OLIVETO (AT)   S. STEFANO BELBO (CN)

CASCINA L'ARBIOLA
REG. SALINE, 56
14050 S. MARZANO OLIVETO (AT)
TEL. 0141/856194

CA' D'GAL
S.DA VECCHIA, 108
FRAZ. VALDIVILLA
12058 S. STEFANO BELBO (CN)
TEL. 0141/847103

The Terzano family owns and runs this attractive estate with skill and passion, concentrating on the promotion of the traditional Barbera wine of this zone, which borders on the great Barbera areas of Agliano and Vinchio. And it is the barbera vine that has given Domenico, Carla and their son, Roberto, their best results, staking their claim to a place in the first rank of the territory's wineries. As wine consultant, they certainly have the right man for the job – Giuliano Noé, a veritable guru of Barbera. We shall begin our round-up with the flagship wine of the extensive Cascina L'Arbiola range, the Barbera d'Asti Superiore La Romilda IV '98, which again earned the Two Glasses it was awarded in the last edition of the Guide. Its bright, intense ruby hue releases heady fragrances of spices that mingle with nuances of toasty oak. These aromas lead into delicious notes of cherry preserve. The palate is juicy and rich in flavour, with a soft, well-balanced entry of mouth-watering fruit. Also excellent is the Monferrato Rosso Dom, which blends barbera with pinot nero and cabernet, two varieties that have gained a firm foothold in the Asti area. Today, the estate's six hectares under vine produce 30,000 bottles a year but there are plans for further expansion, with a consequent increase in production. We tasted a number of other wines, awarding a full Glass to the Barbera d'Asti La Carlotta and the Moscato d'Asti Ferlingot, while the Barbera L'Arbiolin and the sauvignon-based Monferrato Bianco gained mentions.

Alessandro Boido's Moscato d'Asti Vigna Vecchia has loads of personality. Again this year, it is one of the best moscato-based wines from a corner of Piedmont that has always obtained excellent results from this aromatic variety. The '99 version is a lustrous straw-yellow with an elegant nose that brings out the grape's varietal character with originality and style. Cool notes of pear and peach are joined by wild fennel and nutmeg, with a hint of elderflower providing the keynote. The front palate is generously chewy, the abundant carbon dioxide ensuring a refreshingly lively palate that leads in to a long, long finish rich in luscious fruit. There are no complaints about the standard Moscato, either. Vibrant straw-yellow in the glass, it has a less subtle but laudably forthright nose that mingles fruit and flowers in a bouquet dominated by roses and peaches. While offering plenty of weight on the palate, it is perhaps a little too effervescent but gets back on track in the finish, which balances flavours and aromas delightfully The freisa-based Langhe Rosso Pian del Gäje '97 has a deep ruby hue with garnet highlights that introduces an attractive, country-style nose of wild berries, mint and sun-dried earth. Its presence on the palate is immediately obvious on entry and it goes on to reveal sturdy tannins and a slightly bitterish finish where the fruit is again to the fore. The Dolcetto '99 has a moderately intense hue and a slightly ambivalent nose that nonetheless offers attractive black cherry notes. It has decent weight in the mouth. Finally, the Ca' d'Gal Chardonnay is well-made if unchallenging.

● Barbera d'Asti Sup.		
La Romilda IV '98	🍷🍷	4
● Monferrato Rosso Dom '98	🍷🍷	5
● Barbera d'Asti La Carlotta '98	🍷	4
○ Moscato d'Asti Ferlingot '99	🍷	3
● Barbera del M.to L'Arbiolin '99		3
○ Monferrato Bianco Le Clelie IV '99		4
● Barbera d'Asti Sup.		
La Romilda II '96	🍷🍷	4
● Barbera d'Asti Sup.		
La Romilda III '97	🍷🍷	4

○ Moscato d'Asti		
Vigna Vecchia '99	🍷🍷	4
● Langhe Rosso Pian del Gäje '97	🍷	4
○ Moscato d'Asti		
Vigneti Ca' d'Gal '99	🍷	3
● Dolcetto d'Alba		
Vigneti Ca' d'Gal '99		3
○ Langhe Chardonnay '99		3

S. STEFANO BELBO (CN)

PIERO GATTI
LOC. MONCUCCO, 28
12058 S. STEFANO BELBO (CN)
TEL. 0141/840918

In the spring of 2000, Piero Gatti passed away. He was one of Moscato's greatest champions and leading figure in winemaking in this area. In the early 80s, Piero and a group of wine producers set up I Vignaioli di Santo Stefano, one of the finest Moscato cellars around. After a couple of years, Piero and his wife Rita decided to leave I Viagnaioli and set up on their own. Today, the estate continues unswervingly along the path mapped out by Piero, thanks to Rita, who over the years learned from her husband all the tricks of the trade. All the wines we tasted were impressively made, from the Moscato to the Brachetto, the Verbeia (80 percent barbera and 20 percent freisa) and the Freisa La Violetta. The Moscato is labelled "Piemonte" instead of "Moscato d'Asti" as this leaves the estate greater liberty in deciding when to harvest. The nose reveals notes of apples and pears while the palate is gratifyingly full-flavoured. The ruby colour of the Verbeia '98 is a touch too transparent, the nose easy-going and approachable. There is plenty of weight and good structure in the palate, which follows through firmly without missing a beat. Then we tried the Freisa La Violetta, a medium ruby wine that offers notes of strawberry, raspberry and crusty bread in a well-balanced, attractively uncomplicated nose. The palate is robust and mouth-filling, slowly revealing dry tannins and powering through to a slightly austere but thoroughly satisfying finish. The Brachetto '99 is cherry red with purple highlights, introducing a clean nose that brings out the personality of the aromas. The palate is nice and pleasantly smooth.

○	Piemonte Moscato '99	🍷🍷	3*
●	Langhe Freisa La Violetta '99	🍷	4
●	Piemonte Brachetto '99	🍷	4
●	Verbeia '98	🍷	4

S. STEFANO BELBO (CN)

SERGIO GRIMALDI - CA' DU SINDIC
LOC. S. GRATO, 15
12058 S. STEFANO BELBO (CN)
TEL. 0141/840341

The town of Santo Stefano Belbo has always been a byword for top quality Moscato. The two versions produced by Sergio Grimaldi – Ca' du Sindic and a standard wine - account for most of the winery's output, the rest being made up of Barbera and a little Brachetto. Ca' du Sindic, Grimaldi's flagship Moscato, has a fairly lively straw-yellow colour and a very mature, fatty nose with hints of pear, peach and fresh aromatic herbs (sage and catnip). The palate has breadth and plenty of character, the marked sweetness being nicely offset by a moderate effervescence that lends freshness and drinkability. The finish mirrors nose and palate attractively. The non-cru Moscato is bright straw-yellow in the glass, revealing aromas of pear, very ripe apricot and fast-drying rose petals. The palate has lots of character and sparkle, the notes of fruit and flowers returning in the lingering finish. Grimaldi's Barbera d'Asti '98 is pale ruby with faint garnet highlights. Balmy notes prevail on the nose, forcing the cherry fruit to play second fiddle. In the mouth, it offers satisfactory texture and a bright keynote of acidity. The finish follows through well but lacks a little length. The eye-catchingly purple-hued Brachetto has a subtly elegant fruit-and-flower nose. Sweet on the palate, it has average weight and firm, refreshing sparkle leading into a graceful finish where the fruit and flower aromas are joined by light tannins. Finally, the Barbera Vivace merits a mention for its irresistibly outgoing personality.

●	Barbera d'Asti '98	🍷	3
○	Moscato d'Asti '99	🍷	3
○	Moscato d'Asti Ca' du Sindic '99	🍷	3
●	Piemonte Brachetto Ca' du Sindic '99	🍷	4
●	Piemonte Barbera Vivace '99		3

S. STEFANO BELBO (CN)

I VIGNAIOLI DI S. STEFANO
FRAZ. MARINI, 12
12058 S. STEFANO BELBO (CN)
TEL. 0141/840419

S. STEFANO BELBO (CN)

TENUTA IL FALCHETTO
VIA VALLE TINELLA, 16
FRAZ. CIOMBI
12058 S. STEFANO BELBO (CN)
TEL. 0141/840344

You can always bank on the Vignaioli of Santo Stefano when it comes to making first-quality Moscato. Each year, their consistently reliable wines achieve the far from easy objective of balancing ripe fruit and rich extract with freshness and finesse on the nose. The goal is a challenging one and there is little margin for error. To put it another way, a well-made Moscato is a wine whose stunning aromatic simplicity springs from the rigorous management of vineyard and cellar, two absolutely indispensable conditions if the product is going to be successful. Naturally warm, generous vintages, such as those of the last few years, can undermine the aromas of the moscato grape so every harvest – even the best – has to be very carefully timed. The '99 Moscato from the Vignaioli di Santo Stefano is a rather intense straw-yellow. As ever, the nose is very stylish, this year foregrounding the warmth, rather than the freshness, of its aromas. Ripe, clean notes of pear and peach are veined with nuances of mint and tomato leaf, providing a delicious overall balance. In the mouth, the wine's rich texture is immediately obvious, the marked sweetness being nicely offset by the sustained effervescence.

Of the many wines presented this year by the Forno family, it is the very interesting, Two Glass, Moscato d'Asti Tenuta del Fant that stands out. A quiet straw-yellow in colour, it mingles very ripe fruit with lemon and elderflowers on the nose, over delicate notes of sage. The discreet sparkle provides a effective counterpoint to the sweetness of the palate, which slowly reveals a pleasant note of acidity. Then the long finish recapitulates the aroma of the moscato fruit. The Moscato Ciombi scored only a few points below the Tenuta del Fant, impressing tasters with its lustrous straw-yellow colour, nose of fresh aromatic herbs, bananas, pears and flowers. Sustained effervescence on the palate ensures balance and a sober freshness while the lingering finish follows through nicely. The Chardonnay Incompreso '98 has a deep straw-yellow colour and good breadth on the nose, where attractive notes of tropical fruit and wild herbs tend to succumb to the sweetish oak. The palate is juicy and moderately concentrated, opening out into a broad mid-palate and a satisfying finish dominated by caramel and vanilla from the oak. A brightish straw-yellow in the glass, the Arneis '99 comes up with hints of apple and wild flowers over notes of super-ripeness on the nose while the palate has nice texture, a zesty tang and a pleasant bitterish finish. Although the Barberas are well-made, they could have been cleaner-tasting. The Lurei is robust while the Bricco Paradiso is a typically forthright country-dweller's tipple. Finally, the Dolcetto Soulì Braida also left the panel with a good impression.

○	Moscato d'Asti '99	🍷🍷	4
○	Piemonte Moscato Passito	♈♈	6

○	Moscato d'Asti Tenuta del Fant '99	🍷🍷	3*
●	Barbera d'Asti Sup. Lurei '98	🍷	5
○	Langhe Arneis '99	🍷	4
○	Langhe Chardonnay Incompreso '98	🍷	5
○	Moscato d'Asti Tenuta dei Ciombi '99	🍷	3
●	Barbera d'Asti Sup. Bricco Paradiso '98		5
●	Dolcetto d'Alba Soulì Braida '98		3
●	Barbera d'Asti Sup. Bricco Paradiso '97	♈♈	5

SAREZZANO (AL)

SCURZOLENGO (AT)

MUTTI
LOC. S. RUFFINO, 49
15050 SAREZZANO (AL)
TEL. 0131/884119

CANTINE SANT'AGATA
REG. MEZZENA, 19
14030 SCURZOLENGO (AT)
TEL. 0141/203186

On several occasions, we have been told how pleased and surprised Dino Mutti was to read our assessment last year. Dino has always made good wines. Now it seems that he has understood – and perhaps even accepted – the change in policy his son, Andrea, has imposed on the estate. For a producer who has always been faithful to his own sound, but perhaps a little too Tortona-centred, ideas, this is no small step. Now, we can state that the winemaking renaissance in the Colli Tortonesi has found a stalwart in the Mutti estate, which has flanked the classic local grapes, especially barbera and timorasso, with several hectares planted to international varieties. The reasons are environmental – some vineyards are unsuitable for the cultivation of local varieties – as well as geographical or soil-related. And it was Sull'Aia, a wine based one of these "foreign" varieties, that obtained the highest mark this year. Are you looking for an elegant, monovarietal Sauvignon, deliciously oily but not sweet, balanced and exceptionally well-made? Then Sull'Aia is your bottle. Only a few points behind came Timorasso Castagnoli, with a nose that opens with minerally notes mingling with, camomile, peach and whitecurrant. The well-structured palate, with its hint of acidity, follows through nicely, as the deep straw-yellow colour hinted it would. We found the San Ruffino to be a little out of sorts, perhaps because we tasted it too soon. But it is a serious Barbera, sold as a Colli Tortonesi Rosso. Although it still has to develop fully and find its true identity, both on nose and palate, it has notes of roasted coffee beans. The Rosso Rivadestra is an altogether more interesting proposition. Concentrated and sinewy in the mouth, it has yet to find a point of balance. On the nose, clean grassy and balmy notes prevail.

Claudio and Franco Cavallero, the two brothers who today run the Cantine Sant'Agata, in existence since the beginning of the twentieth century, have implemented a major change in estate policy over recent years. More attention is being paid to quality and new vineyards have been planted, particularly of ruché, which will come onstream in 2001. A new temperature-controlled building will rationalise cellar operations in the next few months. Claudio is an oenologist and over the last two years, he has turned out some eminently respectable wines, especially from the traditional grapes of these lovely hillslopes a few kilometres outside Asti, right in the heart of Monferrato. His Barbera, Grignolino (we are a stone's throw from Portacomaro) and the 16-17,000 bottles of Ruché have all helped to make Cantine Sant'Agata better-known among the cognoscenti. Scurzolengo lies in the geographical centre of the seven towns where ruché is grown. Since it obtained DOC status about 15 years ago, the variety has been enjoying steadily growing popularity. Franco Cavallero looks after the commercial side and has taken the brothers' wines all round the world, from Japan to Central America. Almost 90 percent of the 150,000 bottles produced annually go for export, the remainder being sold mainly in Turin and Asti. We particularly liked the Ruché di Castagnole Monferrato 'Na Vota this year. Its flower-rich nose is dominated by roses and the generous, mouth-filling palate has an attractively spicy finish. Other noteworthy offerings were the Monferrato Monterovere, a blend of 60 percent barbera grapes with 30 percent cabernet and ten percent nebbiolo, and the Barbera d'Asti Superiore. The estate's Cortese and Grignolino were also very tempting. Still to be released are the major '98 Barbera selections, Cavalé and Piatin, and the Monferrato Rosso Genesi, from 50 percent barbera and 50 percent raisined ruché fruit. We'll be back for those next year.

O Colli Tortonesi Bianco		
Sull'Aia '99	♟♟	3*
● Colli Tortonesi Rosso		
Rivadestra '98	♟♟	4
O Colli Tortonesi Bianco		
Timorasso Castagnoli '98	♟	3
● Colli Tortonesi Rosso		
S. Ruffino '98	♟	4
● Colli Tortonesi Rosso		
Rivadestra '97	♟♟	4
● Colli Tortonesi Rosso		
S. Ruffino '97	♟♟	4

● Monferrato Rosso		
Monterovere '98	♟♟	4
● Ruché di Castagnole M.to		
'Na Vota '99	♟♟	4
● Barbera d'Asti Sup. '98	♟	3
O Cortese dell'Alto M.to Ciarea '99	♟	3
● Grignolino d'Asti Miravalle '99	♟	3
● Barbera d'Asti Sup. Cavalé '97	♟♟	4
● Monferrato Rosso Genesi '96	♟♟	5
● Ruché di Castagnole M.to		
'Na Vota '98	♟♟	4
● Barbera d'Asti Sup. Piatin '97	♟	4
● Monferrato Rosso		
Monterovere '97	♟	4

SERRALUNGA D'ALBA (CN)   SERRALUNGA D'ALBA (CN)

LUIGI BAUDANA
FRAZ. BAUDANA, 43
12050 SERRALUNGA D'ALBA (CN)
TEL. 0173/613354

FONTANAFREDDA
VIA ALBA, 15
12050 SERRALUNGA D'ALBA (CN)
TEL. 0173/613161

Luigi and Fiorina Baudana have been growing grapes on their four and a half hectare property since 1975 but they only started vinifying in 1996. Since then, they have built up a range of fine wines, turning out 25,000 bottles a year of Barolo, Barbera, Dolcetto, Chardonnay and the Langhe Rosso and Langhe Bianco blends that include international varieties such as merlot and sauvignon. In its very first vintage, the Barolo Cerretta Piani strolled away with a Two Glass rating thanks to a nose that strikes a successful balance of modernity and tradition and the sustained structure of the palate. Deep garnet-ruby, shading slightly into orange at the edge of the glass, it presents a nose of liqueur cherries and cocoa powder over complex notes of balsam and toasty oak. On the palate, it makes its presence felt right from the entry, the rather austere phenolics underpinning the body. The warm, lingering finish follows through well. The estate's standard Dolcetto has an engagingly up-front nose of very ripe wild berries over warm, creamy notes. The full-flavoured palate also lives up to expectations with plenty of breadth and nice grip. The Dolcetto selection from the Sörì Baudana vineyard is even more concentrated. Mouth-fillingly dense and soft on the palate, it is also awesomely long. A fine example of a Serralunga Dolcetto, it manages to temper the characteristic hardness of the area's wines with the fullness of its palate. Headily complex aromas are the first thing you notice about the Langhe Rosso Lorenso, then the austere palate confirms that this is a wine made by an expert. Finally, a little lower down the scale, but nonetheless interesting, were the Chardonnay and the Barbera d'Alba Donatella.

Over 100 hectares under vine and 800,000 bottles a year of Barolo alone. Vineyards like La Rosa, Lazzarito and Gattinera at Serralunga, and La Villa at Barolo. A score of employees who live with their families in the mediaeval village that once belonged to the count of Mirafiori. All this adds up to an enormous potential that, until recently, lay dormant. Then the estate realised it could use Fontanafredda as an image-driving vehicle and in 1999, appointed Giovanni Minetti as general manager and Danilo Drocco as the technical supremo. The new management team's impact is evident in our first tastings of the new vintages now being released. Even though the '96 Barolos were not vinified under Drocco's supervision, they are still exciting. The Lazzarito is the one that is drinking best now. Its bright, enticing colour introduces attractively intense aromas with a hint of violets and a subtle note of burnt rubber. Uncompromising on the palate, it unveils good length in the finish. We were also pleasantly surprised by the standard Barolo, 100,000 bottles of which are made every year from grapes harvested at Serralunga. The excellent raw material is beautifully vinified. The La Villa was up to the same high standards while the La Rosa and La Delizia will need more time in the cellar. We'll be back for them next year. The Chardonnay, Barbera, Nebbiolo and Barbaresco are all professionally made but the Dolcetto di Diano is the wine that best embodies the approach of the estate's new oenologist. It is an archetypal Serralunga Dolcetto with notes of almond and a well-rounded, alcohol-rich body. To round off our visit, we raised a toast with the excellent Gatinera Brut '91 and the fine '94 Contessa Rosa.

● Barolo Cerretta Piani '96	♟♟	6
● Dolcetto d'Alba '99	♟♟	3*
● Dolcetto d'Alba Sörì Baudana '99	♟♟	3*
● Langhe Rosso Lorenso '98	♟♟	4
● Barbera d'Alba Donatella '98	♟	4
○ Langhe Chardonnay '99	♟	3
● Barbera d'Alba Donatella '96	♟♟	4
● Barbera d'Alba Donatella '97	♟	4
○ Langhe Bianco Lorenso '98	♟	4

● Barolo La Villa '96	♟♟	6
● Barolo Lazzarito '96	♟♟	6
● Barolo Serralunga '96	♟♟	6
● Diano d'Alba Vigna La Lepre '99	♟♟	3*
○ Gatinera Brut Talento '91	♟♟	5
● Barbaresco Coste Rubin '97	♟	5
● Barbera d'Alba Papagena '98	♟	4
○ Contessa Rosa Brut '94	♟	5
○ Langhe Chardonnay Ampelio '99	♟	3
● Nebbiolo d'Alba Marne Brune '98	♟	4
● Barolo Vigna La Rosa '95	♟♟	6
○ Gatinera Brut Talento '90	♟♟	5
● Barolo Galarej '95	♟	6
● Barolo La Villa '95	♟	6

SERRALUNGA D'ALBA (CN)   SERRALUNGA D'ALBA (CN)

GABUTTI - FRANCO BOASSO
B.TA GABUTTI, 3/A
12050 SERRALUNGA D'ALBA (CN)
TEL. 0173/613165

ETTORE GERMANO
LOC. CERRETA, 1
12050 SERRALUNGA D'ALBA (CN)
TEL. 0173/613528

The Boasso family is the only one to vinify in the prestigious Gabutti vineyard at Serralunga. Franco, his wife Marina, and their two sons, Ezio and Claudio, own six hectares and produce 25-30,000 bottles a year of Barolo, Barbera and Dolcetto. Their style is traditional. Although the Barolo Gabutti '95 that we presented in last year's edition of the Guide suffered a little from the difficult vintage, the '96 version bounced right back with a well-merited Two Glass rating. The fairly intense garnet-ruby hue is followed up by a nose of great breadth and personality, with hints of rhubarb, dried flowers, wild berries and hay over salty notes. The front palate is soft and juicy, while the tannins make their presence increasingly felt in the mid palate, perfectly offset by the warmth of the texture, and there is plenty of muscle in the convincing finish. This year, the Gabutti is joined by a second-label Barolo, which means that the fruit for the premium cru can be selected with even greater rigour. The initial results are very promising. The garnet hue shades into orange on the rim while the nose is redolent of liqueur wild berries, cocoa, dried flowers and leather. There is good weight in the mouth, although the mid palate wavers slightly before picking up again for a sprightly finish where the notes of cocoa and liqueur fruit emerge again. The Dolcetto earned One Glass. This year it has been released as Meriane, the name of the vineyard next to Gabutti where the grapes are grown. Fairly deep in colour, it reveals a slightly mature nose with notes of fruit, mint and spices. There is decent weight on the palate, as well as a certain austerity, and a hint of bitterness in the finish.

Sergio and Ettore Germano make a fine range of wines in a balanced style. Their Barbera Vigna della Madre '98 is a very intense garnet and offers a nose of breadth and harmony, with notes of black berries, toasty oak, juniper and hay. The palate is full-bodied, the slightly tense but firm mid palate leading into a long, open finish tinged with hints of mint and fruit. We were particularly impressed by the Prapò Barolo. Its vivid garnet-ruby tells that this is a wine of great concentration. The nose of style and distinction hints at blackcurrant, toasty oak, almonds, bramble and menthol. On the palate, the follow through from the entry to the warm finish is uncompromising, sustained and vigorous, leaving balmy, spicy notes lingering on the palate. The Barolo Ceretta is ruby shading into garnet, with orange at the rim, introducing a nose of fruit preserve, coffee and cakes. There is plenty of character in the somewhat uncompromising palate, where the slightly mouth-drying tannins and the sustained acidity augur well for the wine's future in the cellar. Another thoroughly convincing wine is the Dolcetto Pra di Pò, which has a vibrant, youthful colour in the glass. Its nose reveals notes of cherry, almond and wild grasses while the firm, satisfying palate is rounded off by a long, grass-and-fruit finish. The vibrant hue of the Balàu '98 highlights a delightfully fruit-rich nose of bilberry and strawberry over sweet oak-derived notes of vanilla and liquorice. Stylish and invigorating, the palate concludes with a gratifyingly long finish. As ever, the Dolcetto Lorenzino is a very agreeable bottle. Our tasting concluded with the estate Chardonnay, an uncomplicated, very refreshing wine.

● Barolo '96	🍷🍷	5
● Barolo Gabutti '96	🍷🍷	6
● Dolcetto d'Alba Meriane '99	🍷	3
● Barolo Gabutti '90	🍷🍷	6
● Barolo Gabutti '93	🍷🍷	6
● Barolo Gabutti '95	🍷	6

● Barbera d'Alba Vigna della Madre '98	🍷🍷	4
● Barolo Cerretta '96	🍷🍷	6
● Barolo Prapò '96	🍷🍷	6
● Dolcetto d'Alba Vigneto Pra di Pò '99	🍷🍷	3*
● Langhe Rosso Balàu '98	🍷🍷	4
● Dolcetto d'Alba Vigneto Lorenzino '99	🍷	3
○ Langhe Chardonnay '99		3
● Barbera d'Alba Vigna della Madre '97	🍷🍷	4
● Barolo '93	🍷🍷	6
● Barolo Cerretta '93	🍷🍷	6
● Barolo Cerretta '94	🍷🍷	6
● Barolo Cerretta '95	🍷🍷	6
● Barolo Prapò '95	🍷🍷	6
● Langhe Rosso Balàu '97	🍷🍷	4

SERRALUNGA D'ALBA (CN)

SERRALUNGA D'ALBA (CN)

LUIGI PIRA
VIA XX SETTEMBRE, 9
12050 SERRALUNGA D'ALBA (CN)
TEL. 0173/613106

VIGNA RIONDA - MASSOLINO
P.ZZA CAPPELLANO, 8
12050 SERRALUNGA D'ALBA (CN)
TEL. 0173/613138

A triumphantly successful compromise between modernity and Nebbiolo tradition. That's how you could describe this estate's Barolo. The two vineyard selections, Marenca and Margheria, will be joined by a small quantity of Vigna Rionda, beginning with the '97 vintage. They are aged partly in new barriques, partly in barriques used for the second or third year, and partly in large barrels, according to Giampaolo Pira's unique formula. Harmony is the over-riding characteristic of the three Barolos we sampled this year so let's begin with the most impressive. That was the Vigna Marenca '96, a vibrant garnet wine with an enticingly broad nose that mingles intense, elegant fruit with the spicy, balmy nuances of the wood. Aromas of mint and eucalyptus usher in clean notes of mulberry and raspberry over nicely restrained vanilla. On the palate, the wine is vigorous, following through unhesitatingly to a long, relaxed finish redolent of liquorice. The Margheria '96 is also intense in colour, with an orange-tinged rim and a nose only a whisker less stylish than the Vigna Marenca. Its morello cherry fruit and sweet spice aromas introduce an austere palate, with prominent tannins and a satisfying finish. We also liked the standard '96 Barolo very much indeed. In previous years, Giampaolo Pira has only released his vineyard selections but this wine, aged entirely in large barrels, has an appealingly vivid garnet hue and nose of laudable complexity and finesse. Raspberry, mint, rosemary and liquorice mingle over an intriguingly mineral note of dry earth to introduce a broad palate of substance and sinew, and a finish dominated by delicious tannins. The Dolcetto is a very nice wine, although it tries to act a little like a Barolo. All in all, this was a very convincing performance by a winery that is on the way up.

Franco and Roberto Massolino – both trained oenologists -, their father Giovanni and uncle Renato run this winery, founded in 1896. Their 20-hectare estate turns out 100,000 bottles a year. A newcomer to the range is the Barbera Gisep, named after the brothers' grandfather. Its deep purplish ruby colour heralds a nose packed with rich blackcurrant fruit and subtle overtones of cakes and almond paste. The palate is solid and full-bodied, well-sustained by the tannins through to the long, satisfying finish. Piria is a limited-production (only 1,500 bottles) barbera and nebbiolo blend with an outstandingly vivid colour. On the nose, there are aromas of black berry preserve and vanilla mingling with faint gamey notes and the tannins lend the palate plenty of weight. The wine ends with a vigorous finish of lingering cocoa and liquorice. Our panel was very impressed by the three Barolos presented, awarding Three Glasses to the seriously excellent Parafada. Obtained after relatively short maceration and in part barrique-aged, it has a concentrated colour and nose of berry fruit and dried flowers over earth and autumn leaves. The texture in the mouth is warm, and the structure rock solid. The Margheria and the standard Barolo age in large barrels, reflecting their traditional style. Crushed flowers, wild berries and spices dominate the Margheria's nose while its palate is generous yet austere, returning to the flower-and-spice theme in the finish. The second-label Barolo offers salty notes over a background of strawberry, raspberry and coffee on the nose. The palate is warm, alcohol-rich and packed with lively tannins. The elegantly oaked Chardonnay is redolent of ripe fruit and in the mouth reveals a bright, interesting texture. And to round things off for another year, we sampled a rather delightful Moscato.

●	Barolo '96	♟♟	6
●	Barolo Vigna Marenca '96	♟♟	6
●	Barolo Vigna Margheria '96	♟♟	6
●	Dolcetto d'Alba '99	♟	3
●	Barolo Vigna Marenca '95	♟♟	6
●	Barolo Vigna Margheria '95	♟	6

●	Barolo Parafada '96	♟♟♟	6
●	Barbera d'Alba Gisep '98	♟♟	5
●	Barolo '96	♟♟	5
●	Barolo Margheria '96	♟♟	6
○	Langhe Chardonnay '98	♟♟	4
●	Langhe Rosso Piria '97	♟♟	6
○	Moscato d'Asti di Serralunga '99	♟	3
●	Barolo Parafada Ris. '90	♟♟♟	6
●	Barolo Vigna Rionda Ris. '90	♟♟♟	6
●	Barbera d'Alba Margheria '97	♟♟	4
●	Barolo Margheria '95	♟♟	6
●	Barolo Parafada '95	♟♟	6
●	Barolo Vigna Parafada '93	♟♟	6
●	Barolo Vigna Rionda '93	♟♟	6

SERRALUNGA DI CREA (AL)   SPIGNO M.TO (AL)

TENUTA LA TENAGLIA
S.DA SANTUARIO DI CREA, 6
15020 SERRALUNGA DI CREA (AL)
TEL. 0142/940252

CASCINA BERTOLOTTO
VIA PIETRO PORRO, 70
15018 SPIGNO M.TO (AL)
TEL. 0144/91223 - 0144/91551

Thanks to the tireless efforts of the owners and consultants Curtaz and Pagli, La Tenaglia is again living up to the great winemaking tradition of this ravishingly beautiful hill country. Women run things round here. Daughter Erica looks after the cellar and the granddaughter already has a new barbera vineyard named after her. We could see a touch of Tuscany in the beautifully made '99 Grignolino, the Monferrato wine of wines. The colour, slightly deeper than most Grignolinos, tells of careful selection and ripe, ripe fruit. There are stylish aromas of berry fruit, pepper, nutmeg and autumn leaves on the clean, broad nose and the palate is surprisingly soft and warm. Add a decently long finish and mellow tannins and you'll see why it earned its Two Glasses. The Giorgio Tenaglia '98 is a paragon of a Barbera. Almost impenetrably black in the glass, its elegant nose reveals notes of cherry, spices and vanilla before the outstandingly soft, juicy palate has plenty of freshness to take you through to a long, tangy finish. The Barbera Emozioni '98 is even blacker in colour, if that is possible. There is a little too much oak on the nose but it opens out when left to breathe. In the mouth, it is concentrated, fresh-tasting and long. The oak-aged Chardonnay Oltre '98 is a deep, lustrous straw-yellow. The nose is almost excessive in its complexity, mingling ripe apples and pears, butter and hazelnut. Full-bodied and muscular on the palate, it concludes with an impressively long finish. We liked the Barbera Bricco Crea '99, a ruby red wine with youthful purple highlights. The true-to-variety Chardonnay '99 is also attractively fresh-tasting. However, the estate has decided not to release the Syrah Paradiso '98 until next year.

The Traversa family's property is situated about 400 metres above sea level in a lovely, if isolated, spot on the border between Piedmont and Liguria. The soil types here are dominated by calcareous tufa and sand, like those found in the hinterland of Liguria. Until the early twentieth century, this area was grape country, although today it is better known for Robiola di Roccaverano cheese. As viticulture was gradually abandoned, the woods grew back. The vineyards of Cascina Bertolotto cover about 15 hectares, forming a natural amphitheatre that rises prettily from the valley to the winery. The altitude and excellent ventilation enjoyed by the plots help to keep the grapes free of mould, enabling the estate to harvest very late. We thought the Barigi, a blend of equal parts of favorita and cortese, best captured the fragrances of the location. Its straw-yellow hue releases a bouquet of green apples and pine resin while the mid palate is a riot of flowers. There is an interesting note of lemon zest in the finish. Muïette is a Dolcetto made with grapes left to dry for a few days in cases. Fermentation is carried out in a traditional wooden vat more than 100 years old. By time-honoured tradition, the vat is cleaned with boiling water and peach leaves. The moderately intense ruby hue introduces aromas of raspberry, almond and hay. There is plenty of fruit on the palate but the finish is a little on the short side. The One Glass awarded to the Dolcetto d'Acqui La Cresta was well-merited. The Brachetto Il Virginio flaunts rose petal aromas that bring out the wine's varietal character to the full while the nicely poised sweetness and subtle, persistent sparkle ensure that the palate is equally attractive.

● Barbera d'Asti Emozioni '98	🍷🍷	6
● Barbera d'Asti Giorgio Tenaglia '98	🍷🍷	5
● Grignolino del M.to Casalese '99	🍷🍷	3*
○ Piemonte Chardonnay Oltre '98	🍷🍷	6
● Barbera d'Asti Bricco Crea '99	🍷	3
○ Piemonte Chardonnay '99	🍷	4
● Barbera d'Asti Emozioni '96	🍷🍷	6
● Barbera d'Asti Emozioni '97	🍷🍷	6
● Paradiso '96	🍷🍷	5
● Paradiso '97	🍷🍷	5
● Barbera d'Asti Giorgio Tenaglia '97	🍷	4

● Dolcetto d'Acqui La Muïette '98	🍷🍷	4
● Brachetto d'Acqui Il Virginio '99	🍷	4
● Dolcetto d'Acqui La Cresta '99	🍷	3
○ Monferrato Bianco Il Barigi '99	🍷	3
● Barbera del M.to I Cheini '97	🍷	4
● Dolcetto d'Acqui La Cresta '98	🍷	3
● Dolcetto d'Acqui La Muïette '97	🍷	4

STREVI (AL)

STREVI (AL)

BANFI VINI - VIGNE REGALI
VIA VITTORIO VENETO, 22
15019 STREVI (AL)
tel. 0144/363485

MARENCO
P.ZZA VITTORIO EMANUELE, 10
15019 STREVI (AL)
TEL. 0144/363133

The Banfi label has absolutely no need of introduction. The name is synonymous with premium wines, often in awesomely large quantities. We tasted the wines from the Banfi estate at Strevi, in the heart of moscato and brachetto country, and from their vineyards at Novi Ligure, in the Gavi DOCG zone. The Gavi Principessa Gavia '99 is the essence of typicity. Simple but beautifully made, it has faint aromas of hay and hawthorn but its strong points are freshness and robust acidity. Banfi Brut '96 is a good wine selling at a competitive price. Gold in colour, it has lingering perlage and aromas of yeast and crusty bread over attractive fruit. The rich, buttery palate is well-sustained by acidity. As ever, the moscato and brachetto-based sweet wines are excellent. It was the Acqui Brachetto Vigneto La Rosa that stood out, its headily persuasive aromas of roses and musk and delicious palate make it one of the best wines in its category. The '99 version of the Asti Spumante is equally interesting, its broad, fruit-rich nose evoking distinct notes of sage while the sweetness of the palate is never overstated. Another intriguing wine was the oak-aged Dolcetto d'Acqui Argusto '98. Its nose of very ripe berry fruit preserve leads into a fresh palate with loads of grip.

The estate run with such passion by the Marenco sisters is located near Alessandria, in the heartland of Moscato. Indeed, there have even been proposals to create a Strevi subzone to promote local production. The Marencos have planted much of their 60 or so hectares to Moscato and Brachetto, Piedmont's great DOCG dessert varieties. But they also produce dry wines, and their Dolcetto d'Acqui '99 Marchesa easily earned One Glass. Ruby with a distinct purple rim, it releases intense aromas of berry fruit with a faint grassy note. Fresh-tasting, with tannins that have yet to mellow, it signs off with an almondy note in the finish. The Barbera d'Asti '97 Ciresa, aged in small casks, is another admirable dry red. Its attractive ruby hue ushers in berry fruit and toasty notes on the nose. These are mirrored on the palate, whose marked toastiness is backed up by good acidity and moderate structure. Moving on to the dessert wines, we picked out the Brachetto Pineto, and not for the first time. Fresh-tasting and long on the palate, it has the characteristic Brachetto nose of roses. The Moscato Scrapona was almost as good. Its medium straw-yellow is veined with delicate bubbles. The nose has good length while the sweet, buttery tropical-fruit palate never cloys. The Brachetto Passito Pineto Passrì '98 is also worth investigating and earned its One Glass mainly for the generous breadth of its nose, which evokes dried roses and violets. Finally, we mustn't forget the Carialoso. It is obtained from the rare local carica l'asino grape, now saved from almost certain extinction. Although the palate lacks direction, it can offer intriguing vegetal notes.

●	Acqui Brachetto d'Acqui		
	Vigneto La Rosa '99	♟♟	4
○	Talento Banfi Brut		
	Metodo Classico '96	♟♟	5
○	Asti '99	♟	3
●	Brachetto d'Acqui Spumante '99	♟	4
●	Dolcetto d'Acqui Argusto '98	♟	4
○	Gavi Principessa Gavia '99	♟	3
○	Tener Brut		3
○	Gavi Vigna Regale '97	♟♟	4
○	Talento Banfi Brut		
	Metodo Classico '95	♟♟	5
●	Dolcetto d'Acqui Ardì '98	♟	3

●	Brachetto d'Acqui Pineto '99	♟♟	4
●	Barbera d'Asti Ciresa '97	♟	4
●	Brachetto Passito Pineto		
	Passrì '98	♟	6
●	Dolcetto d'Acqui Marchesa '99	♟	3
○	Moscato d'Asti Scrapona '99	♟	3
○	Carialoso '99		3
●	Barbera d'Asti Ciresa '96	♟	4

TORINO

TREISO (CN)

FRANCO M. MARTINETTI
VIA S. FRANCESCO DA PAOLA, 18
10123 TORINO
TEL. 011/8395937

ORLANDO ABRIGO
LOC. CAPPELLETTO, 5
12050 TREISO (CN)
TEL. 0173/630232

Franco Martinetti is one of Piedmontese viticulture's gentlemen and an insatiably inquisitive lover of good food. For him, winemaking is the never-ending search for an ideal. That explains the almost obsessive perfectionism of a winemaker with no vineyard or cellar, who dreams up his creations in an office in downtown Turin before actually making them in his native Monferrato. In recent years, Martinetti's philosophy has led to some superb Barbera d'Asti wines in Montruc and Bric dei Banditi, wonderfully successful marriages of barbera and cabernet sauvignon like Sul Bric, and the cortese-based Minaia, into which goes ten percent dried fruit. While he waits to uncork his '97 Barolo, which will be ready next year, he has allowed himself the luxury of visiting Monleale, near Tortona, to rediscover timorasso, an ancient but almost totally forgotten variety. And with a willing accomplice in Walter Massa, a young grower who has never lost faith in timorasso, Martinetti has created the somewhat self-indulgently named Martin, a white wine limited to fewer than 3,000 bottles. The first edition of this wine shows all the potential of the variety when vinified with care but it was the other Martinetti white that really took our breath away. The Minaia '98, which is no longer labelled as Gavi DOCG, is truly magnificent. Straight away, the golden straw-yellow colour speaks volumes for its concentrated fruit. Nose and palate are near-perfect in style and elegance. Never before have wood and fruit found such a harmonious union. Three indisputable Glasses for one of Piedmont's great whites. Elegance and finesse are the hallmarks of this cellar. If you need proof, try the '98 vintages of Sul Bric and Barbera d'Asti Montruc.

Abrigo's most impressive product this year is a powerful yet approachable Barbaresco, the Montersino '97, entirely barrique-aged for the first time. Deep garnet in the glass, with a firm, youthful rim, fresh-fruit notes of fragrant raspberry and mulberry are laced with walnut, cloves and cocoa in the slightly rustic but vigorous nose. The front palate offers loads of juicy fruit, well-sustained through the mid palate by the unobtrusive tannins that also enhance the warm, lingering fruit-and-spice finish. Abrigo's other Barbaresco, the Rongallo, is another winner. Rich and tannic, it balances spice and fruit notes delightfully. Both Barberas were also very good. The Vigna Roreto '98 has an intense colour that shades into purple at the rim and a sweet nose of cocoa, liqueur cherries and fig leaves. The palate has weight, body and complexity. In contrast, the Mervisano '97 offers a cherry and spice nose over a faintly mineral keynote while the palate has nice density, the clearly perceptible tannins adding zest to the long finish. The merlot-based Livraie has good structure but is still in thrall to the wood. This year, the Abrigo estate has added Très, a fresh, unoaked Chardonnay, to its range. Obtained by cold maceration on the skins, the '99 version is bright straw-yellow with aromas ranging from flowery notes to banana and fresh aromatic herbs. In the mouth, it is up-front and uncomplicated. The Chardonnay Rocca del Borneto is more complex and intriguing, although we would have liked to see a little more length.

O Minaia '98	????	6
O Colli Tortonesi Bianco Martin '98	??	6
● Barbera d'Asti Sup. Montruc '98	??	6
● Monferrato Rosso Sul Bric '98	??	6
● Barbera d'Asti Bric dei Banditi '99	?	4
● Barbera d'Asti Sup. Montruc '96	???	6
● Barbera d'Asti Sup. Montruc '97	???	6
● Sul Bric '94	???	6
● Sul Bric '95	???	6
O Gavi Minaia '97	??	5
● Monferrato Rosso Sul Bric '97	??	6

● Barbaresco Vigna Montersino '97	??	6
● Barbaresco Rongallo '97	??	5
● Barbera d'Alba Mervisano '97	??	4
● Barbera d'Alba Vigna Roreto '98	??	3*
● Langhe Rosso Livraie '97	?	5
O Langhe Chardonnay Rocca del Borneto '97	?	4
O Langhe Chardonnay Très '99	?	3
● Barbaresco '95	??	6
● Barbaresco Vigna Montersino '96	??	6
● Langhe Rosso Livraie '96	??	5

TREISO (CN)

TREISO (CN)

CA' DEL BAIO
VIA FERRERE, 33
12050 TREISO (CN)
TEL. 0173/638219

FIORENZO NADA
LOC. ROMBONE
12050 TREISO (CN)
TEL. 0173/638254

Thanks to help from all the family, Giulio Grasso manages to turn out enviably reliable Barbarescos. Since Ca' del Baio won a place in the Guide two years ago, Giulio's star wines, one barrique aged, the other fined in large barrels and both from the Asili di Barbaresco cru, have been gaining Two Glass scores or better in our tastings. That cannot be taken for granted, even in good years like '96 and '97, while in difficult vintages such as '95 it takes exceptional winemaking skill. The unbarriqued Asili Slavonia '97 has an attractively deep garnet ruby colour and a warm, ripe nose with hints of fruit preserve, menthol and dry flowers. Soft and broad on entry, the palate leads demurely but determinedly into a long finish that nicely echoes the nose. The Asili Barrique is remarkably intense in colour while the nose blends young notes of strawberry and raspberry with more complex nuances of vanilla and rhubarb. The texture on the palate is substantial rather than sumptuous but the sure-footed mid palate leads into a thoroughly satisfying finish. The moderately intense straw-yellow Moscato '99 has a delicately complex nose of pear, peach and elderflower over faint hints of super-ripeness. Balance and depth are the keynotes on the palate before the long, stylish finish concludes in a profusion of fruit. The very well-made Nebbiolo '98 has a clean nose and fills the mouth nicely before closing on a note of cocoa. Sadly, the moderately concentrated Chardonnay Sermine is dominated by its oak. But the '98 Barbera d'Alba Giardin again shows just how good a winemaker Giulio Grasso is.

Bruno Nada has done it. His Barbaresco Rombone '97 has claimed Three Glasses in its first year on the market. Rombone is one of the loveliest vineyards in Treiso. Nearly all the plants face south on the same ridge as the Manzola and Valeirano crus. The wine they produce has all the personality of the great Langhe Nebbiolos, even though it is vinified in small barrels of French oak. In previous years, tastings from the barrel convinced us this was an exceptional product and we could see that Bruno was very happy with the way things were going. At blind tastings, we noted the intense ruby red shading into garnet, the complex, generous aromas of mild spices and chocolate over red berries and an outstandingly intense, stylish palate with sweet, close-knit tannins leading in to a long, balanced finish. The Barbaresco '97 was another contender for Three Glasses. Although slightly paler in hue, it reveals crisp notes of ripe fruit and liquorice on the nose. Despite its relative youth, this is an irresistibly quaffable wine with a great future ahead of it. Next in line was the '97 Seifile, a fine wine although not up to the spectacular standards set by the '96. Almost impenetrably dark, its intense aromas of morello cherry, violets and vanilla introduce a sweet, soft and very warm palate that has plenty of length. Finally, we tasted the delightful Dolcetto '99. The very favourable vintage has produced ripe fruit aromas and a moderately well-balanced palate of great warmth and presence.

● Barbaresco Asili '97	￼￼	5
● Barbaresco Asili Barrique '97	￼￼	5
● Barbera d'Alba Giardin '98	￼￼	4
○ Langhe Chardonnay Sermine '99	￼	4
● Langhe Nebbiolo '98	￼	4
○ Moscato d'Asti '99	￼	3
● Barbaresco Asili '95	￼￼	5
● Barbaresco Asili '96	￼￼	5
● Barbaresco Asili Barrique '95	￼￼	5
● Barbaresco Asili Barrique '96	￼￼	5

● Barbaresco Rombone '97	￼￼￼	6
● Barbaresco '97	￼￼	6
● Dolcetto d'Alba '99	￼￼	4
● Langhe Rosso Seifile '97	￼￼	6
● Langhe Rosso Seifile '95	￼￼￼	6
● Langhe Rosso Seifile '96	￼￼￼	6
● Seifile '93	￼￼￼	6
● Barbaresco '92	￼￼	6
● Barbaresco '93	￼￼	6
● Barbaresco '94	￼￼	6
● Barbaresco '95	￼￼	6
● Barbaresco '96	￼￼	6
● Seifile '94	￼￼	6

TREISO (CN)

TREISO (CN)

PELISSERO
VIA FERRERE, 19
12050 TREISO (CN)
TEL. 0173/638136 - 0173/638430

VIGNAIOLI ELVIO PERTINACE
LOC. PERTINACE, 2
12050 TREISO (CN)
TEL. 0173/442238

Giorgio Pelissero has finished restructuring his cellar and the 2000 vintage saw the inauguration of his new winemaking centre, which is the last word in design and automation. The cellar temperature and rotofermenter speeds are computer-controlled, and can be fine-tuned on-site or even remotely with a simple phone call. Currently, the winery's output is around 100,000 bottles a year, one third of which is Barbaresco, and recent acquisitions have brought the estate's area under vine to a total of 20 hectares. But let's talk about the wines. Pick of the bunch is the Three Glass Vanotu '97, a wine whose deep ruby colour promises a phenomenal concentration of fruit. Sweet vanilla and Barbaresco spice dominate the nose while the entry on the palate is explosive, the powerful intensity backed up by close-knit tannins that lend warm and length. We gave just slightly lower marks to the Barbaresco '97, which needs less time in the cellar than the Vanotu. Its toasty, strawberry-fruit nose introduces a well-structured palate with distinct hints of liquorice. Next came the surprising Barbera I Piani '99, of which the estate makes 30,000 bottles. Its dark, concentrated colour accompanies a nose of fruit preserve and new wood and a sensationally soft, well-balanced palate. And at a sensationally low price. The generous, concentrated Dolcetto Augenta '99 with its liquorice finish and the muscular Langhe Nebbiolo '99 were utterly convincing. Finally, we liked the fruity, alcohol-rich Dolcetto Munfrina '99 and the unusual flower and spice personality of the Favorita '99.

Vignaioli Elvio Pertinace is a co-operative winery that vinifies grapes from 13 member growers who have about 60 hectares of vineyards. The winery produces 180,000 bottles a year, of which 80,000 are Dolcetto and 70,000 Barbaresco. Currently, the enterprise is run by the young Cesare Barbero, who has been working for some years to improve the already impressive quality of its products. In its third year of production, the delicately barrique-aged Langhe Chardonnay San Stefanetto '98 has earned a place in the Guide and the Barbera d'Asti Gratia Plena '98, made with grapes from a recently acquired plot at Agliano, gained One Glass for its generous body and attractive style. Best of the Barbarescos, in our opinion, were the Nervo and the Castellizzano. The fruit-rich, warm and spicy Nervo offers hints of roses and satisfying flavour while the markedly more austere Castellizzano comes up with notes of earth and leather amid a welter of big and as yet untamed tannins The standard Barbaresco earned a Glass for its balmy nose, classic palate and dry finish. Another One Glass award went to the Marcarini, still a little closed but with a very nice after-aroma of violets. The Langhe Pertinace '97 was also up to scratch. A dark-hued blend of nebbiolo, barbera and cabernet, its bilberry and bramble fruit mingles pleasingly with toasty notes of barrique-derived oak. The three Dolcettos are also worth investigating. The standard version is very well-made, considering the number of bottles produced. Its fresh, uncomplicated nose leads into a palate that lacks a little breadth but certainly not balance. The Nervo and Castellizzano vineyard selections are slightly more interesting. The Nervo is fruity and stylish, the Castellizzano less suave and more pugnaciously direct.

● Barbaresco Vanotu '97	🍷🍷🍷	6
● Barbaresco '97	🍷🍷	6
● Barbera d'Alba I Piani '99	🍷🍷	4
● Dolcetto d'Alba Augenta '99	🍷🍷	4
● Langhe Nebbiolo '99	🍷🍷	4
● Dolcetto d'Alba Munfrina '99	🍷	3
○ Langhe Favorita '99	🍷	3
● Barbaresco Vanotu '95	🍷🍷🍷	6
● Barbaresco '95	🍷🍷	5
● Barbaresco '96	🍷🍷	5
● Barbaresco Vanotu '93	🍷🍷	6
● Barbaresco Vanotu '96	🍷🍷	6
● Dolcetto d'Alba Augenta '98	🍷🍷	4

● Barbaresco Castellizzano '97	🍷🍷	5
● Barbaresco Nervo '97	🍷🍷	6
● Barbaresco '97	🍷	5
● Barbaresco Marcarini '97	🍷	5
● Barbera d'Asti Gratia Plena '98	🍷	4
● Dolcetto d'Alba '99	🍷	3
● Dolcetto d'Alba Castellizzano '99	🍷	3
● Dolcetto d'Alba Nervo '99	🍷	3
○ Langhe Chardonnay S. Stefanetto '98	🍷	4
● Langhe Pertinace '97	🍷	5
● Barbaresco Castellizzano '96	🍷🍷	5
● Barbaresco Nervo '96	🍷	5

VERDUNO (CN)

VERDUNO (CN)

VERDUNO (CN)

F.LLI ALESSANDRIA
VIA BEATO VALFRÉ, 59
12060 VERDUNO (CN)
TEL. 0172/470113

BEL COLLE
FRAZ. CASTAGNI, 56
12060 VERDUNO (CN)
TEL. 0172/470196

We were looking forward to the release of the Barolo Monvigliero '96, after Gian Alessandria claimed Three Glasses for the previous year's version, the best wine from Verduno in an indifferent vintage. But the '95's success has not been repeated, although the wine is still very good. Its deep garnet hints at a generous wine but the fruit on the nose is slightly masked by overstated smoky notes that jeopardise its harmony. The thoroughly satisfying broad, dryish palate has loads of chewy fruit and structure. The standard Alessandria Barolo earned Two Glasses. The rich garnet hue shades only slightly into orange at the rim while notes of hay on the nose gradually give way to delicious strawberry and bilberry fruit, with hints of violets and toasty oak. On the plate, the soft entry builds in intensity thanks to firm tannin and a broad texture. The dry, warm finish signs off with notes of cherry and cocoa. The cherry and almond paste nose of the vibrant-hued Barbera '98 is a little compromised by unruly gamey notes. Invigorating and full-bodied on the palate, it offers hints of liquorice in the lingering finish. The Dolcetto '99 has a fairly intense colour and a rather mature but nonetheless interesting nose of strawberry, raspberry, mint and cream. The modest structure of the palate is compensated by good balance and a burgeoning softness before the neat, orderly finish. The pale-hued Pelaverga mingles fruit and spice on the nose while its smooth palate rounds off with a hint of tannin. Finally, the fruit on the nose of the Favorita is a shade too ripe but the youthful, easy-going palate is very drinkable.

Paolo Torchio's estate at Verduno can be relied on for good, traditional wines from both sides of the river Tanaro, Barolo, Barbaresco and Roero. His '96 ruby-red Barolo Monvigliero shades into garnet, with hints of orange towards the rim. Red berry preserve emerges on the nose over complex notes of spices and nutmeg. The entry tells you this will be an austere wine, then the solid mid palate follows through without missing a beat to a deliciously long finish. The concentrated colour of the barrique-aged Barbera le Masche has virtually no rim and its wood-derived aromas blend nicely with notes of black cherry and bilberry, nuanced with tobacco, pepper and hay that add impressive depth. There is lots of breadth in the chewy palate, and sufficient sinew to carry it through to a finish that reveals hints of liquorice and caramel. The garnet-ruby Barbaresco Roncaglie unveils a classic nose of strawberry, bilberry, juniper and leather. Then the juicy-fruit palate develops attractively to a long, well-structured finish. Moderately intense colour and a slightly rustic nose of wild berries, peach and spices are the distinguishing features of the Roero Monvijé. The palate unfolds well but could perhaps do with a little more muscle. The Pelaverga is a winner. Fairly intense in colour, it comes up with notes of cherry, raspberry and pepper on the nose while the firm, well-sustained palate reveals a typically tannic vein in the finish. Finally, the fresh, uncomplicated Arneis is a very nicely made wine.

● Barolo '96	▼▼	5
● Barolo Monvigliero '96	▼▼	6
● Barbera d'Alba '98	▼	4
● Dolcetto d'Alba '99	▼	3
● Verduno Pelaverga '99	▼	3
○ Langhe Favorita '99		3
● Barolo Monvigliero '95	▼▼▼	6
● Barbera d'Alba '97	▼▼	4
● Barolo Monvigliero '93	▼▼	6

● Barbaresco Roncaglie '97	▼▼	5
● Barbera d'Alba Le Masche '97	▼▼	4
● Barolo Monvigliero '96	▼▼	6
● Roero Monvijé '98	▼	3
● Verduno Pelaverga '99	▼	3
○ Roero Arneis Vigneti in Canale e S. Vittoria '99	▼	3
● Barbaresco '96	▼▼	5
● Barolo Monvigliero '95	▼▼	5
● Barolo Vigna Monvigliero '93	▼▼	5
● Barbaresco '95	▼	5
● Nebbiolo d'Alba Bricco S. Cristoforo '97	▼	4

VERDUNO (CN)

VERDUNO (CN)

COMMENDATOR G. B. BURLOTTO
VIA VITTORIO EMANUELE, 28
12060 VERDUNO (CN)
TEL. 0172/470122

CASTELLO DI VERDUNO
VIA UMBERTO I, 9
12060 VERDUNO (CN)
TEL. 0172/470125 - 0172/470284

The Barolo Cannubi '96 is a wine with terrific personality. Its Two Glass rating shows just how far this estate has come, thanks to the efficiency of Giuseppe Alessandria, his wife Marina Burlotto and their son Fabio. You can see that personality in the wine's close-knit, garnet-shaded ruby colour. Notes of autumn leaves and cocoa combine in a nose of good complexity with interesting briny hints. The front palate highlights the rich fruit, developing unwaveringly thanks to invigorating tannins that add volume to a very long finish. The standard Barolo was only a whisker less impressive. The intense colour is firm almost to the edge of the glass while the generous nose of flower and spices is enhanced by iodine and rhubarb-laced fruit. The fullness and austerity of the palate are obvious on entry, then firm tannins emerge to carry it through to a long, long finish, vibrant with the elegant intensity of flowers. Barbera Boscato '98 is every inch a Two Glass wine. An excellent interpretation of the Barbera style, its intense garnet-shaded ruby and broad, well-balanced nose where sweet spice notes just about gain the upper hand, are richly eloquent of its class. Softness and breadth are the hallmarks of the very well-structured palate, whose satisfying finish is redolent of cocoa and liquorice.

The home of this winery is a lovely 18th-century villa that once belonged to King Carlo Alberto. Here, wine-lovers will find a range of products that embraces the traditional styles of both Verduno and Barbaresco. For this year's Guide, Gabriella Burlotto and Franco Bianco have come up with a very exciting Pelaverga. Pale garnet, its intense aromas of pepper and cloves lead in to a fresh palate with lots of body. Satisfyingly, the spicy notes return in the finish. The Barbera Bricco del Cuculo is a touch pale in colour and perhaps lacks a little elegance on the nose of red berries, spice and menthol. The front palate is robust, developing well thanks to solid support from the phenolics while the dry, pleasantly long finish discloses an after-aroma of cocoa. The ruby red of the Barbaresco Rabajà is a touch too translucent and has orange highlights at the rim. The nose is forward but interestingly complex, with notes of fruit preserve, dry grass and truffle. The chewy palate is underpinned by vigorous tannins that sustain the warm, liquorice finish. We gave the Faset a slightly lower mark for its rather over-evolved colour and less interesting nose. It is also fairly austere in the mouth. However, the Barolo Monvigliero impressed. Moderately intense in colour, it unveils a nose of dry flowers, leather and fruit preserve. There is plenty of weight on the palate, where tannins are well to the fore. Last but not least, the Barolo Massara offers good body in a distinctively severe style.

● Barbera d'Alba		
Vigneto Boscato '98	🍷🍷	4
● Barolo '96	🍷🍷	6
● Barolo Vigneto Cannubi '96	🍷🍷	6
● Barbera d'Alba		
Vigneto Boscato '97	🍷🍷	4
● Barolo Vigneto Cannubi '95	🍷	6
● Barolo Vigneto Monvigliero '93	🍷	6
● Barolo Vigneto Monvigliero '95	🍷	6

● Barbaresco Rabajà '97	🍷🍷	6
● Barolo Monvigliero '96	🍷🍷	6
● Verduno Pelaverga '99	🍷🍷	4
● Barbaresco Faset '97	🍷	6
● Barbera d'Alba		
Bricco del Cuculo '98	🍷	4
● Barolo Massara '96	🍷	6
● Barbaresco Rabajà '96	🍷🍷	6
● Barbaresco Rabajà '93	🍷🍷	6
● Barbaresco Rabajà '95	🍷🍷	6
● Barolo Monvigliero '93	🍷🍷	6
● Barbaresco Faset '96	🍷	6
● Barolo Massara '95	🍷	6
● Barolo Monvigliero '95	🍷	6

VIGNALE M.TO (AL)

VIGNALE M.TO (AL)

GIULIO ACCORNERO E FIGLI
CA' CIMA, 1
15049 VIGNALE M.TO (AL)
TEL. 0142/933317

BRICCO MONDALINO
REG. MONDALINO, 5
15049 VIGNALE M.TO (AL)
TEL. 0142/933204

It has been another year to remember for the Accornero family, who have made further investments on their estate, including new bed and breakfast accommodation. Ermanno and Massimo have also decided to label their flagship wine as Monferrato DOC. The decision is a commitment to the territory and a tribute to their roots at a time when other producers seem to have lost their way. Mario Ronco makes his contribution in the cellar to the winery's continuing gains in quality, symbolized by the flawless Barbera Bricco Battista '98, a Three Glass wonder. Its impenetrably compact ruby red introduces aromas of flowers, jam and spices, that come together in a full yet elegant nose nicely nuanced by wood. On the palate, it is simply huge, the full, sweet flavour lingering endlessly. The pitch-black Centenario '97 is another very fine wine. There is great personality in the nose of roasted coffee, cocoa, tamarind and stewed prunes while its power and harmony in the mouth tell you this is one for the cellar. The Barbera Giulìn '98 is a textbook example of vinification in stainless steel. Ruby red, with a nose opening onto notes of grass and red berries, it has an intense, fresh-tasting and satisfyingly long palate. The colour of the '99 Grignolino Bricco del Bosco announces superior fruit, the rich, varietal nose is laced with pepper and spices while the front palate is warm, leading into balanced acidity with seriously good body and structure. Next, there is the new Fonsìna, a '99 Monferrato Bianco blend of chardonnay and cortese. Its rich straw-yellow releases aromas of tropical fruit, banana and apple. The wine is full-flavoured, ripe and oily in the mouth, where softness wins out over tanginess. Next year, the Casorzo Passito Pico '98 will be ready for release and the estate's Malvasia Dolce Brigantino is worth keeping an eye on.

Mauro Gaudio's estate has now grown to 17 hectares, six being rented, which he has planted with the classic Monferrato varieties. His Barbera Il Bergantino is vinified with a longish maceration of about 20 days, and then ages for a year in small oak casks, one fifth of which are new. You can see at a glance from the deep ruby colour that this is a heavyweight. Warm, inviting aromas of walnut and ripe cherry are followed up by a palate of awesome structure and intensity, although the finish has a bit of a sting in its tail. The Barbera Gaudium Magnum is a limited selection of the best barriques of the Bergantino and is bottled exclusively in one and a half-litre magnums. Its style is a carbon copy of the Bergantino's but the execution is much less aggressive. The very drinkable Grignolino is pale ruby in colour, releasing hints of almond, blackcurrant and pepper on the nose. The refreshing, fruit-rich palate has an agreeably long spicy finish. Mauro's Malvasia Molignano is a lively dessert wine with a rich, cherry hue. Flowery notes of roses and violets mingle with pear and peach on the nose while the stylishly understated palate is perked up by a pleasant sparkle. We left the Grignolino Bricco Mondalino '99 until last. It is the estate's premier Grignolino selection and goes into the bottle later than the others. As usual, it turned out to be one of the year's best Grignolino's, with outstanding density achieved by a late harvest of the finest fruit on the property.

● Barbera del M.to Sup.		
Bricco Battista '98	🍷🍷🍷	5
● Grignolino del M.to Casalese		
Bricco del Bosco '99	🍷🍷	3*
● Monferrato Rosso Centenario '97	🍷🍷	6
● Barbera del M.to Sup. Giulìn '98	🍷🍷	4
● Casorzo Brigantino '99	🍷	3
○ Monferrato Bianco Fonsìna '99	🍷	4
● Barbera del M.to		
La Mattacchiona '99		3
● Monferrato Freisa		
La Bernardina '99		3
● Barbera d'Asti Bricco Battista '97	🍷🍷🍷	5
● Barbera d'Asti Bricco Battista '96	🍷🍷	5
● Monferrato Rosso Centenario '96	🍷🍷	6

● Barbera d'Asti Il Bergantino '98	🍷🍷	4
● Barbera d'Asti		
Sel. Gaudium Magnum '98	🍷🍷	6
● Grignolino del M.to Casalese		
Bricco Mondalino '99	🍷🍷	4
● Grignolino del M.to Casalese '99	🍷	3
● Malvasia di Casorzo		
Molignano '99	🍷	3
● Barbera d'Asti		
Sel. Gaudium Magnum '97	🍷🍷	6
● Barbera del M.to		
Sel. Gaudio Amilcare '98	🍷🍷	4
● Grignolino del M.to Casalese		
Bricco Mondalino '98	🍷🍷	4
● Barbera d'Asti Il Bergantino '97	🍷	4

VIGNALE M.TO (AL) VIGUZZOLO (AL)

COLONNA
CA' ACCATINO, 1
FRAZ. S. LORENZO
15049 VIGNALE M.TO (AL)
TEL. 0142/933239

CASCINA MONTAGNOLA
S.DA MONTAGNOLA, 1
15058 VIGUZZOLO (AL)
TEL. 0131/898558

Alessandra Colonna has inaugurated the estate's new wine shop, but the real news is the arrival in the cellar of Beppe Caviola with his winemaking techniques and vineyard management policies. As we wait for the new wines to be released, we wanted to see how the new winemaker would handle grignolino, Monferrato's classic variety. The Sansìn '99 has an eye-catchingly vibrant cherry colour, and red berry aromas of bilberry and raspberry over pepper to follow. The palate is soft and concentrated yet there are still plenty of long, sweet tannins to beef it up. But the estate's flagship label is the cask-conditioned Barbera Alessandra '97, almost black in colour with intense notes of hay, mineral and toastiness on the nose. Close-knit and fruity on the palate, it has good length and a certain oak-derived astringency. The Mondone '97, from cabernet, pinot nero and barbera, was less impressive than the previous vintage. Its demure but very pleasant palate is preceded by a sweet vanilla-and-oak nose and a purple-tinged ruby hue. The Barbera La Rossa '98 also flaunts a coal-black colour. The fruit-themed nose hints at the soft yet down-to-earth palate, rounded off by an attractive bitterish finish. The Colonna Monferrato Rosso Bigio '99, from 100 percent pinot nero fruit, is a rich garnet and evokes aromas of strawberry, ripe red berries and pear drops on the nose. In the mouth, it is backed up nicely by attractive tannins. Then came the '99 Chardonnay Passione, vinified in the wood. Golden straw-yellow in colour, it unveils all the intensity of tropical fruit, with minerally notes coming through the butteriness of the soft, balanced palate before the faintly bitter finish. The Armonia '99 is a bright greenish straw-yellow, with subtle overtones of apples, pears and vanilla. It is soft on the palate, with nuances of caramel and oak.

This estate at Viguzzolo includes a 19th-century villa where Donatella Giannotti, her husband Bruno Carvi and oenologist Giovanni Bailo keep things running smoothly. The cellar still has to be definitively restructured but already boasts everything the three need to vinify the grapes from their four hectares of croatina, cortese, chardonnay and above all barbera. We were very impressed by the excellent '99 Chardonnay Risveglio. Made in the Burgundy style, with fermentation in new wood, malolactic fermentation and stirring on the fine lees, its straw-yellow hue is flecked with golden highlights. The range of aromas on the nose is stunning, passing from lime and acacia blossom to banana and mango fruit, yeast and crusty bread over an attractively balsamic keynote. The rich, buttery palate is backed up by moderate acidity and took the wine well past the minimum Two Glass score. The '99 Cortese Vergato is an altogether simpler affair, fresh, fragrant and with an almondy finish. The best of the reds was the stainless steel-aged Barbera Superiore '98 Amaranto. Its lustrous ruby red shades into purple at the rim and the nose has all the traditional Barbera aromas, from flowers, to red berries, hay and musk. There is refreshing acidity to underpin the palate along with sweet, fruity tannins. Two Glasses and no discussion. The Barbera Superiore '98 Rodeo, aged in small casks, has more serious pretensions. Its dark, vibrant ruby leads into aromas of dried roses, red berries and blackcurrant, with a delicately balmy note. The warm, mouth-filling palate has great structure as well as unassertive tannins and acidity. Finally, there was a mention for the Pigmento '98, a monovarietal croatina with a nice tannin kick.

● Barbera del M.to Alessandra '97	▼▼	5
● Grignolino del M.to Casalese Sansìn '99	▼▼	3*
○ Piemonte Chardonnay Passione '99	▼▼	4
● Barbera del M.to La Rossa '98	▼	3
● Monferrato Rosso Bigio '99	▼	3
● Monferrato Rosso Mondone '97	▼	5
○ Piemonte Chardonnay Armonia '99	▼	3
● Monferrato Rosso Mondone '96	♈♈	5
● Monferrato Rosso Bigio '97	♈	3

● Colli Tortonesi Barbera Sup. Amaranto '98	▼▼	3*
● Colli Tortonesi Barbera Sup. Rodeo '98	▼▼	5
○ Risveglio Chardonnay '99	▼▼	4
● Pigmento '98	▼	3
○ Vergato Cortese '99	▼	2*

VINCHIO (AT)

VIVERONE (BI)

CANTINA SOCIALE
DI VINCHIO E VAGLIO SERRA
REG. S. PANCRAZIO, 1
14040 VINCHIO (AT)
TEL. 0141/950903

LA CELLA DI S. MICHELE
VIA CASCINE DI PONENTE, 21
13886 VIVERONE (BI)
TEL. 0161/98245

In today's world of wine, where outstanding individual winemakers rule the roost, it is a pleasure to note the consistently fine work carried out by some co-operative wineries. This is one of them. Since 1959, it has brought together and assisted a large group of producers to turn out an extensive range of wines that many experts have noted admiringly. Total production stands at about 400,000 bottles a year and further expansion is in the pipeline. As before, the pick of the bunch was the Barbera d'Asti Superiore Vigne Vecchie '98, the result of careful selection in the vineyard and a tried and trusted ageing technique in small oak casks. The ruby colour is virtually impenetrable, and the wine releases aromas of jam, liquorice and pepper. The palate is delicious and muscular, and the finish lingers nicely. Another interesting wine is the Barbera d'Asti Superiore '98, only about 20 percent of which is aged in barriques. On the nose, there are dusky notes of ripe fruit and minerally hints while the palate is full-bodied and well-balanced. The Freisa '99 offers an inviting entry on the nose, with crisp notes of cherry and fresh spices, following through on the palate with intriguing finesse. One Glass, too, for the Grignolino d'Asti '99, a whistle-clean, true-to-type wine of good intensity, and the Monferrato Bianco '99, from müller thurgau fruit, with its clear aromas of white peach, good development and refreshing flavour. Finally, we thought the sheer drinkability of the Cortese Dorato and the in-your-face style of the Barbera Vivace were worth a mention.

The ancient Benedictine monastery, symbolized by the Romanesque bell-tower dating from 1157, stands on the glacial slopes of the Serra d'Ivrea, on a splendid site overlooking the lake of Viverone. It is here that Leo Enrietti and his competent, committed wife, Fernanda, put down their roots 25 years ago. In a landscape of olives, palm-trees and vines, they have dedicated their efforts to the rediscovery of the erbaluce grape and the exploration of its winemaking potential. It is a rare delight to arrive here after coming up the hill from the lake, crossing the vineyards and entering the courtyard, which was once the monastery's cloister, through the lovely brick entrance. On one side are the cellars, where modern technology is employed to produce about 40,000 bottles every year, and on the other is the tasting room and taverna where – if you have phoned ahead to book – you can purchase the estate's wines. And this year, they are again of enviable quality. The established wines, the Erabluce di Caluso Cella Grande and the tank-method Spumante Brut Cella Grande di San Michele, easily hold onto the One Glass they achieved in previous editions. This year, they are joined by a Cella Grande Tardif from part-raisined erbaluce grapes harvested late in December 1998. This first vintage doesn't put a foot wrong and will be an excellent accompaniment for cakes, sweets and cheeses. The Tardif will only be made if the vintage is suitable. In fact, the first release is of only 2,000 half-litre bottles.

● Barbera d'Asti Sup.		
Vigne Vecchie '98	♟♟	5
● Barbera d'Asti Sup. '98	♟	3
● Grignolino d'Asti '99	♟	3
○ Monferrato Bianco '99	♟	3
● Monferrato Freisa '99	♟	3
● Barbera del M.to Vivace '99		3
○ Cortese dell'Alto M.to Dorato '99		3
● Barbera d'Asti Sup.		
Vigne Vecchie '96	♟♟	5
● Barbera d'Asti Sup.		
Vigne Vecchie '97	♟♟	5
● Barbera d'Asti Sup. '97	♟	3
● Barbera d'Asti Sup.		
Vigne Vecchie '95	♟	5

○ Brut Cella Grande di S. Michele	♟	3
○ Cella Grande Tardif '98	♟	5
○ Erbaluce di Caluso		
Cella Grande '99	♟	3

OTHER WINERIES

The following producers obtained good scores in our tastings with one or more of their wines:

PROVINCE OF ALESSANDRIA

Domenico Ghio, Bosio, tel. 0143/684117
Dolcetto di Ovada Sup. Drac Rosso '97

La Caplana, Bosio, tel. 0143/684182
Gavi Vignavecchia '99

Alberti, Castellania, tel. 0131/837298
Colli Tortonesi Barbera Veëdra '97

Liedholm, Cuccaro M.to, tel. 0131/771916
Barbera d'Asti '98

Roberto Gemme, Gavi, tel. 0143/682250
Gavi di Gavi Fontanassa '99

Produttori del Gavi, Gavi, tel. 0143/642786
Gavi Primuva '99

Santa Seraffa, Gavi, tel. 0143/643600
Gavi '99

Cantina Sociale Tre Castelli,
Montaldo Bormida, tel. 0143/85136
Dolcetto di Ovada Sup. Colli di Carpeneto '98

La Marchesa, Novi Ligure, tel. 0143/743362
Gavi Etichetta Nera '99

Valditerra, Novi Ligure, tel. 0143/321451
Gavi Sel. Valditerra '99

Verrina, Prasco, tel. 0144/375745
Dolcetto di Ovada Vigna Oriali '99

Saccoletto, S. Giorgio M.to, tel. 0142/806509
Barbera del M.to Vigneto I Filari Lunghi '98

La Zerba, Tassarolo, tel. 0143/342259
Gavi '99

Claudio Mariotto, Tortona, tel. 0131/868500
Colli Tortonesi Barbera Vho '98

Livio Pavese, Treville, tel. 0142/487045
Barbera d'Asti Sup. Podere S. Antonio '98

Il Mongetto, Vignale M.to, tel. 0142/933469
Barbera d'Asti Vigneto Guera '98

La Scamuzza, Vignale M.to, tel. 0142/926214
Barbera del M.to Vigneto dell'Amorosa '98

PROVINCE OF ASTI

Trinchero, Agliano Terme, tel. 0141/954016
Barbera d'Asti Vigna del Noce '98

La Giribaldina,
Calamandrana, tel. 0141/718043
Barbera d'Asti Sup. Cala delle Mandrie '97

Hohler, Cassinasco, tel. 0141/851209
Barbera d'Asti Pian del Bosco Barrique '98

Villa Fiorita,
Castello di Annone, tel. 0141/401231
Barbera d'Asti Sup. Il Giorgione '97

Renzo Beccaris,
Costigliole d'Asti, tel. 0141/966592
Barbera d'Asti Sup. S. Lorenzo '97

Cascina del Frate,
Costigliole d'Asti, tel. 0141/966494
Barbera d'Asti Sup. '98

Luigi Nebiolo,
Costigliole d'Asti, tel. 0141/966030
Barbera d'Asti S. Martino '97

Rosso, Costigliole d'Asti, tel. 0141/968437
Barbera d'Asti Sup. Cardin '98

Valfieri, Costigliole d'Asti, tel. 0141/966881
Barbera d'Asti '99

Cantina Sociale di Nizza M.to,
Nizza M.to, tel. 0141/721348
Barbera d'Asti Sup. Ceppi Vecchi '97

Chiappone, Nizza M.to, tel. 0141/721424
Barbera d'Asti Barrique '98

Gazzi, Nizza M.to, tel. 0141/793512
Barbera d'Asti Praiot '98

Guasti, Nizza M.to, tel. 0141/721350
Barbera d'Asti Sup. Barcarato '97

La Nunsiò, Nizza M.to, tel. 0141/721531
Barbera d'Asti La Nunsiò '98

Castello del Poggio,
Portacomaro, tel. 0141/202543
Barbera d'Asti Val del Temp '98

Ca' d'Carussin,
S. Marzano Oliveto, tel. 0141/831358
Barbera d'Asti Sup. Carlo Ferro '97

Mondo, S. Marzano Oliveto, tel. 0141/834096
Barbera d'Asti Vigna del Salice '98

PROVINCE OF CUNEO

Mauro Sebaste, Alba, tel. 0173/262954
Barolo Vigna Prapò '96

Poderi Sinaglio, Alba, tel. 0173/612209
Dolcetto di Diano d'Alba Sörì Bric Maiolica '99

Musso, Barbaresco, tel. 0173/635129
Barbaresco Rio Sordo '97

F.lli Barale, Barolo, tel. 0173/56127
Barolo Castellero '96

Damilano, Barolo, tel. 0173/56105
Barolo '96

Cornarea, Canale, tel. 0173/979091
Roero Arneis '99

Porello, Canale, tel. 0173/978080
Roero Bric Torretta '98

Enrico Serafino, Canale, tel. 0173/967111
Roero Pasiunà '98

Marchisio, Castellinaldo, tel. 0173/213226
Castellinaldo Barbera d'Alba Barrique '98

Marsaglia, Castellinaldo, tel. 0173/213048
Roero Sup. Marina '98

Gigi Rosso,
Castiglione Falletto, tel. 0173/262369
Barolo Arione '96

Paolo Monte, Diano d'Alba, tel. 0173/69231
Diano d'Alba Cascina Flino Vigna Vecchia '99

Oddero, Diano d'Alba, tel. 0173/69169
Dolcetto di Diano d'Alba Sorì Sorba '99

Boschis, Dogliani, tel. 0173/70574
Dolcetto di Dogliani Vigna Sorì S. Martino '99

La Fusina, Dogliani, tel. 0173/70488
Dolcetto di Dogliani Vigna Muntà '99

Bruno Porro, Dogliani, tel. 0173/70371
Dolcetto di Dogliani Ribote '99

Eraldo Revelli,
Farigliano, tel. 0173/797154
Dolcetto di Dogliani S. Matteo '99

Accomasso, La Morra, tel. 0173/50843
Barolo Rocche '96

Dosio, La Morra, tel. 0173/50677
Barolo Fossati '96

Rocche Costamagna,
La Morra, tel. 0173/509225
Barolo Rocche dell'Annunziata '96

Aurelio Settimo, La Morra, tel. 0173/50803
Barolo Rocche '96

Stroppiana,
La Morra, tel. 0173/50169
Barolo Vigna S. Giacomo '96

Osvaldo Viberti, La Morra, tel. 0173/50374
Barolo Serra dei Turchi '96

Podere Ruggeri Corsini,
Monforte d'Alba, tel. 0173/78625
Barbera d'Alba Armujan '98

Taliano, Montà d'Alba, tel. 0173/976512
Roero Ròche dra Bòssora '98

Cantina del Glicine, Neive, tel. 0173/67215
Barbaresco Marcorino '97

Cascina Crosa, Neive, tel. 0173/67376
Barbaresco Cascina Crosa '97

Castello di Neive, Neive, tel. 0173/67171
Barbaresco La Rocca di S. Stefano '97

Punset, Neive, tel. 0173/67072
Barbaresco Campo Quadro '97

Chiarle, Neviglie, tel. 0173/630162
Moscato d'Asti '99

Vit. di Rodello, Rodello, tel. 0173/617159
Dolcetto d'Alba Vigna Deserto '99

Cappellano,
Serralunga d'Alba, tel. 0173/613103
Barbera d'Alba Gabutti '97

Ada Nada, Treiso, tel. 0173/638127
Barbaresco Cichin '97

PROVINCE OF TORINO

Cooperativa della Serra,
Piverone, tel. 0125/72166
Erbaluce di Caluso '99

LIGURIA

In the firm conviction that "memory is the only Paradise from which we cannot be thrown out", we would like to devote a few lines to an unforgettable wine personality who died in January 2000. The oenologist, Pietro Trevia, was a man who always believed his principles to be more important than his ambitions. A champion of winemaking methods that aimed to preserve and express the full potential of the fruit at his disposal, he made a major contribution to raising the quality of the wines of the Riviera del Ponente. For many producers, Pietro was a stimulating consultant who pointed out the way forward with his disinterested advice. This is the way we remember him: always ready to put his views on the line, and convinced that being right or wrong is merely an insignificant detail. But now let's move on to Liguria's premium wines. Riccardo Bruna's hard work and tenacity have pulled off a minor miracle of quality with his Pigato U Bacan while his other two excellent Pigatos, Le Russeghine and Villa Torachetta, complete an outstanding hat trick. The Cascina delle Terre Rosse confirms that it is a leading producer, obtaining a Three Glass award for the first time. A source of great satisfaction not only for the estate, but also for Ligurian wine in general. The owner, Vladimiro Galluzzo, has extracted every ounce of quality from his magnificent fruit, earning our unanimous plaudits. His Pigato '99 is stunning while the Vermentino and the Pigato Selezione '98 fully live up to our expectations. There is much experimentation going on with Pigato in an attempt to express fully the potentialities of a unique grape variety and of an equally special area. The chosen route to making longer-lived wines has taken its toll in terms of youthful rough edges because the market demands whites from the latest vintage a mere five or six months after the harvest. However, the benefits of longer bottle-ageing will eventually convince restaurateurs and consumers alike. It is no surprise that certain wineries believe in allowing grape and terroir to have their say and are striving to make the very best, most cellarable wines they can. Among these, the Maria Donata Bianchi estate is concentrating on Vermentino and Pigato, as are the Tenuta Colle dei Bardellini, the Tenuta Giuncheo and – with Rossese di Dolceacqua – Mandino Cane. Back among the whites, Lupi's Vignamare and Terre Rosse's Arcana blends, both fermented in barriques, are well-established success stories. In the Albenga area, Anfossi's progress manifests itself in two standard-label wines – the Vermentino and Pigato – with marked personality while Vio and La Vecchia Cantina have a strong suit in their Vermentinos. To the west, in the Province of La Spezia, there is a welcome comeback in the shape of Forlini e Cappellini with their well-typed and skilfully made Cinque Terre, and Walter De Batte towers over the competition with his currently unbeatable Cinque Terre Sciacchetrà. Our friends in the Colli di Luni area also offer us evolution and, indeed, revolution. There is one accolade after another for Il Torchio's Vermentino and Linero, high ratings for La Pietra del Focolare, which impressed us with its basic Vermentino and the special Solarancio selection, and finally, a heartfelt commendation for the Vermentino of Roberto Giacomelli.

ALBENGA (SV)

ALBENGA (SV)

ANFOSSI
VIA PACCINI, 39
FRAZ. BASTIA
17030 ALBENGA (SV)
TEL. 0182/20024

FAUSTO DE ANDREIS
REG. RUATO, 4
FRAZ. SALEA
17030 ALBENGA (SV)
TEL. 0182/21175

In western Liguria, the prehistoric settlements, and the later ones of the Liguri Ingauni, are to be found on the routes used to transfer animals to and from summer pastures, and along the roads that served trade stimulated by the formation of farming communities. Today, taking full advantage of the fertile Albenga Plain, Mario Anfossi and Paolo Grossi's estate of around 25 hectares produces a large number of headily perfumed jars of basil, olives in brine, olive paste, artichoke spread and artichokes preserved in oil. This varied range of delicious Mediterranean condiments and preserves is destined for the markets of Lombardy, Emilia Romagna and Tuscany, or to be sold in countless delicatessens and wine shops both in Italy and abroad. The same outlets also sell the wines from the company's cellars. Year after year, quality is dependable and admirably high. The ratings achieved by the latest vintage are no exception. The basic versions of the two whites both scored over 80 points. We were particularly struck by the rich-coloured Vermentino, which offers a commendably rounded and intense range of aromas, including Mediterranean scrubland, aniseed, and pear, followed by a consistent, well-balanced and long palate. The Pigato, too, is a success, with its complex, pervasive bouquet of peach, banana, apricot, hazelnut and mineral notes. On the palate, it unveils a warm, soft, silky flavour that is perhaps a shade lacking in freshness but is undoubtedly attractive. The Le Caminate vineyard selection reveals over-evolved nutty hints, as well as a palate which has plenty of alcohol but is lacking in grip, and ends on an off-key bitterish note.

Fausto de Andreis is a man who enjoys a good debate or a new challenges so that's why he considers his Pigato, or rather Spigàu, as he has chosen to call it, to be a wine that should be aged without any hurry. Retasting some of his previous vintages confirmed the exciting cellar potential that this white can often have. Fausto's vineyard at Salea is in one of the most important subzones around Albenga and he has only one hectare under vine. It is a source of frustration for de Andreis, who would like to expand his estate and concentrate on wine but purchasing land in the area is out of the question – there is none for sale. For the time being, he grows flowers as well as grapes. His Spigàu does not enjoy DOC status, which is a deliberate choice on the part of the producer. Fausto is convinced that the denomination is merely a certificate of origin, and not a guarantee of excellence. Successful wines – he maintains – are well-made, have a distinctive personality, and have an identifiable affinity with their area of production. This is the implacable logic of a man who refuses to accept the regulations unquestioningly and who prefers to let his products speak for him. At the time of our tasting, Fausto's Spigàu was still a bit green and closed on the nose at first, opening up later to show fruity aromas and notes of camomile. On the palate, there is a certain complexity, which will probably find full expression over the next few months, as well as the robust structure heralded by the colour. It is not an immediately attractive wine but it certainly does not disappoint. The dry, zesty, enjoyable flavour has a subtle underlying hint of bitterness.

○ Riviera Ligure di Ponente Pigato '99	🍷🍷	3*
○ Riviera Ligure di Ponente Vermentino '99	🍷🍷	3*
○ Riviera Ligure di Ponente Pigato Le Caminate '98		3

○ Spigàu '99	🍷	3

ALBENGA (SV)

ALBENGA (SV)

CASCINA FEIPU DEI MASSARETTI
LOC. MASSARETTI, 8
FRAZ. BASTIA
17030 ALBENGA (SV)
TEL. 0182/20131

LA VECCHIA CANTINA
VIA CORTA, 3
FRAZ. SALEA
17030 ALBENGA (SV)
TEL. 0182/559881

There are two theories about the origin of the name "Pigato". The more scholarly hypothesis traces the word back to the Latin "picatum", indicating wine aromatized with resin and pitch. The other explanation involves a local dialect word, "piga", referring to the rust-coloured markings that often appear on the berries of this variety. Pippo Parodi always was – and still is – rightly considered to be the champion of this cultivar, which is very similar to vermentino and was indeed often confused with it almost until the end of the 19th century. Gruffly good-natured and a proud representative of the true Ligurian spirit, Pippo has earned this white variety a considerable reputation in Liguria and beyond through his search for quality. Now that he has handed over most of the work to his daughters and sons-in-law, he and his wife, Bice, supervise from behind the scenes, making sure that the property's wine continues to display the characteristics that have made it famous. The vineyard is at Massaretti, where the soil is predominantly sandy, and the vine stock is gobelet-trained, Guyot-trained or cordon-trained and spur-pruned in the traditional manner. From around five hectares planted with pigato, rossese, barbera, dolcetto and brachetto, the Parodis produce about 50,000 bottles. Their Pigato '99 earned its One Glass for a fine straw-yellow colour, a crisp, if hardly complex, nose of country herbs and peach fruit. The frank, straightforward flavour echoes the sensations on the nose and is attractively tangy and subtle, even if it is still trying to find a perfect balance.

For some time now, La Vecchia Cantina has been one of the most dependable names on Liguria's Riviera di Ponente, and a producer that consistently turns out a high level of quality. That's why we were puzzled last year to find tasted wines that were lacking in definition. Not every year is the same and misfortunes along the way are sometimes inevitable. But this time round, Umberto Calleri once again proves himself to be a skilled interpreter of Vermentino and Pigato, western Liguria's classic duo of varietal wines. His four hectares of vineyard, the farm portion of the estate, lie in the flatlands and hill country at Salea while the small but well-equipped winery is in the comfortable residence near the main farm building. Production methods here are in line with the techniques used by all winemakers who put quality first. There is minimum use of fertilizers, grass grows between the rows, the bunches are thinned out, fermentation is temperature-controlled and ageing is in stainless steel. The Vermentino is the more interesting wine. It won the panel over with its personality and its appealing progression on both nose and palate. It has an intense straw-yellow colour and broad yet fresh and inviting aromas of peach, pear and citron fruit, together with honey and hazelnuts. The flavours echo the aromas of the nose on a rich, round, full-bodied palate that offers warmth and good structure, and a leisurely, rising finish. The Pigato is well worth investigating, even though nose is only moderately intense and faintly balsamic, with hints of sage, but the reasonably concentrated palate has decent breadth.

O Riviera Ligure di Ponente		
Pigato '99	♀	4

O Riviera Ligure di Ponente		
Vermentino '99	♀♀	4
O Riviera Ligure di Ponente		
Pigato '99	♀	4

CAMPOROSSO (IM)

CASTELNUOVO MAGRA (SP)

TENUTA GIUNCHEO
LOC. GIUNCHEO
18033 CAMPOROSSO (IM)
TEL. 0184/288639

GIACOMELLI
VIA PALVOTRISIA, 134
19030 CASTELNUOVO MAGRA (SP)
TEL. 0187/674155

Tenuta Giuncheo is only a few kilometres from Camporosso but while the town is only 25 metres above sea level, the estate is 200 metres higher up. The property was bought eight years ago by a Swiss couple, Arnold and Monica Schweizer. These intelligent, enlightened entrepreneurs put their faith in Marco Romagnoli, a man equally at home in vineyard or cellar, where the contribution of renowned oenologist, Donato Lanati, should not be underestimated. Marco has self-effacingly and tenaciously got on with the job. When significant results are obtained year after year, it means that chance or improvisation are not factors, so we note with pleasure that Tenuta Giuncheo is back in the Guide on merit. We were totally won over by Le Palme, a Vermentino selection. Its seductive, intense nose unveils aromatic herbs and spring flowers that giving way to hints of citrus fruit and boiled sweets;. There is good weight on the palate, as well as concentration, depth, rich alcohol warmth and nice length. The standard-label Vermentino, too, was generally appreciated for its wealth of subtle but well-expressed fragrances. The palate stands out for its impressive – perhaps even excessive – softness, which is only partly offset by the acidity. It's fairly full-bodied but the taste components do not really come together. The well-managed, quaffable basic Rossese is up to its usual standard. It is a medium-bodied wine with a reasonably intense nose that mingles fruit and balsamic notes. On the palate, the fruit is sustained by attractive alcohol warmth and good length. When the panel was visiting, the Pian del Vescovo vineyard selection of Rossese was still ageing while the Vermentino Eclis will stay for even longer in the wood.

After a few years in the wilderness and a One Glass wine last year, here at last is true recognition for the Giacomelli winery, which this time round joins the Two Glass club. There are only a few hectares of vineyard that produce a few thousand bottles of honest-to-goodness Colli di Luni Bianco, made from vermentino, albarola and trebbiano, a sangiovese and canaiolo-based Rosso, and a really fine monovarietal Vermentino. The one presented by Roberto Giacomelli at this year's tasting is at the top of its class. It's very well made and impressively quality-focused. The deep straw-yellow colour has brilliant highlights and ushers in firm, pervasive aromas of spring flowers, tropical fruit and myrtle, with a subtle underlying honeyed note. It is agreeably forceful on the palate. The fruit is long, rich and juicy, with good balancing acidity, and echoes the sensations on the nose, closing with a characteristic almondy finish. A more than satisfactory result, particularly if we remember that, at least on the Riviera di Levante, '99 was by no means a memorable vintage. The vineyards are situated on hillslopes at 250 metres above sea level and face south. Roberto, who uses only grapes from his own vineyards, was able to keep tight control over the whole production process, making several passes though the vineyards at harvest time and picking only perfectly ripe grapes. He therefore obtained separate lots of grapes which he fermented individually before blending the final products. A significant contribution also came from the experienced Giorgio Baccigalupi, an oenologist who is well-known and highly thought of in Levante winemaking circles. It was he who helped Roberto to maintain fully the quality and typicity achieved in the vineyard.

○ Riviera Ligure di Ponente Vermentino Le Palme '99	▼▼	4
○ Riviera Ligure di Ponente Vermentino '99	▼	3
● Rossese di Dolceacqua '99	▼	3
○ Riviera Ligure di Ponente Vermentino Eclis '98	♈♈	5
● Rossese di Dolceacqua Vigneto Pian del Vescovo '97	♈	4
● Rossese di Dolceacqua Vigneto Pian del Vescovo '98	♈	4

○ Colli di Luni Vermentino '99	▼▼	3*
○ Giacomelli Bianco '99		2
● Giacomelli Rosso '99		2

CASTELNUOVO MAGRA (SP)   CASTELNUOVO MAGRA (SP)

IL TORCHIO
VIA PROVINCIALE, 202
19030 CASTELNUOVO MAGRA (SP)
TEL. 0187/674075

OTTAVIANO LAMBRUSCHI
VIA OLMARELLO, 28
19030 CASTELNUOVO MAGRA (SP)
TEL. 0187/674261

A nice brace of Two Glass wines for an estate that has been reviewing its production methods over the last three years and is now fixing its sights firmly on quality and reliability, albeit after some ups and downs. The fact that some new hillside vineyards have come on-stream, together with longer macerations and the judicious use of refrigeration, have enabled owner Giorgio Tendola to produce two Il Torchio wines from the latest vintage that both scored over 80 points. The Linero, made from 70 percent vermentino along with albarola and trebbiano, is a bright straw-yellow colour. Its clean bouquet combines scents of Mediterranean scrubland, lime and acacia blossom, and plums, and the fruit in the mouth reflects the aromas on the nose. The palate is broad and well-structured, with an attractive almondy finish that offsets the hint of residual sugar. The flagship Vermentino has a deep, intense hue and a delicatel nose with hints of spring flowers and aromatic notes where Mediterranean scrubland emerges distinctly. All this is brought into focus by a subtle smoky note. A positive entry on the palate offers a good balance of tanginess and softness. Although a little light on acidity, there is good length and it has an appealing style. A wine that will definitely benefit from bottle-age. In contrast, the sangiovese, merlot and syrah-based Rosso Riserva is still rather unbalanced, with over-assertive tannins. It fails to convince partly because of its rather too simple style and partly because of its light, evanescent aromas. This youngster will have to grow up before it achieves the results so often obtained by the two whites.

This estate is a Guide fixture and again this year confirms that it is one of the most interesting wineries in the Colli di Luni subzone. The tenacity and passion with which Ottaviano and Fabio Lambruschi are seeking to improve their wines are the stuff of legend. Sadly, the gods are sometimes over-generous with the rain so all the pair's hard work may produce results that are no more than satisfactory. The three wines we tasted all achieved One Glass ratings. Although substantially well-made, they scored no higher because concentration suffered as a result of wet weather during the vintage. The Sarticola obtained the highest score. Its up-front nose offers notes of country herbs and spring flowers. On the palate, it is refreshing, reasonably well-balanced and silky, in spite of a touch of greenness that will disappear with a little bottle-age. On the other hand, the longest-established selection, the Costa Marina, seems a little unknit. The nose hints only fleetingly at floral and aromatic notes and the fruit on the palate is light in structure, with a slightly exaggerated almondy vein. Balsamic aromas, as well as scents of Mediterranean scrubland and notes of hydrangea, are evident in the standard-label Vermentino while its no-nonsense flavour reveals marked, but quite typical, notes of citrus. We were favourably impressed by a cellar tasting of the new, soon-to-be-released red. It is the brainchild and passion of Fabio, and is coming along very nicely. In fact, it has even overcome the initial reluctance of Fabio's father, Ottaviano, a dyed-in-the-wool white wine man.

O Colli di Luni Vermentino '99	ŸŸ	3*
O Linero '99	ŸŸ	3*
● Colli di Luni Rosso Ris. '98	Ÿ	4

O Colli di Luni Vermentino '99	Ÿ	3
O Colli di Luni Vermentino Costa Marina '99	Ÿ	3
O Colli di Luni Vermentino Sarticola '99	Ÿ	3

DIANO CASTELLO (IM)

DOLCEACQUA (IM)

Maria Donata Bianchi
Via delle Torri, 16
18010 Diano Castello (IM)
Tel. 0183/498233

Giobatta Mandino Cane
Via Roma, 21
18035 Dolceacqua (IM)
Tel. 0184/206120

Emanuele Trevia's estate, which has been expanding gradually as the new plantings have come on-stream, has made significant strides forward. The winery, already partly renovated a few years ago, will now be transferred to a new, more spacious site to optimize the workflow and there will also be a purpose-built tasting room. Alongside vermentino and pigato, the traditional grape varieties of the zone, new red cultivars have been introduced, which will enable an innovative wine (probably a grenache-based blend) to be added to a range dominated by whites. Emanuele's intuition and planning for the future are helping to maintain a high level of quality across the range, which includes a Pigato that put up an impressive show at our tastings. A concentrated structure and well-expressed typicity are among its most attractive qualities. The perfect harmony of sensations on the nose and palate, a lively, zesty flavour and the attractive balance, as well as a vibrant straw-yellow colour, complete an admirable taste profile. It will be interesting to follow the evolution of this Pigato over the next few months. The fresh-tasting Vermentino is as persuasive as ever. Its delicate floral and fruity notes are echoed on the palate, which offers ample structure, light, well-modulated acidity, and an underlying bitter note of almonds. All in all, a very inviting, easy-drinking wine. The two Ereticos, the Vermentino and the Pigato, were fermented and aged in small Allier oak casks. As they are still ageing, we'll be back for them next year.

Mandino Cane is a spry, dynamic 71-year-old with the spirit and enthusiasm of a much younger man. This small estate, which turns out 10,000 bottles a year, caused a stir among makers of Rossese di Dolceacqua by calling into question the prevailing philosophy, rooted in outdated habit rather than in any real tradition. In fact, "tradition" was frequently – and incorrectly – invoked as the justification for some pretty dubious products. For now, the range focuses on two crus, which reflect the differences between the single-vineyard wines and the basic Rossese. However, experiments are under way with syrah and viognier, which should form the basis for future wines. The marked varietal characteristics that one always finds in Mandino Cane's bottles can be put down to his commitment to using the bare minimum of technical intervention during vinification and ageing. The resulting reds have a satisfyingly rich texture that combines good alcohol with prominent acidity. The vineyards of Arcagna provide the grapes selected for the Rossese Superiore named after the are. The '99 version, released in November, stands out for its intensity and fullness on the nose, where you can detect hints of strawberries, brambles, redcurrants and Parma violets. The persistence on the palate is equally impressive, and the well-defined, full, rounded flavour drives through to an attractive bitter finish. The Morghe vineyard selection, a Rossese Superiore of considerable power, also scored well. The aromas of the rich bouquet are echoed perfectly on the palate and although it is more austere than the Arcagna, and at first rather subdued, the mid palate is more approachable and open. But it never loses sight of its very own distinctive and sophisticated style so our congratulations go to Mandino.

○ Riviera Ligure di Ponente		
Pigato '99	🍷🍷	4
○ Riviera Ligure di Ponente		
Vermentino '99	🍷	4
○ Eretico Pigato '97	🍷🍷	5
○ Eretico Vermentino '97	🍷🍷	5

● Rossese di Dolceacqua Sup.		
Vigneto Arcagna '99	🍷🍷	4
● Rossese di Dolceacqua Sup.		
Vigneto Morghe '99	🍷🍷	4
● Rossese di Dolceacqua Sup.		
Vigneto Morghe '98	🍷🍷	4
● Rossese di Dolceacqua Sup.		
Vigneto Arcagna '98	🍷	4

DOLCEACQUA (IM)

FINALE LIGURE (SV)

TERRE BIANCHE
LOC. ARCAGNA
18035 DOLCEACQUA (IM)
TEL. 0184/31426

CASCINA DELLE TERRE ROSSE
VIA MANIE, 3
17024 FINALE LIGURE (SV)
TEL. 019/698782

This is a solid, family-run estate where the various responsibilities are shared by Paolo Rondelli, who looks after sales, his brother-in-law Franco Laconi, whose vineyard management philosophy of "use only a little but use the best", and the respected Piedmontese winemaker, Mario Ronco. Their quality across the board is good, but two wines stood out in particular, the Arcana Bianco and the Rossese di Dolceacqua Bricco Arcagna. The former, made from pigato and vermentino fermented in partly new barriques, has an eloquent vitality, loads of class and great style. Its brilliant, intense colour introduces a rich nose of coffee and chocolate aromas that give way to notes of fruit, honey and musk. The well-balanced palate mirrors the bouquet and shows a certain amount of complexity. Soft yet well-structured, it has a fresh underlying acidity to bring it to life. The Bricco Arcagna has a penetrating nose veined with smoky notes from the oak that mingle with hints of roses, violets and red berry fruit. It offers an inviting softness on the front palate, and then shows good concentration and nice length in its development. The rossese and cabernet sauvignon Arcana Rosso is also good. Attractive fruit on the nose is rendered even more intriguing by oaky notes and while the fruit on the palate is not particularly fleshy, it has good balance and appealing length. The basic Rossese di Dolceacqua is more straightforward. A little reticent on the nose and with a rather light body, it is still a nice wine that has you reaching for a second glass. The Vermentino harbours no surprises. The nose has prominent fruit laced with honey and pine resin. The entry on the palate is soft and there is good thrust through to the finish. The Pigato is of a similar standard, its subtle, fresh aromas recalling spring flowers, sage and musk. It may not be especially long on the palate but it is very tidily made.

Vladimiro Galluzzo's estate is in the heart of the verdant Manie plateau. The vineyards, which are laid out in semi-circles, are looked after like suburban gardens. Vladimiro is one of Liguria's finest wine producers and a man who has always taken quality-led decisions on everything, from the type and density of his plantings to yields, not forgetting the way he manages his vines, which is practically organic. Quality is also the keynote of his modern, functional and aesthetically pleasing winery. Vladimiro's wines reflect his personality. They are well-balanced, approachable, very pleasant and technically irreproachable. We tasted some extraordinary wines this year but the star is the '99 Pigato, a white with outstanding structure and great ageing potential. Straw-yellow in colour, it has an intriguingly subtle bouquet, rich in nuances of Mediterranean shrubland, basil, apricots and honey. The very full, satisfying flavour echoes the aromas of the nose with great elegance, good thrust, splendid weight in the mouth and a long finish. This is the Pigato that brought a Three Glass award to Liguria again after several lean years. The '98 Pigato, obtained from scrupulously selected fruit and released a year after the harvest, is almost up to the same standard. On the nose, the aromatic richness of the fruit gradually gives way to sweetish notes of honey, musk and ripe peaches. The palate has good body and concentration, as well as nice balance and freshness. The Vermentino is also very good, showing all its customary finesse and personality. Another success is the L'Acerbina, from 100% lumassina fruit, that delights the nose with heady scents of spring meadows, hay and a hint of almonds. It has soft, inviting fruit on the palate, along with an evident and appealing tanginess. So, congratulations to Vladimiro Galluzzo. His success this year will be a shot in the arm for the region's viticulture.

O Arcana Bianco '98	♟♟	5
● Rossese di Dolceacqua Bricco Arcagna '98	♟♟	5
● Arcana Rosso '98	♟	5
O Riviera Ligure di Ponente Pigato '99	♟	4
O Riviera Ligure di Ponente Vermentino '99	♟	4
● Rossese di Dolceacqua '99	♟	4
O Arcana Bianco '97	♟♟	5
● Arcana Rosso '97	♟♟	5
● Rossese di Dolceacqua Bricco Arcagna '97	♟♟	5

O Riviera Ligure di Ponente Pigato '99	♟♟♟	4
O Riviera Ligure di Ponente Pigato Sel. '98	♟♟	4
O Riviera Ligure di Ponente Vermentino '99	♟♟	4
O L'Acerbina '99	♟	3*
O Le Banche '97	♟♟	5
● Solitario '97	♟♟	6
O Passito Terre Rosse '95	♟	6

IMPERIA

ORTONOVO (SP)

COLLE DEI BARDELLINI
VIA FONTANAROSA, 12
LOC. S. AGATA
18100 IMPERIA
TEL. 0183/291370

LA PIETRA DEL FOCOLARE
VIA DOGANA, 209
19034 ORTONOVO (SP)
TEL. 0187/662129

"The Year of Vermentino". That could be suitable title for a film about the '99 vintage at the Colli dei Bardellini estate, for that was the star variety. Even the more aristocratic Pigato was put in the shade. The estate's top-scoring bottle was the Vigna U Munte selection. It has a lustrous straw-yellow colour with good depth, leading in to an expansive, subtle and very pervasive nose with distinctly aromatic notes that are followed by hints of peaches and spring flowers (broom). The palate is well-balanced, full-bodied and warm, underpinned by a citrusy vein, and the finish is clean and long. The standard-label Vermentino is also good, although the colour is less intense and the nose less concentrated. Nevertheless, the aromas open out well to reveal attractively fresh notes of citron, aniseed and Mediterranean shrubland. The palate is full-flavoured, lingering and dry, over a pleasantly bitterish note. The Pigato La Torretta, a third of which spends some time in new or used wood, earns One Glass. Its straw-yellow is faintly flecked with gold while the nose combines varietal notes of ripe peaches and apricots with prominent pine resin aromas, all laced with light toasty hints. On the palate, the various components are still rather unknit, though the balance is good. The standard Pigato is undemanding and has no great pretensions. The nose is light and acidity dominates the palate. It should be remembered that the estate's consultant is the hugely respected Giuliano Noè.

Two wines sailed blithely through the 80-point barrier and another rated 70-plus with similar ease. Not bad for a small estate which has only been up and running for three years. Stefano Salvetti and his wife Laura have very clear ideas. Even though they are still searching for a distinctive winemaking style, they give their wines that special imprint and personality that are indispensable for achieving results of note. Their most interesting wine is the Solarancio. Made from a selection of the best grapes from the Sarticola and Bacchiano vineyards, it benefits from a brief maceration of the must on the skins, but sees no wood. Its straw-yellow colour is clear and concentrated, ushering in subtle yet generous aromatic hints of Mediterranean scrubland and autumn leaves. On the palate, it is silky, rich and well-balanced, with a long, crisp finish. The standard Vermentino is good, too, its enticing nose combining floral notes of camomile with aromatic and resinous nuances over gooseberry fruit. Elegant rather than powerful on the palate, it manages to appeal although is lacks a bit of structure. The other vineyard selection, the Villa Linda, scored only slightly lower. It comes from the Becco plot, a name used last year for the wine as well. Villa Linda is the result of a more complex winemaking process that involves blending three wines made with different vinification techniques: "normal" temperature-controlled fermentation without the skins; fermentation in barrique; and ageing on the lees with regular stirring, "bâtonnage". The vibrant straw-yellow in the glass unveils rich, slightly evolved aromas of honey, peach, sage and vanilla. The fruit on the palate has admirable texture and reasonable balance and the alcohol is well to the fore.

O Riviera Ligure di Ponente Vermentino '99	YY	3*
O Riviera Ligure di Ponente Vermentino Vigna U Munte '99	YY	4
O Riviera Ligure di Ponente Pigato Vigna La Torretta '99	Y	4
O Riviera Ligure di Ponente Pigato '99		4

O Colli di Luni Vermentino Solarancio '99	YY	3*
O Colli di Luni Vermentino '99	YY	3*
O Colli di Luni Vermentino Villa Linda '99	Y	3

PIEVE DI TECO (IM)

RANZO (IM)

TOMMASO E ANGELO LUPI
VIA MAZZINI, 9
18026 PIEVE DI TECO (IM)
TEL. 0183/36161 - 0183/291610

A MACCIA
VIA UMBERTO I, 56
FRAZ. BORGO
18028 RANZO (IM)
TEL. 0183/318003

Again this year, the range of wines from this Pieve di Teco-based estate is more than satisfactory, confirming a laudable, ongoing commitment to quality. The Lupis have engaged the services of Donato Lanati, an aristocrat among oenologists, and are working hard to bring out the best in the indigenous varieties of the Riviera Ligure di Ponente DOC zone – vermentino, pigato and ormeasco – as well as Rossese di Dolceacqua. The Vignamare, a blend of pigato and vermentino partly fermented in barriques, is a wine with no shortage of character or personality. A vibrant straw yellow, it combines breadth and elegance on the nose, confirming this favourable first impression in the leisurely, full-bodied palate that speaks volumes for its cellarability. The other whites are also well-managed. The Pigato Le Petraie boasts an attractive nose, with fruit aromas set against a floral backdrop of wistaria. The palate mirrors the nose, evincing reasonable concentration and softness. The basic Pigato is equally good. Rather closed at first on the nose, it then unveils floral notes nuanced with fresh figs. The palate is instantly approachable, bringing together balance, finesse and roundness. The Vermentinos are well-crafted. The basic version has pleasantly intense varietal aromas laced with minty notes. The tangy, inviting palate could do with a more robust structure, though. In contrast, the Le Serre selection has faintly balsamic notes on the nose, followed by hints of flowers and citron. The palate is refreshing, nicely balanced, and attractively quaffable. Lastly, the Ormeasco Le Braje, the winery's leading red, scored well. It is an interesting interpretation of this green-stalked version of dolcetto, which is charming and easy to drink, in spite of its heavy-duty fruit on both nose and palate.

There are not many women making wine in Liguria but Loredana Fiorito stands out among them. She is one of the region's leading players and her professionalism and perseverance have for some years now guaranteed her a well-deserved profile in our Guide. Loredana's small winery is very conscious of its origins and demonstrates this by carrying on the centuries-old Ligurian tradition of combining viticulture with the production of extra-virgin olive oil. But since we are talking about Pigato, wine is anything but an afterthought. The roughly three hectares under vine are situated near Ranzo, in a particularly favourable hillslope area. The grapes are cosseted in the vineyard, where organic methods are employed, and then Rossano Abbona, a 30-year-old wine technician who really knows his job, takes over in the cellar. The Pigato has definite potential, which has yet to express itself fully. Enviably correct and very well-made, it could perhaps do with a bit more personality. It has to be admitted, though, that the quality is spot-on yet again this year. The brilliant straw-yellow leads us into a broad but elegant nose, with initial nuances of pine resin and wild herbs that give way to pineapple and pear fruit. These aromas find their echo on the palate, which has good length and satisfying concentration. On the palate, the presence of the fruit, accompanied by lively acidity, is very appealing, as is the progression through to a varietal finish with the classic Pigato bitter note. The Rossese is rich in fruit on nose and palate, displaying a reasonably full-bodied flavour and good balance. In short, a velvety, quaffable wine.

○ Vignamare '98	♟♟	4
● Riviera Ligure di Ponente Ormeasco Sup. Le Braje '98	♟	4
○ Riviera Ligure di Ponente Pigato '99	♟	4
○ Riviera Ligure di Ponente Pigato Le Petraie '99	♟	4
○ Riviera Ligure di Ponente Vermentino '99	♟	4
○ Riviera Ligure di Ponente Vermentino Le Serre '99	♟	4
● Riviera Ligure di Ponente Ormeasco Sup. Le Braje '96	♟♟	4
○ Vignamare '97	♟♟	4

○ Riviera Ligure di Ponente Pigato '99	♟	3
● Riviera Ligure di Ponente Rossese '99	♟	3

152

RANZO (IM)

RIOMAGGIORE (SP)

BRUNA
VIA UMBERTO I, 81
FRAZ. BORGO
18028 RANZO (IM)
TEL. 0183/318082

WALTER DE BATTÈ
VIA PECUNIA, 168
19017 RIOMAGGIORE (SP)
TEL. 0187/920127 - 0347/6019704

Riccardo Bruna's excellent results are not some kind of serendipitous happenstance. They are the direct consequence of his deep-seated, ongoing commitment to quality. Making premium products means investing money, time and effort but what really matters to Riccardo is challenging himself to get even better wines from grapes he – correctly – considers to be outstanding. His four hectares lie partly at Ortovero and partly at Ranzo, both excellent Pigato-growing areas, and he makes two wines. Starting this year, however, Riccardo has added a special cuvée. This is a meticulous selection of part super-ripe grapes, with corresponding extract and sugar levels, which is aged in vats and then in the bottle for one year. His daughters, who lend a hand at the winery when necessary, have named it "U Bacan", ("The Boss"), obviously alluding to their father. It came very close to winning our Three Glass accolade, and displays excellent overall harmony. The lovely, vibrant straw-yellow hue introduces fresh, stylish aromas of fruit, musk, pine resin and honey. The broad, full-bodied palate is well-balanced and satisfying, with a long, almondy note to provide a counterpoint. The Le Russeghine vineyard selection is also very attractive, blending well-defined notes of herbs and Mediterranean scrubland with measured nuances of fruit. On the palate, the solid structure, excellent depth, and impressive fruit come out, taking you through to a long finish. The Pigato Villa Torrachetta performed handsomely as well. A fairly broad bouquet with prominent notes of summer flowers, peaches and honey gives way to a generous, intriguingly tangy flavour. The well-made, deliciously drinkable Rossese completes the range.

The Sciacchetrà from the '97 vintage is majestic and very exciting. It becomes harder and harder each year to find new adjectives to describe a wine that Walter coaxes until it expresses itself to the full, acquiring a wonderfully unique personality. Its warm amber hue is enhanced by subtle reddish highlights while the broad spectrum of aromas reveals an elegant finesse that is sustained by enough dynamism to give it an enviable persistence. The palate conjures up aromas of dried apricots, peaches, raisins and figs, mingling with walnuts; then there are fainter hints of spices, vanilla and chestnut honey. In the mouth, it is stunning in its vigour and authority, and reveals rare balance. Stylishly sweet, tangy and warm, the palate is endowed with just the right degree of sinew by its intriguing tannins. Add superb length to the description and you have a real thoroughbred, with a price to match! The dry version is equally splendid. Its hallmark softness lends its breadth and an unctuous richness. As you can imagine, this is a very special white with a complex nose. This is a wine "vinified" in the vineyard – Walter thins out the bunches ruthlessly to obtain quite spectacularly concentrated fruit – rather than the cellar, where the only aim is to preserve what Mother Nature has provided. A final curiosity. In collaboration with Guido Porrati, owner of the "Bottega dei Sestieri", Walter has created a very unusual "inebriated" cheese called Trancantu, aged in the pomace of his precious Sciacchetrà.

O Riviera Ligure di Ponente Pigato Le Russeghine '99	♥♥	4*
O Riviera Ligure di Ponente Pigato U Bacan '99	♥♥	5
O Riviera Ligure di Ponente Pigato Villa Torrachetta '99	♥♥	3*
● Riviera Ligure di Ponente Rossese '99		3
O Riviera Ligure di Ponente Pigato Le Russeghine '98	♀♀	3

O Cinque Terre Sciacchetrà '97	♥♥	6
O Cinque Terre '99	♥♥	5
O Cinque Terre '98	♀♀	5
O Cinque Terre Sciacchetrà '95	♀♀	6
O Cinque Terre Sciacchetrà '96	♀♀	6

RIOMAGGIORE (SP)

FORLINI E CAPPELLINI
VIA RICCOBALDI, 45
FRAZ. MANAROLA
19010 RIOMAGGIORE (SP)
TEL. 0187/920496

At first sight, the Cinque Terre looks like an enormous architectural model comprising an infinite number of horizontal planes resting on low dry stone walls. Over the last few years, many holdings have been abandoned and, sadly, the area has taken on the appearance of a wilderness and become an inviting habitat for wild boar. In these parts, there are very few growers still active, pursuing a backbreaking occupation which yields Lilliputian production volumes. Two of the survivors are Alberto Cappellini and Germana Forlini, a likeable and resilient couple united not only by marriage but also by their shared passion for viticulture. They have been encouraged by the increasing involvement of their son, Giacomo, in the winery. Even though his day job is working for the Electricity Board, he now looks after the winery's sales operation. This team, their excellent fruit, and vinification techniques that have undergone considerable improvement – the must now spends longer on the lees and filtration is less drastic – have produced from the most recent vintage, after some years of ups and downs, 8,000 bottles of a good Cinque Terre white. In the glass, the wine is a bright yellow with lively greenish highlights, its delicate but persistent nose is utterly typical, offering well-defined notes wild herbs, elderflower, vine blossom and subtle hints of brine. The dry, tangy, warm palate has a fairly soft, persistent flavour with good balance and echoes perfectly the aromas on the nose.

O Cinque Terre '99	🍷	4

VENDONE (SV)

CLAUDIO VIO
FRAZ. CROSA, 16
17032 VENDONE (SV)
TEL. 0182/76338

Viticulture in Liguria is, by its very nature, a tough and unglamorous activity, ideally suited to someone as practically minded and laconic as Claudio Vio. His is a small estate of five hectares, only two of which are planted to vine. It is located in the village of Vendone, in the Arroscia valley. Claudio produces a number of bottles – 15,000 – which elsewhere would be considered derisory, but which here, in this region wedged between the mountains and the sea, represents a great deal of sweat and toil. He owns some outstanding sites which bear ancient names – Barbigione, Valle, Costa della Crosa and Ronco Bruciato – and which enjoy magnificent south-facing aspects. Claudio is a passionate, intelligent grower and winemaker who employs low yields and up-to-date equipment and techniques to produce some very fine wines indeed. The last vintage was kinder to the Vermentino and the result can be seen in Claudio's persuasive Two Glass wine. A bright straw-yellow in colour, with distinct "legs", it offers a clean nose that, after an initial and perfectly normal whiff of sulphur dioxide, opens to reveal an interesting array of aromas. Aromatic herbs, spring flowers (broom and aniseed) blend with just a whisper of peach fruit. The dry, warm palate echoes these aromas, offering tangy acidity, notable structure and good length over an attractive bitterish undertone. In contrast, the Pigato can do no better than One Glass. A deep straw-yellow in the glass, it opens out into a rather brash bouquet with very pronounced notes of nutmeg, balsam and pine needles. There is a lack of balance, too, on the palate, which has a decidedly bitterish twist to the finish.

O Riviera Ligure di Ponente Vermentino '99	🍷🍷	3*
O Riviera Ligure di Ponente Pigato '99	🍷	3

OTHER WINERIES

The following producers obtained good scores in our tastings with one or more of their wines:

PROVINCE OF GENOVA

Enoteca Bisson
Chiavari, tel. 0185/314462
Golfo del Tigullio Bianchetta Genovese
U Pastine '99,
Golfo del Tigullio Rosso Il Musaico '99

Enoteca Bruzzone
Genova Bolzaneto, tel. 010/7455157
Val Polcevera Bianchetta Genovese '99

F.lli Parma, Ne, tel. 0185/337073
Golfo del Tigullio Vermentino I Canselé '99,
Golfo del Tigullio Bianchetta Genovese
Vigna dei Parma '99

PROVINCE OF IMPERIA

Rocca di San Nicolao
Chiusanico, tel. 0183/52850
Riviera Ligure di Ponente Pigato
Vigna Proxi '99,
Riviera Ligure di Ponente Vermentino
Vigna Proxi '99

Montali & Temesio
Diano Marina, tel. 0183/495207
Riviera Ligure di Ponente Vermentino
Vigna Sorì '99

Antonio Perrino
Dolceacqua, tel. 0184/206267
Rossese di Dolceacqua '99

Laura Aschero
Pontedassio, tel. 0183/293515
Riviera Ligure di Ponente Pigato '99,
Riviera Ligure di Ponente Vermentino '99

Lorenzo Ramò
Pornassio, tel. 0183/33097
Riviera Ligure di Ponente Ormeasco '99,
Riviera Ligure di Ponente Ormeasco
Sciac-trà '99

Alessandri
Ranzo, tel. 0182/53458
Riviera Ligure di Ponente Pigato
Costa de Vigne '99

Giovanna Maccario
S. Biagio della Cima, tel. 0184/289947
Rossese di Dolceacqua Sup.
Vigneto Posaù '98

PROVINCE OF LA SPEZIA

Fattoria Il Chioso
Arcola, tel. 0187/986620
Colli di Luni Vermentino Stemma '99,
Colli di Luni Rosso Gran Baccano '98

Il Framiò
Castelnuovo Magra, tel. 0187/670319
Colli di Luni Rosso '98

Cooperativa Agricola di Riomaggiore, Manarola, Corniglia, Vernazza e Monterosso
Riomaggiore, tel. 0187/920435
Cinque Terre Costa de Campu
di Manarola '99

Il Monticello
Sarzana, tel. 0187/621432
Colli di Luni Rosso Poggio dei Magni '98,
Colli di Luni Vermentino Podere Paterno '98

Santa Caterina
Sarzana, tel. 0187/610129
Colli di Luni Vermentino '99,
Colli di Luni Bianco '98,
Colli di Luni Rosso '98,
Ghiaretolo '98

PROVINCE OF SAVONA

Cantine Calleri
Albenga, tel. 0182/21710
Riviera Ligure di Ponente Ormeasco '99,
Riviera Ligure di Ponente Pigato
Soleasco '99,
Riviera Ligure di Ponente Pigato '99,
Riviera Ligure di Ponente Vermentino
I Musazzi '99

LOMBARDY

Oenological Lombardy is moving quickly down the road to quality and competitiveness. The nine wines awarded Three Glasses in this year's Guide represent the region's best performance to date. In other words, Lombard estates are working hard to compete with the best wine regions in Italy and become serious players on the international scene. You only need visit one of Lombardy's traditional growing areas to see for yourself. Winery facilities are constantly being renovated and, particularly, winemaking equipment is everywhere being replaced. Old vineyards with large-volume training systems, and those not designed for quality, are disappearing from the scene. Oenologists and agronomists, once the advisers of a few enlightened producers, are now commonplace, even at small and medium-sized wineries. The results of all this effort are evident. They are there in the glass for all to see, and we could only record them in the Guide. Franciacorta, as usual, leads the list with five of the nine top awards. Though a well-deserved success, it was almost a foregone conclusion. In few areas of Italy is there the same passion and zeal for sheer achievement. Beyond the number of prize-winning wines, we should point out the improvement growth in the overall quality of the zone's wineries. Our panels used the same evaluation criteria as in the past but the abundance of Two Glass wines in Franciacorta bears witness to the fact that grower-producers there are not content merely to muddle through. Instead, they work harder with each new harvest to gain a place in the front rank. Something similar is happening in Valtellina. This zone used to have a reputation for being very conservative and too attached to tradition, in the worst sense of the word. In this edition, however, Valtellina has picked up three accolades. This is a strong signal. It means that producers up there in the hills have become aware of their great potential. They are beginning to see that a promising future lies within their grasp. The formula is very simple and Valtellina's wineries are applying it scrupulously. Vineyards are being restructured on strict quality-oriented criteria and careful management of fermentation, and ageing in good quality wood, is now the order of the day. Now we come to the Oltrepò Pavese, which this year celebrates its first Three Glass wine. It is the Oltrepò Pavese Metodo Classico from Monsupello, a winery that has made great efforts over the last few years to reach this objective. One triumph may not be very much, considering the immense potential of the zone, but it is a start. We are certain that many producers on the far side of the river Po will take the hint and rise to the challenge. Finally, the eastern part of the region, though it produced no top ratings, is proving to be a competitive zone and very attentive to what is happening in the world of wine. Many wineries there have shown they have ambitious plans for the medium term. We look forward to the results.

ADRO (BS)

ADRO (BS)

COLA
VIA SANT'ANNA, 22
25030 ADRO (BS)
TEL. 030/7356195

CONTADI CASTALDI
VIA COLZANO - FORNACI BIASCA, 32
25030 ADRO (BS)
TEL. 030/7450126

This beautiful estate at Adro, the property of Battista and Stefano Cola, has a great resource in the 12 hectares of beautiful vineyards on the slopes of Monte Alto that guarantee excellent raw material for the cellar's wines and Franciacortas. Again this year, thanks to the invaluable consultancy of oenologist Alberto Musatti, the panel's verdict on the range is flattering. The Cola family's flagship bottle is an excellent Franciacorta Extra Brut '96. Full-bodied, elegant and firm, with an attractive all-round softness, it releases stylish and pleasantly ripe aromas of rennet apples on the nose and palate, where its vigour and body come through. This is a Franciacorta with clean, up-front aromas and significant potential for development in the bottle. The Franciacorta Brut has a lovely, deep straw-yellow colour and a sweet nose characterized by hints of yeast, elegant but perhaps a bit over-evolved. On the palate, it shows good body, structure and delicacy, the well-rounded flavour signing off on notes of ripe fruit and toastiness. The Terre Bianco '99 is refreshing and offers striking aromas of tropical fruit on the nose. Its soft, lingering palate puts it among the best of the vintage. The Terre Bianco Tinazza has a lovely fruity richness. It is succulent, but perhaps slightly lacking in acid vitality. Other good quality wines are the Tamino red and the basic Terre Rosso.

Contadi Castaldi was created less than ten years ago but it has already become a shining star in the Franciacorta constellation. Unlike most of the producers in the DOC zone, this cellar, which belongs to the Terre Moretti group that also owns Bellavista, has no vineyards of its own. Or at least, nothing like enough to supply its needs. Credit for its success goes to its brilliant management, made up of Martino De Rosa, the winery administrator, and Mario Falcetti, the oenologist in charge of the technical side of things. Just like the great Champagne makers, Contadi Castaldi, too, buys grapes from the best locations in Franciacorta, from small producers whose progress has been scrutinized all year by its team of experts. This, along with the modern, well-equipped cellars at Adro, give an annual production of more than 300,000 excellent-quality bottles. The Satèn '95 is exemplary in this sense. One of the best Franciacortas we tasted this year, it is a very elegant wine, complex and harmonious both on nose and palate, where it echoes with the same ripe apricot, artemisia and vanilla already detected by the nose. The soft, complex palate finishes with quick flashes of apple and, again, apricot jam. It almost collected a Three Glass rating. The Terre di Franciacorta Bianco Mancapane '98 is an excellent Chardonnay, with a fresh, intense nose where notes of medicinal herbs finish with a rich vein of fruit and hints of vanilla. It is equally firm and refreshing on the palate, offering a clean, lingering fruitiness that is not covered up by the new wood. From the sweet Pinodisé to the Franciacorta Brut, the rest of the wines in the range were all excellent.

O	Franciacorta Brut	♆♆	4
O	Franciacorta Extra Brut '96	♆♆	5
O	T. d. F. Bianco '99	♆	2*
O	T. d. F. Bianco V. Tinazza '98	♆	3
●	T. d. F. Rosso '98	♆	2*
●	T. d. F. Rosso Tamino '98	♆	3
O	Franciacorta Brut	♈♈	4
O	Franciacorta Extra Brut '92	♈♈	4
O	Franciacorta Extra Brut '94	♈♈	4
O	Franciacorta Extra Brut '95	♈♈	4
O	T. d. F. Bianco Sel. '93	♈♈	3*
O	T. d. F. Bianco Sel. '94	♈♈	3*
O	T. d. F. Bianco V. Tinazza '95	♈♈	3*
●	T. d. F. Rosso Tamino '95	♈	3
●	T. d. F. Rosso Tamino '97	♈	3

O	Franciacorta Brut	♆♆	5
O	Franciacorta Satèn '95	♆♆	5
O	Pinodisé	♆♆	6
O	T. d. F. Bianco Mancapane '98	♆♆	5
⊙	Franciacorta Rosé	♆	5
O	Franciacorta Zéro	♆	5
O	T. d. F. Bianco '99	♆	4
●	T. d. F. Rosso '98	♆	4
O	Franciacorta Magno Brut '95	♈♈	6
O	Franciacorta Satèn	♈♈	5
O	Franciacorta Zéro	♈♈	5
O	Pinodisé	♈♈	6
O	T. d. F. Bianco '96	♈♈	3*
O	T. d. F. Bianco Mancapane '97	♈♈	5

ADRO (BS)

CORNALETO
VIA CORNALETO, 2
25030 ADRO (BS)
TEL. 030/7450507 - 030/7450565

BEDIZZOLE (BS)

CANTRINA
VIA COLOMBERA, 7
25081 BEDIZZOLE (BS)
TEL. 030/6871052

Adro-based Cornaleto is one of the historic wineries of Franciacorta. Founded in 1968, it boasts around 18 hectares of vineyards in a splendid position, on lean, stony terrain from which comes its name. "Cornaleto", in the Brescia dialect, means something like "stony ground". Luigi Lancini, the owner, has put energy and commitment into his winery and, with the collaboration of oenologist Cesare Ferrari, trotted out an interesting range of wines from the area. The Franciacorta Pas Dosé '91 shows a lovely, deep, golden colour, a very delicate perlage, a gloriously evolved, complex nose and a palate that hints at pleasant, super-ripe notes. It is a butter-rich, complex wine with a palate that reveals balsamic notes of incense and bay leaf. Aged on the lees in bottle for more than five years, it is now at the peak of its career. Less fascinating is the Franciacorta Brut, which has a slightly over-ripe note, even if it can point to sweet notes of apricot and apple. A somewhat heavy-handed dosage ends up by penalizing its freshness and drinkability. The most outstanding of the still wines is the Terre Rosso della Vigna Sarese '96, which has a lovely dark ruby colour, rich fruit on the nose and softness on the palate. The winery's other selections are also good, from the Rosso Baldoc to the classic Poligono, all aged in small casks of new oak. Of the whites, we enjoyed the fresh fruitiness of the Vigna Saline '98.

The Sole di Dario is the best wine produced by the Cantrina winery, owned by Cristina Inganni, which has six hectares of vineyards planted at 6,000 vines per hectare. It is a half and half blend of sauvignon and sémillon, with the addition of ten percent Rhine riesling. The bunches raisin on rush mats for three months and are then soft-pressed. The must is fermented in new barriques where it is then left to age for two years. With its yellow-amber colour, the Sole '97 has a subtle aroma of sweet vanilla and nutmeg spices, with hints of ripe pineapple and honey. The flavour is sweet and soft yet well-supported, with a crisp finish of tropical fruit preserves. The Corteccio Pinot Nero 1998, aged for a year in barriques and left for six months in stainless steel vats, is concentrated and has very perceptible varietal notes that recall blackcurrants and morello cherries, but the tannins have still to mellow out. It will improve with ageing in the bottle but at the moment, it remains below the threshold of Two Glasses. The Riné Bianco Benaco Bresciano '99, from riesling renano (55 percent), chardonnay (40 percent) and sauvignon, is good, though a bit tart. The lively acidity of the riesling, fermented in stainless steel, will have to harmonize better with the complexity of the chardonnay fermented and aged six months in barriques. It needs bottle age, too. The Groppello '99 Cantherius is also very decent.

O	Franciacorta Pas Dosé '91	🍷🍷	5
●	T. d. F. Rosso Sarese '96	🍷🍷	4
O	Franciacorta Brut	🍷	5
⊙	Franciacorta Rosé '91	🍷	5
O	T. d. F. Bianco V. Saline '98	🍷	4
●	T. d. F. Rosso '98	🍷	4
●	T. d. F. Rosso Baldoc '97	🍷	5
●	T. d. F. Rosso Poligono '97	🍷	5
O	Franciacorta Brut '89	🍷🍷	5
O	Franciacorta Extra Brut	🍷🍷	4
O	Franciacorta Pas Dosé '90	🍷🍷	5
●	T. d. F. Rosso Poligono '90	🍷🍷	3*
O	T. d. F. Bianco Corno Nero '93	🍷🍷	4
O	T. d. F. Bianco V. Saline '94	🍷🍷	3
●	T. d. F. Rosso Cornaleto '90	🍷🍷	3

O	Sole di Dario '97	🍷🍷	4
O	Benaco Bresciano Bianco Riné '99	🍷	3
●	Garda Pinot Nero Corteccio '98	🍷	4
●	Garda Cl. Groppello Cantherius '99		3
●	Garda Pinot Nero Corteccio '97	🍷🍷	4
O	Sole di Dario '96	🍷🍷	4
O	Garda Chardonnay '97	🍷	2*

CAMIGNONE (BS)

IL MOSNEL
VIA BARBOGLIO, 14
25040 CAMIGNONE (BS)
TEL. 030/653117

Since they took over the reins of the family winery, Lucia and Giulio Barzanò have marked Mosnel with the incredible drive that has taken this family concern into the top echelons of winemaking in Lombardy. The more than 40 hectares under vine, all adjacent and well-located on the hillside of San Giorgio in Camignone, and a first rate technical staff including agronomist, Pierluigi Villa, and oenologists, Alberto Musatti and Flavio Polenghi, enable the winery to aim high. The range of labels presented is generous, perhaps over-generous, and takes as its point of reference Franciacorta. The winery still sells an excellent '90 vintage that on re-tasting confirms its great shape. But it is the '93 that we really enjoyed this year. It has elegantly mature notes of yeast and grilled bread on the nose while on the palate it expresses the softness and freshness of the fruit, concluding with a nice long finish. The Satèn '96 dissolves elegantly and persuasively on the palate into notes of vanilla, peach and apricot, and the Brut rolls out a solid structure and good balance. Moving along to the still wines, the white Campolarga '99 has lively notes of tropical fruit, fresh acidity and nice structure. The Pinot Nero '97 has a delicate body and elegantly shows off the varietal aromas of the grape. The red selection from the Fontecolo vineyard has soft tannins and good concentration. Also attractive and well-managed were the white Sulìf and the two standard-label Terre di Franciacortas. There is even a successful sweet wine, the Sebino Passito, from chardonnay grapes, which offers good balance and finesse.

CANNETO PAVESE (PV)

BRUNO VERDI
VIA VERGOMBERRA, 5
27044 CANNETO PAVESE (PV)
TEL. 0385/88023

The heroic efforts of the young Paolo Verdi are bearing good fruit. The Riserva Cavariola '97, a blend of mainly croatina with uva rara, vespolina and barbera aged in Slavonian and French oak, is even better than the '96. Concentrated and rich, it is developing a particularly complex bouquet of tertiary aromas. Alongside this is the Barbera Campo del Marrone, from vineyards in the hills at Canneto and Castano. Modern vinification and appropriate wood-ageing have led to completely satisfactory results in the '97 and '98 vintages. In the younger wine, the prevailing notes are those of violets and morello cherries while the '97 unveils leather and tobacco. But both have fullness, balance and intensity, all wrapped up in a rustic, country-style elegance. The Bonarda '99 Possessione di Vergomberra is unfiltered and was lightly re-fermented in the bottle. It has a purple hue, an attractive blackberry bouquet and a lively, dry, fruity, and pleasantly tannic taste. The Moscato Vivace di Volpara '99 is among the best to come out of a vintage that was anything but exceptional for this wine in the Oltrepò Pavese. Its unusual aroma comes from the ten percent malvasia di Candia in the blend. The Brut Classico Vergomberra '97 is worth investigating. And finally the Buttafuoco Paradiso '97 and Riesling Renano Vigna Costa '99 are also very good.

O	Franciacorta Brut '93	🍷🍷	5
O	Franciacorta Satèn '96	🍷🍷	5
O	T. d. F. Bianco Campolarga '99	🍷🍷	3*
●	T. d. F. Rosso Fontecolo '96	🍷🍷	4
O	Franciacorta Brut	🍷	4
O	Franciacorta Extra Brut	🍷	5
O	Passito Sebino '98	🍷	6
●	Pinot Nero '97	🍷	6
O	T. d. F. Bianco '99	🍷	3
O	T. d. F. Bianco Sulìf '98	🍷	4
●	T. d. F. Rosso '98	🍷	3
O	Franciacorta Brut	🍷🍷	4
O	Franciacorta Brut '91	🍷🍷	5
O	Franciacorta Brut Nouvelle Cuvée	🍷🍷	4
O	Franciacorta Extra Brut	🍷🍷	4

●	O. P. Barbera Campo del Marrone '97	🍷🍷	3*
●	O. P. Barbera del Marrone '96	🍷🍷	3*
O	O. P. Brut Cl. Vergomberra '97	🍷🍷	4
●	O. P. Rosso Cavariola Ris. '97	🍷🍷	4
●	O. P. Bonarda Vivace Possessione di Vargomberra '99	🍷	3
●	O. P. Buttafuoco Paradiso '97	🍷	3
O	O. P. Moscato Volpara '99	🍷	3
O	O. P. Riesling Renano Vigneto Costa '99	🍷	3
●	O. P. Bonarda '98	🍷🍷	3*
O	O. P. Riesling Renano Vigneto Costa '96	🍷🍷	3*
O	O. P. Riesling Renano Vigneto Costa '98	🍷🍷	3*
●	O. P. Rosso Cavariola Ris. '96	🍷🍷	4

CAPRIOLO (BS)

CAPRIOLO (BS)

LANTIERI DE PARATICO
VIA SIMEONE PARATICO, 50
25031 CAPRIOLO (BS)
TEL. 030/736151

RICCI CURBASTRO
VIA ADRO, 37
25031 CAPRIOLO (BS)
TEL. 030/736094

This edition of the Guide records another valid performance by the Franciacortas from Lantieri de Paratico estate at Capriolo. One of the emerging vineyards in the area, Lantieri de Paratico, with its 15 hectares under vine and good technical advice, has fixed its sights firmly on excellence. The Franciacorta Arcadia '96 confirms its reputation as a prestigious cuvée. Produced from a blend of 70 percent chardonnay and 30 percent pinot nero that stays on the lees in bottle for more than three years before disgorgement, it has a lovely, bright straw-yellow colour run through with greenish highlights, a delicate perlage and aromas of ripe tropical fruit, pineapple, vanilla and a hint of violets. In the mouth, it is fresh-tasting and caressing, offering good structure. The palate echoes the delicious fruit notes on the nose and the finish lingers. The Satèn is just as pleasant, with its sweet, classic aromas, and full body on the palate, which delicately reflects the tones of apricot preserves and mace. Fresh-tasting and harmonious, the palate signs off with notes of vanilla. The Extra Brut intelligently weds a firm structure with fresh, fruity traces and finishes with delicate vanilla nuances. It is not unlike the Brut, where the fruity component is cleanly expressed, on the nose as well as the palate, along with classic hints of yeasts and toast that pervade the mouth on fresher tones. The Colzano white, reviewed last year, is refreshing and has good structure. The bouquet is characterized by ripe fruit tones but recovers freshness on the palate. The two Terre di Franciacortas, the Bianco and the Rosso, are also up to their usual good standards.

Riccardo Ricci Curbastro leads this family winery with skill, tenacity and creativity. Over the last few years, the cellar has undergone a period of great growth in quality, production and image. Busy on several fronts — Riccardo is also the president of FederDoc and Agriturist after having also been president, until a short while ago, of the Consorzio Vini della Franciacorta — he has been able to surround himself with talented collaborators, such as oenologists, Alberto Musatti and Owen J. Bird, and presented the panel with a broad, carefully selected range of wines from the area. His Pinot Nero '97 has a lovely rich, ruby colour and intense, elegant aromas of cassis and bilberry that fuse with the spicy and toasty tones of new wood. In the mouth, it is concentrated, soft and full, the rich, lingering fruit shading into notes of vanilla and cakes. The Franciacorta Satèn is rich and succulent, bringing to minds apricots and spring flowers on the nose, and unveils a fresh, balanced, caressing and very long palate. The Extra Brut '96 has a stylish perlage and aromas of yeast and toasty bread that finish with a clean, soft fruitiness, in a fresh-tasting overall framework. The new red from the winery, the Sebino '99, made from merlot, barbera and cabernet sauvignon grapes, is soft, full and rich with exuberant aromas of red berry fruit, while the Brolo dei Passoni, a Chardonnay made from partially dried grapes, flaunts a rich breadth of aromas, well-controlled sweetness and a remarkable overall delicacy. But from the Terre di Franciacorta selection and Rosso Santella del Grüm through to the Bianco Vigna Bosco Alto, every wine from this estate is a genuine expression of the terroir.

O	Franciacorta Brut	YY	5
O	Franciacorta Brut Arcadia '96	YY	6
O	Franciacorta Extra Brut	YY	5
O	Franciacorta Satèn	YY	5
O	T. d. F. Bianco '99	Y	3
●	T. d. F. Rosso '98	Y	3
O	Franciacorta Brut '90	YY	4
O	Franciacorta Brut '91	YY	4
O	Franciacorta Brut '96	YY	5
O	Franciacorta Brut Arcadia '95	YY	5
O	Franciacorta Extra Brut	YY	4
O	T. d. F. Bianco Colzano '95	YY	3*
●	T. d. F. Rosso '96	Y	3
●	T. d. F. Rosso Colzano '96	Y	4

O	Brolo dei Passoni '97	YY	5
O	Franciacorta Satèn	YY	4
●	Pinot Nero Sebino '97	YY	5
●	Sebino Rosso '99	YY	2*
O	Franciacorta Brut	Y	4
O	Franciacorta Démi Sec	Y	4
O	Franciacorta Extra Brut '96	Y	5
O	T. d. F. Bianco '99	Y	2*
O	T. d. F. Bianco Vigna Bosco Alto '98	Y	4
●	T. d. F. Rosso '98	Y	2*
●	T. d. F. Rosso Santella del Gröm '97	Y	4
O	Brolo dei Passoni '96	YY	5
O	Franciacorta Extra Brut '93	YY	4
O	Franciacorta Satèn '92	YY	4
●	Pinot Nero Sebino '96	YY	5

CASTEGGIO (PV)

Riccardo Albani

Strada San Biagio, 46
27045 Casteggio (PV)
tel. 0383/83622

Two of the three wines presented by this estate thoroughly deserved their Two Glass rating while the third just failed to make the cut. Undoubtedly a result for Riccardo Albani, who cultivates 12 hectares of vineyards in Casteggio growing just five varieties – barbera, croatina, uva rara, pinot nero and Rhine riesling – in an area where every conceivable grape type is cultivated on dozens of different vineyards, creating an enormous confusion in the market. While we wait for the new Pinot Nero, still being aged, the best wine is the Rosso Riserva '97 Vigne della Casona. Aged for a year in medium-sized and small oak barrels, it matures for a further year and a half in bottle before release. The ruby colour is tinged with garnet highlights, introducing a nose of morello cherry jam, autumn leaves and vanilla, then an elegantly full-bodied palate. The Riesling Renano '99, vinified with a brief cold maceration of the must on the skins and matured only in stainless steel vats, has an outstanding varietal aroma of roses, pears and mineral notes, which will evolve into a more complex bouquet, and a fresh, clean, lingering flavour. It is almost a shame to drink it now when you think what it will become with more time in the cellar. The sparkling Bonarda '99, re-fermented in a pressure tank in the spring following the harvest, is not as rich as the '98 version but is pleasant enough thanks to its berry aromas – particularly mulberries – and its lively, uncompromising taste.

○	O. P. Riesling Renano '99	🍷🍷	3*
●	O. P. Rosso Vigna della Casona Ris. '97	🍷🍷	4
●	O. P. Bonarda Frizzante '99	🍷	3
●	O. P. Bonarda '98	YY	3*
●	O. P. Pinot Nero '98	YY	4
○	O. P. Riesling Renano '98	YY	3*
●	O. P. Rosso Vigna della Casona Ris. '96	YY	4
○	O. P. Riesling Renano '97	Y	3
●	O. P. Rosso Vigna della Casona Ris. '95	Y	4

CASTEGGIO (PV)

Cantina di Casteggio

Via Torino, 96
27045 Casteggio (PV)
tel. 0383/806311

Already mentioned in the past for several wines worthy of attention, the Cantina Sociale di Casteggio makes its entrance in the Guide with a full profile. A historic co-operative founded in 1907, it has become a respected producer in every sense of the word, with 460 members who cultivate 1250 hectares of vineyards and produce grapes for still wines, sparklers and spumantes. In the difficult '99 harvest, oenologist Renato Defilippi did his best. We particularly liked the still Malvasia from the vineyards on the middle and upper slopes of Casteggio and Borgo Priolo. The skilfully fermented grapes have a greenish straw-yellow colour, leading in to an intense aroma of sage and basil, and a dry, soft, fresh-tasting palate with a long, aromatic finish. The Moscato '99 is almost as good. Brought to life by slight secondary fermentation in a pressure tank, it is sweet without being cloying, and scented with peach, clary and tea. Other good whites are the Sauvignon '99 from the vineyards of Borgo Priolo, Borgoratto and Montalto, with clear hints of fig and pear leaves. The Pinot Nero Brut Classico, which stays for 36 months on the second fermentation lees, is clean and tangy with a clear aroma of golden delicious apples, butter and toasted bread. The Bonarda '98 stands out among the reds. The fruit comes from vineyards on the lower slopes of Casteggio and the wine is part aged in small oak barrels. It has notes of vanilla that underline the varietal aromas of mulberry and morello cherry.

○	O. P. Malvasia '99	🍷🍷	2*
○	O. P. Moscato '99	🍷🍷	2*
●	O. P. Bonarda '98	🍷	2*
○	O. P. Pinot Nero Brut Cl.	🍷	3
○	O. P. Sauvignon '99	🍷	2*

CASTEGGIO (PV)

LE FRACCE
VIA CASTEL DEL LUPO, 5
27045 CASTEGGIO (PV)
TEL. 0383/82526

Roberto Gerbino has come from Piedmont to take over cellar management at Le Fracce. He is totally committed to maintaining the high levels of this splendid, "integrated organic winery", which belongs to the Fondazione Bussolera. Despite problems caused by the bizarre, to say the least, vagaries of the weather in 1999, the wines have turned out well. We begin with the Riesling Renano '99 from the vineyards of San Biagio and Mairano di Casteggio. It has aromas of flowers (rose) and pear and apple fruit, as well as a firm palate with acidity that gives it backbone. Two uncontested Glasses. La Rubiosa '99 is better than just good. A tank method Bonarda sparkler with an intense aroma of grapes and bitter almond, it reveals a frank, fruity, lively palate. The Oltrepò Pavese Rosso '98 Bohemi, named after a thoroughbred racehorse that belonged to the lawyer to whom the Fondazione Bussolera is dedicated, is a little green but has good structure. It promises great things but needs ageing in the bottle. There are no objections however to the pinot nero-based Cuvée Bussolera, fermented without the skins and re-fermented in large containers according to the method patented by Francesco Martinotti at the end of the 19th century. This is an elegant, clean-tasting Brut with overtones of crusty bread. The list ends with the Pinot Grigio '99, which has a good varietal aroma without however possessing the fullness and complexity of the preceding year's version.

CASTEGGIO (PV)

TENUTA PEGAZZERA
LOC. PEGAZZERA, 151/153
27045 CASTEGGIO (PV)
TEL. 0383/804646

The Tenuta Pegazzera, with around 50 hectares of vineyards in excellent locations and tended by an agronomist with the experience of Pierluigi Donna, could – and should – have done better. Its wines are well-managed and fairly good but nothing more. Only the spumantes reach exceptional levels thanks to the guiding hand of an old master, Corrado Cugnasco, an oenologist who has worked for many years in Franciacorta and elsewhere. Let us take, for example, the Rosso del Cardinale '98, dedicated to Cardinal Federico Borromeo since the estate was once the property of the Collegio Borromeo in Pavia. This should be one of the outstanding products of Pegazzera but it is not full-bodied or complex enough. The same could be said for the Petrae '98, from pinot nero vinified on the skins, and for the Ligna, a Cabernet Sauvignon '97. We move on, in the hope that the great potential of the grapes will be brought out more fully in the future, and come to a positive note. The non-vintage Oltrepò Pavese Pinot Nero Brut Classico Pegazzera has a very good, elegant, lingering perlage, a pale and bright gold colour, and a very pronounced aroma of dried bay leaf, ripe apples and toasted bread. The flavour is dry, elegant, well-balanced and clean. Only a few points behind comes the Brut "Metodo Martinotti" (re-fermented in pressure tanks) '98. Attractive on the eye, it has an aroma of wild berries and yeast, with a soft, agreeable taste. Finally, just a mention for the Bianco del Cardinale '98, from chardonnay grapes, and the '99 Pinot Nero sparkler fermented without the skins.

●	O. P. Bonarda La Rubiosa '99	♈♈	3*
○	O. P. Brut Cuvée Bussolera	♈♈	4
○	O. P. Riesling Renano '99	♈♈	3*
○	O. P. Pinot Grigio '99	♈	3
●	O. P. Rosso Bohemi '98	♈	4
●	O. P. Bonarda '94	♈♈	4
●	O. P. Bonarda '95	♈♈	4
●	O. P. Bonarda La Rubiosa '98	♈♈	3*
○	O. P. Pinot Grigio '93	♈♈	4
○	O. P. Pinot Grigio '95	♈♈	4
○	O. P. Pinot Grigio '97	♈♈	4
○	O. P. Pinot Grigio '98	♈♈	3*
○	O. P. Riesling Renano '96	♈♈	4
○	O. P. Riesling Renano '98	♈♈	3*
●	O. P. Rosso Cirgà '97	♈♈	4

○	O. P. Pinot Nero Brut Cl.	♈♈	4
○	O. P. Pinot Nero Brut '98	♈	3
●	O. P. Pinot Nero Petrae '98	♈	3
●	O. P. Rosso Cardinale '98	♈	3
●	O. P. Cabernet Sauvignon Ligna '97		4
○	O. P. Cahardonnay Bianco del Cardinale '98		4
○	O. P. Pinot Nero in bianco '99		3
○	O. P. Pinot Nero Brut Cl. '92	♈♈	4
○	O. P. Moscato '98	♈	3
●	O. P. Pinot Nero '97	♈	3

CASTEGGIO (PV)

CASTELLI CALEPIO (BG)

RUIZ DE CARDENAS
STRADA DELLA MOLLIE, 35
27047 CASTEGGIO (PV)
TEL. 0383/82301

IL CALEPINO
VIA SURRIPE, 1
24060 CASTELLI CALEPIO (BG)
TEL. 035/847178

"I believe I am", claims Ruiz de Cardenas, "one of the few producers with a non-agricultural background - I am a former engineering industry worker from Milan though at this point I have been producing wine for almost twenty years – who does not use other vineyards and wineries. From the very beginning, I have dedicated myself personally not only to making each agricultural and oenological decision but also to the most important cellar operations. My consultants, the oenologist Scaglione, and agronomist, Zatti, are professional, highly respected collaborators but, for better or worse, each choice is my responsibility". De Cardenas is right. The choices in the winery are his alone, both for better (frequently) and for worse (sometimes). That's why each year there are alternating positive and negative notes, reflecting the lack of continuity typical of small wineries with small vineyards (five hectares). This time, the most successful product is the Extra Brut Classico vintage 1995, which remained in contact with the lees in bottle for more than 36 months. It is very evolved both in aroma and on the palate but is also solid, complex and very impressive. The Blanc de Blancs '98 is also good. A monovarietal chardonnay turned into a sparkler with the classic method, it is being released onto the market for the first time. There is another new entry among the reds, the Pinot Nero '97 Vigna Miraggi, aged in Vosges and Allier barriques. In the past, the grapes for this cru were used for the Baloss, an unoaked Pinot Nero that was unexceptional without the contribution of the wood.

Brother Ambrogio da Calepio, called "Il Calepino", who in 1500 compiled the "Lexicon Latinum Calepinus", lends his name to this 15-hectare estate owned by Franco and Marco Plebani. The vines stand on soil of glacial origin, known as "surie", at Castelli Calepio and produce 150,000 bottles of white, red and spumante wines. Sparkling wines are a substantial part of the estate's output, around 60,000 bottles, and they are all produced by the classic method. The best is the Riserva di Fra Ambrogio 1993, made from 70-30 chardonnay and pinot nero base wine, 15 percent of which is aged in barriques. After bottle fermentation, it is left for five years in contact with the second fermentation lees (disgorgement took place in February 2000). It has an evanescent white mousse, a subtle, lingering perlage and a bright golden yellow colour. The bouquet is complex and developed, with dominant notes of crusty bread and dried bay leaf. The flavour is firm and full and there is a lovely finish of ripe, golden delicious apples and cakes. Only a notch or two lower is the Extra Brut '95, which underwent disgorgement in January 2000. Carefully selected grapes, again chardonnay and pinot nero, and 48 months of ageing on the second fermentation lees have given it elegant tertiary aromas and a dry, clean flavour. The Brut 1995 "Linea 2000" is very pleasant, softer and more stylish glass. Of the still wines, the Valcalepio Bianco '99 is not bad, offering fruit and flower aromas and a good compositional balance.

○	O. P. Extra Brut Cl. '95	♈♈	4
○	O. P. Brut Cl. Blanc de Blanc '98	♈	4
●	O. P. Pinot Nero Vigna Miraggi '97	♈	4
○	O. P. Brut Cl. Réserve '93	♈♈	4
●	O. P. Pinot Nero Baloss '97	♈♈	3*
●	O. P. Pinot Nero Brumano '92	♈♈	4
●	O. P. Pinot Nero Brumano '96	♈♈	4
○	O. P. Extra Brut Cl.	♈	4
●	O. P. Pinot Nero '94	♈	3

○	Brut Classico Ris.		
	Fra Ambrogio '93	♈♈	5
○	Extra Brut M. Cl. '95	♈♈	4
○	Brut M. Cl. Linea 2000 '95	♈	4
○	Valcalepio Bianco '99	♈	3
○	Brut Classico Ris.		
	Fra Ambrogio '89	♈	5
○	Brut M. Cl. '91	♈	5
○	Extra Brut M. Cl. '90	♈	5
●	Valcalepio Rosso '92	♈	2*
●	Valcalepio Rosso Surie '90	♈	4

CAZZAGO S. MARTINO (BS)

MONTE ROSSA
FRAZ. BORNATO
VIA MARENZIO, 14
25040 CAZZAGO S. MARTINO (BS)
TEL. 030/725066

Monte Rossa has taken its place over the last few years as one of the leading estates in Franciacorta. The winery created by Paolo Rabotti and Paola Rovetta more than 30 years ago is now in the hands of the tenacious, passionately dedicated Emanuele. Nothing has been left to chance in the ongoing renewal of cellar equipment and replanting of vineyards, and the results are tangible. The Monte Rossa range is one of the most complete and reliable in the area and for the third year in row, the estate has claimed our top award. Yet again, the champion is the Satèn. Produced from a blend of chardonnay and pinot bianco, this wine seduces you with its elegance and delicacy, its clean style obvious in every detail. It has a brilliant straw-yellow colour, a fine, delicate, dense perlage and complex aromas of apples, pears, yeast, vanilla and toasty bread. It is delicately effervescent on the palate, caressing the taste buds like a true Satèn, and expressing a perfect balance between fresh, fruity tones and a softness that in the end translates into a long, fragrant finish. The Cabochon '95 has great structure and, just like all the Monte Rossa Franciacortas, boasts delicacy, complexity and elegance, even if a shade more concentration would have won it our top accolade. The Brut, with its soft keynote of apples and pears, is perhaps the best standard Franciacorta in this edition of the Guide. But other wines as well, from the Sec to the Rosé – non-vintage this year – all confirm the incontrovertible calibre of this winery.

CAZZAGO S. MARTINO (BS)

RONCO CALINO
VIA SCALA, 88
25040 CAZZAGO SAN MARTINO (BS)
TEL. 035/317788

A new estate in the Franciacorta region makes a creditable entrance into the Guide. Ronco Calino, owned by Paolo Radici, an entrepreneur from Bergamo, boasts ten hectares of vineyards around Cazzago San Martino. Aside from the vineyards, Radici also acquired some woodland and a lovely villa that was once the property of the celebrated pianist, Arturo Benedetti Michelangeli. The technical director of the estate is oenologist, Francesco Polastri, who can count not only on his undisputed skill but also on excellent raw material and a superbly equipped cellar. This year, Ronco Calino debuts with a range of wines that are, to say the least, excellent. The Franciacorta Brut is soft and full, fruity and elegant, and boasts great balance of palate and nose, and very good length. The Bianco Sottobosco '98 has a deep straw-yellow colour, an intense stylish nose marked by sweet notes of ripe apples and pears, and shows good balance on the palate. The careful use of wood, good structure, and aromatic length are all apparent in the mouth. The Pinot Nero L'Arturo '98, a tribute to Benedetti Michelangeli, introduces itself with a good, deep ruby colour. It has a lovely intense, sweet nose, rich in aromas of raspberry, bilberry and currants, while the palate is delicate and elegant . It reveals balance and finesse, as well as rounded tannins, and never wavers from the varietal characteristics of the grape. The Terre Rosso has good density and structure. The palate offers rich juicy fruit and aromas of well-ripened morello cherries, closing with a long, soft finish. Finally, we found the Terre Bianco from the '99 vintage of good quality, refreshing, inviting and fruity.

O Franciacorta Satèn	♉♉♉	5
O Franciacorta Brut	♉♉	5
O Franciacorta Brut Cabochon '95	♉♉	6
O Franciacorta Sec	♉♉	5
⊙ Franciacorta Rosé '95	♉	5
O T. d. F. Bianco Ravellino '99	♉	4
O Franciacorta Extra Brut Cabochon '93	♉♉♉	5
O Franciacorta Satèn	♉♉♉	5
O Franciacorta Brut Cabochon '90	♉♉	5
O Franciacorta Brut Cabochon '92	♉♉	5
O Franciacorta Brut Cabochon '94	♉♉	5
O Franciacorta Extra Brut '90	♉♉	5
O Franciacorta Extra Brut '92	♉♉	5
O Franciacorta Extra Brut '93	♉♉	5
● T. d. F. Rosso Cep '95	♉♉	3*

O Chardonnay Sottobosco '98	♉♉	4
O Franciacorta Brut	♉♉	5
● Pinot Nero L'Arturo '98	♉♉	5
● T. d. F. Rosso '98	♉♉	3*
O T. d. F. Bianco '99	♉	3

CHIURO (SO)

NINO NEGRI
VIA GHIBELLINI, 3
23030 CHIURO (SO)
TEL. 0342/482521

CHIURO (SO)

ALDO RAINOLDI
VIA STELVIO, 128
23030 CHIURO (SO)
TEL. 0342/482225

This is the sixth time that the Sforzato 5 Stelle has crossed the Three Glass threshold. It is not surprising, considering the potential of the terroir and the indisputable professional skill of a great oenologist like Casimiro Maule. It is a fact that the "5 Stelle style" has opened the way for the improvement of winemaking standards throughout Valtellina, contributing with its terroir-driven example to the birth of more complex and more elegant wines. In the '98 version, the 5 Stelle unveils richness and complexity, an intense garnet colour, and aromas of dried prunes, cocoa and roasted hazelnuts. It has great concentration and density on the palate, combined with a long finish laced with full, fragrant echoes. Less round, but just as characteristic, is the Sfursat '97 with toasty notes, hints of raisins and a liquorice finish. The very individual 1897 Centesima Vendemmia is produced from nebbiolo grapes. The headily vinous nose is redolent of tamarind and resin. It was a great year for a classic, the Valtellina Nino Negri Riserva '95, whose intense aromas of cloves and fruit preserves leads in to a full-bodied, caressing palate. Very good indeed, in fact the best tasted, was the Sassella Le Tense '97. Concentrated, impeccably stylish and with a very evident, attractive fruitiness. The Inferno Mazer '97 went no higher than One Glass since it is unfocused on the nose. The same goes for the Grumello Vigna Sassorosso '96, perhaps in part because of the poor vintage. The well-made Valgella Fracia Oro '96 took Two Glasses. Finally, the Ca' Brione '99 is a happy combination of nebbiolo, sauvignon and chardonnay. Its aromas are deep and musky, and there is good balance on the palate, which offers considerable weight and sweetness.

Congratulations to Peppino Rainoldi for the constant improvement in the quality of his wines and felicitations, too, to his nephew Aldo, a very young oenologist who works enthusiastically alongside his uncle. This year, again, the wines presented were all of high quality, earning good scores and a considerable collection of glassware. What is more, the performance of the Sforzato Ca' Rizzieri '97 was extraordinary enough to merit a place in the Three Glass stratosphere. A monovarietal nebbiolo, fermented in new wood for at least 15 months, this Sforzato is truly elegant on the nose, with intense aromas of chocolate and spices. Sumptuous and vibrant on the palate, its softness mingles perfectly with the oak to lead through to a clean, sweet, lingering finish. The Sfursat '97 is a very good, individual wine with hints of leather and lots of concentration on the palate. The Crespino '97 is a serious bottle with a deliberately modern style. It offers aromas of black berry fruit and rain-soaked earth, followed by a succulent palate with firm structure. The two Sassellas, the '95 Riserva and '96 standard version, are noteworthy as perfect examples of terroir-driven wines. Produced from nebbiolo fruit, they manage to seduce without going over the top, their clean aromas and refined palates bespeaking a sure-footed winemaking style. The Inferno Barrique '96 is the best of this type we tasted. Aromatically complex, it has a full-bodied and elegantly concentrated flavour. Finally, the nebbiolo-based Ghibellino '98, fermented without the skins, unfurls sweet and floral aromas, then a well-rounded, coherent palate.

● Valtellina Sfursat 5 Stelle '98	♟♟♟	6
● Valtellina 1897 Centesima Vendemmia '97	♟♟	5
● Valtellina Sfursat '97	♟♟	5
● Valtellina Sup. Nino Negri Ris. '95	♟♟	5
● Valtellina Sup. Sassella Le Tense '97	♟♟	4
○ Vigneto Ca' Brione Bianco '99	♟♟	4
● Valtellina Sup. Valgella Fracia Oro '96	♟	4
● Valtellina Sup. Grumello Vigna Sassorosso '96	♟	4
● Valtellina Sup. Inferno Mazer '97	♟	4
● Valtellina Sfursat 5 Stelle '97	♟♟♟	6

● Valtellina Sfurzat Ca' Rizzieri '97	♟♟♟	6
● Valtellina Sfurzat '97	♟♟	5
● Valtellina Sup. Crespino '97	♟♟	5
● Valtellina Sup. Inferno Ris. Barrique '96	♟♟	4
● Valtellina Sup. Sassella '96	♟♟	3*
● Valtellina Sup. Sassella Ris. '95	♟♟	4
○ Bianco Ghibellino '98	♟	4
● Valtellina Sfurzat Ca' Rizzieri '95	♟♟♟	5
● Valtellina Sfurzat '94	♟♟	4
● Valtellina Sfurzat '96	♟♟	5
● Valtellina Sfurzat Ca' Rizzieri '96	♟♟	6
● Valtellina Sup. Crespino '95	♟♟	4
● Valtellina Sup. Crespino '96	♟♟	5
● Valtellina Sup. Inferno Ris. '94	♟♟	4

CICOGNOLA (PV)

COCCAGLIO (BS)

MONTERUCCO
VALLE CIMA, 38
27040 CICOGNOLA (PV)
TEL. 0385/85151

BETTINZANA - CASCINA RONCO BASSO
VIA BUSSAGHE, 14
25030 COCCAGLIO (BS)
TEL. 030/7721689

The Valentis have been making wine for generations, and now turn out around 100,000 bottles a year using exclusively grapes harvested on the 15 hectares of their property at the entrance to the Scuropasso valley. In the last edition of Guide, we were favourably impressed by the Metellianum '96, a Rosso Riserva from barbera and croatina grapes, aged in barriques for two years. But the '97 did not have such good luck this year. In all the bottles examined there were strong notes of reduction that compromised our appreciation of the wine. The Barbera '98, slightly sparkling after re-fermentation in a pressure tank, passed the Two Glass threshold thanks to its intense fragrance of violets, cloves and spices and the tangy sincerity of the palate. More or less at the same level is the Bonarda '98 Vivace Vigna Il Modello. Its hints of wild berries, autumn leaves and bitter almonds come together in an entrancing combination. The sparkling Pinot Nero Primi Fiori '99, fermented without the skins, is pleasant and easy drinking with a nice hint of ripe redcurrants and yeasts. The sparkling Sangue di Giuda '99, from 60 percent croatina, 30 percent barbera and 10 percent uva rara, is a sweet red made to be drunk young and chilled with fruit tarts, peaches or chestnuts. Finally, the non-vintage Brut Classico, from pinot nero grapes with 15 percent chardonnay, is reasonably attractive.

The Bettinzana family is into its third generation of winemakers. Even if Angelo and Enrico, the brothers now directing this small but promising cellar, spend most of their time looking after their main business activities, all their free hours are devoted to the production of Franciacorta and the other still wines of this area. The proof is that they have added more land to their approximately two hectares under vine on the southern slopes of Monte Orfano near the monastery of Our Lady of the Annunciation, buying a plot even higher up the same mountain. Recently, they built a modern cellar below ground level and have pushed production up to roughly 30,000 bottles a year. The wine that impressed us most at the tasting this year was the Franciacorta Brut '95, which has a lovely, bright straw-yellow colour with greenish highlights introducing soft, intense aromas of ripe fruit, vanilla and apricot preserves. On the palate, the wine shows good structure and a softly refreshing, caressingly effervescent palate rich in notes of flowers and cakes. The Franciacorta Brut is a worthy companion. It has a lustrous colour, delicate perlage and an elegant nose of yeasts and hawthorn blossom while the palate reveals fullness of flavour, a clean fruitiness and above all excellent balance. The Bettinzanas, who avail themselves of the advice of oenologist, Corrado Cugnasco, also produce good versions of Terre di Franciacorta Bianco and Rosso.

● O. P. Barbera Frizzante '98	♟♟	2*	
● O. P. Bonarda Vivace Vigna Il Modello '98	♟♟	2*	
○ O. P. Pinot Nero in bianco Primi Fiori '99	♟	2*	
● O. P. Sangue di Giuda '99	♟	2*	
○ O. P. Brut Classico		4	
● O. P. Barbera '97	♟♟	2*	
○ O. P. Brut Classico '93	♟♟	4	
● O. P. Rosso Metellianum Ris. '96	♟	3	
● O. P. Sangue di Giuda '98	♟	2*	

○ Franciacorta Brut	♟♟	4	
○ Franciacorta Brut '95	♟♟	5	
○ T. d. F. Bianco '99	♟	3	
● T. d. F. Rosso '98	♟	3	

COCCAGLIO (BS)

TENUTA CASTELLINO
VIA S. PIETRO, 46
25030 COCCAGLIO (BS)
TEL. 030/7721015

COCCAGLIO (BS)

LORENZO FACCOLI & FIGLI
VIA CAVA, 7
25030 COCCAGLIO (BS)
TEL. 030/7722761

The Tenuta Castellino of the Bonomi family takes its name from the beautiful Art Nouveau construction in the middle of the estate. We are at Coccaglio, on the southern side of Franciacorta, on the slopes of Monte Orfano, where the property's 12 hectares of vineyards enjoy superb locations. Thanks to the very experienced technical staff, and the consultancy of oenologist, Cesare Ferrari, the cellar produces wines of considerable interest every year. At our tasting this year, the Franciacorta Brut '95 earned a place among the best vintage sparklers from the area. It has a deep straw-yellow colour with elegant greenish highlights, a creamy mousse and delicate perlage. The entry on the nose is intense, with a wealth of fruity, spicy and sweet aromas. The soft, full-bodied palate is well-balanced and elegant in its hints of peach and ripe apricot, which are enlivened by a touch of citrus and rennet apples. The Satèn reinforces its reputation as a very sound product. The nose offers rich notes of cakes and aromatic herbs while the palate is fresh, well-rounded and vibrant, showing lovely harmony and good length. Another label we heartily recommend is the Capineto red, a Bordeaux blend that, thanks to an excellent harvest in '97, exhibits a lovely deep ruby colour and aromas of ripe red berry fruit of rare spontaneity. The palate faithfully echoes the aromas on the nose, adding concentration and a remarkable overall balance that is enhanced by a well-judged touch of new wood that contributes balsamic notes. The Franciacorta Brut is as pleasant as ever while the white Solicano '98 seems below par. The two Terre di Franciacortas, the Bianco and Rosso, are of good quality.

Even if it is not one of the largest estates in the area, Faccoli of Coccaglio has made a name for itself with knowledgeable aficionados because of the excellent standards of its products and the consistent quality is has shown over the years. At the helm of the estate founded by Lorenzo Faccoli, who moved here from Le Marche many years ago, we now find his two sons, Claudio, who is also president of the Consorzio dei Vini di Franciacorta, and his brother Gianmario. The tastings this year gave us the chance to appreciate the Franciacorta Extra Brut from 1990. This is a big, full-flavoured, complex wine, incredibly refreshing for its age, which unfurls elegant, intense sensations of ripe fruit on both nose and palate, where it shows great balance and length. The Franciacorta Brut has a lovely, deep straw-yellow colour and aromas that are remarkably soft, proffering intense, delicate notes of yeast and butter. The palate has rich fruit, with flavours of apple, ripe peach and vanilla. There is a long finish that leaves the mouth pleasantly fruity and fresh. The Franciacorta Rosé also reveals good quality, with its delicate hints of bilberry and redcurrants. Both the not very full-bodied Franciacorta Extra Brut and the Terre di Franciacorta Bianco '99 seemed pleasant and well-managed.

	Wine	Rating	Score
●	Capineto '97	▼▼	4
○	Franciacorta Brut '95	▼▼	5
○	Franciacorta Satèn	▼▼	5
○	Franciacorta Brut	▼	5
○	T. d. F. Bianco '99	▼	3
○	T. d. F. Bianco Solicano '98	▼	4
●	T. d. F. Rosso '98	▼	3
○	Franciacorta Brut '93	ΨΨ	5
○	Franciacorta Crémant	ΨΨ	5
○	Franciacorta Satèn	ΨΨ	5
○	Franciacorta Satèn '92	ΨΨ	4
○	Franciacorta Satèn '93	ΨΨ	5
○	T. d. F. Bianco Solicano '95	ΨΨ	3*
○	T. d. F. Bianco Solicano '96	ΨΨ	4
○	T. d. F. Bianco Solicano '97	ΨΨ	4

	Wine	Rating	Score
○	Franciacorta Brut	▼▼	4
○	Franciacorta Extra Brut '90	▼▼	6
○	Franciacorta Extra Brut	▼	4
⊙	Franciacorta Rosé	▼	4
○	T. d. F. Bianco '99	▼	3
○	Franciacorta Brut	ΨΨ	4
○	Franciacorta Extra Brut	ΨΨ	4
○	Franciacorta Extra Brut '89	ΨΨ	6
○	Franciacorta Brut	Ψ	4
○	Franciacorta Extra Brut	Ψ	4
⊙	Franciacorta Rosé	Ψ	4
○	T. d. F. Bianco '94	Ψ	2*
○	T. d. F. Bianco '96	Ψ	2*
○	T. d. F. Bianco '97	Ψ	3
○	T. d. F. Bianco '98	Ψ	3

CODEVILLA (PV)

COLOGNE (BS)

MONTELIO
VIA D. MAZZA, 1
27050 CODEVILLA (PV)
TEL. 0383/373090

LA BOSCAIOLA
VIA RICCAFANA, 19
25033 COLOGNE (BS)
TEL. 030/715596 - 030/7156386

Mario Maffi is truly a brilliant oenologist, a maestro both in the vineyards and the cellar. His blue-ribbon wine is the Comprino, a monovarietal Merlot that is about to be authorized across the entire Oltrepò Pavese but for now is legally present only on the historic Montelio estate. It was here, on this more than 150-year-old property that merlot was planted more than 50 years ago, before the first DOC zones were created. The Comprino Legno '98, aged in barriques, is rather better than the very good '97. Deep ruby in colour, it has a fruity, spicy bouquet and a rich, warm, long palate. There is a second, unoaked, version of this wine. The varietal notes of the grape are very much to the fore in the '98 version. Staying with the reds, the Riserva Vigna Solarolo '96 is outstanding. A 40 percent barbera, 40 percent croatina and 20 percent pinot nero blend aged in oak, it has a deep garnet colour and a full nose of autumn leaves, vanilla and liquorice while the palate is warm, full and vigorous. The Pinot Nero '96 Costarsa is soft and mature, offering more finesse than vigour and a varietal nose of blackcurrant jam over a garnet colour with orange highlights. The still Barbera '98 and sparkling Bonarda '99 are both good. Best of the whites is the Giostra '98, from super-ripe müller thurgau grapes vinified with cold maceration. We confirmed Two Glasses awarded last year to this fine example of cellarability. For those who prefer younger wines, Montelio offers the Müller Thurgau and Cortese '99, both refreshing and enjoyable.

La Boscaiola, the beautiful estate of Nelson and Giuliana Cenci, makes its Guide debut. Nelson, who has practised medicine all his life, bought this small holding with five hectares under vine to spend the weekends in the country. Then, almost as a game, he began producing wine. Over the past few years, since he retired, he has been pursuing the activity with commitment and professionalism. The cellar was fitted out with modern equipment, and technical advice was sought from an expert oenologist, Cesare Ferrari. Today, as the manager of this small winery that turns out around 55,000 bottles a year of Franciacorta and still wines, Nelson is assisted by his daughter, Giuliana, who has also caught the bug and is inspired by laudable ambition. The results of our tastings prove that Giuliana has got it right. The Franciacorta '96 is among the best from that year. The panel found it harmonious and delicate, with a nose that unveils delicate aromas of yeasts and ripe fruit against a seductive hint of aromatic herbs. On the palate, it has remarkable elegance and balance, the apples and pears coming together admirably with the vegetal tones of honeysuckle, mingling with peach and apricot. The long, rising finish leaves an elegant after-aroma of vanilla and yeast. The Giuliana C. is a Bordeaux blend that shows notable finesse, good concentration and soft aromas of ripe red berry fruit fusing with spicy tones of wood, tobacco and cocoa. The Terre Bianco Giuliana C. is impressive for its very attractive aromas of croissants and ripe fruit. There is also a nice hint of vanilla that pervades both nose and palate, which is harmonious, fruit-rich and full-bodied, shading into intriguing notes of white chocolate. Finally, the well-balanced Terre Rosso Ritorno '98, with its ripe tannins, is a worthy complement to the range. A very impressive first showing.

● Comprino Rosso '98	♟♟	3*
● Comprino Rosso Legno '98	♟♟	4
● O. P. Rosso Ris.		
Vigna Solarolo '96	♟♟	4
○ Brut La Stroppa	♟	4
● O. P. Barbera '98	♟	3
● O. P. Bonarda Frizzante '99	♟	3
○ O. P. Cortese '99	♟	3
○ O. P. Müller Thurgau '99	♟	3
● O. P. Pinot Nero Costarsa '96	♟	4
● Comprino Rosso '95	♟♟	4
● Comprino Rosso '97	♟♟	4
● O. P. Barbera '97	♟♟	3*
● O. P. Pinot Nero '90	♟♟	4
● O. P. Pinot Nero '93	♟♟	4

○ Franciacorta Brut '96	♟♟	5
● Sebino Giuliana C. '98	♟♟	3*
○ T. d. F. Bianco Giuliana C. '98	♟♟	3*
● T. d. F. Rosso Ritorno '98	♟	4

CORTEFRANCA (BS)

CORTEFRANCA (BS)

BARONE PIZZINI
FRAZ. TIMOLINE - VIA BRESCIA, 3/A
25050 CORTEFRANCA (BS)
TEL. 030/984136

F.LLI BERLUCCHI
LOC. BORGONATO
VIA BROLETTO, 2
25040 CORTEFRANCA (BS)
TEL. 030/984451

Barone Pizzini, at Timoline near Cortefranca, is rapidly moving up the quality charts and has decided to elbow its way into the select group of top Franciacorta estates. With 33 hectares under vine and a first-class technical staff, including vineyard manager, Pierluigi Donna, Roberto Cipresso, who supervises vinification of the still wines, and Alberto Musatti overseeing the Franciacortas, Barone Pizzini turns out 250,000 bottles a year. This time, the still wines stole the scene from the Franciacortas. The San Carlo '98, a blend of 25 percent cabernet franc and 35 percent cabernet sauvignon with merlot, is a red with grand elegance and concentration that deserved its excellent score. It has a dark ruby colour, a rich, concentrated nose with aromas of red and black berry fruit, and on the palate shows significant structure, great balance, soft tannins and perfectly gauged wood. The Pinot Nero from the same year was also a revelation. It unfurls very stylish fruit that centres on notes of cassis and raspberry, an outstanding varietal identity on nose and palate, where it flaunts a superb balance of wood and fruit, elegant structure and a finish that is very reminiscent of certain bottles from the other side of the Alps. The Franciacorta Brut boasts a deep straw-yellow colour with greenish highlights, a creamy mousse and a floral, fruity nose refined by a touch of vanilla. On the palate, it is full, elegant, well-balanced and delicate. The Franciacorta Extra Dry seduces with its hints of ripe apple and cakes and the Satèn reveals a polished elegance while the Franciacorta Bagnadore I '95 has concentration and complexity but is penalized by notes that are over-evolved with respect to its actual age. The other wines are all very good indeed.

With more than 52 hectares of vineyards and an annual production of around 350,000 bottles, the estate of the Berlucchi brothers is one of the historic names in Franciacorta, where this family has ancient roots. Cesare Ferrari is in charge of winemaking and for years has regularly delivered excellent quality Franciacorta cuvées as well as a good range of still wines. The best wine from the estate this year is the Franciacorta Brut Satèn '96, which has a lustrous straw-yellow colour, creamy mousse and a delicate perlage. It has nice aromas of ripe apples and pears with fresh hints of citrus and a touch of vanilla and crusty bread. Soft on the palate and fresh in acidity, it unveils a firm, balanced, delicate structure. The Franciacorta Brut '96 won plaudits for its good overall harmony and the delicacy of its aromas, but lacks the full-bodied quality and roundness of the '93 vintage put on the market last year to celebrate thirty years of DOC wines in Franciacorta. This year, the Terre di Franciacorta Rosso Dossi delle Querce '95 seems very interesting. It shows good concentration, softness, even in its tannic structure, and recalls a cabernet franc with its notes of red berry fruit and fresh vegetal tones. The Terre di Franciacorta Rosso '98 is less complex, offering only moderate structure, but is well-balanced and refreshing, but it can also show hints of newly mown grass and capsicum. On the other hand, the Dossi delle Querce Bianco '97 and Terre Bianco '99 both fell a bit below our expectations, being penalized by a rather too assertive acid vein.

O Franciacorta Brut	♥♥	5
O Franciacorta Extra Dry	♥♥	5
O Franciacorta Satèn	♥♥	5
● Pinot Nero '98	♥♥	5
● San Carlo '98	♥♥	5
O Franciacorta Brut Bagnadore I '95	♥	5
⊙ Franciacorta Rosé	♥	5
O T. d. F. Bianco '99	♥	3
● T. d. F. Rosso '98	♥	3
O Franciacorta Brut	♥♥	4
O Franciacorta Brut Bagnadore V '93	♥♥	5
O Franciacorta Extra Brut		
Bagnadore V '92	♥♥	5
O Franciacorta Satèn	♥♥	5

O Franciacorta Brut Satèn '96	♥♥	5
● T. d. F. Rosso		
Dossi delle Querce '95	♥♥	4
O Franciacorta Brut '96	♥	5
O T. d. F. Bianco '99	♥	3
O T. d. F. Bianco		
Dossi delle Querce '97	♥	4
● T. d. F. Rosso '98	♥	3
O Franciacorta 30 anni di Doc '93	♥♥	6
O Franciacorta Brut '91	♥♥	4
O Franciacorta Brut '92	♥♥	4
O Franciacorta Brut '93	♥♥	4
O Franciacorta Brut '94	♥♥	4
O Franciacorta Brut '95	♥♥	5
⊙ Franciacorta Rosé '92	♥♥	4

CORTEFRANCA (BS)

CORTEFRANCA (BS)

GUIDO BERLUCCHI & C.
LOC. BORGONATO
P.ZZA DURANTI, 4
25040 CORTEFRANCA (BS)
TEL. 030/984381 - 030/984293

MONZIO COMPAGNONI
FRAZ. NIGOLINE
C.DA MONTI DELLA CORTE
25040 CORTEFRANCA (BS)
TEL. 030/9884157

If Berlucchi in Italy means classic method spumante, this is due to the enterprise and great skill of oenologist Franco Ziliani who, at the beginning of the 60s, with a group of friends, set up this winery. Today, it is a major grower-producer, completely owned by the Berlucchi family, and every year turns out several million bottles that are successfully exported all over the world. The estate's range is vast and our preference this year was again for the Cellarius Brut Riserva, with its lovely lustrous green-flecked straw-yellow colour and delicate perlage. Made with chardonnay and pinot nero grapes from Alto Adige, Franciacorta and the Oltrepò, it has fresh aromas of yeast and crusty bread mingling with inviting floral tones. On the palate, it is round and caressing, hinting at nuances of golden delicious apples and white peaches. The Cuvée Imperiale Brut '95 has impressively rich aromas and a remarkable complexity of toasty and mineral overtones. It reveals great elegance on the palate, even if a touch more "fat" would, to our way of thinking, have been helpful. The rest of the Berlucchi line is up to its customary high standards, in fact, it's even better than usual. But special mention should be made of the labels from the Antica Cantina Fratta, a winery that belongs to the Ziliani family, comprising Franco, and his children, Arturo, Paolo and Cristina. The Zilianis' cellar is in Monticelli Brusati, in the heart of Franciacorta, and their Franciacorta Brut is characterized by a nose of croissant, butter and cakes leading in to a balanced, harmonious palate. The Franciacorta '95 we tasted last year confirms its excellent performance, offering rich, fruity pulp, freshness and nice length.

Since 1995, Marcello Monzio Compagnoni has successfully divided his time between his two estates, one in Cenate di Sotto, in the Valcalepio area, and the other in Cortefranca, in Franciacorta. Here, the dynamic Marcello has rented the Monti della Corte property from its noble owners and now grows his fruit on its 40 well-exposed hectares in Nigoline and Torbiato, on the slopes of Monte Alto. The range of labels is very extensive and the average standard of production is excellent. This year, we were impressed by two Franciacortas, the Satèn and the Brut. The former is soft and persuasive on nose and palate, presenting fruit-rich tones and slightly evolved notes on the palate that develop in complexity, with an elegant, harmonious finish. The Brut has a more traditional style where the accent is on structure and hints of yeast, biscuits and crusty bread. There is good texture on the palate, which is well-balanced and lingering. Another good mark goes to the white Ronco della Seta '99, from chardonnay and pinot bianco grapes aged for several months in barriques. This is a wine with generous fresh, fruity notes on the very clean nose, where the aromas are redolent of golden delicious apple, flowers and a touch of vanilla. The palate shows structure and great balance. The Chardonnay Bianco della Seta '98 is just as irresistible but even more concentrated and lingering. The excellent Rosso di Luna is one of the best labels in Valcalepio. A Bordeaux blend of remarkable concentration, it is fruity, elegant and ages well. The Don Quijote, a pleasant red "passito" from dried moscato di Scanzo grapes, displays elegant hints of rose and sweet spices. The two Valcalepios are also good this year.

O	Cellarius Brut Ris.	♈♈	5
O	Cuvée Imperiale Brut '95	♈♈	5
O	Franciacorta Antica Cantina Fratta	♈♈	4
O	Cuvée Imperiale	♈	4
O	Cuvée Imperiale Brut Extrême	♈	4
⊙	Cuvée Imperiale Max Rosé	♈	4
O	T. d. F. Bianco Antica Cantina Fratta '99	♈	3
O	Cellarius Brut Ris.	♈♈	5
O	Franciacorta Antica Cantina Fratta '95	♈♈	5
O	Franciacorta Brut Antica Cantina Fratta	♈♈	4

O	Franciacorta Brut	♈♈	5
O	Franciacorta Satèn	♈♈	5
O	T. d. F. Bianco della Seta '98	♈♈	5
O	T. d. F. Bianco Ronco della Seta '99	♈♈	3*
●	Valcalepio Rosso di Luna '98	♈♈	5
●	Don Quijote	♈	5
O	Franciacorta Extra Brut	♈	5
●	T. d. F. Rosso Ronco della Seta '98	♈	3
O	Valcalepio Bianco Colle della Luna '99	♈	3
●	Valcalepio Rosso Colle della Luna '98	♈	3
O	Franciacorta Brut	♈♈	4
O	Franciacorta Extra Brut	♈♈	5
O	Moscato di Scanzo Don Quijote '96	♈♈	5
●	Rosso di Nero '97	♈♈	5
O	T. d. F. Bianco Ronco della Seta '98	♈♈	4

CORVINO SAN QUIRICO (PV)   DESENZANO DEL GARDA (BS)

TENUTA MAZZOLINO
VIA MAZZOLINO, 26
27050 CORVINO SAN QUIRICO (PV)
TEL. 0383/876122

PROVENZA
VIA DEI COLLI STORICI
25015 DESENZANO DEL GARDA (BS)
TEL. 030/9910006

The '97 was celebrated as the "vintage of the century" but the '98, at least in the Oltrepò, produced even better results. The Noir '98, a Pinot Nero from selected grapes fermented on the skins and vinified with prolonged maceration before ageing for twelve months in Allier and Tronçais barriques, has a ruby colour that is almost too intense for the category. The aromas of cassis and wild rose, with hints of leather and autumn leaves, introduce a full, rich palate that is already very harmonious and delicious. Not bad, for a wine that still has to age in the bottle. The standard Pinot Nero '97, though good, is not up to the same level. The Corvino '98 is interesting. A Cabernet Sauvignon, in this edition of the Guide it easily merits Two Glasses for its complex, elegant character. The cask-conditioned Chardonnay Blanc '98 is also good. All that held it back from a better score was the slight lack of balance in its oak-derived notes.

The trebbiano di Lugana that, according to ampelographers, might be a verdicchio, can produce long-lived whites with a great structure and complexity. This is the case with the Lugana '97 Selezione Fabio Contato, which sports a label signed by the owner of the Provenza di Desenzano estate. The 30 hectares under vine produce a total of 400,000 bottles of whites, reds and spumantes every year. Bunches selected from the oldest vineyards are vinified with cold-maceration and then aged for 24 months in new barriques. It has a brilliant green-gold colour, a rich, complex bouquet of vanilla, almond blossom, ripe white peaches and mineral overtones, and a concentrated flavour that is elegantly full-bodied and very long. The wood is a little too prevalent but further ageing in the bottle will improve the overall balance. This is not a monovarietal trebbiano di Lugana for the blend does have ten percent chardonnay but it is a very successful addition. The same blend is also used for the Cà Molin '98, which was vinified in the same way but spent less time in barriques (only six months). For those who prefer refreshingly fragrant varietal notes, Provenza offers the Cà Maiol '99, a monovarietal trebbiano di Lugana vinified in stainless steel. The red Negresco '98, a Garda Classico aged for 18 months in small oak casks, is a cut above the already good '96 we tasted last year. As for the rest of the range, the Garda Chiaretto '99 is delicate, floral and fresh while the two Sebastian and Ca' Maiol Bruts, the former a cuve close sparkler and the latter a metodo classico, are very respectable.

● O. P. Cabernet Saugnon		
Corvino '98	♟♟	4
● O. P. Pinot Nero '97	♟♟	4
● O. P. Pinot Nero Noir '98	♟♟	5
○ O. P. Chardonnay Blanc '98	♟	4
○ O. P. Chardonnay Blanc '96	♟♟	4
● O. P. Pinot Nero '96	♟♟	4
● O. P. Pinot Nero Noir '89	♟♟	6
● O. P. Pinot Nero Noir '90	♟♟	6
● O. P. Pinot Nero Noir '95	♟♟	5
● O. P. Cabernet Sauvignon		
Corvino '94	♟	4
○ O. P. Chardonnay Blanc '97	♟	4

● Garda Cl. Rosso Negresco '98	♟♟	4
○ Lugana Cà Maiol '99	♟♟	3*
○ Lugana Sup. Cà Molin '98	♟♟	4
○ Lugana Sup.		
Sel. Fabio Contato '97	♟♟	5
⊙ Garda Classico Chiaretto '99	♟	3
○ Lugana Brut Cl. Cà Maiol '96	♟	4
○ Lugana Brut Sebastian	♟	3
○ Lugana Sup. Cà Molin '97	♟♟	4

ERBUSCO (BS)

ERBUSCO (BS)

★ BELLAVISTA
VIA BELLAVISTA, 5
25030 ERBUSCO (BS)
TEL. 030/7762000

★ CA' DEL BOSCO
VIA CASE SPARSE, 20
25030 ERBUSCO (BS)
TEL. 030/7766111

In the tastings this year, Vittorio Moretti's Bellavista confirmed its breeding and the well-merited fame it has been universally accorded for more than 20 years. Bellavista is one of Italy's most acclaimed labels in the world of premium-quality wines and there are few other wineries capable of presenting such a vast range of products so faithful to the different wine types and terroirs of Franciacorta. Mattia Vezzola, an oenologist and manager of the estate, has produced a massive Franciacorta Gran Cuvée Brut '96 that the panel unanimously awarded Three Glasses. It is a perfect expression of the soft, persuasive "Bellavista style". A brilliant straw-yellow in colour, it offers delicious aromas of ripe apples and pears, flowers and vanilla. The broad, complex palate is whistle-clean and beautifully balanced, with a deliciously caressing mousse redolent of juicy fruit, vanilla and peach jam. The Gran Cuvée Pas Operé '95 flaunts elegant scents of ripe apricots and yeasts on the nose. In the mouth, it is meaty, fruity and very refreshing, ending on a delicate, slightly bitter note that recalls aromatic herbs. The Bianco del Convento dell'Annunciata '97 is one of the best vintages since this wine was launched. It is a very mature Chardonnay whose straw-yellow is flecked with greenish highlights that introduce intense, sweet aromas of ripe fruit, roses, gooseberries and hawthorn. On the palate, it is elegant, soft and complex. The rest of the range, from the Solesine '98, a Bordeaux blend, to the Chardonnay Uccellanda '97, through to the Satèn, are of an average standard that it would be an understatement to call merely "high".

Not for the first time, in this edition of the Guide Ca' del Bosco has distinguished itself with a range of extraordinary wines, and confirmed its place as one of the brightest stars in the Italian oenological firmament, not just Franciacorta. Maurizio Zanella, the magician behind this Erbusco-based winery, works with total dedication and commitment, supported by a firs-class technical staff, including expert oenologist, Stefano Cappelli. The Cuvée Annamaria Clementi '93, which was erroneously included in the list of wines under last year's Guide profile, has all you could wish for in a great Franciacorta – finesse, elegance, fruit and complexity. The perlage is very delicate, the mousse creamy. The rich, stylish nose releases crisp notes of juicy apples and pears, with hints of spice. On the palate, you will appreciate the weight, the complex harmony, the roundness, the long finish and the clean definition of the fruit. The Chardonnay '98 is also extraordinary, indeed it is one of the best vintages since the legendary '93, which incidentally is still drinking superbly. The '98 version has a bright straw-yellow colour and aromas of butter, vanilla, peach and ripe apricots that meld into the delicate smoky nuances of new wood. Another Three Glasses for the trophy cupboard. The Pinèro '98 almost manages to gain a similar distinction, confirming that this wine, too, enjoyed one of its best vintages ever. The Maurizio Zanella from the same year has a deep, intense colour and concentrated aromas where red and black berry fruit meld with herbal notes and oaky tones. Equally good is the Franciacorta Brut '96, with its perfect balance and generous aromas of yeast and gingerbread laced with a soft, refreshing fruity component. And the rest of the range is no less excellent.

○ Franciacorta Gran Cuvée Brut '96	♟♟♟	6
○ Franciacorta Cuvée Brut	♟♟	4
○ Franciacorta Gran Cuvée Pas Operé '95	♟♟	6
○ Franciacorta Gran Cuvée Satèn	♟♟	5
● Solesine '98	♟♟	5
○ T. d. F. Bianco Convento dell'Annunciata '97	♟♟	5
○ T. d. F. Bianco Uccellanda '97	♟♟	5
⊙ Franciacorta Gran Cuvée Rosé	♟	4
○ T. d. F. Bianco '99	♟	4
○ Franciacorta Extra Brut Vittorio Moretti Ris. '91	♟♟♟	6
○ Franciacorta Gran Cuvée Brut '93	♟♟♟	5
○ Franciacorta Gran Cuvée Brut '95	♟♟♟	6

○ Franciacorta Cuvée Annamaria Clementi '93	♟♟♟	6
○ T. d. F. Chardonnay '98	♟♟♟	6
○ Franciacorta Brut	♟♟	5
○ Franciacorta Brut '96	♟♟	6
⊙ Franciacorta Brut Rosé	♟♟	6
○ Franciacorta Dosage Zéro '96	♟♟	6
○ Franciacorta Satèn '96	♟♟	6
● Maurizio Zanella '98	♟♟	6
● Pinèro '98	♟♟	6
○ T. d. F. Bianco '99	♟♟	4
● T. d. F. Rosso '98	♟♟	4
○ Franciacorta Cuvée Annamaria Clementi '91	♟♟♟	6
○ T. d. F. Chardonnay '96	♟♟♟	6

ERBUSCO (BS)

CAVALLERI
VIA PROVINCIALE, 96
25030 ERBUSCO (BS)
TEL. 030/7760217

ERBUSCO (BS)

FERGHETTINA
VIA CASE SPARSE, 4
25030 ERBUSCO (BS)
TEL. 030/7760120 - 030/7268308

Since the wine world began talking about Franciacorta, the estate of Giovanni and Giulia Cavalleri has become one of the area's biggest names. Over the last few years, several of the most interesting cuvées have been come from its perfectly tended vineyards at Erbusco and the Cavalleri's produce equally serious still wines as well. In this edition, unfortunately, there was no commanding peak that would have crowned another year of effort and commitment to ever higher quality across the entire range. But if anything can console the Cavalleris, it is that the overall standard of their production this year is better last year's. At our tasting, the product that stood out from the vast range of labels was the Franciacorta Pas Dosé '95, a thoroughbred blanc de blancs, rich in structure and complexity and characterized by elegant floral and fruity notes on the nose, where a delicate hint of camomile and candied citrus peel peeps through. In the mouth, it is full-bodied, very fresh, harmonious and reasonably long. The Satèn is truly delicious, conjuring up delicious notes of ripe fruit and quince while the Brut Collezione '95, though obviously a wine of breeding, fell a handful of points short of a Three Glass score because of its slight lack of balance on the palate. Although space is limited, we must also mention the excellent Merlot Corniole '97, which unveils intense notes of raspberry and bilberry and offers concentration, definition and softness on both nose and palate. But then the entire Cavalleri range is excellent.

Just a few years ago, when Roberto Gatti decided to set up his own winery after long experience gained over many years working in one of the most prestigious cellars in Franciacorta, he had very clear ideas. His cellar would have to be among the very best, and would be successful where others had had serious difficulties. For Roberto was aiming for quality in still wines, which are much harder to make than sparklers on the Franciacorta terroir. Now, as we take stock, we have to recognize that Roberto has performed very well in both areas. His cuvées are well respected while his whites and reds are simply some of the finest that Franciacorta has to offer. For proof, just taste the excellent Baladello, a Merlot from '97 aged in small, new barrels. It has a dark, ruby colour and sweet aromas of very ripe red and black berry fruit, run through with a very varietal light, grassy note, and then later there emerge notes of cocoa, spice and balsam. It has soft tannins and an exceptional concentration of fruit that softens into a remarkably deep, lingering finish. The Chardonnay Favento unveils great finesse. It has a lovely, deep straw-yellow colour and a stylish, intense nose dominated by soft notes of tropical fruits, vanilla and slight oaky tones. There is nice weight and freshness in the mouth, where elegant notes of apple, white plum and peach fruit emerge in an authoritative, lingering palate. The Terre Bianco and Terre Rosso, though slightly less concentrated than the two vineyard selections, both won very respectable Two Glass ratings. A result that few other wineries in Franciacorta can point to.

●	Corniole Merlot '97	🍷🍷	6
○	Franciacorta Collezione Brut '95	🍷🍷	6
⊙	Franciacorta Collezione Rosé '95	🍷🍷	6
○	Franciacorta Pas Dosé '95	🍷🍷	6
○	Franciacorta Satèn	🍷🍷	6
○	T. d. F. Bianco '99	🍷🍷	4
●	T. d. F. Rosso '98	🍷🍷	4
●	T. d. F. Rosso Tajardino '97	🍷🍷	5
○	Franciacorta Brut	🍷	5
○	T. d. F. Bianco Seradina '98	🍷	5
○	Franciacorta Collezione Brut '86	🍷🍷🍷	6
○	Franciacorta Collezione Brut '93	🍷🍷🍷	6
○	Franciacorta Collezione Brut '94	🍷🍷🍷	6
○	Franciacorta Brut	🍷🍷	5
○	Franciacorta Pas Dosé '94	🍷🍷	5

○	Franciacorta Brut	🍷🍷	5
●	Merlot Baladello '97	🍷🍷	6
○	T. d. F. Bianco '99	🍷🍷	3*
○	T. d. F. Bianco Favento '98	🍷🍷	4
●	T. d. F. Rosso '98	🍷🍷	4
○	Franciacorta Satèn	🍷	5
○	Franciacorta Brut	🍷🍷	4
○	Franciacorta Satèn	🍷🍷	4
●	Merlot Sebino '96	🍷🍷	4
○	T. d. F. Bianco '95	🍷🍷	2*
○	T. d. F. Bianco '98	🍷🍷	3*
○	T. d. F. Bianco Favento '97	🍷🍷	4
●	T. d. F. Rosso Merlot '95	🍷🍷	4
●	T. d. F. Rosso '96	🍷	3
●	T. d. F. Rosso '97	🍷	3

ERBUSCO (BS)

ENRICO GATTI
VIA METELLI, 9
25030 ERBUSCO (BS)
TEL. 030/7267999 - 030/7267157

Gatti at Erbusco is a winery with young ideas, a lot of enthusiasm and a great desire to move up the charts in the Franciacorta hit parade. Lorenzo Gatti and his wife Sonia, along with Enzo Balzarini and his wife Paola, Lorenzo's sister, make up the very efficient team that shares all the responsibilities of the estate. Their 13 hectares of vineyard are looked after with tender loving care and, thanks to a policy of low yields and high planting density, produce excellent quality fruit. Year after year, we have dutifully recorded the constant progress of this winery and the current edition of the Guide is no exception. Quality continues to improve and the Franciacorta Brut is one of the best the panel tasted this year. It has a golden straw-yellow colour, a full, ripe, complex nose of wax, cakes, yeast and vanilla and a dense, full-flavoured yet subtle palate with a lingering fruity finish. The Chardonnay Gatti Bianco '98 is delicate, intense, concentrated and elegant. Superbly handled new wood enhances its fine aromas. The Gatti Rosso is equally skilfully oaked. A Cabernet Sauvignon, it has found in the '98 vintage one of its most felicitous expressions. The dark, dense ruby colour ushers in a deep, intense bouquet of black berry fruit with elegant tones of toasty oak. On the palate, there is good structure and density, with an oily richness and great length that allow delicious varietal tones and velvety tannins to shine through. And the Terre di Franciacorta Bianco and Rosso are among the best in their category. Not bad!

○	Franciacorta Brut	🍷🍷	4
●	Gatti Rosso '98	🍷🍷	4
○	T. d. F. Gatti Bianco '98	🍷🍷	4
●	T. d. F. Rosso '98	🍷🍷	3*
○	T. d. F. Bianco '99	🍷	3
○	Franciacorta Brut	YY	4
○	Gatti Bianco '96	YY	4
○	Gatti Bianco '97	YY	4
●	Gatti Rosso '90	YY	5
●	Gatti Rosso '91	YY	4
●	Gatti Rosso '95	YY	4
●	Gatti Rosso '96	YY	4
○	T. d. F. Bianco '95	YY	2*
○	T. d. F. Bianco '96	YY	2*
●	T. d. F. Rosso '95	YY	2*

ERBUSCO (BS)

SAN CRISTOFORO
VIA VILLANUOVA, 2
25030 ERBUSCO (BS)
TEL. 030/7760482

We have always been very supportive of this small but growing Franciacorta winery, from the time Mario Filippini was its owner and produced high-quality Terre di Franciacorta Bianco and Rosso at very interesting prices. Now that it has been acquired by Bruno Dotti, a young, enthusiastic grower, the vineyard has expanded to eight hectares and the number of bottles produced annually is now almost 60,000. Although the level of quality has risen noticeably, prices – happily – have not. And a further bonus is the excellent Franciacorta that has been added to the still wines in the range. The sparkler we tasted this year has a nice straw-yellow colour flecked with greenish highlights and a very delicate, lingering perlage. On the nose, it offers soft, sweet fruit, almost in the style of a Satèn, with hints of apple, pear and quince. The palate reveals a hefty dosage that very nearly takes it out of the Brut category but the result is a full-bodied and harmoniously rounded wine, impeccably re-fermented, that finishes unhurriedly on notes of vanilla. The Merlot San Cristoforo Uno '98 is also thoroughly good. It has a lovely, dark ruby colour introducing intense aromas of berry fruit, fresh herbs and vanilla with spicy notes of well-integrated new oak. The palate confirms these impressions and unfurls a soft, concentrated, succulent and delicately tannic progression. The Terre Rosso is almost as good. Inviting, and with remarkably well-rounded tannins, it shows nice weight and memorable length. As ever, the Terre Bianco is attractive.

○	Franciacorta Brut	🍷🍷	4
●	San Cristoforo Uno '98	🍷🍷	4
●	T. d. F. Rosso '98	🍷🍷	3*
○	T. d. F. Bianco '99	🍷	3
○	Franciacorta Brut	YY	4
○	T. d. F. Bianco '98	YY	3*
●	San Cristoforo Uno	Y	4
●	T. d. F. Rosso '97	Y	3

ERBUSCO (BS)

GODIASCO (PV)

UBERTI
VIA E. FERMI, 2
25030 ERBUSCO (BS)
TEL. 030/7267476

CABANON
LOC. CABANON, 1
27052 GODIASCO (PV)
TEL. 0383/940912

This year, Agostino and Eleonora Uberti take home another very respectable result. Their Franciacorta Brut Comarì del Salem '95 stood out from the crowd at a blind tasting and sailed comfortably into the Three Glass band. It is a powerful, complex wine but one that still has all the elegance and clean aromas that are the hallmark of the Uberti style. The deep, brilliant straw-yellow ushers in aromas of ripe apples and pears, yeast, vanilla and gingerbread. On the palate, the effervescence is perfectly integrated into the flavour thanks to a very long period of lees contact. It has density, concentration and finesse, showing soft fruit that avoids sliding into over-ripe tones but meld seamlessly into a firm structure that at times seems almost austere. And what length! The Satèn Magnificentia wasn't far behind in fullness and complexity but its soft palate and rich, round structure give it a distinct personality of its own. The Bianco dei Frati Priori '98 is one of its greatest versions ever. The concentration, rich fruit and fine oak aromas put it on a par with the very best Chardonnays. This year, the Francesco I is also in great shape. Elegant, fruity and harmonious like few other Franciacorta Bruts, it combines outstanding freshness and a full body that never threatens to oppress. All the rest of the Uberti range is excellent, perhaps with the sole exception of the Chardonnay Maria dei Medici '98, which wasn't quite up to its usual high standards.

We have always felt that typicity should be considered in a dynamic, rather than a static, sense. However, the massive injections of cabernet into DOC wines where the grape is not allowed distorts the wine type. This can be a good thing from the point of view of quality, so long as DOC status is relinquished and "vino da tavola" is put on the label. But if a wine, even an excellent one like La Botte n.18 from the Mercandelli family, calls itself "Oltrepò Pavese Rosso" and there is a distinct presence of cabernet in the wine, it can not be evaluated as belonging to a DOC zone that permits only barbera, croatina, uva rara, ughetta and pinot nero. This is the reason why, again, La Botte n.18 Cuore di Vino is not reviewed in the Guide. It will be included when it is labelled "vino da tavola" or when (and if) the DOC regulations are changed. And now moving on to the other wines from Cabanon. The Piccolo Principe '97, a Barbera from the oldest vines on the estate, is aged first in new barriques then in oak barrels, and later further matured in the bottle. The resulting wine comes close to excellence. Two Glasses also go to the Bonarda Vivace, the Riesling Renano and the Pinot Grigio, all from the '99 vintage. Two more Glasses were awarded to the Oro '97, a passito from sauvignon, sémillon and muscadelle (the grape used for Sauternes) aged for three years in small oak barrels. The Barbera '97 Prunello is good, if a bit harsh because the tannins are still unbending. The estate's other flagship wines were not ready for release, but a cellar tasting revealed plenty of promise.

O Franciacorta Extra Brut Comarì del Salem '95	♈♈♈	6
O Franciacorta Brut Francesco I	♈♈	5
O Franciacorta Magnificentia	♈♈	5
☉ Franciacorta Rosé Francesco I	♈♈	5
O T. d. F. Bianco dei Frati Priori '98	♈♈	5
● T. d. F. Rosso dei Frati Priori '98	♈♈	5
O Franciacorta Extra Brut Francesco I	♈	5
O T. d. F. Bianco Augustus '99	♈	3
O T. d. F. Bianco Maria Medici '98	♈	5
● T. d. F. Rosso Augustus '98	♈	3
O Franciacorta Brut Comarì del Salem '93	♈♈♈	6
O Franciacorta Extra Brut Comarì del Salem '88	♈♈♈	6
O Franciacorta Magnificentia	♈♈♈	5

● O. P. Barbera Piccolo Principe '97	♈♈	5
● O. P. Bonarda Vivace '99	♈♈	3*
O O. P. Passito Oro '97	♈♈	5
O O. P. Pinot Grigio '99	♈♈	3*
O O. P. Riesling Renano '99	♈♈	3*
● O. P. Barbera Prunello '97	♈	4
● O. P. Bonarda Ris. '91	♈♈	4
O O. P. Riesling Renano '98	♈♈	3*
● O. P. Ris. Bonarda '90	♈♈	4
● O. P. Rosso Ris. Infernot '91	♈♈	5
● O. P. Rosso Ris. Infernot '90	♈♈	5
O Opera Prima Cabanon Blanc '93	♈♈	4
O Opera Prima Cabanon Blanc '96	♈♈	4
O Opera Prima Cabanon Blanc '97	♈♈	4
O Opera Prima Cabanon Blanc '98	♈♈	3*

GRUMELLO DEL MONTE (BG)

CARLOZADRA
VIA CANDOSSE, 13
24064 GRUMELLO DEL MONTE (BG)
TEL. 035/832066 - 035/830244

"Making spumante classico", says Carlo Zadra, "is relatively simple. But it's difficult to choose the right bases for the cuvée. They have to be wines with plenty of sinew and special aromatic and taste profiles. They also have to be long-lived and improve over time in contact with their own second fermentation lees". In fact, Zadra-label spumantes are a fine example of longevity. Mature but well-sustained, they draw depth and subtlety from autolysis of the yeasts. The Millesimato Tradizione 1992, disgorged on 5 June 1999, is now at the peak of its development. The chardonnay that predominates in the cuvée has aromas of honey and incense while the pinot nero and meunier contribute hints of jam and hay. All this is underlined by notes of sweet vanilla and mace spice derived from the initial ageing in oak. The flavour is full, well-balanced and soft, with around the average quantity of residual sugar laid down for extra dry category. The Liberty, disgorged on 18 October 1999, is particularly pleasant and persuasive. Made from white grapes only (chardonnay and pinot bianco), it reveals dominant notes of dried flowers and croissant. Dryer, the Brut Nondosato vintage 1993, was disgorged in June '99 and is very elegant, with a solid full body. The Donna Nunzia '99 is intensely aromatic, dry and very refreshing, and comes from moscato giallo del Trentino grapes.

GRUMELLO DEL MONTE (BG)

TENUTA CASTELLO DI GRUMELLO
VIA FOSSE, 11
24064 GRUMELLO DEL MONTE (BG)
TEL. 035/4420817 - 035/830244

Colle del Calvario Valcalepio Rosso confirms itself as the flagship wine of this estate. A cold-blended Bordeaux mix with 80 percent cabernet sauvignon aged for a year in part new barriques, it has a dark garnet colour in the '97 version and a markedly vanillaed aroma, although the morello cherry typical of Valcalepio is also present. In the mouth, it is dry, warm and well-balanced. The oak-aged Valcalepio Rosso '98 is quite good, even if it is less rich and complex. With regard to the Aurito '98, a barrique-fermented monovarietal chardonnay from the Bergamo area, we are forced to repeat the comments we made last year about the '97 vintage. Small oak barrels, so fashionable nowadays, are one of the tools winemakers can use to create whites and reds with greater structure but if the wine tastes too much of oak, and the varietal tastes and aromas are smothered, their adoption is a mistake. The wine becomes heavy and difficult to drink. Now, class, take this lesson to heart. Without all the vanilla, the Aurito would be worth Two Glasses but as things stand, it will have to settle for just One. Finally, the new Celebra Moscato Nero Passito di Scanzo '97 is a distinguished bottle with an intense, penetrating bouquet of raisins and bitter clove and cinnamon spice. The bittersweet flavour, however, is a little too astringent.

O Carlozadra Cl. Brut Nondosato '93	ŸŸ	4
O Carlozadra Cl. Extra Dry Liberty	ŸŸ	5
O Carlozadra Cl. Extra Dry Tradizione '92	ŸŸ	5
O Donna Nunzia Moscato Giallo '99	ŸŸ	3*
O Carlozadra Cl. Brut '93	♀♀	5
O Carlozadra Cl. Brut '92	♀♀	4
O Carlozadra Cl. Brut '95	♀♀	4
O Carlozadra Cl. Brut Nondosato '92	♀♀	5
O Carlozadra Cl. Brut Nondosato '94	♀♀	5
O Carlozadra Cl. Extra Dry Tradizione '92	♀♀	5
● Don Ludovico Pinot Nero '93	♀♀	4

● Valcalepio Rosso Colle del Calvario '97	ŸŸ	4
O Chardonnay della Bergamasca Aurito '98	Ÿ	4
● Moscato di Scanzo Passito Celebra '97	Ÿ	6
● Valcalepio Rosso '98	Ÿ	3
O Aurito '92	♀♀	4
O Chardonnay della Bergamasca Aurito '96	♀♀	4
● Valcalepio Rosso Colle del Calvario '90	♀♀	4
● Valcalepio Rosso Colle del Calvario '96	♀♀	4

MONIGA DEL GARDA (BS) MONTALTO PAVESE (PV)

COSTARIPA
VIA CIALDINI, 12
25080 MONIGA DEL GARDA (BS)
TEL. 0365/502010

CA' DEL GE'
VIA CA' DEL GE', 3
27040 MONTALTO PAVESE (PV)
TEL. 0383/870179

Brothers Imer and Mattia Vezzola have managed to amaze us with an idiosyncratic version of Chiaretto del Garda. Basically, they have returned to the old tradition of barrel fermentation to create a wine with a very special character and exceptional longevity that they have dedicated to the memory of Pompeo Gherardo Molmenti. It was Molmenti, a Venetian senator, who returned from a journey to Bordeaux and hired French advisors to bring the Gallic winemaking philosophy across the Alps to his estate in Moniga. That was how, in the early 20th century, the forerunner of the '98 Costaripa Chiaretto Molmenti was born. Produced from a careful selection of groppello, marzemino and barbera, this wine ferments in oak. It has a pale, old rose colour, a bouquet of dried flowers, red berry fruit and vanilla, and a sinewy, slightly salty warm flavour with a faint bitterish note in the finish. It is an exception to the general rule of approachable, easy-to-drink rosé wines but it is well worth the effort of hunting down a bottle. Another excellent wine is the Maim '97, absolutely the best monovarietal Groppello tasted this year, the result of a tiny yield per hectare and 12 months in small oak barrels. The Riesling Pievecroce '98 is also excellent, and drinking beautifully right now. The Marzemino Le Mazane '99, Groppello Vigneto Le Castelline '97, Garda Classico Rosso Campo delle Starne, Brut Classico Costaripa and Chiaretto '99 are also all good.

This time Enzo Padroggi, the "padron", or owner, of Cà del Ge', restrained himself a little. This year he "only" sent a dozen wines as opposed to the sixteen or eighteen of the past few years. From the point of view of quality, there is still the same fluctuation between some very satisfactory wines and others that are more debatable. However, keeping tabs on all these different types cannot be easy. The best wine is the Barbera '97 Vigna Varmasì, a deep ruby wine flecked with garnet that offers a bouquet of morello cherry jam, cinnamon and cloves, and a vigorous, firm, pleasantly rugged flavour. We had already tasted the Brut Classico '92, obtained entirely from pinot nero, last year. Now it is coming to the end of its ageing cycle but has held up well, as is confirmed by its Two Glass rating. The still Müller Thurgau from the '99 vintage is fresh and clean, with an intense flower and fruit varietal aroma. The still Pinot Nero, fermented without the skins, has a nose of apple and peach. In the mouth, it is a little lemony but very pleasant nonetheless. The Riesling Italico '99 is uncomplicated and easy drinking, with a slightly bitter finish of green almond. Again from '99, the still Barbera, the slightly sparkling Chardonnay (couldn't the Chardonnay at least have been spared the bubbles?) and the slightly sparkling Moscato are all decent.

⊙ Garda Classico Chiaretto Molmenti '98	♟♟	5
● Garda Classico Groppello Maim '97	♟♟	5
○ Garda Riesling Pievecroce '98	♟♟	4
● Benaco Bresciano Marzemino Le Mazane '99	♟	4
○ Brut Classico Costaripa	♟	4
⊙ Garda Bresciamo Chiaretto Vino di una Notte '99	♟	3
● Garda Cl. Rosso Campo delle Starne '98	♟	4
● Garda Classico Groppello Vigneto Le Castelline '97	♟	4

● O. P. Barbera Vigna Varmasì '97	♟♟	4
○ Müller Thurgau '99	♟	3
○ O. P. Pinot Nero in bianco '99	♟	3
○ O. P. Riesling Italico '99	♟	3
● O. P. Barbera '99		3
○ O. P. Chardonnay Vivace '99		3
○ O. P. Moscato Vivace '99		3
● O. P. Barbera Vigna Varmasi '90	♟♟	4
○ O. P. Pinot Nero Brut Cl. '92	♟♟	3*
○ O. P. Riesling Italico '98	♟♟	2*
● Croatina Rivuné Pasì '91	♟	5
● O. P. Barbera Vigna Varmasi '95	♟	4
● O. P. Pinot Nero Albaron '96	♟	3
● Tormento Rosso '93	♟	4
● Tormento Rosso '95	♟	5

MONTALTO PAVESE (PV)   MONTICELLI BRUSATI (BS)

DORIA
CASA TACCONI, 3
27040 MONTALTO PAVESE (PV)
TEL. 0383/870143

LO SPARVIERE
VIA COSTA, 2
25040 MONTICELLI BRUSATI (BS)
TEL. 030/652382

Giuseppina Sassella Doria and her son, Andrea, are hard at work in their vineyards, bringing back many old varieties – some of which are making contributions of unsuspected importance – and experimenting with "new" grape varieties, at least for the Oltrepò DOC zone, under the guidance of agronomist, Pierluigi Donna. The undoubted potential of the grapes has finally been realized by the new cellar manager, Daniele Manini, who holds a degree in agriculture and has moved to the Oltrepò from Lazio. Beppe Bassi, an oenologist as skilful as he is creative, acts as consultant. The results are brilliant, to say the least. The Pinot Nero Querciolo '98 has returned to its former splendour. Aged in Nevers and Allier oak barriques, it is a bright garnet in hue, and unveils aromas of violets, blackcurrants and vanilla. Velvet-soft on the palate, it reveals a harmony that it combines with longevity. The Querciolo '95 still holds up well and confirms its Two Glass status. The Roncobianco '98, a Riesling Renano part cold-macerated and fermented in oak, has clean notes of tropical fruit and gunflint, underlined by a measured touch of vanilla. The Pinot Nero Brut Querciolo, made by the "metodo Martinotti lungo", involving nine months in a cuve close on the lees, is a straw-yellow colour, with admirable perlage and aromas of hazelnut and artemisia. The palate offers an elegant flavour of fresh almonds. The slightly sparkling Bonarda '99 is approachable and easy to drink while the Roncorosso '97, Oltrepò Pavese Rosso, will do well after a bit longer in the bottle.

The cellar of Ugo Gussalli Beretta, a leading business figure in Brescia, and his wife, Monique Poncelet, this year collected a series of flattering reviews from the panel, and not for the first time. With 28 hectares under vine in the Monticelli Brusati subzone, Lo Sparviere now turns out 120,000 bottles a year. Oenologist Francesco Polastri has created a very carefully planned range of wines that has its strong point in the Franciacorta. The flag-bearer for the estate this year is the Franciacorta Extra Brut. It has a deep straw-yellow colour and a nose marked by sweet nuances of vanilla that shade into floral notes and then again to yeast, toasty bread, ripe peaches and apricots. In the mouth, it has good structure, a full body and a complexity reminiscent of wines from the other side of the Alps. The long, confident finish is almost austere. The Franciacorta Brut is very clean and stylish. Rich in fruit on both the nose and palate, it can point to decent concentration and a certain elegance, hinting at peach and ripe apple in the polished, harmonious palate. The Terre di Franciacorta Rosso Il Sergnana in the '96 version is rich, full and soft-structured, also revealing discreet alcohol. Its laudable complexity and fruit-rich fullness earned it a comfortable Two Glasses. Interesting, but we felt lacking a little depth and not so well-constructed, is the Vino del Cacciatore '97. It can offer soft tannins and good continuity on the palate. The Terre Bianco '99 is rich in fresh notes of tropical fruit. Soft, and well put together on the palate, it wasn't far off a Two Glass rating.

○ O. P. Pinot Nero Brut Querciolo	♀♀	4
● O. P. Pinot Nero Querciolo '98	♀♀	4
○ O. P. Riesling Renano Roncobianco V. Tesi '98	♀♀	4
● O. P. Bonarda Vivace '99	♀	3
● O. P. Rosso Roncorosso V. Siura '97	♀	4
● O. P. Bonarda '98	♀♀	3*
○ O. P. Pinot Nero Brut	♀♀	4
○ O. P. Pinot Nero in bianco Querciolo '97	♀♀	4
● O. P. Pinot Nero Querciolo '91	♀♀	5
● O. P. Pinot Nero Querciolo '93	♀♀	5
● O. P. Pinot Nero Querciolo '95	♀♀	5
● O. P. Rosso Roncorosso V. Siura '93	♀♀	4
● O. P. Rosso V. del Masö '91	♀♀	4

○ Franciacorta Brut	♀♀	5
○ Franciacorta Extra Brut	♀♀	5
● T. d. F. Rosso Il Sergnana '96	♀♀	5
○ T. d. F. Bianco '99	♀	3
● T. d. F. Rosso Vino del Cacciatore '97	♀	4
○ Franciacorta Brut	♀♀	4
○ Franciacorta Extra Brut	♀♀	5
○ Franciacorta Extra Brut	♀♀	4
○ T. d. F. Bianco Ris. '95	♀♀	3*
○ Franciacorta Brut	♀	4
○ T. d. F. Bianco '97	♀	3
○ T. d. F. Bianco Barrique '96	♀	4
● T. d. F. Rosso '96	♀	4
● T. d. F. Rosso Vino del Cacciatore '95	♀	3

MONTICELLI BRUSATI (BS)   MONTÙ BECCARIA (PV)

VILLA
VIA VILLA, 12
25040 MONTICELLI BRUSATI (BS)
TEL. 030/652329

IL MONTÙ
VIA MARCONI, 10
27040 MONTÙ BECCARIA (PV)
TEL. 0385/262252

With 12 wines submitted for our tasting, eight of which scored better than Two Glasses, Alessandro Bianchi's Villa establishes itself as one of the most important producers in Franciacorta. An estate policy focused on absolute quality, serious investment in the vineyards and cellar equipment, a love of detail and a technical staff of proven skill, have all helped Villa to reach this goal. Only the supreme prize of a Three Glass score is missing to crown their efforts but we are certain that it will not be long in arriving. The label that came closest to the prize again this year is the vintage Satèn, which has a lovely, lustrous green-flecked straw-yellow colour. Sweet on the nose, it unfurls well-defined fruit notes of pear and peach, followed by vanilla and yeast, with intensity and finesse. In the mouth it is round, delicate and full-bodied, coherently re-proposing the flavours of ripe fruit, jam and cake already proffered on the nose. The Franciacorta Brut '96 also shows evidence of a skilled hand. Although not particularly complex, it is fat, soft, fruity and full-bodied, with elegance and freshness, a concentration of fruit, and remarkable harmony. The Cabernet Bianchi Roncalli '97 has a dark, dense ruby colour, a sweet nose of ripe red and black berry fruit, and complex, elegant hints of new oak. It reveals a close-knit, soft palate with clean, sweet and juicy cherry and ripe plum fruit, cocoa, very elegant tannins and a lingering finish. The other wines from the vast range presented by Villa are perfectly made and fully reflect the great winemaking tradition of Franciacorta.

In Montù Beccaria on 20 April 1902, the first co-operative winery in the Oltrepò Pavese was set up, but it later had to close after a series of ups and downs. Abandoned for years, it has been revived by a group of private businessmen who have completely restored the premises and so, in 1998, the Cantina Storica Il Montù opened its doors. It includes a modern cellar for the production of wines and spumantes, a distillery with a double copper still for making grappa, and a restaurant. The technical director is oenologist Riccardo Ottina, who produces an interesting range of whites, reds and metodo classico spumantes from the grapes harvested on his 80 hectares of vineyards in Valle Versa. The most impressive wine is the Malvasia Passito '99, from super-ripe grapes harvested in late November. After soft pressing, the sugar-rich must is fermented in small Allier oak casks. The result is an original dessert wine with a golden yellow colour, an aroma of dried roses, sage and vanilla, and a sweet, rich, almost creamy flavour. Though the oak leaves rather too evident a mark, the aromas of the Malvasia hold their own. In contrast, the oak wins out in the Chardonnay '97. If we could have tasted a few more varietal notes, we would have been much happier. The Bonarda '97 Vigna del Vespero is also more than merely good, having aged for 20 months in Allier and Tronçais oak. The non-vintage Pinot Nero Brut Classico rounds off the list of wines presented. We liked its fresh fragrance but it lacks complexity.

O	Franciacorta Brut '96	♟♟	4
O	Franciacorta Brut Sel. '94	♟♟	6
O	Franciacorta Cuvette Sec '96	♟♟	5
O	Franciacorta Extra Brut '96	♟♟	4
⊙	Franciacorta Rosé Démi Sec '96	♟♟	5
O	Franciacorta Satèn '96	♟♟	6
●	Rosso Bianchi Roncalli Sel. '97	♟♟	6
●	T. d. F. Rosso Gradoni '97	♟♟	4
O	T. d. F. Bianco '99	♟	3
O	T. d. F. Bianco Marengo '98	♟	4
O	T. d. F. Bianco Pian della Vigna '99	♟	4
●	T. d. F. Rosso '98	♟	3
O	Franciacorta Satèn Brut '95	♟♟	5
O	Franciacorta Vita Nova Brut '93	♟♟	6

O	O. P. Chardonnay '97	♟♟	4
O	O. P. Malvasia Passito '99	♟♟	4
●	O. P. Bonarda Vigna del Vespero '97	♟	4
O	O. P. Pinot Nero Brut Cl.	♟	4

MONTÙ BECCARIA (PV) MORNICO LOSANA (PV)

VERCESI DEL CASTELLAZZO
VIA AURELIANO, 36
27040 MONTÙ BECCARIA (PV)
TEL. 0385/60067

CA' DI FRARA
LOC. CASA FERRARI, 1
27040 MORNICO LOSANA (PV)
TEL. 0383/892299

The Vercesi brothers maintain a high level of quality year after year, with more than a few high points of excellence, and there are several high-scoring wines in this edition of the Guide. We begin with the Orto di San Giacomo '97, Oltrepò Pavese Rosso, made from very ripe grapes and left for a year in barriques. A dark, lustrous ruby colour, it has elegant tones of vanilla and cinnamon spice with toasty notes of almond and cocoa. The flavour is concentrated, with remarkable balance and vigour. It will definitely improve with bottle age so it is almost a shame to drink it now, considering what it will become in the future. The same thoughts are prompted by the Bonarda Fatila '97, which is outstandingly rich. At the moment it is a bit closed on the nose but promises a complex bouquet. It makes up for this with great fullness on the palate and a flavour that is already delicious. The Vespolino '99, made entirely from vespolina grapes (also called ughetta), eased in to the Two Glass band thanks to its intense aroma of green pepper and wild berries and a clean, refreshingly tangy taste. Better than merely well-made, the Oltrepò Pavese Pinot Nero in bianco Gugiarolo '98, fermented without the skins, is a fruit-rich, floral tipple. Finally, the Oltrepò Pavese Rosso '99 Pezzalunga is good, though a little tart.

For years, Luca Bellani's Cà di Frara – in the local dialect, this is the name of the village of Casa Ferrari near Mornico Losana – has been producing the best Pinot Grigio in the entire Oltrepò Pavese. A lustrous greenish gold, it has a broad aroma of roses, pineapple and ripe pears, and a full, powerful palate that is very fruity without being heavy, and offers a long, aromatic finish. As delicious as it is unique, it recalls certain wines from Trentino, the Collio and Alsace. Bellani says that the grape deserves all the credit for it is harvested when fully ripe from a vineyard planted in the late 70s in a valley where medium-textured, crystalline chalky soil – it is no accident that the village is called "Oliva Gessi", or "Olive Chalk" – emerges through a sandy top layer. It could be the nature of the soil or it could be the site climate, but the fact is that the Pinot Grigio '99 is a notch higher in quality than the already very good '98 and '97 editions. The Riesling Renano Apogeo '99, however, is "only" good for it refuses to open as it should, although it will probably improve in the bottle, and the Malvasia Il Raro '99 is on the same level. Among the reds, the Pinot Nero Il Raro '98 is worth a closer look. Aged for a year in small oak barrels, it offers an elegant, soft fullness on the palate. Equally good, in its own category, is the Bonarda '98 La Casetta, from very old vines and 50 percent oak-fermented. In closing, we confirm the high score awarded in the past to the Rosso Io '97.

● O. P. Bonarda Fatila '97	♟♟	4	
● O. P. Rosso Orto di S. Giacomo '97	♟♟	4	
● Vespolino '99	♟♟	3*	
○ O. P. Pinot Nero in bianco			
Gugiarolo '98	♟	3	
● O. P. Rosso Pezzalunga '99	♟	3	
● O. P. Bonarda Fatila '90	♟♟	4	
● O. P. Bonarda Fatila '91	♟♟	4	
● O. P. Pinot Nero Luogo dei Monti '95	♟♟	4	
● O. P. Pinot Nero Luogo dei Monti '96	♟♟	4	
● O. P. Pinot Nero Luogo dei Monti '97	♟♟	4	
● O. P. Rosso Orto di S. Giacomo '96	♟♟	4	
● O. P. Bonarda Fatila '96	♟	4	
● O. P. Rosso Pezzalunga '98	♟	3	

● O. P. Bonarda La Casetta '98	♟♟	4	
○ O. P. Pinot Grigio V. T. '99	♟♟	4	
○ O. P. Pinot Nero Il Raro '98	♟♟	4	
○ O. P. Malvasia Il Raro '99	♟	4	
○ O. P. Riesling Renano Apogeo '99	♟	3	
○ O. P. Chardonnay '97	♟♟	3*	
○ O. P. Malvasia Il Raro '98	♟♟	4	
○ O. P. Pinot Grigio V. T. '95	♟♟	4	
○ O. P. Pinot Grigio V. T. '97	♟♟	4	
○ O. P. Pinot Grigio V. T. '98	♟♟	4	
● O. P. Pinot Nero Il Raro '97	♟♟	4	
○ O. P. Riesling Renano '95	♟♟	3*	
○ O. P. Riesling Renano Apogeo '98	♟♟	3*	
● O. P. Rosso Io '97	♟♟	4	

OME (BS)

POLPENAZZE DEL GARDA (BS)

MAJOLINI
LOC. VALLE
VIA MANZONI
25050 OME (BS)
TEL. 030/6527378

CASCINA LA PERTICA
FRAZ. PICEDO, 24
25080 POLPENAZZE DEL GARDA (BS)
TEL. 0365/651471

We wrote last year that La Majolini is a winery whose quality is improving fast. The Majolini brothers are making major investments in the estate, in cellar construction as well as in the vineyards and technical staff. After our tastings this year, we can only record further growth in the average quality levels. If last year it was the Franciacorta '92 that made a favourable impression, this year the Satèn was without a doubt the wine that was most appreciated by the panel. It has a lovely deep straw-yellow colour with greenish highlights and opens up sweet and broad on the nose, where hints of yeasts, butter and toffee emerge, shading into more complex, biscuity notes. In the mouth, it is refreshing, thick and full, rich in fruit, caressingly effervescent, with a lingering finish. The '94 vintage is characterized by hints of honey and roasted hazelnuts on the nose. These evolve in the glass into complex, elegant tertiary aromas that lead in to a full palate with a twin theme of citrus freshness and the rounder sensations of quince jam. The Franciacorta Brut is also excellent. Full and concentrated in colour, it releases inviting aromas of yeast and crusty bread while in the mouth it offers elegant structure and a fresh vein of fruit. The Dordaro '98, aged in barriques, is more concentrated and full than the previous year's. It unveils sweet notes of spice and ripe cherries, round tannins and a fresh vegetal vein that recalls a Cabernet. The panel had no trouble in awarding Two Glasses. The Ruc di Gnoc '98 Rosso, Ronchello Bianco and basic Terre di Franciacorta are all well-managed.

Open enthusiasm is what Ruggero Brunori, a young industrialist in the engineering sector from Brescia, feels for his small but well-equipped cellar on Lake Garda. The object of his passion is the Cascina La Pertica, at Picedo near Polpenazze, where he produces an admirable selection of wines produced from biodynamically cultivated vineyards. He has even called one of the great Italian winemakers as his consultant. In the last few years, Franco Bernabei has helped make significant improvements, especially in red winemaking. And we'll begin our tasting with the best of these, the Zalte '98, a blend of cabernet sauvignon and merlot that expresses itself with elegance and balance. It has intense aromas of red berry fruit, with light balsamic and grassy notes. On the palate, it is full with good concentration, revealing itself to be very coherent and technically irreproachable. The oak from the ageing barriques is not intrusive and its most evident feature is its finesse. The metodo classico Spumante Brut is also very good. Made from chardonnay grapes, it is therefore a "blanc de blancs" and possesses all the finest characteristics of this wine type. Fruity aromas with notes of yeasts and white damsons, a delicate but lingering flavour and a note of pleasant, refreshing acidity all come through. Finally, we come to the Garda DOC wines. The Le Sincette Rosso '98, obtained from groppello, marzemino, sangiovese and barbera grapes, is uncomplicated and easy to drink. The rosé fermented version called Chiaretto comes from identical grapes but belongs to the '99 vintage. Finally, the Garda Chardonnay '99 is fruity but a little anonymous, and is perhaps the least convincing wine of the range.

O	Franciacorta Brut	🍷🍷	5
O	Franciacorta Brut '94	🍷🍷	5
O	Franciacorta Satèn '96	🍷🍷	5
●	T. d. F. Rosso Dordaro '98	🍷🍷	5
O	T. d. F. Bianco '99	🍷	3
O	T. d. F. Bianco Ronchello '99	🍷	4
●	T. d. F. Rosso Ruc di Gnoc '98	🍷	3
O	Franciacorta Brut	🍷🍷	4
O	Franciacorta Brut '92	🍷🍷	5
●	T. d. F. Rosso Dordaro '90	🍷🍷	4
●	T. d. F. Rosso Ruc di Gnoc '91	🍷🍷	4
●	T. d. F. Bianco Ronchello '93	🍷	4
O	T. d. F. Bianco Ronchello '98	🍷	4
●	T. d. F. Rosso Dordaro '96	🍷	4
●	T. d. F. Rosso Ruc di Gnoc '92	🍷	4

O	Le Sincette Brut	🍷🍷	5
●	Le Zalte Rosso '98	🍷🍷	5
⊙	Garda Chiaretto Le Sincette '99	🍷	3
●	Garda Classico Rosso		
	Le Sincette '98	🍷	3
O	Garda Chardonnay		
	Le Sincette '99		3
●	Garda Bresciano Rosso		
	Le Sincette Ris. '96	🍷🍷	3*
●	Le Zalte Rosso '90	🍷🍷	4
●	Le Zalte Rosso '92	🍷🍷	4
●	Le Zalte Rosso '94	🍷🍷	4
●	Le Zalte Rosso '97	🍷🍷	4
●	Le Zalte Rosso '95	🍷	4

PONTIDA (BG)

CANTINA SOCIALE VAL SAN MARTINO
VIA BERGAMO, 1195
24030 PONTIDA (BG)
TEL. 035/795035

While waiting for the extremely promising Valcalepio Rosso Riserva '97 to reach maturity, the Cantina Sociale Val San Martino presents its wines from the last two harvests at very competitive prices. This year, two whites particularly impressed us. One is dry and the other is a sweet dessert wine. The first is the Incrocio Manzoni 6.0.13, created at the beginning of the 30s, at the Agricultural Institute in Conegliano by Professor Luigi Manzoni, who crossed two noble varieties, Rhine riesling and pinot bianco. This is a vine that deserves to be used more widely for the production of both still and sparkling wines. The Incrocio Manzoni 6.0.13 della Bergamasca '99 from Val San Martino has a vivid gold-green colour, a fragrant aroma of peaches, roses and artemisia, and a dry, tangy, well-balanced flavour with a crisp finish of apples and bananas. The other top white is the new Moscato Giallo from slightly raisined grapes. This attractively floral, fruity bottle is a good dessert wine. Drink it soon, while it still has lots of freshness. Continuing with the whites, both the Valcalepio '99 and Chardonnay della Bergamasca '99 are pleasant and easy drinking. Then moving on to the reds, the Valcalepio '98 is not bad but is evolving a bit too fast while the dry, tangy Cabernet '98 seems to be holding up well. We shall close this profile with the enjoyable Moscato Nero Passito '98, which offers good varietal expression.

○	Incrocio Manzoni 6.0.13 '99	🍷🍷	2*
○	Moscato Giallo Passito della Bergamasca '99	🍷🍷	3*
●	Cabernet della Bergamasca '98	🍷	2*
○	Chardonnay della Bergamasca '99	🍷	2*
●	Moscato Nero Passito '98	🍷	5
○	Valcalepio Bianco '99	🍷	2*
●	Valcalepio Rosso '98	🍷	2*
○	Valcalepio Bianco '98	🍸🍸	2*
●	Valcalepio Rosso Ris. '95	🍸🍸	3*
●	Cabernet della Bergamasca '97	🍸	2*
○	Incrocio Manzoni 6.0.13 '98	🍸	2*
●	Valcalepio Rosso '97	🍸	2*

POZZOLENGO (BS)

TENUTA ROVEGLIA
LOC. ROVEGLIA, 1
25010 POZZOLENGO (BS)
TEL. 030/918663

The Tenuta Roveglia was set up during the 30s thanks to the enthusiasm for the countryside of Federico Zweifel, a Swiss textile magnate. Over the years, it has grown to extend over an area of more than 100 hectares, 47 of which are under vine. Presently, it is the property of Sara, Vanessa and Babetli Azzone, great-grandchildren of the founder, who have entrusted the vineyards and cellar to the care of manager Paolo Fabiani and oenologist Cesare Ferrari. The quality of the wines has its ups and downs. Profiled in the 1999 Guide, the estate only merited a mention in Other Wineries last year but returns this year with a full profile thanks to a higher level of quality that we hope will remain reasonably constant. The top wine here is the Lugana Superiore Vigne di Catullo '98, a 100 percent trebbiano di Lugana from vines more than 40 years old with a limited yield of 60-70 quintals per hectare. Vinified in stainless steel, with no more than a 50 percent must to fruit ratio, it stays on the yeasts until November and is aged unhurriedly in bottle before release. It is tangy, full and harmonious, with lovely aromas of peach and bitter almond. Also well-made is the Filo di Arianna '98, another Lugana Superiore from old vines, fermented in barriques where it remains until the January following the harvest. Released after ten months or so in vats and three or four months in the bottle, it has a nicely understated hint of oak that underlines the varietal notes without covering them. The standard Lugana from the '99 vintage is still a bit green and lemony but is destined to improve in a short time. The Spumante Brut is very well-managed.

○	Lugana Sup. Filo di Arianna '98	🍷🍷	4
○	Lugana Sup. Vigne di Catullo '98	🍷🍷	4
○	Lugana '99	🍷	3
○	Lugana Brut '98		4
○	Lugana Sup. Vigne di Catullo '95	🍸🍸	3*
○	Lugana Sup. Vigne di Catullo '97	🍸🍸	4
○	Lugana '95	🍸	2*
○	Lugana '97	🍸	2*
○	Lugana Brut	🍸	3
○	Lugana Sup. Filo di Arianna '96	🍸	4

ROCCA DE GIORGI (PV)　RODENGO SAIANO (BS)

ANTEO
LOC. CHIESA
27043 ROCCA DE GIORGI (PV)
TEL. 0385/48583 - 0385/99073

MIRABELLA
VIA CANTARANE, 2
25050 RODENGO SAIANO (BS)
TEL. 030/611197

After a period of disconcerting highs and lows, Anteo is settling down to a satisfying continuity in terms of quality. The Bruts are well up to the fine reputation of this winery, best known for making spumante. It has almost 29 hectares of vineyards on a single plot on the chalky, marly hills 350 metres above sea level at Rocca de Giorgi. The non-vintage Brut Classico, from a cuvée of 70 percent pinot nero and chardonnay, which spent more than 36 months on the lees, collected Two Glasses. Its delicate perlage introduces a complex bouquet of toast, spices and faint notes of citrus, then a fresh, tangy, clean taste. The Pinot Nero Nature Classico, again with three years on the lees but with only 20 percent chardonnay, is dry without being harsh. Clean-tasting, it unfurls elegant touches of crusty bread. The Brut Classico Selezione del Gourmet '94, with 80 percent pinot nero that gives a delicious aroma of berry fruit, has held up well and confirms last year's One Glass. The Blanc de Noirs "metodo italiano lungo", with a year on the lees in a pressure tank, and the Pinot Nero Martinotti, named after the inventor of the Italian tank method of spumante making, are both well-made and get One very full Glass. The same goes for the bright, fruity Moscato di Volpara '99 La Volpe e l'Uva. The Giublot '97, an unusual blend of barrique-aged cabernet sauvignon, pinot nero and bonarda di Rovescala, gained Two Glasses. It will certainly improve in the bottle.

The reason there is a spumante called Wertmüller Brut in the Mirabella range is that Enrico Job, set designer and husband of film director, Lina, is one of the partners in the winery. At our tasting this year, the Wertmüller Brut and the Franciacorta Non Dosato '93 are the products that were most admired. The first, produced from a cuvée of 60 percent chardonnay and pinot bianco aged for four years on the lees, has a creamy mousse and a delicate, continuous perlage. On the nose, it offers rich, sweet notes of ripe fruit and jam, yeast and toasty bread. In the mouth, it is soft and almost aromatic, revealing a generous dosage, almost excessive for a Brut, but it turns out to be a very pleasant glass thanks to the intensity of the fruit and the intriguing nuances of camomile and flowers that pervade its aromas. The Franciacorta Non Dosato '93 has delicately developed, elegant tones. On the nose, it is not powerful but is very well put together, proffering fruit-rich tones and subtle spicy hints. The palate is round, soft and evolved. Definitely a wine to uncork straight away. The Franciacorta Brut has a lovely brilliant greenish straw-yellow colour and a full nose that lacks a little definition. On the palate, it is elegant and soft, with a lean body, and finishes with pleasant touches of fresh almond. The Franciacorta Rosé is a well-typed product but not very interesting while nice results came from the two Terre di Franciacorta selections, obtained from the Palazzina (the white) and Maniero vineyards (red). The former offers convincing structure and notes of soft tropical fruit while the second parades hints of red berry fruit in a very full structure. Both the Terre di Franciacorta Bianco and Rosso are of good quality.

O O. P. Pinot Nero Brut Cl.	♈♈	4
O O. P. Pinot Nero Cl. Nature	♈♈	4
● Rosso Giublot '97	♈♈	4
O O. P. Moscato La Volpe e L'Uva '99	♈	3
O O. P. Pinot Nero Brut Blanc de Noirs	♈	3
O O. P. Pinot Nero Brut Martinotti	♈	3
O O. P. Pinot Nero in bianco Ca' dell'Oca '95	♉♉	4
O Quattro Marzo Bianco '98	♉♉	3*
● O. P. Bonarda Staffolo '98	♉	3
O O. P. Pinot Nero Brut Cl. Sel. Gourmet '94	♉	5
● O. P. Pinot Nero Ca' dell'Oca '93	♉	4
● O. P. Pinot Nero Il Floreale '98	♉	3
● Rosso Giublot '96	♉	4

O Franciacorta Non Dosato '93	♈♈	4
O Wertmüller Brut	♈♈	5
O Franciacorta Brut	♈	4
☉ Franciacorta Rosé	♈	4
O T. d F. Bianco '99	♈	2*
O T. d F. Bianco Palazzina '98	♈	3
● T. d F. Rosso '98	♈	2*
● T. d F. Rosso Maniero '98	♈	3
O Franciacorta Brut	♉♉	4
O Franciacorta Brut	♉♉	4
O Franciacorta Brut '90	♉♉	5
O Franciacorta Non Dosato '91	♉♉	5
O T. d F. Bianco Barrique '95	♉♉	4
O Wertmüller Brut	♉♉	5
● T. d F. Rosso Barrique '95	♉	4

ROVESCALA (PV)

ROVESCALA (PV)

F.LLI AGNES
VIA CAMPO DEL MONTE, 1
27040 ROVESCALA (PV)
TEL. 0385/75206

MARTILDE
FRAZ. CROCE, 4/A1
27040 ROVESCALA (PV)
TEL. 0385/756280

The Cristiano brothers and Sergio Agnes from Rovescala have established themselves as producers of extraordinary Bonardas but this time they were in too much of a hurry. Some of their best wines are not yet ready for the market. We are referring to the Bonarda '99 Campo del Monte, Cresta del Ghiffi and Vignazzo, which should all be left to re-ferment in the bottle and for now are as flat as pancakes. When the yeasts begin to metabolize the residual sugars, these wines will perk up and then it will be another story altogether. This means we will be taking another look at them for the 2002 Guide. The only outstanding Bonarda '99 is the Possessione del Console, from a rare clone called the "pignolo" with a pinecone-shaped, compact bunch and small, irregular grapes. Purple in colour, it has notes of plum and very ripe mulberries, and a robust flavour with an uncompromising rustic nobility. The Poculum '98 is a resounding success. A barrique-aged red table wine from an unspecified blend (although the base seems to be bonarda), it has a purplish black colour, a very intense bouquet of vanilla, liquorice, dried plums, mulberry and violet, and a superbly concentrated, warm flavour. It will be interesting to follow its development... if there are any bottles left. Almost as good is the Millenium '97, another Bonarda, which is ageing very well because of its great structure. The Barbera '99 is forthright and tangy in its simplicity.

Martilde is a winery with a range of wines that is a little too extensive and in consequence displays the lack of continuity in quality that characterizes many producers in the Oltrepò. The first bottle we opened, the Zaffo '94, seemed over-evolved. The second, the Ghiro Rosso d'Inverno '96 was not quite so tired, but nearly, while the third, from the '99 vintage, had an attractive young aroma but no great pretensions. The fourth and last bottle, the Ghiro Rosso d'Inverno '97, turned out to be the best, with a ruby colour, an aroma of autumn leaves and a full, fresh taste with a clean finish of jam and bitter spices. The Pinot Nero Martuffo '96, which was excellent in the last edition of the Guide, is now beginning to go downhill. However, the Pinot Nero '99 promises good things, although it is still a little green and immature at the moment. The Barbera '97 La Strega, la Gazza, il Pioppo is very pleasant, with a fruity, slightly grassy background that blends in well with the overall aromatic profile. The other Barbera, the Diluvio '94, is good, but should be drunk fairly soon since it is almost at the peak of its development. The Malvasia Piume '99 is refreshing, fruity and a bit lemony, but with a clean note of sage. Finally, the Riesling Italico Gelo '99 is pleasant, but not as good as the '98.

● O. P. Bonarda		
Possessione del Console '99	▼▼	3*
● Rosso Poculum '98	▼▼	4
● O. P. Barbera '99	▼	3
● Loghetto '98	♈♈	3*
● O. P. Bonarda Campo del Monte '97	♈♈	3
● O. P. Bonarda Campo del Monte '98	♈♈	3*
● O. P. Bonarda Cresta del Ghiffi '98	♈♈	3*
● O. P. Bonarda Millenium '97	♈♈	5
● O. P. Bonarda		
Possessione del Console '97	♈♈	3
● Rosso Poculum '97	♈♈	4
● O. P. Barbera '98	♈	2*
● O. P. Bonarda Vignazzo '98	♈	3

● O. P. Barbera		
La Strega, la Gazza, il Pioppo '97	▼▼	5
● O. P. Bonarda		
Ghiro Rosso d'Inverno '97	▼▼	5
● O. P. Barbera Diluvio '94	▼	4
● O. P. Bonarda '99	▼	3
○ O. P. Malvasia Piume '99	▼	4
○ O. P. Riesling Italico Gelo '99	▼	3
● O. P. Bonarda '98	♈♈	3*
● O. P. Pinot Nero Martuffo '96	♈♈	4
○ O. P. Riesling Italico Gelo '98	♈♈	3*
● O. P. Barbera Diluvio '95	♈	4
● O. P. Bonarda Zaffo '93	♈	4
○ O. P. Malvasia Piume '98	♈	4

S. MARIA DELLA VERSA (PV)   S. PAOLO D'ARGON (BG)

CANTINA SOCIALE LA VERSA
VIA F. CRISPI, 15
27047 S. MARIA DELLA VERSA (PV)
TEL. 0385/798411

CANTINA SOCIALE BERGAMASCA
VIA BERGAMO, 10
24060 S. PAOLO D'ARGON (BG)
TEL. 035/951098

La Versa began producing spumante in 1907. Now, almost 95 years later, it makes serious quantities of the product. There are 3,000,000 bottles of spumante classico ageing in the cellars and every year, it turns out a further 3,000,000 bottles of metodo italiano spumante, including Pinot Nero, Riesling and Moscato. As a symbol of this special talent for sparklers, it recently erected at the entry of Valle Versa a large sculpture of a bottle by Carlo Mo who, in the words of Giovanni Arpino, is one of the few artists who knows how to place sculptures in large spaces. It is worth a trip to see it. The wine here that took our top award is the Brut Classico Mis en Cave '96. The dosage is integrating harmoniously and adds elegance to the stylish base wine thanks to highly successful bottle fermentation. The two cuve close "metodo italiano" Bruts from the '99 harvest, the Pinot Nero and the Riesling Italico, are easy drinking and fragrant, with well-defined varietal notes. Moving on to the reds, Two Glasses went to the Donelasco '97, the cellar's traditional Rosso Riserva that has now been restored to its former splendour. We found the Oltrepò Pavese Rosso '97 Pentagonon interesting. It is developing well, although it still needs to evolve in the bottle, and we also liked the new line from the Cantina di Montescano, part of the La Versa group. Excellent as always is the barrique-aged Lacrimae Vitis La Soleggia '96, Moscato Passito.

The most important estate in the province of Bergamo, the Cantina Sociale di San Paolo d'Argon, with around 100 hectares of vineyards belonging to its 150 members, continues to put out good, and at times excellent, wines at low prices. Nowadays, that is no mean feat. The Valcalepio Rosso Riserva '97, a Bordeaux blend with a predominance of cabernet sauvignon, comes from a particularly favourable year and aged for three years in 25-hectolitre barrels. It is elegantly full, with distinct aromas of bitter spices. The Rosso '98 "Selezione 2000" is pleasant but still a bit austere, although it shows a bit more concentration than the standard-label Valcalepio Rosso '98. Fresh, tangy and harmonious, with a bouquet of flowers and fruit, the Valcalepio Bianco '99 is among the best of its type. The Pinot Bianco della Bergamasca is simpler, with a pleasant hint of green tobacco leaves. There is an interesting new item in the dessert wine category, the Aureo '99, from partially dried moscato giallo grapes. It has a lovely bright gold colour, an intense aroma of honey, sweet flowers and fruit, and a sweet, persuasive taste, balanced by nice acidity that gives it freshness. Also good is the Moscato Nero Passito di Scanzo '98, with nice, aromatic length and a clean finish of liquorice and cinnamon. Among the other products, One Glass goes to the Merlot della Bergamasca '99, which is grassy and sincere.

○ O. P. Moscato Passito		
Lacrimae Vitis La Soleggia '96	🍷🍷	5
○ O. P. Pinot Nero Brut		
Mise en Cave '96	🍷🍷	4
● O. P. Rosso Ris. Donelasco '97	🍷🍷	4
○ O. P. Pinot Nero Brut '99	🍷	3
○ O. P. Riesling Italico Brut '99	🍷	3
● O. P. Rosso Pentagonon '97	🍷	3
○ O. P. Moscato Passito		
Lacrimae Vitis '92	🍷🍷	6
○ O. P. Moscato Passito		
Lacrimae Vitis '93	🍷🍷	6
○ O. P. Moscato Passito		
Lacrimae Vitis '95	🍷🍷	5
● O. P. Pinot Nero Vigna del Ferraio '93	🍷🍷	4

○ Moscato Giallo Passito		
Aureo '99	🍷🍷	2*
○ Valcalepio Bianco '99	🍷🍷	2*
● Valcalepio Rosso Ris. '97	🍷🍷	3*
● Merlot della Bergamasca '99	🍷	2*
● Moscato di Scanzo Passito '98	🍷	5
○ Pinot Bianco della Bergamasca '99	🍷	2*
● Valcalepio Rosso '98	🍷	2*
● Valcalepio Rosso 2000 '98	🍷	3
○ Valcalepio Bianco '98	🍷🍷	2*
○ Pinot Bianco		
della Bergamasca '98	🍷	2*
● Valcalepio Rosso Ris. '95	🍷	3

SANTA GIULETTA (PV)

ISIMBARDA
LOC. CASTELLO
27046 SANTA GIULETTA (PV)
TEL. 0383/899256

SCANZOROSCIATE (BG)

LA BRUGHERATA
VIA MEDOLAGO, 47
24020 SCANZOROSCIATE (BG)
TEL. 035/655202

Luigi Meroni's Isimbarda — 36 hectares of vineyards at Santa Giuletta and Mornico Losana, near the country house that was property of the noble Marchesi Isimbardi — leads with the reds this year. However, the whites, a still '99 Riesling Italico and a Pinot Nero fermented without the skins, have some problems. At the top of the classification is the Rosso Riserva Montezavo '98. A blend of barbera, croatina, uva rara and vespolina grown on the slopes of Monte Zavo at Santa Giuletta, it comes from old vines and more recent plantings at 6,000 vines per hectare yielding one kilo of grapes per plant. The bunches are de-stemmed and vinified on the skins, with two weeks' maceration in modern fermenting vats. The wine ages for a year and a half in small oak barrels. It is not filtered and then it is left for almost eight months in the bottle before release. The deep ruby colour introduces a nose of red berry fruit and vanilla, and rich, warm flavour, warm and well backed up by fine tannins and good acidity. Equally authentic is the Rosso '98, from barbera, croatina, uva rara and pinot nero from the Vigna del Tramonto plot. It offers good colour, excellent structure and an aroma of jam with slight spicy hints. The Pinot Nero '98, aged for a year in half new barriques, has a clean, varietal bouquet of currants and autumn leaves but is still a bit hard. It should mellow out in the bottle, though. The Bonarda Vivace '99 is frank and fragrant. It may not have the power of the '98 but it still drinks well, like the sparkling Barbera from the same vintage.

La Brugherata, owned by Patrizia Merati, is one of the leaders in Valcalepio with a limited but very high-quality production. From grapes harvested on five hectares of vineyards, completely renovated by agronomist Pierluigi Donna, the estate winemaker, Sergio Cantoni, produces a series of truly excellent red and white wines. Pride of place goes to the Doglio '96 Valcalepio Rosso Riserva, which floated effortlessly into the Two Glass band thanks to its elegant balance. The cabernet and merlot Rosso di Alberico '97 and Rosso Vescovado '98 are both very sound. Outstanding among the whites is the Alberico '99, a chardonnay with a fair amount of oak to underline its varietal flavours of golden delicious apple, bay leaf and almond blossom. It also has good body, braced by a backbone of satisfying acidity. The Valcalepio Bianco Vescovado '99 is simpler, fresher and more immediate. Also nice is the Moscato di Scanzo Passito Doge '97, which was not aged in barrels to preserve the dried rose, sage and acacia honey aromas of the grape. There is important news for the near future, with recent plantings of cabernet sauvignon and the construction of a larger cellar completely below ground in the centre of the winery premises.

	Wine	Glasses	Score
●	O. P. Rosso Vigna del Tramonto '98	YY	4
●	O. P. Rosso Ris. Montezavo '98	YY	5
●	O. P. Barbera Frizzante '99	Y	3
●	O. P. Bonarda Vivace '99	Y	3
●	O. P. Pinot Nero '98	Y	5
●	O. P. Barbera '98	YY	3*
●	O. P. Bonarda Vivace '98	YY	3*
●	O. P. Rosso '96	YY	3*
●	O. P. Bonarda Vivace '97	Y	3
○	O. P. Pinot Nero in bianco '96	Y	3
○	O. P. Riesling '98	Y	3
○	O. P. Riesling Italico '96	Y	3
○	O. P. Riesling V. Belvedere '97	Y	3

	Wine	Glasses	Score
○	Bianco di Alberico '99	YY	4
●	Rosso di Alberico '97	YY	4
●	Valcalepio Rosso Ris. Doglio '96	YY	4
●	Valcalepio Rosso Vescovado '98	YY	3*
●	Moscato di Scanzo Passito Doge '97	Y	6
○	Valcalepio Bianco Vescovado '99	Y	3
○	Bianco di Alberico '98	YY	4
○	Valcalepio Bianco Vescovado '98	YY	3*
●	Valcalepio Rosso Ris. Doglio '94	YY	4
●	Valcalepio Rosso Vescovado '96	YY	3*
●	Moscato di Scanzo Passito Doge '96	Y	6
○	Valcalepio Bianco Vescovado '97	Y	3
●	Valcalepio Rosso '95	Y	3
●	Valcalepio Rosso Ris. Doglio '95	Y	4

SIRMIONE (BS)

CA' DEI FRATI
FRAZ. LUGANA
VIA FRATI, 22
25010 SIRMIONE (BS)
TEL. 030/919468

TEGLIO (SO)

FAY
LOC. S. GIACOMO
VIA PILA CASELLI, 1
23030 TEGLIO (SO)
TEL. 0342/786071

The Dal Cero family are specialists at premium-quality white winemaking. The Brolettino Lugana '98, a trebbiano di Lugana from the I Frati and Ronchedone vineyards, begins its fermentation in stainless steel and ends it in barriques. The resulting wine is rich, complex, long-lived and capable of maturing further in the bottle. No less excellent is the Pratto Benaco Bresciano '98, from barrique-fermented trebbiano di Lugana and chardonnay plus sauvignon blanc fermented only in stainless steel. Its bright, gold colour leads in to a very intense flower and fruit bouquet of jasmine and peach, with aromatic notes of sage, lifted by oak-derived vanilla. The palate is full, concentrated, sinewy and long. Two Glasses also deservedly went to the Tre Filer '97. The same grapes from Pratto were raisined for three months on rush mats and then soft pressed. The must completes its fermentation, begun in stainless steel, in barriques. What emerges is an excellent sweet white with a fruit and spice personality more suited to foie gras and blue cheese than cakes. The range of whites is completed by the Lugana I Frati '99, which is tangy but a bit acerbic, and the Lugana Brut Classico Cuvée dei Frati, whose pressure is limited to four and a half atmospheres in the style used for Crémant wines. The Ronchedone '97 is well-made. A blend of groppello, marzemino, sangiovese, barbera, cabernet and merlot grapes vinified with prolonged maceration, it ages for 14 months in barriques. Lastly, the Chiaretto '99 is uncomplicated and attractive.

An excellent result for Cantina Fay at the tastings this year. That success is due, among other things, to the farsighted vision of mayor-oenologist, Sandro Fay, who has actively involved his two young, promising children, Marco and Elena, in the management of the cellar. Their strategy is clear-headed, combining serious investment in both the cellar and vineyards with the quest for elegance and above all, a terroir-driven expression of the local grapes' varietal characteristics. It is no coincidence, then, that a wine like the Sforzato Ronco del Picchio '97 came within a whisker of a Three Glass rating, proving its great potential. It offers very delicate aromas and good breadth on the crisp, long palate, with its soft, well-developed tannins. Definitely a bottle to tuck away in the cellar for a few years. Less concentrated, but just as individual, is the Sforzato '97 with its generous, fruity aromas, juicy, warm palate and leisurely finish. The Valgella Carteria '97 is by now thoroughly consistent in quality, with notes of super-ripeness on the nose, a mouth-filling palate and good concentration. The Valgella Ca' Morei '97 is dense in colour, revealing fruity aromas laced with attractive spiciness. The palate, too, is elegant and vigorous, showing that the particular vineyard where these nebbiolo grapes are grown is a very special cru. Lastly, the Sassella Il Glicine '97 is sincere with aromas of hay and an intense, structured, well-rounded palate that reveals sweet notes in the finish.

○	Pratto '98	♟♟	5
○	Lugana Il Brolettino '98	♟♟	4
○	Tre Filer '97	♟♟	5
●	Ronchedone '97	♟	4
◉	Garda Bresciano Chiaretto '99	♟	3
○	Lugana Brut Cl. Cuvèe dei Frati	♟	5
○	Lugana I Frati '99	♟	3
○	Pratto '96	♟♟♟	4*
○	Lugana Il Brolettino '97	♟♟	4
○	Pratto '97	♟♟	5
○	Tre Filer '90	♟♟	5
○	Tre Filer '95	♟♟	5
○	Tre Filer '95	♟♟	5
○	Tre Filer '96	♟♟	5

●	Valtellina Sforzato '97	♟♟	5
●	Valtellina Sforzato Ronco del Picchio '97	♟♟	6
●	Valtellina Sup. Valgella Ca' Morei '97	♟♟	5
●	Valtellina Sup. Valgella Carteria '97	♟♟	5
●	Valtellina Sup. Sassella Il Glicine '97	♟	4
●	Valtellina Sforzato '94	♟♟	4
●	Valtellina Sup. Sassella Il Glicine '94	♟♟	4
●	Valtellina Sup. Valgella Carteria '96	♟♟	4

TIRANO (SO)

TORRICELLA VERZATE (PV)

CONTI SERTOLI SALIS
P.ZZA SALIS, 3
23037 TIRANO (SO)
TEL. 0342/710404

MONSUPELLO
VIA SAN LAZZARO, 5
27050 TORRICELLA VERZATE (PV)
TEL. 0383/896043

Claudio Introini never disappoints. Though unable to repeat last year's Three Glass triumph, the skilled Sertoli Salis oenologist has made two wines that easily passed muster for Two Glasses. One of the brace is the Sforzato Canua '98, from a much less interesting vintage than the preceding one, but still a wine that unfurls plenty of charm on the nose, where notes of walnutskin, tamarind and spices have yet to find a point of balance. The very concentrated palate is rich, offering soft tannins and distinct sweet notes that hint at chocolate. In contrast, the Corte della Meridiana '97 comes from an historic vintage and therefore shows great power and elegance. Obtained from nebbiolo grapes, some of which are dried and added later following an old tradition of "rinforzo", or "fortifying", this wine has intense aromas of wild berries with notes of cinnamon and liquorice. On the palate, it is silky, broad and generous, with a sweet, coherent finish. The Sassella '97 also put up a good show. A classic example of a wine that faithfully reflects its variety, it has a deep, balsamic nose, with light notes of dried rose petals. Harmonious on the palate, it reveals meaty pulp and attractive flavours of fruit. The nose of the Saloncello '99 was not entirely convincing when the panel tasted and the palate, too, was rather thin. The Torre della Sirena '99 is aromatic, and in some respects vegetal, with an unusual palate that has interesting notes of citrus and a fresh-tasting, acidic finish.

The packed trophy cupboard at Monsupello puts Carlo and Pierangelo Boatti's winery in the front rank of wine production in the Oltrepò. This is due to the almost obsessive attention given the vineyards and the care taken in the cellar not to jeopardize the wealth of aromas and flavours in the grape. The banner wine of Monsupello is the Chardonnay Senso, which reached a truly remarkable level in the '98 vintage. The grape comes from a family of French and Italian clones planted 20 years ago at a density of 4,000 vines per hectare and yielding 70 quintals. The bunches, harvested by hand twice depending on the degree of ripeness, are soft pressed. The must from the first pressing, removed from the lees at low temperature, ferments in new barriques of Allier, Tronçais, Nevers and Vosges oak. The wine is left for about eight months in the wood, and then spends a long period in bottle before release. Senso '98 is a brilliant gold, with a very full bouquet of vanilla, hazelnut, flowers and fruit introducing a rich, aristocratic palate. Don't miss it. But the long-awaited Three Glass award was taken by the Pinot Nero Nature, a spumante of great elegance. Its dense, very delicate perlage is followed up by well-rounded, complex aromas, with a lovely minerally nuance, and a deliciously mature, full-bodied palate with a extraordinary length. There is a long list of other excellent wines, which we shall run through here. Metodo classico spumantes include the Pinot Nero Brut and Pinot Nero Brut '95. The whites are the Chardonnay, Pinot Grigio, the Pinot Nero in bianco I Germogli and the still developing Riesling Renano '99. The slightly sparkling rosé is the Pinot Nero Rosato I Germogli. The reds are the very mature Pinot Nero 3309 '95, Rosso La Borla '96 and the slightly sparkling Rosso Great Ruby '99, Bonarda '99 and Barbera Magenga '99. Finally, there is a dessert wine, the Passito La Cuenta. Our congratulations.

	Wine	Glasses	Score
●	Valtellina Sforzato Canua '98	♈♈	6
●	Valtellina Sup. Corte della Meridiana '97	♈♈	5
●	Valtellina Sup. Sassella '97	♈♈	4
●	Il Saloncello '99	♈	4
○	Torre della Sirena '99	♈	4
●	Valtellina Sforzato Canua '97	♈♈♈	6
●	Valtellina Sforzato Canua '94	♈♈	5
●	Valtellina Sforzato Canua '95	♈♈	5
●	Valtellina Sforzato Canua '96	♈♈	6
●	Valtellina Sup. Corte della Meridiana '94	♈♈	4
●	Valtellina Sup. Corte della Meridiana '95	♈♈	4

	Wine	Glasses	Score
○	O. P. Pinot Nero Cl. Nature	♈♈♈	4*
●	O. P. Bonarda Vivace '99	♈♈	4
○	O. P. Chardonnay '99	♈♈	4
○	O. P. Chardonnay Senso '98	♈♈	5
○	O. P. Pinot Grigio '99	♈♈	4
●	O. P. Pinot Nero 3309 '95	♈♈	5
○	O. P. Pinot Nero Brut Cl.	♈♈	4
○	O. P. Pinot Nero Brut Cl. '95	♈♈	4
●	O. P. Rosso Great Ruby '99	♈♈	4
●	O. P. Rosso La Borla '96	♈♈	4
○	Passito La Cuenta	♈♈	6
●	O. P. Barbera Magenga '99	♈	4
○	O. P. Pinot Nero in bianco I Germogli '99	♈	4
◉	O. P. Pinot Nero Rosato I Germogli '99	♈	4
○	O. P. Riesling Renano '99	♈	4

VILLA DI TIRANO (SO)

ZENEVREDO (PV)

CASA VINICOLA TRIACCA
VIA NAZIONALE, 121
23030 VILLA DI TIRANO (SO)
TEL. 0342/701352

TENUTA IL BOSCO
LOC. IL BOSCO
27049 ZENEVREDO (PV)
TEL. 0385/245326

Needless to say, we are very happy to award our Three Glass accolade to a wine like Domenico Triacca's Prestigio Millennium '97. It is the first time in Valtellina that a wine other than a Sforzato has gained such an award. Of course, there is a certain similarity with Sforzato, if we remember that the bunchstems of the nebbiolo from which this wine is made are cut before the harvest, leaving the grapes to raisin on the vine for 20 to 25 days. However, the result is unique and surprising. A wine with lots of personality that faithfully mirrors the characteristics of its territory and vineyard of origin. The nose is well-balanced in its aromas of flowers and crushed fruit and the palate enthrals with its harmony and body, before signing off with a long, sweet finish. The Prestigio '98 is elegant, but perhaps less complex, with notes of hay on the nose and a palate that is soft, long and fruity. Fruitiness is also a characteristic of the Riserva Triacca '96, which is tangy, with well-defined and well-balanced tannins. The Sforzato '97, from perfectly raisined grapes, has pleasant notes of liqueur cherries and remarkable structure, with soft tannins and a lingering finish. The Sauvignon Del Frate '99 is surprisingly characterful and well-structured. As it did last year, it impresses with its varietal notes on the nose. A lovely golden yellow in colour, it shows nice texture and considerable intensity on the palate.

With as much as 132 hectares of specialized vineyards in the hills of Zenevredo and San Zeno, and a 6,000-square metre cellar with state-of-the-art equipment, it is clear that Zonin group has cut no corners when investing at the Tenuta Il Bosco. Given all this commitment, it seemed only right to expect impressive results, and positive feedback for the image of the entire Oltrepò. Now, the results are there but the wines tasted this year seemed to us to be "merely" good, with few real peaks. The Teodote '98, Oltrepò Pavese Rosso, after six months in barriques, will improve with bottle ageing but it remains inferior to the 1997. On the other hand, the Malvasia '99 is excellent. A sparkler, thanks to light re-fermentation in a cuve close, it has a golden straw-yellow colour and an intense aroma of musk and acacia blossom, followed by a bright, fresh-tasting and delicately bitterish palate. The Bonarda Vivace '99, with its fragrant bouquet and attractively soft, fruit-rich palate, convinced us more than its still stablemate, the Bonarda '98 Podere Poggio Pelato, which is a little closed on the nose and has a bitter finish that is almost too well-defined. Of the spumantes, the Pinot Nero Brut Classico Millesimato '94 was an easy Two Glass winner after spending more than 48 months on the lees. It's an elegant, complex and very harmonious wine. The other Brut Classico, the non-vintage Regal Cuvée, again from pinot nero, is also good, fruity and very convincing.

●	Valtellina Prestigio Millennium '97	ΨΨΨ	5
○	Sauvignon Del Frate '99	ΨΨ	4
●	Valtellina Prestigio '98	ΨΨ	5
●	Valtellina Sforzato '97	ΨΨ	5
●	Valtellina Sup. Ris. Triacca '96	ΨΨ	4
○	Sauvignon Del Frate '98	ΨΨ	4
●	Valtellina Prestigio '94	ΨΨ	4
●	Valtellina Prestigio '95	ΨΨ	4
●	Valtellina Prestigio '96	ΨΨ	5
●	Valtellina Sforzato '96	ΨΨ	5
●	Valtellina Sforzato Il Corvo '94	ΨΨ	4
●	Valtellina Sup. Ris. Triacca '90	ΨΨ	4
●	Valtellina Sup. Ris. Triacca '91	ΨΨ	4
●	Valtellina Sup. Ris. Triacca '94	ΨΨ	4

○	O. P. Malvasia Frizzante '99	ΨΨ	2*
○	O. P. Pinot Nero Brut Cl. '94	ΨΨ	4
●	O. P. Bonarda Vivace '99	Ψ	2*
○	O. P. Brut Cl. Regal Cuvée	Ψ	4
●	Rosso Teodote '98	Ψ	4
●	O. P. Bonarda Poggio Pelato '98		3
○	O. P. Brut Cl. '92	ΨΨ	2*
○	O. P. Brut Cl. Regal Cuvée	ΨΨ	4
○	O. P. Malvasia '98	ΨΨ	3*
○	O. P. Moscato '95	ΨΨ	2*
●	Rosso Teodote '97	ΨΨ	4
●	O. P. Barbera Teodote '96	Ψ	4
●	O. P. Bonarda '95	Ψ	2*
●	O. P. Bonarda '98	Ψ	2*
○	O. P. Pinot Nero Brut Philéo	Ψ	3

OTHER WINERIES

The following producers obtained good scores in our tastings with one or more of their wines:

PROVINCE OF BERGAMO

Lurani Cernuschi,
Almenno San Salvatore, tel. 035/642576
Valcalepio Rosso '98

Tenuta degli Angeli,
Carobbio degli Angeli, tel. 035/951489
Extra Brut degli Angeli

Le Corne, Grumello del Monte, tel. 035/830215
Valcalepio Bianco '99

Pecis, San Paolo d'Argon, tel. 035/959104
Valcalepio Rosso '98

La Tordela, Torre dei Roveri, tel. 035/580172
Valcalepio Moscato Passito '98

Medolago Albani,
Trescore Balneario, tel. 035/942022
Valcalepio Rosso Ris. '96

PROVINCE OF BRESCIA

B. Tognazzi, Caionvico, tel. 030/2692695
Botticino Vigna Cobio '97

La Torre, Calvagese, tel. 030/601034
Garda Cl. Rosso Sup. Il Torrione '97

Bettoni Cazzago,
Cazzago San Martino, tel. 030/7750875
Franciacorta Brut Tetellus '94

CastelFaglia,
Cazzago San Martino, tel. 059/908828
Franciacorta Brut Monogram

Mario Gatta, Cellatica, tel. 030/2772950
Cellatica Rosso Sup. Negus '97

Visconti, Desenzano, tel. 030/9120681
Lugana S. Onorata '99

Principe Banfi, Erbusco, tel. 030/7750387
Franciacorta Brut

Vezzoli Attilio, Erbusco, tel. 030/7267601
Franciacorta Brut

Berardi,
Molinetto di Mazzano, tel. 030/2620152
Garda Classico Chiaretto '99

Monte Cicogna,
Moniga del Garda, tel. 0365/503200
Garda Classico Sup. Don Lisander '96

Cantine Valtenesi e Lugana,
Moniga del Garda, tel. 0365/502002
Garda Classico Chiaretto '99

Castelveder,
Monticelli Brusati, tel. 030/652308
Franciacorta Brut

La Montina,
Monticelli Brusati, tel. 030/653278
Franciacorta Brut '96

La Guarda, Muscoline, tel. 0365/372948
Garda Marzemino '97

Le Marchesine,
Passirano, tel. 030/657005
Franciacorta Brut Secolonovo '95

La Cascina Nuova,
Poncarale, tel. 030/2540058
Capriano del Colle Rosso '97

Le Chiusure, Portese S. Felice Benaco,
tel. 0365/626243
Benaco Bresciano Rosso Mal Borghetto '97

Marangona,
Pozzolengo, tel. 030/919379
Garda Cl. Rosso Sup. Corte Ialidy '98

Bersi Serlini,
Provaglio d'Iseo, tel. 0365/9823338
Armonia del Grigio '99

Pasini Produttori,
Raffa di Puegnago, tel. 030/266206
San Gioan Rosso I Carati '96

Pusterla, Rovato, tel. 030/7702927
Pusterla Bianco '98

Ca' Lojera,
S. Benedetto di Lugana, tel. 045/7551901
Lugana Vigna Silva '98

PROVINCE OF MANTOVA

Lebovitz, Governolo, tel. 0376/668115
Lambrusco dei Concari '99

Stefano Spezia,
Mariana Mantovana, tel. 0376/735012
Lambrusco Provincia di Mantova Blu '99

Ricchi, Monzambano, tel. 0376/800238
Garda Chardonnay Meridiano '99

Gozzi – Colombara,
Olfino di Monzambano, tel. 0376/800377
Rosso Prov. di Mantova Vigna Magrini '97

C. S. di Quistello, Quistello, tel. 0376/618118
Lambrusco Mantovano Banda Blu '99

PROVINCE OF MILANO

Panigada – Banino,
S. Colombano al Lambro, tel. 0371/89103
San Colombano Ris. La Merla '97

Pietrasanta,
S. Colombano al Lambro, tel. 0371/897540
Collina del Milanese Verdea '99

Enrico Riccardi,
S. Colombano al Lambro, tel. 0371/897381
San Colombano Rosso Roverone '98

PROVINCE OF PAVIA

Percivalle, Borgo Priolo, tel. 0383/871175
O. P. Barbera Costa del Sole '98

Barbacarlo, Broni, tel. 0385/51212
O. P. Rosso Montebuono '98

C. S. Broni, Broni, tel. 0385/51505
O. P. Rosso '96

Travaglino, Calvignano, tel. 0383/872222
O. P. Pinot Nero Brut Cl. '96

Fiamberti, Canneto, tel. 0385/88019
O. P. Rosso Ris. Monte Acutello '97

F.lli Giorgi, Canneto, tel. 0385/262151
O. P. Pinot Nero Brut Cl. G. Giorgi '96

Quaquarini, Canneto, tel. 0385/60152
O. P. Buttafuoco Vigna Pregana '97

Bellaria, Casteggio, tel. 0383/83203
O. P. Barbera Olmetto '98

Clastidio Ballabio, Casteggio, tel. 0383/83243
O. P. Bonarda '98

Frecciarossa, Casteggio, tel. 0383/804465
O. P. Riesling Renano '99

Monteguzzo, Cigognola, tel. 0385/85366
O. P. Rosso Monteguzzo '97

La Costaiola,
Montebello della Battaglia, tel. 0383/83169
O. P. Riesling Renano Attimo '99

Casa Re,
Montecalvo Versiggia, tel. 0385/99986
Bianco Pian del Re '98

Torti Dino - Castelrotto,
Montecalvo Versiggia, tel. 0385/99762
O. P. Bonarda '99

Torti Pietro,
Montecalvo Versiggia, tel. 0385/99763
O. P. Pinot Nero '97

Cantine Scuropasso,
Pietra de' Giorgi, tel. 0385/85143
O. P. Pinot Nero Brut Cl.

Litubium,
Retorbido. tel. 0383/374485
Rosso Stuoiato '98

F. Bazzini,
Rovescala, tel. 0385/75205
O. P. Bonarda Picco Del Sole '97

Vanzini,
San Damiano al Colle, tel. 0385/75019
O. P. Pinot Nero Brut

Bagnasco,
San Maria della Versa, tel. 0385/278019
O. P. Sangue di Giuda '99

Montini, S. Giuletta, tel. 0383/899231
O. P. Moscato Passito Eventi '98

Torrevilla,
Torrazza Coste, tel. 0383/77083
Brut Cl. La Genisia

PROVINCE OF SONDRIO

Nera, Chiuro, tel. 0342/482631
Valtellina Sforzato '95

Mamete Prevostini,
Mese, tel. 0343/41003
Valtellina Sforzato Albareda '98

Bettini,
San Giacomo di Teglio, tel. 0342/786068
Valtellina Sfursat '97

Plozza, Tirano, tel. 0342/701297
Valtellina Sfurzat Vin da Ca' 94

TRENTINO

The relationship Trentino has with its wines is far from simple, despite the terrain, which is mountainous and well suited to the production of high quality fruit. It is no accident that more than half the 223 municipalities in Trentino have officially registered vineyards which provide an annual harvest of a million quintals of grapes for the various Trentino DOCs. The growers are thriving and well equipped - many have studied at the prestigious Istituto Agrario in San Michele all'Adige - and all can count on help from one of the most efficient and well-financed technical services organisations in Italy. Trentino's privileged status as an autonomous region means that the viticultural sector has substantial funds at its disposal specifically to promote both quality and image. This year we tasted a good 393 rigorously selected wines, with excellent results. Both the number of wines with awards and the average level of quality have risen. Nevertheless, the usual problems remain. The problems to do with quantity persist. Often, yields are set right up to the maximum limit permitted by DOC regulations and the very last bunch of grapes possible goes into the press. The mass market commercial strategies dictated by the co-operatives impose high yields while guaranteeing good returns for their thousands of members spread all over the territory. In contrast, individual growers who bottle their own wines can reduce yields on their own initiative. Few of them do so. That is, with the exception of this year's award winners, of course. Producers such as Carlo Guerrieri Gonzaga or Nicola Balter, Marco Donati or Marco Manica, and the Zanoni brothers of Maso Furli are all convinced of the need for quality. Even the Giulio Ferrari sparkling wine can be included in this category. It is, after all, a reserve selection from a small vineyard owned by the winemaking Lunelli family, and carefully designed to express a unique character. The conclusion of our tastings was that the Teroldego wines were extremely good. Much better than usual, in fact. The Pinot Biancos have made a real comeback. All the sparkling wines were good, confirming spumante Trento as a prestigious category and the Bordeaux blends were excellent. More disappointing, on the other hand, were the Pinot Neros, and the Marzeminos, which did not rise above the "interesting, but nothing exceptional" level. All the wines (almost all, anyway) were technically well made. So what was missing? A sense of common purpose is rare. Winemaking in Trentino lacks that "je ne sais quoi" that would reinforce, improve and consolidate levels of quality. But in general, things look quite encouraging.

ALA (TN)

AVIO (TN)

LA CADALORA
FRAZ. SANTA MARGHERITA
38060 ALA (TN)
TEL. 0464/696300

CANTINA SOCIALE DI AVIO
VIA DANTE, 14
38063 AVIO (TN)
TEL. 0464/684008

Over the years, the lower Vallagarina valley has come to resemble a "New Frontier" of Trentino wines, turning out interesting reds and keeping faith with local traditions. It's a pretty area lying near the southern borders of the region, with a climate which benefits from that growers' friend, the Ora breeze from Lake Garda. It was the Ora, which blows in the afternoons, that inspired the Tomasi family when they named their winery La Cadalora. This particular "New Frontier" winery has Cabernet at the top of the list of its red wines. The '97 has a deep ruby red colour, an intense bouquet of blackcurrants and black cherries, and is smooth and full-bodied. The same winemaking skill can be seen in the other wines selected. Pinot Nero Vignalet has a vibrant colour and a good bouquet - perhaps a little thin because of the nature of the '98 vintage and not totally rounded out. The Sanvalentino red is young and needs bottle age. It is made of international grape varieties and some other more distinctly local ones. In fact, La Cadalora has decided to promote an interesting but forgotten local grape called "foia tonda" or "casetta", vinified either as a monovarietal or blended with cabernet and merlot. The red Majere wine has some rough edges in its taste profile. The whites, however, are limpid, with greenish reflections, and open up well on the palate More fruity (apples and pears) than floral, they flaunt fresh vegetal hints that do not detract from the full flavour of either the Chardonnay or the Pinot Grigio. Pronounced aromatic hints of spices and wild roses make the Sauvignon a little "heavy".

The Cantina Sociale co-operative winery at Avio has begun a project aimed at promoting the marzemino varietal, the most famous grape in Vallagarina. It's an ambitious project that involves the genetic invigoration of the marzemino vine through grafting and crossing with marzemino "vitis mater" rootstocks, discovered by Professor Attilio Scienza on remote Greek islands and confirmed by recent DNA analysis. This may be "futuristic" viticulture but the Avio Co-operative is looking even further ahead. The aim is to make a truly great red wine. Which explains the attention given to the cordon-trained cabernet and merlot vines in the Campi Sarni vineyards, a particularly suitable area lying at the foot of Avio castle where viticulture has been practised for the past millennium. It is grapes from this location that have enabled the "Co-op" to gain its reputation as an up-and-coming winery. The Trentino Rosso Riserva '97 has a deep ruby red colour, mineral hints on the nose, and is well-balanced and long finishing. The Pinot Nero is lightweight and loosely structured, better on the nose than the palate, as is quite common with Trentino Pinot Neros. Because of the vintage, the Trentino Bianco is less successful than in previous years - freak weather before the harvest reduced the aromatic qualities of the grapes. The Vendemmia Tardiva, however, has held up well. A full-bodied and truly well made wine.

● Cabernet Sauvignon '97	🍷🍷	4
○ Chardonnay '99	🍷	3
● Majere '97	🍷	4
● Pinot Nero Vignalet '98	🍷	4
● Sanvalentino '99	🍷	4
○ Pinot Grigio '99		3
○ Sauvignon '99		3
○ Trentino Pinot Grigio '98	🍷🍷	3*
● Majere '97	🍷	4
○ Trentino Chardonnay '98	🍷	3
● Trentino Marzemino Sanvalentino '98	🍷	3
○ Trentino Sauvignon '98	🍷	3

● Trentino Rosso Ris. '97	🍷🍷	4
○ Trentino Vendemmia Tardiva '98	🍷🍷	4
● Trentino Pinot Nero '98	🍷	3
○ Trentino Bianco '98	🍷	3
● Trentino Marzemino '99	🍷	2*
○ 11 Novembre '97	🍷🍷	4
● Trentino Pinot Nero '97	🍷🍷	3*
● Trentino Rosso Ris. '96	🍷🍷	4
● Trentino Enantio '98	🍷🍷	2*
● Trentino Rosso '96	🍷🍷	3*
● Trentino Marzemino '97	🍷	2*
● Trentino Marzemino '98	🍷	2*
○ Trentino Pinot Grigio '98	🍷	2*
● Trentino Pinot Nero '96	🍷	3

AVIO (TN)

TENUTA SAN LEONARDO
FRAZ. BORGHETTO ALL'ADIGE
LOC. SAN LEONARDO, 3
38060 AVIO (TN)
TEL. 0464/689004

AVIO (TN)

VALLAROM
LOC. MASI, 21
38063 AVIO (TN)
TEL. 0464/684297

Another award-winning year for the San Leonardo red. The '97 is full-bodied and enviably elegant. Yet again this year, few Trentino producers have been able to endow their wines with as much balance, depth and complexity as Carlo Guerrieri Gonzaga does with this wine. The vintage will be remembered as an outstanding one. It would have been unthinkable to put a foot wrong, and Carlo didn't. Now the result of all that hard work is in the bottle, ready to set people talking. Deep, bright, ruby red in colour, with youthful purple tinges, it releases a sensual bouquet that emerges only gradually, fascinating with its fruit-driven richness and floral overtones. Aromas of ripe blackberries, white plums, oriental spices, violets, coffee and plain chocolate are all there. The first sensation on the palate is one of great balance, the breeding that only the greatest wines possess. Rich, deep and extraordinarily complex in its progression on the palate, it culminates in an immeasurably long finish of crystalline purity. Sip this '97 slowly. There won't be a '98. The Merlot is deliberately made to be more easily drinkable, but is just as enjoyable. The moderately deep ruby red colour leads into a nose of blackcurrants, raspberries and black pepper with intense, well-defined balsamic nuances. Medium weight on the palate, with an excellent attack, it unveils plenty of body on the mid palate and good length in finishing. Congratulations to the producer and all the technical staff of this model winery.

Vallarom is under different management. Nothing dramatic, however. It is just a changeover in the generations. The Scienza family remain in charge but it is now young Filippo who looks after the vineyards and the cellars. A qualified oenologist with experience in several other wineries, Filippo is helped by his wife Barbara. They are an enthusiastic couple, ready to carry on the work begun by their uncle, Professor Attilio Scienza (now busy down in Bolgheri), with a programme of their own devising to relaunch this attractive Vallagarina "maso" mountain estate. They have changed the labels on the bottles, reduced the yields per hectare, and cut down on the number of grape varieties in the vineyards, paying special attention to foreign varieties, cabernet in particular. In fact, it is the Bordeaux-style Campi Sarni, named after the Vallagarina's most famous vineyard site, that hits the quality spot. A red of some distinction with a good bouquet, it contains hints of spicy oak, plums, pepper and chocolate, and has a particularly long and smooth finish, thanks to a finely judged blend of cabernet franc, cabernet sauvignon and merlot of various clonal origins. Another success for the Cabernet Sauvignon, vinified together with very small proportions (less than 5%) of petit verdot and malbec. It has a deep colour, well-evolved aromas, good tannins and a balanced overall structure. Still on the reds, we are sure that the Pinot Nero Vigneto Ventrat will soften out from its current oaky angularity, while the Chardonnay Vigneto Lavine has all the Scienza hallmarks. Very expressive of the grape and well-structured at the same time, it offers marked hints of vanilla and toasted hazelnuts. The Marzemino Vigneto Capitello is complex, albeit rather heavy on the alcohol.

● San Leonardo '97	♥♥♥	5
● Trentino Merlot '98	♥♥	4
● San Leonardo '88	♥♥♥	5
● San Leonardo '90	♥♥♥	5
● San Leonardo '93	♥♥♥	5
● San Leonardo '94	♥♥♥	5
● San Leonardo '95	♥♥♥	5
● San Leonardo '96	♥♥♥	5
● Trentino Cabernet '93	♥♥	3*
● Trentino Cabernet '94	♥♥	3*
● Trentino Merlot '92	♥♥	3*
● Trentino Merlot '95	♥♥	3*
● Trentino Merlot '96	♥♥	3*
● Trentino Merlot '97	♥♥	3*
● Villa Gresti '93	♥♥	3*

● Campi Sarni '98	♥♥	4
● Trentino Cabernet Sauvignon Vign. Belvedere '98	♥♥	4
○ Trentino Chardonnay Vigneto Lavine '98	♥♥	4
● Trentino Marzemino Vign. Capitello '99	♥	4
● Trentino Pinot Nero Vign. Ventrat '98	♥	4
○ Campi Sarni '96	♥♥	4
● Trentino Cabernet Sauvignon Ris. '94	♥♥	4
● Trentino Cabernet Sauvignon Ris. '95	♥♥	4
○ Trentino Chardonnay '95	♥♥	4
○ Trentino Chardonnay Ris. '96	♥♥	4
○ Trentino Pinot Bianco '95	♥♥	3*

CALLIANO (TN)

VALLIS AGRI
VIA VALENTINI, 37
38060 CALLIANO (TN)
TEL. 0464/834113

The trading name chosen by SAV, the Società Agricoltori Vallagarina, for its superior wines evokes a bucolic image and, at the same time, the name of the denomination of the valley vineyards between Rovereto and Trento. The area is traversed by the River Adige, an area of wide plains and gentle hills, all covered with vineyards and many dominated by imposing castles, such as the remarkable Castel Beseno. Vallis Agri selects individual grape lots delivered to the co-operative by members who have agreed to work exclusively on a quality basis. The results are very positive. The wines have a distinct Trentino character and – a rare case in Vallagarina – the whites are almost better than the reds. In the land of Marzemino, this is no mean achievement. We tasted a Nosiola with good length. Light in alcohol, it has ripe fruit, a full body and plenty of flavour. The Pinot Bianco is very good too. Complex and well evolved, it reveals interesting hints of thyme on the nose and good length. The Pinot Grigio, however, is no more than acceptable. Clean, slightly sharp and rather predictable. There's more. The Cabernet Sant'Ilario '96 is good enough, but too vegetal perhaps. The other Bordeaux-blend wine, the Rosso '97, is all right, but one-dimensional and still closed. The Marzemino dei Ziresi – a near-legendary wine with quite a following amongst local fans of the variety - is one of the best of its type, even though it falls short of its immense reputation.

CIVEZZANO (TN)

MASO CANTANGHEL
LOC. FORTE
VIA MADONNINA, 33
38045 CIVEZZANO (TN)
TEL. 0461/859050

Five eager wines were put in the lists, all made in Piero Zabini's unmistakable style. Excellent wines indeed, but they just missed out by a fraction on the top awards. But let's be clear about it, these are very good wines. Starting with the Chardonnay Vigna Piccola. Technically perfect, it has a good green-tinged colour and copper gold highlights, and is both complex and clean. This is the company's most successful wine, vinified in the remarkable bastions of a former Austro-Hungarian fort, where, once upon a time during the Great War, enormous cannons stood guard. Today's oenological target is the Pinot Nero, the favourite wine of this ebullient vigneron, who has succeeded in teaching himself how to make wine after years of work as a chef and restaurateur. Only Zabini could have made a wine that shows such class, softness and length in the difficult 1998 vintage. Nothing more could have been done in such a year. The poor vintage accounts for the weakness of the Cabernet Sauvignon Rosso di Pila, which is nevertheless drinking superbly. It has a genuine porphyry red colour (the quarry at Pila was famous for this marble) - a very attractive bouquet, full flavour, good structure and robust tannins. Merlot Tajapreda is vinous, fresh, youthful and designed to be drunk young. We reckon the Sauvignon Solitaire is, however, more complex. It's a bright, lively wine, clean on the nose and full-bodied on the palate.

O	Trentino Nosiola '99	♟♟	3*
O	Trentino Pinot Bianco '99	♟♟	3*
●	Trentino Cabernet Sauvignon Sant'Ilario '96	♟	4
●	Trentino Marzemino dei Ziresi '99	♟	3
O	Trentino Pinot Grigio '99	♟	3
●	Trentino Rosso '97	♟	4
●	Trentino Cabernet Sauvignon Sant'Ilario '95	♟♟	4
●	Trentino Marzemino dei Ziresi '96	♟♟	3*
O	Trentino Moscato Giallo '97	♟♟	3*
●	Trentino Marzemino dei Ziresi '93	♟	4
O	Trentino Moscato Giallo '98	♟	3

O	Trentino Chardonnay Vigna Piccola '99	♟♟	4
●	Trentino Pinot Nero Zabini '98	♟♟	5
●	Trentino Cabernet Sauvignon Rosso di Pila '98	♟	5
●	Trentino Merlot Tajapreda '99	♟	4
O	Trentino Sauvignon Solitaire '99	♟	4
●	Trentino Cabernet Sauvignon Rosso di Pila '95	♟♟	5
●	Trentino Cabernet Sauvignon Rosso di Pila '96	♟♟	5
●	Trentino Cabernet Sauvignon Rosso di Pila '97	♟♟	5
O	Trentino Chardonnay Vigna Piccola '98	♟♟	4

FAEDO (TN)

FAEDO (TN)

GRAZIANO FONTANA
VIA CASE SPARSE, 9
38010 FAEDO (TN)
TEL. 0461/650400

POJER & SANDRI
LOC. MOLINI, 4/6
38010 FAEDO (TN)
TEL. 0461/650342

Fontana and Faedo – two "F"s that make all the difference. Fontana is a little winery that is a small miracle of entrepreneurship, enthusiasm, imagination, revival of local tradition, love of wine and devotion to local history. Graziano Fontana has been bottling his own wine for only a few harvests. He never believed he would reach this point so quickly, building an attractive winery and finding his place in the ranks of top quality Trentino producers so soon. Just a few thousand bottles of hand-crafted wines, but all with their maker's hallmark. They are the fruit of Graziano's viticultural research and his passion as a self-taught winemaker. There's nothing artificial here. Wine is made as an expression of Nature and of the seasons that bring the grapes to ripeness. Some seasons are benign, others less generous. These are the good points, and the failings, of Fontana's wines. The last vintage of the century masked the potential quality of the grapes from Faedo. The whites were certainly superior in quality, but they lacked freshness. The Chardonnay is powerful on the palate, its structure is sustained by good acidity that balances the soft roundness without over-emphasising the subtle aromas of almonds and tart apples. The Sauvignon suffers from the vintage, for it is simple and lacks bouquet. The same is also true of the fresh Müller Thurgau and the Traminer. So the Lagrein has to make up for the whites. In fact, this red wine is up to its usual remarkable standard, the crowning glory of Graziano's bravura performance, and richly deserving our Two Glass award.

Trentino wines owe a lot of their success to these two producers. Without their dedication and revolutionary insights, it would have been difficult for this province to have acquired its present oenological fame and prestige. Quite apart from their personal achievements, Mario Pojer and Fiorentino Sandri have always been involved in local wine-related debates and have helped several of their colleagues from other wineries to create an identity for winemaking in the Trentino. In human terms, these are qualities beyond price. All their wines are now fully mature creations, and continue to be so. Take the eleven wines that we tasted here. They are all worth a close look. Classy and characterful, these bottles are made with exemplary technique, and have real quality. No fewer than seven of them go right to the top of their individual categories, starting with an Extra Brut sparkling wine, a cuvée of two different years ('95 and '96). Skilfully blended, it has great body and lashings of style. Then there's the Essenzia, a late-vintage wine imitated by many other wineries that is complex, rich and well-rounded on the palate. The Traminer and the Müller-Thurgau both have delicate bouquets and impress with their balance on the palate. The Bianco Faye is full-flavoured with a complex bouquet and a fine golden colour. Then come the reds. The pair's famous, aromatic, big-hearted wine, Rosso Faye, is made as a Bordeaux blend with additions of local grapes. It scores very highly and only just missing out on a Three Glass award. Both the Pinot Neros are very good, the young fresh bottle from last year's harvest, and the cru version, which is more subtle, showing beneficial ageing. It is an example to winemakers both in Trentino and beyond. The Chardonnay, Nosiola and Sauvignon are all fresh, attractive and very drinkable. Three typical wines from the Pojer & Sandri school.

	Wine		Score
●	Trentino Lagrein di Faedo '98	♟♟	4
O	Trentino Chardonnay di Faedo '99	♟	3
O	Trentino Müller Thurgau di Faedo '99	♟	3
O	Trentino Sauvignon di Faedo '99	♟	3
O	Trentino Traminer di Faedo '99		3
O	Trentino Chardonnay di Faedo '97	♟♟	3
●	Trentino Lagrein di Faedo '95	♟♟	3*
●	Trentino Lagrein di Faedo '96	♟♟	3
●	Trentino Lagrein di Faedo '97	♟♟	4
O	Trentino Müller Thurgau '96	♟♟	3*
O	Trentino Müller Thurgau '97	♟♟	3
●	Trentino Pinot Nero '94	♟♟	4
O	Trentino Sauvignon di Faedo '95	♟♟	3*
O	Trentino Sauvignon di Faedo '96	♟♟	3*
O	Trentino Sauvignon di Faedo '97	♟♟	3

	Wine		Score
O	Bianco Faye '97	♟♟	4
O	Cuveé Extra Brut	♟♟	5
O	Essenzia Vendemmia Tardiva '98	♟♟	5
●	Rosso Faye '97	♟♟	5
O	Trentino Müller Thurgau '99	♟♟	3*
●	Trentino Pinot Nero '97	♟♟	4
O	Trentino Traminer '99	♟♟	3*
●	Pinot Nero '99	♟	3
O	Trentino Chardonnay '99	♟	3
O	Trentino Nosiola '99	♟	3
O	Trentino Sauvignon '99	♟	3
●	Rosso Faye '93	♟♟♟	5
●	Rosso Faye '94	♟♟♟	5
●	Rosso Faye '95	♟♟	5
●	Rosso Faye '96	♟♟	5

ISERA (TN)

ISERA (TN)

CANTINA D'ISERA
VIA AL PONTE, 1
38060 ISERA (TN)
TEL. 0464/433795

DE TARCZAL
LOC. MARANO
VIA G. B. MIORI, 4
38060 ISERA (TN)
TEL. 0464/409134

Cantina d'Isera has put forward ten wines, all part of the general renewal programme of the last few years. There's one obvious conclusion: yet again quality pays, and the wines have benefited in all respects from the adoption of quality criteria. Isera is run on sound principles. Prudence and the protection, almost molly-coddling, of its signature Marzemino wine in the face of mass market pressures have recreated its original allure. As we've always said, the Marzemino Etichetta Verde is the jewel in the crown. Rich-flavoured, fresh, and with a deliberate bitter twist to the finish, it is full-flavoured and long-finishing at the same time. The standard Marzemino is fine, but not quite as good. We liked the Bordeaux-blend Novecentosette, named after this dynamic co-operative winery's foundation year (1907). It is a full-bodied red with a slightly spicy nose softened by a bouquet of fresh cherry and morello cherry fruit. There is good extract on the palate and the tannins are smooth. Still in the red category, the Merlot and the Cabernet are both good, the former perhaps slightly superior to the Cabernet for its overall attractiveness. The whites are all good, particularly the Chardonnay and the Moscato Giallo.

The company has the discreet charm of a long history. Centuries of agricultural activity have justified the existence, and ennobled even, generations of de Tarczal winemakers, hard-working and faithful interpreters of local oenological and cultural traditions. Isera, where their roots are, and wine in general have been the beneficiaries. In fact, this was the first winemaking company to gain a licence in the 18th century to supply the market at a more than local scale. Ruggero de Tarczal is a natural aristocrat of the vineyards. A figure from a bygone age, he succeeds in combining the attributes of a mature manager with the noble qualities of his forebears. A modern traditionalist, you could say. Once again this year, his Marzemino Husar is a full-bodied, opaque, big wine, more richly-extracted than normal, but still perfectly within the bounds of typicality for the variety. Only made in the best years, the red Pragiara needs some more time in the bottle. It's so vigorous and full of life that it doesn't seem to have settled down yet. Everything is there, but it will reward patience. The Chardonnay and the Pinot Bianco are both very drinkable and a definite improvement. The latter has a deep golden colour and is more attractive than usual. Full of extract, it delivers a wide range of aromas and loads of flavour. The Chardonnay is made in the same fashion. Perhaps a little lighter on the palate, it still had good complex rennet apple and sage fruitiness and the acidity is nicely offset by alcohol-rich smoothness and residual sugars.

● Trentino Marzemino		
Etichetta Verde '99	♀♀	3*
● Trentino Rosso		
Novecentosette '97	♀♀	3*
● Trentino Cabernet '99	♀	3
○ Trentino Chardonnay '99	♀	3
● Trentino Marzemino '99	♀	3
● Trentino Merlot '98	♀	3
○ Trentino Moscato Giallo '99	♀	3
● Trentino Marzemino		
Etichetta Verde '98	♀♀	3*
● Trentino Merlot '95	♀♀	2*
● Trentino Rebo '98	♀♀	3*
● Trentino Rosso		
Novecentosette '96	♀♀	3*

○ Trentino Chardonnay '99	♀♀	3*
● Trentino Marzemino d'Isera		
Husar '99	♀♀	4
○ Trentino Pinot Bianco '99	♀♀	3*
● Pragiara '97	♀	4
● Trentino Marzemino d'Isera '96	♀♀	3*
● Trentino Marzemino d'Isera		
Husar '98	♀♀	4
● Trentino Marzemino di Isera		
Husar '97	♀♀	4
● Trentino Merlot Campiano '97	♀♀	4
● Trentino Cabernet Franc '97	♀	3
● Trentino Cabernet Sauvignon '95	♀	3
● Trentino Cabernet Sauvignon '97	♀	3
● Trentino Marzemino di Isera '97	♀	3

ISERA (TN)

ENRICO SPAGNOLLI
VIA G. B. ROSINA, 4/A
38060 ISERA (TN)
TEL. 0464/409054

LASINO (TN)

PISONI
LOC. PERGOLESE
VIA S. SIRO, 9
38070 LASINO (TN)
TEL. 0461/563216

The Spagnolli family from Isera have been cellarmasters for more than half a century and their prestige grows from vintage to vintage. This is thanks to the fact that they select individual bunches while still on the vine, both from the vineyards husbanded by supplier growers and from the plots managed by Luigi Spagnolli personally - small parcels of clayey soil with splendid locations on the sun-soaked slopes of the Adige river. The last harvest of the 20th century did not do justice to the house speciality, marzemino, because of freak summer weather conditions. So it's the Bordeaux-blend Tebro, that stands out - a firm, elegant, well- evolved, and long-finishing wine. The Müller-Thurgau distinguishes itself, too, with its pale straw-yellow colour, bouquet of mint and spices, and fresh, flavoursome palate. The Traminer has a fine, well-defined bouquet even if it's unexpectedly lean on the palate, perhaps because of difficulties with the vintage. The Marzemino has the same problem but it's still a successful red. It has a good deep violet colour and is better on the fruity, vinous palate than the nose. Even the reliable Pinot Nero has suffered slightly, despite the scrupulous care taken when growing the fruit at the family-owned, Guyot-trained vineyard at Patone. The rest of the wines, from the Chardonnay to the fine, dry Moscato Giallo, are true to type and very drinkable.

If there were a gene for viticulture, the Pisoni family would have been carrying it for centuries for their winemaking experience stretches back over almost half a millennium. Faithful custodians of rural tradition in the Valle dei Laghi area, the zone with seven lakes bounded by Trento, the Brenta Dolomites and Lake Garda, the Pisonis have been making wine since time immemorial. Once upon a time, they were the only family allowed to do so by decree of His Eminence the Archbishop, and the precious liquid was used as communion wine. Now the latest generation of the family has brought with it a welcome new spirit of innovation. The full-bodied, complex Vin Santo is now less cloying, more balanced, and with a good weight to it. The Sarica is an intriguing wine. Deep ruby red in colour with marked hints of pepper on the nose, it is full-bodied, elegant, and spicy on the palate, thanks both to the use of oak and the particular grape varieties used – including syrah. The Nosiola is fresh and very drinkable, a good wine with a very particular personality that is most evident in the characteristic bitter twist to the finish. The San Siro is well made with a good palate. A Bordeaux blend, its quality gets better and better every year. Finally, a vote of approval for the Trento sparkling wine (as well as being distillers, the Pisoni family were also among the pioneers of sparkling wine in Trentino). Matured in an impressive rock-hewn tunnel, the Trento spumante is a good clean wine with an elegant perlage and a broad palate.

○	Trentino Müller Thurgau '99	♈♈	3*
●	Trentino Rosso Tebro '98	♈♈	4
●	Trentino Marzemino '99	♈	3
●	Trentino Pinot Nero '98	♈	3
○	Trentino Chardonnay '99		3
○	Trentino Moscato Giallo '99		3
●	Trentino Pinot Nero '97	♈♈	4
●	Trentino Rosso Tebro '96	♈♈	4
●	Trentino Rosso Tebro '97	♈♈	4
○	Trentino Traminer Aromatico '97	♈♈	3*
●	Trentino Marzemino '98	♈	3
○	Trentino Moscato Giallo '98	♈	3
○	Trentino Müller Thurgau '98	♈	3
●	Trentino Pinot Nero '96	♈	4
○	Trentino Traminer Aromatico '98	♈	3

●	Sarica '98	♈♈	4
○	Trentino Vino Santo '92	♈♈	5
○	Trentino Nosiola '99	♈	3
●	Trentino Rosso San Siro '98	♈	3
○	Trento Brut Ris. '92	♈	4
○	Trentino Vino Santo '90	♈♈	5
○	Trentino Bianco San Siro '98	♈	3
○	Trentino Nosiola '98	♈	3
●	Trentino Rebo '97	♈	4
○	Trento Talento Brut	♈	4

LASINO (TN)

LAVIS (TN)

PRAVIS
VIA LAGOLO, 26
38076 LASINO (TN)
TEL. 0461/564305

NILO BOLOGNANI
VIA STAZIONE, 19
38015 LAVIS (TN)
TEL. 0461/246354

The three partners in the Pravis company have two fixed aims: to revive the traditions of Trentino winemaking, and to develop new strategies for the future. Both these aims are bound up in basic oenological research into the seasonal cycles of the vineyard and vinification with minimum technological intervention. They strive to make wines with real personality, each reflecting the nature of the grape varietal, especially when they use long-forgotten grape types, revived in the name of historical research into the role of growers in the past. This is how the "Franconia Project" began. Its aim is to re-introduce the Franconia grape variety into the Valle dei Laghi area. The Destrani, in fact, is made from franconia fruit, and is a unique red, most attractive and very drinkable. Another grape-from-the-past is the groppello, used for El Filò, an honest, rustic red, rich in alcohol and made to be enjoyed straight away. Fratagrande is a successful Bordeaux-blend, including cabernet sauvignon from the Lower Sarca Valley. This thoroughbred is one of the best Trentino Cabernets we have tasted. The syrah-based Syrae is also excellent. Spicy and full-bodied, it is now one of the region's classic wines. The Müller Thurgau San Thomà is an attractive tipple with sage and mint flavours. The Nosiola Le Frate is straightforward in a traditional mould, the copper-highlighted Pinot Grigio Polin is an interesting wine and satisfyingly full on the palate. Lastly, the Schiava Sort'Magre is also enjoyable, albeit in a simple, straightforward style.

Diego Bolognani is always striving for perfection, a laudable aim for an expert producer who in recent years has turned his attention more to the vineyard than the cellar. This back-to-basics approach, focusing on the grape rather than the wine, uses the experience and knowledge acquired in the winery to benefit the vines. The result is new vineyards, of red varieties only, with vines that will show their worth in a few years' time. Test micro-vinifications have been successful and in the meantime, the winery produces technically perfect products, thanks to winemaking methods elaborated and patented by Diego and his brothers. The 1999 vintage produced a large crop of grapes from the Cembra Valley, especially müller thurgau. So it is no accident that it was a Müller Thurgau that we liked most. It is one of the best that has ever been presented for tasting in the Cembra Valley's annual oenological competition for Alpine-grown Müller Thurgaus. A lovely pale straw-yellow colour with greenish reflections, it reveals an aromatic bouquet with an attractive bitter twist. The Chardonnay is very similar. Leaner in style than usual, it has all the usual elegance and is very well-managed. Both the Pinot Grigio and the Nosiola are very drinkable, although the former is perhaps somewhat one-dimensional in structure, and lacks in finish, while the Nosiola is definitely rough at the edges. Lastly, the Moscato Giallo is let down by a year that was unkind to this variety.

● Syrae '98	🍷🍷	4
● Trentino Cabernet Fratagranda '98	🍷🍷	4
○ Trentino Müller Thurgau St. Thomà '99	🍷🍷	3*
● Destrani '99	🍷	3
● El Filò '98	🍷	3
○ Trentino Nosiola Le Frate '99	🍷	3
○ Trentino Pinot Grigio Polin '99	🍷	3
● Valdadige Schiava Sort'Magre '99	🍷	2*
● Syrae '96	🍷🍷	4
● Syrae '97	🍷🍷	4
● Trentino Cabernet Fratagranda '95	🍷🍷	4
● Trentino Cabernet Fratagranda '97	🍷🍷	4
● Trentino Rebo Rigotti '97	🍷🍷	3*
○ Vino Santo Le Aréle '84	🍷🍷	5

○ Trentino Chardonnay '99	🍷🍷	3*
○ Trentino Müller Thurgau '99	🍷🍷	3*
○ Trentino Nosiola '99	🍷	3
○ Trentino Pinot Grigio '99	🍷	3
○ Trentino Moscato Giallo '99		3
○ Müller Thurgau della Val di Cembra '96	🍷🍷	3*
○ Trentino Moscato Giallo '96	🍷🍷	3*
○ Trentino Moscato Giallo '97	🍷🍷	3*
○ Trentino Müller Thurgau '97	🍷🍷	3*
○ Trentino Müller Thurgau '98	🍷🍷	3*
○ Trentino Nosiola '98	🍷🍷	3*
○ Trentino Pinot Grigio '96	🍷🍷	3*
○ Trentino Sauvignon '97	🍷🍷	3*
○ Trentino Sauvignon '98	🍷🍷	3*

LAVIS (TN)

LAVIS (TN)

CASATA MONFORT
VIA GARIBALDI, 11
38015 LAVIS (TN)
TEL. 0461/241484

CESCONI
LOC. PRESSANO
VIA MARCONI, 39
38015 LAVIS (TN)
TEL. 0461/240355

Lavis and wine go together naturally. Documents relate how almost every house in the area used to have its own cellar-winery, all of them open to the public for direct sales, especially when quantity was more important than quality. Times have changed, yields per hectare have been limited, the peasant farmers have become growers who now supply the local co-operative, or they have acquired new experience as cellarmasters. Which is what happened to brothers Lorenzo and Michele Simoni, who for the last few years have selected other people's grapes for vinification (including, of course, grapes from their own small family-owned vineyards). They have brought a young oenologist, Dario Tonnazzoli, into the company and year by year their wines continue to improve. The wines have deep colours and are full-bodied in structure. We tasted a full-flavoured Chardonnay with rich golden highlights, lots of fruit on the nose, a full body and a rich palate. Another pleasant surprise was the green-flecked Pinot Grigio with a smooth bouquet of ripe pears and good acidity on the palate. The Müller Thurgau is another attractive, full-bodied wine and a champion in its class. This is one of the Simonis' regular successes, thanks to its marked aromatic qualities and its finely judged backbone acidity. The other white, the Traminer, is good enough, but perhaps leaner than many previous versions. Lastly, the Lagrein is a fine, eminently drinkable wine, clean on the palate and slightly tannic.

The Cesconis may not have managed to repeat last year's success but they still have a place on the winners' podium. Probably it was the poor vintage, in part at least, that influenced the final result. The wine that did impress us for its grace, elegance and aromatic concentration was the Olivar, a tangy blend of white grape varieties. The Pinot Grigio has good structure with attractive green acidity that also comes out on the nose. Full-bodied and richly fruity, it has good balance and a long finish. The Chardonnay is most attractive and really does smell of golden delicious apples while the Sauvignon has pronounced vegetal hints and the usual traces of elderflower on the nose. The Nosiola is richer than usual. The Traminer is clean, with sharp aromatic qualities, and spicy with just the right acidity. The real news is the Cesconis' first red wine releases. The Cabernet has a deep colour and an impressive bouquet that is much bigger than the subsequent palate, probably because the vines where the grapes come from in the company's splendid Lower Sarca Valley estate, near Lake Garda, are so young. The Merlot wines have the same characteristics in both versions. The first is made for easy drinking soon after the harvest – fruity, lively and very attractive. The second Merlot is barrel-fermented and not yet ready to drink, since it is still at the experimental stage. Patience is the order of the day. We must wait for the vines to come round. Certainly, the Cesconis aren't in any hurry. They've built a new modern winery. They've made further refinements to their vineyard management. And soon, they'll be back at the top of their class.

O	Trentino Chardonnay '99	♇♇	3*
O	Trentino Müller Thurgau '99	♇♇	3*
O	Trentino Pinot Grigio '99	♇♇	3*
●	Trentino Lagrein '98	♇	4
O	Trentino Traminer Aromatico '99	♇	3
O	Trentino Brut M. Cl.	♈♈	5
O	Trentino Chardonnay '95	♈♈	3*
O	Trentino Chardonnay '93	♈	4
●	Trentino Lagrein '91	♈	4
●	Trentino Lagrein '95	♈	3
●	Trentino Marzemino '92	♈	4
●	Trentino Marzemino '93	♈	3
O	Trentino Müller Thurgau '93	♈	4
O	Trentino Pinot Grigio '95	♈	3
O	Trentino Traminer Aromatico '95	♈	3

O	Olivar '99	♇♇	4
●	Trentino Cabernet '98	♇♇	4
O	Trentino Chardonnay '99	♇♇	4
●	Trentino Merlot '98	♇♇	4
O	Trentino Nosiola '99	♇♇	4
O	Trentino Pinot Grigio '99	♇♇	4
O	Trentino Sauvignon '99	♇♇	4
O	Trentino Traminer Aromatico '99	♇♇	4
●	Merlot '99	♇	3
O	Trentino Pinot Grigio '98	♇♇♇	4*
O	Olivar '98	♈♈	4
O	Trentino Nosiola '98	♈♈	3*
O	Trentino Pinot Bianco '98	♈♈	4
O	Trentino Sauvignon '98	♈♈	4
O	Trentino Traminer Aromatico '98	♈♈	4

LAVIS (TN)

LAVIS (TN)

VIGNAIOLO GIUSEPPE FANTI
P.ZZA CROCE, 3
LOC. PRESSANO
38015 LAVIS (TN)
TEL. 0461/240809

LA VIS
VIA CARMINE, 12
38015 LAVIS (TN)
TEL. 0461/246325

The line of hills that benefit from the sun at Lavis can rightly be called "wine country". The bottles that come out of the tiny Fanti company are proof of this. The company is run by a young winemaker, Alessandro Fanti, who studied oenology at San Michele all'Adige and was born into the profession for his father, Giuseppe Fanti, was noted for his skill in the vineyards. Just four hectares of vineyards are under cultivation and modern management practices are employed. Guyot training is used rather than the traditional pergola technique, rootstock is planted at greater densities and exclusively eco-friendly treatments are employed, all to produce better grapes. The wines have structure, character, and notable quality. Especially the Chardonnay Robur, vinified in small oak casks. Deep golden yellow colour, it has a good aromatic bouquet, intense fruit and is sure to be long-lived. The same goes for the Portico, a Bordeaux-blend of equal proportions of cabernet franc and merlot, aged for 27 months in barrique. This wine of great structure is impressive in every aspect. It may be slightly vegetal but it is still very successful. Vineyard innovations have allowed the Fantis to make an unusual white, the Incrocio Manzoni, perhaps the best one we have ever tasted. It has spicy notes that are reminiscent of Alsace and excellent acidity on the palate. The Nosiola is good, too. It's a typical wine of the Pressano zone that Alessandro Fanti makes according to the precepts of local tradition to produce an easy-drinking style. Pale straw-yellow colour, it reveals traditional hints of fresh nuts on the nose (hence the dialect name "Nosiola", which means hazelnut), as well as spring flowers.

No fewer than three wines out of ten tasted at La Vis went into the final tastings for the Three Glass awards. A target that was so near, yet so far. What went wrong? The difficult 1998 vintage. Often the efforts needed to make great wines backfire on the best, just when everything seems in order. We're sorry too, because, and we say this quite sincerely, the three La Vis wines are really excellent. The two versions of Ritratto, the red and the white blend, are expertly made. They suffer from a vintage that produced grapes that were a little too "green". The white Ritratto is full-flavoured, with good fruit and balance, and an almost honey-like finish. Its obvious vegetal hints are compensated only in part by an excellent assemblage. The red Ritratto is clean, soft and attractive. The Mandolaia obtained from late-harvested traminer, sauvignon, chardonnay and pinot grigio, is very good, yet again. An ideal dessert wine, it is long and creamy and stays in the mouth forever. From the Ritratti range, the Cabernet and the Pinot Nero are rightly classed amongst Trentino's finest. They are one notch better than many similar wines, as are the Chardonnay and the Pinot Grigio. There were high marks at the tasting for both the Lagrein Maso Baldazzini and a new Chardonnay in the Ceolan range, labelled "Alto Adige" because the grapes come from a grower in the commune of Salorno, in South Tyrol. Finally, the Arcade sparkling wine has a delicate perlage and is clean and full on the palate.

○	Incrocio Manzoni '99	♀♀	3*
●	Portico Rosso '97	♀♀	4
○	Trentino Chardonnay Robur '98	♀♀	3*
○	Trentino Nosiola '99	♀	3

○	A. A. Chardonnay Ceolan '99	♀♀	3*
○	Mandolaia '99	♀♀	5
○	Ritratto '98	♀♀	4
●	Ritratto '98	♀♀	5
●	Trentino Cabernet Sauvignon Ritratti '98	♀♀	4
○	Trentino Chardonnay Ritratti '99	♀♀	4
●	Trentino Lagrein Maso Baldazzini '99	♀♀	3*
○	Trentino Pinot Grigio Ritratti '99	♀♀	4
●	Trentino Pinot Nero Ritratti '98	♀♀	4
○	Trento Brut Arcade	♀♀	4
●	Ritratto '91	♀♀♀	4*
○	Trentino Pinot Grigio Ritratti '95	♀♀♀	4*
●	Ritratto '97	♀♀	5

LAVIS (TN)

MASO FURLI
VIA FURLI, 32
38015 LAVIS (TN)
TEL. 0461/240667

MEZZOCORONA (TN)

MARCO DONATI
VIA CESARE BATTISTI, 41
38016 MEZZOCORONA (TN)
TEL. 0461/604141

A pleasant surprise backed up by proof. The wines made by Marco and Giorgio, the Zanoni brothers, have established their place in the Trentino winemaking firmament. But success hasn't changed the habits of this fine farming family whose knowledge of viticulture has been handed down from generation to generation. Their vineyards are kept like gardens and each vine is treated almost as if it were a family friend. The Zanonis have only been bottling their own wine for three vintages. They make just a few thousand bottles of white wine only, with no concern for commercial or speculative considerations, despite the pressures of the market. The Traminer is exemplary in every aspect of its bouquet and palate. It left all other similar Trentino wines standing, thanks to its crystalline lucidity, crisp aromas and a well-developed palate that is almost opulent in character, but well supported by underlying acidity. The Sauvignon is very good, too. Rich on the nose with characteristic hints of elderflower, peppers and peaches, it is full-bodied and very appealing on the palate. But it was the Chardonnay that won the most approval, gaining top marks for its lustrous, limpid colour, its delicately fruity nose, full, round, ripe palate and attractive finish. Three very well-deserved Glasses. Three wines, each one better than the last, from an estate that can surely be counted on, because it knows how to combine enthusiasm with expertise, and quality with territory. And flies in the face of the mania for quantity that prevails (alas) in many other Trentino wineries.

We were expecting it. Sneaky old Marco Donati was planning a great coup, the presentation of a blockbuster wine that would give the world something to remember him by. Perhaps even using a mediocre vintage, so as to better show off his skills, and to demonstrate the quality of wines from his home territory, Mezzocorona, down on the Rotaliano plain, the kingdom of Teroldego. We knew it was coming. And the Sangue del Drago (meaning "Dragon's Blood"), Marco's best Teroldego '98 cuvée, is spot on target. Appropriately blood red in colour with violet tinges, it proffers delicate mineral hints on the nose and secondary aromas of violets and spices. The palate is full-bodied and rich, combining the happy softness of the mid palate with the firmer tannins on the finish to make a wine that is both easy to drink and well-structured at the same time. A powerful Three Glasses winner. The deft touches of this grower-producer show through in the other wines we were given to taste. First of all comes the Vino del Maso, a blend of lagrein, teroldego and merlot that evinces balance, elegance and power. The Nosiola is a success again, and is indeed one of the best of its vintage, the full body and lovely balance vying with those of much grander wines. The standard Teroldego has an intense ruby red colour and is an attractive long-finishing wine with a clean flavour and a bouquet of raspberries. Drink it cool and young. All in all, the successful products of the passion and skill of an enthusiastic, open-minded, big-hearted winemaker.

○ Trentino Chardonnay '99	▼▼▼	3*
○ Trentino Sauvignon '99	▼▼	3*
○ Trentino Traminer Aromatico '99	▼▼	3*
○ Trentino Sauvignon '98	♀♀	3*
○ Trentino Traminer Aromatico '98	♀♀	3*
○ Trentino Chardonnay '98	♀	3

● Teroldego Rotaliano		
Sangue del Drago '98	▼▼▼	4*
● Teroldego Rotaliano '99	▼▼	3*
○ Trentino Nosiola '99	▼▼	3*
● Vino del Maso Rosso '98	▼▼	4
● Teroldego Rotaliano		
Sangue di Drago '96	♀♀	4
○ Terre del Noce Bianco '95	♀♀	3*
○ Terre del Noce Bianco '96	♀♀	3*
○ Terre del Noce Bianco '98	♀♀	4
● Teroldego Rotaliano '96	♀	3
● Teroldego Rotaliano '98	♀	3
○ Trentino Chardonnay '98	♀	3
● Trentino Moscato Rosa '98	♀	3
● Vino del Maso Rosso '98	♀	3

MEZZOCORONA (TN)

MEZZOCORONA (TN)

F.LLI DORIGATI
VIA DANTE, 5
38016 MEZZOCORONA (TN)
TEL. 0461/605313

MEZZACORONA
VIA IV NOVEMBRE, 127
38016 MEZZOCORONA (TN)
TEL. 0461/605163 - 0461/616399

It surprised us to see that the Methius '93 failed by a whisker to gain a Three Glass score at our tasting. In the run-up comparative tastings, it had consistently done well and was always in the group of top Trentino sparkling wines. It was acclaimed for its marvellous aromatic intensity, for its delicate, ever-lasting perlage, its full flavour and rich style. Without a doubt, brothers Carlo and Franco Dorigati and their friend and winemaker, Enrico Paternoster, will have the chance to repeat the extraordinary success of last year very shortly. If that was the story with the sparkling wine, things went better with the still wines. To start with, the Pinot Grigio is really good. Rich and juicy on the palate, and well-rounded in all respects, it hints at tropical fruit on the nose and offers refreshing acidity on the palate. It's also very good value, considering its quality. Diedri, the top-of-the-range Teroldego, is balsamic, well-evolved and powerful. A wine with a future and the pride of the Dorigati cellars. It's a deep, dark big wine that needs time to reach its potential. The clean, uncomplicated Teroldego from the latest vintage, however, is made to drink straight away, almost in the "vin nouveau" style. And talking of simple wines, the Lagrein Kretzer, or rosé, is most enjoyably fresh and fruity.

Another top level performance from the Rotari Riserva '95 sparkling wine from MezzaCorona, a confirmed thoroughbred in the sparkling wine arena, and not only in the context of Trentino wines. Such prestige is not acquired by chance. MezzaCorona have focused on sparkling wines. In fact, they have even constructed an entire new purpose-built cellar as big as four football fields and perhaps the most technologically advanced in Europe. In the space of just a few years, this co-operative has revolutionised the image and the market for Trentino wines, spearheading sales – of Rotari in particular – in faraway markets, without, however, abandoning their concern for the flagship wines of the area, Teroldego and Pinot Grigio. The Teroldego we tasted, the Riserva '97, more than held its own, thanks to an excellent colour, a fine aromatic bouquet, and a rich palate. A good result, considering the quantities produced. Quantity and quality also rub shoulders happily in the well-made and very attractive Pinot Grigio Selezione Maioliche. The Chardonnay Selezione Maioliche is quite good, too, produced in a soft, fruity international style, like the Cabernet sold under the same label. The "metodo classico" Arte Italiana sparkling wine is scrupulously made according to the precepts of the Trento DOC.

●	Teroldego Rotaliano		
	Diedri Ris. '98	♈♈	5
○	Trentino Pinot Grigio '99	♈♈	3*
○	Trento Methius Ris. '93	♈♈	5
●	Teroldego Rotaliano '99	♈	3
◉	Trentino Lagrein Rosato '99	♈	3
○	Trento Methius Ris. '92	♈♈♈	5
●	Teroldego Rotaliano '97	♙♙	3*
●	Teroldego Rotaliano		
	Diedri Ris. '96	♙♙	5
●	Teroldego Rotaliano		
	Diedri Ris. '97	♙♙	5
●	Trentino Rebo '97	♙♙	3*
○	Trento Methius Ris. '90	♙♙	5
○	Trento Methius Ris. '91	♙♙	5

●	Teroldego Rotaliano Ris. '97	♈♈	3*
○	Trento Rotari Ris. '95	♈♈	4
●	Trentino Cabernet Maioliche '98	♈	3
○	Trentino Chardonnay Maioliche '99	♈	3
○	Trentino Pinot Grigio Maioliche '99	♈	3
○	Trento Rotari Brut Arte Italiana	♈	3
●	Teroldego Rotaliano Ris. '94	♙♙	3*
●	Teroldego Rotaliano Ris. '96	♙♙	3*
●	Trentino Cabernet Sauvignon		
	Oltresarca '94	♙♙	3*
○	Trentino Traminer Aromatico '97	♙♙	3*
○	Trento Rotari Brut Arte Italiana	♙♙	3*
○	Trento Rotari Brut Arte Italiana	♙♙	3*
○	Trento Rotari Brut Ris. '94	♙♙	4

MEZZOLOMBARDO (TN)

MEZZOLOMBARDO (TN)

CANTINA ROTALIANA
C.SO DEL POPOLO, 6
38017 MEZZOLOMBARDO (TN)
TEL. 0461/601010

FORADORI
VIA DAMIANO CHIESA, 1
38017 MEZZOLOMBARDO (TN)
TEL. 0461/601046

The Cantina Rotaliana is rightly considered the "mother" of Teroldego, since it has harvested and vinified the variety for almost a century. Oenologist Luciano Lunelli, a man of few words but great skill, is the architect of the Cantina's success and continuing improvements in quality. New cellars will be the next step. He is an all-round oenologist and an excellent sparkling wine maker but Teroldego is his first and most abiding passion. He himself selects the grape consignments for the cellars and into which vat each lot will go. But he is far from satisfied. Lunelli has now turned his attention to the vineyards, renting some on behalf of the co-operative. One of these is the monastery vineyard right in the heart of the historic town centre, near the monks' church. Blessed grapes, for a really fantastic wine. Our apprehensive tastings last year were our first. This year came explosive confirmation. What we tasted, anonymously of course, impressed us all. Only its youth prevented this wine from gaining a higher classification. Teroldego Rotaliano Pieve Francescana is a complete wine, deep and richly extracted, which will get even better with time. We make this judgement having tasted previous vintages and having tried a barrel sample of next year's edition. We'll come back to this wine. The standard Teroldego and the Riserva '97 are excellent, as usual and the whites – the Pinot Bianco and the Pinot Grigio – are good too.

Elisabetta Foradori is unique in the Trentino wine scene. Unique for her temperament, for her managerial abilities, for her intuition in the vineyards and for her expertise in the cellars. Her wines – or rather her wine, singular, because she devotes most of her attention to her Teroldego – is lavishly praised and imitated by hordes of winemakers. Elisabetta goes on experimenting with her self-appointed speciality, which doesn't mean that it always repays the loving care it receives. The '98, for example, the one we are concerned with now, is a vintage without any great merits. It is no coincidence that several of the more famous Teroldego labels, made only in the best vintages, were not made this year. Let's start with the Elisabetta's Granato, a monovarietal Teroldego. There is all the usual highly individual power, precision and aromatic bouquet. It's only the grassy style that marks it down. The "standard" Teroldego is anything but standard. Year by year, it gets better because it is based on a rigorous selection of grapes from various vineyard parcels in the Foradori-owned estate (14 hectares in total), the best in the Campo Rotaliano. These are almost 50 year-old vineyards managed according to rigid biodynamic principles. The wine is immediately attractive on the nose with its characteristically inviting aromas of violets and spices, well-integrated into the fresh fruit component. On the palate, it has fine structure, rich alcohol and a well-balanced mid palate before the long, elegant finish. Talking of elegance, the estate's only white, the Myrto '99 (50% chardonnay, 25% pinot bianco, and 25% sauvignon) is a full-bodied wine, limpid and lustrous with subtle hints of vanilla, good length and a soft, rich palate. Three wines, six Glasses. We look forward to awarding even more in future vintages.

● Teroldego Rotaliano Pieve Francescana '97	♟♟	4
● Teroldego Rotaliano Ris. '97	♟♟	3*
● Teroldego Rotaliano '99	♟	2*
○ Trentino Pinot Bianco '99	♟	2*
○ Trentino Pinot Grigio '99	♟	2*
● Teroldego Rotaliano '97	♟♟	2*
● Teroldego Rotaliano '98	♟♟	2*
● Teroldego Rotaliano Ris. '93	♟♟	3*
● Teroldego Rotaliano Ris. '95	♟♟	3*
● Teroldego Rotaliano Ris. '96	♟♟	3*
● Teroldego Rotaliano '96	♟	2*
● Teroldego Rotaliano '94	♟	2*
● Teroldego Rotaliano Ris. '94	♟	3
● Trentino Lagrein '97	♟	3

● Granato '98	♟♟	5
○ Myrto '99	♟♟	4
● Teroldego Rotaliano '99	♟♟	4
● Granato '91	♟♟♟	5
● Granato '93	♟♟♟	5
● Granato '96	♟♟♟	5
● Teroldego Rotaliano Sgarzon '93	♟♟♟	4*
● Teroldego Rotaliano Sgarzon '94	♟♟♟	4*
● Ailampa '97	♟♟	4
● Granato '97	♟♟	5
● Karanar '97	♟♟	4
○ Myrto '98	♟♟	3*
● Teroldego Rotaliano '97	♟♟	3*
● Teroldego Rotaliano '98	♟♟	3*
● Teroldego Rotaliano Sgarzon '96	♟♟	4

NOGAREDO (TN)

CASTEL NOARNA
FRAZ. NOARNA
VIA CASTELNUOVO, 1
38060 NOGAREDO (TN)
TEL. 0464/413295

NOMI (TN)

CANTINA SOCIALE DI NOMI
VIA ROMA, 1
38060 NOMI (TN)
TEL. 0464/834195

Not even the old feudal lords of the castles in Vallagarina could exercise an influence over the seasons. Castel Noarna belongs to the Zani family, and it is here that young Marco has created one of the most beautiful wineries in the region. The wines are frank, honest, and faithful to their vintage, which means they have paid the price of the capricious '98 harvest. The Campo Grande, an imposing Chardonnay, shows clear varietal hints of banana together with a decent structure, but is let down a little by its finish. The same goes for the Bianco di Castelnuovo. It is slightly closed on the nose, with hints of almonds and apple pips. Faintly spicy and fresh-tasting, it is a distinctly agreeable tipple. In contrast, the Casot, a Nosiola from old vines surrounding the castle, comes across as full on the nose and rich on the palate. Vibrantly fruity, inviting and straightforward on the front palate, it unfurls a clean progression with delicate vanilla touches in the finish. This is a good half-way house on the road to the winery's most important red wine, the Romeo. This carefully nurtured Cabernet from individually selected bunches of grapes is the Zanis' flagship wine. It is no accident that the wine is called after the jolly nickname of a family that once came from Mantua and has now adopted the Rovereto area as its home. The Romeo '97 has a bright, ruby red colour, of medium intensity. The bouquet is elegant and crisply fruity. There is good structure on the palate, with a well-developed mid palate and a finish with pronounced tannins that have yet to soften. This is a red that will in all probability get better with time. Marco Zani is in no hurry. Better vintages are on their way. We're (pretty) sure they are, too.

It was a fabulous Merlot that gained this winery admission into the Guide last year. This year a different wine provides the justification for Cantina di Nomi's re-appearance in the Guide, the chardonnay-based white called Résorso Le Comete, which stands out for a broad bouquet, as well as delicacy and balance on the palate. It is also proof of the dynamism of an organisation that believes in synergy and in exchanging winemaking experiences with other wineries, not only in Trentino, since one of the members is a grower-producer in Camporeale, on the borders of the provinces of Palermo and Trapani in Sicily. Traditionally enough for the area, red wines are the Nomi co-operative's strong point. The Marzemino is correct enough, with good aromas on the nose, a well-developed palate and a markedly fruity flavour. Merlot predominates in the Bordeaux-blend Rosso Résorso '98. It unfurls a broad aristocratic bouquet with hints of cherries and there is plenty of power on the generous palate, which has a leisurely finish. We were expecting more, perhaps, from some of the whites, the Müller Thurgau, the Pinot Grigio, the Pinot Bianco and in particular from the ambitious Meditandum ad 2000. These are simple, unpretentious wines that should – the late-harvest Meditandum in particular – have more character to them and a touch more gentle power, perhaps. They should be a bit more like the excellent Bianco Résorso Le Comete '99.

● Trentino Cabernet Romeo '97	🍷🍷	5
○ Trentino Nosiola Casot '99	🍷🍷	4
○ Bianco di Castelnuovo '98	🍷	3
○ Trentino Chardonnay Campo Grande '98	🍷	4
○ Bianco di Castelnuovo '97	🍷🍷	4
● Trentino Cabernet Romeo '93	🍷🍷	4
● Trentino Cabernet Romeo '94	🍷🍷	4
● Trentino Cabernet Romeo '96	🍷🍷	4
● Trentino Cabernet Sauvignon Mercuria '97	🍷🍷	3*
○ Trentino Chardonnay '97	🍷🍷	3*
○ Trentino Chardonnay Campo Grande '97	🍷🍷	4
○ Trentino Nosiola '98	🍷🍷	3*

○ Trentino Bianco Résorso Le Comete '99	🍷🍷	4
● Trentino Rosso Résorso Le Comete '98	🍷🍷	4
○ Meditandum ad 2000	🍷	4
○ Trentino Pinot Bianco Antichi Portali '99	🍷	3
○ Trentino Müller Thurgau '99		3
○ Trentino Rulander Antichi Portali '99		3
● Trentino Merlot Le Campagne '97	🍷🍷	4
● Trentino Rosso Résorso '97	🍷🍷	4
● Trentino Marzemino Le Fornas '98	🍷	3
○ Trentino Pinot Bianco Valbone '98	🍷	3

RAVINA (TN)

ROVERÉ DELLA LUNA (TN)

LUNELLI
VIA MARGON, 19
38040 RAVINA (TN)
TEL. 0461/972503 - 0461/972311

GAIERHOF
VIA IV NOVEMBRE, 51
38030 ROVERÉ DELLA LUNA (TN)
TEL. 0461/658527

The Lunellis have made rapid progress. In just a handful of harvests, all vinified independently of the famous Ferrari sparkling wine establishment, Marcello Lunelli, the young heir to the spumante empire, has carved out a prominent position among emerging new wineries. Lunelli wines have the charm of handcrafted products. Every detail is given scrupulous attention, starting in the vineyards. Their Rosso Maso Le Viane is made from grapes from the highly prestigious Campi Sarni area, the vineyard bowl under Avio castle. It missed a Three Glass score by a whisker, probably because of the youth of the current vineyard plantation. The wine is majestic, profound in character with perfect balance on the palate. There are hints of berry fruit, blackcurrants and cherries, with some slight traces of eucalyptus on the back palate. The Pinot Nero Maso Montalto won Two Glasses easily. The fruit comes from a site is on the slopes of Mount Bondone, the mountain above Trento, and the wine is probably the most complex and interesting of its type we have tasted recently. Very elegant and understated, it displays good overall balance and velvety softness, despite a structure that is anything but lightweight. Then there are the white wines. Chardonnay Villa Gentilotti is balanced, "banana-y", and easy to drink. Chardonnay Villa Morgon is more structured and complex. Finally, our tasting notes are full of praise for the fresh, full-flavoured Sauvignon Villa San Niccolò, from vineyards planted right on the edge of the city itself, on the side of Trento that catches the sun.

A border winery, Gaierhof straddles the divide between the provinces of Trento and Bolzano, two neighbouring entities that despite their propinquity are, oenologically speaking, quite different. The Togn family have benefited from this accident of geography and have succeeded in drawing the best from each of the two regions. Gaierhof is a famous name, as well-known abroad as it is in Italy, thanks to a reputation built up by years of hard work. Diversifying the range of wines made, careful grape selection, and a constant regard for maintaining typicity have all helped to improve the selection presented. The Maso Poli Pinot Grigio is perhaps the best of its type in Trentino. An attractive golden yellow in colour, it has crisp notes of pears and golden delicious apples on the nose, a good follow-through to the palate, and a long, well-sustained, lingering finish. The Sorni '99 is as good as ever. A blend of nosiola, chardonnay and müller thurgau grapes, it is both fruity and floral at the same time, with a full-flavoured and well-defined finish. The other wines are interesting. The Pinot Nero is clean and vinous, but perhaps a little lean. The late-vintage Moscato Rosa is smooth, full-flavoured and charming while the Chardonnay Costa Erta, in contrast, is good enough but lacks complexity. The grapes come from Maso Poli again and the name comes from the Trentino dialect expression "coste erte" for the steep slopes where the vineyards are planted. On the subject of altitudes, the Müller Thurgau dei Settecento cuvée is named for the altitude of its vineyard (700 metres above sea level) and confirms its reputation as one of the best of its type, either in Trentino or in Alto Adige.

O	Trentino Chardonnay		
	Villa Gentilotti '98	🍷🍷	4
O	Trentino Chardonnay		
	Villa Margon '98	🍷🍷	4
●	Trentino Pinot Nero		
	Maso Montalto '97	🍷🍷	4
●	Trentino Rosso Maso Le Viane '97	🍷🍷	5
O	Trentino Sauvignon		
	Villa San Nicolò '99	🍷🍷	4
O	Trentino Chardonnay		
	Villa Gentilotti '97	🍷🍷	4
O	Trentino Chardonnay		
	Villa Margon '97	🍷🍷	4
●	Trentino Pinot Nero		
	Maso Montalto '96	🍷🍷	4

O	Trentino Müller Thurgau		
	dei Settecento '99	🍷🍷	4
O	Trentino Pinot Grigio Maso Poli '99	🍷🍷	4
O	Trentino Chardonnay		
	Costa Erta '99	🍷	4
●	Trentino Moscato Rosa '99	🍷	5
●	Trentino Pinot Nero Maso Poli '98	🍷	4
O	Trentino Sorni Bianco		
	Maso Poli '99	🍷	3
●	Trentino Moscato Rosa '97	🍷🍷	4
O	Trentino Müller Thurgau		
	dei Settecento '98	🍷🍷	3*
O	Trentino Sorni Bianco		
	Maso Poli '93	🍷🍷	4
●	Teroldego Rotaliano '97	🍷	3

ROVERETO (TN)

ROVERETO (TN)

NICOLA BALTER
VIA VALLUNGA II, 24
38068 ROVERETO (TN)
TEL. 0464/430101

LETRARI
VIA MONTE BALDO, 13/15
38068 ROVERETO (TN)
TEL. 0464/480200

Nicola Balter picked up Three Glasses for his Barbanico, a powerful, vigorous red wine with lots of character. This blend of cabernet sauvignon, merlot and lagrein is a wine in the family tradition. The choice of grapes, their percentage in the blend, and the name of the wine all owe their origin to Franco Balter, the innovative winemaker and founder of this fine hillside winery. The son and heir has not forgotten his father's lessons. The Barbanico '97 is a serious red wine, full-bodied and well-developed with an intense, extremely elegant bouquet of vanilla, chocolate and tobacco that reveals subtle undertones of berry fruit. Its presence on the palate is commandingly concentrated, with stunning breadth and depth. The Cabernet Sauvignon '97 is also excellent. A deep ruby red with a rich, elegant nose of considerable breadth, it evokes distinct notes of ripe berry fruit leading into a vigorous palate of substantial structure that progresses sure-footedly into a smooth, straightforward finish. The Balter Brut is tangy and delicious. Above all, this utterly reliable product sells for a very competitive price. The Rossinot '99 is a jolly rosé with good character and a fresh acidity that makes it very drinkable, while the Sauvignon is a little closed and hasn't revealed all its quality yet.

Even with 50 vintages under his belt, Leonello Letrari still has all the enthusiasm of a young producer. He still likes to surprise, and he does it in the way he knows best. By presenting a new wine. A red he's "always meant to make", bottled in fact expressly to celebrate his incredible tally of harvests. Half a century of hard work and achievement goes into the Ballistarius, a Bordeaux-blend red. The power and vigour of the cabernet is the key factor in the wine's redoubtable taste profile, which is tempered by the softness of the merlot. It's a red with lashings of character, vibrant and full-bodied, powerful on the nose, and with a long finish. New wines apart, there are other good quality products to investigate. The Marzemino Selezione is one of the best of its type, offering excellent structure, good backbone and balanced alcohol. The varietal Cabernet Sauvignon has a graceful touch. The full aromas reveal characteristic vegetal hints and the finish on the palate is leisurely. The Letraris also make two smooth, elegant white wines. The Incrocio Manzoni is well-balanced and can point to good acidity while the traditional-style Pinot Grigio has a wealth of pear fruit. The full-bodied, attractively balanced spumante is an established success while the late-vintage Dolce Vitae and the pretty, very well-managed Moscato Rosa, are two rarities for the connoisseur with a sweetish tooth.

	Wine	Glasses	Score
●	Barbanico '97	♈♈♈	5
●	Trentino Cabernet Sauvignon '97	♈♈	4
○	Trento Balter Brut	♈♈	4
☉	Rossinot '99	♈	3
○	Trentino Sauvignon '99	♈	4
○	Clarae '95	♀♀	4
○	Clarae '96	♀♀	4
●	Trentino Cabernet Sauvignon '91	♀♀	4
●	Trentino Cabernet Sauvignon '95	♀♀	4
●	Trentino Cabernet Sauvignon '96	♀♀	4
○	Trentino Chardonnay '97	♀♀	3*
○	Trentino Sauvignon '98	♀♀	3*
○	Trento Balter Brut	♀♀	4
○	Trento Balter Brut	♀♀	4

	Wine	Glasses	Score
●	Ballistarius '98	♈♈	5
○	Incrocio Manzoni 6.0.13 '99	♈♈	3*
●	Trentino Cabernet Sauvignon '96	♈♈	4
●	Trentino Marzemino Sel. '99	♈♈	4
●	Trentino Moscato Rosa '97	♈♈	5
○	Trento Brut Letrari	♈♈	4
○	Valdadige Pinot Grigio '99	♈♈	3*
○	Trento V. T. Dolce Vitae '97	♈	4
●	Trentino Marzemino '98	♀♀	3*
●	Trentino Marzemino Sel. '97	♀♀	3*
●	Trentino Moscato Rosa '93	♀♀	6
●	Trentino Moscato Rosa '94	♀♀	6
●	Trentino Moscato Rosa '95	♀♀	6
●	Trentino Rosso Maso Lodron '95	♀♀	3*
○	Trento Brut Letrari Ris. '95	♀♀	4

ROVERETO (TN)

ROVERETO (TN)

LONGARIVA
LOC. BORGO SACCO
VIA ZANDONAI, 6
38068 ROVERETO (TN)
TEL. 0464/437200

ARMANDO SIMONCELLI
LOC. NAVESEL, 7
38068 ROVERETO (TN)
TEL. 0464/432373

Marco Manica celebrates 25 years in the business in style with a Three Glass award for one of the ten jewels he presented to the panel. The Pergole is a wonderful wine made from pinot bianco grapes. It is a minor masterpiece of elegance and style. A shimmering greenish gold in colour, and subtly fragrant on the nose, it unveils a perfect balance on the palate, and an incredible wealth of flavour. No one was more surprised at this success than the producer himself. In fact, Marco Manica has always been more confident about his Cabernet, Merlot and Pinot Nero, and in fact has a well-established name as a maker of red wine. That's why it's no accident that the five red wines he submitted for tasting won ratings only marginally inferior to the winning Pinot Bianco. Burgundian in style, the Zinzèle is excellent, from the elegant nose of wild berry fruit to the fresh, full-flavoured, long-finishing palate. The Marognon is a powerful wine with excellent structure. Obtained from cabernet grapes, it has an elegant, slightly gamey, edge to it that makes it most original. The Quartella '97 is a typical Trentino Cabernet, a medium ruby red in colour, clean and elegant on the nose with hints of blackberry jam nuanced with spice, and a palate that is all softness and subtlety. The Tre Cesure Riserva '97 is made in the same style. It offers good extract, a nice background of ripe fruit, and good weight and character. The Marzemino '98 is, however, not as good as usual because of the poor vintage. Of the other whites, the most interesting is the Graminè, a Pinot Grigio the colour of burnished copper that resembles a rosé in the glass. It delights with a tangy palate and good length. Perer, the chardonnay cuvée, really does have the varietal pear aroma, even if the palate is slightly acidic. The Pinot Grigio is fresh and fruity, and the Cascari Sauvignon's strong suit is its smoky, vegetal aromas.

Best of the bunch this year from Carmelo Simoncelli's winery was the Marzemino. We might have guessed. Marzemino has been this producer's star wine for some time. Violet-tinged red in colour, it unveils an intensely grapey nose while the palate is fruity with a most attractive bitter twist. That the vineyards on the banks of the old Adige river port are ideal for red grape growing is easy to see after tasting the Navesèl, a Bordeaux-blend of great merit in its '97 version and a perfect marriage of body and elegance. Big in structure, full-bodied and broad, it packs plenty of tannins without being at all aggressive. The Lagrein has a similar weight and a comparable tasting profile. Technically well-made, powerful and very drinkable. Of the whites, the Pinot Bianco has a subtle, pale colour and is fairly intense on the nose, the crisply defined bouquet broadening out into scents of pears and ripe apples. The keynote on the palate is an attractive hint of almonds. The Chardonnay is firmly fruity in style with toasted bread and yeast on the nose but the palate is less than elegant, because of the vintage. Simoncelli's sparkling wine, the Trento Talento, is soft and well-balanced, shot through with a vein of ripe fruit and honey, although the finish is slightly lean.

○	Trentino Pinot Bianco Pergole '99	🍷🍷🍷	3*
○	Trentino Pinot Grigio Graminè '99	🍷🍷	3*
●	Trentino Cabernet Quartella '97	🍷🍷	4
●	Trentino Cabernet Sauvignon Marognon Ris. '97	🍷🍷	4
●	Trentino Pinot Nero Zinzèle '96	🍷🍷	4
●	Trentino Rosso Tre Cesure Ris. '97	🍷🍷	4
○	Trentino Sauvignon Cascari '99	🍷	4
○	Trentino Chardonnay Perer '99	🍷	3
●	Trentino Marzemino '98	🍷	3
○	Trentino Pinot Grigio '99	🍷	3
○	Trentino Pinot Grigio '98	🍷🍷	3*
○	Trentino Sauvignon Cascari '98	🍷🍷	4
●	Trentino Merlot Tovi '96	🍷🍷	4

●	Trentino Marzemino '99	🍷🍷	3*
●	Trentino Rosso Navesèl '97	🍷🍷	4
○	Trentino Chardonnay '99	🍷	3
●	Trentino Lagrein '99	🍷	3
○	Trentino Pinot Bianco '99	🍷	3
○	Trento Brut M. Cl.	🍷	4
○	Trentino Chardonnay '95	🍷🍷	3*
●	Trentino Lagrein '97	🍷🍷	3*
●	Trentino Lagrein '98	🍷🍷	3*
●	Trentino Marzemino '96	🍷🍷	3*
●	Trentino Marzemino '97	🍷🍷	3*
●	Trentino Marzemino '98	🍷🍷	3*
●	Trentino Rosso Navesèl '91	🍷🍷	3*
●	Trentino Rosso Navesèl '97	🍷🍷	3*
○	Trento Brut M. Cl.	🍷🍷	4

Endrizzi

Loc. Masetto, 2
38010 S. Michele all'Adige (TN)
tel. 0461/650129

Paolo Endrici has the approach of a top executive, the flair of an artist and a desire to create wines with real personality, as if they were works of art, along the lines of the avant-garde performances that are sometimes staged in the country-life museum he has created in what used to be his wine cellars. In recent years, the Endricis have acquired hillside terrain on the slopes of the mountain that start at San Michele all'Adige, sweeping towards Faedo and lovely Castello Monreale. The new cellars are full of new-wave wines, made from small parcels of grapes, almost all of which come from company-owned vineyards. These wines, or at least the ones that were submitted for tasting for this Guide, all probably still need a few more months of bottle-age. They are still too lively, Well-made and promising, perhaps, but still unformed. The one we liked most, without a doubt, was the Teroldego Maso Camorz, a '98 Riserva with a vibrant colour and a firm backbone of acidity in the palate to enhance its taste profile. The Masetto Nero is a little thin and still developing, the consequence of a poor vintage. The other wines are all good and attractive, from the fresh, clean Masetto Bianco, right up to the two Collezione wines, the Chardonnay and the Cabernet Sauvignon.

●	Teroldego Rotaliano Maso Camorz '98	🍷🍷	4
○	Masetto Bianco '98	🍷	4
●	Masetto Nero '98	🍷	4
●	Trentino Cabernet Sauvignon Collezione '97	🍷	4
○	Trentino Chardonnay Collezione '98	🍷	4
●	Teroldego Rotaliano Maso Camorz '97	ΥΥ	4
●	Teroldego Rotaliano Sup. Sel. '96	ΥΥ	4
●	Trentino Moscato Rosa Collezione '94	ΥΥ	5
●	Trentino Pinot Nero Pian di Castello '97	ΥΥ	4

Azienda Vitivinicola dell' Istituto Agrario Provinciale

Via Edmondo Mach, 1
38010 S. Michele all'Adige (TN)
tel. 0461/615252

For almost 130 years, San Michele all'Adige has been the oenological school par excellence. It has trained generations of wine technicians, educated cohorts of farmers from Trentino and Alto Adige, experimented with viticultural techniques, vinified new grape varieties, and even policed wine frauds and counterfeits. An institution that, in short, must keep up with the times in order to stay at the cutting edge in the new millennium. Let's start with the cellars, where Enrico Paternoster has taken over as manager. He's an alumnus of the Istituto and an inspired new broom with proven experience. The improvement in the wines is tangible. Every single one that was submitted to our tastings was outstanding, characterful, and could have been used as a model in the classroom. The Trentino Bianco Castel San Michele '99 is immediately likeable. It is full-flavoured, with crisp aromas and an intriguingly complex nose. On the palate, it manages to be smooth and vibrant at the same time, progressing invitingly through to the finish. The Chardonnay is good, although perhaps dominated by a touch of acidity. It is headily aromatic but still a little too young. The Pinot Bianco is truly excellent. Rich and full-bodied, its structure is a hymn to elegance, making it perhaps the most successful of the wines the institute produces. It's even better than the nonetheless spot-on Pinot Grigio, a fresh, tangy wine with hints of williams pears. Of the reds, it is the Rebo that deserves special praise. A wine based on a varietal identified by Rebo Rigotti, who worked at the Institute in the 30s, crossing marzemino and merlot to get a vibrantly coloured, alcohol-rich wine that is elegant and easy to drink. All in all, Paternoster's arrival has brought a breath of fresh air to these hallowed, centuries-old barrel cellars.

○	Trentino Bianco Castel S. Michele '99	🍷🍷	3*
○	Trentino Pinot Bianco '99	🍷🍷	3*
●	Trentino Rebo '99	🍷🍷	3*
○	Trentino Chardonnay '99	🍷	3
○	Trentino Pinot Grigio '99	🍷	3
○	Prepositura Atesino '96	ΥΥ	3*
○	Spumante Riserva del Fondatore '89	ΥΥ	5
●	Trentino Castel San Michele '93	ΥΥ	4
●	Trentino Merlot '95	ΥΥ	4
●	Trentino Merlot '96	ΥΥ	4
●	Trentino Rebo '97	ΥΥ	3*
●	Trentino Rosso Castel S. Michele '95	ΥΥ	4

S. MICHELE ALL'ADIGE (TN)   TRENTO

ZENI
FRAZ. GRUMO
VIA STRETTA, 2
38010 SAN MICHELE ALL'ADIGE (TN)
TEL. 0461/650456

CAVIT
CONSORZIO DI CANTINE SOCIALI
FRAZ. RAVINA
VIA PONTE, 31
38040 TRENTO
TEL. 0461/381711

The Zeni brothers go from strength to strength. Roberto has even gained the ultimate accolade from his colleagues by being elected president of the association that includes all the smaller Trentino producers, some eighty winemakers in total, often microscopic in dimension. Not an easy task, but an important one, which Roberto intends to fulfil with the same zeal as he devotes to in his beautiful winery at Grumo, near the river Adige. Here, he vinifies grapes from vineyards all over the valley, whether hillside "maso" plots or riverside parcels of land, with the same care and attention. Grape selection is one concern, but both brothers are oenologists, so vineyard technique and cellar practice, always aimed at maintaining typicity, are also important. This year we tasted a new wine. The Trento spumante is a Brut that is making its debut after being conceived in the early 1990s. Just a few thousand bottles were made and it is being released only now. The results include a lively perlage, good depth of flavour, intense aromas of nuts, full body, elegance and a long, long finishing. Two effortless Glasses and the panel's congratulations. We also particularly liked the Müller Thurgau, which is fresh, fruity and slightly resinous, with good secondary aromas, as well as the Pinot Bianco Sortì. Our true-to-type tasting notes mention a golden delicious apple nose, softness and easy drinkability on the palate. The Nosiola is young and attractive. This 1999 version has a characteristic, albeit barely perceptible, hint of nuts in the taste profile. Of the reds, the Teroldego Pini '99 is an up-front wine, ready to drink now, and quite deliberately made in a youthful, fruity style. Finally, there's a good Moscato Rosa '99, which is subtle and elegant on both nose and palate.

This well-established Consorzio groups together many of Trentino's co-operatives. Beside quality, Cavit likes to talk about figures, pointing out its ever-expanding markets, the quantity of wine produced, and the huge increase in its net worth. So it is no surprise that no fewer than 18 different wines were submitted for our tastings. The total score for these wines was more than 1,400 points, with an average score of 77.5 points for each wine. Which means that each wine was worth an average of "almost Two Glasses". Four of them easily passed the test. The best? Without a doubt, the Teroldego Maso Cervara, from the small, pretty holding on the banks of the Noce river, between Mezzolombardo and the road for the Valle di Non. The terroir here has given this wine a unique character over the past few years. The bouquet unveils well-defined spicy aromas, and there is rich extract on the palate, leading in to a long finish that lends elegance to the natural vigour of the variety. The Teroldego Bottega de' Vinai is lively and youthful, with hints of violets and plums on the nose. Elegant and more subtle than racy in style, it is a most attractive tipple. Praise is also due to the Lagrein Bottega de' Vinai. Similar to the Teroldego (the grapes are, in fact, genetically identical), it offers a deep garnet colour, a full, open nose, and a soft, silky finish. These are thoroughbred reds, worthy of the Trentino region. They vie with the Firmato, this versatile company's top-of-the-range spumante and its most successful product. The other wines are well-managed, above all the Müller Thurgau and the oak-aged Chardonnay. Lastly, the full-bodied Vendemmia Tardiva '97 displays both elegance and good depth of flavour.

O Trentino Müller Thurgau		
Le Croce '99	♈♈	3*
O Trentino Pinot Bianco Sortì '99	♈♈	3*
O Trento Brut M. Cl. '93	♈♈	4
● Teroldego Rotaliano Pini '99	♈	3
● Trentino Moscato Rosa '99	♈	4
O Trentino Nosiola Maso Nero '99	♈	3
● Teroldego Rotaliano '97	♈♈	4
● Teroldego Rotaliano Pini '93	♈♈	4
● Teroldego Rotaliano Pini '95	♈♈	4
O Trentino Müller Thurgau		
Le Croce '97	♈♈	4
● Trentino Pinot Nero Spiazol '97	♈♈	4
● Teroldego Rotaliano '98	♈	3
● Trentino Moscato Rosa '98	♈	4

● Teroldego Rotaliano		
Bottega de' Vinai '99	♈♈	3*
● Teroldego Rotaliano		
Maso Cervara '97	♈♈	4
● Trentino Lagrein		
Bottega de' Vinai '97	♈♈	3*
O Trento Brut Firmato '96	♈♈	4
O Trentino Chardonnay		
Maso Torresella '98	♈	4
O Trentino Müller Thurgau '99	♈	3
O Trentino Vendemmia Tardiva '97	♈	4
O Trento Graal Brut Ris. '93	♈♈♈	4*
● Trentino Marzemino		
Maso Romani '97	♈♈	4
O Trento Graal Brut Ris. '95	♈♈	4

TRENTO

CESARINI SFORZA
FRAZ. RAVINA
VIA STELLA, 9
38040 TRENTO
TEL. 0461/382200

Back in the Guide, and deservedly so, this historic spumante wine company was one of the first in the Trentino region to concentrate its production exclusively on wine with a fizz. These are sparkling wines made with the "metodo classico", and also wines refermented with methods developed and patented by the company itself. Management is securely in the hands of Filippo Cesarini Sforza, a young man determined to bring the company's reputation back to the heights it once commanded for so many years. The cellars are the responsibility of Mauro Merz, an expert oenologist and experienced maker of sparkling wines who has lost no time in upgrading the quality of the range. The past has not been entirely forsworn. Which is why Cesarini Sforza has brought out a new super Riserva dei Conti Brut, a spumante left on the lees for no fewer than ten years before its recent disgorgement. Filippo and Mauro have thus created a flagship wine that embodies the company's intentions. Rich in flavour, full-bodied and mature, it has a steady, delicate perlage and aromas of acacia blossom, apples and wild berries, with a full, complex flavour. The Trento Brut '97 is also excellent. An elegant, uncompromising wine that will cellar magnificently, it unveils an even, delicate perlage and a soft, mouth-filling palate. The Brut Riserva is well-managed and more than acceptable.

○ Brut Riserva dei Conti	▼▼	4
○ Trento Brut '97	▼▼	4
○ Brut Riserva	▼	3
○ Brut Riserva	▽▽	4
○ Brut Riserva dei Conti	▽▽	4
○ Trento Brut	▽▽	5
○ Blanc de Blancs	▽	4
○ Brut Ris. Aquila Reale '92	▽	5
● Trentino Lagrein Villa Graziadei '94	▽	3

TRENTO

★ FERRARI
VIA DEL PONTE DI RAVINA, 15
38040 TRENTO
TEL. 0461/972311

The wines made to see in the new Millennium may be innumerable, but uncorking a bottle of Ferrari is always a pleasure. Especially if the glass is then filled with the latest disgorgement of the Riserva del Fondatore Giulio Ferrari '92. An extraordinary sparkling wine that is fabulously opulent and, above all, stylish to a fault. Excellence of this calibre is rare. It has elegance, length, a well-sustained flavour, steady perlage, complex aromas, smooth toastiness, a broad palate and a taste profile that finds a splendid balance between maturity and clean, refreshing acidity. All this power is kept well under control by the cellarmaster, the noted spumante expert, Mauro Lunelli. The Perlé Millesimato '96 also deserves praise. Made from a rigorous selection of chardonnay grapes and aged on the lees for at least 40 months, it has a creamy, elegant perlage, and is delicate, fresh and floral on the nose. The palate is mature in every respect, a worthy companion to the more famous Riserva del Fondatore. The experience and the skill of the Lunellis can be seen throughout the range. We particularly liked the Perlé Rosé '95, a blush Brut where pinot nero aromas intrigue and seduce with rare success. The standard Brut is just as good as ever. You would never suspect that it is made by the hundreds of thousands of bottles. The other two wines, the Maximum and the Incontri, are easy-drinking, with aromas of white fruit on the nose. However, they are still in the true Ferrari style, albeit for other sectors of an ever more demanding market.

○ Giulio Ferrari '92	▼▼▼	6
○ Trento Brut	▼▼	4
○ Trento Brut Maximum	▼▼	4
○ Trento Brut Perlé '96	▼▼	5
⊙ Trento Brut Perlé Rosé '95	▼▼	4
○ Trento Ferrari Incontri	▼▼	3*
○ Giulio Ferrari '86	▽▽▽	6
○ Giulio Ferrari '88	▽▽▽	6
○ Giulio Ferrari '89	▽▽▽	6
○ Giulio Ferrari '90	▽▽▽	6
○ Giulio Ferrari '91	▽▽▽	6
○ Giulio Ferrari '87	▽▽	6
○ Trento Brut Perlé '93	▽▽	5
○ Trento Brut Perlé '94	▽▽	5
○ Trento Brut Perlé '95	▽▽	5

TRENTO

VOLANO (TN)

VIGNETI DELLE MERIDIANE
LOC. CASTELLER, 6
38100 TRENTO
TEL. 0464/419343

CONCILIO
ZONA INDUSTRIALE 2
38060 VOLANO (TN)
TEL. 0464/411000

Old maps – dating from 1491! – show that the Teroldego vine did not originate in the Rotaliana plain, where it is so proudly cultivated now, but on the slopes overlooking Trento. It may even be possible that its home is the very conical hill upon which now sits the Le Meridiane winery. That is where they make a truly magnificent Teroldego called Cernidor, perhaps the most elegant of all the Teroldegos we have recently tasted and a wine that shows all the viticultural and winemaking skill of the highly experienced, acknowledged red wine specialists in charge of the company. Full-bodied, with substantial alcohol and ready to drink now, this is everything the Teroldego fan needs. In a similar style, and just as good an example of the 1997 vintage, is the Merlot Vigneto San Raimondo. It proffers a very attractive aromatic bouquet, enriched with subtle hints of toasty new wood, and a taste profile that successfully plays softness off against acidity. The Cabernet Vigneto San Bartolomeo (from the same vintage) is only marginally less good. A big, well-rounded and very well-made wine, it flaunts a clean finish that is ever so slightly harsh. The white wines, however, are less impressive. They are clean, technically well-made, and have typical Trentino aromas but signally fail to fascinate. A good example is the Chardonnay Vigneto Fontana Santa. Deep golden yellow in colour, it lays out a good spread of clean, crisp aromas on the nose but totally lacks expression on the palate. The Sauvignon Camp dei Frai is evidently has the makings but it is still closed and vegetal in character. Even after a year in the bottle, both nose and palate play their cards very close to the chest.

Enterprise, tradition and technology. These are the elements that have led to Concilio's success. Used to competing in a market much bigger than the local one, Concilio is a dynamic Vallagarina producer that makes wines with care and dedication in a distinctly traditional Trentino style. Today, the estate's range show how the unique Trentino style of making wines can succeed in a kaleidoscopic international context. This is obvious when one tastes the Chardonnay. It tempts the eye immediately with its lustrous, limpid golden colour and is equally impressive on the nose. There are aromas of ripe apple fruit, certainly, but pineapple and bananas come through as well. The palate is excellent, showing good structure, a sustained mid palate, and good length. There was a good result for the Müller Thurgau, too. Fresh and fruity, it revealed characteristic varietal acidic grip. On the other hand, the Pinot Grigio seemed a little one-dimensional to the panel. Probably, it was the fault of the poor vintage but the wine still manages to retain the grape's essential characteristics. The Pinot Nero Riserva Novaline has a nice bouquet and good fruit, and is as lively as it is elegant on the palate. The other reds are all worth investigating. The Merlot, the Cabernet and the Bordeaux-blend Rosso Mori Vecio are all very well-managed. Finally, a note of praise for the Enantio, a red wine made with the "lambrusco a foglia frastagliata" ("cut-leaf lambrusco") grape, a variety indigenous to Vallagarina, made to satisfy the demand for something a little different. It is fresh, very fruity, and as gluggable as they come.

● Teroldego Atesino Cernidor '97	♚♚	4	
● Trentino Merlot Vigneto San Raimondo Ris. '97	♚♚	4	
● Trentino Cabernet Sauvignon Vigneto San Bartolomeo Ris. '97	♚	4	
○ Trentino Chardonnay Vigneto Fontana Santa '98	♚	4	
○ Trentino Sauvignon Camp dei Frai '98	♚	4	
○ Sauvignon Atesino '97	♛♛	4	
● Teroldego Atesino Cernidor '96	♛♛	4	
● Trentino Merlot Vigneto San Raimondo Ris. '95	♛♛	4	
● Trentino Merlot Vigneto San Raimondo Ris. '96	♛♛	4	

○ Trentino Chardonnay '99	♚♚	3*	
○ Trentino Müller Thurgau '99	♚♚	3*	
● Trentino Pinot Nero Novaline Ris. '97	♚♚	4	
● Enantio '98	♚	3	
● Trentino Cabernet Sauvignon Novaline Ris. '97	♚	4	
● Trentino Merlot Novaline Ris. '97	♚	4	
○ Trentino Pinot Grigio '99	♚	3	
● Trentino Rosso Mori Vecio '98	♚	4	
○ Trentino Chardonnay '98	♛♛	3*	
● Trentino Merlot Novaline Ris. '96	♛♛	4	
○ Trentino Pinot Grigio '98	♛♛	3*	
● Trentino Rosso Mori Vecio '97	♛♛	4	

OTHER WINERIES

The following producers in the province of Trento obtained good scores in our tastings with one or more of their wines:

Alessandro Secchi,
Ala, tel. 0464/696647
Trentino Merlot '98
Trentino Pinot Nero '98,

Cantina di Toblino,
Calavino, tel. 0461/564168
Trentino Cabernet '98,
Trentino Nosiola '99

Gino Pedrotti,
Cavedine, tel. 0461/564123
Trentino Vino Santo '88

Maso Bergamini,
Cognola, tel. 0461/983079
Bianco Maso Bergamini '98,
Trentino Moscato Rosa '99

Arcangelo Sandri,
Faedo, tel. 0461/650935
Trentino Müller Thuragu '99

Renzo Gorga, Folgaria, tel. 0464/721161
Trentino Marzemino Paradaia '98

Abate Nero,
Gardolo, tel. 0461/246566
Trento Brut,
Trento Brut M. Cl. Abate Nero Ris. '96

Conti Bossi Fedrigotti,
Isera, tel. 0464/439250
Conte Federico '94,
Trentino Cabernet '97,
Trentino Marzemino '99

Rosi,
Isera, tel. 0464/486057
Trentino Rosso Esegesi '97

Molino dei Lessi,
Lavis, tel. 0461/870275
Cabernet Sauvignon dei Sorni '97

Maso Martis,
Martignano, tel. 0461/820394
Trentino Chardonnay '99,
Trento Brut Riserva '94

Cipriano Fedrizzi,
Mezzolombardo, tel. 0461/602328
Teroldego Rotaliano Due Vigneti '97

Battistotti,
Nomi, tel. 0464/834145
Trentino Marzemino '99,
Trentino Moscato Rosa '99

Grigoletti,
Nomi, tel. 0464/834215
Trentino Chardonnay L'Opera '99,
Trentino Merlot Antica Vigna '97

Dalzocchio,
Rovereto, tel. 0464/413461
Trentino Chardonnay '98

Giulio Poli,
Santa Massenza, tel. 0461/350443
Schiava Valle dei Laghi '99

Bailoni,
Trento, tel. 0461/911842
Teroldego Rotaliano '99,
Trentino Chardonnay '99,
Trentino Müller Thurgau '99

ALTO ADIGE

"Onward and upward". This slogan from an old Italian advertising campaign is also the most appropriate way of summing up in a single phrase what is taking place on the Alto Adige wine scene. Again this year, there are 52 individual entries in our Guide while the number of Three Glass wines rises to 17. Not bad at all, really. If our arithmetic is to be trusted, then almost one in three of the producers present hit the target. It's an impressive result but one that conveys an idea of the general level of quality in Alto Adige, born of a happy mix of co-operative wineries, large commercial estates and small to medium–sized wineries offering a wealth of styles and wine types that is almost unequalled in Italy or abroad. Here, you can find great indigenous grape varieties like lagrein and gewürztraminer, as well as international grapes from different oenological traditions, such as pinot bianco, sauvignon, chardonnay, riesling, sylvaner, kerner, veltliner and müller thurgau, or red grapes like pinot nero, cabernet and merlot. All of them manage to find extraordinary expression thanks to the very wide range of soil types and climatic conditions, which can offer completely different scenarios a relatively short distance apart. So, from the sun-drenched hillsides of Cortaccia and Caldaro, you pass within the space of only 50 or at most 60 kilometres to the vine-growing districts of the Valle Isarco DOC zone, an area where conditions are almost prohibitive for viticulture. There is everything from potent, California-style Cabernets, to perfumed, high-acid Veltliners and almost aromatic Sylvaners that recall whites from Baden or Wachau. Everything is backed up by extremely efficient winery operations, by oenologists who here go under the name of "Kellermeister", and by producers as serious and competent as you will find anywhere in the world. This year, we awarded Three Glasses to enthusiastic growers such as Peter Pilger, Josephus Mayr and Franz Haas, as well as to the large Colterenzio co-operative winery, to brilliant producers and managers like Martin Foradori of Hofstätter, or Elena Walch of Castel Ringberg & Kastelaz. Each of these, in his or her own way, represents the top level of quality which it is currently possible to achieve in their given zone. The results, then, are frankly positive. Our notes were very flattering after our visit to the Chamber of Commerce in Bolzano for the Guide tastings where at least 100 of the over 500 wines sampled were truly outstanding. There is perhaps no other region of Italy capable of such consistency. We therefore strongly urge you, too, to enjoy these fantastic wines and visit their producers, many of whom offer cellar-door sales. Let yourself be seduced by a region where many different cultures meet and where, finally, they have learned to co-exist in a civilized manner.

ANDRIANO/ANDRIAN (BZ)   APPIANO/EPPAN (BZ)

CANTINA PRODUTTORI ANDRIANO
VIA DELLA CHIESA, 2
39010 ANDRIANO/ANDRIAN (BZ)
TEL. 0471/510137

JOSEF BRIGL
FRAZ. CORNAIANO
VIA S. FLORIANO, 8
39057 APPIANO/EPPAN (BZ)
TEL. 0471/662419

The Cantina Produttori Andriano offers us a fairly wide selection of wines each year but one that is always very reliable. The heart of the range is represented by the whites, many of which come from the subzone of Terlano, to the west of Bolzano. Yet this year, the best products were two reds, the Lagrein Scuro '98 and the Cabernet '98, from the winery's premium Tor di Lupo line. These are both powerful, concentrated red wines. The Lagrein impresses with the way it brings out the classic varietal characteristics and because technically, it is a very skilful piece of winemaking. Moving on to the whites, the Chardonnay and the Sauvignon, again from the Tor di Lupo line, are as good as ever. The former is aged in small oak casks and in fact the wood is perhaps a little too obvious on the nose. The Sauvignon is very varietal but suffers a little from the not particularly successful vintage, which makes it a tiny bit intractable on the palate. The Terlano Pinot Bianco Classico Sonnenhof '99 is pleasant and quite attractively priced. It is a linear, well-made and reasonably elegant wine. All the other wines presented were decent, with the Terlano Müller Thurgau '99 standing out in the value for money stakes and the Schiava Sancta Giustina '99 for its fragrant easy-drinking style.

This is one of the largest wineries in Alto Adige. For some years now, it has also been a dependable brand with a wide selection of wines, almost all of which are of a more than acceptable standard. This has a positive effect on Alto Adige wine as a whole, which can benefit from the distribution network of a company that manages to export its wines just about everywhere on the planet. Of the wines we tasted this year, we were particularly struck by the elegant and typically varietal Sauvignon '99. It may not be a blockbuster but it is irreproachable from a technical point of view. Then there is a long list of sound products, including the oak-aged Chardonnay Thurnerhof '99. The wood tends to mask the fruit a little on the nose but it is already displaying appreciable quality and fairly good concentration. The Lagrein Scuro '97 is not bad, either. Well-typed and reasonably varietal in style, it has medium depth on the palate. It comes from a very good vintage and this is abundantly evident in the wine. All the other wines were pleasant and well-made, although a special mention must go to the Lago di Caldaro Scelto Classico Haslhof '99, which is becoming one of Brigl's specialities.

● A. A. Cabernet Tor di Lupo '98	♟♟	5
● A. A. Lagrein Scuro Tor di Lupo '98	♟♟	4
○ A. A. Chardonnay Tor di Lupo '98	♟	4
○ A. A. Gewürztraminer '99	♟	2*
● A. A. Merlot Siebeneich '98	♟	4
● A. A. Santa Maddalena '99	♟	3
● A. A. Schiava S. Giustina '99	♟	2*
○ A. A. Terlano Müller Thurgau '99	♟	2*
○ A. A. Terlano Pinot Bianco Cl. Sonnenhof '99	♟	3
○ A. A. Terlano Sauvignon Preciosa Tor di Lupo '99	♟	3
○ A. A. Chardonnay Tor di Lupo '97	♟♟	4
● A. A. Lagrein Scuro Tor di Lupo '97	♟♟	4
● A. A. Merlot Siebeneich '97	♟♟	4

○ A. A. Sauvignon '99	♟♟	3*
○ A. A. Chardonnay '99	♟	3
○ A. A. Chardonnay Thurnerhof '99	♟	4
○ A. A. Gewürztraminer Windegg '99	♟	3
● A. A. Lago di Caldaro Scelto Haslhof '99	♟	3
◉ A. A. Lagrein Rosato '99	♟	3
● A. A. Lagrein Scuro '97	♟	3
● A. A. Merlot Windegg '97	♟	3
○ A. A. Müller Thurgau '99	♟	3
● A. A. Santa Maddalena Reierhof Monika Brigl '99	♟	3
○ A. A. Sauvignon '98	♟♟	3*
● A. A. Pinot Nero Haslhof '97	♟	4

APPIANO/EPPAN (BZ)

APPIANO/EPPAN (BZ)

CANTINA PRODUTTORI SAN MICHELE
APPIANO/ST. MICHAEL EPPAN
VIA CIRCONVALLAZIONE, 17/19
39057 APPIANO/EPPAN (BZ)
TEL. 0471/664466

CANTINA PRODUTTORI SAN PAOLO/
KELLEREIGENOSSENSCHAFT ST. PAULS
VIA CASTEL GUARDIA, 21
39050 APPIANO/EPPAN (BZ)
TEL. 0471/662183

Barely a year after last year's triumph – three Three Glass wines and the Guide's Winery of the Year title – the San Michele Appiano co-operative confirms its standing in the front rank of Alto Adige producers. The showing this year was certainly positive but not one that can be compared to the triumphs of 2000. But this has rather more to do with the quality of the '99 vintage than with the ability of Kellermeister Hans Terzer, or any lapses of concentration in the winery. There is, however, the usual spectacular Sauvignon Sanct Valentin. Perhaps it is a little subtler this year but it is just as brilliantly varietal and elegant as in the past and sailed through to another Three Glass award. The '97 Cabernet, perhaps the best yet from this winery, is very good and a clear signal that Terzer can no longer just be considered a white wine specialist. Then there is a whole series of exemplary, well-made, elegant, dependable wines. The two Chardonnays, the Sanct Valentin '98 and the Merol '99, are excellent, with the latter beginning to look like rather more than just a younger brother of the Sanct Valentin. The oak is handled perfectly in both, so that the varietal characteristics shine through, and both are satisfyingly easy to drink. Then there are the following well-made wines from the Sanct Valentin line, the Pinot Nero '97, the Pinot Grigio '98 and the Gewürztraminer '99. The last of these is less complex than the '98 version but still very well-crafted. Finally, there are the less demanding wines, the rather lightweight Riesling Montiggl '99, the Pinot Bianco Schulthauser '99, also very much a product of this poorish vintage, and the Sauvignon Lahn '99, which is varietal, but less concentrated than usual.

No one could say that the wines of the Cantina Produttori San Paolo are not well-made, or that they reveal any particular fault or other. They are as sound as they come and the standard of the winemaking is beyond reproach. But perhaps they are just a shade too simple, or lack a bit of character and concentration. At least, that was the case with the wines submitted to us this year. This is no doubt due in part to the vintages on show for this edition of the Guide. The '99 harvest was not a great one for whites nor was '98 anything special for reds. Nonetheless, we still got the impression that these wines lack a little bit of grip and gusto. They are well-made, in a textbook sort of way, but they do not really have sufficient impact. The panel was never tempted to leap out of its collective chair and cry, "Just get a taste of this!". It is equally true that criticising, as we do, is the easy part. It is not so simple to make great wines every year. However, there are some perfectly decent products available here at the Cantina Produttori San Paolo. The Sauvignon Gfilhof in the Exklusiv line is a good wine, offering a certain structure and reasonable varietal aromas. The Pinot Grigio Egg-Leitn is fairly interesting, too. It is also very varietal, with ripe pear notes on the nose and decent concentration on the palate. All the other wines are in line with the average standard for the region, which, as we mentioned in the introduction, is rather high. We gave slightly higher marks to the Lagrein Scuro DiVinus than to the other reds. Perhaps unsurprisingly, it was the only '97 on offer.

○ A. A. Sauvignon St. Valentin '99	♟♟♟	4*
● A. A. Cabernet Sauvignon St. Valentin '97	♟♟	5
○ A. A. Chardonnay Merol '99	♟♟	3*
○ A. A. Chardonnay St. Valentin '98	♟♟	4
○ A. A. Gewürztraminer St. Valentin '99	♟♟	4
● A. A. Pinot Nero St. Valentin '97	♟♟	5
○ A. A. Pinot Bianco Schulthauser '99	♟	3
○ A. A. Riesling Montiggl '99	♟	3
○ A. A. Sauvignon Lahn '99	♟	3
○ A. A. Chardonnay St. Valentin '97	♟♟♟	4*
○ A. A. Gewürztraminer St. Valentin '98	♟♟♟	4*
○ A. A. Sauvignon St. Valentin '97	♟♟♟	4*
○ A. A. Sauvignon St. Valentin '98	♟♟♟	4*

○ A. A. Chardonnay DiVinus '99	♟	4
● A. A. Lagrein Scuro DiVinus Ris. '97	♟	5
● A. A. Merlot DiVinus '98	♟	5
○ A. A. Pinot Grigio Exklusiv Egg-Leitn '99	♟	4
○ A. A. Sauvignon Exklusiv Gfilhof '99	♟	4
○ A. A. Terlano Pinot Bianco Exklusiv Plötzner '99	♟	4
● A. A. Lagrein Scuro Exklusiv Gries Ris. '95	♟♟	4
● A. A. Lagrein Scuro Exklusiv Gries Ris. '96	♟♟	5
● A. A. Merlot DiVinus '97	♟♟	5
○ A. A. Pinot Bianco '98	♟♟	3*

APPIANO/EPPAN (BZ)

KÖSSLER - PRAECLARUS
SAN PAOLO/ST. PAULS
39057 APPIANO/EPPAN (BZ)
TEL. 0471/660256 - 0471/662182

This is a very innovative winery, with a particularly varied range, including some wines that are unusual in the slightly austere, conservative panorama of Alto Adige winemaking. In origin, the estate was one of the region's top producers of sparkling wine. The Praeclarus Brut and the Noblesse Riserva have always been among the best products of the zone. This year, the '91 vintage of the 70 percent chardonnay and 30 percent pinot nero Noblesse Riserva is quite spectacular. However, there is lots of news – and several new wines – this year. It is worth pausing to sample the excellent Alto Adige Bianco '99, aged for three months in barriques and made from a blend of 50 percent chardonnay, 30 percent sauvignon and 20 percent pinot bianco. It is elegant and concentrated yet very easy to drink. Then there are the three premium reds. The Merlot-Lagrein Ebner '97 is very well-balanced and unveils good, weighty extract. The Cabernet-Merlot St Pauls '97 is perhaps the most classic of the Kössler wines and the Cabernet Kössler & Ebner, also a '97, is stylish but not enormously well-structured. The other bottles are a series of well-crafted, easy-drinking wines, like the extremely fruity Pinot Nero Kössler & Ebner or the fragrant and attractive Terlano Pinot Bianco Spiegelleiten '99. More predictable in style, but still well-made, are the Gewürztraminer Joannisbrunnen '99, which has a slightly dilute aromatic profile, and the straightforward, quaffable Schiava St. Justina, another '99.

APPIANO/EPPAN (BZ)

STROBLHOF
FRAZ. S. MICHELE
VIA PIGANO, 25
39057 APPIANO/EPPAN (BZ)
TEL. 0471/662250

Stroblhof started making its own wines back in the 19th century. They were a Schiava and the Pinto Bianco Strahler, the two typical varieties of the zone. Then 30 years ago, the first gewürztraminer and pinot nero vines were planted and it was the pinot nero that was eventually to make this small estate's name. With the '85 and '88 vintages, it managed to grab the limelight and in the '90, Stroblhof presented a Pinot Nero of extraordinary quality. After a period of difficulty, sisters Rosmarie and Christine Hanny, together with Rosemarie's husband, Andreas Nicolussi-Leck, cellar manager and responsible for the winery since 1995, today run a thriving business. This year, we were particularly amazed by the Pinot Nero Riserva '97, a stunning example of a great Pinot Nero from a great vintage. Pale ruby in colour, it has a very intense, complex nose, with typically elegant fruitiness. On the palate, it is rich, powerful and well-balanced. It missed out on a Three Glass rating by the merest of whiskers. The Pinot Bianco Strahler '99 is a minor classic of Alto Adige winemaking. It has a straw-yellow hue with golden highlights, and a very intense varietal nose of apple fruit aromas with faint toasty notes from the wine's partial ageing in barriques. The flavour is very correct, fresh and tangy. The Gewürztraminer '99, one of the very best in its category in the previous vintage, did not, unfortunately, really impress us this year, even though we tasted it on two separate occasions. It seemed a bit straightforward and lacking in complexity compared to its illustrious forebears. Lastly, the fairly rich, full-bodied Chardonnay '98 was good.

○	A. A. Bianco '99	♥♥	5
●	A. A. Cabernet Kössler & Ebner '97	♥♥	4
●	A. A. Cabernet-Merlot S. Pauls '97	♥♥	5
●	A. A. Merlot-Lagrein Ebner '97	♥♥	5
○	A. A. Spumante Praeclarus Noblesse Ris. '91	♥♥	6
○	A. A. Gewürztraminer Joannisbrunnen '99	♥	4
●	A. A. Pinot Nero Kössler & Ebner '97	♥	5
●	A. A. Schiava Weingut St. Justina '99	♥	3
○	A. A. Spumante Praeclarus Brut	♥	5
○	A. A. Terlano Pinot Bianco Spiegelleiten '99	♥	3

○	A. A. Pinot Bianco Strahler '99	♥♥	3*
●	A. A. Pinot Nero Ris. '97	♥♥	5
○	A. A. Chardonnay '98	♥	3
○	A. A. Gewürztraminer '99	♥	4
○	A. A. Gewürztraminer '97	♀♀	4
○	A. A. Gewürztraminer '98	♀♀	4
○	A. A. Pinot Bianco Strahler '97	♀♀	3*
○	A. A. Pinot Bianco Strahler '98	♀♀	3*
●	A. A. Pinot Nero Ris. '91	♀♀	4
●	A. A. Pinot Nero Ris. '96	♀♀	5
●	A. A. Pinot Nero Strahler Ris. '90	♀♀	5
○	A. A. Chardonnay '97	♀	4
●	A. A. Pinot Nero Ris. '93	♀	4
●	A. A. Pinot Nero Ris. '95	♀	5

BOLZANO/BOZEN

BOLZANO/BOZEN

ANDREAS BERGER THURMHOF
VIA CASTEL FLAVON, 7
39100 BOLZANO/BOZEN
TEL. 0471/288460

CANTINA CONVENTO MURI-GRIES
P.ZZA GRIES, 21
39100 BOLZANO/BOZEN
TEL. 0471/282287

A small selection of wines of outstanding quality. That, in a nutshell, is our report on the products that this famous Bolzano-based winery presented us with this year. Particularly exciting were the two Lagreins, the real speciality of this producer. The '98 is rich and elegant, with intense aromas that are already quite complex. Its fruit literally explodes on the palate with wonderful force and concentration. It just missed a third Glass but came in the top three wines in its category and vintage. The Lagrein Scuro Riserva '97 is even more impressive, with its impenetrable colour and its intense spicy bouquet that reveals marked pepper and bilberry notes. It displays excellent body on the palate, as well as abundant, compact tannins, which are reasonably well-integrated into the general structure of the wine. The Passarum is very interesting. It is a white "vino da tavola" which does not, therefore, declare its vintage on the label. It offers scents of ripe apricots and a full-bodied, concentrated but perhaps slightly one-dimensional flavour. However, it is a wine of excellent structure that could even be cellared for a few years. The range is completed by the Sauvignon '99, which is a very correct, pleasant and fairly varietal white, but nothing more.

Alto Adige's big chance to be numbered, finally, among the most important wine-producing regions of Europe is called Lagrein Scuro, or Dunkel, as they say in these parts. It is an extraordinary wine that when well-executed can stand shoulder to shoulder with the best Rhône valley Syrahs. The abbey of Muri-Gries is undoubtedly the best producer of this remarkable wine. The Lagrein Scuro Riserva '97 is perhaps the finest Lagrein ever made in the region. It has everything, starting with an almost impenetrable colour, which leads in to its spicy and fruity aromas, with notes of freshly ground pepper, bilberries and tobacco. Then the palate shows an intense, powerful, rich flavour, with compact, but not at all aggressive, tannins and an amazingly long finish. This is a great wine that comes from a very specific area, situated just south of Bolzano. Here you will find gravel soils, pergolas that are progressively giving way to the more efficient Guyot system of training, and masterly use of new oak barrels. There are no hidden secrets. This wine is accompanied by the only slightly less complex Lagrein Scuro '98, the delicious Alto Adige Terlano Pinot Bianco '99, the fragrant and straightforward Lagrein Rosato, or Kretzer, also a '99, and the Alto Adige Pinot Grigio, another '99 that is perhaps the least characterful and certainly the least convincing of the abbey's wines this year. So, the very likeable Benedictine monks of Muri-Gries, true wizards when it comes to interpreting Lagrein, have again, deservedly, joined our Three Glass club.

● A. A. Lagrein Scuro '98	♟♟	4
● A. A. Lagrein Scuro Ris. '97	♟♟	5
○ Passarum	♟♟	5
○ A. A. Sauvignon '99	♟	3
● A. A. Cabernet '93	♟♟	4
● A. A. Cabernet Wienegg Ris. '94	♟♟	4
● A. A. Lagrein Scuro '95	♟♟	5
● A. A. Cabernet '91	♟	4
● A. A. Cabernet Sauvignon Weinegg Ris. '95	♟	5
● A. A. Santa Maddalena '93	♟	3

● A. A. Lagrein Scuro Ris. '97	♟♟♟	6
● A. A. Lagrein Scuro '98	♟♟	4
○ A. A. Terlano Pinot Bianco '99	♟♟	4
⊙ A. A. Lagrein Rosato '99	♟	3
○ A. A. Pinot Grigio '99	♟	3
● A. A. Lagrein Abtei Ris. '96	♟♟♟	5
● A. A. Cabernet Ris. '91	♟♟	5
● A. A. Lagrein Abtei Ris. '92	♟♟	5
● A. A. Lagrein Abtei Ris. '94	♟♟	5
● A. A. Lagrein Ris. '90	♟♟	4
● A. A. Lagrein Scuro Gries '95	♟♟	4
● A. A. Lagrein Scuro Gries '97	♟♟	2*
● A. A. Lagrein '91	♟	4
● A. A. Lagrein '92	♟	4
● A. A. Lagrein Scuro Gries '98	♟	4

BOLZANO/BOZEN

BOLZANO/BOZEN

CANTINA DI GRIES
P.ZZA GRIES, 2
39100 BOLZANO/BOZEN
TEL. 0471/270909

CANTINA PRODUTTORI
SANTA MADDALENA
VIA BRENNERO, 15
39100 BOLZANO/BOZEN
TEL. 0471/972944

This is one of the most important wineries producing Lagrein Scuro. Gries, on the southern outskirts of Bolzano, is in fact the heartland of production for this ancient and traditional Alto Adige red. This year, though, the Cantina di Gries is not among the handful of producers who obtain our highest accolade. The wine that came closest to a Three Glass rating is the Lagrein Scuro Baron Carl Eyrl Riserva '97, in which the oak and the fruit are very successfully integrated. It displays good structure and concentration but is not dominated by slightly too strong overtones of vanilla on the nose and palate, as is the case with the Prestige Line '97, whose tasting profile is rather too marked by the oak of the barriques. The Lagrein Scuro Grieser '98, one of the winery's standard products, is almost preferable to the Prestige Line version. It does not possess the concentration of its big brother but it is rather more coherent and elegant. But then power is not, nor should it ever be, the only criterion for judging a wine. The Mauritius, made predominantly from cabernet grapes, is as good as ever. This time around it is the '97 that is on show, the product of a particularly favourable vintage for the zone. The Merlot '98, on the other hand, is less exciting than last year and perhaps it is for this reason that it appears under the Collection Otto Graf Huyn label and not in the Prestige Line, the cellar's top range. It is well-made but a little dilute, with slightly overbearing acidity. Lastly, there are the more simple wines, with a good Terlano Pinot Bianco '99, which is better than the Collection Fritz Dellago version, and a decent Santa Maddalena Tröglerhof, also from the '99 vintage.

The Lagrein Taberhof from the Cantina Produttori Santa Maddalena is one of the best red wines from Alto Adige. In the course of a vertical tasting organised by Stephan Filippi, the winery's "Kellermeister", we were able to note how the '92 and the '95 are now fabulous wines, on a par with many of the world's most famous reds. You have to give it a bit of time. The mineral complexity only really shows through after five years, but isn't that equally true of a Barolo or a Pommard? All of this preamble is by way of explaining that the '98 version of the Taberhof is still a very youthful wine. There is lots of fruit and vanilla on the nose, as well as concentrated, but not yet perfectly balanced flavours. The panel liked this wine a great deal anyway, considering it in terms of potential. It seemed quite capable of shouldering the responsibility of a Three Glass accolade, so we duly awarded it one. Besides, the whole range on offer from this winery is of real interest. The Santa Maddalena Huck am Bach '99 for example, is delicious. It is a fantastic, youthful and very fragrant red, as easy-drinking and delicious as they come. The Chardonnay Kleinstein '99 and the Sauvignon Mockhof '99 are both good, giving the lie to this winery's reputation as being a producer of only red wines. The concentrated, elegant Lagrein Scuro Perlhof '98 is very sound. All the other wines are agreeable, including a noteworthy basic '99 Pinot Bianco, which is straightforward and fragrant, and the characteristic Santa Maddalena Classico '99. The Müller Thurgau is less rich, but still well-made.

●	A. A. Lagrein Scuro Grieser '98	🍷🍷	4
●	A. A. Lagrein Scuro Grieser Baron Carl Eyrl Ris. '97	🍷🍷	5
●	A. A. Lagrein Scuro Grieser Prestige Line Ris. '97	🍷🍷	5
●	Mauritius '97	🍷🍷	5
●	A. A. Merlot Otto Graf Huyn Ris. '98	🍷	5
○	A. A. Pinot Bianco Fritz Dellago '99	🍷	3
●	A. A. Santa Maddalena Cl. Tröglerhof '99	🍷	3
○	A. A. Terlano Pinot Bianco '99	🍷	3
◉	A. A. Lagrein Rosato '99		2
●	A. A. Santa Maddalena '99		3

○	A. A. Lagrein Scuro Taberhof '98	🍷🍷🍷	5
○	A. A. Chardonnay Kleinstein '99	🍷🍷	4
●	A. A. Lagrein Scuro Perlhof '98	🍷🍷	4
○	A. A. Pinot Bianco '99	🍷🍷	3*
●	A. A. Santa Maddalena Cl. Huck am Bach '99	🍷🍷	3*
○	A. A. Sauvignon Mockhof '99	🍷🍷	4
●	A. A. Santa Maddalena Cl. '99	🍷	2*
○	A. A. Valle Isarco Müller Thurgau '99	🍷	3
●	A. A. Cabernet Mumelterhof '94	🍷🍷🍷	3*
●	A. A. Cabernet Mumelterhof '95	🍷🍷🍷	4*
●	A. A. Cabernet Mumelterhof '97	🍷🍷🍷	5
●	A. A. Lagrein Scuro Taberhof Ris. '95	🍷🍷🍷	4*
●	A. A. Santa Maddalena Cl. Huck am Bach '98	🍷🍷	4

BOLZANO/BOZEN

BOLZANO/BOZEN

FRANZ GOJER GLÖGGLHOF
FRAZ. ST. MAGDALENA
VIA RIVELLONE, 1
39100 BOLZANO/BOZEN
TEL. 0471/978775

THOMAS MAYR E FIGLI
VIA MENDOLA, 56
39100 BOLZANO/BOZEN
TEL. 0471/281030

Five wines presented this year, and five Two Glass awards. A notable success for Franz Gojer, the winemaking dynamo behind the small producers in the famous Santa Maddalena zone. Three and a half hectares of vineyard are cultivated by Franz and his family, with a commercial production of around 35,000 bottles and the Santa Maddalena is the winery's flagship product. The standard version, the Santa Maddalena Classico '99, is extremely agreeable and very fruity, with cherry notes and rose overtones. It is fragrant, flavoursome and delightfully easy to drink. The Santa Maddalena Rondell '99 has a ruby red colour and very intense, elegant, fruit aromas and more concentrated, softer and fuller fruit on the palate. The rich, powerful Lagrein Scuro '99, an extremely concentrated, tannic wine, is the basic Lagrein. A highly attractive wine at a very reasonable price indeed. The barrique-aged Lagrein Scuro Riserva '98 is a truly outstanding red. A concentrated ruby in colour, it displays a very intense bouquet, with notes of berry fruit, mulberry and vanilla. The flavour is rich and tannic, with faintly bitterish hints, and offers a pleasant fruity finish. The wine that impressed us most this year, however, is the Merlot Spitz '98, the estate's first release of this particular product. It is made almost entirely from merlot, although there is also five percent lagrein, and matures in small barrels. It has an extremely concentrated opaque ruby colour and offers intense aromas of wild berries, with light vegetal notes. On the palate, it reveals great structure, soft fruit, balance and excellent length. A technically perfect Merlot, with great class and personality.

The real heroes of the Alto Adige viticultural scene are often almost unknown growers of very traditional grape varieties, deeply rooted to their particular terroir. Many of these growers are members of the several fine quality co-operative wineries in the zone, so we shall probably never be able to find out about them, their work or the wines produced from their grapes. Some growers, though, produce and bottle their own wines, sometimes obtaining excellent results. These were our thoughts as we were tasting the delicious Santa Maddalena Rumperhof '99 from the Thomas Mayr e Figli winery. A straightforward, fragrant and delightfully quaffable red. It is made from schiava and lagrein grapes grown in the Santa Maddalena Classico zone which takes its name from a hill of the same name. This summit, completely covered with pergola-trained vines, lies just to the north of the city of Bolzano. Just try it at cellar temperature with a home-cured "speck" smoked ham, cut into little cubes and served with local bread and horseradish sauce. Ten minutes of total pleasure. Who says that all wines have to be powerful and concentrated to be good? The '98 Lagrein Scuro S. (does this stand for "Selezione"?) is also good, confirming the impression we had from the '97 version. All the estate's other wines are decent. The Schiava '99 is delicate and easy to drink while the Lagrein Scuro '99 is characteristic and well-balanced. Overall, then, this estate confirms its worth, demonstrating how even some of the region's small producers can make a very positive contribution to the Alto Adige's high-quality winemaking sector.

● A. A. Lagrein Scuro '99	🍷🍷	3*
● A. A. Lagrein Scuro Ris. '98	🍷🍷	4
● A. A. Merlot Spitz '98	🍷🍷	4
● A. A. Santa Maddalena Cl. '99	🍷🍷	2*
● A. A. Santa Maddalena Rondell '99	🍷🍷	2*
● A. A. Lagrein Scuro Ris. '96	🍷🍷	5
● A. A. Santa Maddalena Cl. '95	🍷🍷	3*
● A. A. Santa Maddalena Cl. '97	🍷🍷	3*
● A. A. Santa Maddalena Cl. '98	🍷🍷	3*
● A. A. Santa Maddalena Rondell '93	🍷🍷	4
● A. A. Santa Maddalena Rondell '95	🍷🍷	3*
● A. A. Santa Maddalena Rondell '98	🍷🍷	3*
● A. A. Santa Maddalena Rondell '96	🍷	3
● A. A. Santa Maddalena Rondell '97	🍷	3

● A. A. Lagrein Scuro S. '98	🍷🍷	4
● A. A. Santa Maddalena Cl. Rumplerhof '99	🍷🍷	3*
● A. A. Lagrein Scuro '99	🍷	3
● A. A. Schiava '99	🍷	2*
⊙ A. A. Lagrein Rosato '99		2
● A. A. Lagrein Scuro '93	🍷🍷	3*
● A. A. Lagrein Scuro '95	🍷🍷	3*
● A. A. Lagrein Scuro Ris. '92	🍷🍷	5
● A. A. Lagrein Scuro Ris. '94	🍷🍷	4
● A. A. Lagrein Scuro Ris. '96	🍷🍷	4
● A. A. Lagrein Scuro S. '97	🍷🍷	4
● A. A. Santa Maddalena Cl. Rumplerhof '98	🍷🍷	3*
● Creazione Rosa '95	🍷🍷	5

BOLZANO/BOZEN

BOLZANO/BOZEN

HEINRICH PLATTNER - WALDGRIES
SANTA GIUSTINA, 2
39100 BOLZANO/BOZEN
TEL. 0471/973245

GEORG RAMOSER
LOC. S. MADDALENA
39100 BOLZANO/BOZEN
TEL. 0471/975481

The hill of Santa Giustina, on which the Waldgrieshof vineyards lie, is situated in the Santa Maddalena Classico zone just outside Bolzano. The history of the Plattner family is a fine example of the centuries–old tradition shared by many Alto Adige growers. Father and son team, Heinrich and Christian Plattner, have available, in their five hectares of vines and in their historic winery, all the agronomic and technical prerequisites for making premium-quality wines. Apart from the Santa Maddalena, it is the Lagrein and the Cabernet Sauvignon that get the most attention at the Plattner winery but of course we should not forget the sweet wines that have become the feather in the estate's cap. Again this year, we found the Lagrein Scuro Riserva '98 to be fantastic. A very concentrated ruby in colour, it has scents of berry fruit and cocoa on the nose, and is full-bodied, rounded and elegant on the palate, where there is also slight rustic roughness. The Cabernet Sauvignon '98 is splendid, too. An intense ruby colour and a very varietal nose, with black cherry notes and aromas of toasted oak, lead in to the well-structured fruit and good length of the palate. Moving on to the sweet wines, pride of place goes to the Peperum '98, one of the best dessert wines in the zone. Made from moscato giallo grapes, it has a brilliant golden colour and very intense, complex perfumes with caramel notes, and very full, yet elegant structure on the palate. The Moscato Rosa '98 displays less aromatic tones compared to the previous vintage but is similarly elegant and very true to type. The Santa Maddalena Classico '99 is correct, fragrant and makes very pleasant drinking. The Terlano Pinot Bianco '99, on the other hand, seems to us, as we also remarked last year, the least convincing wine in the range.

Lots of hard work and a very definite idea of what wine is all about have enabled young Alto Adige grower-producer, Georg Ramoser, to become firmly established as one of the region's finest producers. In '82, he took over the management of Untermoserhof, the old family farm, founded in 1370. He now cultivates four hectares of vines, with a production of around 30,000 bottles a year. The wines that are closest to Ramoser's heart are the Santa Maddalena and the Lagrein. Matured in oak barrels of different sizes, they are both very well-structured, with ripe, tangily fruity aromas. These wines are a bit closed when young, but have excellent ageing potential. Extremely limited yields in the vineyard are just one of the prerequisites for making wines of this quality. The Santa Maddalena Classico Untermoserhof '99 has an intense ruby hue, a complex, fresh, fruity bouquet and a juicy, full-bodied flavour. The Lagrein Riserva '98, from grapes grown on clay and gravel soil, is fermented in stainless steel and matured in barriques. It does not possess the grandeur of its predecessor from the '97 vintage but it is still a very fine wine. It has a deep ruby colour and an intense bouquet of mulberries and cherries. On the palate, it is elegant and subtle, yet powerful, with youthful, slightly over-aggressive tannins to the fore. Over the last few vintages, Ramoser has become particularly fond of another variety, merlot, of which he planted a plot of around half a hectare in '92. The '98 release is an excellent red. An impenetrable ruby in colour, it offers complex aromas of mulberries and pencil lead, with a well-integrated overtone of oak as well. Very full and rich in the mouth, too, it is highly quaffable, with lingering fruit and a very impressive finish.

● A. A. Lagrein Scuro Ris. '98	▼▼	4
● A. A. Moscato Rosa '98	▼▼	4
○ Peperum Bianco '98	▼▼	4
● A. A. Cabernet Sauvignon '98	▼▼	4
● A. A. Santa Maddalena Cl. '99	▼	2*
○ A. A. Terlano Pinot Bianco '99	▼	2*
● A. A. Cabernet Sauvignon '94	♀♀	5
● A. A. Cabernet Sauvignon '95	♀♀	5
● A. A. Cabernet Sauvignon '96	♀♀	5
● A. A. Lagrein Scuro '95	♀♀	4
● A. A. Lagrein Scuro Ris. '96	♀♀	4
● A. A. Lagrein Scuro Ris. '97	♀♀	5
● A. A. Moscato Rosa '97	♀♀	5
○ A. A. Pinot Grigio '98	♀♀	3*
● A. A. Santa Maddalena Cl. '98	♀♀	3*

● A. A. Lagrein Scuro Untermoserhof Ris. '98	▼▼	4
● A. A. Merlot Untermoserhof '98	▼▼	4
● A. A. Santa Maddalena Cl. Untermoserhof '99	▼▼	2*
● A. A. Lagrein Scuro Untermoserhof Ris. '97	♀♀♀	4*
● A. A. Lagrein Scuro Untermoserhof Ris. '96	♀♀	4
● A. A. Merlot Untermoserhof '97	♀♀	5
● A. A. Santa Maddalena Cl. Untermoserhof '97	♀♀	3*
● A. A. Santa Maddalena Cl. Untermoserhof '98	♀♀	3*

BOLZANO/BOZEN

BOLZANO/BOZEN

HANS ROTTENSTEINER
VIA SARENTINO, 1/A
39100 BOLZANO/BOZEN
TEL. 0471/282015

HEINRICH ROTTENSTEINER
LOC. S. MADDALENA
39100 BOLZANO/BOZEN
TEL. 0471/973549

The report on Hans Rottensteiner's wines in this year's Guide is a very favourable one but before we talk about the products themselves, the first thing we have to do is to point out an error we made in the 2000 edition. The Santa Maddalena Premstallerhof '98 in fact, finished up in another producer's entry and did not therefore appear, as it should have done, among the products presented by Rottensteiner. We offer our apologies for this oversight both to him and to our readers. Returning to the matter in hand, though, we find the same Santa Maddalena Premstallerhof, this time from the '99 vintage, and it is right on form. One of the very best Santa Maddalenas overall, it reveals great typicity and a fragrant, immediately appealing style. The extremely varietal Pinot Nero Mazon Riserva '97 is very good, too. The nose unveils scents of strawberries and blackcurrants and a flavour that, with only a bit more concentration, would have won it a Three Glass rating. The '97 Lagrein Scuro Riserva is as interesting as ever. Initially somewhat closed because of its extreme youthfulness, at subsequent tastings it improved steadily until it gained a Two Glass score. The other wines presented for tasting were all sound, with the Pinot Bianco in particular proving to be a very faithful interpretation of the variety's most attractive characteristics.

Even if he only makes three wines, and even if there are only a few bottles available, we want to dedicate an individual profile again to Heinrich Rottensteiner and his historic Obermoserhof estate, the true heart of Santa Maddalena. But this is not really an extravagance. Rottensteiner produces excellent wines and this year, with the Lagrein Grafenleiten Riserva '97, he even made it to our final taste-offs for the Three Glass awards. So, our congratulations go to this skilful, honest grower. But let's get back to that fantastic Lagrein. It is wonderful, although if you really want to nitpick, it is just a shade rough around the edges. However, there is power and concentration to spare. The aromas are varietal and spicy, with very well-defined bilberry notes. It literally explodes on the palate, although it seems a little tousled owing to the sheer abundance of fruit and extract. If you are a lover of traditional Lagreins, then this is the wine for you. We also tasted a pre-release sample of the '98, which was excellent, too. You can expect great things from this wine next year as well. The other two wines we judged seemed very correct. The '99 Sauvignon does not possess extraordinary body but it is varietal and fairly elegant. The Santa Maddalena Classico is a light red which has a pleasant, exemplary easy-drinking style.

● A. A. Lagrein Scuro Grieser Select Ris. '97	ΨΨ	4
● A. A. Pinot Nero Mazzon Select Ris. '97	ΨΨ	5
● A. A. Santa Maddalena Cl. Premstallerhof '99	ΨΨ	3*
○ A. A. Pinot Bianco '99	Ψ	3
○ A. A. Pinot Grigio '99	Ψ	3
○ A. A. Müller Thurgau '99		3
● A. A. Cabernet Select '96	ΨΨ	5
● A. A. Cabernet Select Ris. '93	ΨΨ	5
● A. A. Lagrein Scuro Grieser Select Ris. '96	ΨΨ	4
● A. A. Pinot Nero Mazzon Select Ris. '93	ΨΨ	5

● A. A. Lagrein Scuro Grafenleiten Ris. '97	ΨΨ	5
● A. A. Santa Maddalena Cl. '99	Ψ	3
○ A. A. Sauvignon '99	Ψ	3
● A. A. Lagrein Scuro Obermoser Grafenleiten '93	ΨΨ	3*
● A. A. Lagrein Scuro Obermoser Grafenleiten '96	ΨΨ	4
● A. A. Santa Maddalena Obermoser '93	ΨΨ	3*
● A. A. Santa Maddalena Obermoser '94	Ψ	3

BRESSANONE/BRIXEN (BZ) BRESSANONE/BRIXEN (BZ)

KUENHOF - PETER PLIGER
LOC. MARA, 110
39042 BRESSANONE/BRIXEN (BZ)
TEL. 0472/850546

MANFRED NÖSSING - HOANDLHOF
WEINBERGSTRASSE, 66
39042 BRESSANONE/BRIXEN (BZ)
TEL. 0472/832672

Our congratulations to Peter and Brigitte Pliger. The first Three Glass accolade for one of Kuenhof's wines is their well-deserved reward for a truly extraordinary product. The call of the land and a passion for nature prompted Peter Pliger to take over the abandoned vineyards of the family estate in the Isarco valley, just outside Bressanone. Here, conditions are at the limit for the cultivation of vines, in terms of latitude, average temperature and altitude above sea level. But thanks to these characteristics and a soil rich in schist, the wines from this area are distinctive. And Pliger's whites perhaps represent the finest examples of the category. Our Three Glass award went to the Kaiton '99, a white table wine made exclusively from riesling renano. It is an intense, full-bodied, complex white of great structure, which is still youthful and shows great potential for the future. It's a Riesling that can easily stand comparison to its better-known siblings from Austria and Germany. With their great structure and extract, all of Kuenhof's wines need time to mature and express themselves to the full. The '99 Sylvaner, the wine that Pliger considers to be his most important, is delicious, with aromas of lucerne and spring flowers, and a complex, rich, full-bodied palate. The Grüner Veltliner '99, to our knowledge, the only one in Italy, has a golden straw colour. It is fresh and herbaceous on the nose with concentrated aromas of green tomatoes and citrus fruits, and it has a rich and full-bodied flavour, underpinned by a pleasant vein of counterbalancing acidity. The Gewürztraminer '99 was still very closed at the time of our tastings but should open up with a few months' bottle-age.

We welcome Manfred Nössing into the circle of new, promising Alto Adige grower-producers, at least as far as the Guide is concerned. Nössing was one of the most pleasant surprises at our tastings this year. Young, full of ideas and energy, he bought the estate from his father a couple of years ago. It stands on the slopes to the east of Bressanone, in a very sunny location at 640 metres above sea level. The Isarco valley is above all a white wine area and Manfred presented us with four whites, all displaying excellent varietal typicity, a Sylvaner, a Kerner, a Müller Thurgau and a Gewürztraminer. The Sylvaner, a greenish-gold straw-yellow in colour, is intense and vegetal on the nose, with notes of hay and pears, and a very rich, fresh, full-bodied palate. The rare Kerner has a yellow colour tinged with green. Very characteristic and intense, it releases a delicate herbaceous aroma and good acidity. The Müller Thurgau, a varietal that expresses itself particularly well here in the Valle Isarco zone, also has a greenish straw-yellow colour. All of these wines easily passed the Two Glass threshold in our tastings. We found the Gewürztraminer below par with respect to its stablemates for the bouquet is still rather closed. It has good weight but is pretty straightforward. It is a pity that Nössing did not offer us his red wine for tasting. It is made from blauer zweigelt , an Austrian variety that he planted in '95. The first edition was the '97 vintage, released under the name of Espan, and the few available bottles of this red immediately caused a sensation. No one could believe that this variety could grow and give such interesting results in this zone. We look forward to tasting it next year.

O Kaiton '99	▼▼▼	4*
O A. A. Valle Isarco Sylvaner '99	▼▼	4
O A. A. Valle Isarco Veltliner '99	▼▼	4
O A. A. Valle Isarco Gewürztraminer '99	▼	4
O A. A. Valle Isarco Gewürztraminer '98	♀♀	4
O A. A. Valle Isarco Sylvaner '97	♀♀	4
O A. A. Valle Isarco Sylvaner '98	♀♀	4
O A. A. Valle Isarco Veltliner '93	♀♀	4
O A. A. Valle Isarco Veltliner '97	♀♀	4
O A. A. Valle Isarco Veltliner '98	♀♀	4
O Kaiton '97	♀♀	4
O A. A. Valle Isarco Gewürztraminer '97	♀	4

O A. A. Valle Isarco Kerner '99	▼▼	4
O A. A. Valle Isarco Müller Thurgau '99	▼▼	3*
O A. A. Valle Isarco Sylvaner '99	▼▼	4
O A. A. Valle Isarco Gewürztraminer '99	▼	4

CALDARO/KALTERN (BZ)

Cantina Viticoltori di Caldaro/Kaltern

Via delle Cantine, 12
39052 Caldaro/Kaltern (BZ)
tel. 0471/963149

Helmuth Zozin, the Kellermeister responsible for the Cantina Viticoltori di Caldaro, does an excellent job. Even if the principal wine here is the Lago di Caldaro Classico, the great passions of this winemaker are the more richly structured reds, and especially Cabernet and the Pinot Nero. We'll begin with the fragrant, intense, subtle and very concentrated Cabernet Sauvignon Campaner Riserva '98, with its sweetish and very elegant scents of well-integrated berry fruit and oak. It's a lovely wine at a very competitive price. Its big brother, the renowned Cabernet Sauvignon Pfarrhof Riserva is in the '97 version. A complex wine, with intense blackcurrant fruit, it is full-bodied and rich on the palate, with ripe, soft tannins and outstanding length. But our Three Glass accolade goes this year to a great Gewürztraminer, the Campaner '99, which is in a class of its own. Deep golden yellow in colour, it has very intense, complex aromas of honey and roses. There is soft, well-balanced fruit on the palate, with an attractive aftertaste and a lovely, lingering finish. The basic Gewürztraminer '99 is an excellent example of its category, even if it does not, obviously, express itself at the exalted level of the Campaner. Fragrant on the nose, with hints of roses, mint and apples, it offers sweetish full-flavoured fruit on the palate. The two Pinot Neros, the Saltnerhof '98 and the Riserva from the same vintage, are good and very varietal. The Lago di Caldaro Classico Pfarrhog '99 is one of the best of its type. The other whites, however, are a bit disappointing and fall short of the winery's usual standards of quality. So, with this minor caveat, the year's overall result was a stunning one for the Cantina Viticoltori di Caldaro.

○	A. A. Gewürztraminer Campaner '99	🍷🍷🍷	4*
●	A. A. Cabernet Sauvignon Campaner Ris. '98	🍷🍷	4
●	A. A. Cabernet Sauvignon Pfarrhof Ris. '97	🍷🍷	5
○	A. A. Gewürztraminer '99	🍷🍷	3*
●	A. A. Lago di Caldaro Pfarrhof '99	🍷🍷	3*
●	A. A. Pinot Nero Ris. '98	🍷🍷	5
●	A. A. Pinot Nero Saltnerhof '98	🍷🍷	4
○	A. A. Chardonnay Wadleith '99	🍷	3
●	A. A. Lago di Caldaro Scelto Cl. Sup. Pichlof '99	🍷	3
○	A. A. Müller Thurgau '99	🍷	2*
○	A. A. Pinot Bianco Vial '99	🍷	3

CALDARO/KALTERN (BZ)

Castel Sallegg - Graf Kuenburg

V.lo di Sotto, 15
39052 Caldaro/Kaltern (BZ)
tel. 0471/963132

We fall prey to a sort of taster's schizophrenia when we sample the wines of Castel Sallegg. We like the reds very much indeed but all the whites leave us so perplexed that we have decided to suspend judgement on them. We find them to be excessively mature, almost to the point of being oxidized. We may simply have had some poor bottles, or perhaps it is the estate's winemaking philosophy to go for a style that calls for super-ripe grapes. In either case, we prefer not to express an opinion in points. But on the red front, everything is hunky dory. The wines are rich, potent and show good varietal character. In short, they're excellent. The Merlot Riserva '96, in spite of its far from exciting vintage, displayed extraordinary concentration. The '95 Moscato Rosa is again outstanding. At one time, this was one of the winery's standard-bearers before its quality slipped. Now, at last, it is returning to form. It is still a little bit too evolved but in terms of structure and richness, it is absolutely peerless. The Lagrein and the Cabernet are successful. Both are satisfyingly varietal and technically very well-made. Slightly less impressive are the Rosso Conte Kuenburg, a non-vintage blend of several grape varieties, and the Lago di Caldaro Bischofsleiten '99, from which we might have expected a tiny bit more. Castel Sallegg is actually located at Caldaro itself and this wine should, in our opinion, represent better the typical character of its terroir.

●	A. A. Cabernet Ris. '97	🍷🍷	5
●	A. A. Lagrein Ris. '98	🍷🍷	4
●	A. A. Merlot Ris. '96	🍷🍷	5
●	A. A. Moscato Rosa '95	🍷🍷	6
●	Rosso Conte Kuenburg	🍷🍷	6
●	A. A. Lago di Caldaro Scelto Bischofsleiten '99	🍷	4
●	A. A. Cabernet '90	🍷🍷 (empty)	4
●	A. A. Cabernet '95	🍷🍷 (empty)	5
○	A. A. Gewürztraminer '98	🍷🍷 (empty)	4
●	A. A. Merlot '95	🍷🍷 (empty)	5
●	A. A. Merlot '97	🍷🍷 (empty)	5
●	A. A. Moscato Rosa '91	🍷🍷 (empty)	6
●	A. A. Moscato Rosa '93	🍷🍷 (empty)	6
●	A. A. Moscato Rosa '90	🍷🍷 (empty)	6

CALDARO/KALTERN (BZ)

Graf Enzenberg
Tenuta Manincor
S. Giuseppe al Lago, 4
39052 Caldaro/Kaltern (BZ)
tel. 0471/960

There is no new version of that explosive Cabernet Sauvignon Cassiano '97 to which we awarded Three Glasses last year. It was an immense wine, even though it was very difficult to track down. There is an IGT wine with a similar name from the '98 vintage but it is only a far cry from that wonderful '97. This time around, the range presented to us by the Graf Enzenberg winery is sound but not as impressive as last year. It is the whites in particular, both of them oak-conditioned, that are interesting. The Sieben Aich '99, a blend of several different grapes, and the Chardonnay Cuvée Sophie '99 are the wines in question. Both are well-made and not excessively dominated by the oak. They show good concentration even if they are not wildly full-bodied. The Chardonnay is a good expression of the variety's characteristics. Interesting, and certainly one of the best examples of its type, is the Lago di Caldaro Scelto '99, the ace up the estate's sleeve. It has good structure and a certain elegance. All the other products are less convincing, with a barely decent Pinot Nero and a Moscato Giallo and La Rosa di Manincor that are far from exciting. They are disappointingly thin, dilute and straightforward.

○	A. A. Chardonnay Cuvée Sophie '98	▼▼	5
●	A. A. Lago di Caldaro Scelto '99	▼▼	4
○	Sieben Aich '99	▼▼	5
●	A. A. Pinot Nero Mason '98	▼	5
●	Cassiano '98	▼	6
○	A. A. Moscato Giallo '99		3
⊙	La Rosa di Manincor '99		3
●	A. A. Cabernet Sauvignon Cassiano '97	▽▽▽	5
●	A. A. Lago di Caldaro Scelto '98	▽▽	4
●	A. A. Pinot Nero Mason '97	▽▽	5
○	A. A. Terlano Pinot Bianco '98	▽	4

CALDARO/KALTERN (BZ)

Prima & Nuova/Erste & Neue
Via delle Cantine, 5
39052 Caldaro/Kaltern (BZ)
tel. 0471/963122

The Prima & Nuova winery of Caldaro has passed its hundredth anniversary, having been founded in 1900. With 570 members and 315 hectares of land under vine, it is one of the most important and largest producers of quality wine in Alto Adige. The growers of this co-operative gave themselves the best possible birthday present, in the shape of their Cabernet Puntay Riserva '97, which fully deserves our Three Glass accolade. It is a great red. Dark ruby in colour, with intense fruit aromas, it unveils well-integrated oak on the nose and powerful, concentrated, rich and well-rounded fruit in the mouth. Also excellent is the Gewürztraminer Puntay '99, which came first in its category in the 2000 International Gewürztraminer Symposium. Its deep golden colour ushers in a very concentrated bouquet with ripe scents of roses, cloves, grapefruit and lychees. On the palate, it is refreshing and zesty, with a complex and well-balanced structure. We also tasted some other extraordinary products from Prima & Nuova, particularly the '97 Anthos. It's a dessert wine made from moscato giallo, gewürztraminer and sauvignon grapes specially selected and dried for six months. Full-flavoured, rich and sweet, it reveals complex aromas of dried fruits and hints of botrytis. Three of the winery's other whites are also outstanding. The culprits are the rich, well-typed Pinot Bianco Brunar '99, the riper and more exotic Pinot Bianco Puntay '99, and the Chardonnay Salt '98 with its delicately peach fruit fragrance. The Chardonnay Puntay '99 and the Sauvignon Stern '99 are both good, though we found them less appealing. The Sauvignon in particular is complex but a bit over-evolved. The Lago di Caldaro Scelto Puntay '99 is heady and attractively quaffable while the Pinot Nero Mezzan '98 is sound.

●	A. A. Cabernet Puntay Ris. '97	▼▼▼	5
○	A. A. Gewürztraminer Puntay '99	▼▼	4
○	A. A. Chardonnay Salt '99	▼▼	3*
○	A. A. Pinot Bianco Brunar '99	▼▼	3
○	A. A. Pinot Bianco Puntay '99	▼▼	3
○	Anthos '97	▼▼	5
○	A. A. Chardonnay Puntay '98	▼	4
●	A. A. Lago di Caldaro Scelto Puntay '99	▼	3
●	A. A. Pinot Nero Mezzan '99	▼	4
○	A. A. Sauvignon Stern '99	▼	3

CALDARO/KALTERN (BZ)

JOSEF SÖLVA - NIKLASERHOF
VIA BRUNNER, 31
39052 CALDARO/KALTERN (BZ)
TEL. 0471/963432

Another new entry in the Guide, and, in a sense, a newly discovered gem, although the Niklaserhof estate has been producing wine for years now. But for quite some time, it was known only to a few "cognoscenti" and it is only recently that the family's wines have become more widely recognized. This is perhaps because Josef Sölva, for years in charge of the Alto Adige consultancy centre for fruit and vine cultivation, has retired and now has more time to devote to his vineyards. His son, Dieter, has taken over responsibility for the actual winemaking. A couple of wines struck us as being very interesting. We were particularly impressed our tasting by the Sauvignon '99. It has a concentrated straw-yellow hue and is rather vegetal on the nose, with overtones of tomato leaves. Soft, rounded, rich and salty on the palate, it unveils good underlying acidity. Coming from grapes grown at fairly high altitudes of 550-600 metres above sea level, it offers exceptional value for money and it is a pity that only 2,000 bottles were made. Another excellent representative of its category is the Lago di Caldaro Scelto Classico '99, an agreeably fruity, fresh and quaffable wine. The Lagrein-Cabernet Klaser '97 is a vibrant, concentrated ruby in colour and offers aromas of wild berries and coffee mingling with toasty notes while on the palate it is rich and well-structured, though a bit edgy and not entirely harmonious. The white Justinus Kerner '99, the only wine of this type from the zone, is very interesting and characteristic. Lastly, the Pinot Bianco '99 is satisfactory.

CARDANO/KARDAUN (BZ)

JOSEPHUS MAYR
ERBHOF UNTERGANZNER
VIA CAMPIGLIO, 15
39053 CARDANO/KARDAUN (BZ)
TEL. 0471/365582

One of the greatest satisfactions during our endless round of tastings is when we manage to reward a serious, committed producer, whether small-scale or one of the big boys. What is important is that the grower in question should be a true believer for whom wine is a way of life. Quality should be the goal. And the wines have to have a personal style that makes them utterly distinctive. In these few words, we have drawn you a portrait of Josephus Mayr and have also explained why we were so happy to give him a Three Glass award. His Lagrein Scuro Riserva '97 is one of the finest reds we tasted for this edition of our Guide. Complex, powerful, chewy, it is obviously the product of ripe grapes and superb winemaking. It should also be remembered that Mayr's vineyards are not in the true classic zone for the variety, which is Gries. They are on the slopes to the north of Bolzano, adjacent to those of Santa Maddalena. And it happens that the second interesting wine presented to us by Mayr was the Santa Maddalena Classico '99, another wine that naturally appealed to us lovers of fragrant reds that don't take body to excess. Two very special wines are the Lamarein, made from partially dried lagrein grapes, a sort of Amarone drinkalike, and the Composition Reif, a blend of several red varieties. They are good, unusual wines but they have less typicity and their roots in the terroir are less evident. The Lagrein Rosato is as fruity and up-front as usual. Then the very young Chardonnay '99 is attractive and varietal, even though it still has a distinctly oaky note. In conclusion, we should like to offer Josephus Mayr a warm welcome to the Three Glass club. It is a distinction he thoroughly deserves.

● A. A. Lago di Caldaro		
Scelto Cl. '99	♥♥	2*
○ A. A. Sauvignon '99	♥♥	2*
● A. A. Lagrein-Cabernet Klaser '97	♥	4
○ A. A. Pinot Bianco '99	♥	2*
○ Bianco Justinus Kerner '99	♥	2*

● A. A. Lagrein Scuro Ris. '97	♥♥♥	5
● A. A. Santa Maddalena Cl. '98	♥♥	3*
● Composition Reif '98	♥♥	5
● Lamarein '98	♥♥	6
○ A. A. Chardonnay '99	♥	3
⊙ A. A. Lagrein Rosato '99	♥	3
● A. A. Cabernet Sauvignon '95	♀♀	5
● A. A. Cabernet Sauvignon '96	♀♀	5
● A. A. Lagrein Scuro '98	♀♀	3*
● A. A. Lagrein Scuro Ris. '95	♀♀	5
● A. A. Lagrein Scuro Ris. '96	♀♀	5
● A. A. Santa Maddalena Cl. '98	♀♀	3*
● Composition Reif '95	♀♀	5
● Composition Reif '97	♀♀	5
● Lamarein '97	♀♀	5

CERMES/TSCHERMS (BZ)

CHIUSA/KLAUSEN (BZ)

GRAF PFEIL WEINGUT KRÄNZEL
VIA PALADE, 1
39010 CERMES/TSCHERMS (BZ)
TEL. 0473/564549

CANTINA PRODUTTORI
VALLE ISARCO/EISACKTALER
LOC. COSTE, 50
39043 CHIUSA/KLAUSEN (BZ)
TEL. 0472/847553

Two delicious, well-typed and well-made wines represent once again this year, the calling card of this tiny but extremely high quality winery in the Merano area. The Pinto Bianco, fermented and matured in small oak casks, has, after an initial period in which the vanilla-like notes were rather dominant, gained greater complexity on the nose and has achieved a really notable level of integration between the fruit and the oak. It has become, in fact, one of the best Pinot Biancos in Alto Adige. The Schiava '99 is very impressive, indeed: it is almost a small-scale Pinot Nero with its extraordinary cellaring potential, a quality that one does not normally find in wines of this type. We had the opportunity to taste the '90 and '95 vintages and we remained dumbstruck when we saw the evolution that these wines had undergone. This aspect is worth underlining with particular attention because it could be an as yet undiscovered quality of this rather uncomplicated grape variety that is so widespread in Alto Adige. The Sagittarius, made from cabernet and merlot, is interesting; this too was a bit closed at first, but at later tastings, it displayed much greater class. The other wines in the range were less convincing, and particularly the Pinot Nero which pays the consequences of a vintage, '98, that was not particularly good in this zone.

The Isarco valley wine producers co-operative is a splendid enterprise. It receives and vinifies the grapes of growers who, every year, have to face the challenges of a hostile climate. Here we are very close indeed to the geographical limit of vine growing and the weather is far from generous. Harvests start much later than on the other side of the Adige river and even for the white grapes you have to wait until at least the very end of September, when rain can be quite a problem. In spite of this, you can see from the ratings that the co-operative does a good job and quality is the norm. This year we tasted an excellent Pinot Bianco that came, however, from areas further south. Its generic Alto Adige DOC label doesn't bear the Valle Isarco denomination. Then there was one of the best non-oak fermented Pinot Grigios around, which displayed exemplary varietals aromas. Finally, we enjoyed a long series of more traditional wines from this area, Sylvaner, Kerner, Veltliner, Müller Thurgau and finally the singular and eminently quaffable Klausner Laitacher red. All are '99s and all are very well-typed, fruity and technically very well-made. The Sylvaner Dominus '98, a barrique-aged white, is less satisfying as the fruit is in thrall to the oak. Remember that this is almost an experimental wine. It does not detract from the overall value of a very sound range.

○ A. A. Pinot Bianco '99	🍷🍷	3*
○ A. A. Sauvignon '99	🍷🍷	5
● A. A. Schiava '99	🍷🍷	3*
● Sagittarius '97	🍷🍷	5
● A. A. Pinot Nero '98	🍷	5
○ Justinus '98	🍷	5
○ A. A. Pinot Bianco '96	🍷🍷	4
○ A. A. Pinot Bianco Et. Nera '98	🍷🍷	4
● A. A. Pinot Nero '95	🍷🍷	5
● A. A. Schiava '98	🍷🍷	3*
○ Dorado '94	🍷🍷	5
○ Dorado '95	🍷🍷	5
○ Dorado '97	🍷🍷	5
● Sagittarius '95	🍷🍷	5
● Sagittarius '96	🍷🍷	5

○ A. A. Valle Isarco Pinot Bianco '99	🍷🍷	3*
○ A. A. Valle Isarco Pinot Grigio '99	🍷🍷	3*
○ A. A. Valle Isarco Gewürztraminer Aristos '99	🍷	3
○ A. A. Valle Isarco Kerner '99	🍷	3
○ A. A. Valle Isarco Klausener Laitacher '99	🍷	3
○ A. A. Valle Isarco Müller Thurgau Aristos '99	🍷	3
○ A. A. Valle Isarco Sylvaner Aristos '99	🍷	3
○ A. A. Valle Isarco Veltliner '99	🍷	3
○ A. A. Valle Isarco Sylvaner Dominus '98		4

CORNAIANO/GIRLAN (BZ)   CORNAIANO/GIRLAN (BZ)

CANTINA PRODUTTORI
COLTERENZIO/SCHRECKBICHL
STRADA DEL VINO, 8
39050 CORNAIANO/GIRLAN (BZ)
TEL. 0471/664246

CANTINA PRODUTTORI
CORNAIANO/GIRLAN
VIA S. MARTINO, 24
39050 CORNAIANO/GIRLAN (BZ)
TEL. 0471/662403

It is very hard to know where to begin when documenting the triumphal march of Colterenzio's wines this year. They are all excellent. We'll start with the bottles that won Three Glass awards but there were others that also deserve attention in their various categories. The Chardonnay Cornell '98 is one of the best versions ever. Complex, varietal and persistent, it combines elegance with power, and finesse with concentration. All in all, then, a minor Bâtard-Montrachet from the vineyards of Alto Adige. Finally, we have a great white whose fruit is not excessively masked by vanillaed notes from new oak. The Cabernet Sauvignon Lafoa '97 is also superb, with its remarkable concentration and its varietal character that shuns excessively herbaceous notes. It has balsamic and fruity aromas as well as compact yet soft tannins. A masterpiece. But we cannot stop there. Wine-lovers will also want to try the wines in the Praedium range, the Sauvignon Prail, the Pinot Bianco Weisshaus, and the Chardonnay Coreth, all from the '99 vintage. To say they are correct and varietal does not do them justice. They also offer excellent value for money and their quality is not far short of that shown by the Lafoas or the Cornells, which are considerably more expensive wines. Again from the Praedium line, we would draw your attention to the Merlot Siebeneich Riserva '97 and the Pinot Nero St Daniel Riserva '97, which finally managed to convince. There remain to be mentioned the Bianco and Rosso Cornelius wines and the Sauvignon Lafoa '99. They are, of course, excellent but that is only to be expected, for they are not exactly sold at giveaway prices.

The Cantina Produttori Cornaiano/Girlan is one of the most prestigious producers in Alto Adige. This year, the range they presented to us was even more satisfying than usual, thanks partly to a masterly version of the Schiava Gschleier, the '98, which has to be the greatest Schiava we have ever sampled in our many years of tastings. It reached our final taste-off and only just missed out on a Three Glass award. But the main thing is that this is a truly remarkable wine. It is hard to say whether a Schiava could ever aspire to be part of the first rank of Italian wines but the fact is that for this edition of the Guide, we gave the idea very serious consideration. If it performs as well in the future, we may even give it the green light. The rest of the range is not at all bad, either. Look out, in particular, for an excellent '99 Chardonnay released under the Vinum label, for some good Sauvignons and Pinot Grigios and the delicate, linear Schiava Fass N.9 from the '99 vintage. The two Pinot Neros, the Trattmanhof from the Mazon subzone and the Patricia Selection. are less impressive but here the vintage must take most of the blame. Both are very well-made but slightly dilute. They show promise, though, at least in terms of technique. The other wines are merely fair. We can recall better versions of the Pinot Bianco Plattenriegel than this year's '99 and the barrel-fermented '98 Chardonnay is a tiny bit over-oaked so that its varietal characteristics are masked.

○ A. A. Chardonnay Cornell '98	♀♀♀	5
● A. A. Cabernet Sauvignon Lafoa '97	♀♀♀	6
○ A. A. Chardonnay Coreth '99	♀♀	3*
● A. A. Merlot Siebeneich '97	♀♀	4
○ A. A. Pinot Bianco Weisshaus '99	♀♀	3*
● A. A. Pinot Nero St. Daniel Ris. '97	♀♀	4
○ A. A. Sauvignon Lafoa '99	♀♀	5
○ A. A. Sauvignon Prail '99	♀♀	3*
● Cabernet-Merlot Cornelius Rosso '97	♀♀	6
○ Cornelius Bianco '98	♀♀	5
● A. A. Cabernet Sauvignon Lafoa '92	♀♀♀	6
● A. A. Cabernet Sauvignon Lafoa '94	♀♀♀	6
● A. A. Cabernet Sauvignon Lafoa '95	♀♀♀	6
○ A. A. Chardonnay Cornell '97	♀♀♀	5

○ A. A. Chardonnay Vinum '99	♀♀	3*
○ A. A. Gewürztraminer '99	♀♀	3*
○ A. A. Sauvignon '99	♀♀	3*
● A. A. Schiava Fass N. 9 '99	♀♀	3*
● A. A. Schiava Gschleier '98	♀♀	4
○ A. A. Chardonnay '98	♀	4
○ A. A. Pinot Bianco '99	♀	3
○ A. A. Pinot Grigio '99	♀	3
● A. A. Pinot Nero Mazon Trattmannhof '98	♀	5
● A. A. Pinot Nero Patricia '98	♀	5
● A. A. Cabernet Sauvignon Ris. '97	♀♀	5
● A. A. Lagrein Ris. '97	♀♀	5
● A. A. Schiava Fass N. 9 '98	♀♀	3*
● A. A. Schiava Gschleier '97	♀♀	4

CORNAIANO/GIRLAN (BZ)

CORNAIANO/GIRLAN (BZ)

K. MARTINI & SOHN
VIA LAMM WEG, 28
39050 CORNAIANO/GIRLAN (BZ)
TEL. 0471/663156

JOSEF NIEDERMAYR
VIA CASA DI GESU, 15
39050 CORNAIANO/GIRLAN (BZ)
TEL. 0471/662451

As reliable as ever. That admittedly brief comment admirably sums up the wines produced by this fine Cornaiano cellar, which has been well-run for many years now and which often deservedly earns its own profile in the Guide. There is no news here except for the occasional increasingly positive note. In a year when the Lagrein Scuro Maturm is absent – we reported on the '97 version last year and the next vintage is not ready yet – Gabriel Martini still managed to earn two Two Glass ratings with the Sauvignon Palladium '99 and the delicious Schiava Palladium '99. These wines are perhaps a bit one-dimensional but they are very stylish from the technical point of view. This means they show exemplary adherence to their respective varietal characteristics, something we consider as important for winemakers as the correct use of grammar and syntax is for writers. There is also a series of other impeccably made wines, such as the Pinot Bianco Lamm, the Chardonnay Palladium and the Lago di Caldaro Classsico Felton, all from the '99 vintage. Then there is an acceptable basic Gewürztraminer, also a '99, and the two premium reds, the Lagrein Scuro Rueslhof and the Lagrein Cabernet Coldirus Palladium, both '98s. These suffer from the not particularly favourable year, showing rather too much dilution considering the theoretical – and indeed commercial – values that they ought to express. The basic Pinot Grigio '99, though at best a wine without any particular pretensions, is a bit under par. It is a little acidic and thin.

His place in the Hall of Fame of pioneers in the field of Alto Adige dessert wines is assured. With the white Aureus '98, Josef Niedermayr and his courageous winemaker, Lorenz Martini, have again created an oenological gem. This wine, made from partially dried chardonnay, pinot bianco and sauvignon grapes, is truly delicious. It has an intense golden yellow colour and displays extraordinary complexity on the nose. Honey, botrytized notes and caramel are evident, as well as exotic fruit nuances. On the palate, it is powerful yet well-balanced, harmonious and measured. It has to be one of Italy's finest dessert wines. The Lagrein aus Gries Riserva '97 is also one of the finest in its category. An intense, concentrated ruby in hue, it offers subtle fruitiness on the nose, with slightly vegetal hints of eucalyptus. The full-bodied, tangy flavour lingers unhurriedly on the palate. The Euforius '98, the very first red blend ever produced in Alto Adige back in '82, is the house's elegant, fragrant and beefy special red selection. The Pinot Nero Riserva '98 is very well-typed and offers good fruit on the nose. The Santa Maddalena Classico Egger-Larcherhof '99, a red of notable structure and an easy-drinking style, is well-typed and well-made. Moving on to the whites, apart from the rich, zesty Sauvignon Allure '99, we did not find any wines with particularly incisive character. In some cases, the Terlano Hof zu Pramol, the Sauvignon Lage Naun and the Gewürztraminer Lage Doss, Lorenz Martini will have to do an even better job to obtain the same standard you find in his premium sparkler, the Comitissa. The winery's newly-restructured cellar will no doubt give him plenty of opportunity to fulfil that goal.

○ A. A. Sauvignon Palladium '99	🍷🍷	3*	
● A. A. Schiava Palladium '99	🍷🍷	3*	
● A. A. Cabernet-Lagrein Palladium Coldirus '98	🍷	5	
○ A. A. Chardonnay Palladium '99	🍷	3	
○ A. A. Gewürztraminer '99	🍷	2*	
● A. A. Lago di Caldaro Cl. Felton '99	🍷	3	
● A. A. Lagrein Scuro Rueslhof '98	🍷	5	
○ A. A. Pinot Bianco Lamm '99	🍷	3	
○ A. A. Pinot Grigio '99		2	
● A. A. Cabernet-Lagrein Palladium Coldirus '97	🍷🍷	5	
● A. A. Lagrein Scuro Maturum '95	🍷🍷	5	
● A. A. Lagrein Scuro Maturum '97	🍷🍷	5	

○ Aureus '98	🍷🍷🍷	5	
● A. A. Lagrein Gries Ris. '97	🍷🍷	4	
● A. A. Pinot Nero Ris. '98	🍷🍷	4	
● A. A. Santa Maddalena Cl. Egger-Larcher Hof '99	🍷🍷	3*	
○ A. A. Sauvignon Allure '99	🍷🍷	4	
● Euforius '98	🍷🍷	4	
○ A. A. Gewürztraminer Lage Doss '99	🍷	4	
○ A. A. Sauvignon Lage Naun '99	🍷	3	
○ A. A. Terlano Hof zu Pramol '99	🍷	3	
○ Aureus '95	🍷🍷🍷	5	
● A. A. Lagrein Gries Ris. '96	🍷🍷	4	
○ Aureus '97	🍷🍷	5	
● Euforius '97	🍷🍷	5	

CORNAIANO/GIRLAN (BZ)

IGNAZ NIEDRIST
VIA RONCO, 5
39050 CORNAIANO/GIRLAN (BZ)
TEL. 0471/664494

A really fine Riesling from the '99 vintage opens the range presented by Ignaz Niedrist, one of the leading lights of the Alto Adige wine production scene. It is a Riesling that is a shade more restrained and southern in style than those from Valle Venosta. We might call it the best of the less "northern" interpretations of the variety from South Tyrol. It has a varietal bouquet, with grapefruit notes on the nose, which will evolve into more smoky and mineral aromas with time. On the palate, it is full and quite concentrated. It also has a good vein of acidity but this does not dominate the palate. It could perhaps do with a bit more guts and grip to be a truly great Riesling but we think that this slight failing can be put down to the terroir rather than the winemaker. It did, however, get through to our final taste-offs and only just failed to gain a Three Glass rating. The Merlot '98 is also very good. In a not particularly favourable year for reds, it manages to express particularly precise varietal characteristics and a satisfying structure on the palate. It is not enormously complex but is very well-made. Above all, the oak is kept well under control, a factor of fundamental importance in a good Merlot. The Terlano Sauvignon '99 is good but not up to the same standard as the previous version. While fleshy and potent, it is a touch over-evolved for its age. The range is completed by the Pinot Nero'98, made from a grape variety that is always a source of joy and torment for any producer who tries his hand at it. It reveals rather dominant, toasty oak on the nose and reasonable concentration on the palate. A great Pinot Nero, though, should be decidedly more complex and varietal. Quite clearly, '98 was not a great vintage and we look forward to rather more convincing performances from this wine.

●	A. A. Merlot '98	▼▼	5
○	A. A. Riesling Renano '99	▼▼	4
●	A. A. Pinot Nero '98	▼	5
○	A. A. Terlano Sauvignon '99	▼	4
●	A. A. Pinot Nero '91	▽▽	5
●	A. A. Pinot Nero '92	▽▽	4
●	A. A. Pinot Nero '93	▽▽	4
●	A. A. Pinot Nero '95	▽▽	4
●	A. A. Pinot Nero '96	▽▽	4
○	A. A. Riesling Renano '93	▽▽	4
○	A. A. Riesling Renano '95	▽▽	4
○	A. A. Riesling Renano '96	▽▽	4
○	A. A. Terlano Sauvignon '98	▽▽	4
●	A. A. Lagrein Berger Gei '93	▽	4

CORTACCIA/KURTATSCH (BZ)

CANTINA PRODUTTORI CORTACCIA
STRADA DEL VINO, 23
39040 CORTACCIA/KURTATSCH (BZ)
TEL. 0471/880115

There is no doubt about it. The selection of wines presented to us by the Cantina Produttori di Cortaccia and its director, Arnold Terzer, was something special. There were many wines that showed great quality and only a few disappointments but on the whole we can say that we were very satisfied indeed. As usual, the extraordinary Cabernet Freienfeld, this time in the exciting '97 version, took centre stage with its customary panache. Elegant and balsamic, it is concentrated on the palate, with ripe, compact tannins perfectly enveloped by soft, extract. Also showing well were the oak-matured Chardonnay Eberlehof '98, the Cabernet Kirchhügel '98, a less imposing version of the Freienfeld at a much more affordable price, and the Cabernet-Merlot Soma '98. The last of these was a wine the panel had never tasted before and even in a far from exceptional vintage, offered a well-knit varietal style. The Schiava Grigia Sonntaler '99, yet another fragrant, up-front and quaffable red, is quite delicious. The wines in the less prestigious lines are also worth investigating. Not bad at all – but this comes as no surprise – is the Lagrein Scuro Forhof '98. The Chardonnay Felsenhof and the Sauvignon Milla, both '99s, are satisfactorily varietal and technically very well-made. The Pinot Nero Vorhof '98 was a bit disappointing, turning out to be thin, rather dilute and fairly short. Pinot nero is a difficult variety to deal with at the best of times, and '98 was not a particularly wonderful year, so it might have been better to skip this vintage altogether. With its fine reputation at stake, the Cantina di Cortaccia could certainly have permitted itself to do so. What is indisputable is that this Pinot Nero is not worthy of such a prestigious range.

●	A. A. Cabernet Freienfeld '97	▼▼▼	6
●	A. A. Cabernet Kirchhügel '98	▼▼	4
●	A. A. Cabernet-Merlot Soma '98	▼▼	5
○	A. A. Chardonnay Eberlehof '98	▼▼	5
●	A. A. Schiava Grigia Sonnntaler '99	▼▼	3*
○	A. A. Chardonnay Felsenhof '99	▼	3
●	A. A. Lagrein Scuro Forhof '98	▼	4
○	A. A. Müller Thurgau Hofstatt '99	▼	3
○	A. A. Sauvignon Milla '99	▼	3
●	A. A. Pinot Nero Vorhof '98		5
●	A. A. Cabernet Freienfeld '92	▽▽▽	5
●	A. A. Cabernet Freienfeld '95	▽▽▽	6
●	A. A. Merlot Brenntal '95	▽▽▽	5
●	A. A. Merlot Brenntal '97	▽▽▽	5

CORTACCIA/KURTATSCH (BZ)

Tiefenbrunner

Loc. Niclara
Via Castello, 4
39040 Cortaccia/Kurtatsch (BZ)
tel. 0471/880122

One of the major regrets we have after our blind tastings of Alto Adige wines is to discover that Herbert and Cristof Tiefenbrunner have still not succeeded in earning a Three Glass award. We have known the estate for years and are full of admiration for its father and son owners. We believe that they are, and have been for some time now, one of the most reliable cellars in the South Tyrolean winemaking scene. Yet their wines always seem to lack a bit of concentration and thrust. They are perfectly made from a technical point of view but could do with a bit more soul. Again this year, at least a couple of them were very good. The Cabernet Sauvignon Linticlarus '97, for example, is very interesting. On the nose, it has balsamic tones and wild berry aromas, as well as well-modulated oak. It is good on the palate, too, but the finish is a little dilute. The straightforward Chardonnay Castel Turmhof '99 is splendidly linear, elegant and easy to drink. The Feldmarschall '99 is very distinctive, as usual. Obtained from müller thurgau, perhaps with the addition of some moscato giallo, it is almost aromatic. The Pinot Nero Linticlarus '97 is among the best of its type this year. It may not be particularly explosive but it is thankfully varietal and well-made, without any odd or unpleasant reductive smells. The Sauvignon Kirchleiten '99, another example of a technically well-crafted wine, is interesting and not excessively vegetal. All the other wines are fair, with the only mild disappointment being the Linticlarus Cuvée '98, from lagrein, cabernet sauvignon and pinot nero. We liked the '97 very much indeed but the subsequent version is penalized by the poor vintage.

●	A. A. Cabernet Sauvignon Linticlarus '97	🍷🍷	5
○	A. A. Chardonnay '99	🍷🍷	3*
●	A. A. Pinot Nero Linticlarus '97	🍷🍷	5
○	A. A. Sauvignon Kirchleiten '99	🍷🍷	4
○	Feldmarschall von Fenner zu Fennberg '99	🍷🍷	5
○	A. A. Chardonnay Linticlarus '97	🍷	4
○	A. A. Gewürztraminer '99	🍷	3
●	A. A. Lagrein Linticlarus '98	🍷	5
●	A. A. Lagrein Scuro '98	🍷	4
●	Linticlarus Cuvée '98	🍷	5
●	A. A. Cabernet Sauvignon Linticlarus '96	YY	5
●	Linticlarus Cuvée '97	YY	5

CORTINA/KURTINIG (BZ)

Peter Zemmer - Kupelwieser

Strada del Vino, 24
39040 Cortina/Kurtinig (BZ)
tel. 0471/817143

These two wineries, under the same ownership, are perhaps not among the most fashionable labels in Alto Adige, but that is a real pity. In fact, year after year, the bottles made both by Zemmer and Kupelwieser show that they are two of the region's most reliable winemakers. This year's best releases were Zemmer's Merlot '98 and the Lagrein Intenditore '98 made by Kupelwieser, two excellent reds worthy of any of the big-name producers in South Tyrol. The two Chardonnays, Kupelwieser's '99 and Kemmer's '98, were both aged in wood and very convincing. Above all, they were not overwhelmed by excessive vanilla. A little less concentrated than the Intenditore version, the Lagrein Scuro '98 made by Zemmer was both linear and varietal. All the other wines in the vast range we tasted this year were admirable; all, at the very least, were correct and dependable. In particular, we should mention the Chardonnay '99, not fermented in wood, and the Pinot Bianco '99, both under the Zemmer label, as well as the Müller Thurgau Intenditore '99 and the fragrant Santa Maddalena, also from '99, from the Kupelwieser line. But these are only a few of the wines released by these two firms that, we repeat, are a reliable source for well-made bottles. The wines are especially interesting in terms of their price/quality ratio.

○	A. A. Chardonnay Kupelwieser '99	🍷🍷	3*
○	A. A. Chardonnay Barrique Z. '98	🍷🍷	4
●	A. A. Lagrein Scuro Intenditore '98	🍷🍷	5
●	A. A. Merlot Zemmer '98	🍷🍷	5
●	A. A. Lagrein Scuro Z. '98	🍷🍷	4
○	A. A. Müller Thurgau Intenditore '99	🍷	3
○	A. A. Chardonnay Zemmer '99	🍷	3
○	A. A. Chardonnay Barrique Z. '97	🍷	4
○	A. A. Pinot Bianco Zemmer '99	🍷	3
●	A. A. Santa Maddalena '99	🍷	3
●	A. A. Pinot Nero Zemmer '98	🍷	5
●	A. A. Cabernet-Lagrein Z. '97	🍷	5
○	A. A. Chardonnay Barrique '96	YY	4
●	A. A. Lagrein Scuro '97	YY	4
●	A. A. Merlot '97	YY	5

EGNA/NEUMARKT (BZ)

LUN
VIA VILLA, 22/24
39044 EGNA/NEUMARKT (BZ)
TEL. 0471/813256

Lun proved itself to be in great form again with the wines presented us for this edition. After two seasons in the purgatory of Other Wineries, it is back with a bang. Everyone in the Alto Adige wine world knew that this winery was on its way up after a shift in the set-up of its ownership provided it with better management. But let's get to the wines. The classic Sandbichler Weiss, this time the '99 version, is excellent, as usual. It is a blend of Riesling and Pinot Bianco and displayed delicate and elegant aromas. In the mouth it was fresh and very easy to drink. Another really good wine was the Pinot Nero Riserva '97, a red version (Rot) of the Sandbichler, the flagship of this traditional firm. The wine is one of the best in the South Tyrol and comes from one of the most convincing harvests of the last few years. The other two top-of-the-line whites were delicious. The Sauvignon Albertus Lun '99 was varietal and very linear in the mouth. The aromatic and fragrant Gewürztraminer had surprising concentration and elegance. In all, four wines presented, and four wines winning Two Glasses is a wonderful accomplishment. Lun's star is shining brightly once again in the Alto Adige firmament. Now that's good news.

○	A. A. Bianco Sandbichler Weiss '99	🍷🍷	4
○	A. A. Gewürztraminer '99	🍷🍷	4
●	A. A. Pinot Nero Sandbichler Rot Ris. '97	🍷🍷	5
○	A. A. Sauvignon Albertus Lun '99	🍷🍷	4

MARLENGO/MARLING (BZ)

CANTINA PRODUTTORI BURGGRÄFLER
VIA PALADE, 64
39020 MARLENGO/MARLING (BZ)
TEL. 0473/447137

In spite of the fact that this co-operative winery, which is situated close to Merano, did not show its most representative wine, the Pinot Nero Tiefenthalerhof, the range presented to us this year was well up to scratch. For once, it is the whites that are the winery's best wines, in particular the Pinot Bianco Guggenberg and the Chardonnay Tiefenthaler, both '99s. These are fruity, varietal offerings that may not be terribly complex but are superbly made. They also offer exemplary value for money, a factor that is always well worth bearing in mind with such wines. The absolutely delightful Meranese Schickenburg is also very sound and impressive. Another '99, it is a fragrant, easy-drinking red and, in its own way, a minor masterpiece. We'll close with the wines that we found rather less convincing. The MerVin Süss '95, a white fermented and matured in barrique, seemed to us a bit too evolved on the nose and was rather dominated by its oaky notes. We had already tasted a similarly-named wine a few years ago, from the '97 vintage, and that version was appreciably fresher. The Gewürztraminer and the Moscato Giallo Schickenburg, both '99s, are fair, but no more than that. They are pleasant and well-made but reveal less varietal character and, especially, less concentration than one might have wished for.

○	A. A. Chardonnay Tiefenthaler '99	🍷🍷	3*
●	A. A. Meranese Schickenburg '99	🍷🍷	3*
○	A. A. Pinot Bianco Guggenberg '99	🍷🍷	3*
○	A. A. Gewürztraminer '99	🍷	3
●	A. A. Merlot-Lagrein '98	🍷	5
○	A. A. Moscato Giallo Schickenburg '99	🍷	3
○	MerVin Süss '95	🍷	5
●	A. A. Cabernet-Merlot '96	YY	5
●	A. A. Lagrein-Cabernet MerVin '96	YY	5
●	A. A. Meranese Schickenburg '98	YY	3*
●	A. A. Pinot Nero Tiefenthalerhof '96	YY	5
●	A. A. Pinot Nero Tiefenthalerhof '97	YY	5

MARLENGO/MARLING (BZ)   MELTINA/MÖLTEN (BZ)

POPPHOF - ANDREAS MENZ
MITTERTERZERSTRASSE, 5
39020 MARLENGO/MARLING (BZ)
TEL. 0473/447180

VIVALDI - ARUNDA
CIVICO, 53
39010 MELTINA/MÖLTEN (BZ)
TEL. 0471/668033

You can't win 'em all, as they say, and even the consummately skilled Andreas Menz can't guarantee a Three Glass accolade every time round. But he can rely on a long tradition and on his vineyards. When the vintage is merely fair, like the '98, it can happen that the wines are a tiny bit less concentrated, more dilute and, let's face it, less convincing. Still, Menz's '98s are well-made, decidedly varietal and very representative of their terroir, the Marlengo subzone that is so famous for its reds even though its latitude is near enough that of Burgundy. And so we have here a good '98 version of the Cabernet, which may not possess the explosive fruit of the previous vintage but which is very enjoyable. Above all, it was made without longer maceration and greater extraction than the structure of the wine itself might warrant. The '98 was a lesser vintage than '97 and the wine reflects the difference in quality. This, too, is a way of expressing the true "goût de terroir". The '98 Pinot Noir is also passable, with its characteristic varietal style. It is obviously a bit lean and dilute but it is a very honest wine, as befits Andreas Menz's style and philosophy. What can we say in conclusion? Perhaps just that it would be nice to see more up-front, honest producers like Menz. He has the courage never to pretend his wines are what they are not. Menz brings you what nature brought him. An approach that merits our respect and a full Guide profile.

The Alto Adige sparkling wine sector is not among Italy's most famous. The producers are nearly all small to medium-sized wineries, true artisans of bubbly-making that you find elsewhere perhaps only among the "récoltants-manipulants" of Champagne. The most representative of the South Tyrol contingent is definitely Josef Reiterer, grower and winemaker at Meltina/Mölten, a small village that looks out over the whole of the Terlano district, to the west of Bolzano. From his vineyards situated at between 600 and 1,000 metres above sea level, Reiterer harvests the grapes from which he produces his sparkling wines. These are predominantly chardonnay, but he also grows a little pinot nero and pinot bianco. His results are typical of smaller-scale producers in the sparkling wine sector. Sometimes, when the vintage is favourable, his bottles are excellent while on other occasions, they are a little less good. In this case, though, the actual winemaking skills are not in question because Reiterer is a master. That said, this is one of those years when his products impressed us less than usual. The Arunda Riserva '94, one of the gems in his range, is very good. It displays structure and complexity and there is not the faintest sign of any loss of fruit and freshness in spite of the fact that it is now seven years old. A very well-made sparkling wine. All the other wines are sound, if not particularly exciting. Their bouquets are as intense, complex and attractive as ever but on the palate they are slightly unknit, the acidity coming through a little too strongly. In some cases, the oak in which the base wines were aged is also a bit too prominent, particularly in the Spumante Extra Brut Cuvée Marianna.

● A. A. Cabernet '98	♥♥	5
● A. A. Pinot Nero '98	♥	5
● A. A. Cabernet '97	♥♥♥	5
● A. A. Cabernet '95	♥♥	5
○ A. A. Pinot Bianco '97	♥♥	3*
● A. A. Pinot Nero '97	♥♥	5

○ A. A. Spumante Brut Arunda Ris. '94	♥♥	5
○ A. A. Spumante Blanc de Blancs Arunda	♥	5
○ A. A. Spumante Brut Vivaldi	♥	5
○ A. A. Spumante Extra Brut Vivaldi	♥	5
○ A. A. Spumante Extra Brut Vivaldi Cuvée Marianna	♥	5
○ A. A. Spumante Extra Brut Arunda	♥♥	5
○ A. A. Spumante Extra Brut Vivaldi	♥♥	5
○ A. A. Spumante Extra Brut Vivaldi '95	♥♥	5
○ A. A. Spumante Extra Brut Vivaldi Cuvée Marianna	♥♥	5

MERANO/MERAN (BZ)

CANTINA PRODUTTORI DI MERANO/
MERANER KELLEREI
VIA S. MARCO, 11
39012 MERANO/MERAN (BZ)
TEL. 0473/235544

The outstanding quality of the Merlot Freiberg '97, the wine to which we gave our Three glass award last year, and which is now almost impossible to track down, was obviously no accident. The Meraner Kellerei, in fact, presented us this year with a series of very interesting wines and, in one case, came very close to earning our top accolade again. The wine we were particularly struck by was the Cabernet Sauvignon Graf von Meran Riserva '97, a majestically rich red. It is very varietal and well-made but perhaps not quite complex enough to obtain a third Glass. If you should happen to find a bottle, though, do not pass up the opportunity to try it. Also of considerable interest are the Sissi '98, a sweet white with marked aromatic notes, and the deliciously fragrant, though understandably rather straightforward, Meranese Wachstum St. Valentin '99. The Cabernet-Merlot Graf von Meran '97, the less well-structured and less powerful sibling of the Cabernet Sauvignon Riserva, is not bad at all, either. However, it just goes to show how these slightly secondary zones for wine production in Alto Adige – and we are well away from the region's viticultural heartland – have a genuine, powerful vocation for producing red wines. Probably not all of the potential of this small subzone around Merano has yet been fully exploited. From a rapid survey of the district, though, it seems that the most favourable sites for cabernet and merlot could produce some gems. To conclude, we should like to mention briefly a decent enough Pinot Bianco, the Pfanzer '99, and the Pinot Nero Zenonberg '98, which is no exception to the rule that says the vintage in question was not one for making great reds from pinot nero grapes.

MONTAGNA/MONTAN (BZ)

FRANZ HAAS
VIA VILLA, 6
39040 MONTAGNA/MONTAN (BZ)
TEL. 0471/812280

We are very pleased to have finally been able to give our Three Glass award to the skilful, intelligent Franz Haas. He earns it for an absolutely delicious wine, an extraordinary '99 Moscato Rosa, further embellished by a splendid label designed by the artist, Schweizer. It is a paragon of a wine and merely to describe it as varietally characteristic does not do it justice. In fact, it represents a minor stylistic revolution. A fresh, lively Moscato Rosa, its grapes were not dried for particularly long and the aromas eschew the obviously oxidative notes that derive from a late harvest. A masterpiece of its kind, this wine will make it impossible for Moscato Rosas ever be the same again, or at least that's what we hope. This star's supporting cast, if we may call them that, are a number of excellent other products that give us a clear picture of Franz Haas's way of working. The simple yet extremely well-typed Gewürztraminer '99 came very close to meriting a Three Glass rating. The Merlot '97 remains, in our opinion, the best of the reds released by Haas. The Pinot Bianco '99 demonstrates the very best characteristics of this grape. It is fruity, fairly uncomplicated and easy to drink, revealing irreproachable winemaking technique. Less convincing, paradoxically, are the wines in which Haas loses sight of his terroir, and the varietal expression of the grapes, to head off along other paths. Thus the Manna and the Istante, both from the '98 vintage and respectively a white and a red matured in barriques, are merely sound. They could have been made by anyone with decent winemaking skills and good fruit to work with. The character and the extraordinary ability that Haas demonstrates in bringing out in his wines the most sublime expression of the grape variety, and of the soil they grow on, is something else altogether.

● A. A. Cabernet Sauvignon		
Graf Von Meran Ris. '97	♟♟	6
● A. A. Cabernet-Merlot		
Graf Von Meran '97	♟♟	5
● A. A. Meranese Wachstum		
St. Valentin '99	♟♟	3*
○ Sissi '98	♟♟	5
○ A. A. Pinot Bianco Pfanzer '99	♟	3
● A. A. Pinot Nero Zenoberg '98	♟	5
● A. A. Merlot Freiberg '97	♟♟♟	5
● A. A. Lagrein Scuro		
Segenpichl '97	♟♟	4
○ Sissi '97	♟♟	5
● A. A. Cabernet-Merlot		
Graf Von Meran '95	♟	4

● A. A. Moscato Rosa Schweizer '99	♟♟♟	5
○ A. A. Gewürztraminer '99	♟♟	3*
● A. A. Merlot Schweizer '97	♟♟	5
○ A. A. Pinot Bianco '99	♟♟	3*
● Istante '98	♟	5
○ Mitterberg Manna '98	♟	5
● A. A. Merlot Schweizer '93	♟♟	4
● A. A. Moscato Rosa '96	♟♟	5
● A. A. Moscato Rosa '97	♟♟	5
● A. A. Moscato Rosa Schweizer '95	♟♟	5
● A. A. Pinot Nero Ris. '91	♟♟	5
● A. A. Pinot Nero Schweizer '95	♟♟	5
● A. A. Pinot Nero Schweizer '97	♟♟	5
● Istante '97	♟♟	5
○ Mitterberg Manna '97	♟♟	5

NALLES/NALS (BZ)

NALLES/NALS (BZ)

CANTINA PRODUTTORI NALLES
NICLARA MAGRÉ/KG NALS,
MARGREID, ENTIKLAR
VIA HEILIGENBERG, 2
39010 NALLES/NALS (BZ)
TEL. 0471/678626

CASTEL SCHWANBURG
VIA SCHWANBURG, 16
39010 NALLES/NALS (BZ)
TEL. 0471/678622

The wines from the Cantina Produttori Nalles & Magré-Niclara are being presented in a new way this year. The winery's managers have made a more precise division of their products into three distinct quality ranges, they have revamped their trademark, and they have completed the job of modernizing the winery. Gerhard Kofler, who has been the oenologist in charge here for only a few years, works hard with commitment and enthusiasm, and the results can be seen in the increasingly good quality of his wines. There are three products that we especially liked this year. The Pinot Bianco Sirmian '99 has a deep yellow colour, subtle, apple fruit aromas, and a fresh, well-typed, very zesty flavour: it is an excellent example of a fine Pinot Biancos from Alto Adige. The Chardonnay Baron Salvadori '98, from the winery's top range, is fermented and aged in barriques and is a different style of wine altogether. Golden in hue, it displays a lovely ripe fruitiness on the nose, with aromas of bananas and toasty notes. Full-bodied and buttery on the palate with a touch of saltiness, it rounds off with good length on the finish. The excellent Merlot-Cabernet Baron Salvadori Anticus '98 has an intense ruby colour with the faintest hint of garnet, as well as characteristic, slightly herbaceous aromas on the nose, nuances of coffee and sweetish oak hints. On the palate, it displays fine, rich fruit, with well-integrated tannins and appealing structure. The '99 whites that impressed, earning well-deserved commendations, were the Terlano Sauvignon Mantele, the Gewürztraminer Baron Salvadori, the Pinot Grigio Punggl and the Müller Thurgau, all technically perfect and highly quaffable wines. The Schiava Galela '99 is also well-typed. Lively and fresh as usual, it has good fruit and weight on the palate.

At Castel Schwanberg, there were two wines that got through to our final taste-offs for the Three Glass awards, the Cabernet Sauvignon Castel Schwanburg Riserva and the Lagrein Scuro Riserva, both '97s, and then a long sequence of products that are at least decent and well-made. That's a thumbnail sketch of Dieter Rudolph Carli's cellar, one of Alto Adige's historic producers and today still one of the most famous. We were presented with a rather large range this year, including big, rich reds, the winery's speciality, as well as simple, fruity and always beautifully made whites. There was no flash of brilliance to warrant a Three Glass award but the winery's reliability and consistent quality are indisputable. The Lagrein Scuro Riserva '97 is the real surprise here. It is an imposing, concentrated and very well-typed wine, slightly lacking in complexity, but otherwise very good indeed. The two Cabernet Sauvignons, the Castel Schwanburg and the Riserva, both '97s, are rounded and mouth-filling, with intensely balsamic aromas on the nose. The former, the more prestigious version, is more elegant and a little more concentrated but the two wines are fairly similar in terms of quality this year. The vintage was a pretty good one so there are fewer differences between them than usual. The white that impressed us most was the Terlano Sauvignon '99. It is full-bodied and offers a long, clean finish. The aromas are precise and positive but not particularly complex. All the other wines are sound, with the Pinot Nero '97 perhaps a tiny bit dilute, especially on the palate.

● A. A. Cabernet-Merlot		
Anticus Baron Salvadori '98	🍷🍷	5
○ A. A. Chardonnay		
Baron Salvadori '98	🍷🍷	4
○ A. A. Pinot Bianco Sirmian '99	🍷🍷	3*
○ A. A. Gewürztraminer		
Baron Salvadori '99	🍷	4
○ A. A. Müller Thurgau '99	🍷	3
○ A. A. Pinot Grigio Punggl '99	🍷	3
● A. A. Schiava Galea '99	🍷	3
○ A. A. Terlano Sauvignon Cl.		
Mantele '99	🍷	3
○ A. A. Chardonnay '98	🍷🍷	3*
○ A. A. Pinot Grigio Punggl '98	🍷🍷	3*
● A. A. Schiava Galea '98	🍷🍷	3*

● A. A. Cabernet		
Castel Schwanburg '97	🍷🍷	6
● A. A. Cabernet Sauvignon Ris. '97	🍷🍷	4
● A. A. Lagrein Scuro Ris. '97	🍷🍷	4
○ A. A. Pinot Grigio '99	🍷	4
● A. A. Pinot Nero '97	🍷	5
○ A. A. Riesling '99	🍷	4
○ A. A. Terlano '99	🍷	4
○ A. A. Terlano Pinot Bianco '99	🍷	4
○ A. A. Terlano Sauvignon		
Castel Schwanburg '99	🍷	5
● A. A. Cabernet		
Castel Schwanburg '90	🍷🍷🍷	6
● A. A. Cabernet		
Castel Schwanburg '96	🍷🍷🍷	6

NATURNO/NATURNS (BZ)

SALORNO/SALURN (BZ)

Tenuta Falkenstein
Franz Pratzner
Via Castello, 15
39025 Naturno/Naturns (BZ)
tel. 0473/666054

Haderburg
Loc. Pochi, 30
39040 Salorno/Salurn (BZ)
tel. 0471/889097

Franz Pratzner's tiny winery continues to produce some jewels of handcrafted winemaking. These are real wines, which express the area from which they come, and which reflect the differences between vintages as few others do This is the charm but also sometimes the handicap of estates like Tenuta Falkenstein. It is why last year, the Riesling managed to win a Three Glass award whereas this year it just failed to repeat the performance. Still, it's an outstanding white with a seductive power that derives from a noble grape grown in optimum conditions and from winemaking methods that aim to bring out the wine's personality rather than put on a show of ultra-refined technical bravura. The '99 has aromas of citrus fruit that are already fairly complex but which are certain to become even more minerally as time goes on. Its fruit structure is less concentrated than that of the '98 but it remains one of Alto Adige's very best Rieslings. The Pinot Bianco is very good. It is fleshy, varietal and delightfully rustic on the nose, showing itself to be another very genuine wine, with great character. The Gewürztraminer is also less varietal than the '98 but in particular it displays less depth than the previous version. However, it is a highly attractive, aromatic white. The Sauvignon was a surprise with its overwhelming, slightly exotic, aromas and intense, persistent flavour. The only relatively disappointing wine was the Pinot Nero '98, which was rather too pale in colour and was fairly dilute on the palate. It doesn't seem as if Pratzner is very happy with this variety but we will be very happy to be proved wrong in the future. In the world of wine, certainties tend not to last for very long.

This is an excellent year for the Haderburg estate. Luis and Christine Ochsenreiter were the first in Alto Adige, back in '76, to make Metodo Classico sparkling wines on a thoroughly professional basis and today, they are more than ever the benchmark for spumante-makers in the region. After the Spumante Hausmannhof '90, which last year displayed perhaps the highest level of quality ever obtained in Alto Adige, this time around they again presented two very stylish spumantes indeed. The Pas Dosé Riserva '93 is complex and mature, with buttery and yeasty overtones, and the Hausmannhof Brut '91, an intense, full-bodied sparkler, has inviting aromas of honey, ripe fruit and crusty bread, followed up by a rich, rounded palate. But Luis Ochsenreiter is a maestro with still wines, too. Pinot nero may be a grape that is extremely difficult to deal with, both in the vineyard and in the winery, as we all know, but Luis has achieved some truly remarkable results. The Pinot Nero Hausmannhof '98 is a pale ruby in colour, leading in to an intense nose with aromas of fruit, coffee and toasted oak. On the palate, it is full-bodied, powerful and tannic. The Pinot Nero Hausmannhof Riserva '97 is complex and fruity, with a noticeable new oak tone and a full yet stylish structure. These are two richly charcterful Pinot Neros. The Chardonnay Hausmannhof '98 displays a very intense, fruity style with exotic fruit notes and an elegant, well-integrated toasty nuance. Unfortunately, at the time of our tastings, the Sauvignon Hausmannhof '99 still seemed rather closed but it did reveal promising flinty aromas and a full palate with good acidity. The Gewürztraminer Blaspichl '99, which had been very good in the previous vintage, was not ready when we visited this year.

O	A. A. Sauvignon '99	🍷🍷	4
O	A. A. Valle Venosta Gewürztramlner '99	🍷🍷	4
O	A. A. Valle Venosta Pinot Bianco '99	🍷🍷	3*
O	A. A. Valle Venosta Riesling '99	🍷🍷	4
●	A. A. Valle Venosta Pinot Nero '98	🍷	4
O	A. A. Valle Venosta Riesling '98	🍷🍷🍷	4*
O	A. A. Valle Venosta Gewürztramlner '98	🍷🍷	4
O	A. A. Valle Venosta Pinot Bianco '97	🍷🍷	3*
O	A. A. Valle Venosta Pinot Bianco '98	🍷🍷	3*
●	A. A. Valle Venosta Pinot Nero '95	🍷🍷	5
O	A. A. Valle Venosta Riesling '97	🍷🍷	3*
O	Falkensteiner '97	🍷🍷	5
●	A. A. Valle Venosta Pinot Nero '97	🍷	4

O	A. A. Chardonnay Hausmannhof '99	🍷🍷	3*
●	A. A. Pinot Nero Hausmannhof '98	🍷🍷	4
●	A. A. Pinot Nero Hausmannhof Ris. '97	🍷🍷	5
O	A. A. Spumante Haderburg Pas Dosé '93	🍷🍷	4
O	A. A. Spumante Hausmannhof '91	🍷🍷	6
O	A. A. Sauvignon Hausmannhof '99	🍷	4
O	A. A. Gewürztraminer Blaspichl '98	🍷🍷	4
●	A. A. Pinot Nero Hausmannhof '95	🍷🍷	5
O	A. A. Sauvignon Hausmannhof '96	🍷🍷	5
O	A. A. Sauvignon Hausmannhof '97	🍷🍷	5
O	A. A. Spumante Haderburg Pas Dosé '91	🍷🍷	5
O	A. A. Spumante Hausmannhof '90	🍷🍷	6

STAVA/STABEN (BZ)

TENUTA UNTERORTL-CASTEL JUVAL
JUVAL, 1B
39020 STAVA/STABEN (BZ)
TEL. 0473/667580

TERLANO/TERLAN (BZ)

CANTINA DI TERLANO
VIA SILBERLEITEN, 7
39018 TERLANO/TERLAN (BZ)
TEL. 0471/257135

The wines that Martin Aurich submits for tasting are always good and well-made. They come from the splendid vineyards of the Unterortl estate, near Stava. Here, we are in Valle Venosta, 20 kilometres to the west of Merano, in a zone that is becoming a new focal point for high-quality viticulture in Alto Adige. This is a vine-growing area that is particularly suited to the most aristocratic white varieties but is also good for pinot nero, which expresses itself with good typicity here. Aurich's most impressive wine, though, is the Riesling '99, a white with real varietal character. Its aristocratic, complex aromas usher in a forthright palate with fairly marked acidity and more than decent length. It is elegant, subtle and well-defined, a fine example of good winemaking and respect for the characteristics of the riesling grape. Slightly lighter and less well-knit than the '98 is this year's version of the Pinot Bianco, another flagship product of this small but superbly equipped winery. Its so-called "backbone" of acidity is perhaps a little too unyielding but a few months' bottle-age should have a positive effect on the overall balance of the wine. We close with the Pinto Nero '98, which is soft on the palate and reasonably varietal on the nose. It lacks a little bit of concentration but is agreeable and fairly elegant.

A spectacular Lagrein Scuro Riserva '97, from Gries, the most traditional zone for this grape variety, brought our top award to the Cantina di Terlano after an absence of more than a decade. It is an impressive red, with complex, spicy, and even mineral aromas. The palate is potent and forthright, with barely noticeable tannins and remarkable body. It has grip and elegance, but above all, it shows what great wines can be made from an absolutely indigenous grape variety such as lagrein. But this is not the only exploit from this extraordinary winery. The Chardonnay '90, for example, is marvellous. Only the label gives away its age. It has a nose of rare complexity, the mineral notes melding into a bouquet that lets you pick out the varietal aromas of the grape from which it was originally made. A miracle, after all these years. The two Sauvignons are splendid. The Winkl '99 is more forward whereas the Quarz '98 is complex and varietal, with almost explosive fruit on the palate. Both have a slight residual carbon dioxide content that makes them prickly on the tongue. Will this become integrated with time in bottle? If so, they will both become considerably more elegant wines than they are today. The Terlano Nova Domus '97 is excellent, even if it does still display marked oaky notes. The Pinot Nero Montigl Riserva '98 is pleasant but a bit rustic. Finally, the Terlano Classico '99, the simplest wine in the range, is coherent but also slightly dominated by its wood.

○	A. A. Valle Venosta Riesling '99	🍷🍷	4
○	A. A. Valle Venosta Pinot Bianco '99	🍷	3
●	A. A. Valle Venosta Pinot Nero '98	🍷	5
○	A. A. Valle Venosta Pinot Bianco '98	🍷🍷	3*
●	A. A. Valle Venosta Pinot Nero '95	🍷🍷	5
●	A. A. Valle Venosta Pinot Nero '97	🍷🍷	5
○	A. A. Valle Venosta Riesling '96	🍷🍷	4
○	A. A. Valle Venosta Riesling '97	🍷🍷	4
○	A. A. Valle Venosta Riesling '98	🍷🍷	4
○	A. A. Valle Venosta Pinot Bianco '96	🍷	4
○	A. A. Valle Venosta Pinot Bianco '97	🍷	4
●	A. A. Valle Venosta Pinot Nero '96	🍷	5

●	A. A. Lagrein Scuro Gries Ris. '97	🍷🍷🍷	5
○	A. A. Terlano Chardonnay '90	🍷🍷	6
○	A. A. Terlano Nova Domus '97	🍷🍷	6
○	A. A. Terlano Sauvignon Quarz '98	🍷🍷	5
○	A. A. Terlano Sauvignon Winkl '99	🍷🍷	5
●	A. A. Pinot Nero Montigl Ris. '98	🍷	5
○	A. A. Terlano Classico '99	🍷	4
○	A. A. Terlano Pinot Bianco '79	🍷🍷🍷	5
○	A. A. Gewürztraminer Lunare '97	🍷🍷	4
●	A. A. Lagrein Porphyr Ris. '95	🍷🍷	5
●	A. A. Lagrein Porphyr Ris. '97	🍷🍷	5
●	A. A. Pinot Nero Montigl '97	🍷🍷	5
○	A. A. Terlano Nova Domus '98	🍷🍷	5
○	A. A. Terlano Sauvignon Quarz '97	🍷🍷	5
○	A. A. Terlano Sauvignon Winkl '98	🍷🍷	5

TERMENO/TRAMIN (BZ)

TERMENO/TRAMIN (BZ)

CANTINA PRODUTTORI DI TERMENO
STRADA DEL VINO, 122
39040 TERMENO/TRAMIN (BZ)
TEL. 0471/860126

PODERI CASTEL RINGBERG
E KASTELAZ ELENA WALCH
VIA A. HOFER, 1
39040 TERMENO/TRAMIN (BZ)
TEL. 0471/860172

We have kept a close, careful eye on the progress and quality of this winery over the last few years. It has now succeeded in positioning itself among the leading producers in its zone. Located on the slopes around Termeno, the ancient cradle of Gewürztraminer wine, it impressed us this year particularly with its native variety. Even the standard Gewürztraminer, the Maratsch '99, is an intense wine, with well-typed, rounded fruit and, what's more, excellent value for money. The Gewürztraminer Nussbaumerhof '99 is a wine of outstanding quality. It has an intense straw-yellow colour, introducing an explosive range of typical rose and lychee aromas, and such rich, full-bodied fruit on the palate that it leaves you open-mouthed (after you've swallowed, of course). Going from one success to another, we come to the feather in this winery's cap, the Gewürztraminer Passito Terminum '98. With its intense golden colour, its highly concentrated aromas and its powerful richness on the palate, a perfect balance of its 210 g/l of residual sugar and its 10.5 g/l of total acidity, it is undoubtedly one of the best sweet wines in Italy. It took our prize as "Sweet Wine of the Year". But we must not ignore the winery's other products. The whites include the excellent the Pinot Grigio Unterebnerhof '99 and the Sauvignon '99, the latter being particularly flavoursome. Among the reds, the Lagrein Urbanhof '98 is surely one of the best Lagreins outside the classic Gries zone. Stylish, and not far off a Three Glass rating, is the Cabernet Riserva '97, with its polished, well-typed fruit aromas reminiscent of morello cherries, blackberries and raspberries and an elegant, refined structure on the palate.

The wines of Elena Walch took home enough Glasses to set up a shop this year. This is proof again of the great strides that this cellar is making, whether or not any of its wines claim Three Glass status. But this time, our top accolade did go to the Cabernet Sauvignon Castel Ringberg Riserva '97, a great red that comes from the splendid vineyards overlooking Lake Caldaro. We can still clearly recall its intense, balsamic aromas, the varietal notes of berry fruit, the well-balanced flavour, the elegant body and the aristocratic, refined style on both nose and palate. It is a splendid, but not overblown, wine whose keynote is finesse. And it is flanked by a whole series of excellent products. These include the always well-typed Gewürztraminer from the Kastelaz estate at Termeno, the Sauvignon of Castel Ringberg at Caldaro, one of the few decent oak-fermented Sauvignons around, the delightful Cabernet Istrice '98, and the rounded, mouth-filling Merlot Riserva '97, again from Kastelaz. Then, there are all the other bottles in a range that has never before been so good or so impressive. These include the fragrant, immediately appealing Chardonnay Cardellino '99, the Pinot Grigio Castel Ringberg, which just missed out on a second Glass, and the always agreeable Pinot Bianco and Riesling, all from the '99 vintage. We'll finish off by offering our most sincere congratulations to one of Alto Adige's great ladies of wine, Elena Walch.

○ A. A. Gewürztraminer Nussbaumerhof '99	♟♟♟	4*
○ A. A. Gewürztraminer Passito Terminum '98	♟♟♟	6
● A. A. Cabernet Ris. '97	♟♟	5
○ A. A. Gewürztraminer Maratsch '99	♟♟	3*
● A. A. Lagrein Urbanhof '98	♟♟	4
○ A. A. Pinot Grigio Unterbnerhof '99	♟♟	4
○ A. A. Sauvignon '99	♟♟	4
● A. A. Pinot Nero Mazzon '98	♟	3
● A. A. Schiava Hexenbichler '99	♟	3
● A. A. Cabernet Terminum Ris. '95	♟♟♟	5
● A. A. Cabernet Renommée '97	♟♟	3*
● A. A. Lagrein Urbanhof '97	♟♟	3*

● A. A. Cabernet Sauvignon Castel Ringberg Ris. '97	♟♟♟	5
● A. A. Cabernet Istrice '98	♟♟	4
○ A. A. Gewürztraminer Kastelaz '99	♟♟	4
● A. A. Merlot Kastelaz Ris. '97	♟♟	5
○ A. A. Sauvignon Castel Ringberg '99	♟♟	4
○ A. A. Chardonnay Cardellino '99	♟	3
○ A. A. Pinot Bianco Kastelaz '99	♟	4
○ A. A. Pinot Grigio Castel Ringberg '99	♟	4
○ A. A. Riesling Renano Castel Ringberg '99	♟	4
○ A. A. Gewürztraminer Kastelaz '97	♟♟♟	4
● A. A. Cabernet Sauvignon Castel Ringberg Ris. '95	♟♟	5
● A. A. Merlot Kastelaz Ris. '96	♟♟	5

TERMENO/TRAMIN (BZ) VADENA/PFATTEN (BZ)

HOFSTÄTTER
P.ZZA MUNICIPIO, 5
39040 TERMENO/TRAMIN (BZ)
TEL. 0471/860161

ISTITUTO SPERIMENTALE LAIMBURG
LOC. LAIMBURG, 6
39051 VADENA/PFATTEN (BZ)
TEL. 0471/969210

Paolo Foradori, who for years has been in charge of this historic winery at Termeno, has handed over the keys of the cellar to his son, Martin. And Martin is showing that no father ever made a wiser decision. The range of wines presented to us, and scores they achieved, are indisputable proof of this. The Gewürztraminer Kolbenhof '99 earned a Three Glass award with ease for it is one of the very best wines in its category. We were thrilled by its fragrant aromas, so characteristic and well-defined that they paint a perfect portrait of the variety. Its structure on the palate is notable for concentration and balance, so it is no exaggeration to call it a masterpiece. But there are lots of wines from Hofstätter that are worth a closer look this year. The Lagrein Scuro Steinraffler '97 is a delicious red with fruity and spicy perfumes, as well as impressive weight. The Yngram '97, a blend of various red varieties, is an elegant, modern wine. The Cabernet Sauvignon Riserva '97 offers brilliant balance and typicity while the standard-label Pinot Bianco and Riesling '99 are wines whose value for money earmarked them for the panel's private cellars. The Alto Adige Bianco San Michele '99's most significant characteristics are its fruity aromas and its agreeable, inviting style on the palate. The basic Chardonnay '99 is well-managed and coherent. In fact, the only slight disappointment was the Pinot Nero S. Urbano '97. It is excellent, as usual, but ran into our customary severity when dealing with wines of this kind. It has body, power and excellent concentration but lacks the winning elegance of certain past vintages.

The Laimburg institute performed very well this year. There were one or two less wines than usual, only seven samples being submitted, but no less than six earned Two Glass ratings and at least two just missed out on a third Glass. Let's begin, then, with the heavyweights. The most impressive, which actually made it to our final taste-offs, was the Cabernet Riserva '97. It is a magnificent red, concentrated and rich, with compact tannins and elegant varietal aromas. It is not wildly complex but is very well-made and the oak already seems to have been absorbed quite well by the fruit. It promises to age very well for at least another ten years or so. Just behind it comes the Lagrein Scuro Riserva '97, which has an impenetrable colour and aromas that are at once spicy and fruity. Here, the oak is a little more in evidence, coming through in an overtone of freshly roasted coffee, but the structure is excellent and the varietal characteristics are nicely signalled, too. But there is more. The minerally, characteristic Riesling '99 is rather special and the aromatic and coherent but nicely concentrated '99 Gewürztraminer is excellent. The Moscato Rosa '97 is also good, even if it is not all that intense on the nose. Moscato Rosa is in fact one of the specialities of this extremely modern winery, owned by the Laimburg research institute for viticulture and winemaking. The only small, but relatively insignificant, quality hiccough came from the Pinot Nero '98, which lacks a little weight. But you could not expect a great deal more from this vintage.

○ A. A. Gewürztraminer Kolbenhof '99	ΥΥΥ	4*
○ A. A. Bianco S. Michele '99	ΥΥ	4
● A. A. Cabernet Sauvignon '97	ΥΥ	5
● A. A. Lagrein Scuro Steinraffler '97	ΥΥ	5
○ A. A. Pinot Bianco '99	ΥΥ	3*
● A. A. Pinot Nero S. Urbano '97	ΥΥ	6
○ A. A. Riesling '99	ΥΥ	3*
● Yngram '97	ΥΥ	5
○ A. A. Chardonnay '99	Υ	3
○ A. A. Gewürztraminer Kolbenhof '98	ΨΨΨ	4*
● A. A. Pinot Nero S. Urbano '93	ΨΨΨ	6
● A. A. Pinot Nero S. Urbano '95	ΨΨΨ	6

● A. A. Cabernet Ris. '97	ΥΥ	5
○ A. A. Gewürztraminer '99	ΥΥ	4
● A. A. Lagrein Scuro Ris. '97	ΥΥ	5
● A. A. Moscato Rosa '97	ΥΥ	6
○ A. A. Riesling Renano '99	ΥΥ	4
○ A. A. Sauvignon '99	ΥΥ	4
● A. A. Pinot Nero '98	Υ	5
○ A. A. Gewürztraminer '94	ΨΨΨ	4*
● A. A. Cabernet Ris. '94	ΨΨ	5
● A. A. Cabernet Ris. '96	ΨΨ	5
○ A. A. Chardonnay Doa '97	ΨΨ	5
● A. A. Merlot '96	ΨΨ	5
● V. A. Pinot Nero '97	ΨΨ	5
○ A. A. Riesling Renano '98	ΨΨ	4
○ A. A. Sauvignon '98	ΨΨ	4

VARNA/VAHRN (BZ)

VARNA/VAHRN (BZ)

CANTINA DELL' ABBAZIA DI NOVACELLA
VIA DELL'ABBAZIA, 1
39040 VARNA/VAHRN (BZ)
TEL. 0472/836189

KÖFERERHOF
VIA PUSTERIA, 3
39040 VARNA/VAHRN (BZ)
TEL. 0472/836649

No wine submitted by the Abbazia di Novacella and its shrewd, dynamic director, Urban von Klebersberg picked up a Three Glass prize this year. However, there is a brand new cellar, a talented oenologist in Celestino Lucin and, above all, a range of reliable, well-made wines. We are sure that this winery will have no trouble in collecting a top award in the next few years and one wine did actually get through to our final taste-off. That was the '99 Sauvignon, produced in the Markhof vineyards, where the Adige and Isarco Rivers flow into each other just south of Bolzano. A varietal, concentrated bottle, it could perhaps do with a little more structure but that is the fault of the vintage. Technically, it is just about perfect. Also good is the Praepositus Bianco '98, from sylvaner, pinot grigio and chardonnay. We tasted it last year and can confirm our assessment. All the other wines showed well, with the Pinot Nero Praepositus '97 leading the field, and the pair of well-typed whites from Valle Isarco, the Sylvaner and the Kerner, putting up a very creditable performance. Bear in mind that the vintage was not an easy one for either the zone or the varieties. Less impressive were the two aromatic wines, the Müller Thurgau and the Gewürztraminer, although it would be more appropriate to call them "semi-aromatic". They are lighter and slimmer than you might hope, but that is only to be expected in Valle Isarco. We are right at the geographical limit of viticulture and sometimes this fact is all too obvious in the wines. It is, in the words of Star Wars, the dark side of this terroir.

The difficulties caused by the climate have always obliged growers in the most northerly wine zones to make decisions that are quality-led. The weather is a hard taskmaster and if you leave too many bunches on the vine, the plant will struggle to ripen the grapes. Then the autumn rains come and the crop will be spoiled. Well, at this historic farm, which is over eight centuries old and which has been the property of the Kerschbaumer family for the past 60 years, they learned that lesson a long time ago. Together with those of the Abbazia di Novacella, these vineyards are the most northerly in Alto Adige. They only way to go is down the road of quality, aiming for low yields and healthy, ripe grapes. The resulting wines are sometimes amazing. This year, we could not really expect exceptional results yet everything actually seems to have worked out for the best. An excellent Pinot Grigio '99, with very typical aromas, especially of pears, and outstanding body, was the first wine to grab the panel's attentions. Then came a '99 Sylvaner with herbaceous and floral tones, and an extremely elegant palate. Finally, the '99 Kerner has citrus fruit notes on the nose and a backbone of acidity that underpins very satisfactory body on the palate. They are three impressive wines with a concentration you would not expect at these latitudes. It just goes to show that sound judgement can bring positive results even here, just a stone's throw from the Brenner Pass. The least interesting of the wines was the slightly thinnish '99 Gewürztraminer but this is a minor quibble.

● A. A. Pinot Nero Praepositus '97	🍷🍷	5
○ A. A. Sauvignon '99	🍷🍷	3*
○ A. A. Valle Isarco Gewürztraminer '99	🍷	3
○ A. A. Valle Isarco Kerner '99	🍷	3
○ A. A. Valle Isarco Müller Thurgau '99	🍷	3
○ A. A. Valle Isarco Sylvaner '99	🍷	3
○ A. A. Sauvignon '97	🍷🍷🍷	4*
● A. A. Lagrein Praepositus '97	🍷🍷	4
● A. A. Moscato Rosa '97	🍷🍷	5
● A. A. Pinot Nero '95	🍷🍷	4
○ A. A. Sauvignon '98	🍷🍷	3*
○ Praepositus '98	🍷🍷	4

○ A. A. Valle Isarco Kerner '99	🍷🍷	3*
○ A. A. Valle Isarco Pinot Grigio '99	🍷🍷	3*
○ A. A. Valle Isarco Sylvaner '99	🍷🍷	3*
○ A. A. Valle Isarco Gewürztraminer '99	🍷	3
○ A. A. Valle Isarco Kerner '98	🍷🍷	3*
○ A. A. Valle Isarco Pinot Grigio '98	🍷🍷	3*
○ A. A. Valle Isarco Sylvaner '98	🍷🍷	3*
○ A. A. Müller Thurgau '98	🍷	3
○ A. A. Valle Isarco Gewürztraminer '98	🍷	3

OTHER WINERIES

The following producers in the province of Bolzano obtained good scores in our tastings with one or more of their wines:

PROVINCE OF BOLZANO

Viticoltori dell'Alto Adige/Südtiroler Weinbauernverband,
Appiano/Eppan, tel. 0471/666060
A. A. Chardonnay Torculum '99,
A. A. Lagrein Scuro Torculum Ris. '97

Egger-Ramer,
Bolzano/Bozen, tel. 0471/280541
A. A. Lagrein Scuro Grieser Kristan Ris. '97

Malojer Gummerhof,
Bolzano/Bozen, tel. 0471/972885
A. A. Cabernet Ris. '97,
A. A. Lagrein Scuro
Gries Weingut Rahmhütt '98,
A. A. Lagrein Scuro Ris.'97,
A. A. Santa Maddalena Classico '99

Loacker Schwarzhof,
Bolzano/Bozen, tel. 0471/365125
A. A. Lagrein Scuro Pitz Thurü '98,
Cuvée Jus Osculi '98

Georg Mumelter,
Bolzano/Bozen, tel. 0471/973090
A. A. Lagrein Scuro Griesbauerhof '98,
A. A. Pinot Grigio Griesbauerhof '99,
A. A. Santa Maddalena Cl. Griesbauerhof '99

Anton Schmid – Oberrautner,
Bolzano/Bozen, tel. 0471/281440
A. A. Lagrein Scuro Grieser '98,
A. A. Lagrein Scuro Ris. '97,
A. A. Merlot '97

Baron Dürfeld de Giovannelli,
Caldaro/Kaltern, tel. 0471/962072
A. A. Lago di Caldaro Scelto Keil '99

Kettmeir,
Caldaro/Kaltern, tel. 0471/963135
A. A. Chardonnay Maso Rainer '99,
A. A. Terlano Pinot Bianco '99

Peter Sölva & Sohn,
Caldaro/Kaltern, tel. 0471/964650
A. A. Lagrein Scuro Desilvas '98,
A. A. Merlot Desilvas '98

Baron Widmann,
Cortaccia/Kurtatsch, tel. 0471/880092
Rot '98

Castello Rametz,
Merano/Meran, tel. 0473/211011
A. A. Cabernet '97,
A. A. Pinot Nero '97,
Chardonnay Cesuret '97

Wilhelm Walch,
Termeno/Tramin, tel. 0471/860172
A. A. Chardonnay Pilat '99,
A. A. Pinot Bianco '99

VENETO

Taking full advantage of the very favourable '95, '97 and '98 vintages, the producers of the Veneto have put up their best performance since we started publishing this Guide to Italian Wines. Fully 16 estates collected a total of 17 Three Glass awards this year, the lion's share, as is by now the norm in this region, again going to the province of Verona. Here, thanks to major DOC zones which are now well-known both in Italy and at an international level, things are hunky-dory. Apart from Amarone, which is increasingly establishing itself as the guiding light for winemaking in the Veneto, it was the Reciotos from Valpolicella that excelled in our tastings. Two of them, from Tommaso Bussola and Venturini, obtained our top accolade but several others earned scores just below the 90-point threshold. Among the producers who made their mark in the production of this style, which is important for both the economy and the image of the Valpolicella area, we would draw your attention to Accordini, Allegrini, Viviani and Begali. Three Soaves earned our major award but only Gini's La Froscà really stood out as exceptional in a difficult vintage like '99. It is also in this part of the Veneto that we find the only winery to win more than one Three Glass rating. The estate concerned is the Fumane-based Allegrini, which again staked its claim to the title of the leading winery in the Veneto, and indeed beyond. But alongside the positive notes, there were also certain incongruities, which to some extent are damping the desire for improvement in important areas like that around Verona. We are talking about the need that certain producers feel to withdraw from the DOCs in which they have made their names. Leading producers like Allegrini and Anselmi, who feel that they can no longer identify with the spirit of their denominations as they now stand, have opted (partly in the case of the former, entirely in the case of the latter) for the less significant IGT status. Another sore point in Veronese winemaking is that of viticulture, still too often focused on quantity rather than quality. Finally, we should also like to remind you that – thanks partly to the entrepreneurial spirit of certain young oenologists – the wines of the co-operatives at Valpolicella and at Soave showed very well this year. Then we noted with pleasure the excellent performance put up by Maculan's wines in the province of Vicenza and the successful results obtained by the Recioto di Gambellaras of Zonin and of Angiolino Maule at La Biancara. Again in the province of Vicenza, at Bassano del Grappa, there is the Vigneto Due Santi, where Stefano Zonta is putting his heart into his winemaking. Further east, towards Venice, we are witnessing the coming of age of some producers in the Colli Euganei, in the province of Padua. Here, Vignalta again obtained our Three Glass accolade, this time with the excellent '98 Gemola. The prestige of the Treviso area was stoutly defended by yet another great interpretation of the Rosso dell'Abazia from dynamic duo Serafini and Vidotto whereas other important wineries are having trouble taking off. Definitely worth watching, though, are the wines of Ornella Molon Traverso and of Bepin de Eto.

BAONE (PD)

BARDOLINO (VR)

IL FILÒ DELLE VIGNE
VIA TERRALBA, 239
35030 BAONE (PD)
TEL. 0429/56243

F.LLI ZENI
VIA COSTABELLA, 9
37011 BARDOLINO (VR)
TEL. 045/7210022

"Far filò" means to carry on the rural oral tradition of story-telling. So "il Filò delle Vigne" refers to the handing down, from vine to vine, and from the older plants to the younger ones, of experience, character and flavours, as well as the progress of the lymph as it is transformed into the succulence of the grapes. This estate is located in an ideal position for producing wine. It lies to the south-east of Monte Cecilia, in the heart of the Colli Euganei Natural Park, an area rich in vegetation and plants of every sort, and a haven for birds and wild animals. The winery, which belongs to Nicolò Voltan and Gino Giordani, has 17 hectares under vine, with an annual production of around 60,000 bottles. Winemaking is supervised by the young but knowledgeable oenologist Andrea Boaretti, who is a point of reference for the new wave of winemakers in the Colli Euganei. The vines are cordon-trained and spur-pruned, double-arch cane-trained, or trained in the Casarsa variation of the Sylvoz system. There is also an ampelographical collection, created in association with the Oenological School at Conegliano, which is packed with indigenous varieties of considerable educational interest. There are also extensive olive groves, belonging to the moraiolo, raza and leccino varieties, and the extravirgin oil produced here is good. The excellent Borgo delle Casette, from 70 percent cabernet sauvignon and 30 percent cabernet franc, with a yield of 28 hectolitres per hectare, is aged for 18 months in barrique, remains in stainless steel for a further 18 and is then bottled without filtering. The Vigna Cecilia di Baone, which matures only in stainless steel, is a very precise expression of cabernet franc, revealing hints of red peppers, tobacco and spring flowers. The Pinot Bianco is also very sound. Straw-yellow in colour with green highlights, it offers hints of wild strawberries, walnuts and hazelnuts.

The Zeni estate dates way back to 1870 but, unusually, it continued to sell its wine in bulk to Switzerland until 1985. In the 80s, however, Gaetano "Nino" Zeni started to bottle his wines, building up business and bringing it to the approximately 800,000 bottles of today. This volume is split over three lines, the basic Zeni brand, Vigne Alte, made from specially selected grapes, and Marogne, the company's flagship range. There are 25 hectares at Bardolino and three at Gargagnago in Valpolicella while long-standing contract suppliers provide the rest of the fruit. The Zeni Wine Museum, set up at the company's headquarters, is of notable cultural interest:. With its detailed descriptions and its wealth of historic tools and other objects, it presents an extraordinary overview of the world of grape and wine production, and will be of particular interest to younger visitors. The long series of wines presented, from which the two special selections of Amarone were missing, nevertheless included a thoroughly decent Amarone '97. An almost opaque ruby in colour, it combines freshness with notes of ripe fresh berry fruits and bottled fruit. It is rounded, warm and full-bodied on the palate. The Soave Vigne Alte is delicious, with its hints of peaches and almonds, supple body and attractive acidulous vein. The Valpolicella Marogne is very sound, too. Ruby shading into garnet in colour, it has a floral and peppery bouquet. On the palate, where finesse rather than power is the keynote, there are flavours of red berry fruit and liquorice. The Bianco di Custoza is commendable for its bouquet of apples and peaches, good body and sound balance. The tangy and fruity Bardolinos are of good quality, only the Classico Superiore showing below par. The Valpolicella Classico Superiore and the Garda Garganega Vigne Alte gained honourable mentions. The Recioto '97, tasted last year prior to release, performed well, too.

● Colli Euganei Cabernet		
Borgo delle Casette Ris. '96	♟♟	5
● Colli Euganei Cabernet		
Vigna Cecilia di Baone Ris. '97	♟	5
○ Colli Euganei Pinot Bianco '99	♟	4

● Amarone della Valpolicella Cl. '97	♟♟	6
○ Soave Cl. Sup. Vigne Alte '99	♟♟	3*
☉ Bardolino Chiaretto Cl. '99	♟	2*
● Bardolino Cl. Vigne Alte '98	♟	3
● Bardolino Marogne '98	♟	4
○ Bianco di Custoza Vigne Alte '99	♟	3
● Recioto della Valpolicella		
Vigne Alte '97	♟	6
● Valpolicella Cl. Sup. Vigne Alte '98	♟	3
● Valpolicella Marogne '98	♟	4
● Bardolino Cl. Sup. '98		2
○ Garda Garganega Vigne Alte '99		3
● Valpolicella Cl. Sup. '98		2
● Amarone della Valpolicella Cl. '88	♟♟♟	6

BASSANO DEL GRAPPA (VI) BREGANZE (VI)

VIGNETO DUE SANTI
V.LE ASIAGO, 174
36061 BASSANO DEL GRAPPA (VI)
TEL. 0424/502074

MACULAN
VIA CASTELLETTO, 3
36042 BREGANZE (VI)
TEL. 0445/873733

Stefano Zonta is learning from experience and the progress is evident throughout the whole of his range. The wines now boast a cleaner style and he has gained greater confidence, both in managing the vineyards and in the winery, where he intervenes as little as is humanly possible. The '99 confirmed itself as a particularly good vintage for whites, starting with the Prosecco, which is floral and appealing. The Breganze Bianco is attractive, from its colour and aromas of flowers, apples, and hay through to its richness and power on the palate. The Malvasia is a classic and will be a pleasant surprise for anyone who has not yet had the chance to try this wine. Its nose is predictably exuberant. Sage, cloves and apples are just some of the sensations that take you in to a dry, long palate reminiscent of apples. If it were just a little more crisp and elegant, it would be a truly great wine. The Breganze Rosso '98 combines both ripeness and freshness. Its smoky nose offers a succession of spice, redcurrant jelly and clove nuances while on the palate it is easy-drinking in the best sense of the word. The Vigneto Due Santi, made predominantly from cabernet sauvignon, represents the company's top selection. Both colour and nose immediately suggest intensity and richness. Elegance and depth go hand in hand in a bouquet with marked hints of wild berries, stylish oak, citrus fruits and tobacco. On the palate, the oak is well-integrated and gives way to a nice fruity aftertaste. What is extraordinary about this wine is its balance, which combines very rich fruit and uncommonly fine-grained tannins, a sign of its excellent cellar potential over the next few years.

Maculan's new winery is beginning to take shape. It's a real Château-style affair with welcoming hospitality rooms and rationalized structures for receiving and vinifying the grapes, and for subsequently ageing the wine. In the meantime, we noted the marked progress in the white wines, which are much more convincing in recent years. The newest release, Pinot & Toi – "Pinot" stands for Pinot Bianco and Grigio and "Toi" for Tocai – is just an introduction to a praiseworthy Breganze di Breganze, which displays aromas of hay and apples on the nose and packs plenty of character on the palate. No longer dominated by often excessive oaking, the Chardonnay Riale opens up with super-ripe fruit notes and delights the palate with its balance of fruit and acidity. The other Chardonnay comes from the Ferrata vineyard and takes a bit of time to reveal its charms. After a few minutes, though, it has sorted itself out and enfolds you with aristocratic aromas of honey, butter and hazelnuts. The well-modulated oak adds complexity to the tightly-knit, refined and spicy palate. The delicious Dindarello is as exemplary as ever while the Torcolato confirms the high quality it has shown over the past few years. Moving over to the reds, we find one of the best versions ever of the Palazzotto, with its bouquet of blackcurrants and cloves and good meaty flavour. The Merlot Marchesante is on great form, proving to be well-balanced, soft and muscular at the same time. All that remains is for us to talk about Maculan's "grand vin", the Fratta which amazed us so much last year. The '98, still tough owing to its youth, has intense, mineral aromas, in which the fruit and the toastiness of the oak meld perfectly. The flavour is rich and intriguing, displaying lots of fascinating nuances. A wonderfully made, full-bodied and complex wine – perhaps the estate's best ever – which again earns our Three Glass accolade.

O	Breganze Bianco '99	🍷🍷	3*
●	Breganze Cabernet		
	Vigneto Due Santi '98	🍷🍷	5
O	Malvasia Campo di Fiori '99	🍷	3
O	Prosecco	🍷	3
●	Breganze Cabernet		
	Vigneto Due Santi '95	🍷🍷	4
●	Breganze Cabernet		
	Vigneto Due Santi '96	🍷🍷	4
●	Breganze Cabernet		
	Vigneto Due Santi '97	🍷🍷	4
O	Breganze Sauvignon		
	Vigneto Due Santi '98	🍷🍷	4
●	Breganze Cabernet '96	🍷	3

●	Fratta '98	🍷🍷🍷	6
●	Breganze Cabernet Sauvignon		
	Palazzotto '97	🍷🍷	5
O	Breganze Chardonnay Ferrata '98	🍷🍷	5
O	Breganze Chardonnay Riale '98	🍷🍷	4
O	Breganze Torcolato '98	🍷🍷	6
O	Breganze di Breganze '99	🍷	3
●	Breganze Merlot Marchesante '98	🍷	5
O	Dindarello '99	🍷	5
O	Pino & Toi '99		3
O	Acininobili '91	🍷🍷🍷	6
●	Breganze Cabernet Sauvignon		
	Ferrata '94	🍷🍷🍷	6
●	Cabernet Sauvignon Ferrata '90	🍷🍷🍷	6
●	Fratta '97	🍷🍷🍷	6

CAVAION VERONESE (VR)

LE FRAGHE

LOC. COLOMBARA, 3
37010 CAVAION VERONESE (VR)
TEL. 045/7236832

Le Fraghe is situated in the little village of Colombara at Cavaion Veronese, between Lake Garda and the Adige valley, on morainic hillsides that are particularly favourable for the cultivation of vines. The first wines were vinified here in 1984, the year that marks the foundation of the estate as it now stands. Today, it is run by Matilde Poggi, a determined woman with very clear ideas about the wines she wants to make from her 28 hectares of vineyards. These are divided up between three sites, at Cavaion, Affi and Rivoli, which are three different DOC zones, Bardolino, Garda and Valdadige. The varieties grown range from the indigenous corvina, rondinella and garganega to the international cabernet and chardonnay. Total production is 70,000 bottles, sold at extremely fair prices. We tasted the cabernet-based Quaiare '97 while it was still ageing but we can assure you that it will be an outstanding wine. In the meantime, the '96 version fully confirmed its quality. We can also tell you that the Chardonnay '99 is very promising, which goes to show that the extensive work that has been carried out in the vineyards is providing the foundation for a rosy future at this estate. The '98, which we are reviewing this year, has a light touch of oakiness, as well as aromas of hazelnuts, citrus fruits and a mineral note. It is attractive and fairly long on the palate. The Garganega offers hints of herbaceousness, peaches and golden delicious apples. The '99 Bardolino, made with 30 percent partially dried grapes, is a very characterful wine. The aromas of spices and freshly mown grass on the nose are followed by a palate that, apart from youthful tannins, offers cherry and liquorice overtones. The fresh, appealing Bardolino Chiaretto is a mouthful of sheer delight.

⊙	Bardolino Chiaretto '99	🍷	3
●	Bardolino Cl. '99	🍷	3
○	Garganega del Veneto '99	🍷	3
○	Valdadige Chardonnay '98	🍷	3
●	Valdadige Quaiare '96	ΥΥ	4

CINTO EUGANEO (PD)

CA' LUSTRA

VIA S. PIETRO, 50
FRAZ. FAEDO
35030 CINTO EUGANEO (PD)
TEL. 0429/94128

Year after year, Ca' Lustra has demonstrated such an ability to make progress and to take quality-led decisions that you can happily rank its wines with the very best from the Veneto. Besides, there is no doubt that owners Franco Zanovello and Ivano Giacomin, with oenologist Francesco Polastri, are guarantees of serious professionalism. The view from the Buon Retiro Ca'Lustra is one of the most breathtaking in the Colli Euganei and the decision to open the estate to visitors, particularly school groups, and its close links with the local catering college bode well for its future as an educational resource. At present, the estate extends over 30.5 hectares, 21 of which are under vine. The plants are cordon-trained and spur-pruned, at a density of between 3,000 and 5,000 plants per hectare. The soils are a mixture of sand and limestone, the former coming from volcanic rock and the latter from marine sedimentation. Total output is 170,000 bottles a year. The whites performed very impressively indeed, especially the Vigna Linda, an excellent Incrocio Manzoni Bianco. This was followed by the zesty and full-bodied Pinot Bianco and Ca' Lustra's best Sauvignon to date. The Chardonnay Vigna Marco is excellent while the Colli Euganei Bianco is much more than merely satisfactory. Most notable of the reds were the two Cabernets, the Colli Euganei and the Girapoggio. The Colli Euganei Rosso and the Merlot are very appealing and there is also a forceful Barbera (yes, this grape variety is also grown here). The Colli Euganei Fior d'Arancio is perfumed, aromatic and delightfully bright.

○	Colli Euganei Chardonnay Vigna Marco '99	🍷🍷	4
○	Colli Euganei Pinot Bianco '99	🍷🍷	3*
○	Incrocio Manzoni Vigna Linda '99	🍷🍷	4
○	Sauvignon del Veneto '99	🍷🍷	3*
●	Barbera del Veneto '98	🍷	4
○	Colli Euganei Bianco '99	🍷	3
●	Colli Euganei Cabernet '98	🍷	3
●	Colli Euganei Cabernet Girapoggio '98	🍷	4
○	Colli Euganei Chardonnay '99	🍷	3
●	Colli Euganei Merlot '99	🍷	3
●	Colli Euganei Rosso '99	🍷	3
○	Colli Euganei Spumante Fior d'Arancio '99	🍷	3

COLOGNOLA AI COLLI (VR)   DOLCÉ (VR)

TENUTA SANT'ANTONIO
VIA CERIANI, 23
FRAZ. S. ZENO
37030 COLOGNOLA AI COLLI (VR)
TEL. 045/7650383

ARMANI
VIA CERADELLO, 401
37020 DOLCÉ (VR)
TEL. 045/7290033

The Castagnedi brothers own 20 hectares in the Illasi valley at 120 metres above sea level and another 20 in the Mezzane valley, at 320 metres, on volcanic or limestone soils. Another fundamental reason for their success is their friendship with oenological consultant, Celestino Gaspari, a man who combines great expertise with a profound knowledge of the Valpolicella zone. The estate's handsome and spacious new winery is being completed at Mezzane. It has been built with an eye on one of the zone's particular features, the practice of partially drying the grapes, which calls for large, well-ventilated drying rooms. The varieties grown are garganega, trebbiano di Soave and sauvignon blanc at Illasi, and corvinone, corvina, rondinella, cabernet, merlot, chardonnay and small quantities of other varieties at Mezzane. The training systems used are mainly cordon training with spur pruning, and Guyot. In the '99 vintage, production reached 80,000 bottles. The property also sells extravirgin olive oil. As was the case last year, there are two outstanding wines from Tenuta Sant'Antonio, the Cabernet Capitello and the Amarone Campo dei Gigli. The Cabernet, for which the grapes are dried for about 20 days, has a deep, opaque ruby colour. The nose displays complex herbaceous fragrances and hints of mint and tobacco while the palate offers sensations of ripe berry fruits, with vanilla, chocolate and spices. The Amarone, after three years' ageing in Slavonian oak barrels, also presents a very deep colour. Its generous bouquet unveils notes of cherries, spices and cocoa. On the palate, the wine is warm, mouth-filling and long, with hints of liquorice and pencil lead. Finally, the Valpolicella Monti Garbi and the Chardonnay Capitello only just missed out on Two Glass ratings.

It seems that the indigenous foja tonda variety has always been grown in the Val Lagarina, where it has settled in perfectly, unlike nearly all the other grape types that arrived from the Middle East to spread to their present production zones. For several years now, Albino Armani has devoted his time and enthusiasm to the re-discovery and promotion of this variety. To further his campaign, new vineyards obtained from careful clonal selections will be planted in the spring of 2001, in accordance with strict quality-driven criteria. The latest version of the Foja Tonda confirmed last year's good performance, thanks to its rich, complex and idiosyncratically aromatic style, accompanied by a modern palate where the skilful use of oak does not prevent the primary aromas from showing through. We would also draw your attention to the Corvara, made from 50 percent cabernet sauvignon and 50 percent corvina and merlot. Its long maturation in barrique adds complexity on the nose and a marked tannic vein that only requires further bottle-age to meld with the wine's very good, fleshy fruit. The whites performed well, particularly the Sauvignon Campo Napoleone and the Chardonnay Piccola Botte. We liked the zestiness and pungent aromatic quality of the former, and the fruity and floral notes in the Chardonnay, which contrast well with the wine's fairly marked oakiness. Notes of rennet apples and citrus fruits, as well as good acidity, are the main characteristics of the appealing Chardonnay Vigneto Capitel.

●	Amarone della Valpolicella		
	Campo dei Gigli '96	♟♟	6
●	Cabernet Sauvignon		
	Vigna Capitello '98	♟♟	6
○	Chardonnay Vigna Capitello '98	♟	4
●	Valpolicella Sup. Monti Garbi '98	♟	4
●	Cabernet Sauvignon		
	Vigna Capitello '97	♟♟♟	6
●	Amarone della Valpolicella		
	Campo dei Gigli '95	♟♟	6
●	Cabernet Sauvignon		
	Vigna Capitello '95	♟♟	6
○	Passito Colori d'Autunno '95	♟♟	5
○	Passito Colori d'Autunno '96	♟♟	5
●	Valpolicella Sup. Monti Garbi '97	♟	4

●	Corvara Rosso '97	♟♟	5
●	Foja Tonda Rosso '98	♟♟	4
○	Sauvignon Campo Napoleone '99	♟	3
○	Trentino Chardonnay		
	Vigneto Capitel '99	♟	4
○	Valdadige Chardonnay		
	Piccola Botte '99	♟	4
●	Foja Tonda Rosso '97	♟♟	4
●	Corvara Rosso '96	♟	4

FOSSALTA DI PORTOGRUARO (VE)   FUMANE (VR)

SANTA MARGHERITA
V.LE ITA MARZOTTO, 8
30025 FOSSALTA DI PORTOGRUARO (VE)
TEL. 0421/246111

★ ALLEGRINI
VIA GIARE, 9/11
37022 FUMANE (VR)
TEL. 045/6832011 - 045/7701138

The origins of this company date back to 1935, when Conte Gaetano Marzotto purchased from the aristocratic Stucky family a farm of over 1,000 hectares, 140 of which were under vine. His original intention was to combine agriculture with his industrial interests but in 1979, Santa Margherita acquired a momentum of its own, becoming increasingly involved in the wine business with acquisitions in Alto Adige, Franciacorta and Chianti Classico. Who has never drunk, or at least seen a bottle of the Pinot Grigio which has, over the years, become emblematic of the company? A well-made, pleasant wine, it takes on greater significance if you consider that 5,000,000 bottles of it are produced. We were able to witness during our visit how the firm's attention to quality is increasing, reflecting Santa Margherita's position in the market and the winemaking potential it possesses. If Italy wishes to compete with tough competition from abroad, then even large producers and distributors must make quality their first priority and not delegate the production of premium bottles to small and medium-sized operations. The Malbech Laudato created an excellent impression, and almost rated Two Glasses. An intense ruby in colour, it offers a lovely, elegant bouquet with hints of cherries, plums and blackberries. It has good tannins and an attractively full flavour. The barrique-fermented Chardonnay Ca' d'Archi is of a similar standard. A golden yellow in hue, it unveils vanilla, hazelnut and citrus fruit notes followed up by a refreshing, well-structured palate. The Luna dei Feldi, the Cabernet Sauvignon Ca' d'Archi and the Merlot Versato are all good. The Müller Thurgau is a bit closed on the nose but is sound on the palate. The Refosco and the Cabernet Franc from Lison-Pramaggiore are youthful and refreshingly quaffable.

When discussing Allegrini, you can easily fall into the trap of just talking about the wines themselves. These are important, excellent and even, sometimes, perfect but that would only give an incomplete picture. To get a more precise idea of the estate, you need to talk about it with Franco himself and understand why he wants to take a stand and promote his area, as well as the modern, though tradition-imbued, philosophy that underlies his approach to winemaking. And you have to talk to him about corvina, too, a great grape in which Allegrini believes wholeheartedly, to the extent of taking the painful decision to withdraw his two Valpolicella Superiores from the DOC. From the '97 vintages onwards, they become IGT wines. Let's begin with the two Three Glass products. The La Poja '96, though lacking the power of the '95, is a wine of great depth, with spicy and gamey notes that, coupled with its concentration and firm tannins, promise great ageing potential. From the same vintage comes the Amarone, whose modern profile means that it suffers even less from the poorish quality of the vintage. It has an extremely elegant, mineral style and offers fruit that does not immediately reveal the partially dried grapes from which it was made. Ripe and succulent, it is surprisingly refined for an Amarone. The La Grola and Palazzo della Torre stood up well when compared with wines from other areas. The elegance and cleanliness of their fruit make these two very dependable wines. The Recioto, a paradigm of finesse and elegance, is as splendid as ever. In fact, it is one of Valpolicella's classic sweet wines. Allegrini hits the spot every time and even the straightforward Valpolicella Classico easily obtained a Two Glass score thanks to its finesse and its well-balanced, easy-drinking style.

● A. A. Cabernet Sauvignon Ca' d'Archi '97	♟	5
○ A. A. Chardonnay Ca' d'Archi '98	♟	5
● Laudato Malbech del Veneto Orientale '96	♟	4
○ Luna dei Feldi Vigneti delle Dolomiti '99	♟	4
● Versato Merlot del Veneto '98	♟	3
○ A. A. Müller Thurgau '99		4
● Lison-Pramaggiore Cabernet Franc '98		3
● Lison-Pramaggiore Refosco P. R. '98		3
○ Valdadige Pinot Grigio '99		3

● Amarone della Valpolicella Cl. '96	♟♟♟	6
● La Poja '96	♟♟♟	6
● La Grola '97	♟♟	5
● Palazzo della Torre '97	♟♟	5
● Recioto della Valpolicella Cl. Giovanni Allegrini '97	♟♟	6
● Valpolicella Cl. '99	♟♟	4
● Amarone della Valpolicella Cl. '95	♟♟♟	6
● Amarone della Valpolicella Cl. '93	♟♟♟	6
● La Poja '93	♟♟♟	6
● La Poja '95	♟♟♟	6
● Recioto della Valpolicella Cl. Giovanni Allegrini '93	♟♟♟	6
● Recioto della Valpolicella Amarone Cl. Sup. '91	♟♟♟	6

FUMANE (VR)

LE SALETTE
VIA PIO BRUGNOLI, 11/C
37022 FUMANE (VR)
TEL. 045/7701027

Franco Scamperle and his wife, Monica had great results at the last tastings and they have thrown themselves into running their family estate with renewed energy in order to consolidate the unquestionable leap forward they have made over the last few years. The wine that impressed us most was the Recioto Pergole Vece, which offers a very broad spectrum of aromas, with floral hints of iris and ripe fruit tones which then veer towards unexpected mineral notes. It is creamy and close-knit on the palate, where the fruit evolves in a well-sustained crescendo. The Amarone La Marega, from a vintage deemed inadequate for producing the Pergole Vece selection, received the Scamperles' full attention and is a wine which is all about elegance and approachability. Its fruity aromas are simultaneously fresh and ripe while its fullness and balance on the palate, with firm tannins underpinning the softness of the fruit, demonstrate how you can make a good wine even in indifferent years. Of the two Valpolicella Superiores, we were more impressed by the Ca' Carnocchio, which comes from a vineyard used exclusively for Valpolicella. This means that it is not stripped of the best grapes which normally go to make Amarone. On the nose, it displays clean, positive aromas of crushed red berry fruits while on the palate, the slight roughness that gives it personality is combined with elegance and balance. The creamy, minerally Passito Bianco is also well-made while the '99 Valpolicella is an exercise in lightness and pleasant quaffability.

GAMBELLARA (VI)

LA BIANCARA
C.DA BIANCARA, 8
36053 GAMBELLARA (VI)
TEL. 0444/444244

A strenuous defender of an area which has for too long been a source of unexceptional wines, Angelino Maule draws from his own passion the strength, imagination and humility that enable him to overcome the limitations of a grape like garganega, which is by nature rather unforthcoming in its aromatic profile. Yet the happy combination of the Gambellara zone and this cantankerous grape can give rise to some absolutely extraordinary products, if they are made by a craftsman who knows how to extract depth and character from his terroir. A superb example is the great Recioto '97, which can line up with the very best of Italy's sweet wines. Drying is carried out with meticulous and patient care, and the skilfully measured combination of each of the wine's elements, as well as grapes of outstanding quality, make for a perfect equilibrium of the sugars and the acidity. Taibane, a monovarietal garganega, is the name of a late-vintage wine which regales the nose with an exciting succession of aromas such as honey, apricots, hazelnuts and cooked pears. The palate echoes these notes and the residual sugars are well balanced by a delicate acidulous vein that prolongs the finish. The floral, clean Gambellara I Masieri is very decent while the Sassaia catches your attention with its finesse and the persistent progression of the palate, which offers attractive minerally notes and hints of almonds and citrus fruits, as well as an extremely well-defined flavour. The 100 percent garganega Pico de Laorenti is a very different proposition. The result of a much freer hand in the cellar, it finally lives up to its aspirations this year. The well-integrated oak acts as a foil for a bouquet of tropical fruit, mint, flowers and spices, setting off its long, ripe, deliciously crisp flavour. The Masieri Rosso, an unusual blend of merlot and lagrein cultivated in this zone, is worthy of an honourable mention.

O	Cesare Passito Bianco '97	🍷🍷	5
●	Amarone della Valpolicella Cl. La Marega '96	🍷🍷	5
●	Recioto della Valpolicella Pergole Vece '97	🍷🍷	6
●	Valpolicella Cl. Sup. Ca' Carnocchio '97	🍷🍷	4
●	Valpolicella Cl. Sup. I Progni '97	🍷	3
●	Valpolicella Cl. '99		2
●	Amarone della Valpolicella Cl. Pergole Vece '95	🍷🍷🍷	6
●	Amarone della Valpolicella Cl. La Marega '95	🍷🍷	5
●	Amarone della Valpolicella Cl. Pergole Vece '93	🍷🍷	6

O	Gambellara Cl. Sup. Sassaia '99	🍷🍷	3*
O	Pico de Laorenti '98	🍷🍷	4
O	Recioto di Gambellara '97	🍷🍷	6
O	Taibane '96	🍷🍷	5
O	Gambellara Cl. I Masieri '99	🍷	2*
●	Masieri Rosso '98		2
O	Recioto di Gambellara '95	🍷🍷	5
O	Recioto di Gambellara '96	🍷🍷	5
O	Recioto di Gambellara Ris. '92	🍷🍷	6

GAMBELLARA (VI)

ZONIN
VIA BORGOLECCO, 9
36053 GAMBELLARA (VI)
TEL. 0444/640111

ILLASI (VR)

ROMANO DAL FORNO
VIA LODOLETTA, 4
FRAZ. CELLORE
37031 ILLASI (VR)
TEL. 045/7834923

Although the Zonin family has deep roots in the Gambellara denomination, it has invested profitably in several other Italian wine areas, from Piedmont (Castello del Poggio) to Lombardy (Tenuta Il Bosco), Tuscany (Castello D'Albola), Friuli and Sicily. To reinforce the brand image and highlight the differences between the various lines, they have hired one of Italy's most knowledgeable and gifted winemakers, Franco Giacosa. He has worked hard on improving the vineyards with the aim of exploiting the potential of each of the various subsidiaries to the utmost. As usual, we are grouping together the wines of Zonin's three estates in north-east Italy in this Guide profile, which covers Giangio in Gambellara, Maso Laito in Valpolicella and Ca' Bolani in Friuli. Ca' Bolani's range of whites is very decent indeed, with the 50 percent chardonnay and 50 percent tocai Opimio taking pride of place. Its good structure succeeds in showing off the two varieties' full-bodied charms to best effect. The rich, attractively aromatic Sauvignon is very good, too, while the Pinot Grigio is more straightforward. The best of the reds are the Conte Bolani, from 60 percent merlot and 40 percent cabernet sauvignon, which is stylish and elegant but a bit lacking in body, and the Cabernet Franc, in which the tannins have still not quite found a point of balance. From Gambellara comes the winery's finest new product, the Recioto di Gambellara. This is an excellent dessert wine, whose power is revealed right from the colour in the glass. It has an intense nose with hints of citron and aromatic Mediterranean herbs while the flavour is fleshy and mouth-filling to the point of opulence. The Gambellara Il Giangio is pleasant, although it suffered from the poor quality of the vintage. The Amarone '96 comes from a rather poor year and merits no more than a mention, as does the '98 Valpolicella.

It is not easy to talk about Romano Dal Forno and what he has accomplished. He deserves our most sincere compliments but we wouldn't like our words of praise to sound trite. We'll let his wines speak, then. Instantly recognizable among thousands, they are capable of arousing great excitement but also some perplexity, especially in wine-lovers who have difficulty in comprehending Dal Forno's innovative, and extremely untraditional style. These wines tell us a great deal about the man who made them and his constant search for perfection. His methods leave themselves open to criticism and force Romano himself to constantly question his own convictions. The last few Amarones he has produced are obvious examples of this evolution, their evident change of style aiming to exalt the fragrance of the fruit with a shorter drying period for the grapes and more parsimonious use of wood. The overwhelming concentration which is their hallmark will increasingly be guaranteed by careful management and low yields in the vineyards, which in some cases reach a density of 11,000 vines per hectare. The wines presented this year do not require any particular comments, except to note that the two vintages of Amarone, '94 and '95, follow the path forged by the Amarone '93 towards a style based on elegance, freshness and directness on the nose, without compromising on the body, warmth and infinite length of past versions. These are two great expressions of Amarone, and both deserve very high ratings. Our preference goes to the '95, though, which is even more deep and harmonious than previous selections and unhesitatingly earns our top Three Glass award. It is fair to say that the two vintages of Valpolicella the panel tasted, the '95 and '97, represent a preview of the profound changes which this wine, too, will undergo, destined as it is, in Dal Forno's scheme of things, to aspire to the heights of the Amarone.

O	Friuli Aquileia Sauvignon		
	Ca' Bolani Aristòs '99	♟♟	4
O	Opimio Ca' Bolani Aristòs '99	♟♟	4
O	Recioto di Gambellara		
	Podere il Giangio Aristòs '97	♟♟	5
●	Conte Bolani Ca' Bolani Aristòs '97	♟	5
O	Friuli Aquileia Pinot Grigio		
	Ca' Bolani Aristòs '99	♟	4
O	Prosecco Spumante Brut	♟	2
●	Amarone della Valpolicella		
	Maso Laito '96		5
●	Friuli Aquileia Cabernet Franc		
	Ca' Bolani Aristòs '97		4
O	Gambellara Cl. Podere Il Giangio '99		2
●	Valpolicella Cl. Maso Laito '98		3

●	Amarone		
	Vigneto di Monte Lodoletta '95	♟♟♟	6
●	Amarone		
	Vigneto di Monte Lodoletta '94	♟♟	6
●	Valpolicella Sup. '95	♟♟	6
●	Valpolicella Sup. '97	♟♟	6
●	Amarone		
	Vigneto di Monte Lodoletta '90	♟♟♟	6
●	Amarone		
	Vigneto di Monte Lodoletta '91	♟♟♟	6
●	Amarone		
	Vigneto di Monte Lodoletta '93	♟♟♟	6
●	Recioto della Valpolicella		
	Vigneto di Monte Lodoletta '94	♟♟	6

ILLASI (VR)

SANTI
VIA UNGHERIA, 33
37031 ILLASI (VR)
TEL. 045/6520077

Santi is one of the jewels in the Gruppo Italiano Vini's crown. This group, which is the leading wine producer in Italy both in terms of the overall number of bottles produced and of turnover, owns various estates scattered among the major wine-producing areas of the country. Santi, along with Conti Formentini in Friuli, Nino Negri in Lombardy and Machiavelli in Tuscany, is one of the group's model subsidiaries. The recent efforts towards improving quality have been notable, both in terms of the winemakers involved – Marco Monchiero and his team, for instance, have been working at Santi for some years now – and with respect to the investments made both in the winery and in the vineyard. The final results are particularly evident in two very interesting wines that easily passed the Two Glass threshold. The Amarone della Valpolicella Proemio '97 repeats the successful performance of the '95 selection, making the most of one of the vintages of the decade in Valpolicella. This wine is by no means muscular but is extremely enjoyable for its elegance and finesse. The nose is fruity and sweet, with dried black cherry notes lightly tinged with oak. It is soft and clean on the palate, with a persistent fruity note on the back palate that sets its character apart from that of other Amarones. The Soave Sanfederici '99 is also very good and is less influenced by the fermentation barriques than last year's version. It is a very interesting white, which makes a good pair with the rather more straightforward Soave Monteforte. A well-deserved Glass goes to the Lugana Malibeo, offered for tasting for the first time, and to the Le Solane and Le Caleselle Valpolicella Classicos, while the Bardolino Ca' Bordenis earns an honourable mention.

ILLASI (VR)

TRABUCCHI
LOC. MONTE TENDA
37031 ILLASI (VR)
TEL. 045/7833233 - 049/650129

Thanks to the notable resources which they possess both in the vineyards and in the winery, the Trabucchis are succeeding in their aim of guaranteeing consistently high quality. The wines tasted this year are proof of this, starting with the two Valpolicellas, the San Colombano and the Terre del Cereolo. The San Colombano, made from grapes which have been lightly dried and aged partly in large oak barrels and partly in pre-used barriques, has a fine, bright colour and offers positive scents of ripe cherries and tea leaves. Its stablemate, the Terre del Cereolo, is the result of a strict selection of grapes from vineyards in the Cereolo zone and of a slightly longer period of drying. In this case, ageing at the winery takes place exclusively in barriques. The outcome is a wine with a very rich nose that displays extremely attractive notes of chocolate and tobacco, and very great concentration on the palate. The Amarone, which is noteworthy more for its elegance than its power, is just as admirable a wine, as are the '96 and '97 Reciotos. The '96, making the most of a poor vintage, manages to be temptingly delicious while the '97, taking advantage of what was undoubtedly better fruit, offers an elegant yet generous spectrum of aromas and a full-bodied flavour. The Passito Sparavieri, made from garganega grapes, is an inviting amber in colour, displaying fairly complex aromas with floral and citrus notes, the good acidity on the palate giving it freshness. The version that we tasted this year was the '97, erroneously listed in last year's Guide (it should have been the '95).

● Amarone della Valpolicella Proemio '97	♟♟	6
○ Soave Cl. Sanfederici '99	♟♟	4
○ Lugana Malibeo '99	♟	4
○ Soave Cl. Monteforte '98	♟	3*
● Valpolicella Cl. Le Caleselle '99	♟	3
● Valpolicella Cl. Le Solane '98	♟	3
● Bardolino Cl. Vigneto Ca' Bordenis '99		3
● Amarone della Valpolicella '90	♟♟	6
● Amarone della Valpolicella Proemio '95	♟♟	6

● Amarone della Valpolicella '97	♟♟	6
● Recioto della Valpolicella '97	♟♟	5
● Valpolicella Sup. Terre del Cereolo '97	♟♟	5
● Valpolicella Sup. Terre di S. Colombano '97	♟♟	4
○ Passito Sparavieri '97	♟	5
● Recioto della Valpolicella '96	♟	5
● Amarone della Valpolicella '95	♟♟	6
● Amarone della Valpolicella '96	♟♟	6
● Recioto della Valpolicella '95	♟♟	5
● Valpolicella Sup. Terre di S. Colombano '96	♟♟	4
○ Passito Sparavieri '95	♟	5

LAZISE (VR)

LAMBERTI
VIA GARDESANA
37017 LAZISE (VR)
TEL. 045/7580034

Lamberti's grapes are actually grown in some of the most beautiful farms in the best vine-growing zones of the area around Verona while the company's headquarters at Lazise houses the ageing cellars and the facilities for welcoming guests. The name of the firm, founded on the shores of Lake Garda in 1964, derives from that of one of the oldest families in Verona. The Lambertis were also among the city's leading families and struggled for supremacy against the powerful house of Della Scala. The Torre dei Lamberti, in Verona's Piazza delle Erbe, has been one of the city's landmarks for centuries. The winery owns 110 hectares in Bardolino at Tenuta Preella and Villa Cordevigo, in the Classico zone, and 60 in Valpolicella at Tenuta Pule at San Pietro in Cariano. Vinification takes place at the Preella and Pule properties whereas bottling – and Lamberti produces some 8,000,000 bottles a year – is all carried out at the highly functional winery at Pastrengo. There are many ranges produced, from the cheaper ones to catering labels for restaurants. We tasted the top line, the one produced with grapes from Lamberti's own estates, skipping the various ranges made from bought-in grapes and wines. All the samples we tasted obtained One Glass ratings and the Soave Santepietre once again proved to be one of the best wines on the entire list. Equally attractive were the Bardolino Chiaretto Santepietre, with its attractively fruity aromas and freshness on the palate, the Bardolino Classico and the Orchidea Platino, a Bianco di Custoza that is always one of the best in its category. In contrast, the Amarone has a little less individuality, and doesn't really get the best out of the excellent '95 vintage.

●	Amarone Corte Rubini '95	🍷	5
⊙	Bardolino Cl. Chiaretto Santepietre '99	🍷	2*
●	Bardolino Cl. Santepietre '99	🍷	2*
○	Bianco di Custoza Orchidea Platino '99	🍷	3
○	Soave Cl. Santepietre '99	🍷	3
●	Amarone Corte Rubini '93	🍸	5

LAZISE (VR)

LE TENDE DI FORTUNA E LUCILLINI
LOC. LE TENDE
FRAZ. COLÀ
37017 LAZISE (VR)
TEL. 045/7590748

This estate has been run for just over ten years by its two young owners, Mauro Fortuna, who personally looks after production, and Beatrice Lucillini, who is in charge of the commercial side of things. They are constantly seeking to create an identity for themselves in an area that straddles both the Bianco di Custoza and Bardolino DOC zones and which all too often tends to produce wines rather lacking in personality. Year after year, they try to learn from their experience to achieve the tough objectives they have set themselves. This has pushed them to gain a dependable level of quality so all that is missing is the constant presence of a star wine in their range. We are sure that Mauro and Beatrice will fill this gap by taking some even more courageous decisions, including reducing the range of their products so as to channel their efforts rather more productively. The wines tasted this year bear out what we say above. The Cicisbeo, without the help of a really good vintage, lacks that little bit of freshness which would have made it more well-balanced. It still earned a decent rating, though not as good as last year's. The less ambitious Sorbo degli Uccellatori has all its usual delicacy. Slightly over-assertive oak handicapped the Lucillini, which we have appreciated more on other visits. We found the Custoza Oro interesting for its complex nose and good fleshy fruit on the palate. We preferred the simpler version of Bardolino and in fact it is the style that better expresses this denomination's true vocation. Greater persistence and finesse would have enabled the Amoroso, a white dessert wine, to rise above being merely pleasant.

○	Amoroso '98	🍷	4
●	Bardolino Cl. '99	🍷	2*
○	Bianco di Custoza Lucillini '99	🍷	3
○	Bianco di Custoza Oro '99	🍷	3
●	Garda Cabernet Sauvignon Cicisbeo '98	🍷	4
●	Garda Cabernet Sauvignon Sorbo degli Uccellatori '98	🍷	4
●	Bardolino Cl. Sup. '98		3
●	Cicisbeo '95	🍸🍸	5
●	Cicisbeo '97	🍸🍸	4
○	Amoroso '97	🍸	4
●	Cicisbeo '96	🍸	4

MARANO DI VALPOLICELLA (VR)

MARANO DI VALPOLICELLA (VR)

GIUSEPPE CAMPAGNOLA
VIA AGNELLA, 9
FRAZ. VALGATARA
37020 MARANO DI VALPOLICELLA (VR)
TEL. 045/7703900

MICHELE CASTELLANI E FIGLI
VIA GRANDA, 1
FRAZ. VALGATARA
37020 MARANO DI VALPOLICELLA (VR)
TEL. 045/7701253

This company has a rather interesting history that deserves to be told. Carlo Campagnola began the winemaking adventure at the end of the 19th century then, in 1907, he was awarded a prize at the Verona Wine Exhibition for the best "recciotto". This was the spur that led to his business really taking off and to his combining, over the course of the years, his work as a wine man with the role of tavernkeeper. When Carlo died, the responsibility for all of his activities fell on the shoulders of his wife Caterina Zardini, who found herself with nine children and 100 hectares of land to look after. Over time, this large estate was broken up and today the Campagnolas are in fact left with only three hectares. The vital thing, though, is that the original spirit has stayed alive. Luigi and his son Giuseppe, a dynamic promoter of Campagnola's wines, have been keeping a watchful eye on around 60 contract growers for over 50 years now. Today, major extension works are taking place at the winery to bring it into line with present production needs. The firm now produces 6,000,000 bottles a year, including DOC wines from Valpolicella, but also makes many other styles from the rest of the Veneto. The oenologist for the past 30 years has been Gaetano Pasqua. The Valpolicella Superiore Le Bine, a name which means "rows of vines", made with fruit from vineyards at Purano, is delicate and stylish, with notes of tobacco and bottled fruit. It has good tannins and a flavoursome finish. The Amarone Caterina Zardini is excellent, with its ripe cherry fruit and spicy overtones leading in to a full, rounded, warm palate. The Corte Agnella, made from corvina grapes, is very appealing. This is a wine whose best feature is its nose but which is enjoyable on the palate, too. The Bianco di Custoza and the Soave are refreshing and attractive. Finally, the Recioto Casotto del Merlo was a bit disappointing. It is rather too straightforward and lacking in expressiveness for a wine of this type.

After splitting up with his brother, Sergio Castellani was left, essentially, with the winery and the brand name but most of the vineyards had gone. He therefore had the problem of purchasing plots in an area which was enjoying a boom. Castellani decided to buy new property a little at a time, rather than have to make do with less than perfect sites. His Ca' del Pipa line is very decent indeed. Now released for the second time, it comes exclusively from a splendid south east-facing hill, situated at an altitude of between 150 and 300 metres above sea level. In the wide range of wines on offer, the most successful are the ones made from partially dried grapes. The Recioto Campo Casalin is full-bodied and juicy with extremely stylish and supple fruit on the palate. Though complex and rich, it is still graceful and attractively understated. The Amarone Campo Casalin is super-ripe on the nose, with vegetal and chocolate overtones, while the palate is again rich and full-bodied, clean and long. The other Amarone, the Ca' del Pipa, reveals even more depth. Very intense aromas of roasted hazelnuts and ripe fruit alternate on the nose and the warm, alcohol-rich palate is soft, and has excellent thrust. The Recioto Ca' del Pipa is an exciting wine from a good vintage. After opening with elegant notes of dried flowers and ripe red berry fruit, the progression on the palate is gradual, persistent and increasing intense. The Valpolicella Superiores and the non-DOC wines are also well-made, providing further proof of the Castellani winery's high quality and reliability.

Wine	Rating	Score
● Amarone della Valpolicella Cl. Caterina Zardini '97	▼▼	6
● Valpolicella Cl. Sup. Vigneti di Purano Le Bine '98	▼▼	3*
○ Bianco di Custoza '99	▼	1*
● Corte Agnella Corvina Veronese '98	▼	3
○ Soave Cl. Sup. Vigneti Monte Foscarino Le Bine '99	▼	2*
● Recioto della Valpolicella Cl. Casotto del Merlo '98		4
● Amarone della Valpolicella Cl. Caterina Zardini '95	▽▽	6

Wine	Rating	Score
● Amarone della Valpolicella Cl. Campo Casalin I Castei '97	▼▼	6
● Amarone della Valpolicella Cl. Le Vigne Ca' del Pipa '97	▼▼	6
● Recioto della Valpolicella Cl. Campo Casalin I Castei '97	▼▼	6
● Recioto della Valpolicella Cl. Le Vigne Ca' del Pipa '98	▼▼	6
● Cabernet Sauvignon Ca' del Pipa '97	▼	5
● Cabernet Sauvignon I Castei '97	▼	4
● Valpolicella Cl. Sup. Ripasso Ca' del Pipa '97	▼	4
● Valpolicella Cl. Sup. Ripasso I Castei '97	▼	4

MARANO DI VALPOLICELLA (VR) MARANO DI VALPOLICELLA (VR)

CORTE RUGOLIN
LOC. RUGOLIN, 1
FRAZ. VALGATARA
37020 MARANO DI VALPOLICELLA (VR)
TEL. 045/7702153

F.LLI DEGANI
VIA TOBELE, 3/A
FRAZ. VALGATARA
37020 MARANO DI VALPOLICELLA (VR)
TEL. 045/7701850

Elena and Federico Coati demonstrate yet again the excellent results of which they are capable. It is good to see two young, responsible and very modest people who work with such seriousness and enthusiasm. The estate that the brother and sister team have been running since their parents, Bruno and Silvia, with great foresight, entrusted it to them, consists of five hectares at Marano and five more rented at Negrar, Sant' Ambrogio and Castelrotto, all lying within the Valpolicella Classico zone. Production ranges from 25,000 to 30,000 bottles a year, and is sold mainly abroad. The estate's wines, made with the assistance of oenologist Luigi Andreoli, are the standard ones for this DOC zone, plus a white dessert wine, also a traditional type in the area. We'll begin our notes with the dessert wine, the Passito Veronese Aresco, named after a Latin word meaning "to dry". It has a golden yellow colour with amber highlights. On the nose, there are hints of citrus fruit, especially tangerines, dried flowers and apricots, and the same aromas return on the palate, along with quince, figs, nuts and honey. The Recioto has a floral nose, overlaid with gooseberries, chocolate and plums. The palate reveals hints of cherry jam and rum baba. A truly delightful wine. The Valpolicella di Ripasso is garnet ruby, leading in to a nose of predominantly youthful, toasty notes, with a hint of smokiness along with nuances of leather and tobacco. A little bit of bottle-age will undoubtedly do wonders for its balance and personality. The young Valpolicella is refreshing yet warm. Only the Amarone Monte Danieli is missing from our roll-call. This will be the splendid '97 vintage, as the Coatis skipped the '96, which they did not consider up to par.

The Degani property began to devote its energies to viticulture at the beginning of the 20th century but it was not until around 1970 that brothers Angelo and Sante, who ran the family estate at the time, gave a serious kick start to the vinification and selling of its wines in the Verona area. In 1988, young Aldo joined the company, assisted by his brothers Luca, responsible for winemaking, and Zeno in the vineyards. Together, they took up the challenge of further establishing their products in various markets. The Deganis look after some six hectares of land in the Valpolicella Classico zone, divided between Sant' Ambrogio and Valgatara, at Marano. The grapes they cultivate are the traditional ones for the zone – corvina, rondinella, molinara and sangiovese. In the simple and functional winery, there is an atmosphere of honest-to-goodness hard work and a practical approach that is reflected in the wines, starting with the young Valpolicella, a fresh, fruity, easy drinking tipple. In contrast, the Valpolicella Superiore, coming as it does from the excellent '97 vintage, displays a generous nose with hints of spices, leather and even printer's ink. On the palate, it is stylish and elegant. The Amarone '95 is worth investigating for its warm, mouth-filling, well-structured palate. The Amarone La Rosta, on its first appearance, is also very impressive. The dense ruby colour ushers in balsamic aromas with undertones of juniper and spices. The chewy fruit, backed up by prominent tannins, takes you through to a long finish. Lastly, we come to the two Reciotos. Their main qualities are their approachability, their rich fruit and their sweet, jammy aromas.

O Aresco Passito Veronese '98	🍷🍷	6
● Recioto della Valpolicella Cl. '98	🍷🍷	6
● Valpolicella Cl. Sup. di Ripasso '98	🍷🍷	4
● Valpolicella Cl. '99		3
● Amarone della Valpolicella Cl.		
Vigneto Monte Danieli '95	🍷🍷	6
● Recioto della Valpolicella Cl. '97	🍷🍷	5

● Amarone della Valpolicella Cl. '95	🍷🍷	5
● Amarone della Valpolicella Cl.		
La Rosta '95	🍷🍷	6
● Valpolicella Cl. Sup. '97	🍷🍷	4
● Recioto della Valpolicella Cl. '97	🍷	5
● Recioto della Valpolicella Cl. '98	🍷	5
● Valpolicella Cl. '99	🍷	3
● Amarone della Valpolicella Cl. '93	🍷🍷	5
● Amarone della Valpolicella Cl. '94	🍷🍷	5
● Recioto della Valpolicella Cl. '95	🍷🍷	4
● Recioto della Valpolicella Cl. '96	🍷🍷	4

MARANO DI VALPOLICELLA (VR)   MARANO DI VALPOLICELLA (VR)

GIUSEPPE LONARDI
VIA DELLE POSTE, 2
37020 MARANO DI VALPOLICELLA (VR)
TEL. 045/7755154

NOVAIA
VIA NOVAIA, 3
37020 MARANO DI VALPOLICELLA (VR)
TEL. 045/7755129

In the commune of Marano di Valpolicella, at around 350 metres above sea level, wines are produced which, thanks to the prevailing mesoclimatic conditions, are more notable for their elegance than for their power. The products made by Giuseppe Lonardi, owner of the winery that bears his name as well as of the small restaurant which he runs with his family in the centre of the village, are no exception to this rule. The Privilegia, made from cabernet franc re-fermented in February thanks to the addition of partially dried corvina grapes, is right back on form. Concentrated in colour, it offers a broad, complex gamut of aromas, hampered only by a slightly excessive oaky note. The tannic palate leads into a fine aftertaste of ripe cherries. The range of wines was very sound indeed. The Lonardi Amarone repeats its good results of last year, winning appreciation for the depth of its nose, which releases its aromas quite slowly, and for its elegance and balance on the palate. Both the Reciotos achieved excellent ratings. The Recioto Classico '98 stands out for its up-front, jammy fruit notes and for its easy-drinking style while the Recioto Classico Le Arele '97 has an elegant bouquet and well-balanced sweetness on the palate. The fairly lean entry on the palate prevents the Valpolicella Superiore '97 from scoring as highly as the previous wines though it does have a rich, complex spectrum of aromas. The only negative note comes from the young Valpolicella, which is handicapped by a difficult vintage and is no more than satisfactory.

For some years now, the Vaona brothers have been pursuing a policy that will radically transform their estate. It has led them to replant their own eight hectares of vineyards with new systems which will be more efficient in terms of quality. This process of change has also had an effect on the winery, whose renovation has not only made it more attractive to look at but also more efficient, thanks to the purchase of new machinery and the substitution of the old wooden barrels with better-quality barriques. The wines we tasted this year, though again showing their usual elegance, were generally too lean, which rather penalized them. Although it presented a refined and interesting array of aromas, the '96 Amarone was clearly a victim of a poor vintage – one of the most problematic in recent years – which limited its progression on the palate. The same goes for the Recioto, whose style is based on freshness and immediacy. We very much look forward to tasting the more ambitious new version, which will spend a period of time in oak. Hints of black cherries in syrup and balsamic notes characterized the intriguing nose of the Valpolicella Superiore, giving way to a vibrant freshness on the palate. The Valpolicella Classico '98 is straightforward and well-managed. Knowing, as we do, the great potential of this estate and the capabilities of Cesare and Giampaolo Vaona, we are convinced that, after the changes have been completed and given more favourable vintages, these wines will return to the level of excellence to which for some years now the brothers have accustomed us.

● Amarone della Valpolicella Cl. '96	ΨΨ	5
● Privilegia '97	ΨΨ	5
● Recioto della Valpolicella Cl. '98	ΨΨ	5
● Recioto della Valpolicella Cl. Le Arele '97	ΨΨ	5
● Valpolicella Cl. Sup. '97	Ψ	3
● Valpolicella Cl. '99		2
● Amarone della Valpolicella Cl. '95	♀♀	5
● Recioto della Valpolicella Cl. '96	♀♀	4
● Amarone della Valpolicella Cl. '93	♀	5
● Recioto della Valpolicella Cl. '97	♀	4
● Recioto della Valpolicella Cl. Le Arele '95	♀	5

● Amarone della Valpolicella Cl. '96	Ψ	5
● Recioto della Valpolicella Cl. '98	Ψ	5
● Valpolicella Cl. '98	Ψ	2
● Valpolicella Cl. Sup. '97	Ψ	4
● Amarone della Valpolicella Cl. '95	♀♀	5
● Amarone della Valpolicella Cl. '94	♀	5

MEZZANE DI SOTTO (VR) MEZZANE DI SOTTO (VR)

CORTE SANT'ALDA
VIA CAPOVILLA, 28
LOC. FIOI
37030 MEZZANE DI SOTTO (VR)
TEL. 045/8880006

BRUNO SARTORI
VIA S. GIOVANNI DI DIO, 19
37030 MEZZANE DI SOTTO (VR)
TEL. 045/8880089

Within the space of 15 years, Marinella Camerani has made the estate that she has named after her daughter Alda into one of the very best in Valpolicella. With her forthright, no-nonsense character, she has succeeded in implementing this time-consuming, arduous task with great care and application. Her 15 hectares of vines are on limestone soil and are situated at altitudes which vary between 250 and 350 metres above sea level. The varieties planted are predominantly the classic grapes of Valpolicella – corvina, rondinella, molinara and corvinone, along with a small proportion of white grapes as well. The subzone is Val di Mezzane, an area also renowned for its cherries. For some years now, Marinella has been able to count on the crucial support of her partner, Cesar Romar, a Peruvian who is becoming increasingly passionately interested in winemaking. There are two very special wines this year, the Amarone '95 and the Valpolicella Mithas '97. The Amarone has an intense ruby colour and offers herbaceous notes as well as aromas of morello cherries and bottled fruit. The palate, where we find nuances of chocolate and coffee, is well-knit and the long finish displays finesse, elegance and power. This magnificent Amarone earned Marinella Camerani her second Three Glass award. The Valpolicella Mithas is one of the best we have ever tasted. Its generous, fruity bouquet, full body and chewy fruit are its major features. The Recioto is also remarkable, and the Valpolicella Superiore is excellent. We shall also be keeping an eye on the evolution of the Retratto, a blend of late-vintage chardonnay and sauvignon fermented and aged in barrique.

The Bruno Sartori estate appeared in the Other Wineries section last year but now gains its own well-deserved entry in our Guide. Acquired in 1949, it began production under the La Nave name in the 70s. It was 1993 that saw the next step forward, with the creation of a range that aimed to achieve the new level of quality imposed by contemporary developments in the market for wine. After some experimentation, the '96 vintage witnessed the release of these new wines, looked after today by Bruno and his son Marco, who is a trained oenologist. The wines come from three sites located in the Val di Mezzane valley in the Soave and Valpolicella zones to the north-east of Verona. In all, there are 12 hectares under vine, six at Mezzane planted to soave, one of garganega in the Valpolicella zone and five at San Briccio, near Lavagno, for the reds. We'll begin with the Soave and the Recioto di Soave, a '98 and a '97 respectively. The Soave, principally from garganega grapes with some trebbiano di Soave, is aged in barrique. It offers delicate, sweetish notes on the nose and has an attractive fruity flavour. The Recioto, made entirely from garganega, matures for 18 months in barrique. Golden yellow shading into amber in colour, it unveils aromas of flowers, pineapple and beeswax. On the palate, there are notes of pear and apricot jam, melding into a mouth-filling fusion of acidity and buttery richness. Moving on to the reds, the panel enjoyed the Valpolicella, aged for 20 months in oak and for ten in bottle. Ruby verging on garnet in colour, it reveals notes of vanilla, herbs and tobacco on the nose. The palate offers hints of berry fruit, in a delicate body. The Amarone has an opaque red hue. Delicate, elegant, evolved and gently spicy on the nose, it has a warm, velvety, full-bodied flavour, with overtones of prunes.

●	Amarone della Valpolicella '95	▼▼▼	6
●	Valpolicella Sup. Mithas '97	▼▼	5
●	Recioto della Valpolicella '97	▼	5
○	Retratto '99	▼	4
●	Valpolicella Sup. '97	▼	4
●	Amarone della Valpolicella '90	♀♀♀	6
●	Amarone della Valpolicella '92	♀♀	6
●	Amarone della Valpolicella '93	♀♀	6
●	Amarone della Valpolicella '94	♀♀	6
●	Amarone della Valpolicella Mithas '90	♀♀	6
●	Valpolicella Sup. Mithas '96	♀♀	5
●	Recioto della Valpolicella '96	♀	5

●	Amarone della Valpolicella Roccolo Grassi '96	▼▼	6
○	Recioto di Soave La Broia '97	▼▼	5
○	Soave Sup. La Broia '98	▼▼	4
●	Valpolicella Sup. Roccolo Grassi '97	▼	5

MIANE (TV)

GREGOLETTO
VIA S. MARTINO, 1
FRAZ. PREMAOR
31050 MIANE (TV)
TEL. 0438/970463

MONSELICE (PD)

BORIN
VIA DEI COLLI, 5
35043 MONSELICE (PD)
TEL. 0429/74384

Miane is located halfway between Conegliano and Valdobbiadene. Nearby, in the small village of Premaor, stands the winery of Luigi Gregoletto, one of the area's historic producers. Gregoletto has always believed both in diversifying his product line and in promoting the cause of indigenous varieties such as verdiso. This family-run company has around 30 hectares at its disposal – 15 at Rua di Feletto and the rest in Premaor and Refrontolo. Overall, after buying additional grapes, Gregoletto produces roughly 200,000 bottles a year, sold principally in north-eastern Italy although some are distributed to the rest of the country and abroad. During our visit, we were pleased to note that the Gregolettos were creating a library containing specialist books on viticulture and winemaking but also covering other subjects, proof positive of a cultural sensibility which does credit to the family. Again, the best wine is the Albio, a prototype in the past for the Colli di Conegliano Bianco denomination and now one of its finest versions. An intense straw-yellow in colour, it is elegant and redolent with apple, citrus fruit, almond and peachskin aromas. Its flavour is minerally, full-bodied and long. The '95 Colli di Conegliano Rosso is ruby, verging towards garnet. On the nose, it reveals notes of grass, hay, leather, tobacco and flowers while on the palate it is acidity and tannin that predominate, leaving an aftertaste of damsons. We would draw your attention to the Prosecco Tranquillo, again one of the most persuasive examples of its type. Carrying on through the range, all the wines listed below are linear, correct and appealing. Worth highlighting, apart from the characterful Verdiso, are the Prosecco Extra Dry, the Cabernet and the Merlot.

The Borin winery was founded in 1963 at Monticelli, at the side of the enchantingly picturesque road that leads to Arquà Petrarca, in other words in the southernmost part of the Colli Euganei. Grower and university lecturer, Gianni Borin, and his wife, Teresa, look after the vineyards and winemaking with great enthusiasm. The property is planted at 3,000 vines per hectare on sedimentary limestone soils both on hillslopes and flatland sites. Around 20 of the 26 hectares are under vine and production totals 110,000 bottles a year. The grapes grown range from pinot bianco, to cabernet, merlot and the indigenous corbinella padovana for the reds. This year the wines showed decidedly well. There was an excellent result on its first release for the Cabernet Riserva Mons Silicis. A purplish ruby in colour, it reveals herbaceous fragrances with nuances of mint, and the palate has good body and length. The same can be said of the Colli Euganei Fior d'Arancio Passito. A golden yellow in colour, its bouquet offers hints of honey, hazelnuts, figs, orange marmalade and dried leaves. The Colli Euganei Cabernet Vigna Costa is very well fashioned. Garnet in hue, it offers spicy sensations of red peppers, pencil lead, liquorice and prunes on the nose. The Colli Euganei Chardonnay Vigna Bianca is appealing. With its handsome golden straw colour, it unveils floral scents and hints of walnuts and hazelnuts. The palate is full-bodied and quite alcoholic. The Colli Euganei Vigna dei Mandorli and the Merlot Vigna del Foscolo are both well-made. The Pinot Bianco Vigna Arlecchino is refreshing and pleasantly quaffable. The Corbinello is really rather curious, with its alcohol-rich yet fruity style while the Fior d'Arancio Spumante is true to type.

○	Colli di Conegliano Bianco Albio '99	♀♀	3*
●	Cabernet dei Colli Trevigiani '98	♀	3
●	Colli di Conegliano Rosso Gregoletto '95	♀	5
●	Merlot dei Colli Trevigiani '98	♀	3
○	Prosecco di Conegliano Extra Dry	♀	3
○	Prosecco di Conegliano Tranquillo	♀	3
○	Verdiso dei Colli Trevigiani '99	♀	3
●	Cabernet '95	♀♀	3
●	Colli di Conegliano Rosso Gregoletto '94	♀	4

●	Colli Euganei Cabernet Mons Silicis Ris. '97	♀♀	4
○	Colli Euganei Bianco Vigna dei Mandorli '99	♀	3
●	Colli Euganei Cabernet Sauvignon Vigna Costa '98	♀	3
○	Colli Euganei Chardonnay Vigna Bianca '98	♀	3
○	Colli Euganei Fior d'Arancio Passito '97	♀	5
●	Colli Euganei Merlot Vigna del Foscolo '99	♀	3
○	Colli Euganei Fior d'Arancio Spumante		3

MONTEBELLO (VI)

DOMENICO CAVAZZA & F.LLI
VIA SELVA, 22
36054 MONTEBELLO (VI)
TEL. 0444/649166

The good news comes this year from the reds, all made with grapes from the Colli Berici. As a firm believer in a certain period of ageing in wood and in bottle, Giancarlo Cavazza bottled the '97s in July 2000, with the result that they were not quite ready for the panel. Later samplings gave us a clearer picture of their taste profiles, confirming their quality and potential. The Capitel Santa Libera label is used for the reds that are easy drinking and intended for consumption soon after purchase. The best is the Cabernet, with its rich nose of spices, leather, blackcurrants and roasted almonds. It has even more gutsy fruit on the palate, although the tannins dry the finish a bit. More immediate, but also agreeably fruity, is the Merlot, which should be enjoyed while still in this ebullient, youthful phase. Cicogna is the more serious range and includes a rather exuberant Cabernet. On the nose, there are hints of fine oak, spices, leather and plums, and the freshness on the palate is surprising. Even better is the excellent Merlot, a thoroughbred that offers an opulent, pervasive and sweetly ripe nose. On the palate, the fruit is well-structured and rich in extract. The tannins are soft but quite evident and the elegant finish offers hints of cocoa and blackberries. The single-vineyard La Bocara is a selection from the Gambellara DOC. A light, delicate, floral garganega-based wine, it would have convinced the panel more if it had been able to show a bit more personality and depth. The Dulcis Millenium comes from sauvignon grapes pressed in November. It is a jolly, easy-drinking wine with fresh, fruity appeal. The Recioto Capitel has greater weight and structure, and a nose of candied lemon peel, apricot and vanilla. Its flavour, however, is not so positive and we would like to have seen a little more elegance and freshness.

MONTEBELLO (VI)

DAL MASO
VIA SELVA, 62
36054 MONTEBELLO (VI)
TEL. 0444/649104

Dal Maso earns another entry in this year's Guide thanks to a more than satisfactory performance. Of course, there is no really outstanding wine that might generate some excitement among the panel and in fact, despite the considerable potential of the zone, the Dal Maso wines often seem rather anonymous, if technically impeccable and indeed rather well-made. What is called for now is to go a step further, and give each product its own personality and character. This year the top wines were missing, in particular the Recioto, which is still ageing, and an interesting Merlot from the Colli Berici. As a result, the overall scores suffered. We'll be talking about those two wines in next year's edition of the Guide. The Ca' Cischele, a vineyard selection from Gambellara, has improved substantially. It has a fine golden yellow hue and offers notes of peach, jasmine and almonds. The palate is pleasantly rich and supple, with hints of green almonds. Next, the delicious Sauvignon offers grip and an original style which has very little to do with the clichéd characteristics of this varietal. Its tangy nose, characterized by scents of tomato leaves and tropical fruit, is followed by a palate that perfectly echoes the aromas on the nose, also revealing decent body and good acidity. In contrast, the Chardonnay from the same range is less convincing. It has little personality and the palate has insufficient breadth of flavour, remaining rather flabby. The only red the panel tasted was the Cabernet Casara Roveri. A palish ruby in colour, it offers a very simple nose with hints of vanilla, strawberry boiled sweets, roasted almonds and gamey notes. The palate has medium depth, with tannins that tend to dry out the finish.

● Colli Berici Cabernet Cicogna '97 ♥♥		4
● Colli Berici Merlot Cicogna '97 ♥♥		4
● Colli Berici Cabernet		
Capitel S. Libera '97	♥	3
● Colli Berici Merlot		
Capitel S. Libera '97	♥	3
○ Colli Berici Sauvignon		
Capitel S. Libera '99	♥	3
○ Dulcis Millenium '98	♥	4
○ Recioto di Gambellara		
Capitel S. Libera '98	♥	4
○ Gambellara Cl. La Bocara '99		2
● Colli Berici Cabernet Cicogna '96 ♥		4

● Colli Berici Cabernet		
Casara Roveri '98	♥	4
○ Colli Berici Chardonnay		
Casara Roveri '99	♥	2
○ Colli Berici Sauvignon		
Casara Roveri '99	♥	2
○ Gambellara Cl.		
Vigneti Ca' Cischele '99	♥	1*
○ Recioto di Gambellara Cl.		
Riva dei Perari '98	♥♥	5

MONTEFORTE D'ALPONE (VR)

Roberto Anselmi

Via S. Carlo, 46
37032 Monteforte d'Alpone (VR)
tel. 045/7611488

After having fought for years to get Soave better known in the world's markets, and having invested his time, resources, and enthusiasm in the task, Roberto Anselmi has admitted defeat. From this year, his wines will no longer be released as Soave. In contrast to the prevailing philosophy in the zone, especially as regards flatland growers whose goal is, almost without exception, quantity at all costs, Anselmi gives first priority to expression of terroir. He has sought for years to improve his viticultural practices by using only the best hillside sites, by planting at increasingly high densities of up to 7,000 vines per hectare, and by substituting traditional pergola training with the lower-yielding spur-pruned cordon and Guyot training. He has also equipped his winery with state-of-the-art technology. The estate vinifies grapes from 70 hectares of vineyards, half of which are owned by Roberto and a good 30 of which are in the famous Foscarino subzone, from which he obtains a little under 500,000 bottles. The most impressive wine in the range is the Capitel Foscarino. An intense straw-yellow in colour, introducing attractive scents of green apples, it has nice full fruit on the palate and a harmonious, persistent finish. The fruit for the I Capitelli '98 was given a shorter period of drying to obtain greater freshness, and has therefore less richness than usual. It does, however, gain in elegant finesse on the finish. The San Vincenzo is of a medium-to-good standard, its easy-drinking style being its major quality. The Capitel Croce '98, with its brilliant golden colour, is still strongly influenced by the time it spent in oak, and has balsamic aromas of average complexity. On the palate, it offers reasonably well-structured fruit that needs a few months in bottle to knit. The Realda '98, a Cabernet Sauvignon, is still intractable and less rich than the usual juicy fruit mouthful you are usually offered by this wine.

○	Capitel Foscarino '99	🍷🍷	4
○	I Capitelli '98	🍷🍷	6
○	Capitel Croce '98	🍷🍷	4
●	Realda Cabernet Sauvignon '98	🍷	5
○	San Vincenzo '99	🍷	3
○	Recioto dei Capitelli '87	YYY	6
○	Recioto dei Capitelli '88	YYY	6
○	Recioto di Soave I Capitelli '93	YYY	6
○	Recioto di Soave I Capitelli '96	YYY	6
●	Realda Cabernet Sauvignon '96	YY	4
○	Recioto di Soave I Capitelli '97	YY	5
○	Soave Cl. Sup. Capitel Croce '97	YY	4
○	Soave Cl. Sup. Capitel Foscarino '98	YY	4

MONTEFORTE D'ALPONE (VR)

Carlo Bogoni

Quartiere Aldo Moro, 1
37032 Monteforte d'Alpone (VR)
tel. 045/6100385

Oenologist Carlo Bogoni and his wife Beatrice Portinari manage a 15-hectare estate at Monteforte d'Alpone in the Soave Classico zone. With this new entry in the Guide, the Bogonis join the group of young producers who are bringing new life-blood to this very famous denomination. To trace the Bogoni estate's origins, you will have to go back to 1850 and Napoleone Bogoni. The first vines were planted in the 1950s and the property took shape in its present form in the second half of the 80s. The estate comprises vineyards on the plain, the grapes and wine from which are sold on, and hillslope plots, particularly the three hectares of the La Ponsara parcel, from which the best wine comes. The Soave Classico is very good indeed. Straw-yellow in colour with golden highlights, it offers a nose of citron and apricots, which re-emerge on the palate along with suggestions of apples and almonds. The fruit is well-balanced and persistent and above all, this is a genuine value-for-money wine. The result achieved by the La Ponsara is also significant. A wine with a bright, intense, colour, it has a faintly aromatic bouquet with hints of camomile flowers. It is medium-bodied, with marked acidity and a finish reminiscent of bitter almonds. The Recioto is unusual, bringing to mind Vin Santo with its amber hue and notes of figs, nuts and coffee. The rich palate has good length. The list is completed by the Degorà, a Cabernet Sauvignon from the increasingly interesting Colli Berici zone. Ruby shading into opaque garnet in the glass, it has a grassy nose with overtones of red peppers and notes of autumn leaves and mushrooms. Firmly braced by good tannins, it unveils an acidity and body that will meld even more seamlessly with some bottle-age.

●	Degorà Cabernet Sauvignon '97	🍷🍷	4
○	Soave Cl. Sup. '99	🍷🍷	3*
○	Recioto di Soave '96	🍷	4
○	Soave Cl. Sup. La Ponsara '98	🍷	3

CA' RUGATE

VIA MEZZAVILLA, 12
FRAZ. BROGNOLIGO
37032 MONTEFORTE D'ALPONE (VR)
TEL. 045/6175082

The Tessari family's Ca' Rugate estate is recognized for its high quality and for the dependability of its wine. At present, Amedeo looks after the vineyards and sales while Gianni is in charge of vinification, at least until young Michele starts working full time at the winery. This family team is certainly not resting on its laurels. For the first time, they planted a few rows of chardonnay this year. Nor are they content with their 18 hectares of garganega. They have also decided to try their hand at vinifying corvina and rondinella from the Illasi zone. The result is around 20,000 bottles of young Valpolicella, which is pleasant and easy to drink, as well as just under 3,000 rather more interesting bottles of Valpolicella Superiore, aged for 12 months in half new, half 1-year-old barriques. The Superiore has sufficient body and persistence to make it rank among the best in its denomination. However, the estate's star wines remain its Soaves. The Classico has a finesse and complexity which few other wines in this price bracket can boast. The Monte Fiorentine displays greater personality and length, and also considerable potential for maturing in the bottle. The Monte Alto, fermented and aged in oak, is a Soave that expresses all the complex floral, honey and vanilla aromas, and richness on the palate, of the world's great whites. In contrast, the Recioto di Soave succumbs to the over-assertive aromas and flavours yielded by the oak, despite considerable concentration. Unfortunately, we shall have to wait until next year to express an opinion on the Bucciato, as it only went into bottle after our tastings were over.

○	Soave Cl. Sup. Monte Alto '99	🍷🍷	4
○	Soave Cl. Sup. Monte Fiorentine '99	🍷🍷	3*
●	Valpolicella Sup. Rovere '98	🍷🍷	4
○	Recioto di Soave La Perlara '98	🍷	5
○	Soave Cl. '99	🍷	3*
○	Soave Cl. Sup. Monte Alto '96	🍸🍸🍸	4
○	Soave Cl. Sup. Bucciato '98	🍸🍸	3
○	Soave Cl. Sup. Monte Alto '98	🍸🍸	4
○	Soave Cl. Sup. Monte Fiorentine '98	🍸🍸	3

FATTORI & GRANEY

VIA ZOPPEGA, 14
37032 MONTEFORTE D'ALPONE (VR)
TEL. 045/7460041

Giovanni and Antonio Fattori, the former an expert in viticulture, the latter an oenologist with a diploma from Conegliano, have been producing high quality wines for over 20 years. They specialize in whites, which they normally sell to the area's leading bottlers. This is the Fattoris' principal activity but since 1997, at the suggestion of Antonio's English-born wife, Sarah Graney, they have been producing a small quantity of Soave to bottle under their own label. Using part of the grapes from the 25-hectare family estate located at Motto Piane di Roncà, the Fattoris now make around 60,000 bottles, split between their standard Soave, Soave Motto Piane and Pinot Grigio. The results immediately met with critical acclaim and confirmed the Fattoris' skills. All that is lacking now is demand from the Italian market, which is always a bit reluctant to take a chance on new producers, whereas abroad Fattori & Graney is already a well-respected brand. Making the most of the not particularly favourable '99 vintage, Antonio has obtained an excellent Soave Motto Piane. This is a first release, which immediately takes centre stage with its complex, full-bodied and appealing style. It has been aged in both small and large oak barrels and has real personality. More linear, the acidity not entirely balanced by the fruit, is the basic Soave, a white whose agreeable quaffability is matched by an extremely fair price. As we wait for the Recioto di Soave, which will be released next year, the range is rounded off by a well-made Pinot Grigio, whose fruity nose gives way to an exuberant flavour.

○	Soave Cl. Sup. Motto Piane '99	🍷🍷	4
○	Pinot Grigio delle Venezie '99	🍷	3
○	Soave Cl. Sup. '99	🍷	2*

MONTEFORTE D'ALPONE (VR)

MONTEFORTE D'ALPONE (VR)

SANDRO E CLAUDIO GINI
VIA G. MATTEOTTI, 42
37032 MONTEFORTE D'ALPONE (VR)
TEL. 045/7611908

LA CAPPUCCINA
VIA S. BRIZIO, 125
FRAZ. COSTALUNGA
37032 MONTEFORTE D'ALPONE (VR)
TEL. 045/6175840 - 045/6175036

Construction work is nearing completion at the new Gini cellar, one of the most beautiful and functional in the zone and one in which temperature and humidity controls are superfluous. The production of fine wines, however, carries on. The Gini brothers obtained our highest accolade with the magnificent Soave La Froscà '99. It is a real masterpiece, its splendid straw-yellow hue revealing golden highlights and tinges of green. The intense fragrance of ripe fruit is overlaid with apricot and mineral nuances of great complexity and finesse. The palate is powerful, rich and extremely well-structured, with great length and balance on the finish. A thoroughly deserving Three Glass winner. The Recioto Renobilis scored almost as highly. The colour of old gold, it unfurls rich, complex notes of sultanas and nuts enhanced by a spicy note. The palate, though well-knit, full-bodied and persistent, lacks a touch of personality. The estate's top-scoring wine has often come from the very old vines of the Salvarenza site, some of which are over 80 years old. Though very good this year, it does not yet reveal its usual complex aromas but these will no doubt evolve over the next couple of years. The Col Foscarin '97 is at its normal level but does not have the fragrant complexity or the harmonious flavour of the Renobilis. The standard Soave is more straightforward and deliciously quaffable. The vineyards of sauvignon, chardonnay and pinot nero, grown high up in the hills and cordon-trained in the Burgundian manner, with a very high planting density, deserve a special mention. The still very youthful Maciete Fumé already reveals classic smoky and peachy aromas. The Chardonnay Sorai is more full-flavoured and powerful, with aromas of butter and roasted hazelnuts while the Pinot Nero still needs some fine-tuning.

The Tessari family is responsible for the present success of the more than 100-year-old La Cappuccina, which now produces 180,000 bottles annually from its 28 hectares. The vineyards, distributed around the family house and a chapel built for Capuchin friars in the 15th century, and are cultivated with great respect for the environment. In this traditionally-minded area, the Tessaris are considered innovators, with their Guyot and cordon-trained vineyards, over 25 percent of which are dedicated to black varieties (cabernet franc, cabernet sauvignon and merlot). This year, however, the reds did not really impress us. The Madégo '98 is light even in colour, and the Campo Buri '97, too, is less powerful and concentrated than usual. The traditional wines are better, starting with the '99 Soave. Its aromas are fairly straightforward but it has an attractive softness on the palate that is rare in wines at this price level. The Fontégo, with ten percent chardonnay, displays reasonable freshness and on the nose offers elegant mineral notes in addition to hints apples and pears. There is attractive acidity on the palate, as well as – for now – a fairly austere style. The San Brizio has gained considerable richness from its barrique ageing but its mineral and lemony aromas and the wine's well-knit texture on the palate, which comes through even more firmly on the long finish, are entirely due to low yields and the skills of the winemaker. The Recioto di Soave, which still represents a weak link for many producers, is always dependable at La Cappuccina. From grapes dried until the latter half of February, the Tessaris make a wine with an old gold hue, intense aromas of dried fruit and honey and an attractive, well-balanced sensation of sweetness on the palate.

O Soave Cl. Sup. La Froscà '99	♟♟♟	4
O Chardonnay Sorai '98	♟♟	5
O Recioto di Soave Renobilis '96	♟♟	6
O Sauvignon Maciete Fumé '98	♟♟	5
O Soave Cl. Sup. Contrada Salvarenza Vecchie Vigne '99	♟♟	5
O Recioto di Soave Col Foscarin '97	♟♟	6
● Pinot Nero Sorai Campo alle More '97	♟	5
O Soave Cl. Sup. '99	♟	3
O Soave Cl. Sup. Contrada Salvarenza Vecchie Vigne '96	♟♟♟	5
O Soave Cl. Sup. Contrada Salvarenza Vecchie Vigne '98	♟♟♟	5
O Soave Cl. Sup. La Froscà '97	♟♟♟	4

O Recioto di Soave Arzìmo '98	♟♟	5
O Soave Cl. Sup. S. Brizio '98	♟♟	4
O Soave Sup. '99	♟♟	3*
● Cabernet Franc Campo Buri '97	♟	5
O Soave Sup. Fontégo '99	♟	4
● Cabernet Sauvignon Madégo '98		4
● Cabernet Franc Campo Buri '95	♟♟♟	5
● Cabernet Franc Campo Buri '96	♟♟	4
O Recioto di Soave Arzìmo '96	♟♟	5
O Soave Cl. Sup. S. Brizio '97	♟♟	4

MONTEFORTE D'ALPONE (VR)   MONTEFORTE D'ALPONE (VR)

UMBERTO PORTINARI
VIA S. STEFANO, 2
FRAZ. BROGNOLIGO
37032 MONTEFORTE D'ALPONE (VR)
TEL. 045/6175087

PRÀ
VIA DELLA FONTANA, 31
37032 MONTEFORTE D'ALPONE (VR)
TEL. 045/7612125

Umberto Portinari started bottling his own wine in 1990, after some years learning the basics of the trade. Today, with the collaboration of Luciano Dal Bosco, he produces around 25,000 bottles from the four hectares he owns, two on the plain at Albare and two at Ronchetto, on the hill of Brognoligo. A true enthusiast, Umberto is constantly beavering away in his minuscule winery, experimenting with new types of fermentation and storage tanks. In particular, he devotes a great deal of care and attention to his vineyards. This year, we are writing up just two wines, the Soaves, because the dessert wines are still ageing and will be released at a later date. The Vigna Albare Doppia Maturazione Ragionata '99, of which 7,000 bottles were produced, is particularly striking for the great ripeness of the grapes. The flow of sap to some of the bunches is interrupted by cutting the shoot so that those berries start to dry in the vineyard, whereas the rest of the fruit ripens normally, albeit for rather longer than usual. The resulting wine has a very intense straw-yellow colour, with rich, but not particularly elegant, aromas of apples, pears and almonds. On the palate, it is full, rich and long, with a faint hint of bitter almonds on the finish which is typical of garganega. The Vigna Ronchetto is paler and very bright, offering almondy notes with mineral hints on the nose. The fruit on the palate is well-structured, firm and austere yet refined, and leads into a long, characterful finish. Umberto continues to experiment with sweet wines, ageing one in the classic Tuscan half-barriques and even bottling some without adding sulphur dioxide. Lastly, from the 7,000 square metres planted to chardonnay come the grapes for a dessert wine that takes its inspiration from Vin Santo.

This medium-sized winery, which produces 100,000 bottles from its nearly ten hectares under vine, is run by the Prà brothers. Sergio looks after the vineyards while Graziano is in the cellar, which is rather too small for present needs but will soon be enlarged. The Pràs' basic strategy is to bring down yields per hectare to obtain riper, more concentrated fruit and to intervene as little as possible during vinification. In this way, garganega's rich array of aromas and flavours can find full expression. The three Soaves, though quite different in character, are very similar to each other in quality. The best this year is the Monte Grande, fermented and aged in large barrels in the German fashion. It has a rich, vibrant straw-yellow colour and offers hints of ripe fruit and almonds on the nose, with a mineral touch that gives it added complexity. The palate is rich, powerful and tangy, with a long well-balanced finish, making it a wine of great class and personality. The Colle Sant'Antonio is produced only in certain vintages – the '92, '94 and '95 were not released, for example – and the '97 comes from a special selection of garganega part dried on racks and then fermented and aged in barrique. Its colour is a magnificent bright gold and its aromas of ripe fruit, honey and spices are made even more complex by just a hint of oxidation which translates into delicious notes of chestnuts. The palate is very powerful, complex and full-flavoured, with a long finish. In fact, the only minor fault is a slight lack of freshness. The Soave Classico displays floral and mineral scents and good weight on the palate, as well as a crisp acidity that makes deliciously quaffable. Compared to the Soaves, the Recioto is rather less exciting.

O Soave Sup. Vigna Albare Doppia		
Maturazione Ragionata '99	🍷🍷	3*
O Soave Cl. Sup.		
Vigna Ronchetto '99	🍷	3
O Soave Sup. Vigna Albare Doppia		
Maturazione Ragionata '97	🍷🍷🍷	4
O Recioto di Soave '95	🍷🍷	4
O Recioto di Soave Oro '97	🍷🍷	5
O Soave Cl. Sup.		
Vigna Ronchetto '98	🍷🍷	3
O Soave Sup. S. Stefano '97	🍷🍷	4
O Soave Sup. Vigna Albare Doppia		
Maturazione Ragionata '98	🍷🍷	3

O Soave Cl. Sup. '99	🍷🍷	3*
O Soave Cl. Sup.		
Colle S. Antonio '97	🍷🍷	4
O Soave Cl. Sup.		
Vigneto Monte Grande '99	🍷🍷	4
O Recioto di Soave Le Fontane '96	🍷	5
O Soave Cl. Sup.		
Vigneto Monte Grande '98	🍷🍷	3

NEGRAR (VR)

CAV. G.B. BERTANI
LOC. NOVARE
FRAZ. ARBIZZANO
37024 NEGRAR (VR)
TEL. 045/6011211

Bertani's new project of turning Villa Novare into a real Valpolicella "Château" is coming to fruition and there are now two wines available under this label. Villa Novare, one of the most beautiful villas in the Valpolicella area, is set in an idyllic landscape with a garden, small lakes and waterfalls. It is one of the few "brolos" in the area (the name refers to a property completely surrounded by walls, like "clos" in French). The 50 hectares at Bertani's disposal, planted with the classic grapes of the Verona area, corvina, molinara and rondinella, as well as cabernet sauvignon, are capable of producing wines with great richness and body. The area under vine is constantly being enlarged and transformed. The new terraces, from which you can see the centre of Verona, are an amazing spectacle. The wines presented this year represent a clear signal of Bertani's potential. On its second release, the 100 percent cabernet sauvignon Albion repeated the gratifying performance of last year. Though it perhaps displays slightly less elegance, it is, if anything, even more full-bodied. The Amarone della Valpolicella '93 is, however, the real star. Rich and well-knit, it exemplifies the classic style of Bertani's Amarone, which is a cut above other similar products because it is always aged for longer than other Valpolicella Amarones. Also excellent is the Valpolicella from the Ognisanti vineyard on the Villa Novare estate, a red that seduces you with its finesse and body. Le Lave, made from garganega, chardonnay and sémillon, is a characterful, internationally styled white and the Soave is a charmingly easy-drinking wine. The Secco Bertani is as reliable as ever, and the Bardolino is attractive.

NEGRAR (VR)

TOMMASO BUSSOLA
VIA MOLINO TURRI, 30
FRAZ. S. PERETTO
37024 NEGRAR (VR)
TEL. 045/7501740

If you go up the Negrar valley and turn east, you come to the little village of San Peretto, the most easterly point in the Valpolicella Classico DOC zone, right on the border with Valpantena. Here, you will find the estate of Tommaso Bussola, which looks out over the Negrar, practically dominating the entire valley. It is in this slightly out-of-the-way spot that Tommaso's projects take shape, as he busies himself among the barriques and tonneaux in his cellar, always searching for a shade more complexity, concentration and character. His Amarone demonstrates how you can make a fine wine that is strictly traditional in style, without succumbing to the siren song of modernity. Its scents of dried flowers mingle with hints of leather and balsamic nuances while in the mouth it is complex, well-defined and almost palate-scaldingly rich in alcohol. The Recioto BG, which is usually notable for its supple, easy-drinking style, this year has greater depth. In contrast to its very delicate, floral nose, it is pungent and peppery on the palate, with a fine balance between acidity, tannins, sweetness and extract that makes it really delicious. Tommaso's star wine, however, and the one which again earned our Three Glass award, is the Recioto TB, a product that will amaze even the most sceptical of tasters. Absolutely impenetrable in appearance, it is dense, minerally and still quite closed on the nose thanks to its staggering concentration. Its impact in the mouth is stunning. Suggestions of chocolate, coffee and ripe, fleshy red berry fruit immediately swamp the palate and only relax their grip a good while later. The Valpolicella Superiore, which mirrors the style of the Amarone but with greater élan, is also extremely well-made.

● Albion Cabernet Sauvignon		
Villa Novare '98	🍷🍷	6
● Amarone della Valpolicella		
Cl. Sup. '93	🍷🍷	6
○ Le Lave '98	🍷🍷	4
● Valpolicella Cl. Sup. Vigneto		
Ognisanti Villa Novare '97	🍷🍷	4
● Bardolino Cl. '99	🍷	3
● Catullo Rosso '97	🍷	4
○ Soave Cl. Sup. '99	🍷	3
● Valpantena Secco Bertani '98	🍷	4
● Albion Cabernet Sauvignon		
Villa Novare '97	🍷🍷🍷	6
● Amarone della Valpolicella '85	🍷🍷🍷	6

● Recioto della Valpolicella Cl.		
TB '97	🍷🍷🍷	6
● Amarone della Valpolicella Cl.		
BG '96	🍷🍷	6
● Recioto della Valpolicella Cl.		
BG '98	🍷🍷	5
● Valpolicella Cl. Sup. TB '97	🍷🍷	5
● Recioto della Valpolicella Cl		
TB '95	🍷🍷🍷	6
● Amarone della Valpolicella Cl.		
Vigneto Alto '95	🍷🍷	6
● Recioto della Valpolicella Cl.		
BG '97	🍷🍷	5
● Recioto della Valpolicella Cl.		
Selezione '96	🍷🍷	6

NEGRAR (VR)

NEGRAR (VR)

CANTINA SOCIALE VALPOLICELLA
VIA CA' SALGARI, 2
37024 NEGRAR (VR)
TEL. 045/7500070

LE RAGOSE
VIA RAGOSE, 1
FRAZ. ARBIZZANO
37024 NEGRAR (VR)
TEL. 045/7513241

The Cantina Sociale della Valpolicella was founded at the beginning of the 20th century, at the initiative of seven local gentlemen. It was originally situated in the ancient Villa Novare at Negrar. Shortly after the Second World War, it moved to San Vito and, later in 1987, to its present site. Comprising around 200 members who cultivate 500 hectares of vineyards, it has a production capacity of 6,000,000 bottles a year. The training system most widely in use is the single or double pergola, with a high density of vines per hectare, on hillside terrain principally constituted of limestone and marl. The vines are, on average, 20 years old, and 60 percent of the wine produced is exported. The winery's technical director is the admirable Daniele Accordini, whose competence and enthusiasm are beyond dispute. The Domini Veneti brand denotes the top selections in the range. As usual, the wines are very decent indeed. The outstanding product is the Amarone Manara, whose splendid label was designed by the artist Milo Manara himself. The wine has a dense colour and shows great elegance and length. The fine nose reveals hints of tobacco while the palate is mouth-filling and voluptuous. The Amarone Domini Veneti is also very good, particularly when you remember that fully 200,000 bottles of it are made. The Amarone Vigneti di Jago offers a generous bouquet, solid structure and the promise of excellent ageing potential. Lastly, we come to the winery's other premium products, the Domini Veneti Vigneti di Moron and Manara Reciotos, the La Casetta di Ettore Righetti Valpolicella, and the Campi Raudii, made from corvina and merlot.

Le Ragose is never in any hurry to release its wines onto the market and only does so when the time is absolutely right. We are therefore only now returning to give our report on the Recioto, which has been absent from our ratings for the last few years. The '96 has a particularly intriguing bouquet, in which distinctive herbal notes are mingled with more varietal suggestions of cherry preserves and cocoa. Its powerful palate closes on hints of morello cherry stones. The Rhagòs '96, more than a classic Recioto, resembles a very soft, rounded Amarone. It is full-bodied and fairly dry, with a well-calibrated residual sugar content. The young Valpolicella put up an average showing whereas the Le Sassine '97 has a forthright and agreeable style. The as yet unreleased Superiore Marta Galli '97, however, has much greater depth. The Cabernet Garda '97 confirms the traits that have made it so appealing over the years, a nicely restrained, well-crafted style, and great quaffability. If in poor years Le Ragose's Amarones betray a greater lack of ripeness than those from some other producers, in good vintages they offer extreme elegance and finesse. The '95 makes the most of this delicately balanced profile and surprises you with its refined persistence. One after the other, it yields hints of spices, liqueur morello cherries, cherry stones and liquorice. The flavour seduces you with its well-sustained evolution on the palate. In contrast, the Amarone '96 from the Marta Galli line, which spends some time in barrique and has a more modern style, is quite different. It has a splendid youthful colour, but the nose and palate still have to find a length. It is broader and more alcoholic than the '95, but does not have the same concentration. Lastly, the Raghòs Bianco, made from partially dried grapes (50 percent garganega, 20 trebbiano and 30 chardonnay), is a pleasant wine.

● Amarone della Valpolicella Cl.		
Domini Veneti '97	♟♟	5
● Amarone della Valpolicella Cl.		
Manara '95	♟♟	6
● Amarone della Valpolicella Cl.		
Vigneti di Jago Selezione '97	♟♟	6
● Recioto della Valpolicella Cl.		
Manara '97	♟♟	6
● Campi Raudii Rosso		
Domini Veneti '97	♟	4
● Recioto della Valpolicella Cl.		
Vigneti di Moron '98	♟	5
● Valpolicella Cl. Sup. La Casetta		
di Ettore Righetti Domini Veneti '97	♟	4

● Amarone della Valpolicella Cl. '95	♟♟	5
● Amarone della Valpolicella Cl.		
Marta Galli '96	♟♟	6
● Garda Cabernet Le Ragose '97	♟♟	4
● Recioto della Valpolicella		
Rhagòs '96	♟♟	6
● Recioto della Valpolicella Ris. '96	♟♟	5
○ Rhagòs Bianco '99	♟	5
● Valpolicella Cl. Sup.		
Le Sassine '97	♟	4
● Valpolicella Cl. '99		3
● Amarone della Valpolicella Cl. '86	♟♟♟	6
● Amarone della Valpolicella Cl. '88	♟♟♟	6
● Amarone della Valpolicella Cl. '90	♟♟	6
● Amarone della Valpolicella Cl. '94	♟♟	6

NEGRAR (VR)

NEGRAR (VR)

ROBERTO MAZZI
VIA CROSETTA, 8
FRAZ. S. PERETTO
37024 NEGRAR (VR)
TEL. 045/7502072

GIUSEPPE QUINTARELLI
VIA CERÉ, 1
37024 NEGRAR (VR)
TEL. 045/7500016

We are delighted to announce the return of this estate to the Guide, thanks to a series of very decent wines indeed. Roberto Mazzi, a graduate in agricultural studies and teacher, started up his business in the 60s. Since the late 80s, he has been joined by his sons, Stefano and Antonio, who are gradually taking over the reins of the company. You can tell straight away that they have a great passion for viticulture and winemaking, as well as the self-confidence to produce good wines. They own five and a half hectares of vineyards in the Calcarole, Villa and Poiega plots and one and a half at Jago. At present, their production comes to around 50,000 bottles, of which 70 percent is sold in Italy. The Mazzis benefit from the invaluable consultancy of oenologist Flavio Prà and also run a small restaurant which is open at weekends. Simple yet elegant, it is warm and welcoming, and the food is well-prepared. The Amarone Punta di Villa, a deep ruby in colour, has a very fine bouquet of dried flowers, tobacco and chocolate. These sensations are echoed on the elegant, velvety palate. The Valpolicella Vigneto Poiega spends 18 months in tonneaux and large barrels, and is not filtered. Floral and fruity, it offers notes of cherries and plums on the nose and a well-balanced, lingering flavour of liquorice. The Libero '96, made from cabernet, sangiovese and nebbiolo, has gamey aromas with hints of autumn leaves and tar. The fruit on the palate is chewy, minerally, warm and mouth-filling. The young Valpolicella unveils hints of freshly mown grass, wild cherries and pepper, with appreciable elegance. It is well-rounded and has a satisfyingly full flavour, albeit with prominent acidity.

It was well worth the wait. Yet again, the sumptuous unfolding of the impressively deep bouquets of Quintarelli's wines awed the panel and sent their olfactory receptors into unforgettable ecstasy. These wines evoke the reds of Titian's paintings, the heady scents of Italian gardens, the sweeping notes of "The Four Seasons" and the brooding power of Giorgione's "Tempest". You might feel these exalted similes sit uneasily with a mere wine but when the taste buds are overwhelmed by the sensations that Giuseppe Quintarelli's can deliver, you have to find new ways to talk about the experience. Even the decidedly high prices become rather less important, at least for those who can afford them. With the wines he presented in 2000, Quintarelli confirms his place as a grand master of raisining, who can extract from his fruit a softness, a richness and a succulent sweetness that are absolutely extraordinary. The refinement, charm and elegance of the Recioto Riserva '90 make this wine quite unique. Its sweetness and concentration on the palate are reminiscent of the perfect ripeness of the grapes themselves, to which the skilful use of oak has added allure and a silky texture. The '93 Amarone is extremely refined and evolved, richly spicy and velvety. This is a great wine that had no trouble whatsoever in picking up one of our Three Glass accolades for the Quintarelli winery. The Alzero, a Cabernet made from partially dried grapes, shows absolutely extraordinary concentration and power, although we do sometimes find it difficult to come to terms with a wine as singular, and perhaps even eccentric, as this. The Valpolicella, with its gamey aromas and hints of chocolate and autumn leaves, seems a bit over-evolved, while the Rosso del Bepi '94, a year in which the Amarone was not produced, did not particularly impress.

● Amarone della Valpolicella Cl.		
Punta di Villa '96	▼▼	6
● Libero Rosso Veronese '96	▼▼	5
● Valpolicella Cl. Sup.		
Vigneto Poiega '98	▼▼	4
● Valpolicella Cl. '99	▼	3

● Amarone della Valpolicella Cl.		
Sup. Monte Cà Paletta '93	▼▼▼	6
● Recioto della Valpolicella Cl.		
Ris. '90	▼▼	6
● Alzero Cabernet Franc '94	▼▼	6
● Valpolicella Cl. Sup. '93	▼	6
● Rosso del Bepi '94		6
● Alzero Cabernet Franc '90	♈♈♈	6
● Amarone della Valpolicella Ris. '83	♈♈♈	6
● Amarone della Valpolicella Ris. '85	♈♈♈	6
● Amarone della Valpolicella '84	♈♈♈	6
● Amarone della Valpolicella '86	♈♈♈	6
● Amarone della Valpolicella '90	♈♈	6
● Amarone della Valpolicella '91	♈♈	6

NEGRAR (VR)

SARTORI
VIA CASETTE, 2
37024 NEGRAR (VR)
TEL. 045/6028011

This estate celebrated its 100th anniversary in 1998. Its story begins when Cavaliere Pietro Sartori, the founder, bought a small property at Tomenighe di Mezzo, near Negrar. The winery, which is still owned by the same family, has witnessed major growth both in terms of quantity and quality over the last ten years. This is in part thanks to the efforts of the fourth generation, Andrea, Paolo, and Luca, the sons of Pierumberto and Franco who were at the helm in the 50s. Production, which exceeds 10,000,000 bottles, comprises three ranges, the basic line, accounting for 40 percent of total volume, the classic wines (another 40 percent) and the top line of special selections, which make up 20 percent of output, or over 1,000,000 bottles. The wines are partly bought in for the basic and classic ranges, whereas the vineyard selections come from grapes from trusted growers or from the family's own vineyards, ten hectares of which surround the fine Villa where the winery has its headquarters. The 20-hectare site of Montegradella, at San Pietro, and La Carega, a 30-hectare plot in the Lugana zone, are rented. The wines tasted and reviewed all belong to the top Sartori range and it was the Soave and the Amarone that stood out. The former has a straw-yellow colour, with intense aromas of apples and pears. Its sustained acidity on the palate acts as a good foil to the full fruit. The Amarone, on the other hand, benefits from the excellence of the '97 vintage. It has a dense colour and clean, sweetish, black cherry jam aromas. The entry on the palate is excellent, and the mid palate progresses with persistent, mouth-filling dynamism. The Valpolicella Montegradella is good and the Recioto, the corvina and rondinella-based Regolo and the Cent'Anni, from corvina, rondinella and merlot, produced to celebrate the Sartori centenary, are all very pleasant.

○	Soave Cl. Sup. Vigneti di Sella '99	🍷🍷	3*
●	Amarone della Valpolicella Cl. '97	🍷🍷	5
●	Valpolicella Cl. Sup. Vigneti di Montegradella '97	🍷	3
●	Cent'Anni '97	🍷	5
●	Recioto della Valpolicella '97	🍷	6
●	Regolo '96	🍷	4

NEGRAR (VR)

VILLA SPINOSA
LOC. JAGO
37024 NEGRAR (VR)
TEL. 045/7500093

This estate, which has vinified its own grapes since 1990, is managed with a sure hand by Enrico Cascella Spinosa, a descendant of the Spinosa family which has been in the Valpolicella area since the 19th century. The 15 hectares of vineyards which the cellar draws on are the Jago (at Negrar), Figari and Marano plots. The soils are limestone-based and the vines stand between 230 and 300 metres above sea level. In the old vineyards, the classic corvina, rondinella and molinara grape varieties are grown. The newer sites have a growing presence of corvinone and small proportions of cabernet sauvignon (for drying) and sangiovese. Since 1990, the vines have been trained along rows, with 4,000 plants per hectare. At present 25,000 bottles are produced. Villa Spinosa itself, with its cellar, is a very handsome building constructed in the 18th and 19th centuries. At the time of our tastings, the '96 Amarone and the '98 Recioto were still in the process of ageing and so they will be judged next year. Re-tasting the previous vintages of these wines fully reconfirmed their ratings, with the Recioto showing on tip-top form. Let's move on to the Valpolicellas. The Jago '97, obtained using the "ripasso" method (adding unpressed skins to the wine after fermentation), has a ruby hue shading into garnet. The first impression on the nose is a pleasing hint of cheese, which gives way to notes of dried flowers, herbal tea and black cherry. There is a good balance of acidity, tannins and alcohol, and the palate is full-bodied and long. The Antanel, matured in stainless steel and for a few months in large oak barrels, has a ruby colour, and aromas of hay, raspberries and tobacco. On the palate, which is warm and with a finish reminiscent of liquorice, it is the tannins that come to the fore.

●	Valpolicella Cl. Sup. Jago '97	🍷🍷	3*
●	Valpolicella Cl. Antanel '98	🍷	3
●	Amarone della Valpolicella Cl. '95	🍸🍸	6
●	Recioto della Valpolicella Cl. '97	🍸🍸	5

NEGRAR (VR)

NERVESA DELLA BATTAGLIA (TV)

VIVIANI
VIA MAZZANO, 8
37024 NEGRAR (VR)
TEL. 045/7500286

SERAFINI & VIDOTTO
VIA ARDITI, 1
31040 NERVESA DELLA BATTAGLIA (TV)
TEL. 0422/773281

In the northernmost part of the Negrar valley, at Mazzano, you will find the small but dynamic winery of Claudio Viviani, virtually standing guard over Valpolicella Classico's highest vineyards, as if it were on the look-out for aromas, elegance and finesse inconceivable lower down on the plain. It is the search for these characteristics that is spurring Claudio to make wines whose greatness lies in their balance and refinement, without necessarily going after traits which are perhaps easier to obtain in Valpolicella, such as opulence and over-the-top concentration. The estate's two most important wines are emblematic of this philosophy. The Recioto has a floral, generous, intriguing bouquet with faint balsamic hints. The fruit opens up gradually yet unhesitatingly on the palate, where the sweetness is beautifully counterbalanced by the consistent sustaining acidity. The finish is long and perfectly focused. The more heady and mouth-filling Amarone was also aged for two years longer than the Recioto. Its aromas mingle dried flowers and crushed fruit while on the palate there is an even greater effort to achieve overall balance. Here, the warmth of the alcohol is set off by compact tannins and remarkably dense extract while spiciness and hints of tertiary notes give a clear indication of the wine's glorious cellarability. With this Amarone, Villa Spinosa deservedly enters the select circle of producers on whom we have bestowed our Three Glass award. There is a more evident balsamic note and an undertone of garden herbs in the Valpolicella Superiore, which has a deliciously soft, mouth-filling flavour with notes of mint and cocoa, whereas the Valpolicella Classico's most appealing characteristics are its delicacy and freshness.

In Italy, the term "Bordeaux blend" is often used for any wine made using cabernet and merlot grapes, ignoring the fact that Bordeaux has, for centuries, represented a great deal more. Above all else, Bordeaux means elegance but also implies an austerity and balance of a wine's acidity, fruit and tannins to create supreme complexity and finesse on the palate. This is the type of wine which Antonello and Francesco seek to produce every year, and each year they take full advantage of the fruit which Nature puts at their disposal to make it. Some vintages will have greater power, others will be lighter and more elegant, but in the end the product will have to conform to their principles. The promisingly dark-hued Rosso '98 is going to be a hit with the pair's many fans. The nose is deep and complex, with a marked youthful, mineral tone which then gives way to exciting, alternating sensations of spices and flowers. On the palate, it is quite delicious. Delicate on entry, it gradually reveals its perfect harmony in the sensations on the nose. The finish is excellent and very long. To understand this estate's winemaking philosophy, it is well worth trying the Phigaia, which is a perfect example of a "second wine". Though obviously more straightforward than the Rosso, it is has plenty of elegance and personality. The Pinot Nero is also a great success, offering a bouquet rich in floral and spicy nuances, while the abundantly signalled breadth on the palate is accompanied by a positive vein of acidity which makes the wine very attractive to drink. The Bianco is good, too. Juicy but never cloying, it looks as if it has an interesting future ahead of it.

● Amarone della Valpolicella Cl.		
Casa dei Bepi '95	▼▼▼	6
● Recioto della Valpolicella Cl. '97	▼▼	5
● Valpolicella Cl. Sup. '97	▼▼	4
● Valpolicella Cl. '99	▼	2*
● Amarone della Valpolicella Cl.		
Casa dei Bepi '93	▽▽	5
● Amarone della Valpolicella Cl.		
Casa dei Bepi '94	▽▽	6
● Recioto della Valpolicella		
La Mandrela '93	▽▽	5
● Recioto della Valpolicella Cl. '96	▽	5

● Il Rosso dell'Abazia '98	▼▼▼	6
● Phigaia After the Red '98	▼▼	4
● Pinot Nero '98	▼▼	6
○ Il Bianco dell'Abazia '99	▼	4
● Il Rosso dell'Abazia '93	▽▽▽	6
● Il Rosso dell'Abazia '94	▽▽▽	6
● Il Rosso dell'Abazia '95	▽▽▽	6
● Il Rosso dell'Abazia '96	▽▽▽	6
● Il Rosso dell'Abazia '97	▽▽▽	6
● Pinot Nero '97	▽▽	5

PESCHIERA DEL GARDA (VR)   PESCHIERA DEL GARDA (VR)

OTTELLA
LOC. OTTELLA, 1
FRAZ. S. BENEDETTO DI LUGANA
37019 PESCHIERA DEL GARDA (VR)
TEL. 045/7551950

ZENATO
VIA S. BENEDETTO, 8
FRAZ. S. BENEDETTO DI LUGANA
37019 PESCHIERA DEL GARDA (VR)
TEL. 045/7550300

A new wine has been added to Ottella's product range this year, the Prima Luce, a white dessert wine. It is a Moscato Giallo, made exclusively from grapes grown on the morainic hillsides near Lugana and then vinified after a few months of partial drying. The wine stays in oak for a couple of years and production is small but the quality – even of this first release – is very promising indeed. Its rich, complex spectrum of aromas offers a swathe of appealing sensations, with marked notes of citrus fruits, especially citrons, flowers and a distinctive smoky overtone that comes from its maturation in barrel. The promise of the nose is thoroughly fulfilled on the palate, where the fruit is well-sustained and long. The Campo Sireso, the winery's top red, made from merlot, cabernet sauvignon and corvina, is up to its usual high standard. The quality of the grapes, as always selected with great care, has enabled the spiciness of the oak to integrate beautifully with the fruit, which is well-expressed and fragrant. On the palate, the roundness and concentration of the fruit counterbalance the tannins, which are in any case ripe and soft. Of the company's three Luganas, the oak-conditioned Molceo was still undergoing maturation and so will be presented for tasting next year. The ever-reliable Le Creete selection appeals with its combination of richly-textured fruit and easy-drinking style and, lastly, the basic Lugana is enjoyable, if a little bit below par. The Gimè, a white made from incrocio Manzoni and chardonnay, offers a broad wealth of aromas and a precise, piquant flavour. The Rosso Ottella is straightforward and well-made.

Zenato distinguished itself this year with the high standard of quality across its entire wide range of products. Not only is the Amarone Riserva Sergio Zenato one of the best wines in its category, but all the other estate wines earned Two Glass ratings, or came very close to doing so. This is the result of skilled management and an unflagging commitment to investing both in the vineyards and in the winery. Low vineyard yields have given the Amarone Riserva unusual concentration, yet without detracting from its freshness or immediacy of appeal. On the nose, there is intense ripe fruit and sweet spice while soft fruit and velvety tannins characterize the flavour. The length is excellent, as is the way in which the wine's aromas are echoed on the palate. Though produced in relatively large quantities, the standard Amarone is not greatly inferior to the Riserva. It merely lacks some of its concentration and richness. The Valpolicella Superiores impressed us with the ease and elegance with which they managed to express their considerable fruit, successfully combining complexity and charm. The same comment applies to the two wines made from Bordeaux varieties, the Cabernet Sauvignon from the Santa Cristina estate and the Merlot, both given extra complexity on the nose and a soft, well-balanced flavour thanks to the shrewd use of oak. The two Luganas were among the best from their denomination. We marginally preferred the Santa Cristina Vigneto Massoni because of its greater personality. The Soave Vigneto Colombara is not quite as good as last year, though it is still a very decent bottle indeed.

● Campo Sireso '98	▼▼	4
○ Prima Luce Passito '97	▼▼	5
○ Gimè Bianco '99	▼	3
○ Lugana '99	▼	3
○ Lugana Le Creete '99	▼	4
● Rosso Ottella '99	▼	3
● Campo Sireso '96	♈♈	4
● Campo Sireso '97	♈♈	4
○ Lugana Sup. Il Molceo '98	♈♈	4

● Amarone della Valpolicella Cl. '95	▼▼	6
● Amarone della Valpolicella Cl.		
Riserva Sergio Zenato '95	▼▼	6
● Cabernet Sauvignon		
S. Cristina '97	▼▼	4
○ Lugana S. Cristina		
Vigneto Massoni '99	▼▼	4
● Merlot '97	▼▼	3*
● Valpolicella Cl. Sup. '97	▼▼	3*
● Valpolicella Cl. Sup. Ripassa '97	▼▼	4
○ Lugana S. Benedetto '99	▼	3
○ Soave Cl. Sup.		
Vigneto Colombara '99	▼	3*
● Amarone della Valpolicella Cl.		
Sergio Zenato '88	♈♈♈	6

REFRONTOLO (TV) S. AMBROGIO DI VALPOLICELLA (VR)

VINCENZO TOFFOLI
VIA LIBERAZIONE, 26
31020 REFRONTOLO (TV)
TEL. 0438/894240

ALEARDO FERRARI
VIA GIARE, 15
FRAZ. GARGAGNAGO
37020 S. AMBROGIO DI VALPOLICELLA (VR)
TEL. 045/7701379

On its second appearance in the Guide, the Toffoli estate confirms its good showing of last year, and indeed improves its overall ratings. Vincenzo can consider himself proud of his sons Sante, Luciano and Gabriele for the energy and innovation that they have brought to the business. In this regard, one of the important changes has been the conversion to organic cultivation of the five hectares of family-owned vineyards. Another seven hectares are rented, giving a total of 50,000 bottles, produced under the watchful eye of the Toffolis' friend and oenologist, Daniele Novak. We strongly urge you to go and visit Refrontolo. The wines, quite naturally, reflect the characteristics of this delightful area, which abounds in woods and vineyards. The Prosecco Extra Dry is an excellent starting point. Its keynotes are finesse, incredible lightness of touch and the sheer joy that drinking this lovely wine inspires. Other examples are the two Frizzante wines. Obviously, they have no great pretensions but they are, quite simply, both hugely enjoyable. For the record, our preference goes to the organic version by a whisker. This zone, with the advent of the Colli di Conegliano DOC, has witnessed a significant new interest in dessert wines. The Refrontolo Passito, made from marzemino grapes, is excellent. An intense ruby in colour, it displays aromas of red berry fruits and tobacco. On the palate, there are hints of morello cherry jam and prunes, in an overall taste profile of laudable freshness. The Prosecco and the very forthright, characterful Verdiso are both very good. The Amaranto dei Vanai Rosso is sound and well-made.

Aleardo Ferrari's property is in a state of slow but continuous evolution, both in the winery and also out of doors in the vineyards, where gradually he is replacing the old pergolas with new training systems and new clones which are more suitable for producing top-quality wines. The range is increasingly focused on catering for a market that demands products of a very high standard. The bottles presented this year bear witness to the improvements in the range, with the exception of the young Valpolicella. Actually, this is a category which, at present, does not get the attention it deserves either from producers·or consumers. Although not from a particularly good vintage, the '96 Amarone impressed us with its richness and concentration on the palate, hinted at by its deep colour and intense aromas that include extremely tempting notes of black cherry nuanced with overtones of strawberry and raspberry jam. Another wine that we found to be much improved over previous vintages is the Recioto. Its habitually elegant style has gained density on the palate, which has not, however, detracted from its immediacy or balance. The Valpolicella Bure Alto easily merits its One Glass rating. After a slightly lacklustre first impression, it becomes cleaner and reveals full fruit and finesse. The sensations of depth that are evident on the nose give a clear indication of the well-structured fruit that then emerge on the palate.

● Colli di Conegliano Passito di Refrontolo '99	♔♔	5
○ Prosecco di Conegliano Extra Dry	♔♔	3*
○ Prosecco dei Colli Trevigiani Passito '99	♔	5
○ Prosecco di Conegliano Frizzante	♔	2*
○ Prosecco di Conegliano Frizzante Biologico	♔	2*
○ Verdiso dei Colli Trevigiani Passito	♔	5
○ Verdiso dei Colli Trevigiani Sel. Vincenzo	♔	2*
● Amaranto dei Vanai Rosso dei Colli Trevigiani		2

● Amarone della Valpolicella Cl. '96	♔♔	6
● Recioto della Valpolicella Cl. '98	♔♔	5
● Valpolicella Cl. Sup. Bure Alto '98	♔	4
● Amarone della Valpolicella Cl. '94	♔♔	6
● Valpolicella Cl. Sup. Bure Alto '97	♔♔	4
● Amarone della Valpolicella Cl. '95	♔	6
● Recioto della Valpolicella Cl. '97	♔	5

S. AMBROGIO DI VALPOLICELLA (VR)

MASI
VIA MONTELEONE
FRAZ. GARGAGNAGO
37020 S. AMBROGIO DI VALPOLICELLA (VR)
TEL. 045/6800588

Masi, owned by the Boscaini family, is one of the largest wine-producing groups in the Veneto. It turns out 3,000,000 bottles a year, to which will be added another couple of million from their estate in the Lison-Pramaggiore DOC zone of a red and a white dubbed Modello delle Venezie, and can thus compete on equal terms with the Italy's most renowned producers. The thing that is special about this winery is that it offers exclusively quality wines and scales some seriously high peaks with certain special reserves of Amarone. There are two lines on offer. The Masi-label range includes wines produced both from the company's own grapes and from bought-in fruit from Serègo Alighieri, the estate owned by Conte Pieralvise, the last descendant of the poet, Dante. We tasted a lot of wines this year and all put up good performances, especially the Amarone Vaio Armaron Serègo Alighieri '95 and the Amarone Campolongo di Torbe '95. While we look forward to reviewing the Amarone Mazzano, which is always released after a longer period of ageing, the Vaio Armaron, from one of the finest vintages of the decade, is the bottle that most impressed us. It has a bright colour and well-defined, ripe aromas, followed by considerable elegance and concentration on the palate. The Campolongo di Torbe is of a similar standard but a shade less complex. Two well-deserved Glasses also go to the corvina, oseleta and rondinella-based Toar, a red which triumphantly shows off the characteristics of the local grapes. The Bianco delle Possessioni, from garganega and sauvignon, and the Soave Classico Colbaraca stand out among the whites while the Brolo di Campo Fiorin scored higher than the Valpolicella Classico from Serègo Alighieri. Lastly, the Recioto Amabile degli Angeli displays an unusually rich, sweet style.

S. AMBROGIO DI VALPOLICELLA (VR)

RAIMONDI VILLA MONTELEONE
FRAZ. GARGAGNAGO
37020 S. AMBROGIO DI VALPOLICELLA (VR)
TEL. 045/7704974

In June 2000, at precisely the time we were in Valpolicella for our tastings, we heard the sad news that Professor Anthony Raimondi had passed away. The author of this review, sadly, never had the opportunity to meet him but from my conversation with his widow, Lucia, I was able to discover what a fine human being he was and what a void he left both in the world of wine and in that of medicine, his primary occupation. Just a few years before, he had become actively involved in wine, which had always been his great passion. He set himself the ambitious goal of producing a great Amarone of unique style and character, keeping one eye on tradition but also paying particular attention to elegance. Lucia, who always shared in his passion and his work, now intends to pursue the same objectives, in accordance with her husband's philosophy and with the help and support of the family. And from that point of view, the results of our tasting were very comforting. The Amarone '95 made the most of an excellent vintage, offering a precise but complex array of aromas that unfolds to reveal spicy sensations, then ripe fruit notes, and finally floral hints. On the palate, the tannins are balanced by the warmth of the alcohol, which in turn is held in check by the good length of the palate. The same considerations apply to the Amarone '97, which only requires a little bit more bottle-age. The Valpolicella Campo San Vito '97, an elegant, rich example of a "ripasso" wine (unpressed skins are added to the to the wine after fermentation to enhance flavour and alcohol), met with general acclaim whereas the '96 suffered as a result of the poor vintage. The Valpolicella Campo Santa Lena '97 displays a light, agreeable style.

● Amarone della Valpolicella Cl.		
Campolongo di Torbe '95	♗♗	6
● Amarone della Valpolicella Vaio		
Armaron Serègo Alighieri '95	♗♗	6
● Toar '96	♗♗	5
○ Bianco delle Possessioni		
Serègo Alighieri '99	♗	4
● Il Brolo di Campo Fiorin '96	♗	4
● Recioto della Valpolicella Cl.		
Amabile degli Angeli '97	♗	6
○ Soave Cl. Sup. Colbaraca '99	♗	3
● Valpolicella Cl. Sup.		
Serègo Alighieri '97		4
● Amarone della Valpolicella Cl.		
Mazzano '93	♗♗♗	6

● Amarone della Valpolicella Cl.		
Campo S. Paolo '95	♗♗	6
● Amarone della Valpolicella Cl.		
Campo S. Paolo '97	♗♗	6
● Valpolicella Cl. Sup. S. Vito '97	♗♗	5
● Valpolicella Cl. Sup. S. Vito '96	♗	5
● Valpolicella Cl. Sup.		
S. Lena '97	♗	4
● Amarone della Valpolicella Cl. '94	♗♗	6
○ Passito Bianco di Gargagnago '95	♗♗	5
● Valpolicella Cl. Sup. S. Vito '95	♗♗	4
● Recioto della Valpolicella Cl. '95	♗	6
● Valpolicella Cl. Sup.		
S. Lena '95	♗	4

S. BONIFACIO (VR)

S. FIOR (TV)

INAMA
VIA IV NOVEMBRE, 1
37047 S. BONIFACIO (VR)
TEL. 045/6104343

MASOTTINA
VIA BRADOLINI, 54
LOC. CASTELLO DI ROGANZOLO
31010 S. FIOR (TV)
TEL. 0438/400775

Stefano Inama is a charismatic and controversial figure who has obliged just about everyone to come out and take a stand on the present and future of Soave. In the meantime, he has brought his own winemaking style to maturity, an approach that is based on very full ripeness of the fruit, maceration on the skins, oak-ageing for the top wines and overall sensations of brightness and liveliness. Stefano's wines age very well and, indeed, it is hard to evaluate them in the first few months. Do give them sufficient time for their character to come out. A casual tasting of the splendid '98 Du Lot was very edifying in this respect for the panel. The very clean and measured Vin Soave '99 offers hints of melon and jasmine, and the palate has good length. The Foscarino '99 reveals unusually rich, complex aromatic sensations. Apart from the characteristic almonds, it shows tropical fruit and there is rich, fleshy, yet elegant fruit on the palate. Here, tradition and modernity go hand in hand and the garganega variety is coaxed to surpass its usual limits. The Chardonnay aged in stainless steel is delicate and lively. The Campo dei Tovi still has to integrate properly with the oak but already shows plenty of fleshiness or concentration. The Vulcaia displays not very varietal notes of pears, peaches and vegetables. On the palate, it is gutsy and full-bodied, with lots of ripe fruit. The Bradisismo project, which aims to forge a position for this wine among Italy's premium reds, is getting up to speed. We noted a significant improvement over the first release, which displayed a certain edginess and rather inelegant vegetal tones. Elegance on the other hand, is the keynote of the '98 which complements a complex bouquet with an extremely fine, velvety flavour and a finish in which fine tannins accompany sensations of cherry liqueur chocolates. The Cuveé Speciale of the '97 Soave Vin Soave merits a One Glass rating.

For some time now, the Dal Bianco brothers' company has been distinguishing itself with its ability to reconcile large volume with quality, which, in some cases, is of a very high standard indeed. The whole production philosophy, from the vineyards to the advanced technology in the winery, as well as the firm's notable human resources, are all focused unswervingly on obtaining the very best. So again this year, the wide range of Masottina wines we tasted impressed with their reliable quality. The Colli di Conegliano Bianco '98 showed great personality and notable structure. The oak, well tempered by the fleshiness of the fruit, has given it a greater aromatic complexity, reining in the immediacy and fruit-rich notes of last year's version. This year, the new Ai Palazzi-label wines have been added to the list, comprising a Cabernet Sauvignon Riserva and a Merlot Riserva, both Piave DOCs. We like the Cabernet Sauvignon's traditional style and its richness on both nose and palate. The Prosecco Extra Dry, after a not particularly elegant initial impression, makes up for it with a broad spectrum of aromas, ranging from wistaria to ripe fruit. Its flavour is full-bodied and well-balanced, showing vibrant acidity and a zesty style. The Cartizze is well-typed and appealing while the Incrocio Manzoni confirms itself to be a very elegant wine, with acacia honey notes and a soft, velvety, yet also very refreshing flavour. The Colli di Conegliano Rosso '98 was not released in time for our tastings and so will be reviewed next year.

● Bradisismo Cabernet Sauvignon del Veneto '98	▼▼	6
○ Chardonnay Campo dei Tovi '99	▼▼	5
○ Soave Cl. Sup. Vigneti di Foscarino '99	▼▼	4
○ Soave Cl. Sup. Vin Soave '99	▼▼	3*
○ Chardonnay '99	▼	3
○ Sauvignon Vulcaia Fumé '99	▼	5
○ Soave Cl. Sup. Vin Soave Cuvée Speciale '97	▼	3
○ Vulcaia Après '98	▼	5
○ Sauvignon Vulcaia Fumé '96	♀♀♀	5
○ Soave Cl. Sup. Vigneto Du Lot '96	♀♀♀	5
● Colli Berici Cabernet Bradisismo '97	♀♀	6
○ Sauvignon Vulcaia Fumé '97	♀♀	5

○ Colli di Conegliano Bianco '98	▼▼	4
● Piave Cabernet Sauvignon ai Palazzi Ris. '97	▼	4
○ Cartizze	▼	5
○ Incrocio Manzoni 6.0.13 '99	▼	3
● Piave Merlot ai Palazzi Ris. '97	▼	4
○ Prosecco di Conegliano Extra Dry	▼	3
○ Piave Pinot Bianco '99		2
○ Pinot Spumante Brut		3
● Colli di Conegliano Rosso '97	♀♀	5

S. GERMANO DEI BERICI (VI)   S. MARTINO BUON ALBERGO (VR)

VILLA DAL FERRO LAZZARINI
VIA CHIESA, 23
36040 S. GERMANO DEI BERICI (VI)
TEL. 0444/868025

MARION
VIA BORGO, 1
FRAZ. MARCELLISE
37036 S. MARTINO BUON ALBERGO (VR)
TEL. 045/8740021

Villa dal Ferro Lazzarini makes a very welcome return to the Guide, auguring well, we believe, for results in the future. The prerequisites are all there, from the specific characteristics of the terroir, the volcanic subsoil and the winery's strong roots in tradition to the more modern contribution of innovative winemaking processes and clear new objectives. Undoubtedly, Alfredo Lazzarini, who founded the company in 1962, would be very proud of what his daughters, Angiola and Pamela, are achieving, with the crucially important consultancy of oenologist, Donato Lanati. After a great deal of preparatory work, a three and a half-hectare vineyard has just been planted at a density of 5,000 vines per hectare. Merlot is the major variety here, along with cabernet, riesling renano, gewürztraminer, and chardonnay. The idea is to produce a great red and a great white, with the legendary Campo del Lago of the '70s very much in mind. Another six hectares, with very old vines, make up the total vineyard area. The winery complex is located in the grounds of the majestic mid 16th century villa, built by the architect Sammicheli in the Palladian manner. Pamela and Angiola present a Cabernet Riserva which matures for five years in oak barrels and for one in bottle. It is a real wine-lover's wine, which shuns opulence to focus on expression of the grape variety, and on finesse and elegance. It is also very drinkable. The '97 Campo del Lago is again of a very high standard. Garnet-ruby in colour, it offers hints of leather, liquorice and damsons while on the palate, it is meaty and lingering. The Cabernet Le Rive Rosse is also reliable, with its scents of cherries and raspberries, good tannins and lip-smacking hints of liquorice. The Bianco del Rocolo, made from pinot bianco, is pretty decent, too.

In a general picture of improving quality in the province of Verona, new producers of note and worth continue to emerge. One of these is Marion, which steps into the limelight with self-confidence and character on its first appearance in our Guide. The Campedelli family purchased this large 15th–16th century farm complex, which was in a very precarious condition, in 1988. It had once belonged to the noble Marioni family, one of whose descendants was called Marion, and consists of a main house, an oratory dedicated to Saint Francis and some porticoes. The entire complex is surrounded by walls, inside which the vineyards are laid out. The Campedellis began to re-structure the property and work on re-developing the vineyards, which had been producing Soave and Valpolicella for the local co-operative winery. The encounter in '94 between Stefano, the eldest son of Rosa and Guerrino Campedelli, and oenologist Celestino Gaspari was the major turning point in the running of the estate. One area was set apart to create a quality-led project whose first fruits are just now becoming available. The four hectares involved produce 15,000 bottles of two wines, a Valpolicella and a Cabernet Sauvignon. We tasted both the '96s and the '97s, which are the wines currently on release. These are bottles which make a very clear statement. Powerful and concentrated, they also reveal delicacy and elegance. Their intense colour leads in to rich bouquets and palates where spices mingle with long, abundant fruit. In the case of the '97s, there is a powerful lift in the lingering finish to demonstrate the extraordinary quality of the vintage. In the cellar, we also tasted an excellent Passito Bianco from garganega and trebbiano toscano, which is still ageing.

●	Colli Berici Cabernet Ris. '93	¶¶	6
●	Colli Berici Merlot Campo del Lago '97	¶¶	6
●	Colli Berici Cabernet Le Rive Rosse '97	¶	5
○	Colli Berici Pinot Bianco del Rocolo '99	¶	4

●	Cabernet Sauvignon del Veneto '96	¶¶	5
●	Cabernet Sauvignon del Veneto '97	¶¶	5
●	Valpolicella Sup. '96	¶¶	5
●	Valpolicella Sup. '97	¶¶	5

S. PIETRO DI FELETTO (TV)   S. PIETRO IN CARIANO (VR)

BEPIN DE ETO
VIA COLLE, 32/A
31020 S. PIETRO DI FELETTO (TV)
TEL. 0438/486877

STEFANO ACCORDINI
VIA ALBERTO BOLLA, 9
FRAZ. PEDEMONTE
37029 S. PIETRO IN CARIANO (VR)
TEL. 045/7701733

The Colli di Conegliano Rosso '97 Croda Ronca, which we had already sampled and enjoyed a few months previously, prior to its release, confirmed all of its potential at our actual tasting. Indeed, it revealed even greater finesse, thanks to the longer period of maturation. You get an indication right from the nose of its superb quality and the extreme ripeness of the fruit. It unveils clear sensations of wild berries and prunes, together with complex, inviting aromas of cocoa, tobacco and hay. The palate is full-bodied and powerful, with tannins that are close-knit yet soft. The richness of the fruit and the robust alcohol enhance the wine's softness, which is balanced, though, by nicely judged fresh acidity. The Greccio Colli di Conegliano Bianco '98 is this winery's other top product. Thanks to cold maceration on the skins, it is a handsome golden yellow that tempts you to sample the nose, where there are intense floral and fruity aromas laced with mineral and vegetal notes. The palate impresses with the richness of both the soft fruit and the acidity, which find an admirable point of balance in the robust body. The Prosecco Extra Dry is notable for its very distinctive gamut of aromas. Citrus fruit and hazelnut notes mingle before opening out into sensations of flowers and acacia honey. The palate is rich and well-balanced. Finally, the Incrocio Manzoni 6.0.13 is always agreeable, with its delicately aromatic style and forthright flavour.

The Accordini family's cellar resembles a California-style "boutique winery". From the compact tasting room, to the areas where the vinification takes place and the cellar itself where the wines are aged in wood, everything is on a scale that befits a production that has to try very hard to reach 30,000 bottles a year. The Accordinis, who started off as tenant farmers, today own just over three hectares of specialized vineyards in the little village of Bessole, near Negrar. The family consists of Stefano and Giuseppina, their sons Tiziano and Daniele, and their respective wives. Stefano and Tiziano look after the vineyards and sales, while Daniele, an oenologist at the Valpolicella co-operative winery, is responsible for winemaking. The unchallenged star in the Accordini firmament is the Amarone Il Fornetto '95, which displays a particularly bright and dense colour and an excitingly exuberant nose where you will find gentle hints of toast and coffee cream, a souvenir of the over two years it spent in new barriques. These are rendered even sweeter by notes of strawberry and raspberry jam. The Il Fornetto again claimed the Three Glass award it obtained with the '93 vintage. The Amarone Acinatico '96 is much less concentrated, but demonstrates majestic balance and a style perfectly in keeping with the rainier vintage. The Recioto Acinatico '98 fully lives up to our expectations. It offers a complex nose of fruit bottled in brandy, spices and cocoa, as well as a powerful but well-balanced flavour. The Passo '97, made from lightly dried corvina, cabernet and merlot grapes, is similarly successful. Also striking, if slightly less so, are the Valpolicella Acinatico '98, in which the oak is not yet fully integrated, and the Bricco delle Bessole '97 made from partially dried garganega grapes and fermented in barrique. The Valpolicella '99, on the other hand, is less impressive.

O Colli di Conegliano Bianco		
Il Greccio '98	♥♥	3*
● Colli di Conegliano Rosso		
Croda Ronca '97	♥♥	6
O Incrocio Manzoni 6.0.13 '99	♥	3
O Prosecco di Conegliano Extra Dry	♥	3
O Prosecco di Conegliano Frizzante	♥	3
O Prosecco di Conegliano		
Tranquillo '99		2
● Colli di Conegliano Rosso '96	♥♥	6
O Faè Passito Bianco '95	♥♥	5

● Amarone della Valpolicella Cl.		
Vigneto Il Fornetto '95	♥♥♥	6
● Amarone della Valpolicella Cl.		
Acinatico '96	♥♥	6
● Passo '97	♥♥	5
● Recioto della Valpolicella		
Acinatico '98	♥♥	5
O Bricco delle Bessole Passito '97	♥	5
● Valpolicella Cl. '99	♥	3
● Valpolicella Cl. Sup. Acinatico '98	♥	4
● Amarone della Valpolicella Cl.		
Acinatico '95	♥♥♥	6
● Amarone della Valpolicella Cl.		
Vigneto Il Fornetto '93	♥♥♥	6
● Passo '96	♥♥	5

LORENZO BEGALI
VIA CENGIA, 10
37029 S. PIETRO IN CARIANO (VR)
TEL. 045/7725148

BRIGALDARA
VIA BRIGALDARA, 20
FRAZ. S. FLORIANO
37029 S. PIETRO IN CARIANO (VR)
TEL. 045/7701055

Unlike those large or small producers who rely on big-name oenologists that may have little or nothing to do with a unique area like Valpolicella, the uncompromising and intuitive Lorenzo Begali has chosen to rely on his own small store of experience and on his friends. In fact, his results, which improve with every vintage, seem to be proving him right. Even in a year which everyone acknowledged was poor ('96), Lorenzo demonstrated that he could still get the very best from his vineyards. Thanks to meticulous grape selection during the harvest, and to careful monitoring during drying, he managed to produce some wines of excellent quality. The standard Amarone is rich and minerally, with attractive floral hints on the nose. The entry on the palate is warm yet clean while the close-knit tannins provide good backbone and the progression on the palate is well-sustained. The Monte Ca' Bianca is a much more complete wine. The nose is still rather closed but reveals mineral and balsamic nuances as well as notes of ripe fruit. The oak has integrated perfectly with the fruit, giving a warm and sensual, almost southern Italian feel to the wine. The Recioto, Lorenzo's great passion, is the best ever. It displays authentic class which has no need of justification. The floral attack on the nose is uncompromising. Skilfully handled oak melds into an elegant, yet full-bodied, complex and creamy palate with an amazingly bright, forward style. The Valpolicella Superiore has an attractive fleshy palate while the Valpolicella Classico's most appealing characteristics are its fruitiness and balance.

The engagingly picturesque Brigaldara estate lies in the foothills of San Pietro in Cariano. From the vineyards of Stefano Cesari's property, you can admire the beautiful countryside of Valpolicella and, even though you are only a few metres away from a busy main road, you could be in another world altogether. The handsome residence where Stefano's family lives, which also houses the recently renovated winery, is surrounded by 20 hectares of land, of which 15 are under vine. The varieties planted are the classic ones of the zone (corvina, rondinella and molinara), offering a potential production of around 85,000 bottles a year of Amarone, Recioto and Valpolicella. The wines presented this year were among the best from the entire Valpolicella zone, thanks to the fact that, in the last couple of years, the hillside vineyards that were previously being redeveloped came on-stream. Our tasting notes begin with a splendid '96 Amarone which is one of the most interesting of its type, in spite of the problems of the vintage. On both nose and palate, it is elegant rather than massively powerful, with mouth-filling fruit and slightly prominent oak. All in all, an excellent interpretation of Amarone. We then go on to the Recioto della Valpolicella. This, too, earns Two Glasses without any problem, showing an intense colour and aromas of cherries. Soft and rounded on the palate, it reveals a sweetness that manages not to overwhelm the wine's firmly structured fruit. We close with the Valpolicella Il Vegro '98, a wine that Brigaldara releases after an extra year's ageing. This version has a very attractive style with a fine, clean bouquet and a well-balanced, complex palate.

● Amarone della Valpolicella Cl. '96 ❛❛		5
● Amarone della Valpolicella Cl.		
Vigneto Monte Ca' Bianca '96	❛❛	6
● Recioto della Valpolicella Cl. '98	❛❛	5
● Valpolicella Cl. '99	❛	2
● Valpolicella Cl. Sup. La Cengia '98	❛	4
● Amarone della Valpolicella Cl.		
Vigneto Monte Ca' Bianca '95	❜❜	6
● Recioto della Valpolicella Cl. '95	❜❜	5
● Recioto della Valpolicella Cl. '96	❜❜	4
● Recioto della Valpolicella Cl. '97	❜❜	5
● Amarone della Valpolicella Cl. '93	❜❜	6

● Amarone della Valpolicella Cl. '96	❛❛	5
● Recioto della Valpolicella '98	❛❛	5
● Valpolicella Il Vegro '98	❛❛	3*
● Amarone della Valpolicella Cl. '93	❜❜	5
● Amarone della Valpolicella Cl. '95	❜❜	5
● Recioto della Valpolicella '93	❜❜	5

S. PIETRO IN CARIANO (VR)   S. PIETRO IN CARIANO (VR)

LUIGI BRUNELLI
VIA CARIANO, 10
37029 S. PIETRO IN CARIANO (VR)
TEL. 045/7701118

ANGELO NICOLIS E FIGLI
VIA VILLA GIRARDI, 29
37029 S. PIETRO IN CARIANO (VR)
TEL. 045/7701261

The Campo Inferi vineyard owned by Luigi Brunelli owes its rather ominous name, meaning "Field from Hell", to its tortuous layout, which makes it particularly hard to work. After last year's successful release of the Campo del Titari, Luigi this year produced a new Amarone named Campo Inferi, and made exclusively with grapes from that plot. It is a traditional-style Amarone, garnet in colour and aged in large oak casks. The inviting, intriguing nose offers temptingly decadent hints of raisins and ripe figs over a rich, delicate and well-defined note of chocolate and an attractive overtone of liqueur cherries. In the mouth, its velvety tannins enhance the softness of the opulent, mouth-filling fruit. The Amarone Campo del Titari again showed its class, albeit in a more modern style and rather easily earned another Three Glass award to go with the one the '96 obtained last year. The vibrant, concentrated colour gives you notice that this is a great Amarone. Its generous, complex aromas reveal fresh, fragrant notes of red berry fruits and vegetal nuances of newly-mown hay, walnuts and tobacco. On the palate, it is powerful and long, with lots of ripe tannins, a balance underpinned by good acidity. The impeccably made basic Amarone is a lesser bottle than the preceding wines but stands out for its cleanness, finesse and austerity. Other noteworthy wines in the range include the Valpolicella Pariondo '97 and the garganega-based Bianco Carianum '98. The Recioto '97 and the Bianco Passito Re Sol '97, which we tasted last year, appear to have benefited considerably from their time in bottle.

In this zone, viticulture can be a reasonable source of income but it takes a winemaker with great insight and acumen to turn the occupation into a thriving business. Angelo Nicolis has been selling wine in bulk since 1951 and has been bottling his own wines since 1978. Today, the firm is run by Angelo's numerous children, especially by Giuseppe in the cellar, Giancarlo in the vineyards and Massimo, in charge of export sales. There are two quite separate vineyard, 20 hectares at San Pietro in Cariano, in the heart of Valpolicella Classico, and 15 at Lazise, in the Bardolino Classico area. Over the last few years, the Nicolis family has been busy building a new winery, one of the largest, at around 2,000 square metres, most efficient and technically advanced in the zone. That is probably why we had a few minor doubts in our tastings this year, which meant lower scores for the winery than in previous editions of the Guide. The Custoza, Bardolino Chiaretto and Bardolino from Garda, for example, could still do with a little fine-tuning. The difficult '96 vintage did not permit Nicolis to carry out a separate vinification for the Amarone Ambrosan selection and so all of the partially dried grapes went into the standard Amarone. It offers less concentration but has an attractively spicy nose that is particularly appealing. The Ca' Girardi, made from partially dried garganega and trebbiano grapes, is very good. It stands out for its balance on the palate and its interestingly complex nose. The Valpolicella Superiore and the new Testal, aged in French oak and obtained from a blend of partially dried corvina together with cabernet sauvignon and merlot, both earn One Glass ratings.

● Amarone della Valpolicella Cl.		
Campo del Titari '97	∏∏∏	6
● Amarone della Valpolicella Cl. '97	∏∏	6
● Amarone della Valpolicella Cl.		
Campo Inferi '97	∏∏	6
○ Bianco Carianum '98	∏	3
● Valpolicella Cl. Sup. Pariondo '97	∏	3
● Corte Cariano Rosso '98		3
○ Pariondo '98		3
● Amarone della Valpolicella Cl.		
Campo del Titari '96	∏∏∏	6
● Amarone della Valpolicella Cl. '96	∏∏	5
○ Passito Re Sol '97	∏	4
● Recioto della Valpolicella Cl. '97	∏	4
● Recioto della Valpolicella Cl. '96	∏	4

○ Ca' Girardi '95	∏∏	5
● Amarone della Valpolicella Cl. '96	∏	6
● Testal '97	∏	5
● Valpolicella Cl. Sup. Seccal '97	∏	4
● Bardolino Cl. '99		3
☉ Bardolino Cl. Chiaretto '99		2
● Valpolicella Cl. '99		2
● Valpolicella Cl. Sup. '97		3
● Amarone della Valpolicella Cl.		
Ambrosan '93	∏∏∏	6
● Recioto della Valpolicella Cl. '97	∏∏	6
● Amarone della Valpolicella Cl.		
Ambrosan '95	∏∏	6

S. PIETRO IN CARIANO (VR) S. PIETRO IN CARIANO (VR)

F.LLI SPERI
VIA FONTANA, 14
FRAZ. PEDEMONTE
37029 S. PIETRO IN CARIANO (VR)
TEL. 045/7701154

F.LLI TEDESCHI
VIA VERDI, 4/A
FRAZ. PEDEMONTE
37029 S. PIETRO IN CARIANO (VR)
TEL. 045/7701487

The Speri family has always believed in the importance of vineyard and terrain. For that reason, they have purchased, over the years, some 60 hectares in the premium zones of Valpolicella Classico at Fumane, Negrar and San Pietro in Cariano to become one of the area's major landowners. The vine training system used is the "pergola veronese", with a much higher than average planting density, and constant supervision of the vineyards themselves. The grapes are vinified at the recently restructured winery, though this has already proved rather too small, and construction work on a new facility has now begun. Ageing of the wines takes place partly in large Slavonian oak barrels and partly in French oak tonneaux. As regards the wines presented this year, we were very excited as usual by the Amarone Sant'Urbano. It has an impenetrable colour and very intense aromas, with notes of spices and jam that combine power with finesse. On the palate, it is mouth-filling and rich, with excellent tannins and an interminable finish. It is a marvellous Amarone – indeed, it always is in top vintages – and sailed through to another Three Glass award. Of the two Valpolicellas, we preferred the Sant'Urbano, albeit by the merest of whiskers, to the La Roverina because its greater body and length suggest superior ageing potential. With the release of the La Roggia '97 being postponed, the Recioto I Comunai '97 was on offer. The grapes for it are pressed at the end of January and it is then aged for two years in 30-hectolitre Slavonian oak barrels. It has a ruby colour shading into deep purple, with a very intense, fruit-rich nose of black berry fruit preserve that also reveals a hint of cocoa and spices. It is ample and full-bodied on the palate, with good balance and excellent length.

From this year, brother and sister Riccardo, the winemaker, and Antonietta, in charge of sales, have been joined by Sabrina, a researcher in food technology at the college in San Michele all'Adige. The company controls some 35 hectares of vineyards, of which seven are family-owned. Nearly all stand on hillslope sites and they yield 350,000 bottles a year. The Tedeschis have long had a reputation for their Amarone and in fact, the Monte Olmi selection has been made from one of their own vineyards since 1964. It is a tradition the winery continues to uphold. The Amarone Capitel della Fabriseria '97, whose grapes are dried – as they are for the Monte Olmi – under controlled conditions of temperature and humidity, came out top. This fourth release, after the '83, the '88 and the '95, impressed us with its opaque purple-ruby colour and elegant, complex notes of plum jam which combine with aromas of spices and dried flowers. The powerful, ripe, full-bodied palate is rounded off by a long, soft, well-balanced finish. The Monte Olmi is only slightly less concentrated. It is not quite so dense in the glass but offers a wealth of aromatic nuances ranging from bottled fruit to hints of cloves. A touch less mellow on the palate thanks to its more overt tannins, it is nevertheless rich and persistent. The basic Amarone is even less concentrated, but still good. The Rosso della Fabriseria, produced from Amarone grapes with five percent cabernet sauvignon, and aged for 12 months in new barriques, needs time to express its full potential. The Recioto Monte Fontana '97 has a very dark colour and exceptionally intense aromas which are not yet fully knit. Nor is its splendidly opulent fruit on the palate matched by comparable finesse. The two Valpolicellas and the Capitel San Rocco are decently made.

● Amarone della Valpolicella Cl.	
Vigneto Monte Sant'Urbano '95 ♟♟♟ 6	
● Recioto della Valpolicella Cl.	
I Comunai '97 ♟♟ 5	
● Valpolicella Cl. Sup.	
Sant'Urbano '97 ♟♟ 4	
● Valpolicella Cl. Sup.	
La Roverina '98 ♟ 3	
● Amarone della Valpolicella Cl.	
Vigneto Monte Sant'Urbano '90 ♟♟♟ 6	
● Amarone della Valpolicella Cl.	
Vigneto Monte Sant'Urbano '93 ♟♟♟ 6	
● Recioto della Valpolicella Cl.	
La Roggia '94 ♟♟♟ 6	

● Amarone della Valpolicella Cl. '97 ♟♟ 6	
● Amarone della Valpolicella Cl.	
Capitel della Fabriseria '97 ♟♟ 6	
● Amarone della Valpolicella Cl.	
Capitel Monte Olmi '97 ♟♟ 6	
● Recioto della Valpolicella Cl.	
Capitel Monte Fontana '97 ♟♟ 6	
● Rosso della Fabriseria '98 ♟♟ 5	
● Capitel S. Rocco	
Rosso di Ripasso '97 ♟ 4	
● Valpolicella Cl. Sup.	
Capitel dei Nicalò '97 ♟ 3	
● Valpolicella Cl.	
Capitel delle Lucchine '99 3	
● Rosso della Fabriseria '97 ♟♟♟ 6	

S. PIETRO IN CARIANO (VR)   S. PIETRO IN CARIANO (VR)

MASSIMINO VENTURINI
VIA SEMONTE, 20
FRAZ. S. FLORIANO
37029 S. PIETRO IN CARIANO (VR)
TEL. 045/7701331 - 045/7703320

VILLA BELLINI
VIA DEI FRACCAROLI, 6
LOC. CASTELROTTO DI NEGARINE
37029 S. PIETRO IN CARIANO (VR)
TEL. 045/7725630

The Venturini family cultivates some ten hectares of vines in the hills of San Floriano. Here we are in the noblest part of Valpolicella, where the exposure and slopes of the vineyards call for terracing and yields are naturally very low. The still very exuberant personality of the wines is well tempered by Daniele and Mirco, whose goal in the winery is not to foreground the fruit but rather to place the accent on harmony and balance. Thanks to these characteristics, the Venturinis' wines are among the best in Valpolicella and the cellar earned our Three Glass accolade for the first time with the '97 Recioto Le Brugnine. This is great news for this part of the province of Verona, and goes to confirm the high standard of quality achieved by the best producers in Valpolicella. It offers crisply defined sensations, starting with its aromas of blackberries and flowers and continuing with the well-sustained palate flavour in which the sweetness is skilfully calibrated on the delicately persistent finish. A very fine bottle, much superior to the basic Recioto from the same vintage. One of the selections, the Semonte Alto, has yielded a Valpolicella Superiore of excellent potential. "Ripasso", or the addition of skins after fermentation, has not made the Amarone any heavier. In fact, it has enhanced its complexity with hints of liquorice, berry fruit, coffee and cherries. The flavour is satisfying too, as is the extreme cleanliness of the fruit. The Amarone, from a difficult vintage, does not try too hard to be powerful. The style quite rightly tends to stress freshness, even if the alcohol is a bit overwhelming. A very youthful colour leads into a nose that reminds you of liqueur black cherries, walnut liqueur and spices. The palate is silky and it is only on the chocolate-nuanced finish that the tannins from the oak show through.

Ten years after their first harvest, Cecilia Trucchi and Marco Zamarchi continue along their chosen path as winemakers with the same enthusiasm and renewed passion. Their aim is to stay firmly rooted in tradition but without rejecting the more modern Verona style of winemaking in which supple fruit and balance are the keynotes. The renewal of the vineyards continues unabated and Marco has given up his day job in order to be able to devote all his time to the estate. The interesting impressions that we had last year of the wines that were still ageing were entirely confirmed by the products presented for tasting, and particularly by the '95 Amarone. Closed at first on the nose, with gamey and vegetal overtones, it gradually opens up to reveal ripe, tasty fruit. Spices and aromatic herbs complete the spectrum of fragrances while the palate is even tauter and more crisply defined, without compromising on roundness or balance. A perfect marriage of modernity and tradition. The cellars' goal was balance with the '99 Valpolicella, too, instead of merely going for a run-of-the-mill, easy-drinking style. So, this characterful wine, although it comes from a year which promised relatively little, refuses to settle for agreeable but unexciting fruitiness. The Superiore is deeper and more minerally. Its tertiary notes of dried flowers and leather are more redolent of a traditional style.

● Recioto della Valpolicella Cl.		
Le Brugnine '97	♥♥♥	5
● Amarone della Valpolicella Cl. '96	♥♥	5
● Valpolicella Cl. Sup.		
Semonte Alto '97	♥♥	3*
○ Il Castelliere Passito Bianco '97	♥	5
● Recioto della Valpolicella Cl. '98	♥	5
● Valpolicella Cl. '99		2
● Amarone della Valpolicella Cl. '93	♀♀	5
● Amarone della Valpolicella Cl. '94	♀♀	5
● Amarone della Valpolicella Cl. '95	♀♀	5
● Recioto della Valpolicella Cl. '96	♀♀	5
● Recioto della Valpolicella Cl.		
Le Brugnine '95	♀♀	5
● Recioto della Valpolicella Cl. '97	♀	4

● Amarone della Valpolicella Cl. '95	♥♥	6
● Valpolicella Cl. Il Brolo '99	♥	3
● Valpolicella Cl. Sup. Il Taso '97	♥	4
● Amarone della Valpolicella Cl. '93	♀♀	5
● Amarone della Valpolicella Cl. '94	♀♀	5
● Recioto della Valpolicella Cl. '95	♀♀	5

SALGAREDA (TV)

ORNELLA MOLON TRAVERSO
VIA RISORGIMENTO, 40
FRAZ. CAMPODIPIETRA
31040 SALGAREDA (TV)
TEL. 0422/804807

The energy and innovative spirit which are part and parcel of Ornella Molon and Giancarlo Traverso's characters are qualities that also drive the wines which we have been enjoying for years. We hope that these will eventually be tasted – and imitated – by as many producers as possible in the Piave DOC zone. Giancarlo and Ornella know full well that on these soils, the rocky, sedimentary terrain of Campodipietra, it is best to plant at high densities per hectare so that each plant will produce very little fruit if you want to make a rich, full-bodied wine. This is the goal that they are pursuing on the 12 hectares they own and the 28 which they rent. We hope that their success will contribute, as has happened in other areas, to the renaissance of an area, much of whose potential remains unexpressed. Founded in 1982, the estate has gradually taken shape and today it can point to the stunning architectural complex of Doge Giustinian's 16th-century country villa, which now houses the company's headquarters and winery. The indefatigable Molon-Traverso team has recently broadened its range of activities by purchasing a property in the Colli Orientali del Friuli, which is managed with great enthusiasm by their young son, Stefano. They are skilfully assisted in their efforts by oenologist, Simone Casazza, and consultant, Luca D'Attoma. And now for the wines, released under two labels, a standard range and the selections we shall be describing here. Not for the first time, the Merlots from the '96 and particularly the '97 vintages are among the very best. The Chardonnay is excellent and the Vite Rossa and the Cabernet are very good. The indigenous Raboso is idiosyncratic but interesting and the Sauvignon '99 is refreshing and aromatic. Finally, the sweet Bianco di Ornella offers rich fruit and good persistence.

● Piave Cabernet Ornella '97	🍷🍷	4
○ Piave Chardonnay Ornella '99	🍷🍷	4
● Piave Merlot Ornella '97	🍷🍷	4
○ Bianco di Ornella '96	🍷	4
● Piave Merlot Ornella '96	🍷	4
● Piave Raboso Ornella '95	🍷	4
○ Sauvignon Ornella '99	🍷	4
● Vite Rossa '96	🍷	5
● Piave Merlot Ornella '95	🍸🍸	4
○ Traminer '98	🍸🍸	4
● Vite Rossa '95	🍸🍸	5

SELVAZZANO DENTRO (PD)

LA MONTECCHIA
VIA MONTECCHIA, 16
35030 SELVAZZANO DENTRO (PD)
TEL. 049/637294

Enthusiastic young wine man, Conte Giordano Emo Capodilista, is striving both to improve the quality of his wines and the image and standards of the Colli Euganei zone as a whole. To do so, he continually experiments with different vinification methods, which this year have led to a new version of the estate's dessert wine. He is also constantly on the lookout for particularly suitable viticultural zones to be developed. One such site is the few hectares of vineyard on the hill of Montecastello, near Baone, which has been purchased this year and also partly re-planted. The idea is to create, in the future, two vineyard selections of the Rosso, the Montecchia and the Montecastello. The first will come from the northernmost part of the Colli Eugani DOC zone and the other from the most southerly area, to underline their different styles in the context of the same type of wine. The real strength of this estate's bottles is their identification with the terroir, whose predominant characteristics they express. This is highlighted in the two Colli Euganei Rossos, with their typical salty and gamey aromas and notes of geranium, which then give way to a soft, stylish palate. We preferred the Montecchia selection for its greater complexity and richness. The Merlot has elegantly integrated oak that does not prevent the fruit from coming through. Greater personality on the palate would have helped it to live up to the excellent promise of the nose. The Cabernet Franc Godimondo is again pleasant and immediately appealing, but also has nice juicy flesh on the palate. Of the two vintages of the Moscato Passito on offer, the more recent, the '98, is fresher thanks to a shorter drying period and a more restrained use of oak. The Chardonnay Montecchia is simple and well-typed.

● Colli Euganei Merlot Bandiera '98	🍷🍷	4
● Colli Euganei Rosso Montecchia '97	🍷🍷	5
○ Colli Euganei Chardonnay Montecchia '99	🍷	4
○ Colli Euganei Moscato Fior d'Arancio Passito '97	🍷	5
○ Colli Euganei Moscato Fior d'Arancio Passito '98	🍷	5
● Colli Euganei Rosso '97	🍷	3
● Godimondo Cabernet '99	🍷	4
● Raboso '98	🍷	4
○ Colli Euganei Moscato Fior d'Arancio Passito '96	🍸🍸	4

SOAVE (VR)

SOAVE (VR)

CANTINA DEL CASTELLO
CORTE PITTORA, 5
37038 SOAVE (VR)
TEL. 045/7680093

CANTINA DI SOAVE
V.LE VITTORIA, 100
37038 SOAVE (VR)
TEL. 045/6139811

The wines of the Cantina del Castello, of which Arturo and Silvana Stocchetti are the enthusiastic and energetic proprietors, continue to improve in quality. Situated right in the centre of Soave, in a mediaeval building once owned by the counts of Sambonifacio, it has 13 hectares under vine at Monteforte d'Alpone, where the majority of the vineyards lie, and Soave, in other words the two towns whose territories constitute the Soave Classico production zone. The 13,000 bottles produced each year also include relatively few bottles of a traditional "sur lies" Recioto with natural fermentation in the bottle, which is very pleasant and the apple of Arturo's eye. Coming to the wines themselves, we'll begin with the Soave Classico. Intense and fruity, it reveals good body and is underpinned by inviting acidity and its excellent price-quality ratio also helped it to earn a Two Glass rating. The Monte Pressoni, which comes from the hilly zone of the same name, is worth investigating. It has a very fine bouquet and displays well-structured fruit. The Monte Carniga is all about elegance, even though it is also has plenty of depth. The Acini Soavi, obtained from late-vintage garganega grapes, is made with a slight maceration of the fruit and ages in 15-hectolitre barrels for one year. Yellow, shading into bright gold, in colour, it offers floral and cinnamon spice overtones on the nose. There is good balance of tannins and acidity, and suggestions of almonds emerge on the lingering finish. There are two Reciotos, the traditionally-styled Corte Pittora and a barrique-aged version. Both, sadly, lack the freshness that would be proof positive of a further step forward in quality for this estate.

The potential of this co-operative winery, one of the largest in Italy, can be summarized in statistics that also indicate, however, that this producer has yet to express itself to the full. Among the figures which give a real idea of its overall capacity is the number of member growers, fully 1,200, who cultivate over 3,500 hectares in the most important denominations of the Verona area. As is the case with several producers in the province of Verona, the Cantina di Soave produces wines from all the viticultural areas of the zone and today, thanks to excellent management, the Cantina is laying the foundations for a very successful future. The new company operational centre, located at Borgo Covergnino near the castle, and outside the walls of the town itself, will be inaugurated in April during Vinitaly 2001. It is a very functional complex, with cellars for barrique-ageing dug into the rock, a large hall for conventions and some experimental vineyards where the members will be able to follow courses in viticulture. The products of the Cantina di Soave range from very cheap wines to more refined products, of which the Rocca Sveva selection represents the top line. The wines tasted this year proved to be very interesting, with the traditional reds from Valpolicella – the co-operative has a subsidiary winery at Cazzano di Tramigna, in the enlarged Valpolicella zone – showing best of all. The excellent modern-style Valpolicella Classico Rocca Sveva '98 offers good depth and a full body, but is rather too rigorous in its typicity. The very rounded and velvety Amarone della Valpolicella '94 is a fine product. Finally, the '99 Soaves, the Recioto di Soave and the Garda Cabernet Sauvignon all easily merit One Glass ratings.

O Soave Cl. Sup. '99	♀♀	3*
O Soave Cl. Sup. Acini Soavi '98	♀♀	5
O Soave Cl. Sup. Monte Pressoni '99	♀♀	4
O Soave Cl. Sup. Monte Carniga '99	♀	4
O Soave Cl. Sup. Monte Pressoni '98	♀♀	4

● Amarone della Valpolicella Rocca Sveva '94	♀♀	6
● Valpolicella Cl. Rocca Sveva '98	♀♀	3*
● Garda Cabernet Sauvignon Rocca Sveva '98	♀	3
O Recioto di Soave Cl. Rocca Sveva '98	♀	5
O Soave Cl. Castel Cerino '99	♀	3
O Soave Cl. Rocca Sveva '99	♀	3

SOAVE (VR)

COFFELE
VIA ROMA, 5
37038 SOAVE (VR)
TEL. 045/7680007

The estate of Giuseppe Coffele and his son, Alberto, has roots which go back to the 19th century, but in the 1970s, it required all of Giuseppe's stubbornness to put the estate, by then well-nigh abandoned, back on its feet. This he did initially by re-landscaping and replanting the vineyards and then a few years later, by renovating the winery as well. Today, young Alberto's is the principal guiding hand, while Giuseppe, who maintains his strong bond with the terroir, is still the moving spirit behind the viticultural side of things. Coffele's clean and forthright wines are the perfect expression of the cellar philosophy and the Soave Ca' Visco is an excellent example. The result of severe grape selection, it has an elegant nose with scents of flowers and a marked minerally quality. The progression of the palate is absolutely delightful and mirrors the sensations on the nose while the wine's splendid overall balance suggests that it has an interesting future ahead of it. The basic Soave is more straightforward and immediately appealing, but its clean, refreshing style is accompanied by a certain individuality, the hints of fresh hazelnuts, almonds and aromatic herbs making for a highly attractive and even voluptuous glass of wine. The Recioto Le Sponde is definitely worth trying. Along with exuberant, exotic fragrances of banana, hazelnuts and flowers, it offers an extremely appealing flavour. Supple and complex, it has a sweetness that never threatens to cloy. The Chardonnay Castrum Icerini benefits from a brief stay in wood that gives it a delicate, creamy flavour, with quite a marked peachy note.

SOAVE (VR)

MONTE TONDO
VIA S. LORENZO, 89
37038 SOAVE (VR)
TEL. 045/7680347

This estate's goal is to form part of the small group of top producers in the denomination. Gino Magnabosco began his career as a winemaker in his spare time, patiently laying the foundations of an edifice based on a down-to-earth attitude and hard work. The results have not been slow to arrive. Gino's wines are convincing, his clientele is responding with enthusiasm, and now his original modest winery is no longer big enough. However, the new one is almost ready and the state-of-the-art winemaking equipment is geared to getting the best from his grapes, grown on the best-exposed hillsides in Soave and Monteforte. The Soave Spumante Brut '99 is one of the best in its category. It stands out thanks to its well-made style and its elegance on the palate. The Soave Classico Superiore Monte Tondo '99 is an excellent standard-label wine. Complete and well-managed, it offers a nose of ripe pears and cakes as well as a palate underpinned by refreshing acidity. You can't expect from this clean, uncomplicated wine the complexity that you find in the Casette Foscarin '99. Its extra dimension comes from specially selected fruit, longer maturation and a brief spell in new oak. On the nose, there is a barely perceptible hint of vanilla and the bouquet is filled out with fine almondy scents and exotic fruit notes. The flavour is very ripe, tangy and persistent, with delicate nuances of pear and almonds on the finish. This wine also ages very well. Re-tasting the previous vintage confirms Gino's skill at handling a difficult vinification technique like oak fermentation. We'll conclude on a sweet note with the Recioto '98. An intense golden yellow in colour, it displays hints of oak, baked apples and nuts on the nose. It is glycerine-rich on the palate and the sweetness is perhaps a little over-assertive. It's a wine that could have done with a touch more acidity.

O	Recioto di Soave Cl. Le Sponde '98	🍷🍷	5
O	Soave Cl. Sup. '99	🍷🍷	3*
O	Soave Cl. Sup. Ca' Visco '99	🍷🍷	4
O	Chardonnay Castrum Icerini '99	🍷	4
O	Recioto di Soave Cl. Le Sponde '97	🍷🍷	5
O	Soave Cl. Sup. Ca' Visco '98	🍷🍷	4

O	Soave Cl. Sup. Casette Foscarin '99	🍷🍷	3*
O	Recioto di Soave '98	🍷	4
O	Soave Cl. Sup. Monte Tondo '99	🍷	2*
O	Soave Spumante Brut '99	🍷	3
O	Soave Cl. Sup. Casette Foscarin '98	🍷🍷	3
O	Recioto di Soave Cl. Spumante '97	🍷	4

SOAVE (VR)

LEONILDO PIEROPAN
VIA CAMUZZONI, 3
37038 SOAVE (VR)
TEL. 045/6190171

Leonildo Pieropan, the grandfather of the present owner, founded this firm in 1890. Its headquarters is right in the centre of Soave, in the ancient Palazzo Pulici, whose origins date back to 1460 and which was the childhood home of the writer Ippolito Nievo. From 1970 onwards, young Leonildo, or Nino as he was known, began to buy land in the best subzones of the Soave area, the hills of Calvarino, Pigno, Becco, Boiolo, where La Rocca is situated, and Tondo. His awareness of the importance of the vineyards also led him to change from chemical to organic fertilizers, and he started to apply strict selection criteria to guarantee the very best possible quality. In the meantime, his determined and enthusiastic wife, Teresita, began to take on an important role, becoming responsible for the sales and marketing of the wines. Today, a new generation of Pieropans, represented by their sons Andrea and Dario, is becoming involved in the management of the estate with the same tenacity and diligence as its predecessors and it seems that the future has some pleasant surprises in store in the red wine department as well. The bottles presented this year were, as usual, of excellent quality, beginning with the fresh, inviting and extraordinarily quaffable Soave Classico. The Calvarino is very intense, fruity, full-bodied and long while The La Rocca displays even greater class. Subtle and elegant, with notes of vanilla, flowers, apples and pears on the nose, it has really persuasive fruit and good structure on the palate. Our Three Glass award goes to this particularly stylish interpretation of Soave. The Passito della Rocca is potent and complex, with a spicy nose that offers hazelnut notes. On the palate, there are apricot jam and almond tones in an overall context of freshness and balance.

SOAVE (VR)

SUAVIA
VIA CENTRO, 14
FRAZ. FITTÀ
37038 SOAVE (VR)
TEL. 045/7675089

The original name of the town of Soave was Suavia. This was also the name of a tribe from Swabia that founded the town during the Lombard era. Since 1887, this property has belonged to the Tessari family. Giovanni and Rosetta, together with their gritty, competent daughters, cultivate ten hectares of vineyards from which they produce around 50,000 unfailingly excellent bottles. This year, we noted a very appreciable improvement, resulting in one of the best performances in the Soave zone. The Classico Superiore has a bright straw-yellow colour. Intense and fruity on the nose, with hints of peach and green notes, it shows remarkable body and good acidity. From a vineyard planted in 1946 comes the splendid Monte Carbonare, whose fermentation takes place mainly in stainless steel but also, to a small extent, in barrique. The end product is a wine with a generous bouquet, offering mineral scents of fresh exotic fruits, and which is well-balanced and persistent in the mouth. The Le Rive, a subzone of Fittà, also from an old vineyard planted in 1951, is splendid. This exceptional expression of garganega ferments and matures for around eight months in barrique and offers sensations of vanilla, apricots and hazelnuts in its full, yet fine and elegant flavour. This showing by Le Rive won Suavia our Three Glass award and enabled the cellar to take an important step forwards. Lastly, the Recioto La Boccara is outstanding. Yellow tinged with gold in the glass, it has a nose of honey, fruit in syrup and cakes while the excellent balance of sweetness and acidity emerges satisfyingly on the palate.

O	Soave Cl. Sup. La Rocca '98	🍷🍷🍷	5
O	Passito della Rocca '97	🍷🍷	6
O	Soave Cl. Sup. '99	🍷🍷	3*
O	Soave Cl. Sup. Calvarino '99	🍷🍷	4
O	Recioto di Soave Le Colombare '97	🍷	5
O	Passito della Rocca '88	🍷🍷🍷	6
O	Passito della Rocca '93	🍷🍷🍷	6
O	Passito della Rocca '95	🍷🍷🍷	5
O	Soave Cl. Sup. Vigneto Calvarino '98	🍷🍷🍷	4
O	Soave Cl. Sup. Vigneto La Rocca '95	🍷🍷🍷	4
O	Soave Cl. Sup. Vigneto La Rocca '96	🍷🍷🍷	4

O	Soave Cl. Sup. Le Rive '98	🍷🍷🍷	5
O	Recioto di Soave La Boccara '98	🍷🍷	5
O	Soave Cl. Sup. '99	🍷🍷	3*
O	Soave Cl. Sup. Monte Carbonare '99	🍷🍷	4
O	Soave Cl. Sup. Le Rive '96	🍷🍷	4
O	Soave Cl. Sup. Monte Carbonare '98	🍷🍷	4

CAVALCHINA
LOC. CAVALCHINA
FRAZ. CUSTOZA
37066 SOMMACAMPAGNA (VR)
TEL. 045/516002

LE VIGNE DI SAN PIETRO
VIA S. PIETRO, 23
37066 SOMMACAMPAGNA (VR)
TEL. 045/510016

The 30-hectare Cavalchina estate owned by the Piona family lies in the hills of Custoza, in the province of Verona. The family also owns a lovely property of 50 hectares at Monzambano in the province of Mantua. As from this year, we are including the entry under the Veneto region, rather than Lombardy, because all the wines are actually vinified at the Cavalchina cellar. The range of wines produced is wide and includes all the types from the two zones, with special emphasis on the products of the Garda denomination. It is from that DOC zone that the two most interesting products on the entire 16-strong list both come. The Faial, a red made from 80 percent partially dried and super-ripe merlot grapes, is excellent. It has a deep, almost impenetrable colour introducing an intense nose with very evident notes of ripe red berry fruit. The palate is broad, warm and mouth-filling, and only slightly marked by the wood on the faintly bitterish finish. The Cabernet Sauvignon Vigneto Il Falcone, which contains 10-15 percent merlot added to the cabernet sauvignon, is as outstanding as ever this year. Deep garnet in colour, it offers marked scents of vanilla that combine with those of blackberry preserve in its stylishly elegant bouquet. The powerful, warm, well-balanced fruit on the palate gives way to a long, clean aftertaste. The best of the whites is the Bianco di Custoza Amedeo with its fine, fruity perfumes and full, persistent flavour. The agreeably fruity Sauvignon Valbruna shows a soft, harmonious style. The Bardolino Santa Lucia is a success and the two sweet wines are intriguing, with our preference going to the white version, the Le Pergole del Sole '98, produced from müller thurgau grapes.

From his property at Sommacampagna, Carlo Nerozzi looks out over the Po valley and the last spurs of the morainic hills that slope down from Lake Garda. Here, since 1979, the year in which his father Sergio bought the estate, Carlo has devoted his own efforts and energy to producing high quality wines. From the ten hectares of specialized vineyards planted both with indigenous varieties – garganega, trebbiano toscano, tocai friulano, cortese and malvasia for the whites; corvina, rondinella, negrara, molinara, sangiovese and barbera for the reds – and with the international cabernet sauvignon, pinot nero and riesling varieties, he obtains just over 100,000 bottles of only a few types of wine. In fact, Carlo is trying to decide whether to reduce their number even further. The estate's real war-horse is the Refolà, a massively structured red made mainly from cabernet sauvignon, with the addition of small percentages of other varieties. Some of the grapes are lightly dried for 30 days and after fermentation the wine goes into barriques, 50 percent of which are new, where it matures for 12 months. The final result is a wine of great elegance and notable concentration and body, which does not really give away the fact, especially on the nose, that it contains some briefly dried fruit. The Due Cuori, a Passito made from moscato grapes, is excellent. It has a deep golden colour and offers typically Mediterranean fragrances, characterized by a very distinctive aromatic note. It has great weight on the palate and is long and mouth-filling. The Bardolino Chiaretto and the Bardolino are both very pleasant but the Bianco di Custoza Sanpietro is a bit too evolved.

○ Bianco di Custoza		
Amedeo Cavalchina '99	♈♈	3*
● Garda Cabernet Sauvignon		
Vigneto Il Falcone La Prendina '97	♈♈	4
● Garda Merlot Faial La Prendina '97	♈♈	5
○ Le Pergole del Sole Cavalchina '98	♈♈	5
● Bardolino Sup.		
S. Lucia Cavalchina '99	♈	3
● Garda Merlot La Prendina '97	♈	3
○ Garda Riesling Paroni		
La Prendina '99	♈	3
○ Garda Sauvignon Valbruna		
La Prendina '99	♈	3
⊙ Bardolino Chiaretto Cavalchina '99		2
○ Bianco di Custoza Cavalchina '99		2

○ Due Cuori Passito '97	♈♈	5
● Refolà Cabernet Sauvignon '97	♈♈	6
● Bardolino '99	♈	3
⊙ Bardolino Chiaretto '99	♈	3
○ Bianco di Custoza Sanpietro '98		4
○ Sud '95	♈♈♈	6
○ Due Cuori Passito '96	♈♈	5
● Refolà Cabernet Sauvignon '93	♈♈	6
● Refolà Cabernet Sauvignon '94	♈♈	6
● Refolà Cabernet Sauvignon '96	♈♈	6

SUSEGANA (TV)

CONTE COLLALTO
VIA XXIV MAGGIO, 1
31058 SUSEGANA (TV)
TEL. 0438/738241

TORREGLIA (PD)

VIGNALTA
VIA DEI VESCOVI, 5
FRAZ. LUVIGLIANO
35038 TORREGLIA (PD)
TEL. 0429/777225

Along the road that leads from Treviso to Conegliano, the view opens out very gently over the hills that surround the Castle of San Salvatore, pride of the noble Collalto family. Theirs is the story of a presence here in the Marca Trevigiana that goes way back to before the year 1000. Documents from the 10th and 11th centuries show that the family's viticultural activities helped to shape the bucolic beauty of the hills. The area under vine is almost 120 hectares, split up across the Prosecco, Colli di Conegliano and Piave DOC zones. The wide range of grape varieties includes the red and white incrocio Manzoni, the result of research conducted by Professor Manzoni, head of the oenological institute at Conegliano from 1930 and 1940, and the wildbacher, originally from Styria in Austria. The estate is run by Manfredo while the technical director for several years now has been Adriano Cenedese, assisted by Mirco De Pieri, who is responsible for the management of the vineyards. The estate produces a wide range of wines and, as usual, they are offered at very fair prices. The best score was obtained by the Colli di Conegliano Bianco. Its intense nose offers hints of green leaves, and is aromatic and floral while there is good length on the palate, which is redolent of pears. The Prosecco Extra Dry is fragrant and the Incrocio Manzoni Bianco is fruity. The Pinot Grigio and the Chardonnay are both very appealing while the Incrocio Manzoni Rosso is as exuberant and youthful as ever. The Wildbacher reveals hints of freshly mown grass, autumn leaves and cherries. The Merlot and the Cabernet del Piave reveal a pleasant, refreshing style. Finally, the Colli di Conegliano Rosso displays greater complexity on both the nose and palate.

In 1986, when Vignalta was founded, the Colli Euganei DOC was not particularly noted for quality. It was only their tenacity and enthusiasm that enabled Lucio Gomiero and Franco Zanovello to find success and since 1994, they have been joined by a new partner, Graziano Cardin. The geographical position, the climate, the volcanic origin of the soil and the different altitudes at which the vineyards are planted offer the potential for obtaining well-structured, cellarable reds and whites. The winery is in the village of Marlunghe, near Arquà Petrarca. Production capacity is around 300,000 kilograms of red grapes and 150,000 of white, and the property covers a total of 55 hectares, distributed over seven different municipalities in the DOC zone. The varieties grown range from the traditional moscato to the red grapes of Bordeaux and the whites from Burgundy. Besides, a project has been set in motion which, over the next ten years, will involve the reproduction and experimentation of indigenous varieties such as marzemina bastarda, pattaresca and corbinella. The aim will be to promote the specific characteristics of a viticultural area that has been famous since classical times. After the powerful '97 version, the '98 vintage gave us yet another rich and substantial Gemola. What is particularly striking about it is the fusing of its components. The balance they create will in a few years take the wine to even greater heights. It easily earned our Three Glass accolade with one of the best performances ever put up by this extraordinary red. And the '99 Sirio is perhaps the best ever, too. The standard version is very good and the Oro is quite stunning. It has an excitingly aromatic and floral bouquet, a full body and a very subtle, long finish. The same goes for the Moscatos, and especially the Alpianae, a great sweet wine. The other products are all very good and make their contribution to a really splendid range.

O Colli di Conegliano Bianco '99	♟♟	3*
● Colli di Conegliano Rosso '96	♟	4
● Incrocio Manzoni 2.15 '99	♟	3
O Incrocio Manzoni 6.0.13 '99	♟	3
● Piave Cabernet '99	♟	3
O Piave Chardonnay '99	♟	3
● Piave Merlot '99	♟	3
O Pinot Grigio dei Colli Trevigiani '99	♟	3
O Prosecco di Conegliano Extra Dry	♟	3
● Wildbacher '99	♟	3
● Piave Cabernet Ris. '94	♟♟	5
● Piave Cabernet Ris. '95	♟♟	5
● Wildbacher '98	♟	3

● Colli Euganei Rosso Gemola '98	♟♟♟	6
O Colli Euganei Chardonnay '98	♟♟	5
O Colli Euganei Fior d'Arancio Alpianae '98	♟♟	5
O Colli Euganei Moscato '99	♟♟	4
O Sirio '99	♟♟	4
O Sirio Oro '99	♟♟	4
O Colli Euganei Pinot Bianco '99	♟	4
O Colli Euganei Pinot Bianco Agno Casto '99	♟	5
● Colli Euganei Rosso '98	♟	4
● Colli Euganei Cabernet Ris. '90	♟♟♟	6
● Colli Euganei Rosso Gemola '95	♟♟♟	6
● Colli Euganei Rosso Gemola '97	♟♟♟	6
● Colli Euganei Rosso Gemola '96	♟♟	5

VALDOBBIADENE (TV)

VALDOBBIADENE (TV)

DESIDERIO BISOL & FIGLI
VIA FOL, 33
FRAZ. S. STEFANO
31049 VALDOBBIADENE (TV)
TEL. 0423/900138

F.LLI BORTOLIN SPUMANTI
VIA MENEGAZZI, 5
FRAZ. S. STEFANO
31049 VALDOBBIADENE (TV)
TEL. 0423/900135

In the Valdobbiadene area, Bisol stands for two important things – tradition and modernity. Tradition means roots while modernity implies an understanding of the evolution of wine, of tastes and of new markets. Eliseo Bisol started his activity as a winemaker and distiller in the second half of the 19th century. The period after the end of the Second World War, especially the 50s and 60s, saw the emergence and consolidation of sparkling wine production in the Valdobbiadene area and in the last twenty years, a combination of technical progress, greater attention to quality and the entry of new generations of winemakers has given Prosecco a leading position in the wine market. For the Bisols, the arrival of young Gianluca on the scene has had the effect of introducing new vitality, contributing significantly to the excellent results that have been achieved. There are two new products among the wines presented, the Prosecco Desiderio di Bisol 2000 and the Cuvée Tertium Millennium '85. The former, which comes from one of the very best subzones, Santo Stefano, is a product of the splendid '97 vintage. Made exclusively from prosecco grapes, its fermentation takes place in Allier oak barriques, an unusual process for this type of wine, but an undoubted success. Bright straw-yellow in colour, it unveils aromas of crusty bread and flowers leading in to a creamy palate with hints of nuts on the nicely balanced, lingering palate. The Cuvée Tertium Millennium '85, also from a stunning year, amply deserves its Two Glass rating. We can sum up our comments on the other wines by saying that they are all praiseworthy, with particularly high marks going to the Prosecco Vigneti del Fol.

In the Treviso archive of the Venetian Republic, there are records of a certain Zan Bortolin. In 1542, he lived at Santo Stefano di Valdobbiadene and cultivated 17 plots of land, which allowed him to produce 20.5 "conzi" – a Venetian measure – of wine. This ancient account naturally stimulates our curiosity, while more recent reports tell that between the two World Wars, Valeriano Bortolin, whose name is the same as that of the present owner, started to promote the estate by taking part in wine shows and competitions in various Italian cities. The wine was all sold within the Veneto itself, partly in demijohns and partly in bottle. But it was 1950 that marked the real beginning of the modern F.lli Bortolin Spumanti company as we know it today. In that year, the cellar started to make Charmat method sparkling wines and the winery was equipped with the first pressurized fermentation tanks and a modern bottling line. Continuing modernization will be the keynote in the future too, when production will be 350,000 bottles, obtained both from the 20 hectares of the company's own vineyards as well as from those of producers in the zone with whom Bortolin has a long-standing relationship. Other producers supply about 50 percent of the fruit. The best wine this year was the Prosecco Rù, one of the very best Proseccos the panel tasted on its rounds. The wine displays marked fruity scents reminiscent of apples, and has a mellow, persistent flavour. Close in its wake comes the very fresh, intense, clean-tasting Prosecco Extra Dry. The Prosecco Brut is also excellent. The salient characteristic of the Cartizze is its fragrance while the Prosecco Dry reveals an attractive creaminess. The Colli di Conegliano Bianco, made from incrocio Manzoni bianco, chardonnay and pinot bianco, offers notes of peaches and apples and is very attractive on the palate. Lastly, the Spumante Vigneto del Convento merits an honourable mention.

○	Cuvée Tertium Millennium '85	🍷🍷	6
○	Prosecco di Valdobbiadene		
	Desiderio Bisol 2000 '97	🍷🍷	5
○	Prosecco di Valdobbiadene		
	Extra Dry Vigneti del Fol '99	🍷🍷	4
○	Cartizze '99	🍷	5
○	Prosecco di Valdobbiadene		
	Brut Crede	🍷	4
○	Prosecco di Valdobbiadene		
	Dry Salis	🍷	4
○	Spumante Jeio Cuvée Brut	🍷	4
○	Talento Brut Bisol '96	🍷	5
○	Talento Cuvée del Fondatore		
	Eliseo Bisol '94	🍷	6

○	Prosecco di Conegliano Rù	🍷🍷	3*
○	Prosecco di Valdobbiadene		
	Extra Dry	🍷🍷	3*
○	Cartizze	🍷	4
○	Colli di Conegliano Bianco '99	🍷	3
○	Prosecco di Valdobbiadene Brut	🍷	3
○	Prosecco di Valdobbiadene Dry	🍷	3
○	Spumante Brut		
	Vigneto del Convento		3

VALDOBBIADENE (TV)

VALDOBBIADENE (TV)

BORTOLOMIOL
VIA GARIBALDI, 142
31049 VALDOBBIADENE (TV)
TEL. 0423/975794

CANEVEL SPUMANTI
VIA ROCCAT E FERRARI, 17
LOC. S. BIAGIO
31049 VALDOBBIADENE (TV)
TEL. 0423/975940

Bortolomiol is one of the best known producers of Prosecco. The family's origins date back to the 18th century, when the business was run by Bartolomeo Bortolomiol. The generations followed one another until Giuliano Bortolomiol expanded the company to its present size. Having graduated from the Oenological School of Conegliano, he began making sparkling wines in 1949. Tireless and full of initiative, Giuliano was a founder-member of the Confraternita del Prosecco and in 1962, he was instrumental in setting up, with other producers, the Mostra Nazionale dello Spumante trade fair. Today, he is helped by his daughters and son-in-law, Daniele Buso. Naturally, the roughly 10 hectares of vineyards owned by the family provide only a tiny part of the grapes necessary for the firm's production of 1,500,000 bottles, which is supervised by oenologist Gianfranco Zanon. The remaining fruit comes from long-standing contract growers. The Cartizze made a very good impression. Straw-yellow with green highlights, it unfurls intense floral perfumes and a rich fruitiness, in which hints of apples and pears are evident. There is also remarkable body and length. Our next highest score went to the Prosecco Banda Rossa. Forthright in style, with crusty bread notes, it is well-balanced and extremely delicate, offering hints of golden delicious apples. The Riserva del Governatore, made from prosecco, pinot and chardonnay, is very interesting. On the nose, there are suggestions of rennet apples and almonds while there is notable acidity to balance its good fruit on the palate. The Tranquillo, Brut and Dry Proseccos all deserve an honourable mention.

From the hill of San Biagio, at about 300 metres above sea level, you feel you can almost reach out and touch the peak of Cartizze. It's one of those panoramas that leave you spellbound and it is on this very spot that Canevel Spumanti's new winery is being built. The beauty of the scenery and the company's efficient and up-to-date winemaking plant are two of the principal features of a cellar that for over twenty years now, has been a benchmark for the zone. Some new products have been added to the range this year, including the Prosecco Frizzante Vigneto San Biagio, obtained from fruit grown on the same hill on which the winery itself is located, and the Prosecco Extra Dry Vigneto del Faè, produced with grapes from the estate's own holdings in the Refrontolo district. The Vigneto San Biagio distinguished itself with the elegance of its fruit and floral aromas, as well as with its fine balance on the palate, buoyed up by good persistence. The Faè made a good impression with its vegetal, citrus and hazelnut notes on the nose and its fresh, linear flavour, which displays a distinctive, austere style. However, the Prosecco Extra Dry Il Millesimato was the wine that caught the panel's fancy, thanks to an extremely agreeable character that neither lacks complexity on the nose nor crispness on the palate. The Cartizze is attractive, if somewhat unexciting, but the '99 version of the Prosecco Brut is not one of its best. Moving on to the still wines, we liked the Prosecco because of the elegance of its aromas, which are however insufficiently backed up by fruit on the palate. The Colli di Conegliano Bianco reveals the richness of its fruit on both nose and palate in a nicely gradual progression.

O	Cartizze	🍷🍷	5
O	Prosecco di Valdobbiadene		
	Extra Dry Sel. Banda Rossa	🍷	4
O	Riserva del Governatore		
	Extra Brut	🍷	4
O	Prosecco di Valdobbiadene Brut		3
O	Prosecco di Valdobbiadene Dry		3
O	Prosecco di Valdobbiadene		
	Tranquillo		3

O	Prosecco di Valdobbiadene		
	Extra Dry Il Millesimato '99	🍷🍷	4
O	Cartizze '99	🍷	4
O	Colli di Conegliano Bianco '99	🍷	3
O	Prosecco di Valdobbiadene		
	Extra Dry Vigneto del Faè '99	🍷	4
O	Prosecco di Valdobbiadene		
	Frizzante Vigneto S. Biagio '99	🍷	3
O	Prosecco di Valdobbiadene		
	Tranquillo '99	🍷	3
O	Prosecco di Valdobbiadene		
	Brut '99		3

VALDOBBIADENE (TV)

Col Vetoraz

Via Tresiese, 1
Fraz. S. Stefano
31049 Valdobbiadene (TV)
tel. 0423/975291

Col Vetoraz is the name of the hill where this estate is located. It is a wonderful viewpoint from which to admire an enchanting panorama of prosecco vineyards those of the prestigious Cartizze subzone. Nine hectares actually owned by the firm, four rented hectares and strict selection of grapes from other growers in the area represent Col Vetoraz's solid production base. It is then up to the experience and skill of agronomist, Paolo De Bortoli, and oenologist, Loris Dall'Acqua, to turn this succulent fruit into lively sparkling wines. The various selections presented for tasting included the Millesimato, a superb interpretation of this Prosecco that skilfully and even-handedly combines the crucial quality factor of intensity of fruit, fragrance, finesse and persistence. The Extra Dry scored very nearly as highly and both the Cartizze and the Brut are certainly extremely well-made. Finally, the Tranquillo Tresiese showed itself to be a refreshing, attractive wine. This is an excellent overall performance and it puts Col Vetoraz up there in the zone's top rank. In fact, it is a thoroughly dependable cellar. Every year, it turns out a range of very interesting products indeed, some of which sail comfortably over the Two Glass threshold.

O Prosecco di Valdobbiadene Dry Millesimato '99	🍷🍷	4
O Prosecco di Valdobbiadene Extra Dry	🍷🍷	3*
O Cartizze	🍷	5
O Prosecco di Valdobbiadene Brut	🍷	3
O Prosecco di Valdobbiadene Tranquillo Tresiese '99	🍷	3

VALDOBBIADENE (TV)

Nino Franco

Via Garibaldi, 147
31049 Valdobbiadene (TV)
tel. 0423/972051

The Franco winery was started up after the First World War by Antonio, whose immediate goal was to produce good wines. His son, Nino, followed in his footsteps, developing the business and improving the quality of the products. Then comes the era of Primo, initially working alongside his father, Nino, then on his own. Once he had graduated from the Oenological School at Conegliano, Primo gave the cellar's image and technical know-how a firm boost, making it into one of the leading players in Prosecco's current success in top restaurants and wine shops. Well aware that the final result depends on the quality of the grapes, Primo and a number of other growers in the zone stressed the importance of bringing out the very best in the prosecco variety. At the same time, he began a series of experiments in his Grave di Stecca vineyard using old clones, aimed at giving the final product even greater personality. An excellent result was achieved in our tastings by the Prosecco Rustico, of which no less than 400,000 bottles are produced. This very pleasant wine has an invitingly fruity style, with overtones of pineapple. The Prosecco Brut offers a handsome, bright straw-yellow colour, introducing sensations of apples and peaches. and is underpinned by a delicious acidulous vein. The fragrant, juicy Cartizze, whose fruit as ever is very ripe indeed, lacks a little bit of freshness. The Prosecco Primo Franco is decidedly flavoursome, intense and faintly aromatic, as well as creamy and long on the palate. Finally, there is the Primo Brut Metodo Italiano, a Charmat method chardonnay-based wine with a long second fermentation. The nose displays hints of yeast and green notes while the fruit-rich, full-bodied palate offers suggestions of almonds.

O Prosecco di Valdobbiadene Primo Franco	🍷🍷	4
O Cartizze	🍷	5
O Primo Brut Metodo Italiano	🍷	3
O Prosecco di Valdobbiadene Brut	🍷	3
O Prosecco di Valdobbiadene Rustico	🍷	3

VALDOBBIADENE (TV)

VALDOBBIADENE (TV)

LE COLTURE
VIA FOLLO, 5
FRAZ. S. STEFANO
31049 VALDOBBIADENE (TV)
TEL. 0423/900192

ANGELO RUGGERI
VIA FOLLO, 18
FRAZ. S. STEFANO
31049 VALDOBBIADENE (TV)
TEL. 0423/900235

In the world of Valdobbiadene wine, the fragmentation of the vineyards has led to a fairly widespread practice of purchasing grapes from other growers, rather than personally looking after plots that are inevitably scattered across the entire territory of the municipality. So, the estate of brothers Cesare and Renato Ruggeri goes very much against the trend. Reluctant to sever the strong ties that bind their family to the land, they prefer to shuttle back and forth along the country roads and tracks to tend their over 40 hectares of vineyards, most of which are in Valdobbiadene although some are situated at San Pietro di Feletto and on the hillslopes of Soligo. The almost obsessive attention that Le Colture lavishes on its vineyards and the subsequent TLC in the winery have made this estate one of the most important in the DOC zone, and whose wines are a benchmark for quality. This is certainly the case with the Prosecco Dry Funer, which proffers a rich nose, with intense notes of jasmine, and which then broadens out very elegantly over the entire palate, its flavour delightfully distributed and underpinned by the carbon dioxide. The Prosecco Extra Dry, has mature, ripe tones and is also splendid. In the mouth, it unveils nuances of sweet roasted almonds that caress the palate unhurriedly. The Cartizze offers greater complexity and a touch of sweetness that never cloys. The Brut, with its classic aroma of pears, is agreeable but lacks the weight of the Cartizze. The Prosecco Tranquillo and the Incrocio Manzoni are notable for their cleanliness and easy-drinking style.

The production process for Prosecco does not take place all at one go. The still wine, usually several hectolitres at a time, is transferred to a series of temperature-controlled stainless steel tanks and, every so often, re-fermentation of one or more of these tanks is carried out. It is not hard to imagine how extraordinarily difficult it is for a producer to keep the quality of all his bottles constant as they will come from vinification processes that often take place several months apart. Brothers Remigio and Vittore, thanks to the special care they take with the spumante process, succeed in achieving that reliability. Confirmation is to be found in the bottles that we taste each year for they are invariably among the best in their category. The brothers have a particularly skilled touch with the slightly sweeter styles like Cartizze, which has an inebriating bouquet with scents of almonds and golden delicious apples. The rich palate unfolds gradually with an exquisite note of liquorice on the finish that is both enticing and highly individual. In the Dry Funer, the accent is rather more on the finesse of the wine's sensations. Hints of spring flowers and aromatic herbs emerge with great delicacy and the palate follows a similar progression. It is delicate and appealingly fresh, the sparkle lending a satisfying suppleness. The Prosecco Brut combines a fresh, inviting bouquet with a clean, trenchant attack on the palate, as befits a truly bone-dry sparkler, whereas the Extra Dry is remarkable for its vegetal tones and an unusual rustic quality.

○ Cartizze	♈♈	4
○ Prosecco di Valdobbiadene		
Dry Funer	♈♈	3*
○ Prosecco di Valdobbiadene		
Extra Dry	♈♈	3*
○ Incrocio Manzoni 6.0.13 '99	♈	3
○ Prosecco di Valdobbiadene Brut	♈	3
○ Prosecco di Valdobbiadene		
Tranquillo Masaré '99		3

○ Cartizze	♈♈	4
○ Prosecco di Valdobbiadene		
Dry Funer	♈♈	3*
○ Prosecco di Valdobbiadene Brut	♈	3
○ Prosecco di Valdobbiadene		
Extra Dry	♈	3

VALDOBBIADENE (TV)

VALDOBBIADENE (TV)

RUGGERI & C.
VIA PRA FONTANA
31049 VALDOBBIADENE (TV)
TEL. 0423/975716

SANT'EUROSIA
VIA DELLA CIMA, 8
FRAZ. S. PIETRO DI BARBOZZA
31049 VALDOBBIADENE (TV)
TEL. 0423/973236

The passion and meticulous attention that Paolo Bisol dedicates to his work in the winery are merely the logical conclusion of a path that begins much further back, in the vineyard plots cultivated by this Valdobbiadene-based producer's faithful contract growers. Those plots produce the fruit which for quite some time now has enabled Paolo to achieve a production volume of around 1,400,000 bottles a year. All of it comes from grapes vinified in-house for the cellar has no need to buy in any must or wine whatsoever. Frequent visits are made in the vineyard. The cellar is constantly busy with experiments to get the very best out of each vintage without forcing Nature's hand. And, of course, Paolo himself oversees him every step in the winemaking process. All these factors make Paolo the shrewd yet passionate producer he is, in spite of the substantial quantity of wine he makes. Emblematic of all this dedication and care is the Prosecco Extra Dry Giustino B., which stuns you with the richness of its perfumes. Broad, sinuous notes of spring flowers and citrus fruit are also evident on the palate, where they mingle with notes of aromatic herbs and a marked mineral tone, the whole progression being underpinned by an elegant mousse. The wine's lovely balance ensures that it will age well, as we were able to confirm when we re-tasted the previous vintage. It offers a cellarability that is quite unexpected in such an exquisitely delicate, elegant wine. The Santo Stefano, with its ripe, exotic tones, is as exuberant as ever and contrasts with the Cartizze, which is fresher and more mineral, revealing a taut progression on the lingering palate. The Extra Dry Giall'Oro, one of the cellar's bankers, combines ripe tones with lively acidity while the crisp, dry Brut has excellent persistence.

Extracting the very best from each vintage, without gilding the lilies that Nature has actually offered, is a fair description of the principle objective that Giuseppe Geronazzo has set himself. The pursuit of perfection in the vineyard is followed by the diligent and careful transformation of the grapes into the most elegantly measured and well-balanced wine possible, with particular attention to the second fermentation of the wine, a hallmark of all this cellar's products. That is what lies behind the Prosecco Extra Dry from Sant'Eurosia, a wine that wins you over gradually with the delicacy of its floral perfumes and the evident almondy note typical of the variety. Then there are hints of flowers and nuances of apricots that emerge beautifully on the palate, delightfully accompanied by a discreet prickle. The finish, too, is very clean and elegant. Even more measured is Giuseppe's real passion, the Prosecco Brut, which seeks to convey the very spirit of the grape without recourse to sweetness. The wine displays clean, positive sensations of flowers, apples and pears. Here, too, a hint of almonds gives the dry, forthright flavour a certain richness. The Cartizze is a considerable success, just missing out on a Two Glass rating. Its elegant, clean bouquet is matched by splendid creaminess on the palate, along with an unobtrusive sweetness. The Prosecco Tranquillo, which balances fresh, elegant sensations with toasty notes, is also interesting.

O	Cartizze	🍷🍷	4
O	Prosecco di Valdobbiadene Brut	🍷🍷	3*
O	Prosecco di Valdobbiadene Dry S. Stefano	🍷🍷	4
O	Prosecco di Valdobbiadene Extra Dry Giall'Oro	🍷🍷	3*
O	Prosecco di Valdobbiadene Extra Dry Giustino B. '99	🍷🍷	4
O	Prosecco di Valdobbiadene Tranquillo Le Bastie '99	🍷	3

O	Prosecco di Valdobbiadene Brut	🍷🍷	3*
O	Prosecco di Valdobbiadene Extra Dry	🍷🍷	3*
O	Cartizze	🍷	4
O	Prosecco di Valdobbiadene Tranquillo	🍷	3

VALDOBBIADENE (TV)

VALEGGIO SUL MINCIO (VR)

TANORÉ
VIA MONT, 3
FRAZ. S. PIETRO DI BARBOZZA
31049 VALDOBBIADENE (TV)
TEL. 0423/975770

CORTE GARDONI
LOC. GARDONI, 5
37067 VALEGGIO SUL MINCIO (VR)
TEL. 045/7950382

Tanorè, called after the nickname of Renato and Sergio Follador's father, confirms its serious standing again this year. Our visit to the winery left us a very positive impression of having conversed with industrious, determined winemakers who are conscious that the high quality of their bottles derives from their terroir and from the location of their seven hectares under vine in the subzones of San Pietro di Barbozza, Santo Stefano and Guia, all genuine Prosecco crus. The Follador family – quite a common surname in this area – has been in the area for around a century and its members are personally involved in work both in the vineyard and in the winery. Production, which can of course vary according to the vintage, is normally around 100,000 bottles, with 70 percent obtained from the Folladors' own grapes and 30 percent from purchased fruit. The wines are sold primarily in Italy, predominantly to private customers, but the cellar has small export markets in Germany, Holland, Switzerland and Japan as well. The Prosecco Selezione offers an exemplary version of this wine, rich in fruit, well-balanced and persistent. The Extra Dry is no less a bottle, with its soft fragrance and elegant style. As usual, the Cartizze was a big hitter, unfurling intense floral scents redolent of wisteria. On the palate, which offers notes of pear, it is creamy, very delicate and long. The Tranquillo has a straw-yellow colour with a subtle green tinge and a herbaceous nose with hints of rennet apples. There is good body and faintly almondy fruit on the palate, and its freshness makes it a great aperitif. The Brut is agreeable and well-made.

Corte Gardoni is one of the star producers of Bianco di Custoza and Bardolino, located as it is in an area where these DOCs overlap, with Lake Garda to the north and the Po valley to the south. The family's agricultural traditions date back to the 17th century and they have had their own estate since 1980. Their property extends over an area of 50 hectares, of which 25 are planted to vine, and the cellar turns out 200,000 bottles a year. Gianni Piccoli and his sons are the driving spirits behind the property. Gianni operates in an area known for its youthful, forward wines. His efforts have enabled him not only to make exemplary products in that style but also to try out more complex, characterful bottles as well. These endeavours have borne fruit in wines like the white I Fenili. Made from late-vintage garganega blended with tiny proportions of other varieties, and aged for two years in barrique, it flaunts a brilliant golden yellow hue. The bouquet is generous, intense and subtle, with an explosive fruitiness that yields nuances of orange, citron, pineapple, peach and pear. On the palate, it is elegant and supple, yet full-bodied and attractively persistent. We re-tasted the '93 and '89 vintages. Both are on top form, showing genuine vivacity and grace, especially the older vintage, which is so rich in flavour that it makes a particularly vivid impression. Another wine that lies beyond the bounds of the DOC is the Rosso di Corte, a Bordeaux-style blend of cabernet sauvignon and merlot. Ruby tending towards deep garnet in colour, it offers overtones of minerals, hay and tobacco and a full flavour of cherries, plums and liquorice. We were amazed when we sampled the '92. Despite the anything but exciting vintage, it still has a fresh and deliciously flavoursome style. The Bianco di Custoza is as decent as ever, as are the various versions of Bardolino.

O Cartizze		♟♟	5
O Prosecco di Valdobbiadene Extra Dry		♟♟	3*
O Prosecco di Valdobbiadene Extra Dry Sel.		♟♟	4
O Prosecco di Valdobbiadene Brut	♟		3
O Prosecco di Valdobbiadene Tranquillo	♟		3

O I Fenili '96		♟♟	5
● Rosso di Corte '97		♟♟	5
☉ Bardolino Chiaretto '99	♟		3
● Bardolino Cl. Le Fontane '99	♟		3
● Bardolino Sup. '98	♟		3
O Bianco di Custoza '99	♟		3
● Rosso di Corte '92		♟♟	5
● Rosso di Corte '96		♟♟	5
O I Fenili '93		♟♟	5
O I Fenili '95	♟		5

VERONA

VERONA

GIACOMO MONTRESOR
VIA CA' DEI COZZI, 16
37124 VERONA
TEL. 045/913399

PASQUA
VIA BELVIGLIERI, 30
37131 VERONA
TEL. 045/8402111

Montresor is a winery with a historic past, a fine villa and exceedingly capacious cellars. The headquarters are at Verona while the vineyards themselves sprawl across the 100 hectares of the estate's own four properties, Cavalcaselle at Castelnuovo del Garda, La Mandorla at San Giorgio in Salici di Sona, Corte Quaiara, also in San Giorgio in Salici di Sona, and Siresol at San Peretto di Negrar. Here, they grow the grapes for their most important wines, the range of single-vineyard bottlings and a number of special selections. The Montresors also own other estates, Domenico de Bertiol in the Prosecco DOC zone, and Wallenburg, at Trento. The best of the wines tasted was the Passito Terranatia, made from sauvignon and garganega grapes. It has a lively golden colour and an elegant bouquet, with citron and oaky notes in evidence. Rich and harmonious on the palate, it reveals attractive, well-balanced and not too sweet fruit. The Santomio, a full-bodied red made from cabernet and merlot, was of similar quality. You can see this wine's potential as soon as you pick up the glass for its attractive purplish colour ushers in a fruity nose with hints of black cherries and berry fruit before the palate delights with its rich, mouth-filling flavour. The Cabernet Sauvignon Vigneto Campo Madonna has a more attractive nose than palate, where its rather restrained fruit is overwhelmed by the oak. The Arcaio '98, a red in which the local corvina variety is blended with an international one, cabernet, is agreeable enough but its tannins are still a bit unforgiving. Well-deserved One Glass ratings go to the Recioto Re Teodorico and the more well-structured whites, the Soave Castello di Soave, the Sauvignon Sansaia and the Bianco di Custoza Monte Fiera.

Pasqua, founded in 1925, is one of the biggest producers in the Veneto. Today, the winery's fortunes lie in the hands of Carlo, Umberto and Giorgio, who all joined the group in the 60s. Recent developments in viticulture, and especially in oenology, have not caught the Pasquas off-guard. Towards the end of the 80s, they set up Cecilia Beretta, an estate that was destined to produce the company's top wines. Investments and research continued, culminating in the current collaboration with Luca D'Attoma. The Pasquas' philosophy is to make high-quality wines from carefully selected grapes and the new technical team, led by Giancarlo Zanel, has set about taking drastic measures in the vineyards, boosting the viticultural potential significantly. The results will become evident over the course of the next few vintages while today we can taste the wines from the years that brought the second millennium to a close. From Cecilia Beretta comes the excellent Amarone Terre di Cariano '95, which fully confirms the potential of the label. Again from the Cecilia Beretta estate, we have an agreeable blend of corvina and rondinella, Mizzole, which is still a bit green on the finish. The wine we liked best from the Pasqua range is the Morago, a '97 Cabernet Sauvignon made in a modern idiom, with a longish spell in barrique and further ageing in the bottle. It is an elegant wine, with a mouth-filling flavour. The range of Montegrande, Sagramoso and Brognoligo Soaves is excellent and all obtained One Glass scores. Pick of the Valpolicellas was the Casterna while the Amarone Villa Borghetti '96 suffered as a result of that year's rather poor vintage.

● Santomío Rosso '98		🍷🍷	5
○ Terranatia Passito '98		🍷🍷	5
● Arcaio Corvina Cabernet '98		🍷	4
○ Bianco di Custoza			
Vigneto Monte Fiera '99		🍷	4
● Cabernet Sauvignon			
Vigneto Campo Madonna '97		🍷	4
● Recioto della Valpolicella			
Re Teodorico '98		🍷	5
○ Sansaia Sauvignon '99		🍷	4
○ Soave Cl. Castello di Soave '98		🍷	3
○ Bianco di Custoza '99			3
○ Lugana '99			3
● Valpolicella Cl.			
Capitel della Crosara '98			3

● Morago Cabernet Sauvignon '97		🍷🍷	5
● Amarone della Valpolicella Cl.			
Terre di Cariano Cecilia Beretta '95		🍷🍷	6
● Mizzole Cecilia Beretta '97		🍷	4
○ Soave Cl. Brognoligo			
Cecilia Beretta '99		🍷	2
○ Soave Cl.			
Vigneti di Montegrande '99		🍷	3
○ Soave Sup. Sagramoso '99		🍷	4
● Valpolicella Cl. Sup.			
Vigneti di Casterna '97		🍷	4
● Amarone della Valpolicella Cl.			
Villa Borghetti '96			6
● Valpolicella Cl. Vigneti in Marano			
Villa Borghetti '97			3

VIDOR (TV)

VIDOR (TV)

ADAMI
VIA ROVEDE, 21
FRAZ. COLBERTALDO
31020 VIDOR (TV)
TEL. 0423/982110

DE FAVERI
VIA SARTORI, 21
FRAZ. BOSCO
31020 VIDOR (TV)
TEL. 0423/987673

Walking with Franco Adami around the hillsides of Valdobbiadene is always an experience. When he sees his vineyards, his eyes light up and he starts to describe them to you inch by inch, explaining each nuance of green and the different slopes and exposures. You are quickly made aware of the Adami family's almost sensuous relationship with the land and its fruits. The experience is quite overwhelming. Admiring the Giardino vineyard, one of Valdobbiadene's historic crus, planted by Franco's grandfather, it is impossible to resist the untamed appeal of a landscape that has been given a measure of order thanks to human intervention. It is in this natural amphitheatre that the estate's finest grapes ripen, ready to be transformed into a Prosecco Dry of great finesse at the skilled hands of Franco and Armando. The wine has a bouquet of spring flowers, jasmine and almonds and a crisp entry on the palate. The fruit then evolves gradually and persistently, delightfully accompanied by the prickle of carbon dioxide. All in all, a connoisseur's Prosecco. The Prosecco Extra Dry, another of the firm's classic wines, offers ripe fruit notes on the nose and a mouth-filling, silky flavour. Its sensations of fresh almonds and hazelnuts seem to go on forever. The Prosecco Brut is truly splendid, succeeding as it does in melding its rich, elegant fruit with the naturally high acidity of the Brut style. The palate is broad and extraordinarily velvety. Finally, the Cartizze offers delicate perfumes that open up gradually and a well-sustained, creamy progression on the palate.

Forthright, clean aromas, combined with well-focused typing, are the linchpins of the Lucio De Faveri production philosophy. The wines from the latest vintage bear this out, beginning with the Prosecco Dry in the distinctive black bottle. Its intense aromas of flowers, of ripe exotic fruit, almonds and hazelnuts unfold with finesse and attractive depth. On the palate, the prickly carbon dioxide blends well with sweetness from the residual sugar and well-balanced acidity. The persistent, attractive finish holds up well and never cloys. Another very decent product from this company is the black bottle Prosecco Brut which, as ever, is one of the best of its type. Its bouquet opens up gradually, initially offering sensations of flowers and ripe fruits and then unleashing citrus notes. On the palate, the distinct effervescence and crisp acidity really bring out the freshness of the wine, which is nicely balanced by the good fruit and higher than average residual sugar for a Brut. The nice persistence is hampered only by a slightly bitter finish. Intense notes of spring flowers and ripe fresh fruit salad emerge on the nose of the Prosecco Extra Dry, which is extremely pleasant and very quaffable. The palate echoes the nose, melding the flavours well with the effervescence, which in turn is well integrated into the fleshiness of the fruit. Though it is a bit rustic, we rather liked the new version of the Prosecco Frizzante Colli Trevigiani Selezione Spago, in the now traditional black bottle, the livery that distinguishes De Faveri's premium range. We appreciate the winery's desire to give due consideration to a product category that does not always get the attention it deserves.

O Cartizze	🍷🍷	4
O Prosecco di Valdobbiadene Brut Bosco di Gica	🍷🍷	3*
O Prosecco di Valdobbiadene Dry Giardino '99	🍷🍷	4
O Prosecco di Valdobbiadene Extra Dry dei Casel	🍷🍷	3*
O Incrocio Manzoni 6.0.13 Le Portelle '99	🍷	3
O Prosecco di Valdobbiadene Tranquillo Giardino '99	🍷	3

O Prosecco di Valdobbiadene Dry Sel. '99	🍷🍷	4
O Prosecco di Valdobbiadene Extra Dry	🍷🍷	3*
O Prosecco di Valdobbiadene Brut Sel.	🍷	4
O Prosecco Frizzante Colli Trevigiani Sel. Spago	🍷	3
O Prosecco di Valdobbiadene Brut		3

VIDOR (TV)

VILLAGA (VI)

SORELLE BRONCA
VIA MARTIRI, 20
FRAZ. COLBERTALDO
31020 VIDOR (TV)
TEL. 0423/987201

CONTE ALESSANDRO PIOVENE
PORTO GODI
VIA VILLA, 14
FRAZ. TOARA
36020 VILLAGA (VI)
TEL. 0444/885142

Sisters Ersiliana and Antonella Bronca are leading players in a new trend which is starting to take hold in the Conegliano-Valdobbiadene area. You could call it "beyond Prosecco" for the aim is to diversify and give the zone a quality image for other wines, apart from its prestigious and renowned sparklers. A Colli di Conegliano DOC zone has been created to regulate production of one red, one white and two dessert wines. Prosecco, of course, continues to provide the bulk of production at Sorelle Bronca, which is located at Colbertaldo di Vidor, an area with numerous archaeological sites where once there were ancient settlements. Great merit goes to the Benedictine monks who promoted the arts of vine growing and winemaking in this area in the Middle Ages. Livio Bronca also succeeded in instilling in his daughters a great passion for vines and wine, an enthusiasm shared by the indefatigable Piero, Antonella's husband. With great foresight, the Broncas have invested in vineyards, purchasing around 13 hectares at Rua di Feletto near Conegliano. It is from these plots that they obtain above all their Colli di Conegliano Rosso, a blend of cabernet, merlot and marzemino. The '97 has a garnet-ruby colour and offers hints of vanilla, violets and cherries. It has good balance, sensations of juniper berries, persistence and a finesse that is its main distinguishing trait. The Colli di Conegliano Bianco is lively but still has plenty of body. A greenish straw-yellow in hue, it proffers aromatic notes of wistaria, as well as displaying overtones of tomato leaf, citrus fruit and almonds. The Proseccos, both in the Brut and Extra Dry Spumante versions as well as in the Frizzante, are fragrant and fruity. The Livio Bronca Brut is refreshing and ideal for drinking throughout the meal while the Delico and the Ardesco are sound and pleasant.

The Porto Godi estate dates back to the 16th century but you can see that Tommaso Piovene is not resting on the laurels of a noble and glorious past when you note his shrewd investment in the winery and his well-managed new plantings. Our tasting this year started off with the well-made, temptingly juicy and quaffable Tocai Rosso, the grapes for which come from century-old vineyards. The Riveselle, a 100 percent garganega, is attractively floral while the Pinot Bianco Polveriera reveals a bouquet of apples, flowers and cakes that leads in to good weight on a palate that, however, lacks freshness on the finish. There are two versions of Sauvignon. The Fostine is more classically varietal in its aromas, which range from tomato leaf to peach and elderflower. It is thoroughly convincing on the palate, unveiling good fleshy fruit and satisfying acidity. The very ambitiously conceived Campigie is made from super-ripe grapes. Six months in new oak brings out ripe fruit notes that combine with a subtle, complex mineral tone while the texture can only improve with an appropriate period in the cellar. The real potential of the Colli Berici DOC, however, lies in its red varieties. To prove the point we have the excellent, intriguingly sinuous Merlot Fra i Broli. The colour is vibrant as is the bright nose, which charms with its fragrant notes of stewed strawberries and raspberries, tobacco and oak. Slightly edgy tannins in no way detract from the tasty and persistent fruit. The Cabernet Pozzare, on the other hand, is less than entirely harmonious for the oak is slightly over-assertive. We preferred the jolly, uncomplicated Polveriera, an ideal accompaniment for a summer barbecue.

● Colli di Conegliano Rosso		
Ser Bele '97	▼▼	5
○ Colli di Conegliano Bianco		
Ser Bele '99	▼	4
○ Livio Bronca Brut '98	▼	4
○ Prosecco di Valdobbiadene Brut	▼	3
○ Prosecco di Valdobbiadene		
Extra Dry	▼	4
○ Prosecco di Valdobbiadene		
Frizzante	▼	3
● Piave Cabernet Ardesco '98		4
○ Prosecco di Valdobbiadene		
Delico		3
● Colli di Conegliano Rosso		
Ser Bele '96	♀♀	4

● Colli Berici Merlot Fra i Broli '98	▼▼	4
○ Sauvignon Campigie '99	▼▼	4
● Colli Berici Cabernet Polveriera '99	▼	3
○ Colli Berici Pinot Bianco		
Polveriera '99	▼	3
○ Colli Berici Sauvignon		
Vigneto Fostine '99	▼	3
● Colli Berici Tocai Rosso '99	▼	3
● Colli Berici Cabernet		
Vigneto Pozzare '98		4
○ Colli Berici Garganega		
Riveselle '99		2
● Colli Berici Cabernet		
Vigneto Pozzare '97	♀♀	4
● Colli Berici Merlot Fra i Broli '97	♀	4

OTHER WINERIES

The following producers obtained good scores in our tastings with one or more of their wines:

PROVINCE OF PADOVA

Dominio di Bagnoli,
Bagnoli di Sopra, tel. 049/5380008
Friularo Bagnoli Cl. V. T. '97

Pigozzo - Urbano Salvan,
Due Carrare, tel. 049/525276
Colli Euganei Rosso '97, San Marco '97

PROVINCE OF TREVISO

Carpené Malvolti,
Conegliano, tel. 0438/364611
Prosecco di Conegliano Extra Dry

Merotto,
Farra di Soligo, tel. 0438/898195
Prosecco di Valdobbiadene Dry
Colle Molina

Dall'Armellina, Mareno di Piave
tel. 0438/308878
Incrocio Manzoni 6.0.13 '99

Case Bianche,
Pieve di Soligo, tel. 0438/841608
Colli di Conegliano Bianco
Costa dei Falchi '99

Astoria Vini,
Refrontolo
tel. 0423/665042
Prosecco di Valdobbiadene Tranquillo
Vigna Val de Brun '99

Sanfeletto,
S. Pietro di Feletto
tel. 0438/486832
Prosecco di Conegliano Tranquillo

Bernardi,
Susegana
tel. 0438/781022
Colli di Conegliano Bianco '99

Montesel,
Susegana, tel. 0438/781341
Prosecco di Conegliano Extra Dry Montesel

Bruno Agostinetto,
Valdobbiadene, tel. 0423/972884
Prosecco di Valdobbiadene Tranquillo '99

Cantina Produttori di Valdobbiadene,
Valdobbiadene, tel. 0423/982070
Prosecco di Valdobbiadene Extra Dry
Val d'Oca

Ciodet,
Valdobbiadene, tel. 0423/973131
Prosecco di Valdobbiadene Extra Dry

Col de' Salici,
Valdobbiadene
tel. 055/243101
Prosecco di Valdobbiadene Brut,
Prosecco di Valdobbiadene Extra Dry

Rivalta,
Valdobbiadene
tel. 0438/971017
Prosecco di Valdobbiadene Extra Dry,
Prosecco di Valdobbiadene Bru

Valdo,
Valdobbiadene, tel. 0423/972403
Prosecco di Valdobbiadene Extra Dry
Cuvée del Fondatore

Giorgio Cecchetto,
Vazzola, tel. 0438/28598
Piave Raboso '96,
Sauvignon Marca Trevigiana '99

Spumanti Dal Din,
Vidor, tel. 0423/987295
Prosecco di Valdobbiadene Extra Dry

Bellenda,
Vittorio Veneto
tel. 0438/920025
Chardonnay Colli Trevigiani Rourò '98

PROVINCE OF VENEZIA

Bosco del Merlo,
Annone Veneto, tel. 0422/768167
360 Ruber Capite '97

Santo Stefano,
Fossalta di Piave, tel. 0421/67502
Piave Chardonnay '99

Teracrea, Portogruaro, tel. 0421/287041
Malvasia del Veneto '99

Mosole,
S. Stino di Livenza
tel. 0421/310404
Lison-Pramaggiore Merlot Ad Nonam '96

PROVINCE OF VERONA

Guerrieri Rizzardi,
Bardolino, tel. 045/7210028
Amarone della Valpolicella Cl. Calcarole '95

Lenotti, Bardolino, tel. 045/7210484
Valpolicella Cl. Le Crosare '98

Corte S. Arcadio,
Castelnuovo del Garda, tel. 045/7575331
Bianco di Custoza La Boschetta '99

Tenuta Valleselle - Tinazzi,
Cavaion Veronese, tel. 045/7235394
Amarone della Valpolicella Ca' de Rocchi '97

Fasoli,
Colognola ai Colli, tel. 045/7650741
Recioto di Soave S. Zeno '97

Vicentini,
Colognola ai Colli, tel. 045/7650539
Soave Sup. '99

F.lli Giuliari, Illasi, tel. 045/7834143
Amarone della Valpolicella Cl.
Piccola Botte '96

Paolo Boscaini e Figli,
Marano di Valpolicella, tel. 045/7701334
Amarone della Valpolicella di Marano '96

Ca' La Bionda,
Marano di Valpolicella, tel. 045/6837097
Amarone della Valpolicella Cl. '97

San Rustico,
Marano di Valpolicella, tel. 045/7703348
Amarone della Valpolicella Cl.
Vigneti del Gaso '95

Cantina Sociale di Monteforte,
Monteforte d'Alpone, tel. 045/7610110
Soave Cl. Sup. Clivius '99

Montecrocetta,
Monteforte d'Alpone, tel. 045/7610963
Soave Cl. Sup. I Boschetti '99

Aldegheri,
S. Ambrogio di Valpolicella
tel. 045/6861356
Amarone della Valpolicella Cl. '96,
Le Pietre di S. Ambrogio '97

Brolo di Musella,
S. Martino Buon Albergo, tel. 045/8740211
Amarone della Valpolicella '96,
Valpolicella Cl. Sup. '97

Fornaser,
S. Pietro in Cariano, tel. 045/7701651
Amarone della Valpolicella Cl.
Monte Faustino '95

Santa Sofia,
S. Pietro in Cariano, tel. 045/7701074
Amarone della Valpolicella Cl.
Ris. del Millennio '95

Tommasi,
S. Pietro in Cariano, tel. 045/7701266
Valpolicella Cl. Sup. Ripasso '98

Bisson,
Soave, tel. 045/7680775
Soave Cl. Sup. '99

Tamellini,
Soave, tel. 045/6190491
Soave Cl. Sup. '99,
Recioto di Soave Vigna Marogne '98

Daniele Zamuner,
Sona, tel. 045/6081090
Spumante Brut Villa La Mattarana Ris. '93

F.lli. Bolla,
Verona, tel. 045/8670911
Soave Cl. Sup. Tufaie '99,
Recioto della Valpolicella Cl. '98

Cantina Sociale della Valpantena,
Verona, tel. 045/550032
Amarone della Valpolicella Falasco '95,
Valpolicella-Valpantena Ritocco '98

PROVINCE OF VICENZA

Miotti,
Breganze, tel. 0445/873006
Breganze Torcolato '97

Frigo,
Cornedo Vicentino, tel. 0445/951334
Colli Berici Cabernet Le Pignole '99

Conti Da Schio,
Longare, tel. 0444/555032
Colli Berici Pinot Bianco '99

FRIULI VENEZIA GIULIA

Most of the white wines we tasted for this edition of the Guide were from the '99 vintage, which signalled the end of a quite extraordinary year with no parallel in living memory, according to many of the region's more experienced winemakers. The mild spring concluded with moderate rainfall in April and May. June and early July were exceptionally warm. The rain fell little and often before the temperature began to drop in the second half of July. Warm weather then returned in August. Temperatures were high during the day but occasional showers during the night continued to the end of the month. As a result, conditions were ideal for the grape harvest. The fruit was supremely ripe and the results were almost a foregone conclusion, although some cellars had problems with stuck fermentations. But the fundamental problem for many of the wines of '99 was the high sugar content of the grapes, which led, particularly in hillslope vineyards, to products that rarely had less than 13 percent alcohol and on occasion more than 14 percent, especially in the case of Sauvignons. However, many whites have outstanding character and are destined for a long and brilliant future while the reds have incredible structure. The region-wide improvement in quality posed a number of sometimes painful problems for those whose task it was to decide which producers would have a full Guide profile, which would be relegated to the list of Other Wineries, and which would be left out altogether. Whereas a few years ago, a total of three Glasses overall was sufficient to gain entry into the Guide, that is no longer the case. In consequence, some estates with high-profile ranges have been discarded in favour of winemakers who have been able to come up with exceptional results. One obvious effect of the stunning 1999 vintage is an increase in the number of wines awarded Three Glasses. This year, 20 whites carried off the accolade, as opposed to last year's 17, and there are now four top-scoring reds Some of these Olympians are consistently excellent performers, like Dorigo, Livio Felluga, Le Due Terre, Le Vigne di Zamò, Livon, Miani (with two Three Glass wines), Rocca Bernarda, Ronco del Gelso, Russiz Superiore, Schiopetto, Venica, Villa Russiz and Vinnaioli Jermann. Others are welcome returns, including Borgo San Daniele, Kante, Edi Keber, La Castellada and Lis Neris. But in this introduction, we want to focus on the newcomers: Roberto Picech with his Collio Bianco Jelka '99, Roberto Scubla with Bianco Pomédes '98, Franco Toros with Collio Merlot Selezione '97, Vigna del Lauro for Collio Sauvignon '99 and Volpe Pasini with their Pinot Bianco Zuc di Volpe '99. Nor can we allow to pass unobserved the fact that Italy's – and the world's – most highly rated consultant winemakers are now routinely active in Friuli, testifying to the commitment to quality of the region's producers. Finally, there is another trend under way that opens up interesting new prospects. A number of estates have changed, or are about to change, hands, having been acquired by companies or individuals from outside Friuli. We are referring to Italian-Americans like Bastianich and Nocerino as well as players of the calibre of Folonari, Frescobaldi, Traverso-Molon and Zonin, all serious wine professionals who are demonstrating – with hard cash – that they believe in the future of Friulian wines.

BAGNÀRIA ARSA (UD)

TENUTA BELTRAME
LOC. ANTONINI, 6/8
FRAZ. PRIVANO
33050 BAGNÀRIA ARSA (UD)
TEL. 0432/923670

Cristian Beltrame may be young but his approach is that of an experienced professional. He is one of a group of local producers who are working to promote the image of the Aquileia DOC zone and for years now, the Tenuta Beltrame has been releasing premium wines from its beautiful country manor base. The Sauvignon again convinces with its initial aromas on the nose of red pepper and rue giving way to peach. Elegant and stylish on entry, the palate reveals a note of grapefruit in the finish. Next was the almost "Tuscan" Cabernet Sauvignon Riserva. The impenetrable ruby in the glass leads in to pervasive, well-balanced aromas of black cherries, prunes and Peruvian bark that tell you this is a major red. The fruit on the palate lasts through to the finish, accompanied by hints of coffee, gamey notes and tannins of a silky smoothness. The Merlot Riserva is another very creditable wine. Its ripe plum, new-mown grass and coffee nose is echoed by a well-managed, albeit rather predictable, palate. The Beltrame Tazzelenghe has a sweet, spicy nose and ripe berry fruit in the mouth but lacks length. We tasted the other vintage reds just after they had gone into the bottle. The Merlot and the Cabernet stood out. There are persuasive aromas of plum jam, tobacco, hay and coffee in the nose of the Merlot but the mulberry and plum fruit is slightly compromised by over-assertive tannins. The Cabernet's nose is rustic while the progression on the palate moves forward convincingly. The Beltrame Pinot Bianco offers characteristic varietal notes of green apple and good weight on the palate. The Chardonnay, although it flaunts impressively intense aromas of banana, pineapple, tropical fruit and vanilla, is a little one-dimensional in the mouth. Finally, the elegant Tocai has the variety's trademark aromas of crusty bread and red delicious apples but lacks breadth.

● Friuli Aquileia Cabernet Sauvignon Ris. '97	▼▼	4
○ Friuli Aquileia Sauvignon '99	▼▼	3*
● Friuli Aquileia Cabernet Sauvignon '99	▼	3
○ Friuli Aquileia Chardonnay '99	▼	3
● Friuli Aquileia Merlot '99	▼	3
● Friuli Aquileia Merlot Ris. '97	▼	4
○ Friuli Aquileia Pinot Bianco '99	▼	3
○ Friuli Aquileia Tocai Friulano '99	▼	3
● Tazzelenghe '97	▼	4
● Friuli Aquileia Cabernet Franc '99		3
○ Friuli Aquileia Pinot Grigio '99		3
● Friuli Aquileia Refosco P. R. '99		3

BERTIOLO (UD)

CABERT
VIA MADONNA, 27
33032 BERTIOLO (UD)
TEL. 0432/917434

Since 1960, Cabert (a contraction of "Cantina di Bertiolo") has been vinifying grapes supplied by its members in the Grave zone. The 800,000 bottles made every year are the responsibility of winemaker Daniele Calzavara, who for a few years now has been assisted by consultants from New Zealand and Australia. Cellar innovations and a consultancy project to improve members' vineyard management are the new developments this year, which again is a memorable one. Two wines – the Traminer Aromatico and the Pinot Grigio – earned their spurs. The Traminer's Two Glasses were awarded for its gold-flecked straw-yellow colour and the complexity of its almost buttery aromas of wild roses, musk, apricot and ripe yellow plums. Apricot and peach fruit are prominent on the front palate, then there is plenty of thrust in the broad, rich development to take you through to a long, long finish that is redolent of roses. Intriguing notes of candied orange peel meld attractively with notes of ripe fruit and hazelnut on the nose of the Pinot Grigio, to be mirrored on the palate, where they are joined by nuances of vanilla. The Merlot Riserva has a fine entry on the nose, its spicy pepper, cinnamon and liquorice emerging against a background of plum jam. The palate is dominated by ripe fruit that mingles nicely with the fairly open tannins, although the finish could have been longer. One Glass for the Bertiul Rosso. Made with pinot nero from the vineyards of two of the members, it ages for 18 months in one-year-old wood. Mature aromas of leather over ripe berry fruit on the nose are echoed on the palate, which is a little lacking in interest. And to finish, the Verduzzo Friulano earned a mention in despatches.

○ Friuli Grave Pinot Grigio '99	▼▼	3*
○ Friuli Grave Traminer Aromatico '99	▼▼	3*
● Bertiul Rosso	▼	4
● Friuli Grave Merlot Ris. '94	▼	3
● COF Merlot '99		3
⊙ Friuli Grave Rosato '99		2
○ Friuli Grave Verduzzo Friulano Casali Roncali '99		3
○ COF Picolit '94	▽▽	6
● Friuli Grave Cabernet Sauvignon Ris. '94	▽▽	4

BUTTRIO (UD)

BUTTRIO (UD)

LIVIO E CLAUDIO BUIATTI
VIA LIPPE, 25
33042 BUTTRIO (UD)
TEL. 0432/674317

CONTE D'ATTIMIS-MANIAGO
VIA SOTTOMONTE, 21
33042 BUTTRIO (UD)
TEL. 0432/674027

As scrupulous a producer as Claudio Buiatti wasn't going to stay for very long in the obscurity of the "Other Wineries" section. And in fact, his range of wines this year amply justifies a full Guide profile. Claudio, who has an agricultural technician's diploma from the college at Cividale, combines his knowledge with a passion for the eight hectares of hillside vineyards he farms at Buttrio. He and his wife, Viviana, produce 65 percent white and 35 percent red wines, almost all of which are sold in Italy. The panel was very taken with the '99 Sauvignon, with its crisp, intense notes of tomato leaf on the nose. The aromas are echoed on the palate, where they are joined by elderflower and pennyroyal in a body that is both buttery and fresh-tasting. The Refosco '98 also won Two Glasses for the length and breadth of its complex, spicy nose, the thrust of the palate, its rich wild berry fruit and leisurely finish. When it had had time to breathe, the Pinot Bianco unfurled stylish aromas of apple on the nose and exceptional breadth on the palate, as well as a clean and very refreshing aftertaste. The Pinot Grigio's best point is its fresh-fruit nose. The palate, however, is undermined by excessive acidity. For the Cabernet, it was the palate that tipped the balance. A well-structured and full-flavoured wine, it blends wood-derived aromas delightfully with grassy notes and black cherries that lend allure to the finish. And there was a mention for the outstandingly well-managed Tocai Friulano.

Congratulations are due to Alberto d'Attimis-Maniago for his excellent results. But then we were looking for a quantum leap in quality from this estate, which has been farming its superbly located hillslope vineyards for more than 400 years. The Cabernet is a thoroughbred. Its slight lack of finesse on the nose actually enhances the palate, where the well-balanced aromas of berry fruit and large oak casks carry it forward with determination. There are interesting very green highlights in the Ribolla Gialla, leading you into intense, elegant aromas of acacia blossom, white peach and smoky notes. Then its markedly varietal palate alternates freshness and white peach in a skilfully managed, well-sustained succession. Made from grapes allowed to raisin on the vine, the Picolit unveils very elegant aromas of stewed apple, candied orange peel, wild roses and dried figs. These are reflected on the palate, where the wine develops seamlessly, concluding with a sophisticated fruity finish. The Verduzzo Tore delle Signore is another dessert wine. The orange-highlighted hue reveals aromas of acacia blossom, white plum and peach, which are mirrored on the palate with elegant overtones of peach juice and fresh-squeezed oranges. The finish is sweet. The Sauvignon's aromas of ripe tomato and vanilla mingle enticingly on the nose, to return on the palate with nuances of elderflower. The acidic finish is refreshingly zesty. We retasted the Vignaricco Rosso '95 and were pleased to note how well it is developing.

●	COF Refosco P. R. '98	ΤΤ	3*	●	COF Cabernet '98	ΤΤ	3*
○	COF Sauvignon '99	ΤΤ	3*	○	COF Picolit '99	ΤΤ	6
●	COF Cabernet '98	Τ	3	○	COF Ribolla Gialla '99	ΤΤ	3*
○	COF Pinot Bianco '99	Τ	3	○	COF Chardonnay '99	Τ	3
○	COF Pinot Grigio '99	Τ	3	○	COF Malvasia '99	Τ	3
○	COF Tocai Friulano '99		3	●	COF Refosco P. R. '99	Τ	3
				○	COF Sauvignon '99	Τ	3
				●	COF Tazzelenghe '97	Τ	4
				○	COF Verduzzo Friulano Tore delle Signore '99	Τ	4
				○	Vignaricco Bianco '95	Τ	4
				●	COF Merlot '98		3
				○	COF Pinot Grigio '99		3
				●	Vignaricco Rosso '95	Υ	4

BUTTRIO (UD)

BUTTRIO (UD)

★ GIROLAMO DORIGO
VIA DEL POZZO, 5
33042 BUTTRIO (UD)
TEL. 0432/674268

DAVINO MEROI
VIA STRETTA DEL PARCO, 7
33042 BUTTRIO (UD)
TEL. 0432/674025

Girolamo Dorigo is assisted by his son, Alessio, who looks after production, and the estate staff has been expanded by the arrival of Roberto Cipresso. Some of last year's winemaking experiments are now standard practice and the legendary Dorigo Picolit, from grapes dried for two months in an old loft, is still top of the class. Its aromas range from honey to jasmine, white melon, citron, vanilla and orange blossom, and are accompanied by stupendous concentration and length. There were Three Glasses for the classic Dorigo Chardonnay, with notes of figs, pineapple and apricot and a mellow, fresh-tasting palate, and very high marks also went to the Montsclapade. Its mulberry and pepper aromas emerge from a structure instantly reminiscent of the warm, meaty merlot grapes grown in the hills at Buttrio. The exuberantly juicy, fruit-rich Pignolo, with its heavy-duty tannins, was another big scorer. The remaining wines were all top-notch: a ripe-fruit Tocai with a warm, lingering palate and a Tazzelenghe which, despite its name ("Tongue-cutter") and a hint of volatility, has great structure and a very attractive hint of acidity. In the Ribolla, milky aromas and wild roses are to the fore while the Sauvignon has an elegant entry on the nose, taking you into a palate with a touch of softness to mellow out the robust acidity. The Pinot Grigio is stylish, fresh-tasting and well-structured. The only wine that left us disappointed was the Ronc di Juri. Its fine range of aromas is let down by over-evolved notes and a palate that can't quite stay the course.

Last year, this estate was something of a revelation, albeit one brought about by careful planning, and this time round we are happy to confirm that the good times continue to roll. There were few wines on offer. Quite rightly, Paolo wants to extend cellar ageing and when the panel visited, last year's late releases were available but not the new wines, which have yet to go on sale. What we did taste was excellent, starting with a Picolit that lived up to its noble ancestry. Its almost syrupy nose of elderflower and yellow plum jam leads into a warm, silk-smooth palate packed with extract. The Tocai, too, was a winner again this year, the intense musky nose taking you into a palate of balsamic notes over a persuasively rich texture backed up by good weight and fresh acidity. Next came the merlot and cabernet franc Ros di Buri, a wine that opens steadily after a low-key attack. It's hard to believe the winery considers it a second-label Dominin. Ros di Buri is lively and forthright, with markedly spicy notes and a tannic contribution that gives it a pleasantly rustic style. And to finish, there was the wine that we liked best of all. Paolo's Dominin is so austere it is almost statuesque, despite a question mark over the colour. The warm mulberry and raspberry fruit is enticingly pervasive and the long, dense yet well-balanced palate follows through impeccably.

○	COF Chardonnay		
	Vigneto Ronc di Juri '98	♟♟♟	6
○	COF Picolit Vigneto Montsclapade '98	♟♟	6
●	COF Pignolo di Buttrio		
	Vigneto Ronc di Juri '97	♟♟	6
○	COF Sauvignon Vigneto Ronc di Juri '99	♟♟	4
○	COF Tocai Friulano		
	Vigneto Montsclapade '99	♟♟	4
●	Montsclapade '97	♟♟	6
●	Tazzelenghe di Buttrio '97	♟	6
○	COF Pinot Grigio Vigneto Montsclapade '99	♟	4
○	COF Ribolla Gialla Vigneto Ronc di Juri '99	♟	4
○	Ronc di Juri '98	♟	5
○	COF Chardonnay Vigneto Ronc di Juri '97	♟♟♟	6
●	Montsclapade '96	♟♟♟	6

○	COF Picolit '98	♟♟	6
●	COF Rosso Ros di Buri '98	♟♟	4
○	COF Tocai Friulano '98	♟♟	4
●	Dominin '97	♟♟	5
○	COF Bianco Blanc di Buri '98	♟♟	4
○	COF Picolit '97	♟♟	6
●	Dominin '96	♟♟	5
●	COF Refosco P. R. '97	♟	4
●	COF Rosso Ros di Buri '97	♟	4

BUTTRIO (UD)

BUTTRIO (UD)

MIANI
VIA PERUZZI, 10
33042 BUTTRIO (UD)
TEL. 0432/674327

PETRUCCO
VIA MORPURGO, 12
33042 BUTTRIO (UD)
TEL. 0432/674387

We've used up all our superlatives but what else is there to describe Enzo Pontoni's wines? How can you talk about him except as a paragon? We're going to have to be repetitive because Enzo is a winemaker who should be held up as a role model. His dogged but unpretentious firmness is very engaging, as is his obsessive dedication to the vineyard, which comes from another age when nature ruled triumphant over technology. And here we're talking vines tended every single day to produce two or three bunches per plant. So it's no surprise that the wines were again stunning, the best scoring well over 90 points. Let's start with the reds. The Miani Rosso, a blend of merlot, cabernet sauvignon and tazzelenghe, has fruit you could cut with a knife. Its gloweringly dark, purple-tinted colour releases aromas of blackcurrant, cherry, balsamic wood, leather and liquorice. The palate, to be savoured in reverential silence, is mouth-filling, mellow, incredibly dense and very long. You can tell the same hand made the Merlot, where hints of raspberry jam mingle with vanilla. Warm and velvet-smooth on the palate, its unbelievably concentrated texture is nuanced with notes of fir shoots. The top Miani white is the Tocai, a syrup-thick, alcohol-rich glass of acacia blossom, peach and thyme. Sweet, fresh-tasting, juicy, firm-textured and persuasive, its elegant palate offers buttery notes and a bitterish twist in the finish. Next, the Chardonnay regales the nose with a tropical fruit salad and the trademark Miani complexity on the palate where softness, balance, weight and length combine perfectly. Last came the peach and vanilla sugar Ribolla, another wine with a long, long finish.

Around 20 of the 30 hectares owned by Lina and Paolo Petrucco are planted to vine and the couple produce an average of 100,000 bottles every year. Their vineyards stand in superb hillslope locations at Buttrio, next to, or only a short distance from, the Petrucco's residence-cum-winery. The cellars are superbly fitted out and supervised by winemaker Flavio Cabas with skill and imagination. This the year of Ribolla Gialla for the Petruccos. The nose ranges from beeswax to dry flowers, with sweet notes from fruit harvested when it was perfectly ripe. In the mouth, which mirrors the nose to a T, there is an extraordinarily harmonious mingling of the variety's typical acidity with rich notes of apple and yellow plum. Sauvignon is often one of the cellar's best products and this year it again earned Two Glasses, with characteristic notes of rue and tomato leaf on the nose and a full-flavoured buttery texture in the mouth. A lively yet elegantly rich and vibrantly long wine. The Merlot Vigna del Balbo '98 comes from a vineyard that is more than 50 years old. But the vintage was a difficult one for reds in much of Friuli and as a result, the wine has uncharacteristic hints of spice and geraniums on the nose. In contrast, the weight on the palate is seriously impressive. Vintage-related problems dog the Refosco, too, but its fresh, spice-rich nose is admirably reflected on the palate. There is a coppery vein to the colour of the Pinot Grigio, which unveils a stunningly elegant bouquet of apple and acacia honey. The palate has fruit in spades and the finish is fresh so it scored at the top end of the One Glass band. Acidity makes the palate of the Tocai a little lean but helps to imbue the nose with appreciable finesse.

●	COF Rosso '97	❚❚❚	6
○	COF Tocai Friulano '99	❚❚❚	6
○	COF Chardonnay '99	❚❚	6
●	COF Merlot '97	❚❚	6
○	COF Ribolla Gialla '99	❚❚	6
○	COF Bianco '96	♈♈♈	6
○	COF Bianco Miani '97	♈♈♈	6
●	COF Merlot '94	♈♈♈	6
●	COF Rosso Miani '96	♈♈♈	6
○	COF Sauvignon '96	♈♈♈	6
○	COF Tocai Friulano '96	♈♈♈	6
○	COF Tocai Friulano '98	♈♈♈	6
○	COF Sauvignon '98	♈♈	6
●	Refosco P. R. Vigna Calvari '96	♈♈	6
●	Rosso Miani '95	♈♈	6

○	COF Ribolla Gialla '99	❚❚	3*
○	COF Sauvignon '99	❚❚	3*
●	COF Merlot Vigna del Balbo '98	❚	4
○	COF Pinot Grigio '99	❚	3
●	COF Refosco P. R. '98	❚	3
○	COF Tocai Friulano '99	❚	3
○	COF Chardonnay '99		3
●	COF Cabernet Franc '97	♈♈	3
●	COF Merlot Vigna del Balbo '96	♈♈	4
●	COF Merlot Vigna del Balbo '97	♈	4
○	COF Picolit '97	♈	6

CAPRIVA DEL FRIULI (GO)

Castello di Spessa

Via Spessa, 1
34070 Capriva del Friuli (GO)
tel. 0481/639914

The castle at Spessa is a superb manor house, restructured in the late 19th century and now owned by businessman Loretto Pali. The cellar dates back to the 14th century. The building has been linked by a passageway to a nearby air-raid shelter built 15 metres underground during the 30s. Its constant 13°C temperature means today it is an ideal barrique ageing cellar. Patrizia Stekar runs the business, in tandem with Paolo Della Rovere, while the 30 hectares of the estate and the cellar are supervised by oenologist Domenico Lovat and wine technician Alberto Pelos. We'll start with the Conte di Spessa '95, a blend of 75 percent merlot with cabernet sauvignon and cabernet franc, aged in French barriques. Plums, dry leaves and notes of musk and autumn leaves emerge in the generous nose. The entry on the palate is self-assured, full-flavoured, well-structured and very long. The Pinot Bianco di Santarosa '97, which spent almost a year in barriques, is another international-class wine. Its golden colour introduces elegant, beautifully melded notes of vanilla and apple on the nose while the palate is rich, long and close-textured, with excellent breadth. Then came the Pinot Bianco '99, a fruit-rich, very appealing tipple with great length. When our panel visited, the Sauvignon '99 was drinking much more readily than the Sauvignon Cru '99, which is obtained from three separate vintages. Both have plenty of alcohol and their best feature is their dense, concentrated palate, where tomato leaves are well to the fore. The Tocai greets you with a bountiful nose of pear, herbs and tea while the Pinot Grigio is a particularly elegant example of the genre. The last wine we tasted was the textbook Ribolla Gialla.

○	Collio Pinot Bianco '99	🍷🍷	4
○	Collio Pinot Bianco di Santarosa '97	🍷🍷	5
○	Collio Pinot Grigio '99	🍷🍷	4
○	Collio Ribolla Gialla '99	🍷🍷	4
●	Collio Rosso Conte di Spessa '95	🍷🍷	5
○	Collio Sauvignon '99	🍷🍷	4
○	Collio Tocai Friulano '99	🍷🍷	4
○	Collio Sauvignon Cru '99	🍷	5
○	Collio Pinot Bianco '97	ΨΨΨ	4
●	Collio Rosso Conte di Spessa '93	ΨΨ	5

CAPRIVA DEL FRIULI (GO)

Giovanni Puiatti

Via Aquileia, 30
34070 Capriva del Friuli (GO)
tel. 0481/809922

Giovanni Puiatti, son of the great Vittorio, tends 24 hectares under vine at Romans d'Isonzo and four at Ruttars in the Collio, renting six more at Mossa in the same DOC zone. Our overall impression is that the estate still needs to find its direction, both for its wines from the flatlands and for those produced in the hills. This is confirmed by the Collio Sauvignon P '99. Unforthcoming at first, it opens on a nose of tomato leaf, joined by elderflower on the palate. The overall impression is one of balance and harmony, and there is satisfying length in the finish. The varietal characteristics of the Sauvignon Isonzo lack definition but there is plenty of fruit, which is reminiscent of green apple on the palate. Next the Pinot Grigio, fermented without the skins, is a straw-yellow with bright greenish reflections. The stylish nose of fruit salad heralds robust acidity in the mouth which makes the palate a little uninteresting. The Collio Chardonnay P '99 also needs time to open up but then it offers crisp varietal notes of yeast and crusty bread, which are echoed deliciously on the palate. We were hoping for better things from the Merlot and Cabernet Franc Isonzo '99 but the Puiatti creed of shunning wood for steel has perhaps meant that the vintage's immense potential was not exploited to the full. Nevertheless, both wines are well-managed and worth an honourable mention.

○	Collio Sauvignon P '99	🍷🍷	5
○	Collio Chardonnay P '99	🍷	4
○	Friuli Isonzo Pinot Grigio '99	🍷	3
○	Friuli Isonzo Sauvignon '99	🍷	3
●	Friuli Isonzo Cabernet Franc '99		3
●	Friuli Isonzo Merlot '99		3
○	Collio Sauvignon P '98	ΨΨ	5

CAPRIVA DEL FRIULI (GO)

Roncùs

Via Mazzini, 26
34070 Capriva del Friuli (GO)
tel. 0481/809349

Marco Perco and his wife Laouar Nour continue to search for new ways of improving their products. Progress is constant and although their wines need a little time to give of their best, two – the Tocai and the Roncùs Bianco – were serious contenders for Three Glasses, coming within a whisker of the top award. The Tocai's green and gold livery ushers in an explosion of pear, apple, rue, melon, wild roses and crusty bread on the nose, then the palate unfurls elegant notes of pear and peach fruit. There is remarkable breadth in the rich mid palate before the almond finish takes its leisurely leave. The Roncùs is a blend of pinot, malvasia and ribolla. Its auspiciously bright straw-yellow colour is confirmed by intense, alluringly integrated notes of white peach, melon and confectioner's cream on the nose. The full-flavoured, fruit-rich palate reveals hints of peach that linger in the finish. Ripe pear and almond are the keynotes on the nose of the Pinot Bianco. They are echoed nicely on the palate, which could have had more breadth, but the apple and pear finish is satisfyingly long. Vineyard management and cellar techniques were geared to bring out the Mediterranean, ripe-fruit style of the Sauvignon, which unleashes heady aromas of melon, yellow peach, ripe tomato and tobacco. These are mirrored faultlessly on full-flavoured, long palate. Finally, the Roncùs Merlot is just as good as the whites, beginning with the raspberry and cherry aromas through to the impressive progression of the palate from notes of plum on entry to a rich, effortlessly long finish.

○	Collio Tocai Friulano '99	🍷🍷	4
●	Merlot '99	🍷🍷	4
○	Pinot Bianco '99	🍷🍷	4
○	Roncùs Bianco '99	🍷🍷	5
○	Sauvignon '99	🍷🍷	4
○	Roncùs Bianco '97	YY	5
●	Val di Miez '97	YY	5

Russiz Superiore

Via Russiz, 7
34070 Capriva del Friuli (GO)
tel. 0481/80328 - 0481/99164

At Russiz Superiore, we found another white worthy of the Guide's Three Glasses. This time, it is Tocai, the local variety that seems to have drawn new inspiration from the debate surrounding its name. The Russiz Superiore Tocai is exemplary in its elegance. Rapturous notes of tarragon, sage and damson unfold over a basso continuo of warm, vivacious alcohol and acidity, further enhanced by hints of tobacco and bitter almonds. Just below the crucial 90-point cut-off came the Sauvignon, another vigorous and equally concentrated wine with lashings of extract and great length. The third pearl in the collection was the Pinot Bianco. It may look like a concession to the international market but in Friuli this grape variety has found its second home. For confirmation, savour the elegant weight on the palate and the creamy, fruit-rich structure of the beautifully made Russiz Superiore version. The Pinot Grigio is another serious white. Its lovely nose offers pear, plum and hay, followed by a slightly minerally palate that balances acidity and softness before closing on a leisurely note of almonds. The reds, too, are good and the panel's reactions were similar. The spice-rich Merlot is dense and muscular, auguring well for a long future in the cellar. We expected the Russiz Superiore Cabernet Franc to be the best in the region and it was. Its soft texture and generous, well-sustained fruit evoke the elegance of a bygone age and to round off the tasting, the Rosso Riserva reveals aromas of yeast, confectioner's cream, cloves and strawberry flan, closing on a robust note of tannins.

○	Collio Tocai Friulano '99	🍷🍷🍷	4
●	Collio Cabernet Franc '98	🍷🍷	5
●	Collio Merlot '98	🍷🍷	5
○	Collio Pinot Bianco '99	🍷🍷	4
○	Collio Pinot Grigio '99	🍷🍷	4
●	Collio Rosso Riserva degli Orzoni '96	🍷🍷	6
○	Collio Sauvignon '99	🍷🍷	4
●	Collio Rosso Riserva degli Orzoni '93	YYY	6
●	Collio Rosso Riserva degli Orzoni '94	YYY	6
○	Collio Sauvignon '98	YYY	4
●	Collio Rosso Riserva degli Orzoni '95	YY	6

CAPRIVA DEL FRIULI (GO) CAPRIVA DEL FRIULI (GO)

★ Mario Schiopetto
Via Palazzo Arcivescovile, 1
34070 Capriva del Friuli (GO)
Tel. 0481/80332

★ Villa Russiz
Via Russiz, 6
34070 Capriva del Friuli (GO)
Tel. 0481/80047

Mario Schiopetto's eight hectares at the Podere dei Blumeri, in the Colli Orientali, have won Three Glasses for the Sauvignon '99, which outperformed another two products, both from the Collio zone, the Tocai '99 and the Sauvignon Tarsia '98. But let's take a look at the champion. Its brilliant colour reveals Schiopetto's masterful house style of elegance combined with clean-tasting intensity, the long, mouth-filling palate flaunting crisp notes of peach, citrus, elderflower and tomato leaf. Next, there are clear notes of pear and almond in the complex nose and palate of the Tocai Collio. Persuasive, full-flavoured and with loads of rich fruit, it has excellent length and great style. The Sauvignon Tarsia '98 is a newcomer to the range. Ageing in Slavonian oak has left a marked note of toastiness, which blends well with the aromas of tomato leaf and smoke characteristic of the variety. This is a fresh-tasting Sauvignon that has remarkable structure and nice length. The Pinot Bianco Amrità is a great wine, concentrated, soft and fresh-tasting on the palate. In fact, you wouldn't know this full-flavoured wine had ever seen the inside of a barrel. Similar in character, its fruit and flowers only slightly superior to the Amrità, is the Blanc des Rosis, a blend of tocai, pinot bianco, sauvignon and malvasia that is vinified exclusively in stainless steel. Next, we tried the Pinot Grigio dei Colli Orientali, another superlative wine with a nose of tropical fruit and vanilla. The aromas are mirrored on the long palate, where the admirable thrust is backed up by refreshing acidity. The Schiopetto Two Glass line-up is completed by a Malvasia with delicate aromas of yellow plums and jasmine, a fruit-rich, buttery Pinot Bianco and a warm, complex, full-flavoured Sauvignon, all from the Collio DOC zone.

When there are four wines from the same winery vying for Three Glasses, that tells you all you need to know about the way things are run. At Villa Russiz, the credit must go to manager Gianni Menotti and, in part, to the Istituto Cerruti which owns the estate. The Sauvignon de La Tour is back with a vengeance this year. Its extremely robust alcohol is matched by the structure and the astounding dry extract. The nose is broad, complex and elegant while in the mouth the wine reveals power, body and a close-knit texture, with tomato leaf, elderflower and peach taking you through to the seemingly endless finish. Three Glasses without a doubt. Crisp notes of apple greet you on the nose of the Pinot Bianco before the apricot, spring flowers and hawthorn emerge to introduce a warm, lingering palate of considerable sophistication. The Pinot Grigio highlights apple and cider on the nose and these are picked up in the smooth, well-sustained palate. The finish has good length. Heady alcohol and aristocratic aromas of mulberry and spices are the visiting card of the Merlot Graf del La Tour. In the mouth, the clean progression is underpinned by remarkable weight, elegant tannins and a note of coffee in the very long finish. Among the "ordinary" Two Glass wines, it was the unusually buttery Malvasia that stood out with its apricot fruit and full flavour. The polished Villa Russiz Ribolla Gialla has a generous nose of yellow plums and flowers. In the mouth, its apple fruit is nicely backed up by fresh varietal acidity. Next we sampled the classic Tocai Friulano '99, a tangy, fresh-tasting wine with the variety's trademark bitter almond finish as well as robust alcohol. Then came the Villa Russiz Riesling, one of the few in Friuli that manages to bring out the Rhineland variety's characteristic petrol and raw damson aromas. Finally, sage and yellow pepper are the aromas that emerge from the alcohol-rich, refreshingly acidic Sauvignon.

O COF Sauvignon Podere dei Blumeri '99 ♟♟♟	4
O Blanc des Rosis '99 ♟♟	5
O COF Pinot Grigio Podere dei Blumeri '99 ♟♟	4
O Collio Malvasia '99 ♟♟	4
O Collio Pinot Bianco '99 ♟♟	4
O Collio Pinot Bianco Amrità '98 ♟♟	5
O Collio Sauvignon '99 ♟♟	4
O Collio Sauvignon Tarsia '98 ♟♟	5
O Collio Tocai Friulano '99 ♟♟	4
● Collio Cabernet Franc '98 ♟	4
O Collio Pinot Grigio '99 ♟	4
O Collio Tocai Friulano Pardes '98 ♟	5
● Rivarossa '98 ♟	4
O Collio Pinot Bianco Amrità '96 ♟♟♟	5
O Collio Pinot Bianco Amrità '97 ♟♟♟	5

O Collio Sauvignon de La Tour '99 ♟♟♟	5
O Collio Malvasia Istriana '99 ♟♟	4
● Collio Merlot Graf de La Tour '97 ♟♟	6
O Collio Pinot Bianco '99 ♟♟	4
O Collio Pinot Grigio '99 ♟♟	4
O Collio Ribolla Gialla '99 ♟♟	4
O Collio Tocai Friulano '99 ♟♟	4
O Collio Riesling '99 ♟	4
O Collio Sauvignon '99 ♟	4
● Collio Merlot Graf de La Tour '93 ♟♟♟	6
O Collio Sauvignon de La Tour '91 ♟♟♟	5
O Collio Sauvignon de La Tour '94 ♟♟♟	5
O Collio Sauvignon de La Tour '97 ♟♟♟	5
O Collio Sauvignon de La Tour '98 ♟♟♟	5

CARLINO (UD)

CIVIDALE DEL FRIULI (UD)

EMIRO CAV. BORTOLUSSO
VIA OLTREGORGO, 10
33050 CARLINO (UD)
TEL. 0431/67596

DAL FARI
VIA DARNAZZACCO, 20
33043 CIVIDALE DEL FRIULI (UD)
TEL. 0432/731219 - 0432/706726

Carlino lies in Friuli's most recent DOC zone, where there are evident difficulties in producing wines that live up to the region's reputation. That's why Clara and Sergio Bortolusso are putting so much effort – in the vineyard and in the cellar – into the quest for quality. With the aid of a young wine technician, Luigino De Giuseppe, they have been keeping yields from their 38 hectares, planted at about 3,500 vines per hectare, well down to enhance the concentration and aroma of their wines. And after last year's success, they are back in the Guide again with a memorable Tocai. Its vibrant straw yellow offers intense aromas of crusty bread and yellow apples, which return on the clean, well-sustained palate. There is plenty of length and a refreshing touch of acidity in the finish. The Pinot Bianco is varietal in personality, with a delicate, elegant nose of white flowers and yellow apple, which are also present in the smoke-veined palate. The Bortolusso Merlot signs in with a fruity, sweet nose, stylishly laced with redcurrant and cherry aromas that intensify in the exceptionally soft palate. The winery has been experimenting with raisining the grapes for its Verduzzo on the vine for a number of years. The results have been encouraging and this year's version is a golden wine with striking aromas of wild roses, honey and yellow apple that meld into an overall impression of elegance and balance. The palate is a little weaker, the honey and rose entry being followed by a rather breathless finish. Finally, the Bortolusso Sauvignon almost earned a Glass but was let down by a dullish palate after it had enticed us with a promising peach and elderflower nose.

Dal Fari is a young winery – the first vintage they vinified was 1988 – but one that is aiming for quality. The passion of Renzo Toffolutti, a qualified engineer, and his wife Laura is clear from the way they run their estate and from the calibre of their consultants, agricultural technician Valentino Giurato and Fabio Coser. The wines they presented this year are good, although there is still margin for improvement. One wine that is certainly going to cellar well is the Rosso d'Orsone, a blend of 55 percent cabernet sauvignon, 15 percent cabernet franc, 25 percent merlot and 5 percent schioppettino, aged in the wood for 36 months. Its elegant notes of mulberry and coffee lead into a palate that echoes the nose satisfyingly although lacking a little complexity. We liked the forthright yet delicate aromas of redcurrant, mulberry and damson fruit in the Merlot, as well as its nuances of Parma violets, and the refreshing mint and chocolate palate with its still somewhat over-assertive tannins. The Schioppettino, obtained from an ancient local variety, is still very young. The nose highlights plums, raisins and the characteristic schioppettino spice while the as yet fairly intractable palate reveals a skilful balance of fruit and oak. True to the varieties in the blend (mainly chardonnay with sauvignon, tocai and riesling, part oak-aged), the Bianco delle Grazie unveils delicious aromas of ripe banana, boiled sweets, melon and white peach. The same aromas return on the rather straightforward palate. Next came the Pinot Grigio, its distinctive aromas focusing on acacia blossom, red delicious apple and white plums. It also has a nice clean finish. Last was the Chardonnay. Mediterranean in style, it offers marked notes of tropical fruit on the palate, which has an attractively rich texture.

O	Friuli Annia Tocai Friulano '99	♟♟	2*
●	Friuli Annia Merlot '99	♟	2
O	Friuli Annia Pinot Bianco '99	♟	2
O	Friuli Annia Verduzzo Friulano '99	♟	3
O	Friuli Annia Sauvignon '99		2
O	Friuli Annia Pinot Grigio '99		2

O	COF Bianco delle Grazie '98	♟	3
O	COF Chardonnay '99	♟	3
●	COF Merlot '98	♟	4
O	COF Pinot Grigio '99	♟	3
●	COF Rosso d'Orsone '96	♟	5
●	COF Schioppettino '98	♟	4
O	COF Tocai Friulano '99	♟	3
O	COF Sauvignon '99		3
●	COF Cabernet '98		4
O	COF Bianco delle Grazie '97	♟♟	3
●	COF Merlot '97	♟♟	4
●	Rosso d'Orsone '93	♟♟	5
●	COF Rosso d'Orsone '95	♟	5

CIVIDALE DEL FRIULI (UD) CIVIDALE DEL FRIULI (UD)

DAVIDE MOSCHIONI
VIA DORIA, 30
LOC. GAGLIANO
33043 CIVIDALE DEL FRIULI (UD)
TEL. 0432/730210

PAOLO RODARO
VIA CORMONS, 8
FRAZ. SPESSA
33043 CIVIDALE DEL FRIULI (UD)
TEL. 0432/716066

We've been following the career of Michele Moschioni, born in 1967, for some time. He and his father Davide have 11 hectares under vine which go against the general trend in that they are planted mainly to red grapes from local varieties. In fact, the current 75-25 red-to-white ratio will soon become 85-15. Davide looks after the vineyards while Michele rules the roost in the cellar, where he raisins a variable percentage of red fruit to achieve the desired concentration of sugars. He uses ambient – not cultured – yeasts and makes a base cuvée that is added to the must from the pressing. Its yield is never more than 40 percent of the weight of fruit. Fermentation is in barriques, which are only used twice. The Schioppettino and Pignolo age in the wood for two winters, the Refosco and Celtico (merlot and cabernet sauvignon) for only one, before they go into the bottle without filtration. Reds from the '98 vintage were sold unbottled because of the low quality of the fruit. The result is that Moschioni wines are impressively structured and very muscular. Take the Pignolo '96. A nose of unripe plum, liqueur cherries and raisins heralds a dense palate of juicy fruit that is perfectly balanced by the substantial tannins. The Pignolo had a low-key year in '97 but the '97 Schioppettino, another local variety, has a concentrated nose of rosemary, raspberry juice and berry fruit as well as a powerful, fresh-tasting and very long palate. Tobacco, dry flowers and raisins are on the nose of the Celtico '99, a beautifully broad wine on the palate which has the beef and alcohol to make it an interesting wine for the cellar. Finally, we tried the '99 Refosco. Soft-textured and long on the palate, it stands out for its serious alcohol.

The Rodaros have been growing grapes and making wine since 1946, first to supply their small bar and then, in the 60s, for sale direct to the public. That experience is reflected in the consistently high quality of the wines from this estate, which is due above all to Paolo Rodaro's efforts in the cellar. The Picolit missed Three Glasses by the skin of its teeth. Old gold and amber in the glass, it unfurls rich, sweeping aromas of honey, fig tart and dried fruit. The entry on the palate is very sweet, then becoming buttery, indeed almost oily, and full-bodied. The finish, which is perhaps a shade cloying, goes on forever. The eminently varietal Verduzzo has aromas of stewed apple, ripe apricot and candied orange peel on nose and palate. Next, the Tocai rolls out its varietal aromas of almond and rue, with a hint of lemon, as soon as you raise the glass. The palate is well-managed and the nuances of almond and pear linger attractively. The Sauvignon makes an excellent first impression on the nose with its intense, lingering notes of yellow peach, melon, rue and elderflower. It doesn't quite live up to this high standard on the very well-made palate, and signs off on a note of red pepper. Next came the Pinot Grigio, its aromas of russet pears and minerals mirrored perfectly on the palate. The finish, where hints of dried spring flowers come through, is admirably long. There was confirmation of how good the Ronc white is. A blend of pinot bianco, chardonnay and tocai friulano, it yields up aromas that range from pear, to almond, to crusty bread and vanilla. The palate, where pear comes through, is warm and long and it has an almondy finish. Finally, the Pinot Bianco came close to a Two Glass score. Its colour is vibrant and the nose offers notes of crusty bread, elderflower, green apple and hedgerow. Fruity and full-flavoured on the palate, it signs off in an attractive flourish of apple.

● COF Rosso Celtico '99		🍷🍷	5
● COF Pignolo '96		🍷🍷	6
● COF Schioppettino '97		🍷🍷	6
● COF Pignolo '97		🍷	6
● COF Refosco P. R. '99		🍷	5

O COF Picolit '98		🍷🍷	6
O COF Pinot Grigio '99		🍷🍷	3*
O COF Sauvignon '99		🍷🍷	4
O COF Tocai Friulano '99		🍷🍷	3*
O COF Verduzzo Friulano '99		🍷🍷	3*
O Ronc '99		🍷🍷	4
O COF Pinot Bianco '99		🍷	3
O COF Ribolla Gialla '99		🍷	3
O COF Chardonnay '99			3
O COF Sauvignon Bosc Romain '96		🍷🍷🍷	5
O COF Verduzzo Friulano Pra Zenâr '98		🍷🍷	5
O Ronc '98		🍷🍷	4

CIVIDALE DEL FRIULI (UD)   CORMONS (GO)

RONCHI DI FORNAZ
VIA DELLA FORNAZ, 17
33043 CIVIDALE DEL FRIULI (UD)
TEL. 0432/701462 - 0432/730292

BORGO DEL TIGLIO
VIA S. GIORGIO, 71
FRAZ. BRAZZANO
34071 CORMONS (GO)
TEL. 0481/62166

For some years now, Giovanni Crosato, an expert oenologist whose attention is sometimes distracted by his duties as mayor of one of the towns in the Collio, has been renting the vineyards of Ronchi di Fornaz. There are 12 hectares all told, and despite the fact that they face south, they are often swept by the cold or cool winds that create its unique mesoclimate. The fruit has to be vinified sensitively and, thanks to a planting pattern of 3,000 20-year-old (or older) vines per hectare, the results are often of exceptional quality. Lucia, Giovanni's wife, lends a hand, as does the expert Luciano Toti in the vineyards. We thought the Pinot Grigio '99 was very interesting, its lovely gold-flecked colour introducing an intense, concentrated nose. The prominent fruit opens out on the palate to meld with the glycerine in a broad, well-sustained structure with very good length. Then came the Bianco Fumé, a very successful blend of pinot bianco and pinot grigio. The nose is dominated by apple and pear over an enticingly rich background of fruit, precisely echoed on the front palate, which progresses with poise and firmness through to the long finish. The very fresh-tasting Chardonnay has marked acidity on the palate but is nevertheless inviting and pleasant to drink, fully deserving its One Glass. The cabernet sauvignon, merlot and refosco Rosso Fornaz '97 is unexpectedly sweet on both nose and palate, catching you unawares with its strawberry and raspberry fruit.

The most pleasant surprise at Borgo del Tiglio this year was the Malvasia Selezione. Nicola Manferrari is one of the men behind the revival of Tocai — some of his Tocai Ronco della Chiesa selections, one of Italy's finest whites, have gone down in history — and again, he has come up with a superb, irresistibly alluring wine. In fact, his Malvasia '97 is one of the cult wines of the year. This raisined, creamy and elegantly aromatic wine is remarkable for its lovely ripe fruit with hints of grape and mango. The two Chardonnays – vineyard selections bear a label with a black background – both accompany their tropical fruit aromas with attractive toasty notes, then regale you with a warm, fascinatingly complex palate of impeccable length. The Selezione foregrounds a delicious acidity that ensures the wine will age effortlessly for the next few years. The Studio di Bianco, a blend of tocai, riesling and sauvignon, also has an outstandingly complex nose of citrus, hedgerow and milky nuances leading in to a long, refreshingly zesty palate that recalls the same aromas. However, the tocai-based wines – Ronco della Chiesa and the second-label Tocai - were less convincing. While they are both good, they never scale the heights we have come to expect from Nicola Manferrari. Finally, the Rosso is workmanlike but not exceptional, although here the vintage is probably to blame.

O	Bianco Fumé '99	🍷🍷	4
O	Pinot Grigio '99	🍷🍷	4
O	Chardonnay '99	🍷	4
●	Rosso Fornaz '97		5

O	Collio Chardonnay '98	🍷🍷	5
O	Collio Chardonnay Sel. '98	🍷🍷	6
O	Collio Malvasia Sel. '97	🍷🍷	6
O	Collio Studio di Bianco '98	🍷🍷	6
O	Collio Bianco Ronco della Chiesa '98	🍷	6
●	Collio Rosso '95	🍷	6
O	Collio Tocai Friulano '98	🍷	5
O	Collio Tocai Ronco della Chiesa '90	🍷🍷🍷	6
O	Collio Chardonnay Sel. '96	🍷🍷	6
●	Collio Rosso '93	🍷🍷	6
●	Collio Rosso '94	🍷🍷	6
●	Rosso della Centa '93	🍷🍷	6
●	Rosso della Centa '94	🍷🍷	6

Borgo San Daniele

Via S. Daniele, 16
34071 Cormons (GO)
tel. 0481/60552

Alessandra and Mauro Mauri call Pinot Grigio a "technological" wine and an ambassador for the region. Their version has superbly elegant aromas, with hints of roses, orange and melon. These are echoed on the palate, where they are joined by yellow peach in a delicious progression of remarkable breadth and rich texture. To round off, the fruit on the nose returns in the leisurely finish. Three Glasses, then, for a wonderful, innovative wine. The Gortmarin was also up there around 90 points. A Bordeaux blend with an impenetrable colour, it unfurls rich aromas of mulberry jam, cassis, pipe tobacco and milky coffee on the nose. The palate impresses with its softness and concentration, the mulberry, cassis, coffee, Peruvian bark and mint lingering in the finish. Tocai and pinot bianco vinified in stainless steel, together with wood-fermented sauvignon and chardonnay, go into the blend for the butter-soft Arbis Blanc, which offers aromas of orange, apricot and pear on nose and palate. As usual, the Borgo San Daniele Tocai is one of a kind. Vineyard and cellar management policies conspire to keep its grassy and almondy varietal hints well under control. The result is a sunny, Mediterranean wine that purists might frown at but is undeniably excellent. There are dried roses, melon, peach and citrus fruits on the nose while the finish is laced with sweet almond. Lingering peach and citrus come through on the warm, rich palate.

○	Friuli Isonzo Pinot Grigio '99	▼▼▼	4
○	Friuli Isonzo Arbis Blanc '99	▼▼	4
○	Friuli Isonzo Tocai Friulano '99	▼▼	4
●	Gortmarin '97	▼▼	5
○	Friuli Isonzo Tocai Friulano '97	▽▽▽	4
●	Arbis Rosso '97	▽▽	5
●	Lucky Red '94	▽▽	6
○	Arbis Blanc '98	▽	4

CORMONS (GO)

Branko - Igor Erzetich

Loc. Zegla, 20
34071 Cormons (GO)
tel. 0481/639826

Igor Erzetich is a young wine technician who started out at Volpe Pasini. Having served his apprenticeship, as it were, he decided to go it alone and vinify his own grapes. Despite his youth, Igor is taking things cautiously and for the '99 vintage – the second he has bottled – he has produced 17,000 units. With just over four hectares in one of the finest subzones around Cormons at his disposal, Igor uses varying proportions of five-hectolitre French tonneaux whose influence on the finished product is barely perceptible. We liked what he was making last year but caution is the Guide's watchword so we were looking for confirmation. And since three of the four wines Igor presented were awarded Two Glasses, he certainly earned a full Guide profile this time round. His Chardonnay opens on polished notes of apple over yeast but it is the superbly balanced palate, which echoes the nose delightfully, that convinces with its length. A soft, alluring wine for the cellar. What strikes you about the Tocai Friulano is the rich, elegant nose, with emphatic notes of pear and ripe fruit. Dry and well-sustained, the palate has all the refreshing tang of serious acidity. Fresh, stylish notes of elderflower characterise the nose of Igor's Sauvignon while the palate makes its substantial alcohol felt in a rich, fresh-tasting thrust that opens out in the finish to an accompaniment of ripe citrus and mint. Finally, the Pinot Grigio, too, came close to earning a second Glass, particularly for its full palate and fresh aromas of apple, wild rose and wild strawberries on the nose.

○	Collio Chardonnay '99	▼▼	4
○	Collio Sauvignon '99	▼▼	4
○	Collio Tocai Friulano '99	▼▼	3*
○	Collio Pinot Grigio '99	▼	4

CORMONS (GO)

MAURIZIO BUZZINELLI
LOC. PRADIS, 20
34071 CORMONS (GO)
TEL. 0481/60902

Maurizio Buzzinelli is constantly busy with the search for new ways to improve the quality of the grapes from his nine hectares under vine in the excellent Pradis di Cormons subzone of the Collio and six in the Isonzo DOC zone, in the low-lying countryside near Cormons. For some time, he has been vinifying in wood, releasing the wine under the Ronc dal Luis label. Our tasters feel that Maurizio has now reached Guide status and his best result is with the Collio Bianco Frututis, obtained from mainly tocai, malvasia and picolit vinified in five-hectolitre casks and 30 percent sauvignon fermented in stainless steel. There is absolutely no hint of toastiness. Instead, the rich, sweet fullness is obvious from entry on the nose. A stylish wine, it follows through deliciously on the well-structured palate and offers hints of peach and apple in the admirable finish. The Sauvignon scored only a whisker lower. Up-front tomato leaf aromas and a rich structure, followed by grapefruit and elderflower in the finish, add up to a very fine wine. Then came Maurizio's Müller Thurgau, the best wine from the variety produced in Friuli during the last vintage. The nose combines fresh grassy notes with spring flowers and sweet, ripe hints of yellow flowers and melon. These return on the palate, which has just the right degree of acidity. The Pinot Grigio has a lustrous hue and faint onion-skin highlights to show that it underwent a brief maceration on the skins. The pear and mineral nose is typical of the variety while the palate is dominated by fruit-rich freshness. Finally, the Ribolla Gialla is also utterly varietal, although the '99 vintage has an unusually rich nose of dried flowers and plums. In the mouth, it delivers the classic kick of acidity.

O	Collio Bianco Frututis '99	🍷🍷	4
O	Collio Sauvignon '99	🍷🍷	3*
O	Collio Müller Thurgau '99	🍷	3
O	Collio Pinot Grigio '99	🍷	3
O	Collio Ribolla Gialla '99	🍷	3
O	Collio Tocai Friulano '99		3

CORMONS (GO)

PAOLO CACCESE
LOC. PRADIS, 6
34071 CORMONS (GO)
TEL. 0481/61062

This year, as ever, Paolo Caccese has turned out a range of fine quality whites that reflect his dedication to winemaking. What is missing is a star, a true flagship wine, but we suspect that Paolo's reluctance to trim a few labels from his list is a limiting factor. He is simply too busy keeping up standards across the range. Top of the class this time round was the Pinot Bianco, a wine that the Pradis subzone, where the Caccese vineyards are located, is famous for. Paolo's version is a polished wine with hints of fresh apple and enticing sweet notes on both nose and palate, where they are joined by nuances of crusty bread to remind you that the variety is often blended with its cousin, chardonnay. The finish is sumptuously full. The Malvasia has a fresh attack with notes of rose petal on the nose leading into a pour-me-another-one palate. It's a perfect wine for delicate fish dishes. Paolo continues to make a Müller Thurgau and we have to acknowledge that it is worth its One Glass, especially for its freshness on the nose, where barely ripe apple and plum emerge. Sadly, it has an Achilles' heel in the finish, which is on the short side. Another "foreigner" is the Riesling, which unveils classic notes of petrol and unripe damson. These are mirrored on the palate, which is backed up by acidity and a faintly sweetish note from residual glycerine. The other wines listed here are all well-managed and worth their mention, the Sauvignon, the Traminer Aromatico, the Pinot Grigio and the sweet La Veronica.

O	Collio Pinot Bianco '99	🍷🍷	4
O	Collio Malvasia Istriana '99	🍷	4
O	Collio Müller Thurgau '99	🍷	4
O	Collio Riesling '99	🍷	4
O	Collio Pinot Grigio '99		4
O	Collio Sauvignon '99		4
O	Collio Traminer Aromatico '99		4
O	La Veronica '98		6
●	Collio Cabernet Franc '98	🍸🍸	4

CORMONS (GO)

Cantina Produttori di Cormons

Via Vino della Pace, 31
34071 Cormons (GO)
tel. 0481/60579 - 0481/62471

We sometimes think that Luigi Soini might have muttered as he read last year's Guide, "Do you really believe I don't know how to make a wine you're going to like?" Whatever the case, he ran out the usual long list of labels this year with surprising results, except for two or three wines, such as the Traminer and the Pinot Nero, that still leave us unconvinced. In the past, many of the wines failed to come up to our minimum standard for a mention but this year the problem was a lack of space. So, rather than exclude thoroughly well-made wines, the best of which are listed below, we'll use the profile to provide general information on the winery and help readers gain a better understanding of its production. This is a cellar that has about 200 members who cultivate 300 hectares under vine to produce 2,000,000 bottles every year. All members are provided with supervision and assistance in the field, from site selection to vineyard management - with the help of a meteorological monitoring network – through to the harvest, which must be manual. The techniques are designed to produce fruit that is healthy for both the environment and the producer. According to the cellar's own estimates, over 80 percent of the grapes used are grown organically. Last but not least, we should also mention the cultural activities promoted by the winery. For example, the Vigneto della Pace, or "Peace Vineyard", is one of the world's top five collections of vine varieties. The wine it produces is a very fine, if rather unusual, product, especially if tasted two or three years after the vintage.

○	Collio Collio '99	▼▼	3*
○	Collio Pinot Bianco '99	▼▼	3*
○	Collio Sauvignon '99	▼▼	3*
○	Vino della Pace '97	▼▼	6
○	COF Ribolla Gialla '99	▼	3
○	Collio Pinot Grigio '99	▼	3
●	Friuli Aquileia Refosco P. R. '99	▼	3
○	Friuli Isonzo Chardonnay '99	▼	3
●	Friuli Isonzo Madreterra '99	▼	3
○	Friuli Isonzo Pinot Grigio '99	▼	3
○	Friuli Isonzo Sauvignon '99	▼	3

CORMONS (GO)

Carlo di Pradis

Loc. Pradis, 22/bis
34071 Cormons (GO)
tel. 0481/62272

Boris and David Buzzinelli gave their successful winery a new look, at least in marketing terms, when they decided to label the wines obtained from their six hectares of Collio vineyards as Carlo di Pradis. It is a tribute to their father and a means of avoiding confusion with the estate owned by cousin Maurizio. Their Isonzo DOC wines will continue to be released under the BorDavi label. Thanks to their generously proportioned cellar, Boris and David can work in comfort and their labours have been rewarded with a white and a red of quite exceptional quality. The Collio Pradis Bianco is a blend of tocai friulano, malvasia, pinot bianco and sauvignon that completed its fermentation in five-hectolitre oak casks, where it aged for the following six months. The wood is still very prominent but the nose offers crisp notes of ripe yellow plums, summer fruit salad and dried flowers. Apple and citrus freshness have the upper hand over toastiness in the mouth, particularly in the delicious finish. The Buzzinelli Merlot '97 is another winner, especially for its splendid nose, which ranges from wild berries to notes of plum and cherry tart in an ever-changing panorama. In the mouth, the still assertive tannins leave you with an impression of immaturity but there is more than enough complexity to convince you that this is a bottle with a future. The Sauvignon '99 hints at nettle and medicinal herbs before the palate unveils its intense, fresh-tasting and very attractive progression. Finally, the Tocai, which had still to settle when we tasted, promises to develop reasonably well.

○	Collio Bianco Pradis '98	▼▼	3*
●	Collio Merlot '97	▼▼	4
○	Collio Sauvignon '99	▼	3
○	Collio Tocai Friulano '99		3
○	Collio Bianco Vigneti di Pradis '97	▽▽	3
○	Collio Pinot Grigio Vigneti di Pradis '98	▽▽	3
○	Collio Sauvignon Vigneti di Pradis '98	▽▽	3
●	Collio Merlot Vigneti di Pradis '95	▽	4

CORMONS (GO)

CORMONS (GO)

COLLE DUGA
LOC. ZEGLA, 10
34071 CORMONS (GO)
TEL. 0481/61177

MAURO DRIUS
VIA FILANDA, 100
34071 CORMONS (GO)
TEL. 0481/60998

Commitment and sheer hard work have enabled Damian Princic to confirm the encouraging trends we highlighted on our visit for the preceding edition of the Guide. The just over six hectares of vineyard scattered around the cellar take their name from Colle Duga, the hill where they are located, and are sufficient to allow Damian to be rigorously selective and get the finest possible results from the 12,000 bottles he has produced again this year. It is interesting to note that the small cellar stands only a few metres from the Slovene border. Damian's Collio Bianco is fantastic. Half chardonnay, fermented and aged in barriques, and half stainless steel-vinified sauvignon and tocai friulano, it is complex and stylish, with apple dominating the nose. The structure on the palate is full-bodied and fruit-rich, the texture is close-knit and the finish is mouth-filling. The Tocai Friulano also has a wonderful, alcohol-rich nose where pear and almond notes remind you what grape goes into it. The varietal notes return on the palate, broadening out into a long, long finish. Like the Collio Bianco, it is a wine to keep an eye on for the future. You can just make out the influence of partial ageing in wood in the Chardonnay in the smoky, vanilla notes of the polished and beautifully balanced nose. The palate progresses sure-footedly towards a warm, intense finish of banana and citrus fruits. It's true that '98 was not a great vintage for reds and the Colle Duga Merlot is no exception. Nevertheless, skilful vinification, with ageing for about a year in small oak casks, has produced a wine that offers hints of cherry and plum tart on the nose and a palate that re-elaborates the theme against a backdrop of refreshing acidity. A wine that thoroughly deserves its One Glass rating.

What can we say about this irresistible Friulian winemaker, who was born in 1959? He has surpassed himself. For Mario has made seven Two Glass wines from his nine hectares in the Collio and Isonzo DOC zones with no outside consultants, vinifying the grapes in the cellar of his own home. Congratulations are definitely in order. Let's begin with the Vignis di Siris blend, which scored very well indeed. Made from tocai, sauvignon and pinot bianco, part-aged in small oak casks, it unfurls a generous nose of melon, mandarin and banana, with vanilla and white chocolate in the finish. The well-sustained palate echoes the same aromas before signing off on a lovely warm note. Both Tocais were intense on the nose and refreshing on the palate. Mario's Collio Tocai is more of a varietal wine, with notes of crusty bread and pear on the nose and an almondy twist in the finish while the Isonzo version has a Mediterranean personality, with citrus, almond and white peaches prevalent. The Pinot Bianco is instantly recognizable for its varietal character and evident richness. Next, we tasted the Pinot Grigio, its sweet aromas of red delicious apple and yellow peach returning on the palate, where the wine reveals a refreshing thrust and a long, apple-scented finish. It is well-known that Riesling is not an easy wine to make in Friuli but Mauro Drius has come up with a rather special version that is redolent of pineapple and grapefruit, over nuances of dried flowers and camomile. The long palate is well-balanced and refreshing, revealing attractive notes of grapefruit. In a year that has been anomalous for Sauvignons, many of which have little to offer nose or palate, Mauro's version earned Two Glasses for its typicity and alluring hints of acacia blossom and elderflower.

O Collio Bianco '99	ΨΨ	4
O Collio Chardonnay '99	ΨΨ	3*
O Collio Tocai Friulano '99	ΨΨ	3*
● Collio Merlot '98	Ψ	4
● Collio Merlot '97	ΨΨ	4

O Collio Sauvignon '99	ΨΨ	3*
O Collio Tocai Friulano '99	ΨΨ	3*
O Friuli Isonzo Bianco		
Vignis di Siris '99	ΨΨ	3
O Friuli Isonzo Pinot Bianco '99	ΨΨ	3*
O Friuli Isonzo Pinot Grigio '99	ΨΨ	3*
O Friuli Isonzo Riesling '99	ΨΨ	3*
O Friuli Isonzo Tocai Friulano '99	ΨΨ	3*
O Friuli Isonzo Malvasia '99	Ψ	3
● Friuli Isonzo Cabernet '98		3
● Friuli Isonzo Merlot '98		3

CORMONS (GO)

★ LIVIO FELLUGA
VIA RISORGIMENTO, 1
FRAZ. BRAZZANO
34071 CORMONS (GO)
TEL. 0481/60203 - 0481/60052

Livio Felluga, one of the founding fathers of Friulian oenology, was born at Isola d'Istria, where his family had been growing refosco and malvasia for generations. He emigrated to Friuli, where he managed several large cellars before he realized that it was crucially important to buy up the vineyards that farmers, attracted away from the fields by the newly built factories, were beginning to sell off. That was how Livio built up a solid estate of 135 hectares and in the late 50s became one of the first producers round here to bottle. The Felluga wine that usually walks off with Three Glasses is the Terre Alte but this time the top award went to the Refosco '97, a success that is pleasingly reminiscent of the original Felluga vineyards in Istria. The fine wood on the nose is judged with consummate skill, backing up the varietal aromas of spices, pepper, jam and wild berry tart. The palate has serious tannins and body, outstanding structure, loads of alcohol and great length. There were Two very full Glasses for the Rosazzo Bianco Terre Alte '98. A blend of tocai, pinot bianco and sauvignon, it hints – almost imperceptibly – at a brief, partial, sojourn in the wood. There are notes of walnut, honey, elderflower and peach as well as firm alcohol on the nose while the palate is stylish, well-balanced and long. The golden Picolit Riserva '95 offers milk of almonds, apricot and banana on the nose before the voluptuously intense palate sashays in with its buttery sweetness, excellent length and elegant hints of vanilla. There are hints of vanilla, roses, redcurrant and wild berries in the Rosazzo Sossò Riserva '97. Warm on the nose, it is soft on the front palate before unveiling awesome structure. There was a mention, too, for the chardonnay and ribolla Shàrjs, which hints at confectioner's cream and ripe apple over a rich, full and utterly satisfying flavour. And to finish off, the Tocai Friulano was also excellent.

CORMONS (GO)

EDI KEBER
LOC. ZEGLA, 17
34071 CORMONS (GO)
TEL. 0481/61184

Edi Keber, the likeable and courageous winemaker from Zegla near Cormons, has done it again. We weren't sure whether we should award Three Glasses just to his Tocai or to the Collio Bianco as well. In the end, we focused our attention on the wine that brooked no argument. But let's go back for a minute. Why is Edi courageous? It's because he has abandoned the traditional Friulian winemaker's multiple-label philosophy by opting for only two varietals – Tocai and Merlot – and two blends, a white Collio Bianco and the red Collio Rosso. Edi looks after the eight hectares that lie around his restructured cellar himself. And the icing on the cake is that he keeps prices very low so buyers are assured of superb value for money. Here is his Tocai Friulano '99. Its bright straw yellow has clear greenish highlights, leading into a concentrated, open nose dominated by pear and apple, with hints of almond. The palate is structured, warm, tangy and full. the balance is extraordinary and the long finish delightfully fruit-rich. The tocai, ribolla, pinot bianco and malvasia Collio Bianco scored only a mark or two lower. Its aromas are reminiscent of some Indian teas, veined with honey, herbs and pennyroyal and the superb fruit of the palate is obvious right from the attack. Well-balanced and sinewy in the mouth, it reveals robust, well-integrated alcohol and a very leisurely finish. And to finish on a high note, Edi's Collio Rosso is a blend of all the (not very many) varieties that he grows. Ripe red berry fruit is to the fore on the nose while the entry on the palate is soft to the point of sweetness. The mid palate is drier, mellowing out into a tannic finish of wild cherries.

● COF Refosco P. R. '97	▼▼▼	5
○ COF Picolit Ris. '95	▼▼	6
○ COF Rosazzo Bianco Terre Alte '98	▼▼	5
● COF Rosazzo Sossò Ris. '97	▼▼	6
○ COF Tocai Friulano '99	▼▼	4
○ Shàrjs '99	▼▼	4
○ COF Sauvignon '99	▼	4
○ COF Pinot Grigio '99		4
● Vertigo '98		4
○ COF Bianco Terre Alte '95	♈♈♈	5
○ COF Rosazzo Bianco Terre Alte '96	♈♈♈	5
○ COF Rosazzo Bianco Terre Alte '97	♈♈♈	5

○ Collio Tocai Friulano '99	▼▼▼	4
○ Collio Bianco '99	▼▼	4
● Collio Rosso '99	▼▼	4
○ Collio Tocai Friulano '95	♈♈♈	4
○ Collio Tocai Friulano '97	♈♈♈	4
● Collio Merlot '97	♈♈	5
● Collio Rosso '97	♈♈	4
○ Collio Tocai Friulano '98	♈♈	4
● Collio Rosso '98	♈	4

CORMONS (GO)

CORMONS (GO)

RENATO KEBER
LOC. ZEGLA, 15
34071 CORMONS (GO)
TEL. 0481/61196 - 0481/639844

LA BOATINA
VIA CORONA, 62
34071 CORMONS (GO)
TEL. 0481/60445

We'll make it clear from the start that this year the panel tasted only three wines from Renato Keber. Two scored One Glass ratings and one earned Two Glasses. Other winemakers might have been pleased with such an outcome but for Renato, the results were definitely a disappointment. However, the Keber policy is to make wines for the cellar so we should wait for a while before trying the bottles from the '99 vintage, which was undoubtedly superior to the '98. We should remind readers that Renato gives the name Grici, meaning the peak or upper part of a hill, to his best products and the selections that he ferments and ages on the lees in new barriques, without sulphur dioxide, for almost a year. His Collio Bianco Beli Grici '98, a blend of mainly pinot bianco, chardonnay and ribolla gialla, flaunts a complex nose of mixed fruits and fruit salad without a trace of oak-derived aromas. The substantial, full-flavoured yet fresh-tasting palate echoes the nose deliciously. The Chardonnay offers distinct golden highlights in the glass while sweet notes of toasted oak come out on nose and palate, where the finish yields hints of apricot, banana and yeast. All in all, a young wine that will reward those who have the patience to wait for it to develop. In contrast, the Pinot Grigio '98 is drinking well now. Varietal notes, especially of tropical fruit and apple with faint minerally overtones, emerge on the nose, accompanying the attractive, well-sustained thrust on the palate.

La Boatina, a 60-hectare estate of which 20 hectares are planted to vine, is owned by Loretto Pali and lies on the southernmost slopes of the Collio. Here, as at Castello di Spesso, management of the winery has been entrusted to Patrizia Stekar, Paolo Della Rovere and winemaker Domenico Lovat. That's the secret of the label's steady improvement and enviable reliability. The '99 vintage was a good one for the Ribolla the winery produces from a very exciting local variety. It's a great wine to serve with fish because the fruit ripens reluctantly, maintaining a high level of acidity. In '99, however, all the grapes ripened and the La Boatina Ribolla Gialla is outstandingly good, obtaining a very comfortable Two Glass rating, particularly for its elegant, satisfying nose whose aromas range from dried spring flowers to golden delicious apple. Then a full-flavoured, buttery palate impresses with its remarkable balance. A swift glance at the other La Boatina wines, starting with the stainless steel-vinified Bianco Pertè, obtained from sauvignon, tocai, pinot bianco and other local varieties, which releases elegant hints of pear, apple and almond on both nose and palate. In the polished, long Pinot Bianco, it is golden delicious apple that takes centre stage while the mixed fruit of the Pinot Grigio's nose is compromised on the palate by over-enthusiastic acidity. The Chardonnay is well-rounded, broad and generous with its fruit, which emerges over yeasty notes. In the mouth, it is fresh and long. The came the Tocai, with a close-knit texture and impressive structure introduced by pear on the nose. On the palate, very ripe yellow plum dominates. The Sauvignon is less demanding but nonetheless pleasant and well-managed. But the Poicol Maggiore, a blend of merlot, cabernet sauvignon and cabernet franc, has still to find a balance for its vanilla, spices and grassy notes.

○	Collio Pinot Grigio '98	♟♟	4
○	Collio Bianco Beli Grici '98	♟	4
○	Collio Chardonnay Grici '98	♟	4
●	Collio Merlot Grici '97	♟♟	5
○	Collio Tocai Friulano '98	♟♟	3

○	Collio Ribolla Gialla '99	♟♟	4
○	Collio Bianco Pertè '99	♟	5
○	Collio Chardonnay '99	♟	4
○	Collio Pinot Bianco '99	♟	4
○	Collio Pinot Grigio '99	♟	4
○	Collio Sauvignon '99	♟	4
○	Collio Tocai Friulano '99	♟	4
●	Collio Rosso Picol Maggiore '96		5

CORMONS (GO)

CORMONS (GO)

STANISLAO MAVRIC
LOC. NOVALI, 11
34071 CORMONS (GO)
TEL. 0481/60660

ROBERTO PICECH
LOC. PRADIS, 11
34071 CORMONS (GO)
TEL. 0481/60347

The Mavric winery was created in 1926 by Giovanni Mavric, father of the current owner, Stanislao, who took over in 1972. Stanko, as he is called, immediately set about boosting quality by keeping yields down. He replanted almost all of the property's six hectares, packing in more plants per hectare and adopting a vineyard management policy that, together with his extended and restructured cellar, has enabled the Mavric winery to claim a full Guide profile. Although we like the '98 Pinot Grigio, the '99 was even more rewarding, in particular for its unusual elegance on the nose, where apple has the upper hand over tropical fruit. These aromas are mirrored on the full-flavoured palate, making this an extremely drinkable bottle. The alcohol-rich Sauvignon offers intense fruit aromas that are less than typical but very clean. The palate is deliciously full. There are interesting aromas, ranging from vanilla sugar to apple, in the nose of the Pinot Bianco. In the mouth, it is refreshing, complex, warm and attractively long. Warmth is also the keynote of the Chardonnay – the label tells you it has 14° alcohol – but it can also offer varietal notes of crusty bread and yeast. The palate is well-balanced, thanks to nicely judged acidity, and the finish signs off with notes of melon, golden delicious apple and banana. Moving on to the reds, it was the Merlot that caught our attention with its berry fruit nose laced with fresh green overtones. These are followed up by a well-rounded, warm and full-flavoured palate. The Mavric Cabernet is made the way they like it in Friuli. Its gamey nose introduces a palate with hints of hay and new-mown grass. This is an earthy wine with decent structure. Finally, the Tocai and Pinot Nero are both well-made.

Roberto Picech has always accepted the opinions expressed in the Guide, even when he has not been in full agreement. Son of the legendary Egidio Picech, known as "il ribél", or "the rebel", Roberto has spent the last year looking after his father and working in the five hectares of vineyards the family has in the heart of Pradis, one of the finest Collio subzones, or in the cellar, where they turn out 20,000 bottles each year. For the past few years, Roberto has been trying to pin down the personality of his Collio Bianco Jelka – named after his mother – by trying wood with different toastings and ageing for a longer or shorter period but the blend is always the classic Cormons mix of tocai, malvasia and ribolla. And this time, he has hit the Three Glass jackpot. A background note of toastiness takes nothing away from the apple, yellow plum and pear fruit and spring flowers that regale the nose. The same aromas come through magnificently on the palate, where the close-knit texture is supported by serious alcohol and a wonderfully long finish. Roberto nearly made it two jackpots in a row with his Collio Rosso '97, a blend of mainly merlot, with one third cabernet sauvignon and a small proportion of cabernet franc. The intense nose of fresh red berries, tobacco, raspberry and bitter chocolate usher in a full, rich, warm palate with loads of fruit and fine tannins. His Pinot Bianco is another stunner, its elegant apple coming through over notes of crusty bread before the rich yet refreshing palate drives satisfyingly through to the finish without hesitation. Then the extraordinary Malvasia revealed its yellow fruit on the nose and a concentrated, dry, fruit-rich palate. Only the Tocai had to make do with One Glass. There was a hint of rumbustious alcohol in the finish to upset a warm palate, where pear is well to the fore.

○	Collio Pinot Grigio '99	♥♥	3*
●	Collio Cabernet Franc '99	♥	3
○	Collio Chardonnay '99	♥	3
●	Collio Merlot '99	♥	3
○	Collio Pinot Bianco '99	♥	3
○	Collio Sauvignon '99	♥	3
●	Collio Pinot Nero '99		3
○	Collio Tocai Friulano '99		3

○	Collio Bianco Jelka '99	♥♥♥	4
○	Collio Malvasia '99	♥♥	4
○	Collio Pinot Bianco '99	♥♥	4
●	Collio Rosso Ris. '97	♥♥	5
○	Collio Tocai Friulano '99	♥	4
○	Passito di Pradis '96	♥♥	6

CORMONS (GO)

ISIDORO POLENCIC
LOC. PLESSIVA, 12
34071 CORMONS (GO)
TEL. 0481/60655

Isidoro Polencic has 22 hectares under vine, most of them in the Collio, although a small part lies in the Isonzo DOC zone. His functional and professionally equipped cellar can comfortably handle the roughly 1,500 hectolitres of wine he makes. A significant contribution comes from his son, Michele, who looks after the vineyards and cellar, and daughter Elisabetta, who takes care of administration and customer relations. The '99 Pinot Grigio was again the estate's best wine. Stylish, complex and intensely fruity on the nose, it reveals a palate rendered lean by a hint of green despite its substantial alcohol. Next came the Pinot Bianco, its crisp, pervasive nose dominated by apple. Its stunning attack on the palate wavers only slightly towards the finish. But the Sauvignon is more convincing. Tomato leaf and elderflower prevail on the nose, to be mirrored precisely on the attractively fresh palate. We noted some barely ripe notes on the nose of the Tocai Friulano, over intense aromas of williams pears. The aromas return on the tangy palate, which has admirable acidity in the finish. The Oblin Blanc, named after a brook that skirts the vineyard, is a blend of ribolla, sauvignon and chardonnay: Its amber-highlighted colour introduces a complex, stylish nose of tea, confectioner's cream and herbal tea. These notes come through again on the palate, which has a finish of fresh camomile. Next, the ribolla, malvasia, tocai and chardonnay Collio Bianco offers an attractive nuance of ripe apple on the nose while the very long palate is redolent of fresh golden delicious apple. And to conclude, the Oblin Ros '97 is an intense, spicy Bordeaux blend with wood and liquorice in the finish.

CORMONS (GO)

ALESSANDRO PRINCIC
LOC. PRADIS, 5
34071 CORMONS (GO)
TEL. 0481/60723

Sandro Princic is the son of the legendary Doro, one of the founding fathers of Friulian oenology and still today – at nearly 90 years old – capable of identifying a great wine with one glance and brief sniff of the glass. Equally legendary is Sandro's hospitality, a speciality in which he gets magnificent support from Grazia. The Princic vines stand on the hills at Pradis, a superb location in the Collio near Cormons. For years, we have been saying that Sandro could make great reds as well as his habitually fine whites. Proof has been provided by the Princic Merlot '98 for not many producers were able to squeeze a top-rank red from that particular vintage. The nose privileges stewed cherries while the mixed berry fruit on the palate combines with good texture and a solid structure that takes you into a long, soft finish. Sandro's Pinot Bianco is a classic. Stylish apple and spring flowers on the nose introduce a palate with a close-knit texture for a wine that is full-bodied, warm and very long. Nor is the Tocai Friulano any less impressive. The nose of sweet Dutch pipe tobacco mingling with pear and very ripe apple is echoed perfectly on a palate that unfolds an endlessly array of fruit aromas. The finish is leisurely. The Malvasia has such an intense entry on the nose that it is redolent of toastiness, even though this is a wine vinified exclusively in steel. Its Lucullan feast of summer fruit on nose and palate is brought to a neat close by a hint of acidity in the finish. In the Sauvignon, red pepper is the prevalent aroma and the palate has a firm, fresh-tasting structure. The Cabernet Franc '97 proved to be utterly true to type, parading the notes of new-mown grass and black cherry that some tasters find elegant and others condemn as lacking in savoir faire.

O	Collio Pinot Grigio '99	♂♂	4
O	Oblin Blanc '98	♂♂	5
O	Collio Bianco '99	♂	4
O	Collio Pinot Bianco '99	♂	4
O	Collio Sauvignon '99	♂	4
O	Collio Tocai Friulano '99	♂	4
●	Oblin Ros '97	♂	5
O	Collio Chardonnay '99		4
O	Collio Pinot Grigio '98	♂♂♂	4
O	Oblin Blanc '97	♂	5

●	Collio Merlot '98	♂♂	4
O	Collio Malvasia '99	♂♂	4
O	Collio Pinot Bianco '99	♂♂	4
O	Collio Tocai Friulano '99	♂♂	4
●	Collio Cabernet Franc '97	♂	4
O	Collio Sauvignon '99	♂	4
O	Collio Pinot Bianco '95	♂♂♂	5
O	Collio Tocai Friulano '93	♂♂♂	5
●	Collio Merlot '97	♂♂	4

CORMONS (GO)

CORMONS (GO)

DARIO RACCARO
VIA S. GIOVANNI, 87/B
34071 CORMONS (GO)
TEL. 0481/61425

RONCADA
LOC. RONCADA, 5
34071 CORMONS (GO)
TEL. 0481/61394

Dario Raccaro is a producer who scores low for hectares under vine and number of bottles produced but who is right up there at the top in terms of quality. We can only express our admiration and respect, noting that although he presented a limited number of wines, his haul of Glasses was quite remarkable. One of Dario's bankers over the years has been his Tocai Friulano, perhaps because he rents one of the best vineyards in Brazzano, near Cormons. The '99 version is rich in williams pear and almond notes on the nose, flaunting exceptional elegance on the palate, where the fruit is underpinned by serious structure and tangy acidity. The Raccaro Collio Bianco, a blend of tocai grapes with malvasia, sauvignon and wood-aged picolit, has a bouquet of fruit that ranges from apple to pear and yellow plum, in addition to dried flowers. As for the Tocai, the palate enhances and concentrates the fruit, melding it into the chewy texture and rounding off with an enfolding finish. Although still young, the oak-aged Merlot '99 already has an attractive nose of cherry tart and prunes. The warm, long palate mirrors this fruit, revealing interesting but as yet intractable tannins. Last on the list was the Malvasia. Its flowery, fresh aromas lack a little refinement but the palate is warm, soft and broad, with nicely judged and very refreshing acidity. So there you are. A limited range from a small winery where quality is king and value for money is guaranteed.

The Roncada winery has belonged since 1953 to the Mattioni family, who have 22 hectares under vine in the low-lying part of the Collio zone. Their 19th-century mansion has had a cellar since it was built, testifying to the fact that winemaking was already part of the normal routine at the time. Oscar Biasi, who has been the Roncada wine technician for almost 20 years, expertly supervises the 14 varieties grown on the estate. This year's Pinot Bianco is excellent, its complex, fresh nose of rich fruit dominated by apple. The front palate is full and rich with very ripe fruit while the finish has good length. Another top-notch wine is the Cabernet Sauvignon '98. Intense and full on the nose, where there are attractive hints of oak, its aromas are echoed precisely in the attack on the palate, where the very ripe berry fruit opens up at once, accompanied by nuances of autumn leaves. The structure is decent and the finish lingers. It is increasingly unusual to find Müller Thurgau in Friuli (and good thing, too, in our opinion), but the Roncada version is very acceptable. Warm yet at the same time light, it has elegance, freshness and length on the palate. The Ribolla Gialla scored high in the One Glass band thanks to a soft, persuasive nose, redolent of warm bread, spring flowers and plums, mirrored beautifully on the palate, which unveils a hint of acidity in the finish. The Pinot Grigio was another thoroughly convincing product, from its faintly copper-flecked colour to its rich nose of fruit salad, glycerine-sweet structure and length on the palate. One of the wines that came close to winning One Glass was the Franconia – another disappearing variety – and the Merlot '98 also merited a mention in dispatches. In contrast, the Tocai Friulano and Chardonnay were decently made but little more.

O	Collio Bianco '99	▼▼	3*
●	Collio Merlot '99	▼▼	4
O	Collio Tocai Friulano '99	▼▼	3*
O	Collio Malvasia '99	▼	3
●	Collio Merlot '97	♀♀	3
●	Friuli Isonzo Cabernet Franc '97	♀♀	3
O	Collio Bianco '98	♀	3

●	Collio Cabernet Sauvignon '98	▼▼	4
O	Collio Pinot Bianco '99	▼▼	3*
O	Collio Müller Thurgau '99	▼	3
O	Collio Pinot Grigio '99	▼	3
O	Collio Ribolla Gialla '99	▼	3
O	Collio Chardonnay '99		3
●	Collio Merlot '98		3
O	Collio Tocai Friulano '99		3
●	Franconia '98		4

CORMONS (GO)

CORMONS (GO)

RONCO DEI TASSI
LOC. MONTE, 38
34071 CORMONS (GO)
TEL. 0481/60155

RONCO DEL GELSO
VIA ISONZO, 117
34071 CORMONS (GO)
TEL. 0481/61310

Fabio and Daniela Coser have involved the whole family in the running of this 13-hectare estate, seven and a half of which are planted to vine. Although Fabio is busy with his other winery, which this year distinguished itself with a Three Glass award, and with his consultancy work, the Cosers managed to put together a range in which only the Tocai failed to come up to Two Glass standards. It goes to show just how far this wine technician has come with his five labels (three monovarietals and two blends). Coser's Tocai is outstanding for freshness – despite a hefty structure – on both nose and palate, It also reveals a remarkable wealth of aromas. High marks, too, for the Pinot Grigio. Its apple and pear aromas are laced with robust alcohol and the palate is a perfect balance of fruit and acidity, rounded off with great length. The Sauvignon is stylish and unassertive, its delightfully intense nose offering elderflower and tomato leaf aromas. These are echoed on the palate, where peach and grapefruit emerge in the finish. The Collio Bianco Fosarin, blended from steel-fermented tocai and malvasia and wood-vinified pinot bianco, opens with a light toasty aroma that is followed by hints of apricot, banana and ripe apple. On the palate, these notes meld seamlessly with an alcohol-rich texture that never threatens to overpower. We had been looking forward to the Collio Rosso Cjarandon '97, a blend of merlot, cabernet sauvignon and cabernet franc. We were not disappointed. On the nose, there are notes of strawberry jam, wild berries, autumn leaves and a hint of moss. The soft palate develops unhurriedly, broadening out with persuasive, well-sustained momentum.

Giorgio Badin is both owner and winemaker at this estate, which extends over 15 hectares of vineyards situated around the cellar, all lying within the Isonzo DOC zone. When we called to taste the wines, however, they were going through a difficult period. Although ready only a few months after the vintage, thanks to hyperoxygenation of the must, they reduce considerably at the beginning of the following summer for a couple of months. That's why it is important not to fire off too hasty a judgement that we might regret when the Guide comes out. This year, it was the Pinot Grigio Sot lis Rivis '99 that earned Three Glasses. It offers a rich, concentrated nose of fruit that broadens out continuously while the aromas on the palate are ripe and well-balanced. The acidity is superbly judged and structure ensures that this is a wine to tuck away in your cellar. Only a few points below came the golden-hued Sauvignon. Its palate is quite incredibly full yet elegant and the varietal notes come through clearly. Rich fruit is also the trademark of the Bianco Latimis, obtained from tocai friulano, pinot bianco and riesling. The brilliant colour leads you into a palate that is soft yet fresh, rich and astoundingly long. Giorgio Badin is one of the few winemakers in Italy whose Riesling can give you the characteristic varietal aromas of petrol and raw damson while the wine is still young. These are backed up in the mouth by outstanding structure and a buttery texture. Riesling-lovers will want to add a bottle or two to their stocks. The estate Tocai is another wine that will improve in the cellar and the Chardonnay '98 is also successful. A high One Glass score went to the Merlot '98 and the Cabernet Franc '99 just scraped over the same threshold. Finally, the '98 Pinot Grigio Sot lis Rivis is wonderful. Pity it's so hard to find!

O	Collio Bianco Fosarin '99	🍷🍷	4
O	Collio Pinot Grigio '99	🍷🍷	4
●	Collio Rosso Cjarandon '97	🍷🍷	5
O	Collio Sauvignon '99	🍷🍷	4
O	Collio Tocai Friulano '99	🍷	4
O	Collio Bianco Fosarin '96	🍷🍷🍷	4
O	Collio Sauvignon '98	🍷🍷🍷	4
O	Collio Bianco Fosarin '98	🍷🍷	4
●	Collio Rosso Cjarandon '96	🍷🍷	4

O	Friuli Isonzo Pinot Grigio Sot lis Rivis '99	🍷🍷🍷	4
O	Friuli Isonzo Bianco Latimis '99	🍷🍷	4
O	Friuli Isonzo Pinot Grigio Sot lis Rivis '98	🍷🍷	4
O	Friuli Isonzo Riesling '99	🍷🍷	4
O	Friuli Isonzo Sauvignon '99	🍷🍷	4
●	Friuli Isonzo Cabernet Franc '99	🍷	4
O	Friuli Isonzo Chardonnay '99	🍷	4
●	Friuli Isonzo Merlot '98	🍷	5
O	Friuli Isonzo Tocai Friulano '99	🍷	4
O	Friuli Isonzo Sauvignon '98	🍷🍷🍷	4
O	Friuli Isonzo Tocai Friulano '95	🍷🍷🍷	5
O	Friuli Isonzo Tocai Friulano '97	🍷🍷🍷	4
O	Isonzo Tocai Friulano '94	🍷🍷🍷	5

CORMONS (GO)

OSCAR STURM
LOC. ZEGLA, 1
34071 CORMONS (GO)
TEL. 0481/60720

Over the years, Oscar and Dunja Sturm have demonstrated their commitment to maintaining high standards of quality. The family originally came from Andritz, near Graz in Austria, but they have been living in Friuli for over two centuries. The 11 hectares of Sturm vineyards are scattered over the hillslopes and flatlands around the cellar, which is therefore strategically placed for the grape harvest. Inside the well-equipped and carefully organized cellar, skilful vinification, both in steel and in barrique, ensures excellent results. And again this year, the Chardonnay Andritz, expertly aged in oak half-barriques, turned out to be the finest of the estate's limited range of excellent wines. It has fresh, concentrated aromas that open on notes of ripe banana over yeast. Progression on the palate is broad, full-bodied and generous, finishing on a hint of refreshing acidity. The Pinot Grigio is strikingly elegant, its well-sustained, complex nose offering a wealth of apple, pear and mango fruit before the tangy palate protracts your pleasure in a lingering finish. Lustrous colour and an unassertive nose are the first impressions left by the attractively balanced Sauvignon. Delicate and enticing in the mouth, it marries freshness with characteristic varietal notes of elderflower that stay right through to the finish. And to finish off, there was the Tocai Friulano. Clean and complex on the nose, it is dominated by an intense chorus of pear, apple and almond that returns on a palate where a hint of milk of almonds adds personality. The finish is well-balanced and refreshing, thanks to its robust acidity.

○	Chardonnay Andritz '99	🍷🍷	3*
○	Collio Pinot Grigio '99	🍷🍷	3
○	Collio Sauvignon '99	🍷🍷	3
○	Collio Tocai Friulano '99	🍷🍷	3
○	Chardonnay Andritz '98	ΥΥ	3
●	Merlot Andritz '96	ΥΥ	4
●	Refosco P. R. '97	Υ	3

CORMONS (GO)

SUBIDA DI MONTE
LOC. MONTE, 9
34071 CORMONS (GO)
TEL. 0481/61011

Recently, Gigi Antonutti has been delegating more and more of the work at the winery he founded in 1972 to his sons, Cristian and Andrea. Cristian looks after winemaking while Andrea is in charge of sales. Many of the vineyards on the eight-hectare estate that surrounds the cellar have been replanted more densely with suitable clones and the results should be apparent very soon. The cellar itself is already fully equipped for premium-quality production. We thought the Collio Rosso Poncaia '97 was particularly successful this year. It's a Bordeaux-style blend of merlot, cabernet sauvignon and cabernet franc aged in large and small oak casks for 18 months. The colour is attractively deep and there are notes of cloves and plum over autumn leaves on the nose. "Meaty" is the word for the palate, which has good length and only slightly aggressive tannins in the finish. The Bianco Sotrari is obtained from sauvignon, traminer and riesling grapes macerated on the skins for about ten hours. Mint tea aromas grace the fresh, lively and pleasantly coherent palate. On the nose, stylish elderflower aromas dominate the Sauvignon but the real eye-opener is the degree of harmony achieved by the alcohol, close-knit texture and acidity on the palate. Williams pear and alcohol-rich warmth emerge on the nose of the Pinot Grigio, to be echoed on a refreshing palate that is the merest shade lean in the finish. In the glass, the Tocai is stunning and on the nose its rich aromas of fruit mingle complexity with elegance. In fact, it is only the excessive acidity on the palate that detracts from this fine product. The reds of '99, a Cabernet Franc and a Merlot, are distinctly young. But they are well-made and definitely worth a mention.

●	Collio Rosso Poncaia '97	🍷🍷	5
○	Collio Bianco Sotrari '99	🍷	2
○	Collio Pinot Grigio '99	🍷	3
○	Collio Sauvignon '99	🍷	3
○	Collio Tocai Friulano '99	🍷	3
●	Collio Cabernet Franc '99		4
●	Collio Merlot '99		3
●	Collio Cabernet Franc '97	ΥΥ	4
●	Collio Cabernet Ris. '95	ΥΥ	5
●	Collio Merlot Ris. '95	ΥΥ	4

CORMONS (GO)

TIARE - ROBERTO SNIDARCIG
VIA MONTE, 58
34071 CORMONS (GO)
TEL. 0481/60064

For years, Roberto Snidarcig worked with his father at Dolegna. The he moved to the central part of the Collio zone, where he rented a cellar at Mossa and has a contact address at the "trattoria" his wife Sandra runs on Monte Quarin at Cormons. Roberto manages his cellar with enthusiasm. Although set up in 1985, it is only in recent years that the winery has acquired an estate of seven and a half hectares. Now it has taken off and currently produces 60,000 bottles a year. Unfortunately, Roberto follows the regrettable Friulian habit of proposing as many as 12 different labels so it is almost impossible to find his products in the shops. The flagship wine is the Tocai Friulano Collio, only 1,300 bottles of which are released. Notes of almondskins and sweet Dutch pipe tobacco emerge on the nose while the palate is forthright, warm and long. Roberto's Cabernet Sauvignon Isonzo is equally good. The nose of rose, confectioner's cream and alcohol leads into an austere yet well-balanced palate with plenty of fruit and length. His Ribolla Gialla has a generous nose of yellow plums and flowers, which are mirrored on the palate and complemented by fresh varietal acidity. The Chardonnay Collio, 8,000 bottles of which were released this year, is remarkable for the generous alcohol that renders it deliciously soft. In contrast, only 700 bottles of Del Collio Cuvée Bianco were made by vinifying chardonnay, pinot grigio and sauvignon grapes and ageing the wine in Slavonian oak for six months. There are hints of vanilla, apple and talcum powder on the nose. These return on the palate, enhanced by fruit aromas. Another convincing wine was the Ronco delle Tiare, a '97 red from cabernet sauvignon, merlot and schioppettino. Its mulberry aromas lead in to a palate of vanilla and black cherry.

CORMONS (GO)

FRANCO TOROS
LOC. NOVALI, 12
34071 CORMONS (GO)
TEL. 0481/61327

Wine-lovers who have been following Franco Toros will not be surprised at this year's Three Glass award for his magnificent Merlot '97. In fact, he came very near to a second top rating with his Sauvignon. Franco has nine hectares planted at 5,000 vines per hectare, almost all in a single lot that backs onto his home-cum-cellar, which was completely restructured a only few years ago. It was the parcel on the hillside at Cormons that yielded the spectacularly good Merlot and unlike other Toros versions of the wine, the '97 was aged in oak for a couple of years. Stunningly concentrated, stylish and muscular, with a cornucopia of fruit, it hits nose and palate like a train, overpowering the senses with its structure, density, softness and sheer strength. The Sauvignon marries intensity with crisp notes of elderflower on the nose while the palate reveals breadth, body and richness, hints of citrus fruit emerging in the leisurely finish. Two wines – the Pinot Bianco and the Tocai Friulano – scored high in the Two Glass bracket. The long, complex Pinot Bianco has a close-knit texture alluringly offset by a vein of refreshing acidity whereas the Tocai Friulano foregrounds pear, apple and almond that return on the mellow palate with just the right degree of zesty acidity. On the nose, the Chardonnay '99 has a milky note over a complex backdrop of ripe fruit. The aromas are reflected on the palate, which offers a fresh, butter-rich progression packed with fruit. Fruit is also to the fore in the Pinot Grigio, which impresses with its apple, mango and kiwi fruit aromas and full-bodied palate. Finally, the Cabernet Franc tempts the palate with prune aromas and a dry, tannic finish.

○	Collio Tocai Friulano '99	♼♼	3*
●	Friuli Isonzo Cabernet Sauvignon '98	♼♼	3*
○	Collio Bianco Cuvée '99	♼	4
○	Collio Chardonnay '99	♼	3
○	Collio Ribolla Gialla '99	♼	3
●	Ronco della Tiare '97	♼	4
●	Collio Cabernet Franc '99		3
○	Collio Sauvignon '99		3

●	Collio Merlot Sel. '97	♼♼♼	6
○	Collio Chardonnay '99	♼♼	4
○	Collio Pinot Bianco '99	♼♼	4
○	Collio Pinot Grigio '99	♼♼	4
○	Collio Sauvignon '99	♼♼	4
○	Collio Tocai Friulano '99	♼♼	4
●	Collio Cabernet Franc '99	♼	4
●	Collio Merlot '97	♼♼	4
○	Collio Chardonnay Ris. '97	♼	5

CORMONS (GO)

CORNO DI ROSAZZO (UD)

VIGNA DEL LAURO
LOC. MONTE, 38
34071 CORMONS (GO)
TEL. 0481/60155

VALENTINO BUTUSSI
VIA PRA' DI CORTE, 1
33040 CORNO DI ROSAZZO (UD)
TEL. 0432/759194

The Vigna del Lauro winery rents seven hectares of vineyards at Lucinico, San Floriano del Collio and Cormons in the Collio zone, as well as owning one and a half hectares in the Isonzo DOC zone. It constitutes the second string – the first is Ronco dei Tassi – to Fabio Coser's redoubtable winemaking bow. This year, Vigna del Lauro earned Three Glasses for its superlative Sauvignon. There are golden highlights in the colour while the clean, stylish nose is intriguingly complex with its elegant note of tomato leaf. In the mouth, it is full-bodied, buttery, glycerine-sweet, warm and very long. The Collio Bianco, from tocai friulano, pinot bianco, malvasia and ribolla gialla part aged in wood, scored a few points less. The nose is mesmerizing, revealing flowers and fruit over toastiness and the lingering palate is well-balanced and fresh-tasting. A complex nose of pear, peach and almond is the visiting card of the Tocai Friulano, leading in to a rich, zesty palate that has great length. What the panel liked best about the Pinot Grigio was the palate. The nose is unexciting but in the mouth it unveils rich aromas of tropical fruit and apple over decent texture with reasonable length. This is the first time Coser has released his Chardonnay Isonzo. We appreciated the generous fruit and up-front acidity but found it lacked a little length. To round off, there was the complex Merlot '97, its rustic wood-derived aromas mingling with red berry tart on the nose. Tannins that have yet to mellow penalize the palate for the time being. Wait for a couple of years, though. This is a wine that has what it takes.

Angelo Butussi and his family run this thriving winery, where they cultivate more than 12 hectares of vineyards in the Colli Orientali and Grave DOC zones. Currently, they are adding a new building for tastings and cellar door sales. Last year, Angelo hit the headlines when he purchased two small bottles of Picolit – one full – dating from the early 19th century but now it's time to talk about the present. The Ribolla Gialla is a stunningly elegant wine that releases profound, complex aromas of spring flowers, echoed on the palate. Sadly, the variety's characteristic acidity detracts from balance of the finish. In contrast, Angelo's Sauvignon is much more cogent in the mouth. The nuances of elderflower are fairly concentrated on the nose but they open out spectacularly in the mouth, backed up by a more than decent structure that lingers in a finish where peach and ripe grapefruit provide the keynotes. The Tocai Friulano has an elegant, intense and fairly complex nose of pear and apple, followed by good thrust on the palate. There's plenty of fruit and the finish unveils a hint of toastiness, even though this is a wine that has never seen oak. Pink, onion-skin highlights tinge the colour of the Pinot Grigio, a fresh-tasting and not uninteresting wine whose fruit is more impressive on the nose than in the mouth. Next, we sampled the Verduzzo, another wine with an intriguing colour, this time of old gold. A fresh note of mint overlays the variety's trademark apple while the palate is sweet and very agreeable. Toastiness comes through strongly on the nose of the Picolit, accompanied by hints of tobacco and ripe yellow fruit, while the palate is refreshing, fruit-rich and "amabile" sweet.

O	Collio Sauvignon '99	▼▼▼	3*
O	Collio Bianco '99	▼▼	3*
O	Collio Tocai Friulano '99	▼▼	3*
●	Collio Merlot '97	▼	4
O	Collio Pinot Grigio '99	▼	3
O	Friuli Isonzo Chardonnay '99	▼	3
O	Collio Bianco '98	♀♀	3
O	Collio Tocai Friulano '98	♀♀	3

O	COF Ribolla Gialla '99	▼▼	3*
O	COF Sauvignon '99	▼▼	3*
O	COF Tocai Friulano '99	▼▼	3*
O	COF Picolit '98	▼	6
O	COF Pinot Grigio '99	▼	3
O	COF Verduzzo Friulano '99	▼	3
●	COF Cabernet Franc '99		3
O	COF Chardonnay '99		3
●	Friuli Grave Merlot '99		3
O	Friuli Grave Pinot Bianco '99		2

CORNO DI ROSAZZO (UD)

CA DI BON
VIA CASALI GALLO, 1
33040 CORNO DI ROSAZZO (UD)
TEL. 0432/759316

Even though Ca' di Bon walked away with a good clutch of One Glass awards, this was a lean year for Ameris and Gianni Bon, whose wines have in the past accustomed us to better things. Their vines extend over nine hectares in the adjoining Colli Orientali, Grave del Friuli and Collio DOC zones. Only part of their wine is bottled but even that portion, in line with local custom, is sold under as many as 14 different labels. The best bottle this year was the Chardonnay '99. Its alluring nose offers apple and yeast aromas, leading in to a refreshing, fruit-rich palate with a generous, well-sustained, stylish structure. The Tocai Friulano is also an elegant wine overall, revealing crisp pear and apple on the nose and a lively, fresh-tasting palate that soon has you reaching out for a second glass. Ronc dal Gial means "rooster hill" and the wine that bears this name is a blend of merlot, cabernet franc and refosco fruit from the '97 vintage, aged in French barriques for two years or so. In the interesting nose, you can make out Virginia pipe tobacco, red berry tart, plums and black cherry then the relatively straightforward palate offers abundant fruit and rather assertive tannins. To round off the Ca' di Bon One Glass wines there was Angelo's Schioppettino, where distinct aromas of black cherry and raspberry meld with restrained hints of spices. All the other wines we tasted were well-made, including the Ronco del Nonno white, a blend of tocai friulano, sauvignon and pinot bianco.

CORNO DI ROSAZZO (UD)

EUGENIO COLLAVINI
VIA FORUM JULII, 2
LOC. GRAMOGLIANO
33040 CORNO DI ROSAZZO (UD)
TEL. 0432/753222

The superior quality of Manlio Collavini's wines comes as no surprise. The new estate philosophy is crystal clear and Manlio himself is so impatient to produce world-class wines that he gives the impression of wanting to tell Mother Nature herself to get a move on. You can see at a glance that the cellar was designed with quality as the priority. Fruit comes from the small estate and is also bought-in. At least one third of purchases come from high-density plots of vines more than 20 years old, and thus will yield superior wine. But Ribolla Gialla Turian '99 comes from the estate's own property and is the best in its class from the vintage, combining polished aromas of spring flowers and apple on the nose. This is followed up by a well-sustained, refreshing and beautifully balanced palate where the same aromas come through. Elegance is also the distinguishing feature of the Sauvignon Poncanera del Collio. Its tomato leaf and white peach aromas on the nose and front palate lead into citrus fruit, with grapefruit to the fore, and a long, delicious finish. Manlio's Tocai Friulano has crisp apple and pear on the nose, supremely balanced fruit and acidity in the mouth and an almond twist in the aftertaste. The nose of the Isonzo Chardonnay dei Sassi Cavi '99 evokes yeast, vanilla and milky coffee before the full palate of apricot and banana impresses you with its length. There's a hint of onion skin in the colour of the Pinot Grigio Collio while hints of ripe apple and pear lace the long, fresh aromas on nose and palate. Despite the challenging vintage after problems with excessive rainfall, both the Merlot and Cabernet del Collio '98 are very solid wines, as is the spicy Refosco Pucino. Finally, the Il Grigio, a Charmat-process spumante from chardonnay, pinot and prosecco grapes, is a thoroughly attractive wine.

O	Chardonnay '99	♀	3
O	COF Pinot Bianco '99	♀	3
●	COF Schioppettino '99	♀	3
O	COF Tocai Friulano '99	♀	3
O	Friuli Grave Sauvignon '99	♀	3
●	Ronc dal Gial '97	♀	4
●	COF Cabernet Franc '99		3
●	COF Merlot '99		3
O	COF Pinot Grigio '99		3
O	Ronco del Nonno '99		4
●	COF Refosco P. R. '97	♀♀	3
O	Ronco del Nonno '98	♀♀	4

O	COF Ribolla Gialla Turian '99	♀♀	4
O	Collio Pinot Grigio Collezione Privata '99	♀♀	4
O	Collio Sauvignon Poncanera Collezione Privata '99	♀♀	5
O	Collio Tocai Friulano Collezione Privata '99	♀♀	4
O	Friuli Isonzo Chardonnay dei Sassi Cavi '99	♀♀	3*
●	Collio Cabernet Collezione Privata '98	♀	4
●	Collio Merlot Collezione Privata '98	♀	4
●	Friuli Isonzo Refosco P. R. Pucino '99	♀	3
O	Il Grigio Brut	♀	3
O	Collio Chardonnay dei Sassi Cavi Collezione Privata '98	♀♀	5

318

CORNO DI ROSAZZO (UD) CORNO DI ROSAZZO (UD)

ADRIANO GIGANTE
VIA ROCCA BERNARDA, 3
33040 CORNO DI ROSAZZO (UD)
TEL. 0432/755835

PERUSINI
VIA TORRIONE, 13
LOC. GRAMOGLIANO
33040 CORNO DI ROSAZZO (UD)
TEL. 0432/675018 - 0432/759151

There's a new label on Adriano Gigante's bottles and rather better quality wine inside them. Indeed this year, his Sauvignon came very close to winning Three Glasses. But then Adriano works extremely hard on his 18 hectares of hillslope vineyards near Corno. Quality is his goal, so the results are no surprise. However, we were talking about that Sauvignon. On the nose, it releases elegantly discreet notes of peach, elderflower and hedgerow that return on the palate to linger delightfully. The Gigante Pinot Grigio is free of the rough edges to which the variety is prone. Williams pear and red delicious apple fruit on the nose give way to nuances of flowers and the very fresh palate takes up the theme in a well-sustained progression through to the leisurely finish. We found two Tocais on the list, a standard label and the Storico selection from a vineyard of 60-year-old vines. The first version is true to type on the nose, where characteristic hints of sweet almond and russet pear emerge. These are mirrored on the palate, lingering endlessly in the fresh finish. Although similar in personality, the Storico stands out thanks to a bigger, more powerful nose. Then came the Chardonnay, which easily passed the One Glass threshold with its pervasive aromas of ripe orange and melon fruit, but was held back by a lack of length in the finish. Both Gigante sweet wines were thoroughly decent. The golden-hued Verduzzo offers stewed apple and vanilla while the apricot and apple on the palate are developed with appreciable dynamism. Nose and palate are regaled with dried figs, orange and candied apricot peel by the Picolit. Last, the Merlot is a varietal wine with hints of peppery spice and ripe berry fruit that, however, succumb to the still over-assertive tannins on the palate.

Teresa Perusini has a university degree as a fine arts major. Since 1985, she and her engineer husband, Giacomo de Pace have been running this historic hillslope estate at Corno di Rosazzo, which they inherited from Giampaolo Perusini. In fact, it was Giampaolo who in the 40s and 50s made the first vine selections, propagating the one found to be most suitable. The project involved mainly ribolla and merlot vines, and it is the latter variety that Teresa is concentrating on again today for selection. That must be the reason behind the regular appearance of Ribolla Gialla on our list of Two Glass wines. Its perfect straw-yellow colour has greenish highlights. Then the complex, flower-dominated nose unveils hints of dried herbs, ripe apples and honey. Well-balanced fruit returns on the elegant and full-bodied palate. Although the Merlot Nero '98 was obtained from the selected vines, it shows the limitations of the vintage. Nevertheless, it can offer an intense, generously broad nose reminiscent of red berry tart as well as acidity on the palate that complements the tannins to produce a dry finish. The aromas of the Pinot Bianco are sweet and redolent of ripe apple. The palate is well-sustained and stylish. Next, perhaps thanks to a grape harvest that was carried out in two stages, the Sauvignon unveils clean, well-defined varietal characteristics ranging from tomato leaf to elderflower. Warm and soft in the mouth, where the same aromas return, it is a pleasantly refreshing tipple. The gold-coloured Riesling '98 has developed well. Its varietal notes emerge on the palate especially, with notes of petrol and damson to the fore. These are underpinned by a rich, buttery structure. In contrast, the Pinot Nero wasn't up to our expectations, probably because we tasted it too young.

O COF Pinot Grigio '99	🍷🍷	3
O COF Sauvignon '99	🍷🍷	3
O COF Tocai Friulano '99	🍷🍷	3
O COF Tocai Friulano Storico '99	🍷🍷	4
O COF Chardonnay '99	🍷	3
● COF Merlot '98	🍷	3
O COF Picolit '98	🍷	6
● COF Schioppettino '98	🍷	4
O COF Verduzzo Friulano '98	🍷	4
● COF Cabernet Franc '99		3
● COF Refosco P. R. '98		3
● COF Merlot '97	🍷🍷	3

O COF Ribolla Gialla '99	🍷🍷	3*
● COF Merlot Nero '98	🍷	4
O COF Pinot Bianco '99	🍷	3
O COF Riesling '98	🍷	3
O COF Sauvignon '99	🍷	3
O COF Pinot Grigio '99		3
● COF Pinot Nero '99		3
● COF Merlot Nero '96	🍷🍷	4
● COF Merlot Nero '97	🍷🍷	4
O COF Picolit '97	🍷	6

CORNO DI ROSAZZO (UD)   CORNO DI ROSAZZO (UD)

LEONARDO SPECOGNA
VIA ROCCA BERNARDA, 4
33040 CORNO DI ROSAZZO (UD)
TEL. 0432/755840

ANDREA VISINTINI
VIA GRAMOGLIANO, 27
33040 CORNO DI ROSAZZO (UD)
TEL. 0432/755813

Graziano Specogna, who works mainly in the cellar, and his brother Gianni, in the vineyards, together run this lovely winery on the hillslopes of the historic Rocca Bernarda castle. Currently, the Specognas are working on an exciting range of premium-quality reds. Their Oltre is an oak-aged '96 Merlot that Graziano initially thought was an experiment that had gone wrong. Its stylish nose of berries and plum leads into a meaty cherry-rich palate with a persuasively close-knit texture and lots of length. The Specogna Cabernet '98 is also excellent, its delicate nose of confectioner's cream and red fruit tart taking you in to a clean, nicely sustained palate where the tannins are prominent but not too dry. The copper-flecked Pinot Grigio has a nose of tropical fruit and elderwood. In the mouth, it is concentrated and polished and the fruit-rich, fresh-tasting palate signs off with an attractive note of the initial elderwood. This year, the Specogna Sauvignon is very good indeed. Intense to the point of over-assertion on the nose, which is dominated by varietal elder leaf and tomato leaf, it offers notes of ripe citrus that add complexity. The broad, mellow palate has good thrust that is underpinned by the generous alcohol. Among the One Glass wines was a Merlot '98 with a cherry jam nose that was picked up on the palate, together with a hint of tannins in the finish. The Refosco, also from '98, unveiled crisp spicy aromas and decent alcohol to provide a counterpoint for the abundant berry and plum fruit. The '98 Chardonnay has fresh, deliciously balanced aromas of apricot and apple, developing smoothly on the palate through to the fruit-laced finish. Finally, the Specogna Tocai has serious structure and rather untypical aromas, ranging from peaches to tangerines.

The Visintini estate lies where the Colli Orientali DOC borders on the Collio and Grave zones. Here, the family cultivate 17 hectares of their own vines and six that they rent. The winery logo depicts the tower of the Visintini home and cellar, which dates from 1650. The driving spirit behind the 80,000 bottles of very competitively priced wine that are released each year is young Oliviero, helped by his sister, Cinzia, and father, Andrea. Their Ribolla Gialla has intense, sweet aromas of citrus and muscat grape, a full, balanced palate where yellow plums dominate the fruit and the variety's trademark acidity, somewhat attenuated by the '99 vintage. Tomato leaf and nettle are evident on the nose of the Sauvignon and the same aromas return on the palate, which is refreshing, well-structured and lingering. The '99 Merlot, a fifth of which was aged in large oak casks, has a rich nose of black cherry jam and an intriguingly complex character that echoes the aromas of the nose in a soft, mellow and attractively fresh-tasting palate. The Merlot II Barrique '98 was aged in five-hectolitre casks for 18 months and the wine that emerged has an impressively complex nose with hints of leather and wild berry tart. Generous and fruit-rich on the palate, it also offers robust structure and out-of-the-ordinary length. Last of the Visintini Two Glass wines was the Verduzzo. Its rich golden colour ushers in a classic varietal nose of stewed apple and a sweetish palate with milk of almonds and tannins that come through in the finish. Freshness and style are the distinguishing features of the Pinot Bianco. In contrast, the Pinot Grigio has a copper-tinged colour and notes of rennet apple while the Tocai Friulano impresses with its structure and varietal aromas. The Cabernet is well-made and uncomplicated.

●	COF Cabernet '98	ΨΨ	4
○	COF Sauvignon '99	ΨΨ	3*
●	Oltre '96	ΨΨ	6
○	Pinot Grigio '99	ΨΨ	3
○	COF Chardonnay '98	Ψ	4
●	COF Merlot '98	Ψ	4
●	COF Refosco P. R. '98	Ψ	4
○	COF Tocai Friulano '99	Ψ	3
○	COF Verduzzo Friulano '99		3
●	COF Merlot '97	ΨΨ	4

●	COF Merlot '99	ΨΨ	3*
●	COF Merlot II Barrique '98	ΨΨ	4
○	COF Ribolla Gialla '99	ΨΨ	3*
○	COF Sauvignon '99	ΨΨ	3*
○	COF Verduzzo Friulano '99	ΨΨ	3*
○	COF Pinot Bianco '99	Ψ	3
○	COF Pinot Grigio '99	Ψ	3
○	COF Traminer Aromatico '99	Ψ	3
○	Collio Tocai Friulano '99	Ψ	3
●	COF Cabernet '99		3

CORNO DI ROSAZZO (UD)   DOLEGNA DEL COLLIO (GO)

ZOF
VIA GIOVANNI XXIII, 32/A
33040 CORNO DI ROSAZZO (UD)
TEL. 0432/759673

CA' RONESCA
LOC. LONZANO, 27
34070 DOLEGNA DEL COLLIO (GO)
TEL. 0481/60034

Daniele Zof, who is not long past his 30th birthday, impressed the panel with a range of wines that never dipped below a One Glass rating. With advice from consultant Donato Lanati, this young winemaker looks after his family's nine hectares, with a further six that he rents, enhancing the quality of his products each new vintage. Today, the estate bottles 80,000 units a year, releasing them under 11 labels. Best of the Zof range this time was the Sauvignon. Its bright straw yellow has crisp greenish highlights, leading into a varietal nose of tomato, nettle and lemon zest. These notes are picked up again on the well-structured and beautifully balanced palate, where they are joined by fruit salad, citrus and tangy acidity in the finish. Freshness, together with rennet apple and tropical fruit, is also the keynote of the Pinot Grigio. Then came Daniele's Ribolla Gialla, which marries alcohol with sinewy varietal acidity on the palate after the nose has revealed notes of spring flowers and yellow plums. In the Tocai, the panel noted green apple and mint on the nose, which were echoed on the front palate, although the finish was compromised a little by over-emphatic acidity. Moving on to the reds, we'll begin with the Va' Pensiero '97, a blend of cabernet sauvignon, merlot and schioppettino that aged slowly in oak casks of various sizes. Cherry and prune prevail on nose and palate, where the wine impresses with its structure, well-rounded body and exciting length. On the nose of the Cabernet Franc '99 there are hints of cloves and cherries. These are mirrored on the palate, which has good complexity and length. The Schioppettino has an intriguing range of intense aromas that go from wild rose to pepper and the palate is equally attractive. To finish, we mention the meaty, warm Zof Merlot, whose hints of stewed cherry and black cherry are clearly in evidence on both nose and palate.

Ca' Ronesca has made good progress. Paolo Bianchi, the winery manager, had announced new developments both in the vineyard, where fruit would be harvested riper and yields limited, and in the cellar, where lees contact would be increased. The aim was to obtain softer wines with more structure. So, if we tell you that the Sauvignon Podere di Ipplis came within a whisker of Three Glasses, you'll have the complete picture. This great product has a varietal nose with polished notes of tomato and elder. The front palate has lovely fruit and good body, with apple and peach coming through, and the wine progresses faultlessly to finish slowly on a note of tomato. The Collio version is similar, but with less weight on the palate. The Saramago is a blend of part-dried riesling, malvasia, picolit and verduzzo. Tasters liked the orange, apricot and dried roses on the nose. The palate, sweet on entry, takes you through to a finish of honey and apricot. The characteristically varietal Tocai offers aromas of almond, russet pear and acacia blossom, which return on the rich palate that unveils exceptional length. The Picolit came within an ace of Two Glasses. Its aromas of apricots, tangerines, figs and dates give way to lingering notes of candied orange peel on the palate. The Marnà, a blend of oak-aged malvasia, pinot bianco and chardonnay, showed its mettle once more with notes of roses and wistaria melding into the peach and white chocolate on the nose. The fruit-rich palate culminates in a finish dominated by peach. The other blended white, the Sermar, is a newcomer this year. Obtained from selected tocai, ribolla and pinot bianco grapes, it had only just gone into the bottle when we tasted and so struck us as no more than a well-made product with good fruit and continuity on the palate. Finally, the entry on the nose of the Sariz is an impressive amalgam of cherries and prunes, leading in to a straightforward but well-managed palate.

O COF Sauvignon '99	♀♀	3*
● COF Cabernet Franc '99	♀	3
● COF Merlot '99	♀	3
O COF Pinot Grigio '99	♀	3
O COF Ribolla Gialla '99	♀	3
● COF Schioppettino '99	♀	3
O COF Tocai Friulano '99	♀	3
● Va' Pensiero '97	♀	4
O COF Bianco Sonata '98	♀♀	4
● Va' Pensiero '96	♀♀	4

O COF Sauvignon		
Podere di Ipplis '99	♀♀	4
O Collio Sauvignon '99	♀♀	3*
O Collio Tocai Friulano '99	♀♀	3*
O Saramago '98	♀♀	4
O COF Picolit '98	♀	6
O Collio Bianco Marnà '98	♀	4
O Collio Bianco Sermar '99	♀	4
O Collio Pinot Grigio '99	♀	3
● Sariz '96	♀	4
O Collio Ribolla Gialla '99		3

DOLEGNA DEL COLLIO (GO)

DOLEGNA DEL COLLIO (GO)

LA RAJADE
LOC. RESTOCINA, 12
34070 DOLEGNA DEL COLLIO (GO)
TEL. 0481/639897

VENICA & VENICA
VIA MERNICO, 42
LOC. CERÒ
34070 DOLEGNA DEL COLLIO (GO)
TEL. 0481/60177 - 0481/61264

The La Rajade winery, which owns about seven hectares of vineyards on the Slovene border, in the northernmost part of the Collio DOC zone, has made sauvignon its principal variety. We have come to expect great Sauvignons from Romeo Rossi, the young owner, and this year his Sauvignon '99 was shortlisted for Three Glasses. In fact, it nearly won the top award. Let's start with Romeo's flagship wine. The colour is brilliant, and the wine releases intense aromas of elderflower and tomato leaf, which are superbly echoed right from the entry on the palate, where they are joined by yellow peach. In mid palate, the wine acquires admirable freshness and structure that are well-sustained through to the long, long finish. A high Two Glass wine is the Merlot Riserva '97, with its complex, full nose of warm alcohol and red fruit. The underlying note of wood and absolute continuity from entry to finish ensure the palate is full-bodied, soft and very long. Romeo's cabernet sauvignon and merlot Collio Rosso Stratin can boast very concentrated aromas of wild red berries and tar but the palate lacks complexity and doesn't quite fulfil your high expectations. Last on the list was the Tocai Friulano. The forthright and well-sustained nose hints at pear over almonds before the palate unveils robust structure and a touch of acidity that had yet to settle when we tasted. All in all, things at La Rajade are going well and looking good for the future.

The wines presented by brothers Gianni and Giorgio Venica were awesome. There was one Three Glass giant, seven Two Glass wines and a One Glass bottle in the ten put forward. There can be no doubt that this is a mature estate, which has replanted wisely and kept its cellar well up to scratch. In short, experimentation has now produced results. And when you are talking about Venica & Venica, you've got to mention Gianni's wife, Ornella, the tireless public relations supremo. Some experts maintain that Sauvignon Ronco delle Mele is today the archetypal wine from this variety. The intensity of its tomato leaf, peach and pineapple bouquet is almost overwhelming. Then yellow peach emerges in an irresistibly complex, fresh-tasting yet luxuriant palate that lingers forever. Three unanimous Glasses for a wine with huge personality. Fresh, apple-dominated fruit laced with hazelnut are the main features of the Pinot Bianco, a wine with a warm, alcohol-rich palate. In contrast, the Pinot Grigio marries tropical fruit to apple in its stylish, pronounced aromas while the palate offers hints of citrus fruit. The second-label Sauvignon has notes of elderflower and red pepper, firm structure and good length. Next, we tried the unbelievably complex Tocai Friulano. The nose hints at ripe fruit, straw and nuts, which are echoed on the rich, broad palate and backed up with solid alcohol and vibrant fruit. Dried apple, citrus and fruit salad come together in the intriguingly full-flavoured Chardonnay. Then there was the thoroughly convincing Merlot Perilla '97. Its aromas include cherry tart, spices and liquorice over a robust, refreshing structure. Finally, the Rosso delle Cime '97 is a cuvée of cabernet sauvignon, merlot and refosco. Warm on the nose, where there are nuances of elderflower, its entry on the palate is almost bitter before the wine mellows out in an array of generous fruit.

● Collio Merlot Ris. '97	▼▼	5
○ Collio Sauvignon '99	▼▼	4
● Collio Rosso Stratin '97	▼	5
○ Collio Tocai Friulano '99	▼	3
○ Caprizzi di Marceline	▼▼	4

○ Collio Sauvignon Ronco delle Mele '99	▼▼▼	5
○ Collio Chardonnay '99	▼▼	4
● Collio Merlot Perilla '97	▼▼	5
○ Collio Pinot Bianco '99	▼▼	4
○ Collio Pinot Grigio '99	▼▼	4
● Collio Rosso delle Cime '97	▼▼	5
○ Collio Sauvignon '99	▼▼	4
○ Collio Tocai Friulano Cime '99	▼▼	4
○ Collio Bianco Tre Vignis '98	▼	5
○ Collio Prime Note '98	▼	4
○ Collio Sauvignon Ronco delle Mele '97	▼▼▼	5
○ Collio Sauvignon Ronco delle Mele '98	▼▼▼	5

DUINO-AURISINA (TS) FAEDIS (UD)

KANTE
LOC. PREPOTTO, 3
FRAZ. S. PELAGIO
34011 DUINO-AURISINA (TS)
TEL. 040/200761

PAOLINO COMELLI
VIA DELLA CHIESA, 8
LOC. COLLOREDO DI SOFFUMBERGO
33040 FAEDIS (UD)
TEL. 0432/711226 - 0432/504973

Investment in vineyard and cellar has produced swift results at this winery. It may have been the vintage, or it may be the relaxed composure with which Edi brushes aside other people's scepticism, but there is no denying that his Malvasia is a stunner. Obtained by skilfully blending fruit from vineyards of different ages – 30 percent comes from vines that are more than 70 years old – it is perhaps emblematic of the winery, both for the strong territorial identity of the grape and in the way the wine itself is made. The nose offers evanescent notes of citron, elderflower, lemon balm and vanilla while the elegant, warmly persuasive front palate is backed up as it develops by attractive freshness. This is a particularly subtle and intriguing Three Glass wine. The other Kante products were, as usual, also out of the top drawer, beginning with the Vitovska, which in recent tastings has shown an outstanding propensity for ageing. Yellow plum, tarragon and dried flowers on the nose introduce a delicately dry, clean palate with substantial alcohol and attractive oaky nose to provide contrast. The Chardonnay, too, is traditional in style with its faint raisiny nuances, hints of walnut and pineapple, and a mellow, mouth-filling palate. It was denied a higher score only by what is almost certainly a temporary failure of the palate to come together satisfactorily. The Sauvignon is a lustrous straw-yellow with greenish highlights and unfurls notes of peach, apricot and confectioner's cream. Then an almost arrogant entry on the palate mellows into the elegant progression that is the trademark of all the bottles that emerge from this winery.

Pierluigi Comelli is a man who knows his own mind. Nor is he likely to rest on the many laurels he collects both professionally and as a sportsman. For our part, we can add that this has been another very good vintage for his wines, made under the supervision of Roberto Ottogalli with advice from consultant Fabio Coser. The Comelli white Locum Nostrum, for which chardonnay is blended with a smaller proportion of sauvignon, continues to improve and broke the Two Glass barrier in the '98 version. Aromas of citrus, yellow peach, apricot and banana emerge over toastiness on the nose to return on the palate, never wavering from entry through to the leisurely, broad finish. You can also rely on the Tocai Friulano, which has clean aromas on the nose that range from pear to almond. On the palate, there is good body and structure, a tangy freshness and rich texture. Definitely a serious bottle. For the Chardonnay, it will be better to wait for a year or so since at present the acidity on the palate detracts from the generous fruit, which on the nose is redolent of baked apple. There are distinct copper tinges in the Pinot Grigio, which has a nose nuanced with citrus and a delightfully soft entry on the palate, and signs off with nicely judged acidity in the finish. Even though it comes from a modest vintage for reds, the Merlot '98 is very drinkable. Its attractive cherry and black cherry aromas are present on nose and palate, where the fresh acidity and well-behaved tannins are in perfect accord. Finally, the Sauvignon, called "Superiore" because the yield is less than 80 quintals per hectare, reveals nice varietal notes, especially on the palate, and well-sustained acidity.

O	Carso Malvasia '98	♟♟♟	5
O	Carso Chardonnay '98	♟♟	5
O	Carso Sauvignon '98	♟♟	5
O	Carso Vitovska '98	♟♟	5
O	Chardonnay '90	♟♟♟	6
O	Chardonnay '94	♟♟♟	6
O	Sauvignon '91	♟♟♟	6
O	Sauvignon '92	♟♟♟	6
O	Carso Chardonnay '97	♟♟	5
O	Carso Malvasia '97	♟♟	5
O	Carso Sauvignon '97	♟♟	5
O	Carso Vitovska '97	♟♟	5
●	Carso Terrano '95	♟	4

O	COF Bianco Locum Nostrum '98	♟♟	4
O	COF Tocai Friulano '99	♟♟	3*
O	COF Chardonnay '99	♟	3
●	COF Merlot '98	♟	4
O	COF Pinot Grigio '99	♟	3
O	COF Sauvignon Sup. '99		3
●	COF Merlot '97	♟♟	4

FARRA D'ISONZO (GO)

FARRA D'ISONZO (GO)

BORGO CONVENTI
S.DA COLOMBARA, 13
34070 FARRA D'ISONZO (GO)
TEL. 0481/888004

CASA ZULIANI
VIA GRADISCA, 23
34070 FARRA D'ISONZO (GO)
TEL. 0481/888506

Gianni Vescovo is proud to point out how successfully his daughters Barbara (in sales and marketing) and Erica (in cellar and vineyard) have slotted into the estate's activities. Although reliability is occasionally an Achilles' heel, some of the Vescovo wines are now classics whose quality is assured. One such is the Chardonnay Colle Russian, from the vineyards of the same name at Farra. Fermentation was completed in barriques, where the wine was then aged with masterly skill. Its bright straw yellow is flecked with gold and green. The nose is intriguingly complex, hints of beeswax alternating with citrus, and the warm, soft palate still manages to be fresh as it leads through to the long, fruit-rich finish. Braida Nuova '97, the other flagship wine, is a Bordeaux blend with a stylish nose of red fruit and vanilla, as well as a milky note. Superbly balanced on the palate, it offers nicely judged weight, good structure and a barely perceptible twist of almond in the finish. After tasting the '97, we began to understand the success at the May 2000 auction of the '99, which is still in barrique. We'll be back in a couple of years for a final opinion. It would be fair to call the Sauvignon a typical Borgo Conventi wine. Its varietal aromas of red pepper and tomato leaf usher in a palate that is full-bodied and fresh at the same time before opening out into a long finish. Pear is prominent on the nose of the Tocai, together with a green note. Both return on the palate, which has appreciable length. The fresh, clean palate of the Collio Bianco earned it an honourable mention, which also went to the Chardonnay and Traminer Aromatico from the Isonza DOC zone that the winery releases under the competitively priced I Fiori label.

Bruna Zuliani's estate extends over 23 hectares, 16 of which are planted to vine in the Collio and Isonzo DOC zones. This winery continues to turn out excellent products that offer wonderful value for money. Emanuele Mian is in charge of production, and with Claudio Tomadin, who looks after sales and marketing, he heads a team that runs like clockwork, making about 100,000 bottles a year, mainly for sale abroad. The most successful wine is the Collio Bianco, from 50 percent malvasia fruit with the rest made up of sauvignon and pinot bianco. Its brilliant straw-yellow colour introduces a warm nose of apple and honey. These aromas return on the palate, which is polished, fresh-tasting, full-flavoured and long. Both the Collio and the Isonzo Chardonnays came very close to a second Glass. The Collio version has hints of apple over yeast and is elegantly fruity, full-flavoured and long on nose and palate. Its Isonzo stablemate is a rather fresher-tasting tipple, thanks to its more pronounced acidity, but it still manages to provide reasonable fullness on the palate. The bouquet of the Pinot Bianco Collio is quite outstanding, ranging from apple to mixed citrus juice. Delicately tangy on the palate, it develops attractively through to an inviting finish. Pear and apple aromas emerge in the Pinot Grigio Collio, especially in the lingering aftertaste, while its Collio cousin is more straightforward in structure but still well worth investigating. Finally, the Sauvignon Collio offers an alluring nose laced with peach, tea and medicinal herbs that are mirrored well on the palate. In short, a fresh-tasting wine with satisfying length.

● Braida Nuova '97		🍷🍷	6
○ Collio Chardonnay			
Colle Russian '98		🍷🍷	5
○ Collio Sauvignon '99		🍷🍷	4
○ Collio Tocai Friulano '99		🍷	4
○ Collio Bianco '99			4
○ Friuli Isonzo Chardonnay I Fiori '99			3
○ Friuli Isonzo Traminer Aromatico			
I Fiori '99			3
● Braida Nuova '91		🍷🍷🍷	6
● Braida Nuova '95		🍷🍷	6
○ Collio Chardonnay			
Colle Russian '97		🍷🍷	5
● Braida Nuova '96		🍷	6

○ Collio Bianco '99		🍷🍷	3*
○ Collio Chardonnay '99		🍷	3
○ Collio Pinot Bianco '99		🍷	3
○ Collio Pinot Grigio '99		🍷	3
○ Collio Sauvignon '99		🍷	3
○ Friuli Isonzo Chardonnay '99		🍷	3
○ Friuli Isonzo Pinot Grigio '99		🍷	3
○ Collio Tocai Friulano '99			3
○ Friuli Isonzo Sauvignon '99			3
● Collio Merlot Gospel '97		🍷🍷	4
● Collio Merlot Gospel '96		🍷	4

FARRA D'ISONZO (GO)

COLMELLO DI GROTTA

LUCIANA BENNATI
VIA GORIZIA, 133
34070 FARRA D'ISONZO (GO)
TEL. 0481/888445

When Luciana Bennati died, the Colmello di Grotta winery was inherited by her daughter Francesca Bortolotto, who immediately set about expanding the vineyards and enhancing the quality of the wines. Today, the estate has 21 hectares, equally distributed over the Collio and Isonzo DOC zones. But the wine we liked best was the only non-DOC product, the Rondon '97, a blend of 80 percent cabernet sauvignon and 20 percent merlot, aged in oak for over 18 months. This delicious red offers bramble on the nose before the muscular, full-flavoured palate unveils its structure and a finish adorned by impeccable tannins. Collio got the better of Isonzo by Two Glasses to One in the Chardonnay stakes. Its banana and apricot fruit emerge triumphantly despite a rich toastiness while the Isonzo version is clean and elegantly fresh. The two fresh-tasting Pinot Grigios are redolent of fruit salad, both scoring high in the One Glass band. The Isonzo's nose is more penetrating but the Collio has a more impressive palate. The Tocai Friulano also scored well, thanks to a rich complexity on the nose and an equally broad palate with hints of fruit and hay laced with acacia honey. In the Collio Bianco Rondon, oak-aged chardonnay fruit is to the fore but then the contribution of the stainless steel vinified sauvignon and pinot grigio comes through. Finally, the Collio Sauvignon offers varietal notes of elderflower and tomato leaf. In contrast, the Isonzo version flaunts a note of tobacco in the nose while fresh acidity and alcohol mingle unhurriedly on the palate.

○	Collio Bianco Rondon '99	🍷🍷	3*
○	Collio Chardonnay '99	🍷🍷	3*
○	Collio Tocai Friulano '99	🍷🍷	3*
●	Rondon '97	🍷🍷	4
○	Collio Pinot Grigio '99	🍷	3
○	Collio Sauvignon '99	🍷	3
○	Friuli Isonzo Chardonnay '99	🍷	3
○	Friuli Isonzo Pinot Grigio '99	🍷	3
○	Friuli Isonzo Sauvignon '99	🍷	3
●	Friuli Isonzo Cabernet Sauvignon '97	YY	3
●	Collio Merlot '97	Y	4

FARRA D'ISONZO (GO)

★ VINNAIOLI JERMANN

VIA MONTE FORTINO, 21
FRAZ. VILLANOVA
34070 FARRA D'ISONZO (GO)
TEL. 0481/888080

It's not often that you have the opportunity to taste a Vintage Tunina as outstanding as this '99. Obtained from chardonnay, sauvignon, picolit and other grapes, its brilliant straw yellow shimmers in the glass. The nose alludes to apple, honey, spring flowers, yeast, peach and other aromas in a sumptuous sequence that returns on the palate, whose mellow yet stylish structure is fresh, rich and crowned by a triumphantly long finish. Our Three Glass rating was the only possible conclusion. The '98 version of the same wine scored only a few marks lower. The gold-tinged colour leads in to a sweet, complex nose and a soft palate, where there is a note of fresh fruit and an attractive, lingering aftertaste. The Capo Martino '98 is a blend of pinot bianco and tocai grapes with malvasia and picolit. Its elegant aromas of melon, figs and banana precede fresh apple on the palate, where the fairly close-knit, well-sustained texture is complemented by a lingering finish. This year, Silvio is celebrating 25 years in viticulture and the wine he has dedicated to the occasion is a Pinot Grigio with faint copper highlights, obtained after a brief maceration on the skins. Bottle and label recall the '74 product. Elegant red delicious apple on the nose introduces a fresh-tasting palate with solid structure and a long, fruit-rich finish. The chardonnay-based Dreams '98 has a complex, fresh and velvet-smooth nose. Its soft attack on the palate precedes an attractively well-sustained progression. And to finish off, the Müller Thurgau offers stylish aromas and appealing drinkability on the palate, where fruit prevails over flowers.

○	Vintage Tunina '99	🍷🍷🍷	6
○	Capo Martino '98	🍷🍷	6
○	Müller Thurgau '99	🍷🍷	5
○	Pinot Grigio Special '99	🍷🍷	5
○	Vintage Tunina '98	🍷🍷	6
○	Were Dreams, Now It Is Just Wine! '98	🍷🍷	6
○	Chardonnay '99	🍷	4
○	Sauvignon '99	🍷	4
○	Traminer Aromatico '99	🍷	4
○	Vinnae '99	🍷	4
○	Capo Martino '97	YYY	6
○	Vintage Tunina '95	YYY	6
○	Vintage Tunina '96	YYY	6
○	Vintage Tunina '97	YYY	6

FARRA D'ISONZO (GO)

FARRA D'ISONZO (GO)

VITTORIO PUIATTI
VIA DANTE, 69
34070 FARRA D'ISONZO (GO)
TEL. 0481/888304

TENUTA VILLANOVA
VIA CONTESSA BERETTA, 29
FRAZ. VILLANOVA
34070 FARRA D'ISONZO (GO)
TEL. 0481/888593

It's not easy to find your way through the forest of wines proposed by Vittori Puiatti, the Friulian oenologist who has worked in various parts of Italy, including Tuscany, where he owns the lovely Casavecchia estate in the Chianti Classico DOC zone. In Friuli, Vittorio buys grapes from about 30 growers, as well as vinifying the grapes from his own vineyards. Fortunately, Vittorio's somewhat robustly assertive character is not reflected in his generally very elegant wines. His best product is the Collio Bianco '99, a blend of chardonnay, tocai friulano and sauvignon. Its sophisticated nose is dominated by golden delicious apple, which returns on the fruit-rich, well-balanced palate of this fresh-tasting and very long wine. A couple of points lower, but still well into the Two Glass range, is the Ribolla Gialla. It boasts a full, elegant nose of spring flowers, red delicious apple and yellow plums, which return on the frank, lingering palate. The Pinot Bianco style hinges on the golden delicious apple perceptible in the Puiatti version while the Chardonnay is striking in its complexity and structure. The house slogan is, "Save a tree, drink Puiatti" but a hint of wood might have enhanced even further the appeal of this wine. The Sauvignon is fresh and moderately varietal in style and the Pinot Grigio offers a rich, complex nose over a fairly straightforward palate. Vittorio's Cabernet Sauvignon '99 came close to winning Two Glasses for its cherry and crusty bread aromas and attractive balance on the palate. The Puiattino '99, a white from chardonnay, pinot bianco and tocai friulano fruit, is also intriguing. Apple and fruit salad prevail on the nose and the well-sustained palate has good structure and length.

This winery was founded in 1499 and extends over about 200 hectares in the adjacent Isonzo and Collio DOC zones. After completion of restructuring work in cellar and vineyards, the estate has now built superb conference facilities. For some time, Paolo Cora has been in charge, adopting a quality-first policy that last year produced a Three Glass result. This time round, that exploit was very nearly repeated with a beautifully made Malvasia dell'Isonzo. The nose discloses crisp apple with peach and apricot, flowers, herbs and pears that are echoed by the palate, which manages to balance fresh acidity and alcohol magnificently. Next on the Two Glass list was the Chardonnay Monte Cucco '98. Although vinified and aged in barriques, it reveals not a trace of toastiness, proposing instead varietal aromas of banana and apricot. These are joined on the palate by hints of yeast in a complex, soft structure. There is tomato leaf on the nose of the Sauvignon Monte Cucco '99. In contrast, the palate has hints of citrus and pineapple, its marked acidity remaining in perfect harmony with the alcohol. Brilliant in colour, the Ribolla Gialla Monte Cucco parades pronounced aromas of spring flowers and hawthorn that return on the full-flavoured palate before the wine signs off with a refreshing finish. The impressively stylish Tocai del Collio foregrounds apple aromas, its tempting flavour backed up by well-judged acidity right through to the long finish. The Fraja '95, a Bordeaux blend aged in barriques for 36 months, was released to coincide with the winery's 500th anniversary. Fascinating aromas dominated by red fruit tart and laced with bitter chocolate are followed by lovely fruit on the palate, where mellow tannins emerge in the finish.

O Collio Bianco '99	🍷🍷	5
O Collio Ribolla Gialla '99	🍷🍷	4
● Collio Cabernet Sauvignon '99	🍷	5
O Collio Chardonnay '99	🍷	4
O Collio Pinot Bianco '99	🍷	4
O Collio Pinot Grigio '99	🍷	4
O Collio Sauvignon '99	🍷	4
O Puiattino '99	🍷	2*
● Collio Merlot '97		5

O Collio Chardonnay Monte Cucco '98	🍷🍷	4
O Collio Ribolla Gialla Monte Cucco '99	🍷🍷	4
O Collio Sauvignon Monte Cucco '99	🍷🍷	4
O Collio Tocai Friulano '99	🍷🍷	3
● Fraja '95	🍷🍷	6
O Friuli Isonzo Malvasia Istriana '99	🍷🍷	3*
● Collio Rosso '97	🍷	3
O Friuli Isonzo Pinot Bianco '99	🍷	3
O Friuli Isonzo Pinot Grigio '99	🍷	3
O Menj Bianco '99	🍷	3
O Collio Chardonnay Monte Cucco '97	🍷🍷🍷	4
O Collio Sauvignon Monte Cucco '98	🍷🍷	4

GONARS (UD)

GORIZIA

DI LENARDO
VIA BATTISTI, 1
FRAZ. ONTAGNANO
33050 GONARS (UD)
TEL. 0432/928633

ATTEMS CONTE DOUGLAS
VIA GIULIO CESARE, 36/A
FRAZ. LUCINICO
34170 GORIZIA
TEL. 0481/390206 - 0481/888162

Massimo Di Lenardo has an ambition. He wants to show that premium-quality wines in Friuli don't have to come from hillslope vineyards. With his Tocai, he has all but proved his point. A traditionally solid product, the Di Lenardo Tocai came incredibly close to a Three Glass score. Its vibrant straw-yellow colour ushers in an impressive nose of well-balanced, pervasive aromas of almond, golden delicious apple and yeast. The entry on the palate is uncompromising, with plum and apple to the fore, following through with good breadth and plenty of length in the finish. The Chardonnay Woody ages in casks of American oak. A deep straw-yellow, its consistent toasty notes are nicely offset by pineapple and banana fruit. The creamy palate mirrors the banana of the nose, adding nuances of vanilla, before the lingering finish reveals attractively fresh acidity. The nose of the Sauvignon is varietal and intense, its red pepper and elderflower returning on the fresh, clean-tasting palate. What stands out about the Chardonnay Musque is the well-made style and the prominent notes of banana and pear. The Di Lenardo Pinot Grigio is a high-volume product with initial hints of ripe fruit salad. Then fresh aromas of green apple emerge before the palate impresses with its complexity and freshness, the long finish again hinting at green apple. The Ronco Nolè is a blend of merlot, cabernet franc and sauvignon fruit that is then aged in oak. Although the vintage was unexceptional, it offers a pleasant entry on the nose, where vanilla and milky coffee mingle with ripe red fruit. These aromas return on the palate, which is, however, a little lean. Finally, the sauvignon-based Lis Maris is a very drinkable white.

It was the wish of Attems Conte Douglas, for many years chair of the Consorzio Collio, that his daughter Virginia, who has a degree in modern literature, should take over the historic family cellar with Fabio Coser as consultant. The estate comprises more than 30 hectares of vineyards in the Collio, with one or two more in the Isonzo DOC zone. Annual production is about 170,000 bottles. For some time, the Conte Douglas winery has been expanding its range of labels with the aim of promoting particular vineyard selections and creating its own crus. The most recent vintage could not be called outstanding since none of the cellar's wines obtained a Two Glass rating but the overall quality of the wines listed below is admirable. There are notes of ripe peaches and apricots on the nose of the Malvasia '99. Its coherent, well-sustained palate makes it an excellent accompaniment for fish and seafood. The Tocai Friulano '99 won a high One Glass score for its intense, sweet, alcohol-rich nose of pear and almond, which is followed by a full-bodied, satisfyingly long palate. There are faint hints of onion skin in the colour of the Pinot Grigio Ronco Pelicans, whose nose of warm apple is complemented by an appealingly tangy palate. The warm weather in '99 has given the vintage's Merlot '99 a nose of luscious ripe cherry, mulberry and plums while red fruit comes through in the mouth. This is a velvet-smooth, mouth-filling wine that is in no hurry to sign off. The Collio Bianco Vintage Castel Pubrida '99, a blend of tocai, malvasia and riesling, is still very young but will improve in the cellar. Over-emphatic acidity knocked points off the score of the Sauvignon Ronco Pelicans, which does, however, offer an attractive nose.

O	Friuli Grave Chardonnay Woody '99	🍷🍷	3
O	Friuli Grave Tocai Friulano '99	🍷🍷	2*
O	Friuli Grave Chardonnay Musque '99	🍷	3
O	Friuli Grave Pinot Grigio '99	🍷	3
O	Friuli Grave Sauvignon Blanc '99	🍷	3
O	Lis Maris	🍷	3
●	Ronco Nolè '98	🍷	3
●	Friuli Grave Cabernet '99		3
●	Friuli Grave Merlot '99		3
O	Friuli Grave Pinot Bianco '99		3
●	Friuli Grave Refosco P. R. '99		3
●	Ronco Nolè '97	🍷🍷	3

O	Collio Malvasia '99	🍷	4
●	Collio Merlot '99	🍷	4
O	Collio Pinot Grigio Ronco Pelicans '99	🍷	4
O	Collio Sauvignon Ronco Pelicans '99	🍷	4
O	Collio Tocai Friulano '99	🍷	3
O	Collio Bianco Vintage Castel Pubrida '99		4
O	Collio Riesling Italico '99		4
●	Collio Cabernet Franc Ronco Trebes '98	🍷	4
●	Collio Rosso Vintage Castel Pubrida '98	🍷	4

GORIZIA

GORIZIA

FIEGL
LOC. LENZUOLO BIANCO, 1
FRAZ. OSLAVIA
34170 GORIZIA
TEL. 0481/31072

LA CASTELLADA
FRAZ. OSLAVIA, 1
34170 GORIZIA
TEL. 0481/33670

The '99 vintage was even more difficult than expected. Anyone who failed to take special care during vinification will have been heavily penalized. But brothers, Alessio, Giuseppe and Rinaldo actually managed to improve their scores over '98, even though the potential for significant further improvement is there for the taking. It was the sauvignon, tocai, pinot bianco and ribolla-based Leopold Blanc that stood out in the Fiegl range for its full-bodied and intriguingly complex structure in a palate in total harmony with the nose. Definitely one for the cellar. It finished just ahead of its namesake, the merlot and cabernet franc Leopold Rouge, which has notes of red currant and pot pourri. There is plenty of alcohol but the palate is a little lean and bitterish because of the very assertive tannins. The Chardonnay easily merited One Glass. Pale, fresh and elegant, it is a trim, well-balanced and very stylish wine. The following wines are also very well-managed. The Ribolla Gialla is perhaps a little one-dimensional but it offers fair weight on the palate as well as the usual dry, acidic varietal notes mingling with green apple. The Pinot Grigio has a minerally nose laced with pear and an equally classic dry, fresh-tasting palate with good balance. Its stablemate, the Pinot Bianco, is more attractive in the mouth than on the nose, and is backed up by substantial alcohol and reasonable thrust on the palate. Then came the Sauvignon, a wine that has had to face criticism at some tastings but which nonetheless is a well-typed, skilfully made product. Finally, the Fiegl Tocai was only worth a mention but here we would refer the reader to our initial comments.

Renewal is in the air at the estate run by the Bensa brothers but there is also an awareness that it takes time to find a new point of equilibrium. However, even if strategies are being reviewed, there will be no compromising on quality at this winery, which always wins a large collection of Glasses for very few wines. Nor will there be any corner-cutting on their divine Bianco, a wine that is always at the pinnacle of its category. This year, diehard disciples of the absolute should take careful note of the almost impossible to find '98, which is heaven in a glass. Its aroma of herbs and flowers infused in alcohol leads in to a restrained front palate that soon acquires warmth and power without ever compromising on fullness of flavour or balance. Three Glasses for a masterpiece of potency and harmony. As usual, the La Castellada Chardonnay scored well. Its vibrant straw yellow, suggesting concentration and silky smoothness, ushers in a nose where tropical fruit is flanked by hints of butter and vanilla. Soft and mouth-filling on entry, the rich, mellow palate echoes the nose as it progresses, backed up by attractive acidity. The La Castellada Sauvignon is another wine that should be in every wine-lover's cellar. Elegant and soft, yet never submissive, its milky aromas mingle with plum, rue and red pepper. There was also a triumphant confirmation for the Rosso, a Bordeaux blend with a nose of California prunes that has generous fruit on the palate, where acidity and tannins are kept well under control in an excellent balance. The finish is long and the ever-present fruit emerges yet again. The Ribolla is a little below par, albeit only because the Bensa brothers set themselves such high standards. It has too little fruit and too much wood but it just goes to show that you can't win them all.

O Leopold Cuvée Blanc '98	♔♔	4
O Collio Chardonnay '99	♔	3
O Collio Pinot Bianco '99	♔	3
O Collio Pinot Grigio '99	♔	3
O Collio Ribolla Gialla '99	♔	3
O Collio Sauvignon '99	♔	3
● Leopold Cuvée Rouge '95	♔	5
O Collio Tocai Friulano '99		3
● Leopold Cuvée Rouge '94	♔	5

O Collio Bianco della Castellada '98	♔♔♔	6
O Collio Chardonnay '98	♔♔	6
● Collio Rosso '95	♔♔	6
O Collio Sauvignon '98	♔♔	6
O Collio Ribolla Gialla '98	♔	6
O Bianco della Castellada '92	♔♔♔	6
O Bianco della Castellada '94	♔♔♔	6
O Bianco della Castellada '95	♔♔♔	6
O Collio Chardonnay '94	♔♔♔	6
O Collio Sauvignon '93	♔♔♔	6
O Bianco della Castellada '97	♔♔	6
O Collio Ribolla Gialla '97	♔♔	6
O Collio Sauvignon '97	♔♔	6
● Rosso della Castellada '94	♔♔	6

GORIZIA

GRADISCA D'ISONZO (GO)

PRIMOSIC
LOC. MADONNINA DI OSLAVIA, 3
34170 GORIZIA
TEL. 0481/535153

MARCO FELLUGA
VIA GORIZIA, 121
34072 GRADISCA D'ISONZO (GO)
TEL. 0481/99164 - 0481/92237

Things are humming on the Primosic estate, what with cellar extensions, replanting in the vineyards, with the usual angst over what varieties to go for, and above all the decision to delay until next year release of the new wines, which are adjudged to be outstanding but not yet ready for the market. These are not easily taken decisions, and deserve our respectful admiration. We shall look forward confidently, if impatiently, for the new selections, certain in the knowledge that the wait will be worthwhile. In the meantime, we sampled the Collio Bianco Klin and the Rosso Riserva, two excellent wines that offer the opportunity to appreciate the winemaking skills of the Primosic family. Collio Bianco Klin is a blend of chardonnay, sauvignon and ribolla fermented in new barriques, where it also matures before bottle-ageing. It has a pervasive, lingering aroma of fruit but lacks sufficient structure to take the wood. In contrast, the Rosso Riserva is much more convincing. This merlot-based wine has a vibrant ruby red colour and a nose of dried flowers, liqueur plums and pinewood. The soft, warm palate has good thrust. Tannins and tartaric acid are attractively balanced and there is reasonable length in a finish where fruit is again to the fore.

The Fellugas have left an indelible mark on winemaking in Friuli and the name takes your mind inevitably to the Collio. The Marco Felluga winery is the nerve centre of a production and sales organization that combines big numbers with even bigger wines. The most interesting product is the Carantan, a Bordeaux blend that can stay the course with the best of them. An alluringly complex and superbly drinkable wine, it alternates fruit aromas with autumn leaves, underpinning the palate with wonderful texture that still needs a little time to give its best. The Merlot is another great wine. Although the colour is not especially remarkable, the palate is warm, long, enticingly tannic and laced with delicious vanilla. The third Felluga red, the Cabernet, hints discreetly at notes of grass, accompanied by yeast and fruit tart. Unfortunately, the palate wavers, after a very promising attack. Leaving aside the reds and wines from previous vintages, the top scorer among the whites is an exciting Tocai. It's a serious wine in the classic style, free of rough edges or weak spots, and is flanked by a range of well-managed products. The Chardonnay offers apple and yeast on the palate, progressing from sweet notes to fresh-tasting fruit with a certain lack of thrust. The Molamatta, a blend of tocai, ribolla and pinot bianco, is fruit-rich and fragrant with good alcohol and a fresh, sinewy texture. The Pinot Grigio is clean and coherent, albeit with relatively little to say for itself. The Ribolla unveils notes of tobacco and broom in a dry, almondy palate. Finally, the Sauvignon is last only because the wines are in alphabetical order. Sweet and creamy on the nose, it offers an enticing varietal palate that echoes the aromas of the bouquet.

● Collio Rosso Ris. '97	▼▼	5
○ Collio Bianco Klin '97	▼	5
○ Collio Chardonnay Gmajne '98	▼▼	4
● Collio Merlot Ris. '95	▼▼	5
○ Collio Picolit Ris. '95	▼▼	6
○ Collio Ribolla Gialla Gmajne '98	▼▼	4
○ Collio Sauvignon Gmajne '98	▼▼	4
● Collio Merlot Ris. '96	▼	5

● Carantan '97	▼▼	6
● Collio Merlot '98	▼▼	4
○ Collio Tocai Friulano '99	▼▼	4
○ Collio Bianco Molamatta '99	▼	4
● Collio Cabernet '98	▼	4
○ Collio Chardonnay '99	▼	4
○ Collio Pinot Grigio '99	▼	4
○ Collio Ribolla Gialla '99	▼	4
○ Collio Sauvignon '99	▼	4
● Carantan '96	▼▼	6
○ Molamatta '98	▼	4

GRADISCA D'ISONZO (GO)   MANZANO (UD)

SANT'ELENA
VIA GASPARINI, 1
34072 GRADISCA D'ISONZO (GO)
TEL. 0481/92388

BANDUT - GIORGIO COLUTTA
VIA ORSARIA, 32
33044 MANZANO (UD)
TEL. 0432/740315

The Sant'Elena winery has made a welcome entry into the Guide. Naples-born Dominic Nocerino, who a quarter of a century ago moved to the States, where he imports wines, has been the sole owner of the estate since 1997. He has called in Maurizio Drascek to manage the vineyards and winemaking, with Franco Bernabei as consultant, and the cellars have been completely renovated. Dominic is concentrating on five varieties which are sold under only four labels, so that he can turn out serious quantities of each type. Total production hovers around 130,000 bottles. There are 16.5 hectares on the estate, which rents a further 12. Most lie in the Isonzo DOC zone but there are some parcels in the Collio. In general, the vineyards are planted at a minimum of 5,000 vines per hectare. The Sant'Elena reds are all blends of cabernet sauvignon and merlot, differing in the provenance of the fruit and ageing technique used. For example, Dominic's flagship red, the Tato, spends almost two years in French barriques. The '97 has a deep colour and a fruit-rich, creamy nose. Entry on the palate is fresh and the progression well-sustained, with notes of cherry, mulberry, wild berry fruit and spices. The substantial body is rounded off by a dry finish. The Ròs di Ròl '98 was aged in large casks of Slavonian oak and flaunts a nose dominated by ripe cherry. The soft, clean-tasting, elegant palate has the merest hint of spice and impeccable balance. The nose of the Pinot Grigio is a subtle blend of apple with nuances of honey. The buttery palate has a rich, well-rounded entry before the fresh fruit comes through to linger attractively on the long finish. Finally, the chardonnay and sauvignon Bianco JN impresses with its full, warm palate.

Giorgio Colutta continues the work of getting a winery, created after the break-up of a historic Friulian estate, back on its feet. His plans include the introduction of cellar technology to exploit to the full improvements made in the field and they are being implemented with the help of Marco Simonit, a young vineyard technician who has clear ideas and a solid track record. Riesling and müller thurgau will no longer be produced as monovarietals and new vineyards are to be planted at 5,000 vines per hectare. We particularly like the Bianco Nojâr (the name means "walnut tree"), obtained from a blend of pinot bianco and riesling renano. It has an enticing aroma of red delicious apple which is admirably mirrored on the rich, lingering palate, and there is just enough acidity to perk up the finish. Freshness is also the hallmark of the Tocai Friulano, which proffers apple and spring flowers on the nose, to which the well-sustained, velvety palate adds attractive green notes. The portion of the Refosco dal Peduncolo Rosso that was aged in 15-hectolitre casks and barriques lends a note of tobacco to the variety's trademark spice. The same aromas return on the fresh-tasting palate, which has reasonable length and tannins that are discreetly enhanced by acidity. The tannins in the Cabernet Sauvignon are much more assertive but the red fruit and acidity provide a lovely balance. On the nose, the wine is pervasive and redolent of hay, spices and medicinal herbs. Vinified exclusively in stainless steel, the Chardonnay tempts with a polished style and freshness on nose and palate. And a well-earned mention goes to the Merlot, Cabernet and Selenard, a blend of schioppettino, cabernet sauvignon and refosco.

●	Friuli Isonzo Ròs di Ròl '98	♈♈	5
●	Friuli Isonzo Tato. '97	♈♈	5
○	Pinot Grigio '99	♈♈	3*
○	Bianco JN '98	♈	4

○	COF Bianco Nojâr '99	♈	4
●	COF Cabernet Sauvignon '99	♈	3
○	COF Chardonnay '99	♈	3
●	COF Refosco P. R. '99	♈	3
○	COF Tocai Friulano '99	♈	3
●	COF Cabernet '99		3
●	COF Merlot '99		3
●	COF Rosso Selenard '98		5
○	COF Sauvignon '99		3
●	COF Rosso Selenard '97	♈	5

MANZANO (UD)

ROSA BOSCO
VIA ABATE COLONNA, 20
LOC. ROSAZZO
33044 MANZANO (UD)
TEL. 0432/751522

We are delighted to welcome Rosetta Bosco to our select band of premium producers. And our satisfaction is redoubled because last year, our assessment of Rosa's first "solo" wine was quite uninfluenced by our sincere affection for its maker. It was a Sauvignon that many wine critics praised to the skies, some even managing to ignore the massive oak-derived toastiness that, in our opinion, eclipsed its many merits. Rosa respected our decision while we had no doubt that her many years' experience at the Dorigo winery would guarantee a second vintage worthy of her winemaking skills. That conviction is confirmed by her superb Sauvignon Blanc '99. The pervasive, beautifully balanced nose releases delicate notes of peach, which are mirrored on the fresh, well-structured palate. The hint of sweet wood lends the wine allure and augurs well for the future. Donato Lanati's consultancy is evident above all in the Boscorosso '98, from merlot harvested in the second half of October and selected bunch by bunch after the heavy rain that preceded the vintage. Aged without hurry in oak, it reveals good concentration on the nose, where hints of roast coffee and warm berry fruit are laced with raisiny notes. The firm attack soon broadens out in an astonishing range of fruit, confectioner's cream and spices in the elegant, warm and silky palate. This was very nearly a Three Glass wine.

MANZANO (UD)

WALTER FILIPUTTI
P.ZZA DELL'ABBAZIA, 15
LOC. ROSAZZO
33044 MANZANO (UD)
TEL. 0432/759429

Walter Filiputti is a man who has difficulty accepting the time-horizons of winemaking and agriculture. Our assessments may not always be equal to his aspirations but the general picture is encouraging. This year, two of Walter's reds stole the show, his Filip di Filip '98 and the Ronco dei Domenicani '97. The former is a blend of merlot and cabernet franc with a concentrated nose of wild berries and spices that return on the palate. Tannic and well-structured, it unveils a cornucopia of fruity notes in the mouth. The Ronco dei Domenicani '97 is obtained from cabernet sauvignon blended with 15 percent of local varieties. Barrique-aged for 18 months, it is a strikingly youthful wine with prunes and raspberry prevalent on the nose and a full-bodied palate with a rich entry, plenty of structure and fruit, and very good length. The very successful Sauvignon Suvignis starts with crisp aromas of elderflower, followed up by well-sustained freshness on the palate, where hints of citrus offset the glycerine sweetness and robust alcohol. The Bianco Poiesis, a white from chardonnay and tocai fruit with a little picolit, melds notes of sweet Dutch pipe tobacco with ripe pear and a deliciously close-knit texture. The Filiputti Pinot Grigio has a stunning nose that foregrounds fruit salad and pot pourri. Next came the Ronco degli Agostiniani, a blend of chardonnay and pinot bianco aged in half-barriques. Unfortunately, the prevailing aromas of top of the milk and vanilla hinder appreciation of the fruit underneath. The Ronco del Monastero, obtained from tocai grapes with a proportion of sauvignon, is well-rounded on the palate, where notes of melon and peach come through. The last wine we tasted was the polished, lingering Ribolla Gialla.

● COF Boscorosso '98		🍷🍷	5
○ COF Sauvignon Blanc '99		🍷🍷	5

○ COF Bianco Poiesis '99		🍷🍷	4
● COF Rosso			
Ronco dei Domenicani '97		🍷🍷	6
○ COF Sauvignon Suvignis '99		🍷🍷	4
● Filip di Filip '98		🍷🍷	5
○ COF Bianco			
Ronco degli Agostiniani '98		🍷	6
○ COF Bianco			
Ronco del Monastero '99		🍷	4
○ Pinot Grigio '99		🍷	3
○ COF Ribolla Gialla '99		🍷	4
● Broili di Filip '98			3
○ COF Ramandolo '98			5
● COF 906			
Ronco dei Benedettini '97		🍷🍷	6

MANZANO (UD)

LE VIGNE DI ZAMÒ
VIA ABATE CORRADO, 4
LOC. ROSAZZO
33044 MANZANO (UD)
TEL. 0432/759693

Le Vigne di Zamò is the label that brings together the separately run cellars of brothers Pierluigi and Silvano Zamò. Last year's success has been repeated but this time with a classic Friulian wine, the Tocai Vigne Cinquant'Anni. Obtained from very old vines with a minuscule yield, it stands out as a great product even as you raise the glass, which releases clear notes of pear and almond on the nose. Confirmation comes from the opulent structure on the palate. Luxuriously rich, intensely fruity, full-bodied and tangy, it signs off with the variety's typical almond twist. The Picolit Riserva '95 is another superlative product. Its old gold colour derives from fruit that underwent slow raisining. In fact, you would almost think the wine came from the some island off the south of Italy. The nose regales you with candied citrus peel, almond paste, nuts, walnutskin and liqueur apricots while the mellow, sweet and very rich palate offers lingering notes of pipe tobacco and raisined grapes. The Sauvignon is very well made. Its varietal tomato leaf aromas are stylish and concentrated, leading in to a fresh-tasting palate that mirrors the nose, revealing laudable structure and good length. The Ribolla is more impressive on the palate than the nose. Indeed, in the mouth it is full, rich and warm with all the complexity of this vintage. By now, Ronco dei Roseti has become a classic and the '96 turns out to be superior to the '95. It's a Bordeaux blend to which some native Friulian varieties have been added and which is aged slowly in the wood and the bottle. On the nose, the '96 is reminiscent of printer's ink, alcohol and elderflower. The palate is stylish and well-structured, with pronounced fruit. Although drinking nicely now, the wine is still developing. The Pignolo, a native variety that will age superbly, was marked down for its roughish tannins. But Franco Bernabei, the oenologist who put this great range together, deserves our hearty applause.

MANZANO (UD)

RONCHI DI MANZANO
VIA ORSARIA, 42
33044 MANZANO (UD)
TEL. 0432/740718

Roberta Borghese's wines put this estate at the top of the list in terms of quality. The 45 hectares are distributed over the hills at Manzano and Rosazzo. Most of the winemaking, however, is done at the cellars in Ronchi di Manzano, where all the wines go into the wood. Again this year, Ronchi di Manzano was in the running for Three Glasses, this time with the Tocai Friulano Superiore. A complex, elegant wine with a delicious nose of pear, apple and pipe tobacco, it has serious structure on the well-sustained, full-bodied and very long palate. A wine with attitude. The cellar's sweet whites are always a delight. The Verduzzo Friulano Ronc di Rosazzo, with its old gold colour, has a nose reminiscent of very ripe apricots and apples. In the mouth, almond milk, figs, honey and sultanas emerge in a sweet, beautifully balanced palate. The Rosazzo Picolit puts style first, its fresh, fruit-rich aromas revealing excellent concentration. The sweet, buttery palate has intriguing complexity and outstanding balance. Several of the reds were just as good, beginning with the Cabernet Sauvignon. Its varietal aromas have rich overtones of alcohol and mulberry while the texture on the palate is firm, the wood well-judged and the length remarkable. The Merlot '98 has a broad, meaty nose, accompanied by aromas deriving from large oak casks used for ageing. On the palate, there is great structure, marvellous fruit and only slightly metallic tannins that will soon mellow out. The red Le Zuccule '97 blend keeps red fruit to the fore over toastiness but really lets its hair down on the palate, which is concentrated, alcohol-rich and deliciously long. The long list of One Glass wines includes two that came close to winning a second, the Cabernet Franc and the Refosco '98.

O	COF Tocai Friulano		
	Vigne Cinquant'Anni '99	♟♟♟	5
O	COF Picolit Ris. '95	♟♟	6
O	COF Ribolla Gialla '99	♟♟	4
●	COF Ronco dei Roseti '96	♟♟	6
O	COF Sauvignon '99	♟♟	4
O	COF Bianco Vino di Là '99	♟	3
●	COF Merlot '98	♟	4
O	COF Pinot Grigio '99	♟	4
●	COF Pinot Nero '95	♟	5
●	COF Ronco dei Roseti '95	♟	6
O	COF Ronco delle Acacie '97	♟	5
O	COF Tocai Friulano '99	♟	4
●	Pignolo '96	♟	6
●	Ronco dei Roseti '94	♟♟♟	6

●	COF Cabernet Sauvignon '98	♟♟	3
●	COF Merlot '98	♟♟	3*
O	COF Rosazzo Picolit		
	Ronc di Rosazzo '98	♟♟	5
O	COF Tocai Friulano Sup. '99	♟♟	3*
O	COF Verduzzo Friulano		
	Ronc di Rosazzo '98	♟♟	3*
●	Le Zuccule '97	♟♟	4
●	COF Cabernet Franc '98	♟	3
●	COF Merlot Ronc di Subule '98	♟	4
O	COF Pinot Grigio '99	♟	3
●	COF Refosco P. R. '98	♟	3
O	COF Rosazzo Bianco '99	♟	4
O	COF Sauvignon '99	♟	3
●	COF Merlot Ronc di Subule '96	♟♟♟	5

MANZANO (UD)

MANZANO (UD)

RONCO DELLE BETULLE
VIA ABATE COLONNA, 24
LOC. ROSAZZO
33044 MANZANO (UD)
TEL. 0432/740547

TORRE ROSAZZA
LOC. POGGIOBELLO, 12
33044 MANZANO (UD)
TEL. 0432/750180

All around us are the hills that encircle the abbey of Rosazzo in a unique embrace of history, religion, secular countryside traditions and viticulture going back at least 2,000 years. And the ten hectares of terraced vineyards that comprise Ivana Adami's heaven on earth produce very characterful wines. We'll start with the Narciso Bianco, a blend of barrique-aged pinot bianco and sauvignon with unoaked tocai. Mouth-filling and rich in ripe fruit mingling with confectioner's cream, it offers a fresh, flowery progression sustained by good alcohol. Then there's the Tocai, a textbook interpretation of a classic Friulian wine. The vibrant straw-yellow colour is tinged with greenish highlights, introducing a nose of wistaria and rennet apple. Acidity plays second fiddle to the robust alcohol but the palate is still very lively, finishing on a note of spring flowers. Neither is the Ribolla a wine to ignore. A sprightly, fragrant wine with moderate softness, its has a delightful after-aroma of plum and yeast. The Narciso Rosso is obtained from merlot and cabernet fruit with a yield of about one and a half kilograms per plant, which is subsequently macerated for four weeks and aged in barriques for 14 months. On the nose, it reveals light toastiness, fresh, juicy fruit and appealing spice. The softness of the merlot is for the most part sufficient to offset the tannins but at times the palate is rendered a little too lean by the clash between acidity and astringency on the one hand and supple sweetness on the other.

As we duly take note of the improvement in wines from Torre Rosazza, we cannot help noticing that agronomist Claudio Flaborea and oenologist Giovanni Tomadoni have been joined by Donato Lanati, the famous Piedmontese consultant who is no stranger to Friuli. The estate extends over 80 hectares on the slope to the north of Rosazzo and produces 180,000 bottles under 15 labels. The stars this year are the Sauvignon '99 and the Verduzzo Friulano '98. The Sauvignon has wonderful length, with notes of citron on the nose and a palate where tomato leaf and elderflower come together against a backdrop of citrus. The Sauvignon Silterra '98 has an equally attractive nose of vanilla and elderflower but its acidity makes it leanish on the palate. The Verduzzo is the colour of old gold and has hints of apricot and liqueur fruit. A very sweet wine, it releases a vast range of aromas where figs and dried apricots prevail. The nose of the Merlot l'Altromerlot '97 is reminiscent of wild berry tart, to which the palate adds tones of cherry over a rich, smooth texture. Next, the Chardonnay reveals a varietal range of aromas, including yeast, crusty bread and tropical fruit, following through well from nose to palate. There are pale copper tinges in the colour of the Pinot Grigio. Notes of mineral and pear, and decent acidity, complete the picture. On the nose, the Ribolla Gialla marries spring flowers, fresh fruit and ripe yellow plum in a complex nose that is faithfully reflected on the palate. The wood of the excellent barrique-aged Cabernet Sauvignon Ronco della Torre '97 still tends to mask the intriguing fruit but the finish is attractively long.

O	COF Rosazzo Narciso Bianco '98	▾▾	5
●	COF Rosazzo Narciso Rosso '97	▾▾	6
O	COF Rosazzo Ribolla Gialla '99	▾▾	4
O	COF Tocai Friulano '99	▾▾	4
●	Narciso Rosso '94	▾▾▾	5
●	COF Rosazzo Narciso Rosso '96	▾▾	5
●	Franconia '97	▾▾	4
O	COF Rosazzo Narciso Bianco '97	▾	5

O	COF Sauvignon '99	▾▾	3
O	COF Verduzzo Friulano '98	▾▾	4
●	COF Cabernet Sauvignon Ronco della Torre '97	▾	5
O	COF Chardonnay '99	▾	3
●	COF Merlot l'Altromerlot '97	▾	5
O	COF Pinot Grigio '99	▾	3
O	COF Ribolla Gialla '99	▾	3
O	COF Sauvignon Silterra '98	▾	4
O	COF Pinot Bianco '99		3
●	COF Refosco P. R. '98		3
●	COF Merlot l'Altromerlot '95	▾▾	5
●	COF Merlot l'Altromerlot '96	▾▾	5

MARIANO DEL FRIULI (GO) MARIANO DEL FRIULI (GO)

EDDI LUISA
VIA CORMONS, 19
FRAZ. CORONA
34070 MARIANO DEL FRIULI (GO)
TEL. 0481/69680

MASUT DA RIVE
VIA MANZONI, 82
34070 MARIANO DEL FRIULI (GO)
TEL. 0481/69200

You can't help noting the pride and enthusiasm with which Eddi Luisa talks about his winery. He made a triumphant entry into the 2000 Guide and confirmed his place this year. Behind the success lie densely planted vineyards, with 5,500 vines per hectare, and the hard work in the cellar of sons Michele and Davide, who may be young but are skilled agronomists and winemakers. Although the estate is in a red wine area, and almost all Eddi's standard-label reds earned One Glass, it is the Pinot Grigio that stands out. Obtained from 11-year-old vines, it was vinified without the skins and left on the lees, with frequent stirring, until March. A green-flecked straw-yellow colour ushers in a typical nose of gunflint, red delicious apple and oily, almost buttery, notes. The palate is very soft while the acid-rich finish is very refreshing. But now for the reds. The Cabernet Sauvignon mingles prunes and hay with faintly smoky notes. The entry on the palate has plenty of fruit, progressing with warmth and good length over tannins that still have a little way to go. Moderate breadth and enticing fruit characterize the Cabernet Franc while the Refosco offers an outstanding balance of fruit and tannins as well as varietal fragrances of pepper, tobacco, and mulberry. The only offering from the I Ferretti range, aged in small oak casks, was a Chardonnay. Alluring on the nose, where the oak mingles attractively with ripe banana, it falls away slightly on the palate, which nonetheless mirrors the nose well.

Fabrizio Gallo is a young producer and oenologist whose winery continues to impress. After his inclusion for the first time in last year's Guide, he continues to cut the mustard, particularly with his reds, despite the less than wonderful '98 vintage in Friuli. Fabrizio's Merlot releases aromas of vanilla and talcum powder that give way to mulberry and cherry, then coffee and tobacco that continues through to the finish. The palate lingers, reprising the mulberry and coffee of the nose and adding rich chocolate. There were Two very good Glasses for the Pinot Bianco as well. Its notes of yellow peach, melon and citrus on the nose are rounded off by sweet almond before coming back on the palate, which signs off with a fresh-tasting, flower-themed finish. The second-label Chardonnay is fruity on the citrus-nuanced nose. The attack is almost solar in its determination and the leisurely finish is dominated by yellow peach. The Maurùs, fermented in new barriques, has a similarly convincing structure, enhanced by oak-derived vanilla and milky coffee that are nicely offset by the fruit. The clean nose of the Cabernet '98 offers aromas of wild berries and vanilla. On the palate, the problematic vintage makes itself felt after a stunning entry for there is little breadth, even though the finish is long and generous with its mulberry-dominated fruit. The Sauvignon is stylish and elegant, with nice acacia blossom and white peach on the nose. On the palate, tomato and pear emerge from the delightful fruit and the finish is reasonably long. This is the first year for the red Semidis blend of equal proportions of cabernet franc, merlot and cabernet sauvignon. Its alluring nose of Peruvian bark, plums and wild rose is more tempting than the palate, which is nonetheless well-managed and sustained, with lingering notes of plum.

O Friuli Isonzo Pinot Grigio '99	￥￥	3*
● Friuli Isonzo Cabernet Franc '99	￥	3*
● Friuli Isonzo Cabernet Sauvignon '99	￥	3
O Friuli Isonzo Chardonnay I Ferretti '99	￥	4
● Friuli Isonzo Refosco P. R. '99	￥	3
O Friuli Isonzo Sauvignon '99	￥	3
O Friuli Isonzo Chardonnay '99		3
● Friuli Isonzo Merlot '99		3
O Friuli Isonzo Pinot Bianco '99		3
O Friuli Isonzo Tocai Friulano '99		3
● Friuli Isonzo Cabernet Franc		
I Ferretti '97	￥￥	4
● Friuli Isonzo Merlot I Ferretti '97	￥￥	4
● Friuli Isonzo Refosco P. R.		
I Ferretti '97	￥￥	4

O Friuli Isonzo Chardonnay '99	￥￥	3*
O Friuli Isonzo Chardonnay		
Maurùs '98	￥￥	4
● Friuli Isonzo Merlot '98	￥￥	3*
O Friuli Isonzo Pinot Bianco '99	￥￥	3*
● Friuli Isonzo Cabernet Franc '98	￥	3
O Friuli Isonzo Pinot Grigio '99	￥	3
● Friuli Isonzo Rosso Semidis '98	￥	4
O Friuli Isonzo Sauvignon '99	￥	3
O Friuli Isonzo Tocai Friulano '99	￥	3
● Friuli Isonzo Cabernet		
Sauvignon '97	￥￥	3
● Friuli Isonzo Merlot '97	￥￥	3

MARIANO DEL FRIULI (GO) NIMIS (UD)

★ VIE DI ROMANS
LOC. VIE DI ROMANS, 1
34070 MARIANO DEL FRIULI (GO)
TEL. 0481/69600

DARIO COOS
VIA PESCIA, 1
LOC. RAMANDOLO
33045 NIMIS (UD)
TEL. 0432/790320

None of Gianfranco Gallo's wines earned Three Glasses this year but two took part in the final selections. We want to point out, though, that the wines in question both unfurled a stunningly complex range of aromas on the nose. The best wines this time round were the Pinot Grigio and the Vieris, the former revealing milky notes and a floral bouquet while the latter foregrounds sweet, ripe peach and apricot fruit. Both are dry and well-rounded on the palate, where they can offer impressive weight. The Pinot Grigio is sweet, minerally and composite while the Vieris is more sinewy, vegetal and focused. The Piere revealed a certain discrepancy between acidity and sweetness that left the mid palate somewhat lean. This may well have been due to the period when we were tasting. The panel preferred the stainless steel-vinified version of the Chardonnay for its peach and tangerine nose, almost sweet entry on the palate and seamlessly coherent progression. The Vie di Romans may have rich aromas of toastiness and banana as well as milky notes but it fails to deliver the goods on the palate. As ever, the Flors di Uis is polished and very pleasant. Obtained from malvasia and chardonnay, vinified together after malolactic fermentation, and riesling, its balance, heady aromas and tangy freshness make it a wine that will have you holding out your glass for more. The Voos dai Ciamps '97 Bordeaux blend is very good indeed. A mature, self-possessed wine with loads of character, it is definitely one for the cellar.

Ramandolo is the subzone of the Colli Orientali del Friuli that has been home to the verduzzo friulano grape for centuries. The vineyards are almost invariably to be found on steep slopes and are often protected by netting against the hail that is a constant problem in the area. Dario Coos produces the best verduzzo di Ramandolo because he refuses to plan on the basis of commercial considerations but instead waits until his products are ready for release. Dario's variations on the basic theme of verduzzo di Ramandolo, a grape that although white, has a thick skin and a tannin content to rival many red varieties, have prompted him to delay the release of his barrique-aged and dried grape wines. That leaves us with only the stainless steel vinified Il Longhino to review for the Guide. It has an old gold colour and a concentrated nose of dried figs, hay, dried flowers, apple and liqueur apricots. Sweet on the palate, it regales you with attractively stylish aromas that echo the nose perfectly. All in all, an extremely alluring wine. So now we're going to have to wait a few months to sample the fruits of the '99 harvest, whether late-vintage, dried-grape, cask-conditioned or vinified in steel. They promise to be even better than this lovely Ramandolo Il Longhino.

O	Friuli Isonzo Chardonnay Ciampagnis Vieris '98	♟♟	5
O	Friuli Isonzo Pinot Grigio Dessimis '98	♟♟	5
O	Friuli Isonzo Sauvignon Vieris '98	♟♟	5
●	Friuli Isonzo Rosso Voos dai Ciamps '97	♟♟	5
O	Friuli Isonzo Bianco Flors di Uis '98	♟	5
O	Friuli Isonzo Chardonnay Vie di Romans '98	♟	5
O	Friuli Isonzo Sauvignon Piere '98	♟	5
O	Friuli Isonzo Bianco Flors di Uis '96	♛♛♛	5
O	Friuli Isonzo Sauvignon Piere '93	♛♛♛	5
O	Friuli Isonzo Sauvignon Piere '97	♛♛♛	5
O	Friuli Isonzo Sauvignon Vieris '93	♛♛♛	5
O	Friuli Isonzo Sauvignon Vieris '95	♛♛♛	5

O	COF Ramandolo Il Longhino '99	♟♟	4
O	COF Picolit Romandus '96	♛♛	6
O	COF Ramandolo Romandus '97	♛♛	6
O	COF Ramandolo '97	♛	5
O	COF Ramandolo Il Longhino '98	♛	4

PAVIA DI UDINE (UD)

PIGHIN F.LLI
V.LE GRADO, 1
FRAZ. RISANO
33050 PAVIA DI UDINE (UD)
TEL. 0432/675444

The Pighin estate extends over 140 hectares planted to vine in the Grave DOC zone, and 30 in Collio, and the cellar exports much of its output to a range of non-domestic markets. Unfortunately, the Collio vineyards were planted some time ago and although the winery tries to keep yields down, their products are rarely outstanding, despite the professionalism of wine technician Paolo Valdesolo. But the Sauvignon Casette '98, from ungrafted root stock, is back in the big league. Its nose of green pepper, rue and yellow flowers leads in to a full-flavoured, well-sustained palate with a zesty finish. The Tocai Friulano Casette '98 is a notch or two lower on the scale. The nicely balanced, pervasive nose of pear and apple pips is let down by the pronounced acidity of the palate, which makes the finish seem almost tannic. The base Grave Tocai has citrus and orange blossom aromas, good complexity and a typically almondy after-taste. We liked the elegant bouquet of the Pinot Bianco Grave while the Grave Cabernets were also very appealing. The Cabernet Sauvignon offers notes of cherry and strawberry on the nose and a full, ripe palate whereas the Cabernet's nose of hay, lucerne, pepper, cinnamon and coffee is rounded off by toastiness. Crusty bread comes through on the noses of both the Collio Pinot Grigio and the Pinot Bianco. The Grigio blends this with boiled sweets and almond while the Bianco adds ripe fruit, hazelnut and an alcohol-derived warmth. Tomato leaf and red pepper prevail in the nose of the Collio Sauvignon and the Collio Tocai has the characteristic varietal hints of pear and almond. The Pighin Soreli '98 white, from tocai, sauvignon and pinot bianco, is as always an intriguing wine while the red Baredo '96, a blend of cabernet sauvignon, merlot is refosco, offers, like the previous wine, excellent cellaring potential.

PAVIA DI UDINE (UD)

SCARBOLO
V.LE GRADO, 4
FRAZ. LAUZACCO
33050 PAVIA DI UDINE (UD)
TEL. 0432/675612 - 0432/675150

Valter Scarbolo's wines get better every year, thanks in part to the support of young wine technician, Emilio Del Medico, and consultancy from oenologist Maurizio Castelli. Valter owns nine hectares of his own and rents other plots, as well as buying in selected fruit. His total output is about 90,000 bottles a year. The Scarbolo Chardonnay '99 is a polished, complex product with faint, fresh varietal notes that are warm on the nose and rich in the mouth. Ripe yellow fruit emerges against a backdrop of yeast, with just the right note of acidity in the finish. The Sauvignon is also worth noting for its fresh yet very elegant nose of elderflower and tomato leaf. The solid, warm structure of the palate provides a prelude to an attractively long finish. The Pinot Grigio announces its pedigree right from the nose of ripe apple and yellow plum laced with green notes. These are mirrored on the fresh-tasting and intriguingly complex palate, which has a rich, fruity aftertaste. Refreshingly tangy on the palate, the Tocai is true to type with attractive aromas of pear and almond. Last but not least, we come to the Refosco Campo del Viotto '98, a "riserva" that Valter ages slowly in oak casks and that he views as the prototype for his wines in the next few years. The nose is dominated by black cherry tart, raspberry and spices that return on the palate. A velvet-smooth entry ushers in a fruit-rich mid palate and a finish where the dry tannins are perfectly at home. It looks as if quality is going to continue to improve at the Scarbolo winery.

O Friuli Grave Sauvignon Casette '98	🍷🍷	4
● Baredo '96	🍷	5
O Collio Pinot Bianco '99	🍷	4
O Collio Pinot Grigio '99	🍷	4
O Collio Sauvignon '99	🍷	4
O Collio Tocai Friulano '99	🍷	3
● Friuli Grave Cabernet '98	🍷	3
● Friuli Grave Cabernet Sauvignon '98	🍷	3
O Friuli Grave Pinot Bianco '99	🍷	3
O Friuli Grave Tocai Friulano '99	🍷	3
O Friuli Grave Tocai Friulano Casette '98	🍷	3
O Soreli '98	🍷	4
O Friuli Grave Pinot Grigio '99		3

O Friuli Grave Chardonnay '99	🍷🍷	3*
O Friuli Grave Sauvignon '99	🍷🍷	3*
O Friuli Grave Pinot Grigio '99	🍷	3
● Friuli Grave Refosco P. R. Campo del Viotto '98	🍷	4
O Friuli Grave Tocai Friulano '99	🍷	3
● Friuli Grave Merlot '97	🍷🍷	3
● Friuli Grave Merlot '98	🍷	3
● Friuli Grave Merlot Campo del Viotto '95	🍷	4

PINZANO AL TAGLIAMENTO (PN)   POVOLETTO (UD)

ALESSANDRO VICENTINI ORGNANI
VIA SOTTOPLOVIA, 2
FRAZ. VALERIANO
33090 PINZANO AL TAGLIAMENTO (PN)
TEL. 0432/950107

AQUILA DEL TORRE
VIA ATTIMIS, 25
FRAZ. SAVORGNANO DEL TORRE
33040 POVOLETTO (UD)
TEL. 0432/666428

Alessandro Vicentini Orgnani's estate is a bit of an oddity in the Grave DOC zone since it has a hillslope location and rich soil, and is sheltered by mountains. This unique situation enables Alessandro to propose a range of elegant, stylish wines, thanks also to his hard work in the vineyards, both new and replanted – his merlot vineyard is a jewel – which are managed in line with modern criteria. Put location and honest toil together and premium wine is virtually guaranteed. For the third year running, the Pinot Bianco Braide Cjase, part vinified in wood, claimed Two Glasses, a sure sign of consistency. The lustrous colour tells you this is a serious wine and the impression is confirmed by the nose of white damson, ripe pear and lush buttery notes. After a rich, fruity entry, the palate unveils white damson with good breadth and plenty of substance before the finish rounds off on a note of ripe pear. A very fine wine. The Braide Cjase label includes a Pinot Grigio and a Chardonnay, both very well-made. The Pinot Grigio has golden highlights and a pervasive nose of fruit salad, nicely contrasted by white chocolate and dried spring flowers. Wood-derived vanilla and coffee prevail on the palate then the finish offers reasonably long notes of apple and pear. In contrast, the very varietal Chardonnay has lustrous highlights of gold while nose and palate are redolent of stylish banana and vanilla. Best of Alessandro's steel-vinified wines is the Tocai, from 30-year-old vines. True to type, fresh and very clean on the yeast-dominated nose, it hints at green apple on the palate, which has a refreshing acidity in the finish.

Aquila del Torre dropped out of the Guide after a change of ownership but has now made a comeback. The cellar has been active for decades and stands on a property of about 80 hectares, roughly 30 of which are planted to vine. Work carried out in the early 90s modernized the winery and when the Ciani family left precision metalworking to take over in 1996, the corner had been turned. We particularly appreciate the decision to concentrate on a small number of monovarietal wines and two blends. The flag-bearer white on sale at the moment is the Picolit '97, from dried, late-vintage grapes fermented and aged for seven months in French oak barriques. The nose hints at pear, dried apple, apricot, candied orange peel and dried flowers, all of which return on the palate to take you through to a finish redolent of almond paste. The Merlot Canticum '97, which was also aged in oak casks and barriques, is another fine wine. Red fruit tart comes through on the nose with a hint of wet dog while the palate has personality and structure. The tannins are assertive but not aggressive and the finish is dry. The slight super-ripeness of the fruit in the Tocai Friulano Vocalis is evident on the nose, where very ripe apple and pear emerge in addition to sun-dried apricot. The same aromas are reflected on the palate, where a hint of acidity detracts from the finish. The late-vintage '97 Verduzzo Friulano is a vibrant amber in the glass, releasing sweet, pervasive aromas of varietal rennet apple and following this with a well-balanced, leisurely finish. A mention also goes to the Canticum Bianco '99, a blend of tocai and sauvignon that needs to go into the cellar for a while.

O Friuli Grave Pinot Bianco Braide Cjase '99	♥♥	3*
O Friuli Grave Chardonnay Braide Cjase '99	♥	3
O Friuli Grave Pinot Grigio Braide Cjase '99	♥	3
O Friuli Grave Tocai Friulano '99	♥	2*
● Friuli Grave Cabernet Sauvignon '98		3
O Friuli Grave Pinot Grigio '99		3
O Friuli Grave Sauvignon '99		3

● COF Merlot Canticum '97	♥♥	4
O COF Picolit '97	♥♥	6
O COF Tocai Friulano Vocalis '99	♥	5
O COF Verduzzo Friulano '97	♥	4
O COF Bianco Canticum '99		4

Slow Food®
2001

Slow Food is an international movement which was founded in 1989 and is active in 45 countries worldwide, with 65,000 members and about 550 Convivia (chapters).

Slow Food has a cultural agenda:
It promotes a **philosophy of pleasure**, protects small food producers who make quality products, counters the degrading effects of industrial and fast food culture which standardize tastes, has a **taste education** program for adults and children, works towards **safeguarding** traditional food and wine heritage, provides **consumer information**, promotes tourism that respects and cares for the environment.

Slow Food Events:
Each year Slow Food puts on important food and wine events for food enthusiasts and professionals: the two-yearly **Salone del Gusto** (Hall of Taste) in Turin, Italy; the two-yearly **Cheese** in Bra, Italy; the **Slow Food Festival** in Germany, one of the largest quality food markets in northern Europe; wine festivals such as **Superwhites**; the **World Game of Pleasure**.

Each **Convivium** organizes social meetings, tastings, cooking courses, trips, visits to restaurants, and lectures for its members. The twinning of Convivia from different countries promote the exchange of tastes and knowledge of different cultures.

An Ark to safeguard products and the planet of tastes:
An important project aimed at safeguarding and benefitting small-scale agricultural and food production, which risks dying out. Thousands of different kinds of *charcuterie*, cheeses, animal breeds and plants are in danger of disappearing forever: the homologation of tastes, the excessive power of industrial companies, distribution difficulties and disinformation are the causes of a process which could lead to the loss of an irreplaceable heritage of traditional recipes, knowledge and tastes. The Ark is a scientific research and documentation program which works towards relaunching businesses and outfits with important cultural and economic value.

Taste Education:
The Slow Food Movement has taken action to realize one of the objectives of the **Ark Manifesto** to promote taste education in grade schools. Along with putting on numerous conferences on this subject, Slow Food published an instructional manual for teachers and parents on how to best teach children about enjoying and understanding their taste culture. Slow Food plans many more educational activities around the world during "Weeks of Taste".

Friendly Tables to feed those who need assistance:
Slow Food has also developed aid initiatives in the food field. They include: financial support for a canteen in a hospital for Amazonian Indians in the state of Roraima in Brazil; the building of a kitchen and canteen in schools in Novigrad and Sarajevo; contributions to a project to remove mines from farming land in Nicaragua. From 2001, Slow Food will plan and finance productive activities in the Third World designed to maintain typical production and hence defend biodiversity.

Slow features in-depth and often off-the-wall stories about food culture across the globe, with related lifestyle topics of a truly international scope, unlike anything you've seen before on the newsstand... 160 well-designed pages in full color, with exciting photography and articles by top authors, gourmets, wine experts, and food & travel writers worldwide. Just take your pick: English, German, French or Italian...

The most complete, reliable and influential guide to the best Italian wines. Published by Slow Food and Gambero Rosso, it is now in its 14th edition. It describes the history and production of 1681 vineyards, describes and evaluates 12045 wines, awards 230 wines with "Tre Bicchieri" (Three Glasses): the élite of the great Italian wine-making tradition. Price € 26.86 or $ 24.95

Registration Form

Slow Food is aimed at food and wine enthusiasts, those who do not want to lose the myriad of tastes in traditional foodstuffs from around the world, and those who share the snail's wise slowness. Annual membership includes:
- a personal membership card
- four issues of the quarterly magazine, *Slow*
- the new wine magazine *Slowine*
- the right to attend all events organized by the Slow Food movement throughout the world
- a 20% discount on all Slow Food publications
- further annual benefits (check out our web site for information)

If you have any questions, please feel free to contact us. We are only a FAX, phone call or e-mail away. Phone: ++39 0172 419611 - FAX: ++39 0172 421293 E-mail: international@slowfood.com

I would like to:
❑ become a member   ❑ renew   ❑ start a convivium

....
Full Name
....
(of company or restaurant or other)
....
Street Address   City
....
State/Prov./County   Country   Postal Code
....
Home Tel.   Day Tel.   Fax
....
Profession

I would prefer to receive Slow in: ❑ English   ❑ German   ❑ French   ❑ Italian

Membership fees to join *Slow Food*
European Union   € 50,00
U.S.A. and all other countries $ 60.00

Method of Payment

❑ Cash   ❑ Eurocheque (no personal checks, please)
❑ Credit Card: ❑ Visa   ❑ AmEx   ❑ Mastercard   ❑ Diners

\# |__|__|__|__||__|__|__|__||__|__|__|__||__|__|__|__|

|__|__/|__| ✗ ....
Exp. Date   Signature
....
Cardholder   Amount

POVOLETTO (UD)

TERESA RAIZ
VIA DELLA ROGGIA, 22
LOC. MARSURE DI SOTTO
33040 POVOLETTO (UD)
TEL. 0432/679071

PRADAMANO (UD)

FANTINEL
VIA CUSSIGNACCO, 80
33040 PRADAMANO (UD)
TEL. 0432/670444

The Tosolini brothers' winery confirmed last year's excellent performance. The cellar vinifies fruit from the estate-owned and rented vineyards, as well as bought-in grapes, to produce two distinct ranges. Wines from the Colli Orientali del Friuli are sold under the Teresa Raiz label while Le Marsure line is reserved for Grave products. Annual production hovers around 250,000 bottles. The star this year is the Decano Rosso '97, from a cabernet sauvignon-based blend also containing cabernet franc and merlot. Barrique-aged for 12 months, it is then matured unhurriedly in the bottle. The complex, concentrated aromas ranging from autumn leaves to spices give way to an unexpectedly fresh-tasting palate with firm structure and a genuinely long finish. The Pinot Grigio is clean-tasting and stylish. Entry, on both nose and palate, is very fruity, the green apple and tropical fruit being accompanied by refreshing acidity in the mouth. Tomato leaf dominates the polished, pervasive nose of the Sauvignon. The palate marries freshness and buttery richness, releasing notes of citrus fruit in the long finish. There is a curious note of pipe tobacco mingling with the pear and almond on the nose of the Tocai Friulano. Intriguingly complex, tangy and long on the palate, it also has nice hints of ripe fruit. This year, the Ribolla Gialla isn't up to the usual Teresa Raiz standards. Rather indistinct minerally notes let it down. Finally, a number of Grave wines are more than well enough made to merit a mention, including the Sauvignon Rovel, the Chardonnay and the Refosco.

The work that Marco Fantinel initiated years ago is beginning to bear fruit and we can look forward to further improvements in view of both the recent consultancy agreement concluded with the University of Udine and the inauguration of the spanking new cellar at Tauriano. The Bianco, a blend of sauvignon, tocai, traminer and picolit, proffers stylish, pervasive notes of melon, vanilla, ripe peach and banana. These return on the palate, which progresses sure-footedly, albeit with only moderate breadth, through to a fresh-tasting finish. There are nicely balanced notes of Peruvian bark, violets and wild berries on the nose of the Refosco Sant'Helena, together with enticing hints of smoke. The fruit on the palate is well to the fore, giving way in the finish to pepper and mulberry jam. The Picolit is well worth investigating. The golden-yellow colour is flecked with amber while the raisins, figs, dates and noble rot on the nose are echoed on the warm palate before the finish of dried fruit. The Cabernet Sauvignon Sant'Helena is entirely true to type on nose and palate, where ripe red fruit and spices, particularly white pepper, come through. The wood in which the Pinot Bianco was aged is evident on nose and palate in the notes of vanilla and coffee that emerge over allusions to banana, tangerine and hedgerow. Generous alcohol and notes of yellow peach characterize the Pinot Grigio. Next is the stylish Sauvignon, with its wild rose and elderflower aromas and well-sustained, fresh-tasting palate. The Cabernet Franc is very fruity, soft and long on the palate while the tannins of the very promising Cabernet Sauvignon Borgo Tesis '99 will need more time to mellow.

○ COF Pinot Grigio '99	▼▼	4
● COF Rosso Decano Rosso '97	▼▼	5
○ COF Sauvignon '99	▼▼	4
○ COF Tocai Friulano '99	▼▼	3*
○ COF Ribolla Gialla '99		4
○ Friuli Grave Chardonnay Le Marsure '99		3
● Friuli Grave Refosco P. R. Le Marsure '99		3
○ Friuli Grave Sauvignon Rovel Le Marsure '99		3
● COF Cabernet '98	♀	3
● COF Rosso Decano Rosso '96	♀	5
● Decano Rosso '95	♀	5

○ COF Picolit I Principi '98	▼▼	6
○ Collio Bianco Santa Caterina '99	▼▼	3*
● Friuli Grave Refosco P. R. Sant'Helena '98	▼▼	4
● Collio Cabernet Franc Santa Caterina '99	▼	3
○ Collio Pinot Bianco Sant'Helena '99	▼	4
○ Collio Pinot Grigio Sant'Helena '99	▼	4
○ Collio Sauvignon Sant'Helena '99	▼	4
● Friuli Grave Cabernet Sauvignon Borgo Tesis '99	▼	3
● Friuli Grave Cabernet Sauvignon Sant'Helena '98	▼	4
○ Collio Chardonnay Sant'Helena '99		4
○ Friuli Grave Pinot Grigio Borgo Tesis '99		3

PRATA DI PORDENONE (PN)   PREMARIACCO (UD)

VIGNETI LE MONDE
VIA GARIBALDI, 2
LOC. LE MONDE
33080 PRATA DI PORDENONE (PN)
TEL. 0434/626096 - 0434/622087

BASTIANICH
LOC. CASALI OTTELIO, 7
33040 PREMARIACCO (UD)
TEL. 0432/675612

The estate lies in the elbow formed by the confluence of the rivers Livenza and Meduna at Le Monde, a place name that recalls the fact that this area was once under imperial protection. Cellars and tasting room are housed in a magnificent 18th-century building whose original charm remains intact. Keeping a benevolent eye on all this is Piergiovanni Pistoni Salice, who left Milan years ago to take over the cellar. We may be in the southern part of the Grave DOC zone but the clay and silt soil is ideal for producing premium-quality wines, especially reds, in our opinion. But the wine that won our hearts this year was the Pinot Grigio. Its attractive straw-yellow hue is flecked with greenish highlights and the extremely fresh aromas of peach and hedgerow marry superbly. White peach returns on the very well-managed palate, which also has sumptuous structure. The Chardonnay is very nice, too. There are enticing notes of tobacco and banana on the elegant nose. A well-balanced wine with a firm entry on the palate, which echoes the aromas on the nose, it falls away a little too soon in the finish. We probably didn't time our tasting to suit the Le Monde reds but the Cabernet Sauvignon Riserva '95 stood out for a nose of spicy varietal notes mingling with ripe plums as well as the trademark hay aromas of the estate's reds. The hay and black cherry on the palate are very tempting and the tannins are reasonably mellow. Finally, a long list of Le Monde wines won a Guide mention, the Ca' Salice Rosso leading the pack.

Clear ideas, a well thought-out game plan and the money to back it up. That's what it takes to get first-class results fast. There may also have been a small element of luck involved, too, when Giuseppe Bastianich left his New York restaurants to look after themselves and purchased nine hectares at Buttrio and Premariacco to try his hand at winemaking. The vines are anything from 50 to 70 years old and their wine is incredibly concentrated. When you find out that some of the fruit is harvested only when super-ripe, you realize why the final product is simply enormous. So it is with some justification that Bastianich has added a "Plus" to the label. The vibrant colour of this Tocai Friulano ushers in an extraordinarily opulent, almost sweet, nose that lingers delectably, stewed apple winning out over the oak-derived liquorice. The palate is an ever-expanding symphony of fruit laced with ripe notes reminiscent of carob. The structure is full-bodied and unbelievably complex, with a long, fruit-rich finish. This is a wine with great potential and definitely one for the cellar. Our congratulations go to the winemaking team, Walter Scarbolo, Emilio Del Medico and consultant Maurizio Castelli. This year, Bastianich has released just one other wine, the Vespa '98. It is a red obtained from a merlot-based blend with smaller proportions of cabernet franc, refosco and a soupçon of pignolo. The grapes were vinified separately, macerating for two or three weeks in open-topped vats, fermented and aged in five-hectolitre casks for a year. Red fruit, yeast and herbs come through on the nose and then the palate unveils lovely texture, fruit-rich structure and a very pleasant, tannic finish.

O Friuli Grave Pinot Grigio '99	♥♥	3*
● Friuli Grave Cabernet Sauvignon Ris. '95	♥	4
O Friuli Grave Chardonnay '99	♥	3
O Friuli Grave Bianco Pra' de Gai '99		3
● Friuli Grave Ca' Salice Rosso '98		3
O Friuli Grave Pinot Bianco '99		3
● Friuli Grave Refosco P. R. '99		3
O Friuli Grave Sauvignon '99		3
● Friuli Grave Cabernet Franc '96	♥♥	4
● Friuli Grave Cabernet Franc '97	♥	3
● Querceto '95	♥	5

O COF Tocai Friulano Plus '99	♥♥	5
● Vespa '98	♥♥	5
O COF Tocai Friulano Plus '98	♥♥	5
O Vespa '98	♥♥	5

PREMARIACCO (UD)

DARIO E LUCIANO ERMACORA
VIA SOLZAREDO, 9
FRAZ. IPPLIS
33040 PREMARIACCO (UD)
TEL. 0432/716250

The Ermacora family started growing grapes on the hills near Ipplis in 1922. The soil is a mixture of marl and sandstone and their vineyards at the foot of the Rocca Bernarda hill are sheltered from the cold east winds. Terroir and site climate are ideal for producing premium-quality wines and brothers Dario and Luciano take full advantage. The past vintage promised great things but turned out to harbour one or two unwelcome surprises so the pair have done extremely well to gain high marks for five wines. One of the quintet was the Rîul, a blend of two-thirds merlot grapes with cabernet sauvignon and refosco that spends a year and a half in barriques before being released. The nose reveals intense aromas of mulberry jam, musk, Peruvian bark and tobacco. Then the palate combines gamey notes with ripe fruit deliciously. The tannins have still to mellow out so we will hold fire on a final judgement for the moment. The Ermacora whites are so well-typed they could have come straight out of the textbook. The Pinot Bianco has a nose of green apple, hedgerow and fresh crusty bread that return on the sweet, well-sustained and full-flavoured palate that is in no hurry to sign off. Pear, golden delicious apple and rue are the keynotes on the nose of the fresh, consistent Pinot Grigio. Golden delicious apple again, and almond, introduce the Tocai before yellow plum and white peach come through on the palate, giving way to notes of hedgerow and a long, luxurious almondy finish. The attack of the Sauvignon is almost overwhelming. Ebullient peach, elderflower and ripe tomato follow through from nose to finish in a delicate, flowery finale.

PREMARIACCO (UD)

ROCCA BERNARDA
VIA ROCCA BERNARDA, 27
FRAZ. IPPLIS
33040 PREMARIACCO (UD)
TEL. 0432/716273

For the second year running, the Rocca Bernarda Picolit has earned Three Glasses. The efficient team of enterprising manager, Mario Zuliani, and expert oenologist Marco Monchiero has again coaxed a world-class product from a location historically congenial to the variety (the 1906 treatise on picolit by Giacomo Perusini, owner of the estate at the time, is well worth reading). Golden yellow in colour, it opens on the nose with aromas of stewed apple that give way to hints of orange, tangerine, candied peel, figs and dates, to close with attractive nuances of wild rose. The concentrated palate mirrors the nose perfectly, its buttery richness enhancing them to the full, and the superb finish is magnificently long. The Chardonnay is another very fine wine, mingling rich aromas of ripe banana, melon and candied apricot fruit with macaroon on the nose. The entry on the palate has nuances of hazelnut and yellow peach before citrus notes emerge to linger through to the finish. Vineis is the new Rocca Bernarda white blend, obtained from 40 percent selected oak-aged chardonnay grapes, 40 percent sauvignon and 20 percent tocai. Elegant on the nose, where aromas of acacia blossom, elderflower, almond and crusty bread find an admirable harmony, it is equally convincing on the palate. Initial notes of yellow plum and tomato give way in the finish to aromas of nuts and crusty bread. Citrus, melon and yellow peach aromas on nose and palate give the Sauvignon a distinctly Mediterranean air. And to complete the list, the Tocai is full-bodied and complex, the very fruity Pinot Grigio fully deserved its One Glass rating and the Ribolla Gialla drew favourable comments for its fresh-tasting, varietal personality.

○ COF Pinot Bianco '99	♀♀	3*
○ COF Pinot Grigio '99	♀♀	3*
○ COF Sauvignon '99	♀♀	3*
○ COF Tocai Friulano '99	♀♀	3*
● Rîul Rosso '97	♀♀	5
● COF Refosco P. R. '98	♀	4
○ COF Verduzzo Friulano '99		3
● COF Merlot '97	♀♀	3

○ COF Picolit '98	♀♀♀	6
○ COF Chardonnay '99	♀♀	3
○ COF Sauvignon '99	♀♀	3
○ COF Tocai Friulano '99	♀♀	3*
○ COF Bianco Vineis '99	♀♀	4
○ COF Pinot Grigio '99	♀	3
○ COF Ribolla Gialla '99	♀	3
○ COF Picolit '97	♀♀	6
● COF Merlot Centis '95	♀♀	4
● COF Merlot Centis '96	♀♀	4
● COF Merlot Centis '97	♀♀	4
○ COF Picolit '96	♀♀	6
○ COF Picolit Ris. '94	♀♀	6

PREMARIACCO (UD)

SCUBLA

VIA ROCCA BERNARDA, 22
FRAZ. IPPLIS
33040 PREMARIACCO (UD)
TEL. 0432/716258

One step at a time, Roberto Scubla has restructured his cellar and carried out his projects for the vineyards, assessing the performance of various vine types and finding the right consultants. The results have now arrived. His Pomédes, a blend of late-vintage tocai and pinot bianco with part-dried riesling, walked away with Three Glasses. Its rich bouquet of apple, acacia blossom, citrus and vanillaed confectioner's cream derives from the encounter of the three varieties with the wood. These aromas return in style on the palate, which has all the weight necessary for a leisurely sojourn in the cellar. Scuro is a Bordeaux must blend – Roberto is obviously a believer in fermentation synergy – that stands out for its complexity and solid personality. Cherry and violets on nose, notes of Peruvian bark and liquorice, and a very long, dry finish were the most impressive features of this attractive wine. And here are our tasting notes for the remaining wines. The Tocai is excellent, its soft, well-rounded palate leading through to an almond twist in the finish. The Pinot Bianco has an intriguing nose of baked apple, honey and jam but the palate is a touch bitter and lacks weight. The varietal aromas of the Sauvignon return on the palate in a softer key while the rather assertive Cabernet has firm texture, reminiscent of ripe elderberries. Finally, Roberto's Merlot has an alluring nose of spring hay and liqueur fruit but is still a little immature on the palate. We also retasted last year's Verduzzo Passito Graticcio, which has improved in the interim, and is now drinking superbly.

○	COF Bianco Pomédes '98	🍷🍷🍷	5
●	COF Rosso Scuro '97	🍷🍷	5
○	COF Tocai Friulano '99	🍷🍷	4
●	COF Cabernet Sauvignon '98	🍷	4
○	COF Pinot Bianco '99	🍷	4
○	COF Sauvignon '99	🍷	4
●	COF Merlot '98		4
○	COF Bianco Pomédes '97	🍸🍸	5
○	COF Bianco Speziale '98	🍸🍸	4
●	COF Merlot '97	🍸🍸	4
○	COF Verduzzo Friulano Graticcio '97	🍸🍸	5

PREPOTTO (UD)

IOLE GRILLO

FRAZ. ALBANA, 60
33040 PREPOTTO (UD)
TEL. 0432/713201

In 1974, Iole Grillo bought eight hectares of vineyards on the border of Italy and Slovenia, and of the provinces of Udine and Gorizia. Since 1994, most of the estate's wine has been bottled on-site. Today, Iole's daughter Anna Muzzolini runs the winery and technical assistance in vineyard and cellar comes from Lino Casella, a young, serious professional. Currently, the estate turns out no more than 25,000 bottles a year but there is potential for more. We liked the winery's first experiment with blending, the Bianco Santa Justina, from tocai and malvasia with some sauvignon added to enhance the aromas. Aged for six months in five-hectolitre oak casks, it reveals a stylish nose of tomato leaf and elderflower introducing a rich, full-bodied palate with lingering notes of apple, pear and peach. The Grillo Sauvignon also enjoyed a good vintage. This exclusively steel-vinified version offers pervasive varietal aromas of elderflower laced with mint and peach that return attractively on the warm, rich palate. There is also serious structure and a mouth-filling finish. The Tocai has a well-rounded palate of ripe fruit with a balanced, fresh-tasting flavour. In the Schioppettino '98, we noted concentrated aromas of liqueur cherries and mulled wine (cinnamon and cloves) which are reflected on the palate. An agreeable, inviting wine, despite the rich texture it has acquired after long ageing in large oak casks. The Refosco '98 is also oak-aged. It offers a full, rich, spicy nose and an unusually mellow texture in the mouth. Finally, the Pinot Grigio and Verduzzo '99 are both well worth their mention.

○	COF Bianco Santa Justina '99	🍷🍷	4
○	COF Sauvignon '99	🍷🍷	3*
●	COF Refosco P. R. '98	🍷	3
●	COF Schioppettino '98	🍷	4
○	COF Tocai Friulano '99	🍷	3
○	COF Pinot Grigio '99		3
○	COF Verduzzo Friulano '99		3

PREPOTTO (UD)

LA VIARTE
VIA NOVACUZZO, 50
33040 PREPOTTO (UD)
TEL. 0432/759458

At La Viarte, the '99 vintage is not an easy one to understand. Almost all the wines presented were very closed and reduced on the nose yet on the palate they had serious structure, balance and length. It is as if the winery had decided to go all out for cellarability when the new vinification procedures may still need a little adjustment. We would stress the words "a little" because there are some real blockbusters in this line-up. One such is the Sauvignon, which releases evident aromas of peach and on the palate shows well-sustained thrust, concentration and good personality. The Tocai, too, is warm, muscular, mouth-filling and characteristically almondy. The Pinot Bianco and the Ribolla are in the same vein, although the latter is a touch dilute and lacks harmony. The Pinot Grigio rather overplays the yeasty notes on the nose but the palate, while fairly straightforward, is clean-tasting, coherent, fresh and flowery. Preceding vintages tell a different story, though, for if the Merlot has a rather gamey style, the Siùm is ravishing. A blend of selected verduzzo and dried picolit fruit, barrique-fermented and then left in contact with the lees for a year, it took us all by surprise with its fresh peach, fig and walnut aromas and a gently tannic palate that is elegant and never cloys. The Tazzelenghe was another wine that impressed, its substantial alcohol managing to soften the variety's notorious astringency. The Liende was the better of the two '98 whites with the Roi, a slightly pedestrian but well-made Bordeaux blend, bringing up the rear.

PREPOTTO (UD)

LE DUE TERRE
VIA ROMA, 68/B
33040 PREPOTTO (UD)
TEL. 0432/713189

As we flicked through the notes that Flavio and Silvana Basilicata had given us, we were impressed to see that yields per hectare ranged from a minimum of 30 to a maximum of 45 quintals. It's easy to see, then, why Le Due Terre was able to propose a superlative product – the Sacrisassi Rosso – even in a year when many growers were having difficulty (to put it mildly) with their red grapes. A blend of two local varieties, refosco and schioppettino, it aged for 18 months in large and small oak casks. The nose reveals crusty bread, cherry, pepper and ginger spice and aromatic herbs, leading in to a long, polished palate. The Implicito was also in the running for Three Glasses but it is not an easy wine to appreciate, although some tasters rate it outstanding. A picolit-based white, it has a stylish, dry, pervasive nose rich in alcohol, with nuances of bitter honey and wistaria blossom, while the clean palate offers warmth, vigour, buttery richness and good balance. The Sacrisassi Bianco, from tocai, ribolla gialla and sauvignon, again scored well up in the Two Glass band. Its aromas of petrol, ripe fruit, citrus and flowers are mirrored on the long palate, which has excellent balance. At the insistence of his friends, Flavio agreed to vinify the '98 merlot fruit separately from his blend. The resulting wine releases violets, red fruit and elegant gamey notes before the soft, mellow palate takes you in to a long finish with tannins well to the fore. Last was the fruity, alcohol-rich Pinot Nero, which seemed a little over-evolved after its very soft entry.

O	COF Sauvignon '99	♟♟	4
O	COF Tocai Friulano '99	♟♟	4
O	Siùm '97	♟♟	6
●	Tazzelenghe '96	♟♟	5
O	COF Bianco Liende '98	♟	4
O	COF Chardonnay '98	♟	4
O	COF Pinot Bianco '99	♟	4
O	COF Pinot Grigio '99	♟	4
O	COF Ribolla Gialla '99	♟	4
●	COF Rosso Roi '97	♟	5
●	COF Schioppettino '97	♟	4
●	COF Merlot '97	♟	4
O	COF Bianco Liende '97	♟♟	4
●	Roi '94	♟♟	5
O	Siùm '96	♟♟	5

●	COF Rosso Sacrisassi '98	♟♟♟	5
O	COF Bianco Sacrisassi '98	♟♟	5
●	COF Merlot '98	♟♟	5
O	Implicito '98	♟♟	6
●	COF Pinot Nero '98	♟	6
●	COF Rosso Sacrisassi '97	♟♟♟	5
O	COF Bianco Sacrisassi '97	♟♟	5
O	Implicito '96	♟♟	6
O	Implicito '97	♟♟	6
●	Sacrisassi Rosso '96	♟♟	5
●	Sacrisassi Rosso '94	♟	5

PREPOTTO (UD)

PREPOTTO (UD)

PETRUSSA
FRAZ. ALBANA, 49
33040 PREPOTTO (UD)
TEL. 0432/713192

VIGNA TRAVERSO
VIA RONCHI, 73
33040 PREPOTTO (UD)
TEL. 0432/713072

Last year, we had to make do with a range of well-made, but uninspiring, wines from Gianni and Paolo Petrussi. Happily, this time round their small winery has made significant progress. In addition, some of the wines we tasted last time have come on marvellously, especially the Bianco Petrussa '97. If the Bianco '98 shows a similar improvement, the brothers could usefully delay the release of this wine, which needs time to express its full potential. But the Sauvignon '99 is drinking beautifully now. Its buttery richness is obvious even on the concentrated elderflower-dominated nose. Yellow peach provides the keynote on the palate, which is complex, robust, full-flavoured and long. The garnet-tinged Schioppettino '97 unfurls a nose of walnut, elderflower and cinnamon, then a soft entry introduces a palate of remarkable texture with a dry, tannic finish. The merlot-based Rosso Petrussa is another very fine wine. Its complex nose of berry fruit over nicely gauged wood is mirrored perfectly on the robust, well-structured palate. The Bianco Petrussa '98 is a blend of tocai friulano with smaller proportions of pinot bianco, sauvignon and chardonnay. Its gold-flecked colour heralds a nose of rennet apple and an attractively fresh-tasting palate. Lustrous golden yellow with a nose of honey and pot pourri, the Pensiero '97 tempts with a sweet but never cloying palate. Then we sampled the stylish and very drinkable Pinot Bianco followed by the Tocai, a well-structured wine whose nose of elderflower and sage is reminiscent of the Sauvignon. We rounded off with the Merlot and Cabernet '99, both still too young but worth a mention.

When the Traverso Molon family bought Ronco del Castagneto last year, they certainly didn't expect to have to change the name while a legal dispute over its use wended its way through the courts. Stefano Traverso, his father, Giancarlo, and mother Ornella have decided to carry on regardless, making far-reaching changes to winemaking procedures as well as to the label. With the advice of Luca D'Attoma and the contribution of Lauro Iacolettig, their cellarman and expert vineyard manager, results have not been slow in coming. The Merlot '98 stands head and shoulders above the rest. A yield of less than 50 quintals per hectare, barrique ageing for more than a year and leisurely bottle ageing have produced a wine whose aristocratic nose offers complexity: rich cherry tart aromas laced with plum and mulberry. The full-bodied palate then impresses with its beautiful balance of tannins and wood. The Sauvignon opens slowly on the nose but the palate lets you know straight away it is serious, elderflower and tomato leaf aromas emerging assertively over a glycerine-rich, robustly alcoholic structure before the very long finish. There is good balance, too, on the flower and fruit nose of the Ribolla Gialla. The aromas return on the full-flavoured palate, which is veined with the variety's trademark acidity. The Pinot Grigio also has an outstanding nose of apple, fruit salad and minerally notes while the well-sustained palate offers good breadth. We nearly gave the Chardonnay a second Glass for its sumptuous, warm palate, which has good complexity and length. The Tocai has a classic range of varietal aromas but is let down by a hint of acidity on the palate. And bringing up the rear was the attractive, very drinkable Petali di Rosa, obtained from moscato rosa grapes.

●	COF Rosso Petrussa '97	♙♙	5
○	COF Sauvignon '99	♙♙	3*
●	COF Schioppettino '97	♙♙	5
○	COF Bianco Petrussa '98	♙	4
○	COF Pinot Bianco '99	♙	3
○	COF Tocai Friulano '99	♙	3
○	Pensiero '97	♙	5
●	COF Cabernet '99		3
●	COF Merlot '99		3
●	COF Rosso Petrussa '95	♙♙	5
○	COF Bianco Petrussa '97	♙	4

●	COF Merlot '98	♙♙	5
○	COF Pinot Grigio '99	♙♙	4
○	COF Ribolla Gialla '99	♙♙	4
○	COF Sauvignon '99	♙♙	4
○	COF Chardonnay '99	♙	4
○	COF Tocai Friulano '99	♙	4
⊙	Petali di Rosa '99	♙	5

RONCHI DEI LEGIONARI (GO)

S. FLORIANO DEL COLLIO (GO)

TENUTA DI BLASIG
VIA ROMA, 63
34077 RONCHI DEI LEGIONARI (GO)
TEL. 0481/475480

ASCEVI - LUWA
VIA UCLANZI, 24
34070 S. FLORIANO DEL COLLIO (GO)
TEL. 0481/884140

Tenuta di Blasig is an estate where women call the shots. Skilfully managed by Elisabetta Bortolotto Sarcinelli with the help of her mother, Helga, it has enjoyed the services of talented oenologist, Erica Orlandino, for the past two years. And the all-female team seems to have found its way because this time round, the overall assessments of the panel were significantly higher than in the past. Not a single label failed to make the cut-off. Top marks went to the two reds from the cask-conditioned Gli Affreschi range. The Merlot is a lovely rich violet red and delights with its crisp aromas of Peruvian bark and berries, especially mulberries, pennyroyal and tobacco, which return on the excellent, fruit-rich front palate to give way to hints of Peruvian bark and mulberry that linger through to the finish. Redcurrant, mulberry and plum fruit dominate the nose of the Cabernet while the palate offers deliciously long notes of white chocolate, coffee and mulberries. The Pinot Grigio is being released for the first time this year and very nearly won a second Glass, despite its youth. The straw-yellow colour is dazzlingly brilliant, introducing aromas of pear, apple, dried flowers and varietal notes of mineral. The very stylish palate has good thrust and the pear in the finish is enlivened by tangy acidity. The Chardonnay is also worth investigating. Its lovely straw-yellow colour is flecked with green and the nose reveals ripe fruit. The entry on the palate offers notes of banana and apple that fade slightly in the finish. And then there is a long list of other Guide-worthy bottles from the women of Tenuta di Blasig.

This cellar again confirmed the high standards to which Marjan Pintar has accustomed us, both in the big-league bottles sold under the Ascevi label and in the fruitier, more quaffable wines in the Luwa range. By skilful management of harvest times and maceration, Marjan brings out the characteristic personality of each of his vine types to put together a complete range of products. We were very impressed by two blended wines, the sauvignon, ribolla and chardonnay Vigna Verdana and the Col Martin, obtained from sauvignon, tocai and pinot grigio. The Vigna Verdana has exceptional weight on the palate and robust alcohol, mellowed by a hint of fresh acidity and nuances of medicinal herbs. As in previous years, the Col Martin foregrounds the sauvignon, especially on the nose, where peach and apricot are prominent, while it has good weight and dynamism in the mouth. The Sauvignon was as good as ever and the Pinot Bianco, obtained from late-vintage fruit that underwent an unhurried maceration, is flavoursome, fruity and full-bodied. The grapes for the Chardonnay were harvested early and vinified without the skins, and the resulting wine is fruity, fresh-tasting and very subtle. The Ribolla Gialla Luwa is the outcome of a late September harvest and 48 hours' skin contact. It is actually more convincing than its Ascevi cousin which, after a later harvest, reveals a distinct lack of balance between acidity and softness. Finally, the Luwa Sauvignon came very close to earning a Glass, but for a slightly cloying nose and a lack of ripeness on the palate.

● Friuli Isonzo Cabernet		
Gli Affreschi '98	♈♈	4
● Friuli Isonzo Merlot		
Gli Affreschi '98	♈♈	4
○ Friuli Isonzo Chardonnay '99	♈	3
○ Friuli Isonzo Pinot Grigio '99	♈	3
● Friuli Isonzo Cabernet '99		3
○ Friuli Isonzo Malvasia '98		3
● Friuli Isonzo Merlot '99		3
○ Friuli Isonzo Tocai Friulano '99		3
○ Falconetto Bianco '97	♈♈	4
● Friuli Isonzo Cabernet		
Gli Affreschi '97	♈	4
● Friuli Isonzo Merlot		
Gli Affreschi '97	♈	4

○ Col Martin Luwa '99	♈♈	4
○ Collio Sauvignon Ascevi '99	♈♈	4
○ Vigna Verdana Ascevi '99	♈♈	4
○ Collio Chardonnay Luwa '99	♈	3
○ Collio Pinot Bianco Ascevi '99	♈	3
○ Collio Pinot Grigio Ascevi '99	♈	3
○ Collio Ribolla Gialla Luwa '99	♈	3
○ Collio Ribolla Gialla Ascevi '98		4
○ Collio Sauvignon Luwa '99		3
○ Collio Sauvignon Ascevi '98	♈♈♈	4

Borgo Lotessa
Loc. Giasbana, 23
34070 S. Floriano del Collio (GO)
Tel. 0481/390302

Draga - Miklus
Loc. Scedina, 8
34070 S. Floriano del Collio (GO)
Tel. 0481/884182

There are no changes at Borgo Lotessa as far as winemaking is concerned: Roberto Fratepietro is still in charge. There are no new wines. But the overall level of quality has made giant strides for no wine failed to make the grade this year. There were two wines we particularly liked at this family-run estate in San Floriano, the Chardonnay and the Sauvignon. The first caught our eye with its lovely golden highlights, leading in to a nose of stylish aromas that are echoed on the well-rounded, lingering palate. What sets the Sauvignon apart are its aromas of apple strudel and yellow peach, giving way in the mouth to hints of melon. The palate then broadens satisfyingly into a finish of peach and hay. The Rosso Poggio Crussoli gained a very comfortable One Glass. The nose has notes of white pepper over mulberry and cherry fruit while the palate attractively combines mulberry tart, coffee and tobacco, with mature tannins emerging in the finish. Both of the barrique-aged Margravio blends are of a similar calibre. The sauvignon, chardonnay and pinot grigio Bianco is gold-flecked in the glass with aromas of vanilla, ripe banana and candied apricots that are echoed on the palate. The Rosso, obtained from merlot, cabernet sauvignon and schioppettino, has intriguing notes of talcum powder that marry well with the hints of cherry and raspberry, although the palate is somewhat one-dimensional. The Pinot Bianco is true to type, its intense and very stylish aromas of golden delicious apple introducing vigorous entry on the palate that is let down in the finish by assertive acidity. And to conclude, the Bianco Poggio Crussoli has generous flower and fruit aromas nuanced with pear, apple and spring flowers, as well as a warm finish.

Milan Miklus has now finished work on the new cellar that backs onto his vineyards at Draga. And that is the name he decided to give the wines he started bottling on-site in 1992. For the past couple of years, Milan has also been releasing a range of premium wines, selected from the best fermentation vats and ageing barrels in the winery, and sold under the Miklus label. The Cabernet Sauvignon Miklus '98 was a particular source of satisfaction for the panel. Its broad, intriguing nose offers notes of freshly cut grass, hay and warm black cherry, which return on the soft, full-flavoured and very long palate. The Sauvignon Miklus is an interesting wine, adding unusual notes of dried flowers to the tomato leaf theme. The rich, buttery palate is so soft that it seems almost sweetish while attractive hints of nettle freshen up the finish. Next, it was the turn of the Pinot Grigio Miklus to convince the panel with the ripe golden delicious apple on the nose echoed on the long, full-bodied palate. Only the Miklus Picolit failed to earn a Glass, albeit only by a whisker. Its aromas are fresh and true to type but the palate is a little too straightforward and the sweetness cloys. All of the Draga wines are very well made but, apart from the Pinot Grigio and the Ribolla Gialla, lack the structure to carry off any Glassware.

○ Collio Chardonnay '99	🍷🍷	3
○ Collio Sauvignon '99	🍷🍷	3
○ Collio Bianco Poggio Crussoli '98	🍷	4
○ Collio Pinot Bianco '99	🍷	3
● Collio Rosso Poggio Crussoli '98	🍷	4
○ Il Margravio Bianco '98	🍷	4
● Il Margravio Rosso '98	🍷	4
○ Collio Pinot Grigio '99		3

● Collio Cabernet Sauvignon Miklus '98	🍷🍷	4
○ Collio Pinot Grigio Draga '99	🍷	4
○ Collio Pinot Grigio Miklus '99	🍷	4
○ Collio Ribolla Gialla Draga '99	🍷	4
○ Collio Sauvignon Miklus '99	🍷	4
○ Collio Chardonnay Draga '99		4
○ Collio Picolit Miklus '99		6
○ Collio Sauvignon Draga '99		4

S. FLORIANO DEL COLLIO (GO) S. FLORIANO DEL COLLIO (GO)

CONTI FORMENTINI
VIA OSLAVIA, 5
34070 S. FLORIANO DEL COLLIO (GO)
TEL. 0481/884131

MUZIC
LOC. BIVIO, 4
34070 S. FLORIANO DEL COLLIO (GO)
TEL. 0481/884201 - 0481/884082

For several years, the Gruppo Italiano Vini has been managing the Conti Formentini estate, founded in 1520. The consultancy services of Piedmontese oenologist, Marco Monchiero, have led to a significant improvement in the quality of the roughly 300,000 bottles produced each year, into which goes a proportion of carefully selected bought-in fruit. At the cellar entrance is an intriguing wine museum which boasts a large number of very interesting or unusual exhibits. This year, Sauvignon is spot on. The '99 version has a stylish, almost sweet nose, so ripe is the fruit, while the palate offers crisp notes of yellow pepper, backed up with a sustained acidity that prolongs the attractive finish. Next, the Chardonnay Torre di Tramontana flaunts pervasive notes of vanilla and red delicious apple that return on the palate, where yeast aromas are well complemented by acidity. We very much liked the nose of the Pinot Grigio, with its elegantly rich, intense pear and apple. On the palate, the progression is well-sustained but less interesting than we had expected it to be. Nose won out over palate again in the Merlot Tajut, named after the Friulian word for a glass of wine served in an "osteria", or bar. The Merlot was evidently suffering the effects of a rain-plagued harvest for the richness of the aromas was undermined by poorish structure and a disappointing lack of length. Despite the notorious difficulty of growing the variety in Friuli, the Pinot Nero Torre di Borea is a wine of quality. Black cherry, cherry, raspberry and hints of milky coffee emerge on the nose while the palate is soft, despite the generous quota of rather uninhibited tannins, and reasonably long.

A favourable '99 vintage and a restructured cellar have ensured that Giovanni ("Ivan" to his friends) Muzic has raked in a plentiful haul of Glasses. The estate has ten hectares under vine in the Collio, as well as two more in the Isonzo DOC zone, and turns out around 50,000 bottles a year. The Merlot Primo Legno '97 was aged for a year in French and Slavonian oak casks. On the nose, it is reminiscent of red berry tart and tobacco but fruit dominates the palate. Assertive acidity and tannins in the finish tell you this is still a very youthful product. The Cabernet Sauvignon aged slowly in five-hectolitre oak casks and offers cherry and raspberry aromas on the nose. The palate is alluringly rich and full-bodied, with plenty of complexity and good balance. The Ribolla Giallo is drinking superbly now. Ripe peach and apricot fruit dominate the nose, varietal acidity emerges on the palate and the finish is satisfyingly long. The Sauvignon is not particularly varietal. Nevertheless, its ripe apple and citrus aromas, combined with a palate of tomato leaf over an enticing marriage of fresh acidity and robust alcohol, very nearly earned it Two Glasses. In contrast, the Chardonnay is well-typed. Its nose of yellow peach, crusty bread and yeast is mirrored on the satisfyingly long palate. The Primo Legno white, a new blend of chardonnay and sauvignon with other local varieties, ages in the wood for six months. Toastiness and confectioner's cream come out on the nose but the palate falls away rather too quickly. The Muzic Tocai is coherent and true to type while the Merlot '98 reveals a generous, fruit-rich structure. Finally, the Picolit scores well for its aromas but the almost dry palate is a bit of a disappointment.

O	Collio Sauvignon '99	ŢŢ	3*
O	Collio Chardonnay Torre di Tramontana '98	Ţ	4
●	Collio Merlot Tajut '98	Ţ	4
O	Collio Pinot Grigio '99	Ţ	3
●	Collio Pinot Nero Torre di Borea '98	Ţ	4
O	Collio Chardonnay Torre di Tramontana '97	ŢŢ	4
●	Collio Merlot Tajut '97	ŢŢ	4

●	Collio Cabernet Sauvignon '98	ŢŢ	3*
O	Collio Ribolla Gialla '99	ŢŢ	3*
●	Friuli Isonzo Merlot Primo Legno '97	ŢŢ	4
O	Collio Chardonnay '99	Ţ	3
O	Collio Pinot Grigio '99	Ţ	3
O	Collio Sauvignon '99	Ţ	3
O	Collio Tocai Friulano '99	Ţ	3
●	Friuli Isonzo Merlot '98	Ţ	3
O	Primo Legno '98	Ţ	4
O	Collio Picolit '98		5
●	Friuli Isonzo Merlot Primo Legno '96	ŢŢ	4

S. FLORIANO DEL COLLIO (GO) S. FLORIANO DEL COLLIO (GO)

MATIJAZ TERCIC
VIA BUKUJE, 9
34070 S. FLORIANO DEL COLLIO (GO)
TEL. 0481/884193

FRANCO TERPIN
LOC. VALERISCE, 6/A
34070 S. FLORIANO DEL COLLIO (GO)
TEL. 0481/884215

The quality of Matijaz Tercic's limited production is constantly climbing. Matijaz cultivates four hectares of vines and produces about 22,000 bottles a year, under seven labels, and from ten different varieties. Only the Pinot Grigio, Chardonnay and Sauvignon break the 4,000 bottle barrier. Which, of course, makes them very hard to come by. Bianco Planta, a chardonnay-based wine with ten percent pinot bianco (only 1,500 bottles), is the only oak-aged Tercic white, spending ten months or so in one, two and three-year-old barriques. The final product is a well-balanced wine. Fruit and vanilla meld faultlessly on the nose and the palate is rich, buttery and very long. The Ribolla Gialla can boast a generous nose of flowers and fruit as well as softness and moderate acidity in the mouth. Awesome glycerine and alcohol lend the palate a luxurious roundness. Stylish. Concentrated. Ripe fruit. Those were three of our notes on the nose of the Pinot Grigio, a complex and remarkably fruit-rich glass. The Merlot '97, matured for more than 18 months in barriques of various ages, has a subtle note of wax and wood on the nose that quickly gives way to raspberry and berry fruit. Well-sustained and full-bodied in the mouth, it reveals compact structure and prominent tannins, especially in the finish. Vino degli Orti is a blend of tocai, malvasia and riesling that is redolent of ripe apple and walnuts on the nose. The mellow palate is generously rich and braced by good acidity. We noted yellow flowers and apple in the Chardonnay, as well as attractively tangy citrus in the mouth and a faintly bitterish finish. In contrast, elderflower is the dominant note in the aromas of the Sauvignon, which follows this up with an alcohol-rich palate.

The Terpin family has been farming the Collio for generations. Teodoro – he and his family once worked as tenant farmers – acquired the first few hectares of vineyards and today his son, Franco, looks after them. The Terpins are devotees of the "one step at a time" philosophy and that is why not all of their wine is bottled. For a couple of years, Franco has been experimenting with barriques to make a Collio Bianco, a blend of chardonnay, sauvignon and pinot grigio. Last year's version was a little heavy on toasty oak from new barriques but this year confectioner's cream comes through, laced with sour cream and fruit. The palate is warm (this wine has 14 percent alcohol), complex and deliciously mellow. The Ribolla Gialla, also barrique-aged, is a notch or two above. The elegant flowery nose, reminiscent of apricot, the attractive undertow of toastiness, the rich, soft palate and the appealing note of coffee that returns in the finish all combine to make this an outstanding wine. There is an unusual note of petrol in the Pinot Grigio that returns on the palate, together with pear, apple and a hint of acidity in the finish. It's by no means a typical product but certainly an interesting one. Finally, we sampled the Sauvignon. It has not yet settled down but the characteristic tomato leaf aroma is already perceptible. We adjudged it worthy of a mention for we are sure it will improve in the cellar.

○	Collio Bianco Planta '98	🍷🍷	4
●	Collio Merlot '97	🍷🍷	4
○	Collio Pinot Grigio '99	🍷🍷	3
○	Collio Ribolla Gialla '99	🍷🍷	3
○	Collio Chardonnay '99	🍷	3
○	Collio Sauvignon '99	🍷	3
○	Vino degli Orti '99	🍷	3

○	Collio Bianco '98	🍷🍷	5
○	Collio Ribolla Gialla '99	🍷🍷	5
○	Collio Pinot Grigio '99	🍷	3
○	Collio Sauvignon '99		3
○	Collio Chardonnay '98	🏆🏆	3

S. GIORGIO DELLA RICHINVELDA (PN)   S. GIOVANNI AL NATISONE (UD)

FORCHIR
VIA CIASUTIS, 1/B
FRAZ. PROVESANO
33095 S. GIORGIO DELLA RICHINVELDA (PN)
TEL. 0427/96037

ALFIERI CANTARUTTI
VIA RONCHI, 9
33048 S. GIOVANNI AL NATISONE (UD)
TEL. 0432/756317

Here we have a large winery, producing 800,000 bottles a year, that exploits to the full the potential of the Grave DOC zone, vinifying fruit from three grape-growing centres. Two partners are at the helm. One is oenologist, Gianfranco Bianchini, celebrating his 25th vintage this year and the other is Enzo Deana, who looks after the paperwork. Together, they combine large-scale production with good quality and a serious approach to business. The Forchir Sauvignon l'Altro earned Two Glasses. Obtained from a very old sauvignon vineyard where clonal selection has never been practised, and whose vines are probably no longer available on the market, it was vinified with its own natural yeast in stainless steel vats. The nose is delicate yet pervasive, releasing varietal hints of red pepper. The progression on the palate is intriguingly complex and full while the red pepper in the finish is accompanied by appealingly tangy acidity. The Bianco Martin Pescatore is a blend of barrique-aged chardonnay with riesling and a small proportion of traminer: The straw-yellow hue is flecked delicately with gold and the aromas on the nose range from banana to tropical fruit and vanilla, which return satisfyingly on the palate. Our only criticism is a slight lack of length. The Chardonnay foregrounds red delicious apple on both nose and palate. The Forchir Pinot Grigio has an excitingly intense nose of pear and white peach. Then red delicious apple emerges on the front palate but the minerally varietal finish lacks length. The best of the Forchir reds, in our opinion, is the Cabernet Sauvignon. Its plum and black cherry fruit mingle with milky coffee on the nose, leading in to a well-sustained palate and returning on the finish.

This is a winery on the way up. The investments made in winemaking and in marketing by Antonella and her husband, Fabrizio, have been substantial. Work is still in progress but the results can already be seen. The best Cantarutti wines this year are two new blends. Canto, a wine Antonella has dedicated to herself, is from 60 percent tocai, with sauvignon and pinot bianco vinified separately in stainless steel. The aromas of apple and acacia blossom meld over a close-knit, but very fresh and bright-tasting, texture. The name of the tocai, chardonnay and sauvignon-based Antizio is a conflation of Antonella and Fabrizio while the wine itself offers a long, convincing palate laced with fresh walnut and elderflower. The Carato red, obtained mainly from cabernet sauvignon, is concentrated both in the glass, where there are still youthful highlights, and on the nose, which privileges spicy aromas. The palate is equally convincing, although it needs time to breathe unless you are willing to cellar it for a few months to mellow out the tannins. Good scores also went to the two monovarietal wines, the elegant, alcohol-rich COF Pinot Grigio with its attractive note of yellow plum, and the elderflower and apple Sauvignon, its buttery palate echoing the nose and signing off with a typically sinewy finish. All the other Cantarutti wines easily earned One Glass. The delicate Tocai has a crisp apple aroma, the traditional-style and very drinkable Chardonnay, the unpretentious but well-made Pinot Grigio Grave and the soft, fruity Merlot, with its subtle hint of astringency. Unlike Antonella, we don't believe that the secret of success is finding the right name. Only hard, and often thankless, work can guarantee lasting success.

O	Friuli Grave Sauvignon l'Altro '99	🍷🍷	3*
O	Friuli Grave Bianco Martin Pescatore '98	🍷	3
●	Friuli Grave Cabernet Sauvignon '99	🍷	2*
O	Friuli Grave Chardonnay '99	🍷	3
O	Friuli Grave Pinot Grigio '99	🍷	3
●	Friuli Grave Merlot '99		2
●	Friuli Grave Refosco P. R. '99		2
O	Friuli Grave Traminer '99		3

O	COF Bianco Canto '99	🍷🍷	3*
O	COF Pinot Grigio '99	🍷🍷	3*
●	COF Rosso Carato '96	🍷🍷	5
O	COF Sauvignon '99	🍷🍷	4
O	Friuli Grave Bianco Antizio '99	🍷🍷	3*
●	COF Merlot '97	🍷	4
O	COF Tocai Friulano '99	🍷	3
O	Friuli Grave Chardonnay '99	🍷	3
O	Friuli Grave Pinot Grigio '99	🍷	3
●	COF Schioppettino '97	🍷🍷	4
●	COF Rosso Poema '97	🍷	5

S. GIOVANNI AL NATISONE (UD)

S. GIOVANNI AL NATISONE (UD)

LIVON
VIA MONTAREZZA, 33
FRAZ. DOLEGNANO
33048 S. GIOVANNI AL NATISONE (UD)
TEL. 0432/757173 - 0432/756231

RONCO DEL GNEMIZ
VIA RONCHI, 5
33048 S. GIOVANNI AL NATISONE (UD)
TEL. 0432/756238

Excellent results, particularly in the premium-label range, are fast becoming the order of the day at Livon and the Braide Alte has established itself as a classic. A blend of chardonnay, sauvignon, picolit and moscato giallo, the nose is reminiscent of aromatic herbs, including thyme and mint, which return in the stunningly soft caress of the palate to be enhanced, enriched and even more persistent. A Three Glass wine to die for. But Braide Alte wasn't the only Livon wine on the short list for paradise. Other contenders were the Tocai, which combines a sweet apple and tangerine nose with a fresh, creamy palate; the Ribolla Roncalto, from a recently purchased estate, whose enticingly complex structure is elegant and perfectly balanced; the Sauvignon, a stylish classic with crisp, lingering aromas of rue and tomato; the Refosco Riul, which offers nose and palate clean, rich notes of alcohol preserved black cherries, liquorice and bitter chocolate; and the Tiareblù, a merlot and cabernet blend aged slowly in barriques. The typical aromas of cabernet franc are well to the fore, attractively offset by sweet, juicy berry fruit Then came the long line of runners-up. These range from the Cabernet Arborizza, one of the classic Friulian Cabernet Francs, with its notes of red pepper, stewed raspberries and Peruvian bark, to the aristocratic Verduzzo, its apple and confectioner's cream given a sweetish edge by the phenols, through to the Picolit, with a mouth-filling, vanillaed, acacia blossom palate so glycerine-rich that some will find it cloying. Finally, we tasted the Chardonnay, one of the classic, second-label wines. It is more than good enough to underscore the quality of the premium range and assure us that the general excellence of Livon wines is no coincidence.

Our assessments of wines tasted at the cellar often differ from evaluations of the same wines made later on. Why should this be so? As we chatted to Serena Palazzolo, the owner of Ronco del Gnemiz, we realized we were tasting for that Guide wines that were not yet ready and would only be released in January of the following year. That's why we have included notes on only three wines while the list below features wines tasted in August '99 that went on the market in early 2000. However, the next edition of the Guide will again examine the entire Ronco del Gnemiz range. The Rosso del Gnemiz '97, a Bordeaux blend that usually acquires immense stature after a few years in the bottle, came very close to hitting the Three Glass jackpot. Its intense ruby colour unveils a nose of wild berry tart, plum, spices and alcohol, laced with a youthful green note. The attack on the palate is stunning and the fruit genuinely sumptuous. Great structure, firm tannins and admirable length complete the picture. The Tocai Friulano went into the bottle earlier than usual. It reveals excellent structure in a mellow and very interesting palate. There is good breadth in the fruit aromas and a nice tangy note in the finish. The Verduzzo Friulano '97 is the colour of old gold. On the nose, there are notes of apricots, nuts and a hint of figs while the sweet, fresh-tasting and full-flavoured palate unveils a finish of sweet fruit and candied citrus peel.

O	Braide Alte '98	🍷🍷🍷	6
O	Collio Chardonnay Braide Mate '98	🍷🍷	5
●	COF Refosco P. R. Riul '97	🍷🍷	5
O	Collio Ribolla Gialla Roncalto '99	🍷🍷	5
O	Collio Sauvignon Valbuins '99	🍷🍷	5
O	Collio Tocai Friulano Ronc di Zorz '99	🍷🍷	5
●	Tiareblù '96	🍷🍷	5
O	COF Verduzzo Friulano Casali Godia '98	🍷	5
●	Collio Cabernet Franc Arborizza '97	🍷	5
O	Collio Chardonnay '99	🍷	4
O	Collio Picolit Cumins '97	🍷	6
O	Braide Alte '96	🍷🍷🍷	6
O	Braide Alte '97	🍷🍷🍷	6
O	Collio Sauvignon Valbuins '96	🍷🍷🍷	5

O	COF Tocai Friulano '99	🍷🍷	4
O	COF Verduzzo Friulano '97	🍷🍷	4
●	Rosso del Gnemiz '97	🍷🍷	6
O	Chardonnay '90	🍷🍷🍷	6
O	COF Chardonnay '91	🍷🍷🍷	6
O	COF Chardonnay '97	🍷🍷	5
●	Rosso del Gnemiz '95	🍷🍷	6
●	Rosso del Gnemiz '96	🍷🍷	6
●	COF Schioppettino '97	🍷	5
O	COF Sauvignon '98	🍷	5

S. GIOVANNI AL NATISONE (UD)   S. LORENZO ISONTINO (GO)

VILLA CHIOPRIS
VIA MONTAREZZA, 33
FRAZ. DOLEGNANO
33048 S. GIOVANNI AL NATISONE (UD)
TEL. 0432/757173

LIS NERIS - PECORARI
VIA GAVINANA, 5
34070 S. LORENZO ISONTINO (GO)
TEL. 0481/80105

Villa Chiopris is a Livon-group estate that stands on the border of the Grave and Isonzo DOC zones. The alluvial soil is very stony and covered by a thin layer of fertile soil, washed down from the hills of the more exalted Colli Orientali del Friuli denomination. The cellar has opted for a strategy of producing easy-drinking wines and employs the modern winemaking techniques that serve to enhance precisely these characteristics, including cold maceration, soft crushing, controlled temperature fermentation in stainless steel and maceration on the lees. Since the pleasure of a glass of wine at home often comes from its freshness and fruit-rich flavour (you can't always be opening world-class bottles with a serious pedigree and colossal concentration), we feel it is right to point the spotlight at the clean, well-made products of Villa Chiopris. We'll start with the Tocai, a real find with its elegant sweet tobacco and floral aromas that return to linger deliciously on the palate. Moving on to the Chardonnay, we note tropical fruit, jasmine and a faint hint of hazelnut on the nose. The palate foregrounds papaya, striking an attractive balance of acidity and alcohol-derived softness. Then there is the Pinot Grigio, a little straightforward, perhaps, but perfect with a wide range of seafood dishes, and the label's Sauvignon. The latter's nose mingles broom with tomato leaf, introducing a slightly bitter palate that might belong to a dry Moscato. Of the two reds, we preferred the Merlot. Although a little dilute, it is attractively fresh-tasting and the tannins are very well-behaved.

The wines produced by Alvaro Pecorari are some of the region's finest. This year, the nine Pecorari bottles collected one Three Glass rating, five comfortable Two Glass scores and three effortless One Glass awards. It's a result that reflects the balance and personality of the range for Lis Neris has three labels. The standard line is vinified in stainless steel, the label bearing only the name of the variety. The middle range has both vine type and vineyard on the label and the wines are skilful blends of steel and oak-vinified batches. But the flagship range is vinified exclusively in wood and includes Sant'Jurosa, Dom Picòl and Lis Neris. But let's talk about the wines. Three enthusiastic Glasses went to an unforgettable Pinot Grigio, the Gris. It has a lovely, rich straw-yellow colour that introduces hints of broom, pear and honey. The wonderfully stylish weight on the palate has loads of fruit, overlaid with restrained notes of vanilla and a long silky texture. The steel-vinified Pinot Grigio was also outstanding. Moving on to the Chardonnays, the Sant'Jurosa has attractive, juicy, hazelnut and mango fruit while the moderately intense, but very well-balanced, Jurosa progresses from a sweetish entry to a fresher, more austere mid palate. The appealingly uncomplicated standard-label version has aromas reminiscent of orange. The standard Sauvignon is surprisingly bright and drinkable on the palate, with its notes of yellow plum and tomato leaf. The middle range version is true to type. Dry and sinewy, it unveils aromas of walnutskin and melon. Then to round off the threesome comes the sweet, well-structured Dom Picòl, which however fails to fill the mouth. The Rosso, a blend of merlot and cabernet sauvignon, is "only" worth a One Glass.

O	Friuli Grave Tocai Friulano '99	♟♟	3*
O	Friuli Grave Chardonnay '99	♟	3
●	Friuli Grave Merlot '99	♟	3
O	Friuli Grave Pinot Grigio '99	♟	3
O	Friuli Grave Sauvignon '99	♟	3
●	Friuli Grave		
	Cabernet Sauvignon '99		3

O	Friuli Isonzo Pinot Grigio Gris '98	♟♟♟	4
O	Friuli Isonzo Chardonnay		
	Jurosa '98	♟♟	4
O	Friuli Isonzo Chardonnay		
	Sant'Jurosa '98	♟♟	5
O	Friuli Isonzo Pinot Grigio '99	♟♟	4
O	Friuli Isonzo Sauvignon '99	♟♟	4
O	Friuli Isonzo Sauvignon Picòl '99	♟♟	5
O	Friuli Isonzo Chardonnay '99	♟	4
●	Friuli Isonzo Rosso Lis Neris '97	♟	6
O	Friuli Isonzo Sauvignon Dom Picòl '98	♟	5
O	Friuli Isonzo Sauvignon		
	Dom Picòl '96	♟♟♟	5
O	Tal Lûc '97	♟♟	6
●	Isonzo Rosso Lis Neris '95	♟	6

350

S. LORENZO ISONTINO (GO)   S. QUIRINO (PN)

PIERPAOLO PECORARI
VIA TOMMASEO, 36/C
34070 S. LORENZO ISONTINO (GO)
TEL. 0481/808775

RUSSOLO
VIA S. ROCCO, 58/A
33080 S. QUIRINO (PN)
TEL. 0434/919577

Pierpaolo's best bottle this year is his Baolar, a wine aged in the wood for two years and whose release he delayed. It is a monovarietal Merlot, made with fruit from a classic Isonzo vineyard on stony, well-drained soil. The concentrated ruby in the glass heralds a rich aroma of plum and cassis then the convincingly long, well-balanced palate firms up after a soft, gentle entry, becoming almost austere in the finish. The Pinot Grigio Olivers is just as impressive. The vibrant, copper-tinged, straw-yellow ushers in a nose that opens slowly into aromas of peach and spring flowers against a backdrop of elegant toastiness. The same flower and fruit bouquet in the after-aroma of the subtly convincing palate. Confirmation that recent vintages have been exceptional for Pinot Grigio comes from the steel-fermented standard-label version, which scored well for its admirably clean palate and fresh, sweet nose. A very persuasive glass indeed. The other wines were well up to scratch. The Sorìs has a vibrant golden colour flecked with emerald green and a varietal nose of pineapple, although it goes over the top with notes of pear drops. The texture on the palate is nice and it also offers reasonable length and balance. The fruity version of the Malvasia has sufficient alcohol to support the stylish, but very discreet, aromatic notes. Next, the Pinot Bianco put on a good show, even though it was in a little difficulty since it had only recently gone into the bottle. Then came the Kolàus, a decently varietal Sauvignon. Our only disappointment was the Pratoscuro, a blend of müller thurgau and riesling that has still to settle.

This is the first "Friulian" profile for the Russolo estate. This year, the winery moved to San Quirino, where it has owned vineyards since 1990. The estate of about 16 hectares is run by oenologist Iginio Russolo and his son, Rino, who looks after sales. The vineyards stand on the poor, gravelly, alluvial soil of the "magredi" but the Russolos still managed to come up with a Pinot Nero. The entry on the nose offers cinnamon and pepper spice, coffee, vanilla and wild berry jam before the palate mirrors the same aromas, overlaying them with oak and adding lingering nuances of redcurrant and spices in the finish. Pear, almond and curious mossy notes emerge on the nose of the Tocai, returning on the rich-flavoured palate that signs off with an attractive note of ripe russet pear. There was no denying the Müller Thurgau its One Glass. A complex and very varietal wine, its rich, fresh-tasting palate unveils notes of elderflower, banana and apple. Best of the I Legni range were the Chardonnay and the Merlot. The former has a seriously good entry on the nose, with distinct, well-balanced aromas of honey, banana and ripe apple and pear. These are echoed on the attractively soft palate that loses out, albeit only marginally, to the acidity in the finish. The Merlot is a very successful marriage of mulberry and black cherry aromas on nose and palate, which also throw in varietal hints of hay and coffee. Doi Raps ("two bunches" in Friulian) is an original blend of late-vintage pinot and sauvignon (and moscato, we were tempted to suggest) that delights nose and palate with aromas of melon, elderflower and wild roses. Next came the rich, fruity palate of the Ronco Sesan, an intriguing combination of peach, apricot and white plum. Finally, the Borgo di Peuma red is very professionally made.

● Merlot Baolar '97	▼▼	6
○ Pinot Grigio '99	▼▼	4
○ Pinot Grigio Olivers '98	▼▼	5
○ Chardonnay Sorìs '98	▼	5
○ Friuli Isonzo Pinot Bianco '99	▼	3
○ Malvasia '99	▼	4
○ Sauvignon Kolàus '98	▼	5
○ Pratoscuro '98		5
○ Sauvignon Kolàus '96	♈♈♈	5
● Merlot Baolar '96	♈♈	6
○ Sauvignon '98	♈♈	4
● Refosco P. R. '96	♈	6

○ Friuli Grave Tocai Friulano Ronco Calaj '99	▼▼	3*
● Pinot Nero Grifo '97	▼▼	5
● Borgo di Peuma '97	▼	5
○ Chardonnay I Legni '98	▼	4
○ Doi Raps '98	▼	4
● Friuli Grave Cabernet I Legni '97	▼	4
● Friuli Grave Merlot I Legni '97	▼	4
○ Müller Thurgau Mussignaz '99	▼	3
○ Ronco Sesan '98	▼	3
○ Sauvignon I Legni '98	▼	4
● Friuli Grave Refosco P. R. I Legni '97		4
○ Malvasia Istriana '99		3

SACILE (PN)

VISTORTA
BRANDINO BRANDOLINI D'ADDA
VIA VISTORTA, 87
33077 SACILE (PN)
TEL. 0434/71135

The settlement of Vistorta, on the border between Friuli and the Veneto, belonged until recently to the noble Brandolini d'Adda family. The cottages housed the estate's workers while the main building was the family residence and focus of the farm. Brandino Brandolini, the present estate manager, divided the property into small lots. This has enabled the old village to be repopulated by young families. The estate itself embraces more than 220 hectares, equally distributed between Friuli and the Veneto and divided by a canal that once served to drain a marsh. Today, there are 25 hectares under vine in Friuli, almost exclusively reserved for merlot, with a few rows of carmenère (a cousin of cabernet franc) and syrah. In the '98 vintage, the latter two varieties made up five percent of the Vistorta blend. The experience of Georges Pauli, the oenologist from Château Gruaud-Larose, is crucial in deciding the blends. It should be remembered that only 65 percent of the estate's wine goes into the bottle. The winemaking strategy aims for drinkable wines that can be served with a wide range of foods, rather than body. Ageing capacity and improvement in the cellar are also priorities. We can confirm this after conducting many vertical tastings that reveal just how far previous vintages have come on. But let's look at the Vistorta '98, obtained from fruit harvested before the heavy rain that complicated the vintage in much of the region. Its structure and concentrated fruit are obvious on the nose, where notes of leather and spice emerge, and the delightfully fresh-tasting palate mirrors the same aromas beautifully. All in all, a wine that is drinking deliciously now and has even better prospects.

SAGRADO (GO)

CASTELVECCHIO
VIA CASTELNUOVO, 2
34078 SAGRADO (GO)
TEL. 0481/99742

You can see straight away that Gianni Bignucolo, the winery manager and oenologist, is a passionate and very experienced winemaker. The estate is currently expanding to a total of 40 hectares under vine and laying the foundations for an annual production of 300,000 bottles. The objective is to make wines for the cellar, so late harvesting is essential. We should point out, though, that when we tasted this year, the whites were still closed and reduced, so we will have to hold fire. It was a different story with the reds because the Cabernet Sauvignon and Refosco were actually in the running for Three Glasses. The Cabernet Sauvignon has broad, delicate aromas of bramble, plum jam, tobacco and coffee on the nose, echoed in the concentrated entry on the palate, whose good thrust and breadth take you through to a finish of pennyroyal and roses. The Refosco shows what can be done with a native variety that is so frequently let down by local producers. Black cherry purée, milky coffee, Peruvian bark and mint come through on the nose, which is followed up by mulberry, coffee grounds and tobacco on the broad, masculine palate. Only a notch or two lower came the Cabernet Franc. Its rich nose of cassis, roses and cherries, with hints of tobacco and coffee in the finish, introduces a satisfyingly well-sustained palate that signs off with nuances of coffee and mulberries. The Terrano '99 very nearly earned a Glass. This classic local variety yields a wine that lacks polish when young but mellows with cellar ageing. Then One Glass went to the '97 Carso Rosso Tumino, a blend of cabernet and terrano. Finally, the Traminer was also well worth a Glass, despite excess reduction that was slow to disappear. It is fine interpretation of the variety and has good length.

● Friuli Grave Merlot Vistorta '98	♥♥	4
● Friuli Grave Merlot Vistorta '95	♀♀	4
● Friuli Grave Merlot Vistorta '97	♀♀	4
● Friuli Grave Merlot Vistorta '96	♀	4

● Carso Cabernet Franc '97	♥♥	4
● Carso Cabernet Sauvignon '97	♥♥	4
● Carso Refosco P. R. '97	♥♥	4
● Carso Rosso Turmino '97	♀	4
○ Carso Traminer Aromatico '99	♀	3
● Terrano '99		3
● Carso Cabernet Franc '96	♀♀	4
● Sagrado '95	♀♀	5
● Terrano '97	♀	4

SPILIMBERGO (PN)

TORREANO DI CIVIDALE (UD)

PLOZNER
VIA DELLE PRESE, 19
FRAZ. BARBEANO
33097 SPILIMBERGO (PN)
TEL. 0427/2902

JACUSS
V.LE KENNEDY, 35/A
LOC. MONTINA
33040 TORREANO DI CIVIDALE (UD)
TEL. 0432/715147

It was during the 60s when the Plozner-Maffei family began to grow grapes on their 100 hectares in the flatlands around Spilimbergo. Many years have passed but the overall quality and cellarability of their products remain unchanged. We retasted the Chardonnay Riserva '96 and found it to be even better than it was last year. It has something of a Chablis about it, and you could say the same for the '98 version. This could well be due to the ungenerous soil and the dry site climate that keeps the fruit healthy until it is harvested. Or it might be the skills of oenologist, Francesco Visentini, and manager, Valeria Plozner. Whatever the reason, you can bank on the quality of these wines. The Sauvignon, as ever, is excellent. It offers varietal aromas of tomato leaf, elderflower and spring flowers that return on the palate, enhanced with notes of red pepper and pear. Only moderately well-structured, the ace up this wine's sleeve is its stylish complexity. Rich notes of white plum emerge on the nose of the Pinot Grigio to give way in the finish to the variety's typical minerally notes. These are echoed on the palate in a long finish that reveals a refreshingly tangy acidity. The Tocai is instantly recognizable from its nose of crusty bread and yellow apples through to a palate redolent of almonds and pears, and it rounds everything off with an attractively long finish. Although it comes from a very intractable variety, the Pinot Nero Riserva put on a great show. It's a truly delicious wine, both for its notes of tobacco-laced mulberry and redcurrant, present on the nose and in the mouth, and for the good thrust on a palate backed up by mellow tannins. Finally, the Traminer and Chardonnay both earned a place in the Guide.

This family-owned winery, run by brothers Sandro and Andrea Iacuzzi, extends over ten hectares and produces roughly 50,000 bottles a year. Despite the compact dimensions of the property, the Iacuzzis enjoy experimenting. However, the wines presented to the panel included a serious wood-aged red, a commendably mature Picolit and – unusually for Friuli – a range of very solid reds. The amber-yellow Picolit unveils varietal aromas of apricot, orange and vanilla before giving its best in the broad, buttery palate that passes seamlessly from vanilla to sweet fruit, finishing on a note of walnuts and figs. Lindi Uà is a red blend of merlot, cabernet and refosco with arresting, reasonably intense, Peruvian bark aromas over mulberry jam, tobacco and coffee. The front palate is fruity and full-flavoured, hinting at plums and mulberries, and progresses well through to a finish where the tannins have still to mellow fully. The Verduzzo came close to earning Two Glasses. Its amber-tinged colour heralds pervasive and very varietal notes of stewed apple. These return on a palate that has plenty of thrust and a long finish that foregrounds apple and orange. The Merlot has a very good nose with intense, yet elegant, hints of Peruvian bark, mulberry jam and coffee. The palate falls off a little because of the still roughish tannins but these will mellow out given time. The Iacuzzi brothers' interpretation of Schioppettino, an ancient local Friulian variety, is redolent of Parma violets, mulberries and white pepper. And in conclusion, there were Guide mentions for the Refosco, Tazzelenghe, Tocai Friulano and La Torca, a white blend of müller thurgau and incrocio Manzoni grapes.

○	Friuli Grave Sauvignon '99	🍷🍷	3*
○	Friuli Grave Pinot Grigio '99	🍷	3
●	Friuli Grave Pinot Nero Ris. '97	🍷	4
○	Friuli Grave Tocai Friulano '99	🍷	3
○	Friuli Grave Chardonnay '99		3
○	Friuli Grave Traminer Aromatico '99		3
○	Friuli Grave Sauvignon '98	🍷🍷	3
○	Friuli Grave Chardonnay Ris. '96	🍷	4

○	COF Picolit '97	🍷🍷	6
●	COF Rosso Lindi Uà '96	🍷🍷	4
●	COF Merlot '98	🍷	3
●	COF Schioppettino '98	🍷	3
○	COF Verduzzo Friulano '98	🍷	3
○	La Torca '98		3
●	COF Refosco P. R. '98		3
○	COF Tocai Friulano '99		3
●	Tazzelenghe '97		3

TORREANO DI CIVIDALE (UD)   TORREANO DI CIVIDALE (UD)

VALCHIARÒ
VIA CASALI LAURINI, 3
33040 TORREANO DI CIVIDALE (UD)
TEL. 0432/712393

VOLPE PASINI
VIA CIVIDALE, 16
FRAZ. TOGLIANO
33040 TORREANO DI CIVIDALE (UD)
TEL. 0432/715151

The Valchiarò winery is owned by five friends - Lauro De Vincenti in the chair, Emilio Balutto, Giampaolo Cudicio, Armando Piccaro and Galliano Scandini – who are all engagingly approachable but very serious wine professionals. The results keep coming through and this year they have accumulated a fine collection of Glassware. The estate's plots are in the Chiarò valley, a location by no means ideal for viticulture as the thermometer can drop alarmingly low. But when the vineyards are cultivated with sufficient attention, quality is sure to be the outcome. It was a sweet wine, the Verduzzo Friulano, that gained the highest score thanks to the vein of acidity that steers the palate away from excessive cloying. Its old gold colour introduces aromas of baked apple and sweet Dutch pipe tobacco while the palate mingles the wine's trademark apple with subtly understated varietal tannins. The Merlot '98 still has some way to go but even now can offer sweet fruit aromas and a palate with robust fruit and tannin structure. In contrast, the '98 Refosco is drinking wonderfully now. There are complex sweet and spicy notes on the nose which are echoed on the palate, where gentle tannins support the lingering finish. El Clap, which means "the rock" in Friulian, derives from a blend of oak-aged merlot, cabernet franc and refosco. The aromas are austere, ranging from time-worn wood to plums and raspberry syrup. Its rich, lingering palate reveals substantial structure. The fruity, deliciously elegant Tocai Friulano has attractive texture on the palate while the copper-flecked Pinot Grigio progresses from a sweet fruity nose, with hints of black cherry, to a refreshingly zesty palate. Check out Valchiarò. The impressive quality of the wines is complemented by a very competitive pricing policy.

Emilio Rotolo, the current owner, continues to pour money into the estate in his ongoing quest for quality. Having built and fitted out the cellars, as well as replanting a number of vineyards, Emilio has called in as consultant Riccardo Cotarella, one of Italy's leading oenologists, to work with agronomist Marco Simonit and wine technician Pierpaolo Sirch. A doctor originally from Calabria, Rotolo is partnered by Friulian Rosa Tomaselli, who looks after public relations and the impressive conference and accommodation facilities. Zuc is the Volpe Pasini premium range of wines, all oak-aged in varying proportions, and this year, the '99 Pinot Bianco Zuc secured Emilio his first Three Glass award. The elegant aromas of apple, tobacco and pear with minerally notes, the refreshing entry on the palate and the sure-footed progression of fruit on the palate, accompanied by a close-knit texture and a generous after-aroma, were more than enough to convince the panel. The Tocai Zuc also scored well up in the Two Glass range for its bitter almonds over apple and pear nose, mirrored on a palate that signs off with a lingering finish. And the Chardonnay Zuc '98 is just as good as the Tocai. There are notes of tobacco, vanilla, ripe banana and apricot on the nose and the palate is rich and well-sustained, revealing attractive acidity and hints of milky coffee in the long after-aroma. Next was the Le Roverelle, a blend of oak-aged pinot bianco, chardonnay, sauvignon and picolit that unfurls aromas of vanilla, sweet Dutch pipe tobacco and ripe fruit before revealing great structure and good progression through to the long finish. The Cabernet Zuc '98 is a broad-shouldered wine whose fruit is easily equal to the task of keeping the masterfully judged oak in its place. Finally, the Volpe label Refosco '99 is complex and austere, hinting at spices and red berry tart.

● COF Merlot '98	♟♟	3*
● COF Refosco P. R. '98	♟♟	3*
○ COF Verduzzo Friulano '99	♟♟	3*
● El Clap '96	♟♟	4
○ COF Pinot Grigio '99	♟	3
○ COF Tocai Friulano '99	♟	3
○ COF Bianco La Clupa '97	♟	3

○ COF Pinot Bianco Zuc di Volpe '99	♟♟♟	4
○ COF Bianco Le Roverelle Zuc di Volpe '98	♟♟	5
● COF Cabernet Zuc di Volpe '98	♟♟	4
○ COF Chardonnay Sel. Zuc di Volpe '98	♟♟	4
● COF Refosco P. R. Volpe Pasini '99	♟♟	3*
○ COF Tocai Friulano Zuc di Volpe '99	♟♟	4
● COF Cabernet Volpe Pasini '99	♟	3
○ COF Pinot Grigio Zuc di Volpe '99	♟	4
○ COF Tocai Friulano Volpe Pasini '99	♟	3
○ COF Bianco Le Roverelle Zuc di Volpe '97	♟♟	5
○ COF Chardonnay Sel. Zuc di Volpe '97	♟♟	4

OTHER WINERIES

The following producers obtained good scores in our tastings with one or more of their wines:

PROVINCE OF GORIZIA

Bruno e Mario Bastiani,
Cormons, tel. 0481/60725
Collio Pinot Bianco '99,
Collio Pinot Grigio '99

Albino Kurtin,
Cormons, tel. 0481/60685
Collio Pinot Bianco '99,
Collio Pinot Grigio '99

Magnàs, Cormons, tel. 0481/60991
Collio Tocai Friulano '99,
Friuli Isonzo Chardonnay '99

Ronco di Zegla - Maurizio Princic,
Cormons, tel. 0481/61155
Collio Chardonnay '99,
Collio Tocai Friulano '99

Giovanni - Roberto Ferreghini,
Dolegna del Collio, tel. 0481/60549
Collio Tocai Friulano '99,
Collio Pinot Bianco '99

Francesco Gravner,
Gorizia, tel. 0481/30882
Rosso Gravner '95, Ribolla Gialla '97

Radikon,
Gorizia, tel. 0481/32804
Collio Merlot '93, Oslavje '97

Redi Vazzoler, Mossa, tel. 0432/80519
Collio Chardonnay '99,
Collio Pinot Bianco '99

Lorenzon,
S. Canzian d'Isonzo, tel. 0481/76445
Friuli Isonzo Malvasia Istriana
I Feudi di Romans '99,
Friuli Isonzo Refosco P. R.
I Feudi di Romans '99

Gradis'ciutta,
S. Floriano del Collio, tel. 0481/390237
Collio Ribolla Gialla '99,
Collio Bianco Gradis'ciutta '99

Il Carpino,
S. Floriano del Collio, tel. 0481/884097
Bianco Carpino '98, Collio Ribolla Gialla '98

Edi Gandin,
S. Pier d'Isonzo, tel. 0481/70082
Filare Bianco Vigna Ronchetto '98,
Friuli Isonzo Chardonnay Vigna Cristin '99

PROVINCE OF UDINE

Mulino delle Tolle,
Bagnària Arsa, tel. 0432/928113
Friuli Aquileia Bianco Palmade '99,
Friuli Aquileia Cabernet Franc '99

Flavio Pontoni,
Buttrio, tel. 0432/674352
COF Tocai Friulano '99,
Lippe Rosso '99

Gigi Valle,
Buttrio, tel. 0432/674289
COF Sauvignon '99,
COF Merlot Gigi Valle Ris. '94

Midolini,
Manzano, tel. 0432/754555
COF Cabernet Franc '99,
COF Refosco P. R. '99

Antonutti,
Pasian di Prato, tel. 0432/662001
Friuli Grave Sauvignon Blanc Cru '99,
Friuli Grave Chardonnay Poggio Alto '98

Valerio Marinig, Prepotto, tel. 0432/713012
COF Tocai Friulano '99,
Biel Cûr Rosso '98

Ronco dei Pini,
Prepotto, tel. 0432/713239
COF Pinot Bianco '99,
Limes Rosso '98

Brojli - Franco Clementin,
Terzo di Aquileia, tel. 0431/32642
Friuli Aquileia Riesling '99,
Friuli Aquileia Pinot Bianco '99

Guerra Albano - Dario Montina,
Torreano di Cividale, tel. 0432/715077
COF Pinot Grigio '99,
COF Rosso Gritul '97

PROVINCE OF TRIESTE

Zidarich,
Duino-Aurisina, tel. 040/201223
Carso Rosso '98,
Carso Vitovska '98, Carso Malvasia '98

EMILIA ROMAGNA

After the promising results obtained in the last few years, the Emilia Romagna wine scene is going through something of a lull. This slowdown does not have so much to do with the overall improvement in quality which, as the outcome of our tastings show, continues to be encouraging and indeed, in some cases, extraordinary. There are many companies with several Two Glass wines, and there is renewed interest in wines which, until now, have not offered great results, such as Gutturnio. What has not been achieved this year, though, is a stunning exploit of the kind we have become used to. In the past, some of the region's producers could almost guarantee a Three Glass wine but after the record six Three Glass wines in last year's Guide, we have to make do with just one such prize-winning wine this time round. That blockbuster is the Marzieno, a blend of traditional sangiovese and innovative cabernet sauvignon, a very fine red produced by one of Emilia Romagna's most representative estates, Fattoria Zerbina at Faenza. After some years of frenzied activity, in which this region's top producers have tried to make up for the time lost in going after quantity by concentrating exclusively on quality, we noticed a tiny step backwards this year. Contributing factors are the uncertain quality of some of the vintages on show and, perhaps, the lack of a consolidated personal style in certain wines which, having acquired a successful, distinctive profile, suffer the ill effects of becoming rather too "technical" or of a commitment to body at all costs, producing wines that are more muscular but not sufficiently complex or graceful. After making appropriate improvements in modernizing their cellar techniques, producers now risk failing to follow suit in the vineyard, where many opt for conformity of style rather than aiming for real personality. The wines are correct but rather soulless and, in any case, lack the overall harmony and distinctive character that would enable them to face up to the keen competition of other wines from both Italy and abroad. Let us be quite clear though. The situation is far from desperate, especially considering the major efforts to improve by many estates, which were confirmed at our tastings. Moreover, we are convinced that the Emilia Romagna "system", which in the last few years has espoused the cause of quality in the food and wine sectors, of the rediscovery of regional products, and of wine-based tourism, will know how to react to this situation. Certainly, Cabernet Sauvignon, Merlot and Chardonnay are wines that have given excellent results in Emilia Romagna, but we think that the future of winemaking in this region is still hard to decipher and needs to be planned on a long-term basis. Producers should definitely put their faith in certain, though not all, local grape varieties, provided serious clonal research is carried out on them, and provided that vineyard and winery techniques can be found to highlight the specific characteristics of each grape. There is a need for in-depth study of aromatic profiles, yields per hectare, suitability for ageing in different types of wood and maceration times, to turn these varieties into products with a definite personality which will be elegant ambassadors for their terroir and their territory.

BERTINORO (FC)

BERTINORO (FC)

VINI PREGIATI CELLI
V.LE CARDUCCI, 5
47032 BERTINORO (FC)
TEL. 0543/445183

FATTORIA PARADISO
VIA PALMEGGIANA, 285
47032 BERTINORO (FC)
TEL. 0543/445044

Excellent results for Mauro Sirri and Emanuele Casadei. During 2000, they reaped the rewards of a series of decisions regarding company policy, which needed some time to filter through and bear fruit. These began with the purchase of their own vineyards, which gave them total control over the whole of the production cycle. Neither should we ignore their initially rather timid, then increasingly courageous, experiments with new wood. Finally, we have to take into consideration their application of more ambitious production techniques, associated with their new plantings of so-called international grape varieties, including three hectares of chardonnay. It may well be easy, as some purists maintain, to make good wines from this grape variety but products of the calibre of the '99 Bron e Ruseval, so dubbed after the ancient nicknames of the owners' families, and their first experience with chardonnay grapes, certainly do not abound in the cellars of Romagna. It has perhaps a little too much of a straightforward, textbook nose but benefits from its nine months in barrique, which have yielded a soft, full-bodied, buttery and inviting wine. The Sangiovese Riserva Le Grillaie '97, aged partly in large barrels and partly in barrique, is an ambitious example of its type. The wine offers a spicy nose, which also displays hints of ripe fruit, and is warm, rounded and elegant. The Albana Passito Solara '98 returns to its past level. Characterized by a seductive fusion of alcohol and honeyed sensations, it reveals a finish that is sweet but not cloying. Lastly, the Sangiovese Superiore Le Grillaie '98 is worthy of praise, especially for its notable length on the palate.

A new era has begun in the life of this estate. After being run by Cavaliere Mario Pezzi, the first great ambassador for the wines of Romagna, it is now managed by his daughter, Graziella. The transfer has been carried out without fuss, or upheavals, and in full respect of the estate's winemaking traditions. Indeed, after a period of uncertainty that kept the many fans of this winery on tenterhooks, the estate seems finally to be progressing again along the path towards high quality. The future of the estate therefore seems to be assured by this symbolic handover from one generation to the next. In particular, it ensures that the consumer will continue to find, year after year, wines that recall the glories of the past, with allowances, of course, for the obvious differences between vintages. Our favourite products from this winery are still the reds, starting with the Barbarossa '96, made from the legendary grape of the same name. A light, elegant nose, dominated by hints of black cherry and oak, introduces extraordinarily persistent fruit on the palate, which is the product's most attractive characteristic. Reasonably mellow tannins give rise to notable structure and a satisfying roundness on the palate. The family's other fine red, the '96 Castello di Ugarte, is made from sangiovese. Better known as the Vigna delle Lepri, it entrances you with a garnet-ruby colour that tells you all you need to know about its extract. It reveals its best qualities on the palate, which offers balance and structure but also elegance. The '97 Albana Passito Gradisca is less complex than in previous vintages. On the palate it is fruity and long, though perhaps displaying an over-abundance of alcoholic warmth.

O	Albana di Romagna Passito Solara '98	🍷🍷	4
O	Bron e Ruseval Chardonnay '99	🍷🍷	3*
●	Sangiovese di Romagna Sup. Le Grillaie Ris. '97	🍷🍷	3*
●	Sangiovese di Romagna Sup. Le Grillaie '98	🍷	2*
O	Albana di Romagna Secco I Croppi '99		2
O	Trebbiano di Romagna Poggio Ferlina '99		1

●	Barbarossa '96	🍷🍷	4
●	Sangiovese di Romagna Castello di Ugarte Vigna delle Lepri Ris. '96	🍷🍷	4
O	Albana di Romagna Passito Gradisca '97	🍷	5
●	Sangiovese di Romagna Sup. Vigna del Molino '99		3
O	Albana di Romagna Passito Gradisca '93	🍷🍷	5
●	Barbarossa '95	🍷🍷	5

BERTINORO (FC)

BRISIGHELLA (RA)

GIOVANNA MADONIA
VIA DE' CAPPUCCINI, 130
47032 BERTINORO (FC)
TEL. 0543/444361 - 0543/445085

LA BERTA
VIA PIDEURA, 48
48013 BRISIGHELLA (RA)
TEL. 0546/84998

The annex of the family's villa, which overlooks the historic village of Bertinoro, contains some precious hidden treasures. Down in the cellar, still rather precariously arranged, you will find the few, generously proportioned oak barrels that are no doubt responsible for many of the highly successful wines of the past few years. Here, too, as is often the case, it is the strength and courage of the courteous owner, Giovanna Madonia, that have lifted this family winery above the mere run-of-the-mill. The estate firm may be small but no detail is left to chance, starting with the elegant labels, designed by the owner herself. As for the more substantial aspects – the wines themselves –, these benefit from the contribution of a brilliant member of the new school of Italian oenologists, Attilio Pagli. The estate philosophy is to favour Romagna's own indigenous grape varieties (we are, after all, at Bertinoro), but with one small, rather surprising, exception – the Sterpigno Merlot '98. This is an almost arrogant wine, with intense, persistent aromas of red berry fruit. It is big and rounded but with just the right vein of acidity to suggest that it has a long life ahead of it. Equally good is the Sangiovese Riserva Ombroso '97, with its long, penetrating scents of wood, tobacco and cocoa, as well as outstanding fullness on the palate. Rich in extract, it offers robust tannins and long, delicious, mouth-filling fruit. The Albana Passito Chimera '97 is an elegant and very well-balanced wine, enriched by unobtrusive oak, that unveils seductive botrytized notes and a warm, soft and sweet, but not cloying, palate.

This interesting winery is situated in the verdant hills that mark the boundary between Faenza and Brisighella. The good results currently being achieved may be ascribed, in good part, to young Costantino Giovannini who, having taken over the running of his father's estate, decided to invest economic resources in the property as well as his own inexhaustible human ones. Step by step, he has created a winery that is now a little gem and the final detail is an attractive new tasting room. For the last couple of years, Costantino has also been availing himself of the collaboration of Stefano Chioccioli, to guarantee the necessary level of dependability in his various wines. Costantino is a likeable, reflective character. For years, he has been racking his brain about what to do with the substantial quantity of an unusual grape variety for these parts (alicante) that the estate has in its vineyards. While we wait for his conclusions, we can review the products already on the market. The extraordinary Ca'di Berta '98, a blend of cabernet sauvignon and sangiovese made even finer by ageing in barrique, boasts an intense ruby colour. Its perfumes are persistent and refined, offering suggestions of ripe red berry fruit, while the palate is well-structured, soft and elegant. Robustness and good balance are the hallmarks of the Sangiovese Riserva Olmatello '97 and a powerful flavour and nicely gauged tannins are its most evident characteristics. The Sangiovese Superiore Solano '99 is very interesting indeed, with its sweetish nose, rather reminiscent of Mediterranean herbs. The full flavour reveals tempting notes of cocoa. Trebbiano and chardonnay are the grapes that go into the Pieve Alta '99, a wine of almost aromatic style. Finally, the malvasia-based Infavato '97 offers varietal aromas and a typically bitterish aftertaste.

○ Albana di Romagna Passito		
Chimera '97	🍷🍷	5
● Sangiovese di Romagna Sup.		
Ombroso Ris. '97	🍷🍷	4
● Sangiovese di Romagna Sup.		
Fermavento '99	🍷🍷	3*
● Sterpigno Merlot '98	🍷🍷	5
● Sterpigno Merlot '97	🍷🍷	5
● Sangiovese di Romagna Sup.		
Fermavento '98	🍷	3

● Colli di Faenza Rosso		
Ca' di Berta '98	🍷🍷	5
● Sangiovese di Romagna		
Olmatello Ris. '97	🍷🍷	4
● Sangiovese di Romagna Sup.		
Solano '99	🍷🍷	4
○ Colli di Faenza Bianco Pieve Alta '99	🍷	4
○ Infavato Passito '97	🍷	5
● Colli di Faenza Rosso		
Ca' di Berta '97	🍷🍷	4
● Sangiovese di Romagna		
Olmatello Ris. '95	🍷🍷	4
● Sangiovese di Romagna Sup.		
Solano '97	🍷🍷	4
○ Infavato Passito '96	🍷	4

CASALECCHIO DI RENO (BO)   CASTEL BOLOGNESE (RA)

TIZZANO
VIA MARESCALCHI, 13
40033 CASALECCHIO DI RENO (BO)
TEL. 051/577665 - 051/571208

STEFANO FERRUCCI
VIA CASOLANA, 3045/2
48014 CASTEL BOLOGNESE (RA)
TEL. 0546/651068

Conte Luca Visconti di Modrone keeps a close eye on the activities of this property, with 230 hectares, 35 of which are under vine, from the valley of the Reno up to 250 metres above sea level. But the reins of the estate are in the capable hands of Gabriele Forni. Hard work and passion produce a good-quality range, whose high spot this year is the '98 Cabernet Sauvignon, which took the panel by surprise. On the nose, it offers intense notes of very ripe fruit, together with more mature sensations of liquorice and black pepper. Rounded on the palate, it reveals soft tannins which have been mellowed by the oak used for ageing, which is in no way intrusive. The '99 Barbera is well-made, too. Refreshing and richly aromatic on the nose, it is handsomely crafted and extremely quaffable. These are all wines of great balance, thanks to the skilled attentions of oenologist, Giambattista Zanchetta. As for the whites, the estate is very committed to the indigenous pignoletto variety, offering it for now in two sparkling versions and promising a still wine in the near future. The Pignoletto Brut is one of the few sparklers in the area vinified using the Charmat method (it is an example that is definitely worth following. It displays a lively, youthful perlage and a fragrant, hazelnut nose. Appealing on the palate, it offers well-modulated acidity and good balance. The Pignoletto Frizzante has very fresh, fruity perfumes and a well-integrated fizz which is not too sharp and which makes it very pleasant on the palate. It has a typical, slightly bitter almondy finish. Also among the whites are a Riesling Italico with very characteristic mineral aromas and an austere flavour, and a Sauvignon with an unusual nose that offers, apart from the classic varietal traits, gooseberries, grapefruit and sage. The Pinot Bianco is fruity and well-made.

The wines of Stefano Ferrucci are always good, as well as being rather idiosyncratic. This is particularly true of his major red wines, the Domus Caia and Bottale, thanks to a decision to part-dry the sangiovese grapes for a few months prior to vinification. The results are wines which are different from the standard Sangiovese di Romagna, with a character that some people like and others do not. Whatever your view, these wines certainly stand out. The Domus Caia displays notes on the nose of very ripe, almost jammy fruit, with a hint of freshly roasted coffee in the finish. It is full and soft on the palate, though essentially powerful rather than elegant. The Bottale, aged in 500-litre barrels, immediately offers the nose typical aromas of partially dried grapes, together with a heady whiff of alcohol. It is still tough and monolithic on the palate, with a rather abrupt finish redolent of bitter liquorice, and in fact this is a wine which needs some bottle-ageing. The Centurione, on the other hand, is definitely ready for drinking. It is very clean and full on the nose, if somewhat harsh on the palate. Ferrucci produces three Albanas, the dry La Serena, a sweet Lilaria, and the Domus Aurea, made from partially dried grapes. The first lacks fragrance and body, the Lilaria is well-balanced, with restrained sweetness and distinct sensations of very ripe apples, while the Domus Aurea is a deep amber in colour with lots of alcohol and an attractive note of macaroons. Quite light on the palate, it has a finish which is reminiscent of sweet Normandy cider. We were very impressed by the Vino da Uve Stramature. Made from malvasia grapes dried on the vine for several months, it is elegant yet full on the nose, with delicate botrytis notes which make it even more refined. It is very soft in the mouth, and offers excellent length.

● Colli Bolognesi Cabernet		
Sauvignon '98	♟♟	3*
● Colli Bolognesi Barbera '99	♟	3
○ Colli Bolognesi Pignoletto Brut	♟	4
○ Colli Bolognesi Pignoletto		
Frizzante '99	♟	2*
○ Colli Bolognesi Pinot Bianco '99	♟	2
○ Colli Bolognesi Riesling Italico '99	♟	3
○ Colli Bolognesi Sauvignon '99	♟	3

● Sangiovese di Romagna		
Domus Caia Ris. '97	♟♟	5
○ Vino da Uve Stramature	♟♟	5
○ Albana di Romagna		
Dolce Lilaria '99	♟	3
○ Albana di Romagna Passito		
Domus Aurea '97	♟	5
● Sangiovese di Romagna		
Bottale Ris. '96	♟	6
○ Albana di Romagna Secco		
La Serena '99		2
● Sangiovese di Romagna Sup.		
Centurione '99		3
○ Albana di Romagna Passito		
Domus Aurea '96	♟♟	5

CASTEL S. PIETRO TERME (BO)   CASTELLO DI SERRAVALLE (BO)

UMBERTO CESARI
VIA STANZANO, 1120
FRAZ. GALLO BOLOGNESE
40050 CASTEL S. PIETRO TERME (BO)
TEL. 051/941896 - 051/940234

VALLONA
VIA S. ANDREA, 203
LOC. FAGNANO
40050 CASTELLO DI SERRAVALLE (BO)
TEL. 051/6703058 - 051/6703333

Sometimes quality and quantity – and here, we're talking about 2,000,000 bottles – can go hand in hand. That is in fact precisely what this estate, one of the most interesting in Emilia Romagna, has achieved over the last few years. In any case, the prerequisites for success are all there at Cesari. The winery is pretty much a model of advanced technology and hygiene, the vineyards are tended in an exemplary manner, and there is a well-knit winemaking team under oenologist Maurizio Pausa, and an owner whose exuberant, up-front personality has always been keen to embrace new challenges. Our opinions of the Liano were splendidly confirmed by the '97, a blend of 70 percent sangiovese and 30 percent cabernet sauvignon. Very generous yet precise on the nose, it unfurls positive fruity aromas as well as liquorice and sweet tobacco notes. There is great concentration and softness on the palate and in fact the wine only falls short, perhaps, in its tannins, which are well-amalgamated and nicely rounded, but not particularly dense. The Sangiovese Riserva '97 performed remarkably well. It lost a few points for the nose, but it is rounded and powerful, and very long on the palate. The Sangiovese Ca' Grande '99 is more straightforward, but still well-made. The Malise '99 is a curious bottle, obtained from a blend in which chardonnay fleshes out the pignoletto, giving the wine structure and softness. Decidedly more serious is the Laurento, a Chardonnay aged entirely in barrique. Sadly, the oak tends to overwhelm the exotic hints of banana, mango and papaya fruit, tiring both wine and drinker. The amber-coloured Albana Passito Colle del Re confirms itself as one of the best products of its type. On the nose, buttery notes alternate with dried figs and dates. Its sweetness is appropriately restrained, and its flavour is full and well-balanced, with delicate hints of Peruvian bark on the finish.

The ten hectares of vineyards replanted at Lamezzi di Monte San Pietro will soon come into production alongside the ten at Fagnano which have always belonged to the family. Production should therefore reach 150,000 bottles, and will be able to avail itself of the new underground winery. The 5,000 bottles of Cabernet Selezione '98 are certainly no disappointment. The dense, impenetrable colour leads into a sweetish, long, varietal nose, with hints of figs on the finish. Its rich yet elegant palate displays just the right amount of tannins, giving the wine an immediate appeal. The standard Cabernet Sauvignon, also a '98, manifests similar characteristics, but naturally less structure and intensity. The special selection of Chardonnay '98, fermented and aged in oak, and of which roughly 4,000 bottles were produced, confirms its class. Immediately recognizable thanks to distinct scents of ripe fruit perfectly integrated with the light toastiness of the oak, it unveils a rich, well-balanced palate, with good structure and remarkable length. The '99 Sauvignon and Chardonnay just missed out on Two Glass scores. The Sauvignon has a rich, intriguing nose with ripe fruit-rich and varietal aromas. The fruit on the palate is equally abundant, rich and elegant, echoing perfectly the sensations on the nose. In the Chardonnay, freshness is the dominant perception on the palate, followed by a long finish reminiscent of crusty bread. The still version of Pignoletto was also convincing. Intense and fruity on the nose, it turned out to be rich and soft on the palate, with reasonable depth. In the Frizzante version, we found a complexity on the nose that is uncommon in this style. The palate, too, has a well-defined zestiness that gives real personality to a very successful edition of what is, at first sight, a rather simple wine.

○ Albana di Romagna Passito		
Colle del Re '95	🍷🍷	5
○ Laurento '98	🍷🍷	4
● Liano '97	🍷🍷	5
● Sangiovese di Romagna Ris. '97	🍷🍷	3*
○ Malise '99	🍷	3
● Sangiovese di Romagna Sup.		
Ca' Grande '99	🍷	3
○ Albana di Romagna Secco		
Colle del Re '99		2
● Sangiovese di Romagna '99		2
○ Trebbiano di Romagna Vigneto		
Parolino '99		2
● Liano '96	🍷🍷	5

● Colli Bolognesi Cabernet		
Sauvignon Sel. '98	🍷🍷	4
○ Colli Bolognesi Chardonnay		
Sel. '98	🍷🍷	3*
● Colli Bolognesi Cabernet		
Sauvignon '98	🍷	3
○ Colli Bolognesi Chardonnay '99	🍷	3
○ Colli Bolognesi Pignoletto Sup. '99	🍷	3
○ Colli Bolognesi Pignoletto		
Frizzante '99	🍷	2
○ Colli Bolognesi Sauvignon Sup. '99	🍷	3
● Colli Bolognesi Cabernet		
Sauvignon Sel. '97	🍷🍷🍷	4
● Colli Bolognesi Cabernet		
Sauvignon '97	🍷🍷	3

CASTELVETRO (MO)

CIVITELLA DI ROMAGNA (FO)

VITTORIO GRAZIANO
VIA OSSI, 30
41014 CASTELVETRO (MO)
TEL. 059/799162

PODERI DAL NESPOLI
VIA STATALE, 49
LOC. NESPOLI
47012 CIVITELLA DI ROMAGNA (FC)
TEL. 0543/989637

Perhaps not everyone knows that Vittorio Graziano's vineyard, low cordon-trained and spur-pruned with 5,500 vines per hectare, is a rarity in Emilia, and not only for its lambrusco. Even fewer will know that Vittorio, who is carrying out the work himself in the little free time he has available, is on the point of completing an underground cellar. We are prepared to take bets, however, that no one knows that, for the last ten years, all of the estate's wines have been organic, and are certified as such. In fact, Vittorio has decided not to tell anyone and not even to mention it on any of his labels. Coming to the wines themselves, we'll start with the 12,000 bottles of the quite excellent Grasparossa'99, one of the best vintages ever and one of the very few wines of its type still produced with natural re-fermentation in the bottle. Its attractively rustic nose, with rich fruity and floral scents, is accompanied by a fine, persistent bead. The dense, deep purple-ruby colour suggests that this is a Lambrusco of surprising structure. Rich and soft on the palate, it has a characteristic dose of freshness and tannins, leading in to a dry, reasonably long finish. The Primebrume, a sweet wine made from grasparossa grapes, has a less intense ruby colour than the dry version. This introduces a fragrant, floral nose, a fine perlage and sweet, lively fruit on the palate, where there are also attractively tangy overtones. The Spargolino, obtained from a blend of grapes in which sauvignon predominates, is a white made with re-fermentation in bottle and subsequent disgorgement. It has a rich, if not particularly fine mousse, and a very distinctive nose with ripe notes which are initially herbaceous, and then peach-like. The dry, austere palate has decent structure.

The considerable potential of this firm, located right in the very heart of Romagna alongside a road which leads up over the mountains into Tuscany, still remains mainly unfulfilled. There is some news to relate about the Ravaiolis' estate, such as the hiring of a new technical team in the shape of oenologist Alberto Antonini and agronomist Federico Curtaz, and the scrapping of the old wooden barrels in favour of a more up-to-date production philosophy which favours the use of smaller French oak casks. However, it takes time to effect real changes and some of the old characteristics of the winery's products remain unaltered, such as the jammy, over-ripe tones to be found in some of its wines. This tendency is not particularly unusual in this zone but it does not always make for contented consumers. Moving on to the wines themselves, the sangiovese-based Nespoli'98 is quite interesting even though there is a definite lack of balance between the nose and the palate. Oak from the barriques in which the wine has been aged is rather too predominant. The top wine here remains the Borgo dei Guidi, from sangiovese, cabernet sauvignon and raboso del Piave. This year, it is the '98's turn. A wine with marked tannins, great richness and structure, and good length, it offers the nose attractive hints of autumn leaves and toasted oak. The Damaggio'99, made from chardonnay, is a success, too, revealing soft, warm, fleshy and decidedly buttery fruit.

● Lambrusco Grasparossa			
di Castelvetro '99		♀	3
● Primebrume		♀	3
○ Spargolino Frizzante			3

● Borgo dei Guidi '98		♀♀	5
○ Damaggio '99		♀	3
● Il Nespoli '98		♀	4
● Borgo dei Guidi '95		♀♀	5
● Borgo dei Guidi '97		♀♀	5
● Sangiovese di Romagna Sup.			
Santodeno '98		♀	2
● Il Nespoli '97		♀	4

FAENZA (RA)

FAENZA (RA)

LEONE CONTI
VIA POZZO, 1
TENUTA S. LUCIA
48018 FAENZA (RA)
TEL. 0546/642149 - 0546/27130

FATTORIA ZERBINA
VIA VICCHIO, 11
FRAZ. MARZENO
48010 FAENZA (RA)
TEL. 0546/40022

For some years now Leoni Conti's activities have been in constant, healthy ferment, a state of affairs which, however, has not always helped him to express his full potential. At the moment, though, he seems to be going through a period of stability and self-confidence. Yet, for Leone, the desire to change at least something every year remains irresistible. Some wines disappear from his list. Others change their name. Still others acquire new labels. What remains unchanged, on the other hand, is his passion and his dedication to his work. Similarly unaltered, with regard to previous vintages, is the excellent showing of the estate's flagship wine, the Albana Passito Non Ti Scordar di Me, which is full, mellow, intense and fleshy, with great length. Less good is the Colli di Faenza Bianco Poderepalazzina, a blend of chardonnay and sauvignon fermented in oak, which, though long, seems rather tart and woody. More interesting is the Albana Secco Poderepozzo, which remains one of the best examples of its type. Of the three different Sangiovese di Romagnas presented, the best is the well-crafted, balanced and flavoursome Poderepozzo Le Betulle '98 while in the Contiriserva '97 we found the use of wood rather clumsy. On the nose, there are overwhelming scents of vanilla and liquorice, while on the palate the attenuating influence of the barrique is evident, tending to dry out the fleshiness of the fruit. We have saved until last our comments on the Rossonero, a product whose name betrays Conti's passionate loyalty to the red-and-black jersey of the AC Milan football team. The 1998 vintage was not as successful for syrah, which makes up 90 percent of the blend in this wine, as it was for George Weah. Ultimately, the wine reveals itself to have plenty of muscle but also to be rather rustic and over-tannic. Not exactly a League title candidate.

After the results obtained in our tastings, La Zerbina once again confirms its status as the most interesting producer in Romagna. This is in spite of the fact that one of its finest wines is not available this year because the '97 vintage of the Albana Passito Scacco Matto will only be released in 2001. The performance is the umpteenth demonstration of the great conscientiousness, rigour and care which characterize Maria Cristina Geminiani's running of the estate. Her dedication to study and research, and the wealth of experience she has acquired during the past few years spent at the winery, as well her courteousness and competence in public relations, make Maria Cristina the ideal model of what a modern producer should be. An outstanding vintage of the Marzieno, the '98, opens up the list of Glasses earned by the estate. A blend of 62 percent sangiovese with cabernet sauvignon, it is a wine of great concentration with a very firm tannic texture. Alcohol-rich and austere, yet well-rounded, it only needs a little bit of bottle-age in order to show at its best. Our Three Glass accolade, then, goes to this wine of great breeding and enviable balance. Next, there was the Pietramora '97, another characterful wine with a very deep colour and a splendidly clean, refined nose. It, too, has a powerful flavour – the richness of the tannins is impressive – but is entirely free of affectation. Indeed, it staggers you with its massive concentration and strong personality. The well-balanced and long Torre di Ceparano '98 displays greater backbone and structure than most wines of its type, while the Ceregio '99 is straightforward and correct.

○ Albana di Romagna Passito		
Non Ti Scordar di Me '97	🍷🍷	5
● Sangiovese di Romagna		
Poderepozzo Le Betulle '98	🍷🍷	3*
○ Albana di Romagna Secco		
Poderepozzo '99	🍷	3
● Rossonero '98	🍷	4
● Sangiovese di Romagna Sup.		
Contiriserva '97	🍷	3
○ Colli di Faenza Bianco		
Poderepalazzina '99		3
● Sangiovese di Romagna '99		2
○ Albana di Romagna Passito		
Non Ti Scordar di Me '96	🍷🍷	5
● Rossonero '97	🍷🍷	4

● Marzieno Ravenna Rosso '98	🍷🍷🍷	5
● Sangiovese di Romagna Sup.		
Pietramora Ris. '97	🍷🍷	5
● Sangiovese di Romagna Sup.		
Torre di Ceparano '98	🍷🍷	4
○ Albana di Romagna Passito		
Arrocco '96	🍷	5
● Sangiovese di Romagna Sup.		
Ceregio '99		2
○ Trebbiano di Romagna Dalbiere '99		2
○ Albana di Romagna Passito		
Scacco Matto '96	🍷🍷🍷	5
● Marzieno '95	🍷🍷🍷	5
● Marzieno Ravenna Rosso '97	🍷🍷🍷	5

FAENZA (RA)

FORLÌ

ISTITUTO PROFESSIONALE
PER L'AGRICOLTURA E L'AMBIENTE
VIA FIRENZE, 194
48018 FAENZA (RA)
TEL. 0546/22932

DREI DONÀ TENUTA LA PALAZZA
VIA DEL TESORO, 23
LOC. MASSA DI VECCHIAZZANO
47100 FORLÌ
TEL. 0543/769371

This small winery, run by Sergio Ragazzini, continues to turn out wines of great interest, but in decidedly small quantities. Here, wine is produced almost for fun as well as for reasons of research. The Istituto's own three and a half hectares accommodate 20 different grape varieties, cultivated using the most up-to-date techniques and yielding around 5,000 bottles overall each year. There is more than one path to quality, and we hope, therefore, that these products will emerge from the limited, haphazard market of local country fairs and festivals in order to reach a wider public. The most interesting bottles remain the sweet wines, beginning with the Amabile Persolino Passito Rosso '98 from malbo gentile grapes. Perhaps less fragrant than the previous vintage, but still full-bodied and concentrated, it unveils a delicate, persistent nose and a soft, mouth-filling flavour. This little gem of a dessert wine is redolent of chocolate, nuts, candied fruit and the homemade jams of childhood. The Albana Passito Ultimo Giorno di Scuola '98 has delicate, elegant perfumes whereas on the palate it is warm and well-balanced with notes of peach and apricot fruit and honey, which then give way to a bitter almondy finish. The Varrone '99, made from the burson variety, has a fresh, herbaceous nose, even though it is made from slightly super-ripe grapes. The purple hue is attractive while on the palate it is easy-drinking and a little short, but with an attractive simplicity of style. More ambitious, as evidenced by its strong scent of oak, is the Rosso di Nero '98, made from pinot nero. Its powerful tannins are tempered by the richness of the fruit and by the softness provided by a sustained level of alcohol, giving a final impression of considerable balance.

The pieces of the jigsaw puzzle are all there. Claudio Drei Donà's great passion. The professionalism and hard work of his son, Enrico. An oenologist of the calibre of Franco Bernabei. A winery that is irreproachable in terms of equipment and user-friendliness. And superbly tended vineyards. Yet the overall picture that should emerge from the above doesn't stand out quite as clearly as it ought to. We expected more from La Palazza, which had accustomed us to much more impressive performances. It is true that the '97 Cabernet Sauvignon Magnificat, the estate's top wine, was absent as it was still ageing at the time of our tastings. However, we did try, for the first time, the '95 Graf Noir, an exclusive, Bernabei "designer-label" wine made from sangiovese and cabernet sauvignon, and bottled only in magnums. Well, it has great extract, a dense, opaque, graphite-black colour, a rather closed and not entirely elegant nose, and a powerful, austere palate, with a bitterish aftertaste. All in all, not an absolutely impeccable wine. It has a number of minor defects that, taken individually, could be overlooked but that together brought down its score. The Pruno '96 showed well. It may lack a little something in comparison with previous vintages but it is still a powerful, well-rounded Sangiovese and a fine expression of the variety's potential in Romagna. The Chardonnay Tornese, on the other hand, is under par. The '98 showed much less well than earlier vintages. The oak is well-integrated and refrains from masking the as yet rather latent fruit but overall the wine lacks complexity and personality. The Notturno '98, the estate's house Sangiovese, is well-made and easy to drink.

○	Albana di Romagna Passito		
	Ultimo Giorno di Scuola '98	♟♟	4
●	Amabile Persolino Rosso		
	Passito '98	♟♟	5
●	Rosso di Nero Ravenna		
	Rosso '98	♟	3
●	Varrone Ravenna Rosso '99	♟	1*
●	Amabile Persolino Rosso		
	Passito '97	♟♟	5
○	Albana di Romagna Passito		
	Ultimo Giorno di Scuola '97	♟	4

●	Graf Noir '95	♟♟	6
●	Sangiovese di Romagna Sup.		
	Pruno Ris. '96	♟♟	5
○	Il Tornese Chardonnay '98	♟	5
●	Notturno Sangiovese '98	♟	3
○	Il Tornese Chardonnay '95	♟♟♟	4
●	Magnificat Cabernet		
	Sauvignon '94	♟♟♟	5
○	Il Tornese Chardonnay '97	♟♟	4
●	Magnificat Cabernet Sauvignon '92	♟♟	5
●	Magnificat Cabernet Sauvignon '93	♟♟	5
●	Magnificat Cabernet Sauvignon '95	♟♟	5
●	Sangiovese di Romagna Sup.		
	Pruno Ris. '95	♟♟	5

IMOLA (BO)

TRE MONTI
VIA LOLA, 3
40026 IMOLA (BO)
TEL. 0542/657122 - 0542/657116

LANGHIRANO (PR)

ISIDORO LAMORETTI
STRADA DELLA NAVE, 6
LOC. CASATICO
43013 LANGHIRANO (PR)
TEL. 0521/863590

This winery improves every year, acquiring new winemaking equipment and attaining ever-higher levels of quality. Vinification, too, is kept under constant control, with the primary aim of bringing out the very best from the grape varieties, indigenous or otherwise, that are planted in the company's vineyards. Nowadays, it is mainly young David and Vittorio Navacchia who look after all the phases of production. In a few short years, they have transformed themselves into exceptional entrepreneurs, assisted by the experience of "old" Sergio. The next objective for the estate and oenologist, Donato Lanati, is a major improvement in quality for the native whites. The Albano Secco Vigna della Rocca '99, which spends a brief period in small oak casks, is emblematic of the company philosophy. A warm, rounded wine with a fine oaky aroma, it offers attractive length of flavour. However, the cellar's premium wines remain the reds. The Boldo '99, from cabernet sauvignon and sangiovese, has a still youthful, and not yet entirely well-knit nose, with marked vanilla hints and a pleasant herbaceous tone. The very long, complex fruit on the palate is uncompromising, with soft, well-modulated tannins contributing to a seductive, mouth-filling roundness of flavour. The single-vineyard Sangiovese Thea '98 has a refined, clean aromatic profile and an aristocratic flavour with morello cherry notes. Modern elegance and finesse are the hallmarks of the 100 percent cabernet Turico '99, with its well-defined varietal aromas and long, reflective flavour while the Sangiovese di Romagna Riserva '97 is complex and well-balanced. All the whites are very well-made but the Salcerella '99, from chardonnay and albana, deserves a special mention. It has rich, grassy and fruity scents followed by a well-balanced palate that is backed up by reasonable structure and good alcohol.

Isidoro Lamoretti shows his skills again this year with the two products, the Vignalunga and the Moscato Dolce, which are becoming his estate's flagship wines, especially since they are made from varieties which have no competitors in this zone. The Vignalunga 71 from the '98 vintage confirms the good performance put up by the first two versions released and takes its place as one of the emerging reds from the area. It is a still barrique-aged red made from cabernet sauvignon and a tiny percentage of merlot. It has a deep, concentrated colour, a well-typed bouquet and intense, dry, weighty fruit on the palate. The Moscato, a partially-fermented grape must, is as refreshing and delicious as ever. The traditional-style fizzy Malvasia showed well, even if it reveals a more neutral nose than in the past, whereas the semi-sparkling Sauvignon, while well-managed, seems a little tired. The '98 Colli di Parma Rosso Vigna del Guasto is again a full-bodied, alcohol-rich wine. On the whole, these wines, from 20 hectares of specialized vineyards on the hills at Casatico, stand out as being among the best in the Colli di Parma DOC zone, even if you get the impression that the experiments with the new still wines may partly have distracted the able, enthusiastic Isidoro from giving the traditional semi-sparkling wines all the attention they deserve.

●	Colli d'Imola Boldo '99	▼▼	4
●	Colli d'Imola Cabernet Turico '99	▼▼	4
○	Colli d'Imola Salcerella '99	▼▼	4
●	Sangiovese di Romagna Ris. '97	▼▼	3*
●	Sangiovese di Romagna Sup. Thea '98	▼▼	4
○	Albana di Romagna Secco '99	▼	2*
○	Albana di Romagna Secco Vigna della Rocca '99	▼	3
○	Colli d'Imola Chardonnay Ciardo '99	▼	3
○	Trebbiano di Romagna '99	▼	2
○	Trebbiano di Romagna Vigna del Rio '99	▼	3
●	Colli d'Imola Boldo '97	▼▼▼	5

○	Colli di Parma Malvasia '99	▼	3
●	Colli di Parma Rosso Vigna del Guasto '98	▼	3
○	Moscato '99	▼	3
●	Vignalunga 71 '98	▼	4
○	Colli di Parma Sauvignon '99		3
●	Colli di Parma Rosso Vigna di Montefiore '96	▼▼	3

MODIGLIANA (FC)

MONTE S. PIETRO (BO)

CASTELLUCCIO
VIA TRAMONTO, 15
47015 MODIGLIANA (FC)
TEL. 0546/942486

ISOLA
VIA BERNARDI, 3
FRAZ. MONGIORGIO
40050 MONTE S. PIETRO (BO)
TEL. 051/6768428

Major news at this fine Romagna winery. Part of the company has been bought by Vittorio Fiore, one of the patriarchs of Italian oenology, with a consequent effect on the technical management of the estate. Just as the results of Attilio Pagli's brilliant hand were beginning to be apparent, and Pagli was finally able to produce premium-quality wines thanks to the recent purchase of new winemaking equipment and barrels, the young oenologist has to make way for the imposing figure of the new co-owner, who is obviously destined to take over the reins of the winery. Basically, we are witnessing a return to the time when Fiore fashioned the Ronco wines under the former ownership of the Baldis. Whether or not this latest change at Castelluccio will result in a further improvement in quality remains to be seen over the next few years. What we have for now are the products of a period in which the old and new regimes are rubbing shoulders. We'll begin with the Roncos, the single-vineyard Sangioveses. The austere and powerful Ronco delle Ginestre '97 is a little ill-defined on the nose, yet tannic and with exemplary length of flavour, where there are hints of liquorice and violets. The Ronco dei Ciliegi '97 is well-knit and fruity, the nose being more delicate and the palate more elegant. The Ronco della Simia '97 is unusual with respect to previous vintages. It is oddly rustic on both nose and palate but still possesses great structure and interest. The less prestigious version of Sauvignon from the estate, the Lunaria '98 (the more aristocratic Ronco del Re was not yet ready at the time of our tastings), was also slightly disappointing. Its aromas did not display much precision and alcohol dominated the fruit on the palate. The Sangiovese Superiore Le More '98 is appealing, with its full-bodied flavour of ripe berry fruit and its interesting oaky notes on the nose.

At Isola, everyone pulls together for the common cause. Marco Franceschini, his wife, their children and his parents provide a perfect picture of a genuine family-run estate. They are all involved, now on a full-time basis, in the business of making and selling wine, with the odd brief moment devoted to picking a little of the other varieties of fruit grown on this handsome estate in the middle of the Samoggia valley, set among abbeys, castles and mediaeval towers. This year, the Chardonnay Selezione '99, fermented in medium-sized oak barrels and of which only 2,000 bottles were produced, is the best wine. There is a nice balance between the wood and the fruit on the nose, the positive aromas of ripe fruit being delicately underlined by an attractive hint of vanilla. The crisp fruit on the palate echoes the sensations on the nose, and there is an appealing acidity that contributes freshness and length. The stainless steel-aged Chardonnay is technically clean and well-made. The nose is light yet characteristic and the fruit on the palate is soft and medium-bodied, but well-balanced. As has been the case in other vintages, the Pignoletto Frizzante stands out with its intense notes of ripe apples, its gentle effervescence and its generous fruit in the mouth. The Cabernet Sauvignon is also good. Well-defined and varietal on the nose, it is very soft, alcohol-rich and appealing. There is medium structure on the palate, even though the tannins are perhaps slightly excessive. All in all, an excellent red for everyday consumption. The Pignoletto Superiore is also worth a mention for its light vegetal notes, medium concentration and reasonable length.

● Ronco dei Ciliegi '97	❷❷ 5	● Colli Bolognesi Cabernet	
● Ronco delle Ginestre '97	❷❷ 5	Sauvignon '99	❶ 2*
○ Lunaria '98	❶ 4	○ Colli Bolognesi Chardonnay '99	❶ 2*
● Ronco della Simia '97	❶ 5	○ Colli Bolognesi Chardonnay	
● Sangiovese di Romagna Sup.		Sel. '99	❶ 3
Le More '98	❶ 3	○ Colli Bolognesi Pignoletto	
● Ronco delle Ginestre '90	❸❸❸ 6	Frizzante '99	❶ 2*
● Ronco dei Ciliegi '95	❷❷ 5	○ Colli Bolognesi Pignoletto Sup. '99	3
● Ronco dei Ciliegi '96	❷❷ 5		
○ Ronco del Re '97	❷❷ 5		
● Ronco della Simia '95	❷❷ 5		
● Ronco della Simia '96	❷❷ 5		
● Ronco delle Ginestre '95	❷❷ 5		
● Ronco delle Ginestre '96	❷❷ 5		

MONTE S. PIETRO (BO)   MONTEVEGLIO (BO)

TENUTA BONZARA
VIA S. CHIERLO, 37/A
40050 MONTE S. PIETRO (BO)
TEL. 051/6768324

SAN VITO
VIA MONTE RODANO, 6
FRAZ. OLIVETO
40050 MONTEVEGLIO (BO)
TEL. 051/964521

The Bonzarone, made from cabernet sauvignon, and the merlot-based Bonacciara, the two red wines from the '98 vintage, both obtained excellent results. Your initial impression is that they are in fact twins, both with great weight and breeding. Each displays well-defined aromas of very ripe berry fruit – the grapes must have been picked when absolutely perfect – which in the Bonzarone are combined with elegant, measured hints of spices, above all black pepper. In the Rocca di Bonacciara, the berry fruit is accompanied by even riper notes of plum and blackberry jam. Skilful use of barriques for ageing gives both the wines a sophisticated elegance and great allure, though each has its own individual personality to differentiate it from its stablemate. Owner Francesco Lambertini, who divides time between his overwhelming passion for wine and lecturing at university, consultant oenologist, Stefano Chioccioli, and all of the estate's staff can be happy with the results obtained. Now, they can concentrate even harder on the other wines, and especially the whites. These include this year a very unusual Pignoletto Classico which, having been partly fermented and aged in tonneaux, an innovative practice for the zone, offers slightly toasty sensations which combine with the variety's classic floral notes. The Sauvignon is typically aromatic and varietal. Its balance is enhanced by robust alcohol and it is rich and well-structured on the palate. The Pignoletto Frizzante is very fresh and a little prickly while the Pinot Bianco is measured and attractive. The company's second Merlot, the Rosso del Poggio, on the other hand, is still rather too much the "little brother" of the family, even if it is pleasantly quaffable.

This winery in the small Colli Bolognesi DOC zone has now harvested its 30th vintage. The programme of total replanting has also been completed with the last vineyard of sauvignon, which will come on-stream with the 2001 harvest. Present production is close to 100,000 bottles, of which 65,000 are Pignoletto Frizzante. The Mazzanti Brut Riserva spumante, with a production of little more than 3,000 bottles, comes from chardonnay and pignoletto grapes. The second fermentation is carried out at low temperatures using the prolonged Charmat method. The result is a wine with a light, and not particularly dense bead and faintly vegetal aromas. The fruit on the palate is rounded and of medium length. The Pignoletto in the traditional semi-sparkling version offers a pale straw-yellow colour and a delicate nose with light floral tones. On the palate, it is dry, well-balanced and appealingly enlivened by unobtrusive effervescence. The Cabernet Sauvignon boasts a fine deep ruby colour, introducing an attractive, quite alcoholic and lightly herbaceous nose. On the palate, it is fairly well-balanced, with medium depth, thanks partly to its relatively restrained tannins. A fine example of a red to uncork straight away. An honourable mention, too, for a pleasant Chardonnay, which is characterized on the nose by positive, sweetish, ripe fruit notes that come through only moderately on the palate. The Pignoletto Superiore has a bright straw-yellow colour and light scents of roasted nuts which are echoed on the crisp, dry palate.

● Colli Bolognesi Cabernet Sauvignon Bonzarone '98	♈♈	5
● Colli Bolognesi Merlot Rocca di Bonacciara '98	♈♈	5
○ Colli Bolognesi Pignoletto Cl. Vigna Antica '99	♈	3
○ Colli Bolognesi Sauvignon Sup. Le Carrate '99	♈	3
● Colli Bolognesi Merlot Rosso del Poggio '99		4
○ Colli Bolognesi Pinot Bianco Borgo di Qua '99		3
● Colli Bolognesi Cabernet Sauvignon Bonzarone '97	♈♈♈	5

● Colli Bolognesi Cabernet Sauvignon '99	♈	3
○ Colli Bolognesi Pignoletto Frizzante '99	♈	2*
○ Colli Bolognesi Pignoletto Sup. '99	♈	3
○ Mazzanti Brut Ris. '99	♈	4
○ Colli Bolognesi Chardonnay '99		3

OSPEDALETTO DI CORIANO (RN)   OZZANO TARO (PR)

SAN PATRIGNANO - TERRE DEL CEDRO
VIA S. PATRIGNANO, 53
47852 OSPEDALETTO DI CORIANO (RN)
TEL. 0541/756436 - 0541/362362

MONTE DELLE VIGNE
VIA COSTA, 25-27
43046 OZZANO TARO (PR)
TEL. 0521/809105

With all due modesty, we should like to lay claim to having discovered this very special estate. You will forgive us the sin of presumption but if you can now find the wines of this excellent winery pretty much everywhere in the region, it is probably due not only to their undoubted quality but also to the well-deserved promotion they have enjoyed through our Guide. It should be remembered that only a few years ago the wines of the San Patrignano community were ostracized by fears and an obscurantism which have nothing to do with the world of wine. After a series of variable vintages and varying philosophies of production, it is now oenologist Riccardo Cottarella who dictates the rules to the young and enterprising cellar staff. Again, the use of wood proves decisive and in particular the small French oak casks, dispensed with only a few years ago in favour of stainless steel. Obviously, resources and good winemaking equipment are plentiful here, nor is there any lack of determination to produce wines of high quality. Oak, as we just mentioned, sustains and tempers many of San Patrignano's wines, starting with a white, the Vintàn '99, made from trebbiano grapes. It has an intense colour, a well-defined note of vanilla and is warm and persistent on the palate. The reds are more interesting, especially the Avi '97, whose bouquet is dominated by spicy aromas from the oak. It has marked tannins on the palate, along with ripe fruit and cocoa notes, while the finish is full and rounded, reflecting the wine's aspirations to high quality. The intensity of colour of the Sangiovese Riserva Zarricante '97 is striking. Perhaps less elegant than the Avi, it is nevertheless full-bodied and forward. The Sangiovese Superiore Aulente '98 has delicate aromas and a soft, mouth-filling and very long flavour.

Andrea Ferrari's determination and the fresh commitment of the company as a whole to establish a name for Monte delle Vigne, especially in the realm of still wines, have spawned some interesting new products. The latest wine to come from the cellars at Ozzano Taro is a still '99 Malvasia, only recently drawn off from the barriques, which we tasted prior to its release and to which, of course, we have not yet given a rating. This product, made from those malvasia di Candia grapes that generally go into making the typical semi-sparkling whites of the Colli di Parma, is a barrique-fermented white wine with intensely aromatic varietal perfumes. On the palate, it is rich and mellow but has yet to find its true balance. A novelty, then, that is worth following with great attention because it could create a new style for malvasia in the Colli di Parma zone. The '98 vintage of what is by now a classic Monte delle Vigne wine, the Nabucco, was on show this year. It is a still red made from barbera and merlot and aged in barrique. Thanks to its greater array of aromas and flavours, and a better balance on the palate than last year, it deservedly earned Two Glasses. It has a soft, intense nose whose attractive sensations are confirmed on the palate. The good fruit in the mouth combines well with the oak, which ensures satisfying balance without threatening to predominate. An honourable mention, too, and a One Glass rating, goes to the well-typed Lambrusco. Finally, we should point out that, unhappily, this winery is going through a difficult phase as far as the semi-sparkling DOC whites are concerned. Some are barely decent whereas others, like the Sauvignon, were not even worth a mention in our tastings.

● Sangiovese di Romagna Sup. Avi Ris. '97	🍷🍷	5
● Sangiovese di Romagna Sup. Aulente '98	🍷🍷	3*
● Sangiovese di Romagna Sup. Zarricante Ris. '97	🍷🍷	4
○ Trebbiano di Romagna Vintàn '99	🍷	4
● Sangiovese di Romagna Sup. Zarricante Ris. '96	🍷🍷	4

● Nabucco '98	🍷🍷	5
● Lambrusco dell'Emilia '99	🍷	2
○ Colli di Parma Malvasia Tenuta La Bottazza '99		2
○ Malvasia Dolce '99		3
● Nabucco '96	🍷🍷	4
● Nabucco '97	🍷🍷	4
● Colli di Parma Rosso Tenuta Bottazza '98	🍷	3

PREDAPPIO (FC)

REGGIO EMILIA

PANDOLFA
VIA PANDOLFA, 35
LOC. FIUMANA
47010 PREDAPPIO (FC)
TEL. 0543/940073

ERMETE MEDICI & FIGLI
VIA NEWTON, 13/A
FRAZ. GAIDA
42040 REGGIO EMILIA
TEL. 0522/942135

One only has to glance at the superb 18th-century villa which serves as the estate headquarters in order to get an idea of Pandolfa's solidity and reliability. The winery belongs to the Ricci family, as does the historic villa, much admired by the poet, Giosuè Carducci, but it is the manager, Gimelli, and wine technician, Paolo Inama, who have made it one of the most important concerns on the entire Romagna winemaking scene. To do so, they have availed themselves of tools that are not really typical of local oenological traditions, such as grape varieties like cabernet sauvignon and chardonnay, or small French oak barrels. Nevertheless, their great energy and enthusiasm translates itself into some excellent products, with a considerable gap between the whites, which are interesting but really need more experimentation to shed their imperfections, and the reds, which may be a tad aggressive but really hit the spot. Our first example is the Pezzolo '98, made from cabernet sauvignon and aged in barrique. Its intense colour with purplish highlights leads in to a broad nose whose sensations range from toasty to almondy, as well as displaying varietal notes. The palate is rounded and satisfying, unveiling one after another a whole series of flavours, including liquorice, coffee, chocolate and a slightly over-the-top astringency. The Sangiovese Superiore Pandolfo '99 has down-to-earth, heady aromas and a pleasingly warm, robust flavour. Its "little brother", the Sangiovese di Romagna Canova '99, has a not altogether clean nose but is enjoyable enough on the palate. The Sangiovese Superiore Riserva Godenza '98 is perhaps a little lacking in balance but certainly not in swaggering, full-bodied fruit. On the other hand, the Chardonnay Cavina '99 is correct, well-balanced and refreshing but without any real top notes.

After entering the Guide last year, the Medici company confirms its position at the top of the DOC zone quality tree with its three enviable Lambrusco Reggianos. Medici's own vineyards in the foothills of Montecchio and Cavriago produce the lambrusco salamino that forms the basis for the 100,000 bottles of Concerto, the roughly 600,000 of standard Reggiano and the 20,000 of Assolo, the most recent addition to the range. Yet these three wines represent barely ten percent of the total number of bottles produced and distributed by the company. The Medicis have, for years now, set great store by their ability to select vineyards and soils but they consider equally important the efforts they have lavished on modernizing their cellars and their winemaking equipment. The aim is to produce the very best Lambrusco Reggiano possible while respecting tradition. Moving on to the wines, the one we liked best was the new Assolo, which comes from the I Quercioli vineyard at Cavriago. Dark purple in colour, it has an attractively subdued mousse and medium-bodied, round, tangy fruit. A very satisfying product indeed. The Concerto confirms its reliably good quality. A deep ruby in colour, it has a clean, attractive and well-defined nose and a flavour that is equally well-balanced. The standard version has a more translucent appearance than the two preceding wines but proffers similarly impressive extract and structure. On the nose, there are attractively warm, ripe tones. The Malvasia Secco Daphne, though possessing elegance and balance on the palate, does not offer the varietal precision on the nose evident in previous vintages.

● Pezzolo Cabernet Sauvignon '98 ❦❦		4
● Sangiovese di Romagna Sup.		
Godenza Ris. '98	❦	5
● Sangiovese di Romagna Sup.		
Pandolfo '99	❦	3
○ Cavina Chardonnay '99		2
● Sangiovese di Romagna		
Canova '99		2
● Pezzolo Cabernet Sauvignon '97 ❦❦		4

● Lambrusco Reggiano Secco	❦	1*
● Lambrusco Reggiano Secco		
Assolo	❦	1*
● Lambrusco Reggiano Secco		
Concerto '99	❦	2
○ Colli di Scandiano e di Canossa		
Malvasia Frizzante Secco		
Daphne '99		2

RIVERGARO (PC)

RUSSI (RA)

LA STOPPA
LOC. ANCARANO
29029 RIVERGARO (PC)
TEL. 0523/958159

TENUTA UCCELLINA
VIA GARIBALDI, 51
48026 RUSSI (RA)
TEL. 0544/580144

We shall begin this profile by offering our compliments to Elena Pantaleoni and the estate's winemaker, Giulio Armani. After the hiccough of the '97 vintage, this year's tastings revealed the Cabernet Sauvignon Stoppa to be once again every bit as good as its reputation. The '98 is concentrated in colour and the density of the fruit and the spiciness of the oak perceived on the nose find a mirror image in the polished and concentrated palate. There is, however, just a hint of bitterness in the long finish, which detracts from the wine's overall harmony. Not for the first time, the '98 Malvasia Passito Vigna del Volta shows itself to be a stylish wine. Intense fragrances of fruit in syrup and candied citrus fruit are further enhanced by the soft, mouth-filling palate, which is perked up by good acidity. The red Macchiona, made from barbera and bonarda, also made a great leap forward in quality. After several rather uninspiring vintages, the '98 offers a purplish colour in the glass, intense fruit on the nose and the compact, lively structure of a real thoroughbred. The panel's notes were similar for the Barbera della Stoppa '98. Its enhanced greater fragrance on the nose leads into a palate in which the fruit and the spicy notes are underpinned by sustained acidity. We close our profile with the estate's rare jewel, the Buca della Canne '98, made from botrytized sémillon grapes, and of which only 520 bottles were produced. Its structure seems to be just as concentrated as in the previous vintage but the richness of its aromas and the hint of noble rot are not as intense. Nonetheless, it is silky and elegant, with fragrances of honey, vanilla and exotic fruit.

Uccellina is a small, almost family-scale estate, with great intrinsic potential that crafts, rather than manufactures, its wines. Tenuta Uccellina products stand out for their reliability and cleanness. No obvious errors or defects are to be found here. The vineyards, on the prestigious hill of Bertinoro, and the winery itself, on the flatlands near Ravenna, have in Sergio Ragazzini an attentive custodian. There are some signs of his desire to make changes but these will come only very gradually, with the caution typical of a dyed-in-the-wool Romagna man. Some timid experimentation is taking place and the use of barriques continues to spread. The Ruchetto, this year from the '97 vintage, continues to be the distinctive wine that we have appreciated for some time now. Its deep ruby colour successfully conceals the fact that it is made from pinot nero. It is subtle and elegant on the nose, and skilfully used oak gives it even greater character. On the palate, it offers a flavour of ripe red berry fruit, displaying body and power combined with slightly brusque tannins. A similarly robust character, as well as a traditional profile, are offered by the Sangiovese Riserva '98, whose principal quality is its persistent and gratifyingly quaffable style. Another product at which the estate tries its hand is the Burson, from the '98 vintage, which offers ripe, almost Mediterranean notes. Neither can we forget the Albana Passito '98 which, as every year, is one of the finest wines of its type. It has a golden colour, leading in to a broad, fruity nose and heaps of vigorous fruit, so that it seems both soft yet well-structured. The estate's other sweet wine, the sangiovese-based Regio Rosso Passito '97, is much more than a mere curiosity. Delicate, alcohol-rich and warm, it possesses great balance and elegance.

O Buca delle Canne '98	🍷🍷	5
● Colli Piacentini Cabernet Sauvignon Stoppa '98	🍷🍷	5
O Colli Piacentini Malvasia Passito Vigna del Volta '98	🍷🍷	5
● Macchiona '98	🍷🍷	4
● Colli Piacentini Barbera della Stoppa '98	🍷	4
O Malvasia Passito Vigna del Volta '97	🍷🍷🍷	5
● Stoppa '96	🍷🍷🍷	5
O Buca delle Canne '97	🍷🍷	5
● Colli Piacentini Barbera della Stoppa '97	🍷🍷	4

O Albana di Romagna Passito '98	🍷🍷	4
● Regio Rosso Passito '97	🍷🍷	4
● Ruchetto dell'Uccellina '97	🍷🍷	4
● Sangiovese di Romagna Ris. '98	🍷🍷	4
● Burson '98	🍷	3
O Albana di Romagna Passito '97	🍷🍷	4
● Ruchetto dell'Uccellina '95	🍷🍷	4

S. ILARIO D'ENZA (RE)

S. PROSPERO (MO)

MORO RINALDO RINALDINI
VIA ANDREA RIVASI, 27
FRAZ. CALERNO
42040 S. ILARIO D'ENZA (RE)
TEL. 0522/679190

CAVICCHIOLI
P.ZZA GRAMSCI, 9
41030 S. PROSPERO (MO)
TEL. 059/812411

Rinaldo Rinaldini's range is never short of surprises. Having over the years made a name for his winery, halfway between Parma and Reggio, as a serious producer of Metodo Classico sparkling wines made from white grapes and from several subvarieties of lambrusco, he now takes on well-structured red wines as well. He is turning out around 15,000 bottles of three still reds, which are released alongside the 60-70,000 of Metodo Classico and roughly the same number of Charmat method sparkling wines. By putting their reputation on the line in every vintage, the Rinaldinis have demonstrated how, in a few short years and on soils in vineyards that have for decades been ill-treated by producers and neglected by wine writers, "real miracles can be created", as it says in a Rinaldini advertising leaflet. Alongside some interesting, but not altogether convincing reds, there is the real miracle of the first vintage – the '97 – of the Cabernet Sauvignon Riserva, made from grapes super-ripened on the vine and harvested during the last week in October. It flaunts an unusual breadth of fragrances, ranging from the aromatic nuances of bouquet garni to more vegetal scents such as those of celery and bell peppers and, on the finish, to ripe figs. The mellow, long, well-balanced fruit on the palate is of medium depth, with a gentle, unexaggerated use of oak. The two Lambruscos are well above average. The Vecchio Moro is well-structured and richly fruity, and the almost aromatic Pjcol Ross has considerable body and an unusual, ill-defined but very attractive rusticity on the palate. The white Lambrusco, from fruit vinified without the skins, is also interesting. Fresh and pleasantly herbaceous, we preferred it this year to the Rinaldo Brut, the patriarch of the company's sparkling wines.

The range of wines on offer from Cavicchioli is as irreproachable as ever. We realize that, for a company that produces 12,000,000 bottles a year, wines like the Col Sassoso really do represent the very tip of the iceberg but we feel compelled to offer our congratulations for the 20,000 bottles of one of the best Grasparossas we have ever tasted. Its nose is really distinctive, revealing intense, precise, persistent notes of evolved fruit with nuances of vanilla. The structure and complexity on the palate are also impressive, the echoes of fruit and vanilla being underpinned by a characteristic tannic vein. The Vigna del Cristo, of which 75,000 bottles were produced, has the pretty, pale ruby colour that is typical of a Sorbara. It is almost aromatic on the nose with an intense, persistent fragrance of violets. The flavour is attractively supple, tangy and long. This is a fine example of a modern Sorbara which nonetheless remains within the canons of tradition. The Modena Nuova Cuvée, made using the five subvarieties of lambrusco cultivated in the zone, finds an excellent point of balance for its components. It has a fine, lively perlage, an elegant, floral nose and a tangily fresh, mouth-filling flavour. The Salamino Semisecco and the Grasparossa Amabile are also interesting. The former is characterized by an attractive and very delicate hint of residual sugar which makes it soft on the front palate and almost completely dry on the finish. It is a very original wine which goes particularly well with the fat-rich dishes of traditional Emilian cuisine. The Grasparossa Amabile, though still rather closed on the nose, offers a palate that is harmonious and rich in fruity sensations, among which a distinct note of fragrant golden delicious apples stands out. It reveals delicate sweetness and a reasonably long finish.

● Colli di Scandiano e di Canossa		
Cabernet Sauvignon Ris. '97	♟♟	3*
● Colli di Scandiano e di Canossa		
Vecchio Moro	♟	2*
○ Lambrusco Bianco Metodo		
Classico	♟	2
● Lambrusco Metodo Classico		
Pjcol Ross	♟	2
● Colli di Scandiano e di Canossa		
Cabernet Sauvignon '98		2
○ Rinaldo Brut Chardonnay		
Classico		3

● Lambrusco di Modena		
Nuova Cuvée	♟	2
● Lambrusco di Sorbara		
Vigna del Cristo '99	♟	3
● Lambrusco Grasparossa di		
Castelvetro Amabile Tre Medaglie	♟	2
● Lambrusco Grasparossa di		
Castelvetro Col Sassoso '99	♟	3
● Lambrusco Salamino Semisecco		
Tre Medaglie	♟	2

SALA BAGANZA (PR)

SASSO MARCONI (BO)

VIGNETI CALZETTI
VIA S. VITALE, 47
LOC. S. VITALE BAGANZA
43030 SALA BAGANZA (PR)
TEL. 0521/830117

FLORIANO CINTI
VIA GAMBERI, 48
FRAZ. S. LORENZO
40037 SASSO MARCONI (BO)
TEL. 051/6751646 - 051/845606

One of the finest winemaking concerns in the province of Parma, which again this year offers the best range of wines from the Colli di Parma DOC zone. That is the calling card of this well-known wine producer located in verdant Val Baganza. The owner, Sergio Calzetti, supported as he is by shrewd family management, shuns the siren song of still wines, apart from an experiment with a Colli di Parma Rosso which has had encouraging results. His focus has enabled the property to give lustre to the typical semi-sparkling wines of the area in a way no one else can rival. In addition, the true value of Vignetti Calzetti lies, as the company name itself suggests, in the 18 hectares of specialized vineyards (ten of them family-owned), some of which are located in the splendid, celebrated Boschi di Carrega Regional Park. But let's get to our tasting notes. The '99 vintage of the Malvasia Conventino is again refreshing and floral. The Colli di Parma Rosso Conventino Campo delle Lepri, also a '99, is perhaps the best example of its style. A brilliant ruby red in colour, it is deliciously lively, fruity and intensely flavoured. And well worth an honourable mention, only just missing out on One Glass, is the still version of the same wine from the '98 vintage. Finally, there is the peerless Malvasia Dolce '99, a partially-fermented grape must whose most appealing qualities are its finesse and freshness.

Floriano Cinti, in spite of his youth, is already established as one of the most reliable premium-quality producers in the Colli Bolognesi. His '99 wines are the result of great efforts, both on Floriano's part and on that of oenologist, Giovanni Fraulini, to overcome the adversities of what was a difficult vintage, especially for the early-ripening varieties. All of Cinti's wines obtained One Glass ratings with ease, indeed, some of them came very close to winning Two Glass accolades. While we wait for the '98 Cabernet Sauvignon, which is still in barrique, the only red is the Cabernet Sauvignon '99, which did not see any wood at all. On the nose, you note appealingly fresh berry fruit notes while it is straightforward, well-managed and eminently quaffable on the palate. The best of the whites is the Pignoletto Classico, with its intense yet complex peach and pineapple fruit aromas and rich, full flavour. The Frizzante version has more lemony notes and is a bit firmer on the palate, with the bitter almondy finish that is typical of this variety. The Chardonnay, vinified exclusively in stainless steel, is rounded, full-bodied and persistent, with intense perfumes of exotic kiwi and passion fruit. The Pinot Bianco expresses itself with delicate floral aromas and barely hints at the scent of unripe apples. It evolves on the palate with elegance and attractive balance. The Sauvignon, varietal on the nose without being blowsy, is not particularly intense on the palate but has good length. Our compliments, also, for this producer's commendable habit of indicating on the back label both vinification details and the wine's – generally low – total sulphur dioxide content.

○ Colli di Parma Malvasia Conventino '99	🍷	2*
● Colli di Parma Rosso Conventino Campo delle Lepri Frizzante '99	🍷	2
○ Malvasia Dolce '99	🍷	2
● Colli di Parma Rosso Conventino Campo delle Lepri Fermo '98		2

● Colli Bolognesi Cabernet Sauvignon '99	🍷	3
○ Colli Bolognesi Chardonnay '99	🍷	3
○ Colli Bolognesi Pignoletto Cl. '99	🍷	3
○ Colli Bolognesi Pignoletto Frizzante '99	🍷	2*
○ Colli Bolognesi Pinot Bianco '99	🍷	3
○ Colli Bolognesi Sauvignon '99	🍷	3
● Colli Bolognesi Cabernet Sauvignon '97	🍷	3

SPALLETTI COLONNA DI PALLIANO
VIA SOGLIANO, 100
47039 SAVIGNANO SUL RUBICONE (FC)
TEL. 0541/943446

CASALI VITICULTORI
VIA DELLE SCUOLE, 7
FRAZ. PRATISSOLO
42019 SCANDIANO (RE)
TEL. 0522/855441

The 45 hectares of vineyards belonging to the castle of Ribano are planted predominantly with the traditional grape varieties of Romagna but there are also international cultivars like riesling, chardonnay, merlot, cabernet sauvignon and cabernet franc. The size of Spalletti's holdings allows for the production of a large number of wines, some of which still require some fine tuning, especially as far as their overall balance and bouquets are concerned. A few of the bottles are really splendid, though, particularly some of the reds, which are vigorous and down-to-earth yet full-bodied and satisfying. They are made using production techniques which make no concessions to modern fashion and which still include the use of large old Slavonian oak barrels. Part of the company's success is due, probably, to the collaboration of the ubiquitous Sergio Ragazzini. It is the non-indigenous varieties which provide the happiest surprises, starting with the Monaco di Ribano '98, a skilful blend of cabernet sauvignon and cabernet franc. It offers the herbaceous fragrances of the latter variety, which combine well with the aromas from the oak. On the palate, it is initially a bit edgy and aggressive, but closes with a pleasant, persistent sweetness. The same grape varieties are in the Sabinio '98, which has a more evolved, mature bouquet and which reveals great power on the palate as well as a roundness threatened by slightly excessive tannins. One of the company's standard bearers, the Sangiovese Superiore Rocca di Ribano '98, is disappointing. It confirms in the mouth the faults already suggested on the nose. More interesting, both in terms of its rustic nose and its robust flavour is the Villa Rasponi '97, a Sangiovese Riserva. The Albana Passito Il Maulù is soft, seductive and warm, at last elegantly well-balanced, even if it does reveal a hint of bitterness on the finish.

There has been a change in the ownership but things are very much as before at this company in the hills just outside Reggio Emilia. The Casalis have been joined by some new partners, even though the same family group and the same winemaking staff are still in charge of everyday administration. For the time being, the range of wines remains unchanged, too, though there are some new products on the drawing-board. Again this year, this Scandiano-based firm, which produces 1,000,000 bottles a year, lived up to our expectations. The Acaia, made from malvasia, is a wine that is brilliant in hue, with a delicate, palate-filling perlage. Its nose is intense, varietal and elegant, and the well-balanced, harmonious palate lives up fully to the promise of the bouquet. The Casali Rosa has, for years, been a classic touchstone for those who like the rosé style. This edition is as well-made as ever and it particularly charmed us with its cleanness, its appealing quaffability and just the right balance of acidity and the softness of the fruit. The Bosco del Fracasso, a Charmat wine with a long second fermentation of nine months in tank, is released a year after the harvest and recalls the Lambruscos of yesteryear. Its salient features are medium effervescence, a not altogether precise nose, rounded, well-balanced fruit on the palate, and a tangy, dry finish. Only 5,000 bottles of the Spumante Rosso Metodo Classico Roggio del Pradello are produced. This year it is richer and more full-bodied in comparison with previous vintages but less deliciously gluggable. Its handsome, deep, dense colour gives way to a nose with exotic notes of spices and Peruvian bark. On the palate, the impression of an austere, unusual, richly extracted Lambrusco is reinforced by the prominent tannins.

O Albana di Romagna Passito		
Il Maulù '98	♟♟	4
● Cabernet Rubicone Sabinio '98	♟♟	3*
● Il Monaco di Ribano Cabernet '98	♟♟	5
● Sangiovese di Romagna		
Villa Rasponi Ris. '97	♟	4
O Principessa Ghika '98		3
● Sangiovese di Romagna Sup.		
Rocca di Ribano '98		3
● Sabinio '98	♟♟	3
● Sangiovese di Romagna Sup.		
Rocca di Ribano '97	♟	3

O Acaia Malvasia dell'Emilia		
Frizzante Secco '99	♟	2*
O Colli di Scandiano e di Canossa		
Spumante Villa Jano	♟	3
⊙ Lambrusco dell'Emilia		
Casali Rosa '99	♟	2*
● Lambrusco Reggiano		
Bosco del Fracasso '98	♟	2*
● Lambrusco Spumante		
Roggio del Pradello	♟	3
O Colli di Scandiano e di Canossa		
Metodo Classico Cà Besina '94	♟	4

TRAVO (PC)

IL POGGIARELLO
FRAZ. SCRIVELLANO DI STATTO
29020 TRAVO (PC)
TEL. 0523/957241 - 0523/571610

Paolo and Stefano Perini's estate continues to make progress. From their 13 hectares under vine in the hills of the Val Trebbia, they produce six wines, one of which is new this year. It's Gutturnio Riserva La Barbona '97, which immediately becomes one of the benchmarks for this DOC zone. Concentrated in colour, it offers intense aromas of jam and spices intermingled with vegetal and oaky notes. The rich, substantial fruit on the palate is underpinned by good acidity, which bodes well for the future. The Pinot Nero Le Giastre '98 takes a further step forward over previous vintages. Aromas of blackcurrants and raspberries, swathed in resinous and spicy fragrances, give way to broad, already quite soft, fruit on the front palate. The tannins are well-integrated and the finish is long. The Cabernet Sauvignon Novarei '98 has a deep colour. On the nose, the balsamic hints from the wood marry well with the grape's typical varietal aromas and these sensations are echoed perfectly on the rich yet refreshing palate. In the Gutturnio Valandrea '98, a still rather dumb nose gives way to a supple but quite concentrated flavour, with sweetish notes and a fresh, persistent finish. Let's round things off with the whites. The golden-hued Chardonnay La Piana '99 is much improved. It unveils a broad nose with notes of hazelnuts and candied citrus fruit while the acidity offers a fine foil to the fat, rich fruit on the palate. There is, however, a slightly bothersome hint of bitterness on the finish, which is due to the wine having spent a little too long in wood. In the Sauvignon Quadri '99, the vanilla tones from the oak combine with aromas of citron and celery. These aromas return on the palate, which has tangy fruit and an aftertaste of bitter almonds.

VERNASCA (PC)

LURETTA
LOC. PAOLINI DI BACEDASCO
29010 VERNASCA (PC)
TEL. 0523/895465 - 0523/976500

The intentions of the proprietors here were clear right from the start – to make wines that would stand up to the competition from all-comers and not just in a local context. This is a quite legitimate ambition and one that is shared by many producers. Only a few, however, succeed in transforming ambition into achievement. The outcome of our tastings this year offers us a portrait of a company that is improving exponentially. Four wines obtained Two Glass ratings and two only missed out by a whisker. There are two versions of the Malvasia Boccadirosa from the '99 vintage. The classic edition, one third of which is aged in barrique and the rest in stainless steel, has a delicate nose, with aromas of camomile and basil and satisfying depth on the palate. The version aged entirely in barriques and released only in magnums, dubbed Le Rane, is really surprising. It has a golden-yellow colour and its intense, fragrant aromas give way to a deep flavour with rich tones of exotic fruit, spices and mineral hints. Also very striking is the Chardonnay Selin dl'Armari '99, with its brilliant greenish-gold hue. Vanilla and hazelnuts mingle on the nose with floral notes while the broad yet well-defined flavour reveals a mineral tone. The I Nani e Le Ballerine '99, made from sauvignon grapes, offers hints of sage, tomato leaves and a certain smokiness, sensations also highlighted by satisfying acidity and good length on the palate. The '99 vintage of the Rosso Pantera, made from barbera, bonarda and pinot nero, scored well over the Two Glass threshold. Its aromas of violets, raspberries and blackcurrants lead into a deep, richly spicy and well-nuanced palate which is powerful without being coarse. In the Pinot Nero '98, the oak is attractively integrated with cherry jam notes. The wine may not be particularly persistent but its overall balance makes it very enjoyable.

● Colli Piacentini Cabernet Sauvignon Perticato del Novarei '98	🍷🍷	4
○ Colli Piacentini Chardonnay Perticato La Piana '99	🍷🍷	4
● Colli Piacentini Gutturnio Ris. La Barbona '97	🍷🍷	4
● Colli Piacentini Pinot Nero Perticato Le Giastre '98	🍷🍷	4
● Colli Piacentini Gutturnio Perticato Valandrea '98	🍷	3
○ Colli Piacentini Sauvignon Perticato Il Quadri '99	🍷	3
● Colli Piacentini Cabernet Sauvignon Perticato del Novarei '97	🍷🍷	4

○ Colli Piacentini Chardonnay Selin dl'Armari '99	🍷🍷	5
○ Colli Piacentini Malvasia Boccadirosa '99	🍷🍷	4
○ Colli Piacentini Malvasia Boccadirosa Le Rane '99	🍷🍷	6
● Come La Pantera e I Lupi nella Sera '99	🍷🍷	5
● Colli Piacentini Pinot Nero '98	🍷	4
○ Colli Piacentini Sauvignon I Nani e Le Ballerine '99	🍷	4

VIGOLZONE (PC)

VIGOLZONE (PC)

Conte Otto Barattieri di S. Pietro
Fraz. Albarola
29020 Vigolzone (PC)
Tel. 0523/875111

Cantine Romagnoli
Via Genova, 20
Loc. Villò
29020 Vigolzone (PC)
Tel. 0523/870129

Thanks to the '98 vintage, which was particularly favourable in this area, and to more successful vinification methods, the cellars of Count Otto Barattieri have finally produced some reds of a notably high standard. Best of all is the Merlot '98. Dark, indeed almost black, in colour, it displays ripe berry fruit notes on the nose, followed by a broad, harmonious palate sustained by a good tannic backbone. The Barattieri Rosso '98, made from cabernet sauvignon, also offers a depth and concentration it has never had before. Warm and spicy, it reveals a tiny hint of bitterness on the finish. The Barbera Vignazza Alta '98 is solid and not excessively acidulous, with distinct, but not obtrusive, oak-derived notes. Talking about the Vin Santo Albarola is rather like repeating a lesson learnt by rote, so incredibly reliable is its quality. Produced from malvasia di Candia grapes from the oldest and best-exposed vineyards, it is vinified and then put into chestnut barrels where it remains without undergoing any type of treatment. No sulphur dioxide, no filtration, and no racking. It is bottled after nine years and the few hundred bottles presently on the market are from the '90 vintage. The colour is mahogany brown and the palate merely reinforces the extraordinarily persistent sensations on the nose with its aromas of hazelnuts, figs and zabaglione. The Faggio Rosso Passito, made from old brachetto vines, has a morello cherry colour and floral scents. The fruit on the palate is dense, with notes of strawberry and raspberry jam. In spite of its high alcohol content, it remains remarkably easy to drink.

The Cantine Romagnoli are a well-deserved new entry in our Guide. This is one of the largest companies in the Colli Piacentini with over 200 hectares of property, of which 80 are planted to vine, in the areas around Villò and Carmiano, and a vast range of wines that it distributes all over the world. Of the samples we tasted, two wines stood head and shoulders above the rest. The first was the highly concentrated Cabernet Sauvignon Sonzone '97, with its attractive varietal and balsamic aromas and a long, tangy flavour that recalls berry fruit and spices. The Inno '97, made from barbera, bonarda and 30 percent merlot, might be described as the posthumous legacy of a specific vineyard, which in fact, was grubbed up after this vintage. Probably conceived as a gift, the wine's packaging is particularly attractive but the contents are very decent, too. The herbaceous perfumes, mingled with pepper and nutmeg, are carried through perfectly onto the floral palate with its aromatic, spicy notes. The Gutturnio Riserva Vigna del Gallo '97, an intense ruby in colour, has aromas of ripe cherries, with the spicy notes of bonarda particularly evident on the warm, broad palate which, however, lacks a bit of grip. The Pinot Nero Savara '97, in which the sweetness of the grapes is masked somewhat by the oak, unveils easy, polished fruit on the palate. The Passito Galaverna '91 is made from malvasia and ten percent picolit and, at first glance, reminds you of an Amontillado sherry. It has an amber colour, aromas of salt and tamarind, and a moderately sweet flavour which combines the typical sensations of partially dried grapes with those of ageing-induced oxidation, backed up by appropriate acidity.

● Colli Piacentini Cabernet Sauvignon Barattieri Rosso '98	❦❦	4
O Colli Piacentini Vin Santo Albarola '90	❦❦	6
● Il Faggio Passito '98	❦❦	5
● Merlot Vigneto Pergolo '98	❦❦	4
● Colli Piacentini Barbera Vigneto Vignazza Alta '98	❦	4
O Colli Piacentini Vin Santo '89	❦❦	6
● Colli Piacentini Barbera Vigneto Bocciarelli '97	❦	4

● Colli Piacentini Cabernet Sauvignon Colto Vitato del Sonzone '97	❦❦	4
● Inno al Terzo Millennio '97	❦❦	6
● Colli Piacentini Gutturnio Vigna del Gallo Ris. '97	❦	4
● Colli Piacentini Pinot Nero Colto Vitato del Savara '97	❦	5
O Galaverna '91	❦	6

VIGOLZONE (PC)

LA TOSA
LOC. LA TOSA
29020 VIGOLZONE (PC)
TEL. 0523/870727 - 0523/870168

ZIANO PIACENTINO (PC)

GAETANO LUSENTI E FIGLIA
LOC. CASE PICCIONI DI VICOBARONE
29010 ZIANO PIACENTINO (PC)
TEL. 0523/868479

Anyone who is familiar with Stefano Pizzamiglio's toughness, determination and commitment will not be at all surprised by the results he has obtained. His long experience of experimenting with wood has now convinced him to use it only with great care, in order not to jeopardize clarity and precision in the aromas. A deceptive straw-yellow colour, the result of very soft pressing and the avoidance of all oxidation during vinification, is your first impression of the Malvasia Sorriso di Cielo '99. Its flavour, juicy with tropical fruit notes, is mellow and perfectly balanced, and in spite of the robust alcohol, it is amazingly fresh and positively aromatic. The '99 Sauvignon has aromas of pineapple and elderflower, showing agile, well-proportioned fruit on the palate, which is made even more attractive by just a touch of residual sugar. The Valnure '99, a blend of malvasia, trebbiano and ortrugo, is a charmer. Its precise nose leads into a frank, crisp palate, made even more easy-to-drink by the bubbles. Of Stefano's reds, the Luna Selvatica '98 showed particularly well. It is made from cabernet sauvignon and is aged partly in new barriques and partly in stainless steel. It has an impenetrable colour and a concentrated nose that offers sweet berry fruit aromas. The flavour is rounded and rich in glycerine, with balsamic notes from the oak complementing characteristic varietal tones. The Gutturnio '99 is precise on the nose and offers an excellent, substantial flavour on the palate, which is attractive and remarkably fruity. We close with the Gutturnio Vigna Morello, a special selection of the finest barbera and bonarda grapes. The '99 has an intense violet colour. Its intriguing aromas of strawberry and black cherry are echoed perfectly in the full-bodied flavour, where the fruit broadens out evenly to coat the entire palate.

A big step forward for this estate. After some years in which the wines were sound but unexciting, here at last is the longed-for improvement. This year, the cellar run by Lodovica Lusenti offered some very interesting wines for tasting. Among the whites, the Malvasia di Case Piccioni '99 was making its debut. The typical varietal aromas on the nose give way to a coherent palate of modest depth but with plenty of tanginess and balance, followed by an attractive almondy twist in the finish. In the red department, the still Gutturnio is definitely coming on. The '98 vintage has a nice, intense colour while ripe fruit notes predominate on the nose. These are amply reflected in the full, chewy palate, which is attractively soft and rounded. The Gutturnio Frizzante '99 is also well-made. Fragrant and warm on the nose, it offers a pleasantly spicy and concentrated flavour which makes it enticingly quaffable. The '98 Cabernet Sauvignon Villante, after some pretty disappointing vintages, finally broke through the Two Glass barrier again, this time with remarkable ease. The fine nose offers fruity aromas modulated by spicy and balsamic overtones. These aromas give way to a richly structured palate in which the warmth of the alcohol is tempered by the typical herbaceous notes of the variety. The Filtrato Dolce di Malvasia '99 is as appealing as ever. The aromas reveal distinct varietal notes while the palate is soft and attractively effervescent, with a sweet but not cloying finish. Even better is the Bonarda Amabile '99. Its rich berry fruit aromas are followed up by a forthright, warm palate that has just the right amount of acidity to bring out its more fragrant characteristics.

● Colli Piacentini Cabernet Sauvignon Luna Selvatica '98	▼▼	5
● Colli Piacentini Gutturnio Vignamorello '99	▼▼	4
○ Colli Piacentini Malvasia Sorriso di Cielo '99	▼▼	4
● Colli Piacentini Gutturnio '99	▼	3
○ Colli Piacentini Sauvignon '99	▼	4
○ Colli Piacentini Valnure '99	▼	2*
● Colli Piacentini Cabernet Sauvignon Luna Selvatica '97	▼▼▼	5
● Colli Piacentini Cabernet Sauvignon Luna Selvatica '95	▼▼	5
○ Colli Piacentini Malvasia Sorriso di Cielo '98	▼▼	4

● Colli Piacentini Gutturnio '98	▼▼	3*
● Il Villante Cabernet Sauvignon '98	▼▼	4
● Colli Piacentini Bonarda Amabile '99	▼	3
● Colli Piacentini Gutturnio Frizzante '99	▼	2
○ Colli Piacentini Malvasia di Case Piccioni '99	▼	3
○ Filtrato Dolce di Malvasia '99	▼	3
● Il Villante Cabernet Sauvignon '96	▽	4
● Colli Piacentini Gutturnio '97	▽	3

ZIANO PIACENTINO (PC) ZOLA PREDOSA (BO)

TORRE FORNELLO
LOC. FORNELLO
29010 ZIANO PIACENTINO (PC)
TEL. 0523/861001

MARIA LETIZIA GAGGIOLI
VIGNETO BAGAZZANA
VIA RAIBOLINI, 55
40069 ZOLA PREDOSA (BO)
TEL. 051/753489

A well-deserved debut in the Guide for this young but very representative cellar from the Piacenza area. The 85 hectares of estate-owned land, of which 55 are under vine, in the heart of the Val Tidone are a good starting point. If we add to the equation a winery furnished with state-of-the-art equipment and the advice of consultant oenologist, Donato Lanati, then we can only conclude that Enrico Sgorbati, the young owner, is aiming for the heights. We had a first taste of this winery's true potential from the Gutturnio Riserva Diacono Gerardo '98, a blend of 70 percent barbera and 30 percent bonarda which was up at the top of the Two Glass band. This velvety, complex, elegant and skilfully oaked wine only needs a bit more richness and body to become a real star. The Gutturnio Superiore Sinsäl '99, just bottled at the time of our tastings and with a nose spoiled by salty odours, offers a flavour with good depth and concentration. The Bonarda '99, made spritzy by being re-fermented in pressurized tanks, is fragrantly aromatic and distinctly fruity, with a tangily refreshing finish. Moving on to the still whites, the barrique-aged Chardonnay La Jara '99 offers well-defined but rather insubstantial fruit on the palate. The Vigna Pratobianco '99, a blend of sauvignon, malvasia and chardonnay, flaunts attractively clean and generous floral aromas and a palate that may lack a little weight but is still fluent and enticing. We would also bring a semi-sparkling white, the Chardonnay '99, to your attention. Delicate, with fresh scents of peaches and pears, it has a mellow flavour and a tangy citrus note on the finish.

For at least the last ten years, the wines produced by the Gaggiolis have been some of the best examples of typicity, cleanness and winemaking ability in the area. Much of the merit for this is due to the ideal combination of Maria Letizia's attention to detail and the enthusiastic supervision of her father Carlo, the founder of the winery. The still white wines all earn One Glass ratings with the Crilò again proving itself to be the estate's best white. On the nose, it offers intense, ripe and slightly toasty notes. The rich, well-rounded palate reveals good extract and a dry, tangy finish. The Sauvignon, which comes form the clay terrain of the Vigna Volpara, is interesting too. It can point to a wide gamut of aromas, beginning with precise notes of early-sprouting grass and red peppers, which soften out into gentler hints of budding elderflower. The palate follows through well, with good weight and length. On the nose, the Chardonnay opens up with hints of wild herbs which then evolve into more fruity aromas. The well-defined, consistent flavour reveals distinct yeasty sensations on the finish. The Francia Bianco, the winery's first wine to be fermented in oak, is not bad at all. Made from sauvignon, pignoletto and chardonnay, it displays ripe fruit aromas and well-integrated oak on the nose. These sensations are mirrored on the palate, together with an agreeable hint of oxidation. The Pignoletto Superiore is traditionally styled. Its nose has medium intensity and faint almondy aromas while the palate is soft and the finish has a faintly bitterish note. There was also a good performance from a young Cabernet very much in the house style. Warm and attractive, it shows good, rounded texture and unobtrusive tannins. The Pignoletto Frizzante and the '99 Merlot are both sound.

● Colli Piacentini Gutturnio		
Diacono Gerardo 1028 Ris. '98	🍷🍷	4
● Colli Piacentini Bonarda		
Frizzante '99	🍷	3
○ Colli Piacentini Chardonnay		
Frizzante '99	🍷	2
○ Colli Piacentini Chardonnay		
La Jara '99	🍷	3
● Colli Piacentini Gutturnio Sup.		
Sinsäl '99	🍷	3
○ Vigna Pratobianco '99	🍷	3

● Colli Bolognesi Cabernet		
Sauvignon '99	🍷	4
○ Colli Bolognesi Chardonnay		
Lavinio '99	🍷	3
○ Colli Bolognesi Pignoletto		
Sup. '99	🍷	3
○ Colli Bolognesi Pinot Bianco		
Crilò '99	🍷	3
○ Colli Bolognesi Sauvignon		
Sup. '99	🍷	3
○ Il Francia Bianco '99	🍷	3
● Colli Bolognesi Merlot '99		3
○ Colli Bolognesi Pignoletto		
Frizzante '99		3

OTHER WINERIES

The following producers obtained good scores in our tastings with one or more of their wines:

PROVINCE OF BOLOGNA

Erioli, Bazzano, tel. 051/830103
Colli Bolognesi Sauvignon Ris. '97

Beghelli
Castello di Serravalle, tel. 051/6704786
Colli Bolognesi Barbera '98

Santarosa, Monte S. Pietro, tel. 051/969203
Colli Bolognesi Cabernet Sauvignon
Giò Rosso di Santarosa '97

Bonfiglio, Monteveglio, tel. 051/830758
Colli Bolognesi Pignoletto Passito '98

La Mancina, Monteveglio, tel. 051/832691
Colli Bolognesi Cabernet Sauvignon
Comandante della Guardia Ris. '97

PROVINCE OF FORLÌ

Colombina, Bertinoro, tel. 0543/460658
Sangiovese di Romagna Sup. Ris. '96

PROVINCE OF MODENA

Bellei, Bomporto, tel. 059/818002
Spumante Brut Millennium

Balugani, Castelvetro, tel. 059/791546
Lambrusco Grasparossa di Castelvetro '99

Manicardi, Castelvetro, tel. 059/799000
Lambrusco Grasparossa di Castelvetro
Vigna Ca' del Fiore '99

Chiarli 1860, Modena, tel. 059/310545
Tenuta Generale Cialdini

Civ & Civ, Modena, tel. 059/310222
Lambrusco di Modena Vecchio Ducato

Maletti, Soliera, tel. 059/563876
Lambrusco di Sorbara Sel. '99

PROVINCE OF PARMA

Carra, Langhirano, tel. 0521/863510
Colli di Parma Sauvignon Ris. '99

La Bandina, Langhirano, tel. 0521/355166
Colli di Parma Malvasia '99

Cantine Dall'Asta
Parma, tel. 0521/482406
Colli di Parma Sauvignon '99

Villa Bianca, Traversetolo, tel. 0521/842680
Colli di Parma Rosso Vigna del Tenore '99

PROVINCE OF PIACENZA

Pusterla, Castell'Arquato, tel. 0523/896105
Colli Piacentini Cabernet Sauvignon '98

Tenuta Pernice
Castelnovo Val Tidone, tel. 0523/860050
Collare Rosso '98

Tenuta La Torretta
Nibbiano Val Tidone, tel. 0523/997008
Colli Piacentini Cabernet Sauvignon '98

Molinelli
Ziano Piacentino, tel. 0523/863230
Colli Piacentini Gutturnio Vigna Giacalva '97

Mossi, Ziano Piacentino, tel. 0523/860201
Infernotto '97

Podere Casale
Ziano Piacentino, tel. 0523/868302
Colli Piacentini Malvasia V. T. '97

PROVINCE OF RAVENNA

Treré, Faenza, tel. 0546/47034
Albana di Romagna Secco
Vigna della Compadrona '99,
Sangiovese di Romagna Sup.
Amarcord d'un Ross Ris. '97

Valli, Lugo, tel. 0545/24393
Sangiovese di Romagna
Riserva Della Beccaccia '97

PROVINCE OF REGGIO EMILIA

Venturini e Baldini
Quattro Castella, tel. 0522/887080
Il Grinto Cabernet Sauvignon

F.lli Caprari
Reggio Emilia, tel. 0522/550220
Lambrusco dell'Emilia La Foieta

PROVINCE OF RIMINI

San Valentino, Rimini, tel. 0541/752231
Sangiovese di Romagna Sup. Terra Ris. '96

TUSCANY

There's a profusion of Three Glass awards in Tuscany this year. The grand total is 55, which is far and away the all-time record for the region, and 19 more than last year's. This is an amazing achievement, which has come about because there are now so many areas here that can produce wines of excellence. The Chianti Classico zone, thanks to its red DOCGs and its Supertuscans, gets the lion's share, once again demonstrating what this terroir and the growers that interpret it are capable of. Well over half of the Three Glass awards – 31, in fact – are from this great wine area, which shares with the Langhe in Piedmont the distinction of being the most important in Italy for premium-quality wines, and is the undisputed leader in terms of quantity and its sheer concentration of serious wineries. There are great performances, for example, from Isole e Olena, Fonterutoli, Ricasoli, Antinori and Villa Cafaggio, which have won two Three Glasses each for a series of extraordinary wines. But lots of other producers have also proved they have a technical mastery and consistency of quality that few cellars elsewhere, either at home or abroad, can equal. In addition to Chianti's triumphant results, many other areas have shown themselves to advantage, including some that, until a very few years ago, would never have been thought of as particularly outstanding. We could mention, for example, the Colli Aretini, and even San Gimignano, which this year for the first time received the highest accolade for a Vernaccia Riserva from Giovanni Panizzi. But the northern Maremma is another contender. Quite apart from Sassicaia, this area has now been producing absolutely remarkable wines for some years. Witness the brace of Three Glass scores carried off by Eugenio Campolmi's Le Macchiole and by Ornellaia, which belongs to Ludovico Antinori and now is also part-owned by Robert Mondavi. Montepulciano is holding its own, with five Nobiles and Supertuscans making it to the top, and a pair for Poliziano, one of the most important producers in the zone. The only blot on the Tuscan escutcheon, and not for the first time, is Montalcino, and Brunello in particular. We note that international wine reviews have been assigning stratospheric scores to these wines. The Wine Spectator, for example, gave over 90 to 39 of them, and Robert Parker was not exactly niggardly with his high marks either. That being the case, it may look as though we have it in for Brunello, despite our groups of experts, blind tastings and the fact that personal opinions are the result of at least two rounds of tasting sessions. We feel there may be some unresolved technical problems in the production of many Brunellos, such as old barrels, jaded wines and primitive methods in too many cases. We cannot understand how Brunello has been able to such generally favourable judgements. In our opinion, the praise is counter-productive. Brunello producers are likely to get the impression that all is well when in fact they have a long way to go yet. Montalcino could be giving us the very best Tuscan reds made from sangiovese. The potential is there, in spades. But we feel that it is, on the whole, still just that – potential.

ALBERESE (GR)

AREZZO

POGGIO ARGENTIERA
LOC. BANDITELLA
58010 ALBERESE (GR)
TEL. 0564/405099

FATTORIA SAN FABIANO
BORGHINI BALDOVINETTI
LOC. SAN FABIANO, 33
52100 AREZZO
TEL. 0575/24566

With such a rush of Tuscan estates entering the Guide for the first time each year, usually after a period spent waiting "on the bench" in the Other Wineries section, it has become quite rare for a winery to earn its own profile at first tasting. But that's just what Poggio Argentiera has done with an admirable performance on its debut appearance. The owner, Giampaolo Paglia, seems to be aiming high, as his choice of technical staff shows. The pairing of D'Attoma (consultant oenologist) and Moltard (vineyard specialist) already inspires confidence. But let's get down to the wines. The Morellino CapaTosta '98 is a really pleasing red, made from sangiovese with 5 percent of alicante grapes. The attractively vibrant, dense colour introduces a concentrated nose dominated by notes of black berry fruit and elegant hints of spice. Then a seductive, meaty palate unveils balanced, well-developed tannins. There is just the slightest falling off on the finish, where the oak rather stands out, as does the odd vegetal note. The '98 and '99 versions of the Morellino BellaMarsilia, which have come out together, are more than satisfactory. The '98 vintage is a rich garnet in the glass, offering a bouquet with noticeable notes of tamarind and traces of somewhat precocious development. In the mouth, it has good body but there's an echo of that same forwardness. The '99 seems closer to the mark. The immediately fruity aromas are rich in hints of blackberry jam and the delightfully clean-tasting palate is genuinely refreshing.

Last year's positive impressions of the wines from this large estate (about 650 hectares) near Arezzo have mostly been confirmed. We had noted that there were two distinct styles at work, one traditional and the other more modern. Whatever may have been said of our views on the subject by perhaps less than careful readers, we certainly do not look down our noses at a traditionalist approach if it is well-executed and the wine shows some character. This, however, is not the case with the San Fabiano Vin Santo Cannicci '96, which is actually rather unfocused and harsh. The Chianti '99 seems to have a surer and smoother style The tannins may be a little rustic but there is enough fruit to dominate both nose and palate and it had no trouble in picking up its One Glass. The Chiaro '99 is even better. It's a chardonnay and trebbiano-based white with an intriguing bouquet of attractive citrus – grapefruit stands out – and peach aromas, not to mention good balance on the palate. But the wine we're really excited about is, yet again, the Armaiolo. Last year's release made us sit up and take notice but this year's, the '98, is definitely superior. Indeed, it came dangerously close to a Three Glass score. The dense, intense colour continues all the way to the rim. The nose is a little muffled at first but after a few minutes' breathing, it opens to become pervasive, deep and stylish. Its rich fruit hovers between blackcurrant and blackberry, mingled with faint vegetal notes. On the palate, it is sheer, unalloyed pleasure. The poised, sensually smooth softness is full and caressing, and the finish lingers.

●	Morellino di Scansano CapaTosta '98	🍷🍷	5
●	Morellino di Scansano BellaMarsilia '98	🍷	4
●	Morellino di Scansano BellaMarsilia '99	🍷	4

●	Armaiolo '98	🍷🍷	5
●	Chianti '99	🍷	3
○	Chiaro '99	🍷	3
○	Vin Santo Cannicci '96		5
●	Armaiolo '97	🍷🍷	5

BAGNO A RIPOLI (FI)

FATTORIA LE SORGENTI
VIA DI DOCCIOLA, 8
50012 BAGNO A RIPOLI (FI)
TEL. 055/696004

BARBERINO VAL D'ELSA (FI)

CASA EMMA
FRAZ. CORTINE
50021 BARBERINO VAL D'ELSA (FI)
TEL. 055/8072859

We are very pleased to welcome this newcomer to the Guide. Le Sorgenti lies in an up-and-coming winegrowing area near Florence. The 16-hectare estate has been run by the Ferrari family since 1974. Gabriele Ferrari, the owner, is personally involved in every phase of production, and is assisted by oenologist Paolo Caciorgna of the Matura Group. The Chianti Colli Fiorentini '99 displays a lovely vivid ruby hue. The nose proffers moderately intense fruity and floral tones, with faint vegetal hints. In the mouth, it is uncomplicated but fairly well-balanced, with close-knit, fine-grained tannins. The Chianti Colli Fiorentini '98 has a more forward nose with a pleasing ripe cherry aroma. The palate, after a slightly dilute attack, immediately gathers strength and shows fine overall balance. The tannins are crunchy and delectable. The Sghiras '99 is a 100 percent chardonnay aged briefly in barriques. An attractive brilliant straw-yellow colour introduces a restrained aroma of vanilla and some fluffier hints that finish on a note of honey. The acidity on the palate, although well to the fore, is kept fully under control in a body with medium structure. The Scirus '98, a cabernet and merlot blend, is, in our opinion, the best wine from Le Sorgenti. The colour is an intense ruby, the aromas of blackcurrant and blackberry are well-defined, and the palate is soft, elegant and well-balanced, with a long finish. Lastly, the Vin Santo '94 has an appealing nutty bouquet but is a bit austere in the mouth, and very dry indeed.

The Bucalossi family continues to run its winery in the heart of the Florentine part of Chianti with laudable enthusiasm. Every task is carried out with scrupulous care to make sure that the excellent results keep coming. In the vineyards, replanting continues under the supervision of consultant oenologist, Niccolò D'Afflitto. Once again, Casa Emma wines did well at our tastings, and their merlot struck us as particularly good, coming very close to Three Glasses. But we'll start with the Chianti Classico '98, which has a lovely, limpid, intense ruby colour. Fruit, especially blackcurrant and blackberry, prevails on the nose, mingling with sweet vanilla from well-integrated oak. The Riserva '97 has an extremely concentrated colour that introduces spicy notes of cinnamon and cloves that blend beautifully with rich fruit, and just a hint of tertiary aromas of leather and tobacco. The attack on the palate is determined, full and soft, the tannins amalgamating well into a powerful structure while the finish is a long, satisfying crescendo. The Soloìo '97 is a monovarietal merlot of great breeding. Ripe lively fruit, with blackberry and blackcurrant to the fore, dominates the nose, where spicy notes of vanilla hover in the background. After a vibrant, full-flavoured attack, the palate shows vigour and structure. The tannins, while undeniably present, are well under control and the leisurely finish is a delight.

●	Scirus '98	♟♟	5
●	Chianti Colli Fiorentini '98	♟	3
●	Chianti Colli Fiorentini '99	♟	3
○	Sghiras '99	♟	5
○	Vin Santo '94	♟	5

●	Chianti Classico Ris. '97	♟♟	4
●	Soloìo '97	♟♟	5
●	Chianti Classico '98	♟	4
●	Chianti Classico Ris. '93	♟♟♟	4*
●	Chianti Classico Ris. '95	♟♟♟	4*
●	Soloìo '94	♟♟♟	5
●	Chianti Classico '90	♟♟	3*
●	Chianti Classico '93	♟♟	3*
●	Chianti Classico '96	♟♟	3*
●	Chianti Classico '97	♟♟	4
●	Chianti Classico Ris. '90	♟♟	4
●	Chianti Classico Ris. '94	♟♟	4
●	Chianti Classico Ris. '96	♟♟	4
●	Soloìo '95	♟♟	5
●	Chianti Classico '95	♟	3

BARBERINO VAL D'ELSA (FI) BARBERINO VAL D'ELSA (FI)

★ ISOLE E OLENA
LOC. ISOLE, 1
50021 BARBERINO VAL D'ELSA (FI)
TEL. 055/8072763

LE FILIGARE
LOC. SAN DONATO IN POGGIO
VIA SICELLE
50020 BARBERINO VAL D'ELSA (FI)
TEL. 055/8072796

Paolo De Marchi seems to have taken out a subscription to double Three Glass awards. This is not only the second consecutive year he has won two top ratings but he has also now earned his first Star, which means that he has picked up a total of at least ten of the Guide's highest honours. Of course, De Marchi is an influential player on the Chianti Classico scene. His viticultural ideas put him at the forefront in the zone, and indeed beyond it, while we can only admire his oenological track record and the clean, elegant style that characterises all his wines. A perfect example is the Cepparello '98, released this year. It is an almost 100 percent sangiovese with an intense, varietal bouquet of Parma violets and black cherry that ushers in a stylish aristocratic palate. All this in a vintage which, while good, was not up to the standards of the '97. Praise, too, for the Cabernet Sauvignon '97, from the Collezione De Marchi line. It has the classic Cabernet aromas without the least concession to the obtrusive grassiness so often found in this kind of wine in Chianti. Instead, there are notes of tobacco, leather, red fruit and just a hint of vanilla, then dense tannins kick in and a concentration that would not disgrace a top Bordeaux. The other De Marchi offerings are very good, even though they had to make do with only Two Glasses apiece. The Chianti Classico '98 is one of the best of its kind. The Syrah '97 offers a spicy bouquet and a fairly harmonious structure. Finally, the Vin Santo '94 is a sweet white wine, modern in style, with a forward nose and barrique-derived vanilla, and a sweet, but not at all cloying, alcohol-rich palate.

This estate, a Guide regular for years, has done a little less well than we expected. We cannot fault Carlo Burchi's commitment nor that of oenologist Lorenzo Badini. A short breather, we imagine, from which Le Filigare will soon emerge stronger than ever. The Chianti Classico '98 offers a limpid ruby hue, and a clean if not particularly characterful nose. The palate starts off well and shows definition and balance, although the finish is only moderately long. The Riserva '97 is bright ruby in the glass. The bouquet may be a bit muddled at first, with evident tertiary notes, but it soon opens out into fruit and toasty oak. The entry on the palate is firm and soft, the powerful alcohol keeping the solid, tightly knit tannins in check through to a sure-footed finish that gives great satisfaction. The Podere Le Rocce '97 is well-conceived, starting with its impenetrable ruby hue but the vanilla that lords it over the other aromas indicates that the wine needs more time to finish blending its oak. In the mouth, it is concentrated, rich in extract, succulent and surprisingly lively. The tannins are close-knit but well-integrated, and there's a long, tasty finish.

●	Cabernet Sauvignon '97	♟♟♟	6	●	Podere Le Rocce '97	♟♟	5
●	Cepparello '98	♟♟♟	6	●	Chianti Classico '98	♟	4
●	Chianti Classico '98	♟♟	4	●	Chianti Classico Ris. '97	♟	5
●	Syrah '97	♟♟	6	●	Podere Le Rocce '88	♟♟♟	5
○	Vin Santo '94	♟♟	5	●	Chianti Classico '95	♟♟	4
●	Cabernet Sauvignon '88	♟♟♟	6	●	Chianti Classico '96	♟♟	4
●	Cabernet Sauvignon '90	♟♟♟	6	●	Chianti Classico Ris. '90	♟♟	5
●	Cabernet Sauvignon '95	♟♟♟	6	●	Chianti Classico Ris. '91	♟♟	5
●	Cabernet Sauvignon '96	♟♟♟	6	●	Chianti Classico Ris. '93	♟♟	5
●	Cepparello '86	♟♟♟	6	●	Chianti Classico Ris. '96	♟♟	5
●	Cepparello '88	♟♟♟	6	●	Podere Le Rocce '90	♟♟	5
●	Cepparello '97	♟♟♟	5	●	Podere Le Rocce '91	♟♟	5
●	Chianti Classico '88	♟♟♟	3*	●	Podere Le Rocce '93	♟♟	5
●	Cepparello '94	♟♟	5	●	Podere Le Rocce '94	♟♟	5
●	Cepparello '95	♟♟	5	●	Podere Le Rocce '96	♟♟	5

BARBERINO VAL D'ELSA (FI)

BARBERINO VAL D'ELSA (FI)

CASTELLO DI MONSANTO
VIA MONSANTO, 8
50021 BARBERINO VAL D'ELSA (FI)
TEL. 055/8059000

CASTELLO DELLA PANERETTA
STRADA DELLA PANERETTA, 35
50021 BARBERINO VAL D'ELSA (FI)
TEL. 055/8059003

Producers interested in opening their wineries to the public would do well to take a leaf from Laura Bianchi's book. A visit to Castello di Monsanto makes an indelible impression on the imagination of any wine-lover. Walking past the bottles and barriques in the ageing gallery and admiring the displays of historic labels before passing through into the splendid reception room to emerge finally onto the freshly mown lawn, where the wines are waiting for your approval, is a delightful and memorable experience. So, the fact that this lovely estate is back in the Guide, and with such good results, makes us very happy. It will also please the hard-liners of old-fashioned Chianti Classico that makes a virtue of austerity and scorns crowd-pleasing approachability. The highest marks, however, go to the Nemo '97, a cabernet sauvignon of real breeding, with an enticing sweet nose of lovely ripe fruit. The palate is soft and elegant. It may not have enormous extract but it is well-balanced, and its vanilla-toned finish is a real pleasure. Two Glasses also go to the Chianti Classico Riserva Il Poggio '97, which is a little reluctant to open on the nose, but eventually reveals carnations and glacé cherries. The palate can offer good fruit and fair progression, hampered only by rather insistent wood. One Glass for the Tinscvil '97, a blend of sangiovese and cabernet sauvignon with slightly forward aromas. The Chianti Classico '98, also a little evolved, lacks personality. The Sangiovese Fabrizio Bianchi '97, which is also fairly far along, could be better, too.

This has been something of a mixed year for Castello della Paneretta. There's a good selection of wines but all of them seem to have bouquets that are masked by imperfectly defined aromas. Let's take a closer look. The Chianti Classico '98 has very strong vegetal notes that muffle the fruit on a nose that end with minerally hints. Entry on the palate is muscular, and followed up by succulent fruit with marked acidity and satisfying warmth. The wine goes out on a high note in a delicious finish. The clear, ruby-hued Riserva '97 has rather indistinct aromas, where animal notes mingle with tomato leaf and some fairly inelegant tertiary aromas. The front palate is smooth and reasonably well-balanced but the tannins are a little rough. The Torre a Destra selection, another '97 Riserva, proffers less than stylish toasty notes on the nose and notes of wet dog do nothing to improve matters. The wine is soft and mouth-filling but the tannins soon take over. Le Terrine '97, a canaiolo-based blend, has a vibrant ruby colour and nose that is still closed and not very compelling. In the mouth, however, it is a different story. Well-judged acidity combines attractively with a full body and lots of personality to take you through to a long and very satisfying finish. Lastly, the Quattrocentenario '97, the Paneretta monovarietal sangiovese, won us over. The aromas on the nose are still a bit unforthcoming but stylish, hinting at coffee and chocolate overlaid with subtle suggestions of tobacco and delightful ripe fruit. The attack on the palate is rich, warm and juicy, and there is good breadth and depth to the mid palate, with smooth, tightly knit tannins, and a well-sustained finish.

● Chianti Cl. Il Poggio Ris. '97	♦♦	5
● Nemo '97	♦♦	6
● Tinscvil '97	♦	4
● Chianti Classico '98		4
○ Fabrizio Bianchi Chardonnay '97		5
● Chianti Cl. Il Poggio Ris. '88	♦♦♦	5
● Chianti Cl. Il Poggio Ris. '86	♦♦	5
● Chianti Cl. Il Poggio Ris. '90	♦♦	5
● Chianti Cl. Il Poggio Ris. '93	♦♦	5
● Nemo '85	♦♦	5
● Nemo '88	♦♦	5
● Nemo '90	♦♦	5
● Nemo '93	♦♦	5
● Nemo '94	♦♦	5
● Nemo '95	♦♦	6

● Le Terrine '97	♦♦	5
● Quattrocentenario '97	♦♦	5
● Chianti Classico '98	♦	4
● Chianti Classico Ris. '97	♦	4
● Chianti Classico Torre a Destra Ris. '97		4
● Chianti Classico '95	♦♦	4
● Chianti Classico Ris. '95	♦♦	4
● Chianti Classico Torre a Destra Ris. '95	♦♦	4
● Chianti Classico Torre a Destra Ris. '96	♦♦	4
● Le Terrine '96	♦♦	5
● Quattrocentenario '95	♦♦	5
● Quattrocentenario '96	♦♦	5

BARBERINO VAL D'ELSA (FI) BARBERINO VAL D'ELSA (FI)

FATTORIA CASA SOLA
VIA CORTINE, 5
50021 BARBERINO VAL D'ELSA (FI)
TEL. 055/8075028

QUERCIA AL POGGIO
VIA MONSANTO, 69
50021 BARBERINO VAL D'ELSA (FI)
TEL. 055/8075278

After being absent for a few years, the Gambaro family's Barberino Val d'Elsa estate, Fattoria Casa Sola, is back in the Guide. The vineyards are superbly located at San Donato in Poggio and Isole e Olena, at an average height of 330 metres above sea level and Giorgio Marone is the oenologist. This year, the estate has taken a notable leap forward, particularly with the standard Chianti Classico. We'll start our profile right there, with the Chianti Classico '98, which has a clear, deep and attractively intense ruby colour. Its broad, pervasive nose is strikingly elegant, with complex fruit ranging from blackcurrant to plum, sweet notes of vanilla and a hint of cinnamon. After a splendidly succulent, tangy entry, the palate unveils a full, complex body, very close-knit but fine-grained tannins, good acidity and a long, delightful finish. The Riserva '97 is somewhat less successful. Intriguing pepper and cinnamon spice rubs shoulders with balsamic notes and ripe fruit on the nose but thereafter the palate reveals a slightly jaded, unexciting wine that lacks focus and with excessively astringent tannins. It picks up again in the finish, though, and in fact almost ended up with a One Glass score. The Montarsiccio '97, a sangiovese and cabernet sauvignon blend, has an attractively firm ruby colour, deliciously rich, vivacious, well-defined aromas and a decidedly muscular palate with a fresh, clean flavour that shows good length.

This is the Guide debut for this small estate at Barberino Val d'Elsa, which presented three interesting wines. The real surprise is the Chianti Classico '98. It has a rich, full, brilliant ruby colour which ushers in a bouquet that is bit confused at first. After only a few seconds, though, it opens to unveil lively, intense fruit, in which cherry and blackcurrant are prominent. The attack on the palate is very positive, revealing silky richness, meaty succulence and firm tannins that integrate seamlessly into the structure. There is also a refreshingly acidic tang and a well-sustained finish. The Chianti Classico Riserva '97 came close to carrying off another Two Glasses for Quercia al Poggio. It, too, has a rich, limpid hue and then a wealth of crisp, extremely varied and pervasively intense fruit regales the nose, embellished with faint spicy grace notes. The palate is full-bodied and balanced, then the pleasing and well-conceived finish offers moderate length. The IGT Cataste '97 is a little less distinguished. Wood dominates the nose, with toasty and vanilla notes lording it over the fruit. Oak is in charge on the palate as well. After a soft attack, the wine seems a bit thin. It's not particularly complex or full-bodied but agreeable enough.

● Chianti Classico '98	▼▼	3*
● Chianti Classico Ris. '97	▼	4
● Montarsiccio '97	▼	5
● Chianti Classico Ris. '88	▽▽	4
● Chianti Classico '90	▽	3
● Chianti Classico '91	▽	3
● Chianti Classico '94	▽	3
● Chianti Classico Ris. '90	▽	4
● Chianti Classico Ris. '93	▽	4
● Chianti Classico Sel. di Bacco Ris. '90	▽	4

● Chianti Classico '98	▼▼	4
● Cataste '97	▼	5
● Chianti Classico Ris. '97	▼	4

BOLGHERI (LI)

TENUTA BELVEDERE
LOC. BELVEDERE, 140
57020 BOLGHERI (LI)
TEL. 0565/749735

Marchese Piero Antinori has decided to make a substantial investment of energy and funds in the Bolgheri area. He has planted quite a number of new vineyards, taking the total to 200 hectares, and further plantings will be made in the future to make the estate the largest in the area. It is clear from the way the new vines are planted that size is not the only priority, so the prospects for extraordinary quality in the future are excellent. Meanwhile, the present is far from disappointing. We found that the Guado al Tasso has continued to make progress. It seems firmer than previous versions, and bespeaks more evenly ripened grapes. It lacks only that extra touch of complexity that would make it a great wine but nevertheless unfurls an intense nose of black berry fruit and mulberry jam, without the vegetal aromas that used to jeopardize its performance. The palate still has the delightful softness of previous versions yet isn't at all flaccid, thanks to its enhanced tangy sinew. The Vermentino was surprisingly well received. The panel enjoyed its unusual but attractive, rich bouquet of sage, aromatic herbs and exotic fruit, and its refreshing, well-balanced palate with a long finish that mirrors the nose. The classic rosé, Scalabrone, is up to snuff, with its characteristic raspberry and strawberry nose and fragrant, tasty palate.

BOLGHERI (LI)

LE MACCHIOLE
LOC. CONTESSINE
VIA BOLGHERESE, 189/A
57020 BOLGHERI (LI)
TEL. 0565/766092

What progress this winery has made since 1975, when Eugenio Campolmi first acquired a little vineyard near Bolgheri! Le Macchiole now turns out rich, wonderfully powerful wines. In addition to Paleo Rosso, which was the estate's first product to win general acclaim, there are now other reds with just as much structure. But let's start with the Paleo Rosso, a cabernet that displays real breeding. The '97 has repeated the triumph of the previous vintage, getting its Three Glasses without any trouble. The colour, a vivid ruby red, still shows a youthful purplish tinge. Oak has left its mark on the nose but after a few seconds in the glass, a sumptuous bouquet of roasting coffee, chocolate and blackberry jam emerges. In the mouth, it reveals a marvellously full body, well-integrated tannins and a tactile softness. It's a marvellous achievement, and its two little brothers are not far behind. The Scrio '97, a syrah, is one of the best wines made from this grape in Italy. Its colour is so dark it looks almost black, and the explosive impact of fruit on the nose alternates notes of blackcurrant with hints of pencil lead and Alpine herbs. On the palate, it is big and richly extracted, and the development is full and generous. The house merlot, the Messorio '97, is just as explosive. It, too, is open, muscular, generous, fragrant and incredibly soft, but it is even firmer than the Scrio. Three Glasses on its first time out. We haven't much space left to tell you about the other two excellent offerings. The Paleo Sauvignon '98 has rich notes of citrus and peach, with a buttery yet fresh-tasting palate while the new Macchiole red, a sangiovese, merlot, cabernet and syrah blend, is ripe and juicy. Hardly the sort of wine you'd expect to find at the bottom of a tasting list.

●	Bolgheri Rosso Sup. Guado al Tasso '97	YY	6
○	Bolgheri Vermentino '99	YY	3*
☉	Bolgheri Rosato Scalabrone '99	Y	4
●	Bolgheri Rosso Sup. Guado al Tasso '90	YYY	6
●	Bolgheri Rosso Sup. Guado al Tasso '93	YY	6
●	Bolgheri Rosso Sup. Guado al Tasso '94	YY	6
●	Bolgheri Rosso Sup. Guado al Tasso '95	YY	6
●	Bolgheri Rosso Sup. Guado al Tasso '96	YY	6
●	Bolgheri Rosso Belvedere '96	Y	2*
●	Bolgheri Rosso Sup. Paleo '97	YYY	6
●	Messorio '97	YYY	6
○	Bolgheri Sauvignon Paleo '98	YY	4
●	Le Macchiole '97	YY	5
●	Scrio '97	YY	6
●	Bolgheri Rosso Sup. Paleo '95	YYY	6
●	Bolgheri Rosso Sup. Paleo '96	YYY	6
●	Bolgheri Rosso Sup. Paleo '94	YY	5
○	Bolgheri Sauvignon Paleo '95	YY	4
○	Bolgheri Sauvignon Paleo '96	YY	4
○	Bolgheri Sauvignon Paleo '97	YY	4
○	Paleo Bianco '93	YY	3*
○	Paleo Bianco '94	YY	3*
●	Paleo Rosso '92	YY	2*
●	Paleo Rosso '93	YY	5

BOLGHERI (LI)

TENUTA DELL'ORNELLAIA
VIA BOLGHERESE, 191
57020 BOLGHERI (LI)
TEL. 0565/71811

The third millennium holds no terrors for the Tenuta dell'Ornellaia. This was abundantly clear from our tastings this year, which awarded top honours to two wines and left us with the distinct impression that success of this magnitude is likely to be a regular event in the future. There has also been a structural change in the estate. Mondavi, the celebrated Californian producer, is now a part owner. The Masseto, that archetype of Tuscan merlots, is absolutely outstanding. This exciting wine manages to be fabulously rich and superbly elegant at the same time. What more can we say? We could tell you about the generous complexity of its bouquet, the silky texture of its tannins and the unforgettable finish. But we'll just leave it at that. The Ornellaia '97 is also up to par. It's the best Bolgheri DOC of its vintage and, in all probability, the best Ornellaia ever. Elegance, concentration, depth, admirably enticing tannins, a perfect use of oak and glorious fruit will give you the picture. Its great advantage over past vintages, which were equally stunning, is in the fruit, which was selected to ensure perfect ripeness, and in the exemplary definition of the whistle-clean nose. The third Ornellaia label, Serre Nuove, is making its debut with the '97, and it's a good one. Perhaps a little vegetal and a whisker over-extracted, it is nonetheless firm and vigorous. Le Volte '98 has done better than we expected. It is a simple, grassy wine, but clean, nicely balanced and enjoyable. Finally, the sauvignon blanc, Poggio alle Gazze '99, is good but less distinguished than usual. There are alluring aromas of ripe, well-defined apple and pear, and a pleasing palate, but the finish is a bit one-dimensional.

●	Bolgheri Sup. Ornellaia '97	▼▼▼	6
●	Masseto '97	▼▼▼	6
●	Bolgheri Sup. Serre Nuove '97	▼▼	5
●	Le Volte '98	▼	3
○	Poggio alle Gazze '99	▼	4
●	Masseto '93	▽▽▽	6
●	Masseto '94	▽▽▽	6
●	Masseto '95	▽▽▽	6
●	Ornellaia '93	▽▽▽	6
●	Masseto '92	▽▽	6
●	Masseto '96	▽▽	6
●	Ornellaia '92	▽▽	6
●	Ornellaia '94	▽▽	6
●	Ornellaia '95	▽▽	6
●	Ornellaia '96	▽▽	6

BOLGHERI (LI)

★ TENUTA SAN GUIDO
LOC. CAPANNE, 27
57020 BOLGHERI (LI)
TEL. 0565/762003

Please don't get the idea that we consider Sassicaia some kind of national institution that has to win a top award every year, whatever the outcome of our tastings. This legendary Bolgheri red is subjected to exactly the same scrutiny as any other wine and, like any other wine, it has to prove its worth. The fact is, however, that vintage after vintage, Sassicaia proves itself to be a wine of extraordinary finesse and exceptional quality, especially in its tannins. Hence, yet again, Three Glasses. The '97 is an effortlessly successful example of the style that the Tenuta San Guido has favoured in recent years. Witness the rich but unostentatious extract, well-defined yet intriguing fruit, well-judged and integrated oak and impressively elegant phenols. In comparative tastings, Sassicaia is always instantly recognizable, largely because of its amazingly fine-grained tannins, which are impeccably silky and velvet-smooth. This '97, which is only just at the beginning of its career, is still a little withdrawn. There's a faint green note over the blackcurrant and bramble on the nose. However, the palate has already started to open up and reveal its depth. Well-rounded, soft and full-bodied without being overwhelming, it reveals superlative balance and a remarkably long, perfectly coherent finish. Need we say more?

●	Bolgheri Sassicaia '97	▼▼▼	6
●	Bolgheri Sassicaia '95	▽▽▽	6
●	Bolgheri Sassicaia '96	▽▽▽	6
●	Sassicaia '83	▽▽▽	6
●	Sassicaia '84	▽▽▽	6
●	Sassicaia '85	▽▽▽	6
●	Sassicaia '88	▽▽▽	6
●	Sassicaia '90	▽▽▽	6
●	Sassicaia '92	▽▽▽	6
●	Sassicaia '93	▽▽▽	6
●	Bolgheri Sassicaia '94	▽▽	6
●	Sassicaia '86	▽▽	6
●	Sassicaia '87	▽▽	6
●	Sassicaia '89	▽▽	6
●	Sassicaia '91	▽▽	6

CAPRAIA FIORENTINA (FI)   CARMIGNANO (PO)

ENRICO PIERAZZUOLI
VIA VALICARDA, 35
50056 CAPRAIA FIORENTINA (FI)
TEL. 0571/910078

FATTORIA AMBRA
VIA LOMBARDA, 85
50042 CARMIGNANO (PO)
TEL. 055/486488 - 055/8719049

Some people may be surprised at what Enrico Pierazzuoli has achieved this year. But anyone who has been carefully following this winery recently must have known that sooner or later it would come up with a great wine. Even so, we must admit that the Riserva '97 version of Carmignano Le Farnete is better than even we thought possible. This is a wine with incredibly rich, full fruit. The ravishingly inviting nose offers notes of plum, fresh mulberry jam and hints of coffee. In the mouth, it is voluptuous and soft, without flaccidity, while the very long finish perfectly echoes the bouquet. The tannins and oak are well integrated into the boisterous fruit and the result is irresistible. You could, if you like, say it should be more complex, or reflect its variety more precisely, but these limitations hardly make a dent in a very creditable performance. The very good Chianti Montalbano Riserva, which is similar in conception, reveals a delightful roundness in the mouth, with very lively fruit and tannins that are well under control. The very respectable Chianti Classico Matroneo comes from one of the three estates that Enrico Pierazzuoli runs, the others being Le Farnete at Carmignano and Tenuta Cantagallo near the Monte Albano range. Despite some reduction on the nose, the Matroneo is reasonably concentrated on the palate. The Chianti Montalbano '98 is no more than acceptable.

Another positive year for Beppe Regoli's wines. To tell the truth, some questions from last year do remain unanswered, particularly about the estate's standard-label wine, but the selections have been getting better and better. Their style is very distinct. These are wines that do not follow the fashion of the moment, which is certainly in their favour. In our opinion, they can improve even further, and we hope to see them doing just that in the next few years. We'll start with the wine we liked most, the Carmignano Elzana Riserva '97, which has a very deep, lustrous ruby hue. The positive fruit on the nose includes notes of blackcurrant and bramble with a very stylish spicy finish. The attack on the palate is soft and mouth-filling, and, at first, somewhat austere. Tight-knit tannins are offset by robust alcohol and the rising finish is succulent and very long. The intensely ruby red Vigne Alte Montalbiolo '97 has fruity aromas with faint vegetal hints. There is vigorous acidity on the palate, with assertive tannins that the alcohol has trouble keeping in check. The structure is sound and very full, while the flavour lingers. The Barco Reale '99 offers fresh, attractive aromas of green fruit. Entry on the palate is a little dilute and the structure, although undemanding, is fairly well-balanced. Lastly, the Vin Ruspo '99 has an attractive cherry-ruby hue and bright floral aromas with crisp fruity notes. The tangy acidity in the mouth makes it quite refreshing.

● Carmignano Le Farnete Ris. '97	♟♟♟	5		● Carmignano Elzana Ris. '97	♟♟	4
● Chianti Montalbano Ris. '97	♟♟	4		● Carmignano		
● Carmignano Le Farnete '98	♟	4		Le Vigne Alte Montalbiolo '97	♟♟	4
● Chianti Cl. Matroneo '97	♟	4		☉ Vin Ruspo di Carmignano '99	♟	3
● Chianti Montalbano '98		3		● Barco Reale '99		3
○ Carleto '97	♟♟	4		● Carmignano '89	♟♟	3
● Carmignano Le Farnete Ris. '92	♟♟	4		● Carmignano Elzana Ris. '95	♟♟	4
● Carmignano Le Farnete Ris. '93	♟♟	4		● Carmignano Elzana Ris. '96	♟♟	4
● Carmignano Le Farnete Ris. '94	♟♟	4		● Carmignano Le Vigne Alte Ris. '94	♟♟	4
● Carmignano Le Farnete Ris. '96	♟♟	4		● Carmignano Le Vigne Alte Ris. '96	♟♟	4
● Chianti Montalbano Ris. '93	♟♟	3*		● Carmignano Le Vigne Alte Ris. '90	♟♟	4
● Chianti Montalbano Ris. '94	♟♟	4		● Carmignano '96	♟	4
● Carmignano Le Farnete '97	♟	4		● Carmignano Le Vigne Alte Ris. '95	♟	4
● Chianti Cl. Matroneo Ris. '95	♟	4		● Carmignano		
● Chianti Montalbano Ris. '96	♟	3		Vigna S. Cristina in Pilli '95	♟	4

CARMIGNANO (PO)

CARMIGNANO (PO)

CAPEZZANA
LOC. SEANO
VIA CAPEZZANA, 100
59015 CARMIGNANO (PO)
TEL. 055/8706005 - 055/8706091

PRATESI
VIA RIZZELLI, 10
59011 CARMIGNANO (PO)
TEL. 055/8706400

As we wrote last year, the Tenuta di Capezzana has really changed gear. In very short order, the cellar has won Three Glasses for one of its wines and come close with two others. This across-the-board success is a sign of the renewed vitality of the entire business. The Ghiaie della Furba '98 is a lovely wine, with very bright fruit and splendid balance. Its extremely intense, brilliant ruby hue introduces elegant aromas of redcurrant jam, fresh spice and herbs, with faint vegetal hints. The palate is broad, expansive and wonderfully poised, with firm, silky tannins and admirably integrated oak. The Carmignano '98 is not far behind. Firm, solid and well-supported by the tannic structure, the palate is kept on its toes by the fresh acidity of the sangiovese grape, which is soft yet sharp. It's still a very young wine, but it promises to grow as time passes. We liked the Villa di Trefiano as well. Unlike the other reds, it needs to fine-tune its oak, which is still rather noticeable, but it can offer concentration and distinct personality. The Vin Santo is excellent but that is hardly news. Its very rich nose offers aromas of candied peel, fig and peach jam. The concentrated palate reveals an all-round sweetness nicely balanced by the oak-derived tannins and the finish is long and stylish. Both the Chardonnay, which has aromas of citrus and pear and a refreshing, balanced palate, and the Barco Reale, with its surprisingly full body and pleasing fruit, are worthy of note.

The small Pratesi estate, with its six hectares at Carmignano, near Capezzana, has earned its own entry in the Guide. Bottling began in 1983 but it was the appearance on the scene of Fabrizio Pratesi, in March 1997, that sparked off a determined quest for excellence. Stefano Chioccioli is the consultant oenologist and the replanting that has been going on under his supervision has produced laudable results. The planting density of more than 10,000 vines per hectare is exceptionally tight-packed, the idea being to achieve optimal concentration in the grapes. Things are humming in the cellar, too, for the estate is planning to inaugurate the new premises early in 2001. At the moment, Pratesi produces two wines, the Carmignano, a blend of sangiovese and cabernet sauvignon, and the Lococco, an IGT made from sangiovese alone. It was the Lococco we tasted, and it proved to be a rewarding experience. A lovely dark, deep ruby hue introduces a delightfully elegant bouquet of coffee and chocolate that gives way to a mixture of ripe, concentrated red berries, lifted by faint overtones of vanilla. The entry on the palate is soft. In fact, it is so concentrated that it verges on the creamy. The close-knit tannins are nicely balanced in the robust, if not massive, body. The persistent finish offers delicious toasty notes.

● Ghiaie della Furba '98	▼▼▼	5
● Carmignano Villa di Capezzana '98	▼▼	5
● Carmignano Villa di Trefiano Ris. '97	▼▼	5
○ Vin Santo di Carmignano Ris. '93	▼▼	5
● Barco Reale '99	▼	3
○ Chardonnay '99	▼	2*
● Carmignano Villa di Capezzana Ris. '90	♀♀	5
● Carmignano Villa di Capezzana Ris. '95	♀♀	5
● Ghiaie della Furba '95	♀♀	5
● Ghiaie della Furba '97	♀♀	5
○ Vin Santo di Carmignano Ris. '90	♀♀	5
○ Vin Santo di Carmignano Ris. '92	♀♀	5

● Lococco '97	▼▼	5

CASTAGNETO CARDUCCI (LI)

GRATTAMACCO
LOC. GRATTAMACCO
57022 CASTAGNETO CARDUCCI (LI)
TEL. 0565/763840

Piermario Meletti Cavallari is one of the few people who could tell you anything you want to know about the changes that have taken place in the Bolgheri zone over the past 20 years, from the time when it produced light, almost rosé wines to the era of the great reds. In the last few years in particular, vineyards have sprung up on nearly every vine-worthy inch of the territory. Times have changed, wine has become big business, and we are seeing the end of the age of pioneers like Piermario, whose motivation comes from his heart, not his wallet. Nevertheless, the vines at Podere Grattamacco are still producing exceptional grapes that are turned into seriously good wines. This year our first tasting notes are dedicated to the Grattamacco Bianco, a vermentino-based blend. It was a delightful surprise, although we had had some hints of what was going on last year. Attractive and consistent in every way, it regales the nose with distinct aromas of fruit and summer flowers. The entry in the mouth is fairly sweet, and the palate manages to preserve an admirable roundness as it develops, without sacrificing any of its freshness. A thoroughly enjoyable wine. We have very good things to say about the Grattamacco Rosso as well. The '97 is remarkably rich, bearing witness to the excellent quality of the grapes. The palate has lashings of body, concentration and depth while the robust tannins are wonderfully smooth. It is characteristics like these that make a great wine, and this year it came awfully close to getting its Three Glasses. What held it back, essentially, was its nose, which lacks purity and breadth, although it is much more focused than in previous vintages.

CASTAGNETO CARDUCCI (LI)

MICHELE SATTA
LOC. VIGNA AL CAVALIERE, 61
57022 CASTAGNETO CARDUCCI (LI)
TEL. 0565/773041

This was a cautious year for Michele Satta's wines. Standards have been maintained but there are no major peaks. The main reason for this impression is the absence of the cellar's standard-bearer, the Vigna al Cavaliere, at our tastings. The next edition is scheduled for release in the spring. Meanwhile, the property is expanding, as Satta has planted new vineyards. And work continues on the enlargement of the cellar, which will soon be able to handle winemaking with greater efficiency. There is plenty of energy and enthusiasm at work, even if the results were hard to discern from the tastings. However, we did retaste the Cavaliere '97, which seemed even better this time round. Its elegance, length and balance, augurs well for the '98. The highest ranker this year is the Piastraia, a blend of cabernet, merlot, sangiovese and syrah. It's an interesting wine, with spice taking the lead on the nose, although fruit is there, too, as well as vegetal hints. In the mouth, it is concentrated and nicely balanced. A very agreeable wine all round, in fact. It's as reliable a bottle as you could wish to find, but we wouldn't mind a little more personality in future. The Costa di Giulia, a vermentino and sauvignon blend, has clean, delicate aromas, decent body and a lively, enticingly succulent palate that makes it a good accompaniment for a wide range of dishes. Both the Bolgheri Bianco and the Diambra are well-typed. Of the two, the panel preferred the Bianco but it was a close question.

○	Bolgheri Bianco '99	🍷🍷	4
●	Bolgheri Rosso Sup. Grattamacco '97	🍷🍷	6
●	Grattamacco '85	🍷🍷🍷	5
●	Bolgheri Rosso Sup. Grattamacco '95	🍷🍷	6
●	Bolgheri Rosso Sup. Grattamacco '96	🍷🍷	6
●	Grattamacco '87	🍷🍷	5
●	Grattamacco '88	🍷🍷	5
●	Grattamacco '89	🍷🍷	5
●	Grattamacco '90	🍷🍷	5
●	Grattamacco '91	🍷🍷	5
●	Grattamacco '92	🍷🍷	4
●	Grattamacco '93	🍷🍷	5

●	Bolgheri Rosso Piastraia '98	🍷🍷	5
○	Costa di Giulia '99	🍷	4
○	Bolgheri Bianco '99		3
●	Bolgheri Rosso Diambra '99		3
●	Bolgheri Rosso Piastraia '95	🍷🍷	3*
●	Bolgheri Rosso Piastraia '96	🍷🍷	4
●	Bolgheri Rosso Piastraia '97	🍷🍷	4
●	Vigna al Cavaliere '90	🍷🍷	5
●	Vigna al Cavaliere '95	🍷🍷	4
●	Vigna al Cavaliere '96	🍷🍷	5
●	Vigna al Cavaliere '97	🍷🍷	5
●	Bolgheri Rosso Diambra '94	🍷	1*
●	Bolgheri Rosso Diambra '98	🍷	3
●	Piastraia '94	🍷	3

CASTELLINA IN CHIANTI (SI) CASTELLINA IN CHIANTI (SI)

CASTELLARE DI CASTELLINA
LOC. CASTELLARE
53011 CASTELLINA IN CHIANTI (SI)
TEL. 0577/742903

CECCHI - VILLA CERNA
LOC. CASINA DEI PONTI, 56
53011 CASTELLINA IN CHIANTI (SI)
tel. 0577/743024

This Three Glass award for Paolo Panerai's Castellare could be the first in a series, given the progress they have been making here in recent years. Our top rating goes to a product which is not one of those for which this estate is famous. The wine in question is the Chianti Classico Vigna il Poggiale Riserva '97, made almost exclusively from sangiovese, and it is an admirable example of an authentic Chianti Classico. Its distinct and intensely fruity bouquet, and elegant palate, which although not very concentrated is a model of finesse, are a constant reminder of all that is best about sangiovese (or "sangioveto", as they say in these parts) from the upper Castellina zone. The fine '97 vintage did the rest, giving the wine a sweetness and balance that are hard to equal in comparable Chianti Classicos. The acidity – it's definitely there – seems almost to have been put under a spell, so well does it blend into the wine's structure. The Chianti Classico Riserva '97 is good, but not quite so elegant. While I Sodi di San Nicolò is a worthy wine, it has some rougher edges and perhaps rather less body, but then it is a '96, a year that was much inferior to the subsequent vintage. The Chianti Classico '98 is fair. It's a medium-bodied red with a rather aggressive acid bite, partly because it has only moderate concentration. Finally, the Coniale '96, a cabernet sauvignon, is a bit of a wallflower in the company of these characterful sangiovese-based reds. It gives one food for thought about the role of cabernet in this part of the country.

If you should ever be in need of a Chianti Classico that combines a consistently high standard with a reasonable price and ready availability, at least in Italy, then you ought seriously to consider a bottle from this large and well-known winery. We are paying Luigi Cecchi a very great compliment when we say that he really knows what he is about and that he has enormous respect for his potential customers. For reasons of space, we are again presenting Cecchi and Villa Cerna, the family estate, in the same entry. This makes for quite a collection of tableware, as six wines have won Two Glasses each. While these performances were predictable for such real thoroughbreds as the Spargolo '97, a sangiovese, and the cabernet sauvignon-based Vigneto La Gavina '97, the results of the Chianti Classicos are something of a surprise. The Riserva '97 is exemplary in style and the Villa Cerva Riserva '97 is more complex and concentrated. The two '98s, particularly the Messer Piero di Teuzzo, offer characteristic sangiovese aromas and decidedly generous structure. None of these wines is an international giant but they are all enormously satisfying. Wines from the San Gimignano vineyards worth mentioning include the agreeable Chardonnay Sagrato and the excellent '99 Vernaccia Castello di Montauto. The list ends with a delicious '97 Morellino di Scansano from their Val delle Rose property. A wine to buy by the case. With this kind of fragrance and soft allure, one bottle is just not enough.

● Chianti Classico		
Vigna il Poggiale Ris. '97	▼▼▼	5
● Chianti Classico Ris. '97	▼▼	4
● I Sodi di San Niccolò '96	▼▼	6
● Chianti Classico '98	▼	4
● Coniale '96	▼	5
● Chianti Classico '95	♈♈	4
● Chianti Classico '97	♈♈	4
● Chianti Classico Ris. '96	♈♈	5
● Chianti Classico		
Vigna al Poggiale '95	♈♈	5
● Coniale '94	♈♈	6
● Coniale '95	♈♈	6
● I Sodi di San Niccolò '94	♈♈	6
● I Sodi di San Niccolò '95	♈♈	6

● Chianti Classico		
Messer Piero di Teuzzo '98	▼▼	4
● Chianti Classico Ris. '97	▼▼	3*
● Chianti Classico Villa Cerna Ris. '97	▼▼	4
● Morellino di Scansano Val delle Rose '97	▼▼	3*
● Spargolo '97	▼▼	5
● Vigneto La Gavina '97	▼▼	5
● Chianti Classico Villa Cerna '98	▼	3
○ Sagrato Chardonnay		
Castello di Montauto '99	▼	3
○ Vernaccia di S. Gimignano		
Castello di Montauto '99	▼	3
● Chianti Classico Villa Cerna Ris. '96	♈♈	4
● Spargolo '95	♈♈	4
● Vigneto La Gavina '96	♈♈	5

Concadoro

Loc. Concadoro, 67
53011 Castellina in Chianti (SI)
tel. 0577/741285

Another excellent showing for the Cerasi family's estate. The secret lies in the passion with which they approach every phase of production, in vineyard and cellar. As a result, their rich, meaty wines bear the imprint of the land they come from. "Anonymous" and "ordinary" are not words that spring to mind when tasting. The Chianti Classico '98 has a lovely intense ruby hue and fine aromas of jam, plum and mulberry, enhanced by spicy notes of cinnamon. The attack on the palate reveals complexity, and the progression is smooth, with compact, fine-grained tannins integrated into a juicy full body where the alcohol holds its own against the harder components. The attractive finish is well-sustained. The Riserva '97 strikes the nose first with bottle-ageing aromas, including cocoa blended with mild notes of vanilla. As it opens up, elegant fruit then appears, particularly wild berries, and, to finish, attractive, lingering cloves. In the mouth, it offers notable concentration, with firm, crunchy tannins and well-adjusted alcohol, and the flavour is soft, tangy, long and very attractively balanced. The Vin Santo is the only Concadoro wine we had reservations about. A limpid amber, its nose reveals oxidized notes that have the upper hand over the classic aromas of the wine. There are also some not altogether clean or distinct nuances of dried fruit. The powerful alcohol on the front palate gives an impression of great intensity but is not backed up by a correspondingly full body. The finish is long, although not very soft.

●	Chianti Classico '98	🍷🍷	3*
●	Chianti Classico Ris. '97	🍷🍷	4
○	Vin Santo Cerasi '95	🍷	5
●	Chianti Cl. Vigna di Gaversa '93	YY	4
●	Chianti Cl. Vigna di Gaversa '96	YY	4
●	Chianti Classico '97	YY	4
●	Chianti Classico Ris. '93	Y	4

★ Castello di Fonterutoli

Loc. Fonterutoli
Via Rossini, 5
53011 Castellina in Chianti (SI)
tel. 0577/73571

Castello di Fonterutoli goes from strength to strength. It has become impossible to find wines that are anything less than excellent. Francesco, Filippo and Jacopo Mazzei, who have thoroughly assimilated the experience of their father, Lapo, continue, with the help of Carlo Ferrini, their consultant oenologist, to turn out a stream of great reds. In fact this year, they have carried off two Three Glass awards, which puts them at the top of the class in Tuscany, on an equal footing with Fattoria di Felsina, which has also racked up a total of 14 such accolades. The Siepi '98 is, as usual, a stunner. It may not be quite as concentrated as the '97, but you'd never notice. The foundation of this powerful red is a blend of sangiovese and merlot from – the crucial factor – the extraordinary Siepi vineyard, which has long been considered a sort of Chianti Classico "premier cru". The Chianti Classico Castello di Fonterutoli Riserva '97 is extraordinary as well. It is very concentrated, modern in style, captivating on the nose and soft and lingering in flavour. But if what you want is a quaffable red that won't require a second mortgage, then the Chianti Classico '98 is the wine for you. Delicious and fragrant, it is worth a lot more than it actually costs. Or else, there is the simple, direct Poggio alla Badiola '99, a 100 percent sangiovese which is seductively easy to drink. In fact, you can't help reflecting that you could hardly hope for anything better in Chianti Classico. A range like this would be difficult to match anywhere else.

●	Chianti Classico Castello di Fonterutoli Ris. '97	🍷🍷🍷	5
●	Siepi '98	🍷🍷🍷	6
●	Chianti Classico '98	🍷🍷	4
●	Poggio alla Badiola '99	🍷🍷	3*
●	Chianti Classico Castello di Fonterutoli Ris. '95	YYY	5
●	Concerto '90	YYY	5
●	Concerto '93	YYY	5
●	Concerto '94	YYY	5
●	Siepi '93	YYY	5
●	Siepi '94	YYY	6
●	Siepi '95	YYY	6
●	Siepi '96	YYY	6
●	Siepi '97	YYY	6

CASTELLINA IN CHIANTI (SI)   CASTELLINA IN CHIANTI (SI)

GAGLIOLE
LOC. GAGLIOLE, 42
53011 CASTELLINA IN CHIANTI (SI)
TEL. 0577/740369

LA BRANCAIA
LOC. BRANCAIA
53011 CASTELLINA IN CHIANTI (SI)
TEL. 0577/743084

Gagliole seems to have hit its stride. Its owner, the Swiss lawyer, Thomas Bar, chose the incomparably beautiful Castellina in Chianti landscape as the setting to make wine the way he feels it should be made: in strict observance of the dictates of organic farming. Recently, there have been some big changes. Bar has bought a new property, Casina di Castagnoli, and rented a neighbouring one, Siepi, so he now has a larger area under vine. It all suggests that he means to produce wine of the highest quality. Yet again, only one wine was presented at our tastings. Gagliole Rosso '98 is an IGT made mainly from sangiovese with just a little cabernet sauvignon. In the glass, it flaunts a lively, lustrous ruby hue with limpid highlights. The nose is enticingly generous, the rich, ripe fruit mingling attractively with the wood. In the mouth, there is good body and an even, clear-cut progression underpinned by delicate yet firm, well-developed tannins. It signs off with restrained hints of ripe fruit and vanilla in the long, coherent finish. Two full Glasses!

As regular as clockwork – perhaps in honour of its creator, Bruno Widmehr, who is, after all, Swiss – the new version of Brancaia, a sangiovese and merlot-based red, is consistently excellent. The '98 vintage, which we had expected to find less interesting than the '97, fairly knocked us off our pins. It is one of the few Chianti wines that succeed in uniting softness, grip and concentration in a magical state of balance. This wine, so round it evokes visions of a perfect sphere, is the fruit of vineyards managed for quality and a cellar technique – the consultant is Carlo Ferrini – that approaches perfection. Berries, vanilla, Parma violets and even some balsamic notes greet the nose. On the palate, close-knit tannins blend into a wonderfully full body with a distinctly velvety feel. In a supporting role, but edging towards centre stage, is the Chianti Classico '98. Although from the same good but not extraordinary year, it hardly seems like a wine from a minor vintage. Complex fruity aromas with floral and even some mineral notes introduce a concentrated, full-bodied palate where densely packed tannins mingle with a suggestion of acidic tang. It really is a most interesting wine. Our only regret – for Italian wine-lovers – is that most of La Brancaia's wines are sold abroad. In Italy, it's unusual to spot it in the racks of even the best wine merchants. But then, life can be very unfair sometimes.

● Gagliole Rosso '98	♟♟	5
● Gagliole Rosso '95	♟♟	5
● Gagliole Rosso '97	♟♟	5
○ Gagliole Bianco '96	♟	4

● Brancaia '98	♟♟♟	6
● Chianti Classico '98	♟♟	4
● Brancaia '94	♟♟♟	6
● Brancaia '97	♟♟♟	6
● Brancaia '88	♟♟	6
● Brancaia '90	♟♟	6
● Brancaia '91	♟♟	6
● Brancaia '93	♟♟	5
● Brancaia '95	♟♟	6
● Brancaia '96	♟♟	6
● Chianti Classico '95	♟♟	4
● Chianti Classico '96	♟♟	4
● Chianti Classico '97	♟♟	4

CASTELLINA IN CHIANTI (SI)

Castello La Leccia

Loc. La Leccia
53011 Castellina in Chianti (SI)
tel. 0577/743148

Last year, we gladly welcomed this Castellina estate to the Guide and we are equally pleased to confirm the entry, particularly as La Leccia has done even better this time. This is thanks to the enthusiasm of the young owner, Francesco Daddi (a passion he communicates to everyone who works with him), and also, of course, to the sure hand of experienced oenologist, Franco Bernabei. But let's have a look at the wines. The Chianti Classico '98 has a vivid deep ruby colour. The fruit on the nose is initially slightly muffled but it soon opens out, becoming positive and lively, with some slightly forward secondary aromas. The attack on the palate is unassertive. Balance is the keynote, backed up by fair body and tight-knit, but very smooth, tannins and nicely softening alcohol. The finish is well-sustained, succulent and agreeable. The Riserva '97 is not quite as good. The nose wavers and there are rather inelegant gamey and vegetal nuances undermining the fruit. The tannins are too prominent on the palate and in general the wine lacks delicacy, although it does show grip and flavour. The finish, however, is convincing and reasonably long. The Bruciagna '97 is a monovarietal sangiovese. The initial aromas are elegant notes of coffee, then concentrated jammy fruit kicks in. The attractive entry on the palate is concentrated and substantial, although the fine-textured tannins are still a bit rough. The firm flavour continues through the delightful rising finish.

●	Bruciagna '97	**YY**	4
●	Chianti Classico '98	**YY**	3*
●	Chianti Classico Ris. '97	**Y**	4
●	Chianti Classico '97	YY	3*
●	Bruciagna '96	Y	4
●	Chianti Classico Ris. '96	Y	4

CASTELLINA IN CHIANTI (SI)

Fattoria Nittardi

Loc. Nittardi, 76
53011 Castellina in Chianti (SI)
tel. 0577/740269

Peter Femfert's Fattoria Nittardi has, as usual, produced good, reliable wines. Stylish and well-balanced, they are a flawlessly managed expression of their terroir. This last quality can be taken for granted, since Carlo Ferrini, one of Italy's leading oenologists, is the consultant. Yet again, these Chianti Classicos want just a pinch more concentration to reach the Three Glass level. As usual, they came tantalizingly close. These are, nevertheless, excellent wines, and from a subzone not known for the enormous body of its reds. The Chianti Classico '98, which they have called Casanuova di Nittardi, offers a bouquet of red fruit with a faint nuance of vanilla, also hinting at flowers and, ever so slightly, minerals. The palate starts with alluring softness, underpinned by a delicate tang and just a suggestion of tannins. The finish is fairly long but persistence is not its strong suit. The Chianti Classico Riserva '97 is more concentrated. It still has a fair amount of vanilla on the nose but the attack on the palate is very elegant and gentle. It's a full-bodied red with finesse and an acidity which, although still perceptible, is already well-integrated.

●	Chianti Classico '98	**YY**	4
●	Chianti Classico Ris. '97	**YY**	5
●	Chianti Classico '93	YY	4
●	Chianti Classico '95	YY	4
●	Chianti Classico '96	YY	4
●	Chianti Classico '97	YY	4
●	Chianti Classico Ris. '88	YY	4
●	Chianti Classico Ris. '90	YY	5
●	Chianti Classico Ris. '93	YY	4
●	Chianti Classico Ris. '94	YY	5
●	Chianti Classico Ris. '95	YY	5
●	Chianti Classico Ris. '96	YY	5
●	Chianti Classico '90	Y	3
●	Chianti Classico '92	Y	4
●	Chianti Classico '94	Y	3

CASTELLINA IN CHIANTI (SI)   CASTELLINA IN CHIANTI (SI)

PODERE COLLELUNGO
LOC. COLLELUNGO
53011 CASTELLINA IN CHIANTI (SI)
TEL. 0577/740489

ROCCA DELLE MACÌE
LOC. MACÌE
53011 CASTELLINA IN CHIANTI (SI)
TEL. 0577/7321

Collelungo is well worth another entry in the Guide, to which it was a newcomer last year. The estate started making wine seriously just a few years ago but their enthusiastic labours immediately produced fine results. They've been replanting the vineyard on a rota basis so that the productive area remains steady at about nine hectares. Oenological matters are in the competent hands of their consultant, Alberto Antonini, and considerable investment has gone into the cellar too, where new barriques have appeared. The vineyards are at an altitude of about 500 metres, which contributes to the characteristic terroir-linked flavour of Collelungo's bottles. Both wines presented at our tastings are very good. The deep ruby-hued Chianti Classico Roveto '98 offers very intense tertiary aromas. Closed at first, they then open out to reveal ripe fruit, together with evolved notes of leather. The consistent entry on the palate is uncomplicated. There is only moderate alcohol. While not powerful, the palate is elegant and lifted by a refreshingly delicious acidic tang. The Riserva '97 presents a stylish bouquet of ripe fruit that combines concentration and finesse, and is enhanced by vanilla and smoky tones. The silky, creamy palate grabs your attention straight away, revealing excellent structure and tightly knit, fine tannins while the long finish echoes the aromas of the nose.

We cannot begin our profile of this famous Chianti Classico winery without a word about its founder, Italo Zingarelli, who died last year. A cinema producer (the Bud Spencer – Terence Hill films were his) and a great wine-lover, he decided to create a winery in one of the most beautiful areas in the world. This was how Rocca delle Macìe came into being. His son, Sergio, is now at the helm, but the initial impulse and the first successes were all the work of Italo, his passion and his vision. Italo would have liked this year's wines. We certainly did. A lot. At last, there is a whole Rocca delle Macìe range without blemishes. In fact, three wines made it to our finals, missing their Third Glass by a hair's breadth. The cellar technique is getting better all the time, and we're keeping an eye on them. Their sangiovese and cabernet blend, the Roccato '97, is really interesting. Its delicately fruity aromas, with just a hint of oak, are matched by a wealth of fine-textured, elegant tannins and remarkable body. The Ser Gioveto '97, a pure sangiovese, is just as good. It is less powerful, but right on the mark with a bouquet of red fruit and complex, concentrated structure. The excellent Chianti Classico Fizzano Riserva '97 is a stylish red, typical of the southern Castellina zone. Despite considerable body, it manages to stay soft and quaffable. To round off the list, two Chianti Classicos. The Riserva '97 is well-executed and coherent and the '98, which is simpler, is very true to type.

● Chianti Classico Ris. '97	♟♟	4
● Chianti Classico '98	♟	4
● Chianti Classico Roveto '97	♟♟	4

● Chianti Classico Fizzano Ris. '97	♟♟	5
● Roccato '97	♟♟	5
● Ser Gioveto '97	♟♟	5
● Chianti Classico '98	♟	3
● Chianti Classico Ris. '97	♟	4
● Chianti Classico Fizzano Ris. '93	♟♟	5
● Chianti Classico Fizzano Ris. '96	♟♟	4
● Chianti Classico Ris. '90	♟♟	4
● Roccato '93	♟♟	5
● Roccato '96	♟♟	5
● Ser Gioveto '86	♟♟	5
● Ser Gioveto '88	♟♟	5
● Ser Gioveto '94	♟♟	5
● Ser Gioveto '96	♟♟	5

CASTELLINA IN CHIANTI (SI) CASTELLINA IN CHIANTI (SI)

RODANO
LOC. RODANO, 84
53011 CASTELLINA IN CHIANTI (SI)
TEL. 0577/743107

SAN FABIANO CALCINAIA
LOC. CELLOLE
53011 CASTELLINA IN CHIANTI (SI)
tel. 0577/979232

The Two Glasses we've given the Lazzicante '97, Rodano's splendid barrique-aged merlot, are actually full to overflowing. It makes us wish there were a "plus" or "and a half" we could add to the mark, as you might in a school report. Well, that could be something to think about for the future. Meanwhile, where you see Two Glasses below, please read "Two Glasses Plus". Why not Three then, you ask? Because of a faint note of reduction that disturbs the pervasive and admirably varietal bouquet. This can happen when a wine is either very concentrated or unfiltered (or hardly filtered at all). It is a "rustic" touch that appeals to some but is nevertheless a minor defect. And this is a pity, because on the palate there are not many Italian merlots with such concentration and intensity, a sign that this winery has promise and could come up with a Three Glass product at any time. This little gem is accompanied by a good Chianti Classico '98, an uncomplicated red with typical, if not very complex, aromas and a fairly elegant palate. It's a fine example of a sangiovese from this subzone. Here on the western edge of the DOCG area, where the gently rolling hills are caressed by sea breezes, the wines tend to be softer, alcohol-rich and seductive.

"Modern", "reliable", "the product of excellence-driven vineyard management". These are some of the most apposite descriptions for the wines from San Fabiano Calcinaia. Guido Serio, the owner and moving spirit behind the estate, has managed, thanks also to the wonder-working touch of consultant oenologist, Carlo Ferrini, to carry off Three Glasses for the third time in a row. He has done it, as usual, with a great red. Guido's Cerviolo, this time the '98, is again absolutely stupendous. A blend of sangiovese, merlot and cabernet sauvignon, it is powerful on the palate, with smooth, integrated tannins,. The nose captivates you with lashings of berry fruit and a hint of vanilla. Speaking of vanilla – and barriques – Serio and Ferrini do seem on occasion to be over-addicted to oak. Wood-derived sensations can get out of hand when a wine is young. This is the case with the Cerviolo Bianco '99, as well as with the Chianti Classico Cellole Riserva '97, which should be very good in a couple of years when the oak has been more thoroughly absorbed into the body of the wine. It should give smoky, almost mineral aromas, and will become quite imperceptible on the palate. The Chianti Classico '98, in contrast, is already delightful, proffering a concentrated package of vibrant fruit fragrances and varietal flavours. It's a simpler wine, but well nigh perfectly executed. A very pleasant surprise.

● Lazzicante '97	♥♥	6	
● Chianti Classico '98	♥	4	
● Chianti Cl. Viacosta Ris. '86	♀♀	4	
● Chianti Cl. Viacosta Ris. '88	♀♀	4	
● Chianti Cl. Viacosta Ris. '90	♀♀	4	
● Chianti Cl. Viacosta Ris. '95	♀♀	4	
● Lazzicante '96	♀♀	4	
● Monna Claudia '88	♀♀	5	
● Monna Claudia '95	♀♀	4	
● Monna Claudia '96	♀♀	4	
● Chianti Classico '90	♀	3	
● Chianti Classico '93	♀	3	
● Chianti Classico '94	♀	3	

● Cerviolo Rosso '98	♥♥♥	5	
○ Cerviolo Bianco '99	♥♥	5	
● Chianti Classico '98	♥♥	4	
● Chianti Classico Cellole Ris. '97	♥♥	5	
● Cerviolo Rosso '96	♀♀♀	5	
● Cerviolo Rosso '97	♀♀♀	5	
○ Cerviolo Bianco '98	♀♀	5	
● Cerviolo Rosso '95	♀♀	5	
● Chianti Classico '95	♀♀	3*	
● Chianti Classico '96	♀♀	3*	
● Chianti Classico '97	♀♀	3*	
● Chianti Classico Cellole Ris. '90	♀♀	4	
● Chianti Classico Cellole Ris. '93	♀♀	4	
● Chianti Classico Cellole Ris. '95	♀♀	4	
● Chianti Classico Cellole Ris. '96	♀♀	4	

394

CASTELLINA IN CHIANTI (SI) CASTELLINA MARITTIMA (PI)

Tramonti
Loc. Tramonti
53011 Castellina in Chianti (SI)
tel. 0577/740512

Castello del Terriccio
Loc. Le Badie
Via Bagnoli
56040 Castellina Marittima (PI)
tel. 050/699709

Only one wine, but what depth! Every year, Tramonti presents a single wine at our tastings, but its quality is such that the estate easily keeps its place in the Guide. Work continues apace in the vineyard, partly because the area under vine is being gradually extended in line with a carefully devised plan that promises great things for the future. Then, it will be time to think about whether it there is room for another wine or two. Cellar technique is still based on natural methods, which means labour-intensive winemaking, but the sacrifice is richly repaid by the final results. The Chianti Classico '98 has an intense, vibrant, deep ruby hue. We were struck by the concentration of the nose, whose generous, complex fruit foregrounds blackcurrant, violet and mulberry. Its elegant style allows the spicy nuances to enhancing the secondary aromas without smothering them. The palate is thoroughly enjoyable right from the entry. Dense, creamy and lively in the mouth, the full body is backed up by good acidity and solid, fine-grained tannins while the alcohol is warm and well-judged. The intense, lingering finish is impeccably sustained.

If winning Three Glasses for the fourth year running can be considered normal, then everything is proceeding normally at Terriccio. But the circumstance should not be viewed as inevitable or habitual. In fact, it implies an unremitting commitment to improvement. And indeed the Lupicaia '98, a blend of cabernet sauvignon and merlot, is probably richer in structure than any of its predecessors. Its concentration is extraordinary, which this is exactly why the wine will need more cellar time to express itself to the full. For example, the nose has great depth but is still a little shy about opening up completely. The fruit, though, is perfectly ripe and dominates the hints of cocoa, coffee and eucalyptus. The vigorous attack on the palate is already well-balanced, and soft tannins layer the flavour. The finish is long and complex, with the odd bitterish touch. The Tassinaia '98, made from the same blend with the addition of sangiovese, is more for present pleasure. Characteristic notes of eucalyptus and mint stand out in the bouquet, with both red and black berry fruit. The palate is soft, easy-going and poised, with well-dosed tannins and good length. The Saluccio '98, a chardonnay, is impressively rich on the nose, where citrus fruit, peaches in syrup, honey, vanilla and summer flowers emerge. The palate is fat and full but a little thin, and begins to cloy on the finish. The Rondinaia '99, a chardonnay and sauvignon blend with a nose of tropical fruit and aromatic herbs, and a solid, lingering palate, gets Two Glasses. The sauvignon, Con Vento '99, is fair but not awfully expressive.

● Chianti Classico '98	▼▼	4
● Chianti Classico '96	♈♈	4
● Chianti Classico '97	♈♈	4

● Lupicaia '98	▼▼▼	6
○ Rondinaia '99	▼▼	4
○ Saluccio '98	▼▼	5
● Tassinaia '98	▼▼	5
○ Con Vento '99	▼	3
● Lupicaia '93	♈♈♈	5
● Lupicaia '95	♈♈♈	6
● Lupicaia '96	♈♈♈	6
● Lupicaia '97	♈♈♈	6
● Lupicaia '94	♈♈	6
● Tassinaia '93	♈♈	4
● Tassinaia '94	♈♈	5
● Tassinaia '95	♈♈	5
● Tassinaia '96	♈♈	5
● Tassinaia '97	♈♈	5

CASTELNUOVO BERARDENGA (SI)   CASTELNUOVO BERARDENGA (SI)

FATTORIA DELL' AIOLA
LOC. VAGLIAGLI
53010 CASTELNUOVO
BERARDENGA (SI)
TEL. 0577/322615

CASTELLO DI BOSSI
LOC. BOSSI IN CHIANTI, 28
53019 CASTELNUOVO
BERARDENGA (SI)
TEL. 0577/359330

It is a pleasure to be writing about this estate again, after its year of "exile" from the Guide. We found the wines presented this time much more convincing and admirably expressive of their terroir. We are in the southern part of the Chianti Classico zone, not far from Siena, but also near the bare clay hills known as the Crete Senesi. It is land more suited to producing powerful, full-bodied wines of structure than the quietly elegant Chianti Classico, and Niccolò D'Afflitto, the consultant oenologist, knows how to interpret the terroir. The lip-smacking Chianti Classico '98 offers an intense raspberry fragrance and good weight on the palate, with dense, even tannins and an appropriately long finish. The Riserva '97 exhibits tertiary aromas of leather mingling with rather prominent toasty notes of oak. The entry on the palate is beefy, and the tannic texture smooth. The Cancello Rosso Riserva '97 is even better. The nose is still a little closed and very concentrated, but ripe fruit is already coming through. The palate is elegant, soft and delicious, the slightly aggressive tannins being kept in check by the alcohol. The Logaiolo '97, which very nearly won Two Glasses, is made from what is by now a classic blend hereabouts, sangiovese and cabernet sauvignon, in this case without any time in oak. The only blemish in a pleasing, nicely poised profile is an unruly note of capsicum on the nose. Last on the list is the Rosso del Senatore '98, another sangiovese and cabernet sauvignon. It is well-made, although over-generous vegetal notes detract from the nose.

Much has been happening at Castello di Bossi, the Bacci family estate. There has been a major change of direction. For one thing, the property has acquired new land in Montalcino and has begun to till and replant the vineyards there. Oenological matters are in new hands, too – the very competent ones of Alberto Antonini. The best Castello di Bossi wine this year is the Chianti Classico Berardo Riserva '96. The deep, limpid ruby ushers in fresh minty aromas that meld with pleasingly rich forward notes of Peruvian bark and tamarind. The pleasing impact on the palate shows nice weight and a soft silkiness. The tannins are perfectly integrated and the enjoyable finish lingers impressively. The Chianti Classico '98 is in excellent form. Oak-derived notes enrich the wide range of fruit, which is further enhanced by a floral nuance of violets. There is succulent fruit on the palate, a solid body and an attractively balanced finish. The Girolamo '97, a monovarietal merlot, almost won Two Glasses. Evolved, rather firm, notes of raspberry jam on the nose are mirrored in the attack on the palate, which follows through well, lacking only a touch more tannic support. The finish is lovely. The Corbaia '96, a sangiovese and cabernet sauvignon blend, is not quite up to previous standards. The nose is a little stifled by less than entirely clean sweetish notes. The attack on the palate is powerful but over-assertive tannins soon emerge in a palate dominated by alcohol. The finish, although long, is bitterish.

● Chianti Classico		
Cancello Rosso Ris. '97	♥♥	4
● Chianti Classico '98	♥	3
● Chianti Classico Ris. '97	♥	4
● Logaiolo '97	♥	4
● Rosso del Senatore '98	♥	5
● Chianti Classico Ris. '90	♀♀	5
● Chianti Classico Ris. '94	♀♀	4
● Chianti Classico Ris. '95	♀♀	4
● Chianti Classico '93	♀	3
● Chianti Classico '94	♀	3
● Chianti Classico '95	♀	3
● Chianti Classico '96	♀	3
● Rosso del Senatore '90	♀	5
● Rosso del Senatore '95	♀	5

● Chianti Classico Berardo Ris. '96	♥♥	5
● Chianti Classico '98	♥	3
● Corbaia '96	♥	5
● Girolamo '97	♥	5
● Chianti Classico Berardo Ris. '95	♀♀	5
● Chianti Classico Ris. '94	♀♀	4
● Chianti Classico Ris. '95	♀♀	4
● Corbaia '94	♀♀	5
● Corbaia '95	♀♀	5
● Chianti Classico '94	♀	3
● Chianti Classico '95	♀	3

CASTELNUOVO BERARDENGA (SI) CASTELNUOVO BERARDENGA (SI)

CARPINETA FONTALPINO
LOC. MONTEAPERTI
53019 CASTELNUOVO
BERARDENGA (SI)
TEL. 0577/369219 - 0577/283228

CASTELL'IN VILLA
LOC. CASTELL'IN VILLA
53019 CASTELNUOVO
BERARDENGA (SI)
TEL. 0577/359074

They have lost no time at Carpineta Fontalpino. No sooner had they finished replanting their ten hectares under vine than they set about distancing themselves from the fashion of the moment, and began to aim for genuinely characterful wines. Only one year has gone by since Gioia Cresti's estate first appeared in the Guide and we have already witnessed a significant improvement. This is a serious winery, and certainly worth watching. The Do Ut Des '98, made from their three main red grape varieties (cabernet sauvignon, merlot and sangiovese), easily notched up a Two Glass rating. It has going for it perfectly ripe fruit, balanced acidity and a well-judged use of oak, mainly in the shape of new barriques. The rich, concentrated nose offers black berry fruit over cocoa and coffee and is followed by a palate that lives up to expectations. The attractive sinew, a trademark of the terroir, is complemented by remarkable density and richly extracted tannins that render the progression seamless and close-textured. The long, crisp finish mirrors the bouquet. If it continues at this pace, Do Ut Des will soon be in the running for Three Glasses. Meanwhile it is reassuring to note that the Carpineta Fontalpino second label, the Chianti Colli Senesi '98, is treated with just as much care and attention. It came close to Two Glasses, and was stylistically not unlike the flagship wine. The structure is good, the tannins are soft and it is very easy to like.

When Principessa Coralia Pignatelli della Leonessa remembers to send her wines to our tastings, perhaps through the good offices of her excellent consultant, Giacomo Tachis, we always have some very pleasant surprises. It might be objected that we should remember the princess and her wines, which is perfectly true but not always easy in practice. We have known this estate for years, and we are aware of the enormous potential of its wonderful soil, superbly located vineyards and admirable cellar technique. The wines, too, are often very good but not always quite as good as the list would lead you to expect. But this year, our compliments go to Castell'in Villa. The Santa Croce '90 is a really splendid bottle. This sangiovese-based red is so lively and youthful that it seems almost impossible for it to have come from such a distant vintage, not that there is any doubt about the matter. The complex bouquet is still fruity but also offers mineral and smoky notes. In the mouth, it shows its breeding and elegance, well-integrated if not very sweet tannins, and serious power. The two Chianti Classico Riservas from the new line, Poggio delle Rose, are most interesting. We were able to taste the '94 and the '96. Not stupendous vintages but for that very reason indicative of what the wine will be capable of in more clement years. Both met with the panel's approval for they are soft, complex and well-executed. Above all, these are wines with a personality of their own, utterly indifferent to the current fashion that endlessly recites the mantra of "berry fruit, vanilla and sweet tannins". We await the '97 with some anxiety. Will the princess deem us worthy of it?

● Do Ut Des '98	🍷🍷	4
● Chianti Colli Senesi Gioia '98	🍷	3
● Do Ut Des '97	♀♀	4
● Chianti Colli Senesi Gioia '97	♀	3

● Chianti Cl.		
Poggio delle Rose Ris. '94	🍷🍷	5
● Chianti Cl.		
Poggio delle Rose Ris. '96	🍷🍷	5
● Santa Croce '90	🍷🍷	6
● Chianti Classico Ris. '85	♀♀♀	4*
● Chianti Classico '86	♀♀	3*
● Chianti Classico '87	♀♀	3*
● Chianti Classico '88	♀♀	3*
● Chianti Classico Ris. '82	♀♀	4
● Chianti Classico Ris. '83	♀♀	4
● Chianti Classico Ris. '86	♀♀	4

CASTELNUOVO BERARDENGA (SI)

CASTELNUOVO BERARDENGA (SI)

FATTORIE CHIGI SARACINI
VIA DELL'ARBIA, 2
53019 CASTELNUOVO
BERARDENGA (SI)
TEL. 0577/355113

FATTORIA DI DIEVOLE
LOC. DIEVOLE
53019 CASTELNUOVO
BERARDENGA (SI)
TEL. 0577/322613

After years of refusing to budge from the traditional approach that kept the estate on the sidelines while others were improving standards, Fattorie Chigi Saracini has now taken the plunge and begun to make the most of its considerable potential. The process starts, of course, in the vineyards, which in this case are in a superb viticultural zone, and carries through to the cellar. Extensive new plantings have been planned, mostly of sangiovese, but also of some cabernet sauvignon and merlot. Carlo Ferrini, who by now needs no introduction, has been called in as consultant oenologist so all we need at this point is a little patience. For the moment, things are not going at all badly. The Poggiassai, two parts sangiovese to one cabernet, is up there in the Two Glass zone. We tasted it, and the other Fattorie Chigi Saracini wines, directly after bottling so it was still developing. The aromas need to settle but they already show good rich fruit. The palate offers an attractive meaty texture, firm but not aggressive tannins, and nice length. Many of the same things can be said of the Chianti Superiore, which is not short on structure but does have the odd rough edge that can be put down to its youth. The Chianti Colli Senesi, although a simpler wine, is fruity and agreeable.

Fattoria di Dievole continues to turn out a fine range of wines which are genuinely pleasing and reflect the estate's distinctive style. However, we would also quite like to find, among the estate's many products, a wine that offered greater complexity and could join the very top ranks. But it would seem that estate policy goal is to concentrate on the overall standards of the range, rather than devote any energy to a single flagship wine. The Chianti Classico '98 has a fairly intense bouquet of berry fruit but there is also a vegetal hint and a toasty note of oak. The attack on the palate is forceful, well-balanced and sustained but the wine comes unravelled on the finish, where bitterish notes emerge. The other wines are decidedly better but also rather much of a muchness. The Chianti Novecento, for example, has an indistinct, slightly closed, nose but is much surer of itself on the palate, where concentration, density and good tannic texture are in evidence. The Broccato, a sangiovese, has substance, if not great personality, and is subdued by the rather intrusive oak. Wood is to the fore again in the Plenum but in this case, it is offset by laudably rich, concentrated fruit. The Rinascimento is interesting, however, and more of its own man. Without offering enormous concentration, it progresses elegantly, revealing smooth tannins, leanness and good depth.

● Il Poggiassai '98	♟♟	4
● Chianti Colli Senesi '99	♟	3
● Chianti Superiore '98	♟	3
● Il Poggiassai '97	♟♟	4
● Chianti Colli Senesi '98	♟	3
● Chianti Superiore '97	♟	3

● Broccato '97	♟♟	4
● Chianti Classico Novecento '97	♟♟	4
● Plenum '98	♟♟	5
● Rinascimento '98	♟♟	5
● Chianti Classico '98	♟	3
● Broccato '95	♟♟	4
● Broccato '96	♟♟	4
● Chianti Classico '96	♟♟	3*
● Chianti Classico '97	♟♟	4
● Chianti Classico Novecento '93	♟♟	4
● Chianti Classico Novecento '94	♟♟	4
● Chianti Classico Novecento '95	♟♟	4
● Chianti Classico Novecento '96	♟♟	4
● Chianti Classico Ris. '93	♟♟	4
● Chianti Classico Ris. '95	♟♟	4

CASTELNUOVO BERARDENGA (SI)

★ Fattoria di Felsina
S. S. Chiantigiana, 484
53019 Castelnuovo
Berardenga (SI)
tel. 0577/355117

CASTELNUOVO BERARDENGA (SI)

Le Trame
Loc. Le Bonce
53010 Castelnuovo
Berardenga (SI)
tel. 0577/359116

Another prize for the Felsina trophy cupboard this year, for the estate managed by Giuseppe Mazzocolin collected yet another Three Glass award. The winner, again, was the Fontalloro, a Sangiovese that seldom disappoints in good vintages. As you pick up the '97, it moves in and takes charge, pointing out salient characteristics of both its terroir and its year. Its most striking quality is not splendid harmony, like the '93, or immediacy, the strong point of the '95, but an enormous, almost uncontainable energy. At the moment, the nose lacks a little finesse, but with its very ripe fruit and prominent oak, it performs eloquently on the palate, where the vigorous attack and seamless progression are underpinned by a massive tannic structure. The long finish reveals notes of black berry fruit, spice and chocolate. The Maestro Raro '97, a cabernet sauvignon, is also very good and not far off Three Glasses. The intense bouquet reveals notes of cocoa and blackcurrant, ushering in a muscular, concentrated palate with close-knit tannins. The Chianti Classico '98 is decidedly good and very well executed. Distinct aromas of black berry fruit and a subtle hint of wood lead in to a well-balanced, concentrated, sustained palate that mirrors the nose. The Vigneto Rancia, although a very good wine, is perhaps less impressive than past performances had led us to expect. It is concentrated, full-bodied and persistent but the nose needs more fine-tuning. The chardonnay, I Sistri, is soft and pleasing. The oaky style is a trifle unchallenging and the finish is moderately long.

Many Tuscan estates are called after place-names, which might be a hill, a stream or the ruins of a mediaeval tower and so forth. But the estate that belongs to Giovanna Morganti, an immensely talented, authentic "vigneron", was named Le Trame ("The Intrigues") because she had to plot and scheme to get her hands on it. The property has three hectares under vine and lies in the midst of the sea of vineyards that belong to the enormous San Felice winery. It produces great, and on occasion sublime, fruit. But don't go looking for any cabernet, merlot or syrah here. Giovanna is wedded passionately and faithfully to sangiovese, and the marriage is a sound compromise of traditional values and modern technique. That philosophy starts with the vineyards, which are planted at a density of over 7,000 vines per hectare, but are gobelet-trained. There are a few rows of a local grape, related to sangiovese, which is called fogliatonda. It's a difficult variety to grow but it can produce very fragrant wines. From her distinguished teachers, Giulio Gambelli and Maurizio Castelli, Giovanna has learned the difficult art of making a pure sangiovese reduced to its essence, altogether unlike the depressing crowd-pleasers that could be summed up as "Mega-fruit meets Super-oak". The Chianti Classico '97 has a bright, lustrous ruby hue while the nose offers aromas of wild cherry, sorb-apple and bay leaf mingling with a faint hint of tobacco. The ripe, soft palate is backed up by good acidity and lively, well-extracted tannins. The lingering finale is tidy and satisfying. In short, a genuine Chianti Classico. Well done, Le Trame.

● Fontalloro '97	🍷🍷🍷	6
● Chianti Classico '98	🍷🍷	4
● Chianti Classico Rancia Ris. '97	🍷🍷	5
● Maestro Raro '97	🍷🍷	6
○ I Sistri '98	🍷	4
● Chianti Classico Rancia Ris. '90	🍷🍷🍷	5
● Chianti Classico Rancia Ris. '93	🍷🍷🍷	5
● Chianti Classico Ris. '90	🍷🍷🍷	4*
● Fontalloro '86	🍷🍷🍷	5
● Fontalloro '88	🍷🍷🍷	5
● Fontalloro '90	🍷🍷🍷	5
● Fontalloro '93	🍷🍷🍷	6
● Fontalloro '95	🍷🍷🍷	6
● Maestro Raro '91	🍷🍷🍷	5
● Maestro Raro '93	🍷🍷🍷	6

● Chianti Classico '97	🍷🍷	4
● Chianti Classico '90	🍷🍷	4
● Chianti Classico '92	🍷🍷	4
● Chianti Classico '93	🍷🍷	4
● Chianti Classico '94	🍷🍷	4
● Chianti Classico '95	🍷🍷	4

CASTELNUOVO BERARDENGA (SI)

CASTELNUOVO BERARDENGA (SI)

FATTORIA DI PETROIO
LOC. QUERCEGROSSA
VIA DI MOCENNI, 7
53010 CASTELNUOVO
BERARDENGA (SI)
TEL. 0577/328045

SAN FELICE
LOC. SAN FELICE
53019 CASTELNUOVO
BERARDENGA (SI)
TEL. 0577/359087 - 0577/359088

Fattoria di Petroio is celebrating the new millennium's first Guide with Three Glasses. The award does credit to a winery which, as we noted last year, has staked its all on producing Chianti Classico, without resorting to the usual Supertuscan in order to make a splash. Petroio, the property of Professor Gian Luigi Lenzi and his wife Pamela, consists of 100 hectares, 13 of which are under vine, in the Quercegrossa zone on the western edge of Castelnuovo Berardenga. Their consultant oenologist is Carlo Ferrini, which is tantamount to saying that excellence is guaranteed. The Chianti Classico Riserva '97 is the first peak scaled in a steady climb to quality that would have been difficult to predict a few years ago. This red has shown that it can reconcile conservatives and progressives, satisfying those who love full-bodied, concentrated wines as well as admirers of elegance and quaffability. Completeness and harmony are the keynotes and there is no trace of excess. The nose is full and deep, with clean ripe fruit in evidence. On the palate, it is soft and structured, the silky tannins conferring elegance, and the finish is long, fruity and very refreshing. A quite superlative Chianti. We might add that it has a worthy companion in the Chianti '98, which at first offers sangiovese's typical anchovy notes of reduction but then opens confidently into berry fruit and violets. The palate is poised, showing medium body and a good finish.

We started last year's profile by bemoaning our slight disappointment at San Felice's wines. Well, the estate has taken up the gauntlet and met us at the tasting table where, after almost a decade, the Vigorello has fought back to win Three Glasses. The '97, four parts sangiovese to one of cabernet, was simply irresistible, thanks mainly to the perfect ripe fruit that pervades the nose and palate. Rarely in the past have we found such a close-knit texture in a wine. This is still a young product – the oak has some way to go – but already it offers concentrated aromas of mulberry, spice and citron without the slightest trace of greenness. The warm, vigorous palate unfurls firm, close-knit tannins, leading in to a finish of appealing depth, where the rich fruit again emerges. The Riserva Poggio Rosso '97 does not lag very far behind. It has solid structure, alluring softness, smooth, tight-knit tannins and a firm finish. With just a pinch more of aromatic complexity it would be a great wine. The fairly good Riserva Il Grigio '97 is well-balanced and succulent but did not rate any higher because of marked vegetal notes. The Chianti '98 is slightly grassy and piquant but is nonetheless a clean-tasting, enjoyable tipple. The fruity medium-bodied white, Ancherona '99, is agreeable but a little dull while the Belcaro '99, another white, is more than acceptable. It offers unusual aromas of rose and sage, followed by a rounded, flavoursome palate with a slightly short finish.

● Chianti Classico Ris. '97	♟♟♟	5
● Chianti Classico '98	♟♟	4
● Chianti Classico '90	♟♟	3*
● Chianti Classico '91	♟♟	3*
● Chianti Classico '93	♟♟	2*
● Chianti Classico '95	♟♟	3*
● Chianti Classico '96	♟♟	3*
● Chianti Classico '97	♟♟	3*
● Chianti Classico Ris. '90	♟♟	4
● Chianti Classico Ris. '95	♟♟	4
● Chianti Classico Ris. '96	♟♟	4
● Chianti Classico '94	♟	3
● Chianti Classico Ris. '93	♟	4

● Vigorello '97	♟♟♟	5
● Chianti Classico Poggio Rosso Ris. '97	♟♟	5
○ Ancherona Chardonnay '99	♟	4
○ Belcaro '99	♟	3
● Chianti Classico '98	♟	3
● Chianti Classico Il Grigio Ris. '97	♟	4
● Chianti Classico Poggio Rosso Ris. '90	♟♟♟	4
● Chianti Classico Poggio Rosso Ris. '95	♟♟♟	5
● Vigorello '88	♟♟♟	5
● Chianti Classico Poggio Rosso Ris. '96	♟♟	5
● Vigorello '93	♟♟	5
● Vigorello '95	♟♟	5

CASTELNUOVO BERARDENGA (SI)   CASTELNUOVO DELL'ABATE (SI)

CASTELLO DI SELVOLE
FRAZ. VAGLIAGLI
LOC. SELVOLE
53019 CASTELNUOVO
BERARDENGA (SI)
TEL. 0577/322662

FANTI - SAN FILIPPO
LOC. SAN FILIPPO
B.GO DI MEZZO, 15
53020 CASTELNUOVO
DELL'ABATE (SI)
TEL. 0577/835628

We are reviewing only two offerings from Selvole this year but the wines in question are a monumental Chianti Classico and a Supertuscan, the preponderantly sangiovese-based Barullo '97, that flaunts superb structure. Since this winery is in the process of being restructured and promises great things for the future, we feel it merits its own profile. Guido Busetto, a newspaperman, and his wife Nobuko seem to be restoring to this estate the prestige it rightly enjoyed in the past. It lies in one of the most beautiful parts of Chianti Classico, between Vagliagli and Castelnuovo Berardenga, where climate and terrain conspire to create of some of the greatest sangiovese reds in the whole district. These are powerful, soft wines with a pervasively bewitching range of aromas. "Brunellesque", they call them hereabouts, meaning that they can achieve concentration comparable to that of the finest Brunello di Montalcino wines. But let's get back to Selvole's Chianti Classico '98. As we were saying, it is an impressively rich wine, with rich flavour, good grip and lots of concentration. The nose has generous fruit, with ripe black cherry to the fore, and faint overtones of vanilla, all underpinned by commendable alcohol. The Barullo '97 is slightly less successful, as it is more forward on the nose, but the palate is just as powerful. These are two very fine wines indeed. The Riserva version should be at least as good, so things are looking very promising for Castello di Selvole.

Baldassare Fanti, the ultra-dynamic president of the combined Consorzio del Brunello e del Rosso di Montalcino, devotes some of his considerable enthusiasm to his own estate. In the course of a very few years, he has turned it on its head. An encounter with rising oenologist and agronomist, Stefano Chioccioli, started Fanti thinking about his sometimes over-critical attitude towards his own production methods brought about major changes. The new plantings in the vineyards near the castle of Velona (a fascinating area), are all high-density. There are lots more tonneaux and barriques in the cellar, indeed the more traditional casks are on the way out. These changes will bear fruit in the next few years but it is significant, and also gratifying, to witness such energy in a zone that tends to be rather stick-in-the-mud and slow to embrace positive new ideas. The wines presented this year come from various stages in the winery's history. The Brunello '95 is 'pre-revolutionary', whereas the Rosso di Montalcino '98 belongs to the transitional period. The bright ruby Brunello '95 makes a favourable first impression, foregrounding fruit and pleasing tobacco nuances. On the palate, it reveals its robust alcohol and fairly fine-grained tannins while the underpinning acidity is well-judged and does not stunt the finish. This is a well-executed Brunello in the classic mould. The Rosso di Montalcino '98 has a slightly closed nose but as the wine breathes, there emerge fairly intense notes of incense that cover the expected fruit. It is quaffable and not very rich but refreshingly tangy. The Sant'Antimo '98 does no better that One Glass. It's a very simple, rather acidulous wine.

● Barullo '97	ΥΥ	5
● Chianti Classico '98	ΥΥ	3*
● Chianti Classico Ris. '96	ΨΨ	5
● Chianti Classico '97	Υ	4

● Brunello di Montalcino '95	ΥΥ	6
● Rosso di Montalcino '98	Υ	4
● Sant'Antimo '98	Υ	3
● Brunello di Montalcino '93	ΨΨ	5
● Rosso di Montalcino '96	ΨΨ	4
● Rosso di Montalcino '97	ΨΨ	4
● Brunello di Montalcino '94	Υ	5
● Brunello di Montalcino Ris. '93	Υ	6

CHIUSI (SI)

FICOMONTANINO
LOC. FICOMONTANINO
53043 CHIUSI (SI)
TEL. 0578/21180 - 06/5561283

This year, we were happy to record a significant step forward in the wines from Ficomontanino. Although the symbols below are fairly similar to those assigned in the last few years, the big difference is that the Lucumone, a monovarietal cabernet sauvignon, did not just scrape home into the Two Glass range but actually threatened to end up with Three. This means that from now on, we will be keeping a very close eye on this Chiusi estate. Our tasting notes mention the deep ruby colour, the richly intense aromas of mulberry, oriental spices and pepper, together with some less impressive grassy hints. The palate is balanced, not without elegance, and silky soft in its progression. The tannins are fully integrated but the lingering finish is brought down by vegetal notes. All in all, it is an attractive, well-managed wine that reveals skilful use of the well-amalgamated oak. The wood is, however, a little out of control in the other two wines. Things aren't too bad in the Chianti Tutulus, which comes with a good fruit-rich foundation and delightful spice on the nose. The palate is meaty and attractive, although the oak-derived tannin is a shade too present. But the Porsenna, a sauvignon, is less successful; its admirable roundness of flavour fights a losing battle with the oak.

●	Chianti Colli Senesi Tutulus '98	🍷🍷 (black)	3*
●	Lucumone '98	🍷🍷 (black)	5
○	Porsenna '99	🍷 (black)	4
●	Chianti Colli Senesi Tutulus '95	🍷🍷	3
●	Chianti Colli Senesi Tutulus '96	🍷🍷	3
●	Lucumone '95	🍷🍷	5
●	Lucumone '97	🍷🍷	5
●	Porsenna '97	🍷🍷	4
●	Chianti Colli Senesi Tutulus '97	🍷	3
●	Lucumone '96	🍷	5
●	Porsenna '96	🍷	4
○	Porsenna '98	🍷	4

COLLE VAL D'ELSA (SI)

FATTORIA IL PALAGIO
FRAZ. CASTEL S. GIMIGNANO
LOC. PALAGIO
53030 COLLE VAL D'ELSA (SI)
TEL. 0577/953004

For some years, we have been saying that Fattoria Il Palagio, the Zoni family's holding in San Gimignano, is coming on well. And this year's tastings confirm our good opinion of its wines and of the abilities of its oenologist-manager, Walter Sovran. On the more than 120 hectares under vine at Il Palagio, and at the nearby San Gimignano estate of Abbazia di Monte Oliveto, the Zonis grow chardonnay, sauvignon and sangiovese, in addition to vernaccia. The Vernaccia Gentilesca '99, like its predecessor, won Two Glasses. In fact, we found it to be one of the most interesting Vernaccias of its vintage. It has an attractive straw-yellow colour with elegant greenish highlights, soft fruity aromas with a stylish hint of vanilla, and an agreeably intense, full-bodied and balanced palate that leads in to a long finish on a sweet note of ripe apple and pear. The Sauvignon '99 is, as usual, a very successful wine. A lustrous pale greenish straw-yellow in the glass, it unveils a rich bouquet of varietal notes ranging from tropical fruit to gooseberry, as well as the characteristic varietal aromas of musk and tomato leaf. In the mouth, it reveals a lean, fresh body, rich fruit and pleasant persistence. It's a wine that is on a par with bottles that cost twice as much and more. The Vernaccia from the Abbazia di Monte Oliveto is fresh, fruity, lean-bodied and pleasingly quaffable, as is the Chianti from the Fattoria Il Palagio.

○	Il Palagio Sauvignon '99	🍷🍷 (black)	3*
○	Vernaccia di S. Gimignano La Gentilesca '99	🍷🍷 (black)	4
●	Chianti Colli Senesi Il Palagio '99	🍷 (black)	3
○	Vernaccia di S. Gimignano Abbazia di Monteoliveto '99	🍷 (black)	2*
○	Il Palagio Sauvignon '97	🍷🍷	2*
○	Il Palagio Sauvignon '98	🍷🍷	2*
○	Vernaccia di S. Gimignano La Gentilesca '98	🍷🍷	4
●	Chianti Colli Senesi Il Palagio '98	🍷	2*
●	Chianti Colli Senesi Il Palagio '95	🍷	2*
○	Vernaccia di S. Gimignano Abbazia di Monteoliveto '98	🍷	2*

CORTONA (AR)

Tenimenti Luigi D'Alessandro

Loc. Camucia
Via di Manzano, 15
52044 Cortona (AR)
tel. 0575/618667

It fought fiercely, crossing swords with astoundingly expressive reds, but unfortunately, Podere Il Bosco, the celebrated syrah from Tenimenti Luigi d'Alessandro, was pulled up just a few points short of yet another Three Glass rating. By no means a bad showing, at least for those who consider the quality of a wine instead of just totting the silver in its trophy cupboard. Wine-lovers will in fact find all the characteristics that have made this elegant Tuscan red famous. But the song is sung in a minor key. It has the intense ruby hue, the inviting fruity notes of redcurrant and gooseberry with spicy hints of pepper, the captivatingly generous, mouth-filling palate. So what held it back? Perhaps the tannins, which in the '98 vintage are a little less fine-grained and less developed than usual. The Two Glasses are of course filled to overflowing. The white Podere Fontarca '99, a chardonnay and viognier blend, is a success as well. Its lovely straw-yellow is flecked with golden highlightsl. Its fruit aromas are reminiscent of apricot and ripe pear, nuanced with a distinct oaky tone. The full-bodied, harmonious palate takes you through to a lingering finish. The monovarietal gamay Podere Il Vescovo '99 would be pleasantly fruity, simple and vinous were it not for somewhat uncontrolled volatile acidity. But things are definitely looking up with the excellent Vin Santo '93. A limpid, brilliant yellow, it offers inviting aromas of cakes, dried figs and dates while the palate is succulent and full-bodied, with balanced sweetness and a long-lasting finish.

○	Podere Fontarca '99	🍷🍷	4
●	Podere Il Bosco '98	🍷🍷	5
○	Vin Santo '93	🍷🍷	5
●	Podere Il Vescovo '99		3
●	Podere Il Bosco '95	🍷🍷🍷	5
●	Podere Il Bosco '97	🍷🍷🍷	5
●	Migliara '97	🍷🍷	5
○	Podere Fontarca '94	🍷🍷	4
○	Podere Fontarca '98	🍷🍷	4
●	Podere Il Bosco '94	🍷🍷	5
●	Podere Il Bosco '96	🍷🍷	5
●	Vigna del Bosco '92	🍷🍷	5
●	Vigna del Bosco '93	🍷🍷	4
●	Podere Il Vescovo '97	🍷	3
○	Vin Santo '92	🍷	5

FAUGLIA (PI)

I Giusti e Zanza

Via dei Puntoni, 9
Fauglia (PI)
tel. 0585/44354

In their second year of wine production Paolo Giusti and Fabio Zanza show that they know what they want and have the fighting spirit to compete in the quality stakes. On the estate they acquired, the former Scopicci property, they immediately set about planting, on the advice of their consultant, Stefano Chioccioli, their new vineyards at a staggeringly high density of 10,000 vines per hectare. This bodes well for the body of their wines in future. For the moment, they are working with the vines they found in place but are limiting yields to boost quality. There are only two wines, the Dulcamara (cabernet and merlot) and the Belcore (two parts sangiovese to one of merlot). Both did extremely well, easily netting Two Glasses each. The Dulcamara is their number one label, a status reflected in its price. It has a very dark colour and a rich, concentrated nose that is still developing. At present, black berry fruit rules the roost, together with a substantial dose of oak. The palate is solid, meaty and full-bodied so this is a very promising wine. However, it will need to make peace with its oak to achieve more elegance. The Belcore '98 is exactly what its makers intended it to be – uncomplicated, but beautifully executed. The aromas are immediately attractive, with very enjoyable flower and fruit notes. The balance on the medium-bodied palate is excellent and the wine is a delight to drink.

●	Belcore '98	🍷🍷	4
●	Dulcamara '97	🍷🍷	5

FAUGLIA (PI)

FATTORIA UCCELLIERA
VIA PONTITA, 26
56043 FAUGLIA (PI)
TEL. 050/662747

On the Tuscan coast, that nursery of future stars of the vinous firmament stretching from Lucca to Bolgheri and Scansano in Maremma, the ever-growing demand for wine tempts many producers to release bottles that could do with a few more months' repose in the seclusion of their cellars. Few of those producers have the courage and the wherewithal to skip a year, so when one actually does, it is clear evidence of far-sightedness and trust in the advising oenologist. Thus, the Castellaccio Rosso '98 will not be available for tasting until is released onto the market next year. Two Glasses, meanwhile, go to the Castellaccio Bianco '99, which is no longer a monovarietal chardonnay but has become a blend of sémillon, pinot bianco, sauvignon blanc and chardonnay, since the vines planted in '95 have gradually started producing. Deep straw-yellow in colour, it makes a good impression on the nose with its notes of citrus fruit, hedgerow and peach fusing with a wooded tone. After a toasty attack on the palate, it progresses very well, with notes of cakes balanced by a spirited acid tang, and the finish is appropriately long. There's a good report for the Chianti '98, which came close to getting Two Glasses for its character and spicy bouquet where the fruit is fractionally upstaged by a vegetal note. One Glass also for the chardonnay and trebbiano Ficaia '99, with its fairly soft finish. And so we round off with a lovely dessert wine. Two Glasses go to the Vin Santo Xantos '96, which offers pleasing aromas of shortbread, zabaglione and candied peel, and an elegant, well-ordered palate.

○	Castellaccio Bianco '99	▼▼	4
○	Vin Santo Xantos '96	▼▼	5
●	Chianti '98	▼	3
○	Ficaia '99	▼	3
○	Castellaccio Bianco '96	▽▽	4
○	Castellaccio Bianco '98	▽▽	4
●	Castellaccio Rosso '93	▽▽	4
●	Castellaccio Rosso '95	▽▽	4
●	Castellaccio Rosso '96	▽▽	4
●	Castellaccio Rosso '97	▽▽	4
●	Castellaccio Rosso '92	▽	4
●	Chianti '94	▽	3
●	Chianti '95	▽	3
●	Chianti '96	▽	3
●	Chianti '97	▽	3

FIRENZE

★ MARCHESI ANTINORI
P.ZZA DEGLI ANTINORI, 3
50123 FIRENZE
TEL. 055/23595

It has been quite some time since we last came upon a range of wines as good as this. The Antinoris have really taken our breath away this year. It is also enormously significant that such a large winery should succeed in presenting as many as six such excellent wines. And we are not speaking of selections of a few thousand bottles each but of an output that ranges from over 70,000 for the Solaia to more than 2,000,000 bottles of Villa Antinori Riserva. The most surprising of their wines this time is the Chianti Classico Badia a Passignano Riserva '97, the best version they have ever made and the first Chianti Classico to have won Three Glasses for Antinori. It is elegant, refined and extremely harmonious. An absolutely super bottle. The Solaia '97, from cabernet with 20 percent sangiovese, is as usual a stunner, but this time it is even more concentrated and powerful. Quite simply, Solaia is one of Italy's greatest wines. And then there's the rest of the range. The Tignanello '97, from a memorable vintage, shows a distinction that we haven't encountered since at least the '93, but perhaps even since the '88. The Chianti Classico Tenute del Marchese Riserva '97 is deliciously aristocratic and reveals a softness that suggests a heftier dose of non-native grapes (merlot? cabernet sauvignon?). The Chianti Classico Pèppoli '98 is stylish, less complex and more quaffable. And lastly, we were treated to a sensational version of the Chianti Classico Villa Antinori Riserva, the estate's bread-and-butter wine. Do you remember the '75? Well, that vintage may have been as good as this '97. Piero Antinori, his daughters Albiera, Allegra and Alessia (all of whom work in the family business), and Renzo Cotarella, the managing director and a great oenologist, have reason to be well pleased.

●	Chianti Classico Badia a Passignano Ris. '97	▼▼▼	5
●	Solaia '97	▼▼▼	6
●	Chianti Cl. Villa Antinori Ris. '97	▼▼	4
●	Chianti Classico Pèppoli '98	▼▼	4
●	Chianti Classico Tenute del Marchese Ris. '97	▼▼	5
●	Tignanello '97	▼▼	6
●	Solaia '88	▽▽▽	6
●	Solaia '90	▽▽▽	6
●	Solaia '94	▽▽▽	6
●	Solaia '95	▽▽▽	6
●	Solaia '96	▽▽▽	6
●	Tignanello '85	▽▽▽	6
●	Tignanello '93	▽▽▽	6

FIRENZE

FIRENZE

TENUTE AMBROGIO
E ALBERTO FOLONARI
VIA POR S. MARIA, 8
50122 FIRENZE
TEL. 055/23859001

MARCHESI DE' FRESCOBALDI
VIA S. SPIRITO, 11
50125 FIRENZE
TEL. 055/27141

The first result of the amicable separation of the two branches of the Folonari family is the splitting up of the estates and wine names that once belonged to Ruffino. That is how Ambrogio and Alberto ended up with the Cabreo wines, the Fattoria di Nozzole estate, the Gracciano property at Montepulciano and half of Monte Rossa in Franciacorta. In addition, they have are estates in Friuli and at Bolgheri which have not yet produced wines. The new company is called Tenute Ambrogio e Alberto Folonari , and it is making a cracking Guide debut with Three Glasses, which are as predictable as they are well merited. Step forward Il Pareto '97, the great cabernet sauvignon from the vineyards of Nozzole. It is a masterly wine, and one of the two best versions yet produced (the '90 was the other). We savoured the fruity and balsamic notes on the nose, and density, softness and great elegance on the palate. In fact, the Folonaris could not have made a better start. But that's not all. The two Cabreos, both '98s, are also excellent. The La Pietra, a chardonnay, is less intense than the '97. The wood is integrated and the body is good but not enormous. The Cabreo Il Borgo, a blend of sangiovese and cabernet sauvignon, is elegant and consistent and shows a concentration worthy of its vintage. The Nozzole vines have also given us the stylish Chianti Classico La Forra Riserva '97, which is somewhat light-bodied but very well made, the Chianti Classico '98, which is even and correctly executed, and Le Bruniche '99, mostly chardonnay, a fruity and quaffable white. Well begun!

The name Frescobaldi requires no introduction. This historic estate, rich in tradition, has not rested on its laurels but continues to work as hard as ever to achieve excellence. Recently, they acquired some land in Maremma, the new winemaking frontier of Tuscany, and we look forward confidently to the results. Oenological matters are in the hands of the masterly Niccolò D'Afflitto, who is more than prepared for this exacting task. The wine we liked most is the Mormoreto '97, a Three Glass bottle if ever we saw one. An intense, deep ruby hue leads in to aromas ranging from wild berries to cinnamon, with subtle vegetal notes and elegant balsamic nuances. The attack on the palate is mouth-filling, creamy and balanced, and the tannins are perfectly integrated. High marks, too, for the Nipozzano '97. A fruity nose of clean, inviting cherry is followed by an excellent balance on the palate that makes this a tasty and eminently quaffable wine. The lovely purple Pomino Rosso '97 did well, too. An attractive, very generous fruity bouquet, where notes of cinnamon and cloves rub shoulders with unusual hints of rhubarb, introduces a positive attack on the not very powerful but dense palate. The fruity Pomino Bianco '99 has excessive acidity which stunts the finish. In the Pomino Benefizio '98, the not very eloquent aromas are somewhat below par but the wine reveals grip and meatiness in the mouth. The Chianti Castiglioni '99, a simple, clean red, is interesting this year.

● Il Pareto '97	♙♙♙	6
● Cabreo Il Borgo '98	♙♙	6
○ Cabreo La Pietra '98	♙♙	6
● Chianti Cl. La Forra Ris. '97	♙♙	5
● Chianti Classico Nozzole '98	♙	4
○ Le Bruniche '99	♙	4
● Chianti Cl. La Forra Ris. '90	♟♟♟	4
● Il Pareto '88	♟♟♟	6
● Il Pareto '90	♟♟♟	6
● Il Pareto '93	♟♟♟	6
● Chianti Cl. La Forra Ris. '94	♟♟	4
● Chianti Cl. La Forra Ris. '95	♟♟	4
● Il Pareto '94	♟♟	6
● Il Pareto '95	♟♟	6
● Il Pareto '96	♟♟	6

● Mormoreto '97	♙♙♙	6
● Chianti Rufina Nipozzano Ris. '97	♙♙	5
● Pomino Rosso '97	♙♙	5
● Chianti Castiglioni '99	♙	3
○ Pomino Bianco '99	♙	4
○ Pomino Il Benefizio '98	♙	5
● Chianti Rufina Montesodi '88	♟♟♟	6
● Chianti Rufina Montesodi '90	♟♟♟	6
● Chianti Rufina Montesodi '97	♟♟♟	6
● Chianti Rufina Montesodi '96	♟♟♟	6
● Pomino Rosso '85	♟♟♟	5
● Chianti Rufina Montesodi '95	♟♟	6
● Mormoreto '95	♟♟	6
● Mormoreto '96	♟♟	6

FOIANO DELLA CHIANA (AR)   FOSDINOVO (MS)

FATTORIA SANTA VITTORIA
LOC. POZZO
VIA PIANA, 43
52045 FOIANO DELLA CHIANA (AR)
TEL. 0575/66807 - 0575/966807

PODERE TERENZUOLA
VIA VERCALDA, 14
54035 FOSDINOVO (MS)
TEL. 0187/68943

After a few years down among the Other Wineries, Fattoria Santa Vittoria has deservedly won a Guide profile of its own. This is, we feel, an important step forward for a young estate that is run by the very young Marta Niccolai. Fattoria Santa Vittoria had come close several times before and now the greater consistency of its range has done the trick. Of course, there is still a fair amount of room for improvement and fine-tuning but everything bodes well for the future. Much space is given over to traditional grape varieties, such as sangiovese, canaiolo, trebbiano, malvasia and grechetto but new vineyards are planted to chardonnay, pinot bianco, cabernet sauvignon and merlot. So, there are plenty of options. The most important wine is the Scannagallo, two parts sangiovese to one of cabernet sauvignon, from fairly young vines planted at a good density and yielding no more than two kilos per vine. Maceration in the cellar lasts for at most ten to 12 days, with frequent pumping over the cap. The cabernet and a third of the sangiovese finish their ageing, separately, in barriques. The '98 revealed an admirably clean bouquet with notes of red and black berry fruit, and light wooded nuances while there is good weight and balance on the uncomplicated but very agreeable palate. The dense sweet Vin Santo '95 is very good indeed. The Chardonnay '99 and the red Poggio al Tempio '99 are both more than acceptable while the Grechetto '99 is a little forward but nonetheless perfectly respectable.

"La Petite Alsace" is what young grower-producer Ivan Giuliani likes to call the Caniparola hills in the Colli di Luni zone, a stone's throw from the Ligurian border. This is where he has his vineyards, a sort of mini-laboratory where he experiments with vermentino, including three French clones, merlot and several clones of sangiovese, as well as with some of the rarer native varieties, such as pòllera nera and merla. Ivan's laboratory is scheduled to release in the near future a number of reds. One of these is the Rotonda dei Cipressi, from equal parts of sangiovese and merlot grown in high-density vineyards planted at 6,200 vines per hectare and aged in barriques, and various others, on which experimentation is still proceeding. For the moment, the Vermentino accounts for the lion's share of the estate's production, and its style explains Ivan's nickname for the zone. The Fosso di Corsano '99, made with a percentage of late-vintage grapes and aged in small barrels, had little trouble winning Two Glasses. A vivid straw-yellow introduces intense notes of spring flowers and peachy fruit, with a light hint of honey. The entry on the palate is soft and unctuous, and the body, while not overwhelming, is balanced and pleasingly succulent. The clean finish, with its lingering echoes of honey, has you holding out your glass for a refill.

● Scannagallo '98	▼▼	4
○ Vin Santo '95	▼▼	5
○ Chardonnay '99	▼	3
● Val di Chiana Poggio del Tempio '99	▼	3
○ Val di Chiana Grechetto '99		2

○ Colli di Luni Vermentino Fosso di Corsano '99	▼▼	4
○ Colli di Luni Vermentino Fosso di Corsano '98	♀♀	3*

FUCECCHIO (FI)

GAIOLE IN CHIANTI (SI)

FATTORIA DI MONTELLORI
VIA PISTOIESE, 1
50054 FUCECCHIO (FI)
TEL. 0571/260641

AGRICOLTORI
DEL CHIANTI GEOGRAFICO
VIA MULINACCIO, 10
53013 GAIOLE IN CHIANTI (SI)
TEL. 0577/749489

Fattoria di Montellori really seems to be hitting its stride, as was clear from our tastings. Alessandro Nieri's estate is one of the wineries that need only the endorsement of a first Three Glass award, to which Montellori has come close, to launch their image effectively. This year's most exciting news is the cellar's excellent Sauvignon Blanc, the Sant'Amato, which gives full expression to the variety's characteristics with aromas of tomato leaf, rue flower and lavender. The fresh, balanced palate is backed up by rich aromas. Montellori's best bottle is again their cabernet and merlot blend, the Salamartano. This '98 almost won our highest award, not for the first time. It offers lovely concentration, firmness, perfectly ripe fruit and a dense, lingering finish. Still very young, it should definitely improve with some bottle ageing, which will allow it to integrate its oak properly. The interesting debutante white, Montecupoli '99, shows some personality, a positive progression on the palate and good length, as well as an admirably fresh bouquet. The Castelrapiti, obtained from sangiovese with a little cabernet, doesn't do badly but shows the limited ripeness of the '96 vintage. It is medium-bodied and generally agreeable but cannot disguise a distinct vegetal note. There are no questions about what the Vigne del Moro '98 wants to do. It's a quaffable, no-frills crowd-pleaser but not without a certain appeal. The Chianti '99 is decently made but a bit thin.

This year's real surprise from the range that this famous Chianti wine co-operative presented was the delicious Chianti Classico '98. It's their standard wine, easy to find in many Italian wine shops. Above all, it is a good-quality red that does not cost very much at all. We can still recall its elegantly fruity bouquet with notes of black cherry and plum, and the even, stylish, beautifully balanced palate. The concentration is not brilliant, of course, but perfectly acceptable given the price bracket. On the other hand, its technical execution is truly remarkable. A perfect example of what this type of wine should be. The good Chianti Classico Montegiachi Riserva '97 is a harmonious and mouth-filling red, which again reveals the softness we have come to expect. It proffers aromas of ripe fruit, with some forward notes. Excellent balance is the keynote of the palate, where acidity and tannins are well offset by alcohol. Lastly, the house Supertuscan, the sangiovese and cabernet sauvignon I Vigneti del Geografico '97, is a more concentrated, serious red. It is well executed, and with a little more personality and complexity would have done even better than it did.

● Salamartano '98	ᵀᵀ	6
○ Sant'Amato '99	ᵀᵀ	4
● Castelrapiti Rosso '96	ᵀ	5
○ Montecupoli '99	ᵀ	4
● Vigne del Moro '98	ᵀ	3
● Chianti '99		2
● Castelrapiti Rosso '92	ᵀᵀ	5
● Castelrapiti Rosso '95	ᵀᵀ	4
● Castelrapiti Rosso '93	ᵀᵀ	5
● Salamartano '92	ᵀᵀ	5
● Salamartano '93	ᵀᵀ	5
● Salamartano '94	ᵀᵀ	5
● Salamartano '95	ᵀᵀ	5
● Salamartano '96	ᵀᵀ	5
● Salamartano '97	ᵀᵀ	5

● Chianti Cl. Montegiachi Ris. '97	ᵀᵀ	4
● Chianti Classico '98	ᵀᵀ	3*
● I Vigneti del Geografico '97	ᵀᵀ	5
● Chianti Cl. Montegiachi Ris. '87	ᵀᵀ	3*
● Chianti Cl. Montegiachi Ris. '88	ᵀᵀ	4
● Chianti Cl. Montegiachi Ris. '90	ᵀᵀ	3*
● Chianti Cl. Montegiachi Ris. '94	ᵀᵀ	4
● Chianti Cl. Montegiachi Ris. '95	ᵀᵀ	4
● Chianti Classico '90	ᵀᵀ	2*
● I Vigneti del Geografico '95	ᵀᵀ	5
● I Vigneti del Geografico '96	ᵀᵀ	5
● Chianti Cl. Montegiachi Ris. '96	ᵀ	4
● Chianti Classico '97	ᵀ	3
● Chianti Classico Contessa di Radda '97	ᵀ	3

GAIOLE IN CHIANTI (SI) GAIOLE IN CHIANTI (SI)

★ CASTELLO DI AMA
LOC. AMA
53010 GAIOLE IN CHIANTI (SI)
TEL. 0577/746031

BADIA A COLTIBUONO
LOC. BADIA A COLTIBUONO
53013 GAIOLE IN CHIANTI (SI)
TEL. 0577/749498

Although there are not very many black glasses in evidence below, we must say that we are moderately content with the wines that this famous old estate presented this year. The Chianti Classico Bellavista '97, in particular, is the best version we've tasted recently. We are encouraged by the obvious care that the Chianti Classico receives from Marco Pallanti and Lorenza Sebasti, partners in work and in life who run the winery together. The Bellavista '97, and also the Castello di Ama '97, are elegant, well-executed reds with good concentration. The Bellavista has more to offer in the shape of greater density and a longer finish but both wines represent a turning-point. They are solid, reliable and extremely well-made. In contrast, we felt let down for once by the '96 version of the Vigna l'Apparita, a red that has repeatedly won honours for Castello di Ama in the recent past. Perhaps, given its great tradition, we should have been less critical. However, a wine like this, which is anything but cheap, must expect rigorous scrutiny, whatever the outcome. This year, it simply failed to appeal. We are the first to regret this minor hiccough, which we ascribe to the not very inspiring vintage. But the wine did seem too simple and not awfully concentrated, at least in comparison to earlier versions. The Vigna Il Chiuso, the Castello di Ama Pinot Nero, is good enough, as usual, but a little monotonous. There are gamy notes on the nose and good structure on the palate: our tasting did not inspire panegyrics.

This is a transitional, and hence a rather difficult, year for Badia a Coltibuono. Maurizio Castelli, long their consultant, has resigned and in his place is Luca D'Attoma, another celebrated oenologist, who started with the 2000 vintage. In addition, the new cellar has just been inaugurated and, like all things new, will need to be run in. All this is by way of introduction to the fact that we were expecting a little more from this year's tastings than we found. Two of the principal wines, the Sangioveto and the Chianti Classico Riserva, were '97s so it was not unreasonable to hope for more structure and complexity in both. It has to be said that they are still well-made wines with no technical flaws. The Sangioveto '97 is also not bad at all. It has finesse and texture, good body and even a hint of complexity but it lacks the concentration of the '95 and went no further than Two Glasses. The Chianti Classico Riserva '97 is perhaps still too young. It is anything but muscular and it should be remembered that it comes from the vineyards of the Monti subzone, an area that generally produces rather intense, close-knit wines with hefty extract, at least in outstanding vintages like '97. The other two wines, both '98s, are pleasant if a little uninteresting. One is the standard Chianti Classico, the other the Chianti Classico R.S. The initials stand for Roberto Stucchi, who owns the winery with his sister, Emanuela.

● Chianti Cl. Bellavista '97	♈♈	6
● Chianti Classico Castello di Ama '97	♈♈	5
● Vigna Il Chiuso Pinot Nero '97	♈	6
● Vigna l'Apparita Merlot '96	♈	6
● Chianti Cl. Bellavista '85	♈♈♈	6
● Chianti Cl. Bellavista '86	♈♈♈	6
● Chianti Cl. Bellavista '90	♈♈♈	5
● Chianti Cl. Bertinga '88	♈♈♈	6
● Chianti Cl. La Casuccia '88	♈♈♈	6
● Vigna l'Apparita Merlot '88	♈♈♈	6
● Vigna l'Apparita Merlot '90	♈♈♈	6
● Vigna l'Apparita Merlot '91	♈♈♈	6
● Vigna l'Apparita Merlot '92	♈♈♈	6
● Vigna l'Apparita Merlot '93	♈♈	6
● Vigna l'Apparita Merlot '95	♈♈	6

● Sangioveto '97	♈♈	6
● Chianti Classico '98	♈	4
● Chianti Classico R. S. '98	♈	3
● Chianti Classico Ris. '97	♈	5
● Sangioveto '95	♈♈♈	6
● Chianti Classico Ris. '85	♈♈	4
● Chianti Classico Ris. '88	♈♈	4
● Chianti Classico Ris. '90	♈♈	4
● Chianti Classico Ris. '95	♈♈	5
● Chianti Classico Ris. '96	♈♈	5
● Sangioveto '85	♈♈	6
● Sangioveto '86	♈♈	6
● Sangioveto '88	♈♈	6
● Sangioveto '90	♈♈	6
● Sangioveto '94	♈♈	6

GAIOLE IN CHIANTI (SI)

GAIOLE IN CHIANTI (SI)

BARONE RICASOLI
LOC. BROLIO
53013 GAIOLE IN CHIANTI (SI)
TEL. 0577/7301

CASTELLO DI CACCHIANO
FRAZ. MONTI IN CHIANTI
LOC. CACCHIANO
53010 GAIOLE IN CHIANTI (SI)
TEL. 0577/747018

In '93, it was an ugly duckling. Today it is a magnificent swan soaring into the skies. The Castello di Brolio "Dream Team", consisting of Francesco Ricasoli at the helm, Filippo Mazzei, the can-do general manager of the estate, and a group of extremely competent professionals (Maurizio Ghiori as sales manager, Carlo Ferrini as consultant oenologist and Lucia Franciosi for public relations) has not put a foot wrong. This year's range is one of the very best presented anywhere in Tuscany. Dream wines. The Chianti Classico Castello di Brolio '97 is the first dream, a great red, aromatically complex with notes of berry fruit and leather over light smoky hints. All these nuances are repeated on the palate, which is intense, concentrated and altogether mouth-filling. The tannins are smooth and the alcohol excellently judged. The Casalferro '98, a sangiovese-based wine with a little merlot (and you can tell), is even more complex on the nose, its mineral and wooded tones resting firmly on a foundation of thrilling red fruit. The palate is full-bodied and slightly less complex, but very good. The other wines are all Two Glass winners. The ever fragrant Formulae '98, made mainly from sangiovese, is an extremely fruity and quaffable red while the Chianti Classico Rocca Guicciarda Riserva '97 and the Chianti Classico Brolio '98 are both in great form. The least individual of the lot is the barrique-aged Chardonnay, the Torricella '99, which is powerful and full-bodied, with aromas of vanilla. Good, but we've seen it all before. It could have come from California.

These are the first results of Giovanni Ricasoli's decision to do away with special selections and improve his Chianti Classico Riserva, which thus becomes the flagship of the estate. A far-sighted policy, as we wrote last year, which shows great respect for the terroir. Now that Chianti Classico is a great wine again, returning to its roots like this is a significant gesture. The Chianti '98 is intensely ruby-hued. On the nose, the first perceptions are toasty aromas with notes of incense but as the wine opens out, give way to uncomplicated but clean fruit. The entry on the palate is firm, and the progression is underpinned by pleasant, if not very incisive, acidity. The body has decent structure and the finish is fairly long and flavoursome. The Millennio '97 is rather better. Its lively ruby colour heralds a complex bouquet where iron-rich mineral aromas are at first accompanied by notes of plum and cherry but then make way for spicy tones. After a measured attack on the palate, the wine reveals good balance and an attractively juicy, although not very concentrated, palate and tight-knit tannins. The extremely quaffable Rosso di Toscana '99 is sinewy, fruity, substantial and long. Finally, the limpid amber Vin Santo '94 unveils complex aromas including Peruvian bark, tamarind and almond. After a seductive attack, the palate is generous, mouth-filling, dense and full-bodied.

● Casalferro '98	♟♟♟	5
● Chianti Classico		
Castello di Brolio '97	♟♟♟	5
● Chianti Classico Brolio '98	♟♟	4
● Chianti Classico		
Rocca Guicciarda Ris. '97	♟♟	4
● Formulae '98	♟♟	3*
○ Torricella '99	♟♟	4
● Casalferro '95	♟♟♟	5
● Casalferro '96	♟♟♟	5
● Casalferro '97	♟♟♟	5
● Chianti Classico		
Rocca Guicciarda Ris. '96	♟♟	4

● Chianti Cl. Millennio Ris. '97	♟♟	5
○ Vin Santo '94	♟♟	5
● Chianti Classico '98	♟	4
● Rosso di Toscana '99	♟	3
● Chianti Cl. Millennio Ris. '90	♟♟♟	5
● Chianti Cl. Millennio Ris. '88	♟♟	5
● Chianti Cl. Millennio Ris. '95	♟♟	5
● Chianti Classico '90	♟♟	3*
● Chianti Classico '93	♟♟	3*
● Chianti Classico '95	♟♟	3*
● RF Castello di Cacchiano '90	♟♟	5
● RF Castello di Cacchiano '93	♟♟	4
○ Vin Santo '91	♟♟	5
○ Vin Santo '93	♟♟	5

409

GAIOLE IN CHIANTI (SI)

CASTELLO DI MELETO
LOC. CANTINA
DI PONTE DI MELETO, 1
53013 GAIOLE IN CHIANTI (SI)
TEL. 0577/749217

GAIOLE IN CHIANTI (SI)

IL COLOMBAIO DI CENCIO
LOC. CORNIA
53013 GAIOLE IN CHIANTI (SI)
TEL. 0577/747301

This Gaiole estate presented the panel with an astonishing number of different wines. We are giving it a full profile but their policy leaves us a little puzzled. They appear to be spreading themselves a bit thin with so many labels. The Chianti Classico '98 offers intense, if somewhat muddled, super-ripe and intense fruity aromas. A pleasing fresh acidity is immediately evident on the palate, which also boasts good concentration, but the tannins are not well-amalgamated. The Riserva '97 does better. Unusual notes of aromatic herbs – rosemary, for one – blend with rather harsh vegetal tones on the nose. The attack on the palate is gentle, firm and dense, and the solid tannins are well integrated. The pleasing finish is only moderately long. The Chianti Classico Pieve di Spaltenna '98 displays lively, energetic fruit with enchanting, faintly spicy notes. In the mouth, the wine is nicely judged, not enormous in body, but harmonious, and with an acid tang that merges well with the alcohol. The Rainero '98, a monovarietal sangiovese, offers a bouquet of super-ripe, somewhat coarse fruit with not very refined grassy notes, leading in to a concentrated, even dense, palate which, however, lacks cohesion and balance. The Fiore '97 stands out from the rest of the range. A deep ruby hue introduces intense aromas of black berries and elegant, if slightly heavy-handed, wooded tones. On the palate, it is succulent and full-bodied, with an appropriate balance between alcohol and acidity. The bouquet of the Pieve di Spaltenna Alle Fonti '98 is similarly attractive, with its admixture of fruit and light spice. The firm, big-bodied palate is not altogether harmonious, despite notable power and substance.

This is the second bull's-eye in a row for this tiny Gaiole estate. Werner Wilhelm, the owner, is unwavering in his insistence that all efforts should be focused on creating excellent wines. His extremely able assistants in this endeavour are his young manager and factotum, Jacopo Morganti, and oenologist, Paolo Vagaggini, who provides first-rate advice. The results they have achieved are little short of dazzling. Il Futuro '97, from sangiovese and cabernet sauvignon, is monumental, indeed even better than the splendid '95. The nose is intense and fruity, with undertones of vanilla and minerals while the palate is particularly concentrated, and the close-knit, smooth tannins are completely absorbed into a velvety, soft body. Not far behind it, the Chianti Classico Riserva '97 shows the great qualities of what looks like a historic vintage for this winery. Again, we find elegance, concentration and the textbook use of new wood, together with especially fine-grained tannins and remarkable length. This is a significant second appearance for Il Colombaio di Cenci, which is bound to figure amongst the top producers of the Chianti region in the near future. We are pleased to have contributed to its well-deserved éclat.

● Fiore '97	ΥΥ	5
● Pieve di Spaltenna Alle Fonti '98	ΥΥ	5
● Chianti Classico Pieve di Spaltenna '98	Υ	3
● Chianti Classico Ris. '97	Υ	4
● Rainero '98	Υ	5
● Chianti Classico '98		3

● Il Futuro '97	ΥΥΥ	6
● Chianti Classico Ris. '97	ΥΥ	4
● Il Futuro '95	ΥΥΥ	6
● Chianti Classico '95	ΥΥ	4

GAIOLE IN CHIANTI (SI)

GAIOLE IN CHIANTI (SI)

PODERE IL PALAZZINO
LOC. MONTI IN CHIANTI
53010 GAIOLE IN CHIANTI (SI)
TEL. 0577/747008

S. M. LAMOLE & VILLA VISTARENNI
LOC. VISTARENNI
53013 GAIOLE IN CHIANTI (SI)
TEL. 0577/738186

Alessandro and Andrea Sderci's estate is back in the Guide, as it fully deserves to be. The two wines they released are now excellent, in addition to being as representative of their terroir as they always were in the past. As you will perhaps already have guessed, Il Palazzino is one of that select group of wineries that find being true to their territory a greater good than rapidly achieving a perhaps ephemeral success by taking short cuts. This could hardly be called a profit-driven strategy for it involves sacrifices and occasional disappointments. But if you buy an Il Palazzino wine, you can be certain that there is no sleight of hand. You will be purchasing an authentic sangiovese from the vineyards of Monti. This justifies, at least in part, the wide variation in results from vintage to vintage but it also means that you can find a really thrilling bottle of wine, if you pick your moment. Both the wines we tested this year won Two Glasses. The more impressive of the two is the estate flagship wine, the Grosso Sanese, which offers very individual aromas of berry fruit and walnut with the faintest suggestion of oak. It opens out gently and harmoniously on the succulent, fragrant palate, revealing bright, delicious tannins. The Chianti Classico '98 is not as dense, of course, but is enviably smooth.

The Chianti Classicos from the Lamole subzone in the south-eastern part of Greve are very distinctive. Many are the fruit of gobelet-trained vines, which are traditional here. Elegance and finesse are their strong suits in interpreting the sangiovese grape but they can at times be a bit thin. In fact, they're like those minute old peasant women who are apparently very fragile but are actually as strong as a horse and seem to live forever. The Chianti Classico Campolungo Riserva '95 is built along these lines. It needed years to express itself fully and is now miraculously long-lived. With the passage of time, it has acquired complexity on the nose and integrated the exuberant acidity that dominated the palate for the first few years. All the other wines from this famous estate, which is part of the Marzotto-Santa Margherita Group, are fair. The two versions of Chianti Classico Lamole di Lamole, the '98 and the Riserva '96, reveal further improvements in execution and make a very decent showing, although they both come from mediocre vintages. The Chianti Classico Villa Vistarenni '98, from the vineyards that belong to the Gaiole winery of the same name, is, as usual, an uncomplicated red with primary aromas and a body that could not be called enormous. This version, however, is better than the '97, which was a bit disappointing. And that's good news.

● Chianti Classico '98	♀♀	4
● Chianti Classico Grosso Sanese Ris. '97	♀♀	5
● Chianti Classico Grosso Sanese Ris. '93	♀♀	5
● Chianti Classico Grosso Sanese Ris. '94	♀♀	5
● Chianti Classico '93	♀	4

● Chianti Cl. Campolungo Ris. '95	♀♀	4
● Chianti Cl. Lamole di Lamole '98	♀	3
● Chianti Cl. Villa Vistarenni '98	♀	3
● Chianti Classico Lamole di Lamole Ris. '96	♀	4
● Chianti Cl. Campolungo Ris. '94	♀♀	4
● Chianti Cl. Lamole di Lamole '97	♀♀	3*
● Chianti Cl. Villa Vistarenni '95	♀♀	4
● Chianti Classico Lamole di Lamole Ris. '95	♀♀	4
● Codirosso '95	♀♀	5
● Chianti Cl. Lamole di Lamole '96	♀	4
● Chianti Cl. Villa Vistarenni Ris. '94	♀	4
● Chianti Cl. Villa Vistarenni Ris. '95	♀	4
● Chianti Cl. Villa Vistarenni '97		3

GAIOLE IN CHIANTI (SI)

GAIOLE IN CHIANTI (SI)

MONTIVERDI
LOC. MONTIVERDI
53013 GAIOLE IN CHIANTI (SI)
TEL. 0577/749305 - 02/8378808

RIECINE
LOC. RIECINE
53013 GAIOLE IN CHIANTI (SI)
TEL. 0577/749098

The Longo family's winery in Gaiole is certainly not one of those cellars that stake everything they have on a single label. And Stefano Chioccioli, a name to conjure with among younger Italian oenologists, works hard to produce good results with every wine they make. Two Glasses go to the Chianti Classico Villa Maisano Quello '96. A lively ruby hue and an intense impact on the nose with notes of blackberry and bilberry, and a distinct hint of grassy cabernet, lead in to fresh acidity that livens up the palate and lends allure to a peppery finish. The Questo '96 is a different story. Its mineral and vegetal notes lend personality to the black berry fruit of the bouquet while the palate shows balance and excellent progression. A further Two Glasses were handed out to the Cipressone '96. Its intense fruit and spice nose has a faint vegetal undertone, ushering in a balanced, succulent and very stylish palate. Sangiovese brings its characteristically elegant tannins to the Villa Maisano Riserva '96. The Chianti Classico Riserva '96 offers riper notes on the nose and clean fruit in the mouth that makes it a pleasure to drink. Moving up to the '97s, we find aromas of carnation and cherry in the Chianti Classico Villa Maisano, followed by an agreeably soft palate that offers ripe tannins and good, juicy fruit, although we wouldn't have objected to a little more richness. In contrast, the Chianti Classico '97 is a bit rough and sharp, with medium body and length. Lastly, traditionalists will want to find out more about the dry, sharp-tasting Vin Santo.

The Riecine team is out in full force this year. As many as four wines were presented at our tastings. And it's a good team, as usual, albeit but not quite as triumphant as one might have predicted. The star player, La Gioia '97, a sangiovese, did very well, but failed to reveal the greatness of other vintages. There's no denying the cleanness of the bouquet, which is concentrated and full of fruit that blends pleasingly with toasty oak. In the mouth, it's dense and compact, as well as seductively elegant, which is the La Gioia hallmark. But the finish, although long enough, doesn't have the expected complexity and fades out rather simply. The stylistic consistency of the Chianti Riserva, on the other hand, is simply exemplary. The nose offers well-defined aromas of black berry fruit, violets, spice and tobacco. The compact, well-balanced body is stylish, tripping up just slightly on somewhat austere tannins on the finish. The Chianti '98, which nearly got Two Glasses, is a fine example of a characteristic Sangiovese, with very clean, inviting fruit and flower aromas which carry through to the medium-bodied palate. The range ends well with the Sebastiano '97, a sweet wine in the Vin Santo mode. It may be a little unsure of itself on the nose but the very satisfying palate reveals a sweetness beautifully balanced by refreshing acidity.

Wine	Glasses	Price
● Chianti Cl. Vigneto Cipressone '96	YY	4
● Chianti Cl. Villa Maisano Quello '96	YY	5
● Chianti Cl. Villa Maisano Questo '96	YY	5
● Chianti Cl. Villa Maisano '97	Y	4
● Chianti Cl. Villa Maisano Ris. '96	Y	4
● Chianti Classico Ris. '96	Y	4
● Chianti Classico '97		3
○ Vin Santo	Y	5
● Chianti Cl. Villa Maisano Questo '95	YY	4
● Chianti Classico '96	Y	3
● Chianti Classico Ris. '96	Y	4
● Le Borranine '96	Y	5

Wine	Glasses	Price
● Chianti Classico Ris. '97	YY	5
● La Gioia '97	YY	6
○ Sebastiano '97	YY	5
● Chianti Classico '98	Y	4
● Chianti Classico Ris. '86	YYY	5
● Chianti Classico Ris. '88	YYY	6
● La Gioia '95	YYY	6
● Chianti Classico '97	YY	5
● Chianti Classico Ris. '93	YY	5
● Chianti Classico Ris. '94	YY	5
● Chianti Classico Ris. '95	YY	6
● Chianti Classico Ris. '96	YY	6
● La Gioia '93	YY	5
● La Gioia '94	YY	5
● La Gioia '96	YY	6

GAIOLE IN CHIANTI (SI)   GAIOLE IN CHIANTI (SI)

ROCCA DI CASTAGNOLI
LOC. CASTAGNOLI
53010 GAIOLE IN CHIANTI (SI)
TEL. 0577/731004

SAN GIUSTO A RENTENNANO
FRAZ. MONTI IN CHIANTI
53013 GAIOLE IN CHIANTI (SI)
TEL. 0577/747121

This year we enjoyed a very agreeable series of bottles from Rocca di Castagnoli, which has definitely shifted up a gear. The cellar presented five wines, almost all of which received Two Glasses. For example, the very good Chianti Riserva Capraia is a fitting successor to the lovely '96. This '97 is probably even richer in structure, but it needs more time to settle and achieve full balance. The intense, well-defined aromas include black berry fruit, notes of roasting coffee and a touch of capsicum. Weighty and generous on the palate, it constantly gathers strength on the palate, with layers of robust, if not yet completely absorbed, tannins. On a similar level is the Buriano '97, a cabernet that flaunts admirably ripe fruit without ceding to vegetal tones. Its outstanding structure avoids degenerating into a mere flexing of muscles, instead managing to offer enticing softness and elegance. The Stielle '97, a blend of sangiovese and cabernet, easily won its Two Glasses. Its vigorous, weighty body will need time to finish integrating the oak and tannins. High marks also for the Poggio a' Frati Riserva '97 which, while not particularly muscular, shows remarkably sound fruit and balanced flavour. To finish, the Chianti '98 is more than acceptable. The bouquet could do with some fine-tuning but the palate is admirably harmonious.

This is only the second time Three Glasses have gone to San Giusto a Rentennano, which has long had a solid reputation and some very enthusiastic fans. The Percarlo won our highest award but three other wines came very close in an altogether positive and consistent performance for the Martini di Cigala family estate. The Percarlo '97 is true to its vigorous nature, with intense mineral and spicy aromas and light notes of oak. The attack on the palate is classically emphatic, the progression rich and overwhelming, while the long finish perfectly mirrors the nose. The robust tannins are not yet completely tamed but this is in the nature of the wine. The very good Chianti Riserva '97 is solid and lively in the mouth and the ripe nose unfurls notes of liquorice, tobacco and berry fruit. The excellent Vin Santo '93 has a distinctly individual tone. Aromas of dried fruit, fig and chestnut lead in to a sweet, dense, leisurely palate. The Chianti Classico '98 is obviously simpler but well-executed and agreeable, with a faintly bitter twist in the finish. We close our profile with the estate merlot, the La Ricolma '97, a powerful and energetic red that offers notes of black berry fruit and spice on the nose and a vigorous tannic texture on the palate, leading in to an intense, long finish.

● Buriano '97	▼▼	5
● Chianti Classico Capraia Ris. '97	▼▼	5
● Chianti Classico		
Poggio a' Frati Ris. '97	▼▼	4
● Stielle '97	▼▼	5
● Chianti Classico '98	▼	3
● Buriano '96	♀♀	5
● Chianti Classico Capraia Ris. '96	♀♀	4
● Stielle '96	♀♀	5
● Chianti Classico '97	♀	3

● Percarlo '97	▼▼▼	6
● Chianti Classico Ris. '97	▼▼	5
● La Ricolma '97	▼▼	6
○ Vin Santo '93	▼▼	6
● Chianti Classico '98	▼	4
● Percarlo '88	♀♀♀	6
● Percarlo '85	♀♀	6
● Percarlo '87	♀♀	6
● Percarlo '90	♀♀	6
● Percarlo '91	♀♀	6
● Percarlo '92	♀♀	6
● Percarlo '93	♀♀	6
● Percarlo '94	♀♀	6
● Percarlo '95	♀♀	6
● Percarlo '96	♀♀	6

GAIOLE IN CHIANTI (SI)   GAMBASSI TERME (FI)

SAN VINCENTI
PODERE DI STIGNANO, 27
53013 GAIOLE IN CHIANTI (SI)
TEL. 0577/734047

VILLA PILLO
VIA VOLTERRANA, 24
50050 GAMBASSI TERME (FI)
TEL. 0571/680212

We are in danger of becoming repetitive when we are presented year after year with the wines from San Vincenti, a small estate – only six hectares under vine – that has an immense ability to bring out its terroir. The property is located in an area that has what it takes to produce excellent wine but this, of course, is not enough on its own. The vineyard must be managed by people who know and care about what they are doing. This may seem obvious but it is still worth saying because even in what are considered poor vintages, San Vincenti manages to turn out praiseworthy products. A case in point is the Chianti Classico '98, which has a nose of some depth, redolent with enchanting aromas of blackberry and liquorice. The palate reveals surprising density and concentration and, although not perfectly harmonious, it has genuine character. The Riserva '97 has already acquired greater balance but is less eloquently characterful. There are vegetal hints in the bouquet although the palate is smooth and well articulated. The estate's best wine is, unquestionably, the sangiovese-based Stignano '97, which strolled off with Two very full Glasses for its vibrant, incisive style. It has concentration, a soft, firm palate and a youthful energy that makes it a pleasure to drink. If we were asked to name a fault, then it would have to be the oak, which is clearly perceptible on both the nose, where it adds toasty and spicy notes, and in the mouth, where the finish is dominated by wood-derived tannins.

The California connection (through the owners) is fairly obvious in the way this estate is run, from the grape varieties planted to the methods of vinification, the management style and that of the wines. Villa Pillo, a splendid Palladian pile a stone's throw from San Gimignano, is surrounded by a superb five-hectare park, and a plan is slowly being implemented here to make the estate one of the region's top producers. They did well with their '98s, although Three Glasses remained just out of reach. Better things are hoped for from the '99 vintage. We'll start with the Syrah '98, a round, concentrated red but with slightly overstated oak. Aromas of plum, liquorice and black pepper lead in to a quite substantial and balanced palate with a faintly bitter finish. A rotary fermenter was used to make it and the wine should age well. The Merlot '98 wants just a touch more elegance and a more legible signature of its terroir. The colour is concentrated, and black berry fruit dominates the bouquet, with light vegetal and toasty nuances. The attack on the palate is fresh and fruity, and the lively tannins are a pleasure. The cabernet franc, merlot and syrah Vivaldaia '98 seems a tad undecided on both nose and palate between a forward phase and a vegetal and bitter orange mode. Despite this hesitancy, it is agreeable and original. Lastly, we will simply mention the Vin Santo del Chianti '95, which is sweet but slightly marred by notes of dried mushroom.

● Chianti Classico '98	♛♛	4	● Merlot '98	♛♛	5
● Chianti Classico Ris. '97	♛♛	4	● Syrah '98	♛♛	5
● Stignano '97	♛♛	5	● Vivaldaia '98	♛	5
● Chianti Classico '88	♛♛	3*	○ Vin Santo '95		6
● Chianti Classico			● Syrah '97	♛♛♛	5
Podere di Stignano '96	♛♛	3*	● Cabernet Sauvignon '96	♛♛	5
● Chianti Classico Ris. '85	♛♛	4	● Cabernet Sauvignon '97	♛♛	5
● Chianti Classico Ris. '88	♛♛	4	● Merlot '95	♛♛	5
● Chianti Classico Ris. '95	♛♛	4	● Merlot '96	♛♛	5
● Chianti Classico Ris. '96	♛♛	4	● Merlot '97	♛♛	5
● Stignano '96	♛♛	5	● Syrah '96	♛♛	5
● Chianti Classico '90	♛	3	● Vivaldaia '95	♛♛	6
● Chianti Classico '91	♛	4	● Vivaldaia '97	♛♛	5
● Chianti Classico '97	♛	3	● Borgoforte '94	♛	4
● Chianti Classico Ris. '91	♛	3	● Vivaldaia '96	♛	5

GHIZZANO DI PECCIOLI (PI)

TENUTA DI GHIZZANO
VIA DELLA CHIESA, 1
56030 GHIZZANO DI PECCIOLI (PI)
TEL. 0587/630096

The significant changes in production methods recently introduced at the Tenuta di Ghizzano are beginning to bear fruit. They have gone from the good, reliable bottles of a few years back to excellent wines that bespeak uncompromising effort in vineyard and cellar. The first sign is the ripening time for the grapes, which is now much shorter, and not just because of the recent warm vintages, (not to mention the favourable location of the estate in a zone that benefits from a coastal climate, unlike inland Tuscany). The estate has also made drastic reductions in yield per vine. Their flagship wines, Nambrot and Veneroso, are now consistently outstanding. In very good years, they may even be exceptional. Whatever the vintage, they are most unlikely to disappoint. The Nambrot '98, a monovarietal merlot, gets better every year. This time, it almost broke the Three Glass barrier. Masking its strength (14 percent alcohol) in an elegant structure with silky tannins, it presents a nose with lots of rich fruit and some notes of coffee. The oak is very well integrated and the finish long and expansive. The Veneroso '98, a blend of sangiovese, cabernet and merlot, is equally wonderful, refusing to yield an inch of its customary classic elegance and this time adding succulent concentration, soft tannins and an admirable harmony that is unsettled only by occasional vegetal nuances. The Veneroso '97 is not dissimilar. A very good wine, it is a shade inferior to the Nambrot only in extract and aromatic freshness. Lastly, the fine Chianti '99 is agreeable and well-balanced, with a tad more sinew than usual.

●	Nambrot '98	🍷🍷	6
●	Veneroso '97	🍷🍷	5
●	Veneroso '98	🍷🍷	5
●	Chianti '99	🍷	3
●	Nambrot '96	♀♀	6
●	Nambrot '97	♀♀	6
●	Veneroso '86	♀♀	5
●	Veneroso '88	♀♀	5
●	Veneroso '90	♀♀	5
●	Veneroso '91	♀♀	4
●	Veneroso '93	♀♀	4
●	Veneroso '94	♀♀	4
●	Veneroso '95	♀♀	5
●	Veneroso '96	♀♀	5
○	Vin Santo San Germano '95	♀♀	5

GREVE IN CHIANTI (FI)

CARPINETO
LOC. DUDDA
50020 GREVE IN CHIANTI (FI)
TEL. 055/8549062 - 055/8549086

We were more than satisfied by Carpineto. The wines presented were well conceived, correctly executed and reliable from first to last. They were not, however, successful in communicating a recognizable personality or a sense of terroir, although the two Chiantis are especially well made and the '98 is something of a revelation. The nose is still dumb, but the palate is smooth, intense and juicy, with lovely fruit and deliciously sweet tannins. The Riserva makes a fine showing as well by virtue of its good structure and the balance of underpinning acidity and tannins. Its greatest defect is the intrusive oak but that will probably settle down with more bottle age. The Farnito Cabernet Sauvignon is more questionable. The very dark hue and substantial body are at odds with the excessively vegetal tone that diminishes its harmony and suggests the presence of insufficiently ripe grapes. Last of all, the unpretentious Dogajolo is pleasing and quaffable, despite some rather woody notes.

●	Chianti Classico '98	🍷🍷	3*
●	Chianti Classico Ris. '97	🍷🍷	4
●	Dogajolo '99	🍷	3
●	Farnito Cabernet Sauvignon '97	🍷	5
●	Chianti Classico Ris. '93	♀♀	4
●	Chianti Classico Ris. '94	♀♀	4
●	Dogajolo '93	♀♀	4
●	Dogajolo '95	♀♀	3*
●	Farnito Cabernet Sauvignon '90	♀♀	5
●	Farnito Cabernet Sauvignon '91	♀♀	5
●	Farnito Cabernet Sauvignon '93	♀♀	5
●	Farnito Cabernet Sauvignon '95	♀♀	5
●	Nobile di Montepulciano Ris. '94	♀♀	4
●	Nobile di Montepulciano Ris. '95	♀	4

GREVE IN CHIANTI (FI)

LA MADONNINA - TRIACCA

LOC. STRADA IN CHIANTI
V.LO ABATE, 1
50027 GREVE IN CHIANTI (FI)
TEL. 055/858003

This year, the results are a little under par for this estate belonging to the Triacca family. The Triaccas are grower-producers near Sondrio in their native Valtellina and have quite a foothold in Tuscany, including some first-rate vineyards at Montepulciano. All the Madonnina wines we tasted this time were respectable enough yet they failed to light any fires. It was not a great vintage but we feel sure that they have better things in store. We'll start with the Chianti Classico '98, basically a clean, well-made, straightforward wine with distinct notes of cherry and with light vegetal tones on the nose. An even tannic texture in a moderately structured body leads to a finish of medium length. The Riserva '97 has a more vibrant colour but the aromas lack balance, the fruit is muffled and the nose as a whole is rather forward. The attack on the palate is good and the mid palate has nice weight but the finish doesn't linger. The flagship estate cru, the Chianti La Palaia '97, opens on the nose with very lively grassy tones on an agreeable background of black berry jam. The good acid bite on the palate melds nicely into the well-balanced body which is sound, if not enormous. Il Mandorlo '97, a cabernet sauvignon-based red, releases very marked, intense herbaceous notes on a good fruity foundation. The flavoursome palate shows sinew and is well defined but lacks élan. Predictable and unexciting.

●	Chianti Classico '98	🍷	3
●	Chianti Classico Ris. '97	🍷	4
●	Chianti Classico V. La Palaia '97	🍷	4
●	Il Mandorlo '97	🍷	4
●	Chianti Classico '94	🍸🍸	3*
●	Chianti Classico '95	🍸🍸	3*
●	Chianti Classico Ris. '94	🍸🍸	4
●	Chianti Classico Ris. '95	🍸🍸	4
●	Chianti Classico V. La Palaia '96	🍸🍸	4
●	Chianti Classico '96	🍸	3
●	Chianti Classico '97	🍸	3
●	Chianti Classico Ris. '96	🍸	4
●	Chianti Classico V. La Palaia '95	🍸	4
●	Il Mandorlo '94	🍸	4
●	Il Mandorlo '95	🍸	4

GREVE IN CHIANTI (FI)

LA TORRACCIA DI PRESURA

LOC. STRADA IN CHIANTI
VIA DELLA MONTAGNOLA, 130
50022 GREVE IN CHIANTI (FI)
TEL. 055/490563 - 055/489997

There was a good overall showing for this Chianti Classico estate near Florence. The most promising bottle is the basic vintage Chianti, which stands head and shoulders above the other, perfectly respectable, bottles in the range. The least successful offering was the white, the Solitario '98. A pale straw-yellow colour introduces a tired nose with notes of wood that refuse to integrate with the other aromas. It is appropriately full-bodied but not long enough on the palate. The very good standard-label Chianti Classico has a lovely intense deep ruby hue and an elegant bouquet including ripe wild berries, spicy notes of cinnamon and cloves, and faint tobacco nuances. The balance in the mouth is excellent, the close-knit tannins blending with powerful but not excessive alcohol. The Riserva '97, in contrast, is a little under par. The not entirely clean bouquet reveals almost rubbery and not altogether invigorating, aromas that muffle the fruit. The entry on the palate is good and an initial mouth-filling sensation gives way to soft, well-judged tannins. Lastly, the Lucciolaio '98, a blend of cabernet sauvignon and sangiovese, has a somewhat bitter fragrance, with hints of Peruvian bark upstaging the fruit. In the mouth it progresses well, showing pleasing harmony, simplicity and moderate length.

●	Chianti Classico Il Tarocco '98	🍷🍷	3*
●	Chianti Classico Il Tarocco Ris. '97	🍷	4
●	Lucciolaio '98	🍷	5
○	Solitario '97		3
●	Chianti Classico Il Tarocco '96	🍸🍸	3*
●	Chianti Classico Il Tarocco '94	🍸	3
●	Chianti Classico Il Tarocco '95	🍸	3
●	Chianti Classico Il Tarocco '97	🍸	3
●	Chianti Classico Il Tarocco Ris. '94	🍸	4
●	Chianti Classico Il Tarocco Ris. '96	🍸	4
●	Lucciolaio '95	🍸	5
●	Lucciolaio '96	🍸	5
○	Solitario '97	🍸	3

GREVE IN CHIANTI (FI)

GREVE IN CHIANTI (FI)

MONTECALVI
VIA CITILLE, 85
50022 GREVE IN CHIANTI (FI)
TEL. 055/8544665

PODERE POGGIO SCALETTE
LOC. RUFFOLI
VIA BARBIANO, 7
50022 GREVE IN CHIANTI (FI)
TEL. 055/8546108

Opinions will be divided about the Montecalvi '97. We had predicted that it would be one of the best wines of the year, and here it is with just Two Glasses. Of course, that's not a result to be sneezed at but it has simply not shown the extraordinary personality that it is capable of. It's a sangiovese-based bottle with just a little cabernet sauvignon from spectacular, very low-yielding vineyards and the wine has exceptional richness. The dimensions of the palate, the sheer mouth-filling volume, are stunning and the gathering intensity of the flavour is awesome. It seems unstoppable, and indeed the finish just goes on and on. Unfortunately, we also have to note that the impact on the nose is not altogether edifying. There are some residual reductive notes and animal nuances that conspire to hold the wine back from the heights it ought to attain. We wouldn't like to be misunderstood, though. The aromas are not a serious defect but probably reflect a developmental phase that brings with it rather less elegant notes. And it is here that the personal preferences come into play. For some, the aromas are irrelevant or even a positive characteristic while others will find them unacceptable in a major wine. Whatever the case, a Three Glass wine should leave no room for doubt, however little. It has to be said that we found the Montecalvi '97 to be a truly exciting red and are even more impatient for future versions of a wine that is at once utterly authentic and hard to classify.

Just before Querciabella, the road from Greve to Ruffoli climbs towards an almost Alpine panorama, with a view over vineyards whose oldest vines were planted in the '20s. The great Tuscan oenologist, Vittorio Fiore, was well aware of the store the French set by "vieilles vignes" when he bought this property in '91. And with his considerable experience, he had very clear notions about the use of oak with a grape variety like sangiovese, which is not as well endowed with polyphenolics as some of its international cousins, but does have lots of potentially drying tannins. An appropriate interaction of wine and wood can be achieved with 450-litre tonneaux, and there they are, nicely lined up, in the small, orderly cellar at Poggio Scalette. The wine that emerges from them is a fine example of what sangiovese can do when looked after properly. The '97 Il Carbonaione came very close to winning our top award and we believe it won't be long before it hits the jackpot. A lively, bright ruby hue introduces the concentrated, intense bouquet with notes of ripe black berry fruit and a delicate oak-derived spiciness reminiscent of cigar tobacco. On the palate, after a youthfully boisterous attack, it proves solid and powerful, with satisfying fruit and a broad, clean finish. In short, a masterful Sangiovese.

● Montecalvi '97	♟♟	6		● Il Carbonaione '97	♟♟	6
● Montecalvi '94	♟♟	4		● Il Carbonaione '96	♟♟♟	5
● Montecalvi '95	♟♟	5		● Il Carbonaione '92	♟♟	5
● Montecalvi '96	♟♟	5		● Il Carbonaione '93	♟♟	5
● Montecalvi '93	♟	4		● Il Carbonaione '94	♟♟	5
				● Il Carbonaione '95	♟♟	5

GREVE IN CHIANTI (FI)

CASTELLO DI QUERCETO
LOC. DUDDA, 61
50020 GREVE IN CHIANTI (FI)
TEL. 055/85921

As usual there's a profusion of labels from Castello di Querceto and the results are, on the whole, positive. Late release is an estate policy, to be attributed to their conviction that wines from this area need a relatively long time in the cellar. The Chianti Classico '97 shows a ruby colour verging on garnet. Oak-derived aromas have the upper hand over fruit. The attack on the palate is good and the balance is all it should be. The Cignale '96, a blend of cabernet sauvignon and merlot, is decidedly ruby-hued. The fruity and vegetal notes on the nose are perfectly clean. On the palate, the wine is broad and reveals density and texture as well as stamina. The only thing it lacks is more softness. The red La Corte '96 has a rather tired bouquet with forward fruit. The entry on the palate is very dry, the tannins are roughish and there are slightly bitter notes on the finish. Another famous estate wine, the Querciolaia '96, proffers persistent grassy notes on the nose, filled out by ripe fruit. In the mouth, it is fairly well-balanced and has good texture, with a distinct, lively acidity. The Riserva '95 makes a good showing. The nose is complex and smooth, with aromas of cherry and plum, and although it is still a bit closed it flaunts a pleasing, sober elegance. On the palate, it is impressively concentrated, rich and decisive, with tannins and alcohol that amalgamate well. The Vin Santo shows an attractive amber colour and has atypical notes of celery mixed with nuts on the nose. Although not very complex, it is appropriately soft and offers a long, enjoyable finish.

GREVE IN CHIANTI (FI)

AGRICOLA QUERCIABELLA
LOC. RUFFOLI
VIA S. LUCIA A BARBIANO, 17
50022 GREVE IN CHIANTI (FI)
TEL. 055/853834 - 02/86452793

The headline news from Giuseppe and Sebastiano Castiglioni's Agricola Querciabella concerns their facilities. They have just put the finishing touches to their new, up-to-the-minute cellar, which is so environmentally friendly that you can hardly tell from the outside that anything has happened at all. It will make life much easier for the estate oenologist, Guido De Santi, and also for Giacomo Tachis, who is, unbeknownst to many, their consultant. Meanwhile this splendid estate continues to turn out excellent wines. This year we have given Three Glasses to the best white in Tuscany, the Batàr '98, made mostly from chardonnay. It's a wine of extraordinary breeding, one of the few Italian whites aged in oak that really show balance and are not dominated by notes of super-ripeness and vanilla. Lifted by just the right level of acidity on the palate, it drinks more like a northern wine than one from these latitudes. The Camartina '96 is also very fine, although it comes from quite a tricky vintage, certainly much inferior to '95, which gave rise to one of the best Camartinas ever (if a '95 should ever come your way, don't hold back: it is simply sumptuous at the moment). The '96 is lighter and more dilute, but it is still a seriously good red wine. We were expecting a little more from the Chianti Classico Riserva '97, which is still a bit closed and definitely too young. But it should be borne in mind that Querciabella wines take a while to show what they can do, like thoroughbred racehorses that break away from the field late in the race. The last of the range, the Chianti Classico '98, is good, consistent and elegantly fruity.

● Chianti Classico Ris. '95	♛♛	4
● Chianti Classico '97	♛	3
● Chianti Classico Il Picchio Ris. '95	♛	4
● Cignale '96	♛	5
● La Corte '96	♛	5
● Querciolaia '96	♛	5
○ Vin Santo di Toscana '94	♛	5
● Chianti Classico '95	♛♛	3*
● Chianti Classico Il Picchio Ris. '93	♛♛	4
● Chianti Classico Il Picchio Ris. '94	♛♛	4
● Chianti Classico Ris. '90	♛♛	4
● La Corte '94	♛♛	5
● Querciolaia '90	♛♛	5
● Querciolaia '95	♛♛	5
● Cento '95	♛	6

○ Batàr '98	♛♛♛	5
● Camartina '96	♛♛	6
● Chianti Classico '98	♛♛	4
● Chianti Classico Ris. '97	♛♛	5
○ Batàr '97	♛♛♛	5
● Camartina '88	♛♛♛	5
● Camartina '90	♛♛♛	5
● Camartina '94	♛♛♛	5
● Camartina '95	♛♛♛	6
● Chianti Classico '95	♛♛♛	4*
● Chianti Classico Ris. '95	♛♛♛	5
● Camartina '93	♛♛	5
● Chianti Classico '97	♛♛	4
● Chianti Classico Ris. '96	♛♛	5
○ Vin Santo Orlando '90	♛♛	6

GREVE IN CHIANTI (FI)

GREVE IN CHIANTI (FI)

CASTELLO DI VERRAZZANO
LOC. VERRAZZANO
50022 GREVE IN CHIANTI (FI)
TEL. 055/854243

CASTELLO DI VICCHIOMAGGIO
VIA VICCHIOMAGGIO, 4
50022 GREVE IN CHIANTI (FI)
TEL. 055/854079

To point out that Castello di Verrazzano has become one of the most splendid producers in the Greve zone is, at this point, almost superfluous. Even if Luigi Cappellini's estate didn't pick up another Three Glass award this time, we have had further proof that it is going from strength to strength, and that there are some very good things in store. The three wines presented at our tastings all did well and it was the Bottiglia Particolare '97, made from sangiovese with a touch of cabernet sauvignon, which stood out. It is modern in style, and hence not very striking in personality, but it's unquestionably a fine bottle of wine. The aromas are intense and clean, with a wide range of wild black berries, toasty notes of oak and some – perhaps a few too many – vegetal nuances. The palate is close-knit and concentrated, revealing a solid tannic underpinning. Not does the Chianti Riserva '97 disappoint. Sound fruit comes through clearly on both nose and palate without interference from the oak. The flavour is wonderfully concentrated and well balanced. If these two wines packed a little more aromatic distinction there would be no holding them back. Lastly, the interesting Chianti '98 boasts a clean fragrance and good structure, which is perhaps just a tad over-extracted.

Vicchiomaggio did itself proud this year. The energy of the '97 vintage was exploited to the full – witness the Three Glass accolade collected by the Ripa delle More, and the performance of the Chianti Riserva La Prima, which missed a similar distinction by a hair's breadth. In all, or very nearly all, of the wines we tasted we found a laudable consistency of style, with the accent on harmony and elegance. Obviously, in the case of the two wines mentioned, these characteristics are backed up by first-class structure. For example, the Sangiovese, Ripa delle More '97, unveils rich, full-flavoured fruit, a close-knit and deliciously soft tannic texture and a surprising progression on the palate, where every component melds impeccably into the whole, generating all the complexity and harmony of a great wine. The Chianti La Prima Riserva '97 is similar in character, with very smooth, well-balanced tannins, lovely depth on the palate and well-integrated wood. Both of these champions reveal, in addition to the excellence of their raw material, a masterly vinification technique. The Riserva Petri '97 is another wine that stands out, thanks to its remarkable structure and general harmony, the only defect being the rather unsubtle wood. We found some unoriginal vegetal and vanilla notes in the bouquet of the Chianti San Jacopo '98 but the palate is well put together and the fruity finish fairly long. The rather simple but very well constructed Ripa delle Mandorle '98 is underpinned by an admirable tannic texture. Altogether quite an enjoyable wine.

● Bottiglia Particolare '97	♟♟	6
● Chianti Classico Ris. '97	♟♟	5
● Chianti Classico '98	♟	3
● Chianti Classico Ris. '90	♟♟♟	5
● Sassello '97	♟♟♟	5
● Bottiglia Particolare '90	♟♟	5
● Bottiglia Particolare '95	♟♟	5
● Chianti Classico '91	♟♟	3*
● Chianti Classico '94	♟♟	3*
● Chianti Classico '97	♟♟	3*
● Chianti Classico Ris. '88	♟♟	4
● Chianti Classico Ris. '96	♟♟	4
● Sassello '90	♟♟	5
● Sassello '93	♟♟	5
● Sassello '95	♟♟	5

● Ripa delle More '97	♟♟♟	6
● Chianti Classico La Prima Ris. '97	♟♟	5
● Chianti Classico Petri Ris. '97	♟♟	5
● Chianti Classico San Jacopo '98	♟	4
● Ripa delle Mandorle '98	♟	4
● Ripa delle More '94	♟♟♟	5
● Chianti Classico La Prima Ris. '90	♟♟	5
● Chianti Classico La Prima Ris. '93	♟♟	5
● Chianti Classico La Prima Ris. '88	♟♟	5
● Chianti Classico La Prima Ris. '94	♟♟	5
● Chianti Classico La Prima Ris. '95	♟♟	5
● Chianti Classico Petri Ris. '90	♟♟	5
● Ripa delle More '90	♟♟	5
● Ripa delle More '95	♟♟	5
● Ripa delle More '96	♟♟	5

GREVE IN CHIANTI (FI)

GREVE IN CHIANTI (FI)

VILLA VIGNAMAGGIO
VIA DI PETRIOLO, 5
50022 GREVE IN CHIANTI (FI)
TEL. 055/854661

VITICCIO
VIA SAN CRESCI, 12/A
50022 GREVE IN CHIANTI (FI)
TEL. 055/854210

The constructive criticism we offered Vignamaggio in last year's Guide has been taken up in the best way possible. The cellar presented the entire range at our tasting and, most important, every product pulled its weight, demonstrating the excellent potential of lawyer Nunziante's estate. Actually, the merest of whiskers separated the Obsession '97, a blend of cabernet, merlot and syrah, from Three Glasses. This fruity, direct and instantly engaging red, underpinned by a good structure and soft tannins, develops elegantly and evenly on the palate. But it's not the only wine that caught our fancy. For example, the Vignamaggio '96, which is a very different bottle, did just as well. One rarely finds so much character in a cabernet franc-based product. There's a distinctly mineral tone on the nose, with earthy and pencil lead notes that may not be the last word in elegance but are certainly striking. The palate is warm, powerful, meaty and full-bodied. Then there was a very good Vin Santo that offers a rich bouquet of candied peel, dried fruit and jam aromas, and a sweet, mouth-filling, beautifully poised palate. The Monna Lisa Riserva '97 is held back by its over-abundance of vegetal tones but is very good all the same, revealing nice texture and harmony as well as a certain elegance on the palate. The Chianti Classico Vitigliano has made quite an interesting debut. The structure is very firm, the tannins firmly textured and the oak well-judged. We ended our tasting with two respectable '98 Chiantis. The Terre di Prenzano is the richer of the two while the basic Chianti Classico is more refreshing and has crisper aromas.

This year's range from Viticcio is a mixed bag. The vineyard selections are excellent but the DOC wines are less interesting. That doesn't mean that our view of the work done here by the Landini brothers and oenologists, Vittorio Fiore and Gabriella Tani, is anything other than very positive. The Chianti Classico '98 is the wine that impressed us least. The ruby in the glass introduces aromas that are super-ripe, warm and somewhat disjointed. In the mouth, we found considerable acidity together with prominent, medium-grained tannins. The Riserva '97 was a bit better, although not wildly exciting. Its limpid ruby ushers in pervasive tertiary aromas of tar and leather that stand out against an evolved fruity background. The entry on the palate is very smooth and dilute, then the tannins make their presence felt in the medium-bodied structure. The Riserva Beatrice '97, a very vivid ruby in colour, offers notes of butter and vanilla on a fresh fruity foundation reminiscent of raspberry. The attack on the palate is a bit weak but the wine gradually gathers momentum, unveiling robust tannins. Things start looking up, as we mentioned earlier, with the selections. The Prunaio '97, a monovarietal sangiovese, displays a lovely intense ruby hue. Notes of ripe blackcurrant blend with vanilla and also some vegetal tones on the nose. After a good attack, the mid palate reveals appropriate weight and a nice balance of tannins and alcohol, as well as an acid tang that lends vigour. The rising finish is succulent, mouth-filling and persistent. Lastly, the Monile '97 seemed closed at first but then it opened up with full, warm aromas of plum and cherry enhanced by elegant toasty notes. The entry on the palate is nicely rounded, the progression well-structured and the finish long.

● Chianti Cl. Monna Lisa Ris. '97	▼▼	5
● Chianti Cl. Vitigliano '97	▼▼	4
● Obsession '97	▼▼	5
● Vignamaggio '96	▼▼	6
○ Vin Santo '95	▼▼	5
● Chianti Cl. Terre di Prenzano '98	▼	3
● Chianti Classico '98	▼	3
● Chianti Cl. Monna Lisa Ris. '95	▼▼▼	4*
● Chianti Cl. Monna Lisa Ris. '90	♀♀	4
● Chianti Cl. Monna Lisa Ris. '94	♀♀	4
● Chianti Cl. Monna Lisa Ris. '93	♀♀	4
● Gherardino '90	♀♀	5
● Gherardino '93	♀♀	5
● Gherardino '95	♀♀	5
● Vignamaggio '93	♀♀	5

● Monile '97	▼▼	5
● Prunaio '97	▼▼	5
● Chianti Classico Beatrice Ris. '97	▼	5
● Chianti Classico Ris. '97	▼	4
● Chianti Classico '98		4
● Chianti Classico '97	♀♀	4
● Chianti Classico Ris. '96	♀♀	4
● Monile '93	♀♀	5
● Monile '94	♀♀	5
● Monile '95	♀♀	5
● Monile '96	♀♀	5
● Prunaio '93	♀♀	5
● Prunaio '94	♀♀	5
● Prunaio '95	♀♀	5
● Prunaio '96	♀♀	5

IMPRUNETA (FI)   LUCCA

PODERE LANCIOLA II
VIA IMPRUNETANA
PER POZZOLATICO, 210
50023 IMPRUNETA (FI)
TEL. 055/208324

LE MURELLE
FRAZ. PONTE DEL GIGLIO
LOC. CAPPELLA
VIA PER CAMAIORE TRAV. V
55060 LUCCA
TEL. 0583/394487

The ink of last year's profile, in which we said we expected greater consistency from this estate, had hardly had time to dry when this little Impruneta estate presented us with an outstanding range. Although they make a large number of different wines, the area under vine is limited and the Guarneri family succeed year after year in working wonders in both vineyard and cellar. But we'd better get down to specifics, as there are so many. The Terricci '97, a blend of sangiovese and cabernet sauvignon, makes an excellent impression on the nose with powerful rich fruit that has absorbed the wood beautifully. In the mouth, after a massive attack, the wine is dense, concentrated and creamy. Very high marks also for the Chianti Colli Fiorentini Riserva '97, which is full-bodied and offers lots of ripe fruit, with plum and cherry to the fore. The Riccionero '97, a newcomer, is a monovarietal Pinot Nero which is a little atypical but good all the same. Aromas of wild berries meld seamlessly with spicy notes on the nose. The palate is solid and concentrated, with a robust structure and powerful alcohol. We also liked the Chianti Classico Le Masse di Greve Riserva '97. The fruit on the nose is slightly upstaged by toasty notes but the palate is attractively elegant and well-balance. The Chianti Classico '98 has noticeable vegetal aromas and simple but clean fruit. The palate is stylish and harmonious, with a well-defined finish. The Chianti Colli Fiorentini '98, which is a little rustic on the nose, turns out to have decent structure. Lastly, the chardonnay-based white Terricci '98 is the only wine we found not altogether convincing. The nose fails to hang together and the rather dull flavour lacks concentration.

We note with pleasure that Giampi Moretti, having returned to the Guide last year, has dug in well. In fact, he is advancing strongly. To show that the territory west of Lucca is every bit as good as more celebrated zones, he has presented a new wine, which is already a success and promises great things for the future. He made it with the help of Alberto Antonini, which means with a weather eye on what is going on along the nearby Bolgheri and Maremma coast. The new arrival is a monovarietal cabernet called Niffo '98, with a very intense ruby hue and a nose that belies its youth by flaunting an admirable complexity. The opening displays notes of black berry fruit, flowers, fine spice and cloves. It is sweet, juicy and well defined on the palate, with silky tannins that fade a little in the finish. The Chardonnay and the Sauvignon have exchanged places since last year for this time the Chardonnay has done better, winning its Two Glasses thanks in part to skilfully judged oak. The bouquet is true to type for this grape when the wine is barrique-aged and comes from a hot year. Creamy vanilla and notes of tropical fruit, especially ripe banana, lead in to a palate that is not quite as rich as the nose but has good balance and definition, with a fairly long finish. The Sauvignon '99 proffers a lighter nose of yeast and citrus fruit, with lemon and grapefruit to the fore. These somewhat tart notes are reflected on the rather thin but pleasantly tangy and refreshing palate.

● Chianti Cl. Le Masse di Greve Ris. '97 ▼▼	4
● Chianti Colli Fiorentini Ris. '97 ▼▼	3*
● Riccionero '97 ▼▼	3*
● Terricci '97 ▼▼	4
● Chianti Cl. Le Masse di Greve '98 ▼	3
● Chianti Colli Fiorentini '98 ▼	2*
○ Terricci Chardonnay '98	4
● Terricci '86 ♀♀	4
● Terricci '88 ♀♀	4
● Terricci '95 ♀♀	4
● Terricci '96 ♀♀	4
● Chianti Cl. Le Masse di Greve '96 ♀	3
● Chianti Cl. Le Masse di Greve '97 ♀	3
● Chianti Cl. Le Masse di Greve Ris. '95 ♀	4
● Chianti Colli Fiorentini '96 ♀	2

○ Colline Lucchesi Chardonnay '99 ▼▼	4
● Niffo '98 ▼▼	5
○ Colline Lucchesi Sauvignon '99 ▼	4
○ Colline Lucchesi Sauvignon '98 ♀♀	3*
○ Colline Lucchesi Chardonnay '98 ♀	3

MAGLIANO IN TOSCANA (GR)

LE PUPILLE
LOC. PERETA
58051 MAGLIANO IN TOSCANA (GR)
TEL. 0564/505129

FATTORIA MANTELLASSI
LOC. BANDITACCIA, 26
58051 MAGLIANO IN TOSCANA (GR)
TEL. 0564/592037

Pointing out that Le Pupille is the wine-producing star of Maremma is rather like announcing that Queen Victoria has passed away. People tend to know already. This estate, which belongs to Elisabetta Geppetti and her husband, Stefano Rizzi, has often shown that it is a winery to be reckoned with but this time it has outdone itself. That's not only, as you might suppose, a consequence of the Three Glass distinction earned by the splendid Poggio Valente but also because of the ease with which three other wines very nearly walked off with the same award. We'll start with the Saffredi '98, made from cabernet, merlot and alicante, which came within an inch of repeating the success of last year's version. A full-bodied, rich and well-textured wine with plenty of thrust on the palate, it offers a velvet-smooth tannic texture. The finish is long, succulent and very faintly vegetal. The very good Morellino Riserva '97 has a more reserved style and a firm personality. It's a great Sangiovese, faithful to its terroir, with a soft, almost chewy palate. And what can we say about the Solalto? Wonderful. Fragrant and rich on the nose, with notes of candied fruit, orange peel and honey, it has a sweet and very full-flavoured palate. The white Poggio Argentato '99 has a delightful flowery bouquet and the Morellino '99 does not disappoint either, with its good texture and lively fruit. Then at long last, the Poggio Valente once again provides us with a top-ranking Morellino. An alluringly opulent, fruit-rich wine, it conjures up rich, silky tannins and intriguing aromas of blackberry, coffee and pepper. A concluding note. The estate is about to open its new office complex, which will at long last be worthy of its wines.

This year's tastings confirmed the steady improvement in quality at this well-known Maremma estate, which has long been sending Morellino di Scansano all over Italy, helping to make the wine generally better known. This evangelizing role is now not so important, given the success that the zone has enjoyed and the numbers of producers from other areas who have been attracted to it. Faced with this invasion, the Mantellassi estate has re-adjusted its sights, aiming now at higher quality while keeping prices affordable. All that good work has led to an easy Two Glasses for the Morellino di Scansano Le Sentinelle '97, which is excellent news. The intense ruby has a garnet-tinged rim while the fruit on the nose includes liqueur cherries barely masked by delicious oak. With some more bottle age, the two components will certainly meld. The weight of the palate is nicely offset by the fine texture of the tannins. A notch or two below comes the more traditional Morellino Riserva '97, with greater vigour on the palate and prominent tannins. The Querciolaia '97, although not as good as we hoped, is a very well-managed wine.

● Morellino di Scansano Poggio Valente '98	♥♥♥	5
● Morellino di Scansano Ris. '97	♥♥	4
● Saffredi '98	♥♥	6
○ Solalto '98	♥♥	4
● Morellino di Scansano '99	♥	3
○ Poggio Argentato '99	♥	3
● Saffredi '90	♥♥♥	6
● Saffredi '97	♥♥♥	6
● Morellino di Scansano Poggio Valente '97	♥♥	5
● Saffredi '91	♥♥	5
● Saffredi '93	♥♥	5
● Saffredi '94	♥♥	5
● Saffredi '95	♥♥	5

● Morellino di Scansano Le Sentinelle '97	♥♥	4
● Morellino di Scansano Ris. '97	♥	3
● Querciolaia '97	♥	4
● Morellino di Scansano Ris. '96	♥♥	3*
● Querciolaia '96	♥♥	4
● Morellino di Scansano Le Sentinelle Ris. '95	♥	4
● Morellino di Scansano San Giuseppe '98	♥	4

MANCIANO (GR)

MASSA

LA STELLATA
LOC. STELLATA
VIA FORNACINA, 18
58014 MANCIANO (GR)
TEL. 0564/620190

CIMA
VIA DEL FAGIANO, 1
54100 MASSA
TEL. 0585/830835

Now that it is surrounded by the new estates, large and small, that are springing up like mushrooms in the area, La Stellata looks like just one more Maremma winery but it is in fact one of the oldest producers in the entire territory. Manlio and Clara Divizia make a range of good wines to be drunk straight away without bothering about lengthy cellaring. The classic example, and also the estate's forte, is the celebrated Bianco di Pitigliano Lunaia. The '99 vintage produced an uncomplicated, agreeable wine with a lustrous pale yellow hue. The nose is rather redolent of sulphur dioxide and therefore rather subdued but as the wine breathes the aroma disperses, giving way to straightforward but attractive fruit. The lean, loosely structured body is appropriate to this variety while the delicate fruit flavour takes you through to an evanescent finish. Its red stablemate, the Lunaia Rosso, is more ambitious and fuller-bodied. The '97 has a vivid ruby colour with bright highlights. The bouquet offers aromas of toasty oak and some slightly vegetal notes on a fruity background. The palate is rounded, broad, glycerine-rich and lingering. An attractive red, it is robust and mouth-filling, if not extremely elegant.

This is a triumphal entry into the Guide for Cima, the estate in the Candia hills skilfully run by Aurelio Cima. Aurelio is a young producer who hasn't turned his back on the traditional white wines of his native land but has still managed to shake off the pedantic view that local winemakers should only make local wines. Cima decided to strike out on his own by producing fine wines that were new for the Massa area but could express the potential of the terroir. The wine we were most struck by was his Merlot, the Montervo '98, which had dazzling success at our tastings and cast many much better known bottles into the shade. The colour is extremely vivid and the intense nose, which is still developing, promises lashings of fruit and spicy notes. The palate is full, rich and concentrated, with tannins and oak very well-integrated. The powerful, unflagging dynamism of the palate powers through to a long finish, where a faint vegetal tone manages to emerge. An unusual blend of sangiovese and massaretta goes into the Romalbo, another extremely interesting wine. Concentrated and full-bodied, it takes full advantage of its cask conditioning and the flavour, if somewhat predictable, is out of the top drawer. The Sangiovese '98, a solid red with admirable grip, needs perhaps a little fine-tuning to shake off its modest oak-derived excesses. The three whites are equally successful. Superbly managed, they are beautifully underpinned by fruit and can offer a fair measure of personality, particularly the two Candias.

●	Lunaia Rosso '97	ΨΨ	3*
○	Bianco di Pitigliano Lunaia '99	Ψ	3
○	Bianco di Pitigliano Lunaia '93	ΨΨ	3*
○	Bianco di Pitigliano Lunaia '92	Ψ	3
○	Bianco di Pitigliano Lunaia '94	Ψ	2
○	Bianco di Pitigliano Lunaia '95	Ψ	3
○	Bianco di Pitigliano Lunaia '96	Ψ	3
○	Bianco di Pitigliano Lunaia '97	Ψ	3
○	Bianco di Pitigliano Lunaia '98	Ψ	3
●	Lunaia Rosso '93	Ψ	2

●	Montervo '98	ΨΨ	6
●	Romalbo '98	ΨΨ	6
●	Sangiovese '98	ΨΨ	5
○	Candia dei Colli Apuani '99	Ψ	4
○	Candia dei Colli Apuani Vigneto Candia Alto '99	Ψ	5
○	Vermentino '99	Ψ	4

MASSA MARITTIMA (GR)　　MASSA MARITTIMA (GR)

MASSA VECCHIA
PODERE FORNACE
LOC. ROCCHE, 11
58024 MASSA MARITTIMA (GR)
TEL. 0566/904144

MORIS FARMS
LOC. CURANUOVA
FATTORIA POGGETTI
58024 MASSA MARITTIMA (GR)
TEL. 0566/919135

Fabrizio Niccolaini's wines have their own very distinctive character. There is nothing routine about vinification procedures here. The technique at any given moment tends to reflect the producer's sensitivity and intuition. Nevertheless, this year's tastings showed a greater stylistic consistency throughout, which is partly due to a more measured use of wood. The most notable of the wines is the Cabernet Sauvignon, La Fonte di Pietrarsa, whose generous bouquet has wild black berries to the fore, vegetal undertones and hints of toasty oak. The palate reveals admirable body, a well-sustained, even development and good balance. The scrupulously extracted tannins are fine-grained, hence the wine is at once lively and mature, as well as very easy to drink. But some of the other bottles caught our attention, too. One such was the Monteregio Massavecchia, which made it to Two Glasses. The varied bouquet includes tobacco, autumn leaves, mild oaky notes and a grassy nuance. The soft, supple palate is lean, clean and thoroughly enjoyable. Character is what strikes you about the Matto delle Giuncaie, an aleatico which counters a slight rusticity, perceptible in a mildly bitter finish, with varietal subtlety, aromas of black cherry and spring flowers, and abundant sweet, succulent fruit on the palate. The fresh, appealing Patrizia Bartolini '98 is a late-vintage Sauvignon with an intense fruit and flower nose and a balanced but fairly unexciting palate. Lastly, the Terziere, an alicante, is a bit forward but definitely characterful.

If you travel north from Grosseto on the Via Aurelia, just before Follonica you'll find a view worthy of a Renaissance master. The lovely hill that appears on the Moris Farms label has the estate's splendid vineyards running across its central strip. But it is at Poggio a La Mozza, near Scansano, that the grapes don't seem to need much persuasion from the excellent Adolfo Parentini, who is assisted by experts Attilio Pagli, in the cellar, and Andrea Paoletti, among the vines. The Avvoltore '98, still their top wine, gathered up Two Glasses so easily that it seems pretty likely to make it to Three with the '99. The dark ruby hue has lustrous highlights and offers ripe aromas of cherry, bramble and prune. After a decisive attack, well supported by acid backbone, the palate reveals firm, ripe tannins, good weight and integrated oak. The very fine Morellino Riserva '98 is a Two Glass regular. We found an original note of sage over the perfectly ripe berry fruit background. The entry on the palate is attractively soft, the tannins are ripe and the balance exemplary. The Morellino '99 needs time to settle down. Forward tones on the nose lead in to a bright, roughish palate with sure-footed progression and a consistent finish. The estate also produces the agreeable Massa Marittima Monteregio.

● Il Matto delle Giuncaie '98	▼▼	4
● La Fonte di Pietrarsa '97	▼▼	5
● Monteregio di Massa Marittima '97	▼▼	4
○ Patrizia Bartolini '98	▼	4
● Terziere '97	▼	4
● Il Matto delle Giuncaie '97	♀♀	4
● La Fonte di Pietrarsa '93	♀♀	4
● La Fonte di Pietrarsa '94	♀♀	4
● La Fonte di Pietrarsa '95	♀♀	4
● La Fonte di Pietrarsa '96	♀♀	4
● Terziere '93	♀♀	4
● Le Veglie di Neri '90	♀	4
● Terziere '96	♀	4

● Avvoltore '98	▼▼	5
● Morellino di Scansano Ris. '98	▼▼	4
● Morellino di Scansano '99	▼	2*
● Avvoltore '94	♀♀	5
● Avvoltore '95	♀♀	5
● Avvoltore '97	♀♀	5
● Morellino di Scansano Ris. '94	♀♀	4
● Morellino di Scansano Ris. '97	♀♀	4
● Avvoltore '93	♀	5
● Morellino di Scansano '94	♀	2*
● Morellino di Scansano '95	♀	2*
● Morellino di Scansano '98	♀	2*
● Morellino di Scansano Ris. '93	♀	4

MATRAIA (LU)

MERCATALE VAL DI PESA (FI)

FATTORIA COLLE VERDE
LOC. CASTELLO
55010 MATRAIA (LU)
TEL. 0583/402310

ISPOLI
VIA SANTA LUCIA, 2
50024 MERCATALE VAL DI PESA (FI)
TEL. 055/821613

Fattoria Colle Verde is run by a very dynamic duo. Francesca Pardini devotes her energies to the field of wine tourism, that fast-growing leisure industry phenomenon, while Piero Tartagni is continues to explore the possibilities of the most promising local grape varieties. In fact, the already extensive range of Colle Verde wines has been expanded further with the arrival of the Nero della Spinosa '98, a monovarietal Syrah that picked up Two Glasses on its first time out. The colour is extraordinarily concentrated and the very intense nose with sweet notes of blackberry and blackcurrant jam and bonbons. In the mouth, it is soft, spicy and well-balanced, with still young but ripe tannins, a powerful structure and a long finish. The estate classics, on the other hand, seemed a little under par, especially given the expectations we had for the '97 vintage. The Brania delle Ghiandaie '97, made from sangiovese with a touch of syrah, didn't make it past One Glass. The initially reticent nose takes its time to open, and is weighed down by over-evolved notes. The palate shows some body but the soft attack soon fades into a dry, rough finish. The Terre di Matraja Rosso '98 also has super-ripe notes on the nose and the palate is rather lightweight. Moving on to the whites, the Brania del Cancello '98 has substance but it's going through a slightly inscrutable phase at the moment while the Terre di Matraja Bianco '98 offers attractive aromas of yellow rose and muscat grape, followed by a crisply attractive and well-managed palate. Lastly, we found the Greco delle Gaggie '96, a Grechetto, to be very enjoyable with its intense bouquet of peach jam, sultana and dried fig, and sweet, warm, mouth-filling palate.

After a fine Guide debut last year, this little estate near Mercatale has confirmed our high opinion. A white and a rosé have extended the range of wines but it would seem from the tastings that they should be concentrating on reds. The Chianti Classico '98 looks rich and intense. Its warm bright ruby introduces initial gamey and vegetal aromas that are not entirely clean but these are soon joined by attractively crisp, ripe fruit notes of cherry and plum. The clean, rich palate reveals its enticing succulence straight away and alcohol keeps the tannins in check through to the delicious, rising finish. The Riserva '97 confirms that the vintage was a good one. It flaunts its considerable depth right away in its purple-tinged ruby. Then very ripe, lively fruit blends with subtle, elegant notes of vanilla and toasty oak on the nose. On the palate, it is wonderfully creamy, concentrated and rounded, with a firm but soft body. The Ispolaia is an acceptable rosé with a cherry-red hue and a fresh fragrance of violets and cherries. The weight is good, the finish fair. The Chardonnay '99's golden hue could be a little clearer but the fruity aromas of apple and pineapple, although not very intense, have style. On the front palate, it is medium-bodied and the faint but noticeable prickle should disappear after a few months in the bottle.

O	Greco delle Gaggìe '96	🍷🍷	5
●	Nero della Spinosa '98	🍷🍷	5
O	Brania del Cancello '98	🍷	4
O	Colline Lucchesi Bianco Terre di Matraja '98	🍷	3
●	Colline Lucchesi Rosso Brania delle Ghiandaie '97	🍷	5
●	Colline Lucchesi Rosso Terre di Matraja '98		3
O	Brania del Cancello '97	🍷🍷	4
●	Colline Lucchesi Rosso Brania delle Ghiandaie '95	🍷🍷	4
●	Colline Lucchesi Rosso Brania delle Ghiandaie '96	🍷🍷	4

●	Chianti Classico '98	🍷🍷	3*
●	Chianti Classico Ris. '97	🍷🍷	4
O	Chardonnay '99	🍷	3
⊙	Ispolaia '99	🍷	3
●	Chianti Classico '97	🍷🍷	3*
●	Ispolaia '96	🍷🍷	4

MERCATALE VALDARNO (AR) MERCATALE VALDARNO (AR)

PODERE IL CARNASCIALE
LOC. SAN LEONINO, 82
52020 MERCATALE VALDARNO (AR)
TEL. 055/9911142

FATTORIA PETROLO
LOC. GALATRONA
VIA PETROLO, 30
52020 MERCATALE VALDARNO (AR)
TEL. 055/9911322 - 055/992965

Of course, this property is light years away from those gargantuan estates that churn out hundreds of thousands, if not millions, of bottles of dozens of different wines. But even small producers might learn something from the oenological conscientiousness of Podere Il Carnasciale, which makes only one wine. A great one, we should add. It is called Caberlot, and is available exclusively in magnums. If we really wanted to nit-pick, we might express some reservations about the name. But in every other respect, bar none, it is absolutely first class. For a start, yields in the tiny vineyard, which covers just half a hectare, are so limited that they don't reach 800 grams of fruit per vine. The grape variety is not a cross. It's a genetic mutation of cabernet that has some of the characteristics of merlot – hence the wine's not entirely convincing name. Scrupulous, indeed impeccable, cellar technique does the rest. The result is a splendid red wine that combines power and elegance. The ruby colour is flecked with brilliant highlights and introduces well-defined aromas of bramble, blackcurrant and bitter chocolate. After a lively, well-focused attack, with ripe berry fruit to the fore, the palate opens up into an incredible range of flavours, with remarkably elegant woody tones and a subtle mineral nuance. It is, in short, an excellent wine. So, where are its Three Glasses? As we said last year, they still make too little of it to win our highest award. But in a few years' time the vineyard, and hence the number of bottles, should be larger. Meanwhile, we live in hope.

Tasting the Sanjust family's wines over the last few years makes it clear that there has been constant growth and improvement. Essentially, the strong, genuine (but also brusque) character that was their trademark has not been lost but the Sanjusts have succeeded in moulding the natural energy of their terroir into more graceful forms. And indeed their Sangiovese, the Torrione '98, with its rich and captivating structure, has shed its customary rough edges. It is now a concentrated wine with compelling progression, great balance and plenty of appeal. Only in the finish do some vegetal nuances emerge, and a certain lack of complexity. This is not a problem in the Galatrona '98, once again a very great wine. Like any good Merlot, it is easy to makes friends with and shows a remarkable expansiveness on the palate. What this grape often needs is more of a bite and less softness so that the terroir can emerge to lift it out of anonymity. And the Galatrona succeeds admirably. It has soft roundness but adds great intensity and nice tension on the palate, in a solid tannic structure. The very good Torrione '97 boasts considerable energy, underpinned by powerful tannins and a fine finish. The nose is less expressive since there is rather too much oak-derived sweetness. The Terre di Galatrona, regarded as the runt of the litter, doesn't do at all badly, despite being obtained from second selection sangiovese and merlot grapes. The nose alternates between vegetal nuances and ripe black fruit. In the mouth, it may not be very full-bodied but it is undeniably clean and enjoyable.

● Caberlot '97	ŸŸ	6
● Caberlot '96	ŸŸ	6

● Galatrona '98	ŸŸŸ	6
● Torrione '97	ŸŸ	5
● Torrione '98	ŸŸ	5
● Terre di Galatrona '98	Ÿ	4
● Galatrona '97	ŸŸŸ	6
● Galatrona '95	ŸŸ	6
● Torrione '90	ŸŸ	5
● Torrione '94	ŸŸ	5
● Torrione '95	ŸŸ	5
○ Vin Santo '93	ŸŸ	5
● Chianti Titolato '90	Ÿ	2*
● Terre di Galatrona '97	Ÿ	4
● Torrione '91	Ÿ	5
● Torrione '93	Ÿ	5
● Torrione '96	Ÿ	5

426

MONTALCINO (SI)

MONTALCINO (SI)

ALTESINO
LOC. ALTESINO
53024 MONTALCINO (SI)
TEL. 0577/806208

TENUTA DI ARGIANO
LOC. S. ANGELO IN COLLE, 54
53020 MONTALCINO (SI)
TEL. 0577/844037

The Altesino reds have bounced right back. In last year's Guide, they were overshadowed by the excellent Vin Santo, which was not released this time. But now three wines earned Two Glasses each, testifying to the potential and high general quality of an estate that is, incidentally, quite enchanting and definitely worth the detour (it's a few kilometres from the main road). In the cellar are barrels of various sizes and an imposing display of barriques. The Brunello Montosoli '95 faithfully reflects the characteristics of its terroir and of a vintage whose qualities were certainly exaggerated. The colour is an intense, brilliant ruby that stays firm almost to the rim. The wine needs breathing time before it will release its classic aromas of black cherry and blackberry, which for the time being have still to amalgamate with the oak-derived notes. The density of flavour and weight on the palate are surprisingly good, given that the number one priority at Montosoli is elegance rather than power. And in fact, a typically elegant tang of acidity blends nicely with the fruit. The Brunello '95 is equally impressive, although its characteristics differ. It, too, needs to breathe for a while to unfurl its bouquet of liqueur cherries and hints of vanilla. Prominent acidity and tannins on the palate do not seriously disrupt the general harmony. Of their other wines, we very much liked the Alte di Altesi '97, with its balsamic and spicy aromas and good weight on the palate. The Quarto d'Altesi '97 has noticeable grassy aromas and gets One Glass and the Borgo d'Altesi, with its rather unfocused nose, is worth only a mention.

It came as no surprise that the '98 wines were not as good as the '97s. Everything was pointing that way. But to find Argiano's '98 Solengo on a par with the year's generally modest results did throw us somewhat. After the triumphant performance of the '97 Solengo, which won high praise and Three Glasses, the '98 is rather subdued. It displays an attractive deep ruby hue with brilliant highlights and the initial fruit-rich aromas are well-defined, with prominent oak and lactic nuances that diminish the freshness of the bouquet. In the mouth, it shows good body, bright notes of new oak and a moderately long finish. A good wine, but one that reflects the limitations of its vintage. The Brunello di Montalcino '95 is more convincing. It has a fairly rich ruby hue and a clean fruity fragrance, although the fruit in question is still simple and grapey. It should develop further, though, and the attractive supporting alcohol is firm. The palate opens with notes of ripe berry fruit, progressing well with appropriate weight on the mid palate, finishing with the support of only moderately robust but quite fine-grained tannins. We conclude in a minor key with the '98 Rosso di Montalcino. Essentially well-managed, it is simply not up to the great traditions of Argiano.

● Alte d'Altesi '97	ŸŸ	5
● Brunello di Montalcino '95	ŸŸ	6
● Brunello di Montalcino Montosoli '95	ŸŸ	6
● Quarto d'Altesi '97	Ÿ	5
● Borgo d'Altesi '97		4
● Rosso di Altesino '98		3
● Brunello di Montalcino '93	ŸŸ	5
● Brunello di Montalcino Montosoli '93	ŸŸ	6
● Brunello di Montalcino Ris. '88	ŸŸ	6
● Brunello di Montalcino Ris. '90	ŸŸ	6
● Quarto d'Altesi '95	ŸŸ	6
○ Vin Santo '94	ŸŸ	6
● Alte d'Altesi '96	Ÿ	5
● Brunello di Montalcino '94	Ÿ	6
● Brunello di Montalcino Ris. '93	Ÿ	6

● Brunello di Montalcino '95	ŸŸ	6
● Solengo '98	ŸŸ	6
● Rosso di Montalcino '98		3
● Brunello di Montalcino Ris. '85	ŸŸŸ	5
● Brunello di Montalcino Ris. '88	ŸŸŸ	6
● Solengo '95	ŸŸŸ	6
● Solengo '97	ŸŸŸ	6
● Brunello di Montalcino '88	ŸŸ	5
● Brunello di Montalcino '90	ŸŸ	5
● Brunello di Montalcino '92	ŸŸ	6
● Brunello di Montalcino '93	ŸŸ	6
● Brunello di Montalcino '94	ŸŸ	6
● Brunello di Montalcino Ris. '90	ŸŸ	6
● Brunello di Montalcino Ris. '91	ŸŸ	6
● Solengo '96	ŸŸ	6

MONTALCINO (SI)

★ CASTELLO BANFI
CASTELLO DI POGGIO ALLE MURA
53024 MONTALCINO (SI)
TEL. 0577/840111

MONTALCINO (SI)

FATTORIA DEI BARBI
LOC. PODERNOVI
53024 MONTALCINO (SI)
TEL. 0577/841111

While awaiting the arrival of a successor to Pablo Harri, who left his post as technical director quite a few months ago, the world-famous Banfi estate is not just marking time. The general level of their wines has not fallen away but that is the least we could have expected from the well-oiled machine behind this major oenological designer label. We'll start with a star, the Three-Glass Summus '97, obtained from sangiovese, syrah and cabernet sauvignon. One outstanding merit is its extremely skilful use of wood, which contributes clean and exquisitely balsamic nuances. A dark ruby hue introduces notes of bramble, white pepper and oriental spices on the nose, followed by a close-knit, full palate with well-balanced tannins. Its stablemate, the Excelsus '97, is balanced and full-bodied but on the same level. A Bordeaux blend, it has a soft, grassy palate with nice freshness and reasonable length. The Brunello di Montalcino '95 is drinking deliciously now. The nose is has still to develop completely but has intense, fruity aromas reminiscent of candied peel. On the palate, it offers robust structure, ripe tannins and a long finish. The Rosso di Montalcino '98 is equally successful, with its rich extract, crisp nose of wild berries and round, fruity palate. The '98 Centine, a house classic, did quite well, although it trailed behind the previous wine by a few points. A very soft, round, clean wine, it reveals hints of super-ripeness. Three '97s, the Tavernelle (cabernet), Mandrielle (merlot) and Colvecchio (syrah), are similar in style, proffering clean aromas, balance, nice wood and good fruit. The whites are, as usual, well-made but they tend to be less exciting than the reds.

The varied range of wines presented by this historic Montalcino estate was a little uneven this year. Some Fattoria dei Barbi wines were much more than just correctly executed, showing expressive power and personality, but others were less impressive. This inconsistency is partly explained by the difference in price between the premium range and the standard-label wines. We still feel that they could do more, however. To get down to specifics, the Brunello di Montalcino '95 has an attractive ruby hue with fair depth and the aromas, if somewhat reticent at the moment, are intense. The full-bodied palate, after a slightly acidic attack, offers a mildly super-ripe mid palate and a long finish. They have done better, as is only right, with the special selection from the same vintage, the Vigna del Fiore. A ruby colour with garnet highlights introduces forward notes of cherry jam with nuances of tar and liquorice on the nose. The palate reveals noble alcohol, depth, slightly rough tannins, firm texture and good length. The winery also presented a Brunello Riserva '94, which is actually rather disappointing. The nose is muddled and the palate disjointed. The medium-bodied Rosso di Montalcino '98 offers fairly indistinct fruit aromas and a reasonably well-knit, moderately persistent palate with a tendency to super-ripeness. The more composed Brigante dei Barbi '96 is succulent, already offering rich evolved notes of rain-soaked earth and tobacco, and agreeably tannic on the palate. Finally, the panel thought Brusco dei Barbi '98 was well-made but a little heavy on the oak.

● Summus '97	▼▼▼	6
● Brunello di Montalcino '95	▼▼	5
● Colvecchio '97	▼▼	4
● Mandrielle Merlot '97	▼▼	4
● Rosso di Montalcino '98	▼▼	4
● Tavernelle '97	▼▼	4
● Toscana Centine '98	▼▼	4
○ Sant'Antimo Fontanelle '98	▼	4
○ Sant'Antimo Serena '98	▼	4
● Brunello di Montalcino Poggio all'Oro Ris. '90	♟♟♟	6
● Brunello di Montalcino Poggio all'Oro Ris. '93	♟♟♟	6
● Excelsus '93	♟♟♟	6
● Summus '95	♟♟♟	6

● Brunello di Montalcino Vigna del Fiore Ris. '95	▼▼	6
● Brigante dei Barbi '96	▼	5
● Brunello di Montalcino '95	▼	5
● Rosso di Montalcino '98	▼	5
● Brusco dei Barbi '98		3
● Brunello di Montalcino '93	♟♟	5
● Brunello di Montalcino Vigna del Fiore Ris. '88	♟♟	6
● Brunello di Montalcino Vigna del Fiore Ris. '91	♟♟	6
● Brunello di Montalcino Vigna del Fiore Ris. '93	♟♟	6
● Brunello di Montalcino Ris. '90	♟	6

MONTALCINO (SI)

MONTALCINO (SI)

BIONDI SANTI
VILLA GREPPO, 183
53024 MONTALCINO (SI)
TEL. 0577/848087

CANTINA DI MONTALCINO
LOC. VAL DI CAVA
53024 MONTALCINO (SI)
TEL. 0577/848704

This profile will consider all the wines marketed by Biondi Santi. These include not only the historic Il Greppo and Poggio Salvi labels but also a group of non-DOC wines that are the fruit of collaboration between Jacopo Biondi Santi and Vittorio Fiore. This year's big news is that Jacopo Biondi Santi has acquired an estate in the Morellino di Scansano zone, with headquarters in the castle of Montepò. The two Il Greppo wines presented at our tastings were the Brunello '95 and the Rosso di Montalcino '96. The former is, of course, rigorously traditional. Its ruby hue is shot with garnet and the nose offers notes of cherry and tobacco, although not very deep, while the palate alternates acidity and tannins, rather at the expense of glycerine and alcohol. The Rosso di Montalcino '96 has intense, rather austere, aromas and a fairly close-knit, very drinkable palate. The Brunello Poggio Salvi '95 nearly won Two Glasses. Its vivid ruby hue shows, after initial indecision, a bouquet of black cherry and redcurrant. The palate comes in with a soft attack, then unveils abundant tannins. The fruity and highly drinkable Rosso di Montalcino '98 did equally well. The Montepaone, from cabernet, is good but not outstanding. The aromas are clean, if not fully expressed, and the well-knit palate boasts well-behaved tannins that make the wine very quaffable. The much-publicized Schidione '97 is available only in magnums sporting gold labels but it is so hard to get your hands on that we shall refrain from reviewing it. A solid Two Glasses go to the '95 version of the same wine and the rest of the range is well-managed.

The Cantina di Montalcino is the only wine co-operative in this area. The grapes brought in by member growers are assessed on the basis of physical and chemical parameters, and paid for accordingly. The price varies from 20% above to 20% below the going market rates. This would appear to be a very good system and has been used with success by the co-operatives of Alto Adige. The barrel stock comprises medium to large-sized casks acquired fairly recently but fermentation takes place in temperature-controlled stainless steel vats. The wines are traditional in style, and the Brunello di Montalcino '95 had no trouble picking up its Two Glasses. It is technically well-made in all respects, which says a lot for the winery's cellar technique. The colour is an attractive, fairly vivid ruby, and the well-defined fruit on the nose includes distinct notes of morello and wild cherries that are pervasive, persistent and clean. Muscle is not the strong suit of this Brunello but it has great elegance on the palate, which has fine-grained tannins and no rough edges or hints of bitterness. The Rosso di Montalcino '98 is good albeit, as might be expected, simpler. The ruby hue shades into garnet at the rim, introducing a nose of some complexity, with aromas of cherry and very well-balanced oaky tones. It's extremely smooth in the mouth and the slightly bitter note on the finish in no way detracts from the overall harmony.

●	Brunello di Montalcino '95	🍷🍷	6
●	Schidione '95	🍷🍷	6
●	Brunello di Montalcino Poggio Salvi '95	🍷	6
●	Lavischio Poggio Salvi '96	🍷	4
●	Montepaone '97	🍷	4
●	Rosso di Montalcino '96	🍷	5
●	Rosso di Montalcino Poggio Salvi '98	🍷	4
●	Aurico '96	🍷🍷	6
●	Brunello di Montalcino '94	🍷🍷	6
●	Sassoalloro '95	🍷🍷	5
●	Sassoalloro '96	🍷🍷	5
●	Schidione '94	🍷🍷	6

●	Brunello di Montalcino '95	🍷🍷	6
●	Rosso di Montalcino '98	🍷	4
●	Brunello di Montalcino '93	🍷🍷	6
●	Rosso di Montalcino '96	🍷	4

MONTALCINO (SI)

MONTALCINO (SI)

TENUTA CAPARZO
LOC. CAPARZO
S. P. DEL BRUNELLO KM 1,700
53024 MONTALCINO (SI)
TEL. 0577/848390 - 0577/847166

CASANOVA DI NERI
LOC. CASANOVA
53024 MONTALCINO (SI)
TEL. 0577/834455 - 0577/834029

As usual, we bring you a very favourable report on this solid Montalcino winery, expertly managed by Nuccio Turone with the assistance, for technical matters, of the distinguished oenologist Vittorio Fiore. Every year, Caparzo delivers consistent reliability throughout its range. The number of Glasses awarded may vary from year to year but all the wines are at the very least well-made. Some 22 hectares planted to brunello around the Montalcino area allow the estate to harvest at different times, thus reducing the risk damage to the crop from bad weather. The vineyards are situated in part near the winery itself, hence to the north of Montalcino, and in part in two celebrated crus, Montosoli, which supplies the Brunello La Casa, and Castelgiocondo in the south west. High marks for the Brunello Riserva '94. Despite the poorly regarded vintage, this is a wine with distinct personality and indeed, it is right at the top of its category. The bouquet is rich and well-defined, releasing notes of cocoa, berry fruit and black cherry jam, with a well-integrated note of oak. On the palate, there is a decisive attack, good extract and fine-grained tannins. The panel found the estate's flagship bottle, the Brunello La Casa '95, equally successful. An extremely elegant wine, it unfolds with ripe tannins and good progression on the palate. The finish, although incisive, does not show any great depth. The other Caparzo wines all earned One Glass. We would like to point out the Caparzo Bianco and the Caparzo Rosso, both of which are very quaffable and very attractively priced.

Giacomo Neri's Cerretalto '95 is the best Brunello the panel has tasted in recent years. It is a glorious example, with all the finest features of the category. A powerful, generous wine with an imperious attack and a vitality that it only just manages to keep under control, it unveils generous tannins that are incisive but never aggressive. They back up the impact of the alcohol to carry the palate through to a long finish which releases intense notes of spice, liquorice, black cherry and toasty oak blending with mineral nuances. These Three Glasses prompt us to wonder, regretfully, why more people in Montalcino don't emulate Giacomo Neri by favouring real crus over Riservas, and also why the DOC regulations here specify the minimum length of barrel ageing required instead of leaving it to the producer to decide, vintage by vintage, how long each wine should spend in oak. Neri's other cru, the Tenuta Nuova, came within an ace of Three Glasses with its young, lively fruit and rich, close-knit, beautifully balanced palate. The very good Rosso di Montalcino '98 has an immediately seductive nose of black berry fruit, spice and pepper that stand out thanks to the exemplary cleanness of the wine. The palate is firm and alluring, although the profuse tannins tend to close the finish. A notch or two below, but still very respectable, is Neri's standard Brunello, which offers good ripe fruit with woody notes on the nose. The medium-bodied palate is ever so slightly grassy on the finish.

● Brunello di Montalcino La Casa '95	♟♟	6
● Brunello di Montalcino Ris. '94	♟♟	6
● Brunello di Montalcino '95	♟	6
● Ca' del Pazzo '96	♟	5
○ Caparzo Bianco '98	♟	3
● Caparzo Rosso '98	♟	3
○ Moscadello V. T. '97	♟	5
● Rosso di Montalcino '98	♟	4
● Brunello di Montalcino La Casa '88	♟♟♟	6
● Brunello di Montalcino La Casa '93	♟♟♟	6
● Brunello di Montalcino '93	♟♟	6
● Brunello di Montalcino La Casa '91	♟♟	5
● Brunello di Montalcino La Casa '94	♟♟	6
● Brunello di Montalcino Ris. '88	♟♟	6
● Brunello di Montalcino Ris. '93	♟♟	6

● Brunello di Montalcino Cerretalto '95	♟♟♟	6
● Brunello di Montalcino Tenuta Nuova '95	♟♟	6
● Rosso di Montalcino '98	♟♟	4
● Brunello di Montalcino '95	♟	5
● Brunello di Montalcino '90	♟♟	5
● Brunello di Montalcino '93	♟♟	5
● Brunello di Montalcino Cerretalto Ris. '93	♟♟	6
● Brunello di Montalcino Tenuta Nuova '93	♟♟	6
● Brunello di Montalcino Tenuta Nuova '94	♟♟	6

MONTALCINO (SI)

MONTALCINO (SI)

FATTORIA DEL CASATO
DONATELLA CINELLI COLOMBINI
LOC. CASATO PRIME DONNE
53024 MONTALCINO (SI)
TEL. 0577/849421

CASTELGIOCONDO
LOC. CASTELGIOCONDO
53024 MONTALCINO (SI)
TEL. 055/27141

Donatella Cinelli Colombini presented another fine range of wines this year. The estate is a young one but it profits from the great experience of its owner, so these wines have personality. The two Brunellos she released did very well. We preferred the standard Brunello to the Brunello Prime Donne, so named because the final blend is decided by a group of female tasters. The Brunello Prime Donne '95 has a lustrous, limpid ruby colour. We noted a slight over-abundance of oak-derived tones on the nose, where notes of caramel and toastiness partly submerge the aromas of ripe berry fruit that are fighting to get out. However, time should improve the balance. The palate is more successful, with its firm attack and nicely amalgamated tannins. The beautifully executed, harmonious Brunello '95 is more immediately appealing. A luminous ruby hue introduces its varied range of pervasive aromas, including varietal notes of both wild and morello cherries. The juicy palate is balanced and supple, with remarkably smooth tannins ensuring good thrust through to the long, coherent finish. The Rosso di Montalcino '98, also very good, has a fairly intense ruby hue with purple highlights. The nose offers varietal notes of black and red cherries that lead in to a satisfyingly rich, close-knit palate that drinks very easily and ends on a good rising finish.

The average grower in Montalcino has nothing like ten hectares of DOCG-registered vineyards. In such a fragmented mosaic, the extensive Brunello holdings of Castelgiocondo stand out like a beacon. What with large vineyards and smaller plots, the estate has a total of 134 hectares and it all belongs to the Frescobaldis, relative newcomers from Florence who began making wine here as recently as six or seven hundred years ago. The range presented this year includes some very characterful bottles but there is nothing that is less than well-managed and technically irreproachable. As usual, we'll start with the very successful Brunello di Montalcino '95. It has a particularly vivid ruby colour and a classic nose of bay leaves, violet and black cherry, together with nuances of caramel and new oak. The attack on the palate is firm and succulent, although there is a little hesitation due to sulphur dioxide, leading to a robust, tannic mid palate and a long finish. The panel thought Brunello Riserva '93 was a little shakier. The nose is a tad unfocused and the moderately structured palate is underpinned more by warm alcohol than an abundance of fruit. But things looked up again when we moved on to estate's Merlot, the '97 Lamaione, which unveils a very intense ruby hue with brilliant highlights. The nose has rich fruit that embraces ripe mulberry, redcurrant and bilberry with inviting secondary aromas of cocoa and pencil lead. There is good weight and balance on the broad, generous, soft palate, where the tightly-packed tannins will need time to mellow.

● Brunello di Montalcino '95	♟♟	6
● Brunello di Montalcino Prime Donne '95	♟♟	6
● Rosso di Montalcino '98	♟♟	4
● Brunello di Montalcino '93	♟♟	5
● Brunello di Montalcino Prime Donne '93	♟♟	6
● Brunello di Montalcino Prime Donne '94	♟♟	6
● Brunello di Montalcino '94	♟	6
● Leone Rosso '98	♟	4

● Brunello di Montalcino '95	♟♟	5
● Lamaione '97	♟♟	5
● Brunello di Montalcino Ris. '93	♟	6
● Brunello di Montalcino Ris. '88	♟♟♟	6
● Brunello di Montalcino Ris. '90	♟♟♟	6
● Brunello di Montalcino '93	♟♟	5
● Brunello di Montalcino '91	♟♟	5
● Lamaione '91	♟♟	5
● Lamaione '92	♟♟	5
● Lamaione '94	♟♟	5
● Lamaione '95	♟♟	5
● Lamaione '96	♟♟	5
● Rosso di Montalcino Campo ai Sassi '97	♟♟	4

MONTALCINO (SI)

MONTALCINO (SI)

CENTOLANI
LOC. FRIGGIALI
53024 MONTALCINO (SI)
TEL. 0577/849358 - 0577/849454

CIACCI PICCOLOMINI D'ARAGONA
LOC. CASTELNUOVO DELL'ABATE
B.GO DI MEZZO, 62
53024 MONTALCINO (SI)
TEL. 0577/835616

The Centolani estate has two properties at Montalcino. One is the main estate, Friggiali, and the other is near Castelnuovo dell'Abate. It is here, at the foot of Velona castle, that Centolani has 15 hectares planted to brunello, and where recently some four hectares planted to other varieties, such as merlot and petit verdot, have come on-stream. The cellar turns out two Brunellos and two Rosso di Montalcinos. Both of the '95 Brunellos won Two Glasses, although our preference was very much for the Pietranera. It has an intense ruby colour that stays firm up to the rim, then the broad nose unveils notes of chocolate and berry fruit, with very ripe black cherry and wild cherry to the fore. The admirably balanced palate, with the tannins well integrated into the texture, progresses nicely to a mouth-filling finish. The other Brunello '95 has a different personality. The fruit is less evident on the nose as it is upstaged by wood, and the texture of the palate is insufficient to cover the tannins, which consequently make the finish a bit inflexible. The two Rosso di Montalcinos are very similar and each gets One Glass. They are both a little slow to open on the nose, where they also reveal signs of development, including notes of tobacco and caramel. Both put the emphasis on immediate quaffability but the Friggiali is a little more refreshing.

We are very pleased to welcome Ciacci Piccolomini back to a full profile in the Guide. This year's range was convincing proof that they are making up for lost time, in terms both of the definition of individual wines' aromas and of the overall quality of the entire range. We'll start with the fine Brunello di Montalcino Pianrosso, a local classic. The '95 has an attractive ruby hue and clean aromas that range from wild cherry and damson fruit to alcohol-rich notes. The palate is succulent and full-bodied although the fruit at the moment rather vinous and unexciting. It will benefit from further evolution. Solid tannins back up the firm finish. The Rosso di Montalcino Vigna della Fonte '98 is a little less successful. The varietal notes of bay leaf, violet and black cherry are well-defined on the nose but the flavour is a bit vegetal and the tannins lack subtlety. Things look up again with the '97 Ateo, made from sangiovese with just a little cabernet and merlot. A very vivid ruby colour introduces intensely fruity aromas with distinct notes of new oak, and a rich, full-bodied, robustly tannic palate. But the red that struck us most – and we say this at the risk of being accused yet again of preferring the innovative to the traditional – is the syrah-based Sant'Antimo, Fabius. True, it is lavish with its oak-derived notes but they are harnessed to a firm, well-controlled structure, not massive but rich in extract. This is a juicy, ripe and very fruity wine with elegant, smooth tannins. Congratulations are in order.

● Brunello di Montalcino '95	🍷🍷	5
● Brunello di Montalcino Pietranera '95	🍷🍷	6
● Rosso di Montalcino '98	🍷	4
● Rosso di Montalcino Pietranera '98	🍷	4
● Brunello di Montalcino '90	🍷🍷	5
● Brunello di Montalcino '93	🍷🍷	5
● Brunello di Montalcino Pietranera '93	🍷🍷	6
● Brunello di Montalcino Pietranera '94	🍷🍷	6
● Pietrafocaia '95	🍷🍷	5
● Rosso di Montalcino '93	🍷🍷	3*
● Rosso di Montalcino '97	🍷	4
● Rosso di Montalcino Pietranera '97	🍷	4

● Ateo '97	🍷🍷	5
● Brunello di Montalcino Vigna di Pianrosso '95	🍷🍷	6
● Sant'Antimo Fabius '98	🍷🍷	6
● Rosso di Montalcino Vigna della Fonte '98	🍷	5
● Brunello di Montalcino Vigna di Pianrosso '88	🍷🍷🍷	6
● Brunello di Montalcino Vigna di Pianrosso '90	🍷🍷🍷	5
● Brunello di Montalcino '85	🍷🍷	5
● Brunello di Montalcino Ris. '88	🍷🍷	6
● Rosso di Montalcino '90	🍷🍷	4
● Rosso di Montalcino Vigna della Fonte '95	🍷🍷	4

MONTALCINO (SI)

MONTALCINO (SI)

TENUTA COL D'ORCIA
LOC. S. ANGELO IN COLLE
53020 MONTALCINO (SI)
TEL. 0577/808001

ANDREA COSTANTI
LOC. COLLE AL MATRICHESE
53024 MONTALCINO (SI)
TEL. 0577/848195

While we wait to see what the Banditella cru has in store – it is one of the highest-density vineyards in Montalcino – Col d'Orcia has presented a carefully made, very quaffable range of good-quality wines. The cornerstone is, of course, their Brunello di Montalcino and the '95 is a sound wine, although from such a hyped-up vintage one might have expected a richer bouquet and palate. The ruby colour is moderately intense, with not very brilliant highlights. At first, the nose is a little muffled and indistinct but after a few minutes' aeration, it releases nuances of candied peel and liqueur cherries. There is good weight on the palate, the fruit is fair, the acidity slightly excessive and the finish long, neat and alcohol-rich. We'll skip the Rosso di Montalcino '98, which was not presented for the simple reason that all the stocks have already been sold. Next came the Rosso degli Spezieri '99, a blend of sangiovese, ciliegiolo and malvasia nera, plus a little recently planted merlot, which we found uncomplicated and attractive. A refreshing, alcohol-rich wine, it has good fruit and an easy drinkability. One of the estate's fortes is its Moscadello Pascena. The '97 version is clean and soft, with generous notes of tropical fruit. It may perhaps be a bit unexciting but it does have flavour. We'll finish with the Sant'Antimo Pinot Grigio '99, an interesting experiment which has produced a fairly one-dimensional result. It is very clean and well-made, though.

This year's news at Andrea Costanti's winery – a Guide regular from the first edition – is that there is a new vinification area, temperature-controlled throughout, that is quite separate from the old cellar. The wines presented at our tasting this time show definite progress and the Brunello di Montalcino '95 easily picked up Two Glasses. Its intense, limpid ruby heralds a fruity nose of wild and morello cherries with marked oak-derived aromas that never threaten to overwhelm the fruit. The palate is decently extracted, with a positive attack and very fine-grained tannins. It's an elegant wine, and well worth leaving in the cellar for a few years. This year Costanti is again offering a straight Rosso di Montalcino, the '98 –the entire '97 harvest having gone to make the Brunello – and it, too, gets high marks. The youthful notes of berry fruit mingle nicely with oak-derived tones on the well-balanced nose. Beautifully judged acidity on the palate sustains the body all the way through to the finish, making the wine deliciously quaffable. This is a red with attitude, true to its terroir, and thoroughly earned its Two Glasses. The other Rosso di Montalcino, the Calbello '98, displays notes of coffee and caramel that overshadow the nuances of raspberry. A medium-bodied tipple, it has a refreshing acid tang that makes it irresistibly quaffable.

● Brunello di Montalcino '95	♥♥	6
○ Moscadello di Montalcino		
Vendemmia Tardiva Pascena '97	♥♥	5
● Rosso degli Spezieri '99	♥	3
○ Sant'Antimo Pinot Grigio '99		3
● Brunello di Montalcino		
Poggio al Vento Ris. '85	♥♥♥	6
● Brunello di Montalcino		
Poggio al Vento Ris. '88	♥♥♥	6
● Brunello di Montalcino		
Poggio al Vento Ris. '90	♥♥♥	6
● Olmaia '94	♥♥♥	5
● Brunello di Montalcino		
Poggio al Vento Ris. '93	♥♥	6
● Olmaia '95	♥♥	6

● Brunello di Montalcino '95	♥♥	6
● Rosso di Montalcino '98	♥♥	4
● Rosso di Montalcino Calbello '98	♥	4
● Brunello di Montalcino '88	♥♥♥	6
● Brunello di Montalcino '85	♥♥	6
● Brunello di Montalcino '86	♥♥	6
● Brunello di Montalcino '87	♥♥	6
● Brunello di Montalcino '93	♥♥	6
● Brunello di Montalcino '90	♥♥	6
● Brunello di Montalcino '91	♥♥	6
● Brunello di Montalcino Ris. '83	♥♥	6
● Brunello di Montalcino Ris. '88	♥♥	6
● Brunello di Montalcino Ris. '90	♥♥	6
● Rosso di Montalcino '95	♥♥	4
● Brunello di Montalcino Ris. '93	♥	6

MONTALCINO (SI)

MONTALCINO (SI)

Due Portine - Gorelli
Via Cialdini, 51/53
53024 Montalcino (SI)
tel. 0577/848098

Fanti - La Palazzetta
Fraz. Castelnuovo dell'Abate
B.go di Sotto, 25
53020 Montalcino (SI)
tel. 0577/835631

Those who are familiar with the wines of Montalcino will not be surprised to find in this profile that the area's standard bearer, Brunello, plays second fiddle to reds that ought by rights to be altogether simpler. The reason (or reasons) is in part a mystery. Some distinguished wine connoisseurs blame the anachronistic inflexibility of the DOCG regulations, which prescribe a necessary minimum of barrel time. This period is, however, being slowly but inexorably pared down by the regulators themselves. Others suggest that yields are too high, while still others say that cellar technique is not all it should be. Whatever the reason, for Giuseppe Gorelli's excellent winery the least successful bottle is the Brunello. The '95 does not have any major defects for it is a well-made and very likeable red wine. It does, however, lack character, energy and a certain oomph in its aromas and extract (and it is by no means alone in this). The colour is a moderately intense ruby red, and the aromas are clean, if a little anaemic, with notes of sweet oak. The structure is fair, the mid palate reveals medicinal notes, and the finish is congenial but not exactly seductive. The Rosso di Montalcino '98 has a less complex nose but the palate is much more refreshingly fruity (no surprise there) and the overall balance is more convincing. It, too, gets One Glass, but with a better points rating. What we liked best of all was Gorelli's '98 Rosso di Montalcino Le Potazzine, which takes its name from the new vineyard that supplied the fruit. The impact on the nose is very sweet, thanks to rather marked but very well-handled wood. The palate is richly extracted, with a soft, meaty mid palate, underpinned by lovely acidity. It earned its Two Glasses very comfortably.

Flavio Fanti, the owner of this estate, is one of the most scrupulous grower-producers in Montalcino when it comes to managing his vine stock for quality. While many others are happy with the status quo in their vineyards – they'll have no trouble selling their wine anyway, they feel – Fanti has decided to increase the planting density on his new plots, which total five hectares, to 5,000 vines per hectare. Now we don't want to say that cramming more plants into a small space will necessarily make great wine but if more people in Montalcino followed Flavio's example, many struggling vineyards would enjoy a renaissance. Getting down to the results of our tastings, the first thing to say is that the Rosso di Montalcino has lost ground. This was on the cards because the '98 vintage can't hold a candle to the '97. The Rosso '98 has a lovely ruby hue, fairly muffled, unforthcoming aromas and a succulent, full-bodied palate with rather green tannins and acidity. The Brunello, in keeping with its rank and vintage – the over-hyped but frequently excellent '95 – is in another league. The colour is a full ruby with brilliant highlights and the swathe of aromas is pervasive but still a little closed and in need of further development, although liqueur cherries, jam and spice come through. The wine opens more positively on the full-bodied, balanced palate, where the tannins are a shade lacking in elegance. The long, clean finish is utterly coherent.

● Rosso di Montalcino		
Le Potazzine '98	🍷🍷	5
● Brunello di Montalcino '95	🍷	6
● Rosso di Montalcino '98	🍷	4
● Brunello di Montalcino '89	🍷🍷	6
● Brunello di Montalcino '90	🍷🍷	6
● Brunello di Montalcino '92	🍷🍷	6
● Brunello di Montalcino '93	🍷🍷	6
● Brunello di Montalcino '94	🍷🍷	6
● Rosso di Montalcino '92	🍷🍷	4
● Rosso di Montalcino '93	🍷🍷	4
● Rosso di Montalcino '96	🍷🍷	4

● Brunello di Montalcino '95	🍷🍷	5
● Rosso di Montalcino '98	🍷	4
● Brunello di Montalcino '93	🍷🍷	5
● Brunello di Montalcino '94	🍷🍷	5
● Rosso di Montalcino '96	🍷🍷	4
● Rosso di Montalcino '97	🍷🍷	4

MONTALCINO (SI)

MONTALCINO (SI)

EREDI FULIGNI
VIA S. SALONI, 32
53024 MONTALCINO (SI)
TEL. 0577/848039 - 0577/848127

GREPPONE MAZZI
TENIMENTI RUFFINO
LOC. GREPPONE
53024 MONTALCINO (SI)
TEL. 055/8368307 - 0577/849215

Roberto Guerrini, who has been looking after the family estate for some years, is a university professor and a man of varied interests with a particular weakness for classical music. The Fuligni wines reflect his personality. The terroir lends itself especially well to the quest for elegance. A few of the hectares under vine are reserved for the grapes that go to make the San Giacomo, now rechristened S.J. This is a blend of about 85% sangiovese with a little merlot and the '98 version is attractive but rather green. The cellar is well-equipped and temperature-controlled throughout. The vinification features temperature-controlled stainless steel vats while in the ageing rooms, there are now more large casks, which are preferred to barriques for sangiovese. Future versions of Roberto's Brunello Riserva will be going into the larger ageing casks. The well-executed Brunello '95 won Two Glasses. On the nose, evident notes of oak appear together with distinct aromas of ripe berry fruit. The very elegant palate boasts close-knit, ripe tannins. It's a pity that the finish is a bit closed and over-oaked. The Rosso di Montalcino Ginestreto '98 needs a few minutes to open before releasing its intense, inviting fruity notes. Acidity and tannins are to the fore on the palate, but the wine is very drinkable all the same.

For details about the considerable reorganization of the Folonari family holdings, we refer you to our profile of their principal estate, Ruffino, and to that of the Tenute Folonari near Florence. The wines produced on the Montalcino property, after a few years of ups and downs, are at last worthy of this historic Tuscan winery. The Brunello '95 is fuller-bodied, smoother, and more complex – better, in a word – than its two or three predecessors. The vintage itself, which, as we have said before, was not uniformly excellent, is only part of the story. What seems to have vastly improved is the winemaking style. It has to be said that the Brunello '95 is not altogether focused in its bouquet but the colour is a moderately intense ruby with bright, limpid highlights. The wine opens on the nose with rather closed, indistinct notes, relaxing only after aerating for several minutes. On the palate, however, it is immediately expressive, offering delightful notes of black cherry, blackcurrant, Alpine herbs and pencil lead. There is good weight as well, and the wood is not aggressive. On the notably long finish, there emerges a bitterish note of Peruvian bark. This is an austere Brunello with good, powerful alcohol that will clearly need several years of cellar age to show itself to its best advantage.

● Brunello di Montalcino '95	🍷🍷	6
● Rosso di Montalcino Ginestreto '98	🍷	4
● S. J. '98	🍷	5
● Brunello di Montalcino '87	🍷🍷	5
● Brunello di Montalcino '88	🍷🍷	5
● Brunello di Montalcino '89	🍷🍷	5
● Brunello di Montalcino '90	🍷🍷	5
● Brunello di Montalcino '93	🍷🍷	5
● Brunello di Montalcino '94	🍷🍷	6
● Brunello di Montalcino Ris. '88	🍷🍷	6
● Brunello di Montalcino Ris. '90	🍷🍷	6
● Brunello di Montalcino Ris. '93	🍷🍷	6
● Rosso di Montalcino Ginestreto '95	🍷🍷	4
● Brunello di Montalcino '92	🍷	5
● San Giacomo '97	🍷	5

● Brunello di Montalcino '95	🍷🍷	6
● Brunello di Montalcino Ris. '82	🍷🍷	6
● Brunello di Montalcino Ris. '83	🍷🍷	6
● Brunello di Montalcino Ris. '90	🍷🍷	6
● Brunello di Montalcino '91	🍷	5
● Brunello di Montalcino '93	🍷	5
● Brunello di Montalcino '94	🍷	6
● Brunello di Montalcino Ris. '85	🍷	6
● Brunello di Montalcino Ris. '88	🍷	6
● Brunello di Montalcino Ris. '91	🍷	6

MONTALCINO (SI)

MONTALCINO (SI)

IL MARRONETO
LOC. MADONNA DELLE GRAZIE
53024 MONTALCINO (SI)
TEL. 0577/849382

IL POGGIOLO
LOC. POGGIOLO, 259
53024 MONTALCINO (SI)
TEL. 0577/848412

Il Marroneto is a welcome newcomer to the Guide. Alessandro Mori, who has been managing the family estate for many years, presented just one wine at our tastings, but it's excellent. We had no hesitation in giving it Two Glasses. Its garnet-tinged ruby hue bespeaks a classic style, which is confirmed by the nose of morello cherry and violets, enhanced by very elegant nuances of tobacco. The balance on the palate is quite remarkable, with the soft, fine-grained tannins integrating beautifully into the texture of the wine. The palate is rounded, warm and noble, the long finish mirroring the aromas on both nose and palate. This is not a muscular wine but it is elegant and faithfully reflects its terroir. The small estate, only one and a half hectares in all, is in the northern part of the Montalcino zone at about 400 metres above sea level. The ageing cellar utilizes barrels made of French oak that hold about 25 hectolitres but fermentation takes place in vats of both stainless steel and wood. A very interesting detail is that two kinds of fermentation technique are employed. One is the fairly traditional Montalcino method, involving medium-to-long macerations. The second involves repeated pumping over, to avoid the formation of a cap. A combination of the two techniques, according to Mori, helps to create a distinctive aromatic profile without sacrificing too much extract.

This is the first appearance in the Guide for Rudy Cosimi's estate and we have rarely known a debutante to do so well, and, what's more, in a tricky zone like Montalcino. Quite a number of Glasses have been given to Rudy's wines, particularly to the various versions of Brunello. The average quality of the range is impressive, which suggests that the grapes from his eight DOCG-registered hectares are of excellent quality. The clear stylistic differences of Rudy's three Brunellos are especially striking. The standard Brunello is very traditional. Its brilliant ruby shades into garnet at the rim, introducing a nose of cherry and mulberry jam. The tannins are prominent on the palate but remain well-integrated into the texture of the wine. The Brunello Sassello '95 has more going for it, particularly on the palate, which is very richly extracted, with an abundance of fine-grained tannins. The broad, lingering finish makes this one of the best examples of its vintage. In contrast, the Brunello Beato '95 is completely different. Modern in style, it is aged in barriques and tonneaux and displays an impressively lustrous, deep ruby hue. A curious note of Peruvian bark mingles with the intense wild cherry fruit on the nose, where the wood puts in a very discreet appearance. The admirable palate has excellent tannins and a sure-footed follow-through. All Rudy's other wines are also well-made.

● Brunello di Montalcino '95	♈♈	6

● Brunello di Montalcino '95	♈♈	6
● Brunello di Montalcino Beato '95	♈♈	6
● Brunello di Montalcino		
Sassello '95	♈♈	6
● 10 Anni '97	♈	5
● Bottaccio '97	♈	4
● Rosso di Montalcino '98		4

MONTALCINO (SI)

TENUTA IL POGGIONE
LOC. S. ANGELO IN COLLE
VIA CASTELLO, 14
53020 MONTALCINO (SI)
TEL. 0577/844029

Do we need to say it again? Il Poggione is one of the longest-established wineries in Montalcino. When you could count the local producers on the fingers of one hand, Il Poggione was bottling and labelling wines to tuck away in the cellar for decades. For years now, we have been writing more or less the same things about their products. On the one hand, we praise the winery's merits. Overall quality is excellent for the huge number of bottles it turns out and the style is well-established and reliable, with no concessions to the fashion of the moment, even if this means fewer bottles sold. On the other hand, we note the preference at Il Poggione for a more traditional idiom which, where Brunello is concerned, means a deep structure that privileges alcohol over fruit, neither overstated nor particularly eloquent. The Brunello '95 is very much in the house style. The colour is mid ruby, leading into heady but rather veiled aromas. On the palate, there is plenty of body and an attractive acid tang but the finish is a little dry and nervy. The Rosso di Montalcino '98 gives more play to its fruit, which has a distinctly super-ripe tone. In the mouth, it is tannic and powerful, and also livelier, if simpler, than the Brunello. The San Leopoldo is part of a new project. It is clear that its makers are looking for a more modern profile, both in the choice of grapes – half sangiovese and half cabernet (sauvignon and franc) – and from its fresher, fruitier style. A vivid ruby in the glass, it releases intense aromas of blackcurrant and white pepper, ushering in a beautifully structured, broad palate with a consistent, delicately tannic finish. This is a tremendously well-made red, above all at a very competitive price. To round off, the panel sampled the well-managed Moscadello Frizzante sparkler.

MONTALCINO (SI)

PODERE LA FORTUNA
LOC. PODERE LA FORTUNA
53024 MONTALCINO (SI)
TEL. 0577/848308

After the very successful Brunello '94 – from what was hardly a felicitous vintage in these parts – Podere La Fortuna has released a Brunello '95 that is very good but less brilliant than we had expected. It is now generally agreed that the '95 vintage was remarkable, despite the fact that the grapes did not ripen until much later than usual, so we were hoping for a equally remarkable wine. We don't wish to upset the fans of this small but very serious Montalcino estate of 3.4 hectares planted to Brunello, so we shall say at once that the '95 is a well-made wine that should get much better after a few years in the bottle. This last comment, which many people take for granted, is by no means a foregone conclusion, despite the cachet of Brunello. Indeed there is an increasing tendency among producers to make Brunellos that are ready to drink, if not actually over the hill, when they are released onto the market. But back to the Podere La Fortuna Brunello. A deep, limpid ruby in colour, it offers aromas where caramel, vanilla and spice for the time being have the upper hand over the fruit, which is nonetheless clean and attractive. After a broad, low-key attack, the palate is rounded, and although the oak-derived tones are to the fore, there is no doubting their quality. The coherent finish closes on a delicately bitter note. The Rosso di Montalcino '98 is in many ways similar but displays fresher fruit and greater energy. Its ruby hue is wonderfully vivid, the nose offers aromas of raspberry, black cherry and bay leaf with strong notes of new oak, and the full-bodied palate is positive and well-structured, with a fresh tang of acidity and a lingering finish. It must be one of the best Rosso di Montalcinos from its vintage.

●	San Leopoldo '98	🍷🍷	5
○	Moscadello Frizzante '99	🍷	3
●	Rosso di Montalcino '98	🍷	4
●	Brunello di Montalcino '95	🍷	5
●	Brunello di Montalcino '88	🍷🍷	5
●	Brunello di Montalcino '90	🍷🍷	5
●	Brunello di Montalcino '92	🍷🍷	5
●	Brunello di Montalcino Ris. '88	🍷🍷	6
●	Brunello di Montalcino Ris. '93	🍷🍷	5
●	Rosso di Montalcino '92	🍷🍷	3*
●	Rosso di Montalcino '93	🍷🍷	3*
●	Rosso di Montalcino '95	🍷🍷	3*
●	Brunello di Montalcino '93	🍷	5
●	Brunello di Montalcino '94	🍷	5
●	Brunello di Montalcino Ris. '90	🍷	6

●	Brunello di Montalcino '95	🍷🍷	6
●	Rosso di Montalcino '98	🍷🍷	4
●	Brunello di Montalcino '83	🍷🍷	6
●	Brunello di Montalcino '91	🍷🍷	6
●	Brunello di Montalcino '93	🍷🍷	6
●	Brunello di Montalcino '94	🍷🍷	6
●	Brunello di Montalcino Ris. '93	🍷🍷	6
●	Rosso di Montalcino '95	🍷🍷	4
●	Rosso di Montalcino '96	🍷🍷	4
●	Brunello di Montalcino '85	🍷	6
●	Brunello di Montalcino '92	🍷	6
●	Rosso di Montalcino '94	🍷	4
●	Rosso di Montalcino '97	🍷	4

MONTALCINO (SI)

MONTALCINO (SI)

LA PODERINA
FRAZ. CASTELNUOVO DELL'ABATE
LOC. PODERINA
53020 MONTALCINO (SI)
TEL. 0577/835737

LA TOGATA
VIA DEL POGGIOLO, 222
53024 MONTALCINO (SI)
TEL. 0577/847107 - 06/42871033

La Poderina, the Montalcino estate of SAI, the agricultural branch of a large industrial insurance company, owns about ten DOCG-registered hectares near the road to Castelnuovo dell'Abate. The technical staff, led by Lorenzo Landi, seeks – successfully – to bring out the characteristics of this terroir, which is capable of producing wines of great elegance and harmony. The cellar is beginning to look a bit small for everything that goes on there but they make intelligent use of the space they have, finding a place for barrels of various sizes in Slavonian oak, tonneaux and some barriques. Wines aged in barriques include the Moscadello Vendemmia Tardiva ("late-vintage"), which in its second edition – the '98 – scored very well at our tasting. An intense golden yellow introduces a rich bouquet of pervasive flowery notes and aromas of apricot and yellow peach fruit. The palate is equally exciting. An excellent balance of acidity and residual sugar confers elegance, a close-knit texture and good length. Special praise, too, for the skilful use of wood. The Brunello '95, which by now has its own distinctive style, is just as successful. The colour is lustrous and the nose generous, with concentrated balsamic nuances and perfectly ripe notes of fruit. The sweet, positive attack leads in to a mid palate with good weight while well-judged acidity and tannins ensure that the flavour never cloys. And to round off, the interesting Rosso di Montalcino offers pervasive fruit aromas of raspberry.

La Togata continues to maintain the high standards it has established in recent years. The new centre of operations in Poderuccio has made possible a more functional allocation of space so that the fermentation rooms are now quite separate from the ageing cellar. And soon they are going to build a temperature-controlled environment solely for storing bottled wine. In the cellar, the DOCG and DOC wines repose in great Slavonian oak barrels while the barriques contain the estate's newcomer, Azzurreta, a monovarietal sangiovese dedicated to the daughter of the owners. The 2000 vintage marks the first harvest from the approximately five hectares under vine in Orgiano and Camigliano, an excellent zone with splendid exposure. Three wines were presented this year. The Azzurreta was sacrificed in '97, its grapes going into the Brunello, and the '98 disappointed us slightly. It is a little undefined on the nose and the palate is straightforward and not very exciting. On the other hand, the Brunello, which is now regularly one of the best around, did very well in the '95 version. A clean, intense nose with classic fruity notes leads in to a palate that impresses with its harmony, thanks to good extract and fine-grained, elegant tannins. The finish is very good and is in no hurry at all. The Rosso di Montalcino '98 displays faintly unfocused mineral tones and notes of Peruvian bark on the nose but turns out to be full-bodied and very quaffable.

● Brunello di Montalcino '95	ΨΨ	5
○ Moscadello V. T. '98	ΨΨ	5
● Rosso di Montalcino '98	Ψ	4
● Brunello di Montalcino Ris. '88	ΨΨΨ	6
● Brunello di Montalcino '88	ΨΨ	5
● Brunello di Montalcino Ris. '90	ΨΨ	6
● Brunello di Montalcino Ris. '93	ΨΨ	6
● Brunello di Montalcino '89	Ψ	5
● Brunello di Montalcino '94	Ψ	5
● Brunello di Montalcino '90	Ψ	5
○ Moscadello V. T. '97	Ψ	5

● Brunello di Montalcino '95	ΨΨ	6
● Rosso di Montalcino '98	Ψ	4
● Azzurreta '98		5
● Azzurreta '96	ΨΨ	5
● Brunello di Montalcino '90	ΨΨ	6
● Brunello di Montalcino '91	ΨΨ	6
● Brunello di Montalcino '94	ΨΨ	6
● Brunello di Montalcino '92	Ψ	5
● Rosso di Montalcino '97	Ψ	3

438

MONTALCINO (SI)

MONTALCINO (SI)

Maurizio Lambardi
Podere Canalicchio di Sotto, 8
53024 Montalcino (SI)
Tel. 0577/848476

Lisini
Loc. S. Angelo in Colle
53020 Montalcino (SI)
Tel. 0577/864046

After a brief stay amongst the Other Wineries, largely due to our chronic lack of space, this reliable Montalcino winery is back with a Guide profile of its own. Maurizio Lambardi is a man who doesn't have much small talk but he does demonstrate a great deal of persistence in bringing out the best in his grapes. That's why he is very proud of his newly installed system for controlling and monitoring fermentation temperatures, and of the cellar enlargement in progress, necessitated by an increase both in production and in the use of smaller barrels. The cellar is temperature-controlled and so intelligently planned that Maurizio manages to follow all the stages of production personally. The wines are excellent and the prices very reasonable. This is a particularly cheering fact in Montalcino, where producers in general are unresponsive to the idea of affordable pricing. Both wines won Two Glasses. The Brunello has a brilliant, concentrated ruby hue, followed by fresh fruit on the nose, with notes of morello cherry and cherry jam. The impact on the palate is good, the tannins are solid and the finish is fairly long. The Rosso di Montalcino '98 is a delight, with good weight on the mid palate, thanks to its hefty tannins, and the well-sustained finish echoes the notes of raspberry and cherry on the nose.

It isn't easy to get to the Lisini estate, particularly for city-dwellers who are not fond of dirt roads. All the same, we recommend a visit to this lovely property, which is on the country road from Sant'Angelo in Colle to Castelnuovo dell'Abate. As you go along, keep an eye on the woods and the vineyards that line the road and you may see pheasants, wild boar or porcupines, especially at dusk. In addition, wine-lovers will be able to admire one of the best places to grow Brunello, the Sesta subzone. It is here that Lisini has its ten hectares planted to Brunello, growing excellent grapes on which the consummate oenologist, Franco Bernabei, then works his magic. This year, Lisini's star bottle, the Brunello from their Ugolaia cru, was not presented because the '95 was not quite ready and the producer wisely decided to wait. So, only two wines were available for our tastings, the Brunello '95 and the Rosso di Montalcino '98. The Brunello got only One Glass because of poor definition on the rather unfocused nose, with notes of earth and autumn leaves masking the fruit. Things are better on the palate, where the wine shows elegance and balance. The finish is not overwhelming but it is fairly persistent and quite positive. Curiously enough, given its category, this is a fairly straightforward but extremely enjoyable wine. The Rosso di Montalcino did equally well, with fragrant fruity overtones of cherry amalgamating well with the wood. The tangy acidity makes the finish a little lean but the wine is a very pleasant tipple, nonetheless.

Wine	Glasses	Price
Brunello di Montalcino '95	YY	6
Rosso di Montalcino '98	YY	4
Brunello di Montalcino '88	YY	5
Brunello di Montalcino '93	YY	5
Brunello di Montalcino '90	YY	5
Brunello di Montalcino '91	YY	5
Rosso di Montalcino '90	YY	4
Rosso di Montalcino '91	YY	4
Rosso di Montalcino '92	YY	4
Rosso di Montalcino '93	YY	4
Rosso di Montalcino '95	YY	4
Brunello di Montalcino '87	Y	5
Brunello di Montalcino '89	Y	5
Brunello di Montalcino '92	Y	5
Rosso di Montalcino '96	Y	4

Wine	Glasses	Price
Brunello di Montalcino '95	Y	6
Rosso di Montalcino '98	Y	4
Brunello di Montalcino '88	YYY	6
Brunello di Montalcino '90	YYY	6
Brunello di Montalcino Ugolaia '91	YYY	6
Brunello di Montalcino '87	YY	6
Brunello di Montalcino '89	YY	6
Brunello di Montalcino '91	YY	6
Brunello di Montalcino '93	YY	6
Brunello di Montalcino Ris. '85	YY	6
Brunello di Montalcino Ris. '86	YY	6
Brunello di Montalcino Ris. '88	YY	6
Brunello di Montalcino Ugolaia '90	YY	6
Brunello di Montalcino Ugolaia '94	YY	6
Rosso di Montalcino '90	YY	3*

MONTALCINO (SI)

MONTALCINO (SI)

LUCE
LOC. CASTELGIOCONDO
53024 MONTALCINO (SI)
TEL. 0577/848492

MASTROJANNI
LOC. CASTELNUOVO DELL'ABATE
PODERI LORETO E SAN PIO
53024 MONTALCINO (SI)
TEL. 0577/835681

Much of what we said last year applies again this time round, although the standard wines seem to have improved. That's how we could sum up what we found in the latest range of offerings from the joint-venture estate belonging to Frescobaldi and Mondavi. Their flagship is still Luce, which, if not exciting, does show, in this its fifth vintage, a laudable consistency of style. It has also managed to give more expression to its terroir, although we still find that it lacks the concentration and body that would make it a star. The '97 Luce has a very deep, intense ruby hue. The nose opens on notes of ripe fruit, which are then joined by elegant, well-controlled aromas of vanilla and toasty oak. On the palate, it is soft and moderately mouth-filling and the tannins blend nicely with the alcohol. The Danzante Bianco '99, a blend of pinot grigio and riesling from the Tre Venezie in north-eastern Italy, has a very limpid straw-yellow colour. Strong flowery aromas combine with apple fruit on the passably persistent nose. The palate shows prominent acidity right from the attack, and decent texture. The Danzante Rosso '98, made from sangiovese grapes grown in the Marche region, offers cherry fruit with fairly marked vegetal nuances, in addition to light, pleasant spice. The positive attack leads in to a balanced, attractive progression on the palate but fades rather too quickly.

Some people will turn up their noses when they learn that we think this year's prize wine from Mastrojanni is their new creation, Botrys. This wine, from the '96 vintage, is an assemblage of moscato fruit dried on rush mats and late-vintage malvasia di Candia, barrique-aged for about 15 months before bottling. Aromas of yellow peach and medlar and a flowery undertone of lime blossom tempt the nose. The discreet sweetness on the palate is nicely balanced by acidity. This wine is also a welcome signal of a dynamic estate policy. Mastrojanni is not limiting its attention to traditional wines but seeks to make the most of the enormous potential that the Montalcino area has for non-native grape varieties. Meanwhile the three reds get One Glass each, which is less than we expected. Of course the Mastrojanni champion, the Brunello Schiena d'Asino, was not in the running. The '95 will be released later on. The standard Brunello '95 is garnet-tinged ruby red and needs to breathe for a few minutes before the nose releases its crisp notes of berry fruit. There is not enough softness on the palate to counter the robust tannins, which consequently tend to dry out the finish. It will get better with time, which is, as we have seen, the way with Mastrojanni's wines. The good Rosso di Montalcino '98 has lovely fruit on the nose and medium density on the palate. The San Pio '97, a partly barrique-aged blend of sangiovese and cabernet sauvignon, offers aromas of mulberry, caramel and citron, ushering in a powerful and substantial, if not very elegant, palate.

●	Luce '97	▼▼	6
○	Danzante Bianco '99	▼	3
●	Danzante Rosso '98	▼	3
●	Luce '94	▼▼▼	6
●	Luce '93	▼▼	6
●	Luce '95	▼▼	6
●	Luce '96	▼▼	6
●	Lucente '95	▼▼	5
●	Lucente '96	▼▼	5
●	Lucente '97	▼▼	5
○	Danzante Bianco '98	▼	3
●	Danzante Rosso '97	▼	3

○	Botrys '96	▼▼	5
●	Brunello di Montalcino '95	▼	5
●	Rosso di Montalcino '98	▼	4
●	San Pio '97	▼	4
●	Brunello di Montalcino '90	▼▼▼	6
●	Brunello di Montalcino Ris. '88	▼▼▼	6
●	Brunello di Montalcino Schiena d'Asino '90	▼▼▼	6
●	Brunello di Montalcino Schiena d'Asino '93	▼▼▼	6
●	Brunello di Montalcino '93	▼▼	5
●	Brunello di Montalcino Ris. '90	▼▼	6
●	Brunello di Montalcino Ris. '93	▼▼	5
●	San Pio '93	▼▼	5
●	San Pio '95	▼▼	5

MONTALCINO (SI)

MONTALCINO (SI)

MOCALI
LOC. MOCALI, 273
53024 MONTALCINO (SI)
TEL. 0577/849485

TENUTE SILVIO NARDI
LOC. CASALE DEL BOSCO
53024 MONTALCINO (SI)
TEL. 0577/808269

Amazingly, all the wines that Tiziano Ciacci makes get better every year. These improvements are perhaps less noticeable in the Brunello but they are very obvious in the Rosso di Montalcino. It is also well worth mentioning that his wines are very competitively priced. That the land where he grows his vines is particularly well-suited to viticulture is a necessary, but not sufficient, condition for making good wine. The continual renovation of Ciacci's cellar and barrels, his temperature control system, and his rigorous selection of grapes during harvests are part of the winning approach of this small estate which lies on a hill overlooking the church of Santa Restituta. The '94 Brunello Riserva was not put on sale because the year was such a poor one but Mocali has brought out a new wine, I Piaggioni '98, that is pleasant without being especially outstanding. It has a marked acid vein that is not sufficiently integrated into the texture and is too simple a wine to be worth more than a mention. But the two DOC bottles are both delicious, easily meriting their Two Glasses. The Rosso di Montalcino '98 is much better than the previous year's. At last, it has a good clean nose and the fresh notes of cherries and raspberries mingle well with the wood. The palate confirms this good impression, finding a good full flavour and long finish. The Brunello '95 has a classic, intense ruby colour and a fruity nose on which prunes are evident, as well as the trademark fruit preserve. It makes a good impression on the front palate, where it reveals a broad, warm, lingering progression.

Emilia Nardi keeps her nose to the grindstone and continues to implement the scheduled changes to this estate. The barrel stock has been renovated and the wine is now vinified in temperature-controlled stainless steel vats. Much effort has dedicated to the vineyards. In collaboration with the University of Florence, research is under way into new clones and mass selection and another project under way to recover the grape types in some of the estate's plots that are unrelated to sangiovese. The cellar has also been making a systematic study of the aromas present in their wines. The idea is to have a clear-cut aromatic profile of all Nardi wines that could be used to "brand" future products. They have come a long way and the progress was tangible at our tastings. A completely new Brunello di Montalcino is one of the results of these efforts. It comes from a vineyard in a superb location in the eastern part of the DOCG zone. The name of both vineyard and wine is Manachiara. It has a dense, luminous ruby colour that introduces a rich fruit nose, although at the time of our tasting, it needed a few minutes to open. The palate is full and well-sustained, offering solid, rounded tannins. Not bad for a first showing. The standard '95 Brunello is a very pleasant effort. Entry on the palate is decisive, the mid palate is warm, and the delicious finish echoes the nose. The intensely fruit-rich '98 Rosso di Montalcino is also successful, foregrounding notes of raspberries and cherries.

● Brunello di Montalcino '95	♟♟	5
● Rosso di Montalcino '98	♟♟	3*
● I Piaggioni '98		2
● Brunello di Montalcino '93	♟♟	5
● Brunello di Montalcino Ris. '93	♟♟	5
● Brunello di Montalcino '94	♟	5
● Rosso di Montalcino '97	♟	3

● Brunello di Montalcino '95	♟♟	5
● Brunello di Montalcino Manachiara '95	♟♟	6
● Rosso di Montalcino '98	♟	4
● Brunello di Montalcino '90	♟♟	5
● Brunello di Montalcino '93	♟♟	5
● Brunello di Montalcino Ris. '93	♟♟	5
● Brunello di Montalcino '92	♟	5
● Brunello di Montalcino '94	♟	5
● Rosso di Montalcino '93	♟	4
● Rosso di Montalcino '95	♟	4
● Rosso di Montalcino '96	♟	4

MONTALCINO (SI)

SIRO PACENTI
LOC. PELAGRILLI, 1
53024 MONTALCINO (SI)
TEL. 0577/848662

Brunello di Montalcino has elected its paladins and, without a doubt, one of them is Giancarlo Pacenti, a young but far-seeing winemaker who is not content with merely getting a good price for his wine, as so many of his fellow producers are. Instead, Pacenti is the first to criticize his own bottles and recognize their limitations. In short, he is a man who loves his work and constantly strives to improve his products, even though he gets little help from DOCGs regulations that stipulate a minimum period of ageing in the wood. Giancarlo's '95 Brunello is reticent on the nose at first but on closer examination reveals a strong character founded on superb fruit, backed up, after the hesitant start, with attractive oak-derived vanilla and toastiness. In the mouth, it is even better, demonstrating great energy, equilibrium, a noticeable tannic density and overall compactness. The finish is long and expansive, with a lively note of wood coming through. This is an excellent Brunello with a long life ahead of it. Giancarlo Pacenti's Rosso di Montalcino is, as it has been for some years, one of the best of its kind. It has enviable structure and soft, close-knit tannins that set the pace on the palate. All it needs is time to fine-tune the wood, which is a bit prominent at the moment. But perhaps we are just being hypercritical.

MONTALCINO (SI)

PIAN DELLE VIGNE
LOC. PIAN DELLE VIGNE
53024 MONTALCINO (SI)
TEL. 0577/816066

Guess who owns the 60 hectares under vine at Pian delle Vigne, a good half of which is Brunello? The answer is simple – Antinori, of course. How could this prize-winning, centuries-old Tuscan wine maker, embarking on a campaign to acquire major estates in all parts of Italy, not add Montalcino to the list? Actually, the acquisition of this estate goes back to 1993. Renzo Cotarella, who supervises all Antinori's production, and the owner himself, Piero Antinori, could have sold the '93 and '94 under their own label. Instead, they preferred to wait for a superior vintage that they could see through from start to finish. How good is the '95 Brunello di Montalcino Pian delle Vigne? We thought it was very good. The colour is full and dense, with brilliant highlights. The nose begins with stiff reductive notes and then opens up to reveal attractive notes of liqueur morello cherries, redcurrants, cocoa powder and caramel. The sulphur dioxide reappears on the palate but the extract is rich and ripe, and the aroma disappears after a few minutes. The mid palate is well-sustained, markedly tannic and takes you through to a bitterish finish. This is a promising red wine that should develop complexity in a few years' time. Pian delle Vigne's debut in the Guide is a decidedly positive one.

● Brunello di Montalcino '95	♈♈♈	6
● Rosso di Montalcino '98	♈♈	5
● Brunello di Montalcino '88	♈♈♈	6
● Brunello di Montalcino '89	♈♈	6
● Brunello di Montalcino '90	♈♈	6
● Brunello di Montalcino '91	♈♈	6
● Brunello di Montalcino '93	♈♈	6
● Brunello di Montalcino Ris. '90	♈♈	6
● Rosso di Montalcino '88	♈♈	4
● Rosso di Montalcino '90	♈♈	4
● Rosso di Montalcino '92	♈♈	4
● Rosso di Montalcino '93	♈♈	4
● Rosso di Montalcino '95	♈♈	4
● Rosso di Montalcino '96	♈♈	4
● Rosso di Montalcino '97	♈♈	5

● Brunello di Montalcino		
Pian delle Vigne '95	♈♈	6

MONTALCINO (SI)

MONTALCINO (SI)

PIANCORNELLO
FRAZ. CASTELNUOVO DELL'ABATE
LOC. PIANCORNELLO
53024 MONTALCINO (SI)
TEL. 0577/844105

AGOSTINA PIERI
LOC. PIANCORNELLO
VIA FABBRI, 2
53024 MONTALCINO (SI)
tel. 0577/844163

Silvana Pieri's small property is situated in the southernmost part of the Brunello DOCG zone, and is easy to reach from Sant'Angelo Scalo. The three hectares are planted in classic Brunello fashion. The cellar is equally traditional, as the medium-sized Slavonian oak barrels clearly testify. The renovation of the barrel stock, begun about two years ago, is now complete, and will enable a greater degree of consistency. The winery is run by the family, and their cellar, although not large, is a good example of the rational use of space, as well as being very attractive. The wines are very much terroir-driven and received sufficiently high marks to bring this producer back into our Guide after a couple of years on the sidelines. The '95 Brunello is very successful. It has an attractively intense, but not tremendously concentrated, ruby colour and a crisp nose of classic wild cherry and ripe berry fruit, as you might expect, given the warm area in which the grapes were grown. The palate is convincing, the initial mellow sweetness being nicely balanced by close-knit tannins, then the sure progression leads in to a broad, leisurely finish. All in all, a solid, very satisfying wine. The '98 Rosso di Montalcino did not quite earn its Two Glasses because the nose has a faint reductive note that tends to cover its fruitiness. The wine opens out pleasantly in the mouth, however, where the sweetness of the fruit is clearly present.

Expectations were high for this winery's '95 Brunello. The reason was the great performance of the '95 Rosso di Montalcino, the only wine in its class to get Three Glasses. However, the '95 Brunello failed to earn our top accolade, even though it is one of the best of the year. It has an intense ruby colour, and a clean, complex nose. The wild and morello cherry and mulberry jam fruit is perceptible but struggles to emerge because it is slightly overwhelmed by the toasty notes of the wood in which the wine was aged. In the mouth, the impact is warm, with sufficient alcohol to soften the wine despite its strong tannins, which are, however, laudably fine-grained. The very attractive finish is broad and deep, leaving after-aromas of coffee and vanilla. The new Brunello DOCG regulations have lowered to two years the minimum time that wine must spend in the barrel. This wine would definitely have gained in harmony and freshness had those rules already been in force. The Rosso '98 is less successful. We had hoped for better. True, it is well made, clean, and sincere, but there are vegetal notes of not quite ripe fruit on the nose that restrict its breadth. It does, however, offer a very interesting palate where rich fruit and soft, close-knit tannins emerge. The finish is long and free of any hint of bitterness.

● Brunello di Montalcino '95	▼▼	6
● Rosso di Montalcino '98	▼	4
● Brunello di Montalcino '93	♀♀	5
● Rosso di Montalcino '96	♀	3

● Brunello di Montalcino '95	▼▼	6
● Rosso di Montalcino '98	▼	4
● Rosso di Montalcino '95	♀♀♀	4*
● Brunello di Montalcino '94	♀♀	6
● Rosso di Montalcino '94	♀♀	4
● Rosso di Montalcino '96	♀♀	4
● Rosso di Montalcino '97	♀	4

Poggio di Sotto

Fraz. Castelnuovo dell'Abate
Loc. Poggio di Sopra, 222
53020 Montalcino (SI)
tel. 0577/835502

The manner in which Piero Palmucci and his cellarmaster, Giulio Gambelli, interpret Brunello di Montalcino may not be to everyone's taste but it is undeniably a wine of remarkable personality and character. Certainly, this is a Brunello that does not pander to modern taste (but is there any such a thing as modern taste, or is that a critic's simplification?), nor does it fall into the melancholy routine of powerful fruit and new wood. On the other hand, its austerity of style is a drawback when it is lined up against some of its rounder and softer "colleagues". There is no doubt that the grapes are of excellent quality. The vines enjoy a superb position at Castelnuovo Abate. Vinification and ageing are inspired by strict criteria: fermentation temperatures that are kept high, leisurely maceration and four years or more of ageing in large barrels of Slavonian oak. The most recent Poggio di Sotto Brunello to be put on the market is the '95. It has a moderately deep ruby colour with clear, lustrous, orange-tinged highlights. The alcohol-rich aromas are enriched with enticing hints of jam and liqueur cherries, leading in to a full-bodied palate, with firm tannins in the mid palate and a very long finish. The only wrong note, but a fairly insistent one, is the marked presence of volatile acid, which compromises some of the wine's freshness and its overall integrity. However, this wine fully merits its Two Glasses, in particular for its faithful expression of Brunello's varietal characteristics.

●	Brunello di Montalcino '95	🍷🍷	6
●	Brunello di Montalcino '94	YY	6
●	Rosso di Montalcino '94	YY	4
●	Brunello di Montalcino '91	Y	6

MONTALCINO (SI)

Castello Romitorio

Loc. Romitorio
53024 Montalcino (SI)
tel. 0577/897220

Sandro Chia's winery is a firmly-established part of the Montalcino scene and its strong suits are the reliability and quality of its products. Chia, very much a trend-setter, has many fans who race to collect bottles of Castello di Romitorio because one of their favourite artists has designed the label. Now, to further improve the quality of his wines, he is enlarging the cellar next to the lovely former monastery that houses his offices. Chia has about eight hectares of brunello and a further 12 planted to other vines, including cabernet sauvignon and chardonnay. Only three wines were presented at our tastings this year, as the Chardonnay was not ready in time. The best of the three was the Brunello '95, which scored well over the minimum required to receive its Two Glasses. The close-knit, luminous ruby shades into pigeon's blood, ushering in a broad, intense nose of wild and morello cherries that meld attractively into the sweet spiciness of the wood. The rich fruit makes the palate satisfying and the beefy, ripe tannins are deliciously compact. Another equally good wine is Sandro's Romito del Romitorio '98, a blend of cabernet sauvignon and sangiovese. The nose offers raspberry, geranium and candied peel while the palate is mellow yet concentrated, revealing firm tannins that are still a little over-assertive. It should develop well in the cellar. The medium-bodied, very agreeable Rosso di Montalcino '98 notched up a One Glass score.

●	Brunello di Montalcino '95	🍷🍷	6
●	Romito del Romitorio '98	🍷🍷	6
●	Rosso di Montalcino '98	🍷	4
●	Brunello di Montalcino '93	YY	6
○	Chardonnay '98	YY	5
●	Romito del Romitorio '90	YY	5
●	Romito del Romitorio '96	YY	6
●	Romito del Romitorio '96	YY	5
●	Brunello di Montalcino '88	Y	6
●	Brunello di Montalcino '94	Y	6
●	Rosso di Montalcino '92	Y	4
●	Rosso di Montalcino '96	Y	4

MONTALCINO (SI)

MONTALCINO (SI)

SALICUTTI
PODERE SALICUTTI, 174
53024 MONTALCINO (SI)
TEL. 0577/847003

SALVIONI - LA CERBAIOLA
P.ZZA CAVOUR, 19
53024 MONTALCINO (SI)
TEL. 0577/848499

The former chemist and proprietor of the Salicutti estate, Francesco Leanza, has had a successful year. He entered the Guide last year thanks to an excellent Rosso di Montalcino '97, and we looked forward to this year to see what he had done with his Brunello. The '95 version turns out to be very interesting indeed. It has an intense ruby colour, and reveals a nose on which wood gets the better of the very intense fruit. It makes a powerful first impression in the mouth, lining up plenty of alcohol, and has good weight through the mid palate even though the tannins have not yet been completely absorbed. Another Two Glass winner is the Rosso di Montalcino, among the best in its category from '98. The rich ruby colour is flecked with purple highlights and on the complex nose the hints of morello cherry and mulberry are lifted by balsamic and spicy notes. On the palate, it offers good presence and thrust which are undisturbed by the robust tannins. The use of small wood, as well as barriques and tonneaux, lends Leanza's wines a certain richness on the nose, although on occasion, as in the case of the Brunello, the oak may seem excessive. However, the superb raw material should be capable of integrating the wood, given a bit of time in the bottle. Two Glasses also go to the Dopoteatro, a '98 Cabernet Sauvignon with a well-sustained palate, gentle attack and attractive elegance. It's a brilliant result.

We are beginning with the good news for the many admirers of the wines of this estate, one of the most famous in Montalcino. Giulio and Mirella Salvioni are planting another hectare to vine. The new vineyard is practically right in front of the house which gives the property its name, La Cerbaiola, and stands next to an old vineyard. Obviously, it will need time, but when it comes on-stream, the Salvionis will be able to satisfy more of the demand for La Cerbaiola wine. Their hard work in the vineyards generated enthusiasm for their products right from the very beginning. You could almost say that they created a new kind of Brunello, a "Salvioni-style" wine. However, we have noticed, over the last two years, a shift in the intensely fruity house character, often enhanced by surprising hints of tropical fruit. The '95 Brunello confirms this impression. The nose has a fruity vein that is dominated by oak-derived notes over a vegetal background. It is all very cleanly presented but very far removed from those aromas of tropical fruit that played such a big part in creating the Salvioni's reputation. They are probably at a crossroads so we will have to for the next version to see which way they go. In the mouth, the wine is very nearly on a par with its predecessors. The palate doesn't go for power but aims at a balance of softness with the acidity and tannins in a search for the greatest possible elegance. In fact, the tannins have remarkable finesse and this is combined with a goodly amount of extract. It's a pity that the finish is a little stiff-backed, and so doesn't have the depth which one would expect to find. Also, there is a touch of green that disturbs the general equilibrium.

● Brunello di Montalcino '95	🍷🍷	5
● Dopoteatro '98	🍷🍷	5
● Rosso di Montalcino '98	🍷🍷	4
● Rosso di Montalcino '97	🍷🍷	4

● Brunello di Montalcino '95	🍷🍷	6
● Brunello di Montalcino '85	🍷🍷🍷	6
● Brunello di Montalcino '87	🍷🍷🍷	6
● Brunello di Montalcino '88	🍷🍷🍷	6
● Brunello di Montalcino '89	🍷🍷🍷	6
● Brunello di Montalcino '90	🍷🍷🍷	6
● Brunello di Montalcino '86	🍷🍷	6
● Brunello di Montalcino '91	🍷🍷	6
● Brunello di Montalcino '92	🍷🍷	6
● Brunello di Montalcino '93	🍷🍷	6
● Brunello di Montalcino '94	🍷	6

MONTALCINO (SI)

MONTALCINO (SI)

SOLARIA - CENCIONI
PODERE CAPANNA, 102
53024 MONTALCINO (SI)
TEL. 0577/849426

TENIMENTI ANGELINI - VAL DI SUGA
LOC. VAL DI CAVA
53024 MONTALCINO (SI)
TEL. 0577/80411

As you go up from Torrenieri towards Montalcino, you might see a young woman driving a tractor through the vineyards, or pruning the plants. Patrizia Cencioni is more than just a "wine woman". She's a grower. Her motto is that you can only make a great wine from perfect grapes and the main thing in the cellar is to avoiding ruining all your hard work out of doors. Vinification is done in a modestly functional building while the cellar holds casks of various sizes, although none is bigger than 30 hectolitres. The number of barriques and tonneaux has increased. They are used not only for the Brunello but also for a new, cabernet sauvignon-based wine which will come out for the first time in 2001. Patrizia is totally dedicated to her winery, to the point of actually designing herself the attractive labels of the wines. For the present, she releases only a Brunello and a Rosso di Montalcino, and the '95 version of her Brunello is very good. It has an unflaggingly intense ruby colour and a broad nose of balsamic and fruit notes with clear hints of wild cherries. The influence of the wood is perceptible but not overpowering. Its palate is intense, well-balanced, warm and long. It's a very elegant Brunello, indeed one of the best of the year, with nothing inelegant about it, as a wine from this terroir should be, especially if it is made by a producer like Patrizia. The Rosso di Montalcino '98 is less brilliant. Its nose reveals rather unfocused fruit that tends to be jammy. Correct on the palate, it lays the emphasis on freshness, rather than body.

The vines of Tenimenti Angelini are producing excellent fruit, both figuratively and literally. Of the various holdings owned by this pharmaceutical group, their Montalcino property is probably the best known and appreciated. Some wine professionals may dismiss the wines almost out of hand as being untypical of the area but they are of excellent quality. An unprejudiced observer has to admit that, aside from the nod to international taste represented by the generous use of new oak, the bottles that carry the Val di Suga label have a nose and palate that are faithful to the best Sangiovese tradition. We are convinced, perhaps ingenuously, that a wine freed of the more obvious defects of its category, although perhaps a bit too rich in aromas of new oak, should be encouraged for having made progress rather than blamed for having betrayed its heritage. So that's why there is another Three Glass award, this time for the Vigna al Lago '95. An invigorating, full-bodied wine, there is nothing banal about its fruit. It is light years away from being a "vin nouveau", revealing instead a noble depth on the nose with notes of wild cherries, liqueur cherries and liquorice. The palate also has remarkable intensity, as the generous alcohol is backed up by rich extract and robust breadth of structure. The standard Brunello this year is less forthcoming but still holds its own very well. The warm, clean nose has ripe aromas leading in to a generously complex palate. The '98 Rosso di Montalcino, the child of an unfortunate year, is a bit too simple on the nose, with a roughish palate and a tannic finish.

● Brunello di Montalcino '95	♟♟	6
● Rosso di Montalcino '98	♟	4

● Brunello di Montalcino Vigna del Lago '95	♟♟♟	6
● Brunello di Montalcino '95	♟♟	6
● Rosso di Montalcino '98	♟	4
● Brunello di Montalcino Vigna del Lago '90	♟♟♟	6
● Brunello di Montalcino Vigna del Lago '93	♟♟♟	6
● Brunello di Montalcino Vigna Spuntali '93	♟♟♟	6
● Brunello di Montalcino '90	♟♟	5
● Brunello di Montalcino '93	♟♟	5
● Brunello di Montalcino Ris. '93	♟♟	5
● Brunello di Montalcino Vigna Spuntali '90	♟♟	6

MONTECARLO (LU)

MONTECARLO (LU)

Fattoria del Buonamico
Via Provinciale, 43
55015 Montecarlo (LU)
Tel. 0583/22038

Gino Fuso Carmignani
Loc. Cercatoia
Via della Tinaia, 7
55015 Montecarlo (LU)
Tel. 0583/22381

Much was been hoped for at the Fattoria del Buonamico from the hot vintages of '97, '98, and '99. Hopes were particularly high in an area like the countryside around Lucca that didn't suffer much from the droughts that afflicted other, drier areas of Tuscany. We sampled the wines from '96, which performed admirably, confirming the reliability of Fattoria del Buonamico, which has always been a benchmark in this part of Tuscany. This year, it reinforces its position with two wines that won Two Glasses. Il Fortino '96, a monovarietal Syrah, has a concentrated colour, a clean, elegant nose of ripe dark berries, and a balsamic hint of liquorice over an earthy background. In the mouth, it offers juicy fruit, notable cohesion, good body and a long finish. The other Two Glass success was the Cercatola '96, a blend of sangiovese, cabernet sauvignon, cabernet franc, and syrah, the last of these contributing intriguing notes of plums and black pepper that mingle with the spiciness of the wood. Only an excess of vegetal notes that come through on the palate over touches of wood-derived coffee and spices denied it Three Glasses. The Montecarlo Rosso '99 got its Glass for the cherries on the nose and for its delicious softness in the mouth. The Montecarlo Bianco '99 obtained a similar score for its clean fragrances and enjoyable, balanced taste. Expectations for the L'Oro del Re, obtained from sémillon and sauvignon attacked by noble rot, were high but our appointment with this wine, and with the white Vasario '98, has been postponed until next year.

Gino "Fuso" (which means "out to lunch") lives in a sort of fourth dimension made up of unlikely stories, improbable names, and the imaginary space in which he conducts his activities and into which his visitors and friends are welcomed whenever they come to see him. It is always pleasant to spend a few hours listening to him and tasting his wines. After hearing about Gino's "acoustic method" and possible names for a future merlot, we tried to persuade him not to stop making a barrique-aged white of his, which Gino claims is too much work. Stati d'Animo is a very nice wine which we would be sorry not to have around. The rich straw-yellow '99 has a nose of plums and yellow peaches in which there are touches of spices and Virginia tobacco. The palate, which reflects the nose attractively, is very well-balanced. The '98 For Duke also gets Two Glasses. It has a deep ruby colour and pleasant aromas of plums and fresh cherries that merge well with creaminess from the wood. It is full and decisive in the mouth, revealing sweetish tannins, progressing well with more fruit on a mid palate held back only by slightly lightweight structure. Also good is the Sassonero '99, where the presence of its Syrah is more noticeable in the aromas of black pepper, spices, and ripe plums. It is a more spirited glass and the sustained thrust on the palate makes it pleasing and refreshingly drinkable.

● Cercatoja Rosso '96	￥￥	5
● Il Fortino Syrah '96	￥￥	6
○ Montecarlo Bianco '99	￥	3
● Montecarlo Rosso '99	￥	3
● Cercatoja Rosso '90	￥￥	5
● Cercatoja Rosso '95	￥￥	5
● Fort'Yrah '94	￥￥	5
● Il Fortino Cabernet/Merlot '91	￥￥	5
● Il Fortino Cabernet/Merlot '93	￥￥	5
● Il Fortino Cabernet/Merlot '94	￥￥	5
● Il Fortino Syrah '92	￥￥	5
● Il Fortino Syrah '95	￥￥	5
○ Vasario '95	￥￥	5
○ Vasario '96	￥￥	4

● For Duke '98	￥￥	5
○ Montecarlo Bianco Stati d'Animo '99	￥￥	4
● Montecarlo Rosso Sassonero '99	￥	3
● For Duke '90	￥￥	4
● For Duke '94	￥￥	4
● For Duke '95	￥￥	4
● For Duke '97	￥￥	5
● Montecarlo Rosso Sassonero '97	￥￥	2*
○ Vin Santo Le Notti Rosse di Capo Diavolo '95	￥￥	4
● For Duke '93	￥	4
● For Duke '96	￥	4
● Montecarlo Rosso Sassonero '96	￥	2*
● Montecarlo Rosso Sassonero '98	￥	3

MONTECARLO (LU)

MONTECARLO (LU)

FATTORIA DI MONTECHIARI
VIA MONTECHIARI, 27
55015 MONTECARLO (LU)
TEL. 0583/22189

WANDANNA
VIA DON MINZONI, 38
55015 MONTECARLO (LU)
TEL. 0583/228989 - 0583/22226

After two years, the Cabernet from Montechiari again wins Three Glasses, thus clearly demonstrating that the winery is reaping the benefits of all its hard work and commitment to making premium wine. This is a classic estate that you visit by walking round the vineyards. The vines are planted low and close together, with only a few bunches on each plant. "One kilogram per vine" at Montechiari isn't a slogan. It's the way things are done. Nor are there any secrets about the scrupulous, skilful way work is carried out in the cellar. The Cabernet '97 is not a wine that wins you over with its muscle power. It convinces with the harmony it presents at every phase of tasting. As you raise the glass, the aromas reveal a laudable fusion of fruit and wood which fans out into notes of redcurrants, plums, cocoa powder and aromatic herbs. The flavour is soft, consistent and well-sustained, with moments of real elegance and a very profound finish. The Pinot Nero '97 is also worth investigating. It has a varietal nose of cherries, roses, cinnamon and liquorice followed by nice balance on the palate, where its round body, meek tannins and well-judged acidity impress. The finish is satisfyingly long. The '98 Chardonnay performed well. Its honey and mineral nose is followed by a rich buttery palate with an attractive profile. The sangiovese-based Rosso '97 has an intense nose of berry fruit, violets and toasty oak. Oak is to the fore on the palate, which reveals crisp tannins and good acidity. To finish off, the Montecarlo Bianco '99 is attractive and headily perfumed.

In the Lucca area, especially at Montecarlo, there is a tendency to differentiate the wines with a wide variety of labels. Wandanna is one of the front-runners in the label stakes but it has to be said that their quality has been consistently good, and gets better all the time. This year, they received three Two Glass ratings. As usual, the '97 Virente, a blend of syrah, merlot and ciliegiolo, is a pleasure. The nose unfurls aromas of redcurrants and mulberries while the palate is fresh-tasting, tangy and very juicy, with just a faint burning sensation in the finish. The Terre di Cascinieri Rosso, made from cabernet, sangiovese, syrah, and ciliegiolo, is a very individual wine that has aromas of black berry fruit and faintly minerally notes. In the mouth, it opens softly but quickly picks up with lively acidity. Delicious tannins and good fruit extract underpin the admirable progression. The Terre di Cascinieri Bianco '98 is the third Two Glass wine. It offers a wide range of fruit on the nose, including pears, lychee and roses, but is a bit over-burdened by the wood. The sweet, aromatic palate mirrors the nose, following through to a pleasingly fresh finish. Guide mentions go to the Montecarlo Rosso, Rosato Cerasello, Vermentino, Montecarlo Bianco Terre della Gioiosa, and the unusual Syrah for their uncomplicated but well-managed style.

● Montechiari Cabernet '97	▼▼▼	6
○ Montechiari Chardonnay '98	▼▼	5
● Montechiari Pinot Nero '97	▼▼	6
○ Montecarlo Bianco '99	▼	3
● Montechiari Rosso '97	▼	5
● Montechiari Cabernet '95	♈♈♈	5
● Montecarlo Rosso '96	♈♈	3*
● Montechiari Cabernet '96	♈♈	6
○ Montechiari Chardonnay '96	♈♈	4
● Montechiari Nero '95	♈♈	5
● Montechiari Pinot Nero '96	♈♈	5
● Montechiari Rosso '95	♈♈	4
○ Montechiari Chardonnay '97	♈	4
● Montechiari Rosso '96	♈	4

○ Montecarlo Bianco		
Terre dei Cascinieri '98	▼▼	4
● Terre dei Cascinieri '98	▼▼	4
● Virente '97	▼▼	5
◉ Cerasello '99		2
○ Montecarlo Bianco		
Terre della Gioiosa '99		2
● Montecarlo Rosso		
Terre della Gioiosa '99		2
● Syrah '99		2
○ Vermentino '99		2
● Montecarlo Rosso		
Terre dei Cascinieri '97	♈♈	4
● Virente '95	♈♈	5
● Virente '96	♈♈	5

448

MONTECATINI VAL DI CECINA (PI)　MONTEFOLLONICO (SI)

FATTORIA SORBAIANO
VIA PROVINCIALE TRE COMUNI
56040 MONTECATINI
VAL DI CECINA (PI)
TEL. 0588/30243

VITTORIO INNOCENTI
VIA LANDUCCI, 10/12
53040 MONTEFOLLONICO (SI)
TEL. 0577/669537

Tenaciously and unrelentingly, the Fattoria di Sorbaiano has carved itself out an important wine-making niche in the Pisa-Livorno area, well away from the better-known zones such as Chianti or Montalcino. It was a bit of a surprise this year that their best wine was the Lucestraia, one of the best whites to be found around Montescudaio. It easily carried off Two Glasses but at the same time it gave the impression of being an unfinished masterpiece, lacking only a little will or strength to scale even more prestigious heights. Its straw-yellow colour is flecked with gold and ushers in an inviting nose of ripe fruit, honey, and faint smoky notes. The entry on the palate is so soft it is almost unctuous but it has weight and equilibrium as it progresses into a well-sustained mid palate and a rising finish that lingers well. The Rosso delle Miniere is not ready yet but in its place there is a new red, the Pian del Conte '98. Its has a palate of good juicy fruit and a supple dynamism that takes it through to a decent finish, where still roughish tannins show through. The Montescudaio Rosso '99 has shifted up a gear. A pleasant wine, it unveils a fruity if slightly vegetal nose. The palate is well-sustained, with medium structure and a shortish finish nuanced with pepper. However, the Montescudaio Bianco is not as successful. There is rich tropical fruit on the clean nose but in the mouth, it is unbalanced and somewhat acidulous. Finally, their Vin Santo '92 is made in a very traditional style. Not very sweet on the palate, it has a well-balanced flavour and is moderately long.

Vittorio Innocenti's most important news is that he has moved his cellar to the 17th-century Muccinelli Palace in the atmospheric mediaeval quarter of Montefollonico. Innocenti is rightly proud of his new cellar, which is both architecturally splendid and more functional that the previous one. The increase in the number of small barrels should permit the cellar, according to the proprietor, to speed up the process of ageing the wines. The Montefollonico zone is known for the structure of its wines, which require time to age properly. For this reason, wines and wine guides sometimes have conflicting deadlines. The Acerone '97 is not ready for this year's Guide but the two selections of Vin Santo are marvellous. The Vin Santo '95 has intense aromas of walnutskins, hazelnuts and candied peel. The entry on the palate is elegant, with enough acidity to offset the sugar and produce a broad, deep finish that never threatens to become cloying. The only problem is the meagre number of bottles released. The '90 has a different style. The colour is decidedly amber, and the aromas are more evolved, with prominent notes of marron glacé. In the mouth, it has incredible texture, with a very sweet attack and exciting progression. Over the top? Perhaps, but the parameters are different for a Vin Santo. The red wines showed well, the Nobile di Montepulciano nearly gaining Two Glasses. It has a traditional style, with notes of peach and crushed cherry fruit, and the wood is reasonably well-integrated. The tannins on the palate are a little assertive, which is characteristic of the area. Equally good is the Montepulciano Riserva '96, a successful wine, considering its vintage.

O	Montescudaio Bianco Lucestraia '98	♙♙	4
●	Montescudaio Rosso '99	♙	2*
O	Montescudaio Vin Santo '92	♙	3
●	Pian del Conte '98	♙	3
O	Montescudaio Bianco '99		2
●	Montescudaio Rosso delle Miniere '94	♙♙	4
●	Montescudaio Rosso delle Miniere '95	♙♙	4
●	Montescudaio Rosso delle Miniere '96	♙♙	4
●	Montescudaio Rosso delle Miniere '97	♙♙	4

O	Vin Santo '90	♙♙	6
O	Vin Santo '95	♙♙	6
●	Nobile di Montepulciano '97	♙	4
●	Nobile di Montepulciano Ris. '96	♙	5
●	Nobile di Montepulciano Ris. '88	♙♙♙	5
●	Acerone '90	♙♙	5
●	Acerone '93	♙♙	5
O	Vin Santo '93	♙♙	5
●	Nobile di Montepulciano '89	♙♙	4
●	Nobile di Montepulciano '93	♙♙	3*
●	Nobile di Montepulciano Ris. '90	♙♙	5

MONTEMURLO (PO)

MONTEPULCIANO (SI)

TENUTA DI BAGNOLO
DEI MARCHESI PANCRAZI
VIA MONTALESE, 156
59013 MONTEMURLO (PO)
TEL. 0574/652439

AVIGNONESI
VIA DI GRACCIANO NEL CORSO, 91
53045 MONTEPULCIANO (SI)
TEL. 0578/757872 - 0578/757873

When you talk about growing pinot nero in Italy, you have to mention Tenuta di Bagnolo. Certainly, it is the only estate in Tuscany whose flagship wine is obtained from the grape, and the '98 Villa di Bagnolo once again proves that it is among the best of its kind in the country. It also demonstrates how astounding well this difficult grape has adapted to Montemurlo, where it deserves classification as an official subzone. Yet again, we feel we should underline how important it is with Pinot Nero not to make a hurriedly superficial evaluation. A palate that initially seems very simple often gradually reveals an unexpected complexity. The Pinot Nero from Villa di Bagnolo is that kind of bottle. At first, it is reluctant – even unco-operative – on the nose, where black berry fruit and smoky notes emerge. After breathing for a while, aromas of flowers, spices, and minerals begin to peek through. The palate is rather more approachable and shows an attractively understated softness, complemented by fresh acidity and delicious tannins. There is a new label this year from the estate's other property, the Tenuta di San Donato. This wine, Casaglia '98, is a monovarietal Colorino and nearly walked off with Two Glasses on its debut. A well-made wine, it has laudably crisp aromas and even some style. Which is saying a lot for a Colorino. On the palate, it is solid and rigorous, thanks to still rather aggressive tannins that nevertheless show good quality. To conclude, we sampled the decent and very drinkable Rosso di San Donato '98.

It is a real pleasure to give our top award to an estate that has been of fundamental importance in the oenological history of Montepulciano. The 50&50 '97 is a stunner. Made in collaboration with the Capannelle estate, the wine is a barrique-aged blend of sangiovese (from Capannelle) and merlot (from Avignonese). The very intense red colour shades into violet, ushering in a rich, fruity nose in which wild cherries, black berry fruit and both red and blackcurrants are present. The palate is really outstanding for power and elegance, the sweet entry being followed by a sure-footed progression backed up by delicate tannins. The Desiderio '97 is almost as good and possibly the best version ever released. The blend has been altered slightly and instead of 100% merlot now includes cabernet sauvignon. The nose of rich berry fruit has a faint, not unpleasant, vegetal note. The flavour is good but it will need a bit more time for the tannins to settle down. There is also good news on the white front. The Marzocco '98, a barrique-aged Chardonnay, is very good indeed. The intense straw-yellow colour unfolds notes of ripe peaches and mashed banana while the palate has good balance, intensity and persistence. The '97 Vino Nobile, the Bianco Avignonesi '97 and its Rosso stablemate, are all good. As expected, the Vin Santo '90 is very good and suffers only from a slight reluctance to open on the nose. For all its richness, the L'Occhio di Pernice '88 is not as drinkable as it might be because of its over-abundant residual sugars, which are not adequately offset by acidity.

● Pinot Nero Villa di Bagnolo '98	🍷🍷	5
● Casaglia '98	🍷	4
● San Donato '98	🍷	2*
● Pinot Nero Villa di Bagnolo '89	🍷🍷	5
● Pinot Nero Villa di Bagnolo '91	🍷🍷	5
● Pinot Nero Villa di Bagnolo '92	🍷🍷	5
● Pinot Nero Villa di Bagnolo '93	🍷🍷	5
● Pinot Nero Villa di Bagnolo '94	🍷🍷	5
● Pinot Nero Villa di Bagnolo '95	🍷🍷	5
● Pinot Nero Villa di Bagnolo '97	🍷🍷	5
● Pinot Nero Villa di Bagnolo '90	🍷	5
● Pinot Nero Villa di Bagnolo '96	🍷	5
● San Donato '97	🍷	3

● 50 & 50 Avignonesi e Capannelle '97	🍷🍷🍷	6
● Desiderio '97	🍷🍷	6
○ Il Marzocco '98	🍷🍷	4
○ Vin Santo '90	🍷🍷	6
○ Vin Santo Occhio di Pernice '88	🍷🍷	6
○ Bianco Avignonesi '99	🍷	3
● Rosso Avignonesi '98	🍷	3
● Nobile di Montepulciano '97	🍷	4
○ Vin Santo '88	🍷🍷🍷	6
○ Vin Santo '89	🍷🍷🍷	6
● Merlot '93	🍷🍷	6
● Merlot Desiderio '95	🍷🍷	6
○ Vin Santo '86	🍷🍷	6
○ Vin Santo Occhio di Pernice '87	🍷🍷	6

BINDELLA

Loc. Acquaviva
Via delle Tre Berte, 10/a
53040 Montepulciano (SI)
tel. 0578/767777

Including the recent plantings, Bindella now has 30 hectares under vine, which should be sufficient to satisfy the needs of the many admirers of this important producer. All the new vines are high-density plantings because of the satisfactory results obtained from the older plots planted in this way. The main estate building is one of the most handsome in the zone, with large, comfortable rooms. The barrique cellars and area where fermentation vats stand are temperature-controlled. Two wines are produced at Bindella, a Nobile di Montepulciano and Vallocaia. The '97s are very good, although we were expecting an even better result. In particular, both wines were a little hesitant on the nose. The Nobile has a fine, concentrated ruby colour and an incisive attack on the palate, which reveals attractive tannins, and the sustained finish has good breadth and persistence. The fruit has a hard time emerging, which cost the wine a point or two, but it is still a lovely bottle. The Vallocaia went no further than One Glass. Its purple hue is attractive but the fruit on the nose is held back by an over-stated grassy note. The palate is satisfying, although the tannins will needs more time in the bottle to integrate properly.

●	Nobile di Montepulciano '97	**YY**	5
●	Vallocaia '97	**Y**	6
●	Vallocaia '90	YY	5
●	Vallocaia '94	YY	5
●	Vallocaia '95	YY	5
●	Nobile di Montepulciano '90	YY	4
●	Nobile di Montepulciano '91	YY	4
●	Nobile di Montepulciano '92	YY	4
●	Nobile di Montepulciano '94	YY	4
●	Nobile di Montepulciano Ris. '90	YY	5
●	Vallocaia '93	Y	5
●	Vallocaia '96	Y	5
●	Nobile di Montepulciano '95	Y	4

BOSCARELLI

Fraz. Acquaviva
Via di Montenero, 28
53040 Montepulciano (SI)
tel. 0578/767277 - 0578/767608

This estate, which belongs to the De Ferraris, is one of the best known in Montalcino. The seriousness and attention that the family has devoted to the property have attracted many passionate admirers. Located at Cervognano, in one of the best subzones of Montepulciano, and well-known for producing elegant, powerful wines, Boscarelli has over the years acquired a well-defined style. Their austere, terroir-driven wines are delightful when they first come out, and maintain their quality or even improve over the years. Year after year, the Boscarelli style is obvious in the leading wine, the Nobile di Montepulciano Vigna del Nocio, a product of great personality. In the version presented this year, the legendary (and perhaps over-hyped) '97 vintage, the "Nocio", as it is known to its fans, it is at the top of its category. Although rich and fruity, the aromas are unfortunately a little fuzzy, which cuts back its breadth. But the flavours are a credit to this cellar and its well-known oenologist, Maurizio Castelli, for the palate is austerely elegant and has a wonderful balance of tannins and alcohol. The other Boscarelli wines are less successful. Above all, the reluctance of the Nobile di Montepulciano '97 to open up on the nose left us perplexed, even though it makes a good recovery on the palate, thanks to its poised opulence. The house Supertuscan, the Boscarelli '97, has a very concentrated ruby colour. The nose is interesting, with balsamic notes of mint and eucalyptus over a hint of blackberry jam. In the mouth, it proffers generous tannins, good alcohol, and a long finish.

●	Boscarelli '97	**YY**	5
●	Nobile di Montepulciano Vigna del Nocio '97	**YY**	5
●	Nobile di Montepulciano '97	**Y**	4
●	Nobile di Montepulciano Ris. '88	YYY	5
●	Nobile di Montepulciano Ris. del Nocio '91	YYY	5
●	Boscarelli '95	YY	6
●	Nobile di Montepulciano Ris. del Nocio '93	YY	5
●	Nobile di Montepulciano Vigna del Nocio '95	YY	5
●	Nobile di Montepulciano Vigna del Nocio '96	YY	5

MONTEPULCIANO (SI)

MONTEPULCIANO (SI)

FATTORIA DEL CERRO
FRAZ. ACQUAVIVA
VIA GRAZIANELLA, 5
53040 MONTEPULCIANO (SI)
TEL. 0578/767722

CONTUCCI
VIA DEL TEATRO, 1
53045 MONTEPULCIANO (SI)
TEL. 0578/757006

The Fattoria del Cerro has done well this year. Five of their wines received Two Glasses, and two of those were very high-scoring. Our congratulations go to the oenologist, Lorenzo Landi, who will now be continuing his work here as consultant. The Nobile di Montepulciano Antica Chiusina '97 is simply delicious. A very concentrated ruby in colour, it offers notes of morello cherry and mulberries that blend seamlessly with the wood. The attack on the palate is excellent, revealing an elegantly complex wine with delicate, well-integrated tannins. The finish is equally outstanding, and the aromas on the palate mirror the nose perfectly. No less eye-catching is the Poggio Golo '98, which strikes us as even better than its last version. This monovarietal Merlot has a rich, almost impenetrable ruby hue and a nose that unveils hints of redcurrants and bilberries, as well as an enticing balsamic note of eucalyptus. In the mouth, it is captivating and sweet. The palate has good weight and never cloys, signing off with a broad, deep finish. A cracker of a wine. Not quite as good as the foregoing, but still among the best in its class this year, is the Rosso di Montepulciano '99. The fresh aromas of cherry and raspberry on the nose introduce a very drinkable palate with a fine balance of acidity and tannins. Extra credit goes to the Nobile di Montepulciano Riserva '96 which, despite the poor vintage, easily won Two Glasses for its all-around balance. There may be a tad too much wood on the nose but the floral note of violets comes through well while its seductive drinkability more than compensates for the slight insufficiency of extract. The standard-label wines are all well-managed.

Only one wine was presented at our tasting. Evidently Alamanno Contucci, the fiery president of the Consorzio dei Nobile di Montepulciano, decided to postpone releasing his winery's cru, Pietrarossa, because of the outstanding vintage, 1997. In the magnificent cellar, one of the most striking in Montepulciano, there now repose the products of Contucci's new winemaking policies. He has moved over to large (25-30 hectolitre) barrels of Slavonian oak and French oak tonneaux, while barriques seem to have been abandoned. It seems a long time since this cellar had romantic-looking chestnut barrels painted red and black to the delight of the many tourists who visit the winery. It's less showy now but much more in keeping with modern winemaking, which considers a barrel to be not just a container but also an ageing tool. Renovation here is still not over as the fermentation vats are going to be replaced as well. All this hard work should result in major improvements in the wines, particularly when one considers how good the vine stock is. The Nobile di Montepulciano '97 has a lovely bright ruby colour and a touch of ripe mulberry on the nose as well as the classic cherry aroma of cherries, with oak providing the subtlest of counterpoints. The palate is impeccably well-made, revealing adequate body and fine-grained tannins. The finish is lightish but coherent. Finally, it was a real shame not to taste the Vin Santo, which in recent years has been very convincing.

● Manero '98	▼▼	5
● Poggio Golo '98	▼▼	5
● Rosso di Montepulciano '99	▼▼	3*
● Nobile di Montepulciano Ris. '96	▼▼	5
● Nobile di Montepulciano Vigneto Antica Chiusina '97	▼▼	5
○ Cerro Bianco '99	▼	3
● Chianti Colline Senesi '99	▼	3
○ Vin Santo '93	▼	5
● Nobile di Montepulciano '97	▼	4
○ Bravìolo '99		2
● Nobile di Montepulciano '90	▼▼▼	4*
● Manero '97	▼▼	5
● Poggio Golo '97	▼▼	5

● Nobile di Montepulciano '97	▼	4
○ Vin Santo '86	▼▼	6
○ Vin Santo '90	▼▼	4
● Nobile di Montepulciano '90	▼▼	4
● Nobile di Montepulciano Pietrarossa '90	▼▼	5
● Nobile di Montepulciano Ris. '91	▼▼	4
● Rosso di Montepulciano '98	▼	3
● Nobile di Montepulciano '94	▼	4
● Nobile di Montepulciano '96	▼	4
● Nobile di Montepulciano Pietrarossa '94	▼	4
● Nobile di Montepulciano Pietrarossa '96	▼	4

MONTEPULCIANO (SI)

MONTEPULCIANO (SI)

DEI
LOC. VILLA MARTIENA, 35
53045 MONTEPULCIANO (SI)
TEL. 0578/716878

FASSATI
LOC. GRACCIANO
VIA DI GRACCIANELLO, 3/A
53040 MONTEPULCIANO (SI)
TEL. 06/844311 - 0578/708708

Caterina Dei, the owner of this winery, was not very pleased with how we reviewed her wines in the last edition of the Guide. She did not agree that the gap between her DOC wines and her Sancta Catharina was as wide as we thought. However, the results obtained this year are much the same as in previous years, with the DOC wines unable to match the pace of the estate's Supertuscan, Sancta Catharina, which at this point is a fixture in the top half of our Two Glass category. A barrique-aged blend of prugnolo gentile, syrah and cabernet sauvignon, this thoroughbred has a dark red colour with violet highlights, as well as a broad nose revealing clear hints of citron and pencil lead, with a faint grassy note. It is equally good on the palate, where it reveals a firm entry and good weight, thanks to its delicate tannins. The aromas on the long finish reflect the nose extremely well. The Nobile di Montepulciano '97 is in a lower category. Though better in some respects than the '96, it has not improved sufficiently to gain Two Glasses. Its ruby hue is fairly intense but fades towards the rim. On the palate, there is a not altogether satisfactory green note that tends to mask the cherry fruit. The structure is good but the tannins are not well integrated, leaving the finish without much depth. It is a pleasant enough wine but one which needs greater focus, particularly on the nose, if it is to make the big time.

A good 80 hectares, of which much has been replanted to higher densities, make up the viticultural dowry of this estate which belongs to Fazi Battaglia, a well-known Marche-based company. Of that total, a good 35 are registered in the Montepulciano zone, which shows the owners' commitment to producing this DOC wine. The cellar is put together in a very practical manner and hosts a good number of barriques and tonneaux, which when one also considers that an expert oenologist like Franco Bernabei is their consultant, gives a good indication of the potential. We noticed a change in the winery's style this year. Wood is now used with a lighter hand but this has had contrasting results. The Nobile di Montepulciano '97 Pasiteo has a dark, concentrated red colour that stays firm right to the rim. On the nose, ripe fruit with jammy overtones prevails while progression on the palate shows some hesitancy. The fine-grained tannins are free over bitter notes and so contribute to an agreeable finish which has a certain amount of depth. The Rosso di Montepulciano '99 Selciaia offers fragrant notes of cherries and is a very drinkable wine, thanks to its well-integrated acidity. In contrast, the Torre al Fante '95 was something of a let-down as it has little personality. The nose is unfocused, tannins dominates the palate and the finish is faintly bitter.

● Sancta Catharina '97	♀♀	5
● Nobile di Montepulciano '97	♀	4
● Rosso di Montepulciano '93	♀♀	3*
● Rosso di Montepulciano '94	♀♀	3*
● Sancta Catharina '94	♀♀	5
● Sancta Catharina '95	♀♀	5
● Sancta Catharina '96	♀♀	5
● Nobile di Montepulciano '90	♀♀	4
● Nobile di Montepulciano '91	♀♀	4
● Nobile di Montepulciano '93	♀♀	4
● Nobile di Montepulciano Ris. '90	♀♀	4
● Nobile di Montepulciano Ris. '93	♀♀	4
● Nobile di Montepulciano Ris. '95	♀	4

● Nobile di Montepulciano		
Pasiteo '97	♀♀	4
● Rosso di Montepulciano		
Selciaia '99	♀	3
● Torre al Fante '95		5
● Nobile di Montepulciano '93	♀♀	4
● Nobile di Montepulciano '94	♀♀	4
● Nobile di Montepulciano '95	♀♀	4
● Nobile di Montepulciano '96	♀♀	4
● Nobile di Montepulciano Ris. '93	♀♀	5
● Nobile di Montepulciano		
Salarco '93	♀♀	5
● Nobile di Montepulciano		
Salarco '95	♀♀	5

MONTEPULCIANO (SI)

MONTEPULCIANO (SI)

Fattoria La Braccesca
Loc. Gracciano
S. S. 326, 15
53040 Montepulciano (SI)
Tel. 0578/724252

La Calonica
Loc. Valiano
Via della Stella, 27
53040 Montepulciano (SI)
Tel. 0578/724119

Every year, the Antinori empire in Montepulciano gets bigger. In a few years' time, plans for development will make La Braccesca the biggest privately-owned estate in the area. The Maestrelle estate at Valiano will grow to include a fully 300 hectares under vine. In the near future, work will begin on a new underground ageing cellar. For the present, the wines reach maturity in the old cellar of the Badia di Montepulciano. The La Braccesca wines presented this year won approval at our tastings. The reds are technically impeccable, and are blessed with character and personality. The Nobile di Montepulciano '97 has intense, complex odours with grassy notes complementing the abundant fruit. After a clean, fruit-rich entry, the palate reveals slightly insistent tannins that tend to squeeze the finish. The Merlot '98 is even better. It's a stylish red even though its vegetal aromas are a bit over-done with respect to the ripe fruit. The initial impact on the palate is good, robust, and attractively complex. The tannic structure is fairly stiff at the moment, making it difficult to appreciate the wine's considerable volume. The deliciously appealing, full-bodied Rosso di Montepulciano '99 Sabazio merits just One Glass as its aromas are a little unfocused, at least in the samples that were available to us.

The Valiano area has special climatic characteristics that are due to the influence of Lake Trasimeno, which ensures mild winters and summers that are not too dry. This permits vines to have a fairly constant vegetative cycle. Ferdinando Cattani's estate takes full advantage of this situation, and as a result regularly offers good wines. The new vine stock, which has not yet come on-stream, includes not just sangiovese grapes but also others permitted by the new Nobile DOC regulations, such as cabernet and merlot. La Calonica presented four wines for tasting this year. One, presented for the first time, did so well that it easily merited Two Glasses. The Signorelli '98 is a monovarietal merlot aged in 250-litre barrels of French oak. It has a deep purplish ruby colour and while at first the nose is a bit closed, after breathing for a short time, it displays inviting hints of redcurrants and bilberries. Acidity and tannins are both rather aggressive on the palate but with a bit more bottle-ageing, these excesses should put themselves right. The progression is certainly good, and the finish coherent. This is not a Rambo-style red but it is a very attractive wine to drink. Down a notch or two is the estate classic, the Girifalco. The '98 doesn't show much improvement over previous editions. The morello cherry and cherry-themed fruit on the nose is unexciting while the glycerine and alcohol on the palate fail to amalgamate with the tannins. The two DOC wines are on the same level. The Vino Nobile '97 is slightly superior to the Rosso di Montepulciano, as it should be because of its vintage and pedigree. The Nobile is an agreeable wine without much structure but is well-managed on nose and palate.

● Merlot '98	�♐	6
● Nobile di Montepulciano '97	♐♐	5
● Rosso di Montepulciano Sabazio '99	♐	3
● Merlot '96	♈♈	5
● Merlot '97	♈♈	5
● Rosso di Montepulciano Sabazio '97	♈♈	3*
● Nobile di Montepulciano '90	♈♈	4
● Nobile di Montepulciano '93	♈♈	4
● Nobile di Montepulciano '95	♈♈	4
● Nobile di Montepulciano '96	♈♈	4
● Rosso di Montepulciano Sabazio '98	♈	3
● Nobile di Montepulciano '94	♈	4

● Signorelli '98	♐♐	5
● Girifalco '98	♐	6
● Rosso di Montepulciano '99	♐	3
● Nobile di Montepulciano '97	♐	4
● Girifalco '93	♈♈	5
● Girifalco '95	♈♈	5
● Rosso di Montepulciano '91	♈♈	3*
● Nobile di Montepulciano '90	♈♈	4
● Nobile di Montepulciano '91	♈♈	4
● Girifalco '96	♈	5
● Girifalco '97	♈	6
● La Calonica '98	♈	2*
● Nobile di Montepulciano '93	♈	4
● Nobile di Montepulciano '95	♈	4
● Nobile di Montepulciano '96	♈	4

MONTEPULCIANO (SI)

MONTEPULCIANO (SI)

TENUTA LODOLA NUOVA
TENIMENTI RUFFINO
LOC. VALIANO - VIA LODOLA, 1
53023 MONTEPULCIANO (SI)
TEL. 0578/724032

NOTTOLA
LOC. BIVIO NOTTOLA
53045 MONTEPULCIANO (SI)
TEL. 0578/707060 - 0577/685240

This estate is a part of the Tenimenti Ruffino group and now extends over the not insignificant area of 50 hectares under vine, 30 acres of which are DOC-registered. The property lies partly in Valiano and partly in Gracciano, two of the most famous subzones in Montepulciano. According to tradition, Valiano gives elegance and the Gracciano contributes power and longevity. Ruffino has been replanting the oldest plots with vines experimented at the group headquarters. New high-density vineyards and a modernised cellar will contribute to improving the wines made at Lodola Nuova. The vine types planted also correspond to the demands of the new DOC regulations, which permit cabernet and merlot as well as the traditional sangiovese. The wines presented this year reflect the transitional phase of the cellar. The Nobile di Montepulciano '97 has certainly improved. The aromas are very successful. The nose is a little slow to open but has crisp, generous notes of mulberries and wild cherries. The progression on the palate is captivating, backed up by fine-grained tannins which are neither too sharp nor detached from the alcohol. The finish, though, does not have that breadth and depth required for admission to the Two Glass level. The Rosso di Montepulciano '99 Alauda is fresh and well-made but is perhaps a bit uncertain to the nose. The flavour is more satisfactory and the palate is very refreshing and concentrated for a wine of this category.

After years of relative inertia, the Giomarelli family has decided to go in for renovation. Their new cellar is very functional, with a temperature-controlled ageing area. For the time being, much of it is surplus to requirements, until the new vine stock comes on-stream. In the new vineyards, there are a few hectares of merlot, which comes as no surprise since Riccardo Cotarella, the celebrated oenologist, is now on the staff, and he knows and greatly appreciates the variety's potential. There are also many new barriques and tonneaux, which are destined for the estate's flagship wine, the Nobile di Montepulciano Vigna del Fattore, the grapes for which come from an excellent cru. The '97 version of this wine easily merits its Two Glasses. It has a very dense red colour with purple highlights and a nose dominated by aromas of redcurrants along with strong grassy notes. The thrust on the palate is attractive, with good volume and close-knit, well-grained tannins that amalgamate well with the softer elements. The finish is free of bitter notes and has good depth. It's an admirable wine, yet one that shows some limitations, both in terms of personality and in the way it expresses its terroir.

● Rosso di Montepulciano '99	♀	3
● Nobile di Montepulciano '97	♀	4
● Rosso di Montepulciano '98	♀♀	3*
● Nobile di Montepulciano '93	♀♀	4
● Nobile di Montepulciano '95	♀♀	4
● Nobile di Montepulciano '94	♀	4
● Nobile di Montepulciano '96	♀	4

● Nobile di Montepulciano		
Vigna del Fattore '97	♀♀	5
● Nobile di Montepulciano		
Vigna del Fattore '95	♀♀	5
● Rosso di Montepulciano '93	♀	2*
● Rosso di Montepulciano '96	♀	3
● Nobile di Montepulciano '93	♀	4
● Nobile di Montepulciano '94	♀	4
● Nobile di Montepulciano '96	♀	4
● Nobile di Montepulciano Ris. '91	♀	4
● Nobile di Montepulciano		
Vigna del Fattore '96	♀	5

MONTEPULCIANO (SI)

MONTEPULCIANO (SI)

REDI
VIA DI COLLAZZI, 5
53045 MONTEPULCIANO (SI)
TEL. 0578/757102

MASSIMO ROMEO
LOC. NOTTOLA DI GRACCIANO
VIA DI TOTONA, 29
53045 MONTEPULCIANO (SI)
TEL. 0578/757127

This has been another good year for Redi. All their wines get at least one glass, a significant indication that their whole range is getting better. They also have a new wine this year, the Argo, a very approachable, easy-drinking Sangiovese. A brilliant ruby red in the glass, it has a pleasantly fresh nose and an attractive palate nicely backed up by balanced acidity. There is also good news on the barrel front. The historic cellar in the centre of Montepulciano is no longer full of old, large-capacity chestnut barrels; they have been replaced with barriques and tonneaux. Redi is the technical cutting edge of Vecchia Cantina, the only wine co-operative in the Montepulciano area, and has 970 hectares under vine. Their '98 edition of their only white wine, the Riccio, was not ready at the time of our tastings but their more traditional wines, the Vin Santo '92 and the Nobile Briareo '97, were both more than just well-managed. The Nobile has a deep ruby colour and a broad, intense nose, on which caramel and redcurrant preserves emerge, then lives up to expectation with a mouth of good breadth and density. The amber Vin Santo '92 is very solid, offering notes of walnutskins and apricots on the nose and good balance in the mouth. The Rosso di Montepulciano '99 and the Vino Nobile '97 both easily qualified for One Glass.

Massimo Romeo's wines have a very personal style. He grows his fruit in Gracciano, one of the noblest parts of Montepulciano, and strives to make the best wines he can by limiting yields per hectare, by using various kinds of barrels, from 30-hectolitre giants down to barriques, and by opting for long macerations. Massimo's wines have hallmark aromas which have found numerous fans but also a few detractors. We are among those who like this rather traditional style. The wines tend to be at their best after a few years in the bottle to mellow out their tannins. The Nobile di Montepulciano '97 has an attractive, concentrated ruby colour and a nose that unfurls notes of tobacco, oleander, peaches, apricots, and an appealing grace note of pencil lead. On the palate, the tannins overpower the softer components but on the positive side, there is absolutely no trace of bitterness, and this bodes well for the wine's future. The Lipitiresco '97 is better. Its aromas are very much in the Romeo style, proffering floral notes of oleander and violets and berry fruit with cherry to the fore, enhanced by nicely understated wood. The palate is nice. Its relative austerity is complemented by good weight and prominent, but well-controlled acidity and tannins. This small winery has done a good job all round, preserving its identity without succumbing to pressure from the market place and passing fashions.

O Vin Santo '92	♟♟	6
● Nobile di Montepulciano		
Briareo '97	♟♟	6
● Argo '99	♟	3
● Nobile di Montepulciano '97	♟	4
● Rosso di Montepulciano '99	♟	3
O Riccio '97	♟♟	4
O Vin Santo '90	♟♟	6
● Nobile di Montepulciano		
Briareo '96	♟♟	5
● Rosso di Montepulciano '97	♟	3
● Nobile di Montepulciano '95	♟	4
● Nobile di Montepulciano '96	♟	4
● Nobile di Montepulciano Ris. '95	♟	5

● Lipitiresco '97	♟♟	6
● Nobile di Montepulciano '97	♟	4
● Lipitiresco '90	♟♟	4
O Vin Santo '83	♟♟	6
O Vin Santo '86	♟♟	5
● Nobile di Montepulciano '91	♟♟	5
● Nobile di Montepulciano '95	♟♟	5
● Nobile di Montepulciano Ris. '88	♟♟	5
● Nobile di Montepulciano Ris. '95	♟♟	5
● Lipitiresco '95	♟	5
● Nobile di Montepulciano '96	♟	4
● Nobile di Montepulciano		
Ris. dei Mandorli '94	♟	5

MONTEPULCIANO (SI)

SALCHETO
VIA DI VILLA BIANCA, 15
53045 MONTEPULCIANO (SI)
TEL. 0578/799031

There have been many changes at the Salcheto winery this year. The new cellar is finished and it's splendid. Completely underground and temperature-controlled, it is a great improvement on the old facilities. It holds a few 20 or 30 hectolitre barrels but the barriques and tonneaux are legion. There is a completely separate fermentation cellar, in a building that looks more like a Tyrolese farmhouse than a Tuscan one but it, too, is absolutely functional. There is news from the vineyards as well. Seven more hectares of vines have been planted, bringing the total to 12. There have been some concessions made to international varieties but very few of them, and they consist of small experimental plots. This attention to the search for new possibilities in the vineyards is utterly praiseworthy, considering the size of the operation. There is very positive news about the wines as well. The Nobile di Montepulciano '97 is truly excellent, earning its Three Glasses with authority and panache. It has an intense ruby hue with violet highlights. Black berry fruit is very much in evidence on the nose, as well as the varietal trademark hint of cherries, and the vanilla from the oak is nicely dosed. Both entry and progression on the palate are excellent, the smooth tannins leading through to a slow, seductive finish, laced with the subtlest of wood-derived sensations. This wine is a paragon of focus and harmony. The Rosso di Montepulciano '98, which needs a few minutes to express itself to the full, gained a One Glass rating for its pleasing medium-bodied palate and refreshing acidity.

MONTEPULCIANO (SI)

TENIMENTI ANGELINI
TENUTA TREROSE
FRAZ. VALIANO
VIA DELLA STELLA, 3
53040 MONTEPULCIANO (SI)
TEL. 0578/724018

Three very well merited glasses go to Tenimenti Angelini, a winery which for a number of years has been striving uncompromisingly for high quality. The prize goes to their Nobile di Montepulciano '97 Simposio but the other wines they presented this year are also worthy of note. However, that Nobile Simposio is simply splendid. The product of techniques that are modern without sliding into mere fashion, it brings out the characteristics of the prugnolo gentile grape, which are enhanced by the high quality of the fruit and a careful use of wood. The ruby in the glass is concentrated, introducing complex aromas of morello cherries and mulberries with balsamic notes of eucalyptus and mint, and touches of vanilla and coffee. The splendid poise of the nose is reflected on the palate, where the exceptionally close-knit tannins mingle seamlessly with the other components. The acidity gives freshness to wine but does not hold back the well-sustained progression through to the long, broad finish. The second selection of their Nobile from the same year is also very good. In fact, the Vino Nobile La Villa '97 itself comes quite close to receiving Three Glasses. Pitched in a different key from the Simposio, it follows a more international style, with aromas of citron and blackcurrants which hint at the presence of grapes other than prugnolo gentile, as, indeed, is permitted by the DOC regulations. The palate is very soft and inviting. The Busillis '98, an oak-aged monovarietal Viognier, is also excellent. Fruit-rich and full-bodied, it offers hints of apricot on the nose and lovely weight and balance on the palate. The other wines presented were all nicely managed.

●	Nobile di Montepulciano '97	♟♟♟	5
●	Rosso di Montepulciano '98	♟	3
●	Salcheto '90	♟♟	4
●	Nobile di Montepulciano '91	♟♟	4
●	Nobile di Montepulciano Ris. '93	♟♟	5
●	Nobile di Montepulciano Ris. '95	♟♟	5
●	Rosso di Montepulciano '92	♟	3
●	Rosso di Montepulciano '96	♟	3
●	Nobile di Montepulciano '94	♟	4
●	Nobile di Montepulciano '95	♟	4
●	Nobile di Montepulciano '96	♟	4

●	Nobile di Montepulciano Simposio '97	♟♟♟	6
●	Nobile di Montepulciano La Villa '97	♟♟	6
○	Busillis '98	♟♟	4
○	Renaio '99	♟	3
●	Rosso di Montepulciano '99	♟	3
●	Nobile di Montepulciano '97	♟	4
●	Nobile di Montepulciano La Villa '95	♟♟	5
●	Nobile di Montepulciano Simposio '93	♟♟	5
●	Nobile di Montepulciano Simposio '95	♟♟	5

MONTEPULCIANO (SI)

MONTEPULCIANO (SI)

TENUTA VALDIPIATTA
VIA DELLA CIARLIANA, 25
53040 MONTEPULCIANO (SI)
TEL. 0578/757930

VILLA S. ANNA
FRAZ. ABBADIA
53040 MONTEPULCIANO (SI)
TEL. 0578/708017

Expansion of the cellar at Valdipiatta has been completed in time for the new vineyards that are about to come on-stream. The revamped building is very attractive and blends in very well with its surroundings. The constant improvements at this estate have brought it very close to a Three Glass award for its Nobile di Montepulciano '97. The vibrant ruby colour stays firm to the rim, ushering in a broad, complex nose where morello cherry fruit and violet floral notes blend nicely with hints of wood. It has outstanding presence on the palate, combining well-knit tannins with good length. Perhaps it could have done with a little more finesse but it is certainly one of the best interpretations of Vino Nobile this year. There is good news about the other Valdipiatta wines, as well. The Tre Fonti '97 is an unqualified success. As soon as you pick up the glass, the colour tells you that this blend of cabernet sauvignon, prugnolo gentile and canaiolo will mirror its fruit, and in fact it releases aromas of red and black berries, a hint of citron, and serious cherry fruit. The palate is equally delicious, delivering good balance and well-integrated tannins that guarantee that it is drinking well right now. Il Trincerone '98 is a very nice wine that came very close to getting Two Glasses. From merlot and canaiolo, it is symbolic of the link between native varieties that were sidelined with too much haste and the international grapes that have had such success in Italy in recent years. The Rosso di Montepulciano '99 is also well made. We would like to mention that Miriam Caporali, the owner's daughter, has started working full-time at the winery, and is in charge of public relations. Our best wishes for success in her new job.

The big news at this lovely winery is the arrival of a new technical consultant, Carlo Ferrini. This is an excellent choice, considering the success that Carlo's wines have had elsewhere. The first sign of improvement here is the increase in the number of barriques which will be used for the Vallone and also, at least in part, for the Nobile. As always, with only 12 hectares planted to vine, Villa S. Anna has problems meeting demand. Nevertheless, things are beginning to look up since they are in the process of acquiring new land. We are talking long-term, of course, but then time is always needed in agriculture, especially when you are aiming for quality. Three wines were presented this year, the '96 Vallone having been shelved because the vintage was not considered good enough. All three earned One Glass, although the Nobile di Montepulciano was a cut above the other two, as its vintage and pedigree might suggest. It has an attractively intense ruby hue and morello cherry fruit on the nose mingling with attractive floral notes. The palate is very drinkable, with a refreshing vein of acidity. An undemanding wine, but a well-managed one. The work-horse of the estate, the Chianti Colline Senesi '99, is also well put together. Fragrant and fruity, it is incredibly easy to drink, the only drawback being a slightly bitter finish. The Rosso di Montepulciano '99 was making its debut at our tasting. It opens somewhat slowly on the nose, and is a little hesitant until it manages to breathe, but then it improves on the palate, which is attractively well-balanced and refreshing.

● Tre Fonti '97	♟♟	5
● Nobile di Montepulciano '97	♟♟	4
● Rosso di Montepulciano '99	♟	3
● Trincerone '98	♟	5
● Nobile di Montepulciano Ris. '90	♟♟♟	5
● Tre Fonti '96	♟♟	5
● Trincerone '97	♟♟	5
● Nobile di Montepulciano '94	♟♟	4
● Nobile di Montepulciano '95	♟♟	4
● Nobile di Montepulciano '96	♟♟	4
● Nobile di Montepulciano Ris. '93	♟♟	5
● Nobile di Montepulciano Ris. '95	♟♟	5

● Chianti Colli Senesi '99	♟	3
● Rosso di Montepulciano '99	♟	3
● Nobile di Montepulciano '97	♟	4
● Chianti '94	♟♟	2*
● Chianti Colli Senesi '95	♟♟	2*
● Vigna Il Vallone '95	♟♟	5
● Nobile di Montepulciano '94	♟♟	4
● Nobile di Montepulciano '96	♟♟	4
● Nobile di Montepulciano '93	♟♟	4
● Chianti Colli Senesi '96	♟	3
● Chianti Colli Senesi '98	♟	3
● Vigna Il Vallone '93	♟	5
○ Vin Santo '90	♟	5
○ Vin Santo '93	♟	5
● Nobile di Montepulciano '95	♟	4

MONTEPULCIANO STAZIONE (SI)

★ Poliziano
Via Fontago, 1
53040 Montepulciano
Stazione (SI)
tel. 0578/738171

It gets harder and harder to find new adjectives to say how good a winemaker Federico Carletti is. A benchmark for the whole Nobile area, he presented this year two splendid wines that carried off our top award. Both the Nobile Asinone '97 and the Le Stanze Supertuscan from the same year absolutely mesmerised our tasting panel. Success and recognition, though, have not halted Carletti's ongoing efforts to improve his products. His new cellar now enables work to be done in a more rational fashion but even more changes are currently under way. There are new fermenters to be tried out on the 2000 vintage, in the hope of extracting even sweeter tannins. The Nobile di Montepulciano Asinone '97 is truly exemplary, not only for its terroir-oriented character but also for its style. The fruit on the nose is endlessly subtle and the oak lends excellent balance. On the palate, there is a richness that never cloys, thanks to silky tannins and well-judged acidity, while its finish is broad and long. Le Stanze '97 is on a par with its stablemate, a red that can stand alongside the world's finest Bordeaux blends. Bluish red in colour, the nose offers notes of blackcurrant, cinnamon and citron while the palate has excellent weight, the tannins melding perfectly into the whole. There is also good news about the Vino Nobile '97 which, even though it has a less imposing structure than its big brother, it is still very pleasing and harmonious. The aromatic Morellino Lhosa '99 offers a palate of the customary softness and exemplifies the new way of making Morellino. The Rosso di Montepulciano '99 didn't earn more than One Glass because its nose lacks focus.

●	Le Stanze '98	🍷🍷🍷	6
●	Nobile di Montepulciano Asinone '97	🍷🍷🍷	6
●	Morellino di Scansano Lohsa '99	🍷🍷	3*
●	Rosso di Montepulciano '99	🍷	3
●	Nobile di Montepulciano '97	🍷	4
●	Elegia '95	YYY	5
●	Le Stanze '95	YYY	5
●	Le Stanze '97	YYY	6
●	Nobile di Montepulciano Vigna dell'Asinone '93	YYY	5
●	Nobile di Montepulciano Vigna dell'Asinone '95	YYY	5
●	Nobile di Montepulciano Asinone '96	YY	5

MONTESCUDAIO (PI)

Poggio Gagliardo
Loc. Poggio Gagliardo
56040 Montescudaio (PI)
tel. 0586/630775

Poggio Gagliardo has come out with yet another label, and if all new wines were this good, we would be very happy indeed. The newcomer is called Gobbo ai Pianacci (the name of a vineyard) and it's a Montescudaio DOC, pepped up with a bit of cabernet sauvignon and merlot. Soon, it will be made entirely from these two grapes. Walter Surbone's winery has been broadening its horizons, not least in that it is now run by his son, Andrea. Up until now, they have concentrated almost totally on making the finest possible Sangiovese, in the shape of their Rovo, the '98 version of which was not yet ready at the time of our tastings. The Gobbo '97, however, came out for the first time in the best possible fashion, easily earning its Two Glasses. It has a dark, vibrant, close-knit colour and a nose that is clean, concentrated, fruit-rich and nicely dosed with wood. The palate is full-bodied, well-balanced, lined with soft tannins and endowed with a good long finish. The Montescudaio Vigna Lontana '99 is also very good, revealing intense aromas of tropical fruit and oak-derived smoky notes. On the palate, it is attractively buttery, with good thrust and plenty of length. The Linaglia '99 also did well, showing good breadth on the palate and fresh, intense flower and fruit aromas on the nose. The structure of the Montescudaio Rosso was a surprise. It has the odd vegetal note but is decidedly pleasing. Poggio Gagliardo's attractively lively Montescudaio Bianco rounded off this impressive outing.

○	Montescudaio Bianco Vigna Lontana '99	🍷🍷	4
●	Montescudaio Rosso Gobbo ai Pianacci '97	🍷🍷	5
○	Montescudaio Bianco '99	🍷	3
○	Montescudaio Bianco Linaglia '99	🍷	4
●	Montescudaio Rosso '99	🍷	3
○	Montescudaio Bianco Vigna Lontana '98	YY	4
●	Montescudaio Rosso Malemacchie '92	YY	3*
●	Montescudaio Rosso Rovo '93	YY	4
●	Montescudaio Rosso Rovo '94	YY	4
●	Montescudaio Rosso Rovo '97	YY	5

MONTESPERTOLI (FI)

LE CALVANE
VIA CASTIGLIONI, 1/5
50025 MONTESPERTOLI (FI)
TEL. 0571/671073

MONTESPERTOLI (FI)

POGGIO A POPPIANO
VIA DI POPPIANO, 19
50025 MONTESPERTOLI (FI)
TEL. 055/213084

We are always pleased when wineries like Fattoria de Le Calvane receive public recognition even though they have had to struggle in a less than propitious location. We are even happier when the wine that gets the prize has been already been making very good showings for several years. Put succinctly, Borro del Boscone has been coming close to Three Glasses for some time now, and this year it just could not be denied. This is an magisterial wine that makes full use of the cabernet sauvignon grapes which grow at Le Calvane. It has a dark, deep colour, and makes an immediate impact with its exuberantly rich aromas of redcurrant, mulberry and chocolate. The entry on the palate is well-balanced, combining the vitality of the fruit with substantial yet velvety tannins, and carrying everything through to a broad, lingering finish. Le Calvane winery devotes equal care to the production of all it products and the Chianti Colli Fiorentini Riserva Il Trecione is proof. It's a wine with an astonishing structure, formed with elegance and rigorous style. The aromas are still youthful but the palate has juicy fruit, good balance and nicely judged wood. The Chardonnay Collecimoli is better than you might expect. The vibrant, lively entry on the nose offers intense floral aromas of roses and jasmine, as well as tropical fruit. The palate is well-rounded and attractively balanced, with moderate length. Although intense, sweet, and fairly original, the Vin Santo Zipolo d'Oro is already showing signs of age.

Situated in Montespertoli, this estate owned by Clemente Zileri del Verme makes its Guide debut this year. The 86-hectare estate has 25 hectares under vine and since 1990, replanting has been going on under the supervision of Federico Staderini, who has been putting in the major Bordeaux grapes and paying special attention to the sangiovese selections planted. There are two different wines made here. One is the Flocco, which is mostly cabernet sauvignon with some merlot and sangiovese, and the other is Calamita, a blend of merlot and sangiovese. Both impressed the panel. The Calamita '99 has an invitingly lively ruby colour. The nose offers vivaciously intense fruit aromas and then a fresh, lively entry on the palate with just the right amount of acidity to set off the robust alcohol. The prominent tannins never intrude and the finish is long and enjoyable. More time in the cellar can only improve this wine. The Flocco '97 has a dark ruby colour that is almost impenetrable. The nose reveals wood-derived aromas at first but these then give way to fruit notes of ripe redcurrants. Entry on the palate is immediate, with rich, juicy fruit. The Flocco '98 has a very deep, intense ruby colour. Spices are immediately apparent to the nose, and then comes an attractively elegant, delicate note of fruit. The entry on the palate is soft and silky, nicely concentrated and backed up by well-integrated tannins.

● Borro del Boscone '97	￥￥￥	5
● Chianti Colli Fiorentini Il Trecione Ris. '97	￥￥	4
○ Collecimoli '98	￥	4
○ Vin Santo Zipolo d'Oro '93		4
● Borro del Boscone '91	￥￥	4
● Borro del Boscone '94	￥￥	4
● Borro del Boscone '95	￥￥	5
● Borro del Boscone '96	￥￥	5
● Chianti Colli Fiorentini Il Trecione Ris. '91	￥￥	4
● Chianti Colli Fiorentini Il Trecione Ris. '96	￥￥	4
○ Vin Santo Zipolo d'Oro '92	￥	4

● Calamita '99	￥￥	4
● Flocco '97	￥￥	5
● Flocco '98	￥￥	5

MONTESPERTOLI (FI)　　　MONTOPOLI IN VAL D'ARNO (PI)

FATTORIA CASTELLO SONNINO
VIA VOLTERRANA NORD, 10
50025 MONTESPERTOLI (FI)
TEL. 0571/609198

VARRAMISTA
LOC. VARRAMISTA
VIA RICAVO, 31
56020 MONTOPOLI
IN VAL D'ARNO (PI)
TEL. 0571/468121 - 0571/468122

This Montespertoli winemaker made another good impression this year. Last year we pleaded with them to try to give their products greater consistency and at the tasting, the panel gained the impression that Castello Sonnino was now on the right track. The best bottle was the Sanleone '98. A blend of merlot and sangiovese with a small proportion of petit verdot, it has a concentrated ruby colour in the glass and a nose that is a little slow to open but which eventually reveals sweet fruit that shades into jammy notes. The entry on the palate is concentrated and close-knit, backed up by soft, well-integrated tannins. The Chianti '99 is uncomplicated but utterly reliable. The simple fruit has nice acidity and tannins that are evident but not over-aggressive, together with a finish of medium length. The Riserva Castello di Montespertoli '97 is even better. It has pleasing aromas of fresh fruit, and is clean, robust, and lingering. The Cantinino Vigneto Fezzana '97 has aromas that are sweetish and buttery at first but then reveal notes of plum fruit, followed by a slightly excessive grassy note. The palate is soft, medium-bodied, and spirited. We close with their Vin Santo '96. The clear amber colour leads in to a very broad range of aromas going from hazelnuts to confectioner's cream, together with notes of oxidation that blend in well. The velvety palate offers hints of raisins and a very long, sweet after-aroma.

Without much fanfare, or being noticed in the press, syrah in Tuscany – except of course in those areas where it has been grown for over than a century – has demonstrated a potential that even the growers hardly suspected. The best results have been obtained in Chianti but the Varramista winery, whose vines stand in the Pisan countryside, are a brilliant exception. Since the mid 90s, Federico Staderini, the oenologist who is responsible for the crop, has consistently brought out wines that are crisply defined, aroma-rich and full-bodied without ever being too heavy. As you can see from the grid below, the row of Two Glass awards indicates an admirably consistent level of quality. The winery has not yet received a Three Glass accolade, it is true, but it has never been far off. As ever, the '98 version is an excellent wine, clean, consistent, and very good – in fact, a hair's breadth away from the very top rank. It has a medium ruby colour with bright cherry red highlights and a spicy nose typical of the variety, together with a ripe, inviting fruit richness. The palate is well-balanced and tangily fruity, with an excellent acid-based freshness, lots of elegance and good structure. The long finish concludes in a crisply well-ordered succession of aromatic sensations.

● Sanleone '98	♟♟	4
○ Vin Santo del Chianti '96	♟♟	4
● Cantinino Vign. di Fezzana '97	♟	3
● Chianti '99	♟	2*
● Chianti Titolato		
Castello di Montespertoli Ris. '97	♟	3
● Cantinino Vign. di Fezzana '88	♟♟	4
● Sanleone '93	♟♟	4
● Sanleone '94	♟♟	4
○ Vin Santo del Chianti '95	♟♟	4
● Cantinino Vign. di Fezzana '93	♟	4
● Chianti '98	♟	2*
● Chianti Colli Fiorentini		
Castello di Montespertoli '94	♟	2*
● Sanleone '97	♟	4

● Varramista '98	♟♟	6
● Varramista '95	♟♟	5
● Varramista '96	♟♟	5
● Varramista '97	♟♟	5

PALAIA (PI)

PANZANO IN CHIANTI (FI)

San Gervasio
Loc. San Gervasio
56036 Palaia (PI)
Tel. 0587/483360

Carobbio
Via S. Martino a Cecione, 26
50020 Panzano in Chianti (FI)
Tel. 055/852136

How much influence has the name "Chianti" had, for good or ill, on the wines made in this wonderful zone known as the Colline Pisane? Should you plant native or international vines? The discussion could go on forever. Certainly, producers in these parts keep a close eye on what is going on in Maremma, without giving much away themselves. At any rate, the two Lucas – owner Tommasini and D'Attoma, the oenologist – both, as ever, committed to the quest for quality, are now producing an innovative, merlot-based red. I Renai '98, a very small amount of which will go on sale this year, looks very successful and promises great things for the future. It has a deep ruby colour and the nose is a concentrate of black berries, tinged with spices and coffee from the wood. In the mouth, toasty wood is still very much to the fore but the progression is well-sustained and full of fruit and silky tannins. The more traditional wines are also very good. A Sirio '98 gets a full Two Glasses, placing it once again among the best Sangioveses from the area. It has fruit-rich aromas, nuanced by cabernet-derived herbaceous notes, and elegant, distinctive toasty notes from the wood. In the mouth, it has typical sangiovese acidity, balanced by well-developed tannins. The Chianti Colline Pisane Le Stoppie '99 is also convincing. The nose reveals morello cherries and raspberry jam, while the palate is clean and fresh-tasting. We finished with the rosé Aprico '99, whose bright, vibrant colour is a delight to the eye. It has pleasing aromas of cherries and strawberry jam, and a tangy, consistent palate.

The wines produced here at Carobbio have always been good, and this year, too, results are impressive. Passion and an almost obsessive attention to detail, both in vineyard and in cellar, lie behind that success. The estate's consultant winemaker is Gabriella Tani, an outstanding interpreter of the local terroir. Only one of the flagship selections, the Pietraforte del Carobbio, was missing from our tastings but the rest of the range was on parade, and passed muster with flying colours. The deep, impenetrable ruby of the Chianti Classico '98 introduces a nose where the fruit is still dominated by sweet, but over-assertive wood. The entry on the palate is encouragingly firm, with a nice balance of tannins and alcohol. The '97 Riserve has a satisfyingly rich ruby hue and an intense nose of fruit and prominent grassy notes. The palate has remarkable thrust, good breadth and depth, and nice structure. The Leone di Carobbio '95 is the only bottle that let the side down a little. Its nose is distinctly over-evolved, with rather jammy fruit and notes of prune that fail to integrate with the whole. The soft, silky entry on the palate introduces a very drinkable mid palate and good texture but it somehow lacks brio. The Vin Santo '93 has a limpid orangey hue but the nose is slightly unfocused, with rather veiled notes of dried fruit. The dry palate has decent body and a very creditable finish.

● A Sirio '98	♟♟	5	● Chianti Classico '98	♟♟	4
● I Renai '98	♟♟	6	● Chianti Classico Ris. '97	♟♟	5
☉ Aprico '99	♟	2*	● Leone del Carobbio '95	♟	5
● Chianti Le Stoppie '99	♟	3	○ Vin Santo '93	♟	5
● A Sirio '96	♟♟	4	● Chianti Classico '93	♟♟	4
● A Sirio '97	♟♟	5	● Chianti Classico '94	♟♟	4
○ Marna '97	♟♟	4	● Chianti Classico '95	♟♟	4
☉ Aprico '98	♟	2*	● Chianti Classico '97	♟♟	4
● Chianti Le Stoppie '96	♟	3	● Chianti Classico Ris. '93	♟♟	5
● Chianti Le Stoppie '97	♟	3	● Chianti Classico Ris. '95	♟♟	5
● Chianti Le Stoppie '98	♟	3	● Chianti Classico Ris. '96	♟♟	5
○ Marna '96	♟	4	● Leone del Carobbio '93	♟♟	5
○ Marna '98	♟	4	● Leone del Carobbio '94	♟♟	5
○ Vin Santo '95	♟	4	● Pietraforte del Carobbio '93	♟♟	5
			● Pietraforte del Carobbio '95	♟♟	5

PANZANO IN CHIANTI (FI)

FATTORIA CASALOSTE
VIA MONTAGLIARI, 32
50020 PANZANO IN CHIANTI (FI)
TEL. 055/852725

We've always been are very interested in what the d'Orsi family is up to, as they beaver away in their vineyards and cellar, and when the new vine stock comes on-stream, which should be next year, they're going to need more cellar space. The d'Orsis are not the kind of people who rest on their laurels, and we are very pleased with what they came up with this year. The Chianti Classico '98 has a clear, medium ruby colour. Fruit, mingling superbly with the oak, dominates the nose to produce an overall sensation of elegance and intensity. In the mouth, it is concentrated, substantial, juicy and well-balanced, the acidity and tannins fusing well with softer components. The finish is a well-sustained crescendo, with well-rounded after-aromas. The '97 Riserva betrays a less than felicitous interpretation of the vintage, especially considering how good the Chianti Classico from the same year was. Its deep, ruby colour releases sharp, rather confused aromas where the vegetal notes overwhelm the underlying fruit. The attack on the palate is well-managed and the tannins unfold smoothly but with only moderate intensity. The Don Vincenzo '96 has an impenetrable colour and evolved, jammy fruit aromas offset by attractive vegetal notes that meld with elegant tertiary aromas of cinnamon and other spices. The robust palate offers succulent, chewy fruit, lifted deliciously by the tannins and acidity. This is a wine with plenty of character.

PANZANO IN CHIANTI (FI)

CENNATOIO
VIA DI SAN LEOLINO, 35
50020 PANZANO IN CHIANTI (FI)
TEL. 055/893230 - 055/852134

Cennatoio, with Leandro Alessi at the helm, had a low-key vintage this year and only presented two wines at our tastings. The others will be aged for longer and released at a later date. There is nothing particularly negative about this but the winery has accustomed us to a consistently reliable quality that we would be pleased to find again across the whole range they offer to the public. We'll be talking next year about the wines that came out after our tastings so let's turn now to the wines that were available. The Chianti Riserva O'Leandro '97 has a vibrant ruby colour with garnet highlights. The first aromas on the nose are pleasantly sweet tertiary notes, laced with Peruvian bark, that mingle nicely with the hints of coffee, which in turn give way to the ripe fruit notes of plum jam. In the mouth, the wine has good balance, the tannins and alcohol finding a point of equilibrium in a moderately robust structure. The perfectly sustained finish is coherent rather than explosive. The Etrusco '97 has a rich, dense colour of good intensity ushering in a nose where vibrant fruit reigns supreme, mingling with fainter vegetal nuances that are enhanced by light touches of vanilla and cinnamon. The soft, creamy palate, underpinned by a robust structure with perfectly integrated wood, is a delight. It lacks, perhaps, a little complexity but signs off with a sweet, well-sustained finish.

● Chianti Classico '98	♈♈	3*		● Etrusco '97	♈♈	5
● Chianti Classico				● Chianti Classico O'Leandro '97	♈	4
Don Vincenzo Ris. '96	♈♈	5		● Etrusco '94	♈♈♈	5
● Chianti Classico Ris. '97	♈	4		● Chianti Classico '97	♈♈	3*
● Chianti Classico '95	♈♈	3*		● Chianti Classico Ris. '91	♈♈	4
● Chianti Classico				● Chianti Classico Ris. '93	♈♈	4
Don Vincenzo Ris. '95	♈♈	5		● Chianti Classico Ris. '94	♈♈	4
● Chianti Classico Ris. '94	♈♈	4		● Chianti Classico Ris. '95	♈♈	4
● Chianti Classico Ris. '95	♈♈	4		● Etrusco '93	♈♈	5
● Chianti Classico '93	♈	3		● Etrusco '95	♈♈	5
● Chianti Classico '94	♈	3		● Etrusco '96	♈♈	5
● Chianti Classico '96	♈	3		● Mammolo '93	♈♈	6
● Chianti Classico '97	♈	3		● Rosso Fiorentino '93	♈♈	5
● Chianti Classico Ris. '96	♈	4		● Rosso Fiorentino '95	♈♈	5

PANZANO IN CHIANTI (FI)

PANZANO IN CHIANTI (FI)

★ TENUTA FONTODI
VIA SAN LEOLINO, 87
50020 PANZANO IN CHIANTI (FI)
TEL. 055/852005

IL VESCOVINO
VIA XX LUGLIO, 39
50020 PANZANO IN CHIANTI (FI)
TEL. 055/852907

We should say straight away that the panel awarded Three Glasses to the Flaccianello della Pieve '97 only after much retasting and reflection. At first, the wine seemed a bit closed on the nose and appeared reduced, perhaps because of the very concentrated extract. When a wine has a lot of substance, or "matière", as they say in France, such things happen. But two months later, just as we were putting the Guide to bed, we decided to try it again in a blind tasting with some other wines. As if by magic, the Flaccianello scored well enough for a top award this time. All the characteristic sangiovese aromas were there, including black cherries, Parma violets and other more earthy notes. The palate had enormous structure, bigger in all likelihood than ever before. In other words, it was precisely the wine that we had been expecting to find on our first visit. A little time was all that was needed, and, of course, a little belief in the product. If you should note a hint of reduction on uncorking the bottle, decant it, and the unwanted aromas will be spirited away. Moving on to the rest of the range, the Syrah Case Via '97 is as excellent as its predecessors. Also surprisingly good is the Chianti Classico '98, though its acidity is a bit exuberant. The Chianti Classico Vigna del Sorbo Riserva '97 has less personality than the Flaccianello, and the poorly typed, rather lightweight Pinot Nero Case Via '98 failed to convince.

The two wines presented this year by Riccardo Gosi, the owner of il Vescovino, have very similar styles that blur the differences in their blends. We take this as a sign that first of all, both are terroir-driven wines and second, that there is room to exploit this for further development, even though our overall impression was positive. The aromatic profile of the wines, the Il Vescovino Achilles' heel in the past, still needs attention. All the wines we tasted had traces of reduction on the nose that detracted from their appeal. However, with thorough aeration, these notes were much diminished and the superb substance of the palate persuaded us to include this Panzano-based winery. The Chianti Classico Vigna Piccola '98, for example, reveals remarkable structure full, delicious tannins and fruit that finally manages to come through. The progression on the palate is vibrant, with a tautness that comes from varietal acidity nicely masked by the sheer body of the wine. The Merlotto, a sangiovese with a very small proportion of cabernet sauvignon, has a meaty palate and a long finish. Its sinew should guarantee it a long life in the cellar.

● Flaccianello della Pieve '97	▼▼▼	6
● Chianti Cl. Vigna del Sorbo Ris. '97	▼▼	5
● Chianti Classico '98	▼▼	4
● Syrah Case Via '97	▼▼	5
● Pinot Nero Case Via '98	▼	5
● Chianti Cl. Vigna del Sorbo Ris. '86	♀♀♀	5
● Chianti Cl. Vigna del Sorbo Ris. '90	♀♀♀	5
● Chianti Cl. Vigna del Sorbo Ris. '94	♀♀♀	5
● Flaccianello della Pieve '88	♀♀♀	6
● Flaccianello della Pieve '90	♀♀♀	6
● Flaccianello della Pieve '91	♀♀♀	5
● Syrah Case Via '95	♀♀♀	5

● Chianti Cl. Vigna Piccola '98	▼▼	4
● Merlotto '97	▼▼	5
● Chianti Cl. Vigna Piccola '97	♀♀	3*
● Merlotto '94	♀♀	5
● Chianti Cl. Vigna Piccola '94	♀	3
● Chianti Cl. Vigna Piccola Ris. '96	♀	4
● Merlotto '95	♀	5
● Merlotto '96	♀	5

PANZANO IN CHIANTI (FI)

PANZANO IN CHIANTI (FI)

LA MASSA
VIA CASE SPARSE, 9
50020 PANZANO IN CHIANTI (FI)
TEL. 055/852722

PODERE LE CINCIOLE
VIA CASE SPARSE, 83
50020 PANZANO IN CHIANTI (FI)
TEL. 055/852636

This winery continues its winning ways. Giampaolo Motta has had his sixth consecutive success, and doesn't seem inclined to break his streak. You can't help thinking of those people who judgements of wine depend on the opinions of others or on the presumed merits of a particular vintage. The year makes practically no difference to the wines from La Massa. They may get a point or two more in excellent years, or score a point lower in bad ones, but they are always comfortably above the cut-off for Three Glasses. But what about the supposed capriciousness of sangiovese? Giampaolo seems to have turned it into a thoroughly reliable, well-behaved grape. Naturally, the little bit of merlot present in his more recent versions is a nudge in the right direction but that can't explain everything. Instead, we suggest that his results might well be due to the tiny yields he takes from each vine, the superb Panzano subzone and the enviable locations of his vineyards. Well-judged maceration and excellent quality wood probably also come into the equation, as well. The Giorgio Primo '98 knows exactly what it's doing on the nose, revealing both intensity and precision as it unveils pervasive but not overpowering fruit that gradually gives way to notes of pepper, chocolate and violets. The palate has concentration, fullness and depth but the ace up its sleeve is an awesome combination of complexity and harmony. The Chianti '98 is another miniature masterpiece. There is a faint vegetal sensation at first but the richness of the fruit takes over, driving an attractively full-bodied progression through to a long, very satisfying finish.

It's hard to find a more typical Panzano Chianti Classico than the ones produced at Podere Le Cinciole, and this is particularly true of the Riserva Petresco '97. Violet in the glass, it offers a nose of Parma violets and black cherries with fleeting balsamic notes. The entry on the palate is firm, well backed up by that characteristic Panzano touch of acidity. The tannins are a little edgy and the finish has decent length. It's a lovely, elegant wine, that comes from the fusion of the estate's two vineyard selections, the Vecchie Vigne and the Vigna del Pozzo, which until 1996 had its own label. This is an excellent result for Luca Orsini and Valeria Viganò, a Rome-Milan team both at work and in their private life. Their standard-label wine, the Chianti Classico '98, is more straightforward and leaner. It has plenty of fruit but is rather linear. Although technically impeccable, it is a bit light on concentration. All in all, they are two typical wines, dominated neither by oak nor extract and utterly sincere. They tell the story of their terroir, its strengths and weaknesses, and of their vintages, without artifice or affectation. That point should be stressed, as should the hard, intelligent work that Luca and Valeria have put into making these wines. Uncorking one of their bottles, if you are lucky enough to come across one, is always a thrill.

●	Chianti Cl. Giorgio Primo '98	▼▼▼	6
●	Chianti Classico '98	▼▼	4
●	Chianti Cl. Giorgio Primo '93	♀♀♀	4*
●	Chianti Cl. Giorgio Primo '94	♀♀♀	5
●	Chianti Cl. Giorgio Primo '95	♀♀♀	5
●	Chianti Cl. Giorgio Primo '96	♀♀♀	5
●	Chianti Cl. Giorgio Primo '97	♀♀♀	6
●	Chianti Cl. Giorgio Primo '92	♀♀	5
●	Chianti Classico '92	♀♀	4
●	Chianti Classico '93	♀♀	4
●	Chianti Classico '94	♀♀	4
●	Chianti Classico '95	♀♀	4
●	Chianti Classico '96	♀♀	4
●	Chianti Classico '97	♀♀	4
●	Chianti Classico Ris. '90	♀♀	5

●	Chianti Classico		
	Petresco Ris. '97	▼▼	4
●	Chianti Classico '98	▼	3
●	Chianti Classico '93	♀♀	3*
●	Chianti Classico '94	♀♀	3*
●	Chianti Classico '95	♀♀	3*
●	Chianti Classico		
	Valle del Pozzo Ris. '95	♀♀	4
●	Chianti Classico		
	Valle del Pozzo Ris. '96	♀♀	4
●	Chianti Classico '97	♀	3
●	Chianti Classico		
	Valle del Pozzo Ris. '94	♀	4

PANZANO IN CHIANTI (FI)   PANZANO IN CHIANTI (FI)

FATTORIA LE FONTI
VIA LE FONTI
50020 PANZANO IN CHIANTI (FI)
TEL. 055/852194

MONTE BERNARDI
VIA CHIANTIGIANA
50020 PANZANO IN CHIANTI (FI)
TEL. 055/852400

We'll begin this profile by repeating what we wrote last year. In the best vintages, Le Fonti bottles all its Chianti Classico as Riserva. For that reason, we were unable to comment on last year's standard Chianti and were compelled to ask readers to wait for this year's Guide. Le Fonti had even more reason than usual to follow this strategy for their '97 wines for the vintage at Panzano was an excellent one. Conrad Schmitt continues to work as dedicatedly as ever in both vineyards and cellar so, as usual, we were interested to see the results. The '97 Riserva has a deep, bright ruby colour. The nose has its work cut out unravelling the wine's complexity. First, there are evolved notes that evoke delicious aromas of coffee and vanilla that then give way to vibrant, complex fruit with berries prominent. The entry on the palate is a show-stopper. Its full-bodied concentration unveils soft, close-knit tannins and then progresses to a long, juicy and very attractive finish. A blend of sangiovese with a dash of cabernet sauvignon, the Fontissimo is a very dark, concentrated ruby in colour, proffering ripe, elegant blackcurrant fruit aromas. Well-balanced in the mouth, it has a decent and well-sustained, if not immense, structure. The tannins amalgamate well with the alcohol and its finish is pleasing, though not very long.

The wines that we tasted this year from Monte Bernardi were consistently good. The Aivaliotis family confirmed the positive direction taken by their winery but there isn't one bottle that really stands out. These are well-made wines in the modern idiom, obtained from good-quality fruit. The best of the bunch was the Tzingana which, though a perfectly valid wine, is a very distant relative of the explosive '97. It is a Cabernet-Merlot blend with good texture and lovely tannins, appropriately backed up by oak. The nose is clean, the palate nicely balanced and it has admirable length so has to go down as a very good wine but one lacking a distinctive personality. To avoid repeating ourselves, we will just say that all the wines presented had similar texture, body and length. The Sangiovese Sa'etta '98 stands out for its lively style and well-integrated toasty oak. The Chianti Riserva '97 has poise, a gratifyingly elegant drinkability and substantial dynamism on the palate. A wine with a rather linear tasting profile, its marked vegetal aromas hinder full expression of the terroir. The Chianti Paris '98 is also good, offering well-knit tannins accompanied by uncomplicated but very abundant fruit. It should also be said that this wine has more marked oak aromas than the rest of the range.

● Chianti Classico Ris. '97	♟♟	4
● Fontissimo '97	♟♟	5
● Chianti Classico Ris. '95	♟♟	4
● Chianti Classico Ris. '96	♟♟	4
● Fontissimo '91	♟♟	5
● Fontissimo '95	♟♟	5
● Fontissimo '96	♟♟	5
● Chianti Classico '96	♟	4
● Chianti Classico Ris. '90	♟	3
● Chianti Classico Ris. '91	♟	4
● Chianti Classico Ris. '93	♟	4
● Fontissimo '93	♟	5

● Chianti Classico Paris '98	♟♟	5
● Chianti Classico Ris. '97	♟♟	5
● Sa'etta '98	♟♟	6
● Tzingana '98	♟♟	6
● Tzingana '97	♟♟♟	6
● Chianti Classico '97	♟♟	4
● Sa'etta '97	♟♟	6

PANZANO IN CHIANTI (FI) PANZANO IN CHIANTI (FI)

CASTELLO DEI RAMPOLLA
VIA CASE SPARSE, 22
50020 PANZANO IN CHIANTI (FI)
TEL. 055/852001

FATTORIA SANT'ANDREA
LOC. CASE SPARSE
50020 PANZANO IN CHIANTI (FI)
TEL. 055/8549090

Two years ago we chose the '96 La Vigna di Alceo as our Wine of the Year. It was a great red, made with cabernet sauvignon (mostly) fruit from the vineyard which the owner, Principe Alceo di Napoli, planted just under ten years ago shortly before he died. The estate passed on to his children, Luca and Maurizia, two people whose honesty and commitment to their task make them well worthy of the inheritance. But let's get back to the wine. The '98 Alceo is every bit as good a wine as the '96 or '97. The differences are minimal, for here we are at the very highest level of excellence. There can be no doubt that it is one of Italy's greatest red wines. The concentrated aromas are redolent of berry fruit and pencil lead while the elegant, almost aristocratic, palate unfolds the sweetest of tannins and serious length. The Sammarco '97, made from cabernet and sangiovese, is also very interesting. Rougher and less velvety than the Alceo, it displays determination and character. Above all, the tannins seem a bit aggressive, partly because of the different blend, but it's also a question of planting densities, here about 5,000 plants per hectare as opposed to the 8,500 of La Vigna di Alceo. Obviously less concentrated, but a valid example of its category, is the Chianti Classico Riserva '97 while the Chianti Classico '98 is linear, straightforward and, perhaps, a little bit thin.

The Sant'Andrea winery, known by all in Chianti as Panzanello, is one of those which have been showing the clearest signs of improvement. The owners, Andrea and Iole Sammaruga, who moved from Rome to the vine-clad hills of Tuscany, have hired as their consultant Gioia Crest, a highly competent oenologist. Thanks to the contributions of all three, the cellar has begun to make seriously good wine. One indication is that the Chianti Classico '98 scored better than either the Riserva '97 or the Il Mastio '97, a red made with sangiovese, cabernet and merlot grapes, in spite of the fact that the grapes and the vintage (1997) were, at least on paper, superior. It's a remarkable step forward to make better wine from poorer grapes in a less felicitous year. The Chianti Classico Panzanello '98 is a very well-managed red with medium body. Its fruit aromas have faint vegetal overtones but in the mouth it is full and concentrated, the acidity sustaining its structure very well. The more vegetal and markedly merlot-ish Riserva '97 is a wine that reflects the transition from past to future at Panzanello. It has good body but is not very true to type. The Mastio '97 is also pretty good. Its nose is complex enough but in the mouth it hasn't got very much concentration.

● La Vigna di Alceo '98	♟♟♟	6
● Chianti Classico Ris. '97	♟♟	5
● Sammarco '97	♟♟	6
● Chianti Classico '98	♟	4
● La Vigna di Alceo '96	♟♟♟	6
● La Vigna di Alceo '97	♟♟♟	6
● Sammarco '85	♟♟♟	6
● Sammarco '86	♟♟♟	6
● Sammarco '94	♟♟♟	6
● Chianti Classico Ris. '94	♟♟	5
● Chianti Classico Ris. '95	♟♟	5
● Sammarco '88	♟♟	6
● Sammarco '93	♟♟	6
● Sammarco '95	♟♟	6
● Sammarco '96	♟♟	6

● Chianti Classico Panzanello '98	♟♟	3*
● Chianti Classico Panzanello Ris. '97	♟	4
● Il Mastio '97	♟	4
● Chianti Classico '97	♟♟	3*
● Chianti Classico Ris. '95	♟	4
● Chianti Classico Ris. '96	♟	4

PANZANO IN CHIANTI (FI)

VECCHIE TERRE DI MONTEFILI
VIA S. CRESCI, 45
50022 PANZANO IN CHIANTI (FI)
TEL. 055/853739

PANZANO IN CHIANTI (FI)

VILLA CAFAGGIO
VIA S. MARTINO IN CECIONE, 5
50020 PANZANO IN CHIANTI (FI)
TEL. 055/8549094

Granted, there is no real star performer this year but the overall showing of the Montefili wines is more than satisfactory. The Vigna Regis '98 is a complex white made from chardonnay, sauvignon, and gewürztraminer. It has an intense, golden colour and is ravishingly limpid. Floral notes predominate but they are elegantly accompanied by fruit. The entry on the palate is convincing and delicately mouth-filling. It lacks only a hint of acidity to buck it up and provide backbone. The Chianti Classico '98 has a firm, dark ruby colour. Its aromas are rather evolved, with super-ripe notes of prune. The attack is soft, indeed almost feathery, but then firm, solid tannins kick in, the alcohol supplying a counterpoint. The finish is even, with attractive fruit-rich after-aromas. On the nose, the deep ruby Anfiteatro '97 initially reveals toasty notes from the wood that are not quite in synch with the fruit but still bright and attractive. However, the palate comes together extremely well and lacks only an extra spark to give it more personality. The Bruno di Rocca '97, a blend of sangiovese and cabernet sauvignon, displays balsamic notes on the nose that mitigate the vegetal overtones against a backdrop of cherry and redcurrant fruit. In the mouth, it is creamy and full-bodied, with delicate, even tannins mingling pleasingly with the alcohol. The finish is sweet, leisurely and satisfyingly full.

A stunningly good performance by Villa Cafaggio has shot it into the front rank of Tuscan producers for the new century. Two wines received Three Glasses and all the other bottles presented scored very well. It is tempting to think that the year, 1997, played a significant part in this success but that view would do scant justice to the real merits of Stefano Farkas' estate. In fact, Villa Cafaggio is reaping the harvest of years of hard work and investment both in the vineyards and in the cellar. The Cortaccio '97 is a Cabernet Sauvignon of extraordinary breeding. The fruit is almost perfectly ripe and completely free of vegetal overtones. Its concentration is impressive but so well integrated by the overall harmony that the wine's drinkability actually benefits. The tannins are very close-knit but so firmly integrated by the extract that the palate acquires a velvety smoothness and the oak melds in seamlessly. The San Martin '97 is almost overshadowed by all this magnificence but this splendid Sangiovese is a vibrant, compact red with the tannic texture of a great wine and full-bodied, satisfyingly ripe fruit. The Chianti Classico Riserva '97 is another attractive bottle. It has all the characteristic sinew of Chiantis from Panzano, also showing great depth of flavour and an admirably integrated aromas. Bringing up the rear is the Chianti '98, a pleasing, powerful wine with fruit that is perhaps a little unvaried but is nevertheless generous and very juicy.

●	Anfiteatro '97	♟♟	6	●	Cortaccio '97	♟♟♟	6
●	Bruno di Rocca '97	♟♟	6	●	San Martino '97	♟♟♟	5
●	Chianti Classico '98	♟♟	4	●	Chianti Classico '98	♟♟	4
○	Vigna Regis '98	♟	4	●	Chianti Classico Ris. '97	♟♟	5
●	Anfiteatro '94	♟♟♟	6	●	Cortaccio '93	♟♟♟	6
●	Chianti Cl. Anfiteatro Ris. '88	♟♟♟	6	●	Chianti Cl. Solatio Basilica Ris. '95	♟♟	5
●	Chianti Classico Ris. '85	♟♟♟	6	●	Cortaccio '90	♟♟	6
●	Anfiteatro '93	♟♟	6	●	Cortaccio '94	♟♟	6
●	Anfiteatro '95	♟♟	6	●	Cortaccio '95	♟♟	6
●	Anfiteatro '96	♟♟	6	●	San Martino '90	♟♟	5
●	Bruno di Rocca '92	♟♟	6	●	San Martino '93	♟♟	5
●	Bruno di Rocca '93	♟♟	6	●	San Martino '94	♟♟	5
●	Bruno di Rocca '94	♟♟	6	●	San Martino '95	♟♟	5
●	Bruno di Rocca '95	♟♟	6	●	San Martino '96	♟♟	5
●	Bruno di Rocca '96	♟♟	6				

PELAGO (FI)

TRAVIGNOLI
VIA TRAVIGNOLI, 78
50060 PELAGO (FI)
TEL. 055/8361098

The Busi family winery confirms that it is becoming an increasingly important presence in the Rufina area. In the last two years, they have planted another ten hectares of vines, bringing their total to nearly 70. These are significant numbers, calling for ceaseless vigilance in both vineyard and cellar, but the results achieved are spurring the Busis to continue along the same path. So far, the only problem (if you can even call it that) has been that they have been bringing out their wines a little too soon. But even that has changed this year. In fact, we will be tasting the standard Chianti next year, together with the vineyard selection, the Tegolaia. Let's get on with our tastings. The Gavignano '99 is made from chardonnay grapes with a small amount of sauvignon. It has a lustrous, intense golden colour and a pervasive fruit nose in which pear, mellowed by honey, is prevalent. Entry on the palate is firm, and there is refreshingly lively acidity to take you through to a clean finish. The Chianti Rufina Riserva '98 has a rich, deep ruby colour. Vegetal notes come across first on the nose, giving way to aromas of ripe cherry and plum fruit. The soft, well-rounded palate is almost creamy but its vein of acidity lends remarkable freshness. The Calice del Conte '98 is the second newcomer. A red from merlot and cabernet sauvignon, its aromas are very evolved, evoking slightly rustic stewed fruit and jam with hints of chocolate and coffee. The entry is low-key as the front palate is dominated by warm alcohol before the fine-grained tannins emerge.

●	Chianti Rufina Ris. '98	▼▼	3*
●	Calice del Conte '98	▼	4
○	Gavignano '99	▼	3
●	Chianti Rufina Ris. '97	▽▽	3*
●	Tegolaia '94	▽▽	4
●	Tegolaia '97	▽▽	4
●	Chianti Rufina '96	▽	2*
●	Chianti Rufina '98	▽	2*

PIEVE AL BAGNORO (AR)

VILLA CILNIA
LOC. MONTONCELLO, 27
52040 PIEVE AL BAGNORO (AR)
TEL. 0575/365017

The province of Arezzo is in a state of healthy agitation. Vineyards are expanding all the time and massive investment is being made by small players and by giants like Antinori. New DOC zones such as Cortona, Val di Chiana and Valdarno are coming rapidly into being, the number of wineries has grown, and those already in existence have been infected by the expansion bug. Villa Cilnia, after a period of uncertainty, has now returned to the straight and narrow. The wines are already good but we are hoping for even more improvement. The two Chiantis are both rather interesting, the better of the brace being the Riserva '97. Although it opens on a note of super-ripeness, it then shows fine structure, lashings of fruit, and a finish that is slightly edgy but very promising. The '98 Chianti has a lovely, bright, intense ruby hue. The nose is attractively fruity but there are also faint vegetal notes. Here, too, the palate is youthful, and there is a bit of oak still to be assimilated, but the basic material is good and the finish is reasonably long. Il Vocato, a blend of cabernet sauvignon and sangiovese, is the estate's flagship wine, although we relegated it to the upper half of the One Glass band because we expected more from a '97 Supertuscan. The nose has a good impact, mingling notes of coffee and green peppers. There is substance on the palate, and laudable balance, but you can detect a certain greenness in the fruit. The Chardonnay Mecenate '97 is not bad, but perhaps a bit far along.

●	Chianti Colli Aretini '98	▼▼	3*
●	Chianti Colli Aretini Ris. '97	▼▼	4
○	Mecenate '97	▼	4
●	Vocato '97	▼	4
●	Vocato '93	▽▽	4
●	Chianti Colli Aretini '95	▽	2*
●	Chianti Colli Aretini '96	▽	2*
●	Chianti Colli Aretini Ris. '93	▽	3
●	Chianti Colli Aretini Ris. '94	▽	3
○	Mecenate '95	▽	4
●	Vocato '94	▽	4

PIOMBINO (LI)

PITIGLIANO (GR)

SAN GIUSTO
SALIVOLI
57025 PIOMBINO (LI)
TEL. 0565/41198

TENUTA ROCCACCIA
LOC. ROCCACCIA
58017 PITIGLIANO (GR)
TEL. 0564/617976

Here is a very deserving new entry that enlarges the area in which premium wines are made on the Tuscan coast. Piero Bonti's winery has been productive for many years but, as is often the case in small family businesses, it was only a few years ago that he decided to try his hand at producing first-rank wines. The enterprise is a costly one but at our tastings, the panel had to admit that Bonti's gamble has paid off. The Rosso degli Appiani, made from sangiovese and a small proportion of montepulciano d'Abruzzo, is a wine that we remember as being powerful and robust, but rather rustic. The '97 version is different. It has managed to channel its inherent solidity into a much more satisfying progression of flavours backed up by generous but not over-extracted tannins, ripe yet not evolved fruit, and a long, clean finish. Also prevalently sangiovese-based is the San Giusto '98, which makes its debut this year. It easily merits its Two Glasses, displaying a crisp, concentrated nose of black berry fruit and well-dosed wood. A soft, reasonably full-bodied palate follows, leading in to a fruit-rich finish. The Val di Cornia Bianco San Giusto '99 is a serious wine that offers intense aromas of broom, roses and tropical fruit. The palate is a little straightforward but coherent and attractive nonetheless. The two Bontesco '99s, the Bianco and the Rosso, provide a dignified conclusion to the range, each winning One Glass for clean execution and good overall balance.

Tenuta Roccaccia, which was in the Other Wineries section last year, has earned a full Guide profile this year. The owners, Danilo and Rossano Goracci, showed they can make reds with the best of them, presenting the panel with two that sailed over the Two Glass threshold with points to spare. The Goraccis have been growing grapes for some time, selling them to the local co-operative, and it was only recently that they decided to make their own wine, having taken stock of their skills and the potential of their land. With assistance from oenologist Alberto Antonini, they have got off to a good start, thanks to ideas that are both clear and innovative for the Pitigliano zone. Danilo and Rossano have some 30 hectares under vine in which, besides the traditional varieties, they have planted cabernet sauvignon and merlot. Their new plots are fairly densely planted and the cellar is modern. The two reds presented were the Roccaccia '99 and the Fontenova '98. The first has an intense, dark violet colour and a nose of well-defined fruit, enhanced by the subtle contribution of the oak. The firm front palate progresses smoothly over a close-knit texture with well-integrated tannins. And the very competitive price tag makes it even more attractive. Its stablemate, the Fontenova, is another Two Glass bottle, albeit with a slightly higher score. A blend of ciliegiolo and sangiovese, it is aged for over a year in barriques. The very intriguing aromas are redolent of black and red berry fruit, with overtones of cinnamon. On the palate, it displays excellent progression thanks to its close-knit tannins and plump, juicy fruit. The whites are less successful, and have yet to find their own personal styles.

●	Rosso degli Appiani '97	▼▼	5
●	San Giusto '98	▼▼	4
○	Bontesco Bianco '99	▼	2*
●	Bontesco Rosso '99	▼	2*
○	Val di Cornia Bianco San Giusto '99	▼	3

●	La Roccaccia '99	▼▼	3*
●	La Roccaccia Fontenova '98	▼▼	4
○	Bianco di Pitigliano '99		2
○	Chardonnay '99		3

POGGIBONSI (SI)

POGGIBONSI (SI)

MELINI
LOC. GAGGIANO
53036 POGGIBONSI (SI)
TEL. 0577/989001

FATTORIA ORMANNI
LOC. ORMANNI, 1
53036 POGGIBONSI (SI)
TEL. 0577/937212

Melini is one of the estates that belong to the Gruppo Italiano Vini, and one of the best known in the whole of Chianti. It is also one of the biggest and most important since its 150 hectares under vine enable it to be largely self-sufficient, especially with regard to the most prestigious wines in the range. More than 40 of those hectares comprise the superb La Selvanella vineyard at Radda, almost on the border of the Panzano subzone at Greve. In the last few years, this vineyard has been undergoing a complete overhaul, and the last of the new vines should be planted in 2001. Some of the new stock has already come on-stream and the fruit is having a significant impact on the wine it produces. The Chianti Classico La Selvanella Riserva '97, for example, is still made in the traditional fashion and aged for a year in large barrels. It is proudly true to type but now is also decidedly more concentrated, less edgy and much easier to drink than previous versions. The Montevecchio, the other '97 Riserva, is much more modern. Softer and more velvety, it bears the clear imprint of its barrique ageing. The Chianti Classico I Sassi '98 is a particularly good buy. An uncomplicated, straightforward wine at an affordable price. Finally, the Vernaccia di San Gimignano Le Grillaie '99, the one Melini white, is as interesting as ever, although it lacks the concentration of the '98 edition.

Fattoria Ormanni, owned by engineer Brini Batacchi, made its Guide debut last year and confirms its status this time round with another excellent performance. The Chianti Classico '98 has a lustrous deep ruby colour introducing a nose somewhat dominated by the wood, and slightly jarring vegetal notes. It soon opens out, though, into attractive fruit that gains complexity from refreshing balsamic notes. The palate is a delight from the moderately powerful but precise and dynamic entry through to a reasonably long length. The Riserva '96 has a dark hue and a nose that offers sweet aromas of toasty oak, coffee and chocolate against a background of convincingly serious fruit. The palate opens on a soft note before revealing good, if not massive, structure and nice balance, decent acidity and well-integrated tannins. The Julius '98, a blend of sangiovese with a little merlot, has a rich ruby colour. The nose unveils rich, ripe fruit while the soft front palate leads into a concentrated, silky progression. The tannins fuse well with the alcohol, the acidity is well-judged and the finish flavoursome.

● Chianti Cl. La Selvanella Ris. '97 ♟♟	5
● Chianti Classico		
Montevecchio Ris. '97 ♟♟	5
○ Vernaccia di S. Gimignano		
Le Grillaie '99 ♟♟	4
● Chianti Classico I Sassi '98 ♟	3
● Chianti Cl. La Selvanella Ris. '86 ♟♟♟	4*
● Chianti Cl. La Selvanella Ris. '90 ♟♟♟	4*
● Chianti Cl. La Selvanella Ris. '93 ♟♟	4
● Chianti Cl. La Selvanella Ris. '94 ♟♟	4
● Chianti Cl. La Selvanella Ris. '95 ♟♟	4
● Chianti Cl. La Selvanella Ris. '96 ♟♟	5
● Chianti Classico		
Montevecchio Ris. '95 ♟♟	4
● Merlot '98 ♟♟	4

● Chianti Classico '98 ♟♟	4
● Chianti Classico Ris. '96 ♟♟	4
● Julius '98 ♟♟	5
● Chianti Classico Ris. '95 ♟♟	4
● Julius '97 ♟♟	5
● Chianti Classico Ris. '97 ♟	4

POGGIO A CAIANO (PO) PONTASSIEVE (FI)

LA PIAGGIA
VIA CEGOLI, 47
59016 POGGIO A CAIANO (PO)
TEL. 055/8705401

TENÙTA DI BOSSI
VIA DELLO STRACCHINO, 32
50065 PONTASSIEVE (FI)
TEL. 055/8317830

To win a Three Glass accolade on your second time out in the Guide is to get a result, and no mistake. But then Mauro Vannucci's Carmignano is a wine that brooks no argument, unless you are one of those diehards who think that wines should always be true to type. This wine has a very modern style that makes it similar to other great wines from other regions but then if you want to make a serious bottle, you have to start with superb fruit and age the wine in top-quality barrels, wherever you are. At the same time, it is equally evident that communicating the special characteristics of a terroir is the final step towards making a truly great wine. The Carmignano Riserva '97 lays its cards on the table when you lift the glass and examine its deep, lustrous, dark ruby hue. The richness of the fruit emerges at once on the nose, enfolding the other aromas of coffee, cocoa and spices that mingle deliciously. The long, concentrated palate lives up to all expectations, revealing layer after layer of silky sweet tannins. This masterpiece is produced by Mauro Vannucci and Alberto Antonini, who thus succeed in focusing attention again on the all but forgotten Carmignano subzone.

The Tenuta di Bossi marches on. What we are happiest to report is the excellent quality of the Vin Santo, which, we feel, is a paragon of its kind. In addition, the standard-label Chianti Rufina '98 is the best of the reds presented, an important signal of renewed interest in the wine. It has a dense ruby colour and offers crisp, elegant aromas of ripe fruit. The entry on the palate is mouth-filling, soft and juicy, while the mid palate shows good, if not powerful, structure and nice balance, soft tannins, well-judged alcohol and a long finish. The Riserva '97 has a lovely intense ruby colour but there are rather over-assertive vegetal notes on the nose. The palate lacks substance and the thinnish body reveals fairly raw tannins. The monovarietal cabernet sauvignon Mazzaferrata '96 has a rather unruly nose. Vegetal aromas stand out, mingling with gamey overtones. The progression on the palate is undemanding, with modest body or length. The estate Vin Santo della Rufina '95 has a rich, limpid amber colour and a nose of almonds and hazelnuts, followed by very intense aromas of fruit and nuts. The entrance on the palate is creamy, rich and amazingly mouth-filling. The serious alcohol is superbly amalgamated and the very long finish is delicious and broad. This year, the Bianco offers well-managed but unexciting aromas of apple and a fresh-tasting, faintly fruity palate. Finally, the Rosè dei Goti has an attractive nose but on the palate turns out to be lean and unexciting.

● Carmignano Ris. '97	TTT	5
● Carmignano Ris. '94	♈♈	4
● Carmignano Ris. '95	♈♈	4
● Carmignano Ris. '96	♈♈	4

● Chianti Rufina S. Giuliano '98	▼▼	4
○ Vin Santo Rufina '95	▼▼	4
● Chianti Rufina Ris. '97	▼	4
● Mazzaferrata '96	▼	4
⊙ Rosè dei Goti '99		3
○ Tenuta dei Bossi '99		3
● Chianti Rufina Ris. '90	♈♈	4*
● Mazzaferrata '90	♈♈	4
● Mazzaferrata '92	♈♈	4
● Mazzaferrata '93	♈♈	4
● Mazzaferrata '94	♈♈	4
● Mazzaferrata '95	♈♈	4
○ Vin Santo Rufina '91	♈♈	5
○ Vin Santo Rufina '93	♈♈	4
○ Vin Santo Rufina Ris. '94	♈♈	4

PONTASSIEVE (FI)

PONTASSIEVE (FI)

★ RUFFINO
VIA ARETINA, 42/44
50065 PONTASSIEVE (FI)
TEL. 055/83605

FATTORIA SELVAPIANA
LOC. SELVAPIANA, 43
50065 PONTASSIEVE (FI)
TEL. 055/8369848

As the poet Horace said, "est modus in rebus" ("there is measure in all things"). The Latin tag could well be applied to recent events at this famous Pontassieve estate where Luigi Folonari, from the branch of the Folonari family that bought up the Ruffino interest, has successfully concluded an operation that could have upset the property's existing status quo. However, good sense all round has enabled the break-up to take place without any particular difficulty. Ruffino will keep the Lodola Nuova estate at Montepulciano, Santedame and other properties in Chianti Classico and the title to the lease on Greppone Mazzi at Montalcino (Lodola and Greppone have separate profiles in the Guide). In addition, Ruffino will keep all the old Ruffino wines, the Riserva Ducale and the Riserva Ducale Oro (the '98 versions will be released next year), the Libaio and so on. But if there has been a "modus" (or "measure") with a small "m", there will also soon be a "Modus" with a capital letter. It will be the big surprise of the year 2001, a great cabernet, merlot and sangiovese-based red that will start tongues wagging with a vengeance. But for the time being, we will have to make do with the monumental 1998 version of Romitorio di Santedame, from sangiovese and colorino. It is a powerful, concentrated wine in the style of its immediate predecessors. Then there is an excellent Nero del Tondo '98, from pinot noir, that is the best of its kind made hereabouts for many years. A surprising Chianti Classico Santedame '98 joins the fragrant and very fruity Libaio '99 on the list. The new Ruffino has got off to a very good start, but this is just the beginning.

Not for the first time, we were a bit disappointed by the wines from Selvapiana. All things considered, the results of the tastings were good but the fact is that we are still waiting for that step up in quality which we feel is within this winery's reach. We say this even though we are well aware of the good work that Federico Giuntini has done day after day under the supervision of Marchese Francesco. But let's move on to the panel's notes. The Chianti Rufina '98 has a good dense ruby colour and straightforward ripe fruity aromas of some intensity. The entry on the palate is a little fuzzy and lacking in structure, with acidity well to the fore. Nevertheless, it is a well-made bottle and has a clean, reasonably long finish. The Riserva '97 confirms the excellence of the year, starting with its deep, almost impenetrable ruby hue. The nose is tempted by sweet sensations of wood-derived coffee and vanilla, mingling with lovely redcurrant and bilberry fruit. The front palate is soft, and even creamy, leading in to a seductively silky mid palate with well-balanced, delicate but close-knit tannins. The rising finish is long and enjoyable. The Riserva Bucerchiale '96 has an attractive ruby colour. On the nose, there are notes of ripe plum and cherry fruit, and faint gamey hints. The remarkably meaty entry reveals good grip and is backed up by tannins that still need to mellow and do not yet reveal their full texture. The finish is intense and clean.

● Romitorio di Santedame '98	▾▾▾	6
● Chianti Classico Santedame '98	▾▾	4
● Nero del Tondo '98	▾▾	5
○ Libaio '99	▾	3
● Cabreo Il Borgo '85	♀♀♀	6
● Cabreo Il Borgo '90	♀♀♀	6
● Cabreo Il Borgo '93	♀♀♀	5
● Cabreo Il Borgo '95	♀♀♀	6
● Cabreo Il Borgo '96	♀♀♀	6
○ Cabreo La Pietra '97	♀♀♀	5
● Chianti Cl. Ris. Ducale Oro '88	♀♀♀	5
● Chianti Cl. Ris. Ducale Oro '90	♀♀♀	5
● Romitorio di Santedame '96	♀♀♀	5
● Romitorio di Santedame '97	♀♀♀	6
● Romitorio di Santedame '95	♀♀	5

● Chianti Rufina Ris. '97	▾▾	4
● Chianti Rufina '98	▾	3
● Chianti Rufina Bucerchiale Ris. '96	▾	5
● Chianti Rufina '91	♀♀	3*
● Chianti Rufina Bucerchiale Ris. '90	♀♀	5
● Chianti Rufina Bucerchiale Ris. '94	♀♀	5
● Chianti Rufina Bucerchiale Ris. '95	♀♀	5
● Chianti Rufina Fornace Ris. '94	♀♀	5
● Chianti Rufina Ris. '88	♀♀	4
● Chianti Rufina Ris. '95	♀♀	4
● Chianti Rufina Ris. '96	♀♀	4
○ Vin Santo della Rufina '93	♀♀	5
● Chianti Rufina '97	♀	3
● Chianti Rufina Fornace Ris. '96	♀	5

PORTOFERRAIO (LI)

RADDA IN CHIANTI (SI)

ACQUABONA
LOC. ACQUABONA, 1
57037 PORTOFERRAIO (LI)
TEL. 0565/933013

CASTELLO D' ALBOLA
LOC. PIAN D'ALBOLA, 31
53017 RADDA IN CHIANTI (SI)
TEL. 0577/738019

Acquabona is the only winery on Elba to be profiled in the Guide and, as usual, it does credit to the island. We sincerely hope that sooner or later other estates will join them but up to now, there are none of a sufficiently high level to be included here. This year, we were rather pleased with the tastings, particularly of their Aleatico and of the Acquabona whites in general. The estate policy regarding Aleatico looks increasingly convincing. It spends a long time ageing in the barrel, and then in the bottle, before it is put on the market. The cellar's accumulated knowledge of the grape, and their years of experience, enable them to preserve the characteristic aromas of black cherries and spring flowers, and at the same time to give the wine itself more complexity and balance. The tannins are softer and silkier, the palate acquires greater elegance, and the evident sweetness is never cloying. This bottle is a delight. The Vermentino Acquabona di Acquabona also made a good impression. It has aromas of citrus fruit and apricots, and is well-balanced and very attractive on the palate. The Ansonica also obtained an encouraging report from the panel. It has attractively solid, broad structure and a moderately long but very agreeable finish. The light, fragrant Elba Bianco is well-made but has less personality. In the case of the Rosso Riserva, first impressions on eye and nose are not very promising. It has a washed-out colour and is over-evolved but then it picks up on the palate, where it shows good equilibrium and offers some pleasure.

In one of the most ravishingly beautiful parts of Chianti Classico, you can't help making great wines. Or so it seems again this year. Indeed, perhaps we should say, especially this year, because many of the wines presented were from the excellent '97 vintage. L'Acciaiolo, a red obtained from sangiovese and cabernet sauvignon, usually has an aristocratic aloofness brought about by its unique association of acids and tannins but this time it is smooth and invitingly soft. The Pinot Nero Le Marangole '97 has fairly varietal aromas and good structure but is blessedly free of those aromas of super-ripeness that plague many of Tuscany's other Pinot Neros. Here we find instead a coherent expression of the grape, which is a triumph in itself for any Pinot Nero made so far south. Also encouraging is the Chianti Classico Riserva '97, a well-made wine with good density in the mouth. Predictably, the '98 Chianti is a simpler wine. Although pleasant and fruity, it has just a touch too much acidity. The Fagge Chardonnay '98 is less successful than some previous versions. It is as well-managed as ever but does not have a great deal of concentration. This is a reliable and generally convincing range of wines and shows that Zonin group wineries are continuing relentlessly along the path to quality. And that is good news for Italian wine.

●	Aleatico dell'Elba '97	▼▼	6
○	Acquabona di Acquabona '99	▼	4
○	Ansonica dell'Elba '99	▼	3
●	Elba Rosso Ris. '97	▼	4
○	Elba Bianco '97		3
●	Aleatico dell'Elba '95	♈♈	6
●	Aleatico di Portoferraio '91	♈♈	6
○	Acquabona di Acquabona '97	♈	3
●	Aleatico dell'Elba '96	♈	6
●	Aleatico di Portoferraio '92	♈	6
○	Ansonica Passito '92	♈	5
●	Elba Rosso Ris. '94	♈	2*
●	Elba Rosso Ris. Camillo Bianchi '91	♈	3

●	Acciaiolo '97	▼▼	5
●	Chianti Classico Ris. '97	▼▼	5
●	Le Marangole '97	▼▼	5
●	Chianti Classico '98	▼	3
○	Le Fagge Chardonnay '98	▼	4
●	Acciaiolo '95	♈♈♈	5
●	Acciaiolo '88	♈♈	5
●	Acciaiolo '93	♈♈	5
●	Acciaiolo '96	♈♈	5
○	Le Fagge Chardonnay '91	♈♈	4
○	Le Fagge Chardonnay '93	♈♈	4
○	Le Fagge Chardonnay '95	♈♈	4
○	Le Fagge Chardonnay '96	♈♈	4
●	Le Marangole '95	♈♈	4
●	Le Marangole '96	♈♈	5

RADDA IN CHIANTI (SI)

BORGO SALCETINO
LOC. LUCARELI
53017 RADDA IN CHIANTI (SI)
TEL. 0577/733541

Borgo Salcetino seems definitely to be on the right path and this little estate of 13 hectares, owned by the Friuli-based Livon family, has had another good year. In part, this is thanks to hard work in the vineyards and in part to a replanting programme that involves two hectares each year and increased densities of up to 7,000 vines per hectare. Great attention has been paid to sangiovese and other local grapes but the estate has also planted some international varieties like merlot. The Chianti Classico '98 has a lovely lustrous, concentrated ruby colour and is penalized at first by strong aromas of reduction on the nose. This soon passes and refreshing vegetal notes then emerge, along with full, ripe fruit. The front palate is warm and alcohol-rich, then the tannins come through, a little immature perhaps but very solid. The finish is sweet and simple, but good. The Riserva Lucarello '97 is even better. It has an impenetrable ruby colour, while the nose presents fairly unsubtle notes of oak, suggesting that the barrels may be a bit past their best. Gradually, these aromas disappear to be replaced by complex notes of fruit. The entry on the palate is impressively broad and deep, and the flavour is massive and full-bodied. Alcohol and tannins integrate well, and the acidity slots in perfectly. The sangiovese and merlot Rossole '98 has a slightly closed nose that masks its fruit. After a few minutes in the glass, the complexity of its character comes out in delicate grassy notes and cinnamon spice. On the powerful palate, there is plenty of weight, although it still needs some more time to lose its rough edges. The finish is long and consistent.

RADDA IN CHIANTI (SI)

LIVERNANO
LOC. LIVERNANO, 67/A
53017 RADDA IN CHIANTI (SI)
TEL. 0577/738353

For the second year in a row, Livernano has won our highest award, thus staking its claim to a place in the front ranks of Chianti's most representative producers. They owe their success to the radical steps they have made in the vineyard, which now produce excellent fruit even if the weather is less than entirely clement. Livernano has many merits, some of which are due to its location for the estate's wines are not just powerful. They can also unveil a distinct aromatic profile deriving from their unique terroir. And it is the attack on the nose that makes Livernano, a blend of cabernet, merlot and sangiovese, so fascinating and endows it with such finesse. The complex aromas include blackcurrants, mulberries, violets, pepper and chocolate, all surging to fuse together in a wonderful whole. On the palate, there is remarkable concentration and softness, as well as silky tannins that allow the magical aromas to come through and linger in the leisurely finish. The Sangiovese Puro Sangue is excellent and deserves similarly close attention. Deliciously fresh, its broad aromas embrace flowers, fruit and spices, then the palate turns out to be surprisingly deep and close-knit before signing off with a long, spicy finish. It is a wine that is going places, and is only held back at the moment by the marked note of wood. The Livernano white wine, Anima, from chardonnay and sauvignon, is typical of the Carlo Montanari-owned winery's style, offering depth combined with elegance, though it still needs to develop a tad more personality.

● Chianti Classico '98	▼▼	4
● Chianti Classico Lucarello Ris. '97	▼▼	5
● Rossole '98	▼▼	5
● Chianti Classico '97	♀♀	4
● Chianti Classico Lucarello Ris. '96	♀	5

● Livernano '98	▼▼▼	6
○ Anima '98	▼▼	5
● Puro Sangue '98	▼▼	6
● Livernano '97	♀♀♀	6
○ Anima '96	♀♀	5
● Livernano '96	♀♀	6
● Nardina '95	♀♀	5
● Puro Sangue '95	♀♀	6
● Puro Sangue '97	♀♀	6
○ Anima '97	♀	5

RADDA IN CHIANTI (SI)

Fattoria di Montevertine

Loc. Monte Vertine
53017 Radda in Chianti (SI)
tel. 0577/738009

Recently, we retasted the Pergole Torte Riserva '90, which a few years ago we thought was one of the best Italian wines ever made. Well, it's still in great shape and has intriguingly complex aromas, grip and concentration. The tannins are even still a little over-enthusiastic, which shows how young at heart it is. We continue to think it is a world-class blockbuster and if it had been present at our tastings this year, we would have had to give it Four Glasses, not Three. However, we found ourselves asking why it is that neither the '95 nor this year's wine, the '97, both of which come from vintages that can stand comparison with 1990, are not equally convincing. Are we getting harder of heart? Are we losing our marbles? Are age and alcohol finally catching up with the panel's lucidity? There is, however, no denying that the aromas of all the Montevertine wines seem more evolved, less clear and less elegant than they were in the past. They are still wonderful wines, made with genuine passion, but we felt ever so slightly let down. This time the '97 Montevertine Riserva '97 was perhaps the most coherent on the nose. Simpler than its two partners, it is rather impressively well-made. The Sodaccio '97 offered rich fruit aromas but there were also earthy and faintly gamey notes creeping through. As you might expect, the Pergole Torte '97 was the fattest and most concentrated of the three but the nose was fairly evolved. An excellent wine, but not a great one. At least, in our humble opinion.

● Il Sodaccio '97	TT	5
● Le Pergole Torte '97	TT	6
● Montevertine Ris. '97	TT	5
● Le Pergole Torte '83	YYY	6
● Le Pergole Torte '86	YYY	6
● Le Pergole Torte '88	YYY	6
● Le Pergole Torte '90	YYY	6
● Le Pergole Torte '92	YYY	6
● Montevertine Ris. '85	YYY	5
● Le Pergole Torte '85	YY	6
● Le Pergole Torte '93	YY	6
● Le Pergole Torte '94	YY	6
● Le Pergole Torte '95	YY	6
● Le Pergole Torte '96	YY	6
● Montevertine Ris. '90	YY	6

Podere Capaccia

Loc. Capaccia
53017 Radda in Chianti (SI)
tel. 0577/738385 - 0574/582426

The Querciagrande '97 is great. It's a big, convincing red, full-bodied and complex, and perfectly in line with the best versions of this great Sangiovese from Radda in Chianti. This is a wine that backs up the positive judgements that we continue to express year after year about Podere Capaccia. We have to admit that we were expecting an exceptional performance from this winery in such a favourable year. The slight defects of over-evolved aromas and excessive acidity which were present in the '96 have vanished from the '97. Ripe berry fruit comes through clearly and intensely on the nose while the palate proffers an enticing softness, against an understated backdrop of acidity and tannin-driven grip that gives the wine structure and guarantees it a long life in the cellar. Oddly, the '97 Chianti Classico Riserva is less successful. Much simpler and more dilute than the Querciagrande, it even shows some symptoms of precocious evolution. Unlike its big brother, this bottle doesn't seem to have much ageing potential. Still, there's no need for anyone to tear their hair out, of course. An estate that can come up with a wine like the Querciagrande '97 has already shown it can do the business.

● Querciagrande '97	TT	5
● Chianti Classico Ris. '97	T	5
● Querciagrande '88	YYY	6
● Chianti Classico '90	YY	4
● Chianti Classico Ris. '86	YY	5
● Chianti Classico Ris. '88	YY	5
● Chianti Classico Ris. '96	YY	5
● Querciagrande '86	YY	6
● Querciagrande '87	YY	6
● Querciagrande '90	YY	6
● Querciagrande '91	YY	6
● Querciagrande '92	YY	6
● Querciagrande '93	YY	6
● Querciagrande '95	YY	6
● Querciagrande '96	YY	5

476

RADDA IN CHIANTI (SI)

RADDA IN CHIANTI (SI)

POGGERINO
LOC. POGGERINO, 6
53017 RADDA IN CHIANTI (SI)
TEL. 0577/738958

FATTORIA DI TERRABIANCA
LOC. S. FEDELE A PATERNO
53017 RADDA IN CHIANTI (SI)
TEL. 0577/738544

The wines of Poggerino are all fruit-rich, well-balanced and terroir-driven. Piero Lanza's label is a guarantee, and every wine gives you exactly what you pay for. The Chianti Classico '98 has a well-integrated nose of berry fruit and faint notes of spices. The well-managed palate offers nice length, well-extracted tannins and a discreet touch of characteristic sangiovese acidity to add lift. Isn't this precisely what we expect from a young Chianti? With the Riserva Bugialla '97, you know straight away that it is a very different proposition. The nose heralds outstanding concentration as the aromas open out over a wealth of ripe, but not over-ripe, fruit and a touch of vanilla. The entry on the mouth is firm and full-bodied, picking up the pace as it progresses sure-footedly. The close-knit tannins are bright and well-rounded. This is a wine that is still developing, and one that very nearly won more than the Two Glasses it was awarded. The Primamateria '98, from equal parts of sangiovese and merlot, is a wine of excellent quality that (as its name, meaning "First Fruit", suggests) stakes its claim to fame on its raw material. It may lack a little complexity but it can offer superb-quality fruit, serious weight on the palate and attractive drinkability. The clean, fragrant Rosato Aurora '99 is a fine example of its category.

This winery belongs to Roberto Guldener, who came to Chianti from Switzerland 12 years ago, and continues its steady march towards top quality. The wines are again convincing and show good breeding. To confirm how effective the work done here has been is the new red, Ceppate '97, a truly successful Bordeaux blend which has the makings of a future champion. Its intense, pervasive nose hints at redcurrants and blackberries against a spicy backdrop of white pepper and nutmeg. The broad palate offers chewy fruit and fine-grained tannins that suffuse the palate and the attractively long finish mingles hints of mulberries with refreshing balsamic touches. The Campaccio is also successful. A blend of sangiovese and cabernet sauvignon, it maintains the high standards of previous years. The nose presents grassy notes that mingle well with the cherry and redcurrant fruit. Entry on the palate is soft, progressing with attractive balance. More concentration would have given that extra something we have been anticipating for some time. The Campaccio Selezione Speciale '96 also notched up a few extra points. There is more cabernet in the blend and the palate is a little fuller. Moving on the Sangioveses, we find the Chianti Classico Vigna della Croce Riserva and the Piano del Cipresso. The first is not quite as good as other recent versions. Although it still as enjoyably fruity as ever, its tannins are still rough, which gives the palate an excessive dryness. The Piano del Cipresso offers notes of geraniums and cherries over faint spice. In the mouth, it is soft, not very concentrated, and still needs to settle down.

● Chianti Cl. Bugialla Ris. '97	♥♥	5
● Chianti Classico '98	♥♥	3*
● Primamateria '98	♥♥	5
☉ Aurora '99		2
● Chianti Classico Ris. '90	♥♥♥	5
● Chianti Cl. Bugialla Ris. '94	♥♥	5
● Chianti Cl. Bugialla Ris. '95	♥♥	5
● Chianti Cl. Bugialla Ris. '96	♥♥	5
● Chianti Classico '93	♥♥	3*
● Chianti Classico '94	♥♥	3*
● Chianti Classico '95	♥♥	3*
● Chianti Classico '96	♥♥	3*
● Chianti Classico '97	♥♥	3*
● Vigna di Bugialla '91	♥♥	5
● Vigna di Bugialla '93	♥♥	5

● Campaccio Sel. Speciale '96	♥♥	5
● Ceppate '97	♥♥	6
● Campaccio '96	♥	5
● Chianti Classico		
Vigna della Croce Ris. '97	♥	4
● Piano del Cipresso '96	♥	5
● Campaccio '90	♥♥	5
● Campaccio '93	♥♥	5
● Campaccio '94	♥♥	6
● Campaccio '95	♥♥	5
● Campaccio Sel. Speciale '93	♥♥	6
● Campaccio Sel. Speciale '95	♥♥	6
● Chianti Classico		
Vigna della Croce Ris. '95	♥♥	4
● Piano del Cipresso '94	♥♥	6

RADDA IN CHIANTI (SI)

VIGNAVECCHIA
VIA ROMA, 23
53017 RADDA IN CHIANTI (SI)
TEL. 0577/738090

RADDA IN CHIANTI (SI)

CASTELLO DI VOLPAIA
LOC. VOLPAIA
P.ZZA DELLA CISTERNA, 1
53017 RADDA IN CHIANTI (SI)
TEL. 0577/738066

This small producer in Radda had good results over the whole range, including a newcomer, an interesting cask-aged white. We'll begin with this wine, the Titanium '99, a monovarietal Chardonnay with a rich, gold-flecked straw-yellow colour. The nose unveils a vibrant note of vanilla softened by hints of butter and spices. The palate is warm, mouth-filling and unctuously full-bodied, with toasty overtones that lend elegance to the finish. The Riserva '97 is also very good. It has an impenetrable ruby colour and a nose of plum and mulberry fruit, complemented by notes of oak, leather and tobacco. The powerful entry on the palate packs plenty of alcohol to tame the close-knit tannins and progresses admirably. The Canvalle '97, a blend of cabernet sauvignon with a small proportion of sangiovese, is the least convincing of the line-up. The rich, limpid colour introduces a rather fuzzy nose with over-assertive grassy notes, and hints of capers and gamey overtones that combine to make a rather inelegant whole. The palate reveals medium weight and prominent acidity. The Raddese '97 is a monovarietal Sangiovese that offers marked grassy notes on the nose, with faint nuances of green pepper, that mask its unforthcoming fruit. The palate has good concentration, although the rather exuberant tannins tend to mask the alcohol.

The best-ever Balifico reviewed in the Guide, the '97, introduces the finest performance ever by Castello di Volpaia at our tastings. Not all the reds that come from this estate's vineyards are "competition wines". Castello di Volpaia makes wines in a classic style with elegant aromas and moderate body, characteristics that penalize them in a comparative blind tasting. So this result, with the '97 Balifico leading the way, is even better than it might seem at first glance. But let's talk about the wines. We've already mentioned the Balifico, a sangiovese and cabernet sauvignon blend. It has more body and elegance than any of the previous versions. The Chianti Classico Riserva '97 is clean, fruity and very delicate on the palate. The '97 Coltassala is a largely sangiovese blend. Cogent and elegant, it reveals faint hints of acidity that are still evident on the palate but promises to age with class and dignity. The Chianti Classico '98, is no more than decent for it offers little structure and, though it is technically impeccable, it is, as one would expect, the least distinguished Castello di Volpaia wine. Nevertheless, our visit was very fruitful. There are some very serious wines to be found at Volpaia and we would like to emphasize this point. Castello di Volpaia is one of the best-known wineries in the whole of Chianti so performances like this can only reinforce the positive image of Chianti Classico.

● Chianti Classico Ris. '97	♊♊	4
○ Titanum '99	♊♊	4
● Canvalle '97	♊	5
● Raddese '97	♊	5
● Chianti Classico Ris. '95		0
● Canvalle '93	♉♉	5
● Canvalle '96	♉♉	5
● Chianti Classico '90	♉♉	4
● Chianti Classico Ris. '96	♉♉	4
● Raddese '90	♉♉	5
● Canvalle '92	♉	5
● Chianti Classico '91	♉	3
● Chianti Classico Ris. '90	♉	5
● Chianti Classico Ris. '91	♉	4
● Raddese '96	♉	4

● Balifico '97	♊♊	5
● Chianti Classico Ris. '97	♊♊	5
● Coltassala '97	♊♊	5
● Chianti Classico '98	♊	4
● Balifico '87	♉♉	5
● Balifico '88	♉♉	5
● Balifico '91	♉♉	5
● Chianti Classico '97	♉♉	4
● Chianti Classico Ris. '93	♉♉	4
● Chianti Classico Ris. '94	♉♉	4
● Chianti Classico Ris. '95	♉♉	5
● Coltassala '90	♉♉	5
● Coltassala '91	♉♉	5
● Coltassala '94	♉♉	5
● Coltassala '95	♉♉	5

RAPOLANO TERME (SI)   ROCCALBEGNA (GR)

CASTELLO DI MODANELLA
LOC. SERRE
53040 RAPOLANO TERME (SI)
TEL. 0577/704604

VILLA PATRIZIA
FRAZ. CANA
LOC. VILLA PATRIZIA
58050 ROCCALBEGNA (GR)
TEL. 0564/982028

The wines of Castello di Modanella made a good overall showing. All their samples had a flattering reception at our tastings. Truth to tell, given the continual progress that this winery has made, we expected an even better performance, particularly since three of their four wines presented were from the '97 vintage. As usual, the Cabernet Sauvignon Le Voliere was the pick of the crop but only just, both with respect to the other products and in comparison with previous vintages. A rich, concentrated wine, with a very convincing progression on the palate, it is let down by vegetal notes that detract from the overall balance and by a lack of ripeness in the fruit. The Sangiovese Campo d'Aia '97 has a clean nose of berry fruit and spices, followed up by an attractive, balanced palate sustained by good tannins that emerge particularly in the finish. The Merlot Poggio Mondino '97 also did well. It offers fairly ripe, if not altogether focused, fruit, vegetal and gamey aromas. The palate is more convincing, unveiling good balance, a broad progression and fine length. The Poggio l'Aiole '98 just missed out on Two Glasses, which is a significant result if we remember that it is a monovarietal Canaiolo. The aromas are uncomplicated but clean, with notes of berry fruit and a hint of oak. The palate is coherent, well-balanced and offers reasonable depth.

The long list of wines presented by Villa Patrizia this year showed good overall quality. While it is true that there is no really superlative wine, nor are there any bottles that are less than decent. Their best wine, and also the estate's flag-bearer, is the Orto di Boccio '97, a blend of cabernet, merlot and sangiovese. It has fine texture, which comes through on an intense nose of black berries that is slightly veiled by the wood. In the mouth, the fine-grained tannins sustain the soft progression through to a long finish, revealing one or two youthful rough edges on the way. It easily earned its Two Glasses but to go any higher, it would need more complexity and character. The '96 version of the same wine is less compact and its fruit is less than fully ripe. The palate shows reasonable volume but the tannins are somewhat aggressive. The Morellino Riserva '97 impressed the panel with its tenacity. The nose reveals a few tertiary notes of leather and tobacco, lifted by spice from the wood. There is plenty of chewy fruit on the palate, which also offers good balance and a fairly long finish. The uncomplicated but very appealing Morellino '99 has an intense nose of cherries and raspberries and a fragrant, up-front palate with lots of juicy fruit. Finally, the Malvasia Sciamareti '99 came close to winning Two Glasses. Its aromas on the nose are low-key but the palate is full-bodied and generous.

● Campo d'Aia '97	🍷🍷	4
● Le Voliere Cabernet Sauvignon '97	🍷🍷	4
● Poggio Mondino '97	🍷🍷	4
● Poggio l'Aiole '98	🍷	3
● Campo d'Aia '95	🍷🍷	3
● Le Voliere Cabernet Sauvignon '95	🍷🍷	4
● Le Voliere Cabernet Sauvignon '96	🍷🍷	4
● Campo d'Aia '96	🍷	3
● Poggio l'Aiole '97	🍷	3
● Poggio Mondino '96	🍷	3

● Morellino di Scansano Ris. '97	🍷🍷	4
● Orto di Boccio '97	🍷🍷	5
● Morellino di Scansano '99	🍷	2*
● Orto di Boccio '96	🍷	4
○ Sciamareti '99	🍷	2*
○ Alteta '96	🍷🍷	4
○ Alteta '97	🍷🍷	4
● Albatraia '96	🍷	1*
● Albatraia '98	🍷	1*
● Morellino di Scansano '96	🍷	2*
● Morellino di Scansano '97	🍷	3
● Morellino di Scansano '98	🍷	2*
● Orto di Boccio '94	🍷	4
● Orto di Boccio '95	🍷	4
● Villa Patrizia Rosso '96	🍷	3

ROCCATEDERIGHI (GR) RUFINA (FI)

MELETA
LOC. MELETA
58028 ROCCATEDERIGHI (GR)
TEL. 0564/567155

FATTORIA DI BASCIANO
V.LE DUCA DELLA VITTORIA, 159
50068 RUFINA (FI)
TEL. 055/8397034

We had trouble recognizing the once distinctive style that used to characterize wines from Meleta. Until a few years ago, this was a winery that had the wind in its sails. It was one of the best producers in the area and a credit to its terroir. The results of our tastings this year were satisfactory but we know that Meleta is capable not only of higher quality but also of a wonderful vitality that, unhappily, seems now to be a thing of the past. For the second year in a row, their best wine is the Vin Santo, whose '96 version stays true to its subdued and rigorous, yet very attractive, style. The clean aromas hint at concentration, proffering notes of apricots, almonds, and dried figs. In the mouth, there is decent breadth and elegance, and moderate depth. The Bianco della Rocca '98, a Chardonnay, shows its worth in the lively energy of the palate. The nose is clean and a little pedestrian but it shifts up a gear in the mouth, where it reveals good texture, a well-sustained continuous development and laudable balance, as well as good length. The Merlot Massaio '97 is delicious, aided by the well-balanced progression of flavours on the palate but it has only moderate body, and there are distinct vegetal hints. The decent, but fairly disappointing, Rosso della Rocca '97, from equal parts of cabernet, merlot, and sangiovese, also has marked vegetal aromas. The palate is robust but fails to come together completely. The Sangiovese Pietrello '99 has pleasant aromas of blackberry jam, a rounded, well-balanced palate, and is very easy to drink. The vermentino-based Lucertolo white and the Rocchigiano, a rosé, are lightweight but well-managed.

The Masi family's winery has had another successful year. If there is anything to carp about, it is the way they interpret the terroir. The international varieties they plant make their presence felt, even though the quality of the wines is very high. In time, they might want to develop a more distinctive character for their products. The Chianti Rufina '98 has an intense, limpid ruby colour, a sweet nose of concentrated fruit with touches of vanilla, and is soft, smooth, and inviting in the mouth, its tannins integrating well into the generous structure of the body. The Riserva '97 has a full, firm colour that introduces stylish aromas of chocolate and other, more evolved, notes of tobacco. The presence of rather raw vegetal notes, however, jars somewhat. In the mouth, the initial almost tender softness still allows the powerful tannins to emerge but in fact, this wine is not very representative of its birthplace. I Pini '98 is half sangiovese and half cabernet, and has crisp, intense aromas of mature fruit, including redcurrants and plums, as well as notes of vanilla. The palate is convincing and very full-bodied. The Corto '98 is a blend of sangiovese with some cabernet. It has a ripe nose of fresh fruit enhanced by well-integrated wood. The entry on the palate is spectacular. Full-bodied and richly textured, it unveils a rich and beautifully balanced mid palate of juicy fruit. The less convincing '99 Rosato is fresh on nose and palate but reveals aromas that are not entirely clean. The Vin Santo Rufina '95 has a lovely amber colour, and a nose of chestnuts and dried fruits, but is a little rough on the palate.

O Bianco della Rocca '98	�	5
O Vin Santo '96	�	5
● Massaio '97	�	5
● Pietrello '99	�	3
● Rosso della Rocca '97	�	5
O Lucertolo '99		2
☉ Rocchigiano '99		2
● Merlot '94	�YY	6
● Rosso della Rocca '91	�YY	5
● Rosso della Rocca '92	�YY	5
● Rosso della Rocca '93	�YY	5
● Rosso della Rocca '94	�YY	5
● Rosso della Rocca '95	�YY	5
O Vin Santo '94	�YY	5
O Vin Santo '95	�YY	5

● Chianti Rufina '98	�YY	3*
● I Pini '98	�YY	3*
● Il Corto '98	�YY	3*
● Chianti Rufina Ris. '97	�	3
O Vin Santo Rufina '95	�	3
☉ Rosato '99		2
● Chianti Rufina Ris. '95	�YY	2*
● Chianti Rufina Ris. '96	�YY	2*
● I Pini '96	�YY	3
● I Pini '97	�YY	3*
● Il Corto '96	�YY	3
● Il Corto '97	�YY	3*
● Chianti Rufina '96	♀	2
● Chianti Rufina '97	♀	2*
O Vin Santo Rufina '94	♀	3

480

CASTELLI DEL GREVEPESA
LOC. MERCATALE VAL DI PESA
VIA GREVIGIANA, 34
50024 S. CASCIANO VAL DI PESA (FI)
TEL. 055/821911

FATTORIA CORZANO E PATERNO
FRAZ. S. PANCRAZIO
VIA PATERNO, 8
50026 S. CASCIANO VAL DI PESA (FI)
TEL. 055/8248179 - 055/8249114

This is one of the best-known co-operative wineries in Chianti Classico. Its list of products is almost endless and covers most sectors of the market. We always review the wines destined for the top end of the market but, by and large, everything they produce is both reliable and good value for money. On call this year were wines that did not always come from very good vintages. Nonetheless, the results are reasonably satisfactory, as you can see from a quick glance at the bottom of the page. Their Guado al Luco '96, a blend of sangiovese and cabernet sauvignon, is particularly interesting. It has clean, intense aromas and a full, fairly concentrated palate. It comes from the '96 vintage so we weren't expecting any great power or texture but it put on a good show and easily earned its second Glass. "Convincing", however, is the word for the Chianti Classico Castelgreve Riserva '97, in one of the best versions of recent years. It has good complex aromas, decent equilibrium and a long finish. In the mouth, it may not be very complex but it is decidedly well made. The Chianti Classico Castelgreve '98 is ever-dependable, pleasant and perhaps a bit simple but it is certainly very well typed. Almost on the same level, but with more acidity-driven grip, is the Chianti Classico Castelgreve Clemente VII '98. The only slight disappointment comes from the Coltifredi '96, a 100% Sangiovese from a weak year.

This time Aljoscha Goldsmitt has hit the bull's-eye. His Corzano '97 is a truly great wine in every way. He has fine-tuned the components that made it so intriguing and characterful, producing a wine that is as rich, concentrated and strong as it has always been but with a softness and elegance that were not there in the past. As well as the perfect ripeness of the fruit, the nicely gauged use of oak and the masterful extraction of the silky tannins have played a fundamental role here. Dark and close-knit in the glass, it opens with attractively rich fruit nuanced with coffee on the nose. Then the broad, full-flavoured, mouth-filling palate offers lingering aromas. The varietal notes of sangiovese and cabernet are actually very subtle, melding seamlessly with terroir-derived characteristics in an attractive taste profile. However, it would be wrong for us not mention the excellent Chianti Riserva, which has concentrated notes of black berries, faint vegetal overtones and well-amalgamated wood. The long, elegant palate is well sustained, with the tannins adding bite. The chardonnay-based Aglaia made a good impression on the panel, revealing smoke-veined hints of vanilla and tropical fruits. It has a substantial, very agreeable palate with good balance, although the oak is perhaps over-stated. The Chianti Terre di Corzano '98 is a worthy effort. The finish is a little green but the palate is fleshy and the fruit fragrant.

● Chianti Cl. Castelgreve Ris. '97	♟♟	4	
● Guado al Luco '96	♟♟	5	
● Chianti Cl. Castelgreve '98	♟	3	
● Chianti Cl. Clemente VII '98	♟	4	
● Coltifredi '96	♟	5	
● Chianti Cl. Castelgreve Ris. '88	♟♟	4	
● Chianti Cl. Castelgreve Ris. '90	♟♟	4	
● Chianti Cl. Castelgreve Ris. '95	♟♟	4	
● Chianti Cl. Montefiridolfi '90	♟♟	4	
● Chianti Cl. Vigna Elisa '90	♟♟	5	
● Chianti Cl. Clemente VII '88	♟♟	5	
● Coltifredi '95	♟♟	5	
● Guado al Luco '93	♟♟	5	
● Guado al Luco '95	♟♟	5	
● Chianti Cl. Castelgreve Ris. '96	♟	4	

● Il Corzano '97	♟♟♟	5
○ Aglaia '99	♟♟	4
● Chianti Terre di Corzano Ris. '97	♟♟	4
● Chianti Terre di Corzano '98	♟	3
○ Aglaia '98	♟♟	4
● Chianti Terre di Corzano '97	♟♟	3*
● Chianti Terre di Corzano Ris. '90	♟♟	4
● Chianti Terre di Corzano Ris. '95	♟♟	4
● Il Corzano '88	♟♟	5
● Il Corzano '96	♟♟	5
● Il Corzano '95	♟♟	5
○ Vin Santo '90	♟♟	5
○ Vin Santo '93	♟♟	5
● Chianti '96	♟	3
● Chianti Terre di Corzano '94	♟	3

S. CASCIANO VAL DI PESA (FI) S. CASCIANO VAL DI PESA (FI)

TENUTA CASTELLO IL CORNO
VIA MALAFRANCA, 20
50026 S. CASCIANO VAL DI PESA (FI)
TEL. 055/8248009

LA SALA
VIA SORRIPA, 34
50026 S. CASCIANO VAL DI PESA (FI)
TEL. 055/828111

There is plenty to report about this winery, which lies on the edge of Chianti Classico and belongs to the Frova family. First, they have hired the excellent oenologist, Stefano Chioccioli to look after winemaking. Next, their results with the colorino grape are more interesting than ever, definite proof that the experiments that they began years ago with this variety have been successful. And we'll begin with the Colorino '97, which has a ruby colour so deep it is almost black. The nose starts with elegant notes of coffee and vanilla, enhanced by hints of cloves. In the mouth, it is soft and enticing, the alcohol prevailing over the tannins in an attractively balanced structure, while the rich flavour lingers. The Corno Rosso '99 offers aromas of ripe fruit, such as mulberries and redcurrants, and distinct, well-integrated hints of coffee. The entry on the palate is deliciously smooth and creamy, then moves on to a firm, complex mid palate and a long finish. The Chianti Colli Fiorentini San Camillo '99 is an excellent example of a simple, but very well-made wine. There are evolved notes on the nose, which also has vegetal notes mingling with lively berry fruit. It holds up well on the palate, where it shows plenty of texture and balance, rounding off with a long, convincing finish. The Chianti Classico '98 has a very deep ruby colour leading in to a nose with marked vegetal aromas and refreshing spice. It has good breadth and weight in the mouth, the alcohol and tannins are well balanced, and it signs off with a pleasing finish.

We are particularly fond of this small estate in San Casciano, and the dedication with which Laura Baronti runs things commands respect. Today, if Laura is one of the best winemakers in her area, it is because she consistently produces good wines. The marks awarded this year confirm last time's assessments, although there has again been a small but significant step forward. The Campo all'Albero '97, a blend of sangiovese and cabernet sauvignon, is more concentrated and convincing than the '95 or '96. It is softer and more inviting in the mouth, if a little vegetal to the nose, but it has the intensity and balance of a champion. Well-typed, elegant and almost perfectly poised, the Chianti Classico Riserva '97 is a child of its native soil in a way that few other wines from San Casciano succeed in being. Moderate tannic grip, utterly convincing velvet smoothness and crisp, not excessively complex fruit with a hint of oak are its distinguishing characteristics. It is just the wine it should be. No more, no less. Somewhat thinner, with a fruity nose and straightforward flavour, the Chianti Classico '98 is a shade predictable but still a decent product in a good but not excellent year. Taken all together, this is a range that makes the cellar a shining example of the winemaker's craft. And that, perhaps, is the finest compliment that we could pay it.

● Colorino '97	▼▼	4
● Corno Rosso '99	▼▼	4
● Chianti Classico '98	▼	3
● Chianti Colli Fiorentini San Camillo '99	▼	3
● Colorino '96	♀♀	4
● I Gibbioni '97	♀♀	4
● Chianti Classico '97	♀	3
● Chianti Colli Fiorentini San Camillo '97	♀	3
● I Gibbioni '96	♀	4

● Campo all'Albero '97	▼▼	5
● Chianti Classico Ris. '97	▼▼	4
● Chianti Classico '98	▼	3
● Campo all'Albero '94	♀♀	4
● Campo all'Albero '95	♀♀	4
● Campo all'Albero '96	♀♀	5
● Chianti Classico '96	♀♀	3*
● Chianti Classico Ris. '96	♀♀	4
● Chianti Classico '93	♀	3
● Chianti Classico '95	♀	3
● Chianti Classico '97	♀	3
● Chianti Classico Ris. '93	♀	4
● Chianti Classico Ris. '95	♀	4

S. CASCIANO VAL DI PESA (FI)

FATTORIA LE CORTI - CORSINI
VIA SAN PIERO DI SOTTO, 1
50026 S. CASCIANO VAL DI PESA (FI)
TEL. 055/820123

Principe Ducio Corsini's wines have never come as close to winning Three Glasses as they did this year. We are beginning to realize the true value of products that are still only at the start of a journey they set out on years ago. Soon, we will see sumptuous wines emerging from the dark cellars at Villa Le Corti, between San Casciano and Mercatale. The Chianti Classico Don Tommaso '98 made it to our last round and only just missed a third Glass. There is still a bit too much wood on the nose and the structure is very good but not exceptional. With just a little bit more concentration, the wine will hit the jackpot. This time around, it is penalized by the vintage ('98), which was good but not excellent. However, the panel admired the perfection of the winemaking technique. Particular attention has obviously been paid to fermentation, maceration on the skins and the use of wood. Only a slight lack of body allows a little too much vanilla to come through on the nose. However, the real surprise is the Chianti Classico '98, the cellar's standard-label wine. Deliciously fruity, it has slightly oaky notes on the nose while in the mouth it is soft and full-flavoured. A little gem. It is even more convincing than the Chianti Classico Cortevecchia Riserva '97, which is more predictable, and even old-fashioned, in its conception. It is a good wine that risks being left behind by the progress of the estate's winemaking technique. And that is all that we need to say.

S. CASCIANO VAL DI PESA (FI)

MACHIAVELLI
LOC. S. ANDREA IN PERCUSSINA
50026 S. CASCIANO VAL DI PESA (FI)
TEL. 0577/989001

Only if you actually go to see the Machiavelli vineyards at Sant'Andrea in Percussina on the northern edge of the Chianti Classico zone can you understand why their wines have been receiving such high marks in the last few years. The Vigna di Fontalle, in particular, which has miraculously survived intact from the original Machiavelli's times, is quite spectacular. This goes to show that when the wine has been successful for such a long time, there should be no problems today. All you have to do is continue to work with scrupulous care and make no concessions on quality. And that's why the Chianti Classico Vigna di Fontalle Riserva '97 has again notched up a Three Glass score. It was aged half in large barrels and half in barriques so the oak-derived aromas are well managed and the vanilla is not excessive. Yet it does have a traditional twist in the acidity that is not entirely absorbed by the sweet tannins. In short, it is a wine with attitude. And when a Sangiovese is so much more impressive than the winery's two Supertuscans, the Principe '97, a Pinot Nero, and their less than wonderful Ser Niccolò '97, it means we are talking about a wine with very pronounced characteristics. This is something that you certainly conjure up in the cellar. It comes from the terroir. Hats off to Machiavelli, then, to the Gruppo Italiani Vini that owns it and to oenologist, Nunzio Capurso, one of the grand masters of Italian wine.

● Chianti Cl. Cortevecchia Ris. '97	▼▼	5
● Chianti Classico '98	▼▼	3*
● Chianti Classico Don Tommaso '98	▼▼	5
● Chianti Cl. Cortevecchia Ris. '95	♈♈	5
● Chianti Classico '97	♈♈	3*
● Chianti Classico Don Tommaso '94	♈♈	5
● Chianti Classico Don Tommaso '95	♈♈	5
● Chianti Classico Don Tommaso '96	♈♈	5
● Chianti Classico Don Tommaso '97	♈♈	5
● Chianti Classico '96	♈	4

● Chianti Cl. V. di Fontalle Ris. '97	▼▼▼	5
● Il Principe '97	▼▼	5
● Ser Niccolò Solatio del Tani '97	▼	5
● Chianti Cl. V. di Fontalle Ris. '95	♈♈♈	5
● Il Principe '95	♈♈♈	4*
● Ser Niccolò Solatio del Tani '88	♈♈♈	4*
● Chianti Cl. V. di Fontalle Ris. '88	♈♈	4
● Chianti Cl. V. di Fontalle Ris. '90	♈♈	4
● Chianti Cl. V. di Fontalle Ris. '93	♈♈	4
● Chianti Cl. V. di Fontalle Ris. '94	♈♈	4
● Il Principe '94	♈♈	4
● Il Principe '96	♈♈	5
● Ser Niccolò Solatio dei Tani '87	♈♈	5
● Ser Niccolò Solatio del Tani '93	♈♈	5

S. CASCIANO VAL DI PESA (FI)   S. GIMIGNANO (SI)

FATTORIA POGGIOPIANO
VIA DI PISIGNANO, 28/30
50026 S. CASCIANO VAL DI PESA (FI)
TEL. 055/8229629

BARONCINI
LOC. CASALE, 43
53037 S. GIMIGNANO (SI)
TEL. 0577/941961

With its third top award in four years, Rosso di Sera enters the Olympus of great Italian red wines. It also offers us another opportunity to scotch the idea that there are well-defined good years and bad years. Such blanket judgements are at best superficial and can only be taken as indicative. With the exception of real catastrophes, it's fair to say that careful vineyard management is almost always sufficient to offset the vagaries of the weather. If we factor in the variables of site climate and soil type from vineyard to vineyard, we can conclude that, happily, vintages are different from each other, but not necessarily better or worse. The Rosso di Sera '98, for example, has not lost its basic characteristics of concentration, softness, and rich fruit, but also unveils an elegance and refined execution that are probably superior to its predecessors. It is a textbook example of a modern-style wine with its lavish fruit pulp and massive, yet velvet-smooth, tannins. But it was the oak in the '98 that really impressed the panel. This greater expertise is adequately confirmed in their Chianti Classico '98, which shows a more clearly-defined character than its predecessors. The nose has good breadth, firm fruit well-supported by oak and negligible vegetal notes. The palate is full-bodied and nicely poised, with lively tannins in the very attractive finish.

Baroncini is one of the most important wineries in San Gimignano. It was started in the early '60's by Jaures Baroncini and today is run with determination and success by his children Stefano and Bruna. They have lengthened the list of wines with new varieties, all native to Tuscany. Now the Vernaccia di San Gimignano has been joined by a Brunello di Montalcino, a Chianti, a Nobile di Montepulciano and a Morellino di Scansano. For the time being, though, the winery's heart is still in San Gimignano and again this year, the Vernaccia Dometaia Riserva was the most interesting and representative wine that Stefano and Bruna presented at our tastings. It has a bright straw-yellow colour and intense, fresh aromas in which notes of ripe peach and apple mingle with elegant nuances of flowers. The attractively fresh and fruit-rich palate has good structure, shading into more complex notes and showing faint hints of spice in the finish. The Vernaccia Poggio ai Cannicci Sovestro is fresh, fruity and very agreeable while the trebbiano and malvasia-based Bianco Faina took our fancy with its softly intense aromas, good body and elegantly aromatic finish. The Vernaccia di San Gimignano is well-managed and fruity, and we thought the Cortegiano '98 was also attractively rich and solid. The wines from Aia della Macina, the property in Maremma run by Bruna Baroncini, are good again. The Morellino Riserva Terranera is a remarkably full-bodied, softly elegant red and the Vigneto Roggetone displays convincingly intense fruit and spice on the nose while the palate is rounded and well-structured.

● Rosso di Sera '98	ŢŢŢ	6		● Morellino di Scansano Terranera		
● Chianti Classico '98	ŢŢ	4		Ris. Aia della Macina '97	ŢŢ	4
● Rosso di Sera '95	ŢŢŢ	5		● Morellino di Scansano Vign.		
● Rosso di Sera '97	ŢŢŢ	5		Roggetone Aia della Macina '99	ŢŢ	3*
● Rosso di Sera '96	ŢŢ	5		O Vernaccia di S. Gimignano		
● Chianti Classico '95	Ţ	3		Dometaia Ris. '98	ŢŢ	4
● Chianti Classico '96	Ţ	3		● Cortegiano Sovestro '98	Ţ	4
● Chianti Classico '97	Ţ	4		O Vernaccia di S. Gimignano '99	Ţ	2*
				O Vernaccia di S. Gimignano		
				Poggio ai Cannici Sovestro '99	Ţ	3
				● Chianti '99		2
				● Chianti Colli Senesi S. Vigna		
				S. Domenico Sovestro '99		3
				● Morellino di Scansano Terranera		
				Ris. Aia della Macina '96	ŢŢ	4

S. GIMIGNANO (SI)

CASA ALLE VACCHE

LOC. LUCIGNANO, 73/A
53037 S. GIMIGNANO (SI)
TEL. 0577/955103

This winery, enthusiastically managed by brothers Fernando and Lorenzo Ciappi, is still going through a period of transition. They have 13 hectares under vine in the Pancole zone but the wines we tasted this year do not yet do justice to this estate's potential. The Aglieno '99, a blend of cabernet sauvignon and sangiovese, gets a very full One Glass. It has a nose resplendent in fruit aromas and notes of vanilla, then the palate unveils its exuberant structure. However, the tannins, although fine-grained, are a little over-assertive in the finish. The Chianti Colli Senesi '99 is a model of dependability and drinking pleasure. A perfect wine to quaff, perhaps over a plate of cold meat, it is offered at an extremely honest price. The Chianti Colli Senesi Cinabro '98 has an intense ruby colour, aromas of black berry fruit, and hints of pencil lead and citron. The solid palate has good weight and well-woven tannins that are slightly aggressive at the end. We are certain, though, that a few months' more ageing in the bottle will bring greater equilibrium As for the whites, the Vernaccia I Macchioni returns to a good level, even if '99 wasn't an excellent year. It has a delicate, floral nose, and good balance and softness on the palate which lead in to a delicately bitterish, varietal finish. Down a notch or two we find the barrique-fermented Vernaccia di San Gimignano Crocus '99. Its intense aromas are redolent of sweet vanilla, flowers and almonds. The soft, substantial entry on the palate is almost buttery but the finish is rather short. The Ciappis' Vernaccia '99 is extremely well-made and easy to drink.

●	Aglieno '99	🍷	4
●	Chianti Colli Senesi '99	🍷	2*
●	Chianti Colli Senesi Cinabro '98	🍷	4
○	Vernaccia di S. Gimignano Crocus '99	🍷	4
○	Vernaccia di S. Gimignano I Macchioni '99	🍷	3
○	Vernaccia di S. Gimignano '99		2
●	Chianti Colli Senesi Cinabro '97	🍷🍷	4
○	Vernaccia di S. Gimignano Crocus '98	🍷🍷	3*
●	Chianti Colli Senesi '97	🍷	1*
●	Chianti Colli Senesi '98	🍷	2*
●	Chianti Colli Senesi Cinabro '95	🍷	3

S. GIMIGNANO (SI)

CASALE - FALCHINI

VIA DI CASALE, 40
53037 S. GIMIGNANO (SI)
TEL. 0577/941305

When long ago in 1964, Riccardo Falchini decided to embark on a career in viticulture, he at once realised that quality would have to be his priority if the estate was going to be in the front rank of producers at San Gimignano. With this in mind, he started to make Vernaccia in the modern style, creating excellent wines that in turn influenced other producers. His Vernaccia Riserva '98 is among the most convincing of the year. It has a lovely straw-yellow colour with green highlights and a complex nose that mingles aromas of ripe fruit with vanilla from the wood. On the palate, it is fresh, full-bodied and well-structured, with a lingering finish. The Ab Vinea Doni '99 selection is not reviewed here because it had not yet been bottled at the time of our tastings. The Vernaccia '99 is interesting and correct. The nose unveils floral notes and almonds, which return on the palate, but the finish is slightly dilute. This year's date with the reds was less inspiring than last year's. The Campora '96, a 100% Cabernet Sauvignon, missed Two Glasses by the smallest of margins. The nose is slightly vegetal while there is good structure on the palate which, however, falls away in the finish. Still, the '96 vintage was anything but memorable. The Paretaio '97 is more successful. A red IGT made from sangiovese, it has a persuasive palate even though the structure is not spectacular. The Chianti Colombaia '98 is uncomplicated but well-made while the Vin Santo del Chianti '94 is one of the best in its category. Sweet on the palate, it tempts with sensual notes of figs and hazelnuts.

○	Vernaccia di S. Gimignano Vigna a Solatio Ris. '98	🍷🍷	4
●	Campora '96	🍷	6
○	Falchini Brut M. Cl. '96	🍷	4
●	Paretaio '97	🍷	4
○	Vernaccia di S. Gimignano Vigna a Solatio '99	🍷	2*
○	Vin Santo del Chianti '94	🍷	4
●	Chianti Colli Senesi Titolato Colombaia '98		2
●	Campora '88	🍷🍷	6
●	Campora '90	🍷🍷	6
●	Campora '91	🍷🍷	6
●	Campora '94	🍷🍷	6
●	Campora '95	🍷🍷	6

Vincenzo Cesani

Loc. Pancole, 82/d
53037 S. Gimignano (SI)
tel. 0577/955084

The Cesanis have not been resting on their laurels. Despite the commotion after last year's Three Glass award, they have continued to work hard in their beautiful vineyards at Pancole as if nothing special had happened. Anyone who knows them, and has seen the occasional fatigue-induced wrinkle on their brows, will have realized that their aim is to keep making even better wine. Their Luenzo '98, a blend of sangiovese with a bit of colorino, is actually very good and just missed out on Three Glasses in our finals. It has a deep ruby colour with a violet rim, introducing a nose of intense, persistent red berry fruit with spicy and oak-derived notes of considerable elegance. The palate is fat and well-structured but lacks the fruit-driven complexity, and a little of the concentration, of last year's version. The Vernaccia Sanice '99 is even better than last year's. The lustrous straw-yellow colour is flecked with green highlights, leading in to a fresh nose of elegant flowers laced with a hint of fruit. The palate is noteworthy for its attractive softness, full body and the spicy hints of its perfectly judged wood. The Vernaccia '99 is another characterful wine. The nose blends flowers and golden delicious apples while the soft, sweet palate offers great balance, signing off with a bitterish varietal aftertaste. Finally, the Chianti Colli Senesi '99 is a pleaser, winning One Glass for its intense aromas and good structure.

●	Luenzo '98	▼▼	5
○	Vernaccia di S. Gimignano Sanice '99	▼▼	4
●	Chianti Colli Senesi '99	▼	3
○	Vernaccia di S. Gimignano '99	▼	3
●	Luenzo '97	▽▽▽	5
●	Luenzo '95	▽▽	4
●	Luenzo '96	▽▽	4
○	Vernaccia di S. Gimignano Sanice '98	▽▽	4
●	Chianti Colli Senesi '93	▽	2*
●	Chianti Colli Senesi '94	▽	2*
●	Chianti Colli Senesi '98	▽	2*
○	Vernaccia di S. Gimignano '98	▽	2*

Fontaleoni

Loc. S. Maria, 39
53037 S. Gimignano (SI)
tel. 0577/950193

Franco Troiani's Fontaleoni winery, situated to the north-east of San Gimignano, shot into the Guide in 1996 with well-made wines that established him as an emerging producer of Vernaccia. Then there were some ups and downs but this year Franco and his oenologist, Paolo Caciorgna, convinced us with two excellent Vernaccias and an interesting Rosso di San Gimignano. The Vernaccia '99 has a nose of floral and mineral notes, laced with ripe fruit. Entry in the mouth is attractively soft and the palate reveals a refreshing prickle before closing with a characteristic twist of almond. The Vernaccia Vigna Casanuova '99, of which 20% was fermented in wood, has a brilliant straw-yellow colour. On the nose, there are aromas of almonds and flowers while the palate is sweet, soft, well-balanced and nicely structured but a little short in the finish. The Rosso di San Gimignano '99, a new DOC that came into force in 1998, is made from 90% sangiovese and 10% merlot. The panel thought it was the best Fontaleoni wine presented this year, and it came close to earning Two Glasses. Ruby with violet highlights in the glass, it has intense, well-defined aromas of raspberries and blackberries as well as faint vegetal hints. The attack is soft and sweet, and the progression on the palate is sustained by good backbone, closing with notes of fruit and a hint of astringency. Finally, the Chianti Colli Senesi '99 has an attractive fruit-rich nose but is roughish on the palate.

●	S. Gimignano Rosso La Carretta '99	▼	4
○	Vernaccia di S. Gimignano '99	▼	2*
○	Vernaccia di S. Gimignano Vigna Casanuova '99	▼	3
●	Chianti Colli Senesi '99		2
○	Vernaccia di S. Gimignano Vigna Casanuova '95	▽▽	3*
●	Chianti Colli Senesi '95	▽	1*
○	Vernaccia di S. Gimignano '95	▽	2*
○	Vernaccia di S. Gimignano '96	▽	2*
○	Vernaccia di S. Gimignano Vigna Casanuova '94	▽	2*
○	Vernaccia di S. Gimignano Vigna Casanuova '96	▽	3

S. GIMIGNANO (SI)

Guicciardini Strozzi

Fattoria Cusona
Loc. Cusona, 5
53037 S. Gimignano (SI)
tel. 0577/950028

A parchment from 994 AD proves that the Fattoria di Cusona has been operating for more than a thousand years but there is nothing antiquated about their approach. The vitality that emerged at our tastings was confirmed by a recent visit to the cellar, where new winemaking equipment, more frequent turnover of the barrique stock, the experience of oenologist, Ivaldo Volpini, and the management of Vittorio Fiore have come together in a winning formula. The three IGT wines, Sodole (100% sangiovese), Selvascura (90-95% merlot, the rest colorino) and Millanni (sangiovese, cabernet sauvignon, and merlot) reached the Two Glass level with the greatest of ease. Il Sodole '98 has a nice ruby colour introducing an elegant, well-made nose, in which it clearly reveals its sangiovese origins. The Millanni '98 is equally impressive. Its dense ruby hue ushers in a nose of coffee, black berries and a faint vegetal note mingle delightfully. The full, soft palate then parades its fine, elegant tannins. In contrast, the Selvascura is not all it might be. There is a marked vegetal note on nose and palate, and the wine lacks concentration. The Chianti Titolato '99 was much appreciated for the power of its fruit, and the alcohol that melds beautifully in the structure on the palate. The Vernaccia Riserva '98 was well worth its Two Glasses. A rich straw-yellow in colour, it unfurls a sweet nose with hints of pipe tobacco over its abundant fruit. The soft, warm, close-knit palate then reveals a lively finish with toasty notes and the classic Vernaccia twist of almond. A rather pleasant surprise was the new IGT Vermentino, the Luna Verde '99, which was on its first outing.

●	Millanni '98	🍷🍷	6
●	Selvascura '98	🍷🍷	5
●	Sodole '98	🍷🍷	5
○	Vernaccia di S. Gimignano Ris. '98	🍷🍷	4
●	Chianti Colli Senesi Titolato '99	🍷	3
○	Luna Verde '99	🍷	3
○	Vernaccia di S. Gimignano Perlato '98	🍷	4
○	Vernaccia di S. Gimignano S. Biagio '99		3
●	Millanni '95	🍸🍸	6
●	Millanni '96	🍸🍸	6
●	Millanni '97	🍸🍸	6
●	Selvascura '97	🍸🍸	5
●	Sodole '93	🍸🍸	5

S. GIMIGNANO (SI)

Il Lebbio

Loc. S. Benedetto, 11/c
53037 S. Gimignano (SI)
tel. 0577/944725

Il Lebbio has about ten hectares of vines in the San Benedetto subzone to the north-east of San Gimignano. Although it has had some excellent results, the estate is still experimenting with its product line. Indeed, yet again, the best wines do not include a Vernaccia, the most characteristic local wine. The Polito '97, a red IGT obtained from sangiovese and colorino, is a fine bottle that easily earned its Two Glasses. The fairly intense ruby colour has violet highlights. It introduces a nose that embraces a range of enticing aromas, including mulberries and raspberries fusing delicately with nuances of well-judged oak. On the palate, there is good concentration and lashings of lively fruit while the sweet, firm tannins are backed up by good depth. Another red, I Grottoni '99, is back to its former high level of quality. Made from 40% cabernet sauvignon, 40% montepulciano d'Abruzzo and 20% merlot, it has a violet ruby colour and an interesting nose of raspberries, autumn leaves and very faint vegetal traces. In the mouth, it has a good, full-bodied structure, revealing velvety tannins and soft, rich fruit. The finish is a crescendo of pleasure and the Two Glasses are richly deserved, particularly considering its exceptional price-quality ratio. The Cicogio '99 is somewhat less convincing. Its bizarre name is an anagram of the grapes from which it is made: ciliegiolo, colorino and sangiovese. It has a very deep, concentrated ruby colour but the nose is a little closed. There is good weight, and ripe fruit on the palate but it lacks a little balance and the finish is disappointingly short. Finally, the standard-label Vernaccia '99 got no more than a mention. It has shy, rather uninteresting aromas and a straightforward palate.

●	I Grottoni '99	🍷🍷	3*
●	Polito '97	🍷🍷	4
●	Cicogio '99	🍷	3
○	Malvasia '99		2
○	Vernaccia di S. Gimignano '99		2
●	Cicogio '98	🍸🍸	3*
●	I Grottoni '97	🍸🍸	2*
●	Chianti '97	🍸	2*
●	I Grottoni '98	🍸	3
○	Malvasia '98	🍸	2*

S. GIMIGNANO (SI)

S. GIMIGNANO (SI)

IL PARADISO
LOC. STRADA, 21/A
53037 S. GIMIGNANO (SI)
TEL. 0577/941500

LA LASTRA
LOC. SANTA LUCIA
VIA R. DE GRADA, 9
53037 S. GIMIGNANO (SI)
TEL. 0577/941781

This year Vasco Cetti astonished us with a range of truly characterful wines. It was as if he wanted us to take back what we said last year, when we called his estate, Il Paradiso, one of the unfulfilled promises of the area. His Saxa Calida '98, a Bordeaux blend, came dangerously close to getting Three Glasses. It has a ruby colour that remains dark and close-knit right up to the rim, regaling the nose with rich, impressively deep aromas of ripe, black berry fruit. The palate has power, concentration and equilibrium while the finish deliciously long, if perhaps just a little vegetal. Il sangiovese-based Paterno II° is the apple of Vasco's eye and a very classy wine indeed. A deep ruby in the glass, it has an elegant, complex nose with hints of spices. The palate is richly extracted and the ripe fruit mingles with hints of spices, the well-judged use of oak underlining the fine tannins. It was the Vernaccia Biscondola '98 that stood out among the whites. In fact, it is probably the best version ever. It has a brilliant, almost golden, straw-yellow colour, an intense nose with a wealth of ripe peach and melon fruit, and well-integrated notes of oak. The palate is close-knit, almost unctuously soft, and well-sustained by fruit and acidity. Their standard Vernaccia '99 is well-defined on both nose and mouth while the Docciola '99 is equally convincing, delighting the eye with its flecks of gold, the nose with hints of vanilla, and the palate with a deliciously soft structure. The Chianti Colli Senesi '99 is also good, although there is a hint of astringency in the finish. We were not able to assess the Bottaccio '98 because it was unavailable at the time of our visit.

Nadia Betti and Renato Spanu's La Lastra is one of the most interesting wineries to have emerged in the last few years at San Gimignano. The couple, originally from Trentino and agronomists by profession, moved to this "City of Towers" a few years ago and have been practising there successfully. Bit by bit, they began to vinify their own grapes from a small vineyard they own. Encouraged by their success, they have bought and leased other vineyards. They can now count on fruit from ten hectares under vine, and as one might imagine, tend them with an almost maniacal degree of care. Production, with the assistance of Enrico Paternoster, an oenologist also from Trentino, has now arrived at an annual total of approximately 60,000 bottles and comprises a Vernaccia, a Vernaccia Riserva, a Chianti Colli Senesi and a table wine, the Rovaio. The Rovaio '98 is still ageing so we tasted the excellent '97. It is a blend of one third cabernet sauvignon, one third sangiovese, and oné third merlot that won our hearts with the richness and complexity of its fruit, beautiful concentration and round tannins that integrate deliciously with the structure and new wood. The Vernaccia Riserva has a solid structure, rich, ripe fruit on both nose and palate, and a long finish with a wealth of ripe apple and pear fruit. The Vernaccia '99 is not so imposingly concentrated but it does offer attractive fullness, floral notes and ripe golden delicious apple, and for its good overall balance. Then the Chianti Colli Senesi brings this brief list of excellent wines to a fitting conclusion.

● Paterno II '97	♛♛	5
● Saxa Calida '98	♛♛	5
○ Vernaccia di S. Gimignano Biscondola '98	♛♛	4
● Chianti Colli Senesi '99	♛	2*
○ Docciola '99	♛	3
○ Vernaccia di S. Gimignano '99	♛	2*
● Bottaccio '97	♛♛	4
● Saxa Calida '96	♛♛	4
● Chianti Colli Senesi '97	♀	2*
● Chianti Colli Senesi '98	♀	2*
● Paterno II '94	♀	4
● Paterno II '95	♀	4
● Paterno II '96	♀	4
● Saxa Calida '95	♀	4

● Rovaio '97	♛♛	5
○ Vernaccia di S. Gimignano Ris. '98	♛♛	4
● Chianti Colli Senesi '99	♛	3
○ Vernaccia di S. Gimignano '99	♛	3
○ Vernaccia di S. Gimignano '98	♛♛	2*
○ Vernaccia di S. Gimignano Ris. '95	♛♛	3*
○ Vernaccia di S. Gimignano Ris. '96	♛♛	3*
○ Vernaccia di S. Gimignano Ris. '97	♛♛	3*
● Chianti Colli Senesi '95	♀	4
● Chianti Colli Senesi '96	♀	4
● Chianti Colli Senesi '97	♀	4
● Chianti Colli Senesi '98	♀	2*
● Rovaio '95	♀	4
● Rovaio '96	♀	5
○ Vernaccia di S. Gimignano '97	♀	3

S. GIMIGNANO (SI)

S. GIMIGNANO (SI)

LA RAMPA DI FUGNANO
LOC. FUGNANO
53037 S. GIMIGNANO (SI)
TEL. 0577/941655

TENUTA LE CALCINAIE
LOC. MONTEOLIVETO, 36
53037 S. GIMIGNANO (SI)
TEL. 0577/943007

Gisela Traxler and Herbert Erhenbold continue to demonstrate that they are serious winemakers and bring out excellent wines. This year their Gisèle did not manage to carry off our highest award but that doesn't matter. The '98 is a great wine any way. It is only a little less concentrated and dense in the mouth than its predecessor, and although the tannins are very fine, the wine's finish lacks the irresistible abundance of ripe pulpy fruit that characterised the '97 version. The Bombereto '98, made only from sangiovese, is also a Two Glass contender. The palate is more ready to drink, soft, and pleasurable but doesn't have any great depth. The cellar's approach to white winemaking is very convincing. The Vernaccia Riserva Privato '98 has a straw-yellow colour, and a rich, intense nose of citrus fruit accompanied by delicate notes of flowers and almonds. The entry on the palate is fresh and soft, leading in to a sure-footed, well-balanced evolution nicely sustained by discreet acidity. The Vernaccia Alata '99 gets a Glass. The lustrous straw-yellow ushers in a nose of vanilla, spring flowers and vegetal notes. The attack on the palate is uncompromising yet soft and fresh, following through with good balance and body to a finish that tails off quite quickly. The newcomer "Vi ogni è" has an inscrutable name, a vivid straw-yellow colour, and aromas of tropical fruit, flowers and wood. The palate lacks co-ordination and the follow-through is undermined by the influence of the wood. Finally, the Chianti Colli Senesi '99 earns a Glass for its varietal character and clean style.

The Tenuta Le Calcinaie estate, which lies in Monte Oliveto to the south east of San Gimignano, deservedly re-enters the Guide after an absence of two years. Here in the village of Affittacci, the dynamic young owner, Simone Santini, has about ten hectares under vines, some of which are newly planted at a density of 5,500 vines per hectare, since Simone is aiming for high quality. The experience of the last two vintages, together with the technical help of Andrea Mazzoni, has brought the estate significant results, Two Glasses going to the Vernaccia Vigna ai Sassi in both the '98 and the '99 versions. The '98 has a bright straw-yellow colour leading in to a nose that is at first somewhat reticent. After aeration, it begins to release notes of ripe fruit and vanilla, opening out to fill the palate seductively. The '99 is just as good and is perhaps even better balanced in the mouth. It is full, and at the same time fresh, soft, and fat, the nicely gauged oak coming through clearly. The Vernaccia '99 confirms the technical expertise of the Le Calcinaie cellar, even though the vintage was unexceptional, for this is one of the best in the DOC zone. The Chianti Colli Senesi '98 is also interesting. Its ruby colour ushers in vinous aromas with crisp, intense hints of red berry fruit. In the mouth, it is perhaps a little rustic as the tannins are somewhat intrusive and the finish is bitterish. We shall have to wait until next year to judge the Teodoro '97, a red IGT made from sangiovese and merlot, as it had not yet gone into the bottle at the time of our tastings.

● Bombereto '98	♥♥	5	○ Vernaccia di S. Gimignano '99	♥♥	3*
● Giséle '98	♥♥	6	○ Vernaccia di S. Gimignano		
○ Vernaccia di S. Gimignano			Vigna ai Sassi '98	♥♥	4
Privato Ris. '98	♥♥	4	○ Vernaccia di S. Gimignano		
● Chianti Colli Senesi			Vigna ai Sassi '99	♥♥	4
Via dei Franchi '99	♥	3	● Chianti Colli Senesi '98	♥	3
○ Vernaccia di S. Gimignano			● Chianti Colli Senesi '97	♀	4
Alata '99	♥	3	● Chianti Colli Senesi		
○ Vi ogni è '99	♥	4	Geminiano '94	♀	4
● Giséle '97	♀♀♀	5	● Chianti Colli Senesi		
● Bombereto '97	♀♀	5	Geminiano '95	♀	4
● Bombereto '93	♀	4	● Teodoro '94	♀	4
● Chianti Colli Senesi			● Teodoro '95	♀	4
Via dei Franchi '97	♀	3	● Teodoro '96	♀	4
● Chianti Colli Senesi Via dei Franchi '98	♀	3			

S. GIMIGNANO (SI)

S. GIMIGNANO (SI)

MORMORAIA
LOC. S. ANDREA
53037 S. GIMIGNANO (SI)
TEL. 0577/940096

PALAGETTO
VIA MONTEOLIVETO, 46
53037 S. GIMIGNANO (SI)
TEL. 0577/943090 - 0577/942098

Giuseppe Passoni, a Milanese business man and former rally driver, has put together in recent years one of the most promising and beautiful estates in the area. The Tenuta Mormoraia now extends over 90 hectares, 20 of which comprise its very beautiful vineyards. Passionate, precise, and tireless, "Pino", as Giuseppe is known, continues year after year to enlarge the cellar, to plant new vines, and to make better and better wine with the help of the celebrated Italian oenologist, Franco Bernabei. His Vernaccia Riserva is one of the very finest of the year. It is a full, fresh, well-balanced wine that displays perfect poise as it seduces your senses with its almost sweet aromas of ripe fruit mingling with hints of spices from the wood. His Ostria Grigia '98, a blend of vernaccia and chardonnay, is one of the most elegant and harmonious wines from the area and successfully expresses a fascinating fusion of mineral and ripe fruit aromas, in addition to well-calibrated hints of vanilla and toastiness from the new oak. The Vernaccia '99 has also come out very well, and is among the most interesting ones from this vintage. It has a full body without being too heavy and a nice pulpy texture while remaining fresh-tasting and enjoyable. It came very close to getting its Second Glass. That objective was easily reached by the red Neitea '97, a Supertuscan obtained from 80% sangiovese and 20% cabernet sauvignon. It has concentration, balance, finesse and attractive drinkability, signing off on an intense, lingering note of red berries. Our congratulations.

A new wind is blowing through this winery, which has had another good year, confirming Simone Noccolai's commitment to winning the Guide's top accolade. There are two important bits of news to mention. One is that work in the vineyards has almost been completed. The other is that Simòne has signed up Giacomo Tachis as his consultant. Not for the first time, the wine that impressed us most was the red, Sottobosco '98, which is sangiovese-based with 20% cabernet sauvignon. One of Palagetto's flagship products, it has an intense ruby colour introducing hints of tobacco and leather on the nose that then make way for ripe fruit and vanilla. The palate is close-knit, with plenty of structure, but needs to age more in the bottle to soften its generous dose of oak. The whites produced several good wines, starting with the Vernaccia Riserva '98, which was only a hair's breadth away from confirming its rating from last year. A successful wine, it offers delicate, fresh aromas of almonds and vanilla that are complemented by a well-structured palate and an only moderately long finish. The standard Vernaccia is also attractive, with its fresh, fruity, floral nose. The Vernaccia Vigna Santa Chiara '99 is less expressive but just as well-managed. The Solleone '98, a new sangiovese-based wine, has an intense ruby colour with garnet highlights. The nose proffers hints of liqueur morello cherries as well as over-evolved notes while the palate is soft and well balanced. The finish is well-managed but uninspiring.

● Neitea '97	♟♟	4	
○ Ostrea Grigia '98	♟♟	4	
○ Vernaccia di San Gimignano Ris. '98	♟♟	4	
○ Vernaccia di San Gimignano '99	♟	3	
● Neitea '95	♟♟	4	
● Neitea '96	♟♟	4	
○ Ostrea '95	♟♟	4	
○ Ostrea '96	♟♟	4	
○ Ostrea '97	♟♟	4	
○ Vernaccia di San Gimignano '98	♟♟	3*	
○ Vernaccia di San Gimignano Ris. '97	♟♟	4	
○ Vernaccia di San Gimignano '96	♟	3	
○ Vernaccia di San Gimignano '97	♟	3	

● Sottobosco '98	♟♟	5	
● Solleone '98	♟	4	
○ Vernaccia di S. Gimignano '99	♟	3	
○ Vernaccia di S. Gimignano Ris. '98	♟	4	
○ Vernaccia di S. Gimignano Vigna Santa Chiara '99		3	
● Sottobosco '97	♟♟	5	
○ Vernaccia di S. Gimignano Ris. '97	♟♟	4	
● Chianti Colli Senesi '95	♟	1*	
● Chianti Colli Senesi '98	♟	3	
● Sottobosco '94	♟	3	
● Sottobosco '95	♟	4	
● Sottobosco '96	♟	4	
○ Vernaccia di S. Gimignano Vigna Santa Chiara '98	♟	3	

S. GIMIGNANO (SI)

S. GIMIGNANO (SI)

GIOVANNI PANIZZI
LOC. RACCIANO
PODERE S. MARGHERITA, 34
53037 S. GIMIGNANO (SI)
TEL. 0577/941576 - 02/90938796

PIETRAFITTA
LOC. CORTENNANO
53037 S. GIMIGNANO (SI)
TEL. 0577/943200

At last! Giovanni Panizzi's Vernaccia di San Gimignano Riserva '98 is even better than it has been in other years and fully deserves its Three Glasses. This is a great personal success for Giovanni, the undemonstrative but passionate winemaker who moved here from his native Milan. It is also a success for Vernaccia di San Gimignano in general and arrives at a crucial moment in the history of the wine. We are certain that this award to Giovanni Pannizzi will give new heart and enthusiasm to all those producers who have worked hard in recent years to make world-class Vernaccia, a wine that has extraordinary potential. This Riserva has certainly shown what can be done. It has an intense, vibrant greenish straw-yellow colour and aristocratic aromas of ripe apples and pears that blend perfectly with hints of toastiness and vanilla. The entry is muscular, concentrated and well-balanced, and the progression through to the mid palate is well-sustained and utterly convincing. The rich, juicy fruit is braced by firm acidity, that fades unhurriedly into soft tones of vanilla and spices. Massive. The Vernaccia '99 is as good as ever and both the invitingly fresh red Ceraso and the good Chianti dei Colli Senesi Vertunno are very attractive. We can only hope that Giovanni repeats this performance every year, and that a few other Vernaccias join him.

The Fattoria di Pietrafitta is one of the historic names of Vernaccia di San Gimignano. The estate has about 300 hectares, of which 40 are under vine. The greater part (24 hectares) is planted to vernaccia. The Vernaccia Riserva La Costa '98 was barrique-fermented after a brief period of maceration on the skins. It has a vibrant straw-yellow colour with green highlights leading in to an engaging nose of sweet vanilla and pipe tobacco with a hint of menthol against a backdrop of fruit. The palate unveils impressive structure, softness and freshness, closing on a delicately varietal bitterish note. In short, this is a very respectable Vernaccia. The Vernaccia Borgetto '99 also seemed to the panel to be satisfactory and amply earned its One Glass. It has a straw-yellow colour and has an abundantly fruity nose with floral hints. The attack is vigorous, thanks to acidity that enlivens the softer components, taking you through to pleasantly almondy finish. The San Gimignano Rosso La Sughera '98, a sangiovese with 10% merlot, carried off One Glass without difficulty for its soft palate and decent thrust in the finish. We'll close this round-up with the Vin Santo '93, from trebbiano and malvasia, which well deserved its Two Glasses. It has intense aromas of figs, roasted hazelnuts and candied peel. On the palate, it offers power and a buttery richness, following through sure-footedly on the palate to a finish that mirrors the aromas of the nose.

O	Vernaccia di S. Gimignano Ris. '98	♟♟♟	6
●	Ceraso '99	♟	3
●	Chianti Colli Senesi Vertunno '98	♟	4
O	Vernaccia di S. Gimignano '99	♟	4
●	Chianti Colli Senesi '97	♟♟	4
O	Vernaccia di S. Gimignano Ris. '94	♟♟	5
O	Vernaccia di S. Gimignano Ris. '95	♟♟	5
O	Vernaccia di S. Gimignano Ris. '96	♟♟	5
O	Vernaccia di S. Gimignano Ris. '97	♟♟	5
●	Ceraso '95	♟	3
●	Ceraso '96	♟	3
●	Ceraso '98	♟	3
●	Chianti Colli Senesi '93	♟	2*
●	Chianti Colli Senesi '95	♟	3
●	Chianti Colli Senesi '96	♟	4

O	Vernaccia di S. Gimignano Vigna La Costa Ris. '98	♟♟	4
O	Vin Santo '93	♟♟	4
●	S. Gimignano Rosso La Sughera '98	♟	4
O	Vernaccia di S. Gimignano Vigna Borghetto '99	♟	3

S. GIMIGNANO (SI)

S. GIMIGNANO (SI)

TERUZZI & PUTHOD
LOC. CASALE, 19
53037 S. GIMIGNANO (SI)
TEL. 0577/940143

F.LLI VAGNONI
LOC. PANCOLE, 82
53037 S. GIMIGNANO (SI)
TEL. 0577/955077

Enrico Teruzzi is the producer who has made Vernaccia di San Gimignano known and appreciated on the international market. A lot of water has passed under the bridge since Enrico and his wife, Carmen Puthod, made their first Vernaccia in 1974. This white wine, already well known in the Middle Ages, was going through a bad period. If today it has reached a degree of excellence that at one point seemed unthinkable, much of the credit belongs to Enrico. He had the passion and courage to develop Vernaccia's potential and the initiative to present its qualities to a wide public. This winery has increased in size as its success has burgeoned and today there are 180 hectares under vine. Annual production exceeds 1,000,000 bottles. The Teruzzi & Puthod Vernaccia is the benchmark for this popular white wine, and flaunts floral and fruit aromas on the nose, leading in to a fresh-tasting, well-structured palate. The Vigna a Rondolino vineyard selection is equally rich and intense but has a touch of extra elegance. But the estate's most representative wine is, in our opinion, the Terre di Tufi, which is a predominantly vernaccia (80%) blend aged for several months in barriques of French oak. The '98 has a lovely straw-yellow with greenish highlights. The nose is intense and fresh, with rich notes of fruit that blend attractively with floral hints new wood. The palate is well-structured, broad, nicely balanced, and deep. The progression is well-sustained, shading into a delightful finish of apples, pears, and vanilla. Finally, the estate red wine, the Peperino, is one of the best-made and most enjoyable examples of Sangiovese in the area.

Il Mocali, a barrique-aged Vernaccia and this winery's leading product, again proved to be a true thoroughbred in the '98 edition, earning its Two Glasses without fuss. This confirms the Vagnonis, originally from the Marches, as some of the best interpreters of the terroir at Pancole, one of the most promising zones in the area and the site of their Imocali and Solatio vineyards. Congratulations should also go, however, to oenologist Salvatore Maule, who has been a skilled handler of vernaccia for some years now. The Mocali '98 is an intense straw-yellow colour. The nose presents elegant notes of ripe fruit seamlessly integrated with hints of vanilla from the oak. On the well-rounded palate, there is good structure and nice body while the reasonably long finish reveals the characteristically bitterish varietal aftertaste. The Vagnonis' standard Vernaccia is in the classic mould but suffers from a poor vintage and doesn't quite come up to the usual level. It is a somewhat pale straw-yellow in colour while the nose, a little shy at first, opens out with ripe fruit and floral notes. The palate is fresh-tasting, soft and fairly well-balanced but the finish is slightly diluted. We did not have a chance to try the I Sodi Lunghi '98 red, which had not yet gone into the bottle when we visited, so we will talk about it next year. Neither was the Chianti Colli Senesi '99 ready, so the Vagnoni brothers dusted off the '97 version of their Chianti Colli Senesi Riserva, which failed to inspire much enthusiasm. The colour is somewhat evolved and the palate lacks softness, which is rather surprising, given that the vintage was generally successful in the San Gimignano area.

●	Peperino '99	🍷🍷	3*
○	Terre di Tufi '98	🍷🍷	4
○	Vernaccia di S. Gimignano '99	🍷	3
○	Vernaccia di S. Gimignano Vigna a Rondolino '99	🍷	4
○	Carmen '93	🍷🍷	4
○	Carmen '94	🍷🍷	4
○	Carmen '95	🍷🍷	4
○	Carmen '96	🍷🍷	4
○	Carmen '97	🍷🍷	4
○	Carmen '98	🍷🍷	4
○	Terre di Tufi '94	🍷🍷	5
○	Terre di Tufi '95	🍷🍷	5
○	Terre di Tufi '96	🍷🍷	5
○	Terre di Tufi '97	🍷🍷	5

○	Vernaccia di S. Gimignano Mocali '98	🍷🍷	4
●	Chianti Colli Senesi Ris. '97	🍷	4
○	Vernaccia di S. Gimignano '99	🍷	3
●	I Sodi Lunghi '97	🍷🍷	4
○	Vernaccia di S. Gimignano Mocali '96	🍷🍷	4
○	Vernaccia di S. Gimignano Mocali '97	🍷🍷	4
●	Chianti Colli Senesi '95	🍷	3
●	Chianti Colli Senesi '97	🍷	3
●	Chianti Colli Senesi '98	🍷	3
●	I Sodi Lunghi '93	🍷	3
●	I Sodi Lunghi '95	🍷	4
●	I Sodi Lunghi '96	🍷	4

SAMBUCA DI TAVARNELLE (FI)

Il Poggiolino
Via Chiantigiana, 32
50020 Sambuca di Tavarnelle (FI)
tel. 055/8071635

It is always the Pacini family's Chianti Classico that we find most convincing. We think it speaks well of this winery that it should have such success with Chianti's most typical product. This year at our tastings the Pacinis also presented a rosé, the Poggiolino '99, and we will begin with this, their simplest wine. It has a cherry-pink hue, aromas of cherry fruit with floral nuances and a clean, well-managed and appropriately fresh palate. The Chianti Classico '98 is a wine of breeding. The very dark ruby colour is full and deep while the fruit aromas are intense and lingering, with berry fruit, especially redcurrants, coming through firmly. The attack on the palate is warm and the progression is almost creamy in its soft density. The tannins are firm but the finish, though tasty, is a bit short. The Riserva '97, also impenetrably dark in colour, is at first unfocused on the nose where vanilla from the wood dominates the cherry aromas. In the mouth, it is opulently fat and full-bodied but not perfectly balanced. The tannins develop evenly, taking you through to a sweet finish with hints of mint. Le Balze '96 is a wine that we found less convincing. On the nose, there are vegetal tones mingling gamey notes of wet dog but after a few seconds imperfectly integrated aromas of toasty oak take over. The palate is unexciting. Fluid and medium-bodied, it offers a pleasant enough flavour but no great length.

● Chianti Classico '98	🍷🍷	3*
● Chianti Classico Ris. '97	🍷🍷	4
⊙ Il Poggiolino '99	🍷	3
● Le Balze '96	🍷	4
● Chianti Classico '97	♀♀	3*
● Chianti Classico Ris. '96	♀	4
● Le Balze '95	♀	4

SAN CASCIANO DEI BAGNI (SI)

Giacomo Mori
Loc. Le Case Palazzone
P.zza Sandro Pertini, 8
53040 San Casciano dei Bagni (SI)
tel. 0578/56230

This is a fine Guide debut for a winery situated in an area with no particular name for making excellent wine. Founded in the early 19th century, the Giacomo Mori estate extends over 100 hectares, nearly eight of which are under vine. It has sold its wine in bulk since the 20s but recently a complete replanting programme has been carried out under the supervision of consultant oenologist, Alberto Antonini. Only when this operation was finished did they begin bottling their own wine. The first vintage of the new regime is the '98 and both of the wines presented at our tastings did well. Above all, we appreciated their strong personality and terroir-driven character. The '99 Chianti has a lovely deep, vivid ruby colour. On the nose, it offers clean ripe fruit and jammy aromas. The entry on the palate is solid, with prominent acidity that helps to keep the well-knit tannins in place in the medium structure before ushering in the delicious, rising finish. The Chianti Castelrotto '98 has a vibrant ruby colour and a surprisingly well-defined nose of fresh, inviting aromas that integrate seamlessly with the oak. The entry on the palate is coherent and fairly soft. The structure is satisfying, the tannins firm but not intrusive, the acidity well-judged and the positive finish develops alluringly.

● Chianti Castelrotto '98	🍷🍷	4
● Chianti '99	🍷	3

SAN VINCENZO (LI)

SCANDICCI (FI)

Podere San Michele
Loc. Caduta, 3/a
57027 San Vincenzo (LI)
tel. 0565/798038

Vigliano
Loc. San Martino alla Palma
Via Carcheri, 309
50010 Scandicci (FI)
tel. 055/8727006

Giorgio and Tiziana Socci's winery continues to make steady progress in its own unflustered way, avoiding any imitation of other equally successful producers on the same coast. Their greatest efforts are concentrated on the sangiovese grape, which is unusual around Livorno, an area where more attention is usually focused on cabernet sauvignon and merlot. Their chosen road is a more challenging one but probably offers greater satisfaction as well as more distinctive products. The foundation of their enterprise is, necessarily, careful preparation of the vineyard, where the vines are planted close together and yields are decidedly low. Depending on how the vintage has gone, the Soccis decide on reasonable periods of maceration for their reds, and a shrewd use of barriques, most of which are new. Their two labels are an accurate reflection of the current status of this winery, and of the style it aspires to. This brother and sister team understand very well that real progress can only be made slowly and that there is still ample room for improvement. At our tasting, the Allodio Rosso '98, made from sangiovese with a touch of cabernet sauvignon, put on a good show and, despite the excessive use of oak, has a personality of its own. Apart from wood-derived toastiness, the aromas include striking notes of black berry fruit, oriental spices and aromatic herbs. The juicy palate is well-sustained, with firm tannins, and the finish is sturdy. The other wine, the mainly viognier-based Allodio Bianco '99, also has plenty of personality. Well-rounded and balanced on the palate, it unfurls enticing aromas of summer flowers with peach and apricot fruit.

This little estate, which lies just outside Florence and belongs to the Marchionni family, surprised us with the high quality of its wines, an unusual feat in this area. Thanks to the enthusiasm with which brothers Lorenzo and Paolo work in the vineyards, Vigliano is no longer merely a small producer of red wines for the family and the local market but now makes wines of considerable personality. On their six-hectare property, you will finds sangiovese, cabernet sauvignon, chardonnay and a few merlot vines. The white Bricoli '97 has a lovely golden hue but seems a bit tired on the nose, the smoky notes from the wood tending to overpower the fruit. In the mouth, it is very warm, perhaps a touch flabby, and rich but the palate has no great length. The '98 version is better. Here, the aromas are fresher and hints of aromatic herbs enhance the ripe fruit, which is redolent of bananas. There is a clear vein of acidity on the palate, which has medium body. The Vigna dell'Erta '97, a blend of sangiovese and cabernet, has aromas of ripe cherry and redcurrant fruit, as well as some vegetal notes. The '98 is much more convincing. It has a brilliant ruby colour, a nose of attractive ripe fruit with faint balsamic touches, although the finish lacks a little definition. Entry on the palate is soft and the progression reveals a firm, almost creamy texture, close-knit tannins and a lingering, flavoursome finish.

● Allodio Rosso '98	♥♥	5
○ Allodio Bianco '99	♥	4
● Allodio Rosso '97	♥♥	4
○ Allodio Bianco '98	♥	4

● Vigna dell'Erta '98	♥♥	5
○ Bricoli '98	♥	4
● Vigna dell'Erta '97	♥	5
○ Bricoli '97		4

SINALUNGA (SI)

SINALUNGA (SI)

TENUTA FARNETA
LOC. FARNETA, 161
53048 SINALUNGA (SI)
TEL. 0577/631025

CASTELLO DI FARNETELLA
FRAZ. FARNETELLA
RACCORDO AUTOSTRADALE
SIENA-BETTOLLE, KM 37
53040 SINALUNGA (SI)
TEL. 0577/663520

Farneta's wines are rarely disappointing, and are also very consistent in maintaining their relative quality across the range. Their Sangiovese, Bongoverno, is still at the top of their list and will, we believe, take a major step forward sooner or later. It may happen next year. Since they made a very good wine from a mediocre vintage, the '96, they could well have made an outstanding wine from the excellent '97 harvest. They also need, however, to improve the personality of the wine. The '96 Bongoverno did very well at our tastings, displaying above all an enviable equilibrium and an overall elegance. It is a surprisingly fresh-tasting wine with a neat, well-focused nose. The palate offers moderate concentration but the structure finds an excellent point of equilibrium for its various components and the satisfyingly long finish is only slightly disturbed by a vegetal note. The Bentivoglio '97 is also another very nice wine. Still somewhat closed on the nose, it is reassuringly soft and long in the mouth. The extract is well-judged and never threatens the excellent equilibrium. Of the other wines, the Bianco put on a dignified display with its attractive floral aromas, although it was a little lightweight on the palate, but the Chianti and the Rosato Bonagrazia turned out to be merely well-made.

Things were quiet at La Tenuta di Farnetella this year. The wines that we tasted were not disappointing but two of their major labels, the red Poggio Granoni – the '93 won Three Glasses – and the Sauvignon were not yet ready when we visited. We had to make do, as it were, with the generous range of wines that they did present. Their Chianti Colli Senesi '98 was a surprise, not for the first time. We gave it not only Two Glasses for quality, but also an asterisk because it is excellent value for money. It's a very well-made wine, whistle-clean and rich in fragrances of cherries, wild berries, a green vegetal hint and an intriguing note of white pepper. The medium-bodied palate is well balanced to the point of nonchalant elegance in the way its flavours progress. In contrast, this producer's wager on Pinot Nero has yet to be won. The Nero di Nubi '97 is only partly convincing. It offers varietal aromas of raspberry jam, wild roses and rhubarb and a sophisticated display of soft tannins on the palate but it also betrays distinctly evolved notes of over-ripe fruit and bitterish nuances in the finish. But as we said, making a Pinot Nero is a gamble. The '96 Moscato Rosa, Rosa Rosae has unusual fruit and floral aromas that are not very intense. In the mouth, however, it is lively and pleasant.

● Bentivoglio '97	▼▼	4
● Bongoverno '96	▼▼	6
○ Farneta Bianco '99	▼	2*
⊙ Bonagrazia '99		2
● Chianti Colli Senesi '99		2
● Bentivoglio '89	♀♀	2*
● Bentivoglio '91	♀♀	2*
● Bongoverno '86	♀♀	6
● Bongoverno '88	♀♀	6
● Bongoverno '90	♀♀	6
● Bongoverno '91	♀♀	6
● Bongoverno '92	♀♀	6
● Bongoverno '93	♀♀	6
● Bongoverno '94	♀♀	6
● Bongoverno '95	♀♀	6

● Chianti Colli Senesi '98	▼▼	3*
● Nero di Nubi '97	▼	5
⊙ Rosa Rosae '96	▼	4
● Poggio Granoni '93	♀♀♀	6
● Chianti Colli Senesi '96	♀♀	3
○ Sauvignon '91	♀♀	4
○ Sauvignon '95	♀♀	4
○ Sauvignon '97	♀♀	4
● Chianti Colli Senesi '91	♀	3*
● Chianti Colli Senesi '97	♀	3
● Nero di Nubi '93	♀	5
● Nero di Nubi '94	♀	5
● Nero di Nubi '95	♀	5
○ Sauvignon '96	♀	4

SOVANA (GR)

SOVICILLE (SI)

SASSOTONDO
LOC. PIANI DI CONATI, 52
58010 SOVANA (GR)
TEL. 0564/614218

POGGIO SALVI
LOC. POGGIO SALVI, 221
53018 SOVICILLE (SI)
TEL. 0577/349045 - 0577/45237

Carla Benini and Edoardo Ventimiglia are now very much part of the group of successful new Tuscan wine producers. What is remarkable, though, is that they did not choose to make their wine in an area already renowned for its viticulture but chose instead the little-known zone of Sovana and Pitigliano. As if that wasn't enough, they decided not to plant the usual safe international varieties but instead put their money on ciliegiolo! This is the grape, shunned by nearly everyone else, from which Sassorondo makes its top wine, San Lorenzo. The San Lorenzo '98 is a splendid bottle and you are forced to concede that the vineyards of Sovana represent a "grand cru" of ciliegiolo. The wine has clean, concentrated aromas of blackberries, nettles, brambles and, especially, blasts of black pepper so strong that you would think the wine was made from syrah. In the mouth, it is soft, full and fresh while the pepper in the finish is so insistent it risks becoming monotonous. It could use, perhaps, a bit more complexity but its personality is that of an authentic "vin de terroir". The Sangiovese Franze was very convincing this year. The nose is quite ripe and the palate has great structure, well backed up by close-knit tannins. The Sassotondo Rosso '99, made mostly from ciliegiolo, is a small-scale San Lorenzo. Its pepper and red berry fruit on the nose are followed up by a balanced, attractive and decently long palate. The fruity, substantial Bianco '99 brings up the rear felicitously.

This winery, run by Roberto Bonucci, is back in the Guide after an absence of several years. It is the only representative of an area to the south-west of Siena, which stretches from Sovicille to the edge of prestigious Montalcino. The zone presents very different site climates from those found in the other winemaking territories around Siena. To a certain extent, it is similar to Maremma, whose sea breezes help to ripen its grapes. Although Poggio Salvi has a modern approach to vinification, it is extremely loyal to tradition in its choice of grapes. Sangiovese and other Tuscan varieties dominate the scene, with only one exception. Sauvignon is used with trebbiano to make the Refola. The '99 version of this wine is technically correct, coherent and well balanced. The Chianti '98 is not very convincing. Although it has good weight in the mouth, it shows signs of over-ripeness on the nose. A fairly full Glass goes to the Sangiovese Camp del Bosco '98, which has a good, concentrated nose of black cherry jam, with suggestions of cocoa powder, leather and tobacco. There is good texture and nice complexity on the palate We finish with their wonderfully successful Vin Santo '95, which is austere in character and somewhat dry. It has a crisp, rather severe nose that highlights notes of almonds, walnuts and candied peel. The flavour is full and sober while the elegant progression is well-sustained and the long finish is laudably intriguing.

● Franze '98	▾▾	4	○ Vin Santo '95	▾▾	5
● San Lorenzo '98	▾▾	5	● Campo del Bosco '98	▾	4
● Sassotondo Rosso '99	▾▾	3*	○ Refola '99	▾	3
○ Sassotondo Bianco '99	▾	3	● Chianti Colli Senesi '98		2
● San Lorenzo '97	♈♈	4	● Chianti dei Colli Senesi '91	▾	2*
● Sassotondo Rosso '98	♈♈	3*	○ Refola '93	▾	3
○ Bianco di Pitigliano '97	▾	3	○ Refola '95	▾	3
○ Bianco di Pitigliano '98	▾	3	○ Refola '96	▾	3
● Franze '97	▾	3	● Vigna del Bosco '93	▾	4
● Sassotondo Rosso '97	▾	3	● Vigna del Bosco '94	▾	4

SUVERETO (LI)

SUVERETO (LI)

Lorella Ambrosini
Loc. Tabaro, 95
57028 Suvereto (LI)
Tel. 0565/829301

Gualdo Del Re
Loc. Notri, 77
57028 Suvereto (LI)
Tel. 0565/829888 - 0565/829361

Lorella Ambrosini and Roberto Fanetti began to make wine almost by chance. They began with the vineyards given to them by Lorella's father who, like any good Abruzzo-born farmer, planted his vigorous pergola-trained montepulciano vines, very capable of producing interesting wines, as soon as he arrived in Tuscany. Only later did they realize that making excellent wine means taking serious decisions and near-total dedication. That was why their new vineyards were very differently conceived. Their new vines are densely planted in a spur-pruned system and the new varieties include sangiovese and merlot. Their cellar has been completely renovated to bring it up to the standard required by their new projects. Roberto, with the technical assistance of Claudio Gori, at present keeps tabs on all the phases of production while his wife, Lorella, has discovered the new and unusual vocation of going around the vines and cutting out the excess bunches of grapes. The wines currently on release are influenced only to a limited extent from these changes but without doubt their future wines will benefit much more. As the Riflesso Antico, a 100% montepulciano, was not yet ready to be tasted, we tried their Subertum, a blend of two thirds sangiovese and one third merlot. It is a warm, powerful wine that bears the imprint of its terroir. It has an intense, if not very well-defined, nose that has notes of blackberry and plum jam. Its broad palate is well-supported by alcohol. The tannins tend to dry out the progression but the finish is fruit-rich and satisfyingly long. The Tabarò Bianco is simple, clean and delicious and the Rosso, although a little fuzzy on the nose, shows more character on the palate.

A new wine, the Re Nero, has become part of the Gualdo del Re family. It is a blend, so far as we know without precedent, of equal parts of merlot and pinot nero. As usual, this is a very original choice by Nico and Teresa Rossi, who have raised a considerable number of eyebrows with the decision. The panel's taste test, however, demonstrated the legitimacy of the experiment by placing the wine at the top of the winery's scoresheet. The wine is a particularly convincing fusion of its various constituent elements, so much so that the varietal origins are largely hidden. It has a rich colour and the clean, balanced nose focuses principally on fruit, although there are some carefully measured oak-derived notes. On the palate, it does not show great concentration but it finds good balance and a very appealing drinkability. Re Nero, of which very little was produced, may be purchased in limited quantities only at the winery. The Val di Cornia Riserva '97 is a wine that continues to perplex. It has more structure than any of the other Gualdo del Re wines and the palate evinces good weight, character and tannic texture. It continues to be somewhat muddled on the nose and to show hints of reduction that penalize its rating. While allowing the wine to breathe does improve the situation, we remain convinced that more work needs to be done on the wine's aromas. The Federico Primo, a blend of cabernet, merlot and sangiovese, has a nose dominated by toasty notes of coffee and is pleasant but somewhat dilute in the mouth. Lumen, a pinot bianco, did rather well. It has clean aromas and progression on the palate is deliciously sweet. The Rossi Vermentino, the Vigna Valentina, is sweetish but perfectly acceptable while the Val di Cornia Bianco and Rosso are both well-managed.

●	Subertum '98	♟♟	5
○	Val di Cornia Bianco Tabarò '99	♟	3
●	Val di Cornia Rosso Tabarò '99	♟	3
●	Riflesso Antico '94	♟♟	4
●	Riflesso Antico '97	♟♟	5
●	Subertum '97	♟♟	5
●	Riflesso Antico '93	♟	4
●	Subertum '94	♟	4
●	Subertum '96	♟	5
○	Val di Cornia Bianco Armonia '98	♟	4
○	Val di Cornia Bianco Tabarò '98	♟	3
●	Val di Cornia Rosso Ambrosini '93	♟	2*
●	Val di Cornia Rosso Tabarò '98	♟	3

○	Lumen '99	♟♟	4
●	Re Nero '98	♟♟	5
●	Federico Primo '97	♟	5
●	Val di Cornia Gualdo del Re Ris. '97	♟	5
○	Vigna Valentina '99	♟	4
○	Val di Cornia Bianco '99		2
●	Val di Cornia Rosso '99		2
●	Federico Primo '93	♟♟	5
●	Federico Primo '96	♟♟	5
○	Lumen '98	♟♟	4
●	Val di Cornia Gualdo del Re Ris. '95	♟♟	5
○	Vigna Valentina '95	♟♟	3*

SUVERETO (LI)

SUVERETO (LI)

MONTEPELOSO
LOC. MONTEPELOSO, 82
57028 SUVERETO (LI)
TEL. 0565/828180

TUA RITA
LOC. NOTRI, 81
57028 SUVERETO (LI)
TEL. 0565/829237

This young winery at Suvereto in the province of Livorno manages to make some progress every year. This is perhaps easiest to note by retasting the various versions of Montepeloso's flagship wine, the Nardo, made mostly from sangiovese but with the addition of a little cabernet sauvignon. Its first year, the '94, did little more than suggest the potential the wine offered for expressing its terroir. It was a powerful wine with that boisterous lack of discipline you expect from the young. The '95 had milder tones and was better all around and then the slight dip of the '96 was in keeping with the vintage, a very difficult one for sangiovese-based wines. The '97 had character and complexity, although the nose was still unruly. Now the '98 represents a further step forward by Nardo. Dark and concentrated in the glass, its nose is decidedly more focused than in previous editions, with broad aromas of black berry fruit mingling with spicy and vegetal notes. Entry on the palate is powerful, and the mid palate marches on in close order. Although it falls apart a bit in the finish, it quickly gathers itself together and closes satisfyingly. It is still a very young wine but it has a harmony and a coherence that are very promising. Also very interesting, but even more youthful, is the 100% cabernet sauvignon, the Gabbro '98. It is very powerful, with imposing tannic structure, but definitely needs more time to achieve greater balance and to absorb the prominent toasty notes of the oak. It may be difficult and relatively unapproachable at the moment but we feel that it is on the way to becoming a wine of real finesse.

Rita and Virgilio Bisti's winery has in just a few years re-organized to be able to maintain the high level of their wines and to achieve the planned increase in annual production. Probably it was easier to make great wines than it is to switch from a craft-based approach to winemaking to that of a modern producer with 12 or so hectares under vine and the right equipment to do the job. The Bistis 100% Merlot, the Redigaffi '98, again won Three Glasses for the extraordinary richness it revealed at our tastings. We would like to add that this is not just a run-of-the-mill big wine that impresses anyone who picks up a glass. Its nose maintains the opulent up-front fruit and notes of earth and mineral that it had in the past but now it also manages to bring greater order and focus to bear than it has in recent years. Its mouth is powerfully imperious, pervasive and very long, with a generous helping of extremely fine-grained tannins. The Giusto di Notri '98 came within a hair's breadth of winning Three Glasses, too, for it has made notable progress. The aromas are very interesting and distinctive, unveiling hints of plums, blackberries, nettles, and spices. In the mouth, it is concentrated and soft, revealing silky tannins and a very long finish. The Perlato del Bosco '98 seems a bit reticent but is nonetheless clean on the nose. It has remarkable weight on the palate but fails to express a rounded personality.

● Gabbro '98	▼▼	6
● Nardo '98	▼▼	6
● Gabbro '97	♀♀	5
● Nardo '95	♀♀	5
● Nardo '97	♀♀	6
● Val di Cornia Rosso		
Montepeloso '95	♀♀	4
● Nardo '94	♀	5
● Nardo '96	♀	6
● Val di Cornia Rosso '98	♀	4
● Val di Cornia Rosso		
Montepeloso '94	♀	4

● Redigaffi '98	▼▼▼	6
● Giusto di Notri '98	▼▼	6
● Perlato del Bosco Rosso '98	▼	4
● Giusto di Notri '94	♀♀♀	5
● Redigaffi '96	♀♀♀	6
● Giusto di Notri '92	♀♀	5
● Giusto di Notri '93	♀♀	5
● Giusto di Notri '96	♀♀	5
● Giusto di Notri '97	♀♀	5
● Perlato del Bosco Rosso '96	♀♀	4
● Redigaffi '95	♀♀	6
● Redigaffi '97	♀♀	6
○ Sileno '96	♀♀	4
● Perlato del Bosco Rosso '97	♀	4

TAVARNELLE VAL DI PESA (FI)   TAVARNELLE VAL DI PESA (FI)

FATTORIA LA RIPA
LOC. S. DONATO IN POGGIO
50028 TAVARNELLE VAL DI PESA (FI)
TEL. 055/8072948

PODERE LA CAPPELLA
LOC. S. DONATO IN POGGIO
STRADA CERBAIA, 10/A
50028 TAVARNELLE VAL DI PESA (FI)
TEL. 055/8072727

This is an excellent start in the Guide for Fattoria La Ripa, a Barberino Val d'Elsa-based producer. The estate presented two wines and both earned Two Glasses without breaking sweat. This result is even more significant when you stops to think that they are both DOC wines. This means that this winery has faith in the denomination, as well in its own ability to make wine that is a clear expression of its terroir. The Chianti Classico '98 has an attractively clear pale ruby colour. The nose offers rich, powerful aromas of berry fruit leading in to a medium-bodied palate that reveals juicy pulp and close-knit tannins that fuse well with the alcohol, and a refreshing vein of acidity. The lip-smacking palate takes you through to a delightful, potent finish with plenty of grip. The '97 Riserva has a very intense, deep, luminous hue and a broad gamut of aromas on the nose, ranging from ripe redcurrant and plum fruit to spicy notes of cloves, laced with vegetal and oak-derived nuances. In the mouth, the decisive attack demonstrates the wine's complexity and softness. Richly extracted, the palate reveals seamlessly integrated tannins while the finish is delicious, long and well-sustained.

We ended our notes on La Cappella in the last edition of the Guide with a reminder that we would be back this year to describe a monovarietal Merlot that promised to be an eye-opener. Our expectations are still high but you'll have to be patient for a while yet. The wine is still ageing and we will be able to review it for you next year. The winery provides full-time occupation for Bruno Rossini and his daughter Natascia, both of whom are passionately enthusiastic about their vines. They are kept busy with replanting, re-organizing the cellar and buying new barriques. Those of their wines that we tasted did very well. Their Corbezzolo '98, mostly sangiovese with a small proportion of other grapes, has an intense, deep ruby colour. On the nose, it offers sensations of enticingly rich fruit enlivened by faint vegetal and balsamic touches. Entry on the palate is stunning. It has power, a somewhat rough fullness that is not entirely focused, and great warmth from the substantial alcohol that nevertheless manages to soften the crackling-hard tannins. The finish is long but this wine will need further ageing to find a perfect equilibrium. The Chianti Classico '98, has a lovely, dense, firm ruby colour. The fresh, minty aromas are mellowed delightfully by the rich, elegant fruit. Juicy and succulent on the palate, it offers tannins that are assertive but not harsh, and a deliciously well-sustained finish.

● Chianti Classico '98	▼▼	3*
● Chianti Classico Ris. '97	▼▼	4
● Chianti Classico Ris. '90	♀♀	4
● Chianti Classico '93	♀	3
● Chianti Classico Querciolo '98	▼▼	4
● Corbezzolo '98	▼▼	5
● Corbezzolo '96	♀♀	5
● Corbezzolo '97	♀♀	5
● Chianti Classico Querciolo '96	♀	4
● Chianti Classico Querciolo '97	♀	4

TAVARNELLE VAL DI PESA (FI) TAVARNELLE VAL DI PESA (FI)

MONTECCHIO
VIA MONTECCHIO, 4
50020 TAVARNELLE VAL DI PESA (FI)
TEL. 055/8072907

POGGIO AL SOLE
LOC. SAMBUCA VAL DI PESA
50028 TAVARNELLE VAL DI PESA (FI)
TEL. 055/8071504

The wines of Montecchio have taken on a precise character in recent years. The phrases that keep cropping up in our tasting notes are "cleanly made", "equilibrium", and "elegant drinkability". This year's tastings have confirmed these impressions but with an extra dimension because the vintage in question is the excellent '97. At present, the wines still lack a bit of the character and complexity necessary for them to be called great. Everything seems to be in place, however, to sustain our hopes of really great wines from Montecchio in the future, especially when the grapes from recently planted vines come on-stream. The Chianti Riserva '97 fully reflects all the finest characteristics of bottles from this year. It is a wine that seduces you with its elegance of execution, its excellent balance and depth of taste. The wood is well integrated and in keeping with the dimensions of the wine, which are good but not enormous. Of a similar profile is their Pietracupa '97, a blend of sangiovese with a proportion of cabernet sauvignon whose strong suits are elegance and length in the mouth. Neither bulky nor heavy, it is perhaps a little too simple on the nose but it does express its abundance of fruit very clearly. Also satisfactory, but in a lower category, we find the '98 Chianti. Its aromas are interesting but somewhat atypical, with floral and vegetal notes emerging. The fruit states its case more eloquently on the palate, where the moderate weight is well distributed, and there are faint bitterish hints in the finish.

The Chianti Classico Casasilia '97 is a truly great wine. Its Three Glasses were claimed with disarming facility and reward a cellar that has been doing excellent work for years. This result is no surprise to us because Poggio al Sole has come close on several occasions in the past. The Casasilia is about as complete a wine as you could wish to find. It has a vibrant, dark, close-knit colour and a intense, rich nose with a backdrop of admirably ripe black berry fruit mingling with fresh, spicy notes and a subtle touch of smokiness. The palate deliciously reconciles the broad volume of the close-knit structure with the elegance of its fruit, before concluding with an extremely long finish worthy of a great wine. The Syrah '98 very nearly repeated this exploit. It is similar in style to the Casasilia, and has a beautiful richness of fruit, perfect balance and lovely elegance in the mouth. The wine has an enviably tidy style that is not completely anticipated by the nose, in which pepper and plums are very evident. The Seraselva '97 is good and interesting. From cabernet sauvignon and merlot, it is reined in, as on other occasions, by the hardness of its tannins and oak. Its weight in the mouth and its concentration are praiseworthy, the fruit is exuberant and its finish well sustained. Nevertheless, it is a wine that, although muscular, does not have the elegance and harmony of the others reviewed. Finally, the standard Poggio al Sole Chianti Classico '98 is pleasant, soft, balanced and reasonably long.

● Chianti Classico Ris. '97	🍷🍷	4
● Pietracupa '97	🍷🍷	5
● Chianti Classico '98	🍷	4
● Chianti Classico '96	🍷🍷	4
● Chianti Classico '97	🍷🍷	4
● Chianti Classico Ris. '95	🍷🍷	4

● Chianti Cl. Casasilia '97	🍷🍷🍷	6
● Seraselva '97	🍷🍷	6
● Syrah '98	🍷🍷	6
● Chianti Classico '98	🍷	4
● Chianti Cl. Casasilia '93	🍷🍷	5
● Chianti Cl. Casasilia '94	🍷🍷	5
● Chianti Cl. Casasilia Ris. '95	🍷🍷	5
● Chianti Cl. Casasilia Ris. '96	🍷🍷	5
● Chianti Classico '97	🍷🍷	4
● Chianti Classico Ris. '95	🍷🍷	4
● Seraselva '94	🍷🍷	5
● Seraselva '95	🍷🍷	5
● Seraselva '96	🍷🍷	5
● Syrah '96	🍷🍷	5
● Syrah '97	🍷🍷	5

TERRICCIOLA (PI)

VAGLIA (FI)

BADIA DI MORRONA
LOC. LA BADIA
56030 TERRICCIOLA (PI)
TEL. 0587/658505

CAMPOSILIO
LOC. MONTORSOLI
VIA BASCIANO, 8
50030 VAGLIA (FI)
TEL. 055/696456

The wonderful hospitality offered by the Conti Gaslini Alberti and the great competence of Corrado Dal Piaz make Badia di Morrona a model winery and a pleasure to visit. Its wines increasingly display both a quality and a personality that are exceptional. This year too, however, the appointment with Three Glasses has had to be postponed but just for a short while, we hope. This is a sign that winemaking has its own time-horizons and that it is just as well not to force matters. The Vignalta '97, made with sangiovese grapes from old vines at a very low yield, together with a little canaiolo, gets Two Glasses. It has a garnet ruby colour that is lustrous and intense while the complex nose ranges from cherry jam to vegetal notes, leather and wet dog. In the mouth, it is full-bodied and warm with attractive fine-grained tannins and the finish is well sustained by the oak. Two Glasses also go to the N'Antia '97, made from sangiovese, cabernet and merlot. The dark ruby colour ushers in aromas with prominent notes of black berry fruit, bilberries and plums that are nicely contrasted by the wood. The palate is soft, juicy and broad, with an attractive note of wood that persists on the finish. The delicious San Torpé Felciaio '99, is a trebbiano-based white that bears witness to Dal Piaz's excellent work. It is one of the few such wines that can boast fruit and citrus aromas and a refreshing acid tang. The Chianti Sodi del Paretaio '99 is a distinctive, if not altogether convincing, interpretation of the style with its faintly mineral aromas and good body on the palate, which is, however, in thrall to tannins that are unexpectedly rough for a vintage like the '99. The Chianti Riserva '96 shows signs of age and the palate is bitterish.

Camposilio confirms its status. This year, the only wine presented scored a comfortable Two Glass rating. We note that new vineyards have come on-stream and there are already plans to enlarge their premises. Such projects are inevitable with production rising steadily. Greatly to his credit, Alessandro Rustioni was the first to believe in the potential of this area, which before his arrival was not exactly well known for its wines. But things are beginning to happen and other producers have followed Alessandro's example and are now becoming more quality-oriented. Besides sangiovese, international grapes like cabernet sauvignon and merlot are beginning to provide interesting results, which could well have major repercussions. But to return to the present, the Camposilio Rosso blend has already been enriched with modest proportions of cabernet and merlot. The '97 has an attractively deep ruby hue flecked with violet highlights. On the nose, a refreshing vegetal note emerges and is then lifted by delicate balsamic hints. The intense fruit is reminiscent of ripe mulberry and redcurrant. The weight on the front palate is satisfying and the progression is balanced by the texture of the tannins, with the alcohol providing an appropriate counterpoint. The finish is admirably long.

● N'Antia '97	ΨΨ	5
● Vigna Alta '97	ΨΨ	6
● Chianti Sodi del Paretaio '99	Ψ	2
○ S. Torpè Felciaio '99	Ψ	2*
● Chianti Riserva '96		3
● N'Antia '91	ΨΨ	5
● N'Antia '93	ΨΨ	5
● N'Antia '94	ΨΨ	5
● N'Antia '95	ΨΨ	5
● N'Antia '96	ΨΨ	5
● Vigna Alta '94	ΨΨ	5
● Vigna Alta '96	ΨΨ	6
● Chianti Sodi del Paretaio '94	Ψ	2*
● Chianti Sodi del Paretaio '96	Ψ	2*
● Chianti Sodi del Paretaio '97	Ψ	2*

● Camposilio '97	ΨΨ	5
● Camposilio '95	ΨΨ	5
● Camposilio '96	ΨΨ	5
● Camposilio '94	Ψ	5

VALGIANO (LU)

VINCI (FI)

TENUTA DI VALGIANO
VIA DI VALGIANO, 7
55010 VALGIANO (LU)
TEL. 0583/402271

CANTINE LEONARDO
BIVIO DI STREDA
VIA PROVINCIALE MERCATALE, 291
50059 VINCI (FI)
TEL. 0571/902444

Nowadays, we have the phenomenon of flying winemakers who look after 60 or 70 wineries, so wines often tend to reflect the oenologist's style rather than the characteristics of a terroir. People who follow what is going on in the wine business are no longer surprised at these developments. There are, however, some brave souls who have chosen not to abandon the straight and narrow path of the "native" winemaker who works solely for one cellar. Valgiano's owners, Moreno Petrini and Laura di Collobiano, are in this latter category and their oenologist Saverio Petrilli shows year after year, with the precision of a Swiss timepiece, that their faith in his skills is well founded. The team are now very near to winning our top award. Again, their Scasso dei Cesari was awarded Two brimming Glasses. It has a dense colour and the nose reveals remarkably concentrated aromas of black berries and black cherry jam, laced with delicate, wood-derived spiciness which is remarkably well dosed. Entry on the palate is soft and the tannins are sweet but still young. Then it expands juicily in the mouth and closes with an austere and impressively lingering finish. Those who think that Tuscany does not produce good whites should take a look at the new Valgiano wine, Scasso del Bugiardo, which means "Liar's Downfall" (finding good names for their wines is not one of this estate's strongest points). Made from barrique-fermented vermentino and chardonnay, it has a crisp, attractive nose of grapefruit, ripe medlars and a touch of mint. Lively in the mouth, it offers good texture and a sweet, long finish. Their second-label wines also performed very well. The Rosso Palistorti, pleasantly spicy and ripe but sinewy on the palate, carried off One Glass, as does the Giallo dei Muri, which has notes of citrus fruits, green pears and roses on the nose and a tangy, soft palate.

There's no doubt about it. This winery is well on its way along the road that leads to high quality. The cellar has taken enthusiastically to its new role, which is the one that used to be fulfilled by co-operative wineries, offering assistance to their growers, and at the same time encouraging them to work hard and well in the vineyards. Their two oenologists, Riccardo Pucci, the in-house winemaker, and Alberto Antonin, the consultant, are both expert professionals and, as usual, their special selections are the best products. The Sant'Ippolito '98, a blend of merlot and syrah, is again elegant, delicious and very dense, expressing elegance and finesse on the palate. The San Zio '98 is a monovarietal sangiovese. It has a firm ruby colour and ripe fruit aromas that are almost jammy. Rich, full-bodied and muscular on the palate, it is let down by roughish tannins that are mellowed, however, by the generous alcohol. The finish is powerful, sweet and long. The Ser Piero '99 performed well, too. A chardonnay-based white that has a short spell in barrique, it presents a straw-yellow colour with golden highlights. On the nose, it shows freshness with notes of aromatic herbs and citrus clearly present. The palate proves to have moderate body and nicely balanced acidity. The Vin Santo Tegrino d'Anchiano '95 has a dark amber colour and tempts the nose with warm, ripe aromas of hazelnuts, chestnuts, figs and raisins. The entry on the palate is rounded, fat and soft while the only black mark is for a pleasant but rather short finish. The Chianti '99 is unprepossessing but worth investigating for its very competitive price tag.

● Colline Lucchesi Rosso		
Scasso dei Cesari '98	♈♈	6
○ Scasso del Bugiardo '99	♈♈	5
○ Colline Lucchesi Bianco		
Giallo dei Muri '99	♈	4
● Colline Lucchesi		
Rosso dei Palistorti '98	♈	4
○ Colline Lucchesi Bianco		
Giallo dei Muri '97	♈♈	3*
● Scasso dei Cesari '95	♈♈	4
● Scasso dei Cesari '96	♈♈	4
● Scasso dei Cesari '97	♈♈	5
● Colline Lucchesi		
Rosso dei Palistorti '97	♈	3

● Sant'Ippolito '98	♈♈	5
● SanZio '98	♈♈	4
○ Ser Piero '99	♈	3
○ Vin Santo Tegrino d'Anchiano	♈	4
● Chianti '99		3
● Sant'Ippolito '96	♈♈	4
● Sant'Ippolito '97	♈♈	5
● SanZio '96	♈♈	4
● SanZio '97	♈♈	4
● Chianti '97	♈	2*
● Chianti '98	♈	2*
○ Ser Piero '98	♈	3
○ Vin Santo Tegrino d'Anchiano '93	♈	4
○ Vin Santo Tegrino d'Anchiano '94	♈	4

OTHER WINERIES

The following producers obtained good scores in our tastings with one or more of their wines:

PROVINCE OF AREZZO

SLe Ginestre, Bucine, tel. 055/9918032
Chianti '98,
Chianti San Pancrazio '97

I Selvatici, Montevarchi, tel. 055/9102712
Vin Santo '93

Giacomo Marengo,
Palazzuolo, tel. 0575/847083
Chianti La Commenda Ris. '95

Fattoria di Gratena,
Pieve a Maiano, tel. 0575/368664
Rapozzo da Maiano '97

Tenuta Setteponti,
San Giustino Valdarno, tel. 055/977443
Crognolo '98

PROVINCE OF FIRENZE

I Balzini,
Barberino Val d'Elsa, tel. 055/8075503
I Balzini Rosso '97

Pasolini dall'Onda,
Barberino Val d'Elsa, tel. 055/8075019
San Zanobi '96

Sant'Appiano,
Barberino Val d'Elsa, tel. 055/8075541
Monteloro '98

Spadaio e Piecorto,
Barberino Val d'Elsa, tel. 055/8072915
Chianti Classico '98

Casale, Certaldo, tel. 0571/669262
Sangiovese '97

Fiano,
Certaldo, tel. 0571/669048
Fianesco '98

Il Cavaliere,
Dicomano, tel. 0555/8386340
Chianti Rufina Ris. '97

Piazzano,
Empoli, tel. 0571/999044
Chianti Rio Camerata '99

San Vettore,
Gambassi Terme, tel. 0571/678005
Cabernet Sauvignon '98

Belvedere,
Greve in Chianti, tel. 055/8544823
Chianti Classico '98

Rignana, Greve in Chianti, tel. 055/852065
Chianti Classico '97

Riseccoli, Greve in Chianti, tel. 055/853598
Chianti Classico Ris. '97,
Saeculum '97

Savignola Paolina,
Greve in Chianti, tel. 055/853139
Chianti Classico '98

Terreno,
Greve in Chianti, tel. 055/854001
Chianti Classico Lignanello Ris. '95,

Villa Buonasera,
Greve in Chianti, tel. 055/8547932
Chianti Classico '98

Villa Calcinaia,
Greve in Chianti, tel. 055/854008
Chianti Classico Ris. '97

Castello Il Palagio,
Mercatale Val di Pesa, tel. 055/8218157
Il Palagio '99

Solatione,
Mercatale Val di Pesa, tel. 055/821082
Chianti Classico '97

Castello di Poppiano,
Montespertoli, tel. 055/82315
Tricorno '96

La Gigliola, Montespertoli, tel. 0571/608001
Camporsoli '98

Poggio Capponi,
Montespertoli, tel. 0571/671914
Chianti Montespertoli Petriccio '99

Le Bocce,
Panzano in Chianti, tel. 055/852153
Chianti Classico Ris. '97

Grignano,
Pontassieve, tel. 055/8398490
Chianti Rufina Poggio Gualtieri Ris. 97

Lavacchio, Pontassieve, tel. 055/8317472
Chianti Rufina Ris. '97

Colognole, Rufina, tel. 055/8319870
Chianti Rufina '98

Cigliano,
S. Casciano Val di Pesa, tel. 055/820033
Chianti Classico '98

Il Mandorlo,
S. Casciano Val di Pesa, tel. 055/8228211
Chianti Classico '98

Ripanera,
S. Casciano Val di Pesa, tel. 055/826098
Terra di Ripanera '97

S. Michele a Torri, Scandicci, tel. 055/769111
Chianti Classico Ris. '97

Majnoni Guicciardini,
Vico d'Elsa, tel. 055/8073002
Chardonnay Le Cantine '98

Marchesi Torrigiani,
Vico d'Elsa, tel. 055/8073001
Guidaccio '98

PROVINCE OF GROSSETO

Montecucco, Cinigiano, tel. 0564/999029
Le Coste '98

Coliberto,
Massa Marittima, tel. 0566/919039
Monteregio di Massa M.ma Rosso Thesan '98

Perazzeta,
Montenero d'Orcia, tel. 0564/954065
Montecucco Sangiovese Ris. '98

Serraiola,
Monterotondo M.mo, tel. 0566/910026
Monteregio di Massa M.ma Bianco
Cala Violina '99

Rascioni Cecconello,
Orbetello, tel. 0564/885642
Poggio Capitana '97

I Campetti, Ribolla, tel. 0564/579663
Almabruna '99

Cantina Cooperativa del Morellino,
Scansano, tel. 0564/507785
Morellino di Scansano Roggiano Ris. '97

Provveditore,
Scansano, tel. 0564/599237
Morellino di Scansano Primo Ris. '97

PROVINCE OF LIVORNO

Le Volpaiole,
Campiglia M.ma, tel. 0565/843194
Val di Cornia Rosso '98

Cipriana,
Castagneto Carducci, tel. 05665/877153
Bolgheri Rosso San Martino '98

San Luigi, Piombino, tel. 0565/220578
Fidenzio '97

Martelli e Busdraghi,
Suvereto, tel. 0565/829401
Val di Cornia Rosso Incontri '98

PROVINCE OF LUCCA

Cohens e Gervais,
Lucca, tel. 0583/90431
Sorbus '98

Fattoria del Teso,
Montecarlo, tel. 0583/286288
Vin Santo '89

Vigna del Greppo,
Montecarlo, tel. 0583/22593
Vermentino '99

PROVINCE OF MASSA

Lavandaro,
Fosdinovo, tel. 0187/68202
Vermentino Colli di Luni '99

Scurtarola,
Massa, tel. 0585/833523
Vermentino '98

PROVINCE OF PISA

La Regola,
Montescudaio, tel. 0586/699216
Montescudaio Rosso La Regola '98

Merlini, Montescudaio, tel. 0586/681694
Montescudaio Rosso Guadi Piani '98

Moos,
Soiana, tel. 0587/654180
Fontestina '98

PROVINCE OF SIENA

Campoperi,
Castellina in Chianti, tel. 0577/743062
Chianti Classico Casale Sparviero Ris. '97

Casina di Cornia,
Castellina in Chianti, tel. 0577/743052
L'Amaranto '98

La Castellina,
Castellina in Chianti, tel. 0577/741238
Chianti Classico '98

Poggio Amorelli,
Castellina in Chianti, tel. 0571/668733
Chianti Classico Ris. '97

Fattoria Valtellina,
Gaiole in Chianti, tel. 0577/731005
Convivio '97

Le Miccine,
Gaiole in Chianti, tel. 0577/749526
Chianti Classico Don Alberto Ris. '97

Rocca di Montegrossi,
Gaiole in Chianti, tel. 0577/747267
Geremia '97

Castello di San Polo in Rosso,
Gaiole in Chianti, tel. 0577/746045
Cetinaia '97

Cerbaiona, Montalcino, tel. 0577/848660
Brunello di Montalcino '95

Col di Sole, Montalcino, tel. 0577/355789
Brunello di Montalcino '95

Corte Pavone,
Montalcino, tel. 0577/848110
Brunello di Montalcino '95

La Fiorita, Montalcino, tel. 0577/835511
Brunello di Montalcino '95

La Fornace,
Montalcino, tel. 0577/848465
Brunello di Montalcino '95

La Gerla, Montalcino, tel. 0577/848599
Brunello di Montalcino Vigna degli Angeli '95

La Serena,
Montalcino, tel. 0577/848659
Brunello di Montalcino '95

Oliveto, Montalcino, tel. 0577/835542
Rosso di Montalcino Il Roccolo '98

Pietroso, Montalcino, tel. 0577/848573
Brunello di Montalcino '95

Di Sesta, Montalcino, tel. 0577/835612
Brunello di Montalcino '95

Vitanza, Montalcino, tel. 0577/846031
Brunello di Montalcino '95

Canneto,
Montepulciano, tel. 0578/757737
Nobile di Montepulciano '97

Fattoria di Paterno,
Montepulciano, tel. 0578/798174
Nobile di Montepulciano '97

Fattoria Le Casalte,
Montepulciano, tel. 0578/798246
Nobile di Montepulciano '97

La Ciarliana,
Montepulciano, tel. 0578/758423
Nobile di Montepulciano '97

Lombardo, Montepulciano, tel. 0578/708321
Nobile di Montepulciano '97

Le Fonti, Poggibonsi, tel. 0577/935690
Chianti Classico Ris. '97

Caparsino,
Radda in Chianti, tel. 0577/738174
Chianti Classico Doccio a Matteo Ris. '97

Villa Buoninsegna,
Rapolano Terme, tel. 0577/724380
Villa Buoninsegna '97

Ca' del Vispo, S. Gimignano, tel. 0577/943053
Crueter '98

Rubicini, S. Gimignano, tel. 0577/944816
Vernaccia di S. Gimignano '99

S. Donato, S. Gimignano, tel. 0577/941616
Vernaccia di S. Gimignano '99

S. Quirico,
S. Gimignano, tel. 0577/955007
Vernaccia di S. Gimignano Sel. '99

Signano, S. Gimignano, tel. 0577/940164
Vernaccia di S. Gimignano Sel. '98

MARCHE

Without resorting to hyperbole we can hardly resist proclaiming the continuing rise in the quality standards of Marche wines. Yet Marche is still a region without a strong identity or, more to the point, despite all the developments, it doesn't yet seem to have hit public consciousness. The main point, though, as the pages of this guide show, is that the region's real success isn't a one-off, rather the end of a journey – or, more realistically, a significant first staging post – which the determination and tenacity of the region's producers has gradually attained. Hence the smiles in Marche this year can be measured by the number of estates in the guide (a good 48) and the large number that almost made it and are listed in the appendix; these latter are often, we assure you, deserving of a full entry in their own right. A further parameter is the number of top-scoring wines and on this front the number of glasses gained overall is as impressive as the crowning glory of eight Three Glass awards, double the number gained last year. This is despite the fact that 1999 was not particularly kind to the whites as a result of difficult conditions during the harvest. This means that the productive aplomb demonstrated by Verdicchio dei Castelli di Jesi Casal di Serra from Umani Ronchi, for example, (which gains Three Glasses for the first time) is even more impressive than it otherwise would be. Verdicchio dei Castelli di Jesi Contrada Balciana '98 from Sartarelli – which reminds more than a few tasters of Alsace – and the '98 Verdicchio Podium from Garofoli are both as superb as in previous vintages. A new star is the sensational Verdicchio Passito Tordiruta '97 from Terre Cortesi Moncaro, a sumptuously radiant wine that brings lustre to an exemplary co-operative. It could even become a lynchpin wine for the DOC, leading the way to a new styling for its wines. Moving on to the reds, the Le Terrazze estate at Numana has notched up a personal achievement by gaining two Three Glasses awards, one for its '98 Rosso Conero selection, Sassi Neri, the other for a stunning Rosso Conero, Visions of Johanna. It is cabernet sauvignon grapes, however, that keeps the Boccadigabbia estate in the limelight, with its Akronte gaining Three Glasses for a record fifth time. The '98 Kurni from Oasi degli Angeli also repeats its success of last year by hitting the top slot. Looking a little deeper into this year's tasting results it is only right to mention several wines that showed particularly prominently: Rosso Conero Fibbio '98 from Lanari, Rosso Piceno Regina del Bosco '98 from Dezi (a worthy newcomer), as well as Rosso Piceno '98 GrAnarijS from Rio Maggio, Rosso Piceno Superiore '98 Roggio del Filare from Velenosi and Rosso Conero Dorico '97 from Moroder. There are also several other good new wines from lesser known denominations, and from both new and long-standing estates; you will find them on the following pages.

LANARI
VIA POZZO, 142
FRAZ. VARANO
60029 ANCONA
TEL. 071/2861343

MARCHETTI
VIA DI PONTELUNGO, 166
60131 ANCONA
TEL. 071/897386

The Lanari estate is increasing in size and has another six hectares ready to join the seven already planted, which will double its current annual production of around 40,000 bottles. Its policy remains that of vigorous selection in the vineyard and careful attention to detail in the cellar. As a result, Lanari and oenologist Giancarlo Soverchia continue to improve the quality of their powerful yet elegant reds. The '99 Rosso Conero is a happy exception to most of its counterparts from that vintage, a distinctly unhappy one for the denomination. It has an opaque yet liquid vermilion colour and typical morello cherry, mulberry and plum tones on the nose. It is muscular, full and well-structured on the palate but without asperity and has enough weight to set off the perfumes, leaving an elegant finish. Fibbio '98, a Rosso Conero selection matured in a mixture of new and one-year-old barriques, has an opaque, dark violet colour and a long, intense and heady aroma of ripe cherry and morello cherry jam intertwined with liquorice, tobacco and a wisp of tar. The palate has tremendous structure, with ripe tannins weaving through a succulent texture laced with berry fruit. The finish is very long and satisfyingly complex. This wine is already ready to drink but will last and improve over many years.

Although it is the last few years that have seen Rosso Conero steadily gaining renown for the quality of its red wines, the zone can boast a considerable tradition from several long-standing estates. Among these is Ancona-based Marchetti, which has been producing DOC Rosso Conero for thirty years and whose wines are as well received on export markets as at home. Recently there was a change in the winemaking style. Whereas it used to be the underlying structure and the acid-tannin balance that took pride of place, now more emphasis is placed on the fruit, in line with market trends and more modern thinking. Nevertheless, you can rest assured that this change of tack will not upset the classic longevity of these wines and the '97 Rosso Conero is eloquent confirmation. This year, we retasted both the Rosso Conero '98 (the '99 not yet having been released) and the Riserva Villa Bonomi '97. Each confirmed our impressions last year. The '98 Rosso Conero is full-flavoured, with the classic morello cherry overtones well in evidence. The Villa Bonomi has better defined structure, a more complex bouquet, and is ripe and spicy. It is showing the beginnings of development and its longevity appears assured. The estate also produces two styles of Verdicchio dei Castelli di Jesi, the Classico and the Villa Bonomi selection, which spends a short time in wood. This year, only the basic version was available for tasting and proved to be a fresh, lively tipple with good balance and a zesty palate.

Rosso Conero '99	▼▼	3*
Rosso Conero Fibbio '98	▼▼	5
Rosso Conero '98	▽▽	3
Rosso Conero Fibbio '97	▽▽	5

○ Verdicchio dei Castelli di Jesi Cl. '99	▼	2
● Rosso Conero '98	▽▽	3
● Rosso Conero Villa Bonomi Ris. '96	▽▽	4
● Rosso Conero Villa Bonomi Ris. '97	▽▽	4

ANCONA

APPIGNANO (MC)

ALESSANDRO MORODER
FRAZ. MONTACUTO, 112
60029 ANCONA
TEL. 071/898232

VILLA FORANO
C.DA FORANO, 40
62010 APPIGNANO (MC)
TEL. 0733/57102

The Rosso Coneros produced by the Moroder family recently have continued to demonstrate the pivotal role they play both within the denomination and as undisputed forerunners in the ongoing regional revamp. Alessandro Moroder has been looking after the estate with his wife, Serenella, since 1984, although it has been in the hands of the family since 1837. The cellars have recently been flanked with comfortable accommodation for paying guests. Indeed, a zone like Parco del Conero has all the makings of successful wine tourism: a welcoming attitude towards visitors, highly interesting wines and a fascinating, unspoilt environment. The estate, which has Franco Bernabei as consultant, has released a new vintage of its flagship wine, the Rosso Conero selection Dorico. The '97 is very good indeed, even if takes a little time to impress. The fruit-oak balance is perfect and there is remarkable harmony between its aromas and its elegant flavours. The large number of bottles produced (around 40,000) only does the producer even more credit. The basic Rosso Conero '98 also shows very well with fine concentration and inviting drinkability. Although Rosso Conero is the estate's mainstay, there has always also been a good rosé, the Rosa di Montacuto, and for some years now it has been flanked by an attractive dessert wine, L'Oro di Moroder, made from raisined trebbiano, moscato and malvasia fruit.

The zone where Villa Forano lies, between Appignano and Macerata, is absolutely delightful and the vineyards are interspersed with olive groves and its well cared-for countryside. The estate's owner, Conte Lucangeli, was convinced that the spot would be excellent for wine production and didn't cut any corners when he was investing in the property. He refurbished the beautiful master villa and its gardens, planted new vineyards, took on an able winemaker, Giancarlo Soverchia, and installed the most technologically advanced equipment. To this must be added the creditable decision to exploit indigenous vine varieties to the full. These, carefully nurtured, have shown their propensity to give some really good wines. The varieties involved are maceratino, the base of DOC Colli Maceratesi, sangiovese and montepulciano, these two being used together in Rosso Piceno. The '99 Colli Maceratesi selection, Monteferro, was not available in time for our tastings so we retasted the previous vintage, which is now admirably firm. The current vintage of the estate's base white has a good straw colour, floral perfumes and a zesty, fresh palate. The '98 selection Bulciano di Rosso Piceno is a wine of great power and a textbook example of a wine from the torrid summer of '98 and the extremely ripe grapes that resulted. Its opaque ruby colour introduces a nose with deep, pervasive aromas of liqueur cherries and coffee while the palate is exuberant and full of extract, alcohol and tannin. It will therefore need several months in the bottle for its impressive structure to knit together. The finish is very long with excellent nose-palate consistency.

● Rosso Conero '98	♼♼	3*		● Rosso Piceno Bulciano '98	♼♼	4
● Rosso Conero Dorico '97	♼♼	4		○ Colli Maceratesi Bianco		
○ L'Oro di Moroder	♼	5		Villa Forano '99	♼	2*
⊙ Rosa di Montacuto '99		2		○ Colli Maceratesi Bianco		
● Rosso Conero Dorico '90	♼♼♼	5		Monteferro '98	♼♼	3
● Rosso Conero Dorico '93	♼♼♼	5		● Rosso Piceno Villa Forano '97	♼♼	3
● Rosso Conero '97	♼♼	3				
● Rosso Conero Dorico '95	♼♼	5				

ASCOLI PICENO

Ercole Velenosi
Via dei Biancospini, 11
63100 Ascoli Piceno
tel. 0736/341218

Credit for this estate's success belongs not only to Angela and Ercole Velenosi, who have invested lavishly in both vineyard and cellar, but also to the entire technical staff, led by oenologist Romeo Taraborrelli. Among the wines tasted we must applaud Falerio Vigna Solaria '99 whose customary richness of extract was admirable. The nose reflects the super-ripeness of its grapes, with aromas of summer flowers and ripe fruit. The palate is elegant, with an attractive balance of acidity and alcohol. Aromas of banana, fresh butter and apple characterize the Villa Angela '99, a very fruity and typically zesty un-oaked Chardonnay. Rêve '98, another Chardonnay, this time fermented and aged in small barrels, has a nose of good intensity with overt vanilla spice overlaid with tropical fruit sweetness. The elegant, harmonious palate nicely echoes the nose. Linagre '99, produced mainly from sauvignon, is well-typed, fresh and nicely aromatic. Rosso Piceno Superiore Brecciarolo '97 is a textbook example of the style. Its lovely, lustrous ruby colour ushers in fine aromas of cherry and plum, then a soft, fruity palate that is a pleasure to drink. The uncomplicated Rosso Piceno '98 is lighter and more vegetal, with an attractively clean, even finish. However Roggio del Filare '97 offers a lot more. Firm and elegant, it is probably the best Rosso Piceno Superiore selection Velenosi has ever produced. To finish there is the Velenosi Brut Metodo Classico, a fragrant, long, sparkling wine that is one of the region's best.

○	Falerio dei Colli Ascolani Vigna Solaria '99	▼▼	3*
○	Rêve di Villa Angela '98	▼▼	4
●	Rosso Piceno Sup. Roggio del Filare '97	▼▼	5
○	Villa Angela Chardonnay '99	▼▼	3*
●	Rosso Piceno '98	▼	2*
●	Rosso Piceno Sup. Brecciarolo '97	▼	3
○	Velenosi Brut Metodo Classico	▼	4
○	Linagre Sauvignon di Villa Angela '99		3
●	Rosso Piceno Sup. Roggio del Filare '95	▽▽	5
●	Rosso Piceno Sup. Roggio del Filare '96	▽▽	5

BARBARA (AN)

Santa Barbara
Borgo Mazzini, 35
60010 Barbara (AN)
tel. 071/9674249

A dozen or so years ago Stefano Antonucci took over Santa Barbara and completely overhauled production. As a result, the estate now holds a leading place in the Castelli di Jesi area, distinguishing itself for reds as well as whites, and the range presented by this year was excellent. The '98 Stefano Antonucci selection, a tightly woven red from merlot and cabernet sauvignon, showed particularly well. The colour is dark, the aromas merit serious attention and the palate is full, with obvious development potential. The San Bartolo '98 (from montepulciano and cabernet) is less intense and could be viewed as a good alternative to a young, easy drinking Chianti, while the '99 Pignocco Rosso, from an unusual grape blend, is as attractive as usual and has immediate appeal. Among the Verdicchios, the mainstay of production, the standard-label '99 is clean and not without substance. In fact, it's not far short of the '99 Pignocco selection. The clean, straightforward Nidastore, another Jesi Verdicchio named after its vineyard of provenance, is also good. We move well up the quality scale, though, when we come to the Stefano Antonucci '98 Verdicchio selection. Its colour is bright yellow but its perfumes (citrus fruits with spices and fragrant hints of cake) will need time to develop, as will the palate. The '99 vintage of Verdicchio Le Vaglie is also impressive. Here too, despite the less than brilliant vintage, the wine's intricate mineral and fruit aromas and its unusually deep, complex palate had us wondering whether this was the best version ever to be released. The Muscatell, from moscato, is as well-typed as usual.

●	Rosso delle Marche Stefano Antonucci '98	▼▼	5
○	Verdicchio dei Castelli di Jesi Cl. Le Vaglie '99	▼▼	3*
○	Verdicchio dei Castelli di Jesi Cl. Stefano Antonucci '98	▼▼	4
○	Muscatell '99	▼	3
●	Pignocco Rosso '99	▼	3
●	San Bartolo '98	▼	3
○	Verdicchio dei Castelli di Jesi Cl. '99	▼	2*
○	Verdicchio dei Castelli di Jesi Nidastore '99	▼	3
○	Verdicchio dei Castelli di Jesi Pignocco '99	▼	2*

BARCHI (PS)

BELVEDERE OSTRENSE (AN)

VALENTINO FIORINI
VIA CAMPIOLI, 5
61030 BARCHI (PS)
TEL. 0721/97151

LUCIANO LANDI
VIA GAVIGLIANO, 16
60030 BELVEDERE OSTRENSE (AN)
TEL. 0731/62353

The Fiorini estate presented another fine set of wines this year. Some were from '99, others were selections from earlier vintages. Actually, quality levels are good throughout the entire range, following recent encouraging improvements. These are most evident in the reds, where the collaboration of oenologist Roberto Potentini with Carla Fiorini seems to have had a positive impact. Sant'Ilario '99 has an attractive, clear straw-yellow colour but its aromas are somewhat weak and the deficiencies of the vintage are revealed by its over-edgy and one-dimensional palate. The '99 Tenuta Campioli has yellow plum and citrus aromas. The palate strikes a good balance between body and fruit, and there is sufficient after-aroma to give an excellent finish. Sirio '98, a straightforward Sangiovese dei Colli Pesaresi, has fair breadth of aromas, mainly spicy, and a palate that, while not particularly challenging, is soft, super-clean and well-typed. To finish, there is the excellent Luigi Fiorini (dedicated to Carla's grandfather), from 100 percent Sangiovese aged in small barrels. A splendid vermilion colour and aromas of ripe berry fruit, mulberry and cherry, lead in to a palate whose tannins are still rather unbending but which has a fine layering of berry fruit and sweet spices, all set in a good balance of acidity and structure. It is an extremely elegant wine that reveals great finesse and a long, attractive finish.

Sergio Landi was a dedicated grape grower and a great believer in the winemaking potential of his area when he set up his estate in 1964. It extends over 11 hectares within the zones of Verdicchio dei Castelli di Jesi and Lacrima di Morro d'Alba, and is now in the hands of his grandson Luciano. The wines remain as consistent in quality and style as ever, particularly the standard Lacrima where the emphasis is placed on the aromas and above all on a tannic structure that is a little firmer than its predecessors. Apart from lacrima and verdicchio, Landi has montepulciano and sangiovese planted and the two are blended in equal measure to produce his Rosso Piceno Goliardo. The '99 vintage showed well with a good aroma of red berry fruit (raspberries, morello cherries), a structure that was balanced, although not overly incisive, but offered limited tannic weight. Better, however, is the Lacrima di Morro d'Alba Vecchi Sapori '99 which benefits from a short (four-day) maceration that gives full rein to the variety's joyous youthful aromas. The straight Lacrima '99 has more structure, as expected, but also slightly less intense perfumes, although the colour and concentration are impressive. To finish, Verdicchio dei Castelli di Jesi Classico '99 is well-typed and without pretension.

● Colli Pesaresi Rosso		
Luigi Fiorini '97	♟♟	4
○ Bianchello del Metauro		
Tenuta Campioli '99	♟	3
● Colli Pesaresi Rosso Sirio '98	♟	3
○ Bianchello del Metauro		
Vigna Sant'Ilario '99		2
● Colli Pesaresi Rosso Bartis '97	♟♟	4
○ Monsavium Passito	♟	4

● Lacrima di Morro d'Alba '99	♟	3
● Lacrima di Morro d'Alba		
Vecchi Sapori '99	♟	3
● Rosso Piceno Goliardo '99	♟	3
○ Verdicchio dei Castelli di Jesi		
Cl. '99		2
● Lacrima di Morro d'Alba '98	♟♟	3
● Saturno Passito '98	♟	4

CAMERANO (AN)

CASTEL DI LAMA (AP)

SILVANO STROLOGO
VIA OSIMANA, 89
60021 CAMERANO (AN)
TEL. 071/731104

TENUTA DE ANGELIS
VIA S. FRANCESCO, 10
63030 CASTEL DI LAMA (AP)
TEL. 0736/87429

When the chance came his way, Silvano Strogolo, partly out of self-respect and partly as a gamble, stopped turning out wine in demijohns to sell locally and started to work on producing Rosso Conero of quality. As a result, he has radically revamped the estate's cellar set-up in the past two years, equipping it with the best technology, and brought yields down in the vineyards. These epoch-making changes have brought us Julius and Traiano, two wines of which Strogolo and his oenologist Giancarlo Soverchia will doubtless be very proud. The former is a red, dense and dark purple in colour, with a fruity nose that proffers rich aromas of morello cherry and leather. On the palate, its texture is close-knit and succulent, while the flavours of cocoa and of plum and mulberry jams form a counterpoint to its cottonwool-soft tannins. Traiano, from a selection of montepulciano, has a deep, opaque violet colour. On the nose are the strong scents of morello cherry typical of the variety, as well as dried cherry and the elegant vanilla yielded by small barrels. The palate, redolent of stewed plums, dried violets and cloves, is expansive, magnificently structured and finds an attractive overall balance. The finish is long with an intense after-aroma. These two wines, both already drinking well, will doubtless improve further. It is not difficult to predict even greater success for this estate.

The De Angelis estate has excellent vineyards, situated in the heart of the Rosso Piceno Superiore production zone. The superior quality of the fruit is turned to good account by oenologist Roberto Potentini, and a fine example is provided by Anghelos, a blend of montepulciano, sangiovese and cabernet sauvignon, he has turned into the flagship wine of the estate. Vibrant ruby in colour, the '98 unveils an intense, lingering nose with scents of plum and black cherry, and an extra hint of spiciness from the oak in which it was aged. It is full and fairly mouth-filling on the palate, with ripe tannins and overall it is excellently made. The '97 Rosso Piceno Superiore is just as good. It is ruby red with a rich nose of red berry fruit, most notably cherry. The palate has just the right level of concentration. The tannins are still a little dominant but they are held in check by good structure. The final red to come under the microscope is Rosso Piceno '99. Intense ruby with a light purple rim, it offers fruit on the nose and an attractively easy-drinking palate. We also tasted two whites. Falerio dei Colli Ascolani '99 is a typical example of the style with floral perfumes, a fresh palate and a bitterish aftertaste. Prato Grande '99 is a 100 percent Chardonnay that has fairly intense, fruity aromas and appealing drinkability but is penalised by having too much spritz.

● Rosso Conero Julius '98	ΨΨ	3*
● Rosso Conero Traiano		
Sel. Strologo '98	ΨΨ	4

● Anghelos '98	ΨΨ	4
● Rosso Piceno Sup. '97	ΨΨ	3*
○ Falerio dei Colli Ascolani '99	Ψ	1*
○ Prato Grande Chardonnay '99	Ψ	1*
● Rosso Piceno '99	Ψ	1*
● Anghelos '97	ΨΨ	4

CASTELPLANIO (AN)

CINGOLI (MC)

FAZI BATTAGLIA
VIA ROMA, 117
60032 CASTELPLANIO (AN)
TEL. 0731/813444

TAVIGNANO
LUCANGELI AYMERICH DI LACONI
LOC. TAVIGNANO
62011 CINGOLI (MC)
TEL. 0733/617303

There was a good showing this year by Fazi Battaglia, the company that conceived the celebrated amphora-shaped bottle (sometimes called the "sex bottle" from its sinuous shape) which became the calling card of the Verdicchio zone. Wines come from 340 hectares distributed over 12 vineyards in several municipalities in the Castelli di Jesi area. The technical staff, comprising oenologist Dino Porfiri, agronomists Mario Ghergo and Antonio Verdolini, and consultant Franco Bernabei, continue to experiment. A newcomer to the Verdicchio line-up, an intriguing late-vintage wine, is shortly to emerge, perhaps as soon as next year. Among the already tried and tested Verdicchios are Titulus, the '99 showing as well as usual; the shrewdly selected Le Moie, a product of careful clonal research and endowed with greater breadth of expression; and the Riserva San Sisto '97, fermented and aged in small French oak barrels. The last of these, although still young, already has an aromatic complexity that ranges from tropical fruit to spice and toast. Arkezia Muffo di San Sisto, produced only in certain years when verdicchio is botrytis-affected and manages to develop noble rot, is an IGT that, in this latest release, is better than ever. The '99 Rosso Conero, with its excellent concentration and the purity of its plum and morello cherry tones, was a real surprise. The structured, soft '95 Riserva of Rosso Conero Passo del Lupo, aged with technical aplomb and marked out by the consistency of its nose and palate, also scored well.

The estate is situated at Tavignano near Cingoli and comprises around 230 hectares. Of these, 22 and a half are entirely given over to viticulture. Since taking on Giancarlo Soverchia, an oenologist who is known all over Italy, in 1992, the cellar has turned out a series of seriously interesting wines. As is to be expected in this area, the lion's share of the estate is planted to verdicchio, here at a density of around 3,000 plants per hectare. However, red varieties (mainly montepulciano and sangiovese but also lacrima di morro d'alba and cabernet sauvignon), reach a good 4,400 plants per hectare. As for the wines themselves, top of the list this year is the '99 Verdicchio dei Castelli di Jesi Misco. It is finely-tuned and has good weight on the palate. Sante Lancerio, a selection of verdicchio picked when extremely ripe (and released this year as a non-vintage), was a little disappointing. Although it has good structure, it lacks finesse and the less than perfectly clean aroma results in a lack of definition that carries through to the aftertaste. The Verdicchio Vigneti di Tavignano has also suffered from the rather poor vintage and is less expressive than usual. The rest of the range is as well-typed as ever, especially the Rosso Piceno Tavignano '99, which, although not especially elegant, has good fruit.

O	Arkezia Muffo di S. Sisto	YY	6
●	Rosso Conero '99	YY	3*
●	Rosso Conero Passo del Lupo Ris. '95	YY	5
O	Verdicchio dei Castelli di Jesi Cl. S. Sisto Ris. '97	YY	4
O	Verdicchio dei Castelli di Jesi Cl. Sup. Le Moie '99	Y	3
O	Verdicchio dei Castelli di Jesi Cl. Titulus '99	Y	3
O	Verdicchio dei Castelli di Jesi Fazi Battaglia Brut	Y	3
●	Rosso Conero Passo del Lupo Ris. '94	Y	5
●	Rutilus Marche Sangiovese '98	Y	3

●	Rosso Piceno Tavignano '99	Y	3*
O	Verdicchio dei Castelli di Jesi Cl. Sel. Misco '99	Y	3
O	Verdicchio dei Castelli di Jesi Cl. Sante Lancerio		4
O	Verdicchio dei Castelli di Jesi Cl. Sup. Tenuta di Tavignano '99		2
O	Verdicchio dei Castelli di Jesi Cl. Sel. Misco '98	YY	3
O	Verdicchio dei Castelli di Jesi Cl. Sup. Tenuta di Tavignano '98	YY	3

CIVITANOVA MARCHE (MC)   CUPRA MARITTIMA (AP)

BOCCADIGABBIA
C.DA CASTELLETTA, 56
62012 CIVITANOVA MARCHE (MC)
TEL. 0733/70728

OASI DEGLI ANGELI
C.DA SANT'EGIDIO, 50
63012 CUPRA MARITTIMA (AP)
TEL. 0735/778569

Founded in 1975 by Elvidio Alessandri, Boccadigabbia's real leaning is towards wines from French varieties and in fact cabernet sauvignon is the variety that oenologists Fabrizio Ciufoli and Giovanni Basso use to make the wine that has brought the estate international renown – Akronte. The '97, thanks to favourable weather that the gods only rarely concede, is quite simply fabulous. Its sheer intensity is obvious from your first glimpse of its opaque ruby hue while the nose is an explosion of aromas. Mulberry, varietal hints of red pepper, coffee and chocolate meld into tones that become ever more complex. On the palate, the first impression is of richly extracted tannins that combine with the alcohol in an eruption of power and sweetness. The finish has superlative elegance and great depth. And that's how you win Three Glasses. Girone '96, from pinot nero, is also very good. In the glass, its ruby hue shades into garnet. Vanilla leaps out on the nose with pepper and ginger hints underneath. Similar toasty, spicy notes also emerge from the characterful, elegant palate. Moving on to the whites, we tasted Montalperti '98, from barrique-aged chardonnay. It's a wine with abundant oak toastiness on both nose and palate. Then there was La Castelletta '99, a very drinkable Pinot Grigio with a floral nose. Garbì '99, a blend of chardonnay and trebbiano, was very fresh but a little lightweight. However, the estate also makes wine from indigenous grapes. Saltapicchio '97 has a good ruby colour and aromas of cherry and spices with a trace of Peruvian bark, as well as a palate of good concentration and complexity. Rosso Piceno Villamagna '98 offers aromas of red berry fruits that are echoed on a soft but substantial palate. Finally, the Rosso Piceno '98 is not dissimilar, just a little simpler and more fruity.

Just a year after first entering the Guide, Marco Casolanetti and Eleonora Rossi's small estate with four and a half hectares under vine has already embarked on some radical changes. There have been new plantings of montepulciano at 5-6,000 plants per hectare From the 2000 vintage, they will be concentrating on only one wine, Kurni, and they are well on the way to their longer-term goal of turning this into a great red with tip-top quality to bank on. It will be a just reward for all their painstaking efforts. With the help of oenologist Giovanni Basso, they have already shown themselves capable of producing characterful wines. Kurni, a monovarietal montepulciano from very low-yielding vines, is a wine of great complexity. It has a dark purple, almost black, colour and a viscosity that presages its imposing structure. The nose is full, deep and firm, the aromas of morello cherry and red fruit jam mingling with subtle undertones of tobacco, leather and sweet spices. The initial impression on the palate is of power, structure and opulence. The tannins, while still a touch forward, do not submerge the pervasive fleshiness of the fruit or the flavours of stewed plums, cherry and bitter chocolate. The finish is clean and very long. Overall, the wine is already drinking remarkably well but it will be at its best in a few years' time. It amply deserves its Three Glasses, as did the previous vintage. The other wine, Esedra, from trebbiano, is in its last year of production and was released solely in magnums, like some of the great French wines. Despite this, it does not rate more than One Glass. It remains unfiltered and is slightly cloudy; the aromas are warm and buttery, evoking vanilla and petit fours, but the palate has a touch too much oak. Its vanilla tones mask the structure and produce a one-dimensional taste that is over-generous with its alcohol.

● Akronte '97	♈♈♈	6
● Girone '96	♈♈	6
● Rosso Piceno '98	♈♈	3*
● Rosso Piceno Villamagna '98	♈♈	4
○ La Castelletta Pinot Grigio '99	♈	3*
○ Montalperti Marche Chardonnay '98	♈	5
● Saltapicchio Marche Sangiovese '97	♈	5
○ Garbì '99		3
● Akronte '93	♈♈♈	6
● Akronte '94	♈♈♈	6
● Akronte '95	♈♈♈	6
● Akronte '96	♈♈	6

● Kurni '98	♈♈♈	6
○ Esedra '98	♈	6
● Kurni '97	♈♈♈	6
○ Esedra '97	♈♈	6

CUPRAMONTANA (AN)

CUPRAMONTANA (AN)

VALLEROSA BONCI
VIA TORRE, 13
60034 CUPRAMONTANA (AN)
TEL. 0731/789129

COLONNARA VITICULTORI
IN CUPRAMONTANA
VIA MANDRIOLE, 6
60034 CUPRAMONTANA (AN)
TEL. 0731/780273

The estate has 35 hectares of vineyard situated in particularly good areas (at San Michele, Colonnara, Torre, Carpaneto, Alvareto and Pietrone) in the heart of the Verdicchio dei Castelli di Jesi DOC zone. Even in 1999, when rain and high humidity threatened the final stages of ripening, Giuseppe Bonci and his oenologist Sergio Paolucci came up with two good wines. San Michele has a bright straw-yellow colour, with highlights ranging from greenish to pale gold. The nose has decent depth, with notes of lime blossom and apple, and the stylish palate offers an attractive fruitiness that is well balanced by its fleshy structure. The faintly bitterish finish is one of the variety's hallmarks. Le Case is a Verdicchio that was part-aged in small barrels. Its lustrous straw-yellow hue is tinged with green and the well-defined fragrances of acacia blossom mingle with boisé notes. Reasonable structure and plenty of freshness ensure an appealingly drinkable palate. Barré is a barrique-fermented Riserva from '97. The colour is deep, while the nose yields scents of vanilla and elderflower with a hint of citrus. The full-bodied, muscular palate echoes the nose. The structure is decisive and the finish elegant. Rojano, a "passito", or dried-grape wine, with a warm golden colour, is splendidly rich in the mouth, evoking apricot, ripe yellow plum and hazelnut. Finally, the more than decent sparkling Verdicchio has fresh aromas of hedgerow, reasonable structure and a decidedly attractive price.

Founded in 1959, Colonnara groups around 200 small grape growers within the Verdicchio dei Castelli di Jesi production area. The winery works closely with consultants Cesare Ferrari and Corrado Cugnasco, both from Franciacorta, and verdicchio-based sparkling wine is one of its specialities. Particularly interesting and complex this year is the creamy Colonnara Metodo Classico, which show just how versatile the variety can be, while Colonnara Brut, a cuve close, is up to its usual high standards. Cuprese '99, is a verdicchio selection from vines situated in Cupramontana, Staffolo and Maiolati, and the symbol of the estate from the year dot. The '99 is possibly a little below par or, more to the point, within its usual parameters as far as the vintage will allow. Its aromas are fairly green, the palate medium-bodied with the beginnings of pleasant almondy tones. We also retasted several earlier vintages, which left no doubt as to the wine's ageing potential. The basic '99 Verdicchio, slightly vegetal and fresh-tasting, was also well-typed, and a '97 late-vintage Verdicchio, a newcomer to the range, particularly caught our attention, even though it was not ready in time for this edition of the Guide. Two reds bring this overview to a close. One is a good Tornamagno '96, made from sangiovese grosso, sangiovese montanino and montepulciano aged in French oak barrels, which is characterized by aromas of ripe red berry fruits, and the other is an honest, decently structured Rosso Piceno '97.

O Verdicchio dei Castelli di Jesi			
Cl. Passito Rojano '98	🍷🍷	5	
O Verdicchio dei Castelli di Jesi			
Cl. Sup. Barré Ris. '97	🍷🍷	5	
O Verdicchio dei Castelli di Jesi			
Cl. Sup. S. Michele '99	🍷🍷	4	
O Verdicchio dei Castelli di Jesi			
Cl. Sup. Le Case '99	🍷	4	
O Verdicchio Spumante Brut Bonci	🍷	3*	
O Verdicchio dei Castelli di Jesi			
Cl. Sup. S. Michele '96	🍷🍷🍷	4	
O Verdicchio dei Castelli di Jesi			
Cl. Sup. S. Michele '97	🍷🍷🍷	4	
O Verdicchio dei Castelli di Jesi			
Cl. Sup. Barré Ris. '96	🍷🍷	5	

● Tornamagno '96	🍷🍷	3*	
O Verdicchio dei Castelli di Jesi			
Colonnara Metodo Classico	🍷🍷	4	
● Rosso Piceno '97	🍷	2*	
O Verdicchio dei Castelli di Jesi			
Cl. Sup. Cuprese '99	🍷	3	
O Colonnara Brut	🍷	3	
O Verdicchio dei Castelli di Jesi			
Cl. '99	🍷	2*	
O Verdicchio dei Castelli di Jesi			
Cl. Cuprese Ris. '97	🍷🍷	4	
O Verdicchio dei Castelli di Jesi			
Cl. Sup. Cuprese '98	🍷🍷	3	
● Tornamagno '95	🍷	3	

514

FABRIANO (AN)

Enzo Mecella
Via Dante, 112
60044 Fabriano (AN)
Tel. 0732/21680

FANO (PS)

Claudio Morelli
V.le Romagna, 47/b
61032 Fano (PS)
Tel. 0721/823352

Mecella is an outstanding figure on the regional wine scene. As passionate as he is competent, he scrupulously follows his wines every step of the way. The care with which he selects the grapes and his consistent use of small barrels, despite the difficulties they pose when gauging the oak, are just two of the strong points that we have always appreciated. This quality-first philosophy has sometimes led to difficult decisions, such as not presenting his best wines at tastings until they are absolutely ready. Indeed this year there is no Braccano, no Rubelliano and no Casa Fosca in the Guide. They will await the next edition. However, older vintages of Rosso Conero Rubelliano – richly extracted, austere wines made over ten years ago – eloquently testify to Enzo's abilities. Best of the wines released more recently is without doubt Longobardo '98, from cabernet sauvignon. A garnet-tinged ruby in colour, it has aromas of ripe berry fruit and plum which are reflected in an attractive palate boasting a good base of alcohol and extract. The Verdicchio di Matelica Antico di Casa Fosca '99 selection is a little below its usual standard. There is a touch too much barrique on the nose while in the mouth, although fresh and with a reasonably complex framework, it finishes a little short. The lighter Verdicchio selection, Pagliano '99, showed well within its category. The straw colour leads in to a nose of golden delicious apples and boiled sweets, an enjoyable palate and a finish with verdicchio's typical almondiness.

Claudio Morelli's estate has long been recognized as one of the most consistently dependable in the province of Pesaro. It enjoys well-aspected vineyards, including some plots at Roncosambaccio, a particularly outstanding zone for viticulture. A good part of the estate's energies are concentrated on Bianchello, a wine that is certainly not monumental but which, as a young-drinking white, certainly has its place and is remarkably versatile at partnering foods. This year, the wines have, sadly, not shone, despite being correctly typed. Among the whites, the '99 San Cesareo is herbaceous and a little green, although better fruit comes over on La Vigna delle Terrazze because its acidity is more restrained. The Borgo Torre is sound as is the red Colli Pesaresi Sangiovese Sant'Andrea in Villis '98. The Suffragium '97 is very good, despite slightly restrained tannins, but Sangiovese La Vigna delle Terrazze '98 is disappointing because of a lack of definition on the nose. A retaste of the delightful, if slightly one-dimensional, sweet Solare '97 confirmed the favourable comments it received last year.

● Longobardo Rosso '98	♈♈	3*
○ Verdicchio di Matelica Antico di Casa Fosca '99	♈	3
○ Verdicchio di Matelica Pagliano '99	♈	1*
● Braccano '95	♈♈	4
● Braccano '97	♈♈	4
● Rosso Conero Rubelliano '97	♈♈	4

● Suffragium '97	♈♈	3*
○ Bianchello del Metauro Borgo Torre '99	♈	3
○ Bianchello del Metauro La Vigna delle Terrazze '99	♈	3
○ Bianchello del Metauro S. Cesareo '99	♈	2*
● Colli Pesaresi Sangiovese Sant'Andrea in Villis '98	♈	3
● Sangiovese La Vigna delle Terrazze '98		3
● Colli Pesaresi Sangiovese Sant'Andrea in Villis '97	♀	3
○ Solare Passito '97	♀	4

515

JESI (AN)

LORETO (AN)

MARIO E GIORGIO BRUNORI
V.LE DELLA VITTORIA, 103
60035 JESI (AN)
TEL. 0731/207213

GIOACCHINO GAROFOLI
VIA ARNO, 9
60025 LORETO (AN)
TEL. 071/7820163

Operative since 1956, Mario and Giorgio Brunori's estate has distinguished itself over the years for the excellent character of its Verdicchio dei Castelli di Jesi. The grapes that go into the whites come from vineyards in the San Paolo di Jesi territory, one of the best areas for the variety. This terroir has enabled the creation of the San Nicolò cru, only about 15,000 bottles of which are produced each year. It is a wine that is always elegant and long-lived, even though the '99 reflects the disappointing vintage. Its straw-yellow is tinged with youthful green highlights, and there are scents of spring flowers and almond to the fore on the nose. These aromas are echoed on the mid-weight palate, which has still to knit perfectly. It may need a little cellar time, but class will tell in the long run. The standard-label Verdicchio, with 35,000 bottles produced on average, is on the right lines. Straw-yellow in the glass, it has perfumes reminiscent of acacia blossom and wild herbs while the palate has a fresh swathe of acidity that gives it excellent drinkability. The range is completed by Lacrima di Morro d'Alba '99 (just over 3,000 bottles a year) which, as usual, combines aromas of violet and rose with a simple, direct flavour.

The estate run by Giampiero and Carlo Garofoli, sales director and oenologist respectively, is one of the oldest in the region. It also manages some of the best vineyards in the province of Ancona – vineyards whose superb grapes have been responsible for many award-winning wines. In addition, there is commendable consistency of quality and fair pricing across the range. The '99 Macrina does not betray any of the vintage's weaknesses while Le Rondini '99, from verdicchio, chardonnay and sauvignon, has delicate vegetal perfumes with floral hints on the nose and a very attractive, fresh, zesty palate. The Podium is as magnificent as ever and the '98 again walks away with Three Glasses. Its fairly rich straw-yellow is flecked with subtle hints of green and the nose reveals sensations of spring flowers, mineral tones, and rich, elegant hints of glycerol, with traces of botrytis. The palate is well-knit, full, powerful and very well balanced. The '97 Serra Fiorese, from a splendid vintage, is similarly complex. The hazelnut, almond and apple of the nose also come through on the palate, which has a tightly woven yet soft structure. There is also a hint of vanilla from the wood on the long and stunningly elegant finish. Kòmaros '99 is a rosato from montepulciano that combines freshness and drinkability. The only red presented by the estate this year was Rosso Conero Vigna Piancarda '98, with its typically fragrant aromas of morello cherry and a very fruity, really attractive palate. The '97 Agontano, the more serious Rosso Conero, was not ready when the panel visited. We'll discuss it next year. Finally the Brut Riserva, a classic method sparkling wine – a Garofoli speciality – showed excellently.

● Lacrima di Morro d'Alba '99	♀	2*	
○ Verdicchio dei Castelli di Jesi Cl. '99	♀	2*	
○ Verdicchio dei Castelli di Jesi Cl. S. Nicolò '99	♀	3	
○ Verdicchio dei Castelli di Jesi Cl. S. Nicolò '98	♀♀	3	

○ Verdicchio dei Castelli di Jesi Cl. Sup. Podium '98	♀♀♀	4	
○ Brut Riserva	♀♀	4	
○ Verdicchio dei Castelli di Jesi Cl. Serra Fiorese Ris. '97	♀♀	4	
○ Verdicchio dei Castelli di Jesi Cl. Sup. Macrina '99	♀♀	3*	
⊙ Kòmaros '99	♀	3	
○ Le Rondini '99	♀	3	
● Rosso Conero Vigna Piancarda '98	♀	3	
○ Verdicchio dei Castelli di Jesi Cl. Sup. Podium '97	♀♀♀	4	
○ Verdicchio dei Castelli di Jesi Cl. Sup. Podium '96	♀♀♀	4	

MAIOLATI SPONTINI (AN)

MONTESCHIAVO

VIA VIVAIO
FRAZ. MONTESCHIAVO
60030 MAIOLATI SPONTINI (AN)
TEL. 0731/700385 - 0731/700297

The plans of the Monteschiavo winery at Maiolati Spontini, run by Pierluigi Lorenzetti, are beginning to bear fruit and the range this year is probably the best ever. Certainly the Verdicchio dei Castelli di Jesi Palio di San Floriano is once more up there with the best in the denomination. The grapes are from the Fossato vineyard, at San Marcello, and were left to become slightly super-ripe. Some were aged in stainless steel, some in oak barrels. The resulting wine has depth and freshness, with good development potential. Coste del Molino, although a "minor" wine with respect to the Palio, has depth and personality as well as a tempting price and plentiful availability The base Verdicchio and the Colle del Sole are also very well-typed. The Bando di San Settimo '98, a Verdicchio of understated but complex expression, also performed very well, as did the '98 Riserva Le Giuncare, a richly perfumed wine with a well-knit palate. The Passito Arché, also from verdicchio, is a wine with just the right degree of sweetness. It was the Rosso Conero Conti Cortesi '98 that stood out among the reds, attractively marrying good fruit and softness on the palate. The Lacrima di Morro d'Alba is spot on, offering beautifully articulated flower and fruit perfumes, a lively colour and a full, captivating taste. The biggest red, though, is the Esio, a blend of montepulciano and cabernet in equal proportions. The '98, while still a little vegetal on the nose, has greater weight on the palate than the previous vintage and is nicely balanced.

●	Esio Rosso '98	🍷🍷	4
○	Verdicchio dei Castelli di Jesi Cl. Le Giuncare Ris. '98	🍷🍷	4
○	Verdicchio dei Castelli di Jesi Cl. Bando di S. Settimio '98	🍷🍷	3*
○	Verdicchio dei Castelli di Jesi Cl. Sup. Palio di S. Floriano '99	🍷🍷	2*
●	Lacrima di Morro d'Alba '99	🍷	3
●	Rosso Conero Conti Cortesi '98	🍷	3
○	Verdicchio dei Castelli di Jesi Cl. '99	🍷	2*
○	Verdicchio dei Castelli di Jesi Cl. Colle del Sole '99	🍷	3
○	Verdicchio dei Castelli di Jesi Cl. Coste del Molino '99	🍷	3

MATELICA (MC)

BELISARIO CANTINA SOCIALE DI MATELICA E CERRETO D'ESI

VIA MERLONI, 12
62024 MATELICA (MC)
TEL. 0737/787247

The Belisario co-operative co-ordinates and manages the production of a considerable number of the small growers in the small Verdicchio di Matelica denomination. Roberto Potentini, the director and oenologist, has managed to give his whites commendable consistency of quality, while ensuring each cru retains its own style. Hence, the Cambrugiano '97 is remarkably elegant, with aromas of wisteria, citrus fruits and sweet almond, and a long, balanced palate. The Vigneti Belisario '98 is also pretty powerful on the palate, thanks to the vintage, but has less freshness. Attractive drinkability, good typicity and good value are just some of the plus points of the Vigneti del Cerro '99, which is even more inviting thanks to a nice touch of residual sugar. The Verdicchio Ritratti '99 is floral on the nose but lacks weight and has a rather fierce swathe of acidity on the palate. The dry whites close with the Esino Ferrante '99: well-typed, straightforward and great for casual drinking. However, Belisario also produces a sweet, "passito" dried-grape wine from verdicchio, Carpe Diem. This year's release was the '96. Despite the sensations of stewed fruit and caramel on both nose and palate, the wine is held back by a preponderance of acidity. On the red front, the '97 Rosso San Leopardo has aromas of berry fruit and leather, as well as a reasonably stylish palate, and is definitely an improvement on previous versions. Then the Colferraio '99 is happily unpretentious, from its light ruby colour to its youthful fragrances, unprepossessing structure and fruit-rich flavour. Judgement on the '99 Verdicchio selection Belisario will have to wait for next year's Guide.

○	Verdicchio di Matelica Cambrugiano Ris. '97	🍷🍷	3*
○	Verdicchio di Matelica Vigneti Belisario '98	🍷🍷	3*
○	Verdicchio di Matelica Vigneti del Cerro '99	🍷🍷	3*
○	Esino Bianco Ferrante '99	🍷	1*
●	San Leopardo '97	🍷	3
○	Verdicchio di Matelica Ritratti '99	🍷	1*
●	Colferraio '99		1
○	Verdicchio di Matelica Passito Carpe Diem '96		4

MATELICA (MC)

MATELICA (MC)

LA MONACESCA
C.DA MONACESCA, 1
62024 MATELICA (MC)
TEL. 0733/812602

SAN BIAGIO
VIA S. BIAGIO, 32
62024 MATELICA (MC)
TEL. 0737/83997

Aldo Cifola, who runs this estate founded by his father, wanted to add a major red to his well-established range of fine whites and, with help from his oenologist Roberto Cipresso, that aim has now been realised. Camerte, named in honour of the ancient Marca Camerte territory which had Camerino as its main centre, comes from a 50-50 blend of sangiovese grosso and merlot, aged for around one year in barrique. Although the vines are just five years old, the wine has extreme elegance and class. It is superb on the nose, where raspberry, oak spiciness, toastiness, cedar of Lebanon and herbs all emerge, and remarkably well-balanced on the palate. In short, a major wine that drinks superbly. The rest of the range is a carbon copy of previous years and if an estate's quality can be measured by its ability to turn out good wines vintage after vintage, this must be one of Italy's best producers. Getting down to details, a retaste of Verdicchio di Matelica La Monacesca '98 (distinguishable from the base Verdicchio by the winery name on the label) confirmed that it is still fabulous, proving the panel were right to give it Two Glasses last year. Mirum, a non-oaked selection of 80 percent verdicchio, chardonnay and sauvignon, was also excellent. It has a somewhat shy nose where aniseed, hawthorn and thyme stand out, a palate of outstanding fullness and softness, and a rounded, almondy, very warm finish. The estate also produces a felicitous steel-vinified Chardonnay, the Ecclesia, but it was not ready in time for this year's Guide. Nor were the two '99 Verdicchios, the base version or the La Monacesca.

After a number of quiet years producing wines that were not at all bad but rather unexciting, San Biagio has finally earned a full Guide profile. Owned by Sabina Girotti, it lies at an average height of 460 metres above sea level and extends over 100 hectares, of which 16 are dedicated to vine at an average density of 4,500 plants per hectare. Apart from verdicchio di matelica, the varieties planted are ciliegiolo, merlot, sangiovese and cabernet sauvignon. The wines are looked after by agronomist Fabrizio Armanni and world-famous oenologist Riccardo Cotarella. San Biagio produces just one Verdicchio, a philosophy that goes against current tendencies but brings out the personality of the vintage. There are also two reds, the Bragnolo, from 60 percent ciliegiolo and sangiovese, aged for four months in barriques and six months in stainless steel, and the Grottagrifone, a Bordeaux-style blend, from 60 percent merlot and 40 percent cabernet sauvignon, which is aged for one year in barriques. The average annual production overall is around 50,000 bottles. Moving on to the tasting results, the '98 Verdicchio di Matelica Vigneto Braccano has clear varietal notes of hawthorn and bitter almond, good structure and none of the oxidation that bedevils many of the '98s. The Bragnolo '98 has attractive balanced fruit but the Grottagrifone '98 was the most convincing. Irresistibly classy, the nose combines fruit tones with oak-derived spiciness and an attractive grassy note while the palate is broad, brimming with fruit and delightfully drinkable.

● Camerte '98	▼▼	5
○ Mirum '98	▼▼	4
○ Mirum '94	♀♀♀	4
○ Mirus '91	♀♀♀	4
○ Verdicchio di Matelica		
La Monacesca '94	♀♀♀	4
○ Ecclesia Marche		
Chardonnay '98	♀♀	3
○ Mirum '95	♀♀	4
○ Mirum '97	♀♀	4
○ Verdicchio di Matelica		
La Monacesca '98	♀♀	3

● Grottagrifone '98	▼▼	5
● Bragnolo '98	▼	4
○ Verdicchio di Matelica		
Vigneto Braccano '98	▼	4

MONTECAROTTO (AN)

MONTEGRANARO (AP)

TERRE CORTESI MONCARO
VIA PIANDOLE, 7/A
60036 MONTECAROTTO (AN)
TEL. 0731/89245

RIO MAGGIO
C.DA VALLONE, 41
63014 MONTEGRANARO (AP)
TEL. 0734/889587

Not to beat about the bush, the Tordiruta '97 is one of the best ever verdicchio-based sweet wines. Its lustrous golden yellow ushers in a warmly scented nose with hints of tropical fruit but the astounding range of aromas goes from honey and peach through to vanilla to pineapple. It is equally magnificent on the palate, which has impressive richness, great sweetness and interminable length. There is perfect nose-palate harmony too. It is a pleasure to be able to start like this, rendering just tribute to a great vintage and a great wine that fully deserves its Three Glasses. It is also a great moment for this creditably quality-conscious co-operative, right in the heart of Verdicchio country, which puts such great efforts into this wine. Certainly, the rest of the range doesn't reach such giddy heights but the winemaking is even and correct throughout. ' This is particularly praiseworthy since around 4,500,000 units come off the bottling line every year. The Verdicchio Le Vele '99 is floral on the nose and lingers on the palate while the Verde di Ca' Ruptae '99 is herbaceous, a little low on acidity at first but then displays considerable length. The '97 Vigna Novali flaunts attractive balance and its mature aromas let you know that it is already drinking excellently. Moving on to the reds, the '98 Rosso Conero was a little disappointing but the '97 Riserva and the '97 Barocco were both more convincing. The last of these, obtained from barrique-aged montepulciano and cabernet sauvignon, is balanced and rich in fruit but offers little in the way of tannins, particularly considering its varietal make up.

Simone Santucci's estate is living proof that ideas and hard work can bring about a considerable improvement in quality in a very short time. Only a few years ago ,the estate was an also-ran but now, with the input of oenologist Giancarlo Soverchia, its wines are some of the region's most successful. The vineyards, all in good locations in the area around Montegranaro, contribute to that success. The estate cultivates both indigenous varieties (sangiovese, montepulciano and falerio) and international ones (chardonnay, sauvignon and pinot nero). Let's start with the whites. The Falerio is well-typed, as usual, while the '99 Artias Sauvignon is very elegant, although lacking the power of the '97. The Chardonnay also has good precision of style and is endowed with elegant floral notes, whereas the Rosso Piceno '99 is straightforward but attractively drinkable. Its pricing makes it even more of a good thing. Moving on to the top wines, the strong suit of the beautifully structured Artias Pinot Nero '98 is how well the oak integrates with the varietal tones of red berry fruit while GrAnarijS '98, a monovarietal montepulciano, is one of this year's top Marche reds. It has excellent concentration and a juicy fruit sweetness underpinned by notable alcoholic warmth. It is also way ahead of most of the competition for its beautifully-knit aromas – and that's in a year in which montepulciano often produced wines that were rather jammy on the nose. Our compliments for the whole range.

○	Verdicchio dei Castelli di Jesi Cl.		
	Passito Tordiruta '97	▼▼▼	6
○	Verdicchio dei Castelli di Jesi Cl.		
	Sup. Verde di Ca' Ruptae '99	▼▼	3*
●	Barocco '97	▼	4
●	Rosso Conero Terre Cortesi Ris. '97	▼	3
○	Verdicchio dei Castelli di Jesi Cl.		
	Le Vele '99	▼	3
○	Verdicchio dei Castelli di Jesi Cl.		
	Sup. Vigna Novali '97	▼	4
●	Rosso Conero '98		3
○	Verdicchio dei Castelli di Jesi '99		2

●	Artias Pinot Nero '98	▼▼	4
●	Rosso Piceno GrAnarijS '98	▼▼	4
○	Artias Chardonnay '99	▼	3
○	Artias Sauvignon '99	▼	3
○	Falerio dei Colli Ascolani '99	▼	1*
●	Rosso Piceno '99	▼	2*
●	Rosso Piceno GrAnarijS '97	♀♀	4

MONTEROBERTO (AN)   MORRO D'ALBA (AN)

POGGIO MONTALI
VIA FONTESTATE, 6
60030 MONTEROBERTO (AN)
TEL. 0731/702825

STEFANO MANCINELLI
VIA ROMA, 62
60030 MORRO D'ALBA (AN)
TEL. 0731/63021

For some years now, Carla Panicucci's estate has seemed on the point of achieving the quality necessary to win a full profile in the Guide. And finally here it is, thanks not only to a good all-round range but also to one wine that inspired a chorus of approval. That bottle is Rosso Conero Poggio al Cerro '98, an unexpected little gem of a wine. A vibrant ruby in colour, it reveals a nose with intensely pervasive notes of morello cherry over a broad range of other fruit aromas. On the rich, full-flavoured palate, there are plentiful ripe tannins and the long finish mirrors the aromas of the nose. The Rosso Conero Poggio Montali, another '98, doesn't live up to its cru. Its best feature is its typicity. The estate presented two whites, the Verdicchio dei Castelli di Jesi Classico Superiore '99 and the Fonte ai Frati '99, a blend of verdicchio and sauvignon. Of the two, we preferred the former, with its fresh, fruity palate and its pleasing drinkability. The second does not offer much more than good style. It has attractive notes of spring flowers and eucalyptus on the nose, though, and a palate with lively acidity. In conclusion, Poggio Montali's owner and its consultant oenologist Sergio Paolucci have laid down a good foundation of quality on which the estate should now be able to build.

If Lacrima di Morro d'Alba now has admirers all over the place, much of the credit belongs to the Mancinelli family, who believed in the potential of the variety when no-one else knew, or cared, about it. And this year Stefano, son of the estate's founder, Fabio, decided to flank the unfailingly headily perfumed and well-balanced standard version with a Lacrima that aspires to fine wine status. We were well pleased with the result, Terre dei Goti Rossi. It is a blend of Lacrima from part-raisined grapes and Lacrima given carbonic maceration, the wine then being aged in tonneaux (oak barrels containing a little more than two barriques). As one might expect, it has very intense, powerful fruit aromas enhanced by a discreet hint of wood. It is also a stunner on the palate – chewy, immensely muscular and with a high tannic impact unusual for a Lacrima. It then signs off with a faintly bitter finish. The '99 Rosso Piceno San Michele has its usual fruit and excellent concentration but there is a gamey undercurrent that detracts from its finesse, while the '99 Verdicchio is precise and well-balanced, though with no great power or length. The Terre dei Goti Bianco was rather unfocused at the time of tasting and only moderately interesting, while the more convincing Re Sole, a sweet wine, made yet again from lacrima, is powerful and full of morello cherry, raspberry and blackcurrant fruit.

● Rosso Conero		
Poggio al Cerro '98	🍷🍷	5
● Rosso Conero		
Poggio Montali '98	🍷	3
O Verdicchio dei Castelli di Jesi Cl.		
Sup. '99	🍷	3
O Fonte ai Frati '99		3

● Lacrima di Morro d'Alba		
S. Maria del Fiore '99	🍷🍷	3
● Terre dei Goti Rosso	🍷🍷	5
● Re Sole	🍷	5
● Rosso Piceno S. Michele '99	🍷	2*
O Verdicchio dei Castelli di Jesi		
Cl. '99	🍷	2*
O Terre dei Goti Bianco		3
● Lacrima di Morro d'Alba		
S. Maria del Fiore '97	🍷🍷	2
● Lacrima di Morro d'Alba '98	🍷	3
● Rosso Piceno S. Michele '98	🍷	2

MORRO D'ALBA (AN)

NUMANA (AN)

MAROTTI CAMPI
LOC. S. AMICO, 14
60030 MORRO D'ALBA (AN)
TEL. 0731/618027

CONTE LEOPARDI DITTAJUTI
VIA MARINA II, 26
60026 NUMANA (AN)
TEL. 071/7390116

The estate has around 125 hectares, of which 52 are planted with verdicchio, lacrima and sangiovese. The technologically advanced and well-equipped cellar is new and the consultant oenologist is Roberto Potentini. This set-up has not been slow to bring results for the wines are expressive and characterful, precisely reflecting both their terroir and the grapes that go into them. Salmariano shows good Verdicchio typing with its deep straw-yellow colour, interesting aromas of apple and elderflower, and an evocative, well-structured palate that echoes the nose's fruit tones. The Luzano has greater complexity on the nose, which unfurls intense notes of honey and tropical fruit, and is elegant and balanced on the palate. Orgiolo displays perfect lacrima typicity. The scarlet colour, the rose, violet and cherry aromas, the lightly tannic palate that is nevertheless sufficiently structured to give attractive drinkability are all true to type. The Laurito is a "vino da tavola" from a blend of lacrima and sangiovese. It has a fine, ruby-purple colour, a nose whose floral character reflects the presence of lacrima, a palate with assertive but not invasive tannins, and a beautifully clean finish. Total production of the four wines is currently only 40,000 bottles.

This estate belongs to Conte Piervittorio Leopardi and lies in delightful hilly country on the coast at Numana. The vineyards benefit from sea breezes as well as excellent locations. In 2000, control of winemaking was passed to Giancarlo Soverchia, the celebrated oenologist and expert in the regional wine scene. The estate's range of wines is as diverse as ever but two varieties predominate – sauvignon, a grape in which the estate clearly has great faith, and montepulciano, as you might expect in the Conero area. This year's wines are well up to the standards of the previous vintage. The Sauvignon Bianco del Coppo '99 has fairly good varietal character but loses out on finesse because of gamey nuances on the nose. The Sauvignon Calcare '99 has more balance and is better overall. The two Rosso Coneros, Fructus and Vigneti del Coppo, have remarkable concentration and, in the case of Vigneti del Coppo, good fruit, but suffer from tones of over-ripeness both on the nose, which has hints of jam, and on the palate. Pigmento '96, though, is a fine wine, evolved and complex on the nose, and with a chewy palate that gains thrust from subtle gamey nuances. It is one of the best Rosso Coneros of '96. There is also a sauvignon-based classic method sparkling wine.

O Verdicchio dei Castelli di Jesi Cl.		
Luzano '99	▼▼	2*
O Verdicchio dei Castelli di Jesi Cl.		
Salmariano '99	▼▼	3*
● Lacrima di Morro d'Alba		
Orgiolo '99	▼	3
● Laurito '99	▼	2

O Calcare Sauvignon '99	▼▼	3*
● Rosso Conero Pigmento '96	▼▼	4
O Bianco del Coppo Sauvignon '99	▼	3
● Rosso Conero Fructus '98	▼	3
● Rosso Conero		
Vigneti del Coppo '98	▼	3
O Villamarina Extra Brut '99	▼	4
● Rosso Conero Pigmento '95	♀♀	4
● Rosso Conero		
Vigneti del Coppo '97	♀	3

NUMANA (AN)

OFFAGNA (AN)

FATTORIA LE TERRAZZE
VIA MUSONE, 4
60026 NUMANA (AN)
TEL. 071/7390352

MALACARI
VIA ENRICO MALACARI, 6
60020 OFFAGNA (AN)
TEL. 071/7207606

You can only take your hat off to Antonio and Giorgina Terni, their oenologist, Attilio Pagli, and their agronomist, Leonardi Valentini. They have produced three fabulous wines that show montepulciano deserves to rub shoulders with the world's élite grape varieties. Let's start with the quite excellent base '98 Rosso Conero. It has a clean nose with cherry aromas and vegetal undertones while the palate reveals good structure and stylish flavours. Rosso Conero '98 Sassi Neri has a dark purple hue and there is breadth on the nose, which evokes morello cherry, sweet spices and leather. The palate is meaty and complex, with a full, rounded structure that melds seamlessly with mellow tannins and an after-aroma of jam. The elegant, whistle-clean tasting profile makes this a worthy Three Glass wine. Chaos, obtained from montepulciano, syrah and merlot, has an opaque purple colour, with well-defined "legs". Its has vanilla, white pepper, cocoa and ripe mulberry aromas, leading in to a palate notable for its elegantly soft tannins and its weighty mellowness. But the real star of the estate is Rosso Conero Visions of J, dedicated to Bob Dylan, of whom Antonio Terni is an enthusiastic fan of long standing. It gives the estate a second bite of the cherry as it sailed above the Three Glass threshold. Only 1,500 bottles are made but the wine, from 100 percent montepulciano, is simply extraordinary. It has a blue-tinged purple hue introducing a nose with a formidable array of aromas, including morello cherry, coffee, vanilla, cocoa and spices. The palate has a softness you want to snuggle into and the juicy, stylish palate is sheer elegance. Le Cave '99 has a good nose and a fresh, not particularly full, but pleasing palate.

The Malacari cellars, dating from 1668, lie on the edge of the mediaeval village of Offagna, in a splendid 18th-century villa. Alessandro Starrabba, assisted by oenologist Sergio Paolucci, produces Rosso Conero exclusively from montepulciano, on ten hectares of well-sited vineyard on the Baviera hillside and in south-facing locations at Grigiano. The grapes are collected in small cases, fermentation is carried out in stainless steel and ageing, lasting 12 to 18 months, takes place partly in barrique and partly in large, old oak "botti", or casks. The '97 Rosso Conero has a deep scarlet colour and aromas of violet, cherry and spice. The palate has nice structure, with evident but not intrusive tannins, a plum and mulberry jam flavour and good overall balance. The nose of the '98 Rosso Conero is still a little closed but some berry fruit aromas emerge, while the palate has well-judged tannins and an attractive, soft elegance. Grigiano is a selection of grapes from the territory of the same name. A long maceration and vigorous extraction give it an opaque appearance. There is vanilla and morello cherry on the nose, the palate is full and richly structured, and the elegant finish echoes the fruit notes of the nose.

● Rosso Conero Sassi Neri '98	▼▼▼	5
● Rosso Conero Visions of J '97	▼▼▼	6
● Chaos '98	▼▼	6
○ Le Cave Chardonnay '99	▼▼	3*
● Rosso Conero '98	▼▼	3*
● Chaos '97	♀♀♀	6
● Rosso Conero '97	♀♀	3
● Rosso Conero Sassi Neri '95	♀♀	5
● Rosso Conero Sassi Neri '96	♀♀	5
● Rosso Conero Sassi Neri '97	♀♀	5

● Rosso Conero Grigiano '98	▼▼	4
● Rosso Conero '97	▼	3
● Rosso Conero '98	▼	3

OFFIDA (AP)

OFFIDA (AP)

SAN GIOVANNI
C.DA CIAFONE, 41
63035 OFFIDA (AP)
TEL. 0736/889032

VILLA PIGNA
C.DA CIAFONE, 63
63035 OFFIDA (AP)
TEL. 0736/87525

Lying in Ciafone, one of the best zones in the province, this estate was founded in 1979 by Silvano Di Lorenzo and is now run by his son Giovanni. Assistance comes from the oenologist Narcisi and, since the '99 vintage, from consultant Attilio Pagli. There are 48 hectares in total, of which around 30 are under vine. The proportion of red grapes has been increased recently to allow efforts to be directed towards wines with greater concentration. For now, the reds are substantial and very drinkable. The best example is the '98 Rosso Piceno Superiore selection Rosso del Nonno, which this year is the estate's top wine. It has overt aromas of morello cherry and plum, and a soft palate. A notch below is the '98 Rosso Piceno Superiore Leo Guelfus selection, an elegant, very sippable wine with a good fruity attack but slightly less concentration. Other noteworthy wines from the Leo Guelfus line are the Rosato and, especially, the '99 Falerio, a wine with intense, rich aromas that are partially mirrored on the zesty, nicely poised, albeit not desperately long, palate. The Dulcis in Fundo '98 is good. This botrytized wine has considerable complexity and is probably better enjoyed as an unusual aperitif than at the end of a meal. The Rosso Piceno Superiore '98 is well-typed and well-priced and, finally, the standard-label '99 Falerio is a reliable product.

The Villa Pigna estate, currently with over 300 hectares of vine, is, and always has been, the largest grape producer in Ascoli Piceno, the province that grows over 50 percent of the region's grapes and boasts the largest number of cellars. Villa Pigna offers a wide range of wines, all made under the watchful eye of the young oenologist, Massimo Uriani. It is the reds that generally make most impact and this year, as in the past, the one that stands out is the Rozzano. When we tasted it, the '98 still had an oaky patina but its rich underlying aromas of berry fruits, leather and spice still came trickling through. The palate has good concentration but moderate power. It was also interesting to retaste the '97, which is now more evolved and complete. The '97 Briccaio Vellutato, a montepulciano selection, has slipped a notch, more from a certain leanness on the palate than its nose. However, it remains more substantial than the base '98 Vellutato. Both Rosso Piceno Superiores tasted, the standard version and the Vergaio, were from '97. The premium wine was predictably the more interesting of the pair but even so was a little undemonstrative. As for the whites, the current range includes Colle Malerbi '99, a Chardonnay that is well-typed despite the difficult vintage. The Falerio Pliniano '99 is understandably more structured and has a more interesting nose than the base version. The Rugiasco is a very approachable blend of chardonnay and riesling, and to round off there is the Villa Pigna Brut, a chardonnay-based cuve close sparkler.

● Rosso Piceno Sup.		
Rosso del Nonno '98	♥♥	4
○ Dulcis in Fundo '98	♥	4
○ Falerio dei Colli Ascolani		
Leo Guelfus '99	♥	3
● Rosso Piceno Sup. '98	♥	2*
● Rosso Piceno Sup.		
Leo Guelfus '98	♥	3
○ Falerio dei Colli Ascolani '99		1
☉ Leo Guelfus Rosato '99		1
● Rosso Piceno Sup.		
Leo Guelfus '97	♀	3

● Rozzano '98	♥♥	5
● Briccaio Vellutato '97	♥	3
○ Colle Malerbi '99	♥	3
○ Falerio dei Colli Ascolani		
Pliniano '99	♥	3
● Rosso Piceno Sup. '97	♥	2*
● Rosso Piceno Sup. Vergaio '97	♥	3
○ Rugiasco '99	♥	3
● Vellutato '98	♥	2
○ Falerio dei Colli Ascolani '99		2
○ Villa Pigna Brut		3
● Cabernasco '97	♀♀	5
● Rozzano '97	♀♀	5

OSIMO (AN)

OSTRA VETERE (AN)

UMANI RONCHI
S.S. 16, KM. 310+400, 74
60027 OSIMO (AN)
TEL. 071/7108019

F.LLI BUCCI
VIA CONA, 30
60010 OSTRA VETERE (AN)
TEL. 071/964179 - 02/6570558

Umani Ronchi owns 50 hectares of vineyard in Rosso Conero and 100 in the Castelli di Jesi area, plus a further 40 hectares that are rented. Chardonnay, sauvignon, cabernet sauvignon and merlot grow alongside the dominant verdicchio and montepulciano. The estate is well-known and has had numerous successes in Great Britain, notably with Pelago. This year Umani Ronchi led the field in our tastings too, obtaining Three Glasses for the first time. But the wine is the '99 Casal di Serra, a selection of the region's most traditional white, Verdicchio dei Castelli di Jesi. It is extremely elegant, flaunting a rich yellow hue with golden highlights. The nose has a wealth of fruit nuances, with camomile to the fore. The palate leaves no room for doubt. It is wonderfully poised and stylish, ending in a long, well-sustained finish. Of the other whites, the '97 Verdicchio Riserva Plenio has a delightful fruit-oak balance, a complete absence of any aggressiveness, and good ageing potential. The Le Busche '98, from verdicchio and chardonnay, and the Verdicchio Villa Bianchi '99 are both also very good, while the Bianchello del Metauro '99 is well-typed. The Maximo '97 is excellent and must be one of the best botrytized wines in Italy. The '97 Pelago has less fruity sweetness than the previous vintage. The Rosso Conero San Lorenzo '97 has spice, fruit and tobacco aromas, a concentrated, rich palate and scored almost as highly as the other '97 Rosso Conero selection, Cùmaro. The Montepulciano d'Abruzzo Jorio '98 has a well-textured palate while Medoro '98, from sangiovese, and the estate's new wine, the Lacrima di Morro d'Alba '99 Fonte del Re, both warrant One Glass.

Regular readers of the Guide will know that the Bucci estate doesn't give two hoots for fashion. Independent and qualitatively ahead of the field, it turns out instantly recognizable, very individual wines that will last and evolve over many years. Moreover, Ampelio Bucci is never in a hurry to put his wines on the market. There are 18 hectares of vineyard, 15 of which grow verdicchio. Red grapes – mainly sangiovese and montepulciano – are planted on the remainder. The Verdicchio comes from five vineyards with various aspects at altitudes ranging from 200 to 350 metres above sea level and the grapes from each are vinified separately before blending. Our review starts with a second look at the '95 Riserva di Verdicchio dei Castelli di Jesi Villa Bucci, a white of great elegance and inimitable style, and particularly noteworthy for its longevity and maturity. The new vintage of Villa Bucci, the '97, promises well although it still seems very young, with fresh aromas of hazelnut and camomile, and a low-key acid-alcohol balance. The base Verdicchio dei Castelli di Jesi '98 is less complex but has considerable structure and good varietal character to give it a very drinkable personality. The last wine on the list is the Rosso Piceno Tenuta Pongelli '97, first reviewed last year, which has retained its soft, easy-drinking character.

○ Verdicchio dei Castelli di Jesi		
Cl. Sup. Casal di Serra '99	▼▼▼	3*
○ Le Busche '98	▼▼	4
● Montepulciano d'Abruzzo Jorio '98	▼▼	3*
● Pelago '97	▼▼	6
● Rosso Conero Cùmaro '97	▼▼	5
● Rosso Conero S. Lorenzo '97	▼▼	4
○ Verdicchio dei Castelli di Jesi		
Cl. Plenio Ris. '97	▼▼	4
○ Verdicchio dei Castelli di Jesi		
Cl. Villa Bianchi '99	▼▼	3*
○ Bianchello del Metauro '99	▼	2*
● Lacrima di Morro d'Alba		
Fonte del Re '99	▼	4
● Medoro Sangiovese '98	▼	3

○ Verdicchio dei Castelli di Jesi		
Cl. '98	▼▼	3*
○ Verdicchio dei Castelli di Jesi		
Cl. Villa Bucci Ris. '97	▼▼	5
○ Verdicchio dei Castelli di Jesi		
Cl. Villa Bucci '92	♀♀	4
○ Verdicchio dei Castelli di Jesi		
Cl. Villa Bucci '94	♀♀	4
○ Verdicchio dei Castelli di Jesi		
Cl. Villa Bucci Ris. '95	♀♀	5
● Rosso Piceno Tenuta Pongelli '97	♀	3

PESARO

POGGIO S. MARCELLO (AN)

FATTORIA MANCINI
S.DA DEI COLLI, 35
61100 PESARO
TEL. 0721/51828

SARTARELLI
VIA COSTE DEL MULINO, 24
60030 POGGIO S. MARCELLO (AN)
TEL. 0731/89732 - 0731/89571

At times, the distinction between indigenous and non-native varieties can get very fuzzy at the edges. "Foreign" usually means a variety that has been in circulation for just a few years, often grown with the aim of aping French styles or following an international prototype that shamelessly foregrounds fruit or, even worse, oak. Things are different at Luigi Mancini's Fattoria Mancini. True, he grows pinot nero, a magnificent variety that is most at home in Burgundy, but it has been knocking around Fattoria Mancini for a good 200 years. The clone is so unique and impressive that it has attracted scrutiny by Professor Attilio Scienza, one of the top Italian wine academics. Monovarietal pinot noir gives a fine wine, Impero Rosso, and an unusual white, Impero Bianco. All the estate's wines, though, are worthy of attention this year. The Colli Pesaresi Roncaglia, a blend based on albanella with pinot nero vinified off the skins, stands out for its sweet, wide-ranging palate and balanced fruit. A similar blend, but with the addition of a small proportion of sauvignon, gives Valserpe '98. We first tasted it last year and we are happy to report it has retained its agreeable apricot fruit and soft, full palate. The Impero Bianco '98 is very good, or even excellent. Its lustrous yellow is slightly tinged with pink, ushering in an exemplary fruit-oak balance on a nose resplendent in berry fruit – the pinot nero hallmark. The reds include an attractive '99 Sangiovese, a Montebacchino '98, from 100 percent montepulciano, and the Focara '98, all of which are good. If the '97 Impero, the estate's leading wine, was no more than "good", let down by weakish structure, the '98 was entirely convincing.

Sartarelli's new oenologist, Alberto Mazzoni, is continuing the quality-driven strategy of the estate both in vineyards and cellar. Careful selection means grapes are harvested when rich in sugar and extract, to give Verdicchios whose alcohol content and dry extract match those of fine reds. The base Verdicchio '99 is an extremely well-made wine. It has fruit and flower aromas and a palate with a nice balance of structure, fresh acidity and concentration. The '99 Tralivio is a splendid wine, despite the disappointing vintage. It offers a clear straw yellow colour and a broad range of aromas, notably lime blossom, wistaria and quince. The palate, as usual, has great concentration and a good balance of freshness and breadth, with an almondy finish. Contrada Balciana '98 has the characteristically fruit-rich personality of a wine from a hot year and a late harvest (it went on until the end of October). The style differs a little from previous vintages. The colour is a rich golden yellow, ushering a nose that is initially shy and then opens out to release generous aromas of notes of ripe apple, acacia blossom, thyme, candied citron and musk. The palate has immense power – it has more than 14 percent alcohol – but you'd hardly notice, thanks to a richly extracted texture with just enough residual sugar to provide balance and support the hazelnut and almond finish. Yet again, it takes its place among Italy's top whites and thoroughly deserves its Three Glasses.

○ Impero Bianco '98	🍷🍷	5
● Impero Rosso '98	🍷🍷	4
● Colli Pesaresi Focara '98	🍷	3
○ Colli Pesaresi Roncaglia '99	🍷	2*
● Montebacchino '98	🍷	3
● Sangiovese '99	🍷	2
● Impero Rosso '97	🍷🍷	4
○ Valserpe '98	🍷🍷	3

○ Verdicchio dei Castelli di Jesi Cl. Sup. Contrada Balciana '98	🍷🍷🍷	4
○ Verdicchio dei Castelli di Jesi Cl. Sup. Tralivio '99	🍷🍷	3*
○ Verdicchio dei Castelli di Jesi Cl. '99	🍷	2*
○ Verdicchio dei Castelli di Jesi Cl. Sup. Contrada Balciana '94	🍷🍷🍷	5
○ Verdicchio dei Castelli di Jesi Cl. Sup. Contrada Balciana '95	🍷🍷🍷	5
○ Verdicchio dei Castelli di Jesi Cl. Sup. Contrada Balciana '97	🍷🍷🍷	5
○ Verdicchio dei Castelli di Jesi Cl. Sup. Tralivio '98	🍷🍷	3

525

RIPATRANSONE (AP)

TENUTA COCCI GRIFONI
C.DA MESSIERI, 12
FRAZ. S. SAVINO
63030 RIPATRANSONE (AP)
TEL. 0735/90143

RIPATRANSONE (AP)

LA CANTINA DEI COLLI RIPANI
C.DA TOSCIANO, 28
63038 RIPATRANSONE (AP)
TEL. 0735/9505

If there were a prize for safeguarding wine typicity, Guido Cocci Grifoni would be a prime candidate. Since 1969, he has undertaken innumerable trials and experiments on indigenous varieties. Once he was happy with the reds, he turned his attentions to lesser varieties, such as pecorino and passerina, to further critical acclaim. At this point, his enthusiasms renewed, he released Grifone '97, a Rosso Piceno Superiore that marks a turning point for the estate. Instead of the traditional large, old casks, the wine was aged in barriques. And it has immediately become the marker for the entire range. It has a dark ruby appearance, yields intense aromas of cherry and red berry fruits, and is vigorous in the mouth, with balanced levels of alcohol and structure. The '98 Vigna Messieri cru being absent, although a retaste of the '97 confirmed last year's positive impressions, traditional Rosso Piceno was represented by the Le Torri '97. This is a fair, mid-range wine adhering perfectly to the characteristics of the denomination. First of the whites is the Passerina Brut, a tank method sparkling wine made from passerina, which is as stylish as ever. The '99 vintage of Podere Colle Vecchio, made from pecorino, is a little below par because of over-assertive acidity but the Vigneti San Basso Falerio selection showed well, offering good structure on the palate and elegant floral aromas that make it one of the denomination's best.

It is always a pleasure to be able to list a good co-operative cellar, especially when its entire range is convincing and offers commendable value for money. So it is with La Cantina di Colli Ripani, based at Ripatransone, a mere hop from the sea despite its 494 metre altitude. Up here, the conditions for growing grapes are exceptional. Founded in 1969, the co-operative first made wine in 1977 when it had 150 members. Now it has 510, who together own 1,000 hectares of under vine, planted with practically all the most important varieties of the region, including verdicchio, pecorino, trebbiano, montepulciano, sangiovese, cabernet sauvignon and others. The wines, made under the aegis of consultant Fabrizio Ciufoli, are, therefore, many and varied. Those tasted this year included the Falerio Brezzolino '99, which has generous floral perfumes and a good, well-balanced palate, as well as an excellent Rosso Piceno Riserva Castellano '96 which, though from a so-so vintage, is now drinking better than most Rosso Picenos. The '97 version of the flagship red, Rosso Piceno Superiore Leo Ripanus, obtained from montepulciano and sangiovese with a small amount of cabernet sauvignon, stands out from the crowd. Oak and fruit knit perfectly on the nose, and support a rich, full and already delicious palate that nevertheless makes no secret of its excellent ageing potential. This bottle outclassed wines costing three times as much and must be one of the best-value wines anywhere in Italy.

● Rosso Piceno Sup. Il Grifone '97	▼▼	5
○ Falerio dei Colli Ascolani Vigneti S. Basso '99	▼	3
○ Podere Colle Vecchio '99	▼	4
● Rosso Piceno Le Torri '97	▼	3
○ Passerina Brut		3
○ Podere Colle Vecchio '98	♀♀	4
● Rosso Piceno Sup. Vigna Messieri '95	♀♀	4
● Rosso Piceno Sup. Vigna Messieri '97	♀♀	4
● Rosso Piceno Sup. Vigna Messieri '96	♀	4

● Rosso Piceno Castellano Ris. '96	▼▼	3*
● Rosso Piceno Sup. Leo Ripanus '97	▼▼	3*
○ Falerio dei Colli Ascolani Brezzolino '99	▼	2*

RIPATRANSONE (AP)

LE CANIETTE

C.DA CANALI, 23
63038 RIPATRANSONE (AP)
TEL. 0735/9200

The is the third year that this estate run by Giovanni and Luigi Vagnoni has appeared in the Guide as well as its best ever. That can only be due to the tenacity and competence of its two owners, who never tire of analysing, questioning, experimenting and investing. Let's start with Falerio Veronica '99, which has floral aromas and a palate that has notable structure and staying power, together with a clean finish. The other Falerio selection, the Lucrezia '99, is less convincing on the nose as its aromas are a little indistinct but it makes up for this on the attractively fresh, zesty palate. Indeed, despite '99 being a poorish year, the standard of the wines is more than gratifying. The '98 vintage tended to favour sangiovese and montepulciano-based wines. The '98 Rosso Piceno Rosso Bello has a lustrous ruby colour, aromas of cherry and Peruvian bark on the nose, and a palate with good structure, richness and complexity. The Rosso Piceno Morellone '98 comes from an even more stringent selection of fruit. It can't fail to impress from the first glance at its dark, almost opaque ruby colour. The admirable ripeness of the grapes is initially signalled by the rich, cherry aromas. These are then echoed on an opulent, alcohol-rich and very leisurely palate. And to finish, we find ourselves once more heaping praise on the modern version of Vin Santo di Ripatransone, a wine whose ancient traditions are perpetuated by the estate. Amber in the glass, it has a nose of stewed fruit mixed with just the right degree of oxidation and a palate packed with robust alcohol and perfectly poised sweetness and acidity.

●	Rosso Piceno Morellone '98	🍷🍷	4
●	Rosso Piceno Rosso Bello '98	🍷🍷	3*
○	Vin Santo di Ripatransone Sibilla Delphica	🍷🍷	4
○	Falerio dei Colli Ascolani Lucrezia '99	🍷	2*
○	Falerio dei Colli Ascolani Veronica '99	🍷	2*

S. PAOLO DI JESI (AN)

AMATO CECI

VIA BATTINEBBIA, 4
60038 S. PAOLO DI JESI (AN)
TEL. 0731/779052

In operation since 1960, this estate totals 9 and a half hectares of vineyard, part owned and part leased. Verdicchio, sangiovese, montepulciano and other varieties are grown, mainly on medium-textured, clay-rich soils. Over the years, vinification techniques have been refined, thanks to the efforts of Maurizio Ceci and his oenologist Paolucci. Now, the wines are well-typed and steadily improving in quality. The Verdicchio is exemplary and absolutely typical. It has a lovely straw-yellow colour tinged with green while the nose offers aromas of lime blossom and elderflower that shade into minerally notes. The palate, very full and zesty even in a poor vintage like '99, is firmly structured with a nice acid-alcohol balance. The finish, with its lightly bitter tone, adds a final touch of typicity. The Vignamato is the more robust of the '99s, particularly on the palate, whereas the Valle delle Lame has a more elegant nose. The Vignamato Rosso has an attractive ruby colour and fairly distinct berry fruit aromas leading in to a well-structured palate with substantial tannins and a attractively complementary acidity. The Verdicchio Passito is good too. Its nose is honeyed, with aromas of dried fig and thyme, while the palate is broad, if a little one-dimensional.

○	Verdicchio dei Castelli di Jesi Cl. Sup. Vignamato '99	🍷🍷	2*
○	Verdicchio dei Castelli di Jesi Cl. Valle delle Lame '99	🍷🍷	1*
○	Verdicchio dei Castelli di Jesi Cl. Passito Antares '98	🍷	4
●	Rosso Piceno Vignamato '98	🍷	2

SERRA DE' CONTI (AN)   SERRAPETRONA (MC)

CASALFARNETO
VIA FARNETO, 16
60030 SERRA DE' CONTI (AN)
TEL. 0731/889001

ALBERTO QUACQUARINI
VIA COLLI, 1
62020 SERRAPETRONA (MC)
TEL. 0733/908180

This promising young estate had to face a vine-grower's worst enemy in 1999 – hail. It destroyed part of the crop, preventing the owners from being able to select the fruit as they would have liked but there were enough grapes left from their 20 plus hectares to salvage the vintage. In addition, the year has seen the release of two new wines from Danilo Salustri and Massimo Arcangeli's stable, a fine white, the Cimaio '97, and a red, the Fiorile '99. The latter has a ruby colour and youthful, strawberry aromas. A fresh wine that follows through splendidly from nose to palate, it reveals an attractive vein of acidity that lends it drinkability. The least serious of the whites is the Fontevecchia '99. Straw yellow in the glass, it has a nose that makes little impact as the aromas fail to open out but there are hints of apple and almond. The palate, though, has good structure and is nicely zesty with a typical Verdicchio finish. The '99 selection Gran Casale has clean perfumes but less body than the previous vintage. Fresh, fruity and well extracted, it has the faintly bitter finish typical of the variety. But let's go back to that barrique-aged, verdicchio-based Cimaio '97. Straw yellow with golden highlights, it offers a nose with intense aromas of ripe fruit and vanilla, a full-bodied palate with good backbone, and nice nose-palate consistency.

Vernaccia di Serrapetrona comes from high-altitude vineyards with an extreme climate. Yet the wines disappoint. We have long wanted to see a complete shake-up in the area and renewed stimulus to produce wines worthy of the denomination's celebrated status. But year after year, even the best wines, whether dry or semi-sweet, from a range of wineries have left us having to pray for a greater investment of time and effort in winemaking techniques and management expertise. But finally, this estate, directed by Mauro, Luca and Alberto Quacquarini, with Roberto Potentini contributing his oenological wisdom, is taking a serious look at the wine. Beside the two classic Vernaccia di Serrapetrona Spumante styles, Secco and Amabile, both of which are well-managed – we tasted the '98s as the '99s had not yet been released – there are now three new, more serious wines. Petronio '98 is a monovarietal Vernaccia. Obtained from semi-dried grapes with a slightly lower concentration of sugars than for the sparkler, it undergoes a fairly long maceration and ferments to dryness. It showed very well, with rich perfumes of ripe berry fruit and a satisfying, multi-layered taste. This really is a new look for Vernaccia. We will review the two others, from blends of sangiovese, merlot, cabernet and ciliegiolo, next year.

○ Cimaio '97	▼▼	4
● Fiorile '99	▼	2*
○ Verdicchio dei Castelli di Jesi Cl. Sup. Fontevecchia '99	▼	2*
○ Verdicchio dei Castelli di Jesi Cl. Sup. Gran Casale '99	▼	3
○ Verdicchio dei Castelli di Jesi Cl. Sup. Gran Casale '98	♀♀	3

● Petronio '98	▼▼	5
● Vernaccia di Serrapetrona Amabile '98	▼	4
● Vernaccia di Serrapetrona Secco '98	▼	4

SERVIGLIANO (AP)

FATTORIA DEZI
C.DA FONTE MAGGIO, 14
63029 SERVIGLIANO (AP)
TEL. 0734/750408

SPINETOLI (AP)

SALADINI PILASTRI
VIA SALADINI, 5
63030 SPINETOLI (AP)
TEL. 0736/899534

Stefano Dezi has made a brilliant debut with high-scoring wines that mark out this Piceno estate for notice. Stefano, a real enthusiast, is both traditionalist and innovator as far as denominations are concerned. In fact, Servigliano lies just outside the Superiore part of the Rosso Piceno zone yet both the '97 and the – slightly better – '98 of Dezi's Rosso Piceno Regina del Bosco distinguish the wine as one of the most interesting in the whole region. The '98 is a dark, deep colour, with a nose of ripe berry fruit aromas. It is full and powerful on the palate and a little more elegant on the nose than its predecessor. A third red, the Dezio '99, from sangiovese and montepulciano, is more up-front, as is the Falerio Le Solagne '99, a tastily correct version of the denomination style. But it is with his other white, Le Solagne '99, from late-vintage verdicchio, pecorino and malvasia (all Falerio-denomination varieties but used here in different proportions), that Dezi obtains a truly unique, fascinating wine to give superb fine expression to this central Italian terroir. A vibrant yellow in colour, it has intense perfumes of fruit and herbs, and a vigorous, satisfying palate. The estate's 30 hectares of vineyard are on south-facing, clay-sand soils at around 240 metres. Yields are kept low and the grapes from each area are vinified separately. Such practices bode well for this promising, quality-driven winery.

The wines from this estate are released as two separate lines. The Saladini Pilastri label retains the name and title of the old winery and the results of the more modern approach, introduced by agreement with consultant Roberto Cipresso, form the new Conte Saladino range. Quality is improving throughout, partly thanks to the commitment and painstaking effort of oenologist Domenico D'Angelo. The Saladini Pilastri range now boasts a new Rosso Piceno Superiore, the Vigna Montetinello '97. Conceived with an eye to tradition and aged in 100-hectolitre Slavonian oak casks, it has very good typicity. The aglianico and montepulciano blend of the Pregio del Conte Rosso '98 is intriguing and very successful, as is the 80 percent fiano and falanghina mix for the Pregio del Conte Bianco '99. The latter has lovely citrus aromas and a structured but soft palate. The '99 Falerio Vigna Palazzi, despite the vagaries of the vintage, is once more up there with the denomination's best. From the Conte Saladino range, we started with a second look at the '98 Vigna Piediprato Rosso Piceno selection. It unveils a deep, dark colour, intense aromas and a concentrated, elegant palate. The Rosso Piceno '98 is more immediately drinkable while the Rosso Piceno Superiore Vigna Monteprandone '98 stands out as one of the best wines in the Marche. It has concentrated, complex aromas, where spicy, tobacco tones meld with notes of plum, redcurrant and morello cherry fruit. The palate is full and soft, with notable weight and balance. A benchmark for the denomination.

○ Le Solagne V. T. '99	♥♥	4
● Rosso Piceno Regina del Bosco '97	♥♥	4
● Rosso Piceno Regina del Bosco '98	♥♥	4
● Dezio '99	♥	2
○ Falerio dei Colli Ascolani Le Solagne '99	♥	2

○ Pregio del Conte Bianco Saladini Pilastri '99	♥♥	2*
● Pregio del Conte Rosso Saladini Pilastri '98	♥♥	3*
● Rosso Piceno Sup. Vigna Monteprandone Conte Saladino '98	♥♥	4
○ Falerio dei Colli Ascolani Vigna Palazzi Saladini Pilastri '99	♥	1*
● Rosso Piceno Vigna Piediprato Conte Saladino '98	♥	2*
● Rosso Piceno Sup. Vigna Montetinello Saladini Pilastri '97	♥	3
● Rosso Piceno Sup. Vigna Monteprandone Conte Saladino '97	♥♥	4

STAFFOLO (AN)

FATTORIA CORONCINO
C.DA CORONCINO, 7
60039 STAFFOLO (AN)
TEL. 0731/779494

This estate has roughly seven hectares of vineyard and is run by Lucio Canestrari and his wife Fiorella. For years, it has been known for exemplary consistency of quality and the wines released in 2000 are as well made as ever, both opulent and fresh at the same time. The Gaiospino '98, from super-ripe grapes with a yield of 60 quintals per hectare from the Spescia vineyard, was partially (around 30 percent) fermented in 500-litre oak casks. It has a straw-yellow colour tinged with greenish-gold and the distinct "legs" on the glass hint at its remarkable structure. The nose is full and deep, with hints of quince, pineapple and vanilla, then the palate explodes in a meaty richness. Yellow plum and ripe citrus meld with fresh nuances of cakes. The structure is powerful and the finish is long, intense and elegant. The Bacco '99 is the estate's standard Verdicchio but that doesn't mean it's a minor wine. It has pronounced typicity, both in appearance and in its characteristic flower and herb perfumes, which integrate well with its freshness. The palate is firmly textured and zesty, with fruity overtones, and finishes clean. Staffilo, a more basic Verdicchio, is excellently made. It is maybe a little less captivating in aroma but has remarkable structure. The robust 13.5 percent alcohol content simply fades into the roundness of the close-knit extract. The finish has the variety's characteristic bitterish tang. The '99 whites, the Le Lame and Il Coroncino, will be reviewed next year as they were not bottled in time for our tastings. In any event the estate's philosophy tends to favour late release, when the wines are beginning to drink at their peak.

○	Verdicchio dei Castelli di Jesi Cl. Sup. Bacco '99	▼▼	2*
○	Verdicchio dei Castelli di Jesi Cl. Sup. Gaiospino '98	▼▼	4
○	Verdicchio dei Castelli di Jesi Cl. Staffilo '99	▼	1*
○	Verdicchio dei Castelli di Jesi Cl. Sup. Gaiospino '97	▽▽▽	4
○	Verdicchio dei Castelli di Jesi Cl. Sup. Il Coroncino '98	▽▽	3
○	Le Lame '98	▽	3

STAFFOLO (AN)

FONTE DELLA LUNA
MEDORO CIMARELLI
VIA S. FRANCESCO, 1
60039 STAFFOLO (AN)
TEL. 0731/779307

The wines of Fonte della Luna continue to make steady progress. A series of building projects has resulted in an enlarged, better organized and more efficient cellar. In addition, new, higher density plantings have paved the way for the emergence of finer wines, which are not all verdicchio-based. Indeed, only a few decades ago Staffolo was known more for its red wines so it is not unreasonable for the estate to concentrate on improving the montepulciano that makes its already very fine Rosso Piceno Grizio. The exceptional work in vineyard and cellar carried out by Luca Cimarelli and his oenologist, Giancarlo Soverchia, meant that the '99 Verdicchios avoided most of the problems posed by the vintage. The base Verdicchio, Fonte della Luna, has an attractively lustrous straw-yellow colour, aromas of citrus, hazelnut and apricot, and a sinewy, zesty, structured palate with good fruit and elegance. Fra Moriale is a Verdicchio selection with good typicity. The colour is a vibrant straw yellow highlighted with green and its the lively perfumes are reminiscent of dried flowers and quince. It has considerable body but avoids overshadowing the overall elegance of the palate, which ends on a note of almond. The '99 Grizio, the estate's Rosso Piceno, was not bottled in time for our tastings so we'll come back to it next year.

○	Verdicchio dei Castelli di Jesi Cl. Fonte della Luna '99	▼▼	2*
○	Verdicchio dei Castelli di Jesi Cl. Fra Moriale '99	▼▼	3*
●	Rosso Piceno Grizio '98	▽▽	3
○	Verdicchio dei Castelli di Jesi Cl. Fra Moriale '98	▽▽	3

OTHER WINERIES

The following producers obtained good scores in our tastings with one or more of their wines:

PROVINCE OF ANCONA

Serenelli, Ancona, tel. 071/31343
Rosso Conero '98

Mancini,
Maiolati Spontini, tel. 0731/702975
Verdicchio dei Castelli di Jesi Cl.
Santa Lucia '99

Laurentina, Montecarotto, tel. 0731/89435
Verdicchio dei Castelli di Jesi Cl.
Il Vigneto di Tobia '99

Donatella Paoloni,
Montecarotto, tel. 0731/889004
Verdicchio dei Castelli di Jesi Cl.
Sabbionare '99

San Lorenzo,
Montecarotto, tel. 0731/89656
Verdicchio dei Castelli di Jesi Cl.
Vigneto delle Oche '98

Lucchetti, Morro d'Alba, tel 0731/63314
Lacrima di Morro d'Alba '99

Saltamartini,
Morro d'Alba, tel. 0731/63019
Lacrima di Morro d'Alba Antica Cantina
S. Amico '99

Spinsanti, Osimo, tel. 071/7819885
Camars '99

Marconi, S. Marcello, tel. 0731/267223
Verdicchio dei Castelli di Jesi Cl.
Corona Reale '99

Angelo Accadia,
Serra S. Quirico, tel 0731/85172
Verdicchio dei Castelli di Jesi Cl.
Cantorì '99

La Staffa, Staffolo, tel. 0731/779430
Verdicchio dei Castelli di Jesi Cl. Sup.
La Rincrocca '98

Zaccagnini
Staffolo, tel. 0731/779892
Verdicchio dei Castelli di Jesi Cl.
Salmàgina '99

PROVINCE OF ASCOLI PICENO

Cantina di Castignano,
Castignano, tel. 0736/822216
Gramelot '99

Carminucci,
Grottammare, tel. 0735/735869
Chardonnay Naumachos '99

Aurora, Offida, tel. 0736/810007
Rosso Piceno Sup. Barricadiero '98

Ciù Ciù, Offida, tel. 0736/810001
Rosso Piceno Sup. '98

PROVINCE OF MACERATA

Antonio Canestrari, Apiro, tel. 0733/611315
Verdicchio dei Castelli di Jesi Cl. Lapiro '99

Colle Stefano,
Castelraimondo, tel. 0737/640439
Verdicchio di Matelica Colle Stefano '99

Saputi, Colmurano, tel. 0733/508137
Colli Maceratesi Bianco Castru Vecchiu '99

Bisci, Matelica, tel. 0737/787490
Verdicchio di Matelica Vigneto Fogliano '98

Gino Gagliardi, Matelica, tel. 0737/85611
Pianero '98

Tenuta Montepulischio,
Matelica, tel. 0737/84503
Nearco '98

Azzoni Avogadro,
Montefano, tel. 0733/850002
Rosso Piceno '98

Capinera, Morrovalle, tel. 0733/222444
Chardonnay La Capinera '99

Lanfranco Quacquarini,
Serrapetrona, tel. 0733/908103
Vernaccia di Serrapetrona Secco '99

PROVINCE OF PESARO

Fattoria Villa Ligi, Pergola, tel. 0721/734351
Vernaculum Grifoleto '99

Solazzi, Saltara, tel. 0721/895491
Bianchello del Metauro Villa Romana '99

UMBRIA

Umbrian winemaking has had a landmark year and the Guide has naturally noted the developments. The number of estates submitting wines increased by ten percent and a good six wines gained Three Glasses awards, the region's best result so far. It doesn't take a soothsayer to foretell that, with the progress Umbria's dynamic producers are making, the number just has to rise further. And this is a region that only five or six years ago was accused of being stuck in a time warp. The criticism stung and the producers reacted swiftly and as one. The result is that today their wines are among Italy's best. Similarly, only a few years ago no more than a couple of names from the entire region were held in regard internationally. Today, respect and esteem are coming from around the globe. Here, then, are the prize-winning wines. First on the list is Cervaro della Sala, a wine that even the '98 vintage could not diminish and which remains one of the most starry and consistent of all Italy's whites. It has structure, finesse and elegance, and will mature happily for years in the bottle. The Orvieto area is home to a further two fabulous wines. There is Armaleo, a marvellous red from Palazzone that, while not new to the scene, found an intensity and an ease of expression with the '98 that sets it up among the greats. Then there is Fobiano from Carraia, a Merlot with a small percentage of cabernet sauvignon grapes. Its concentration and soft elegance quite astounded us, and it proves beyond doubt that Orvieto can easily produce reds every bit as fine as its whites. Montefalco is an up-and-coming area gaining world-wide renown and it blasted us with two stunning '97 Sagrantinos, one from Còlpetrone and the other, already famous, from the volcanic Marco Caprai. The fact that these are all repeat performances only goes to underline the consistency of the progress made throughout the zone, a progress that appears unstoppable. Indeed, the top ranks have been swollen by a newcomer, an international style red wine from merlot and pinot nero, from Sportoletti in Assisi. There is also much jostling for position just below the Three Glasses level and we are sure that the next few years will see the arrival of even better wines than those we are applauding today. Moreover, if we had to bet on which area will be the next to take off we would stake our money on the Lake Trasimeno zone where there is a wholesale upgrading of vineyards and cellars in progress, under the supervision of some of the sector's best. One last point. For some years, the important Torgiano winery Lungarotti, a name of major standing on the Umbrian wine scene, seemed to be resting on its laurels. There is now a new consultant oenologist in place and we reckon it is only a matter of time before the estate finds the right formula to express its great potential to the full.

AMELIA (TR)

BASCHI (TR)

CANTINA SOCIALE DEI COLLI AMERINI
LOC. FORNOLE
STRADA AMERINA KM 7.100
05020 AMELIA (TR)
TEL. 0744/989721

BARBERANI - VALLESANTA
LOC. CERRETO
05023 BASCHI (TR)
TEL. 0744/950113 - 0763/341820

Overall, the Cantina Sociale di Colli Amerini's range is as good as usual, even though the group of incredible value for money whites that made this co-operative a talking point seems to be getting progressively slimmer. If we exclude the One Glass for Chardonnay dell'Umbria Amiro '99, there was little else to enthuse us. What's happened to the character and personality of Malvasia La Corte, for example? Where are the freshness and the fruit in the Grechettos? With the reds, however, there is no letdown, just great quality and year-on-year consistency. Colli Amerini Rosso Superiore Carbio '98 gains Two Glasses. It is deep ruby, aromatic, with nose-palate balance, power and personality. The Merlot dell'Umbria Olmeto '98, stylish and full on the nose, rich in redcurrant and plum on the palate with hints of tobacco and coffee, is of similar quality and, moreover, excellent value for money. Colli Amerini Rosso Terre Arnolfe is an attractive, easy-drinking wine with fresh, fruity aromas. Aleatico dell'Umbria Bartolomeo '98, with its aromas of jam and black fruits in syrup, and its sweet but not cloying taste, makes an attractive dessert wine to go with biscuits or cakes. Sangiovese dell'Umbria Torraccio '98 was, however, below par. It had power, structure and virility but a rather indistinct nose. Moscato dell'Umbria Donna Olimpia '99 and Malvasia dei Colli Amerini La Corte '99 are both worthy of mention.

In the absence of Orvieto Classico Superiore Calcaia, it falls to Lago di Corbara '98 Foresco to hold aloft the image of this estate, which is situated in one of Umbria's prettiest spots. After several vintages that left a little to be desired, the '98 Foresco comes right up to the level of the other great reds in the region. It impresses right from the first glance at its very deep ruby hue with bright highlights. The nose has an array of intense aromas, revealing berry fruit, spices, touches of wood and vegetal hints. The palate has good tannic weave and is penetrating, powerful, elegant and harmonious. It gains Two Glasses with ease and gives the distinct impression that future vintages will be even better. The '99 Orvieto Classico Superiore Castagnolo, a white of notable freshness, elegance and balance, also performed well. The marked personality of the Grechetto dell'Umbria came through again on the '99 which was bright in hue with ripe, floral, very clean perfumes and a zesty, intense palate imbued with alcoholic warmth. The oak-aged Moscato Passito Villa Monticelli '98, first tasted last year, remains of interest. Even though its components are not perfectly integrated, overall it is very attractive.

●	Colli Am. Rosso Sup. Carbio '98	❦❦	4
●	Merlot dell'Umbria Olmeto '98	❦❦	3*
●	Aleatico dell'Umbria Bartolomeo '98	❦	4
O	Chardonnay dell'Umbria Amiro '99	❦	2*
●	Colli Am. Rosso Terre Arnolfe '99	❦	2*
●	Sangiovese dell'Umbria Torraccio '98	❦	3
O	Colli Am. Malvasia La Corte '99		2
O	Colli Am. Moscato Donna Olimpia '99		2
●	Colli Am. Rosso Sup. Carbio '94	❦❦	3*
●	Colli Am. Rosso Sup. Carbio '95	❦❦	3*
●	Colli Am. Rosso Sup. Carbio '96	❦❦	4
●	Colli Am. Rosso Sup. Carbio '97	❦❦	4
●	Merlot dell'Umbria Olmeto '97	❦❦	3*

●	Lago di Corbara Foresco '98	❦❦	5
O	Orvieto Cl. Castagnolo '99	❦❦	4
O	Grechetto '99	❦	4
●	Foresco '93	❦❦	4
O	Moscato Passito Villa Monticelli '97	❦❦	6
O	Orvieto Cl. Sup. Calcaia '92	❦❦	5
O	Orvieto Cl. Sup. Calcaia '93	❦❦	5
O	Orvieto Cl. Sup. Calcaia '94	❦❦	5
O	Orvieto Cl. Sup. Calcaia '95	❦❦	5
O	Orvieto Cl. Sup. Calcaia '97	❦❦	5
●	Foresco '95	❦	4
●	Foresco '96	❦	4
●	Foresco '97	❦	4
O	Moscato Passito Villa Monticelli '98	❦	6

BEVAGNA (PG)

F.LLI ADANTI
LOC. ARQUATA
06031 BEVAGNA (PG)
TEL. 0742/360295

Adanti returned to the Guide last year and the quality of the wines remains good this time round. The estate lies in the hilly territory of Arquata and Colcimino at Bevagna and has around 25 hectares of vineyard. There is a wide range of varieties grown, from the international merlot, cabernet and chardonnay to the indigenous sagrantino and grechetto. They even grow some barbera and sangiovese. Mauro Monicchi, the young oenologist in charge, has turned out a successful range of wines, especially with the reds. These are led by the excellent Arquata Rosso '97, from cabernets sauvignon and franc, merlot and barbera. Deep ruby red in colour, it offers an intense nose with rich berry fruit aromas underscored by hints of prune and red pepper. The palate is fruity with elegant, firm tannins. Nispero '98, in its first year of production, also showed well. It is a sangiovese, cabernet sauvignon and barbera-based red of good aromatic intensity, with decent structure and a fairly long finish. The wines from Montefalco are, as ever, well-typed. The Rosso '98 is intense and clean on the nose with flavours redolent of plum and sweet spices. The Sagrantino '98 is soft and warm while the fine Sagrantino di Montefalco Passito '96, fat, weighty and richly extracted, almost reached a Two Glass score.

BEVAGNA (PG)

FATTORIA MILZIADE ANTANO
LOC. COLLE ALLODOLE
06031 BEVAGNA (PG)
TEL. 0742/360371

The continued presence of Milziade Antano's estate in the Guide is a quiet certainty. Once more, the wines are up to expectations and those presented to the panel were of considerable interest. All were red. The two '98 Rosso di Montefalcos come from sangiovese and sagrantino. The basic version is a purple-ruby colour. The nose is intense, persistent and rich in tones of very ripe fruit, mainly plum and morello cherry, while the palate is lightly tannic and shows good complexity. The Riserva, with its extremely lively nose, gains Two Glasses. Well-fruited and complex, it give a first impression of great cleanliness, then flavours of cooked plum and sweet spices follow. There are three Sagrantino di Montefalcos, all from '97. The basic version has a good purple-ruby colour. Its full, complex nose reveals scents of very ripe, plum and morello cherry fruit and spicy tones of black pepper. The powerful, concentrated palate also offers very ripe fruit as well as well-balanced tannins. The Colle delle Allodole selection is excellent, too. It has a deep purple-ruby colour, a nose that is stylish and well-fruited with aromas of bilberry and redcurrant, and a full, penetrating palate with well-judged tannin levels and notable length. The Passito is full, clean and open on the nose, where there is plenty of very ripe fruit, especially prunes. The palate is lightly tannic, with good elegance and complexity.

● Rosso dell'Umbria Arquata '97	▼▼	5
● Nispero Rosso '98	▼	3
● Rosso di Montefalco '98	▼	3
● Sagrantino di Montefalco '96	▼	5
● Sagrantino di Montefalco		
Passito '96	▼	5
● Rosso dell'Umbria Arquata '91	♀♀	4
● Rosso di Montefalco '91	♀	2*
● Sagrantino di Montefalco '90	♀	3
● Sagrantino di Montefalco		
Passito '89	♀	4

● Rosso di Montefalco Ris. '98	▼▼	4
● Sagrantino di Montefalco '97	▼▼	5
● Sagrantino di Montefalco		
Colle delle Allodole '97	▼▼	5
● Rosso di Montefalco '98	▼	3
● Sagrantino di Montefalco		
Passito '97	▼	5
● Rosso di Montefalco '97	♀♀	3*
● Rosso di Montefalco Ris. '97	♀♀	3*
● Sagrantino di Montefalco '95	♀♀	5
● Sagrantino di Montefalco		
Passito '94	♀♀	5
● Sagrantino di Montefalco		
Passito '96	♀♀	5
● Sagrantino di Montefalco '96	♀	5

CANNARA (PG)

CASTEL VISCARDO (TR)

DI FILIPPO
VIA CONVERSINO, 160/A
06033 CANNARA (PG)
TEL. 0742/731242

CANTINA MONRUBIO
FRAZ. MONTERUBIAGLIO
LOC. LE PRESE, 22
05014 CASTEL VISCARDO (TR)
TEL. 0763/626064

The De Filippo winery, situated in hill country halfway between Torgiano and Montefalco, first appeared in the Guide last year. It has a broad range of varieties planted, including grechetto, sagrantino, barbera, sangiovese, montepulciano, cannaiolo, trebbiano and the now essential so-called "international" grapes, cabernet and merlot. The wines presented were of considerable interest, especially the reds. Madrigale '98 showed best of all. From merlot, montepulciano and sangiovese, it has a dark purple-red colour, an intense, powerful nose, and a powerful, cherry and ripe plum fruitiness on the palate, which also vaunts fine-grained tannins. Terre di San Nicola '97, from merlot, montepulciano and barbera, is excellent, too. First impressions on the nose reveal an intense, ripely fruited character, with overt aromas of redcurrant. The palate has good body and is soft, fresh and well supported by its tannins. Colli Martani Sangiovese Properzio '97 and Villa Conversino '99 are both well-typed and easy drinking. The former, ruby red, is full of wild cherry notes on the nose while the palate is intense and long. The young Conversino is livelier, with notable acidic freshness on the palate and a lightly tannic finish. Grechetto Terre di San Nicola '99, fruity and with good complexity on the palate, showed well too.

Among the region's co-operative wineries, that of Monrubio di Castel Viscardo has to be one of the most dynamic and most interesting. Founded in 1957, with the aim of turning the then discredited Orvieto zone into a respectable place to make wine, it currently vinifies the grapes of around 300 member growers. It has benefited from the consultancy of Riccardo Cotarella for several years now and this year it once again has a range of excellent quality wines. The list is led by Palaia '98, a red from merlot, pinot nero and cabernet sauvignon that has a dark purple-red colour. The nose is powerful and intense, with aromas of wild berries and redcurrant. The palate is full and complex, with flavours of red berry fruits and sweet spices. Monrubio '99, with its intense tones of very ripe fruit on both nose and palate, remains an absorbing wine. The various selections of grapes made for the Orvietos resulted in each one having its own, individual style and gave the impression of being the work of a skilled hand. Roio '99 is fresh with fruity tones of white peach and damson. Sanceto '99 is fragrant and easy drinking, if maybe a touch acidic on the finish. Macchia del Pozzo '99 is floral and has subtle hints of apple. However, the Orvieto Classico Superiore Opinioni '98, the result of a joint venture with the Cardeto and Carraia estates, easily carried off Two Glasses. It is straw-yellow in colour and the nose is abundantly floral with attractive undertones of oak while the palate is full, complex, open and clean, and has a carefully judged dose of wood.

● Madrigale '96	🍷🍷	4		○ Oriveto Cl. Sup. Opinioni '98	🍷🍷	3*
● Terre di S. Nicola Rosso '97	🍷🍷	3*		● Palaia '98	🍷🍷	5
○ Colli Martani Grechetto				● Monrubio '99	🍷	2*
Terre di S. Nicola '99	🍷	2*		○ Orvieto Classico Roio '99	🍷	2*
● Colli Martani Sangiovese				○ Orvieto Classico Salceto '99	🍷	2*
Properzio '97	🍷	3		○ Orvieto Macchia del Pozzo '99	🍷	1*
● Villa Conversino Rosso '99	🍷	1*		● Monrubio '98	🍷🍷	2*
● Madrigale '96	🍷🍷	4		○ Orvieto Classico Roio '97	🍷	1*
○ Colli Martani Grechetto				○ Orvieto Classico Roio '98	🍷	2*
Terre di S. Nicola '98	🍷	2*		○ Orvieto Classico Salceto '97	🍷	2*
● Colli Martani Sangiovese				○ Orvieto Classico Salceto '98	🍷	2*
Properzio '97	🍷	3		○ Orvieto Classico Sup. Fiorile '97	🍷	3
● Terre di S. Nicola Rosso '96	🍷	3		○ Orvieto Classico Sup. Soana '98	🍷	2*
● Villa Conversino Rosso '98	🍷	1*		● Palaia '97	🍷	3

CASTIGLIONE DEL LAGO (PG) CITTÀ DELLA PIEVE (PG)

FANINI
C.DA CUCCHI
LOC. PETRIGNANO DEL LAGO
06060 CASTIGLIONE DEL LAGO (PG)
TEL. 075/9528116

DUCA DELLA CORGNA
VIA PO' DI MEZZO
06064 CITTÀ DELLA PIEVE (PG)
TEL. 075/9653210

For years, Dino Fanini has been vinifying his grapes, which come from about 12 hectares of vineyard sited on the hills surrounding Lake Trasimeno, using the most modern of techniques while retaining full respect for tradition. And the fine quality of the wines means that the estate continues to be a Guide regular. The Chardonnay Robbiano is always excellent and this year it is the '98 and '99 that come under the microscope. The '98, sadly no longer available at the estate, has a deep, warm, straw-yellow hue. The nose is intense, powerful and complex, dominated by clean-cut scents of apple and by more delicate hints of spring flowers. The palate is full, with good acidity and excellently judged wood. The '99, although not fully ready at the time of our tastings, has a straw-yellow colour with bright highlights. The nose is clean and open, with the oak still fairly evident. The palate is complex and rich, with inviting flavours of banana, white peach and apricot. Albello del Lago '99, Colli del Trasimeno Bianco, is also good: fresh and fruity on the nose, crisp and fragrant on the palate. Although Morello del Lago has impressed us more in the past, the '97 was still well-typed and its fresh berry fruitiness and great drinkability made it worthy of One Glass.

This consistent co-operative, making wines in the Colli del Trasimeno DOC zone, has consolidated its presence in the Guide this year. Our tastings of the Duca della Corgna line confirmed a slow but constant increase in the quality of the wines, their aromatic definition and their extractive weight. The range comes from a selection of the best grapes from the winery's member growers, vinified by the Cantina del Trasimeno oenologist, Andrea Mazzoni, whose input results in wines of great personality and typicity. Flagship of the winery remains the Colli del Trasimeno Rosso Corniolo. The '98 has excellent structure with complex, elegant, highly nuanced perfumes and a palate of impressive intensity. Red berry fruit, mulberry, bitter chocolate, spices and liquorice are all discernible. The Gamay del Trasimeno Divini Villa '99 is also very good. Its colour is a deep, bright ruby with purple highlights and the spice-tinged nose is decidedly fruity. The palate is intense and full-bodied, with attractive tones of pepper and tobacco. The Grechetto Nuricante '99 is a new wine. It has a good straw-yellow colour, inviting floral, fruity perfumes, and a palate of good structure, reasonable complexity and decent length.

O	Chardonnay Robbiano '98	♟♟ 3*	●	Colli del Trasimeno Rosso		
O	Chardonnay Robbiano '99	♟♟ 3*		Corniolo '98	♟♟	4
O	Colli del Trasimeno Bianco		●	Colli del Trasimeno Gamay		
	Albello del Lago '99	♟ 2*		Divina Villa '99	♟	3
●	Colli del Trasimeno Rosso		O	Colli del Trasimeno Grechetto '99	♟	2*
	Morello del Lago '97	♟ 3	●	Colli del Trasimeno Rosso		
O	Chardonnay Robbiano '96	♟♟ 3*		Corniolo '97	♟♟	3*
O	Chardonnay Robbiano '97	♟♟ 3*	●	Gamay dell'Umbria '97	♟	3
●	Colli del Trasimeno Rosso					
	Morello del Lago '95	♟♟ 3*				
●	Colli del Trasimeno Rosso					
	Morello del Lago '96	♟ 3				
O	Colli del Trasimeno Bianco					
	Albello del Lago '98	2				

CORCIANO (PG)

Pieve del Vescovo
Via G. Leopardi, 82
06073 Corciano (PG)
tel. 075/6978874

It is evident, at least to us, that Pieve del Vescovo is one of the best estates in Colli del Trasimeno. The transfer of the estate from the Tinarelli family to its new owners, the young American industrialists, Joseph Mannello and Frederich Contini, has resulted in no change of direction. The friendly, entrepreneurial Jolanda Tinarelli still runs the estate and the technical side remains in the hands of Riccardo Cotarella. The pair are working with alacrity to renew the vineyards and thus improve grape quality to give the estate the opportunity of gaining a more competitive edge over the next few years. The leading wine is Lucciaio, a Colli del Trasimeno Rosso aged for around one year in barrique. The '98 has had its usual merlot, ciliegiolo, canaiolo and gamay blend souped up with a sizeable proportion of cabernet sauvignon in place of some of the merlot. It has a good deep ruby colour and the nose is redolent of berry fruits with elegant overtones of wood, vanilla and spices. The palate is complex, elegant and soft. Colli del Trasimeno Rosso '99 has a ruby colour with purple tinges and is fruity on the nose. The fresh, fruity, soft palate is deliciously drinkable. Etesiaco, a fresh, zesty well-structured Colli del Trasimeno white also retains its One Glass. One last note. The basic Colli del Trasimeno has gone out of production.

● Colli del Trasimeno Rosso Lucciaio '98	🍷🍷	4
○ Colli del Trasimeno Bianco Etesiaco '99	🍷	3
● Colli del Trasimeno Rosso '99	🍷	2*
○ Colli del Trasimeno Bianco Etesiaco '94	♀♀	2*
● Colli del Trasimeno Rosso Lucciaio '94	♀♀	3*
● Colli del Trasimeno Rosso Lucciaio '95	♀♀	3*
● Colli del Trasimeno Rosso Lucciaio '96	♀♀	4
● Colli del Trasimeno Rosso Lucciaio '97	♀♀	4

FICULLE (TR)

★ Castello della Sala
Loc. Sala
05016 Ficulle (TR)
tel. 0763/86051

It is difficult to describe Castello della Sala, now one of the most important Italian wine concerns, in just a few words. Owned by Marchesi Antinori, it is situated in the northern part of the Orvieto zone and for over a decade it has been producing wines that to call technically perfect would be putting it mildly. Cervaro della Sala, the barrique-aged Chardonnay that is the estate's emblem, notched up its tenth Three Glass award with the '98 vintage. No other Italian white can boast such a performance. So, even if it is not the best Italian white wine in absolute terms, at the very least it has to be the most reliable and consistent of the country's top band. Which is no small matter. This year's prize-winner, the '98, is less powerful than the '97 or the '94. It has intensely fruited perfumes and its vanilla overtones are only just discernible, as are its mineral hints, although these will become more marked with bottle maturation. The palate is full, balanced, concentrated, very elegant and very refined. But Cervaro della Sala was not the only exciting wine presented this year for the Chardonnay della Sala '99 is a sort of scaled down Cervaro. Muffato della Sala '98 is less dense and sweet than the '97 but has more complexity of aroma and is much more drinkable. The '97 Pinot Nero Vigneto Consola is one of the best editions ever. Soft and nicely varietal, it lacks the vagueness on the nose that previous vintages have at times shown. Sauvignon della Sala '99 is an aromatic, attractive white. It may not have remarkably full body but it is a joy to drink. Clearly, the Castello della Sala estate is not just Cervaro della Sala. It is also clear that it remains a bastion of the Italian wine elite.

○ Cervaro della Sala '98	🍷🍷🍷	6
○ Chardonnay della Sala '99	🍷🍷	3*
○ Muffato della Sala '98	🍷🍷	5
● Pinot Nero Vigneto Consola '97	🍷🍷	5
○ Sauvignon della Sala '99	🍷	3
○ Cervaro della Sala '88	♀♀♀	5
○ Cervaro della Sala '89	♀♀♀	5
○ Cervaro della Sala '90	♀♀♀	5
○ Cervaro della Sala '92	♀♀♀	5
○ Cervaro della Sala '93	♀♀♀	5
○ Cervaro della Sala '94	♀♀♀	5
○ Cervaro della Sala '95	♀♀♀	5
○ Cervaro della Sala '96	♀♀♀	5
○ Cervaro della Sala '97	♀♀♀	5
○ Muffato della Sala '93	♀♀♀	5

GUALDO CATTANEO (PG)   MARSCIANO (PG)

CÒLPETRONE
FRAZ. MARCELLANO
LOC. MADONNUCCIA
VIA DELLA COLLINA, 4
06035 GUALDO CATTANEO (PG)
TEL. 0578/767722

UMBRIA VITICOLTORI ASSOCIATI
LOC. CERRO - Z. I.
06055 MARSCIANO (PG)
TEL. 075/8748989

It is as if Lorenzo Landi wanted to leave a powerful memento of his time at Còlpetrone – although he hasn't departed completely, he's still retained as consultant – and did so by producing a Three Glass Sagrantino '97 which, if anything, is even better than the previous vintage. It is an opaque red, with an intense, complex nose yielding black fruit aromas underlined by tobacco and spices, then a full palate with dense tannins, a rare degree of finesse, magnificent fruit and immense length. In short, a marvel of magnificent drinkability. Even its so-called "little brother", the Rosso di Montefalco '98, is a great glass of wine. It is slightly less concentrated than the Sagrantino but still has intense aromas of bilberry and blackcurrant with hints of spice. It is stylish, soft and very attractive in the mouth, in fact a gem of a wine that easily gains a triumphant Two Glasses. The real surprise, though, is the estate's new wine, a Sagrantino Passito. Both the '96 and the '97 were presented although the '96, given the small amount produced, is to all intents only of curiosity value. It is less noteworthy than the '97 as it is a little too volatile but its interest lies primarily it being the first "experimental" release. On the other hand, the moment you pour the '97 into your glass you realise that you are not dealing with any old wine. It is completely black, thick, almost oily. The nose has devastating intensity, like freshly squeezed mulberry and bilberry with cinnamon and clove. The palate is powerful and incredibly full of fruit and stuffing. Had it not had just the merest hint of tannin in excess, it would have reached Three Glasses. In total, Còlpetrone has collected enough Glasses to put it unequivocally among Italy's top estates.

After having been listed among the Other Wineries last year, this consortium of co-operatives now gains a full Guide entry. Grapes come from around 2,500 members with vineyards in the best parts of the region – Montefalco, Orvieto and Colli Perugini. All the wines presented had notable quality, from those simply with exemplary typing to others scaling much higher qualitative peaks. And we start right at the top, with the wine that we found most convincing of all, the Chardonnay dell'Umbria '98, fermented and aged 12 months in barrique. A lustrous, deep straw-yellow in colour introduces a nose with notes of melon and banana fruit, given complexity by hints of butter and vanilla. On the palate, there is an appealing acidity that integrates well into the weave of the wine. Tropical fruit and a pleasant hint of caramel round off the finish. The Colli Perugini Bianco '99, a straightforward, easy-drinking white, is well made. The Rosso di Montefalco '97 is also perfectly executed, with its ruby colour, its fresh nose of berry fruit and its concentrated, balanced, elegant palate. It well deserves its One Glass. The Sagrantino di Montefalco '95 is a very quaffable wine but its nose, with only medium fruit intensity, is not as interesting as one would have hoped and the palate is rather loosely textured, this being echoed on the finish, too. Sangiovese dell'Umbria is also worth mentioning. It has good typicity and attractive drinkability.

● Sagrantino di Montefalco '97	♛♛♛	5
● Rosso di Montefalco '98	♛♛	3*
● Sagrantino di Montefalco Passito '97	♛♛	6
● Sagrantino di Montefalco Passito '96	♛	6
● Sagrantino di Montefalco '96	♛♛♛	4*
● Rosso di Montefalco '95	♛♛	3*
● Rosso di Montefalco '97	♛♛	3*
● Sagrantino di Montefalco '95	♛♛	4
● Rosso di Montefalco '93	♛	3
● Rosso di Montefalco '96	♛	3
● Sagrantino di Montefalco '93	♛	4

○ Chardonnay Vigne Umbre '98	♛♛	2*
○ Colli Perugini Bianco '99	♛	1*
● Rosso di Montefalco Vigne Umbre '97	♛	3
● Sagrantino di Montefalco Vigne Umbre '95	♛	5
● Umbria Sangiovese '98		1

MONTECASTRILLI (TR)

FATTORIA LE POGGETTE

LOC. LE POGGETTE
05026 MONTECASTRILLI (TR)
TEL. 0744/940338

Founded in the 60s when Giorgio Lanzetta, from Abruzzo, bought a plot of land near Montecastrilli and planted a considerable part to vine, Fattoria Le Poggette has now become one of the best estates in the province of Terni. Currently, the estate comprises 450 hectares, 12 of which are under vine. Last year, around six hectares were replanted with a selection of canaiolo and montepulciano d'Abruzzo and it was the reds that gave better results this year. The Umbria Rosso Montepulciano '97 has a very deep, almost opaque, dark purple-red colour. The nose is deep and powerful, with distinct aromas of wild berry fruits, notably mulberry, bilberry and blackcurrant, accompanied by a clean vegetal note. The palate is full and structured, with oak toast evident but, all things considered, well assimilated into the flavours of ripe berry fruit. The estate's latest red, the Canaiolo '98, is also good. It has a pale ruby colour that introduces a harmonious, fragrantly fruit-rich nose with overt strawberry and fresh cherry aromas. The palate has good body, balanced tannins, a lively fruitiness and, overall, excellent drinkability. However, Colli Amerini Rosso Superiore '98 gains no more than a mention as it seemed a little disconnected on the nose and finished a little weakly on the palate.

● Montepulciano '97	**YY**	5
● Canaiolo '98	**Y**	3
● Colli Amerini Rosso Superiore '98		3
● Montepulciano '95	YY	5
● Montepulciano '96	YY	5
● Colli Amerini Rosso Superiore '96	Y	3
● Colli Amerini Rosso Superiore '97	Y	3

MONTEFALCO (PG)

ANTONELLI - SAN MARCO

LOC. SAN MARCO, 59
06036 MONTEFALCO (PG)
TEL. 0742/379158

Never have the Antonelli wines, always reliable and full of character, distinguished themselves as they did this year. Considered one of the soundest wineries in Montefalco, this year the estate came within an inch of gaining Three Glasses. Praise must go to Filippo Antonelli, the estate's enthusiastic and dedicated owner, who, with oenologist Manlio Erba, manages to stamp a distinct estate personality on top of the wines' zonal characteristics. There were two bottles that nearly made the top ranking and the first was the Sagrantino di Montefalco Passito '97. It has a purple-ruby colour and a rich, full nose with aromas of mulberry and prunes. The palate is complex, powerful and elegant, the tannins having found a nice balance. The Sagrantino di Montefalco '97, a Two Glass regular, was no less impressive. It is deep ruby red, with bright tinges, in the glass and offers a broad, powerful nose rich in ripe berry fruit aromas nuanced with black pepper. The palate is long, intense and resplendent in ripe fruit with complex undertones of leather and tobacco. The Rosso di Montefalco '98, a purple-ruby red, is also rich, with good body and soft tannins, but not at the same level. On the white front, the '99 Grechetto Vigna Tonda, with its apple scents and its well-measured use of oak, is as successful as ever. Colli Martani Trebbiano '99, however, gains only a mention as despite its attractive scents of lemon liqueur and broom, it is rather lightweight on the palate.

● Sagrantino di Montefalco '97	**YY**	6
● Sagrantino di Montefalco Passito '97	**YY**	6
○ Colli Martani Grechetto Vigna Tonda '99	**Y**	4
● Rosso di Montefalco '98	**Y**	4
○ Colli Martani Trebbiano '99		2
○ Colli Martani Grechetto Vigna Tonda '97	YY	3*
● Sagrantino di Montefalco '94	YY	4
● Sagrantino di Montefalco '95	YY	4
● Sagrantino di Montefalco '96	YY	4
● Sagrantino di Montefalco Passito '95	YY	4
● Sagrantino di Montefalco '93	Y	4

MONTEFALCO (PG)

ARNALDO CAPRAI - VAL DI MAGGIO
LOC. TORRE
06036 MONTEFALCO (PG)
TEL. 0742/378802 - 0742/378523

MONTEFALCO (PG)

ROCCA DI FABBRI
LOC. FABBRI
06036 MONTEFALCO (PG)
TEL. 0742/399379

This year brings another great showing for the Arnaldo Caprai – Val di Maggio estate. The property has around 80 hectares under vine and is run with grit and zeal by Marco Caprai. And guess what? Surprise, surprise, there is a Three Glass award for this year's release of the Sagrantino 25 Anni selection. The '97 vintage is a dark purple-ruby and the nose is intense and powerful, full of small red berry fruit aromas and hints of fine spices. The palate is rich and long, powerfully fruity with flavours of redcurrant and bilberry, and the firm tannins are excellently compact. Sagrantino di Montefalco '97 is almost as good. Full, elegant, stylish and complex, it combines alcoholic warmth with fruity zip. Rosso di Montefalco Riserva '97 is excellent, too. Broad on the nose with notes of mulberry, sorb apple and black pepper, it is full bodied and elegant on the palate. The Rosso di Montefalco '98 is less complex but is very quaffable. A new wine, Poggio Belvedere '98, has a distinctly fruity character, enhanced by a touch of incense. Among the whites, the most impressive were the Montefalco Bianco '99, full of apple scents and with well-balanced acidity, and the Grechetto Grecante '99, with its notes of spring flowers. Finally, the very dependable Sagrantino di Montefalco Passito '97 is as good as ever. In closing, it seems only right to observe that not only has Caprai attained great expertise in his entire wine production but his was the stimulus that set off the success that the whole of Montefalco is now experiencing. Indeed, producers, such as Caprai, who can show the way ahead have been the most effective antidote to inertia throughout the whole Italian wine scene.

The legitimate ambitions of Rocca di Fabbri – to gain consistency of quality, to produce wines of greater character, to harness their energies to take their wines to higher peaks of quality – are already partly realized. Only the last remains. The wines have not quite got the edge yet, even though the best of them are of very good quality. Head of the team this year is Faroaldo, from sagrantino di Montefalco and cabernet sauvignon in equal parts, and aged 18 months in new barriques. The '97, an excellent vintage in the area, as it was in most of the region, has a very deep ruby colour. The nose has a marked initial impact of pervasive ripe berry fruit then a slightly vegetal tone emerges, followed by the still rather overt stamp of sweet, spicy oak. It is firm and lightly tannic on the palate, with a good dose of alcohol and lively acidity. The Sagrantino di Montefalco '97 is also well made. The colour is deep and concentrated, the nose is fruit-rich with subtle notes of spices, the palate has good body and intensity, and shows good tannins and length. The Rosso di Montefalco '97, with its inviting colour and the considerable intensity of its aromas and flavours, missed Two Glasses by a whisker. The Sagrantino di Montefalco Passito '97 also gains One Glass – a very full one – for its body, good concentration and even considerable elegance. The '98 Sangiovese dei Colli Martani Satiro is simple, easy drinking and well made, worthily carrying off the palm as the best in its category.

● Sagrantino di Montefalco		
25 Anni '97	♔♔♔	6
● Rosso di Montefalco Ris. '97	♔♔	6
● Sagrantino di Montefalco '97	♔♔	6
○ Colli Martani Grechetto		
Grecante '99	♔	3
○ Montefalco Bianco '99	♔	3
● Poggio Belvedere '98	♔	3
● Rosso di Montefalco '98	♔	4
● Sagrantino di Montefalco		
Passito '97	♔	6
● Sagrantino di Montefalco		
25 Anni '95	♔♔♔	6
● Sagrantino di Montefalco		
25 Anni '96	♔♔♔	6

● Faroaldo '97	♔♔	5
● Colli Martani Sangiovese		
Satiro '98	♔	2*
● Rosso di Montefalco '97	♔	3
● Sagrantino di Montefalco '98	♔	5
● Sagrantino di Montefalco		
Passito '97	♔	5
● Pinot Nero dell'Umbria '90	♔♔	5
● Cabernet Sauvignon '90	♔	3
● Colli Martani Sangiovese Satiro '93	♔	2*
● Pinot Nero dell'Umbria '97	♔	5
● Rosso di Montefalco '95	♔	3
● Rosso di Montefalco '96	♔	3
● Sagrantino di Montefalco '90	♔	3
● Sagrantino di Montefalco '96	♔	4

ORVIETO (TR)

ORVIETO (TR)

BIGI
LOC. PONTE GIULIO, 3
05018 ORVIETO (TR)
TEL. 0763/316224 - 0763/316391

CO.VI.O.
FRAZ. SFERRACAVALLO
LOC. CARDETO, 18
05019 ORVIETO (TR)
TEL. 0763/343189 - 0763/341286

Owned by Gruppo Italiano Vini, the century-old Bigi shows no sign of losing its reputation as one of Umbria's better quality estates. And once more, its best wine is the excellent Orvieto Classico Vigneto Torricella, the '99. Its bright straw-yellow leads in to an intense, lingering nose, rich in apple and, particularly, pear aromas. The palate is soft, elegant and full of weighty, complex fruit, with fresh acidity and excellent length. The straight Orvieto Classico '99 is also good and, as with the previous vintage, easily gains One Glass. Its colour is pale straw-yellow, the nose is elegant, subtle, with fruity aromas of apricot and damson and the fresh palate is easy drinking, revealing good acidity and medium length. The Grechetto '99 completes the whites. The straw-yellow hue ushers in an elegant, harmonious nose with full, complex notes of apple and pear. The palate is clean and even. The '99 Sangiovese dell'Umbria is of good quality, as usual. The nose is fruity, evoking strawberry and fresh cherry, and the palate has good body and balanced tannins. Excellent drinking.

The wines of this excellent co-operative show ever more convincingly. All the Orvietos are excellent, starting with the fresh, fruity, delicately acidulous '99 base version. The Superiore Febeo '99 is not dissimilar but more elegant, and with a greater overall harmony. The '99 Classico Superiore Colbadia, the most recent addition to the range, has a well fruited character, reminiscent of ripe peach on both nose and palate. The Matile Bianco '99 and the Umbria Grechetto '99 are both good quality. However, the excellent Orvieto Classico Superiore Opinioni '98, the product of a joint venture with the Carraia and Monrubio wineries, deserves a special mention. It is intense, clean, full-bodied and has a complex array of aromas. The Matile Rosa is attractive. Cherry red in colour and full of fresh cherry tones, it has a nice overall harmony. The range of reds is impressive and all gain Two Glasses. The Pinot Nero has turned out to be a successful gamble. The nose on the '98 is varietal and complex, rich in fruit aromas and gamey notes, stylish and long. The Arciato '98, from merlot, cabernet sauvignon and sangiovese, is also excellent: clean, dense and intense. The Nero della Greca '98, a new wine made from sangiovese and merlot, is dark ruby red with a powerful, elegant, spicy nose and a soft palate with balanced tannins. To finish, the Vendemmia Tardiva is always a sure thing. The current release has a golden straw-yellow colour ushering in a nose of tropical fruit aromas with hints of citrus peel that makes very good impact. The palate is harmonious and long, with elegant hints of acacia honey on the finish.

O Orvieto Classico		
Vigneto Torricella '99	♟♟	3*
O Grechetto dell'Umbria '99	♟	2*
O Orvieto Classico '99	♟	2*
● Sangiovese dell'Umbria '99	♟	2*
O Marrano '93	♟♟	4
O Marrano '94	♟♟	4
O Orvieto Classico		
Vigneto Torricella '98	♟♟	3*
● Sangiovese dell'Umbria '97	♟♟	2*
O Grechetto dell'Umbria '98	♟	2*
O Marrano '97	♟	4
● Sangiovese dell'Umbria '98	♟	2*
● Sangiovese Tenuta Corbara '98	♟	3

● Arciato '98	♟♟	4
● Nero della Greca '98	♟♟	4
O Orvieto Cl. Sup. Opinioni '98	♟♟	3*
O Orvieto Classico Dolce V. T.		
Cardeto '99	♟♟	4
● Pinot Nero '98	♟♟	6
O Grechetto dell'Umbria '99	♟	2*
O Matile Bianco '99	♟	1*
⊙ Matile Rosa '99	♟	1*
O Orvieto Cl. Sup. Colbadia '99	♟	3
O Orvieto Classico Cardeto '99	♟	1*
O Orvieto Classico Sup. Febeo '99	♟	3
● Fantasie del Cardeto Rosso '96	♟♟	3*
O Orvieto Classico Dolce V. T.		
Cardeto '97	♟♟	4

ORVIETO (TR)

DECUGNANO DEI BARBI
LOC. FOSSATELLO DI CORBARA, 50
05019 ORVIETO (TR)
TEL. 0763/308255

ORVIETO (TR)

LA CARRAIA
LOC. TORDIMONTE, 56
05018 ORVIETO (TR)
TEL. 0763/304013

Situated near Lago di Corbara, Decugnano dei Barbi is, traditionally and in terms of quality, one of Orvieto's archetypal estates. It currently has 32 hectares of vine and the capacity to produce 120,000 bottles a year. The able oenologist, Corrado Cugnasco, acts as consultant. The estate's classic method Brut is always among the best of the sparkling wines in the region and the '96 is full and complex, with characteristic notes of crusty bread and elegant overtones of ripe fruit on the nose, and great finesse and length on the palate. Orvieto Classico Superiore Decugnano dei Barbi '99, full of white peach and golden delicious apple fruitiness, is also good. The '99 Orvieto Classico Superiore "IL" is, as usual, well within the Two Glasses band. It has a deep straw-yellow colour, then the nose is intense, complex, elegant, full of ripe fruitiness and harmonious, sweet oak scents. Among the reds, the good, easy-drinking Sangiovese Pojo del Ruspo '98 has a wealth of wild and fresh cherry notes. Just as good is Lago di Corbara '98, which on one front seems a little over-ripe but which has compensating weight and balance on the palate. However, the top red is the '97 selection IL, from sangiovese, montepulciano and canaiolo. The nose is intense and fruity, with overt plum and morello cherry aromas while the palate has good body and fair length. The Orvieto Pourriture Noble '97 is good, but slightly lacking in complexity. It is a golden straw-yellow and the nose has good impact, with pineapple and citrus peel aromas. The palate has medium structure and length but overall we expected more from it.

The La Carraia estate, owned by Odoardo Gialletti and Riccardo Cotarella – a name that has no need of introduction – produces wines of ever greater consistency and interest year after year. This time, the range is of particularly high quality, high enough for the estate to join the Three Glass stratosphere. The wine that gains the honours is the estate's "marker", Fobiano '98. From 70 percent merlot and cabernet sauvignon, with 12 months' barrique ageing, it is a deep ruby red. The nose is intense, very well-focused and full of complex fruitiness and vegetal overtones, with pure tones of morello cherry, mulberry and wild berries enhanced by the sweet spiciness of clove and vanilla. The palate is elegant, powerful, well-fruited, balanced in tannin, complex and full. The Sangiovese dell'Umbria '99 is also good, with a fruity, herbaceous nose giving hints of red pepper and a lightly tannic palate with plenty of body. The Orvieto line is excellent, too. The Poggio Calvelli again gains Two Glasses, this time for the '99 with its intense, balsamic nose recalling tomato leaf and sage, and its full-bodied palate with convincing length. The straight Orvieto Classico is safe as houses. The '99 is fragrant and full-bodied, with an even finish. However, the Orvieto Classico Superiore Opinioni '98, created thanks to a joint venture with the Monrubio and Cadeto estates, warrants a special mention. The colour is straw-yellow, introducing a full, abundantly floral nose and a deep, expressive and complex palate.

● "IL" '97	🍷🍷	5
○ Decugnano dei Barbi Brut M. Cl. '96	🍷🍷	5
○ Orvieto Classico Sup. "IL" '99	🍷🍷	4
● Lago di Corbara '98	🍷	4
○ Orvieto Classico Decugnano dei Barbi '99	🍷	3
○ Orvieto Classico Pourriture Noble '97	🍷	5
● Pojo del Ruspo Barbi '98	🍷	3
● "IL" '93	🍷🍷	5
● "IL" '94	🍷🍷	5
● "IL" '95	🍷🍷	5
● "IL" '96	🍷🍷	5
○ Orvieto Classico Sup. "IL" '98	🍷🍷	4

● Fobiano '98	🍷🍷🍷	5
○ Orvieto Cl. Sup. Opinioni '98	🍷🍷	3*
○ Orvieto Classico Poggio Calvelli '99	🍷🍷	2*
○ Orvieto Classico '99	🍷	2*
● Sangiovese dell'Umbria '99	🍷	2*
● Fobiano '95	🍷🍷	4
● Fobiano '96	🍷🍷	4
● Fobiano '97	🍷🍷	4
○ Orvieto Classico Poggio Calvelli '98	🍷🍷	3*
● Sangiovese dell'Umbria '97	🍷🍷	3*
● Sangiovese dell'Umbria '97	🍷🍷	3*
○ Orvieto Classico '98	🍷	2*

ORVIETO (TR)

TENUTA LE VELETTE
LOC. LE VELETTE, 23
05019 ORVIETO (TR)
TEL. 0763/29090

ORVIETO (TR)

PALAZZONE
LOC. ROCCA RIPESENA, 68
05019 ORVIETO (TR)
TEL. 0763/344921

The more than 95 hectares of the Le Velette vineyards lie in the heart of the Orvieto Classico production zone and stretch over the high plain that abuts the massive outcrop of Orvieto. The estate, run by Corrado and Cecilia Bottai, with Gabriella Tani on the technical side, boasts an ancient Etruscan cellar which was hand-carved from the tufa rock and is still used for ageing the wines. Emblematic of the heights reached by the estate is the Calanco red, from sangiovese and cabernet sauvignon, which put up a strong showing, despite the problematical '97 vintage. It has a dark purple red colour and an intense, elegant nose with complex scents of redcurrant, raspberry and sorb apple. The palate is full and penetrating with balanced tannins and a complex fruitiness. The Gaudio '97, a new red from 100 percent merlot, was most impressive. It is elegant and complex on the nose and full of wild berry fruit aromas, notably mulberry and bilberry. The palate is soft, characterful, harmonious and complex. The Rosso di Spicca '99 has clean aromas and a well-balanced palate. The performance of the whites was also newsworthy. The Traluce '99 is an intensely fruited, elegantly aromatic Sauvignon. Similarly good were the two Orvietos, the Classico Superiore Lunato '99, fresh, crisp and redolent of white peaches, and the Classico Amabile '99, with apple aromas and a well-judged sweetness.

Situated within the Orvieto zone and with around 25 hectares of vine, Giovanni Dubini's Palazzone was one of the first estates to work with Riccardo Cotarella. Now it has notched up its nth great success. Three Glasses are once more awarded to an excellent Armaleo – the '98 – making it three in a row. From barrique-aged cabernets sauvignon and franc, it is a deep purple-red colour. The nose is rich in berry fruit notes, recalling mulberry and blackcurrant, and chocolate. The palate is intense and there is precision in its fruitiness, as there is in the acidity and the tannins, which have great finesse. The range of whites is also good. Orvieto Classico Superiore Campo del Guardiano '98 has inviting scents of white peach and damson on the nose while the palate has good weight and complexity. Then the Orvieto Terre Vineate is tempting, too, with its – as usual – excellent drinkability and very fair price. The Grechetto '99 is very ripe, recalling tropical fruit, mango and papaya, and is long and full on the palate. Another good white is L'Ultima Spiaggia '99, a monovarietal Viognier aged for some months in barrique. Its bright straw-yellow introduces a complex, spicy nose and elegant hints of toastiness. The '99 Muffa Nobile, from 100 percent oak-fermented sauvignon, is slightly below par this year. It was rather one-dimensional on the nose and a little too sweet on the palate, although it still retained plenty of interest.

●	Calanco '97	▼▼	5	●	Armaleo '98	▼▼▼ 5
●	Gaudio '97	▼▼	4	○	Grechetto '99	▼ 3
●	Rosso Orvietano			○	L'Ultima Spiaggia '99	▼ 4
	Rosso di Spicca '99	▼▼	2*	○	Muffa Nobile '99	▼ 5
○	Orvieto Classico Amabile '99	▼	2*	○	Orvieto Cl.	
○	Orvieto Classico Sup. Lunato '99	▼	3		Campo del Guardiano '98	▼ 4
○	Traluce '99	▼	3	○	Orvieto Cl. Terre di Vineate '99	▼ 3
●	Calanco '95	♀♀♀	5	●	Armaleo '95	♀♀♀ 4*
●	Calanco '91	♀♀	4	●	Armaleo '97	♀♀♀ 5
●	Calanco '96	♀♀	5	●	Armaleo '92	♀♀ 5
○	Traluce '96	♀♀	3*	●	Armaleo '94	♀♀ 4
●	Calanco '93	♀	4	○	Muffa Nobile '95	♀♀ 5
●	Rosso di Spicca '97	♀	2*	○	Muffa Nobile '96	♀♀ 4
●	Rosso Orvietano			○	Muffa Nobile '97	♀♀ 4
	Rosso di Spicca '98	♀	2*	○	Muffa Nobile '98	♀♀ 4

PANICALE (PG)

PENNA IN TEVERINA (TR)

LA FIORITA - LAMBORGHINI
LOC. PANICALE
06064 PANICALE (PG)
TEL. 075/8350029

RIO GRANDE
LOC. MONTECCHIE
05028 PENNA IN TEVERINA (TR)
TEL. 0744/993102 - 06/66416440

Ferruccio Lamborghini, the founder of the famous car firm, fell in love with the Umbrian countryside three decades ago and in '71 decided to buy the La Fiorita holding near Lake Trasimeno. It is now run by his daughter, Patrizia, and covers 90 hectares, of which 32 are vineyard, giving an annual production of around 60,000 bottles. The estate continues to hold its place as one of the most interesting in the region, as is shown by the two wines tasted this year, the Colli del Trasimeno Rosso Trescone and the already well-known Campoleone, both from '98. The Trescone, a blend of sangiovese, ciliegiolo and merlot, has a deep ruby colour and a fruit-rich nose, with scents of cherry and wild berries. The spicy, elegant palate has medium intensity and length but the tannins are a little raw. The Rosso dell'Umbria Campoleone '98, from merlot and sangiovese in equal proportions, is decidedly more complex. It has a dark ruby colour and a deep, powerful nose, full of intense vegetal tones and hints of redcurrant and mulberry, with attractive hints of pepper and clove. The palate is powerful, balanced, clean and harmonious, unfolding rich, wild berry fruit and soft, ripe tannins.

Owned by Franco Pastore since 1988, the Rio Grande estate lies in the extreme south of the region. There are around 54 hectares in total, of which 12 were planted with chardonnay and cabernet sauvignon at the beginning of the '90s. Never have the wines been as interesting as they were this year. The best of the range, as usual, is the '98 Umbria Rosso Casa Pastore, a really convincing, fascinating wine that came within a whisker of winning Three Glasses. From 100 percent cabernet sauvignon, it has an attractive, dark purple hue and an intense, penetrating nose, full of the vegetal tones expected from the variety, together with eloquent notes of berry fruit, most notably mulberry, redcurrant and ripe cherry. The palate is powerful and harmonious, with ripe, elegant tannins. Not only is the wine first-rate but it is also excellent value for money. Still with the reds and still at the Two Glass level, there is the fascinating new Poggio Muralto '98, a monovarietal Cabernet Sauvignon. The colour is a purple-ruby red, introducing an intense nose with good complexity and fresh wild cherry and blackberry aromas. The palate is soft, elegant, fresh and fruity. No less impressive is the Chardonnay Colle delle Montecchie '99 with its elegant tones of apple, pear and citrus peel, its subtle floral hints of broom and its warm, complex palate backed up by excellent body and length. Congratulations.

● Rosso dell'Umbria Campoleone '98	▼▼ 5
● Colli del Trasimeno Trescone '98	▼ 3
● Rosso dell'Umbria Campoleone '97	♀♀ 5
● Colli del Trasimeno Trescone '97	♀ 3

● Casa Pastore Rosso '98	▼▼ 4
○ Chardonnay Colle delle Montecchie '99	▼▼ 3*
● Poggio Muralto '98	▼▼ 3*
● Casa Pastore Rosso '95	♀♀ 4
● Casa Pastore Rosso '97	♀♀ 4
○ Chardonnay Colle delle Montecchie '94	♀♀ 3*
○ Chardonnay Colle delle Montecchie '95	♀♀ 3*
● Casa Pastore Rosso '93	♀ 3
● Casa Pastore Rosso '94	♀ 4
● Casa Pastore Rosso '96	♀ 4
○ Chardonnay Colle delle Montecchie '98	♀ 3

PERUGIA

GISBERTO GORETTI
LOC. PILA
STRADA DEL PINO, 4
06070 PERUGIA
TEL. 075/607316

The Goretti brothers' estate is steadily gaining recognition as the most consistent and influential in the Colli Perugini zone. In addition, each year their range of wines – which gain gratifying scores in our tastings – continues to grow. But let's begin at the beginning. We were previously highly impressed by the '95 Colli Perugini Rosso Arringatore but this year's version, the '97, is less exciting. Its colour is a deep ruby, its nose is rich in redcurrant and sorb apple fruit, mingling with hints of vanilla and spices, but the palate lets it down. The fruit is not brilliantly ripe and the body less than fully structured. It is still worth of One Glass but we would hope for better in the future. Instead, the estate's most impressive wine this year was the Chardonnay dell'Umbria '99, which is just a hop away from Two Glasses. It has a good straw-yellow colour and inviting perfumes of yellow peach and tropical fruit. The palate is soft, mouth-filling and long. The Grechetto dell'Umbria '99, whose palate mirrors the nose impeccably, has just a note of acidity on the finish and is also well made. The estate's two basic wines, the Fontanella Rosso '99, with fruit-rich aromas and a clean, rounded taste, and the Fontanella Bianco '99, zesty and honest-to-goodness easy drinking, are both well-typed and attractive.

○	Chardonnay dell'Umbria '99	🍷	2*
●	Colli Perugini Rosso L'Arringatore '97	🍷	4
○	Fontanella Bianco '99	🍷	1*
●	Fontanella Rosso '99	🍷	2*
○	Grechetto dell'Umbria '99	🍷	2*
●	Colli Perugini Rosso L'Arringatore '95	🍸🍸	3*
○	Chardonnay dell'Umbria '97	🍸	2*
○	Chardonnay dell'Umbria '98	🍸	2*
●	Colli Perugini Rosso L'Arringatore '96	🍸	3
●	Fontanella Rosso '97	🍸	2*
○	Grechetto dell'Umbria '97	🍸	2*
○	Grechetto dell'Umbria '98	🍸	2*

SPELLO (PG)

F.LLI SPORTOLETTI
VIA LOMBARDIA, 1
06038 SPELLO (PG)
TEL. 0742/651461

This year the Sportoletti estate peaks with a terrific Villa Fidelia Rosso. In the '98 vintage, Remo and Ernesto Sportoletti, and their consultant, the renowned Riccardo Cotarella, have come up with a wine, made with tremendous care, that offers exceptional depth of aroma and flavour. The appearance dances with purple on an intense, deep ruby base. The nose, in which fruitiness alternates with autumn leaves, is laced with herbaceous and delicately spicy hints and reveals both great depth and definition. The palate is similarly full and is centred on a balanced, ripe and very generous structure. Well-balanced, elegant tannins and an effortlessly long finish bring it triumphantly into the Three Glass category. The Assisi Rosso '99 has an intense, dense ruby hue while the aromas are full although without great complexity. The palate has balance that derives from its gentle first impression, its soft, fruit-rich development in the mouth, and its clean, vanilla-toned finish. The Grechetto di Assisi '99 is floral, fruity and lightly oaky on the nose, its decisive character belying an inviting softness of taste. The Pinot Nero Valle Gloria '98, a new wine, is an attractively deep ruby colour. The aromas are intense but a little off-key and the fruit is of medium intensity on both nose and palate. There are faint notes of toastiness in the finish.

●	Villa Fidelia Rosso '98	🍷🍷🍷	6
●	Assisi Rosso '99	🍷🍷	4
○	Assisi Grechetto '99	🍷	3
●	Pinot Nero '98	🍷	6
○	Villa Fidelia Bianco '98	🍷	5
○	Villa Fidelia Bianco '95	🍸🍸	4
○	Villa Fidelia Bianco '97	🍸🍸	4
●	Villa Fidelia Rosso '91	🍸🍸	4
●	Villa Fidelia Rosso '97	🍸🍸	4
○	Assisi Bianco '98	🍸	2*
○	Assisi Grechetto '98	🍸	2*
●	Assisi Rosso '96	🍸	1*
●	Assisi Rosso '98	🍸	2*
●	Villa Fidelia Rosso '94	🍸	4
●	Villa Fidelia Rosso '96	🍸	5

STRONCONE (TR)

TORGIANO (PG)

LA PALAZZOLA
LOC. VASCIGLIANO
05039 STRONCONE (TR)
TEL. 0744/607735 - 0744/272357

CANTINE LUNGAROTTI
VIA MARIO ANGELONI, 16
06089 TORGIANO (PG)
TEL. 075/9880348

Stefano Grilli's La Palazzola is one of the most successful estates in Umbria and its position is confirmed by this year's high-quality range of wines. Situated in the Stroncone hills, in the province of Terni, it has 14 hectares of vine and, as consultant, a certain . . . Riccardo Cotarella. The estate's best wines, both only millimetres away from a Three Glass score, are the two red selections, the Merlot and the Rubino, two bottles from the class of '98. The former is a dark purplish-ruby red in the glass. Full and powerful on the nose, it is rich in berry fruit, notably wild berries, morello cherry and redcurrant, as well as vegetal notes. The palate is elegant and long, unveiling lashings of red berry fruit and balanced tannins. The Rubino is just as good. Its colour is a good purple-ruby. The nose offers aromas of mulberry, morello cherry and redcurrant fruit. On the palate, it is powerful, elegant and redolent of sweet spiciness. Next, the red Cerquolo '99 has plenty of slightly super-ripe fruit on the nose leading in to a palate of good intensity with balanced tannins. Of the other wines, the '98 Pinot Nero has good varietal character, the Brut La Palazzola '96 has good complexity on the nose, the white Palazzotto '99 offers attractive scents of flowers and quince and the '98 Vendemmia Tardiva is as good as ever, with a complex, elegant nose of pineapple, mango and ripe apricot fruit and a long, full palate with well balanced sweetness.

If certain vintages of Lungarotti's flagship wine, Vigna Monticchio, are memorable – the celebrated '78 Riserva, for example – others are sadly less so and the '92 we tasted this year did not inspire us. It is an austere red, with complex, evolved tones but which suffers from its long ageing first in wood then in bottle. In a vintage like this that is not of the best, the penalty a wine pays for such treatment is weakened fruit. Instead, the wine that showed best this year was the more fully expressive '97 Vessillo. From equal proportions of cabernet sauvignon and pinot nero, it has a good purple-ruby colour and a nose of conviction, with aromas of berry fruit, plum and ripe morello cherry, and its hints of balsam. The palate has good body, richness of fruit, lingering touches of spiciness and good elegance. San Giorgio '92, from cabernet and sangiovese with a small percentage of colorino, has a dark ruby colour of good depth. The nose offers soft aromas of ripe plum with evolved tones that range from liquorice to leather and autumn leaves. The palate proffers decent body and elegantly ripe flavours. The Chardonnay di Torgiano '98 was also attractive, with its deep straw-yellow colour and fresh softness, good fullness and moderate fruit on the palate. The Torgiano Vigna il Pino '98 has a rather over-evolved tone that brings it a scant One Glass. Next year, we should be tasting the first results of Lungarotti's collaboration with the oenologist Lorenzo Landi, which we are sure will bring notable improvements.

O	La Palazzola V. T. '98	▼▼	5
●	Merlot '98	▼▼	5
●	Rubino '98	▼▼	5
●	Cerquolo '99	▼	3
O	La Palazzola Brut M. Cl. '96	▼	4
O	Palazzotto '99	▼	3
●	Pinot Nero '98	▼	4
●	Merlot '97	▼▼▼	5
O	La Palazzola V. T. '96	▼▼	5
●	Merlot '95	▼▼	4
O	Riesling Brut M. Cl. '94	▼▼	4
●	Rubino '95	▼▼	4
●	Rubino '96	▼▼	5
●	Rubino '97	▼▼	5
O	Vino Passito '96	▼▼	5

●	Il Vessillo '97	▼▼	5
●	San Giorgio '92	▼▼	5
O	Torgiano Bianco Torre di Giano Vigna il Pino Ris. '98	▼	4
●	Torgiano Rosso Vigna Monticchio Ris. '92	▼	5
●	Cabernet Sauvignon '95	▼▼	4
●	Il Vessillo '93	▼▼	4
●	San Giorgio '88	▼▼	5
●	Torgiano Rosso Vigna Monticchio Ris. '88	▼▼	5
●	Torgiano Rosso Vigna Monticchio Ris. '90	▼▼	5

OTHER WINERIES

The following producers obtained good scores in our tastings with one or more of their wines:

PROVINCE OF PERUGIA

Vignabaldo – Brogal Vini,
Bastia Umbra, tel. 075/8001501
Rosso di Montefalco '98,
Sagrantino di Montefalco '97,
Torgiano Rosso '97

Eredi Benincasa,
Bevagna, tel. 0742/361307
Sagrantino di Montefalco '95

Il Poggio,
Castiglione del Lago, tel. 075/9589923
Colli del Trasimeno Bianco '99,
Colli del Trasimeno Rosato '99,
Colli del Trasimeno Rosso '98

Podere Marella,
Castiglione del Lago, tel. 075/9659028
Colli del Trasimeno Rosso '96

Poggio Bertaio,
Castiglione del Lago, tel. 075/956921
Umbria Sangiovese Cimbolo '98

Villa Po' del Vento,
Città della Pieve, tel. 0578/299950
Colli del Trasimeno Bianco '99,
Colli del Trasimeno Rosso '98,
Colli del Trasimeno Rosso del Duca '94,
Umbria Riesling '99,
Umbria Rosato '99

Terre dei Trinci, Foligno, tel. 0742/320165
Sagrantino di Montefalco '96

Cantina Intercomunale del Trasimeno,
Magione, tel. 075/840298
Colli del Trasimeno Rosso Erceo '99

Napolini, Montefalco, tel. 0742/379362
Sagrantino di Montefalco '97,
Sagrantino di Montefalco Passito '94

Ruggeri, Montefalco, tel. 0742/379294
Rosso di Montefalco '98,
Sagrantino di Montefalco Passito '96

Scacciadiavoli,
Montefalco, tel. 0742378272
Sagrantino di Montefalco '96,
Sagrantino di Montefalco Passito '96

Virili Piero, Montefalco, tel. 0742/379602
Sagrantino di Montefalco '96,
Sagrantino di Montefalco Passito '96

La Querciolana, Panicale, tel. 075/837477
Colli del Trasimeno Bianco '99,
Colli del Trasimeno Rosato '99,
Colli del Trasimeno Rosso '98

Il Ramaccio,
Petrignano del Lago, tel. 075/9528148
Colli del Trasimento Rosso Assolato '98

Spoletoducale,
Petrognano di Spoleto, tel. 0743/56224
Ducato del Sole '98,
Rosso di Montefalco '97,
Sagrantino di Montefalco, '95

Chiorri, S. Enea, tel. 075/607141
Colli Perugini Bianco '99,
Colli Perugini Rosso '99

Cantina Sociale Tudernum,
Todi, tel. 075/8989403
Sangiovese dei Colli Martani '98,
Sangiovese dei Colli Martani Ris. '97

PROVINCE OF TERNI

Poggio del Lupo,
Allerona, tel. 0763/628350
Rosso di Allerona Cottabo '96

Zanchi, Amelia, tel. 0744/970011
Colli Amerini Malvasia '99,
Colli Amerini Rosso Sup. Sciurio '97,
Umbria Grechetto '99

Podere Vaglie, Baschi, tel. 0744/957425
Orvieto Cl. Sup. Matricale '99,
Umbria Masseo '98

Tenuta di Salviano,
Civitella del Lago, tel. 0744/950459
Lago di Corbara Turlò '98,
Orvieto Classico Sup. '99,
Orvieto Classico Sup. V.T. '98

Sassara, Orvieto, tel. 0763/25119
Orvieto Classico Sup. '99,
Umbria Vantaggio '99

Tordimaro,
Orvieto, tel. 0763/304227
Umbria Selvaia '98,
Umbria Torrello '98

LAZIO

Oh Lazio, what are we going to do about you? Yet again, you dole out joy and pain in equal measure. Nearly every year, there is something to stimulate our enthusiasm and others that make us despair. With all these ups and downs, it is hard to find any pattern. How can you explain wines that vary so hugely in quality from one year to the next? And why does such an oenologically significant region produce just one Three Glass wine? Mind you, there is at least some consistency here as it is Riccardo Cotarella's Montiano, this time the '98, that again takes the honours. We don't want to appear biased but there are pitifully few others who are working seriously to obtain wines whose quality goes beyond mere softness of aroma and taste. We are pleased to record Castel de Paolis among that select few. The wines have improved greatly right across the board and the range is now better than ever, particularly the outstanding, sumptuous Quattro Mori '98. Casale del Giglio is also making steady progress. Sure, there is no world-beater on the list yet but the scores are edging up steadily year after year. It was Paola and Armando De Mauro's Colle Picchioni that came closest – actually very close indeed – to breaking the Three Glass barrier with Vigna del Vassallo '98. Another positive aspect is the existence of producers with substantial market penetration who turn out very respectable wines. The calibre of Fontana Candida in particular never fails to astound us. Two of the "minnows" who deserve a mention are Sergio Mottura and Villa Simone. Their top whites are of similar quality but in diametrically opposing styles. The Mottura Latour a Civitella is fat and powerful while the latter's Vigna dei Preti is fresh, light and fragrant. We'd also like to dedicate a symbolic crown of excellence to Trappolini, who has come out with a first-class Paterno '98. This is a clear sign that, with a bit of care, results will come sooner or later. And while Casale Marchese is still marking time in the Frascati zone, Conte Zandotti is revamping all its wines and giving them greater depth. In Ciociaria, Giovanni Palombo continues to plough his chosen furrow and although his Duca Cantelmi '98 does not quite reach the peaks it at least shows character and interest. Colacicchi in Anagni has not yet released the new vintage of the red Torre Ercolana but the good Romagnolo Bianco provides ample consolation. In short, there is a rich array of wines in the region but, apart from the leading estates we have mentioned, there are no signs of a more general vitality. It is a great pity, especially when you think that there are numerous terroirs and climatic zones throughout the region which are superbly suited to producing top-quality grapes. Why not capitalize on them? Maybe the answer lies in the extreme ease with which Lazio's wines find space on the marketplace, particularly in the medium-low price band. After all, no-one asks much of a Frascati, apart from Giulio Santarelli whose wines seem more of an oddity than an example to follow. But we have faith, and we continue to hope that once the Holy Year razzamatazz and the expectations of easy sales it generated has faded away, the region's producers will start to reflect seriously on their role in the international market and do full justice to the great potential of their territory.

ATINA (FR)

GIOVANNI PALOMBO
C.SO MUNANZIO PLANCO
03042 ATINA (FR)
TEL. 0776/610200

We have DOC! The long yearned-for denomination of Atina has finally arrived. And this year there is a pleasing Atina Cabernet '99 to add to the list of Giovanni Palombo's attractive wines. It is still too young to be a Glassware-winner" but has all it needs to improve with time. In contrast, the '98 Cabernet Duca Cantelmi left us perplexed. Last year, it had us calling its performance miraculous but this year's version is much less concentrated and full, although the caprices of an inclement growing season could well take much of the blame. There is also a prevalence of oak toast that submerges the underlying fruit and spiciness, leaving a slight rasping feel in the mouth. Roberto Mazzer will have to stretch his skills to their limit in the future if his wines are so weather-prone. Colle della Torre '98, though, from 90 percent merlot and cabernet, showed well. It flaunts a fine array of vegetal aromas, fair structure and even better concentration. The early-drinking Rosso delle Chiaie '99 is as well-typed as ever, with ripe tannins well in evidence and a decent structure giving good support. Somigliò as usual topped the whites. From sémillon and sauvignon, it has an intense, penetrating nose with substantial impact and evident varietal aromas. Finally, Bianco delle Chiaie '99, from malvasia and vermentino, is an early-drinking, any-occasion wine.

●	Cabernet Duca Cantelmi '98	▼▼	5
●	Colle della Torre '98	▼▼	4
●	Atina Cabernet '99	▼	4
○	Somigliò '98	▼	3
○	Bianco delle Chiaie '98		2
●	Rosso delle Chiaie '98		3
●	Cabernet Duca Cantelmi '97	▽▽	5
●	Colle della Torre '97	▽▽	4
●	Colle della Torre '97	▽▽	4
●	Rosso delle Chiaie '97	▽	3
●	Rosso delle Chiaie '98	▽	3
○	Somigliò '98	▽	3

BOLSENA (VT)

ITALO MAZZIOTTI
LOC. MECONA-BONVINO
VIA CASSIA KM 110
01023 BOLSENA (VT)
TEL. 0761/799049

A pause for reflection. Flaminia Mazziotti and her husband, Alessandro, decided to delay the release of the Canuleio and Filò Rosso selections, two of their most interesting wines. They will remain in the estate's cool cellars in Bolsena, under the care of technician, Gaspare Buscemi, until their release in 2001. This left us with the estate's base wine, the '99 Est Est Est di Montefiascone, and the white Filò selection, also a '99, to taste. The first of the two has a bright straw-yellow colour, introducing subtle fruity nuances on the nose with an underlying hint of citrus. The palate is fresh and easy drinking, a million miles from the heavy wines of the past. In short, it is well-typed and thoroughly enjoyable. The Filò has more complexity of fruit, on both nose and palate. The colour is a limpid straw-yellow with lustrous highlights. The aromas recall citrus fruits, damson and spring flowers while the palate is fluent, with medium extractive weight, and fairly long with an even finish. It certainly has more depth and conviction than the simpler wine. However, both are well-made and have a refreshing, very attractive streak of acidity.

○	Est Est Est di Montefiascone '99	▼	2*
○	Est Est Est di Montefiascone Filò '99	▼	2*
○	Est Est Est di Montefiascone Canuleio '94	▽▽	4
●	Volgente Rosso '97	▽▽	4
○	Est Est Est di Montefiascone '96	▽	2*
○	Est Est Est di Montefiascone '97	▽	2*
○	Est Est Est di Montefiascone Canuleio '92	▽	3
○	Est Est Est di Montefiascone Canuleio '97	▽	4
○	Est Est Est di Montefiascone '98		2

CASTIGLIONE IN TEVERINA (VT) CASTIGLIONE IN TEVERINA (VT)

PAOLO D'AMICO
LOC. PALOMBO- VAIANO
01024 CASTIGLIONE IN TEVERINA (VT)
TEL. 0761/948868 - 0761/948869

TRAPPOLINI
VIA DEL RIVELLINO, 65
01024 CASTIGLIONE IN TEVERINA (VT)
TEL. 0761/948381

There is a newcomer to the Lazio wine scene. And it isn't an estate that does things by half measures. Husband and wife, Paolo and Noemia d'Amico, decided to invest their resources in making wines of the highest quality, and so they have. They have around six hectares of vineyard near Calanchi Viterbese, in the area once known as Tuscia, and currently make two wines, Falesia and Calanchi di Vaiano, producing around 10,000 bottles a year. Both are whites, both based on chardonnay, and both have been entrusted to the tender loving care of two of the highest calibre experts in the country, Fabrizio Moltard for grape cultivation and Carlo Corino for winemaking. With that sort of background, it is not surprising that results have come quickly. The Falesia '98, which spends 12 months in oak, is an object lesson in how to use barriques without losing varietal character. It has a good deep straw-yellow colour with attractive golden tinges. On the nose, its vanilla tones do not overwhelm the fruit but instead meld with them into a harmonious whole, giving good balance and notable length. The Two Glasses are well deserved. Calanchi di Vaiano '98 is a less demanding wine, focused on freshness and varietal purity. It ages for 12 months in stainless steel vats and then six more in bottle. The nose is particularly attractive, with broad-ranging aromas and elegant touches of white-fleshed fruit. The palate is both tangy and fresh at the same time, and offers an enticing fragrance. The only point of criticism is that these are not exactly bargain basement wines.

During our tastings of Lazio reds, we came across a sample from Trappolini of Castiglione in Teverina that made a great impression on us. It is a stunning release of Paterno, the '98, a wine that had previously been interesting but no more. It has now leapt ahead in the quality stakes, acquiring an exuberance of aromas and a density and breadth of taste it had never before achieved. It collected a very comfortable Two Glasses and deserves abundant praise. The '99 Est Est Est di Montefiascone also has good varietal aromas and a fresh, lively structure. So, too, does the Orvieto S. Egidio '99, which is even more convincing. It has an attractive youthful fruitiness that blends well with the overall harmony of the wine and finishes fairly long. The '99 version of the monovarietal Greco, Brecceto, is much improved. It unveils a good aromatic framework, with typical varietal perfumes, and the palate is zesty and long. Chardonnay dell'Umbria '99, fermented and aged in barrique, was still coming round at the time of our tastings and showed all the edginess of a very young wine. It will need another look once it is ready. However, the aleatico-based Idea '99 is very good, unfurling fragrant fruity aromas underlined by hints of jam and dried rose petals and then a warm, sweet, velvety palate.

O Falesia '98	🍷🍷	5
O Calanchi di Vaiano '98	🍷	4

O Chardonnay '99	🍷🍷	3*
● Idea '99	🍷🍷	4
● Paterno '98	🍷🍷	3*
O Grechetto dell'Umbria Brecceto '99	🍷	3
O Est Est Est di Montefiascone '99		2
O Orvieto Sant'Egidio '99		3
O Chardonnay '98	🍷🍷	3*
● Idea '98	🍷🍷	4
● Paterno '96	🍷🍷	3*
O Grechetto dell'Umbria Brecceto '95	🍷	3
O Grechetto dell'Umbria Brecceto '98	🍷	3
● Paterno '92	🍷	3

CERVETERI (RM)

Cantina Cooperativa di Cerveteri
Via Aurelia, km 42.700
00052 Cerveteri (RM)
tel. 06/9905677 - 06/9905697

We often find ourselves tasting ranges from large wineries that oscillate between genuinely exciting bottles and more modest offerings. Cerveteri is a case in point. We can't bring ourselves be negative but we do have to say that the wines in general were less enthralling than we expected. The whites have lost some of their brio and seem to have an intrinsic weakness of framework. Cerveteri Bianco Fontana Morella '99, for instance, is fairly insubstantial in both colour and structure. Cerveteri Bianco Vigna Grande '99, from malvasia, trebbiano, tocai and others, however, deserves a closer look. The tasty fruitiness we have admired in the past is now given a further lift by an attractively fresh note. Cerveteri Rosso Fontana Morella '99 is as enjoyable as ever, with a fairly youthful style that makes it ideal for those who like their reds less intense. The two new wines that the winery has recently developed both showed very well. The first, Villanova '99, based on malvasia del Lazio, has a delicious fruitiness that is perfectly offset by the smoky, vanillaed sensations infused by a short stay in oak. The other new baby, Tertium '98, which we first tasted as an early release last year, is now showing all its potential and is just fascinating. From malvasia nera, sangiovese and cabernet given some bottle ageing, it has an enviable array of spicy aromas which make a harmonious counterpoint to its stylish tannins. We will comment on the '98 Cerveteri Rosso Vigna Grande next year as it was not ready in time for this year's Guide.

●	Tertium '98	🍷🍷	3
○	Cerveteri Bianco Vigna Grande '99	🍷	2*
○	Malvasia del Lazio '99	🍷	2*
○	Cerveteri Bianco Fontana Morella '99		1
●	Cerveteri Rosso Fontana Morella '99		1
●	Cerveteri Rosso Vigna Grande '95	YY	3*
●	Cerveteri Rosso Vigna Grande '97	YY	3*
○	Cerveteri Bianco Vigna Grande '96	Y	2*
○	Cerveteri Bianco Vigna Grande '97	Y	2*
○	Cerveteri Bianco Vigna Grande '98	Y	2*
●	Cerveteri Rosso Fontana Morella '96	Y	1*
●	Cerveteri Rosso Vigna Grande '94	Y	3
●	Cerveteri Rosso Vigna Grande '96	Y	3
●	Tertium '97	Y	3

CIVITELLA D'AGLIANO (VT)

Tenuta Mottura
Via Poggio della Costa, 1
01020 Civitella d'Agliano (VT)
tel. 0761/914533

Latour a Civitella is a strange name for a wine. But if the wine turns out to be an estate's best, who are we to quibble? It comes from grechetto vinified in stainless steel and then aged in barriques supplied by the famous Burgundy "négociant" Louis Latour. So "Viva Latour". The wine has never been as deep, sumptuous and balanced (at last!) as it is this time round with the '98. Warm vanilla tones diffuse through a sublimely harmonious and fruitily nuanced nose, leading in to a full-bodied, mouth-filling palate. Two Glasses without a moment's doubt. Neither can we ignore the major white made by Mottura, Muffo, which is now available in the '98 version. Year after year, it gains in self-assurance and style. Even the '99 Orvieto Vigna Tragugnano, less full and less fat than the previous vintage, now has an array of aromas that are more appropriate to a wine that strives to be easy-drinking and youthful. The selection Poggio della Costa '99 is very elegant and here, too, firm texture is played off against a pleasing overall harmony. So a big "Well done!" to Sergio Mottura. The next step will be the reds, which he is already working on. Two have been released so far, the Rosso di Civitella '98, from a multi-grape blend, and Magone '98, mainly from pinot nero. The styles of both are still evolving and probably still need a bit of touching up. The potential is all there, though, as is the doggedness of their winemaker. We shall wait and see.

○	Grechetto Latour a Civitella '98	🍷🍷	4
○	Grechetto Poggio della Costa '99	🍷🍷	3*
○	Muffo '98	🍷🍷	3*
○	Orvieto Vigna Tragugnano '99	🍷	2*
●	Magone '98		4
●	Rosso di Civitella '99		3
○	Grechetto Latour a Civitella '96	YY	4
○	Grechetto Latour a Civitella '97	YY	4
○	Grechetto Poggio della Costa '95	YY	3*
○	Grechetto Poggio della Costa '98	YY	3*
○	Muffo '95	YY	4
○	Muffo '97	YY	3*
○	Muffo '94	Y	4
●	Magone '94	Y	4

CORI (LT)

FRASCATI (RM)

PIETRA PINTA
VIA GRAMSCI, 52
04010 CORI (LT)
TEL. 06/9678001

CASALE MARCHESE
VIA DI VERMICINO, 68
00044 FRASCATI (RM)
TEL. 06/9408932

Consumers have never taken a great deal of notice of the wines from Cori, probably because the commercial bias of the zone's producers has prevented it from taking off as a quality wine area. Then the Ferretti brothers turned up and things started to take a different turn. With advice and technical assistance from research institutes in Conegliano and Velletri, they have set about rewriting the zone's history. So far, their leading wine is the red Colle Amato '98. From a blend of cabernet and syrah whose proportions vary from year to year, it has a fair concentration of fruity aromas, interwoven with sensations of spiciness and plain chocolate. The palate is warm, soft and long. Cori Rosso comes from merlot and petit verdot and is partially vinified in small oak barrels. The '98 is reasonably full and has a nose of medium intensity that leads in to a warm palate with flavours of berry fruit. It is well enough styled but the previous vintage was a little more impressive. The same applies to the '99 Chardonnay del Lazio, which has an attractive array of aromas. It is fresh and quaffable but not all that long and lacks the concentration of the '98.

Casale Marchese continues to stick firmly to its production strategy and our misgivings, voiced in last year's Guide, have not yet had any effect. Salvatore Carletti and his family are now several steps along a path that seems to satisfy them, producing a red wine of stature, and leaving their Frascati as it is, with a style that is atypical to say the least. Even Sandro Facca, the architect of this shift in emphasis from white to red, seems to think along the same lines. For our part, we should like to place on record that the red Vigna del Cavaliere did not enjoy particularly good weather conditions in '97. So, while retaining an undeniably firm structure, it has less weight and less length than the '96 and its aromas are also less intense. Nevertheless, it is a distinctive, well-made wine that has every right to take its place with Lazio's best. Rosso di Casale Marchese maintains its standing with the '99 edition. It has an attractive fruitiness and a delightful freshness on the palate, which is warm with stimulating sensations of green pepper and coffee running through it. It finishes fairly long on a note of sweetness. The Frascati Superiore '99 has a most attractive hint of citrus under the more usual, rather exaggerated fruity and floral scents. Finally, the Cortesia '99 continues to lack presence with a barely perceptible sweetness.

● Colle Amato '98	ΥΥ	3*
● Cori Rosso Costa Vecchia '98	Υ	2*
O Chardonnay del Lazio '99		2
● Colle Amato '97	ΨΨ	3*

● Vigna del Cavaliere '97	ΥΥ	4
● Rosso di Casale Marchese '99	Υ	3
O Cortesia di Casale Marchese '99		3
O Frascati Superiore '99		2
O Cortesia di Casale Marchese '93	ΨΨ	3*
O Cortesia di Casale Marchese '94	ΨΨ	3*
O Cortesia di Casale Marchese '95	ΨΨ	3*
O Frascati Superiore '93	ΨΨ	2*
O Frascati Superiore '94	ΨΨ	2*
O Frascati Superiore '95	ΨΨ	2*
● Rosso di Casale Marchese '97	ΨΨ	3*
● Vigna del Cavaliere '96	ΨΨ	4
O Frascati Superiore '96	Ψ	2*
O Frascati Superiore '97	Ψ	2*
● Rosso di Casale Marchese '98	Ψ	3

GROTTAFERRATA (RM)

CASTEL DE PAOLIS
VIA VAL DE PAOLIS, 41
00046 GROTTAFERRATA (RM)
TEL. 06/9413648 - 06/94316025

If Giulio Santarelli's wines are now justifiably taking their place alongside Italy's best, he owes it to the fact that he has never yet had a year when quality has taken a dive. In addition, the range had a great boost when Franco Bernabei came in as consultant winemaker and brought grace and elegance to what had formerly been rather concentrated styles. The Frascati Superiore '99, for instance, is a very good wine that shows balance and lingering aromas and flavours, underscored by notes of fresh fruit. The Vigna Adriana '99 selection is intriguing. There is greater concentration of aromas than before, a firm, yet very elegant weave and considerable length. We had a further pleasant surprise from Selve Vecchie '98, a blend of two parts sauvignon and one part chardonnay, fermented and aged in barrique. Apart from its structure, it is the balance between its varietal aromas of tropical fruit and its vein of vanilla that really make an impact. The red Quattro Mori '98 is marvellous and easily took Two Glasses. With this vintage, the blend of syrah, merlot, petit verdot and cabernet sauvignon has turned out considerably more balanced than before and the wine now offers a firm structure with sensations of spices, cocoa powder and tobacco gently melting together. Both the '99 Cannellino, from indigenous grapes, and the '99 Muffa Nobile, with the aristocratic presence of sémillon clearly distinguishable, are sumptuous and elegantly sweet. The musky notes of dried rose petals on the gently sweet Rosathea '99 are quite captivating. Finally, even Castel de Paolis' two "working-class" wines, the Frascati Superiore Campo Vecchio '99 and Campo Vecchio Rosso '98 show well.

○	Frascati Sup. V. Adriana '99	🍷🍷	5
○	Frascati Superiore '99	🍷🍷	4
○	Muffa Nobile '99	🍷🍷	5
●	Quattro Mori '98	🍷🍷	5
●	Rosathea '99	🍷🍷	5
○	Selve Vecchie '98	🍷🍷	5
●	Campo Vecchio Rosso '98	🍷	3
○	Frascati Sup. Campo Vecchio '99	🍷	3
○	Frascati Sup. Cannellino '99	🍷	5
○	Frascati Sup. V. Adriana '98	🍷🍷 (white)	5
○	Muffa Nobile '94	🍷🍷 (white)	5
○	Muffa Nobile '97	🍷🍷 (white)	5
●	Quattro Mori '94	🍷🍷 (white)	5
●	Quattro Mori '96	🍷🍷 (white)	5
●	Quattro Mori '97	🍷🍷 (white)	5

LE FERRIERE (LT)

CASALE DEL GIGLIO
STRADA CISTERNA-NETTUNO, KM 13
04010 LE FERRIERE (LT)
TEL. 06/5746359 - 06/92902530

It's full steam ahead at Casale del Giglio. In a region where many find it difficult to maintain reliably good quality standards, it is cheering to be able to acknowledge the abilities of Antonio Santarelli and the loyal Paolo Tiefenthaler. Over the years, the pair has consolidated and improved the quality of the estate's wines to the extent that the number deserving of attention is now huge – so huge that we would need several Guide pages to do them justice. Satrico has been restyled and the '99 has an unusual vanilla fragrance. The same goes for the '99 Sauvignon, which has good varietal typing and is fresh and clean. The '99 Chardonnay is a little under par and has less concentration and less impact than in the past. In contrast, there was a particularly good showing from the '97 Antinoo. From oak-aged chardonnay, its toasty, vanilla-like notes marry well with the fruity aromas typical of the variety, and overall it is long and most elegant. The rosé Albiola '99 is as fragrant and fresh as ever. This leads us to the reds, which start with the surprising '98 Shiraz. After a broad, pervasive nose with aromas of berry fruit and spices, the palate maintains the intensity and shows good tannic balance. The '98 Merlot is also very good. Along with the '98 Petit Verdot, it demonstrates that it is quite possible to produce a distinguished wine at a very reasonable price. However, from the more expensive end of the estate's range of reds, it was the Mater Matuta '96 that came out on top. We were struck by its great concentration, its depth and its elegance, which were only partly clouded by a faint hint of gaminess. A note of merit goes also to the excellent Madreselva '96 and Cabernet Sauvignon '97.

○	Antinoo '97	🍷🍷	3*
●	Cabernet Sauvignon '97	🍷🍷	4
●	Madreselva '96	🍷🍷	4
●	Mater Matuta '96	🍷🍷	4
⊙	Albiola '99	🍷	2*
●	Merlot '98	🍷	3
○	Satrico '99	🍷	2*
○	Sauvignon '99	🍷	2*
●	Shiraz '98	🍷	2*
○	Chardonnay '99		2
●	Cabernet Sauvignon '96	🍷🍷 (white)	4
●	Madreselva '94	🍷🍷 (white)	3*
●	Madreselva '95	🍷🍷 (white)	4
●	Mater Matuta '95	🍷🍷 (white)	4
●	Merlot '96	🍷🍷 (white)	3*

MARINO (RM)

MARINO (RM)

PAOLA DI MAURO - COLLE PICCHIONI
VIA COLLE PICCHIONE DI MARINO, 46
00040 MARINO (RM)
TEL. 06/93546329

GOTTO D'ORO
FRAZ. FRATTOCCHIE
VIA DEL DIVINO AMORE, 115
00040 MARINO (RM)
TEL. 06/9302221

The "Cotarella cure" is beginning to work its magic here at Colle Picchioni and a good two of Paola and Armando di Mauro's wines reached our final Three Glass taste-off. It has been some time since that last happened. But more importantly, the entire range is now more consistent and more impressive. even though some of the wines are, or look like remaining, rather undemanding. However, this time cabernet and merlot Vigna del Vassallo '98 really hit the spot. There may still be a proportion of the wine that is aged in large casks but even as it stands, it came over as far more concentrated and complex than in recent years. Now it is the fruit, the more varietal aromas, especially of Merlot, and impressive softness on the palate that prevail. It still needs a little more weight in the mouth to gain a really high score but it is certainly on the right track. Similar considerations apply to Marino Colle Picchioni Oro '99, with its aromas of ripe, almost tropical fruit nuanced with pineapple, white peach and fresh almond. Here at last is a white that is concentrated, soft and easy to drink, without the rustic or bitterish finish that may have been its calling card but was not appreciated by most customers. We finished with the more straightforward, immediate wines, the light, fruity, drinkable Marino Etichetta Verde '99 and Colle Picchioni Rosso '99, principally from montepulciano and merlot, which has slim structure but reasonable elegance.

Good, easy to find and competitively priced. It takes just a few short words to sum up the wines of this large Marino-based co-operative whose celebrated Frascati and Marino whites are exported all over the world. In addition, the average level is not only good but consistent enough, year after year, for us to be able to talk about genuine reliability. With the grapes contributed by members from several hundred hectares of vineyard, we are sure that sooner or later Gotto d'Oro will set up a research and experimentation programme to enable the cellar to turn out more challenging wines, rather as has been done at the Cantina Produttori dell'Alto Adige. Meanwhile, anyone looking for a good, fresh, fragrant glassful, redolent of hedgerow and golden delicious apples, need look no further than the '99 Frascati. If you want a wine to drink with full-flavoured fish dishes or even white meat, there's a good Marino, brimming with spring flowers and ripe peach and apricot fruit, which fits the bill. Then we tasted the sweet Marino, simple as dessert wines go, but still one of the nicest and most successful around. As ideal an accompaniment for petit fours and cakes as it is with mature ewe's milk cheeses. The Castelli Romani Rosso has a slim but perceptible body and is fresh, fruity, lightly tannic and balanced. Just the wine for those who don't like heavy reds. And if you want something red but with a light, refreshing prickle, make a beeline for the Castelli Romani Vivace or the Merlot del Lazio. Obviously, we are not talking about major bottles but these are tried and tested wines that offer uncomplicated drinking pleasure.

O Marino Colle Picchioni Oro '99	🍷🍷	4
● Vigna del Vassallo '98	🍷🍷	5
● Colle Picchioni Rosso '98	🍷	4
O Marino Etichetta Verde '99	🍷	3
● Vigna del Vassallo '85	🍷🍷🍷	5
● Vigna del Vassallo '88	🍷🍷🍷	5
O Le Vignole '93	🍷🍷	4
O Marino Colle Picchioni Oro '97	🍷🍷	4
O Marino Colle Picchioni Oro '98	🍷🍷	4
● Vigna del Vassallo '90	🍷🍷	5
● Vigna del Vassallo '92	🍷🍷	5
● Vigna del Vassallo '93	🍷🍷	5
● Vigna del Vassallo '95	🍷🍷	5
● Vigna del Vassallo '96	🍷🍷	5
● Vigna del Vassallo '97	🍷🍷	5

● Castelli Romani '99	🍷	2*
O Frascati Superiore '99	🍷	2*
O Marino Superiore '99	🍷	2*
O Marino Superiore Dolce '99	🍷	2*
O Castelli Romani Frizzante '99		2
O Malvasia del Lazio '99		2
● Merlot del Lazio Frizzante '99		2
● Castelli Romani '97	🍷	2*
● Castelli Romani '98	🍷	2*
O Frascati Superiore '96	🍷	2*
O Frascati Superiore '97	🍷	2*
O Frascati Superiore '98	🍷	2*
O Marino Superiore '96	🍷	2*
O Marino Superiore '97	🍷	2*
O Marino Superiore '98	🍷	2*

MONTEFIASCONE (VT)   MONTEPORZIO CATONE (RM)

FALESCO
LOC. ARTIGIANA LE GUARDIE
01027 MONTEFIASCONE (VT)
TEL. 0761/825669

FONTANA CANDIDA
VIA FONTANA CANDIDA, 11
00040 MONTEPORZIO CATONE (RM)
TEL. 06/9420066

Here we go again. Not for the first time, Falesco lines up in pole position as the only Lazio estate to take home those Three much sought-after Guide Glasses. And again, it is all down to Montiano. Irrespective of what the weather brings, Montiano keeps abreast of Italy's other great wines. Riccardo Cotarella, who owns this well-known, modern winery and has an understanding of the Viterbo district second to none, has now decided to work with the indigenous rossetto variety and has created a captivating white, the Ferentano '99. It makes a welcome change from the ubiquitous chardonnay, with its refined style in which the oak and the fruit knit together so elegantly. Two Glasses, brimful. Vitiano '99, from cabernet, merlot and sangiovese, has pervasive herbaceous aromas and spicy overtones. It is very attractive indeed, and even shows decent complexity. The '99 Est Est Est Falesco has retained the understated style that is the wine's hallmark, giving more emphasis to its aromatic profile and freshness than to structure. The Poggio dei Gelsi '99 selection has a broad range of fruity nuances which have taken on tropical notes this year. The '99 Grechetto showed as well as the previous vintage. Its brief contact with oak has not compromised the primary aromatic components but actually enhances them instead. It is full-flavoured and long, with an attractively bitterish finish. The '98 version of the Vendemmia Tardiva, from classic local grapes picked when super-ripe, made a good impression. The nose has greater breadth than usual in its aromas of honey, sweet pears and spring flowers. The taste does not cloy, indeed it is remarkably fresh and has undeniable power of expression.

Fontana Candida is a large winery and Franco Bardi is the guiding spirit who makes sure it remains one of the landmarks of the Lazio wine scene. And when a monster winery such as this manages to improve what is generally thought of as supermarket wine like Frascati, then it is no coincidence. Tasting is believing. The '99 Frascati Superiore is Fontana Candida's best ever and has incredible freshness and deep fruitiness. Moreover, its price is still very competitive. Naturally, the Santa Teresa selection is still the company's top wine and always comes out among the leaders in our tastings. The '99 impresses with the fragrance of its aromas, its great freshness and the elegance of its undertones. The Two Glasses are well-merited. Fontana Candida was the first estate to believe in the potential of Malvasia del Lazio and today's wines are the result of years of experimentation. The '99 Malvasia del Lazio from the Terre dei Grifi line is again very good, with a broad swathe of aromas, most notably banana and sage, supported by a soft freshness. The '99 Frascati Superiore from the same line is also very interesting. Careful selection of the grapes has enhanced its aromas, giving a very intense fruitiness beneath overt floral notes and the palate is full and zesty, with a very attractive streak of freshness.

●	Montiano '98	♟♟♟	5
O	Est Est Est di Montefiascone		
	Poggio dei Gelsi '99	♟♟	3*
O	Est Est Est di Montefiascone		
	Vendemmia Tardiva '98	♟♟	4
O	Ferentano '99	♟♟	5
O	Grechetto '99	♟♟	3*
●	Vitiano '99	♟♟	3*
O	Est Est Est di Montefiascone		
	Falesco '99	♟	2*
●	Montiano '94	♟♟♟	5
●	Montiano '95	♟♟♟	5
●	Montiano '96	♟♟♟	5
●	Montiano '97	♟♟♟	5
●	Montiano '93	♟♟	5

O	Frascati Sup. Santa Teresa '99	♟♟	2*
O	Malvasia del Lazio '99	♟♟	2*
O	Frascati Sup. Terre dei Grifi '99	♟	2*
O	Frascati Superiore '99	♟	2*
O	Frascati Sup. Santa Teresa '93	♟♟	2*
O	Frascati Sup. Santa Teresa '94	♟♟	2*
O	Frascati Sup. Santa Teresa '95	♟♟	2*
O	Frascati Sup. Santa Teresa '96	♟♟	2*
O	Frascati Sup. Santa Teresa '97	♟♟	2*
O	Frascati Sup. Santa Teresa '98	♟♟	2*
O	Frascati Sup. Terre dei Grifi '95	♟♟	2*
O	Malvasia del Lazio '95	♟♟	2*
O	Malvasia del Lazio '96	♟♟	2*
O	Malvasia del Lazio '97	♟♟	2*
O	Malvasia del Lazio '98	♟♟	2*

MONTEPORZIO CATONE (RM)   ROMA

VILLA SIMONE - PIERO COSTANTINI
VIA FRASCATI-COLONNA, 29
00040 MONTEPORZIO CATONE (RM)
TEL. 06/3213210 - 06/9449717

CONTE ZANDOTTI
VIA VIGNE COLLE MATTIA, 8
00132 ROMA
TEL. 06/20609000 - 06/6160335

Vigna dei Preti continues to reflect Villa Simone's safe, dependable winemaking style. We have always liked the fragrance and the enchanting freshness of the wine from this vineyard but this year it seemed better than ever. Perhaps Piero Costantini will be surprised at all this emphasis on one wine believing, with considerable justification, that all his wines merit close attention. But since our job involves documenting the evolution of his, and others', wines year by year, it is only right to underline the aspects that we feel distinguish one wine from another. Frascati Superiore Villa Simone '99, for example, continues to be a well-made, well-typed wine but in a lower key than the others in the range. At the other end of the scale, we might compare the Frascati Vigneto Filinardi to a Burgundy "clos", a small parcel subject to variable weather conditions whose wines are not allowed to be "adjusted" by grapes from elsewhere. The '99 is a fine product which we feel will have to age longer than usual to allow its wide range of aromas and flavours to develop fully. The '98 Cannellino has at last been released and is developing excellently. It is full, fat and opulent, with a rich, silky texture, and is very attractive.

After trying the Conte Zandotti wines on several occasions, we had the distinct impression that something in their make-up had changed. In short, each time they seemed better than the last. This is a clear example of just how much certain wines benefit by being given bottle ageing. The estate's Frascatis, produced with determination by oenologist, Marco Ciarla, display remarkable balance. The '99 version of Frascati Superiore is probably the best ever. The colour is a not particularly deep straw-yellow while the aromas are full and elegant, linking with the warmth and softness in the mouth in perfect nose-palate symmetry. The Malvasia del Lazio Rumon '99 has a deep bouquet with clear notes of almond, alongside attractive touches of spice and honey. The palate is firm but fairly open and fresh but never loses the characteristic mellow softness of the style. It is well worth its Two Glasses. The focus of Frascati Cannellino '99 is its elegance and gentle sweetness, flanked by attractive notes of honey and spring flowers. As for the red La Petrosa '99, bottled after six months in large oak casks, it still needs time to come round but is already fairly firm, warm and mouth-filling, with aromas of berry fruit and spices. With a shade more concentration, it will become one of Lazio's great reds.

O Frascati Sup. Cannellino '98	ΨΨ	4
O Frascati Sup. V. dei Preti '99	ΨΨ	2*
O Frascati Sup. Vign. Filonardi '99	ΨΨ	3*
O Frascati Sup. Villa Simone '99		2
O Frascati Sup. Cannellino '91	ΨΨ	5
O Frascati Sup. Cannellino '92	ΨΨ	5
O Frascati Sup. Cannellino '97	ΨΨ	5
O Frascati Sup. V. dei Preti '94	ΨΨ	2*
O Frascati Sup. V. dei Preti '95	ΨΨ	2*
O Frascati Sup. V. dei Preti '97	ΨΨ	2*
O Frascati Sup. Vign. Filonardi '93	ΨΨ	3*
O Frascati Sup. Vign. Filonardi '94	ΨΨ	3*
O Frascati Sup. Vign. Filonardi '95	ΨΨ	3*
O Frascati Sup. Vign. Filonardi '97	ΨΨ	3*
O Frascati Sup. Vign. Filonardi '97	ΨΨ	3*

O Frascati Cannellino '99	ΨΨ	3*
O Frascati Superiore '99	ΨΨ	2*
● La Petrosa '99	ΨΨ	4
O Malvasia del Lazio Rumon '99	Ψ	3
O Frascati Cannellino '95	ΨΨ	3*
O Frascati Cannellino '96	ΨΨ	3*
O Frascati Superiore '94	ΨΨ	2*
O Frascati Superiore '95	ΨΨ	2*
O Frascati Superiore '98	ΨΨ	2*
● La Petrosa '98	ΨΨ	4
O Malvasia del Lazio Rumon '98	ΨΨ	3*
O Frascati Cannellino '94	Ψ	3
O Frascati Cannellino '97	Ψ	3
O Frascati Cannellino '98	Ψ	3
O Frascati Cannellino De Copa '97	Ψ	3

OTHER WINERIES

The following producers obtained good scores in our tastings with one or more of their wines:

PROVINCE OF FROSINONE

Cantina Colacicchi Anagni,
Anagni, tel. 06/4469661
Romagnano Bianco '98

Antonello Coletti Conti,
Anagni, tel. 0775/728610
Cesanese del Piglio Hernicus '99

Marcella Giuliani,
Anagni, tel. 06/44235908
Cesanese del Piglio Alagna '99

Paolo Perinelli,
Anagni, tel. 0775/56031
Cesanese del Piglio '99,
Cesanese del Piglio Casale della Ioria '99

Giuseppe Iucci,
Cassino, tel. 0776/311883
Merlot di Atina Tenuta La Creta '99

La Selva,
Paliano, tel. 0775/533125
Cesanese del Piglio '99,
Passerina del Frusinate '99

Cantina Sociale Cesanese del Piglio,
Piglio, tel. 0775/502355
Cesanese del Piglio Etichetta Oro '99,
Cesanese del Piglio Etichetta Rossa '99

Vigneti Massimi Berucci,
Piglio, tel. 06/68307004
Cesanese del Piglio Casal Cervino '99,
Passerina del Frusinate '99

PROVINCE OF LATINA

Cantina Sociale Cincinnato,
Cori, tel. 06/9679384
Rosso dei Dioscuri '99

Pouchain, Ponza, tel. 06/30365644
Vino di Bianca '99

PROVINCE OF ROMA

Casale Mattia,
Frascati, tel. 06/9426249
Frascati Superiore '99,
Rosso di Casale Mattia '99

Casale Vallechiesa,
Frascati, tel. 06/9417270
Frascati Sup. Vallechiesa '99

L'Olivella,
Frascati, tel. 06/9424527
Frascati Sup. Racemo '99

Pallavicini,
Frascati, tel. 06/9438816
Frascati Superiore '99

Pietra Porzia,
Frascati, tel. 06/9464392
Frascati Sup. Regillo Etichetta Nera '99

San Marco,
Frascati, tel.06/9422689
Frascati Sup. Selezione' 99

Cantina Sociale La Selva,
Genzano, tel.06/9396085
Colli Lanuvini Sup. Fontanatorta '99

Camponeschi,
Lanuvio, tel. 06/9374390
Carato Bianco '99,
Carato Rosso '98,
Colli Lanuvini Superiore '99,

Le Quinte,
Montecompatri, tel. 06/9438756
Montecompatri Colonna Sup.
Casale dei Papi '99,
Montecompatri Colonna Sup.
Virtù Romane '99,
Rasa di Marmorata '99

CO.PRO.VI,
Velletri, tel. 06/9587444
Velletri Bianco Villa Ginnetti '99,
Velletri Rosso Riserva '97

Cesare Loreti,
Zagarolo, tel. 06/9575956
Zagarolo Sup. Vigneti Loreti '99

PROVINCE OF VITERBO

Cantina Sociale di Gradoli,
Gradoli, tel. 0761/456087
Aleatico di Gradoli Ris.

Cantina Sociale Colli Cimini,
Vignanello, tel. 0761/754591
Greco di Vignanello

ABRUZZO AND MOLISE

Looking back through the introductions to the Abruzzo and Molise section over the past few years, we note that we have frequently stressed the overall improvement in the quality of the estates and their wines. Happily, this year's tastings have shown that this trend is continuing. In Abruzzo, there is one producer, Illuminati, who has newly joined the exclusive Three Glass club with the wine Lumen. But more generally, a sort of "virtuous circle" has been triggered where the leading producers are beginning to concentrate on areas that have long been ignored. They are now devoting serious effort to the vineyards and are taking on highly skilled consultants to turn out a finished product that does credit to the grapes it was made from. This is nothing new in the case of Edoardo Valentini, who has spent half a century in his vineyards and cellars. It has also been true, although on a much shorter time scale, of Gianni Masciarelli, the architect of some extraordinary wines this year as he has been in other recent vintages. Their example shows that Abruzzo clearly has the ability to produce wines of supreme class and that all it ought to take for other producers to follow suit is a similar degree of determination. Living proof of this is the amiable Dino Illuminati, based in the north of the Teramo area, whose Lumen scaled the peaks. And it is in the cards for Luigi Cataldi Madonna, Marcello Zaccagnini, Alessio Di Majo and perhaps also Marina Orlandi Contucci, Sabatino Di Properzio of Fattoria La Valentina, Camillo Montori, Enrico Marramiero and Cantina Tollo. At least, these are the producers whose abilities and potential are fueling our expectations. Our tastings have, as expected, confirmed the standing of this group of estates. Gianni Masciarello takes centre stage with two Three Glass wines as well as the Wine of the Year award for the outstanding Montepulciano d'Abruzzo Villa Gemma '95. The "Maestro", Edoardo Valentini, is back with wines to present and they are as good as ever. Since each producer is free to submit whatever he or she likes for tasting, we found ourselves assessing wines straddling four or five different vintages. So perhaps we should mention that, apart from the odd exception, '96 was the worst vintage of the decadè while the run from '97 to 2000 was very good throughout, with the exception of a slight dip in '99. This means that the foundations are all there for those who have the skills and the determination to take their wines' from merely good to great. We have two final observations. The first regards the large number of Other Wineries listed on the last page of this section, some of which – particularly Sarchese Dora from Abruzzo and Borgo di Colloredo from Molise – deserve a full entry but had to be relegated there for reasons of space. The second reason is perhaps even more important. There still does not appear to be any common strategy among producers. Each goes his or her own sweet way, so much so that the proposal to set up a consortium to work on topics such as the identification of subzones is still gathering dust somewhere. That's not quite true. A consortium of the Colline Teramane producers does exist but it has not exactly been utilized fully. And this does nobody any good.

BOLOGNANO (PE)

CICCIO ZACCAGNINI
C.DA POZZO
65020 BOLOGNANO (PE)
TEL. 085/8880195

Zaccagnini's wines get better every year. It all goes to show the value of the serious effort put in, first by the late Ciccio Zaccagnini and now by his demanding and extremely outgoing son, Marcello. The technical side of the winery is in the hands of able oenologist, Concezio Marulli, and recently they have been turning out some highly impressive wines. The new expansion of the vineyard holding brings it to about 45 hectares, scattered across the surrounding area. There is also a new cellar overlooking the Orta Valley. The two most compelling wines are both from the San Clemente line. The Montepulciano d'Abruzzo, one of the best tasted this year, has a concentrated ruby colour and is noteworthy for its fine balance of fruit and oak on both nose and palate. The wine is tightly knit, elegant and has a full, firm finish. The other stunner, the Chardonnay, is strongly varietal and has exemplary aromatic purity. The ripe banana and citrus fruit on the palate is well supported by acidity and integrates well with the oak. There have been improvements in the other wines, too. Most notable of these is the classically styled '98 Montepulciano d'Abruzzo, a "classic" in that it offers firm structure on the palate, abundant tannins and an assertive fruitiness. These characteristics are less evident on Castello di Salle '97 and Capsico Rosso. Bianco di Ciccio, from trebbiano and chardonnay, and the riesling-based Ibisco Bianco are as attractive as usual. Special credit is due for Zaccagnini's work on his Cerasuolos, Myositis in particular, and on the dessert wines, most notably the passito dried-grape wine from moscato, a variety that has been cultivated in the area for centuries.

CAMPOMARINO (CB)

DI MAJO NORANTE
C.DA RAMITELLO, 4
86042 CAMPOMARINO (CB)
TEL. 0875/57208

Molise's leading estate, run by Alessio Di Majo, is on the ascendant, having taken on Riccardo Cotarella as consultant last year. All the wines are praiseworthy, especially the reds, as they have ridden better the caprices of recent vintages. However, Don Luigi, a great wine from montepulciano and aglianico, stands head and shoulders above the rest. It has an intense, pulpy fruitiness with fresh balsamic notes on both nose and palate. The rest of the range is also fresh, well-styled and good drinking. The most obvious example is the inexpensive, tasty Molì, made with the same grapes as Don Luigi, but the warmer, more mature and structured Ramitello Rosso, with its black cherry notes, is also good in its class. Then there is Prugnolo, an elegant wine with depth of flavour and a toasty, vanilla aftertaste. The three whites are also in a modern style, especially the Greco, which has delicate perfumes of ripe citrus fruits and a decently structured palate with a good swathe of acidity. This makes it a wine that is easy to drink without being dull. The Falanghina is less expressive on the nose but the palate is harmonious with an enjoyable taste. It also has a bitterish note on the finish, as does the clean, well-typed Molì Bianco. After a few years on the sidelines, the Apianae dessert wine returns to the limelight with a nose offering aromas of candied fruit and a sweet, well-structured palate.

O Chardonnay Abbazia S. Clemente '99 ♀♀	4
● Montepulciano d'Abruzzo Abbazia S. Clemente '98 ♀♀	5
O Bianco di Ciccio '99 ♀	3
● Capsico Rosso '96 ♀	4
O Ibisco Bianco '98 ♀	3
☉ Ibisco Rosa '99 ♀	3
● Montepulciano d'Abruzzo '98 ♀	3
● Montepulciano d'Abruzzo Castello di Salle '97 ♀	4
☉ Montepulciano d'Abruzzo Cerasuolo '99 ♀	3
☉ Montepulciano d'Abruzzo Cerasuolo Myosotis '99 ♀	3
O Passito Bianco '98 ♀	4
● Passito Rosso '98	4

● Molise Don Luigi '98 ♀♀	5
O Apianae '98 ♀	4
O Biferno Molì Bianco '99 ♀	1*
● Biferno Molì Rosso '99 ♀	2*
● Biferno Rosso Ramitello '98 ♀	3
O Molise Falanghina '99 ♀	3
O Molise Greco '99 ♀	3
● Prugnolo '98 ♀	3
O Apianae '93 ♀♀	4
O Biblos '95 ♀♀	4
● Biferno Rosso Ramitello '96 ♀♀	3*
● Biferno Rosso Ramitello '97 ♀♀	3*
● Prugnolo '97 ♀♀	3*
● Aglianico Contado '97 ♀	3
● Don Luigi '97 ♀	4

COLONNELLA (TE)

LEPORE
C.DA CIVITA
64010 COLONNELLA (TE)
TEL. 0861/70860 - 085/4222835

The Lepore estate, which is about to celebrate its tenth anniversary, is as reliable as they come. The family has always been aware of the need for continuous experimentation and development in both vineyards and cellars. As a result, steady improvements in quality have kept coming. There are currently about 30 hectares of vine and Gaspare Lepore, together with his oenologist, Umberto Svizzeri, and his sales manager, Giampiero Cichetti, can take great pride in having concentrated on indigenous varieties from the beginning, montepulciano in particular for the reds and passerina for the whites. Two wines are produced from each grape, one being more straightforward and the other one barrique-aged. Paradoxically, it was the pair of "basic" versions that showed better, although there is still room for improvement. The '98 Montepulciano d'Abruzzo has a concentrated ruby red colour. The nose is shy at first, then opens to reveal pervasive aromas of ripe cherry. The palate is soft and structured, its fruit nicely highlighted by hints of spiciness. The white Passera delle Vigne has a characteristic pale straw-yellow colour and an engagingly floral nose with aromas of just-ripe citrus fruits. These notes are echoed intensely on the palate, which has a firm acid backbone. The barriqued version, Do, although reasonably successful, has slightly less substance overall and the same could also be said of the Montepulciano d'Abruzzo Re. We await future improvements. The Trebbiano d'Abruzzo is uncomplicated and well-typed but the Cerasuolo has suffered from the problematic vintage.

CONTROGUERRA (TE)

DINO ILLUMINATI
C.DA S. BIAGIO, 18
64010 CONTROGUERRA (TE)
TEL. 0861/808008

Dino Illuminati has finally cracked it. The Three Glasses went to his Lumen wine but they seem more like a lifetime achievement award. There are 70 hectares of vineyard, a dedicated cellar staff working under oenologist, Claudio Cappellacci, and Giorgio Marone as consultant. And the estate's wines are always spot on. The '96 vintage was not one of the best so we will have to wait until the '97 releases for the Montepulciano d'Abruzzo Zanna and the Nicò. With the '97 vintage, Lumen is labelled as a Controguerra DOC wine, which gave its creators a freer hand with the montepulciano and cabernet sauvignon. As a result, it has turned into an extraordinary wine. The colour is a lively, deep ruby and the nose has aromas of mulberry, redcurrant and white damson with touches of fresh cut grass. The palate has a ripe, penetrating fruity base, shot through with hints of coffee. It develops powerfully but evenly in the mouth, and is close-knit and elegant. Montepulciano d'Abruzzo Riparosso, although officially Illuminati's "base" wine, is actually one of his best. It is deep in colour and has plentiful fruit, with a touch of oak adding refinement. The four whites are as attractive as usual, from the warm, evolved barrique-aged Trebbiano d'Abruzzo Daniele to the well-fruited Chardonnay Cenalba, the floral Ciafré and the straightforward Costalupo. Montepulciano d'Abruzzo Cerasuolo Campirosa is also good, with an attractive cherry hue and a fresh, youthful fruitiness, while the botrytized Loré gains Two Glasses for its well-defined aromas of sage, rosemary and citrus, given extra impetus by its sweetness.

● Montepulciano d'Abruzzo '98	▼	3
● Montepulciano d'Abruzzo		
Colline Teramane Re '97	▼	4
○ Passera delle Vigne '99	▼	3
○ Passerina Do '98	▼	4
○ Trebbiano d'Abruzzo '99	▼	3
⊙ Montepulciano d'Abruzzo		
Cerasuolo '99		3
● Montepulciano d'Abruzzo '96	♀	3
● Montepulciano d'Abruzzo '97	♀	3
● Montepulciano d'Abruzzo		
Luigi Lepore '95	♀	5
● Montepulciano d'Abruzzo		
Luigi Lepore Ris. '93	♀	5
● Passito dei Lepore '95	♀	5

● Controguerra Lumen '97	▼▼▼	6
○ Loré Muffa Nobile	▼▼	4
● Montepulciano d'Abruzzo		
Riparosso '99	▼▼	3*
○ Controguerra Chardonnay Cenalba '98	▼	3
○ Controguerra Ciafré '98	▼	3
○ Controguerra Costalupo '98	▼	2
⊙ Montepulciano d'Abruzzo		
Cerasuolo Campirosa '98	▼	2*
○ Trebbiano d'Abruzzo Daniele '97	▼	4
● Montepulciano d'Abruzzo Lumen '95	♀♀	5
● Montepulciano d'Abruzzo		
Riparosso '98	♀♀	2*
● Montepulciano d'Abruzzo		
Zanna Vecchio '95	♀♀	4

CONTROGUERRA (TE)

CAMILLO MONTORI
PIANE TRONTO, 23
64010 CONTROGUERRA (TE)
TEL. 0861/809900

Camillo Montori's long-standing estate is one of those held in highest esteem in the region and Montori himself is an enthralling character, someone who comes up with ideas that can benefit all the producers in the area, and then sees them through to fruition. Even if there have been no fireworks from his wines recently, his 30 hectares or so of vineyard still produce grapes that give bottles of very high quality. Montori's greatest strengths are with his reds, particularly the Montepulciano d'Abruzzo Fonte Cupa, and the '97 has good impact on the nose and an attractive ripe fruitiness which also comes through on the palate, though here integrated with the oak. The structure is impressive, although the definition is not quite perfect and the tannins are just a touch edgy but the finish is decently long. Leneo Moro '97, from montepulciano and cabernet, was not ready in time for our tastings but the '98 Montepulciano d'Abruzzo, a most approachable wine with an easy fruitiness and good drinkability, made a very good impression on the panel. The two leading whites derive from contrasting winemaking approaches. The Trebbiano d'Abruzzo Fonte Cupa is as attractive as usual. Clean and well-focused, it unveils intense scents of ripe fruit, a full palate and enough acidity to give good definition. The Leneo d'Oro '98, from oak-fermented chardonnay and trebbiano, has a more intense, developed colour but both nose and palate seem to lack fruit, allowing the oak to take over. The two Cerasuolos seemed to be showing signs of premature oxidation, no doubt due, at least in part, to the vintage. They will need a second look.

○ Controguerra Leneo d'Oro '98	▼	4
● Montepulciano d'Abruzzo '98	▼	2*
● Montepulciano d'Abruzzo Fonte Cupa '97	▼	4
○ Trebbiano d'Abruzzo Fonte Cupa '99	▼	3
○ Controguerra Fauno '99		2
⊙ Montepulciano d'Abruzzo Cerasuolo Fonte Cupa '99		3
● Leneo Moro '94	▽▽	5
● Leneo Moro '95	▽▽	5
● Montepulciano d'Abruzzo Fonte Cupa '94	▽▽	4*
○ Leneo d'Oro '97	▽	4
● Leneo Moro '96	▽	4
● Montepulciano d'Abruzzo Fonte Cupa '96	▽	4

FRANCAVILLA A MARE (CH)

FRANCO PASETTI
C.DA PRETARO
VIA S. PAOLO, 21
66023 FRANCAVILLA A MARE (CH)
TEL. 085/61875

It looks as if Mimmo and Rocco Pasetti are well on the way to achieving their quality aims. With the new vines at Collecorvino now in production, the holding has reached 40 hectares and the grapes are of high quality, bringing clearly discernible improvements to the wines. Confirmation comes from Montepulciano d'Abruzzo Fattoria Pasetti and the new white, Tenuta di Testarossa. The former has a deep ruby colour and a nose that opens slowly but decisively, giving aromas of ripe red fruit. The palate is full and well-structured, the oak is not intrusive, the finish is long and there is a tang of liquorice on the aftertaste. The Testarossa is from chardonnay, pecorino and trebbiano and, surprisingly, has vague similarities to white Burgundy. Here, too, a lot of skill has obviously gone into the winemaking, the careful use of small and medium-sized barrels giving a balanced amount of oak. This is well-integrated into the wine's citrus and banana notes and its mineral tones, so that there is an elegant overall fluency. Yet again, the Montepulciano d'Abruzzo Tenuta di Testarossa comes tantalisingly close to Two Glasses. Even just after bottling, it already had excellent aromatic definition, with berry fruit aromas intertwining with oak toast, although the concentration was still awry. Similarly, the tannins were a little in disarray on an otherwise full, structured palate. The Trebbiano d'Abruzzo Fattoria Pasetti, with uncomplicated perfumes and good acidity, is attractive and well-styled.

● Montepulciano d'Abruzzo '98	▼▼	3*
○ Tenuta di Testarossa Bianco '99	▼▼	4
● Montepulciano d'Abruzzo Tenuta di Testarossa '97	▼	4
○ Trebbiano d'Abruzzo '99	▼	2*
⊙ Montepulciano d'Abruzzo Cerasuolo '99		2
● Montepulciano d'Abruzzo '96	▽	2*
● Montepulciano d'Abruzzo '97	▽	2*
● Montepulciano d'Abruzzo Tenuta di Testarossa '94	▽	4
● Montepulciano d'Abruzzo Tenuta di Testarossa '95	▽	4
○ Trebbiano d'Abruzzo '98	▽	2*

LORETO APRUTINO (PE)   MIGLIANICO (CH)

★ EDOARDO VALENTINI
VIA DEL BAIO, 2
65014 LORETO APRUTINO (PE)
TEL. 085/8291138

CANTINA MIGLIANICO
VIA SAN GIACOMO, 40
66010 MIGLIANICO (CH)
TEL. 0871/951262 - 0871/950240

That maestro of the vineyard, Edoardo Valentini, continues to shower us with oenological gems. It might seem paradoxical but the way Valentini's wines are made, quite apart from the fact that he keeps a good deal of his technique a strictly guarded secret, has something of the classical world about it. It is not just chance that Edoardo often cites the Pre-Socratic philosophers of ancient Greece who sought the origins of life in the natural elements, earth, water, fire and air. It is the naturalness of the wines that gives them their fascination, their small imperfections enhancing their great character. There's a little residual carbon dioxide, but this happens even to the whites of Leonard Humbrecht, a winemaking wizard if ever there was one. There's a hint of reduction when the bottles are first uncorked, but Edoardo insists that his wines need to be allowed to breather for some time before drinking. You also have to wait for years before the wines show what they're really made of but just try the Trebbiano d'Abruzzo '92. At first, it was heavily criticized. Now, it is a monument of complexity and elegance. But let's have a look at this year's wines. Edoardo brought out his '97 Trebbiano before the '96, which he felt had further to go. And as usual, he was right. The '97 is simpler and appears to be developing faster while the '96 is one of Valentini's great Trebbianos. It will reward anyone who can keep it in the cellar until 2010 many times over. The Montepulciano Cerasuolo '97 is excellent and up to the standard of the great '95. The '94 Montepulciano d'Abruzzo is less concentrated and powerful than some other versions. It is evidently from a mediocre harvest. As the Greeks could have told you, there's no arguing with Nature.

Cantina Miglianico remains one of the most dynamic co-operatives of the region, and one that manages to marry large quantities with ever-improved quality. This is especially true of the less expensive wines. These benefit by the work on grape selection directed by the winery's oenologist, Carmine Mancini, on some of the better sites belonging to the co-operative's 450 members. The less expensive of the two labels, the Montupoli, was, as ever, laudable. The Montepulciano d'Abruzzo Montupoli '98 is the pick of the bunch, a red that marries attractive drinkability with the structure of a premium wine. It has intriguing aromas of ripe red and black cherries shot through with spicy notes of coffee, and a full, balanced fluency in the mouth that is well nigh exemplary. The Trebbiano d'Abruzzo from the same line has a pale straw-yellow colour and aromas of ripe apple and banana but is let down by a palate that, although well-styled, is just too slim. The first-label Trebbiano d'Abruzzo was not submitted for tasting but its red counterpart, the Montepulciano d'Abruzzo Fondatore selection, dedicated to the founder of the estate, was presented and proved to be somewhat below par. There are delicate blackcurrant aromas on the nose with herbaceous undertones but these are squashed by a rather pungent note. The palate has medium weight, tannins that are still astringent and a slightly bitterish finish.

O Trebbiano d'Abruzzo '96	♔♔♔	5
● Montepulciano d'Abruzzo '94	♔♔	6
⊙ Montepulciano d'Abruzzo		
Cerasuolo '97	♔♔	5
O Trebbiano d'Abruzzo '97	♔♔	5
● Montepulciano d'Abruzzo '77	♔♔♔	6
● Montepulciano d'Abruzzo '85	♔♔♔	6
● Montepulciano d'Abruzzo '88	♔♔♔	6
● Montepulciano d'Abruzzo '90	♔♔♔	6
● Montepulciano d'Abruzzo '92	♔♔♔	6
O Trebbiano d'Abruzzo '88	♔♔♔	5
O Trebbiano d'Abruzzo '92	♔♔♔	5
O Trebbiano d'Abruzzo '95	♔♔♔	5
● Montepulciano d'Abruzzo '87	♔♔	6
● Montepulciano d'Abruzzo '93	♔♔	6

● Montepulciano d'Abruzzo		
Montupoli '98	♔♔	2*
O Trebbiano d'Abruzzo		
Fondatore '97	♔	4
O Trebbiano d'Abruzzo Montupoli '99	♔	2*
⊙ Montepulciano d'Abruzzo		
Cerasuolo Montupoli '99		2
● Montepulciano d'Abruzzo		
Fondatore '96	♔	4
● Montepulciano d'Abruzzo		
Montupoli '97	♔	2*
O Trebbiano d'Abruzzo		
Montupoli '98	♔	2*

NOCCIANO (PE)

NOTARESCO (TE)

NESTORE BOSCO
C.DA CASALI, 7
65010 NOCCIANO (PE)
TEL. 085/847345

BRUNO NICODEMI
C.DA VENIGLIO
S. P. 19
64024 NOTARESCO (TE)
TEL. 085/895493 - 085/895135

This profile shows that we have not lost our faith in the wines of one of the oldest wineries in Abruzzo. Indeed, we believe that, thanks to the considerable improvements Giovanni and Nestore Bosco have brought to their wines in the last few years, all that is needed is a tiny extra push on the technical front for the whole range to reach reliably high quality standards. It is better to concentrate for now on the more classic wines, the two traditional versions of Montepulciano d'Abruzzo, as the estate's new bottles are not really up to speed yet. The '97 selection shows that old-style doesn't have to mean old-fashioned. It has a dense, weighty palate with a firm note of alcohol that helps project its notes of black cherry and raspberry. A little tannic, but tightly knit, on the front palate, it then develops evenly, finishing with a faintly bitter tone. The younger wine, the '99, has a ruby colour with tinges of violet, and its fresh fruitiness and gentle balsamic notes give it much more charm. The palate is soft and balanced, although not particularly long. The Pan line, comprising a Montepulciano d'Abruzzo and a Chardonnay, the latter the estate's newest wine, falls somewhere between the two classics. Both are modern in style but, so far at least, without very much personality. The Trebbiano d'Abruzzo, however, is clean, straightforward and well-made, as is Grappolo Rosso, from sangiovese, merlot and montepulciano. A fruity, early-drinking wine, it nevertheless has the structure of a wine with a much more exalted pedigree.

There's been a renewed outbreak of enthusiasm at the Nicodemi residence, probably because Elena and Alessandro, offspring of the late Bruno, who died a few years ago, are now installed on the estate. It is still too early to say how they will adapt the winemaking techniques in order to get back on the quality trail. They seem to have hit a few potholes recently but on the other hand, the estate owns almost 35 hectares, on an ideal site and with state-of-the-art technology to hand. It ought to be set fair, and indeed, this year's tastings showed clear quality improvements. The Montepulciano d'Abruzzo Bacco selection from '97 won Two Glasses. Incidentally, it was a praiseworthy decision to skip '96, one of the worst vintages of the decade. The '97 has a well-defined nose and assertive fruitiness on the attractive but slightly one-dimensional palate, together with spicy notes from the oak. The finish is reminiscent of liquorice. The Trebbiano d'Abruzzo from the same line is also good. It is a bright straw-yellow. The nose has peach and citrus aromas, introducing a soft palate with a gentle acid backbone. The better two of the three wines from the classic line are Montepulciano d'Abruzzo '98, whose decently structured palate makes it, as usual, a very attractive proposition, and the fresh, perfumed Cerasuolo.

● Grappolo Rosso '99	♀	2*
● Montepulciano d'Abruzzo '97	♀	4
● Montepulciano d'Abruzzo '99	♀	2*
● Montepulciano d'Abruzzo Pan '98	♀	4
○ Trebbiano d'Abruzzo '99	♀	2*
○ Chardonnay Pan '98		4
⊙ Montepulciano d'Abruzzo Cerasuolo '99		2
● Montepulciano d'Abruzzo '95	♀	4
● Montepulciano d'Abruzzo '98	♀	2*
● Montepulciano d'Abruzzo Pan '95	♀	5

● Montepulciano d'Abruzzo Bacco '97	♀♀	5
● Montepulciano d'Abruzzo '98	♀	3
⊙ Montepulciano d'Abruzzo Cerasuolo '99	♀	2*
○ Trebbiano d'Abruzzo Bacco '99	♀	3
○ Trebbiano d'Abruzzo '99		2
● Montepulciano d'Abruzzo Bacco '93	♀♀	5
● Montepulciano d'Abruzzo Bacco '94	♀♀	5
● Montepulciano d'Abruzzo '97	♀	2*
● Montepulciano d'Abruzzo Bacco '95	♀	5
○ Trebbiano d'Abruzzo Bacco '98	♀	4

OFENA (AQ)

TENUTA CATALDI MADONNA
LOC. PIANA
67025 OFENA (AQ)
TEL. 085/4911680

Every year, Luigi Cataldi Madonna, who also finds time to teach philosophy at university, manages to make his estate a little more solid and a shade more significant. Montepulciano d'Abruzzo Toni is again in the vanguard of the range. The estate skipped the difficult vintage '96 and therefore released the '97 early. It has a deep, opaque ruby colour and a surprisingly intense nose. First impressions on the palate are of tannin and it then opens out to give softness, fatness and flavours of ripe fruit, chocolate and coffee powder, before coming to an oaky, and rather short finish. While waiting for a version of this wine that will really show what it's made of – and the '98, still ageing, is looking remarkably good – the base version is there, ready to be enjoyed. It has a fine swathe of aromas of mainly ripe fruits, supported on the palate by an assertive structure and a good tannic weave. There are a further two good quality reds. One is the Malandrino, from cabernet and montepulciano, which marries vegetal and ripe morello cherry aromas, and the other is the 100% cabernet Vigna Cona, whose aromatic spectrum makes it one of the most successful versions of recent years. The estate remains unrivalled for its two Cerasuolos and this year's releases are as impressive as ever. The Pié delle Vigne selection is particularly intriguing, marrying red-wine structure with rosé-like approachability. The two whites submitted are also good. Vigna Cona, a Sauvignon with perfectly varietal herbaceous notes, and Trebbiano d'Abruzzo, as fresh, zesty and balanced as ever. There is a third white, Pecorino, but it is still at an experimental stage.

⊙	Montepulciano d'Abruzzo Cerasuolo Pié delle Vigne '99	🍷🍷	3*
●	Montepulciano d'Abruzzo Tonì '97	🍷🍷	5
●	Malandrino '98	🍷	4
●	Montepulciano d'Abruzzo '98	🍷	3
⊙	Montepulciano d'Abruzzo Cerasuolo '99	🍷	2*
○	Trebbiano d'Abruzzo '99	🍷	2*
○	Vigna Cona Bianco '99	🍷	3
●	Vigna Cona Rosso '98	🍷	4
⊙	Montepulciano d'Abruzzo Cerasuolo Pié delle Vigne '98	🍷🍷 (outline)	3*
●	Montepulciano d'Abruzzo Tonì '91	🍷🍷 (outline)	4*
●	Montepulciano d'Abruzzo Tonì '93	🍷🍷 (outline)	5
●	Montepulciano d'Abruzzo Tonì '95	🍷🍷 (outline)	5

ORTONA (CH)

AGRIVERDE
C.DA CALDARI
VIA MONTE MAIELLA, 118
66020 ORTONA (CH)
TEL. 085/9032101

This is the first appearance in the Guide for this new estate, which has been making very respectable wine for a few years now. Its key staff are all young too. The boss, Giannicola Di Carlo, is assisted by Paride Marino and oenologist, Riccardo Brighigna. The strictly organic Agriverde estate possesses around 50 hectares and has a well-equipped cellar adjacent to its visitor accommodation facilities, which enjoy a splendid setting. All the wines tasted were noteworthy and surprisingly good value for money, particularly when you remember that there are another two, even less expensive lines. To start, we tasted the '97 Montepulciano d'Abruzzo, as here too the '96 vintage was passed over. The '97 is intriguing in the way the sensations of ripe black cherry, particularly on the palate, interweave with notes that range over bitter chocolate and coffee, and even rhubarb and cinchona. The '98 Montepulciano d'Abruzzo scored almost as well. It, too, is a bit reticent on the nose and although full and firm it has a more aggressive tannic attack than its "elder brother". The third red is the organically cultivated Natum, enjoyable for its simplicity and its fruitiness on both nose and palate. And if, in the case of the Cerasuolos, we need do no more than mention the numerous awards they have won at wine competitions, a word or two wouldn't go amiss on the straightforward but fresh, floral Trebbiano d'Abruzzo, with its almondy finish, and the Chardonnay Tresor whose varietal characteristics are well marked, underlined by a good acidic backbone and enriched by skilled barriquing.

○	Chardonnay Tresor '99	🍷	2*
⊙	Montepulciano d'Abruzzo Cerasuolo Riseis '99	🍷	2*
●	Montepulciano d'Abruzzo Natum '99	🍷	2*
●	Montepulciano d'Abruzzo Riseis '97	🍷	3
●	Montepulciano d'Abruzzo Riseis '98	🍷	2*
○	Trebbiano d'Abruzzo Riseis '99	🍷	2*

POPOLI (PE)

LORENZO FILOMUSI GUELFI
VIA MARCONI, 28
65026 POPOLI (PE)
TEL. 085/98353

If there's one thing we can say about Lorenzo Filomusi Guelfi, it is that he's one of the most passionate, tenacious and above all enthusiastic of producers. Having seen the refurbishment of his cellars at Tocco di Casaurisa practically through to completion, he can now devote more energy to his favourite occupation, and the one that is most crucial for the estate's success – the vineyards. His intention is to bottle almost the entire production of his ten hectares of vineyard at Ceppete, one of the best subzones in the region. He has two new wines in preparation, a red from montepulciano, destined to become the estate's top wine, and a barrique-aged white. Of the current wines, we particularly liked the Montepulciano d'Abruzzo '98 which, tasted just a few weeks after bottling, was nudging Two Glasses. Ruby red with deep purple tinges, it has well-defined aromas of berry fruit on the nose, which are faithfully mirrored on the palate. The Cerasuolo and the Bianco are also both up to their usual standards. The Cerasuolo has a deep, bright colour, leading in to delicate scents of morello cherry and red flowers on the nose. A good vein of acidity underpins the palate, which echoes the nose's fruity notes, and there is an even, clean finish. The chardonnay, sauvignon and malvasia-based Bianco, although fairly deep in colour, does not have great intensity of aroma. It comes over better on the palate, where there is good acid-alcohol balance, and develops well through the mouth, finishing with nice softness.

○ Le Scuderie del Cielo '99	▼	3
● Montepulciano d'Abruzzo '98	▼	3
⊙ Montepulciano d'Abruzzo Cerasuolo '99	▼	3
● Montepulciano d'Abruzzo '93	▽▽	3*
○ Le Scuderie del Cielo '98	▽	3
● Montepulciano d'Abruzzo '90	▽	3
● Montepulciano d'Abruzzo '91	▽	3
● Montepulciano d'Abruzzo '92	▽	3
● Montepulciano d'Abruzzo '97	▽	3
⊙ Montepulciano d'Abruzzo Cerasuolo '98	▽	3

ROSCIANO (PE)

MARRAMIERO
C.DA S. ANDREA, 1
65010 ROSCIANO (PE)
TEL. 085/8505766

When we took the gamble some time back of giving this winery a full profile in the Guide, we knew we would be seeing good results within a few years. Yet an estate like this, belonging to a young, capable businessman such as Enrico Marramiero, with 30 hectares of vineyard, a beautiful new cellar, and brilliant expertise on both the technical and commercial fronts, should surely be capable of better than just "good". However, the latest releases again reflect the estate's philosophy of producing modern-style wines to satisfy market demands. The '96 Montepulciano d'Abruzzo Inferi defies the miserable vintage and, astonishingly if the truth be told, even manages a deep, purple-tinged colour. The nose is reticent, alcoholic and initially rather edgy but on the well-constructed palate, after the first impression of tannin, there is breadth and ripeness, and quite a long finish. The Trebbiano d'Abruzzo Altare, fermented and aged in small oak, is also good with a deep, bright yellow colour introducing rather atypical aromatics and robust alcohol on the nose. There is well-judged oak enhancing the palate, which has flavours of tropical fruit and a long finish with a bitterish aftertaste. Similar, but rather simpler sensations are also found on the other Trebbiano d'Abruzzo, Anima. Improvements are apparent throughout the low-budget Dama line, with the sole exception of the Cerasuolo, but the new Montepulciano d'Abruzzo Basserese is vegetal and tousled on the nose and overly tannic on the palate. It failed to impress.

● Montepulciano d'Abruzzo Inferi '96	▼▼	5
● Montepulciano d'Abruzzo Basserese '97	▼	4
● Montepulciano d'Abruzzo Dama '97	▼	3
○ Trebbiano d'Abruzzo Altare '98	▼	5
○ Trebbiano d'Abruzzo Anima '99	▼	4
○ Trebbiano d'Abruzzo Dama '99	▼	3
⊙ Montepulciano d'Abruzzo Cerasuolo Dama '99		3
● Montepulciano d'Abruzzo Inferi '93	▽▽	4
● Montepulciano d'Abruzzo Inferi '94	▽▽	4
● Montepulciano d'Abruzzo Inferi '95	▽▽	4

ROSETO DEGLI ABRUZZI (TE)   S. MARTINO SULLA MARRUCINA (CH)

ORLANDI CONTUCCI PONNO
C.DA VOLTARROSTO
VIA PIANA DEGLI ULIVI, 1
64026 ROSETO DEGLI ABRUZZI (TE)
TEL. 085/8944049

GIANNI MASCIARELLI
VIA GAMBERALE, 1
66010 S. MARTINO
SULLA MARRUCINA (CH)
TEL. 0871/85241

The zeal with which Marina Orlandi Contucci is modernizing the estate set up by her father continues to bring rewards, especially since the consultant is Donato Lanati, an oenologist who has no need of introduction and who is working wonders with Abruzzo's red wines. The highest scoring segment of the range confirms Marina's predilection for wines from international varieties. Particularly impressive are those based on cabernet sauvignon. Let us start with Liburnio '97, which has varietal notes of blackcurrant and mulberry, as well as a well-structured palate and a distinctive tannic weave. There is impressive depth giving the wine support through to the finish, which tails off on toasty notes. The Colle Funaro sticks more closely to the textbook style but is just as characterful. The nose is less varied and tannins that still need to settle down are well to the fore on entry but the palate is nonetheless soft, warm and harmonious with sensations of berry fruit evident throughout. All three of the whites are attractive and well-made. Yet in other vintages, even the less favoured ones, they have seemed much fresher and more charming. Only the Trebbiano d'Abruzzo, straightforward but balanced, really distinguishes itself. The Montepulciano d'Abruzzo is deserving of a note apart. It has finally been liberated from the vegetal notes that previously plagued it and this time round its fruit aromas meld perfectly with spicy tones of pepper and ginger. On the palate, it has a rounded, open drinkability that it has never shown in the past.

Last year, we concluded our report on the Masciarelli estate by talking about "excesses". Gianni's behaviour was over the top, his imposing, dazzling wines were too much and so on. Well, our comments are now looking distinctly moderate, and Masciarelli absolutely detests moderation. Just taste his Montepulciano d'Abruzzo Villa Gemma '95! The colour is an opaque, brightly tinged ruby, leading in to ripe mulberry aromas that are intense, complex and pervasive. The palate is fat, incredibly long and immensely powerful yet is still fabulously drinkable. It is simply spectacular, and probably Masciarelli's best Montepulciano d'Abruzzo ever. The Three Glass rating was a mere formality, as was the award of the title, Red Wine of the Year. All this magnificence risks putting the almost equally fantastic Trebbiano d'Abruzzo '98 into the shade. But there is no way a varietal, elegant, powerful wine like this, with its balanced nuances of oak on the nose and sumptuous complexity on the palate, is going to stay in the background. The wine's fans will just adore it. But all the wines that new father Masciarelli produces – our congratulations to him and Marina on their new daughter – reached stupendous heights of quality. In fact, he almost gained a third Three Glass trophy for the brilliant Chardonnay Marina Cvetic '98. It is full, with clean and highly elegant aromas of tropical fruit, has a fat yet fresh palate, and is all too drinkable. A marvel. It is probably worth reminding readers that the estate also produces hundreds of thousands of bottles of exemplary wine, such as its standard Montepulciano '98, the Villa Gemma white and so on. This indicates a solidity and a reliability that is frankly . . . just too much.

● Cabernet Sauvignon		
Colle Funaro '97	🍷🍷	4
● Liburnio '97	🍷🍷	5
○ Chardonnay Roccesco '99	🍷	3
● Montepulciano d'Abruzzo		
La Regia Specula '98	🍷	3
○ Sauvignon Ghiaiolo '99	🍷	3
○ Trebbiano d'Abruzzo		
Colle della Corte '99	🍷	2*
⊙ Montepulciano d'Abruzzo		
Cerasuolo Vermiglio '99		2
● Cabernet Sauvignon		
Colle Funaro '95	🍷🍷	3*
● Liburnio '93	🍷🍷	5
● Liburnio '95	🍷🍷	5

● Montepulciano d'Abruzzo		
Villa Gemma '95	🍷🍷🍷	6
○ Trebbiano d'Abruzzo		
Marina Cvetic '98	🍷🍷🍷	4*
● Cabernet Sauvignon		
Marina Cvetic '95	🍷🍷	5
○ Chardonnay Marina Cvetic '98	🍷🍷	5
● Montepulciano d'Abruzzo '98	🍷🍷	2*
● Montepulciano d'Abruzzo		
Marina Cvetic '98	🍷🍷	4
○ Villa Gemma Bianco '99	🍷🍷	3*
○ Chardonnay Marina Cvetic '97	🍷🍷🍷	4*
● Montepulciano d'Abruzzo		
Villa Gemma '94	🍷🍷🍷	6

SPOLTORE (PE)

TOLLO (CH)

FATTORIA LA VALENTINA
VIA COLLE CESI, 10
65010 SPOLTORE (PE)
TEL. 085/4478158

CANTINA TOLLO
VIA GARIBALDI
66010 TOLLO (CH)
TEL. 0871/961726

The small group of Abruzzo estates that have finally graduated from "up-and-coming" and can be said to have "arrived" most certainly includes the Fattoria La Valentina, owned by Sabatino Di Properzio, a young businessman who is now dedicating his energies almost exclusively to wine. Last year, he took on Luca D'Attoma as consultant and the wines immediately took a further hike in quality. This year's news is a joint venture, set up as a result of Di Properzio's friendship with Stefano Inama. The new enterprise has given birth to a red, Montepulciano d'Abruzzo Binomio '98, which even on its first release is tremendously exciting. It has a dark red colour and perfumes that are all-enveloping, with the fruit interweaving with notes of bitter chocolate and coffee. The palate has similar notes, and a resonance that brings out the ripeness of the tannins meshing with the complex depth of the flavours. Just a few points down the scale is Spelt, another Montepulciano d'Abruzzo selection. Here it is the nuances of pepper and pencil lead that frame the fruity flow of its aromas. A softness of attack, smooth tannins and good length mark out the palate. The standard Montepulciano is fresher and less complex, as well as being excellent value for money. There is a stylistic difference between the two Trebbiano d'Abruzzos. The Vigneto Spilla, from late-picked grapes, refined by a small proportion of chardonnay, is partly vinified in oak and turns out to be the softer and riper of the pair.

The Cantina Tollo wines show clearly that there is nothing to prevent high quality wines being produced in large quantities. Tollo is not the only proof of this. There are numerous other cellars, some very successful, especially in Alto Adige, which, like the province of Chieti, is co-operative territory. Cantina Tollo is one of the largest co-operatives and groups 1,200 members, a number of whom were selected some years back to take part in a series of research projects aimed at producing new, higher profile wines. The credit for this, and the philosophy of making headway in a series of small yet important steps, belongs to Tollo's president, Tommaso Perantuono, and its technical director, Goffredo Agostini. The '97 Montepulciano d'Abruzzo came out very well. It has depth and elegance on the nose, and a structure on the palate that, without going overboard on power, has good balance as a whole. It has even progression through the mouth, with densely packed flavours and appreciable ripeness of fruit. Cagiòlo, a white from barrique-aged chardonnay, is well focused. Here, too, the pendulum has swung in favour of elegance over power and there are delicate notes of banana and candied fruit, supported by a good acidic freshness. While waiting for the release of the two '98 Montepulciano d'Abruzzos, Colle Secco and Colle Secco Rubino, the flag of the second line is kept flying by the Montepulciano d'Abruzzo Valle d'Oro '98 and two wines which have won numerous awards for their ability to combine quality with remarkably good prices, the Trebbiano d'Abruzzo Colle Secco and Cerasuolo Valle d'Oro.

● Montepulciano d'Abruzzo		
Binomio '98	♟♟	5
● Montepulciano d'Abruzzo Spelt '96	♟♟	4
● Montepulciano d'Abruzzo '98	♟	2*
○ Trebbiano d'Abruzzo '99	♟	2*
○ Trebbiano d'Abruzzo		
Vigneto Spilla '99	♟	3
⊙ Montepulciano d'Abruzzo		
Cerasuolo '99		2
● Montepulciano d'Abruzzo Ris. '93	♟♟	3*
● Lusinga	♟	2*
● Montepulciano d'Abruzzo '96	♟	2*
● Montepulciano d'Abruzzo '97	♟	2*
● Montepulciano d'Abruzzo Spelt '94	♟	3
● Punta Rossa	♟	2*

● Montepulciano d'Abruzzo '97	♟♟	4
○ Cagiòlo Bianco '98	♟	4
⊙ Montepulciano d'Abruzzo		
Cerasuolo Valle d'Oro '99	♟	2*
● Montepulciano d'Abruzzo		
Valle d'Oro '98	♟	2*
○ Trebbiano d'Abruzzo		
Colle Secco '99	♟	2*
● Montepulciano d'Abruzzo		
Cagiòlo '94	♟♟	3*
● Montepulciano d'Abruzzo		
Cagiòlo '95	♟	4
● Montepulciano d'Abruzzo		
Colle Secco Rubino '97	♟	2*

TORANO NUOVO (TE) VACRI (CH)

BARONE CORNACCHIA
C.DA TORRI
64010 TORANO NUOVO (TE)
TEL. 0861/887412

BUCCICATINO
VIA FONTANELLE, 7
66010 VACRI (CH)
TEL. 0871/720273

We would like to be there when Piero Cornacchia's estate finally produces a truly great wine. For its size, with over 30 hectares, and its location on high southeast-facing hill slopes, it is among the best in the region. The wines submitted show that the quality of the grapes is exceptional and the idea of producing reds that don't need long ageing is a good one. However, despite the good intentions, none of the wines got close to Two Glasses and only the Montepulciano d'Abruzzo Poggio Varano even looked as if it had the potential to get there. It has a deep ruby colour and marked vegetal notes on the nose, a sign that a little well-selected cabernet has been added to the montepulciano. There is good body on the palate, which has fine nose-palate symmetry. The Montepulciano d'Abruzzo Vigna Le Coste, in common with the Poggio Varano, has a rather rustic feel on the nose, and despite the lively colour, the fruit scents are over-ripe, indeed almost stewed. The palate, though, has good, rounded tannins, medium depth of structure and good balance. The youngest red is stylistically purer and also has a fair bit of character, with clear fruit aromas of cherry, both red and black. The palate is initially a little fragile and the tannins not particularly fine-hewn but it finishes attractively, maintaining good balance. The Trebbiano d'Abruzzo is pleasant and while the usually well-made Cerasuolo has been weakened by the vintage, the Chardonnay is lacking in weight and is ageing just as fast as in previous years.

If Alberto Umberto Buccicatino lacks anything, it is not enthusiasm for his cellar. In his proud, determined manner he has taken just a few years to enlarge his estate and now has 14 hectares under vine backed up by state-of-the-art equipment. The area around Vacri and that close to Villamagna are still little known but all the signs are that they will prove to be of great viticultural interest. We have already listed the Buccicatino estate under Other Wineries several times but the steady increase in the quality of its wines has finally earned it a full profile. This year, the top flights of the range have been enriched by a red, the Montepulciano d'Abruzzo Stilla Rubra '97. It has a lively colour and the nose is intense but, for the moment, the oak is masking the fruit. The palate starts well, continuing with softness and balance propelled by a fairly firm body, and finishes sweet. The Cabernet Sauvignon, which has been our overall preference on other occasions, is certainly a good wine but this time round it seemed a bit raw and "powdery" on the nose. Its palate, though, is nicely rounded, the tannins have no excessively rough edges and the palate finishes with a bitterish tang. The Montepulciano d'Abruzzo '98, with a concentrated colour and clear-cut aromas of ripe black cherry, came over as more balanced and complete. The impression on the palate is mainly of softness, the tannins are ripe and there is good length, with an attractively fruity after-aroma. The Trebbiano d'Abruzzo showed better than in previous years. It has a fairly deep straw-yellow colour, floral tones and a delicate, ripe fruitiness.

● Montepulciano d'Abruzzo '98	❢	2*
● Montepulciano d'Abruzzo Poggio Varano '98	❢	4
● Montepulciano d'Abruzzo Vigna Le Coste '97	❢	4
○ Trebbiano d'Abruzzo '99	❢	1*
○ Controguerra Chardonnay Villa Torri '99		2
☉ Montepulciano d'Abruzzo Cerasuolo '99		1
● Montepulciano d'Abruzzo Poggio Varano '96	❢❢	3*
● Montepulciano d'Abruzzo '97	❢	2*
● Montepulciano d'Abruzzo Poggio Varano '97	❢	4

● Cabernet Sauvignon '98	❢	5
● Montepulciano d'Abruzzo '98	❢	3
☉ Montepulciano d'Abruzzo Cerasuolo '99	❢	2*
● Montepulciano d'Abruzzo Stilla Rubra '97	❢	5
○ Trebbiano d'Abruzzo '99	❢	2*

OTHER WINERIES

The following producers obtained good scores in our tastings with one or more of their wines:

PROVINCE OF CAMPOBASSO

Borgo di Colloredo,
Campomarino, tel. 0875/57543
Biferno Bianco Gironia '99,
Biferno Rosso Gironia '97

PROVINCE OF CHIETI

Spinelli,
Atessa, tel. 0872/897916
Montepulciano d'Abruzzo Tatone '97,
Montepulciano d'Abruzzo Terra d'Aligi '98

Casalbordino,
Casalbordino, tel. 0873/918107
Trebbiano d'Abruzzo Contea di Bordino '99

Citra,
Ortona, tel. 085/9031342
Montepulciano d'Abruzzo Caroso '95,
Montepulciano d'Abruzzo Villa Torre '98,
Trebbiano d'Abruzzo Villa Torre '99

Farnese,
Ortona, tel. 085/9067388
Chardonnay Farneto Valley '99,
Montepulciano d'Abruzzo Opis '96,
Sangiovese Farneto Valley '99

Sarchese,
Ortona, tel.085/9031249
Esmery Brut '93,
Montepulciano d'Abruzzo Pietrosa '98,
Montepulciano d'Abruzzo
Rosso di Macchia '96

Cantina Soc. Frentana,
Rocca S. Giovanni, tel. 0872/60152
Trebbiano d'Abruzzo Terre di Venere '99

Torre Zambra,
Villamagna, tel. 0871/300121
Montepulciano d'Abruzzo Brume Rosse '96,
Montepulciano d'Abruzzo Colle Maggio '97

PROVINCE OF L'AQUILA

Praesidium Enzo Pasquale,
Prezza, tel. 0864/45103
Montepulciano d'Abruzzo '97

PROVINCE OF PESCARA

Chiusa Grande,
Nocciano, tel. 085/847460
Montepulciano d'Abruzzo Perla Nera '96

Chiarieri,
Pianella, tel. 085/971365
Montepulciano d'Abruzzo Hannibal '96

Vinicola Roxan,
Rosciano, tel. 085/8505683
Montepulciano d'Abruzzo Galelle '98,
Montepulciano d'Abruzzo Roxan '98

PROVINCE OF TERAMO

Ferliga,
Ancarano, tel. 0736/899385
Montepulciano d'Abruzzo
Poggio delle Ginestre '98

Di Giovampietro,
Giulianova, tel. 085/8002569
Montepulciano d'Abruzzo Rubens '97

Fael Dario D'Angelo,
Giulianova, tel. 085/8002550
Montepulciano d'Abruzzo Daris '98

Faraone,
Giulianova, tel. 085/8071804
Montepulciano d'Abruzzo
S. Maria dell'Arco '97,
Trebbiano d'Abruzzo Le Vigne '99

Valori, Sant'Omero, tel. 0861/88461
Montepulciano d'Abruzzo '99,
Montepulciano d'Abruzzo
Vigna S. Angelo '99

Pepe, Torano Nuovo, tel. 0861/856493
Montepulciano d'Abruzzo Pepe Nero '98

CAMPANIA

With four wines gaining Three Glasses, Campania has again earned its place on Italy's roll of honour. Feudi di San Gregorio, with two top-ranked wines, remains one of the high spots of today's wine scene in Italy. Villa Matilde has already set its course with absolute resolve for absolute quality, and the stunning showing of its Vigna Camarata is no more than due confirmation of this. Montevetrano continues to be the gem of an estate it always has been. One fundamental point in all this will, however, not be lost on attentive observers. The four wines in question may hail from different parts of the region – Irpinia, Massico and the province of Salerno, respectively – but they have all been "shaped" by the same oenologist, Riccardo Cotarella. He is one of the most brilliant and talented of all Italian winemakers, so much so that to most wine-lovers his name speaks for itself. Given the seemingly infinite potential for quality in the region, though, and its key role in southern Italy, it seems rather limiting to have just one top oenologist making the running. Campania surely needs at least ten professionals of similar class to bring its terroirs and its wines into the international spotlight. Why we are still waiting for their arrival remains a mystery. We are not trying to suggest that the region shoul be overrun by a tidal wave of consultants from all over the place. But a few fresh ideas would not come amiss for the majority of Campanian producers. Neither would the chance to see where their cellars stand compared with what's happening elsewhere, in Italy and abroad,. The oenologists based in the region already have some pretty good wines to their credit. They are also carrying out a fundamental task, that of ensuring the continuance and spread of the region's indigenous varieties. It sometimes appears, though, as if they lack the courage to go the extra mile and come up with a wine that is seriously sensational. Or maybe it is the producers themselves who are resting on their laurels, or who are happy enough with the commercial success of wines like Fiano di Avellino and Greco di Tufo (to name just the best known), wines which no Campanian wine list nor wine shop's shelves can be without. Moreover, top wines apart, this year's tastings have not generally been such as to raise enthusiasms. The '99 vintage has tended to give whites that are a bit restrained and which demonstrate not just the limits of the year but also of winemaking concepts that probably need a good overhaul. In much of Italy, vineyards and cellars are being replanned with the declared objective of aiming not just for high quality but for ultimate quality. It is a definitive moment for the whole national wine sector. And an Italy based on a culture of fine wine is incomplete without a region whose history, climate and terrains, not to mention its wealth of fascinating, indigenous grape varieties, ought easily to put it firmly in the front rank. With a large number of estates and an even larger number of wines.

ATRIPALDA (AV)

MASTROBERARDINO
VIA MANFREDI, 75/81
83042 ATRIPALDA (AV)
TEL. 0825/614111

Of all the wines produced by Antonio, Carlo and Pietro Mastroberardino this year, the one that really bowled us over and that stood head and shoulders above the rest was Fiano d'Avellino More Maiorum '96. No, there's no mistake. The vintage is '96. The leaders of Campania's winemaking revival, the architects of Greco di Tufo's and Fiano di Avellino's international success, not to mention the renowned Taurasi, are often accused of being "violent" with their whites, and of "forcing" them onto the market early, before the end of November, for commercial gain at whatever cost to quality. But this complex, sumptuously rich white wine, released a good three years after the harvest, has revealed a different side to Mastroberardino – a desire to go against the tide and to lead, rather than follow, fashions and trends. But let's come to the wine itself. It has an intense, bright straw-yellow colour. The aromas are soft and complex, showing notable intensity and finesse, and maintain a note of fruitiness that overlies delicate scents of hazelnut and toasted almonds, as well as more overt tones of spring flowers. The palate has good concentration, soft flavours of stewed apples and complex spicy touches. It is a wine that explores new avenues for Fiano and we are confident that it will set people talking. Taurasi Radici '96 still has a youthful appearance, with a purple-tinged ruby colour, and offers elegant aromas of ripe cherry on the nose with delicate nuances of spices, bay and white pepper. The palate has structure, richness of extract, ripe tannins and a soft fruitiness. Of the other wines in the extensive Mastroberardino range, which was not immune to the effects of the disappointing '99 vintage, the red Lacryma Christi and Naturalis Historia, and the Fiano di Avellino came out best.

○	Fiano di Avellino More Maiorum '96	▼▼	5
●	Taurasi Radici '96	▼▼	6
○	Fiano di Avellino '99	▼	4
●	Lacryma Christi Rosso '99	▼	4
●	Naturalis Historia '97	▼	6
●	Taurasi Radici '90	ΥΥΥ	6
○	Fiano di Avellino Radici '95	ΥΥ	4
○	Fiano di Avellino Vignadora '95	ΥΥ	4
○	Fiano di Avellino Vignadora '98	ΥΥ	4
●	Lacryma Christi Rosso '98	ΥΥ	3*
●	Taurasi Radici '93	ΥΥ	5
●	Taurasi Radici '94	ΥΥ	5
●	Taurasi Radici '95	ΥΥ	5
●	Taurasi Ris. '86	ΥΥ	6

CELLOLE (CE)

VILLA MATILDE
S. S. DOMITIANA, 18 - KM. 4,700
81030 CELLOLE (CE)
TEL. 0823/932088

The Avallone siblings, Salvatore and Maria Ida, keep up their determination and their enthusiasm for their work. Together with their consultant Riccardo Cotarella, one of the top names in Italian winemaking, they are starting to realize the full potential of this corner of Campania which a couple of millennia ago was already considered, if not the absolute best, at least one of the best wine areas in the known world. And now, an absolutely stunning Vigna Camarato '97 proves that the '95, which so delighted us, was not simply an isolated episode, and establishes Villa Matilde conclusively as one of the best estates in southern Italy. The '97, from 100 percent aglianico, is also from an excellent vintage. It has a dark red colour tinged with purple. The nose is full and complex, and unveils intriguing aromas of red and black berry fruits, given additional complexity by hints of spiciness, herbs and toasty notes from the new oak. On the palate, power and concentration soften into a rounded amalgam of ripe plum, mulberry and bilberry, set in a tannic weave that is assertive but reveals extraordinary finesse. The wine develops a penetrating breadth in the mouth with a progression of beautifully harmonious, pure flavours that finally tail off on notes of mulberry jam, coffee and tobacco. This is indeed an exceptional red and it also bears elegant witness to the potential of aglianico, or "vitis hellanica", the south's outstanding red variety. The Cecubo from the same year is not far short of this Camarato. It has remarkable soft fullness, elegant symmetry between red fruit and new oak, firm structure and perfect balance. Vigna Caracci, a white from falanghina, is more elegant, fresh and soft than ever, and brings new lustre to the ancient name Falerno – but there are no bottles on the long list that fall short of excellence.

●	Vigna Camarato '97	▼▼▼	6
●	Cecubo '97	▼▼	4
○	Falerno del Massico Bianco Vigna Caracci '99	▼▼	4
●	Aglianico di Roccamonfina '98	▼	3
○	Eleusi Passito '98	▼	4
○	Falanghina di Roccamonfina '99	▼	3
○	Falerno del Massico Bianco '99	▼	3
●	Falerno del Massico Rosso '98	▼	3
⊙	Terre Cerase '99	▼	3
●	Vigna Camarato '95	ΥΥΥ	5
●	Falerno del Massico Rosso '97	ΥΥ	3*
●	Vigna Camarato '85	ΥΥ	6
●	Vigna Camarato '88	ΥΥ	6
●	Vigna Camarato '92	ΥΥ	4

FOGLIANISE (BN)

FORIO (NA)

CANTINA DEL TABURNO
VIA SALA
82030 FOGLIANISE (BN)
TEL. 0824/871338 - 0824/50084

CANTINE DI PIETRATORCIA
LOC. FORIO
VIA PROVINCIALE PANZA, 267
80075 FORIO (NA)
TEL. 081/908206 - 081/997406

Situated on the slopes of Mount Taburno, this important co-operative, with 300 members contributing grapes and over 1,500,000 bottles produced each year, returns to the Guide with a very respectable series of wines. The one that most impressed our tasting panel was Coda di Volpe Amineo '99. It is deep straw-yellow in colour and has fruity aromas of ripe green apple, citron and pink grapefruit. The palate is fat, with fine acidity and length, so it was well worth its Two Glasses. The Greco del Taburno '99 isn't bad, either. On the nose, it has light notes of damson and white peach enhanced by attractive balsamic tones. The palate is pleasant, fruity and full of ripe apple flavour. The Falanghina Folius '99, aged for nine months in barrique, is full of character. Despite the disappointing vintage, it has a deep straw-yellow colour, floral aromas with appley notes, and a palate that shows good body, good aromatic length and a note of oak that does not overwhelm. The basic Falanghina and the Aglianico del Taburno '97 are lower-ranking wines but both are reasonably good. The Aglianico has plum and morello cherry fruitiness but is not absolutely clean on the nose. The palate also has an excessive overlay of oak and lacks elegance. In any event, the wines performed more than decently overall and we hope that their showing will encourage the co-operative's members to work towards even higher quality.

When three families of growers from Ischia joined forces, Pietratorcia was the result. The Iaconos, Regines and Verdes decided to pool their efforts and turn their seven hectares of vineyard to full advantage. The vines are those traditional to the island, biancolella, forastera, per 'e palummo and guarnaccia, and the estate can call on technical assistance from the Agrarian Institute at San Michele all'Adige. Five wines are produced and it was the Rosso Riserva '98, from piedirosso and guarnaccia, aged in new oak barriques, that most impressed us. It has a good purple-ruby colour, leading in to intense aromas of berry fruit and wild berries that are given additional emphasis by hints of pencil lead, printer's ink and an elegant oakiness. The palate is round, soft and full of fleshy fruit. It offers polished, ripe tannins and finishes long with attractive scents of Mediterranean scrub. The oak is currently a little over-invasive but this is simply due to the wine's youth. Further confirmation of the estate's class comes from Ischia Bianco Riserva, a wine with a good deep straw-yellow colour. The nose has aromas of apple and pear which knit well into the soft, vanilla tones of new oak. Oak is also the dominant element on the otherwise beautifully fresh palate but it does not submerge the fruitiness. Instead, the elegant waves of vanilla add approachability and harmony. Although the Ischia Bianco Vigne del Cuotto is not a highly complex wine, it is characterful and well-made. The red Tifeo and the white Vigne di Chignole, however, were slightly below expectations.

O Coda di Volpe Amineo '99	🍷🍷	3*
O Falanghina del Taburno		
Folius '99	🍷	4
O Greco del Taburno '99	🍷	4
● Aglianico del Taburno '97		3
O Falanghina del Taburno '99		3
● Aglianico del Taburno '91	🍸	3
● Aglianico del Taburno Ris. '90	🍸	4
● Aglianico del Taburno '90	🍸	3

O Ischia Bianco Ris. '98	🍷🍷	5
● Pietratorcia Rosso Ris. '98	🍷🍷	5
O Ischia Bianco Sup.		
Vigne del Cuotto '99	🍷	4
O Ischia Bianco Sup.		
Vigne di Chignole '99		4
● Tifeo Rosso '99		3
O Ischia Bianco Ris. '97	🍸🍸	5
● Pietratorcia Rosso Ris. '97	🍸🍸	5
O Ischia Bianco '98	🍸	3
● Ischia Rosso		
Vigne di Ianno Piro '97	🍸	3
O Meditandum '98	🍸	5
● Tifeo Rosso '98	🍸	3

FORIO D'ISCHIA (NA)   FURORE (SA)

D'AMBRA VINI D'ISCHIA
LOC. PANZA
S. S. 270
VIA MARIO D'AMBRA, 16
80075 FORIO D'ISCHIA (NA)
TEL. 081/907210 - 081/907246

CANTINE GRAN FUROR
DIVINA COSTIERA
VIA G. B. LAMA, 14
84010 FURORE (SA)
TEL. 089/830348 - 0336/610544

Andrea d'Ambra now has the running of this long-standing estate fully in hand. He has been replanting, experimenting and getting firmly involved with ensuring the survival of the traditional Ischian varieties. However, this year his wines, we regret to say, were in general not really all that impressive and the reds in particular seem to have lost their way. But let's start on a more positive note with Biancolella Tenuta Frassitelli, which rarely disappoints. The '99 has a pale straw-yellow colour with bright highlights. The nose has scents of apple and citron peel, with hints of tropical fruit, while the palate is attractive, full, deep and rich in fruit, with inviting flavours of pineapple. It gains an easy Two Glasses. Among the reds is a new wine, the Ischia Rosso Dedicato a Mario d'Ambra '98, from equal proportions of guarnaccia and per 'e palummo. High expectations surrounded its release yet it has turned out to be well-styled but no more. It has a ruby colour, then the nose has touches of ripe plum but is a little reduced and has no great finesse. The palate, though, has good body, well-balanced tannins and plentiful berry fruit. Even so, we expected more. The other wines in the range really did not appear to be up to scratch and we would prefer not to comment further. Still, even the best estates can have a year when everything goes belly-up and Andrea is so keen and so competent a winemaker that we are sure that next year he will be back producing the sort of bottles that will do him credit. And delight us.

In a region where consistency of quality is a perennial problem, it is a great pleasure to find an estate that unwaveringly comes out with wines that are more than good. In fact, Gran Furor wines have come to define the character of the Costa d'Amalfi DOC. The property has seven hectares of vine, cultivated organically, producing around 50,000 bottles a year, and the whole production process is followed with extreme care, which means the wines are very reliable. Andrea Ferraioli, an agronomist and oenologist, and his wife, Marisa Cuomo, actually submitted only three wines for tasting. But what wines! Let's start with the Furore Bianco Fiorduva '99, from falanghina, biancolella and ginestrella, and aged for 12 months in barrique. It has a deep straw-yellow colour and a complex nose with aromas of broom, golden delicious apple, citron peel and pink grapefruit. The palate is full and fat with flavours of ripe fruit, highlighted by hints of pineapple. It's a great wine and easily gains Two Glasses. The estate's reds showed just as well. Furore Rosso Riserva '97 has a dark ruby colour and an intense, vegetal and lightly spicy nose ushering in a broad, soft palate with flavours of small berry fruit overlaid with spicy hints, especially cloves, all well-integrated with the oak. What more can we say? Two Glasses again! Its younger brother, the Furore Rosso '99, kept the flag flying. While naturally less concentrated than the Riserva, it has a good ruby colour, a clean, fresh nose and an easy-drinking palate with a vegetal touch and a slightly bitterish finish.

○ Biancolella Tenuta Frassitelli '99	♥♥	4	
● Rosso Dedicato			
a Mario d'Ambra '98	♥	5	
○ Biancolella Tenuta Frassitelli '90	♥♥♥	4	
○ Biancolella Tenuta Frassitelli '98	♥♥	4	
○ Cimentorosso '97	♥♥	3*	
● Ischia Per''e Palummo			
Tenuta Montecorvo '94	♥♥	4	
○ Tenuta Frassitelli '97	♥♥	4	
○ Vigne di Piellero '97	♥♥	3*	
○ Arime '98	♥	4	
○ Biancolella Vigne di Piellero '98	♥	3	
● Ischia Per''e Palummo '98	♥	2*	
● Ischia Per''e Palummo			
Tenuta Montecorvo '98	♥	4	

○ Costa d'Amalfi Furore Bianco			
Fiorduva '99	♥♥	5	
● Costa d'Amalfi Furore Rosso			
Ris. '97	♥♥	5	
● Costa d'Amalfi Furore Rosso '99	♥	3	
○ Costa d'Amalfi Furore Bianco '95	♥♥	3*	
○ Costa d'Amalfi Furore Bianco			
Fiorduva '98	♥♥	4	
● Costa d'Amalfi Furore Rosso			
Ris. '95	♥♥	4	
● Costa d'Amalfi Furore Rosso			
Ris. '96	♥♥	4	
● Costa d'Amalfi Ravello Rosso			
Ris. '95	♥♥	4	

573

CORTE NORMANNA
CONTRADA SAPENZIE, 20
82034 GUARDIA SANFRAMONDI (BN)
TEL. 0824/817004 - 0824/355057

DE LUCIA
C.DA STARZE
82034 GUARDIA SANFRAMONDI (BN)
TEL. 0824/817705

The Falluto brothers came out with a fine array of well-typed, attractive wines this year. Both the range and the quality have increased and there are now a good six listed in the Guide. All come from traditional local grape varieties, both the white falanghina, fiano, greco, malvasia and trebbiano, and the red aglianico, sangiovese and agostinella, with small amounts of cabernet sauvignon. A good starting point is Solopaca Bianco Guiscardo '99, a fresh, attractive wine with pleasant aromas of green apple and grapefruit and an easy-drinking but long palate with a citrus finish. Its red partner, Solopaca Riccardo '99, is also characterful and pleasing. It has a good ruby colour, a clean nose with intense aromas of red fruit, and a soft, well-fruited palate. Staying with the reds, both the '99 and the '98 Aglianico Tre Pietre are enjoyable wines. The '99 has a good ruby colour. The nose has red fruit aromas highlighted by a hint of bergamot while the palate is clean and soft, with good body, balanced tannins and good length. The '98 has a slightly super-ripe character that makes it a little less elegant but it is nevertheless well-made and long. To finish, both Falanghinas are worthy of mention. Not bad overall. Not bad at all.

The De Lucia cousins' estate has once more turned out a comprehensive range of sound wines from the area's Sannio and Solopaca DOC zones. Their efforts, together with those of their consultant Riccardo Cotarella, oenologist of the year in this year's Guide, have brought gratifying results. The wine that really stood out was a red, the Sannio Aglianico Adelchi '98, which gains Two Glasses, as did the previous vintage. It has a deep, bright ruby colour and elegant, intense aromas of mulberry and bilberry, with hints of spiciness and tobacco which knit well with the toasty notes of the oak used for ageing. The palate shows good weight and there are berry fruit flavours well in evidence as well as dense but elegant tannins. Both Solopacas are good, although the '99 white possibly lacks a touch of body and complexity. Even so, it has a good fruity nose with aromas of citron, crisp green apples and sage. The palate follows suit, and has good acidity but finishes a little short. The red, also a '99, has a good ruby colour, aromas of small berry fruit and flavours that recall ripe plums, together with prominent but soft tannins. The '99 Falanghinas, both the basic version and the Ginestraio selection, have good character. The Ginestraio has tones of apple and toasty oak, with the wood in the ascendant. The standard-label version, a simpler wine, has character, good length and plentiful flavour, with attractive notes of white peach and damson. The Sannio Coda di Volpe '99 is also well worth a mention. It all adds up to a good array of Glasses for this up-and-coming estate.

● Sannio Aglianico '99		♀	4
● Sannio Aglianico Tre Pietre '98		♀	4
○ Solopaca Bianco Guiscardo '99		♀	3
● Solopaca Rosso Riccardo '99		♀	3
○ Sannio Falanghina '99			4
○ Sannio Falanghina Palombaia '99			4
● Sannio Aglianico '98		♀	4
○ Sannio Falanghina '98		♀	4
○ Solopaca Bianco Guiscardo '98		♀	3

● Sannio Aglianico Adelchi '98		♀♀	5
○ Ginestraio '99		♀	4
○ Sannio Falanghina '99		♀	3
○ Solopaca Bianco Vassallo '99		♀	2*
● Solopaca Rosso Vassallo '99		♀	2*
○ Sannio Coda di Volpe '99			3
● Sannio Aglianico '97		♀♀	3*
● Sannio Aglianico Adelchi '97		♀♀	4
○ Sannio Falanghina '97		♀♀	3*
○ Sannio Greco '97		♀♀	3*
○ Solopaca Bianco Vassallo '98		♀♀	3*
● Sannio Aglianico '96		♀	3
● Sannio Aglianico '98		♀	3
● Solopaca Rosso Vassallo '97		♀	2*
● Solopaca Rosso Vassallo '98		♀	2*

MANOCALZATI (AV)

D'Antiche Terre - Vega

C.da Lo Piano
S. S. 7 bis
83030 Manocalzati (AV)
tel. 0825/675358

Last year, we were pretty critical about the wines from this estate which, with an annual production of around 300,000 bottles, occupies an important place on the Irpinia wine scene. We are delighted that this year the wines are far more in line with Gaetano Ciccarella, Carmine Cornacchia and Saverio Iandoli's skills and investment of energy. They have 30 hectares of vine planted with aglianico, fiano di Avellino and greco di Tufo, and from these they submitted four wines, with gratifying results across the board. We'll start with the attractive Taurasi '96. It has a light ruby colour and its aromas are clean-cut and elegant, with notes of balsam, bay and ripe small red fruit. The palate is warm, powerful and well-fruited, with close-woven, elegant tannins and touches of spiciness. In short, it is a very fine wine and comes within an inch of Two Glasses. After a slump in '98, the '99 Eliseo di Serra bounced back to reflect the wine's usual high standards. It is a good deep straw-yellow and has subtle pear, damson and ripe apple aromas. There is good body on the palate, with flavours echoing the apple and damson notes of the nose. The progression is soft and elegant, taking you through to a firm, long finish. The Greco di Tufo '99 is not bad at all, either. It is clean, with an intense, attractive minerality and a fresh taste that highlights attractive flavours of balsam and tomato leaf. It is possibly a touch short but it makes up by being easy to drink and very attractive. The Fiano di Avellino '99 also earned its mention. In short, this fine estate has made an excellent comeback.

○	Eliseo di Serra '99	🍷	3
○	Greco di Tufo '99	🍷	4
●	Taurasi '96	🍷	4
○	Fiano di Avellino '99		4
○	Fiano di Avellino '96	YY	4
●	Coriliano '94	Y	3
●	Coriliano '96	Y	2*
●	Coriliano '98	Y	2*
○	Eliseo di Serra '95	Y	3
○	Eliseo di Serra '96	Y	3
○	Fiano di Avellino '95	Y	4
○	Fiano di Avellino '98	Y	4
○	Greco di Tufo '96	Y	3
●	Irpinia Rosso Coriliano '96	Y	2*
●	Taurasi '94	Y	4

MONDRAGONE (CE)

Michele Moio

V.le Regina Margherita, 6
81034 Mondragone (CE)
tel. 0823/978017

Moio di Mondragone is one of the longest-established names in Campanian winemaking. The company was founded as far back as 1880 but rose to prominence with the more recent re-launch of Falerno, the once-famous wine that was produced in this corner of Campania, the "Ager Falernus" to the north of the river Volturno at the foot of Mount Massico, in the age of imperial Rome. Nowadays, Michele Moio is at the helm of the estate. He is assisted by his sons Bruno, the estate manager, and Luigi, a professor of oenology at the University of Naples, who looks after the viticultural side. The Moios tend their six hectares of vineyard personally. They own four, which are planted with primitivo, and lease the other two, where they grow falanghina. From these plots, they produce four good quality wines. The most interesting of the group is Falerno del Massico Primitivo. The '97 has a purple-ruby colour, an intense nose rich in aromas of mulberry, bilberry and sweet spices, and a full, soft, elegant, attractively complex palate, which has flavours of ripe small berry fruit interwoven with echoes of the spiciness found on the nose, plus notes of new oak. The Rosso 57 is a wine whose name celebrates the glories of the famous 1957 vintage, which was exceptional in this area. It, too, is from primitivo and reveals good extractive weight and aromas of ripe red fruit but there is a little edginess on the otherwise attractive palate. The Falanghina '99 has good fresh fruit, balance and a delicately floral finish but the Gaurano, a primitivo-based red, didn't seem quite up to the standards of the rest of the stable.

○	Falerno del Massico Falanghina '99	🍷	3
●	Falerno del Massico Primitivo '97	🍷	4
●	Rosso 57	🍷	4
●	Gaurano		4

MONTEFUSCO (AV)

COLLI IRPINI

VIA SERRA DI MONTEFUSCO
83030 MONTEFUSCO (AV)
TEL. 0825/963972

Colli Irpini, which until last year was listed in the Guide as Montesolæ, is one of the most promising estates in the province of Avellino. It was started up recently, in '95, on the initiative of its owner, Rosa Pesa, who is an agronomist. It soon came to our attention for the good quality and consistency of its wines and now has a production of around 600,000 bottles a year. This year's tastings revealed that, in line with other estates in the zone, the wines were a little under par – no doubt as a result of the unhappy vintage. Nevertheless, it retains its "place in the sun". We found the Fiano di Avellino to be the best of the range and indeed, one of the best '99s of the DOC. It has a good bright straw-yellow colour and its aromas, reminiscent particularly of golden delicious apples enhanced by delicate floral scents, are quite intense, very clean and captivating. The palate is full and has decent fleshy fruitiness, given lively attack by fresh, attractive citrus notes. Its finish is long and complex. The Taurasi '96 is impressive for its deep ruby colour tinged with purple, its full, persistent, clean-cut aromas of spring flowers, and its dry, nicely tannic palate with unusual touches of candied violets that emphasize its personality and a sweet aftertaste. The Greco di Tufo '99 has a bright straw-yellow colour leading in to pleasing aromas of white peach and damson. These are followed by a fruity palate of medium body and good freshness. The estate's other wines are less interesting, with the single exception of the pleasant Falanghina del Sannio '99.

○	Fiano di Avellino '99	🍷	3
○	Greco di Tufo '99	🍷	3
○	Sannio Falanghina '99	🍷	3
●	Taurasi '96	🍷	4
○	Falanghina del Beneventano '99		2
○	Irpinia Fiano '99		2
●	Sannio Aglianico '98		3
○	Splendore '99		2
○	Fiano di Avellino '98	♀	3
○	Irpinia Bianco '98	♀	2*
○	Irpinia Fiano '98	♀	2*
●	Irpinia Rosso Aglianico '97	♀	2*
○	Splendore '98	♀	2*

MONTEFUSCO (AV)

TERREDORA DI PAOLO

VIA SERRA
83030 MONTEFUSCO (AV)
TEL. 0825/968215

Although the wines of Walter, Lucio, Paolo and Daniela Mastroberardino's Terredora estate had enthused us in previous years, last year we noted a drop in quality throughout the range that left us somewhat perplexed. The estate has a good 150 hectares of vineyard situated in some of the best sites in the Greco di Tufo DOC, the Fiano di Avellino DOC and the Taurasi DOCG areas, as well as numerous other vineyards around Irpinia. In addition, the Mastroberardino family has winemaking experience that goes back a very long way. But again this year, the wines did not show brilliantly, although this time round it may have been due to the depressing vintage. The Rosato Rosaenovae '99 was one of the better wines. It is pale pink, tinged with copper, and offers aromas of citron, golden delicious apple and pink grapefruit. The palate is soft, elegant, fresh and most attractive. Taurasi Fatica Contadina '96 is deep ruby in colour and the nose is a little weak, although there are some reasonably complex berry fruit aromas accented by hints of printer's ink. The palate is powerful and tannic but slightly unbalanced and a touch too astringent on the finish. The Aglianico del Principe '99 is very pleasant, full of soft tones of ripe plum and berry fruit jam, but is certainly neither demanding nor complex. Falanghina '99 is an attractive white with fruited and floral perfumes. Clean-bodied and nicely balanced, it is well-typed and very quaffable. A further three wines gained listings. We sincerely hope to be able to write in more positive tones next year. The estate certainly has no lack of potential.

●	Irpinia Aglianico Il Principio '99	🍷	4
○	Irpinia Bianco Falanghina '99	🍷	3
⊙	Irpinia Rosato Rosaenovae '99	🍷	3
●	Taurasi Fatica Contadina '96	🍷	5
○	Fiano di Avellino Terre di Dora '99		4
○	Greco di Tufo Loggia della Serra '99		4
○	Greco di Tufo Terra degli Angeli '99		4
○	Fiano di Avellino Terre di Dora '98	♀♀	4
○	Greco di Tufo Terra degli Angeli '98	♀♀	3*
●	Taurasi Fatica Contadina '94	♀♀	5
●	Irpinia Aglianico Il Principio '97	♀	4
●	Taurasi Fatica Contadina '95	♀	5

MONTEMARANO (AV)   PONTE (BN)

SALVATORE MOLETTIERI
VIA MUSANNI, 19/B
83040 MONTEMARANO (AV)
TEL. 0827/63424

OCONE
VIA DEL MONTE, 56
82030 PONTE (BN)
TEL. 0824/874040

Salvatore Molettieri is the factotum of his small estate in Montemarano. It is Salvatore who looks after the seven hectares of vineyard planted on well exposed slopes at 500-600 metres. It is he who picks the grapes and he who vinifies them to produces around 20,000 bottles a year of top-notch wine. The "secrets" of his success are no more than a passionate involvement in his work, punctilious care at every stage of the production process and a fine palate. Hence even in a year that was not brilliant for the wines of Avellino, with one or two exceptions, Salvatore picked up a good five, well-deserved Glasses with just three wines. We very much liked Cinque Querce Rosso '98. It has a good dark ruby colour with hints of purple. The nose is clean, fresh and inviting, and has aromas of red and black berry fruit that flow round notes of sweet spice. On the palate, it is full, fleshy and expressive, balanced in acidity, soft in its tannins and long. The Taurasi Cinque Querce '96 has intense, stylish aromas with touches of white pepper and a gaminess that adds emphasis to the general soft fruitiness. The palate echoes the nose perfectly and here, too, there are sensations of berry fruit along with ripe, velvety tannins and hints of shrewdly calibrated new oak. The Bianco '99 is fresh, very floral and well-balanced, in fact, well up to its usual high standard.

Aglianico del Taburno Vigna Pezza La Corte is without doubt the wine that is closest to the heart of the passionately keen, cultured Domenico Ocone, who runs this family estate. It has a lovely, intense ruby colour tinged with purple and, although the nose was still a little closed at the time of our tastings, it promised excellently, with small berry fruit aromas that just needed to open out and develop. The palate is dense, powerful, full of ripe tannins and long, reflecting beautifully the berry fruit sensations on the nose. Domenico produces numerous other wines in his modern cellars at Ponte, both from his own grapes and those from a selected group of growers. Working with oenologist Carmelo Ferrara, he has turned out a fine Piedirosso del Taburno. It offers a deep colour that introduces a nose with captivating aromas of ripe cherry. The palate is clean, clearly defined, warm, penetrating, velvet-smooth and finishes on an attractive note of ripe morello cherry. The Aglianico del Taburno '97 is soft and quite densely woven. It has well-focused aromas of berry fruit with vegetal hints but the palate, although showing good body and extractive weight, is spoilt by a somewhat rough, astringent overlay. The Aglianico del Taburno Diomede '97 was not ready in time for our tastings but the cask sample we tried showed that the wine was no lightweight. It is, though, still a long way from attaining balance so we shall delay making judgement until next year. The whites were less exciting but the Greco del Taburno '99 is worth investigating.

● Cinque Querce Rosso '98	🍷🍷	4
● Taurasi Vigna Cinque Querce '96	🍷🍷	5
○ Cinque Querce Bianco '99	🍷	3
● Cinque Querce Rosso '96	🍷🍷	3*
● Cinque Querce Rosso '97	🍷🍷	4
● Taurasi Vigna Cinque Querce '94	🍷🍷	4
○ Cinque Querce Bianco '97	🍷	3
● Taurasi Vigna Cinque Querce '95	🍷	5

● Aglianico del Taburno		
Vigna Pezza la Corte '96	🍷🍷	4
● Aglianico del Taburno '97	🍷	3
● Piedirosso del Taburno '99	🍷	3
○ Greco del Taburno '99		3
● Aglianico del Sannio		
Vigna Pezza la Corte '91	🍷🍷	4
● Aglianico del Taburno '94	🍷🍷	4
● Aglianico del Taburno Diomede '96	🍷🍷	4
● Aglianico del Taburno		
Vigna Pezza la Corte '93	🍷🍷	4
● Aglianico del Taburno		
Vigna Pezza la Corte '95	🍷🍷	4
● Aglianico del Taburno '95	🍷	4
● Piedirosso del Taburno '97	🍷	3

PRIGNANO CILENTO (SA)   QUARTO (NA)

VITICOLTORI DE CONCILIIS
LOC. QUERCE, 1
84060 PRIGNANO CILENTO (SA)
TEL. 0974/831090

CANTINE GROTTA DEL SOLE
VIA SPINELLI, 2
80010 QUARTO (NA)
TEL. 081/8762566

Bruno De Conciliis and his family have taken up viticulture with enthusiasm and, with the valued assistance of oenologist, Francesco Saverio Petrilli, continue to produce a large range of well-crafted wines. The estate has been up and running for just five years but has already provided the impetus for the regeneration – or perhaps "renaissance" is a more accurate term – of winemaking throughout the Cilento area. The estate's philosophy of taking particular care in managing the vineyards, which are planted mainly with aglianico and fiano, and of ensuring that cellar practices are up to date and technically irreproachable, has led to the Zero and Naima reds being among the region's top wines this year. The Zero '98, from aglianico with a small percentage of other traditional varieties, has a dark ruby hue with a purple rim. The aromas are complex, dominated by ripe plum shot through with balsamic and delicately toasty nuances. The palate is powerful and concentrated, unveiling velvety tannins and good intensity of mulberry and blackcurrant fruit. The Naima, also from '98, is a monovarietal aglianico and is an equally deep, dense wine. Its nose has delicate scents of lavender and balsamic notes. While there is no lack of concentration, it does not have the same clarity of expression as Zero and it has not yet lost its slightly astringent finish. From the rest of the large range the fat, soft, Fiano Perella, aged for several months in new oak, Donna Luna, with its fine fruitiness, and the good Aglianico Donna Luna all stand out.

Grotta del Sole deserves a prize for the tremendous work it has done over the past ten years to save numerous ancient grape varieties and traditional regional wines from extinction, and to restore them to the current wine scene. Oenologist Gennaro Martusciello is at the helm of this family estate. There are seven hectares of vineyard, planted with falanghina, and the rest of the grapes are bought in from a team of small growers whose activities are followed closely all year round. Total production is considerable and has now reached 700,000 bottles a year. There are almost 20 wines, which range from Asprinio di Aversa to Lacryma Christi del Vesuvio, and they include such traditional gems as Lettere and Gragnano from the Sorrento peninsula. The latest vintage was not among the best of recent years and the wines reflect this, some quite markedly. Our overall preference went to the Aglianico '98, from grapes grown at Benevento, which has good texture, marked aromas of berry fruit and new wood spiciness. The Montegauro Riserva '96 has a bright, pale ruby colour and delicate fruity aromas of ripe plum and mulberry. The palate reveals good structure and fair balance. Of the wines from the Sorrento peninsula, the Gragnono '99, a blend of piedirosso, aglianico and sciascinoso, is a must. Despite the vintage, it has a fine dark ruby-purple colour, intense aromas of cherry and strawberry, and an attractively spritzy, fruity and delicately tannic palate. The Asprinio di Aversa and Lacryma Christi also showed well.

● Naima '98	ⵙⵙ	5
O Vigna Perella '99	ⵙⵙ	5
● Zero '98	ⵙⵙ	5
● Aglianico Donna Luna '98	ⵙ	4
O Donna Luna Bianco '99	ⵙ	4
O Tempadoro '99	ⵙ	3
● Naima '97	ⵙⵙ	5
● Temparubra '97	ⵙⵙ	2*
● Zero '97	ⵙⵙ	5
O Donna Luna Bianco '97	ⵙ	3
O Donna Luna Bianco '98	ⵙ	3
● RA Passito '97	ⵙ	5
O Tempadoro '98	ⵙ	2*
● Temparubra '98	ⵙ	2*
O Vigna Perella '97	ⵙ	3

● Aglianico '98	ⵙ	3
O Asprinio d'Aversa '99	ⵙ	3
● Campi Flegrei Piedirosso Montegauro Ris. '96	ⵙ	4
● Gragnano '99	ⵙ	3
⊙ Lacryma Christi Rosato '99	ⵙ	3
● Lettere '99		3
O Asprinio d'Aversa '98	ⵙ	3
● Campi Flegrei Piedirosso '97	ⵙ	3
O Fiano di Avellino '98	ⵙ	4
● Gragnano '98	ⵙ	3
O Greco di Tufo '98	ⵙ	4
● Lacryma Christi Rosso '97	ⵙ	4
● Lacryma Christi Rosso '97	ⵙ	3
● Piedirosso '98	ⵙ	4

578

S. CIPRIANO PICENTINO (SA) S. MARCO DI CASTELLABATE (SA)

MONTEVETRANO
VIA MONTEVETRANO
84099 S. CIPRIANO PICENTINO (SA)
TEL. 089/882285

LUIGI MAFFINI
LOC. CENITO
84071 SAN MARCO
DI CASTELLABATE (SA)
TEL. 0974/966345

The '98 vintage continues the seemingly unstoppable series of awards collected by Silvia Imparato for her Montevetrano. Silvia, a sensitive, cultured and refined extrovert who continues to pursue her profession of photography, has always had a great passion for fine wine. So much so that she finally had to find herself a niche in the wine world. With star oenologist, Riccardo Cotarella, as her "partner in crime", she turned her family's lands over to producing a wine that, from its first release, took on legendary status and set new standards for southern Italian winemaking. Enthusiastic reviews on both sides of the ocean have turned Montevetrano almost into a cult wine, hunted down frenetically by its fans. And from the 300 bottles she produced of the '91, Silvia has gradually, with great effort and at no little sacrifice, edged the numbers up to a substantial 17,000. But even if she doubled her output we doubt she could satisfy the demands of the market. The '98 Montevetrano, a blend of cabernet sauvignon, merlot and aglianico, is absolutely fascinating. It is irresistible from the first glance at its concentrated, deep ruby colour with luminous highlights. Then the nose is intense but, more important, elegant as well, and shows a full, well-defined and almost chewy fruitiness, with aromas of small berry fruit and ripe plum interwoven with great finesse into the spicy, vanillaed notes yielded by the oak. The wine's great class is revealed further in the concentrated and powerful yet soft palate, which has great complexity and endless nuances of flavour.

Luigi Maffini continues along his chosen path with great determination. The small fiano vineyard adjacent to his country house has been augmented by others and more are in the process of being purchased. The cellar, too, is being enlarged, by excavating underground, and the estate will shortly have sufficient capacity for its needs. Year by year, the vines are gradually gaining a name for themselves – deservedly so – and this year is no exception to the rule that sees them among the region's best. Kràtos, from fiano with a small proportion of greco, has a fine, bright straw-yellow colour. The nose offers intense, clean aromas of white peach and damson and the palate is good and full, as well as fresh-tasting, fully structured and well balanced. The red Klèos, from aglianico and piedirosso in equal proportions, has a seductively multi-layered structure. As well as a dark, concentrated ruby hue, it has sweet aromas of ripe berry fruit with streaks of spiciness. The palate is firm, compact, soft and fruity, and offers a rich, velvety texture. The most serious and intriguing of Luigi's wines, however, is undoubtedly the Cenito, a red named after the estate's locality. It is a monovarietal Piedirosso, aged in new oak barriques, with a broad spectrum of aromas. Its tones of complex, alluring red and black berry fruit, mainly mulberry and redcurrant, meld into spicy scents of tobacco, liquorice, coffee and cocoa powder. The palate is powerful, harmonious and richly fruited, with prominent notes of plum, revealing rounded tannins and notable length.

● Montevetrano '98	♥♥♥	6
● Montevetrano '93	♀♀♀	5
● Montevetrano '95	♀♀♀	5
● Montevetrano '96	♀♀♀	5
● Montevetrano '97	♀♀♀	5
● Montevetrano '94	♀♀	5

● Cenito '99	♥♥	6
● Klèos '99	♥♥	3*
○ Kràtos '99	♥♥	3*
● Cenito '97	♀♀	5
● Cenito '98	♀♀	6
● Klèos '97	♀♀	2*
● Klèos '98	♀♀	3*
○ Kràtos '97	♀♀	2*
○ Kràtos '98	♀♀	3*

SESSA AURUNCA (CE) SORBO SERPICO (AV)

GALARDI
PROV.LE SESSA-MIGNANO
81030 SESSA AURUNCA (CE)
TEL. 0823/708034

FEUDI DI SAN GREGORIO
LOC. CERZA GROSSA
83050 SORBO SERPICO (AV)
TEL. 0825/986266

The '98 vintage has seen a further impressive series of accolades from both Italy and abroad for Terra di Lavoro, which has become one of Italy's new cult wines. Once Roberto and Maria Luisa Selvaggi, Arturo and Dora Celentano and Francesco Catello combined forces, they moved in a few years from producing two barriques of a wine that was no more than experimental to the 6,000 bottles that are now so feverishly sought after on both sides of the Atlantic. The next vintage will see the quantity rise to 9,000 bottles and the plan is to reach 40,000 bottles by 2005, all coming, as now, from their own grapes. So what started off as a light-hearted gamble, or so it seemed, is now becoming a business with a firm economic foundation. Galardi is an Estate with a capital E. Much of the success has been due to the indispensable contribution of consultant oenologist, Riccardo Cotarella. His work on the '98 has resulted in a wine so deep and dark as to be almost black, with just a hint of purple on the rim. The 80-20 aglianico and piedirosso blend gives an intense, characterful nose with close-knit aromas of ripe, red and black berry fruit that range from mulberry to raspberry and redcurrant. As it opens, it gains complexity from the gradual appearance of notes of tobacco, new oak and bay leaf, followed by pencil lead and a touch of gaminess. The finely hewn palate is dense and powerful, with tannins of great finesse and a sharply defined, joyously vivacious fruitiness that ripples through notes of mulberry jam, caramel, black pepper and toastiness. In short, the wine is full of personality. Unique and quite unforgettable, it is hovering again on the brink of Three Glasses.

The Ercolino brothers' estate is growing at a dizzying rate. In terms of quality that is. The property has over 80 hectares of vineyard in Campania and Puglia, and producing around 1,000,000 bottles annually. This year, 15 wines were submitted for tasting. Of these, two gained Three Glasses and a further three or four were very close. In addition, the average score across the board was remarkably high, testifying to the owners' wisdom in handing over control of the technical side to an oenologist of the calibre of Riccardo Cotarella. Taurasi Piano di Montevergine '96 is a red of considerable power and concentration, qualities that it manages to express with an elegance, a softness and a drinkability that seem almost impossible when you remember the rather rigid, "straight up and down" wines that the area generally turns out. The Fiano di Avellino Pietracalda is a late-vintage wine that has complex, intense notes of tropical fruit, vanilla, citrus peel and cakes. Its palate has a sensuality in the way it softly fills the mouth, unfurling sensations of acacia honey and raisins but also fresh, citrus-like notes and almost infinite length. The Idem '98, from aglianico and piedirosso, is elegant and fluent but also voluptuous in its notes of ripe cherries and mulberry. The perfectly judged dose of new oak adds complexity and length. All the estate's other wines are characterful, from the Greco Cutizzi, another late-vintage wine, the Fiano Privilegio, right through to the more "modest" bottles.

● Terra di Lavoro '98	🍷🍷	6	
● Terra di Lavoro '94	♀♀	5	
● Terra di Lavoro '95	♀♀	5	
● Terra di Lavoro '97	♀♀	5	
● Terra di Lavoro '96	♀	5	

○ Fiano di Avellino Pietracalda V. T. '99	🍷🍷🍷	4*
● Taurasi Piano di Montevergine '96	🍷🍷🍷	6
○ Fiano di Avellino '99	🍷🍷	3*
○ Fiano di Avellino Campanaro '99	🍷🍷	5
○ Greco di Tufo '99	🍷🍷	3*
○ Greco di Tufo Cutizzi V. T. '99	🍷🍷	4
● Idem '98	🍷🍷	5
○ Privilegio '98	🍷🍷	5
● Rubrato '98	🍷🍷	4
● Serpico '97	🍷🍷	6
● Syriacus '98	🍷🍷	5
○ Sannio Falanghina '99	🍷	3
○ Campanaro '98	♀♀♀	5
○ Fiano di Avellino Pietracalda V. T. '98	♀♀♀	4*
● Taurasi '94	♀♀♀	5

TAURASI (AV)

TORRECUSO (BN)

ANTONIO CAGGIANO
C.DA SALA
84030 TAURASI (AV)
TEL. 0827/74043

FONTANAVECCHIA - ORAZIO RILLO
C.DA FONTANAVECCHIA
82030 TORRECUSO (BN)
TEL. 0824/876275

Antonio Caggiano's winery set a record this year. Just behind the stratospheric Feudi di San Gregorio, it is the Campanian estate with the highest average score in our tastings. Five wines were submitted and all gained Two Glasses, an extraordinary result considering the rather iffy wines produced in much of the region last year, especially around Avellino. The key, which Antonio does nothing to keep secret, lies in the vineyards. Caggiano has spent years patiently acquiring land in the best sites and replanting it in line with the most modern criteria. How else can one explain a Guyot-trained vineyard with a density of 8,000 plants per hectare in a zone where everywhere else training is on high cordons at 2,000 or 2,500 plants per hectare? Antonio shares his dreams and his endeavours with another personality, Luigi Moio, lecturer in oenology at the University of Naples, who consults for him on a friendly basis. The result is a series of remarkably high-quality wines, as exemplified by Taurasi Vigna Macchia dei Goti '97. This has a dark ruby colour. The nose offers rich aromas of berry fruit, both fresh and cooked, which support complex, spicy tones of pepper and cloves, and highly complex notes of autumn leaves and leather. The palate is warm, powerful and mouth-filling. The Aglianico from the Salae Domini vineyard is powerful, deep and complex. The Taurì has a ripe, clean fruitiness with excellently judged oak while the white Fiagrè, from fiano and greco, offers alluring citron and grapefruit notes with floral nuances. Mel, a sweet wine of impressive balance and freshness, given emphasis by its pink grapefruit and ripe apricot tones, closes the parade. Onwards and upwards!

Fontanavecchia, owned by Orazio Rillo, was founded in 1980 but is based on a century-old tradition of wine production. The vineyards total about seven hectares, planted predominantly to aglianico. Orazio first bottled his wines in 1990. He now produces about 60,000 bottles annually, which come almost exclusively from his own vineyards. Together with his oenologist, Angelo Pizzi, he is carving out a major role for the estate in the regional wine scene. Confirmation of this comes from the excellent Aglianico del Taburno Vigna Cataratte '96, which has a purplish ruby colour of good depth and an intense, full nose, rich in aromas of mulberry and blackcurrant, with elegant spicy touches. The palate is assertive and warm, with ripe, assertive tannins and flavours of mulberry and ripe cherry, leading to a long, clean finish and a good fruity aftertaste. Fontanavecchia itself is made from aglianico with small quantities of other local varieties, and aged in small French oak barrels. It has an intense ruby colour while the nose displays sweet aromas of ripe plum that flow through more complex notes of tobacco, carob and white pepper. The palate is firmly structured, with a clean, fleshy fruitiness, ripe tannins and fair length. The Aglianico del Taburno '98 also reveals fine quality, with its attractive, youthful, deep ruby colour, its clean, well-defined nose and its nicely full palate. Both the Rosato and the Falanghina are good too.

O Fiagrè '99	♥♥	4	
O Mel '98	♥♥	6	
● Salae Domini '98	♥♥	5	
● Taurasi Vigna Macchia dei Goti '97	♥♥	6	
● Taurì '98	♥♥	4	
O Fiagrè '96	♀♀	3*	
● Salae Domini '96	♀♀	5	
● Salae Domini '97	♀♀	5	
● Taurasi Vigna Macchia dei Goti '94	♀♀	5	
● Taurasi Vigna Macchia dei Goti '95	♀♀	6	
● Taurì '95	♀♀	3*	
● Taurì '96	♀♀	3*	
● Taurì '97	♀♀	4	
O Mel '97	♀	6	
● Salae Domini '95	♀	5	

● Aglianico del Taburno			
Vigna Cataratte '96	♥♥	4	
● Aglianico del Taburno '98	♥	2*	
☉ Aglianico del Taburno Rosato '99	♥	2*	
O Falanghina del Taburno '99	♥	2*	
● Fontanavecchia	♥	4	
● Aglianico del Taburno '96	♀♀	3*	
● Aglianico del Taburno			
Vigna Cataratte Ris. '94	♀♀	5	
● Aglianico del Taburno			
Vigna Cataratte Ris. '95	♀♀	5	
● Aglianico del Taburno '95	♀	3	
☉ Aglianico del Taburno Rosato '97	♀	2*	
● Aglianico del Taburno Rosato '98	♀	3	
O Falanghina del Taburno '98	♀	3	

TUFO (AV)

VITULAZIO (CE)

BENITO FERRARA
FRAZ. S. PAOLO, 14/A
83010 TUFO (AV)
TEL. 0825/998194

VILLA SAN MICHELE
VIA APPIA KM. 198
81050 VITULAZIO (CE)
TEL. 081/666773

This small estate situated at San Paolo, near Tufo, in the province of Avellino, is one of the most cheering discoveries of this year's Guide. The estate was founded by Benito Ferrara but it is now his daughter, Gabriella, and her husband who look after the production of DOC Greco from the three hectares of vineyard. The vines are planted on well-aspected sites on clay and limestone soil, and are Guyot-trained to a density of 5,000 plants per hectare. As a result, they give wines of great distinction. Attilio Pagli and Paolo Caciorgna, who head up the Matura group, act as consultant oenologists. The standard Greco di Tufo is excellent. Bright straw-yellow in colour, it has an intense aroma of ripe white fruits, particularly quince, with delicate floral touches. The palate is full, soft, structured, harmonious, fresh, rich in fleshy fruitiness and long. It clocked up Two Glasses with ease. The Greco di Tufo Vigna Cicogna selection has similar characteristics but has greater concentration and more complexity, on both nose and palate. The nose has elegant mineral notes overlying the fruitiness and its florality is both subtler and more distinct than the standard-label version. The palate is also rounder and deeper, making it a wine of outstanding quality. All this makes for a most impressive debut and puts some of the more famous wines of the zone firmly in their place, even more so when one takes value for money into account. One last point. Production is currently around 22,500 bottles a year. Food for thought.

Villa San Michele, owned by the Galeno family, has stood out for several years now thanks to the quality of its wines, both still and classic method sparkling, all of which come from the estate's 33 hectares of vineyard. The property is situated at Vitulazio, in the province of Caserta, and oenologists Franco Pastore and Maurizio De Simone, with agronomist Bruno Mogavero, spare no effort to get the most from Campania's best traditional varieties, aglianico, piedirosso, greco and falanghina. The '99 Greco impresses, as usual, for its cleanliness and freshness, for its clean-cut aromas of white peach and ripe damson, and for its good weight. The Don Carlos Brut has a fine beading of bubbles, clean perfumes of yeast and golden delicious apples, and a fresh palate that echoes the nose in its appley flavours. These tail off on the back palate to hints of toastiness, bread crusts and an attractive bitterish tang. The Greco Brut is simpler but we found it just as attractive and well-made, with its delicate nuances of vanilla, ripe apple and flowers on both nose and palate. However, the most convincing of the three sparkling wines was again the Demi Sec. It has a notably fine perlage, a nose of good intensity with florality and aromas of fresh white fruit, and a gentle palate with good acid balance. The Piedirosso has a fine palate but is penalized by its nose which is not absolutely clean. Finally, the Aglianico is unbalanced between nose and palate, and is a little too rustic and over-evolved.

○ Greco di Tufo '99	🍷🍷	4
○ Greco di Tufo Vigna Cicogna '99	🍷🍷	4

○ Don Carlos Brut	🍷	4
○ Don Carlos Demi Sec	🍷	4
○ Greco '99	🍷	2*
○ Greco Brut	🍷	4
● Aglianico '98		2
● Piedirosso '99		2
○ Greco '96	🍷🍷	3*
● Aglianico '96	🍷	2*
● Aglianico '97	🍷	3
○ Don Carlos Brut	🍷	4
○ Don Carlos Brut	🍷	4
○ Don Carlos Demi Sec	🍷	4
○ Don Carlos Demi Sec	🍷	4
○ Falanghina '98	🍷	3
○ Greco Brut	🍷	5

OTHER WINERIES

The following producers obtained good scores in our tastings with one or more of their wines:

PROVINCE OF AVELLINO

Marianna,
Grottolella, tel. 0825/627252
Irpinia Bianco Cantico '99,
Taurasi '96

Nicola Romano,
Lapio, tel. 0825/982189
Irpinia Bianco Lapideum '99

La Casa dell'Orco,
Pratola Serra, tel. 0825/967038
Taurasi '96

Di Meo,
Salza Irpinia, tel. 0825/981419
Taurasi '95

Struzziero,
Venticano, tel. 0825/965065
Fiano di Avellino Roseto '99

PROVINCE OF BENEVENTO

Antica Masseria Venditti,
Castelvenere, tel. 0824/940306
Solopaca Bianco Bacalat '99

Ciabrelli,
Castelvenere, tel. 0824/940565
Solopaca Bianco Vigna di Castelvenere '99

Mustilli,
Sant'Agata dei Goti, tel. 0823/717433
Sant'Agata dei Goti Piedirosso '98

PROVINCE OF CASERTA

Coop. Lavoro e Salute,
Galluccio, tel. 0823/925841
Aglianico di Roccamonfina '98,
Falanghina di Roccamonfina '99

I Borboni,
Lusciano, tel. 081/8141386
Coda di Volpe Luna Janca '99

Caputo,
Teverola, tel. 081/5033955
Falanghina Frattasi '99

PROVINCE OF NAPOLI

Cantine Farro,
Bacoli, tel. 081/8545555
Falanghina dei Campi Flegrei '99

Sorrentino,
Boscotrecase, tel. 081/8584194
Lacryma Christi del Vesuvio Bianco '99

La Caprense, Capri, tel. 081/8376835
Capri Bianco Bordo '99

De Falco,
S. Sebastiano al Vesuvio, tel. 081/7713755
Greco di Tufo '99

De Angelis,
Sorrento, tel. 081/8781648
Lacryma Christi del Vesuvio Rosso '99

PROVINCE OF SALERNO

Val Calore,
Castel S. Lorenzo, tel. 0828/944035
Castel San Lorenzo Rosso '99

San Giovanni,
Castellabate, tel. 089/237331 - 224896
Fiano Tresinus '99

Sammarco, Ravello, tel. 089/872774
Costa d'Amalfi Ravello Bianco
Selva delle Monache '99,
Costa d'Amalfi Ravello Rosso
Selva delle Monache '97

Rotolo, Rutino, 0974/830050
Fiano Valentina '99

BASILICATA

This edition of the Guide marks a point of no return for Basilicata. The die is cast and Aglianico enters the new millennium with head held high. Make no mistake, it was not that the wines lacked great reputation and standing before. Anything but. Wine critics and wine lovers have long praised them and drunk them with immense pleasure. Aglianico's tannic attack and its extraordinary ageing potential have often prompted observers to call it the "Barolo of the south". And indeed, when an example from a good vintage gets to about ten years of age, the first sniff, with its wafts of liquorice, tobacco and truffle, not to mention its moderately deep orange-garnet colour, might fool you into thinking it actually is Barolo. That's part of its fingerprint. Previous editions of the Guide have highlighted the significant gap between the two leading producers, D'Angelo and Paternoster, who are Aglianico del Vulture DOC's standard bearers, and all the rest. While the duo turned out wines of ever greater class, other cellars seemed locked into wines that were knocked together with archaic techniques that managed to spoil even excellent quality grapes. Well, that is all becoming history. After last year's gratifying results, Basilicata, with Vulture in leading place, is now very much "battle-ready", so much so that we had difficulty selecting the estates which deserved a full Guide profile. In the end, we had to increase the number of pages dedicated to the region, if only by a fraction, and introduce a list of the more interesting Other Wineries. We are pleased to say that the large number of estates that have thrown themselves enthusiastically into quality production, and the standard of the wines tasted, made this move absolutely essential.

ACERENZA (PZ)

Basilium
C.da Pipoli
85011 Acerenza (PZ)
tel. 0971/741449

Basilium is one of the co-operatives that have muscled their way onto the scene in the past few years. Its wines show that careful attention has been paid both to grape growing and to winemaking. They are light years away from the old, full-bodied but rustic reds that characterized the Vulture district until a short time ago. Here, we have finesse and elegance, irrespective of whether the wine is the flagship Aglianico del Vulture Valle del Trono, or any of the other selections. The '97 Valle del Trono is as good as the previous vintage. It has a dark ruby colour and an intense, deep, sweet nose of great finesse, with aromas of ripe berry fruit, vanilla and roasted coffee. The full, fat, soft palate reveals balance and length, with an excellent interplay of fruit and new oak, tailing off elegantly into an after-aroma of very ripe morello cherry. The Aglianico I Portali '98 has a fresher, more accessible fruitiness but is not to be undervalued. It is a thoroughbred with lashings of structure, also offering velvety tannins and a tightly knit, warm, mouth-filling palate with notes of cakes and berry fruit jam on the full finish. The third Aglianico selection, Pipoli, is again from '98. This has aromas of mulberries and fully ripe cherries, introducing a full, well-structured palate with delicate astringency and convincing balance on the finish. Greco I Portali is fresh, fruity and full of floral fragrances on both nose and palate, recalling ripe apple and pear fruit. It also has a full structure and fair aromatic length.

●	Aglianico del Vulture I Portali '98	▼▼	3*
●	Aglianico del Vulture Valle del Trono '97	▼▼	4
●	Aglianico del Vulture Pipoli '98	▼	2*
○	Greco I Portali '99	▼	2*
●	Aglianico del Vulture I Portali '97	▽▽	3*
●	Aglianico del Vulture Valle del Trono '96	▽▽	4
●	Aglianico del Vulture Pipoli '97	▽	2
○	Greco I Portali '98	▽	2*

BARILE (PZ)

Consorzio Viticoltori
Associati del Vulture
S. S. 93
85022 Barile (PZ)
tel. 0972/770386

In the climate of regeneration which has recently spread through the region, the Consorzio Viticoltori Associati, which brings together the produce of co-operatives and private growers alike, has become one of the most dynamic and qualitatively most promising players around. Oenologist Sergio Paternoster oversees all stages of production, starting with the members' vineyards, and turns out over 200,000 bottles of excellent wine each year. New this year is an Aglianico del Vulture, the Vetusto '97, of such elegance and fascination that it picked up Two Glasses with ease. It comes from some of the area's best vineyards, and from grapes left on the vine for two weeks with the shoots partially cut through so that they are slightly dried when harvested. As a result, the wine is rich and concentrated, from its deep ruby colour onwards. The nose has aromas of mulberry, bilberry and small black berry fruit, with elegant touches of vanilla, spiciness and just a hint of vegetal freshness. The palate is fleshy and structured, unveiling a refined tannic weave, just as one would expect from a good southern red in an excellent vintage. The Aglianico del Vulture Carpe Diem, also from '97, is a more modest proposition but still evokes some of the warmth and fullness of the Vetusto. As fresh and clean as its stablemate, it offers good nose-palate symmetry and decent length. The latest release of the standard Aglianico del Vulture displays its customary good quality, proffering notes of ripe wild cherry and fresh almond, while the delightfully sweet, fresh and aromatic Moscato Spumante, and the aglianico-based Ellenico, a slightly sweet, sparkling red wine, are both worthy of their One Glass status.

●	Aglianico del Vulture Vetusto '97	▼▼	4
●	Aglianico del Vulture '98	▼	3
●	Aglianico del Vulture Carpe Diem '97	▼	4
●	Aglianico Spumante Ellenico	▼	3
○	Moscato Spumante	▼	3
●	Aglianico del Vulture '96	▽▽	2*
●	Aglianico del Vulture Carpe Diem '93	▽▽	3*
●	Aglianico del Vulture Carpe Diem '95	▽▽	3*
●	Aglianico del Vulture '97	▽	2*
●	Aglianico del Vulture '94	▽	2*
●	Aglianico del Vulture Carpe Diem '96	▽	3

BARILE (PZ)

MATERA

PATERNOSTER
VIA NAZIONALE, 23
85022 BARILE (PZ)
TEL. 0972/770224

PROGETTO DI VINO
VIA NAZIONALE, 76
75100 MATERA
TEL. 0835/262851

The official date of birth of this estate is 1925, when Anselmo Paternoster first started to sell bottles of a red wine obtained from his own vines. Today, the estate has over 25 hectares of vineyard, produces 120,000 bottles of wine a year, and is regarded as one of southern Italy's leading estates. A new wine, an Aglianico del Vulture '97 from the Rotondo vineyard, came out on top of the range in our tastings. It is a carefully honed, modern-style red with a good dark ruby colour leading in to intense but soft aromas of perfectly ripe red and black berry fruit and a firmly structured, notably fat palate with an exceptional concentration of fruit. It gains in complexity as it progresses through the mouth and finishes long, leaving a captivating note of vanilla. The '95 release of the estate's classic, Aglianico del Vulture Don Anselmo, is in fine fettle. From a perfect marriage of tradition and modern technology, it has a good dark ruby colour and an intense, sweet, concentrated nose with aromas of ripe berry fruits and more complex spicy tones. The palate is rich and fully structured, with great balance of fruit, tannin and acidity. There is a classic note of morello cherry, which melds into more complex tones of tobacco and new oak on the finish. The basic Aglianico is as engaging and well-made as ever. The '98 version has body, concentration and rich fruitiness, most notably cherry and ripe plum, on both nose and palate. It is harmonious and long, with pepper and spice on the aftertaste. The estate's other wines, from the perfumed fiano-based Bianco di Corte to the slightly sparkling wines, are all very good.

In the heart of Matera's stony territory is a cellar holding a number of barriques containing a very fine red, San Biagio . Progetto di Vino is a new estate, now at its second release with the '98 vintage, and is run by five partners, led by Sante Lomurno. A few years ago, they decided to produce a red wine that could express to the full the great potential of aglianico when grown on the best terroirs in the region. They bought a vineyard in the Vulture zone, where two of the team, expert agronomists Giuseppe Malvasi and Francesco Paolicelli, look after the vineyards. The grapes are vinified in the area and then brought to the old cellars in the church of San Biagio at Matera, which lie ten metres underground. After a year's ageing in barrique and a further year in bottle, the wine is released for sale. The '97 has a good dark ruby colour, ushering in intense aromas of berry fruit, tobacco and oak toast. The full, soft palate has plenty of concentrated fruit, ripe tannins, suppleness and considerable length. The following vintage, '98, has very similar characteristics and here, too, there is cleanliness and finesse in the aromas of ripe red and black berry fruit. A thoroughly elegant wine, it has an immediate approachability that comes from the small percentage of merlot that rounds out the aglianico's firm tannic streak. The wine is long and finishes with delicate hints of spice and vanilla. The estate will soon have a second wine, a Primitivo, which will boost significantly the current production of just a few thousand bottles. The grapes will come from the area of Matera where the primitivo variety has been cultivated for centuries.

●	Aglianico del Vulture '98	♥♥	4
●	Aglianico del Vulture Don Anselmo Ris. '95	♥♥	5
●	Aglianico del Vulture Rotondo '97	♥♥	4
●	Barigliott '99	♥	3
O	Bianco di Corte '98	♥	3
O	Clivus Moscato della Basilicata '99	♥	3
●	Aglianico del Vulture '95	♀♀	3*
●	Aglianico del Vulture '97	♀♀	4
●	Aglianico del Vulture Don Anselmo Ris. '88	♀♀	5
●	Aglianico del Vulture Don Anselmo Ris. '93	♀♀	5
●	Aglianico del Vulture Don Anselmo Ris. '94	♀♀	5

●	San Biagio '97	♥♥	4
●	San Biagio '98	♥♥	4

POTENZA

Tenuta Le Querce

Via Appia, 123
85100 Potenza
tel. 0971/410709

Le Querce is one of the newest wineries to join the ranks of Basilicata's top producers. It was set up in 1997 by the Pietrafesa family, who took over the estate from the Sasso family (a long-standing name in Basilicata winemaking). They have 82 hectares, of which 50 are dedicated to vine. Part of the vineyard area is being replanted and when it reaches full production, the estate should have a potential output of around 300,000 bottles. While this side is taken care of by the agronomist, Professor Valentini, it is Severino Garofano, one of most respected oenologists in southern Italy, who is at the helm in the cellars. There are three versions of Aglianico del Vulture, all from '98. We found the best of the trio to be the Rosso di Costanza selection, aged in new oak. It has a great wealth of very ripe berry fruits aromas with attractive notes of vanilla, coffee, cocoa powder and oak toast. The palate is warm, enveloping, fat, powerful and full of soft flavours of morello cherry and ripe plum. Its tannins are well-rounded and its finish long and assertive. The Viola has a ruby colour, which just begins to turn orange on the rim. There are ripe, complex aromas of leather, coffee and liqueur cherry and then the palate is rich in tannin and alcohol but has good overall balance. The colour of the Federico II is turning slightly more towards orange, introducing mature aromas of liquorice, coffee and cherry jam. The palate is warm and richly tannic, although a little too astringent and evolved. Still, this is an encouraging debut for an estate with great potential.

● Aglianico del Vulture Rosso di Costanza '98	YY	6
● Aglianico del Vulture Federico II '98	Y	5
● Aglianico del Vulture Il Viola '98	Y	4

RIONERO IN VULTURE (PZ)

D'Angelo

Via Provinciale, 8
85028 Rionero in Vulture (PZ)
tel. 0972/721517

Lucio and Donato D'Angelo's estate has long been a point of reference for south Italian winemaking, as well as one of the region's archetypes. And to judge by the results of this year's tastings, its fame is well-merited. Donato acts as the estate's oenologist and obtains the excellent quality grapes on which their reds are based from their 20 hectares of vineyard. Canneto '97, from late-picked aglianico, was well up to expectations, with obvious concentration on both the appearance and the nose, where scents of vanilla and oak toast meld elegantly into aromas of berry fruit jam. On the palate, there is a well-judged dose of new oak that does not mask the opulent fruit. There is also excellent balance and a long, firm finish with a controlled amount of astringency. After several years' absence, the excellent '95 vintage has permitted the return of Aglianico del Vulture Vigna Caselle Riserva to these pages. It gains Two Glasses for its good, deep ruby red colour and its fine aromas of black berry fruit, tobacco and spices as well as a palate of serious depth, where there is softness along with assertive but ripe tannins, good acidity and substantial fruit. Even the basic Aglianico del Vulture, which has balance and a freshness that is immediate but not simplistic, is a wine to be highly recommended.

● Aglianico del Vulture Vigna Caselle Ris. '95	YY	5
● Canneto '97	YY	5
● Aglianico del Vulture '98	Y	4
● Aglianico del Vulture '90	YY (white)	3
● Aglianico del Vulture '95	YY (white)	3
● Canneto '90	YY (white)	5
● Canneto '91	YY (white)	5
● Canneto '93	YY (white)	5
● Canneto '94	YY (white)	5
● Canneto '95	YY (white)	5
○ Vigna dei Pini '94	YY (white)	3
○ Vigna dei Pini '97	YY (white)	3*

587

RIONERO IN VULTURE (PZ) VENOSA (PZ)

ARMANDO MARTINO
VIA LUIGI LA VISTA, 2/A
85028 RIONERO IN VULTURE (PZ)
TEL. 0972/721422

CANTINA RIFORMA FONDIARIA
DI VENOSA
C.DA VIGNALI
85029 VENOSA (PZ)
TEL. 0972/36702

The Armando Martino winery has an average production of around 500,000 bottles and is one of the most firmly established in the Vulture DOC zone. It was founded at the beginning of the 40s and, obviously, is specialized in the production of Aglianico del Vulture. The company owns just three hectares of vineyard, the rest of the grapes being bought in from growers in the zone, and produces a large range of wines, which are made by oenologist, Giovanni Colucci. At the top of the tree is the barrique-aged Aglianico del Vulture Oraziano. The '97 showed particularly well. It unfurls good concentration of colour and has intense aromas of liquorice, coffee and mulberry. The palate is firmly structured, warm, full, soft, balanced and richly fruited, with berry fruit underscored by notes of chocolate and vanilla, and a stylish array of tannins on the finish. It is already drinking well but has several years' ageing in front of it. Carolin '99, from aglianico, is simpler and more immediate in style but is extremely engaging. The ripe fruitiness has overt aromas of peach and redcurrant, and a warm, soft, fleshy palate with an elegant touch of tobacco. A second look at Aglianico del Vulture '97, first tasted for last year's Guide, showed it to be good, balanced and firmly tannic, with berry fruit flavours on the back palate and the beginnings of some more evolved, tertiary notes. The Rosato Donna Lidia, again from aglianico, is rather less alluring this year while the estate's whites still have a touch of rusticity that detracts from their appeal.

Founded in 1957, the Cantina Cooperativa della Riforma Fondiaria di Venosa is now a modern, efficient winery controlling a good 700 hectares of vineyard in the Aglianico del Vulture DOC zone and producing around 240,000 bottles a year. The two fine vintages of '97 and '98 stimulated agronomist, Rocco Manieri, and oenologist, Oronzo Alò, to show just how much potential the property had and, at the same time, showcase their own skills. The Aglianico del Vulture I Vignali '98, produced from vines up to 30 years old, made a great impact on the panel. The colour is dark ruby, the aromas are intense and sweet, and despite its youth there is already concentration, elegance and complexity. The barrique-aged Aglianico del Vulture Carato Venusio '97 is fairly similar on the palate but it is the nose, with its elegant aromas of ripe cherry and tobacco, faithfully echoed on the palate, that gives it its distinctive personality. The Aglianico del Vulture Terre di Orazio is aged in 500 to 700-litre tonneaux and has been named in honour of the Latin poet, Horace, a local boy who made a name for himself. The colour is dark and the nose is intense and full of ripe berry fruit. The assertive palate is stylish yet soft and restrained, with flavours of blackcurrant and vanilla. The range of Aglianicos comes to a close with the basic '97 version. This is actually not a long way short of the premium-label wines in fullness and attractiveness. It loses out only because it is slightly over-evolved, perhaps caused by barrels that were a tad past their best. The red Vignali '99 is well-typed. And value for money is excellent across the board.

● Aglianico del Vulture Oraziano '97	▼▼	4
● Rosso Carolin '99	▼	3
⊙ Donna Lidia Rosato '99		3
● Aglianico del Vulture '93	♀	3
● Aglianico del Vulture '94	♀	3
● Aglianico del Vulture '95	♀	3
● Aglianico del Vulture '97	♀	3
● Aglianico del Vulture Oraziano '93	♀	4
○ Basilicata Chardonnay '98	♀	3
⊙ Donna Lidia Rosato '98	♀	3
● Rosso Carolin '93	♀	2*
● Rosso Carolin '95	♀	2*
○ Basilicata Bianco Oraziano '97		4

● Aglianico del Vulture		
Carato Venusio '97	▼▼	4
● Aglianico del Vulture		
I Vignali '98	▼▼	2*
● Aglianico del Vulture		
Terre di Orazio '98	▼▼	3*
● Aglianico del Vulture '98	▼	2*
● Vignali '99		1
● Aglianico del Vulture '94	♀♀	3*
● Aglianico del Vulture '96	♀	3

OTHER WINERIES

The following producers obtained good scores in our tastings with one or more of their wines:

PROVINCE OF POTENZA

Basilisco,
Rionero in Vulture, tel. 0972/720032
Aglianico del Vulture Basilisco '98

Di Palma,
Rionero in Vulture, tel. 0972//722515
Aglianico del Vulture Nibbio Grigio '98,
Aglianico del Vulture
Nibbio Grigio etichetta Nera '97

C. S. del Vulture
Rionero in Vulture,
tel. 0972/721062
Aglianico del Vulture '96

F.lli Napolitano
Rionero in Vulture,
tel. 0972/721040
Aglianico del Vulture '97

Pisani,
Viggiano,
tel. 0975/352603
Concerto '97
Basilicata Rosso '99

PUGLIA

As Puglia's wine scene makes headway, it does so with, in general, a careful balance of tradition and innovation. Last year, we spoke of the "dynamism" and "vivacity" pervading the region. This year, we need to add adjectives such as "strong", or even "extreme", and we are delighted to do so. Despite the rather depressing vintage of '99, the whole sector showed that it was fully up to speed both technically and managerially. Not only did we have many more wines to taste but the average score also increased across the board. The problematic wines, those archaic wines that oxidized easily and suffered numerous other defects as a result of "rustic", off-the-cuff winemaking, and that were once so common, have now all but disappeared. New wineries and new names have sprung up, often with excellent results. Many of the new protagonists have been businessmen for generations, not necessarily in the wine sector, but all have realized that Puglia is on the brink of a new, definitive stage in its development. Conscious of the immense quality potential of the region, its superb indigenous grapes and the climate and lands so superbly suited to viticulture, they have invested enthusiasm as liberally as resources in the creation of new enterprises. Many have turned to capable, competent oenologists to manage the winemaking and this has often been the decisive, winning, stroke. The great heritage we have often talked about needed only to be turned to account. This is exactly what is now happening. The successes are not always tied to "imported" names either. Puglia is a region that is structuring its progress through a class of well prepared, professional youngsters who understand the value of experience gleaned from the past while being acutely aware of current developments in the wine sector in Italy and, especially, abroad. And so we find new Primitivos that vie with the American Zinfandels. Wonderful, negroamaro-based reds that brook no competition for depth, richness and cleanliness of execution. Some of Italy's best rosés and whites that are beginning to make waves. With so many players jostling for space the scene is starting to look a little complicated - but all the more exciting for it. This year our Three Glass awards go to two wines. One is a classic that needs no presentation, Patriglione. This year's is the '94, a vintage vinified by Cosimo Taurino who, until his recent death, was one of the greats of the Puglian wine scene and one of the architects of the region's wine renaissance. The other is the spectacular Nero from Conti Zecca. This hails from a grape blend that reflects tradition but then endows it with a scintilla of international class. It crowns a decade of continuous hard work and is vindication for all the region's producers, be they small or large, co-operative or private, who have realized that the times when they could stand still have long gone. Indeed, many are already looking ahead, knowledgeably and decisively, towards new and even more ambitious goals . . .

ALEZIO (LE)

ANDRIA (BA)

ROSA DEL GOLFO
VIA GARIBALDI, 56
73011 ALEZIO (LE)
TEL. 0833/281045

RIVERA
C.DA RIVERA
S. S. 98, KM 19.800 ANDRIA-CANOSA
70031 ANDRIA (BA)
TEL. 0883/569501 - 0883/569510

This year's tastings have convinced us that Damiano Calò's Rosa del Golfo is probably Italy's best '99 rosé. Congratulations to Damiano, who has clearly not just taken over from his father but done so with great commitment. The wine has a good, bright, deep pink colour and intense, clean-cut, delightful perfumes of red berry fruit, cherry and wild rose (or did the name influence our nostrils?). The full palate is rich in fresh fruitiness, whose character echoes the nose perfectly and whose flavours taper off only gradually. In short, it's a small marvel. In addition, it would be as adept at partnering white meats as it is with highly flavoured fish and vegetable dishes. A second look at the red Portulano, made from the same grapes as the Rosa – negroamaro with a touch of malvasia nera – and first tasted last year, confirms that it still has good substance. The estate's other rosé, Scaliere '99, is also of fine quality. It doesn't have the fascination of Rosa del Golfo but there is good concentration and freshness in its youthful aromas. Finally, there is Bolina '99, from verdeca, which, to be truthful, let the side down. It is a well-typed white, fruity and well balanced, but somewhat simple.

Rivera's wines have once more gained gratifying scores. The estate, run by Carlo di Corato, has 55 hectares of vines scattered about but mostly within the Castel del Monte DOC zone. Grapes are also brought in from a group of tried and tested growers, which allows the annual production easily to exceed 1,500,000 bottles. The reputation of the estate is founded on the great care taken in vine cultivation and in grape purchase, as well as on the abilities of its oenologist, Leonardo Palumbo. Rivera's star wine this year, as often in the past, is Il Falcone, a highly-structured red made from 70 percent uva di troia and 30 percent montepulciano. The '97 Riserva demonstrates the stylistic aplomb of the estate and is probably the best-ever release of the wine. It has a lively, dark ruby colour leading in to intense, well-defined aromas of ripe red and black fruits, with hints of cocoa powder and coffee beans. It then shows a full, fruity, assertive palate that develops with harmony, revealing tannins of great finesse. Full of fruit, balanced and long, it finishes with attractive balsamic notes. The Aglianico Cappellaccio '97 is another full, fat, powerful red that manages to be intense while displaying nice finesse. The palate is richly tannic and well-imbued with ripe black fruit. Its warmth and power takes you through to a finish with an attractive touch of astringency. The '98 Moscato Piani di Tufara is as appealing as the '97 while the Primitivo Triusco is richly fleshy and strongly varietal. With possibly the sole exception of the Rosato, all the rest of the vast range is of very good quality.

⊙ Salento Rosato Rosa del Golfo '99	¶¶	4
○ Salento Bianco Bolina '99	¶	3
⊙ Salento Rosato Scaliere '99	¶	3
○ Salento Bianco Bolina '95	¶¶	2*
○ Salento Bianco Bolina '96	¶¶	3*
○ Salento Bianco Bolina '97	¶¶	3*
⊙ Salento Rosato Rosa del Golfo '96	¶¶	3*
⊙ Salento Rosato Rosa del Golfo '97	¶¶	3*
⊙ Salento Rosato Rosa del Golfo '98	¶¶	3*
● Salento Rosso Portulano '93	¶¶	2*
● Salento Rosso Portulano '97	¶¶	3*
● Quarantale '88	¶	5
○ Salento Bianco Bolina '98	¶	3

● Castel del Monte Aglianico		
Cappellaccio Ris. '97	¶¶	4
● Castel del Monte Rosso Il Falcone Ris. '97	¶¶	4
○ Moscato di Trani Piani di Tufara '98	¶¶	3*
○ Castel del Monte Bianco		
Dama di Svevia '99	¶	2*
○ Castel del Monte Chardonnay		
Preludio n. 1 '99	¶	3
● Castel del Monte Rosso		
Rupicolo di Rivera '98	¶	3
○ Castel del Monte Sauvignon		
Terre al Monte '99	¶	3
○ Locorotondo '99	¶	2*
● Primitivo Triusco '97	¶	3
⊙ Castel del Monte Rosé di Rivera '99		2

AVETRANA (TA)

BRINDISI

Sinfarosa
S. S. 174, km 3
74020 Avetrana (TA)
tel. 099/9711660

Rubino
Via A. Pigafetta, 3
72100 Brindisi
tel. 0831/571955

Although Sinfarosa didn't manage to repeat its starry showing of last year, when its exceptional Zinfandel '98 shot the estate into the Three Glass elite, it remains one of the more exciting of the new Puglian estates. However, it was unfortunately hit by hail and despite the meticulous care that the estate's owners, Antonio Spedicato, Arcangelo My and Celestino Scarciglia, took with their ten hectares of 40-year-old, bush-trained vines, they could not avoid a slight dip in quality. The difference is hardly noticeable in the '99 Primitivo di Manduria Zinfandel but is just enough to bring it those critical few points below the Three Glass threshold. Even so, it still has a beautiful, almost opaque, dark ruby hue and a full, complex, rich nose with aromas of ripe cherry, chocolate and spices, most notably pepper. The palate is concentrated and fleshy, with tightly woven but beautifully soft tannins. Although the wine does not have quite the expressive power of the '98, it does have the same soft fruitiness on the nose and the notes of jam, vanilla and spices on its long finish. Fabrizio Perrucci, Sinfarosa's oenologist, has also produced a more immediate, easier-drinking '99 Primitivo. This has a good deep ruby colour, rich aromas of ripe cherry and a soft, attractively fruited, assertive but fluid palate. These are all excellent wines that are well worth drinking while we wait for those from the 2000 vintage, which promise to be excellent.

Father and son team Tommaso and Luigi Rubino are the owners of this major estate with a good 160 hectares of spur-pruned cordon-trained vines and total production of 100,000 bottles. There is a brand-new cellar, Luca D'Attoma acts as consultant and Luca Petrelli is the estate's full-time oenologist. The first vintage was the '99 and a good number of mainly red wines were produced, all of fine quality and all exceedingly well-priced. The reds we particularly liked included the Sangiovese Terra dei Messapi '99, a well-structured, easy-drinking, fruit-rich and fresh-tasting wine with soft tannins. The Salice Salentino Terra dei Messapi '99 has a good dark ruby colour introducing sweet, intense aromas of small berry fruit and a palate with good body and a soft, fruity flow. The Salento Rosso Tamerici, from negroamaro, montepulciano and malvasia nera, is noteworthy for its good balance, its inviting, fruity aromas, with an attractively up-front immediacy, and its rounded palate that flaunts nicely ripe tannins. The Salento Rosato Marmorelle '99 is convincingly good, too. It has a full body, fresh, small berry fruit aromas and good length. The '99 Chardonnay has an appealingly bright, pale straw-yellow colour and sweet aromas of ripe fruit with floral touches. The soft palate is light-bodied but not evanescent, and has an attractive streak of fresh fruit.

● Primitivo di Manduria		
Zinfandel '99	▽▽	4
● Primitivo di Manduria '99	▽	4
● Primitivo di Manduria		
Zinfandel '98	▽▽▽	4*
● Primitivo di Manduria '98	▽▽	4

○ Chardonnay		
Terra dei Messapi '99	▽	2*
⊙ Salento Rosato Marmorelle '99	▽	2*
⊙ Salento Rosato Tamerici '99	▽	1*
● Salento Rosso Gallico '99	▽	3
● Salento Rosso Tamerici '99	▽	1*
● Salice Salentino		
Terra dei Messapi '99	▽	2*
● Sangiovese		
Terra dei Messapi '99	▽	2*

CELLINO SAN MARCO (BR)   CELLINO SAN MARCO (BR)

LA MEA
VIA SAN MARCO, 61
72020 CELLINO SAN MARCO (BR)
TEL. 0831/617689

LIBRA
C.DA BOSCO, 13
72020 CELLINO SAN MARCO (BR)
TEL. 0831/619211

This estate, run by Marco Maci, extends over more than 100 hectares in total, most of which lie within the territory of Cellino San Marco. About 90 hectares of the property is given over to vine. There are a couple of things to consider at this point. The first is that there are several significant quality peaks in the huge production and in general, the line shows steady improvement. Hence the estate's entry in the Guide. The second point emerged at our tastings, which showed that alongside wines of undoubted class La Mea has others that are much less successful. With more than 12 wines in production, the moral would seem to be to cut back the range and concentrate on the wines with higher profiles. Among the more interesting of these is the Primitivo del Salento Fra Diavolo '99, which is well-constructed, has considerable concentration and power, and is stylish and long. Vita, from negroamaro and cabernet, is dark ruby in colour. Its aromas of red fruit jam, with hints of liquorice, tobacco and spices, are intense and the palate is warm and powerful. Just as successful and just as captivating is the Dragonero '97, a red from negroamaro blended, to excellent effect, with merlot. It is soft and intense, as dense on the nose and palate as it is on the eye. Notes of chocolate, berry fruit and tobacco give it complexity on both nose and palate, leading through to a warm, long finish. Similar levels of depth and length are to be found in Sire, a monovarietal Negroamaro, and Bella Mojgan, from negroamaro and malvasia nera. The rest of the wines listed below have great character but, quite frankly, the prices asked look a little over-optimistic.

Al Bano Carrisi has always had a great passion for the land and he turns out a carefully crafted range of clean, attractive wines that have been in the limelight for several years now. The estate extends over 200 hectares and has 70 hectares of vineyard, from which oenologist Giuseppe Rizzo turns out grapes of excellent quality. These are mainly negroamaro, chardonnay and sauvignon, together with smaller amounts of other local varieties. The Libra wines steer an even-handed course between regard for tradition and the need to innovate in an increasingly global market. At the top of the range is the classy Platone, '97, a full-bodied red, from equal proportions of negroamaro and primitivo, aged in French oak barriques. It has a dark ruby colour; sweet, intense aromas of mulberry and plum berry fruit with touches of tobacco, chocolate and attractive toasty hints. These usher in a concentrated, dense, long palate, full of soft tannins. The '96 Salice Salentino, first tasted last year, has retained its concentration from its appearance onwards. The nose, with aromas of ripe berry fruit, herbs and liquorice, and more complex spicy touches, deliciously evokes the character of its terroir. The red Nostalgia is based on negroamaro and is a full-bodied, fat, balanced wine, brimming with scents of morello cherry and spice. These mingle with a delicate, fresh herbaceousness and warm, pervasive notes of berry fruit that linger unhurriedly on the finish. All the other wines have nice character, particularly the velvety, mouth-filling Salento Rosso Don Carmelo '96.

● Bella Mojgan '97	ΥΥ	6
● Dragonero '97	ΥΥ	5
● Primitivo del Salento		
Fra Diavolo '99	ΥΥ	5
● Sire '97	ΥΥ	6
● Vita '97	ΥΥ	6
● Copertino Duca d'Atene '97	Υ	5
● Lume di Candela '99	Υ	4
● Salice Salentino Ribò '98	Υ	4

● Salento Rosso Nostalgia '97	ΥΥ	3*
● Salento Rosso Platone '97	ΥΥ	6
○ Salento Bianco Don Carmelo '99	Υ	2*
○ Salento Bianco Felicità '99	Υ	3
● Salento Rosso Don Carmelo '96	Υ	2*
⊙ Salento Rosato Mediterraneo '99		3
● Salento Rosso Nostalgia '96	ΨΨ	3*
● Salice Salentino		
Albano Carrisi '96	ΨΨ	2*
○ Salento Bianco Felicità '98	Υ	3
⊙ Salento Rosato Mediterraneo '96	Υ	3
● Salento Rosso Nostalgia '94	Υ	3

CORATO (BA)

CORATO (BA)

SANTA LUCIA
STRADA COMUNALE SAN VITTORE, 1
70033 CORATO (BA)
TEL. 080/8721168 - 080/7642888

TORREVENTO
LOC. CASTEL DEL MONTE
S. S. 170, KM 28
70033 CORATO (BA)
TEL. 080/8980929

Santa Lucia, currently owned by successful Naples businessmen Giuseppe and Roberto Perrone Capano, has a long history. Founded in 1628, the estate has been involved continuously in viticulture ever since. There are now 15 hectares under vine and these produce around 70,000 bottles a year, with winemaking in the hands of oenologist Luigi Cantatore. The wines are very well-made and provide some of the benchmarks for the Castel del Monte DOC zone. The best to emerge from this year's tastings was the Castel del Monte Riserva '97. It has a good dark ruby colour, which introduces a nose that shows both intensity and finesse, with aromas of ripe berry fruit enhanced by touches of spiciness and vanilla. The palate has body and firm structure, an assertive but refined astringency, good concentration and a fresh finish dominated by notes of bilberry fruit. The '96 Aleatico also has a good dark ruby colour. Its captivating, rich nose offers aromas that suggest a wide range of ripe berry fruit, both fresh and cooked, delicate hints of balsam and a touch Mediterranean scrub. The palate is balanced, sweet, and attractively concentrated, grabbing your attention with a delicate note of tannin, which interweaves enticingly with the wine's general softness and fruity richness. The Castel del Monte Vigna del Melograno '98 is a red with lashings of style. It has reasonable weight, clean notes of fresh almond, mulberry and plum, a nicely structured palate, nice fleshy fruitiness and a delicate herbaceousness on the finish. The estate's other wines are also of good quality.

Francesco Liantonio's estate is one of the most reliable and consistent in Puglia. There are 100 hectares in all, of which 63 are planted to vine, but there are plans to increase the vineyard area. Lino Carparelli, Torrevento's oenologist, produces a vast range of carefully made wines and the cellar releases a total of around 600,000 bottles each year. Vigna Pedale '98, from 100 percent uva di troia, comes well up to expectations. It has a nice dark ruby colour and deep, fresh, berry fruit aromas that are given complexity by delicate herbaceous hints and touches of pencil lead. The fat, soft palate has good structure and balance, a fair array of flavours centred on ripe berry fruit, tannins of a certain finesse and a fairly long finish. It amply deserves its Two Glasses. The '98 Moscato di Trani Dulcis in Fundo repeats the excellent showing of the previous vintage. Softly sweet without cloying, it is as concentrated and rich in aromatic, vanilla-tinged notes of tropical fruit and orange blossom on the nose as it is on the palate. The Castel del Monte '98 has a clean, appealing character, with good body, well-defined aromas and herbaceous touches from the cabernet. All in all, a very attractive wine. Torre del Falco '98, mainly from cabernets sauvignon and franc with uva di troia making up the balance, showed well. Torrevento also markets the wines of the Carparelli brothers' I Pastini estate. We thoroughly appreciated their Primitivo di Tarantino this year and also liked the Murgia Rosso '98.

● Castel del Monte Rosso Ris. '97	▼▼	5
● Puglia Aleatico Dolce '99	▼▼	4
○ Castel del Monte Bianco		
Vigna Tufaroli '99	▼	2*
⊙ Castel del Monte Rosato		
Vigna Lama di Carro '99	▼	2*
● Castel del Monte Rosso		
Vigna del Melograno '98	▼	3
● Murgia Rosso Vigna Pozzo '98	▼	2*
● Castel del Monte Rosso '97	▽▽	2*
● Castel del Monte Rosso Ris. '95	▽▽	3*
● Castel del Monte Rosso '95	▽	2*
● Castel del Monte Rosso '96	▽	2*
● Castel del Monte Rosso Ris. '96	▽	4
● Vigna del Pozzo '97	▽	2*

● Castel del Monte Rosso		
Vigna Pedale Ris. '98	▼▼	3*
○ Moscato di Trani Dulcis in Fundo '98	▼▼	4
● Primitivo del Tarantino I Pastini '99	▼▼	3*
⊙ Castel del Monte Rosato '99	▼	2*
● Castel del Monte Rosso '98	▼	2*
● Murgia Rosso I Pastini '98	▼	3
● Torre del Falco '98	▼	3
○ Castel del Monte Bianco '99		2
● Castel del Monte Rosso '97	▽▽	1*
● Castel del Monte Rosso		
Vigna Pedale Ris. '94	▽▽	2*
● Castel del Monte Rosso		
Vigna Pedale Ris. '96	▽▽	2*
● Primitivo del Tarantino I Pastini '97	▽▽	3*

FASANO (BR)

GUAGNANO (LE)

BORGO CANALE
LOC. SELVA
V.LE CANALE DI PIRRO, 23
72015 FASANO (BR)
TEL. 080/4331351

ANTICA MASSERIA DEL SIGILLO
VIA PROVINCIALE, 37
73010 GUAGNANO (LE)
TEL. 0832/706331

Borgo Canale is a large winery, owned by the Marchitelli family, and produces over 700,000 bottles a year. It has no vineyards. Instead, long-term contracts with reliable growers ensure the supply of grapes. The estate's star is back in the ascendant thanks to very careful management of grape purchases and, particularly, of the cellar, where the young but very able Nicola Carparelli handles production. Again, it is the impressive Primitivo Maestro that leads the estate's array of wines. A concentrated wine, it unfurls clean aromas of berry fruit and spices on the fresh nose. There are inviting flavours of mulberry, ripe plum, morello cherry and white pepper on the palate, which has fair body and good length. There is also an attractive hint of tobacco in the aftertaste. The Rosa di Selva '99 has a good, bright, pink colour and is as fresh and fruity on the nose as it is on the palate. Last year, we found some quality dips in the falanghina and bianco d'Alessano-based Diva and Locorotondo whites, but both '99s restored our faith with their fine freshness and cleanliness. Divo is noteworthy for its structure and skilful touch with the oaking while the Locorotondo, with its aromas of ripe apple and its vein of fresh fruitiness on the palate, is a delight to drink. The lively white Agorà is attractive and well-typed.

Antica Masseria del Sigillo, situated at Guagnano in the heart of the Salento area, is one of the names that have recently emerged with success onto the regional wine stage. It currently has around ten hectares of gobelet and cordon-trained vines, mainly negroamaro and primitivo but, on the wave of the attention it has been receiving, the plantings are increasing. The oenologist is Aronzo Alò, a consultant who operates in Puglia and Basilicata. Now in its second year of activity, Antica Masseria has already made considerable advances in the Italian market but has done even better abroad. There are four wines, all of which showed well in our tastings. The Primitivo Sigillo is a red of great power and concentration. Its attractive dark ruby colour leads in to a nose with intense ripe berry fruit aromas that are given additional pizzazz by elegant touches of printer's ink and white and black pepper. The palate is warm, enveloping, rich in fleshy fruitiness and nicely balanced. It gains Two Glasses, as does Terre del Guiscardo '98, a successful blend of primitivo, merlot and cabernet sauvignon. This has a deep, even colour, an intense nose, rich in ripe plum and mulberry aromas, and a soft, fresh palate with good structure and length, backed up by ripe tannins. The Salice Salentino Il Secondo is a full-bodied, rounded wine made from perfectly ripe grapes. However, it shows better on the palate than on the nose, which is slightly weak. Sigillo Primo Chardonnay also has character. It is fresh, balanced and has good complexity.

O Divo '99	♀	4
O Locorotondo '99	♀	2*
● Primitivo Maestro '98	♀	3
☉ Rosa di Selva '99	♀	2*
O Agorà Bianco '99		2
● Primitivo Maestro '97	♀♀	3*
O Chardonnay del Salento Robur '94	♀	4
O Divo '93	♀	4
O Divo '94	♀	4
O Moscato Dolce Gotha '98	♀	4
● Primitivo Maestro '96	♀	3
☉ Rosa di Selva '98	♀	2*

● Sigillo Primo Primitivo '99	♀♀	2*
● Terre del Guiscardo '98	♀♀	4
● Salice Salentino Il Secondo '98	♀	2*
O Sigillo Primo Chardonnay '99	♀	2*

GUAGNANO (LE)

LATIANO (BR)

COSIMO TAURINO
S. S. 605 SALICE-SANDONACI
73010 GUAGNANO (LE)
TEL. 0832/706490

LOMAZZI & SARLI
C.DA PARTEMIO
S. S. 7 BRINDISI - TARANTO
72022 LATIANO (BR)
TEL. 0831/725898

After two years' absence, Patriglione comes back to reclaim its customary role as the pole star of Puglian winemaking. Much water has passed under the bridge since the '88 Patriglione took everyone by storm. The saddest thing is that the wine's architect, Cosimo Taurino, is no longer with us to celebrate and enjoy the renewed success of a wine he vinified himself. The continuity of the estate is, however, assured by his son, Francesco, who has retained as consultant Severino Garofano, one of the best-known names on the southern Italian wine scene. Indeed, improvements are afoot. Modernization of the winemaking areas is underway, which is bound to be reflected in the quality of the wines sooner or later. Of the current releases, the '94 Patriglione is a fabulous red from 90 percent negroamaro and 10 percent malvasia nera, picked when very ripe. It is powerful, complex and full, with seductive, very ripe berry fruit aromas that percolate through notes of antique wood, leather, tobacco, liquorice, chocolate and spices. The fascinating richness of the nose is reflected perfectly on the palate, which is full of alcohol and extract, and mouth-fillingly sweet with flavours of liqueur cherries and berry fruit. It also shows a certain austerity and a deep vein of elegant astringency. The finish is warm and long, with notes of chocolate and coffee. In short, it is a dazzler of a wine. We feel that the rest of the range has probably suffered a bit from the hiatus at the estate. Some of the wines, although interesting, are not perfectly clean on the nose and others appear over-evolved for their age. We shall, however, await future vintages with optimism.

Lomazzi & Sarli is situated at Latiano in the province of Brindisi. It has been around since 1869 but is currently owned by the Dimastrodonato family. It is a large estate with 120 hectares of land of which over 100 are planted to vine. The annual average production is 500,000 bottles, with red wines taking the lion's share, and the oenologist, Lino Carparelli, looks after winemaking. So far, there are no particular high spots among the wines. Instead, and perhaps just as important, the entire range is very well-typed and great value for money. This base makes an excellent springboard for the wines of greater prominence which we are sure will soon follow. From the wines tasted this year, we particularly liked Primitivo Latias. It has a good dark ruby colour, followed up by clean, intense berry fruit perfumes with touches of Mediterranean scrub, balsam, and possibly even brine. Then comes a warm, soft, fruity palate with a delicate spiciness on the finish. The Salento Rosso Terre di Tacco '98, from negroamaro and malvasia nera, is harmonious on the nose with aromas of ripe plum and tobacco introducing good body, soft tannins and attractive fruitiness. The Aleatico '98 is a well-typed red, full of aromas of berry fruit jam. The taste is not particularly sweet and the fairly intense tannins show nice finesse. The Malvasia Partemio has a fresh, fruity character, with attractive citrus notes on the nose and back palate, but the Brindisi Rosso Solise seemed a little too evolved for its age and the Salento Bianco '99 is not much more than well-typed.

● Patriglione '94	♟♟♟	6
⊙ Salento Rosato Scaloti '99	♟	3
● Salice Salentino Rosso Ris. '97	♟	3
○ I Sierri '99		4
● Patriglione '85	♟♟♟	5
● Patriglione '88	♟♟♟	5
● Notarpanaro '88	♟♟	3*
● Notarpanaro '90	♟♟	3*
● Notarpanaro '93	♟♟	4
● Notarpanaro '94	♟♟	4
● Patriglione '93	♟♟	5
● Salice Salentino Rosso Ris. '88	♟♟	3*
● Salice Salentino Rosso Ris. '90	♟♟	3*
● Salice Salentino Rosso Ris. '93	♟♟	3*
● Salice Salentino Rosso Ris. '94	♟♟	3*

⊙ Brindisi Rosato Solise '99	♟	3
○ Malvasia del Salento Partemio '99	♟	3
● Primitivo del Salento Latias '99	♟	3
● Salento Aleatico		
Dimastrodonato '98	♟	3
⊙ Salento Rosato Terra di Tacco '99	♟	2*
● Salento Rosso Terra di Tacco '98	♟	2*
● Brindisi Rosso Solise '97		3
○ Salento Bianco Terra di Tacco '99		2
● Primitivo del Salento Latias '98	♟♟	3*
● Brindisi Rosso Solise '96	♟	2*
○ Malvasia del Salento Partemio '98	♟	3
● Salento Rosso Terra di Tacco '97	♟	2*

LECCE

LECCE

CANTELE
VIA VINCENZO BALSAMO, 13
73100 LECCE
TEL. 0832/240962

AGRICOLE VALLONE
VIA XXV LUGLIO, 7
73100 LECCE
TEL. 0832/308041

Cantele has an important place on the Puglian wine scene as it successfully combines high-quantity output with good quality. The figures are significant. Although the winery owns no vineyards of its own, it vinifies almost 200 hectares-worth of grapes, mainly chardonnay and negroamaro, which are bought in from a fixed group of growers who have been selected over the years and whose cultivation techniques Cantele oversees and controls. This results in a production of around 2,000,000 bottles a year, which is predominantly destined for export. The concentration on the international scene is reflected in the importance given to Chardonnay, which oenologist Augusto Cantele produces in two styles. The Teresa Manara '99 selection has an attractive, bright, deep straw-yellow colour while the nose is full of ripe apple fruit, vanilla and a light toastiness that comes from the limited use of new wood. On the palate, the wine is dense, structured and balanced, rich in fruity zestiness and satisfyingly long. The Chardonnay del Salento, another '99, is less concentrated but still impresses for its fluency of style, its streak of fresh fruit and the fullness of the palate. We tasted two vintages of the Salice Salentino Riserva, the '97 and the '96, and both showed very well. The younger wine has a dark ruby colour, sweet aromas of berry fruit and jam, and a stylish, fat, soft palate with lots of tannin. The '96 is slightly fatter and more structured. Its oak is well-balanced and there is great elegance and cleanliness throughout. The Primitivo del Salento, the Salento Rosso Teresa Manara and the white and red Salice Salentinos from the Cenobio line are all very good wines.

Owned by sisters Vittoria and Maria Teresa, the Vallone estate extends over 600 hectares, of which a good 150 are planted to vine, making it one of Puglia's most significant agricultural holdings. The quality of the wines has reached impressive levels and, vintage after vintage, Vallone is one of the surest, most reliable names of the region. Part of the credit for this is due to the dynamic estate manager, Donato Lazzari, and long-standing consultant oenologist, Severino Garofano. The flagship of the estate's large range is a brilliant red, Graticciaia, from slightly raisined negroamaro and malvasia nera. It is a wine of extraordinary vigour which seems to concentrate all the warmth and ripening power of the southern sun into its intense perfumes of red and black berry fruit, the elegant notes of Mediterranean scrub and the touches of spice and antique wood. The palate has a powerful attack but as it unwinds, it reveals elegance in its flavours of berry fruit jam, chocolate, toasty oak, vanilla and spices. The Brindisi Rosso Vigna Flaminio '97 has a fine, concentrated ruby colour that ushers in elegant, warm, intense aromas of ripe morello cherry, tobacco and herbs. The soft palate has good backbone, ripe tannins and admirable length. The Salice Salentino Vereto is good and full-bodied but a little too developed for its age while the Vigna Flaminio Rosato keeps up its track record of good quality. Value for money is excellent across the board.

O	Salento Chardonnay Teresa Manara '99	▼▼	4
●	Salice Salentino Rosso Ris. '96	▼▼	4
●	Salice Salentino Rosso Ris. '97	▼▼	4
O	Salento Chardonnay '99	▼	3
●	Salento Primitivo '97	▼	3
●	Salento Rosso Teresa Manara '97	▼	4
O	Salice Salentino Bianco Cenobio '99	▼	3
●	Salice Salentino Rosso Cenobio '96	▼	3
●	Salento Primitivo '96	▽	2*
●	Salento Rosso Cerbinare '92	▽	2*
●	Salento Rosso Cerbinare '96	▽	3
⊙	Salice Salentino Rosato Cenobio '94	▽	2*
●	Salice Salentino Rosso Cenobio '92	▽	2*
●	Salice Salentino Rosso Cenobio Ris. '94	▽	2*

●	Brindisi Rosso V. Flaminio '97	▼▼	2*
●	Graticciaia '95	▼▼	6
⊙	Brindisi Rosato V. Flaminio '99	▼	2*
●	Salice Salentino Vereto '97	▼	2*
O	Salento Bianco Corte Valesio '99		2
●	Brindisi Rosso V. Flaminio '94	♊	2*
●	Brindisi Rosso V. Flaminio '95	♊	2*
●	Brindisi Rosso V. Flaminio '96	♊	2*
●	Graticciaia '92	♊	5
●	Graticciaia '93	♊	5
●	Salice Salentino Rosso '93	♊	2*
●	Salice Salentino Rosso '94	♊	2*
●	Salice Salentino Vereto '95	♊	2*

LEVERANO (LE)

LOCOROTONDO (BA)

CONTI ZECCA
VIA CESAREA
73045 LEVERANO (LE)
TEL. 0832/925613

CANTINA COOPERATIVA
DEL LOCOROTONDO
VIA MADONNA DELLA CATENA, 99
70010 LOCOROTONDO (BA)
TEL. 080/4311644 - 080/4311298

The noble Conti Zecca of Leverano are owners of one of Puglia's largest agricultural estates, with 800 hectares of which a good 320 are under vine. The property has always been famous for the excellent quality of its wines and for their spectacular value for money. At the helm of the cellar is an able, determined, professional oenologist, Fernando Romano. He has invested incredible energy in the estate and, in the space of a few years, has managed to achieve quite remarkable quality levels. However, until this year there was no real peak that could give the measure of the estate's extraordinary potential. Now, though, this great range has turned up one truly great bottle. The Nero. Produced with valuable input from Giorgio Marone, one of the country's most noted consultants, Nero '98 was the best red the panel tasted this year in the entire region, and one of the best in all southern Italy. It is made from a 70-30 blend of negroamaro and cabernet sauvignon, aged almost two years in French oak barriques. It has a deep, all but opaque, ruby colour, leading in to a nose that is full, complex, assertive and clean as a whistle. After your nostrils have enjoyed the intense aromas of ripe black berry fruit, tobacco and spices, all sharply defined and well balanced, it delights your palate with its concentration, structure, harmony and well-constructed complexity. Full of fruit, it unveils a full, fleshy softness and ripe tannins, finishing well with very elegant notes of vanilla, tobacco and red fruit jam, which speaks volumes for its ageing potential. Partnering Nero is an excellent Salice Salentino '97 and a whole raft of other similarly good wines.

With an annual output of 3,500,000 bottles, the Locorotondo co-operative is one of the largest wine producers in the region. Famed for its Locorotondo, the classic white wine of the Itria valley, the winery has recently also started producing a successful range of elegant reds, all made from typical Puglian grape varieties. The range in its entirety is huge, comprising some very good rosés and sparkling wines, as well as whites and reds. The wine that got most attention this year is the red Cummerse '97, from aglianico, uva di troia and cabernet sauvignon grown in the Murgia hills. It has a deep ruby colour, aromas of ripe berry fruit accented with light spiciness, and an attractively astringent palate that shows good body, beautifully soft tannins, fresh fruitiness and fair length. The Casale San Giorgio Rosato is worth investigating for its brilliant hue, the immediacy of its aromas, its acidity and its good weight. The Valle dell'Itria Roccia Rosato is less full but just as fresh. The Locorotondo we liked best is the Vigneti in Tallinajo, which has a bright, green-flecked straw-yellow colour, ripe apple aromas and good fullness on the palate. The Riserva del Presidente '98 is more developed and mature but overall perhaps a little less successful. The straightforward, standard Locorotondo is as well-typed and as enjoyable to drink as ever. Both still and sparkling versions of the Moscato Olimpia are good-quality products, as are all the other wines.

● Nero '98	♟♟♟	5
⊙ Leverano Rosato		
Vigna del Saraceno '99	♟♟	2*
● Salice Salentino Rosso Cantalupi '97	♟♟	2*
○ Leverano Bianco		
Vigna del Saraceno '99	♟	2*
○ Leverano Malvasia		
Vigna del Saraceno '98	♟	4
● Leverano Rosso		
Vigna del Saraceno '98	♟	2*
⊙ Salento Rosato Donna Marzia '99	♟	1*
● Salento Rosso Donna Marzia '97	♟	1*
○ Salice Salentino Bianco Cantalupi '99	♟	2*
● Leverano Rosso		
Vigna del Saraceno Ris. '96	♟♟	2*

⊙ Casale San Giorgio Rosato '99	♟	2*
⊙ Cummerse Rosato '99	♟	3
● Cummerse Rosso '97	♟	4
○ Locorotondo In Tallinajo '99	♟	3
○ Locorotondo		
Ris. del Presidente '98	♟	4
○ Moscato Olimpia '99	♟	3
○ Moscato Spumante Olimpia '99	♟	3
⊙ Roccia Rosato '99	♟	1*
● Roccia Rosso '99	♟	1
○ Locorotondo '99		2
○ Roccia Bianco '99		2
● Casale San Giorgio '97	♟	2*
● Primitivo di Manduria		
Terre di Don Peppe '97	♟	5

598

MANDURIA (TA)

MANDURIA (TA)

CONSORZIO PRODUTTORI VINI
VIA FABIO MASSIMO, 19
74024 MANDURIA (TA)
TEL. 099/9735332

FELLINE
VIA N. DONADIO, 20
74024 MANDURIA (TA)
TEL. 099/9711660

Currently, there is a climate of renewed enthusiasm for Primitivo, and for the wines of Manduria in general. The area's co-operatives and consortia, which a few years back had been restricted to local markets for their wines or had resorted to releasing bulk wine and grape must to other regions, are now back at the heart of things. As part of this, the Consorzio Produttori Vini di Manduria has set up a well thought-out programme for improvements to primitivo, the area's principal variety. That, and up-to-date, carefully controlled winemaking systems allow it to produce a good five styles from the grape, all of very good quality and all excellently priced. The Primitivo Antiche Contrade is one of the estate's leading wines. The '97 version is very dark ruby, almost black, in colour. There is a lovely concentration of red and black fruit aromas on the nose, together with the typical spicy notes of white and black pepper. The palate is dense and zesty, full of fruit, ripe tannins and alcohol, and while it has considerable concentration, it retains balance and good finesse. Moving on to the sweet Primitivos, a more traditional style, the Consortium's Madrigale is one of the most impressive. The '97 has aromas of ripe cherry and black cherry jam, notes that are echoed perfectly on a palate with a balanced vein of sweetness that does not cloy. One step down in concentration, but still stylishly elegant and very attractive, is the '97 Elegia. It has tobacco, leather, liquorice and chocolate on the nose and a warm, structured and mouth-filling palate with a fairly long finish. The Primitivo di Manduria Lirica '97 and the Primitivo di Salento Antiche Contrade '98 are well-typed and very competently made.

The tenacity of the Perrucci brothers, who own this estate, paid off last year with Three Glasses going to their top wine, Vigna dei Feudi '97. This year, though, they had to do battle with a hail-ravaged vintage. The vineyards were hit to the extent that it was impossible to produce the Vigna dei Feudi, a blend of primitivo and montepulciano with small admixtures of cabernet sauvignon and merlot. But our intrepid brothers refused to throw in the towel and, with the help of Roberto Cipresso, their renowned consultant oenologist, who is based in Tuscany but has clients throughout the country, they turned out an excellent Primitivo di Manduria which only just missed Three Glasses. This '99 has a traditional-style colour that, though in essence ruby, appears almost black. It has intense, sweet aromas of red berry fruit, tobacco, Mediterranean scrub and pepper. The palate is warm and mouth-filling, proffering flavours of plum, ripe cherry, chocolate and tobacco which evolve into more complex, developed tones on the finish before fading into a delicate bitterish aftertaste. It has a fine partner in another excellent red, the Alberello, from equal proportions of primitivo and negroamaro. The '99 has a good deep ruby colour and aromas of black berry fruit and cherry jam. The characterful palate has ripe tannins and yields soft, fascinating notes of vanilla and chocolate in the finish. It lacks the intensity and cleanliness of aroma that characterized the previous vintage but it is, nevertheless, a beautifully soft, velvety wine of substance.

● Primitivo di Manduria		
Antiche Contrade '97	🍷🍷	3*
● Primitivo di Manduria Dolce		
Il Madrigale '97	🍷🍷	4
● Primitivo del Salento		
Antiche Contrade '98	🍷	2*
● Primitivo di Manduria Elegia '97	🍷	3
● Primitivo di Manduria Lirica '97	🍷	3

● Primitivo di Manduria '99	🍷🍷	4
● Salento Rosso Alberello '99	🍷	3
● Vigna del Feudo '97	🍷🍷🍷	4*
● Primitivo di Manduria '96	🍷🍷	4
● Primitivo di Manduria '97	🍷🍷	4
● Primitivo di Manduria '98	🍷🍷	3*
● Salento Rosso Alberello '97	🍷🍷	3*
● Salento Rosso Alberello '98	🍷🍷	2*

MANDURIA (TA)

MARUGGIO (TA)

PERVINI
VIA SANTO STASI PRIMO - Z. I.
C.DA ACUTI
74024 MANDURIA (TA)
TEL. 099/9711660

MASSERIA PEPE
LOC. CASTIGNO
74020 MARUGGIO (TA)
TEL. 099/9711660

For some years now, Gregory Perrucci, his oenologist brother, Fabrizio, sister Alessia, and agronomist, Salvatore Mero, have been involved in the major task of renovating numerous growers' old bush-trained vineyards that were under threat of extinction. In fact, the Perruccis head up the Racemi Academy, an organization that brings together various small estates in the area, giving them moral support and practical assistance to keep them afloat. Unfortunately, owing to the violent hailstorms that compromised the harvest, two of these, Casale Bevagna and Antica Masseria Torre Mozza, whose wines made such a favourable impression last year, did not present any for tasting this time. Pervini itself, however, did. There was an excellent soft, warm and spicy Primitivo Archidamo, a well-made Primitivo I Monili with good varietal typing, despite a touch too much development for its age, and an excellent Bizantino Rosso, from negroamaro and primitivo, which is noteworthy for the fullness of its structure and the finesse of its tannins. The red Gorgolano, from primitivo, negroamaro and malvasia nera, and the Bizantino Bianco are both very attractive. Last but not least, the Academy also markets an extraordinary semi-dried grape "passito" wine, produced by the Ferrari winery in Salice Salentino. It comes from a single, "rediscovered" vat that contained a wonderful Primitivo from the '59 vintage, one of the hottest of the century. The wine has such supreme elegance, complexity and depth that it far outclasses most other dessert wines. It is called Solaria Ionica and is a one-off. A never-to-be-repeated experience.

Masseria Pepe is one of the estates that first hit the pages of the Guide last year. It is owned by Alberto Pagano, born in 1911, an figure of extraordinary vitality and enthusiasm. After working all his life as a pharmacist, Alberto recently decided to start vinifying his grapes. The vines face onto the shores of the Ionian sea, their roots clawing into its sandy soil and their growth cooled by its gentle coastal breezes. Last year, the Pepe Primitivos were already amassing gratifying tasting scores and this year, they are again right up with the top-ranking wines of Manduria, the zone where the estate's Maruggio home lies. Duncio '99, which takes its name from the location of the vineyard, just a few metres from the coast, has a thick, dark ruby colour and is concentrated and rich throughout. The nose has enthralling notes of ripe berry fruit, tobacco and chocolate, elegant aromas of Mediterranean scrub and the peppery hints typical of good Primitivo. The palate is rich and impressively structured. First impressions are of warmth and alcohol, then captivating flavours of raspberry and blackcurrant fruit emerge as it opens and gradually the framework, in the form of more complex streaks of toasty oak, coffee and chocolate, becomes apparent. The finish is leisurely. These characteristics brought it to within a hair's breadth of Three Glasses. The Primitivo di Portile, also a '99, shares the voluptuous style of its "big brother" and, even though it is a little less concentrated and complex, its attractive aromas of ripe cherry, cocoa powder and spices make it a wine with lots of appeal for lovers of Primitivo.

● Primitivo di Manduria		
Archidamo '98	▼▼	3*
● Salento Rosso Bizantino '98	▼▼	3*
● Solaria Ionica Ferrari '59	▼▼	6
● Primitivo del Tarantino I Monili '98	▼	2*
○ Salento Bianco Bizantino '99	▼	2*
● Salento Rosso Gorgolano '98	▼	2*
● Finibusterre Antica Maseria		
Torre Mozza '97	♈♈	6
● Primitivo del Tarantino I Monili '97	♈♈	2*
● Primitivo di Manduria		
Archidamo '97	♈♈	3*
● Sole Leone Antica Maseria		
Torre Mozza '96	♈♈	6
● Galante Rosso '97	♈	1*

● Primitivo di Manduria Dunico '99	▼▼	5
● Primitivo II Portile '99	▼▼	4
● Primitivo di Manduria Dunico '98	♈♈	5
● Primitivo II Portile '98	♈♈	4

SALICE SALENTINO (LE)

LEONE DE CASTRIS
VIA SENATORE DE CASTRIS, 50
73015 SALICE SALENTINO (LE)
TEL. 0832/731112 - 0832/731113

Leone de Castris is a star of major proportions on the southern Italian wine scene, not just because of the vast number of bottles produced (2,800,000 a year!) but because of the excellent quality of most of the huge range. And while it did not reach the dizzy heights of last year, this year's '96 release of the flagship wine, the Salice Salentino Donna Lisa Riserva, is still one of the most fascinating reds in the whole region. It has body and power, warmth and pervasiveness, a wealth of spiciness and berry fruit and tannins of considerable finesse, all coming together in glorious harmony. Its cherry and plum aromas mark it out as a wine of the south but it avoids the tertiary aromas and evolved style that many southern wines tend to develop prematurely. In addition, its taste profile is clean and modern. In fact, its only failing is a slight weakness on the back palate, which means that its aromatic length is good but not exceptional. The Salice Salentino Majana '98 has turned out very well indeed. It is warm, penetrating, soft and concentrated. Although not a wine of any great complexity, it has an open attractiveness that makes it irresistible. The '97 Salice Salentino Riserva is one of the best releases of the wine to date. Its up-front but elegant nose is underlined by hints of spiciness, cocoa powder and tobacco. On the palate, it has a dense but elegant weave and beautifully ripe tannins. Then there is the special release, the Anniversary '99 edition of Five Roses, Italy's most famous rosé. This has a freshness and a completeness of expression that makes it a sure-fire winner. The rest of the huge range, all produced by oenologist Leonardo Pinto, is at its usual very high standard of quality.

⊙	Five Roses Anniversary '99	🍷🍷	3*
●	Salice Salentino Majana '98	🍷🍷	2*
●	Salice Salentino Rosso Donna Lisa Ris. '96	🍷🍷	5
●	Salice Salentino Rosso Ris. '97	🍷🍷	3*
⊙	Five Roses '99	🍷	3
●	Primitivo del Salento la Rena '97	🍷	2*
●	Primitivo di Manduria Santera '98	🍷	3
○	Salento Bianco Verdeca Messapia '99	🍷	3
○	Salento Sauvignon Vigna Case Alte '99	🍷	3
○	Salice Salentino Bianco Donna Lisa '99	🍷	4
○	Salice Salentino Bianco Imago '99	🍷	2*
●	Salice Salentino Rosso Donna Lisa Ris. '95	🍸🍸🍸	5

SAN PIETRO VERNOTICO (BA)

TORMARESCA
VIA MATERNITÀ ED INFANZIA, 21
73023 SAN PIETRO VERNOTICO (BA)
TEL. 080/4771392

In recent years, the Antinori family from Florence has been buying up vineyards and estates in Tuscany and various other parts of Italy. The most recent purchases include two holdings in Puglia. One, Tormaresca, comprising about 100 hectares, is at Minervio Murge in the Castel del Monte DOC zone and the other is further south, at San Pietro Vernotico in the Salento zone, where the Antinoris have acquired about 500 hectares. As soon as the first Tomaresco wines were available last year, we were struck by the tremendous freshness of their aromas, their perfect cleanliness throughout and their overall attractiveness. This year, there has been a repeat performance quality-wise. There is also a new wine, the Chardonnay Tormaresca Bianco '99. This has a bright pale straw-yellow colour with greenish tinges. The nose is intense, fresh and rich in scents of peach and fresh apple that meld into an attractive butteriness and the vanilla tones of new oak. The fresh, fruity palate is well-structured, concentrated, varietal and full of flavour, with a slowly fading, gently oaky finish. All in all, it's a gem of a wine and is bound to be incredibly popular, especially when people find out how much it costs. The Chardonnay Sferracavallo '99 has a deep straw-yellow colour and an aroma that is full but dominated by the smoky tones of new oak, which are rather over-assertive. The palate is fresh and medium bodied, with fairly full structure, but here, too, the fruit is a little masked by oak. Puglia Rosso, from aglianico, cabernet sauvignon and merlot, has a mid-depth ruby colour; good ripe fruit aromas, vegetal notes and attractive spicy touches on the nose. Its reasonably structured palate has no great concentration but is well-balanced and very attractive.

○	Tormaresca Bianco '99	🍷🍷	2*
○	Castel del Monte Chardonnay Sferracavallo '99	🍷	3
●	Tormaresca Rosso '99	🍷	2*
○	Tormaresca Bianco '98	🍸🍸	2*
●	Tormaresca Rosso '98	🍸	2*

SANDONACI (BR)

TRICASE (LE)

Francesco Candido
Via A. Diaz, 46
72025 Sandonaci (BR)
Tel. 0831/635674

Castel di Salve
Fraz. Depressa
P.zza Castello, 8
73039 Tricase (LE)
Tel. 0833/771012

Candido is one of the most respected names on the Puglia wine scene. And rightly so, as the estate produces a distinguished range of wines that are marketed at very keen prices. An emblematic example is the Cappello di Prete, a powerful, warm red from negroamaro and malvasia nera that has become a classic of southern Italian winemaking. The new vintage, the '96, is among the best ever produced. It is a dark ruby colour with a nose rich in ripe cherry and plum fruit, which is brought into relief by notes of tobacco, spices and dried roses. The palate is deep, warm, soft and full of good, closely woven tannins. In other words, a great southern red. Candido's most prestigious wine, though, is the Duca d'Aragona, from negroamaro and montepulciano, a wine that pretty much represents the state of the art in Puglia. The '94 has a concentrated, thick, ruby colour and intense, spicy aromas. On the palate, there is all the complexity of a great, traditional, mature Negroamaro, rich in alcohol, tannins and notes of berry fruit jam. New to emerge this year is Immensum '98, a distinguished red from 80 percent negroamaro and 20 percent cabernet sauvignon. Made, as are all the Candido wines, under the guiding hand of consultant oenologist, Severino Garofano, it is right up to the standards of the estate's other wines, disclosing a full body, firm structure, assertive tannins and hints of tobacco and spices on the finish. The rest of the range, from the good Vigna Vinera, an oak-aged Sauvignon, to the Salice Salentino Riserva, is all of good-quality stuff.

It has been an excellent year for Francesco Marra and Francesco Winspeare, the enthusiastic young owners of this up-and-coming estate. Their wines achieved gratifying scores in our tastings and reflect the sense of excitement and regeneration that is currently pervading the region. The most interesting wine without doubt was Lama del Tenente '98, an admirable red from montepulciano, negroamaro, malvasia nera and cabernet sauvignon, aged in small, new oak barrels. It has a thick, dark ruby colour ushering in a warm, intense nose with elegant aromas of ripe berry fruit and spicy notes of considerable finesse. The structured, warm, full-bodied palate is richly pervaded by the sweetness of ripe plum and mulberry fruit and sensations of Mediterranean scrub. The tannins are soft and its fruitiness perfectly clean. It shows fine balance in the mouth and finishes long and in fact came within an inch of Three Glasses. The estate's other two reds are also good, despite coming from the disappointing '99 vintage. The negroamaro-based Rosso del Salento Armecolo has a concentrated ruby colour, intense, clean aromas of red berry fruit and Mediterranean scrub, and a palate of reasonable depth with ripe tannins, raspberry fruit, good spiciness and fair length. The Priante '99, from a blend of the estate's red varieties, has a good dark colour and decent concentration but the nose is veiled by a slight pungency that prejudices its otherwise considerable extractive richness and attractive finish.

● Cappello di Prete '96	♟♟	3*
● Duca d'Aragona '94	♟♟	5
● Immensum '98	♟♟	4
○ Salento Bianco Vigna Vinera '99	♟	3
○ Salice Salentino Bianco '99	♟	2*
● Salice Salentino Ris. '96	♟	2*
◉ Salice Salentino Rosato Le Pozzelle '99	♟	2*
○ Chardonnay del Salento Casina Cucci '99		2
● Cappello di Prete '93	♟♟	3*
● Cappello di Prete '94	♟♟	3*
● Cappello di Prete '95	♟♟	3*
● Duca d'Aragona '92	♟♟	5
● Duca d'Aragona '93	♟♟	5

● Armecolo '99	♟♟	3*
● Lama del Tenente '98	♟♟	4
● Priante '99	♟	3
● Armecolo '98	♟♟	3*
● Priante '98	♟♟	3*
● Il Volo di Alessandro '98	♟	3

OTHER WINERIES

The following producers obtained good scores in our tastings with one or more of their wines:

PROVINCE OF BARI

Botromagno,
Gravina di Puglia, tel. 080/3265865
Gravina '99,
Gravisano '97

Cardone,
Locorotondo, tel. 080/4311624
Murgia Primitivo '96,
Primitivo Primaio '99,
Salento Primitivo '97

Coop. Riforma Fondiaria di Ruvo,
Ruvo di Puglia, tel.080/3601611
Castel del Monte Ris. '96

PROVINCE OF BRINDISI

Due Palme,
Cellino S. Marco, tel. 0831/619728
Salento Primitivo '99,
Salice Salentino '98

Resta,
San Pietro Vernotico, tel. 0831/671182
Salice Salentino '98

PROVINCE OF FOGGIA

D'Alfonso del Sordo,
San Severo, tel. 0882/221444
Bombino Bianco Catapanus '99,
San Severo Rosato Posta Arignano '99

PROVINCE OF LECCE

Masseria Monaci,
Copertino, tel. 0832/947512
Primitivo del Salento I Censi '97,
Simposia '97

Valle dell'Asso,
Galatina, tel. 0836/561470
Galatina Rosso '97

C. S. Leverano, Leverano, tel. 0832/925053
Leverano Vecchia Torre '99

La Corte,
Novoli, tel. 055/9707594
Anfora Zinfandel '99,
Zinfandel '98

Duca Guarini di Poggiardo,
Scorrano, tel. 0836/460288
Primitivo del Salento Vigne Vecchie '99,
Salento Sauvignon Murà '99

Michele Calò,
Tuglie, tel. 0833/596242
Vigna Spano '96

PROVINCE OF TARANTO

C. S. L. Ruggieri – Lizzano,
Lizzano, tel. 099/9552013
Negroamaro '98,
Primitivo del Tarantino '98

Soloperto, Manduria, tel. 099/9794286
Primitivo Bagnolo '98

Miali, Martinafranca, tel. 080/4303222
Aglianico del Vulture '98,
Primitivo di Manduria '98

Cantina Oleificio Sociale di Sava,
Sava, tel. 099/9726139
Primitivo di Manduria Dolce Naturale
Terra di Miele '96,
Primitivo di Manduria Mosaico '96

Pichierri - Vinicola Savese,
Sava, tel. 099/9726232
Primitivo del Tarantino Desiderium '98,
Primitivo di Manduria Tradizione del Nonno '99

CALABRIA

For years now, we have believed in the great potential of this region. It seems to have been created specifically for the cultivation of vineyards, olive groves and citrus fruit groves on every inch of its territory, whether flatland or hillslope. Not to do so would be insane. This year, we have certainly seen lots of effort going on and genuine attempts – at last – at modernization in the wineries but we really can't bring ourselves to say that things are changing significantly. Too much Calabrian wine is still sold in bulk. Elementary errors in vinification are still everyday occurrences in many cellars and the mentality that puts quantity before quality is still prevalent. So, we are not out of the woods yet and there is the ever-present risk that Calabria will remain marginalized from the vital process of image-enhancement, not to mention the improvement of the intrinsic quality of the products, which is underway in other regions of the south, Sicily, Puglia, Campania and now, cautiously, even Basilicata. And while investment is coming into these regions from large national wine companies, who are buying up vineyards and renovating cellars, there is little of this on the horizon for Calabria. Then suddenly you come up against estates such as those of Lento, Odoardi, Librandi and Francesco Siciliani (Fattoria San Francesco) and you are back in a world with a more rational, positive attitude to wine production. You then realize that all is not lost and that it is simply the entrepreneurial attitude, which these producers have and the others do not, that makes the difference. The end result is that the number of Calabrian entries in this year's Guide remains at six, which is far too few. But these six are the only ones who have so far managed to produce premium-quality wines reliably and consistently, and also whose wines are available outside their specific production zone. There is no point in stressing the negative, nor do we want to point the gun at random, but it is surely time for the Calabrian wine sector to change its mentality. Growers must start thinking long term and understand that the era of making ends meet and no more with poor-quality wines is long gone. These days, success lies in organization for medium-sized and large wineries and in intelligently thought-out, hand-crafted, exclusive products of high quality and high added value for the smaller ones. Despite all this, there is some good news. For now, it is just a glimmer but it could lead to major developments. It concerns an ancient, semi-extinct, grape variety called magliocco, which has been rediscovered by Librandi. The bunches are small and few in number but the potential, judging by the magnificent Magno Megonio wine which Librandi has produced from the variety, is fabulous. Magliocco represents a ray of hope for everyone. Within a few years, it should be possible to subject it to clonal selection and scientific study, distributing it, on an experimental basis, throughout the region's better zones. If so, in less than ten years' time we could be seeing the re-appearance of top-notch reds in Calabria, comparable with those that nero d'avola has given Sicily and aglianico has brought to Campania and Basilicata. We are crossing our fingers that the region doesn't waste precious time.

CIRÒ (KR)

CIRÒ MARINA (KR)

FATTORIA SAN FRANCESCO
LOC. QUATTROMANI
S. P. EX S. S. 106
88813 CIRÒ (KR)
TEL. 0962/32228

CAPARRA & SICILIANI
BIVIO S. S. 106
88811 CIRÒ MARINA (KR)
TEL. 0962/371435

For a couple of years now, Francesco Siciliani has had the services of Fabrizio Ciufoli as consultant and for just over one he has had the benefit of a spanking new cellar. And results are beginning to be seen. The wines are obviously better made, to the extent that they are now the finest to be found in the Cirò DOC. The bottle liked best this year was the modern, powerful Donna Madda, which avoids the evolved, oxidized style that still plagues many, too many, other Ciròs. The '98 Ronco dei Quattro Venti is more typical and old-fashioned, and has had to relinquish its position as the estate's leading wine. But it is the standard-label wines that made a very positive impact this year. For Calabria, it is extremely rare to find such well-made wines in the medium-low price band. The three Ciròs, the even, fruity Bianco, the fairly full, very drinkable Rosso, and the unusually stylish Rosato are all attractive, reliable and technically unimpeachable. In addition, they are very easy on the pocket book. At this point, all that remains between Francesco Siciliani and the end of his long journey towards quality is to pick up that third Glass for one of his range of products. Have no doubt, sooner or later he will succeed.

This famous and, in some respects, pivotal Cirò estate returns to the Guide after a year in the outer darkness. This is down to a good showing overall, with Cirò Bianco Curiale '99 representing the high point, backed up by a series of other wines which, all things considered, are not at all bad. Certainly, from an estate of this type and a name of such renown, we would like to have seen rather more but the general situation regarding Cirò production is such that more encouraging results are still a long way off. But let us get back to the wines. We were talking about the Cirò Bianco Curiale '99, a simple but well-made, modern wine that has clean, well-fruited aromas with tropical fruit scents and an even, well-styled palate of structure that even shows some elegance. The Cirò Bianco '99 is more neutral, but still very well-made. The red Ciròs, however, are less exciting and are the result of harvesting practices and vinification techniques that belong to the past. The Classico Superiore Volvito '95 is, as usual, the best of the group and has good concentration despite an acid and tannin sharpness that gives a rawness to the taste which, again, is part of a heritage of a now somewhat obsolete past that is destined to disappear. The other two wines presented, the Classico Superiore '96 and the Classico '98, are more straightforward and less characterful. Simple and a bit rustic in personality, they are rather pale in colour.

●	Cirò Rosso Classico Ronco dei Quattro Venti '98	🍷🍷	4
●	Cirò Rosso Classico Sup. Donna Madda '98	🍷🍷	3*
○	Cirò Bianco '99	🍷	2*
⊙	Cirò Rosato '99	🍷	2*
●	Cirò Rosso Classico '98	🍷	2*
●	Cirò Rosso Classico Ronco dei Quattro Venti '92	🍷🍷	4
●	Cirò Rosso Classico Ronco dei Quattro Venti '97	🍷🍷	4
●	Cirò Rosso Classico Sup. Donna Madda '93	🍷🍷	4
●	Cirò Rosso Classico Sup. Donna Madda '95	🍷🍷	4

○	Cirò Bianco Curiale '99	🍷🍷	3*
○	Cirò Bianco '99	🍷	2*
●	Cirò Rosso Cl. Sup. Volvito '95	🍷	3
●	Cirò Rosso Cl. Sup. '96		3
●	Cirò Rosso Classico '98		2
●	Cirò Rosso Cl. Sup. '92	🍷	2*
●	Cirò Rosso Cl. Sup. Volvito '89	🍷	3
●	Cirò Rosso Cl. Sup. Volvito '91	🍷	3
●	Cirò Rosso Cl. Sup. Volvito '92	🍷	3
●	Cirò Rosso Cl. Sup. Volvito '94	🍷	3
●	Cirò Rosso Classico '90	🍷	2*
●	Cirò Rosso Classico '91	🍷	2*
●	Cirò Rosso Classico '92	🍷	2*
●	Cirò Rosso Classico '93	🍷	2*
●	Cirò Rosso Classico '94	🍷	2*

CIRÒ MARINA (KR)

COSENZA

LIBRANDI
C.DA S. GENNARO
S. S. 106
88811 CIRÒ MARINA (KR)
TEL. 0962/31518 - 0962/31519

GIOVAN BATTISTA ODOARDI
V.LE DELLA REPUBBLICA, 143
87100 COSENZA
TEL. 0984/29961

A great red, the Magno Megonio '98, signals the start of a new era for this famous and widely respected winery. The Librandi brothers and their new consultant, Donato Lanati, have put a lot of effort into the wine, which comes from magliocco, a semi-abandoned variety that is now giving extraordinary results and which could well turn into a leading player on the south Italian quality wine scene. Magno Megonio is named after a Roman centurion who is said to have been a great lover of this area's wines. And this is undoubtedly a bottle that would have made him a happy man. The colour is ruby and not markedly concentrated. The aromas are pervasive, with notes of black cherry and spices, while the palate is soft, concentrated and shows great finesse. It is easy to predict huge success in the future but for now, it is simply the best wine in Calabria. And a third Glass won't be long in coming, provided there is continuity and a few more bottles are produced – current production is tiny. The '96 Gravello, from cabernet sauvignon and gaglioppo, is also very good but a little less concentrated than in this wine's best years. All the other wines are decent, as usual, with Cirò San Felice Riserva '97 just a little more evolved than we would have liked. Critone '99, a fragrant, easy-drinking little white from chardonnay and sauvignon, and the sweet, evolved Le Passule '97, from mantonico, are both well-typed.

Odoardi wines can always count on individuality and character. They come from an area that is distinct from the better known DOC zones of Cirò and Lamezia. Here, we are in the territory of Nocera Tirinese, in the province of Catanzaro, in hill country near to the Tyrrhenian Sea. These lands are home to wines such as Savuto, from classic Calabrian grapes, mainly gaglioppo, greco nero and nerello cappuccio, and Scavigna, both white and red, which instead comes from newer, more international grape varieties such as cabernet, merlot, chardonnay, pinot bianco and riesling. However, the Odoardi wine that made most impact this year was Valeo, a sweet white that is produced from a particular variety of moscato, similar to zibibbo or moscato di Alessandria. On the nose, it is almost like freshly squeezed tropical fruit juice, with its notes of mango, papaya and ripe pineapple while the sweetness on the palate is well-supported by a luxuriant swathe of acidity that tempers any sense of cloying and makes it easy and attractive to drink. Savuto Superiore Vigna Mortilla '98, a more mundane red but one obviously made with excellent technique, is most successful. The two Scavignas, the white Pian della Corte '99 and the red Vigna Garrone '98 were less impressive. Both seemed still very youthful and not as concentrated as previous releases have been. But they could still come round with time.

●	Gravello '96	♟♟	5	●	Savuto Sup. Vigna Mortilla '98	♟♟	4
●	Magno Megonio '98	♟♟	6	○	Valeo '99	♟♟	5
●	Cirò Rosso Cl. Sup.			○	Scavigna Pian della Corte '99	♟	4
	Duca Sanfelice Ris. '97	♟	3	●	Scavigna Vigna Garrone '98	♟	5
○	Critone '99	♟	3	●	Savuto Sup. Vigna Mortilla '88	♟♟	3
○	Le Passule '97	♟	3	●	Savuto Sup. Vigna Mortilla '93	♟♟	4
●	Gravello '89	♟♟♟	5	●	Savuto Sup. Vigna Mortilla '95	♟♟	4
●	Gravello '90	♟♟♟	5	●	Savuto Sup. Vigna Vecchia '87	♟♟	3
●	Gravello '93	♟♟♟	5	●	Savuto Sup. Vigna Vecchia '88	♟♟	4
○	Critone '98	♟♟	3*	○	Scavigna Pian della Corte '97	♟♟	4
●	Gravello '88	♟♟	5	●	Scavigna Vigna Garrone '96	♟♟	4
●	Gravello '91	♟♟	5	●	Scavigna Vigna Garrone '97	♟♟	5
●	Gravello '95	♟♟	5	○	Valeo '93	♟♟	5
○	Le Passule '90	♟♟	3*	○	Valeo '95	♟♟	5
○	Le Passule '95	♟♟	4	○	Valeo '97	♟♟	5

LAMEZIA TERME (CZ)

LAMEZIA TERME (CZ)

CANTINE LENTO
VIA DEL PROGRESSO, 1
88046 LAMEZIA TERME (CZ)
TEL. 0968/28028

STATTI
TENUTA LENTI
88046 LAMEZIA TERME (CZ)
TEL. 0968/456138 - 0968/453655

The range submitted by Salvatore Lento this year is liable to make this winery one of the all time stars of the Calabrian wine scene. The region could well do with the boost, if for no other reason than to show that, with modern cellar equipment and just a bit of care in production, you can make very fine wines from the superb grapes that abound in these parts. Federico II '97, from cabernet sauvignon, and Lamezia Rosso Riserva '94, from gaglioppo, nerello cappuccio, greco nero and other local varieties, are two real gems. They are quite different from each other, the former being very modern, the latter fairly traditional, but despite the diversity in technical approach, they have come out fairly similarly. Each is well-made of its type, revealing itself to be varietal, complex and elegant. The Contessa Emburga '99, from 100 percent sauvignon aged in small casks, is intriguing, unveiling a nice softness and good concentration. All the rest of the range showed well. The Lamezia Greco '99 has a deepish colour and aromas that are surprisingly reminiscent of ripe pineapple. The two Tenuta Romeo Lamezias are less individual but very well-typed, with the red still a little edgy from its swathe of acidity and the white drinking very appealingly even though it is a tad simplistic.

There was no repetition of the quality we saw last year but this estate has retained its full Guide profile because it is one of the wineries that is promising good things for the future. The cellar has a modern set-up, there are around 30 hectares of vineyard and the owners have huge commitment, to their olive cultivation and general agricultural activities as well as wine production. The property embraces a good 500 hectares in total so this is by no means a small-scale undertaking. The slight quality slide may be solely connected with the vintage for it certainly doesn't depend on an overall decline in the estate's activities. In any event, the '99 Lamezia Greco retains One Glass by virtue of its delicate, clean-cut aromas and good overall structure. It is not a particularly complex wine but it is well-made. The '99 Ligeia, from sauvignon and chardonnay, seemed a little more neutral, less varietal and less concentrated than the '98. It is quite a reasonable white and has good winemaking behind it but we would like to see more character. Arvino '98 is simple, light and attractive to drink but nothing more, while a retaste of Cauro '97, from cabernet sauvignon and gaglioppo, first assessed last year, confirmed our original ideas. It has good structure and a ripe berry fruitiness.

	Wine	Rating	Score
●	Federico II '97	ΨΨ	5
●	Lamezia Rosso Ris. '94	ΨΨ	4
○	Contessa Emburga '99	Ψ	4
○	Lamezia Bianco Tenuta Romeo '99	Ψ	3
○	Lamezia Greco '99	Ψ	2*
●	Lamezia Rosso Tenuta Romeo '98	Ψ	3
●	Federico II '96	ΨΨ	4
●	Lamezia Rosso Ris. '84	ΨΨ	3*
●	Lamezia Rosso Ris. '91	ΨΨ	3*
●	Lamezia Rosso '91	Ψ	3
●	Lamezia Rosso '92	Ψ	1*
●	Lamezia Rosso '97	Ψ	2*
●	Lamezia Rosso Ris. '90	Ψ	3
●	Lamezia Rosso Ris. '92	Ψ	3
●	Lamezia Rosso Ris. '93	Ψ	4

	Wine	Rating	Score
○	Lamezia Greco '99	Ψ	3
○	Ligeia '99	Ψ	3
●	Arvino '98		3
○	Ligeia '98	ΨΨ	3*
●	Cauro '97	Ψ	5
○	Lamezia Greco '98	Ψ	3

SICILIA

Sicily's wineries take the Guide by storm this year. With the 32 that have retained full entries are a further 17 with brief listings in the Other Wineries section. Eight bottles earned Three Glasses. It would be difficult to imagine a more encouraging outcome. Nevertheless, there are still many shadows lurking and it shouldn't be thought that Sicily's entire production has been transformed, as if by magic, into sublime nectar. However, the simple fact that several large Italian wine concerns, such as Zonin, Marzotto Santa Margherita and Gruppo Italiano Vini, have invested heavily in the region is an unequivocal sign of the status enjoyed, at least in potential, by the region's vine stock and the wines that it could produce. The success of the new investments, like that of other producers, will depend ever more heavily on management skills because Mother Nature poses no particular problems. She continues to play her part superbly, as she has done for two millennia. In fact, "Sicily" is synonymous with "wine country" and the region continues to produce a good eight million hectolitres, more than Chile or Australia, and competes with Puglia for the title of Italy's largest-producing region. But it is only the premium high-water mark of this tide of Sicilian wine that concerns us and here there have been some sea changes. The formation and success of estates like Planeta, Firriato and Morgante, the continued achievements of Tasca d'Almerita and Donnafugata, the lone battles of Salvatore Murana to create the ultimate Passito di Pantelleria and those of Salvatore "Turi" Geraci to save Faro di Messina from extinction are the first indications of a new direction that has been set in motion and will continue to gain strength in the next few years. Even the restoration of quality-led winemaking at Duca di Salaparuta and its imminent privatisation is a significant element. The sell-off was widely expected and has stimulated great interest in the wine sector – all the country's biggest important names are expected to take part in the auction. With all this going on, the year 2001, the first of the new century, could be the harbinger of a genuine, definitive transformation of the island's wine scene. It is as if a new frontier has opened up. Sicilians have moved on from relying on the easy, trite rhetoric of a "glorious past" to which they can never return and instead are starting to realize that the present is not only a far more promising place to be but a more effective communications tool. And when the moment of this remarkable island and its extraordinary people really does come, we hope we shall be able to say that it was Sicily's food and wines that were the trigger. But for now let us simply enjoy some of these unforgettable wines: Firriato's Camelot, Planeta's Chardonnay, as exotic as ever, the fabulous Faro Palari and the brand-new Don Antonio di Morgante, another minor masterpiece from Riccardo Cotarella, one of the most credible of Italy's flying winemakers. Then there are the repeat stars and the classic wines from the island's Three Glass estates . . . Read on.

ACATE (RG)

ACATE (RG)

CANTINE TORREVECCHIA
C.DA TORREVECCHIA
97011 ACATE (RG)
TEL. 091/6882064 - 0932/990951

CANTINA VALLE DELL'ACATE
C. DA BIDINI
97011 ACATE (RG)
TEL. 0932/874166

It has been a very good year indeed at Torrevecchia. Or perhaps it would be more accurate to say that the decision to go all out for quality, as Giuseppe and Daniela Favuzza, the business-like joint owners of the winery, had long wanted to, is beginning to bear fruit, and plenty of it. Their success this year, however, is also the merit of their dedicated, capable staff, including the efficient sales manager, Silvio Ruffino, the dynamic Santi Buzzotta in charge of marketing, and oenologist Giovan Vito Genna, who is partnered to good effect in the cellars by the Piedmontese consultant wine technician, Daniele Saracco. We, as scrupulous observers, can do no less than report fully on developments. Bianco Biscari '98, from inzolia and chardonnay, and Casale dei Biscari '97, 100 percent nero d'Avola, are once more the estate's top wines. Both are technically irreproachable, the former offering pure, elegant vanilla tones on the nose and the latter good concentration and attractive, intense scents of liqueur fruits and spices. Both are soft and long on the palate. The '99 Frappato is of comparable quality and reveals tempting aromas of morello and wild cherries. The first release of the new Fontanabianca, a '99, from syrah, cabernet sauvignon and merlot, comes over as a good, characterful, concentrated wine with attractive blackcurrant and coffee aromas. The '98 Pietra di Zoe is once more well-typed and well-made. Note that value for money is excellent throughout the range.

The best known wine from this admirable winery, situated in the best part of the Cerasuolo di Vittoria zone, is the red Frappato and this year's, the '99, again came out on top at our tasting. It has good aromas of morello and liqueur cherries, and is soft on the palate, with a broad swathe of flavours. This latest release is without doubt better than last year's and the same goes for the Cerasuolo di Vittorias. Two versions were sent for tasting, both '98s and both had similar characteristics: the classic cherry red colour with very bright highlights, wild berry fruit on the nose and moderate extract on a clean, attractive, easy-drinking palate. Milaro Rosso, a humble footsoldier of a wine and less of an image-definer for the cellar, is also attractive and stands out for its exceptional value for money. The Inzolia is the most attractive of the whites, even though it doesn't exactly scintillate. Bidis '98, an inzolia and chardonnay blend that ages for 12 months in small oak barrels, sadly failed to live up to our expectations.

○ Bianco Biscari '98	♟♟	3*
● Casale dei Biscari '97	♟♟	4
● Fontanabianca '99	♟♟	5
● Frappato '99	♟♟	3*
○ Chardonnay '99	♟	1*
○ Inzolia '99	♟	1*
● Pietra di Zoe '99	♟	1*
● Syrah '99	♟	3
○ Bianco d'Alcamo '99		1
● Cerasuolo di Vittoria '98		2
● Casale dei Biscari '93	♟♟	3*
● Casale dei Biscari '94	♟♟	3*
● Casale dei Biscari '95	♟♟	3*
● Casale dei Biscari '96	♟	4
● Pietra di Zoe '98	♟	1*

● Cerasuolo di Vittoria '98	♟	2*
● Frappato '99	♟	2*
● Milaro '99	♟	2*
○ Inzolia '99		2
● Frappato '97	♟♟	2*
○ Bidis '95	♟	2*
○ Bidis '96	♟	2*
○ Bidis '97	♟	2*
● Cerasuolo di Vittoria '94	♟	2*
● Cerasuolo di Vittoria '95	♟	2*
● Cerasuolo di Vittoria '96	♟	3
● Frappato '95	♟	2*
● Frappato '96	♟	2*
● Frappato '98	♟	2*
● Milaro '97	♟	3

609

CEUSO
VIA ENEA, 18
91011 ALCAMO (TP)
TEL. 0924/507860

DUCA DI SALAPARUTA - VINI CORVO
VIA NAZIONALE, S. S. 113
90014 CASTELDACCIA (PA)
TEL. 091/945201

In France, they are known as "garagistes", that is, small growers, often from Saint-Emilion and Pomerol in Bordeaux, who, from just a few rows of vines and with the bare minimum of equipment, produce a few thousand bottles. Of superb wine. Even their cellars are tiny, often literally the garages that gave rise to their name. But there are "garagisti" in Italy, too, and the Sicilian version is the team of Antonino, Vincenzo and Giuseppe Melia, each with his own, specific role on their mini-estate near Alcamo. They make just one wine, the excellently structured Ceuso Custera. It comes from a single variety, nero d'Avola, grown on the tiny vineyard they tend as if it were a garden, and vinified with sophisticated, state-of-the-art techniques before ageing for just over a year in small barrels of French oak from Allier. This time, it was the turn of the '98 to take the stage. It certainly didn't disappoint, even though it was perhaps just a shade less good than the majestic '97. It, too, has a dark, concentrated ruby colour ushering in aromas of black cherry, spices and new oak. The flavour is assertive, the only downside being a hint of edginess as the variety's characteristically high level of acidity is only partly attenuated by the oak and the softness of the abundant extract.

The signs of an upswing in Duca di Salaparuta wines are unequivocal. On the winemaking front, continued stability is now assured, thanks to the arrival of Giacomo Tachis as consultant. On another front, though, the company is still going through a phase of transition. Its long-awaited privatization by auction, in which many of the world's large wine groups are bidding, continues to be put off. It is due to be finalized shortly, possibly during 2001, but at the time of writing a delay is on the cards. Various articles in the prospectus may have to be revised because of objections from politicians or economists, or both. Still, that's the way things are in Sicily. In fact, sometimes getting an initiative off the ground resembles the Siena Palio horse race, where the riders delay the start time and time again, on occasion for hours. However, if we turn at last to the wines, it gives us great satisfaction to report that the Duca Enrico has improved so much that the '96 very nearly regained Three Glass status. It has not been on form like this since the '92. Powerful, elegant, lacking only the merest touch of concentration, it is a very fine wine indeed. Bianca di Valguarnera '98 merits similar consideration. It is less oaky, better fruited and more elegant than its recent predecessors. The rest of the range is in essence well-typed, whether it be the new Nero d'Avola Triskelè '98, the Corvo Rosso '98, the Colomba Platino '99, the Glicine '99 or the Corvo Bianco '99. Only Terre d'Agala '97, predominantly from frappato, was a little less good than expected as it was more neutral and dilute than usual.

● Ceuso Custera '98	♟♟	5
● Ceuso '96	♟♟	5
● Ceuso Custera '97	♟♟	5

○ Bianca di Valguarnera '98	♟♟	5
● Duca Enrico '96	♟♟	6
○ Corvo Bianco '99	♟	2*
○ Corvo Colomba Platino '99	♟	3
○ Corvo Glicine '99	♟	2*
● Corvo Rosso '98	♟	2*
● Nero d'Avola Triskelè '98	♟	4
● Terre d'Agala '97	♟	3
● Duca Enrico '84	♟♟♟	6
● Duca Enrico '85	♟♟♟	6
● Duca Enrico '86	♟♟♟	6
● Duca Enrico '87	♟♟♟	6
● Duca Enrico '88	♟♟♟	6
● Duca Enrico '90	♟♟♟	6
● Duca Enrico '92	♟♟♟	6

COMISO (RG)

ERICE (TP)

VITIVINICOLA AVIDE
C.DA MENDOLILLA - S. P. 7 KM 1,5
97013 COMISO (RG)
TEL. 0932/967456

FAZIO WINES
FRAZ. FULGATORE
VIA CAPITAN RIZZO, 39
91010 ERICE (TP)
TEL. 0923/811700 - 0923/811701

The Avide wines did well this year. From the owners through to the technical staff, everyone can be well pleased. Seven wines were presented and all gained at least One Glass, which is definitely a result. We'll start with Cerasuolo di Vittoria Barocco '96, from vines grown around Bastonaca and Mortilla, lands which give the wine its classic style of a deep cherry red colour and ripe fruit aromas full of mineral notes. Sigillo '98, a blend of indigenous and international varieties, has aromas of wild berry fruits and leather with touches of chocolate, and is savoury and attractively long on the palate. The '98 Cerasuolo di Vittorio Etichetta Nera is as good as ever, with its warm aromas, balanced tannins and depth of concentration. Among the whites, the inzolia-based '98 Vigne d'Oro shows a distinct improvement over the previous vintage. It unfurls attractive scents of vanilla and ripe banana, and the palate is supported by good structure. Herea Rosso, from nero d'Avola with a small proportion of frappato, and Herea Bianca, from 100 percent inzolia, are both well-typed and easy to drink. To finish, Lacrimae Bacchi, a fragrantly aromatic inzolia-based wine with a velvety, fruit-rich flavour, gains its first Guide mention and One Glass rating.

To tell the truth, we were expecting a little more after Fazio Wines' success last year. We were looking for a consistency that we did not find or, to be more fair, we found only in part. Let's get things straight. These wines are well-styled and proficiently made but, quite simply, they just did not inspire. So much so that of seven wines put forward, we felt only three warranted full reviews. We'll begin with the one that showed best overall, the Cabernet Sauvignon '99, which has a full ruby red colour, aromas of red berry fruit and hints of black pepper, and good structure on the palate with delicate tannins. The Nero d'Avola and the Merlot have faintly fruity aromas and attractive but rather light, almost washed-out flavours. A bit of time in the cellar might perk them up, or at least lend them a little complexity. The whites on show included an attractive Inzolia-Chardonnay with a straw-yellow colour, inviting aromas of summer fruit and a full, balanced flavour. The elegant Sauvignon was equally good, unveiling a deep yellow colour, fruit-rich aromas and good balance of nose and palate. Finally, the Inzolia and the Müller-Thurgau are not overly endowed with body and are made for early drinking.

● Cerasuolo di Vittoria Barocco '96	⬤⬤	4
● Sigillo Rosso '98	⬤⬤	4
○ Vigne d'Oro '98	⬤⬤	3*
● Cerasuolo di Vittoria Etichetta Nera '98	⬤	2*
○ Dalle Terre di Herea Bianco '98	⬤	2*
● Dalle Terre di Herea Rosso '99	⬤	2*
○ Lacrimæ Bacchi	⬤	5
● Cerasuolo di Vittoria Barocco '95	⬤⬤	4
○ Vigne d'Oro '96	⬤⬤	3*
● Cerasuolo di Vittoria Barocco '94	⬤	4
● Cerasuolo di Vittoria Etichetta Nera '96	⬤	2*
● Cerasuolo di Vittoria Etichetta Nera '97	⬤	2*

● Cabernet Sauvignon '99	⬤	4
○ Inzolia-Chardonnay '99	⬤	3
● Merlot '99	⬤	4
○ Sauvignon Blanc '99	⬤	2*
● Torre dei Venti Rosso '99	⬤	3
○ Inzolia '99		2
○ Müller Thurgau '99		2
● Cabernet Sauvignon '98	⬤⬤	4
● Torre dei Venti Rosso '98	⬤	3

GROTTE (AG)

LICATA (AG)

MORGANTE
C.DA RACALMARE
92020 GROTTE (AG)
TEL. 0922/94559

BARONE LA LUMIA
C.DA CASAL POZZILLO
92027 LICATA (AG)
TEL. 0922/891709

No estate can attain such a prestigious, coveted result as a Three Glass rating, and on its first appearance in the Guide at that, unless there is a carefully planned strategy and a clear set of objectives in place. And that's precisely what the Morgante family can point to. They have around 200 hectares at Grotte where their vines, almond groves and arable farmland stand on parched terrain that is subject to high temperatures but also enjoys plentiful, damp breezes when the wind blows from Africa. Antonio and his sons Carmelo and Giovanni divide their time between crop cultivation and marketing. In '94 they decided to re-organize the agricultural side of the business and entrusted their vineyards to the famed oenologist, Riccardo Cotarella. Don Antonio '98, a remarkable monovarietal Nero d'Avola, comes from clay soil at Scintilia and Poggio Biagio. It has a dark ruby colour and aromas that are full and pervasive, with hints of black cherry and vanilla. On the palate, it is powerful, structured and soft, with elegantly tight, concentrated tannins. The other wine produced, another Nero d'Avola '98 with four months barrique ageing, has a ruby colour, deep aromas with subtle touches of balsam and spices, and good nose-palate resonance.

If you ask anyone with a good knowledge of Sicilian wine who has the best nero d'Avola vineyards, there is only one reply – Barone La Lumia. But understanding why these vines have, for many years, given wines that are typical and full of character but, oenologically speaking, rather wobbly is neither easy nor particularly simple. So let's concentrate instead on the fact that this year, at last, two of the estate's wines are made with modern techniques, new wood and a winemaking style that is on a par with the fame and prestige of the cellar. It hardly needs saying that Don Totò '97 comes from nero d'Avola while the white Sogno di Dama '99, following tradition, is made from inzolia. Both are beautifully varietal, elegant wines in which the base grapes are perfectly recognizable and the oak component is no more than a subtle undertone. At last! The range is completed with the two Signorio wines, a red and a white, and the Delizia del Conte '98, another wine in the new style, which has intensely fruity aromas and a balanced, elegant taste. Our sincere congratulations to Barone La Lumia on this new direction.

● Don Antonio '98	♟♟♟	5
● Nero d'Avola '98	♟	3

● Don Totò '97	♟♟	4
○ Sogno di Dama '99	♟♟	4
● Delizia del Conte '98	♟	3
○ Signorio Bianco '99	♟	3
● Signorio Rosso '96	♟	3
○ Signorio Bianco '95	♟	2*
○ Signorio Bianco '97	♟	2*
○ Signorio Bianco '98	♟	3
● Signorio Rosso '93	♟	3
● Signorio Rosso '94	♟	3
● Signorio Rosso '95	♟	3
● Stemma '97	♟	2*

MARSALA (TP)

MARSALA (TP)

MARCO DE BARTOLI
C.DA FORNARA, 292
91025 MARSALA (TP)
TEL. 0923/962093 - 0923/918344

TENUTA DI DONNAFUGATA
VIA SEBASTIANO LIPARI, 18
91025 MARSALA (TP)
TEL. 0923/999555

Marco De Bartoli's long ordeal is finally over. For more than five years, he was writhing in the coils of an over-formal legal system that is blinkered and excessively inflexible, dragging him through the courts with papers flying in all directions and seals affixed to the Vecchio Samperi cellars for presumed administrative irregularities in its registers of wine movements. Thankfully, these have now been removed. For something that could have been resolved in next to no time with a modest fine, De Bartoli found himself deprived of his cellar buildings and all the wine that he had ageing there. Five years during which he was unable to enter his cellars, check the levels of the barrels or test for volatile acidity. That is a long time. Nevertheless, it probably hasn't jeopardized the quality of the wines since they are Marsalas and other high-alcohol styles: oxidation and high levels of volatility are part and parcel of their very nature. We are looking forward to some great offerings from Marco in the future. Actually, we already have some idea of what is to come, having tasted his best Vecchio Samperi ever and a Bukkuram of great density and concentration, despite a touch of residual rusticity. Furthermore, the Marsala Superiore 20 Anni is as excellent as ever and is clearly the best in its category. These three wines suggest Marco De Bartoli will soon be back in a big way. He deserves to be, just as he deserves all our support and esteem.

Giacomo Rallo, master of this long-standing and most Sicilian of estates, decided to submit only his five top wines for tasting this year. By doing so, he clearly intimated the direction in which he is trying to take Donnafugata and the market sectors in which he expects to be active in the near future. His policy is as intelligent as he himself is far-sighted and clear-thinking, and it marks the final stage in an ambitious plan that should enjoy long-term success. This year's version of the barrique-aged Chardonnay, Chiarandà del Merlo, is magisterial and again comfortably carries off Three Glasses. It is quite simply one of the best Italian whites, in absolute terms. Full without being heavy, it reveals oak that is not intrusive and a balanced, almost aristocratic flavour. The aromas are rich in fruit with the merest touch of vanilla that will develop into complex mineral notes as the wine evolves. The Passito di Pantelleria Ben Ryé '99 is superb, too. It lacks only a final touch of complexity that would bring it top honours. The Milleunanotte '96, from 100 percent nero d'Avola, and Tancredi '98, from nero d'Avola and cabernet sauvignon, are both very good but less exciting than their previous release. The '99 Vigna di Gabri, from inzolia and chardonnay, is also a shade less convincing than usual. While richly flavoured, it is a little over-evolved on the nose.

O Marsala Superiore 20 Anni	♈♈	5
O Passito di Pantelleria		
Bukkuram '94	♈♈	5
O Vecchio Samperi	♈♈	5
O Marsala Sup. Oro		
Vigna La Miccia '90	♈♈	4
O Marsala Sup. Oro		
Vigna La Miccia '91	♈♈	4
O Moscato Passito di Pantelleria '91	♈♈	5
O Vecchio Samperi		
Ris. 20 Anni Solera	♈♈	5
O Vecchio Samperi		
Ris. 30 Anni Solera	♈♈	6

O Contessa Entellina		
Chiarandà del Merlo '99	♈♈♈	5
● Milleunanotte '96	♈♈	6
O Passito di Pantelleria Ben Ryé '99	♈♈	5
● Tancredi '98	♈♈	5
O Contessa Entellina		
Vigna di Gabri '99	♈	3
O Contessa Entellina		
Chiarandà del Merlo '98	♈♈♈	5
O Contessa Entellina		
Vigna di Gabri '98	♈♈	3*
● Milleunanotte '95	♈♈	6
O Passito di Pantelleria Ben Ryé '98	♈♈	4
● Tancredi '97	♈♈	5

MARSALA (TP)

MARSALA (TP)

CANTINE FLORIO
VIA VINCENZO FLORIO, 1
91025 MARSALA (TP)
TEL. 0923/781111

CARLO PELLEGRINO
VIA DEL FANTE, 37
91025 MARSALA (TP)
TEL. 0923/719911

More re-tastes and more results that tally with previous assessments, as was the case in last year's Guide, sums up the situation at Florio. The only new element is the new release, the '97, of Morsi di Luce, an excellent, moscato-based, fortified sweet white wine. Its nose is strongly characterized by a light yet distinct vanilla note, from the new oak used for ageing, with overtones of butter and alcohol, as well as the more usual moscato aromas. There is abundant sweetness on the palate but also plenty of concentration from the rich extract, which prevents any sense of cloying. In short, this is a modern, technically unimpeachable, sweet wine that confirms the consistent performance of Florio, a winery and a label that are intimately bound up in the history of Sicilian fortified wines. Of the wines reviewed last year and re-tasted this time round, the Marsala Superiore Vecchioflorio Riserva '91 remains exemplary for typicity, consistency and value for money, and well deserves its second Two Glass rating. Wines like this indicate that Florio is not about to lose the leadership status in image and quality that it has long enjoyed.

Yet again, this major, long-established Marsala house, one of the clutch of Sicilian wineries that manage to combine large quantities with good quality, has come out with a vast number of reliably good wines. Despite the size of the range, managing director Michele Sala and export manager Massimo Bellino, with technicians Gaspare Catalano and Enrico Stella, are about to release even more wines but we are confident that they, too, will be excellent. This year, it is the new Passito di Pantelleria Nes '98 that stands head and shoulders above the rest. It has an attractive amber colour and intense perfumes of dried figs and dates, and then flows over the palate with confidence, harmony and good concentration. It would go perfectly with biscuits or the traditional fig and almond-filled "buccellato" cakes. The delicate, convincing white Gorgo Tondo '99 is also good, as is the red Gorgo Tondo '97, with its overtones of ripe fruit and spices. The equally good Alcamo '99 Fiorile is refined and captivating, and backed up by firm acidity. The Moscato and the Passito di Pantelleria, both from the '99 vintage and both strongly evocative of the delicious zibibbo grapes from which they are made, are always sure things, as are all the Marsalas, from the Vergine Soleras right through to the Superiore Oro and Fine Ruby. As ever, the value for money offered by the entire range is excellent and probably unbeatable.

O	Morsi di Luce '97	♀♀	5
O	Marsala Soleras Oro Baglio Florio '79	♀♀	6
O	Marsala Sup. Targa Ris. '89	♀♀	4
O	Marsala Sup. Targa Ris. '88	♀♀	4
O	Marsala Sup. Vecchioflorio Ris. '91	♀♀	4
O	Marsala Vergine Baglio Florio '85	♀♀	5
O	Marsala Vergine Baglio Florio '86	♀♀	5
O	Marsala Vergine Terre Arse '86	♀♀	4
O	Marsala Vergine Terre Arse '87	♀♀	4
O	Morsi di Luce '95	♀♀	4
O	Marsala Sup. Vecchioflorio '94	♀	3*
O	Marsala Vergine Baglio Florio '87	♀	5
O	Morsi di Luce '92	♀	4

O	Passito di Pantelleria Nes '98	♀♀	4
O	Alcamo Fiorile '99	♀	1*
O	Cent'Are Bianco '99	♀	2*
●	Cent'Are Nero d'Avola Rosso '97	♀	2*
O	Gorgo Tondo Bianco '99	♀	3
●	Gorgo Tondo Rosso '97	♀	3
●	Marsala Fine Ruby	♀	3
O	Marsala Superiore Oro	♀	3
●	Marsala Superiore Riserva Dom Pellegrino	♀	4
O	Marsala Vergine Soleras	♀	3
O	Moscato di Pantelleria '99	♀	3
O	Passito di Pantelleria '99	♀	4
●	Gorgo Tondo Rosso '96	♀♀	3*
O	Passito di Pantelleria '98	♀♀	4

MARSALA (TP)

CANTINE RALLO
VIA VINCENZO FLORIO, 2
91025 MARSALA (TP)
TEL. 0923/721633 - 0923/72163

MENFI (AG)

SETTESOLI
S. S. 115
92013 MENFI (AG)
TEL. 0925/77111

The winery that last year was called Alvis-Rallo has now proudly reverted to the Rallo name and label that played such a significant part in building the quality reputation of Sicilian winemaking. The wines are technically well-made and bear all the hallmarks of the fine fruit that goes into them. Two are especially good. The Grillo '99, aged in small oak barrels, was a great hit with the panel. It has intense ripe fruit aromas with subtle hints of toasted oak and peanut butter. The palate is full, soft and richly sweet, thanks to the alcohol and extract. In short, it is an admirable white that walked away with Two Glasses. The Inzolia-Chardonnay '99 is lighter and more immediate, its oak tones barely discernible and its nose dominated by clean, distinct, fruit aromas. The full, stylish palate has medium concentration. The classic Passito di Pantelleria Mare d'Ambra, which is released as a non-vintage, and the Vesco Rosso '98, from nero d'Avola and cabernet sauvignon, are both as reliable and well-made as ever. The Vesco Rosso in particular, though a little closed on the nose at the time of tasting, has a stylish, even palate.

This giant of Sicilian wine continues to amaze us. Settesoli is a co-operative capable of vinifying 500,000 quintals of grapes a year. It represents a formidable economic resource for the entire area around its base in Menfi and is a textbook example of what co-operative winemaking can achieve in Italy, if the job is done well. Diego Planeta, perhaps the most far-sighted wine entrepreneur in the whole of Sicily, presides and Carlo Corino, a wonderfully down-to-earth oenologist with huge international experience, is the consultant. Their task is assisted by members who do their best to comply with the detailed, enlightened directives on viticulture they regularly receive, knowing that it is this that makes the difference between prosperity and plunging the area back into depression. The results are outstanding. Settesoli's premium line, sold under the Mandarossa label, includes some really exciting wines. The '99 Chardonnay and the '99 Merlot are the most successful but even the Grecanico and the Cabernet Sauvignon, both also '99, while not aspiring to any great complexity, are good-quality bottles, especially with regard to their scrupulously correct varietal typing. All the rest, the Mandarossa red and white, Nero d'Avola and the Porta Palo '99, are well-typed and the Porta Palo, the simplest and cheapest of the lot, has particularly attractive fruity aromas. Overall, these wines make up an exemplary range that we would also recommend to readers for its excellent value for money.

O Grillo '99	¶¶	3*
O Passito di Pantelleria Mare d'Ambra	¶¶	4
O Inzolia-Chardonnay '99	¶	3
● Vesco Rosso '98	¶	3
O Passito di Pantelleria Mare d'Ambra	¶¶	4
O Grillo '98	¶	2*
O Marsala Sup. Ambra Semisecco	¶	3
O Marsala Sup. Semisecco Anima Mediterranea	¶	3
O Moscato di Pantelleria	¶	3
● Nero d'Avola '97	¶	2*
● Vesco Rosso '96	¶	4
● Vesco Rosso '97	¶	3

O Chardonnay Mandrarossa '99	¶¶	3*
● Merlot Mandrarossa '99	¶¶	3*
● Cabernet Sauvignon Mandrarossa '99	¶	3
O Grecanico Mandrarossa '99	¶	3
O Mandrarossa Bianco '99	¶	3
● Mandrarossa Rosso '99	¶	3
● Nero d'Avola Mandrarossa '98	¶	3
● Porta Palo Rosso '99	¶	2*
● Bonera '94	¶¶	3*
O Feudo dei Fiori '97	¶¶	2*
● Nero d'Avola '98	¶¶	3*
● Nero d'Avola/Cabernet '98	¶¶	3*
● Bonera '95	¶	3
● Rosso di Sicilia '97	¶	2*

MESSINA

MILAZZO (ME)

PALARI
LOC. S. STEFANO BRIGA
VILLA GERACI
98137 MESSINA
TEL. 090/694281 - 090/630194

CASA VINICOLA GRASSO
VIA ALBERO, 5
98057 MILAZZO (ME)
TEL. 090/9281082

Turi Geraci continues to wear his panama hat and his white linen suit when, towards the end of September, he climbs into his vintage Jaguar to start out on the tortuous drive to his vineyards and cellar at Santo Stefano Briga. After all, white linen is "de rigueur" if the weather is still hot and this area, between Messina and Taormina, has particularly long summers. It is as September gives way to October that the nerello mascalese and nerello cappuccio varieties start to ripen on the tiny plots of bush vines that are scattered on all sides of the Palari cellar. Palari is also the name of the sumptuous wine that is Turi Geraci's pride and joy, and the one that prompted him to persuade his brother Giampiero to become cellarman so that it would turn out exactly the way he wanted. He also restored the family villa, opened up the cellar again and twisted the arm of Piedmontese winemaker, Donato Lanati, to come down to Sicily to maximize the potential of the scant few thousand bottles of Palari that he manages to produce. It should therefore come as no surprise to learn that Geraci is a fascinating individual. Indeed, with his cultured, old-fashioned, gentlemanly refinement, he seems to have stepped out of some story of Sicily's distant past. But the Palari '98 is a magisterial wine that takes Geraci back to the highest peaks of Sicilian winemaking. Rich, mouth-filling and velvet-smooth, it is tremendously exciting and quintessentially Sicilian. Then there is Geraci's Rosso del Soprano '98, available only in magnums this time. In fact, it is a second-choice Palari, which has been "declassified" in the manner of the great Bordeaux châteaux. Less concentrated and more immediately approachable than the first selection, it is probably available only in magnums because an ordinary bottle would be finished too soon.

Paola and Alessio Grasso should be pleased to see their second consecutive entry in the Guide. New wines have been added to those shown last year, and all are well-made. The grapes come from the countryside around Milazzo and from Castellaro on the island of Lipari. On the red front, the Caporosso '98, from nero d'Avola and nerello mascalese, has a ruby colour leading in to attractive aromas of red berry fruit and toasted oak, and then a perfect symmetry of nose and palate. The first release of the Sulleria, the '99, from nero d'Avola and sangiovese grown at Solaria di Rodi Milici, showed well. It is a little less concentrated than the Caporosso but its bouquet is broad and deep. The Mamertino '98 and the Salina '99, the latter another newcomer, are along the same lines. The whites showed equally impressively. The Sulleria '99, an blend of inzolia, grillo and catarratto, is soft, structured, attractively fruity and quite captivating. The Capobianco '99 is good enough but slightly less impressive than last year's edition while the Mistral '99, from catarratto and inzolia, is attractively fruited and easy drinking. However, the catarratto, grillo and late-vintage inzolia Salina '99 deserves a special mention as it is a particularly fruity, intriguing wine with notable complexity of flavour. The Passito di Pantelleria Ergo is again successful, as intense, attractively aromatic and concentrated in sugars as ever.

● Faro Palari '98	▼▼▼	6
● Rosso del Soprano '98	▼▼	5
● Faro Palari '96	♈♈♈	5
● Faro Palari '94	♈♈	5
● Faro Palari '95	♈♈	5
● Faro Palari '97	♈♈	6
● Rosso del Soprano '95	♈♈	4
● Rosso del Soprano '96	♈♈	4
● Rosso del Soprano '97	♈	4

● Caporosso '98	▼▼	2*
O Passito di Pantelleria Ergo '92	▼▼	5
O Sulleria Bianco Feudo Solaria '99	▼▼	2*
O Capobianco '99	▼	2*
● Mamertino Rosso '98	▼	1*
O Mistral '99	▼	1*
O Salina Bianco '99	▼	1*
● Salina Rosso '99	▼	1*
● Sulleria Rosso Feudo Solaria '99	▼	2*
O Capobianco '98	♈♈	2*
O Passito di Pantelleria Ergo '93	♈♈	4
● Caporosso '97	♈	2*
O Passito di Pantelleria Ergo '95	♈	5

616

MONREALE (PA)

AZIENDE AGRICOLE POLLARA
C.DA MALVELLO
90046 MONREALE (PA)
TEL. 091/8462922

This year's wines from the Pollara estate, which lies a few kilometres from Corleone, were well-typed and well-made. Indeed, the Pollara brothers' wines are always up to scratch although we, like most true wine lovers, continue to hope that at least one of them will leap out in front of the rest and catch the headlines. Six wines won reviews, starting with the Cabernet Sauvignon. A fine ruby in colour, it has an attractive ripe fruitiness, with hints of red pepper, and a well-structured palate. The Nero d'Avola, with its attractively youthful, harmonious flavour drawing complexity from a delicious undertone of spicy oak, was also good. The Pollara whites were satisfactory, too. The best, if only by a small margin, was the Chardonnay Vigna del Corte. More concentrated than the previous release, it has good intensity on nose and palate, light touches of vanilla and a fruitily balanced palate. The Inzolia, with its classic deep straw-yellow colour and fresh perfumes of orange blossom and citrus, was very appealing, as was the Pinot Bianco, its pleasing fruitiness nicely backed up by a clean, herbaceous undertone. The Alcamo finds an enticing balance between its delicate fruitiness, which comes from the quality of the damaschino grapes used, and its impressive structure on the palate, boosted by the power of the catarratto in the blend.

PACECO (TP)

FIRRIATO
VIA TRAPANI, 4
91027 PACECO (TP)
TEL. 0923/882755

Firriato gains a coveted Three Glasses and takes its place as the new star in the Sicilian wine firmament. In the wine firmament of the whole of Italy, actually. The estate, owned by brothers Girolamo and Salvatore Di Gaetano, with Salvatore's dynamic wife, Vinzia, handling PR, had the tasting panel leaping out of their seats with a range of wines that were quite superb, from the most serious right through to the least expensive. All were technically impeccable, produced by a celebrated international team, from Australia, California and New Zealand, led by the British Master of Wine, Kim Milne, with assiduous on-hand assistance from the highly skilled oenologist from Marsala, Giuseppe Pellegrino. The Camelot '98, from cabernet sauvignon and merlot, is the wine that strolled off with a unanimous Three Glasses. It has an opaque ruby colour and a stunning spectrum of aromas, with clear tones of ripe berry fruit and spices overlying particularly elegant balsamic notes. The palate is powerful and of rare concentration, with ripe, gentle tannins that make it a masterpiece of balance and harmony. The other wines showed excellently too, from the white catarratto and chardonnay Santagostino '99 to the red Santagostino '98, from nero d'Avola and syrah) Both the red and white versions of the Altavilla della Corte were much improved, revealing themselves to be more elegant and attractive than in the past while the Etna Rosso '97 put on an equally good show and is the best Etna we have tasted in recent years. All the rest of the estate's production performed very well.

O	Alcamo Principe di Corleone '99	♀ 2*
●	Cabernet Sauvignon Principe di Corleone '97	♀ 3
O	Chardonnay Vigna di Corte '99	♀ 3
O	Inzolia '99	♀ 2*
●	Nero d'Avola '98	♀ 2*
O	Pinot Bianco Principe di Corleone '99	♀ 2*
O	Alcamo Principe di Corleone '98	♀ 2*
●	Cabernet Sauvignon Principe di Corleone '96	♀ 3
●	Cabernet Sauvignon Principe di Corleone '96	♀ 3
O	Chardonnay Vigna di Corte '97	♀ 2*
O	Chardonnay Vigna di Corte '98	♀ 3

●	Camelot '98	♀♀♀ 5
O	Altavilla della Corte Bianco '99	♀♀ 3*
●	Altavilla della Corte Rosso '98	♀♀ 3*
●	Etna Rosso '97	♀♀ 2*
O	Santagostino Bianco '99	♀♀ 4
O	Santagostino Rosso '98	♀♀ 4
O	Bianco d'Alcamo '99	♀ 1
O	Charlotte de Roseville '99	♀ 1*
O	Primula Bianco '99	♀ 1*
●	Primula Rosso '98	♀ 1*
O	Santagostino Bianco '98	♀♀ 4
●	Santagostino Rosso '97	♀♀ 4
●	Altavilla della Corte Rosso '97	♀ 3
●	Etna Rosso '96	♀ 2*
●	Primula Rosso '97	♀ 1*

PALERMO

PALERMO

ABBAZIA SANTA ANASTASIA
VIA MARIO VACCARO, 4
90145 PALERMO
TEL. 091/201593 - 091/201472

AZIENDE VINICOLE MICELI
VIA DENTI DI PIRAINO, 9
90142 PALERMO
TEL. 091/6396111

The expression "falling on your feet" seems to sum up what happened to this Sicilian winery, newly enrolled in the ranks of fame. At the beginning of last year, it lost the consultancy of Giacomo Tachis, world-famous oenologist and for the past three decades the great patriarch of Italian winemaking. However, Tachis involved himself personally in the search for a successor and in his place has come none other than the hugely able Riccardo Cotarella, another winemaker of great renown. As a result, things have gone from good to better for Francesco Lena. Of course, vintages are not always perfect and this year no Abbazia Sant'Anastasia wine gains Three Glasses, as has been the case in each of the past two years. There's definitely a bit too much oak on the aromas of the Baccante and the Zurrica, both '99 whites, which, understandably, are still too dominated by their recent ageing in barrique. There's certainly a less concentrated structure in the '98 Litra, in comparison with the '96 and '97. But all this is due to the caprices of the weather rather than the change of consultant. For there is also the exciting debut of a new red, the Montenero '98, from 100 percent nero d'Avola, a wine that slips in just below Litra in overall quality. Following the best traditions of the estate, the Montenero is elegant and well-made, with closely-woven, stylish tannins,.

Aziende Vinicole Miceli put up a good showing again this year. This important wine producer owns 40 hectares, divided between Castelvetrano and the island of Pantelleria, and has two modern cellars, one at Sciacca and one on Pantelleria. The managing director is Giuseppe Lo Re and the technical side is in the hands of oenologist, Filippo Di Giovanna. The Alcamo '99, a simple, well-made white with delicate fruity perfumes, is pleasant and easy to drink. The '99 Yrnm, a dry white made from zibibbo, is intriguing and conjures up the magic of Pantelleria and the minerally tang of its soils. The Inizio '98, from chardonnay, is also good, offering a bright gold colour and marked aromas of tropical fruit. The rest of the whites are a touch under par. The Sicilian red grape "par excellence", nero d'Avola, is responsible for Fiammato '99, an early-drinking red with cherry and berry fruit notes that can also be enjoyed lightly chilled, and for Nero d'Avola '99. This has a deep ruby colour and aromas of wild berry fruits and morello cherry. It is flavoursome and reveals good texture and concentration. Garighe, a sweet wine from zibibbo, is as alluring as ever while the two sweet wines, the Moscato Passito di Pantelleria Yanir, and the classic Moscato di Pantelleria Tanit, are both attractive, long and well-typed. The new arrival, Nun, another Moscato Passito di Pantelleria, is attractive, aromatic, stylish and enticing.

● Litra '98	♟♟	6	○ Alcamo '99	♟	1*
● Montenero '98	♟♟	5	● Fiammato '99	♟	3
○ Baccante '99	♟	5	○ Garighe Zibibbo	♟	3
● Passomaggio '98	♟	4	○ Inizio '98	♟	3
○ Santa Anastasia Bianco '99	♟	3	● Nero d'Avola '99	♟	2*
● Santa Anastasia Rosso '97	♟	3	○ Passito di Pantelleria Nun	♟	4
○ Zurrica '99	♟	4	○ Passito di Pantelleria Tanit	♟	4
● Litra '96	♟♟♟	5	○ Passito di Pantelleria Yanir	♟	4
● Litra '97	♟♟♟	6	○ Yrnm '99	♟	3
○ Baccante '97	♟♟	5	○ Garighe Zibibbo '98	♟	3
○ Baccante '98	♟♟	5	● Nero d'Avola '97	♟	2*
● Passomaggio '95	♟♟	4	○ Organza '98	♟	2*
● Passomaggio '96	♟♟	4	○ Passito di Pantelleria Tanit	♟	3
● Santa Anastasia Rosso '96	♟♟	3*	○ Passito di Pantelleria Yanir	♟	5
○ Zurrica '97	♟♟	3*	○ Yrnm '98	♟	4

618

PALERMO

PALERMO

RAPITALÀ ADELKAM
VIA SEGESTA, 9
90141 PALERMO
TEL. 091/332088

SPADAFORA
VIA AUSONIA, 90
90144 PALERMO
TEL. 091/514952 - 091/518544

There have been significant improvements in this famous winery since Gruppo Italiano Vino took over ownership and technical direction. The wines are now better executed. They are no longer such as to force us to relegate Rapitalà into the limbo of the "Other Wineries", as has happened in the past. Good news, then. But not everything is roses, or not yet anyway, because alongside newly formulated wines such as whites Casalj and Bouquet '99, and the red Nuhar '98, there are still other bottles awaiting their turn to be put right. The Alcamo Rapitalà Grand Cru '98, for instance. This ought to be the jewel in the estate's crown but in fact, it is a touch too evolved and over-elaborate. The Rapitalà Rosso '98 is a decent wine, elegant and rather stylish. Alcamo Rapitalà '99, the cellar's workhorse made mainly from catarratto, is even and well-typed but without any great depth. What we are seeing is the first stage of recovery with the rest yet to come. Rapitalà is one of the best and largest estates in the Alcamo area so it surely cannot be that difficult to bring the wines up to speed.

After the consistently admirable wines we enjoyed last year, we were expecting great things again from Francesco Spadafora. But he tells us that we'll have to wait another year for more goodies and in fact, his current offerings are well-typed and well-made but not much more. As usual, the reds are two strides ahead of the whites and the most interesting overall is Schietto '98. This is a Cabernet Sauvignon, deep red in colour, with good, spicy aromas overlaid with attractive fruit notes. The full-bodied flavour allows you a glimpse of the excellent underlying structure and this should be a most rewarding wine after a few years of bottle ageing. Just a notch below is the Vigna Virzì '99, from nero d'Avola and syrah, a wine characterized by a decent finesse on both nose and palate. The nero d'Avola, cabernet and merlot Don Pietro '99 was next in line. It has a good ruby colour, attractively fruity aromas and a delicate herbaceousness. Moving on to the whites, the inzolia and chardonnay Divino reveals floral notes on the nose, mingling with aromas that reflect each of the varieties in the blend. Both the Vigna Virzì Bianco and the Alcamo are well-typed, easy drinking wines with good nose-palate symmetry.

○ Alcamo Rapitalà '99	♀	3
○ Alcamo Rapitalà Grand Cru '98	♀	4
○ Bouquet '99	♀	3
○ Casalj '99	♀	3
● Nuhar '98	♀	4
● Rapitalà Rosso '98	♀	3
○ Alcamo Rapitalà Grand Cru '95	♀♀	4
○ Alcamo Rapitalà '97	♀	3
○ Alcamo Rapitalà '96	♀	3
○ Alcamo Rapitalà Grand Cru '96	♀	4
● Rapitalà Rosso '95	♀	3
● Rapitalà Rosso '96	♀	3

● Schietto '98	♀♀	3*
○ Bianco d'Alcamo '98	♀	2*
○ Divino '99	♀	2*
● Don Pietro Rosso '99	♀	2*
○ Vigna Virzì Bianco '99	♀	2*
● Vigna Virzì Rosso '99	♀	2*
● Don Pietro Rosso '95	♀♀	3*
● Don Pietro Rosso '96	♀♀	3*
● Don Pietro Rosso '98	♀♀	2*
● Schietto '97	♀♀	3*
● Vigna Virzì Rosso '98	♀♀	2*
○ Divino '98	♀	2*
○ Don Pietro Bianco '96	♀	2*
● Don Pietro Rosso '94	♀	3
● Vigna Virzì Rosso '95	♀	2*

PANTELLERIA (TP)

PANTELLERIA (TP)

SALVATORE MURANA
C.DA KHAMMA, 276
91017 PANTELLERIA (TP)
TEL. 0923/915231

D'ANCONA
C.DA KADDIUGGIA
91017 PANTELLERIA (TP)
TEL. 0923/913016

You could call him a bit of a guru or you might say he's impervious to the circus of fame that the top producers usually join. Say what you will, Salvatore Murana – "Salvo" to his friends – is the man who has brought the world's wine-lovers to understand and appreciate the great wine that is Moscato Passito di Pantelleria. Whether it is the wonderful, complex Martingana, which in the '97 version is again intensely sweet and stunningly concentrated, or the subtly simpler Khamma, or the fruited, aromatic Mueggen, both from '98, all of Murana's wines are characterful and astoundingly well-executed. These are wines that you don't forget easily, just as you won't forget the passion and pride that drive Salvo's labours in vineyard and cellar, year in year out. Working on Pantelleria is not easy. You are miles from anywhere and so everything is that much more difficult. Even getting an order of bottles to arrive in time is a hassle because it has to arrive by boat, with all the logistical problems that entails, not to mention higher costs. Then nature itself is tough and lack of rain is just the first of the long list of problems. Each year is a trial for a tiny, simply equipped cellar such as Murana's. Nevertheless, his wines are emblematic of the territory and remain firmly etched in the memory of all who drink them. Perhaps the effort is worthwhile after all. So, let's thank Salvatore Murana and thank heaven that he is prepared to carry on producing such splendid dried-grape, or "passito", wines, brimming with Mediterranean sunshine and imbued with character by Salvo's extraordinary dedication and passion.

The D'Anconas are a young couple whose success has meant they have had to define their roles very precisely. Giacomo, the grand craftsman of zibibbo, now concentrates on the technical side, leaving the cordial, serene, self-assured Solidea, whose name graces their celebrated range of wines, to look after public relations. When Solidea is not attending award ceremonies and other events all over the place, she looks after the numerous guests visiting the estate, which includes preparing them a great Pantellerian couscous. The couple have an air of contentment, and this gives us great pleasure. This year they just missed out on Three Glasses but even so, their wines are right out of the top drawer. Technically well-made and distinctive, they are strongly representative of the "Windy Island's" heritage. The '99 Passito Solidea is as outstanding as ever. With really concentrated fruit, it has a bright amber colour and magnificent aromas of honey, dates and figs. The palate is soft and round, and just oozes the fabulous Mediterranean sensuality of the island. The '99 Moscato Solidea is an improvement on the '98 and has attained a quality level that is comparable to the Passito. A delicate, "amabile" semi-sweet wine, it has become a benchmark for Pantellerian Moscato. The Solidea '99, dry Zibibbo, was already showing well at the time of tasting but will doubtless acquire even more pronounced and enticing scents of fruit and fresh flowers with time in the cellar.

O Moscato Passito di Pantelleria Martingana '97	♥♥♥	6
O Moscato Passito di Pantelleria Khamma '98	♥♥	5
O Moscato Passito di Pantelleria Mueggen '98	♥♥	5
O Moscato Passito di Pantelleria Martingana '93	♟♟♟	6
O Moscato Passito di Pantelleria Martingana '94	♟♟♟	6
O Moscato Passito di Pantelleria Martingana '96	♟♟♟	6
O Moscato Passito di Pantelleria Khamma '96	♟♟	6

O Moscato di Pantelleria Solidea '99	♥♥	4
O Passito di Pantelleria Solidea '99	♥♥	5
O Zibibbo Solidea '99	♥	2*
O Passito di Pantelleria Solidea '98	♟♟♟	5
O Bianco Scuvaki '97	♟♟	3*
O Moscato di Pantelleria '	♟♟	3*
O Passito di Pantelleria	♟♟	3*
O Passito di Pantelleria Solidea '93	♟♟	5
O Passito di Pantelleria Solidea '95	♟♟	5
O Scirocco '96	♟♟	2*
O Bianco Sciuvaki '96	♟	3
O Moscato di Pantelleria Solidea '98	♟	4
O Zibibbo Solidea '98	♟	2*

PARTINICO (PA)

CASA VINICOLA CADIVIN
C.DA S. CARLO
S. S. 113 KM 307
90047 PARTINICO (PA)
TEL. 091/8903456

S. CIPIRELLO (PA)

CALATRASI - TERRE DI GINESTRA
C.DA PIANO PIRAINO
90040 S. CIPIRELLO (PA)
TEL. 091/8576767 - 091/8578080

Following in the footsteps of a family tradition started by their father, Francesco, some years back, young, dynamic brothers, Alberto and Diego Cusumano, founded Cadivin, a winery that took us by surprise this year. Limited yields, technologically advanced equipment, scrupulous cellar work and a desire to be up to speed in the marketplace are the elements that form the foundations of this family ensemble's efforts. The technical side has been entrusted to Giuseppe Clemente, an oenologist from Marsala, with Piedmontese Mario Ronco acting as consultant. The Insolia '99 is technically well-made. Its characteristic straw-yellow colour introduces clean fruit aromas and a delicate palate with just the right amount of acidic backbone. The Nadaria '99, from grecanico and inzolia, is equally good. The attractive nose leads in to a fresh-tasting, pleasantly zesty palate. The Nero d'Avola '99 is also attractive, with a concentrated colour and aromas of wild berry fruit and liqueur black cherry well in evidence, followed up by a full, rich, long palate. The Gocce di Bisaccia '99 is a successful blend with a deep ruby colour, rich scents of ripe fruit and spices, and an attractive, soft, warm, enveloping palate offering well-balanced tannins. The '99 Alcamo was not quite ready in time for our tastings and so we found it rather closed. However, it will no doubt improve with a few months in bottle.

As usual, Calatrasi presented us with a whole raft of wines but we were happy to note that they were consistently well-made, modern in style and – with the emphasis on blends of international and typically Sicilian varieties – carefully designed to appeal to modern palates. There was chardonnay with catarratto, merlot with sangiovese (more common in these parts than in Tuscany) and syrah with nero d'Avola. The wines are not particularly complex but few would contest their proficiency of execution and no one could fault their extreme drinkability. The top line, released under the D'Istinto label, includes the Magnifico '98, a blend of several varieties that come together in one glorious, fruit-rich bouquet, redolent of black cherry and plum, concentrating all the power of the Mediterranean terroir from which they come. The rest of the huge range includes many other good-quality wines, which are listed below. Here, we will comment on only two of them, the fruity, varietal, "no-frills" Chardonnay Allora '99, and the delicious D'Istinto Sangiovese-Merlot '99, a hymn to drinking pleasure. All the rest are well-made and reveal decent quality.

●	Gocce di Bisaccia '99	▼	2*	●	D'Istinto Magnifico '98	▼▼ 4
○	Insolia '99	▼	2*	○	Chardonnay Allora '99	▼ 3
○	Nadaria '99	▼	2*	○	D'Istinto	
●	Nero d'Avola '99	▼	2*		Catarratto-Chardonnay '99	▼ 3
○	Alcamo '99		2	●	D'Istinto Sangiovese '99	▼ 4
				●	D'Istinto Sangiovese-Merlot '99	▼ 4
				●	D'Istinto	
					Sangiovese-Nero d'Avola '99	▼ 4
				●	D'Istinto Syrah '98	▼ 4
				○	Terre di Ginestra Bianco '99	▼ 3

SAMBUCA DI SICILIA (AG)   SANTA VENERINA (CT)

PLANETA
C.DA ULMO E MAROCCOLI
92017 SAMBUCA DI SICILIA (AG)
TEL. 0925/80009

BARONE SCAMMACCA DEL MURGO
VIA ZAFFERANA, 13
95010 SANTA VENERINA (CT)
TEL. 095/950520

It looks like we are going to have to repeat ourselves but what else can we do? For the second year running the young Planetas, Francesca, Alessio and Santi, have bagged a brace of Three Glass scores. This puts them right at the top of the tree, and not just in Sicily. Indeed, some of their offerings have already become cult wines like the Chardonnay, for instance, which is completely sold out within weeks of release, despite a production run of 60,000 bottles. This year, it is the '99 that drew praise. It is a great Chardonnay, warm, soft, penetrating, very richly extracted, incredibly long and dominated by tropical fruit aromas. But this time the Merlot also did the business. We had always previously considered it rather over-rated but the '98 is exemplary, with its concentrated palate and its varietal aromas that strongly evoke tobacco and black cherry. The other wines, an unbroken line of Two Glasses, include the Alastro '99, a white from grecanico and chardonnay, well worth spotlighting for its near-perfect technical execution. It is the finest "uncomplicated" wine in Sicily. The Santa Cecilia '98, from nero d'Avola with a little syrah, is very good but not exceptional while the '98 Cabernet Sauvignon, just a touch dilute but elegant and varietal, is rather better. La Segreta Bianco '99 is marvellous but the red version, a '98, is more predictable. When the vines planted by Planeta in the Vittoria subzone come on-stream this year, the estate will be producing 1,000,000 bottles a year. You can be sure there will be even more great things to investigate, as there are on their new website, www.planeta.it.

This famous Etna estate has got its full Guide profile back this year even though we are still not completely convinced by its two basic wines, the Etna Bianco '99 and Etna Rosso '98. They are both rather one-dimensional, the aromas are yeasty and the palates are rather too slim. At least that is our humble opinion. We'd be much happier seeing them perform as they did reliably until a couple of years or so ago. However, there is one wine that received nothing but compliments, and which speaks volumes for the estate's potential, the Tenuta San Michele '97, from cabernet sauvignon. It comes over as one of the best wines in the entire province of Catania. Elegant, varietal and complex on both nose and palate, it is, in short, a knockout, almost an "Etna-grown Sassicaia". It is this wine alone that earned Barone Scammacca del Murgo a place in the Guide again. The estate's noble owner has now returned to Sicily after a career spent travelling the world in the Italian diplomatic service, an experience that will doubtless have taught him how to get the most from his staff. It looks as if he will now be running the estate personally and it will be a pleasure to see him at the helm. We wish Barone Scammaca del Murgo all the success of which he and his estate are undoubtedly capable.

O Chardonnay '99	♟♟♟	5
● Merlot '98	♟♟♟	5
O Alastro '99	♟♟	4
● Cabernet Sauvignon '98	♟♟	5
O La Segreta Bianco '99	♟♟	3*
● La Segreta Rosso '98	♟♟	3*
● Santa Cecilia '98	♟♟	5
O Chardonnay '96	♟♟♟	5
O Chardonnay '98	♟♟♟	5
● Santa Cecilia '97	♟♟♟	5
● Cabernet Sauvignon '97	♟♟	5
O Chardonnay '97	♟♟	5
O Chardonnay '95	♟♟	5
● Merlot '95	♟♟	5
● Merlot '97	♟♟	5

● Tenuta San Michele '97	♟♟	4
O Etna Bianco '99		3
● Etna Rosso '98		3
O Etna Bianco '95	♟♟	2*
● Tenuta San Michele '92	♟♟	4
● Tenuta San Michele '94	♟♟	4
● Tenuta San Michele '95	♟♟	4
O Etna Bianco '96	♟	2*
O Etna Bianco '97	♟	2*
● Etna Rosso '93	♟	3
● Etna Rosso '94	♟	3
● Etna Rosso '96	♟	3
● Etna Rosso '91	♟	3
● Tenuta San Michele '91	♟	4
● Tenuta San Michele '93	♟	4

TRAPANI

VALLELUNGA PRATAMENO (CL)

CANTINA SOCIALE DI TRAPANI
C.DA OSPEDALETTO FONTANELLE
91100 TRAPANI
TEL. 0923/539349

★ TASCA D'ALMERITA
C.DA REGALEALI
90029 VALLELUNGA PRATAMENO (CL)
TEL. 0921/544011 - 0921/542522

The province of Trapani is the one with the greatest density of vineyards in Sicily and the island's up-and-coming winemaking area. The leading local co-operative has now proved itself worthy of its place in the Guide for the second time running, its wines gaining almost identical results to last year. Grapes from the territories of Kinisia, Rocca del Giglio and Valderice are responsible for the monovarietal Cabernet Sauvignon. It is a good, weighty red with intense aromas of redcurrant and plum jam, topped by a delicate herbaceousness. The palate is rich, mouth-filling and finely textured, with balanced tannins. Forti Terre di Sicilia '99, from cabernet sauvignon and nero d'Avola, has good concentration, tannins and balance while the monovarietal Nero d'Avola, which undergoes a period in oak barrels, has lightly herbaceous aromas and gentle balsamic overtones. Finally, the Forti Terre di Sicilia Bianco, from inzolia and chardonnay, has varietal perfumes, good structure and attractive drinkability.

What with reds, whites, rosés and sparklers, there were a good 12 samples from Tasca d'Almerita to assess this year. The '98 Cabernet Sauvignon showed well enough to regain Three Glasses after a "sabbatical" last year. It is less powerful than the '97 or the '90 but is decidedly more harmonious and technically polished, the emphasis having shifted to elegance and balance. The Cabernet Sauvignon '97 is also good but has less ageing potential. Both the Almerita Brut '97, which has evolved, complex aromas, and the Nozze d'Oro '98, one of the best releases of the wine ever, are decidedly accomplished. Among the reds, Rosso del Conte '98 and Rosso Novantasei '98 stand out. The latter has a paradoxical name as "novantasei" means 96 in Italian. In fact, the wine was first made in '96 as a one-off substitute for the Rosso del Conte but turned out to be so successful that the Tascas decided to continue producing it, and to keep its rather odd name. The '98 Chardonnay is a touch under par, being lighter and less complex than usual, but there are no quibbles about any of the other wines. A special mention goes to the Regaleali Rosato '99, which is a star among rosés.

● Forti Terre di Sicilia Cabernet Sauvignon '98	♥♥	3*
● Forti Terre di Sicilia Rosso '99	♥♥	2*
○ Forti Terre di Sicilia Bianco '99	♥	2*
● Forti Terre di Sicilia Nero d'Avola '98	♥	2*
● Forti Terre di Sicilia Cabernet Sauvignon '97	♀♀	3*
● Forti Terre di Sicilia Rosso '98	♀♀	1*
○ Forti Terre di Sicilia Bianco '98	♀	1*

● Cabernet Sauvignon '98	♥♥♥	6
○ Almerita Brut '97	♥♥	5
● Cabernet Sauvignon '97	♥♥	6
○ Nozze d'Oro '98	♥♥	4
● Rosso del Conte '98	♥♥	5
● Rosso Novantasei '98	♥♥	4
○ Chardonnay '98	♥	6
○ Leone d'Almerita '99	♥	3
○ Regaleali Bianco '99	♥	2*
⊙ Regaleali Rosato '99	♥	2*
● Regaleali Rosso '98	♥	3
○ Villa Tasca '99	♥	2*
● Cabernet Sauvignon '90	♀♀♀	6
● Cabernet Sauvignon '95	♀♀♀	6
○ Chardonnay '95	♀♀♀	6

VIAGRANDE (CT)

VITTORIA (RG)

BENANTI
VIA G. GARIBALDI, 475
95029 VIAGRANDE (CT)
TEL. 095/7893533 - 095/7893438

COS
P.ZZA DEL POPOLO, 34
97019 VITTORIA (RG)
TEL. 0932/864042

There have been numerous changes in the Benanti wines this year. Some have been for the better but a few wines in the range have taken a minor dive, mainly because their vintages were nothing special. Their vineyards are high up on the slopes of Mount Etna, some lying at 700-800 metres above sea level, and at such altitudes the weather is not as benign as it is in other parts of Sicily. The best of the range is the Etna Rosso Rosso di Verzella '98. While it does not shine for structure or complexity, it is competently made with well-defined aromas and a balanced, stylish palate. The Lamoremio '97, from cabernet sauvignon, nero d'Avola and nerello mascalese, is also good, although a little rustic on the nose, and there is a touch too much tannin-acid edginess. Both these wines, though, showed better than the '97 Etna Rosso Rovittello, usually considered one of the winery's gems. This revealed a touch of coarseness on the palate and was not absolutely clean on the nose. However, the real news from the estate is that a new range of varietals has been released. It includes a reasonable oak-aged Chardonnay, a fresh, tangy, excellently typed Carricante, a good Nerello Cappuccio, and a Nero d'Avola and a Nerello Mascalese, both of which are tempting and very quaffable. The Etna Bianco Bianco di Caselle '99 and the white Edelmio '97, another new wine, are both fairly good. The Etna Bianco Superiore Pietramarina '97 was not available for tasting but we re-tasted the '96 and confirmed last year's evaluation.

We owe many fabulous wine-related experiences to Titta Cilia and Giusto Occhipinti, the immensely likeable "terrible twins" of the Sicilian quality wine scene. The two are invariably bursting with enthusiasm, full of new ideas and tirelessly industrious. Anyone visiting the estate this year will have found them preparing new wines or acquiring new equipment. And after this brief transition period, the new wines will, as they continue to say with feeling, "reflect our terroir precisely. There will be no pretence or distortion. They will be the pure, unwavering essence of the potential nature has given to our soil". The Sciri is again the estate's top wine and the most eloquent expression of an approach that adheres strictly to the heritage and traditional methods of the Cerasuolo zone. The '97 has a lovely ruby colour that shades into garnet, ushering in a broad, pervasive spectrum of aromas where ripe fruit, cinnamon and liquorice take centre stage. The palate is generous and seductive, epitomizing the warm, Mediterranean terroir from which it comes. The '98 Cerasuolo di Vittoria, from frappato and nero d'Avola, is as inviting as previous vintages, offering captivating aromas and good concentration. Ramì '99, the new name for the inzolia-based Ramingallo, has delicate floral and fruit aromas, notably white damson, and a soft, attractive palate.

● Etna Rosso Rosso di Verzella '98	YY	3*
● Lamoremio '97	YY	5
O Carricante '98	Y	3
O Chardonnay '98	Y	4
O Edelmio '97	Y	4
O Etna Bianco Bianco di Caselle '99	Y	3
● Etna Rosso Rovittello '97	Y	5
● Nerello Cappuccio '98	Y	3
● Nerello Mascalese '98	Y	3
● Nero d'Avola '98	Y	3
O Etna Bianco Sup. Pietramarina '95	YY	4
● Etna Rosso Rovittello '94	YY	5
● Etna Rosso Rovittello '95	YY	5
● Lamoremio '95	YY	5
● Lamoremio '96	YY	5

● Cerasuolo di Vittoria Sciri '97	YY	5
● Cerasuolo di Vittoria '98	Y	4
O Ramì '99	Y	3
● Cerasuolo di Vittoria '94	YY	3*
● Cerasuolo di Vittoria '95	YY	3*
● Cerasuolo di Vittoria '96	YY	3*
● Cerasuolo di Vittoria Sciri '95	YY	4
● Cerasuolo di Vittoria Sciri '96	YY	4
● Cerasuolo di Vittoria		
V. di Bastonaca '95	YY	4
● Le Vigne di Cos Rosso '95	YY	4
O Ramingallo '97	YY	3*
O Ramingallo '98	YY	3*
● Cerasuolo di Vittoria		
V. di Bastonaca '98	Y	2*

OTHER WINERIES

The following producers obtained good scores in our tastings with one or more of their wines:

PROVINCE OF CATANIA

Valle Galfina,
Giarre, tel. 095/933822
Etna Rosso Opheus '99

Barone di Villagrande,
Milo, tel. 095/7082175
Sciara di Villagrande Rosso '97

Vincenzo Bonaccorsi,
Piedimonte Etneo tel. 095/7122801
Etna Rosso Val Cerasa '98

PROVINCE OF RAGUSA

Francesca e Gimbattista Curto,
Ispica, tel. 0932/950161
Curto Fontanelle Rosso '98

Poggio di Bortolone,
Roccazzo,
tel. 0932/921161
Cerasuolo di Vittoria Poggio di Bortolone '98,
Pigi Rosso '98

PROVINCE OF MESSINA

Cantine Colosi,
Messina tel. 090/53852
Passito di Pantelleria '98

Hauner,
Salina, tel. 090/9843141
Malvasia delle Lipari Passita '98

PROVINCE OF PALERMO

Tamburello,
Monreale, tel. 091/8465272
Dagala Rosso '99

PROVINCE OF SIRACUSA

Cooperativa Interprovinciale Elorina,
Noto, tel. 0931/857068
Eloro Rosso Pachino '97

Pupillo,
Siracusa, tel. 0931/494029
Moscato di Siracusa Solacium

PROVINCE OF TRAPANI

Cantine Motia,
Marsala, tel. 0923/737295
Vela Latina Bianco '99

Promed,
Mazara del Vallo,
tel. 0923/670214
Nero d'Avola Tenuta d'Apaforte '96

Marchesi Platamone,
Nubia,
tel. 0923/868114
Grillo Tor di Nubia '99

Abraxas,
Pantelleria, tel. 0923/915157
Passito di Pantelleria

Garche del Barone,
Pantelleria,
tel. 06/30311298
Moscato di Pantelleria Khafur '98

Nuova Agricoltura,
Pantelleria
tel. 0923/691009
Passito di Pantelleria
Le Lave del Kuttinar '98

Cantina Sociale Ericina,
Sperone di Custonaci,
tel. 0923/576588
Castello di Venere Bianco '9

SARDINIA

Producing wine in the south of Italy and on its islands is not as easy as it might seem. Fine, the vineyards receive plentiful warmth, light and aeration but it is water that is often lacking and Sardinia suffers more drought years than most. As a result, many wineries have had to install irrigation systems to get them through the most critical vegetative periods. Last year was yet another one with sparse rainfall. It was also marked by a number of developments on the island's wine scene. New estates, such as Pala di Serdiana, and its attention-grabbing red and white wines made their first appearance and new wines were launched by some of the better known producers. Many of these new products are blends of indigenous and the so-called "imported" varieties. The risk in taking this route is that individual territories can lose their identity, especially when, as so often happens, such decisions are made for purely commercial reasons or simply to follow fashion. We cannot let this trend pass unremarked as it threatens not just Sardinia but all Italy. On the other hand, thank goodness, there are numerous estates going against the tide and concentrating on furthering the specific characteristics of their own varieties. Their philosophy is endorsed by the importers world-wide who are continually looking for fine wines of individuality, not those from the ubiquitous "international" grapes. Currently, it is Sella & Mosca that is stealing a march on the competition. Not only does it have a fabulous red in Marchese di Villamarina but it has also brought out a superb Anghelu Ruju and two outstanding whites, Alghero Terre Bianche and Vermentino di Sardegna La Cala. Another winery enjoying well-merited success is Argiolas. Its Turriga is already on the fast track but its new red Korem has also received critical acclaim and the brilliant Angialis is, in our opinion, one of the best Italian dessert wines. The exceptional ability of Dino Addis is clearly behind the significant improvements in the quality of the wines at the Cantina Sociale Gallura, where, let it also be said, value for money across the board is unbeatable. The Trexenta, Dolianova and Santadi co-operatives also continue to perform well while those of Dorgali, Oliena and Jerzu have come out with some good new reds. Apart from Pala, other up-and-coming wineries are the small Villa di Quartu estate, with a distinctive red called Cepola. Gabbas has broadened its range with a new red while Cherchi's standing seems to have been restored. The wines of Gian Vittorio Naitana, whom we feel is the best producer of Malvasia della Planargia, continue to improve slowly and steadily, suggesting that we should support and encourage his efforts. Remaining in the dessert wine sector, the Vernaccia di Oristanos of Contini, Serra and Puddu stand out proudly from a sea of mediocrity. In the area around Cagliari, Meloni and Picciau are distinguished for their wines from malvasia and nasco. The Loi estate is heavily involved in making serious reds and there are good things, too, from Fattoria Mauritania, Soletta, Arcone and Mancini. Finally, the Santa Maria La Palma, Marrubiu and Mogoro co-operatives are worth watching.

ALGHERO (SS)

ARZACHENA (SS)

TENUTE SELLA & MOSCA
LOC. I PIANI
07041 ALGHERO (SS)
TEL. 079/997700

TENUTE CAPICHERA
LOC. CAPICHERA
07021 ARZACHENA (SS)
TEL. 0789/80612 - 0789/80654

There are still major changes under way in the vineyards at this celebrated estate. Replantings continue but many of the new vines are already flourishing and will soon be ready to add further lustre to the wines. Some, though, are already superb. The '96 Marchese di Villamarina, from 100 percent cabernet sauvignon, is as intense and stylish as previous releases. It may be a little less powerful this time round but has compensating richness in its ripe fruitiness and sensual aromas of balsam, vanilla and Mediterranean scrub. Vermentino di Sardegna La Cala '99 has a fine array of fresh and fruity aromas. Just as impressive is Alghero Terre Bianche '99, which has personality from its inviting floral and fruited notes and enticing subtle aromas of cakes. Vermentino di Gallura Monteoro '99, zesty, full-bodied and with tropical fruit aromas, is very attractive, as is Alghero Arenarie '99, from sauvignon. This wine has fresh, vegetal aromas, a soft, full palate, and good style. The '99 vintage was excellent for the clean, refreshing rosé Alghero Oleandro. It has a particularly lively palate that makes it ideal drinking right through the meal. Raim '97 and Tanca Farrà '95 were among the more interesting of the other wines but were overshadowed by the extraordinary Anghelu Ruju Riserva '92 which has intense aromas, a powerful vein of alcohol and strong tones of walnutskin and liqueur cherries. It is full and warm in the mouth, with good mid-palate definition and a velvety finish.

At the moment, Capichera looks more like a building site than a winery. The Ragnedda brothers are in the middle of a major project to extend their vineyards and enlarge their winemaking capacity, involving the construction of a new red wine cellar. Eight hectares of vermentino, from various Gallura clones, have been planted at Spridda, a few kilometres from Capichera, which is also the site of the new buildings. A further nine hectares are being planted at Surrau, between Arzachena and Palau, another excellent viticultural zone. Here, there will be experimental plantings of red grapes including carignano, cabernet sauvignon and syrah, as well as vermentino. The results of all these endeavours will no doubt benefit not just Capichera but the entire regional wine scene. But the Ragneddas are already high-quality producers, as our tastings confirmed. The '99 Vermentino di Gallura Vigna 'Ngena has gone up a gear and is full, fat and particularly alluring. The '99 version of the straight Vermentino di Gallura is also more characterful on the palate than before and has notable extractive structure. Vermentino di Gallura Vendemmia Tardiva '99, from late-vintage grapes fermented in a mixture of new and partly used barriques, is even more complete in itself. It is richly perfumed, with a clear note of oak toast. The palate is forward, full, soft, silky midway through and has an even, complex finish. All three wines amply merit their Two Glasses. One Glass goes to the red Assajè '99, which has fresh, youthful aromas of fresh, almost perfumed, fruit. It also has up-front flavours and is attractively harmonious on the palate.

○ Alghero Le Arenarie '99	♀♀	3*
● Alghero Marchese di Villamarina '96	♀♀	6
⊙ Alghero Oleandro '99	♀♀	3*
○ Alghero Torbato Terre Bianche '99	♀♀	3*
● Anghelu Ruju Ris. '92	♀♀	4
● Raim '97	♀♀	3*
○ Vermentino di Gallura Monteoro '99	♀♀	3*
● Cannonau di Sardegna '97	♀	2*
○ Vermentino di Sardegna La Cala '99	♀♀	3
● Alghero Marchese di Villamarina '93	♀♀♀	6
● Alghero Marchese di Villamarina '95	♀♀♀	6

○ Vermentino di Gallura Capichera '99	♀♀	5
○ Vermentino di Gallura V. T. '99	♀♀	6
○ Vermentino di Gallura Vigna 'Ngena '99	♀♀	4
● Assajè Rosso '99	♀	4
○ Vermentino di Gallura Capichera '95	♀♀	5
○ Vermentino di Gallura Capichera '98	♀♀	5
○ Vermentino di Gallura V. T. '96	♀♀	5
○ Vermentino di Gallura V. T. '97	♀♀	5
○ Vermentino di Gallura V. T. '98	♀♀	5
○ Vermentino di Gallura Vigna 'Ngena '94	♀♀	4

BERCHIDDA (SS)

CABRAS (OR)

CANTINA SOCIALE GIOGANTINU
VIA MILANO, 30
07022 BERCHIDDA (SS)
TEL. 079/704163 - 079/704939

ATTILIO CONTINI
VIA GENOVA, 48/50
09072 CABRAS (OR)
TEL. 0783/290806

Things are in ferment at the Giogantinu co-operative and we are not just talking about the grape musts. The air is a-buzz with desire to change the old way of working that has previously hampered progress. This is one of the principal wineries in the Gallura district, even if others dwarf it for production volumes. Giogantinu's catchment area includes several important viticultural zones, including some genuine crus, which give superb grapes and wines. These are now being better exploited in a range called Vigne Storiche, which comes from a selection of the better grapes, including some from bush-trained vines. The latest bunch of wines maintains reasonable quality but has felt the effects of a year that was not out of the top drawer. Both the standard and the Superiore versions of the '99 Vermentino di Gallura Vigne Storiche have slightly less robust aromas and are slimmer on the palate than usual. They are still well-made, well-typed wines. They just lack some of the fat of more classic Vermentino from this area. Strangely, the standard Vermentino di Galluras from '99, both the basic version and the Superiore, do have this characteristic. Both have quite intense, fruity aromas with almondy overtones and the palates of both are fresh and attractive. Moving on to the reds, there is a new addition to the Vigne Storiche line, Terra Mala '98. Conceived with the same philosophy as for the whites, it is bursting with ripe fruit aromas and the palate is fat and notably tannic. Nastarrè, a blend of mainly indigenous grapes, also shows well. It is well-typed and well-made, with freshness on the nose and a balanced palate.

There are not many producers left who continue to fight to save wines like Vernaccia di Oristano. Such martyrs tend to live from hand to mouth, producing less and less wine and selling it with increasing difficulty. The Contini estate started out producing Vernaccia and grew by producing Vernaccia, first building then consolidating an enviable reputation that spread far beyond Italy. But forever tilting at windmills is wearing even for those with a firm belief in what they are doing. It is also disheartening to see local councils spending their time and resources on craft fairs rather than projects to safeguard the existence of a product fundamental to the area's economy. Still, we were encouraged by our tasting results, which underlined the potential of this all-Sardinian wine. The '92 Vernaccia di Oristano has notes of dried fruits and vanilla overlying its more classic aromas of almond and walnut. The palate is very warm and soft, and long enough to warrant its Two Glasses. Two Glasses also go to Antico Gregori, a blend of some of the better older vintages. It brims with evolved, lingering aromas and the palate is full and velvety. One Glass went to the most impressive of the reds, the Cannonau di Sardegna Riserva '97, from bush-trained grapes grown at Oliena, one of the best Cannonau zones. The bouquet is rich and intense, with overt aromas of morello cherry and quince leading in to a full palate with balanced tannins and good length. The Vermentino di Sardegna is worthy only of a mention as it is a little weak, slender in its aromas and has marked acidity on the palate. Last year's was better. Niedderra Rosato '99 is attractive and well-typed, revealing delicate, cherry-like aromas.

● Nastarrè '99		▼	1*
● Terra Mala Vigne Storiche '98		▼	4
○ Vermentino di Gallura Sup. '99		▼	2*
○ Vermentino di Gallura Sup. Vigne Storiche '99		▼	4
○ Vermentino di Gallura Vigne Storiche '99		▼	4
○ Vermentino di Gallura '98			1
○ Vermentino di Gallura Vigne Storiche '98		▽▽	4
● Nastarrè '98		▽	1*
○ Vermentino di Gallura Sup. '98		▽	2*

○ Antico Gregori		▼▼	6
○ Vernaccia di Oristano '92		▼▼	3*
● Cannonau di Sardegna Ris. '97		▼	3
☉ Niedderra Rosato '99			2
○ Vermentino di Sardegna '99			2
○ Vernaccia di Oristano Ris. '71		▽▽▽	5
○ Antico Gregori		▽▽	6
○ Elibaria '93		▽▽	2*
○ Karmis '96		▽▽	2*
● Niedderra Rosso '91		▽▽	3*
● Niedderra Rosso '96		▽▽	2*
○ Vernaccia di Oristano '88		▽▽	3*
○ Vernaccia di Oristano Ris. '80		▽▽	3*
○ Vernaccia di Oristano Ris. '90		▽▽	3*

DOLIANOVA (CA)

DORGALI (NU)

CANTINE DOLIANOVA
LOC. SANT'ESU
S. S. 387 - KM. 17,150
09041 DOLIANOVA (CA)
TEL. 070/744101

CANTINA SOCIALE DI DORGALI
VIA PIEMONTE, 11
08022 DORGALI (NU)
TEL. 0784/96143

This winery produces a large, well-diversified range of wines, enabling it to satisfy all sectors of the market. There was a slight downturn in average quality this year, which was due to the performance of the reds. In contrast, the whites improved. Two Glasses went to Moscato di Cagliari '97, the highest scoring wine. It impresses with its intensity and persistence on the nose, which unveils marked scents of sage and Mediterranean scrub. The palate is warm and full, the taste is sweet without being cloying, and it finishes with a clean, attractive note of fruit. The line-up of Dolianova whites began with the Vermentino di Sardegna Dolia '99, which offers fresh, lively aromas with notes of apple fruit while the palate has all the freshness and cleanliness of a well-made wine. Nuragus di Cagliari is also interesting for its attractive perfumes, although it does have a slightly thin palate. The Sibiola Rosato, a mid-bodied, well-typed, easy-drinking tipple, showed a little better. On the red front, we found the Cannonau di Sardegna from the Dolia line appealing. Its bouquet is rich and complex, ranging over fruity and vegetal tones, punctuated by notes of lavender. The wine is still a little astringent, but not rough, on the palate, and is full and well-structured. The Monica di Sardegna is on an upswing. The '98 is as attractive on the nose as on the palate, with delicacy in its aromas and balance to its taste. The cannonau, carignano and montepulciano-based Falconaro, from the Vigne Sarde line, is in a lower key. It has good berry fruit aromas and flavours, and is well-typed and balanced, although offering little in the way of body. The two sparkling wines, the Caralis Brut and the semi-sweet Scaleri, are both as attractive as ever.

In last year's Guide, we referred to the fact that the Cannonau consortium benefits from the consultancy of super-winemaker, Franco Bernabei. To avoid any misunderstandings, we must stress that the wines of the Dorgali co-operative are produced under the direction of its own in-house oenologist, Pignatelli. Here, too, work is being done to identify members' best plots, where many continue to bush-train their vines. There has also been an additional three hectares of vineyard planted, with a range of indigenous grapes, together with others from the lists of authorized and recommended varieties. The winery's latest wine, Fuili, comes from a selection of these and is aged partly in barrels of different woods and different sizes, and partly in stainless steel vats. The '98 has particularly fruity and vegetal aromas with well-defined overtones of green pepper. The palate has a full, firm, well-knit structure that reveals nicely ripe tannins. The '98 vintage of the other IGT produced, the Noriolo, is also very distinctive but more so in the mouth than on the nose, where aromas are of medium intensity and have both vegetal and ripe fruit notes. It is the full, fleshy palate, with its clean, long finish, that best expresses the wine's typically Sardinian character. Cannonau di Sardegna Vigna di Isalle '99 is one of the new-style Cannonaus which, as its name implies, comes from a selected part of the production zone. It is a well-made wine with a fresh, well-fruited, very lightly vegetal nose dominated by raspberry and redcurrant aromas. The flavours are up-front and fresh, and show a lively zestiness rarely found in Cannonaus of the old school.

○ Moscato di Cagliari '97	🍷🍷	4
● Cannonau di Sardegna '98	🍷	2*
● Falconaro '98	🍷	3
● Monica di Sardegna '98	🍷	2*
○ Nuragus di Cagliari '99	🍷	2*
☉ Sibiola Rosato '99	🍷	2*
○ Vermentino di Sardegna Dolia '99	🍷	2*
○ Caralis Brut		3
○ Scaleri Démi sec		3
○ Dolicante '96	🍷🍷	3*
● Falconaro '96	🍷🍷	3*
● Falconaro '97	🍷🍷	3*
○ Moscato di Cagliari '96	🍷🍷	4
● Cannonau di Sardegna '97	🍷	2*
● Falconaro '95	🍷	3

● Fuili '98	🍷🍷	5
● Cannonau di Sardegna		
Vigna di Isalle '99	🍷	3
● Filieri Rosso '98	🍷	2*
● Noriolo '97	🍷	4
● Cannonau di Sardegna '94	🍷	3
● Cannonau di Sardegna Filieri '95	🍷	2*
● Filieri Rosso '96	🍷	2*
● Filieri Rosso '97	🍷	2*
● Filieri Rosso '98	🍷	2*
● Noriolo '97	🍷	4

FLORINAS (SS)

JERZU (NU)

TENUTE SOLETTA
VIA SASSARI, 77
07030 FLORINAS (SS)
TEL. 079/438160

ANTICHI PODERI JERZU
VIA UMBERTO I, 1
08044 JERZU (NU)
TEL. 0782/70028

In a sector such as agriculture, the arrival of a new generation can only be a good thing and in Tenute Soletta, we have a young estate run by youngsters. The estate lies in the south of the Sassari district, where gentle hills dominate the scenery and soils are rich in tufa and limestone. The Soletta siblings currently have around ten hectares of vineyard in production, on three separate plots, planted mainly with indigenous varieties such as cannonau, cagnulari, bovale, vermentino and moscato. There are a further six hectares about to be planted and these will also include incrocio Manzoni, cabernet sauvignon, pinot, chardonnay, syrah and tocai. The vineyards are at 400-500 metres, on well-aspected sites. The cellars have recently been fitted out with modern equipment for vinifying the whites, and barriques of various types for ageing the reds. From the wines tasted, we particularly liked the freshness and the intense, clean-cut fruitiness of the Vermentino di Sardegna Prestizu '99, which is dense, full and long on the palate. The other Vermentino di Sardegna is considerably less impressive, being less assertive on the nose and short in the mouth. On the other hand, the Cannonau di Sardegna Riserva '96 has good style with an evolved nose that offers aromas of balsam and cherry jam, and a lightly tannic palate with similar characteristics. Dolce Valle Moscato Passito '97 is a concentrate of ripe fruit on both nose and palate.

An idea of the possibilities this newly-renamed co-operative offers can be gleaned from a few figures. Over 500 members confer grapes and in a normal year, approximately 40,000 hectares of wine are produced. It is easily the largest winery in the Ogliastra area and the largest red wine producer on the island. But of course, size does not always equate with quality. And perhaps this is one of the factors that have prompted this estate to come up with new, different wines, not just the same old tipples dolled up in a new bottle-shape or label. The brain behind Jerzu's new winemaking philosophy is Franco Bernabei and the most significant of the new wines he has masterminded is Cannonau di Sardegna Riserva '97 Chuerra. It is made from 100 percent cannonau, aged in a mix of large oak barrels and 500-litre French tonneaux for 18 months and then kept in bottle for a while before release. Its nose was still closed when we tasted but the typical, inviting aromas of ripe berry fruit, particularly morello cherry, were already discernible. The bouquet will doubtless become fuller and more characterful as the wine evolves. The wine's youth was also apparent on the palate, where the tannins and acidity were still rather excessive, although kept in control. But it was as clear as day that this was a wine with the quality to slot comfortably into the Two Glass bracket. The Cannonau di Sardegna Riserva '98 is also a fine wine. Although it is younger than the Chuerra, its aromas are more developed and it has considerable fatness and softness on the palate. Cannonau di Sardegna Marghìa '98 is another new wine. It is called a "vintage selection" and comes from cannonau yielding less than 50 quintals per hectare. The fruit on the nose suggests mulberries and there are robust tannins on the palate but overall it is fairly harmonious and easy to drink.

○ Vermentino di Sardegna		
Prestizu '99	▼▼	3*
● Cannonau di Sardegna Ris. '96	▼	4
○ Dolce Valle Moscato Passito '97	▼	4
● Cannonau di Sardegna '92	♀	3
● Cannonau di Sardegna		
Firmadu '91	♀	3
● Cannonau di Sardegna		
Firmadu '96	♀	3
○ Moscato di Sassari '92	♀	4
○ Moscato Passito '96	♀	4

● Cannonau di Sardegna Ris.		
Chuerra '97	▼▼	4
● Cannonau di Sardegna Marghìa '98	▼	4
● Cannonau di Sardegna Ris. '98	▼	3
● Cannonau di Sardegna Ris. '91	♀♀	3*
● Cannonau di Sardegna '92	♀	2*
● Cannonau di Sardegna '93	♀	2*
● Cannonau di Sardegna '95	♀	2*
● Cannonau di Sardegna '96	♀	2*
● Cannonau di Sardegna '97	♀	2*
● Cannonau di Sardegna Ris. '95	♀	3
● Pardu Dolce '91	♀	3
● Radames '97	♀	4

MAGOMADAS (NU)

MONTI (SS)

GIANVITTORIO NAITANA
VIA ROMA, 2
08010 MAGOMADAS (NU)
TEL. 0785/35333

CANTINA SOCIALE DEL VERMENTINO
VIA S. PAOLO, 1
07020 MONTI (SS)
TEL. 0789/44012

There is a serious risk that one of Sardinia's pearls, which also means one of Italy's pearls, is heading for extinction. The Malvasia produced in the Planargia area is in the hands of a few small producers and just one co-operative. The wine has been held back by a lack of winemaking expertise, producers loath to co-operate, and local politicians and bureaucrats whose interests lie elsewhere. Moreover, there are two competing schools of thought on the style that best suits the variety. Should the wine be young or aged? We believe that the more youthful version expresses the varietal characteristics better while more mature examples have the oxidative style that is also typical of Vernaccia di Oristano. And Sherry, for that matter. Naturally, both styles can and should co-exist but apparently, there is neither the desire nor the ability to modify the production regulations so that this can happen. In the middle of this anarchic situation is a young producer, Naitana, who remains unswayed by events and just gets on with producing traditional, but very high quality, Malvasia. He has a selection of tiny plots scattered around the best subzones that yield from as little as 20-30 quintals per hectare up to a maximum of 50 or 60. These he cultivates with love and expertise in equal measure. The weather conditions leading up to the '99 vintage were good and gave small quantities of perfectly ripe grapes. As a result, Planargia Murapiscados '99 has generous, pervasive aromas of apricot and peach. Its taste is delicately sweet and the palate has body and structure but, even more important, a silky softness from a high glycerine content that exalts its excellent typicity.

We have pointed out the versatility of the vermentino grape on numerous occasions and this co-operative, situated on the borders of the Gallura and Logudoro districts, produces considerable quantities of Vermentino, fully exploiting the variety's adaptability with a well-diversified range of wines. To judge by our tastings, the '99 vintage was not one of the best. The winery's flagship wines reflected this most, particularly the Vermentino di Gallura Funtanaliras '99. It has good intensity and delicate fruit and floral aromas but it lacks length. The Vermentino di Gallura S'Eleme '99 has rather weak aromas and not much more than a decently zesty flavour. Vermentino di Gallura Superiore '99, however, is a tad better. It has almondy, ripe fruit scents and is full, powerful and fat on the palate. We were even more disappointed with the reds, especially with the new Galana '97, a blend of cabernet sauvignon, sangiovese, carignano and cagnulari with small proportions of other red varieties, and aged for over a year in oak casks. The aromas are pungently intense and evolved, revealing hints of liquorice and dried flowers. The palate has body and fatness but it is almost overwhelmed by tannin, although this will probably soften in time. We preferred Abbaia, finding it well-typed, balanced and with a reasonable dose of fruit.

O Planargia Murapiscados '99	🍷🍷	4	● Abbaìa '99	🍷	2*
O Planargia Murapiscados '96	🍷🍷	4	O Vermentino di Gallura Funtanaliras '99	🍷	3
O Planargia Murapiscados '97	🍷🍷	4	O Vermentino di Gallura S'Eleme '99	🍷	2*
O Planargia Murapiscados '98	🍷🍷	4	O Vermentino di Gallura Sup.		
			Aghiloia '99	🍷	2*
			● Galana '97		5
			O Vermentino di Gallura		
			Funtanaliras '98	🍷🍷	3*
			O Vermentino di Gallura Sup.		
			Aghiloia '94	🍷🍷	2*
			O Vermentino di Gallura Sup.		
			Aghiloia '96	🍷🍷	2*
			● Abbaìa '96	🍷	1*
			● Abbaìa '97	🍷	1*
			● Abbaìa '98	🍷	1

MONTI (SS)

PEDRA MAJORE
VIA ROMA, 106
07020 MONTI (SS)
TEL. 0789/43185

The Isoni family estate benefits from having vineyards in one of the best areas for Vermentino production. They face south and are surrounded by cork-tree and holm-oak woods which are interspersed with granite outcrops. This is the extraordinary scenery of Gallura, where vines can grow and ripen without much need of attention, one of the factors that enabled the estate to gain organic certification. The cellars, which have been in action for just two years, have a capacity of around 5,000 hectolitres and have been fitted out with modern winemaking equipment. The results obtained so far are encouraging, especially when you remember how young the estate is. The most interesting of the whites is Vermentino di Gallura Hysonj '99. Its aromas are quite intense but we expected the palate to be fuller. Nevertheless, it is a harmonious, balanced wine with very good style. The Vermentino di Sardegna Le Conche '99 is fresher and more immediate and has a more marked, clean fruitiness on the nose too. We found Vermentino di Gallura I Graniti '99 to be a little off-key. Its aromas are a touch too evolved and the palate finishes short. On the other hand, the red Murighessa, made from a blend of nebbiolo, cannonau, bovale sardo and cabernet sauvignon, has good character. It may not have the sumptuousness of a truly great red but its fresh, youthful aromas give it great appeal. It is also well-made, medium-bodied and has a good few years' ageing potential. The Pedra Majore range also includes a white dessert wine, Mirju, which comes from semi-dried moscato grapes and is produced only in particularly good years.

●	Murighessa '99	🍷	3
○	Vermentino di Gallura Hysonj '99	🍷	3
○	Vermentino di Gallura I Graniti '99		3
○	Vermentino di Sardegna Le Conche '99		3
○	Mirju Passito '98	🥂	5
○	Moscato Passito La Eltica	🥂	4
●	Murighessa '98	🥂	3
○	Vermentino di Gallura I Graniti '98	🥂	3

NUORO

GIUSEPPE GABBAS
VIA TRIESTE, 65
08100 NUORO
TEL. 0784/31351 - 0784/33745

The hills between Oliena and Orgosolo, in the heart of the Barbagia district, have a slightly different profile as Giuseppe Gabbas' new cellars rise across their slopes. The decision to rebuild was not taken overnight but came as a result of increased demand for the wines, both abroad and at home. Gabbas always aims to produce great reds that maintain strong links with their origins and respect traditional Sardinian styling. Indeed, all his wines are based on cannonau. Working with his Tuscan oenologist, Giorgio Gori, Giuseppe also insists on extended maceration as part of the winemaking technique, sometimes protracting it for as long as 30 days. Some other winemakers on the island have turned their noses up at this but it is no more than a return to tradition, backed up by improved technical know-how, and it certainly helps to counter the recent invasion of reds rendered insipid and atypical by skimpy macerations. Gabbas' latest releases, while retaining good structure, may have suffered from the developments on the estate, as several vineyards have been in production for only a few years and are not yet giving grapes at their full potential. Cannonau di Sardegna Lillovè '99 is still youthful. The aromas are fairly intense and persist reasonably well. The palate has marked tannins and acidity which will require time to gain balance. The Dule '99, from cannonau, sangiovese and montepulciano, is better. The bouquet is intense, with fresh fruit aromas that are echoed on the palate and there is also considerable body and structure that will allow it to age well. The Arbeskia '97 is the estate's new wine. It comes from 50 percent Cannonau, 40 percent cabernet sauvignon and 10 percent of other indigenous grapes, and is aged in barrique. It showed as well-styled and well-made but a little closed on the nose.

●	Dule '98	🍷🍷	4
●	Arbeskia '97	🍷	5
●	Cannonau di Sardegna Lillovè '99	🍷	3
●	Cannonau di Sardegna Lillovè '96	🥂🥂	3*
●	Cannonau di Sardegna Lillovè '97	🥂🥂	3*
●	Cannonau di Sardegna Lillovè '98	🥂🥂	3*
●	Dule '94	🥂🥂	4
●	Dule '95	🥂🥂	4
●	Dule '96	🥂🥂	4
●	Dule '97	🥂🥂	4
●	Dule '98	🥂🥂	4
●	Cannonau di Sardegna Lillovè '93	🥂	2*
●	Cannonau di Sardegna Lillovè '94	🥂	2*
●	Cannonau di Sardegna Lillovè '95	🥂	2*

632

QUARTU S. ELENA (CA) SANTADI (CA)

VILLA DI QUARTU
VIA GARIBALDI, 96
09045 QUARTU S. ELENA (CA)
TEL. 070/820947 - 070/826997

CANTINA SOCIALE DI SANTADI
VIA SU PRANU, 12
09010 SANTADI (CA)
TEL. 0781/950012 - 0781/950127

Villa di Quartu is a newish estate, although grapes have been produced on the site for several generations. It has been lurking on the sidelines for some time now but this year it has finally gained a first Guide profile. There are around 45 hectares of vine, dotted around the environs of Cagliari, but all on excellent sites with good reputations for dessert wines and Nuragus. And in fact, the '99 vintage, while not exceptional, clearly demonstrated the terrain's potential for making dessert wines. The main aim of the owners is to make the most of the local indigenous grapes, although they are also keen to experiment with several clones of newer varieties. From the classics, Malvasia di Cagliari '97 showed well, with delicate aromas and fair length. The attempts to create new wines from indigenous grapes are also giving promising results. Cepola Bianco '99 has fruity aromas of golden delicious apples and a warm, full palate. Cepola Rosso '98, from monica, bovale, cannonau, cagnulari and barbera sarda, is even more intriguing. It offers an intense, markedly fruity nose with notes of dried figs and walnuts, and a rich, full, fleshy palate with a light mesh of tannins. The white Nuragus di Cagliari '99 and Vermentino di Sardegna '99 are less exciting.

As usual, the Santadi co-operative has a large number of wines on offer. The range begins triumphantly with Villa di Chiesa '99, a vermentino and chardonnay blend so full and ripe that it warranted Three Glasses. The nose is sensual, with aromas of fresh butter and candied apricot while the palate expresses all the warmth of the Mediterranean, confidently backed up by a good acidic backbone. The Carignano del Sulcis Superiore Terre Brune '98 also keeps the house flag flying. The nose is evolved, with touches of oak toast, and the palate is warm and meaty. The other Carignano del Sulcis, the Grotta Rossa '98, is good too, with aromas of ripe fruit and mushrooms but the Carignano del Sulcis Riserva Rocca Rubia '97 is in a lower key. Its rather over-evolved nose releases aromas of wood and carob, and the fairly raw tannins dominate the palate. The Monica di Sardegna Antigua '99 is also below par, with faintish aromas and only moderate length on the palate. However the '98 version of Araja, from carignano and sangiovese, has shifted back up a gear. Its aromas have notes of spices and tobacco while the palate is clean and harmonious. The Carignano del Sulcis Baie Rosso '97 is also rich in aroma, expressing all the power of a big, full-bodied wine on its palate. On the white front, it was the Vermentino di Sardegna Cala Silente '99 that stood out. It has intense, lingering aromas with vegetal and vanillaed notes. The palate is warm and attractively soft so it was a worthy Two Glass winner. The Nuragus di Cagliari Pedraia '99, a wine of excellent style and unusual fullness for its denomination, gained One Glass. The Vermentino di Sardegna Villa Solais '99, delicate and clean on both nose and palate, is also good while Latinia, a dessert wine from nasco, is very well-made.

○ Cepola Bianco '99	?	2*
● Cepola Rosso '98	?	3
○ Malvasia di Cagliari '97	?	4
○ Nuragus di Cagliari '99		2
○ Vermentino di Sardegna '99		2

○ Villa di Chiesa '99	???	4*
● Carignano del Sulcis		
Baie Rosse '97	??	5
● Carignano del Sulcis Sup.		
Terre Brune '96	??	6
○ Vermentino di Sardegna		
Cala Silente '98	??	3*
● Araja '98	?	3
● Carignano del Sulcis Grotta Rossa '98	?	2*
● Carignano del Sulcis		
Rocca Rubia Ris. '97	?	4
○ Latinia '98	?	4
○ Nuragus di Cagliari Pedraia '99	?	2*
● Terre Brune '93	???	6
● Terre Brune '94	???	6

SELARGIUS (CA)

SENORBÌ (CA)

MELONI VINI
VIA GALLUS, 79
09047 SELARGIUS (CA)
TEL. 070/852822

CANTINA SOCIALE DELLA TREXENTA
V.LE PIEMONTE, 28
09040 SENORBÌ (CA)
TEL. 070/9808863 - 070/9809378

Meloni Vini is a winery that has adapted its products to customer demand, not just locally, but in the rest of Italy and non-domestic markets, too. It has various production centres and a range of production lines that embrace the full gamut of Sardinian wine styles. Recently, it has even added an organic range, although the take-off of such produce in Italy has been slow. The Donna Jolanda line, incorporating the dessert wines, is without doubt the one that most fully reflects the traditions of the zone, which was once famous for Girò, Malvasia, Nasco and Moscato. Of these, we tasted the Girò di Cagliari '95. The aromas are somewhat over-evolved and a rather fat sweetness dominates the palate which, in truth, is a bit cloying. Vernaccia di Oristano also forms part of the group. It is full of clean tertiary aromas with a characteristic almondy note and a full, rounded palate. Monica di Sardegna '98 showed very well and in fact collected Two Glasses. There is a delightful attack on the nose, with aromas that tend towards the vegetal. The palate has all the freshness of a wine that is still young but will improve with age. Cannonau di Sardegna Le Ghiaie '96, with aromas of ripe berry fruit and tobacco, and a warm palate supported by lightish tannins, also showed well.

Trexenta is not the only co-operative to have sought to reform its procedures but it benefits particularly from being efficiently managed, with go-ahead youngsters in all the key roles, from the chair to the winemaker, and from the commercial director to the sales manager. As a result, it suffers little from the notorious slowness in making decisions and the reluctance to accept change that bedevils so many co-operatives. The changes set in place here are already bringing improvements, most notably with the reds, where it appears that most attention is being concentrated. In addition, the '96 vintage was a particularly promising one for red wines. Tanca su Conti '96, from cannonau and carignano, and aged around 18 months in barrique, has full, intense, unabashedly fruity aromas and a warm, soft taste. Cannonau di Sardegna Baione '96 almost gained Two Glasses. It, too, has attractive aromas which range from balsamic nuances to fruit and vegetal tones while the palate displays the appealing qualities of a well-typed, harmonious wine. The Monica di Sardegna Duca di Mandas '99, though, was slightly less good than we expected. It is certainly well-made but has also clearly suffered from the troublesome vintage. Still, it is very good value for money. Among the whites tasted was a very good Monteluna Chardonnay '99, which is lively but not superficial, and has good nose-palate symmetry. The Vermentino di Sardegna Tanca Sa Contissa '99 is also attractive but Vermentino di Sardegna Donna Leonora '99 and Nuragus di Cagliari Tenute San Mauro '99 fell below expectations.

● Monica di Sardegna '98	♟♟	2*
● Cannonau di Sardegna Le Ghiaie '96	♟	3
● Girò di Cagliari Donna Jolanda '95	♟	4
○ Vernaccia di Oristano '93	♟	3
● Cabernet di Sardegna '92	♟♟	4
○ Moscato di Cagliari Donna Jolanda '91	♟♟	4
○ Nasco di Cagliari Donna Jolanda '94	♟♟	4
● Cannonau di Sardegna Le Ghiaie '91	♟	3
● Cannonau di Sardegna Le Ghiaie '95	♟	3

● Tanca Su Conti '96	♟♟	4
● Cannonau di Sardegna Baione '96	♟	3
● Monica di Sardegna Duca di Mandas '99	♟	2*
○ Monteluna Chardonnay '99	♟	3
○ Vermentino di Sardegna Tanca Sa Contissa '99	♟	2*
○ Nuragus di Cagliari Tenute San Mauro '99		1
○ Vermentino di Sardegna Donna Leonora '99		1
● Monica di Sardegna '97	♟♟	1*
● Cannonau di Sardegna Baione '95	♟	3
● Monica di Sardegna Duca di Mandas '98	♟	2*
● Tanca Su Conti '95	♟	4

SERDIANA (CA)

SERDIANA (CA)

ANTONIO ARGIOLAS
VIA ROMA, 56/58
09040 SERDIANA (CA)
TEL. 070/740606

PALA
VIA VERDI, 7
09040 SERDIANA (CA)
TEL. 070/740284

Argiolas is getting us used to drinking well. Very well indeed. Wines that seemed to be the exception a few years ago are becoming the rule and practically all are now simply excellent, with some absolutely extraordinary. Turriga is back at the very top of the tree with the '95. The nose is an explosion of powerfully intense aromas that are still in development but already show well-defined berry fruit and vanilla. The palate is quite majestic – concentrated and full, with a long, lingering finish. This wine swept in authoritatively to claim its Three Glasses. The '98 Korem, the second release of this red from cannonau, carignano, bovale and bovaleddu, with small proportions of syrah and merlot, was close on its heels and almost collected Three Glasses as well. It has vanillaed notes on the nose and aromas of cherry while the palate is young, lively, balanced and harmonious. The '98 versions of Cannonau di Sardegna Costera and Monica di Sardegna Perdera racked up similar scores to their '97 versions. The Serralori rosé is fresh and has good impact and then the sumptuous richness of Angialis' aroma and the perfect harmony of its palate puts this beautiful "passito" from nasco and malvasia up with the very best of Italy's sweet wines. The nose is an invitingly concentrated amalgam of Mediterranean scents while the delicacy of its flavour and its velvety smoothness bring elegance to the mouth-filling palate. It won Two Glasses, as did the Argiolas '99, with its rich scents of flowers and vanilla, hints of cakes, and impressive structure and length. The Vermentino di Sardegna Costamolino '99 is delicious, too, with its fresh fruitiness and its attractive palate; Nuragus S'Elegas has a clean nose and delicate aromas. It notched up a slightly lower score.

Pala, situated north of Cagliari, is a newcomer to the ranks of quality wine producers in Sardinia, although it has been in existence for about 50 years. Founded by Salvatore Pala, its grapes were previously sold to other wineries on the island. It is now owned and run by his sons, Enrico and Mario, and it was they who took the decision to start making and bottling their own wine. It wasn't exactly a leap in the dark, though, because the pair had a good idea of how the wine market was moving and were well aware of the potential of their 50 hectares under vine. It goes without saying that they fitted out their cellar with the most up-to-date winemaking and bottling equipment. Our first impressions of the wines were very encouraging and we are confident that the estate will make a significant contribution to the island's fine wine sector. One bottle even made it to within a hair's breadth of Three Glasses. The star's name is S'Arai '98, a wine from cannonau, carignano, barbera sarda and bovale. The bouquet is rich and fruity but its great power shows through to greatest effect on the palate which, despite not yet being fully developed, is full and concentrated. It's also a wine with great ageing potential. The other reds have good character but there is room for improvement. The Cannonau di Sardegna Triente '99 is fairly long but its tannins are still rather stalky. Monica di Sardegna showed better and is well-typed and balanced. Among the whites, we were highly impressed by the attractive Nuragus di Cagliari Salnico '99, which has uncommon fullness for a Nuragus. It unveils a raft of floral aromas that range from sage to tomato leaf, and a full, round, long palate. The Vermentino di Sardegna '99 Crabilis is not quite as fine, but good nevertheless, with lavender-rich floral and vegetal aromas, and a well-balanced palate of medium structure.

● Turriga '95	▼▼▼	6
○ Angialis '97	▼▼	5
○ Argiolas '99	▼▼	3*
● Korem '98	▼▼	5
○ Vermentino di Sardegna Costamolino '99	▼▼	2*
● Cannonau di Sardegna Costera '98	▼	3
● Monica di Sardegna Perdera '98	▼	2*
○ Nuragus di Cagliari S'Elegas '99	▼	2*
⊙ Serralori Rosato '99	▼	2*
● Turriga '90	♈♈♈	6
● Turriga '91	♈♈♈	6
● Turriga '92	♈♈♈	6
● Turriga '93	♈♈♈	6
● Turriga '94	♈♈♈	6

○ Nuragus di Cagliari Salnico '99	▼▼	2*
● S'Arai '98	▼▼	5
● Monica di Sardegna Elima '98	▼	3
○ Vermentino di Sardegna Crabilis '99	▼	3
● Cannonau di Sardegna Trieste '99		3

TEMPIO PAUSANIA (SS)

CANTINA SOCIALE GALLURA
VIA VAL DI COSSU, 9
07029 TEMPIO PAUSANIA (SS)
TEL. 079/631241

In the past, we have been surprised more than once by the consistent quality of the wines from this co-operative. This year's tastings have provided further confirmation of what Dino Addis has achieved. The flagship wines remain the Vermentino di Gallura Superiore Canayli and the Vermentino di Gallura Piras. Both '99s have powerful bouquets, the former of fresh fruit, the latter more floral. They are fat on the palate, easy-going, soft and even elegant, with good length. This year, the '99 Vermentino di Gallura Mavriana, younger brother of the above pair, claimed Two Glasses of its own for its attractive, fresh fruit aromas, which are also reflected on the palate. The Balajana '99, from vermentino aged for several months in barrique, does not disappoint either. It has considerable body and structure yet displays all the finesse of a wine with serious class. Rosato del Limbara Campos '99 is also an exceptional wine with a clean, fairly intense fruitiness on the nose and just the right amount of acid freshness on the palate. As for the reds, Karana '99, from nebbiolo, is already showing well. We get the impression that Addis doesn't have too much difficulty making it. By now, he knows where to find the best grapes and how to vinify them to achieve the immediacy and taste harmony that mark it out. In some vintages, the nebbiolo is suitable for barrique ageing, and goes to make the Dolmen. The '99 harvest yielded such grapes and the wine has a fruity bouquet, if a little closed. It shows better on the palate where its structure, softness and acid-tannin balance are very good. Finally, we would bring to your attention the sparkling Moscato di Tempio with its clean-cut, delicate, grapey perfumes and its stylish, elegant palate.

○	Balajana '99	🍷🍷	4
●	Karana Nebbiolo dei Colli del Limbara '99	🍷🍷	1*
○	Moscato di Tempio Pausania	🍷🍷	4
○	Vermentino di Gallura Mavriana '99	🍷🍷	1*
○	Vermentino di Gallura Piras '99	🍷🍷	2*
○	Vermentino di Gallura Sup. Canayli '99	🍷🍷	2*
⊙	Campos Rosato del Limbara '99	🍷	1*
●	Dolmen '96	🍷	4
○	Balajana '98	🍸🍸	4
●	Karana Nebbiolo dei Colli del Limbara '98	🍸🍸	1*
○	Vermentino di Gallura Piras '98	🍸🍸	1*

USINI (SS)

GIOVANNI CHERCHI
VIA OSSI, 18/20
07049 USINI (SS)
TEL. 079/380273

Sometimes a shake-up can be a jolly good thing. We don't think our comments in last year's Guide gave Giovanni Cherchi that much of a jolt but they must at least have given him food for thought. Vintages are not always the same for everyone and no-one can make blockbusters all the time. Nevertheless, without going into details of the estate's plus and minus points, and despite this year's wines showing considerably better than last year's, we still don't believe that Cherchi's wines are as good as they could be. Overall, though, it has been a reasonably good year for the estate's bottles, both red and white. The cagnulari-based Alghero Cagnulari '99 has intense and very distinctive aromas that lie somewhere between fruity and vegetal. The palate is dry, soft, fleshy and reasonably structured. Luzzana '98, from a cannonau and cagnulari blend aged for several months in cask, has fairly intense aromas, with accentuated floral notes of geranium and vegetal notes of wild herbs. The palate has firm acidity but the tannins are a little withdrawn. On the white front, the Vermentino di Sardegna Tuvaoes has re-surfaced as the estate's flagship. The '99 has an intriguing nose with intense, lingering aromas, particularly confectioner's cream, and a full, fat, zesty palate that finishes long, leaving the mouth clean. Vermentino di Sardegna '99 is almost, but not quite as good. Its aromas show medium intensity but the interest comes mainly from the fresh, soft, well-structured palate.

○	Vermentino di Sardegna Tuvaoes '99	🍷🍷	4
●	Alghero Cagnulari '99	🍷	2*
●	Luzzana '98	🍷	4
○	Vermentino di Sardegna '99	🍷	2*
●	Cagnulari di Sardegna '94	🍸	2*
●	Cannonau di Sardegna '93	🍸	3
●	Luzzana '91	🍸	4
●	Luzzana '93	🍸	4
●	Luzzana '94	🍸	4
●	Luzzana '96	🍸	4
●	Luzzana '97	🍸	4
○	Vermentino di Sardegna '97	🍸	2
○	Vermentino di Sardegna '98	🍸	2*
○	Vermentino di Sardegna Tuvaoes '96	🍸	4

OTHER WINERIES

The following producers obtained good scores in our tastings with one or more of their wines:

PROVINCE OF CAGLIARI

Gigi Picciau, Pirri, tel. 070/560224
Sardegna Semidano '99

Fattoria Mauritania,
Santadi, tel. 070/401465
Antas '98,
Barrua '99

PROVINCE OF NUORO

Loi, Cardedu, tel. 070/240866
Cannonau di Sardegna Cardedo Ris. '97,
Cannonau di Sardegna Sa Mola Rubia '98

Cantina Sociale Oliena,
Oliena, tel. 0784/287509
Cannonau di Sardegna
Nepente di Oliena '98

PROVINCE OF ORISTANO

Cantina Sociale Marrubiu,
Marrubiu, tel. 0783/859213
Arborea Sangiovese '99 Rosso,
Campidano di Terralba '98

Cantina Sociale Il Nuraghe,
Mogoro,
tel. 0783/990285
Cannonau di Sardegna Vigna Ruja '99,
Sardegna Semidano '99

Josto Puddu,
San Vero Milis, tel. 0783/53329
Vernaccia di Oristano '80,
Vernaccia di Oristano '95

F.lli Serra,
Zeddiani, tel. 0783/418276
Vernaccia di Oristano '92

PROVINCE OF SASSARI

Cantina Soc. Santa Maria La Palma,
Alghero,
tel. 079/999008
Alghero Chardonnay '99,
Alghero Sauvignon '99,
Cannonau di Sardegna Le Bombarde '98

Mancini,
Olbia, tel. 0789/50717
Vermentino di Gallura Saraina '99

Arcone,
Sassari, tel. 079/233721
Arcone Rosso '97

INDEX OF WINES

647

653

INDEX OF PRODUCERS

688